POWERS

VOLUME ONE

™

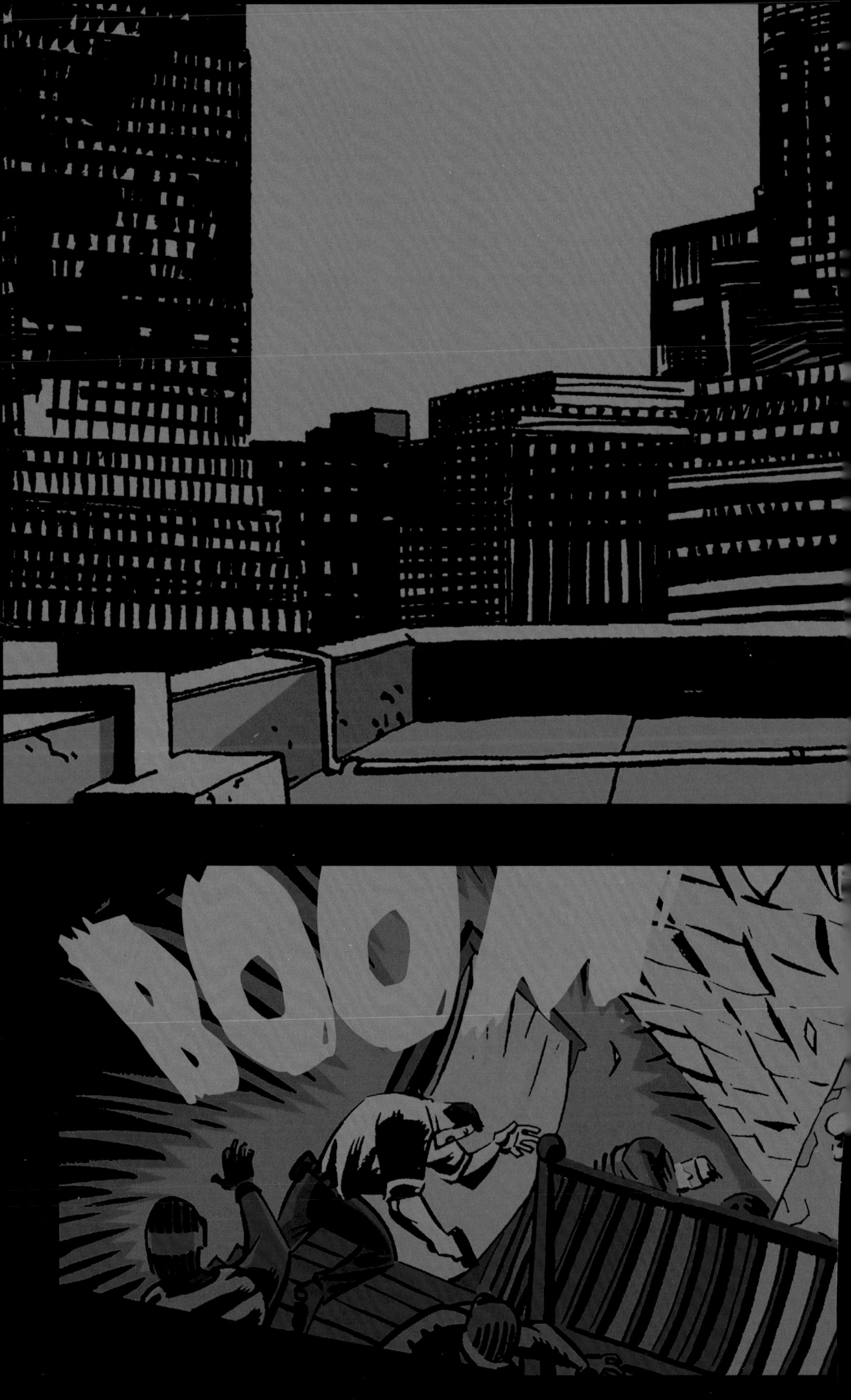
BOOM

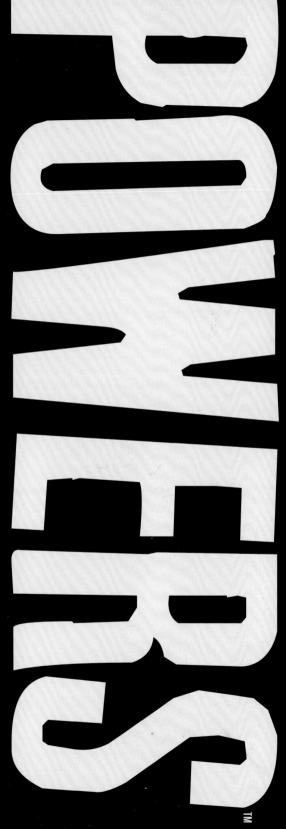

POWERS

Created by
Brian Michael Bendis and
Michael Avon Oeming

Colored and Lettered by
Pat Garrahy with
Brian Michael Bendis

Separation Assists by
Ojo Caliente Studios

Art and Cover
Michael Avon Oeming

Dark Horse Books®

VOLUME ONE

Publisher **Mike Richardson**
Collection Editor **Daniel Chabon**
Assistant Editors **Chuck Howitt-Lease** and **Misha Gehr**

ORIGINAL PRINTING
Publisher **Alisa Bendis**
Editor **Alex Galer**
Publication Design **Curtis King Jr.**

Designer **David Nestelle**
Digital Art Technician **Betsy Howitt**

To find a comics shop in your area, visit comicshoplocator.com.

POWERS Volume One

This volume collects *Powers* #1–#11, the complete *Powers* comic strips from *Comic Shop News*, and the *Powers Coloring/Activity Book*, along with all covers and a sketchbook section.

Published by Dark Horse Books
A division of Dark Horse Comics LLC
10956 SE Main Street
Milwaukie, OR 97222
DarkHorse.com

First edition: September 2022
Ebook ISBN 978-1-50673-033-2
Trade paperback ISBN 978-1-50673-017-2

10 9 8 7 6 5 4 3 2 1
Printed in China

MIX
Paper from responsible sources
FSC® C169962

Names: Bendis, Brian Michael, author. | Oeming, Michael Avon, illustrator. | Garrahy, Pat, illustrator. | Ojo Caliente Studios, contributor.
Title: Powers / created by Brian Michael Bendis and Michael Avon Oeming ; colored and lettered by, Pat Garrahy with Brian Michael Bendis ; separation assists by Ojo Caliente Studios ; art and cover Michael Avon Oeming.
Description: First edition. | Milwaukie, OR : Dark Horse Books, 2022- | v. 1: "This volume collects Powers #1-#11, the complete Powers comic strips from Comic Shop News, and the Powers Coloring/Activity Book, along with all covers and a sketchbook section." | Summary: "In a world where superheroes soar through the sky, follow homicide detectives Christian Walker and Deena Pilgrim on the dirty city streets below. Assigned to the "powers" special cases, they will face the worst their city has to offer. The shocking murder of America's superhero sweetheart, Retro Girl, has the world in mourning. The investigation takes Walker and Pilgrim from the city's seedy underbelly to the gleaming towers that are home to immortal beings. As shocking truths about Retro Girl come to light, Walker finds that to solve this crime, he might have to reveal his own dark secret."-- Provided by publisher.
Identifiers: LCCN 2022012778 (print) | LCCN 2022012779 (ebook) | ISBN 9781506730172 (volume one ; trade paperback) | ISBN 9781506730332 (volume one ; ebook)
Subjects: LCGFT: Detective and mystery comics. | Superhero comics. | Graphic novels.
Classification: LCC PN6728.P66 B463 2022 (print) | LCC PN6728.P66 (eboo | DDC 741.5/973--dc23/eng/20220415
LC record available at https://lccn.loc.gov/2022012778
LC ebook record available at https://lccn.loc.gov/2022012779

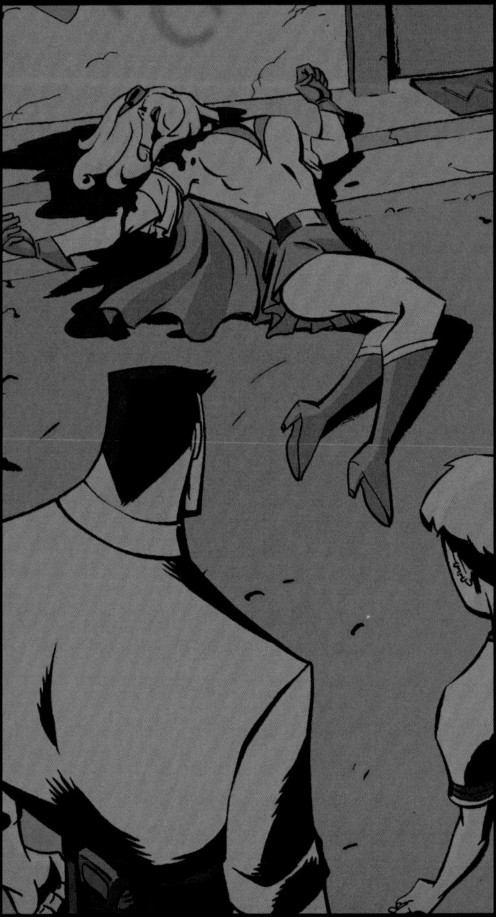

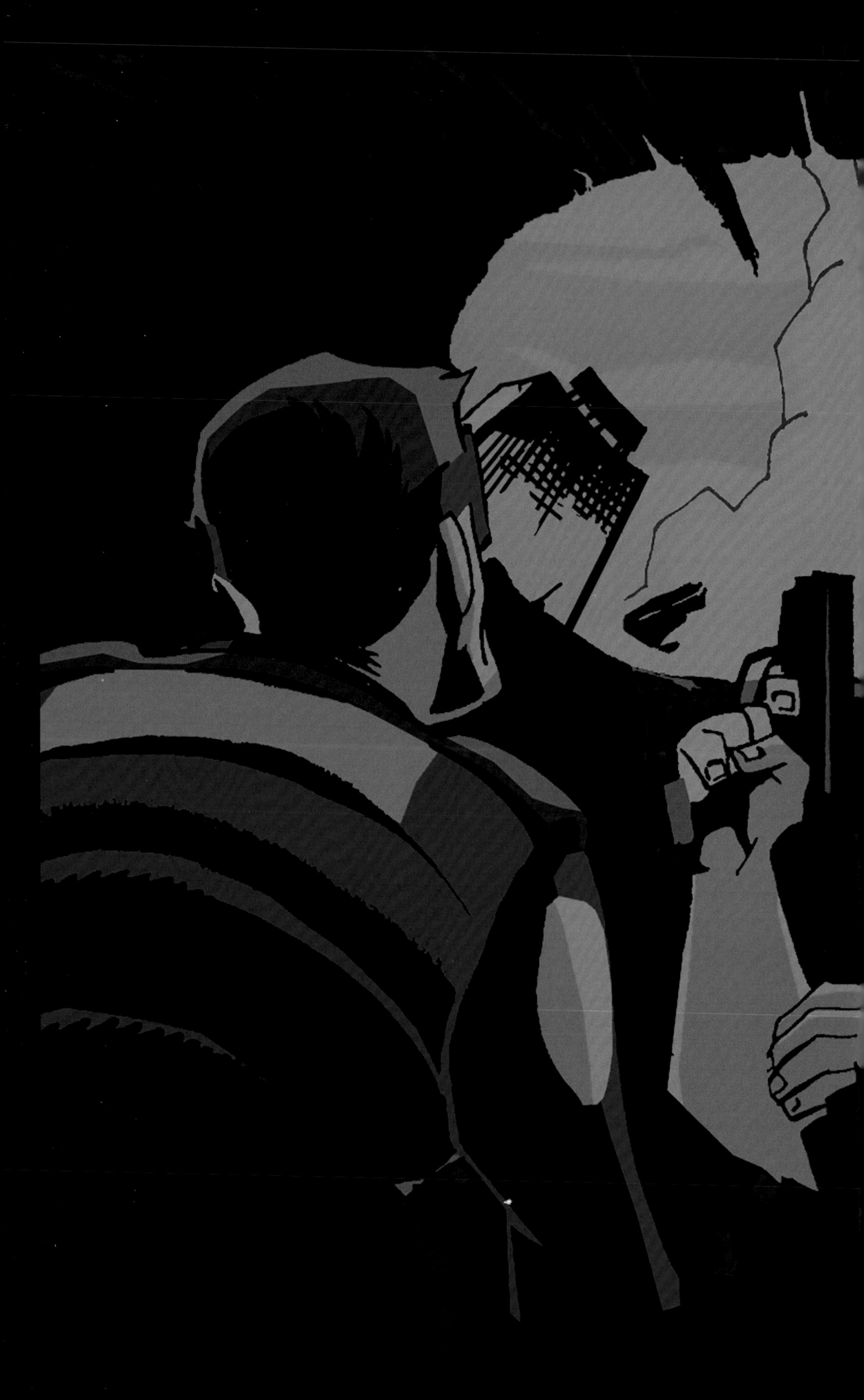

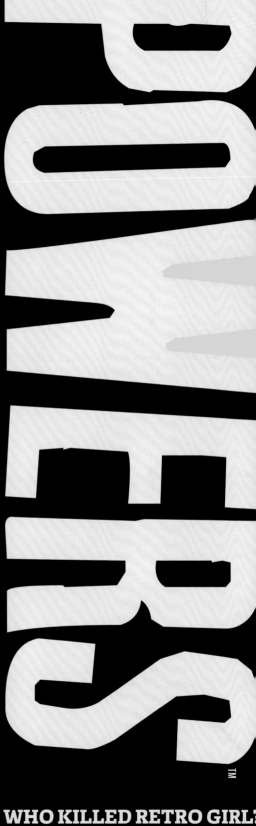

POWERS ™

WHO KILLED RETRO GIRL:
CHAPTER 1

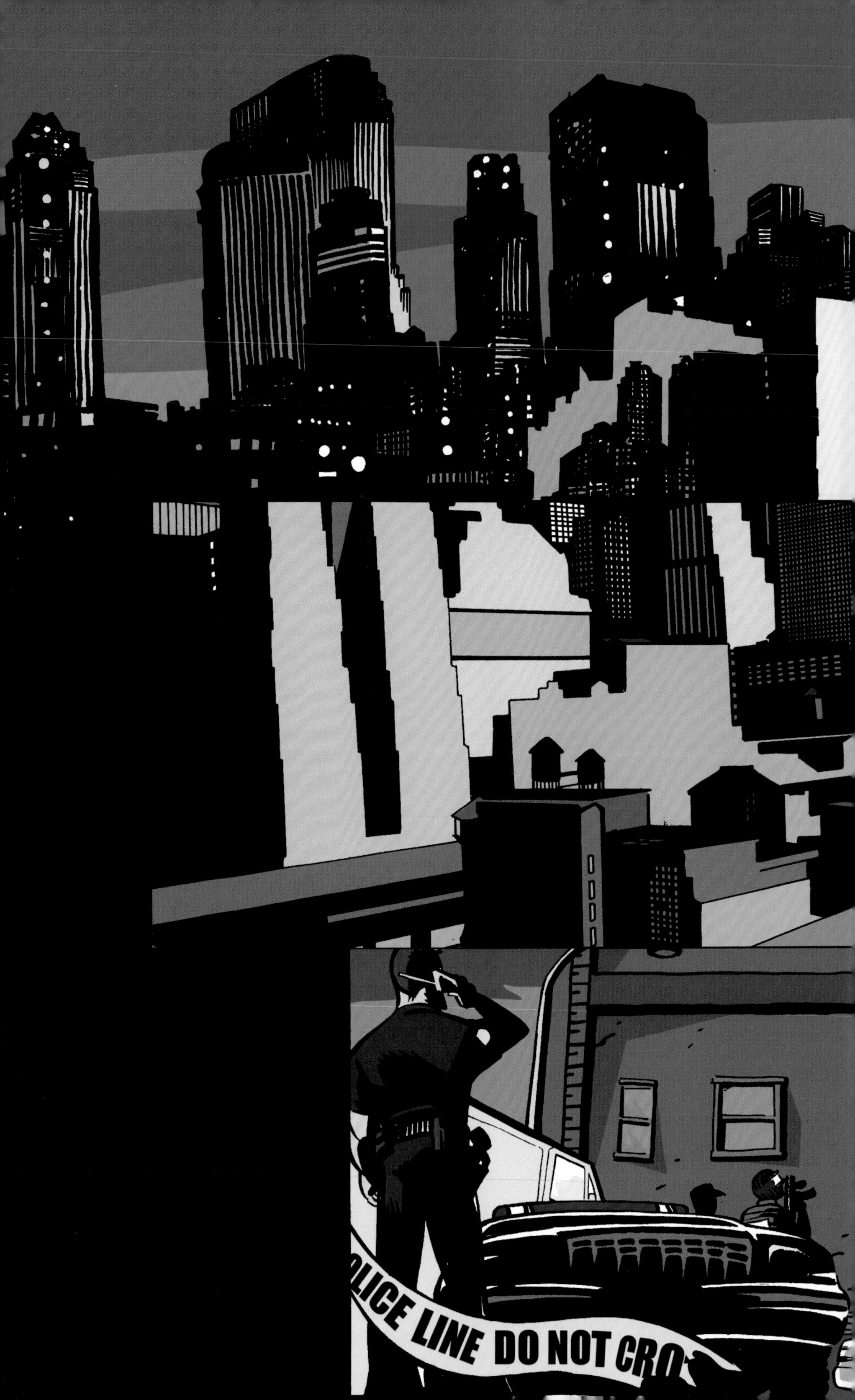
OLICE LINE DO NOT CRO

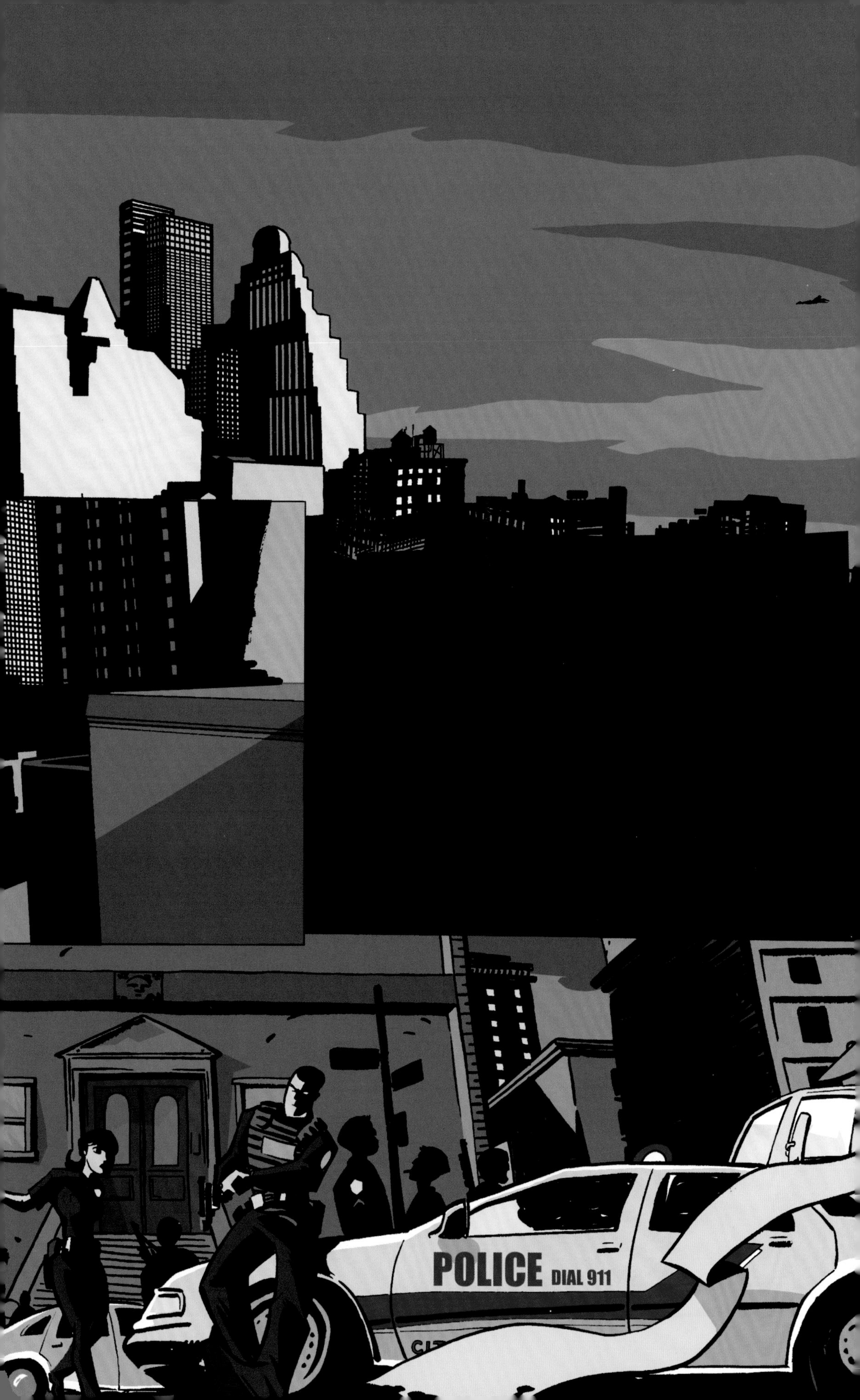
POLICE DIAL 911

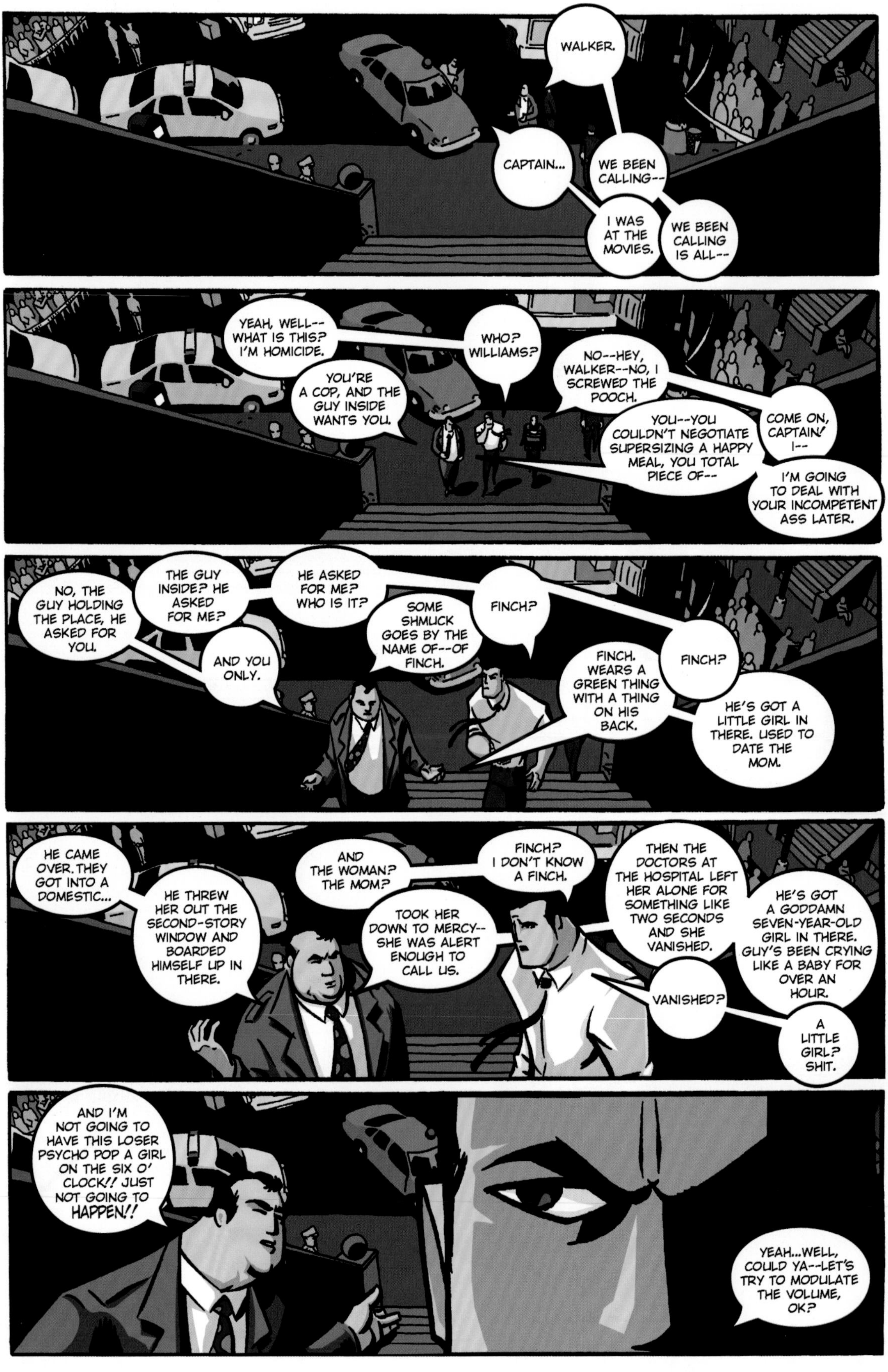
WALKER.
CAPTAIN...
WE BEEN CALLING--
I WAS AT THE MOVIES.
WE BEEN CALLING IS ALL--
YEAH, WELL-- WHAT IS THIS? I'M HOMICIDE.
YOU'RE A COP, AND THE GUY INSIDE WANTS YOU.
WHO? WILLIAMS?
NO--HEY, WALKER--NO, I SCREWED THE POOCH.
YOU--YOU COULDN'T NEGOTIATE SUPERSIZING A HAPPY MEAL, YOU TOTAL PIECE OF--
COME ON, CAPTAIN! I--
I'M GOING TO DEAL WITH YOUR INCOMPETENT ASS LATER.
NO, THE GUY HOLDING THE PLACE, HE ASKED FOR YOU.
THE GUY INSIDE? HE ASKED FOR ME?
AND YOU ONLY.
HE ASKED FOR ME? WHO IS IT?
SOME SHMUCK GOES BY THE NAME OF--OF FINCH.
FINCH?
FINCH. WEARS A GREEN THING WITH A THING ON HIS BACK.
FINCH?
HE'S GOT A LITTLE GIRL IN THERE. USED TO DATE THE MOM.
HE CAME OVER. THEY GOT INTO A DOMESTIC...
HE THREW HER OUT THE SECOND-STORY WINDOW AND BOARDED HIMSELF UP IN THERE.
AND THE WOMAN? THE MOM?
TOOK HER DOWN TO MERCY-- SHE WAS ALERT ENOUGH TO CALL US.
FINCH? I DON'T KNOW A FINCH.
THEN THE DOCTORS AT THE HOSPITAL LEFT HER ALONE FOR SOMETHING LIKE TWO SECONDS AND SHE VANISHED.
VANISHED?
HE'S GOT A GODDAMN SEVEN-YEAR-OLD GIRL IN THERE. GUY'S BEEN CRYING LIKE A BABY FOR OVER AN HOUR.
A LITTLE GIRL? SHIT.
AND I'M NOT GOING TO HAVE THIS LOSER PSYCHO POP A GIRL ON THE SIX O' CLOCK!! JUST NOT GOING TO HAPPEN!!
YEAH...WELL, COULD YA--LET'S TRY TO MODULATE THE VOLUME, OK?

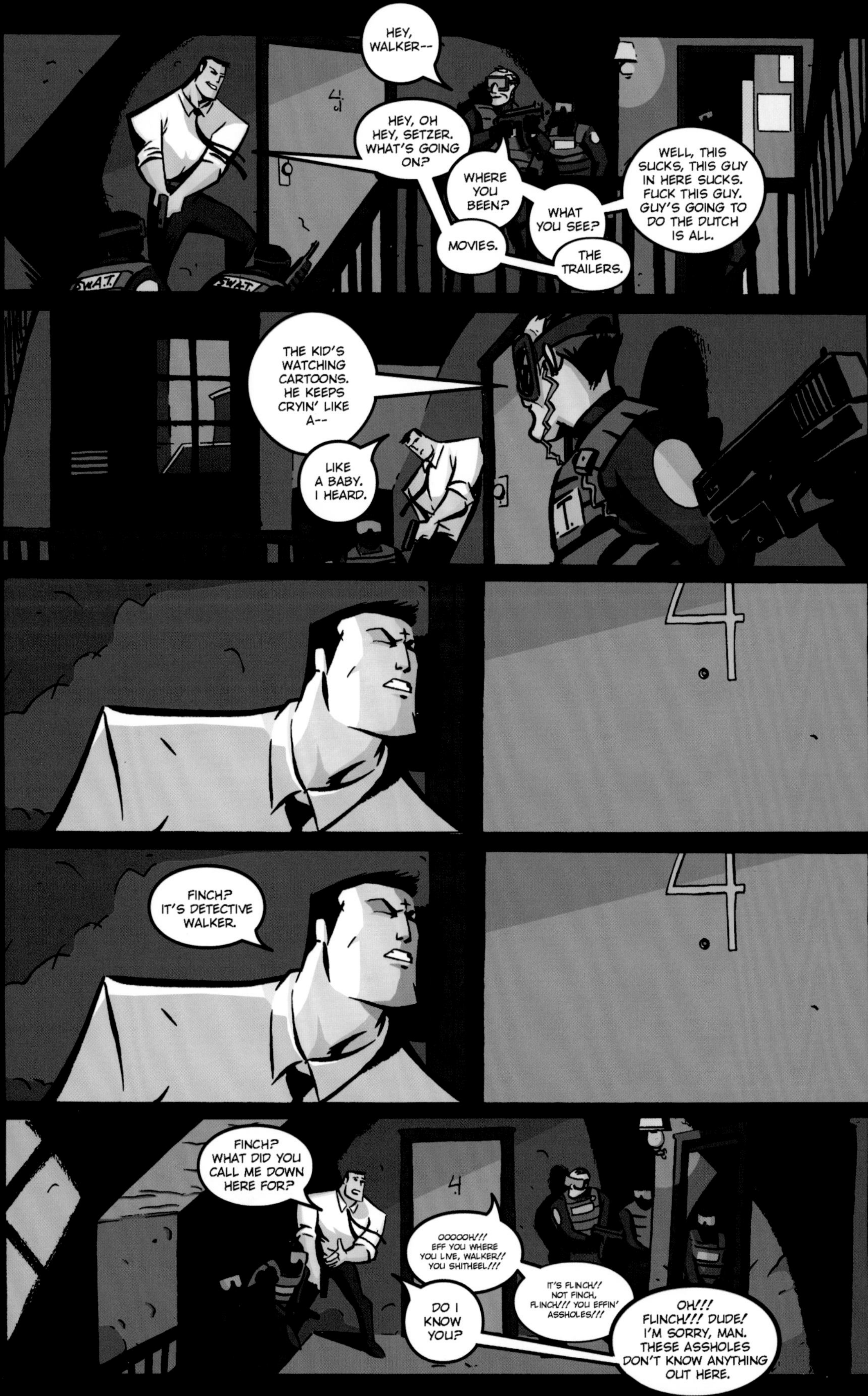
HEY, WALKER--
HEY, OH HEY, SETZER. WHAT'S GOING ON?
WHERE YOU BEEN?
MOVIES.
WHAT YOU SEE?
THE TRAILERS.
WELL, THIS SUCKS, THIS GUY IN HERE SUCKS. FUCK THIS GUY. GUY'S GOING TO DO THE DUTCH IS ALL.
S.W.A.T.
THE KID'S WATCHING CARTOONS. HE KEEPS CRYIN' LIKE A--
LIKE A BABY. I HEARD.
FINCH? IT'S DETECTIVE WALKER.
FINCH? WHAT DID YOU CALL ME DOWN HERE FOR?
OOOOOH!!! EFF YOU WHERE YOU LIVE, WALKER!! YOU SHITHEEL!!!
DO I KNOW YOU?
IT'S FLINCH!! NOT FINCH, FLINCH!!! YOU EFFIN' ASSHOLES!!!
OH!!! FLINCH!!! DUDE! I'M SORRY, MAN. THESE ASSHOLES DON'T KNOW ANYTHING OUT HERE.

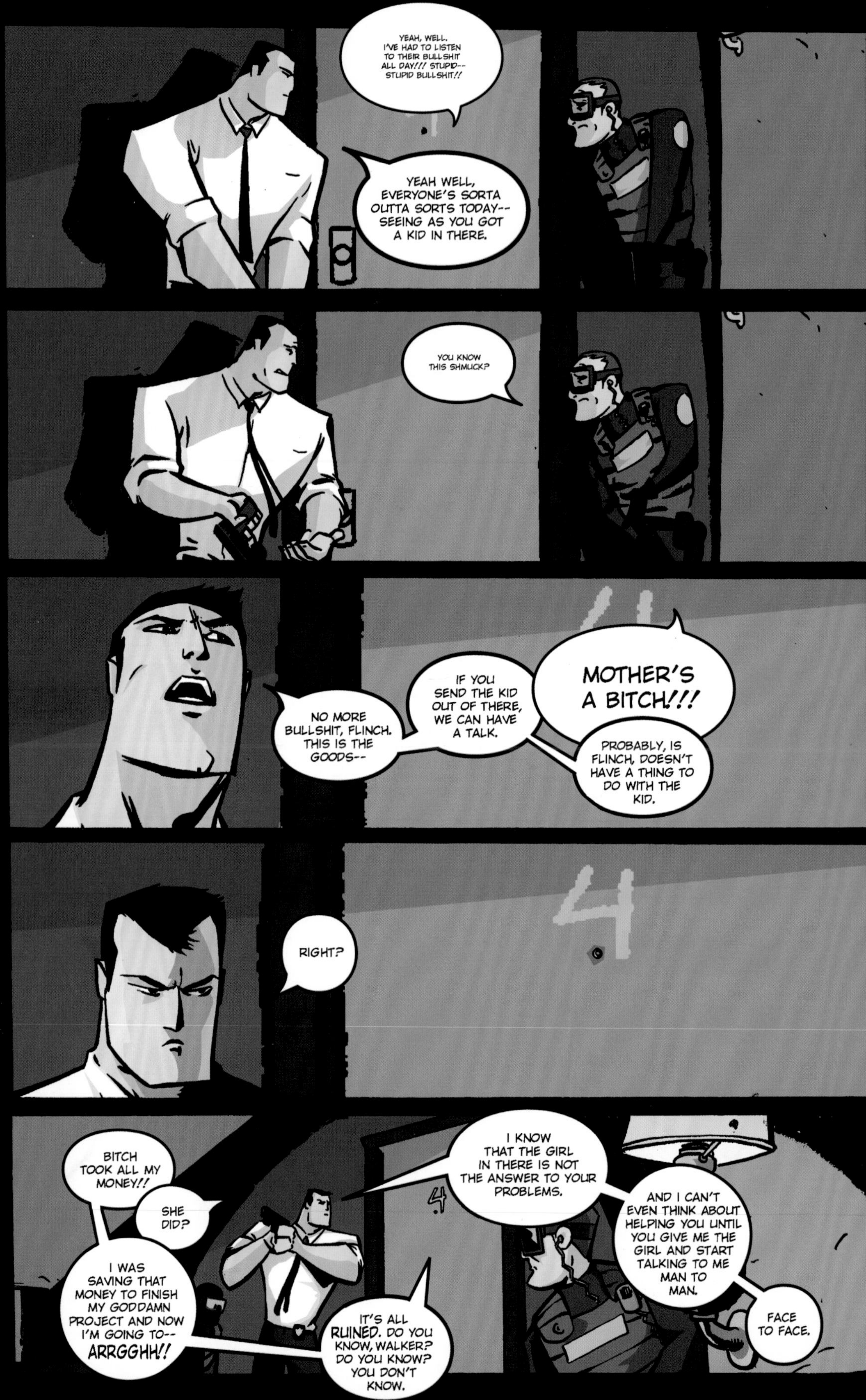

YEAH, WELL. I'VE HAD TO LISTEN TO THEIR BULLSHIT ALL DAY!!! STUPID-- STUPID BULLSHIT!!
YEAH WELL, EVERYONE'S SORTA OUTTA SORTS TODAY-- SEEING AS YOU GOT A KID IN THERE.
YOU KNOW THIS SHMUCK?
NO MORE BULLSHIT, FLINCH. THIS IS THE GOODS--
IF YOU SEND THE KID OUT OF THERE, WE CAN HAVE A TALK.
MOTHER'S A BITCH!!!
PROBABLY, IS FLINCH, DOESN'T HAVE A THING TO DO WITH THE KID.
RIGHT?
BITCH TOOK ALL MY MONEY!!
SHE DID?
I WAS SAVING THAT MONEY TO FINISH MY GODDAMN PROJECT AND NOW I'M GOING TO-- ARRGGHH!!
IT'S ALL RUINED. DO YOU KNOW, WALKER? DO YOU KNOW? YOU DON'T KNOW.
I KNOW THAT THE GIRL IN THERE IS NOT THE ANSWER TO YOUR PROBLEMS.
AND I CAN'T EVEN THINK ABOUT HELPING YOU UNTIL YOU GIVE ME THE GIRL AND START TALKING TO ME MAN TO MAN.
FACE TO FACE.

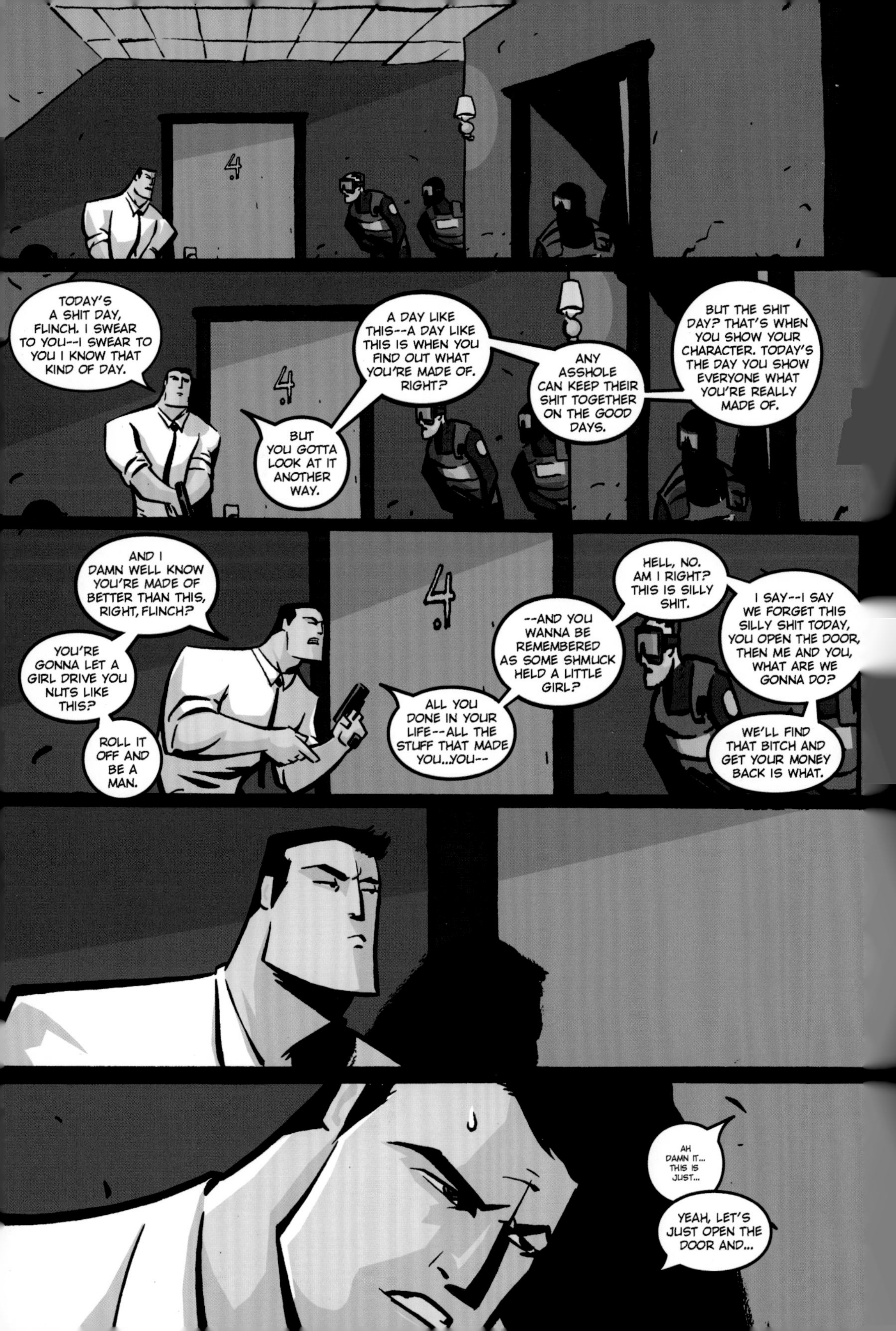
TODAY'S A SHIT DAY, FLINCH. I SWEAR TO YOU--I SWEAR TO YOU I KNOW THAT KIND OF DAY.
A DAY LIKE THIS--A DAY LIKE THIS IS WHEN YOU FIND OUT WHAT YOU'RE MADE OF. RIGHT?
BUT YOU GOTTA LOOK AT IT ANOTHER WAY.
ANY ASSHOLE CAN KEEP THEIR SHIT TOGETHER ON THE GOOD DAYS.
BUT THE SHIT DAY? THAT'S WHEN YOU SHOW YOUR CHARACTER. TODAY'S THE DAY YOU SHOW EVERYONE WHAT YOU'RE REALLY MADE OF.
AND I DAMN WELL KNOW YOU'RE MADE OF BETTER THAN THIS, RIGHT, FLINCH?
YOU'RE GONNA LET A GIRL DRIVE YOU NUTS LIKE THIS?
ROLL IT OFF AND BE A MAN.
ALL YOU DONE IN YOUR LIFE--ALL THE STUFF THAT MADE YOU...YOU--
--AND YOU WANNA BE REMEMBERED AS SOME SHMUCK HELD A LITTLE GIRL?
HELL, NO. AM I RIGHT? THIS IS SILLY SHIT.
I SAY--I SAY WE FORGET THIS SILLY SHIT TODAY, YOU OPEN THE DOOR, THEN ME AND YOU, WHAT ARE WE GONNA DO?
WE'LL FIND THAT BITCH AND GET YOUR MONEY BACK IS WHAT.
AH DAMN IT... THIS IS JUST...
YEAH, LET'S JUST OPEN THE DOOR AND...

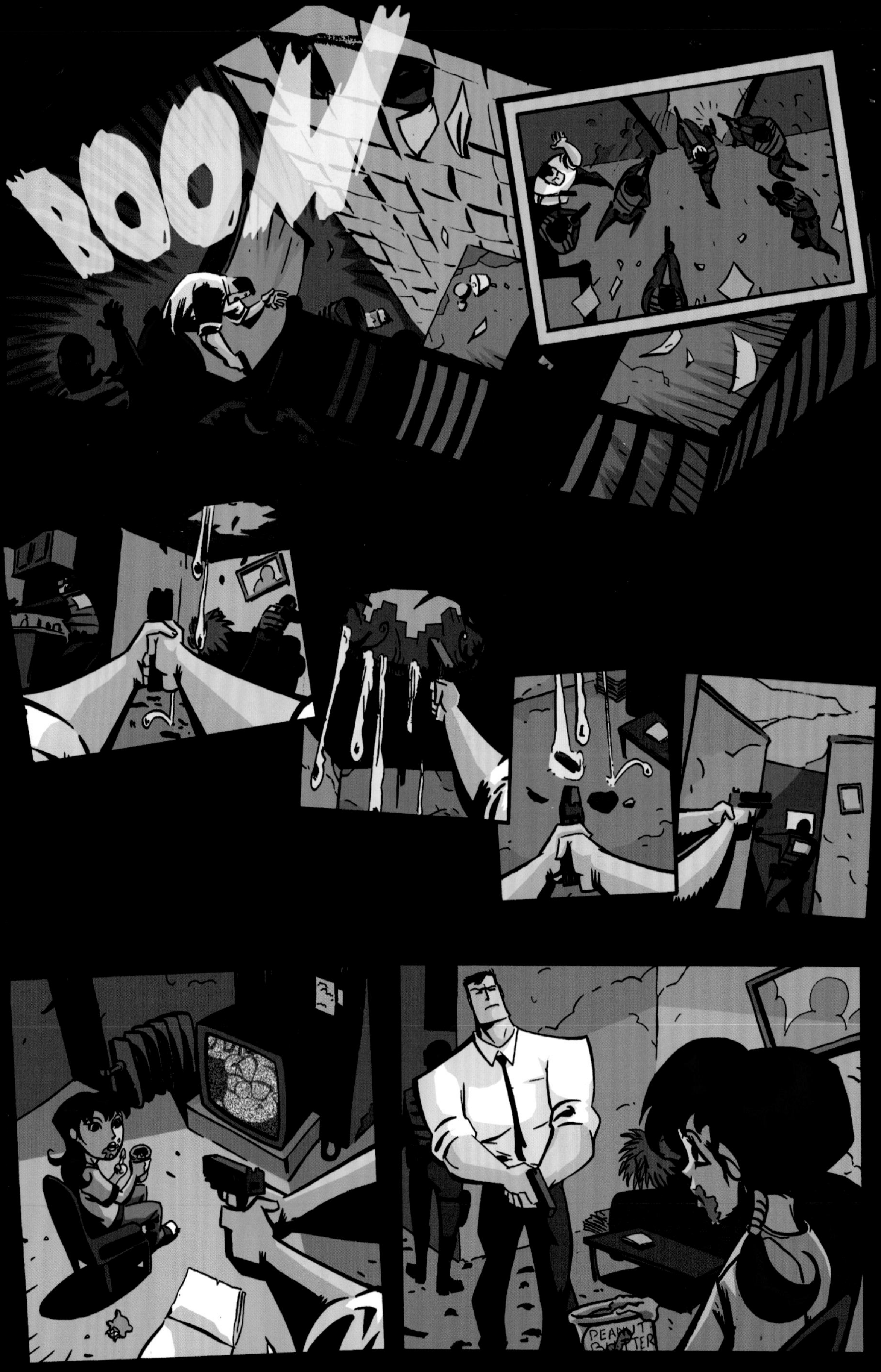
BOOM
PEANUT BUTTER

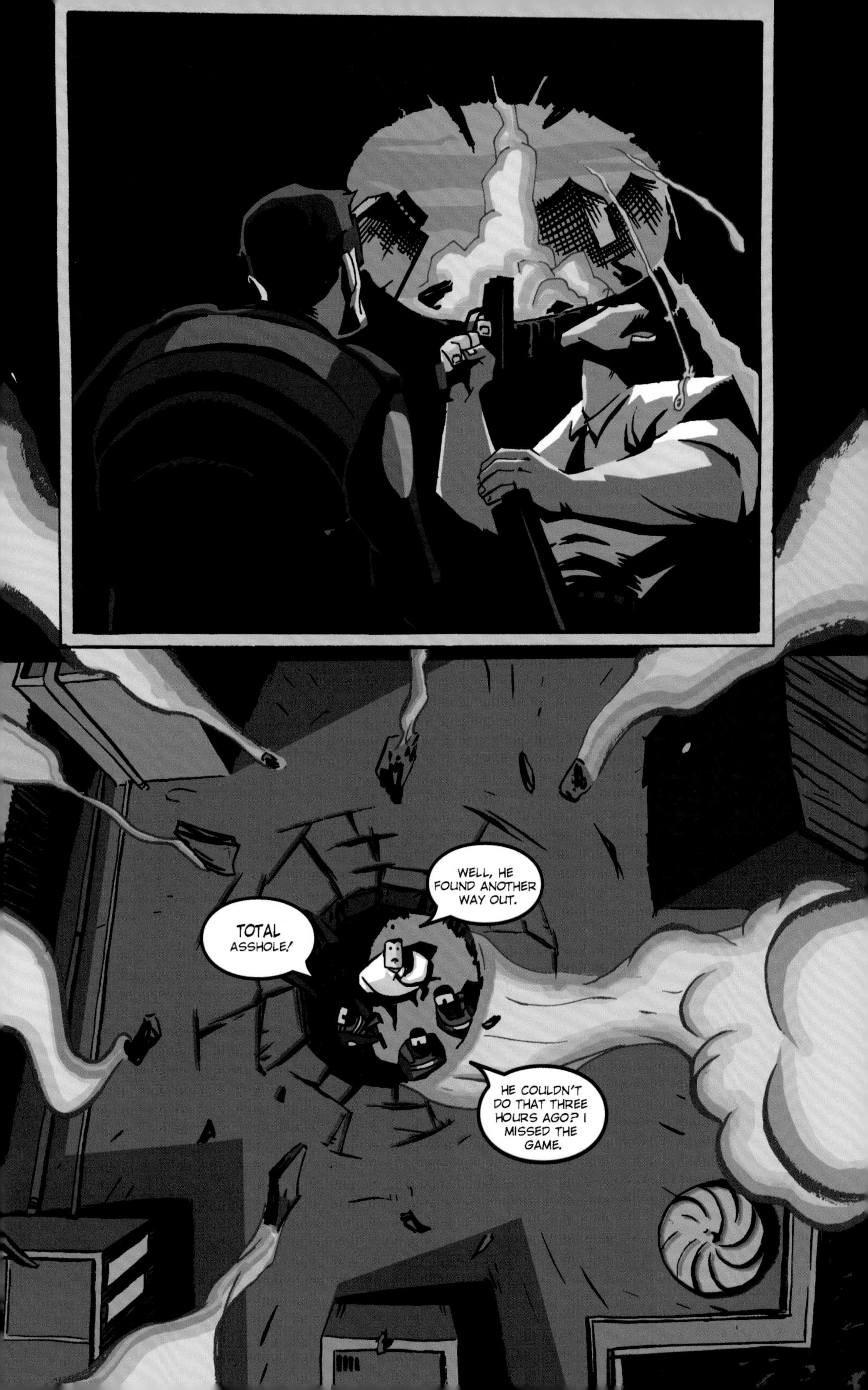
WELL, HE FOUND ANOTHER WAY OUT.
TOTAL ASSHOLE!
HE COULDN'T DO THAT THREE HOURS AGO? I MISSED THE GAME.

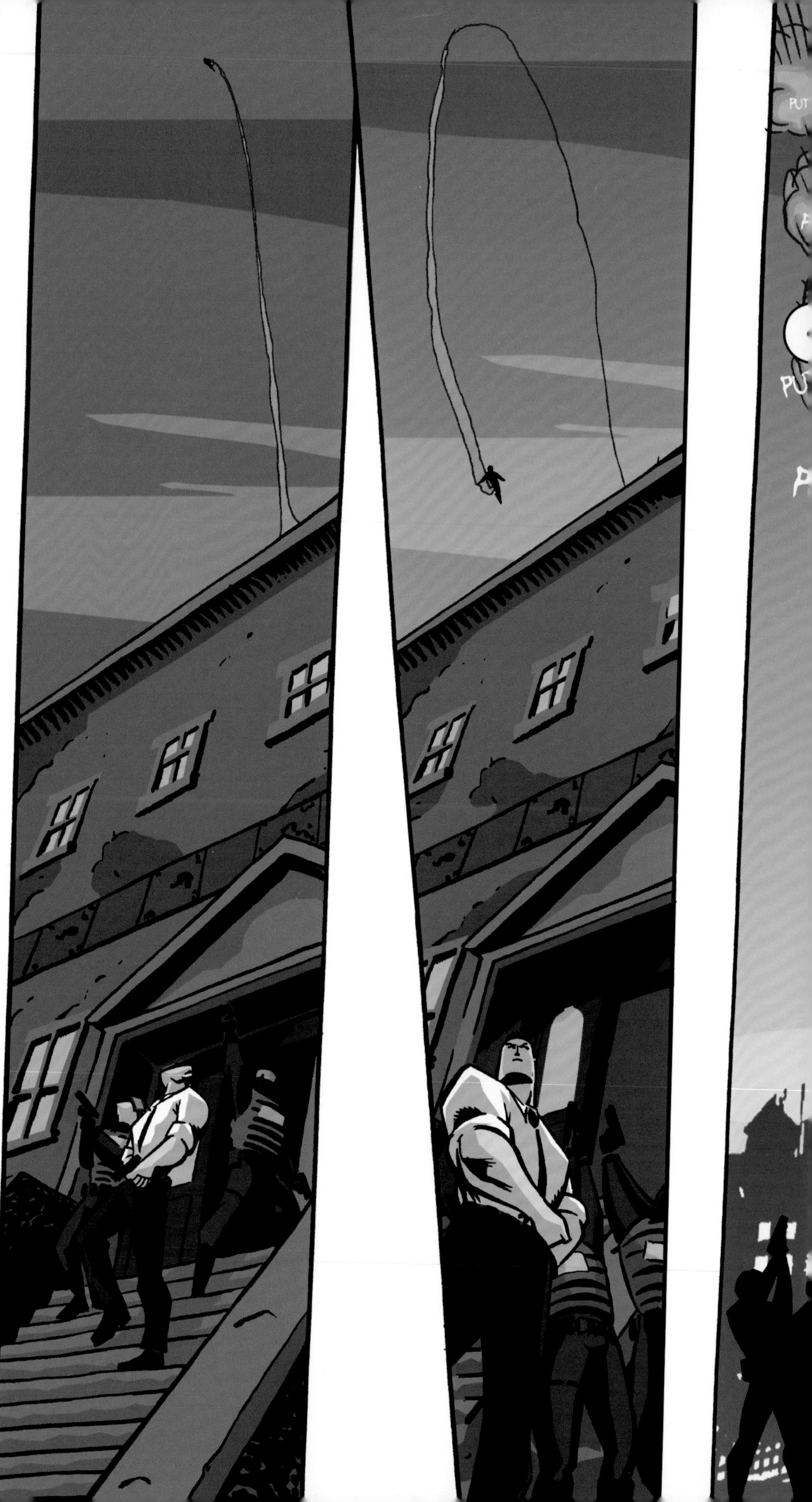
PUT

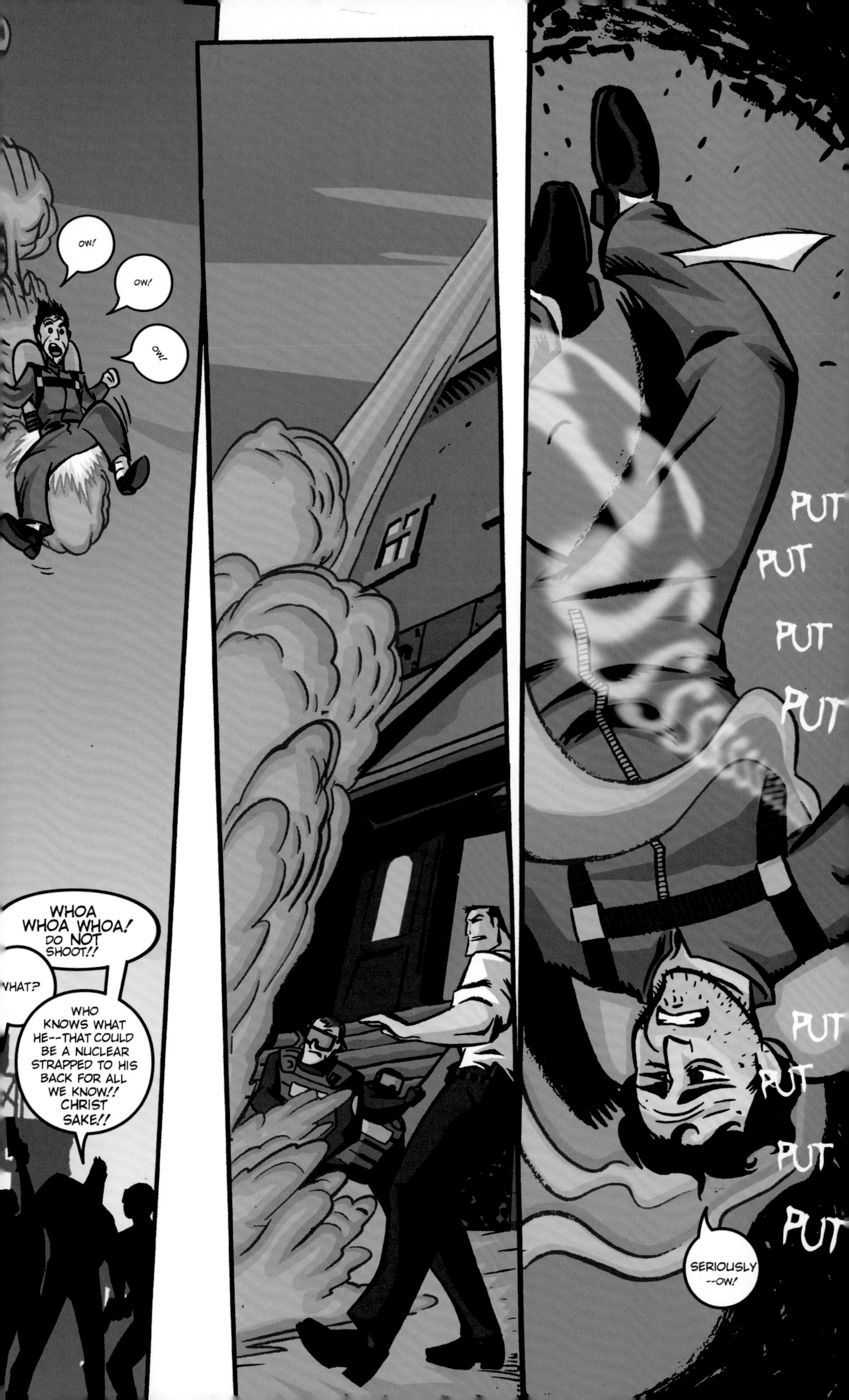
OW!
OW!
OW!
WHOA WHOA WHOA! DO NOT SHOOT!!
WHAT?
WHO KNOWS WHAT HE--THAT COULD BE A NUCLEAR STRAPPED TO HIS BACK FOR ALL WE KNOW!! CHRIST SAKE!!
PUT
PUT
PUT
PUT
PUT
PUT
PUT
PUT
SERIOUSLY --OW!

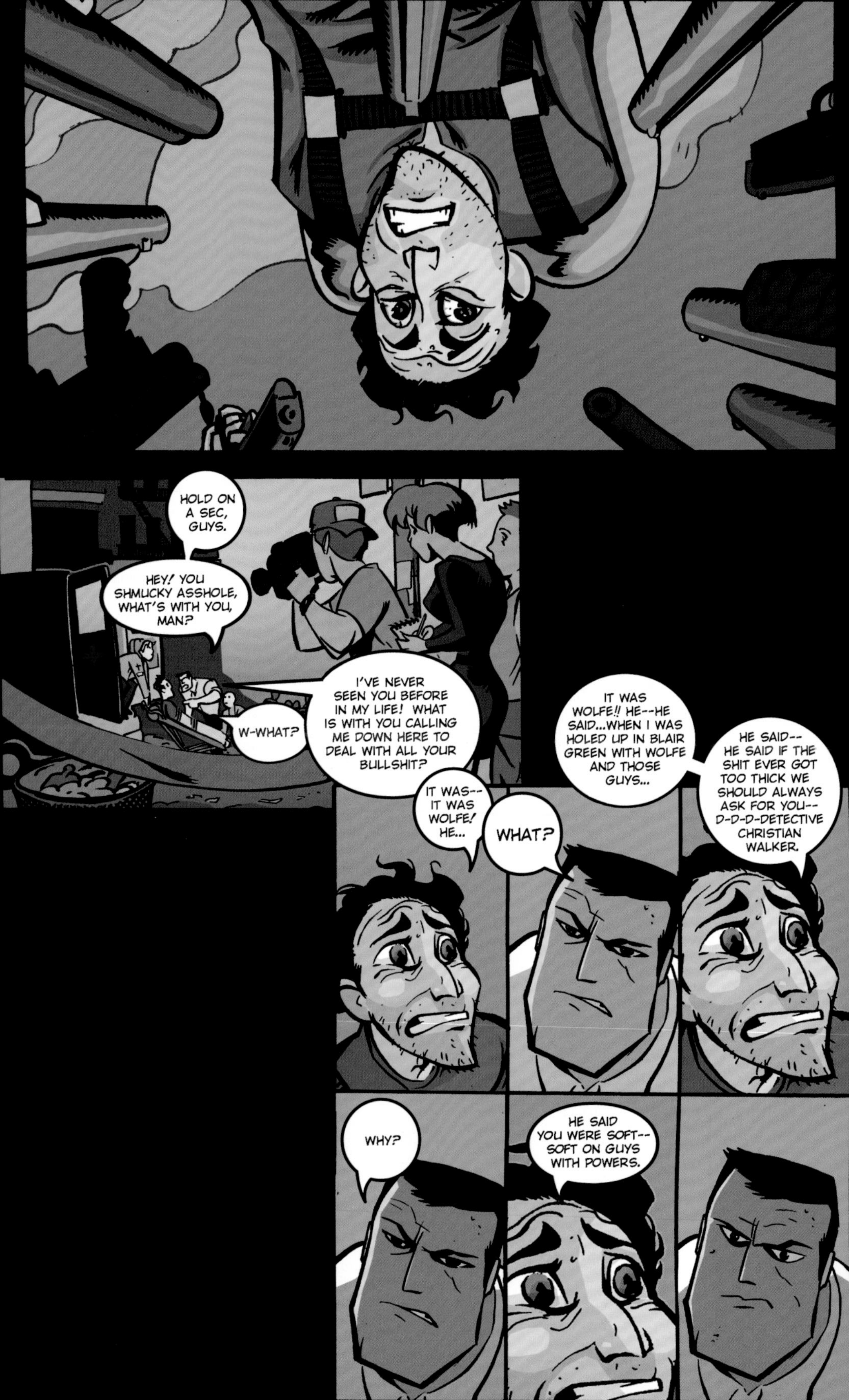
HOLD ON A SEC, GUYS.
HEY! YOU SHMUCKY ASSHOLE, WHAT'S WITH YOU, MAN?
I'VE NEVER SEEN YOU BEFORE IN MY LIFE! WHAT IS WITH YOU CALLING ME DOWN HERE TO DEAL WITH ALL YOUR BULLSHIT?
W-WHAT?
IT WAS-- IT WAS WOLFE! HE...
WHAT?
IT WAS WOLFE!! HE--HE SAID...WHEN I WAS HOLED UP IN BLAIR GREEN WITH WOLFE AND THOSE GUYS...
HE SAID-- HE SAID IF THE SHIT EVER GOT TOO THICK WE SHOULD ALWAYS ASK FOR YOU-- D-D-D-DETECTIVE CHRISTIAN WALKER.
WHY?
HE SAID YOU WERE SOFT-- SOFT ON GUYS WITH POWERS.

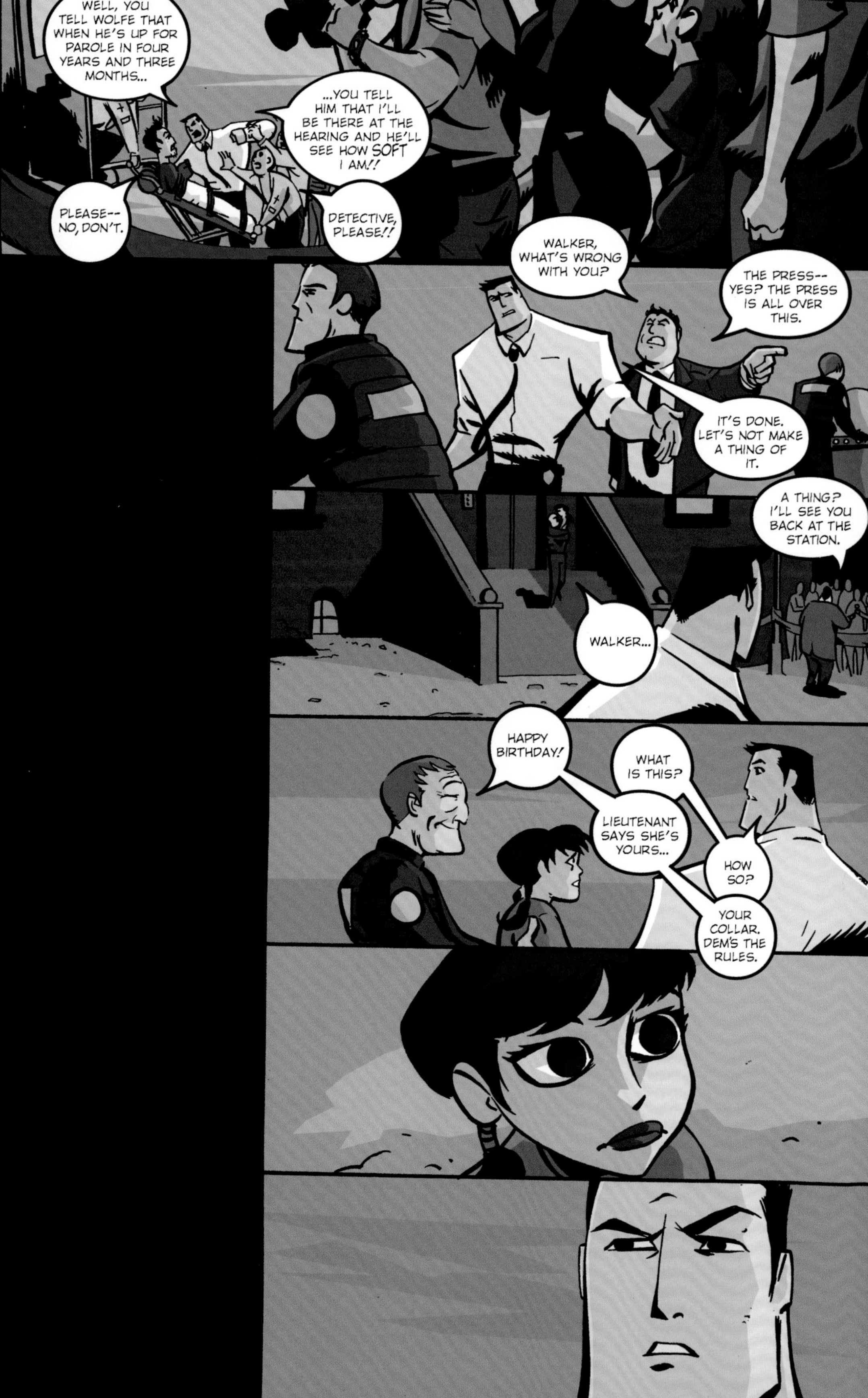
WELL, YOU TELL WOLFE THAT WHEN HE'S UP FOR PAROLE IN FOUR YEARS AND THREE MONTHS...
...YOU TELL HIM THAT I'LL BE THERE AT THE HEARING AND HE'LL SEE HOW SOFT I AM!!
PLEASE-- NO, DON'T.
DETECTIVE, PLEASE!!
WALKER, WHAT'S WRONG WITH YOU?
THE PRESS-- YES? THE PRESS IS ALL OVER THIS.
IT'S DONE. LET'S NOT MAKE A THING OF IT.
A THING? I'LL SEE YOU BACK AT THE STATION.
WALKER...
HAPPY BIRTHDAY!
WHAT IS THIS?
LIEUTENANT SAYS SHE'S YOURS...
HOW SO?
YOUR COLLAR. DEM'S THE RULES.

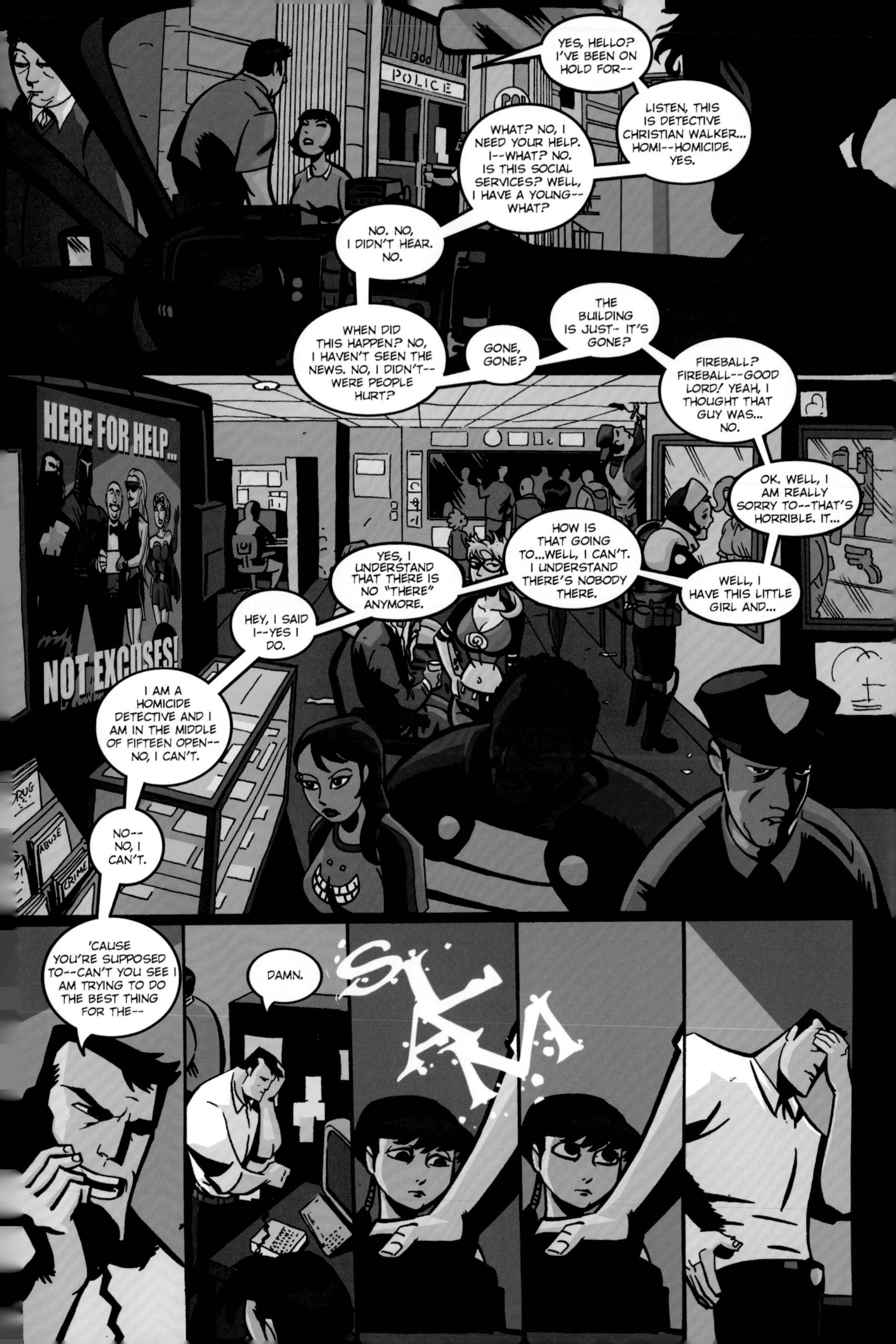

POLICE
YES, HELLO? I'VE BEEN ON HOLD FOR--
LISTEN, THIS IS DETECTIVE CHRISTIAN WALKER... HOMI--HOMICIDE. YES.
WHAT? NO, I NEED YOUR HELP. I--WHAT? NO. IS THIS SOCIAL SERVICES? WELL, I HAVE A YOUNG-- WHAT?
NO. NO, I DIDN'T HEAR. NO.
WHEN DID THIS HAPPEN? NO, I HAVEN'T SEEN THE NEWS. NO, I DIDN'T-- WERE PEOPLE HURT?
GONE, GONE?
THE BUILDING IS JUST-- IT'S GONE?
FIREBALL? FIREBALL--GOOD LORD! YEAH, I THOUGHT THAT GUY WAS... NO.
HERE FOR HELP... NOT EXCUSES!
OK. WELL, I AM REALLY SORRY TO--THAT'S HORRIBLE. IT...
WELL, I HAVE THIS LITTLE GIRL AND...
HOW IS THAT GOING TO...WELL, I CAN'T. I UNDERSTAND THERE'S NOBODY THERE.
YES, I UNDERSTAND THAT THERE IS NO "THERE" ANYMORE.
HEY, I SAID I--YES I DO.
I AM A HOMICIDE DETECTIVE AND I AM IN THE MIDDLE OF FIFTEEN OPEN-- NO, I CAN'T.
DRUG
ABUSE
CRIME
NO-- NO, I CAN'T.
'CAUSE YOU'RE SUPPOSED TO--CAN'T YOU SEE I AM TRYING TO DO THE BEST THING FOR THE--
DAMN.
SLAM

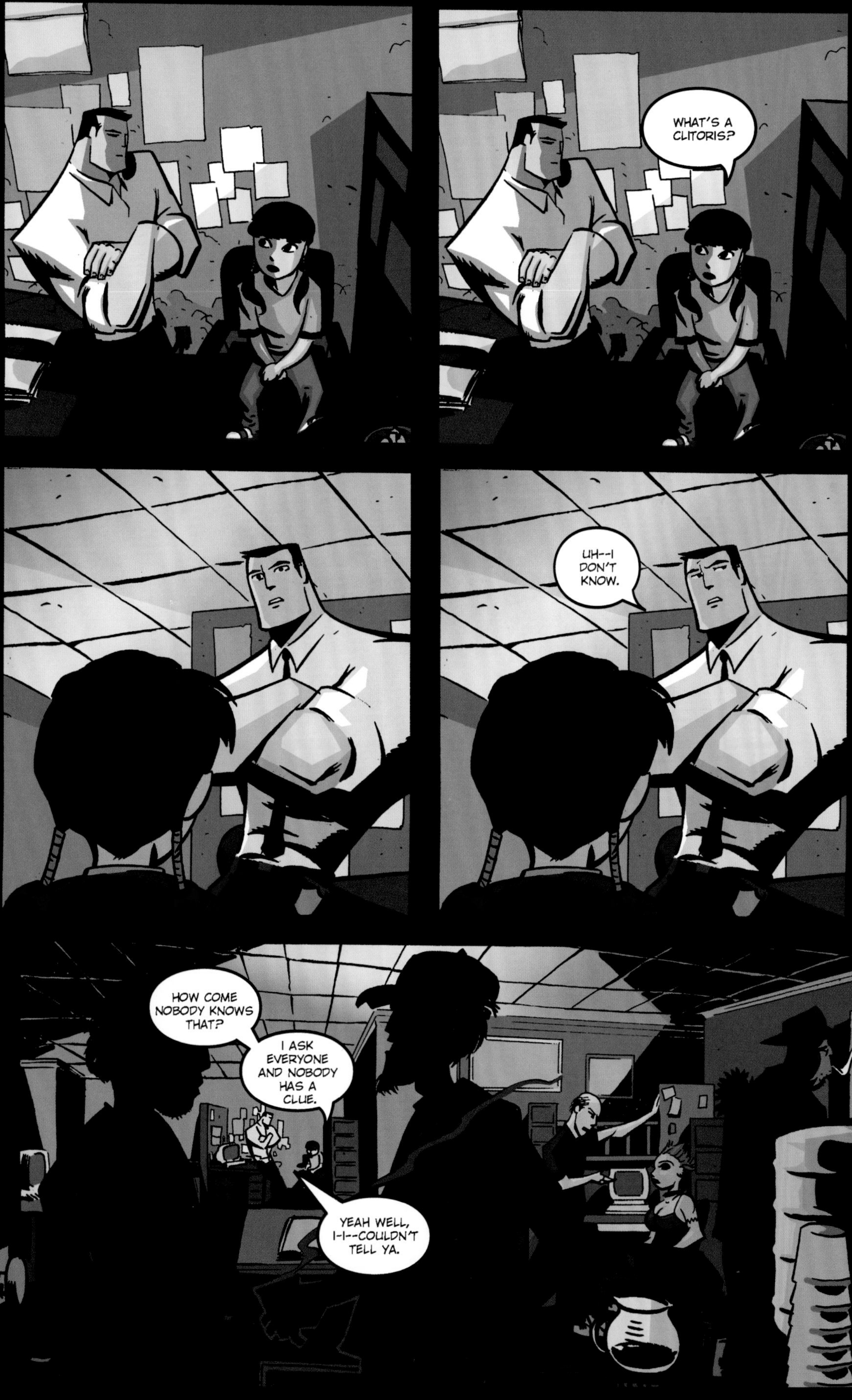
WHAT'S A CLITORIS?
UH--I DON'T KNOW.
HOW COME NOBODY KNOWS THAT?
I ASK EVERYONE AND NOBODY HAS A CLUE.
YEAH WELL, I-I--COULDN'T TELL YA.

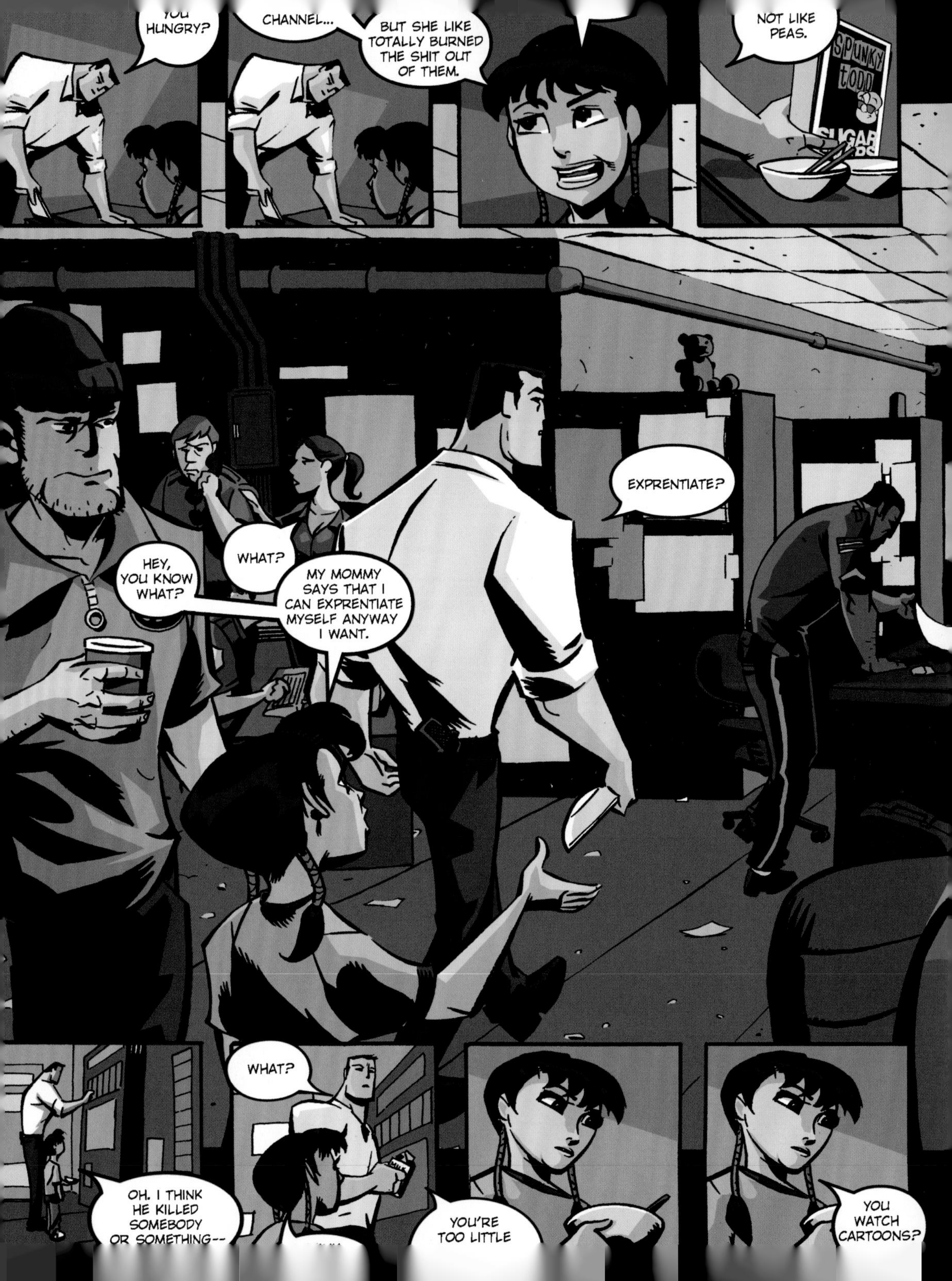
HUNGRY?
CHANNEL...
BUT SHE LIKE TOTALLY BURNED THE SHIT OUT OF THEM.
NOT LIKE PEAS.
SPUNKY todd
SUGAR
HEY, YOU KNOW WHAT?
WHAT?
MY MOMMY SAYS THAT I CAN EXPRENTIATE MYSELF ANYWAY I WANT.
EXPRENTIATE?
WHAT?
OH. I THINK HE KILLED SOMEBODY OR SOMETHING--
YOU'RE TOO LITTLE
YOU WATCH CARTOONS?

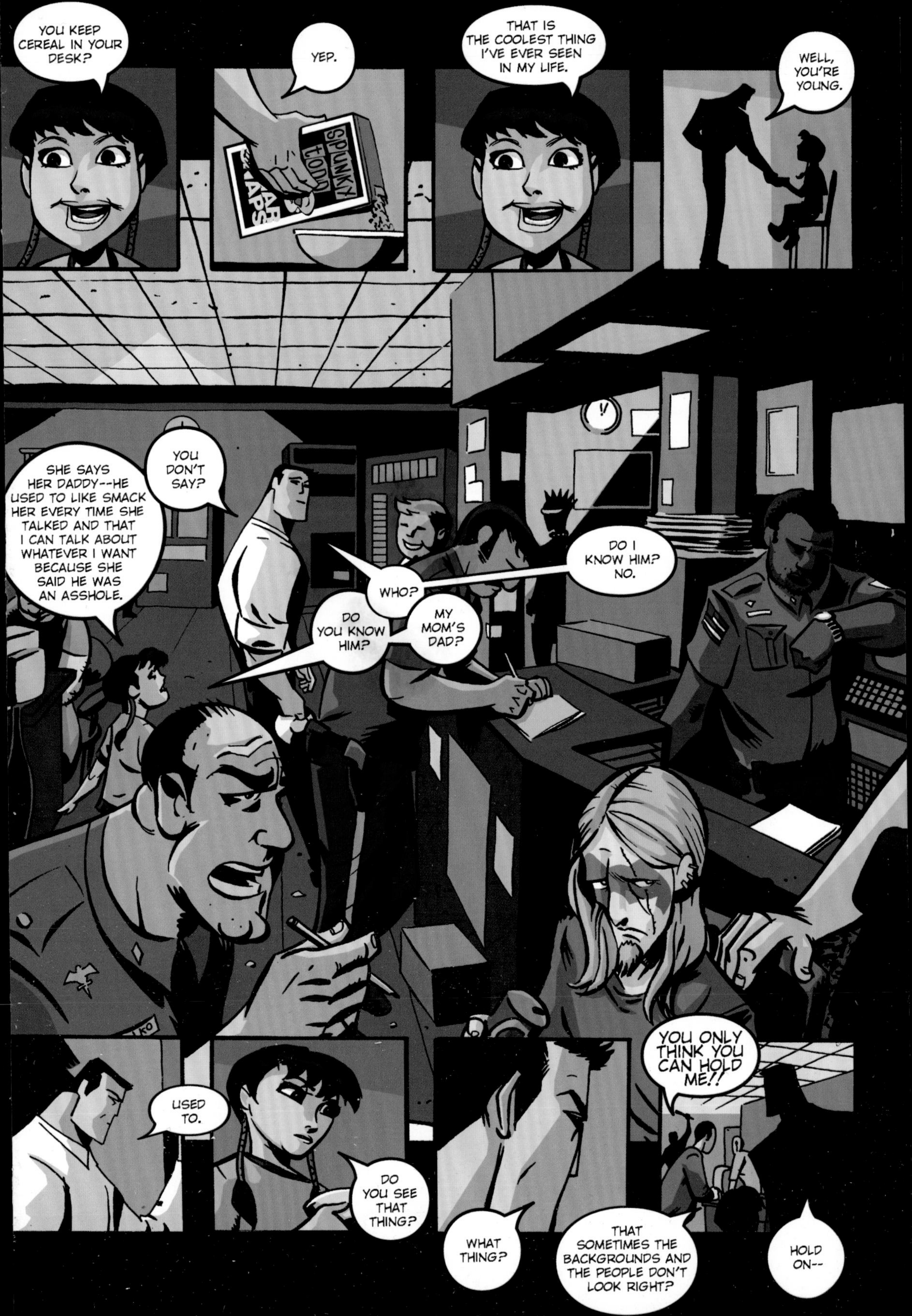
YOU KEEP CEREAL IN YOUR DESK?
YEP.
SPUNKY TODD STAR SNAPS
THAT IS THE COOLEST THING I'VE EVER SEEN IN MY LIFE.
WELL, YOU'RE YOUNG.
SHE SAYS HER DADDY--HE USED TO LIKE SMACK HER EVERY TIME SHE TALKED AND THAT I CAN TALK ABOUT WHATEVER I WANT BECAUSE SHE SAID HE WAS AN ASSHOLE.
YOU DON'T SAY?
WHO?
MY MOM'S DAD?
DO YOU KNOW HIM?
DO I KNOW HIM? NO.
USED TO.
DO YOU SEE THAT THING?
WHAT THING?
THAT SOMETIMES THE BACKGROUNDS AND THE PEOPLE DON'T LOOK RIGHT?
YOU ONLY THINK YOU CAN HOLD ME!!
HOLD ON--

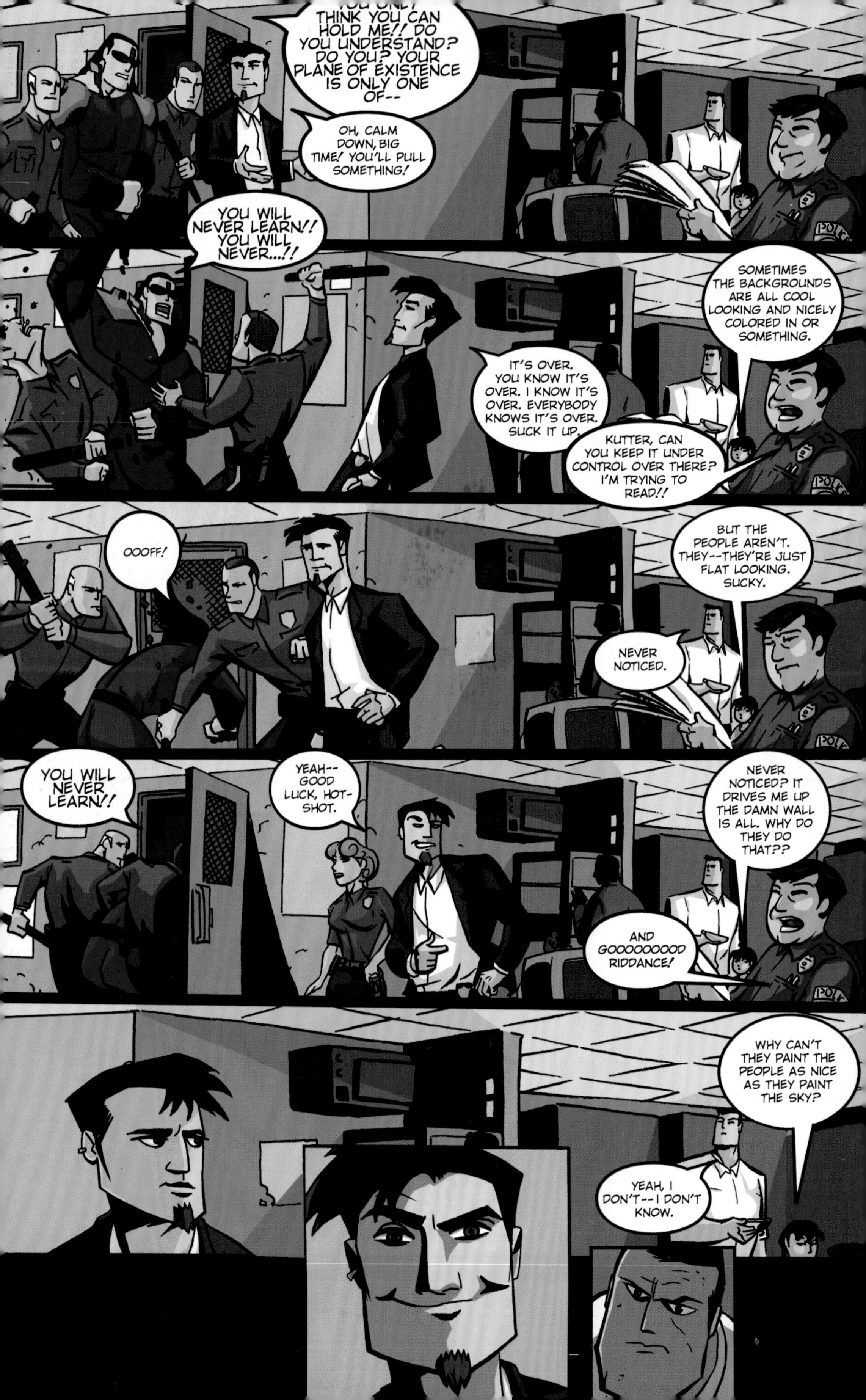

THINK YOU CAN HOLD ME!! DO YOU UNDERSTAND? DO YOU? YOUR PLANE OF EXISTENCE IS ONLY ONE OF--
OH, CALM DOWN, BIG TIME! YOU'LL PULL SOMETHING!
YOU WILL NEVER LEARN!! YOU WILL NEVER...!!
SOMETIMES THE BACKGROUNDS ARE ALL COOL LOOKING AND NICELY COLORED IN OR SOMETHING.
IT'S OVER. YOU KNOW IT'S OVER. I KNOW IT'S OVER. EVERYBODY KNOWS IT'S OVER. SUCK IT UP.
KUTTER, CAN YOU KEEP IT UNDER CONTROL OVER THERE? I'M TRYING TO READ!!
OOOFF!
BUT THE PEOPLE AREN'T. THEY--THEY'RE JUST FLAT LOOKING. SUCKY.
NEVER NOTICED.
YOU WILL NEVER LEARN!!
YEAH--GOOD LUCK, HOT-SHOT.
NEVER NOTICED? IT DRIVES ME UP THE DAMN WALL IS ALL. WHY DO THEY DO THAT??
AND GOOOOOOOOD RIDDANCE!
WHY CAN'T THEY PAINT THE PEOPLE AS NICE AS THEY PAINT THE SKY?
YEAH, I DON'T--I DON'T KNOW.

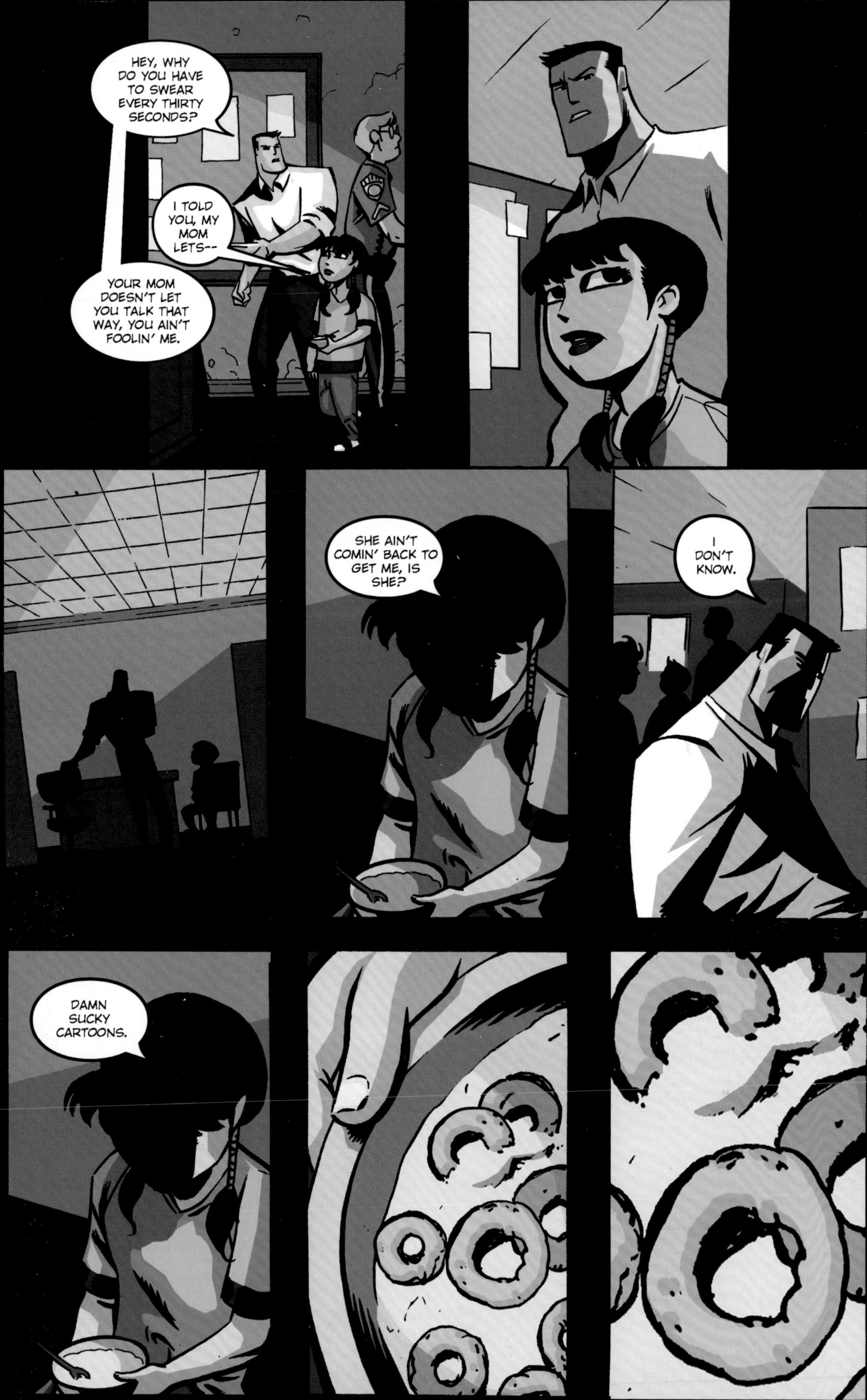
HEY, WHY DO YOU HAVE TO SWEAR EVERY THIRTY SECONDS?
I TOLD YOU, MY MOM LETS--
YOUR MOM DOESN'T LET YOU TALK THAT WAY, YOU AIN'T FOOLIN' ME.
SHE AIN'T COMIN' BACK TO GET ME, IS SHE?
I DON'T KNOW.
DAMN SUCKY CARTOONS.

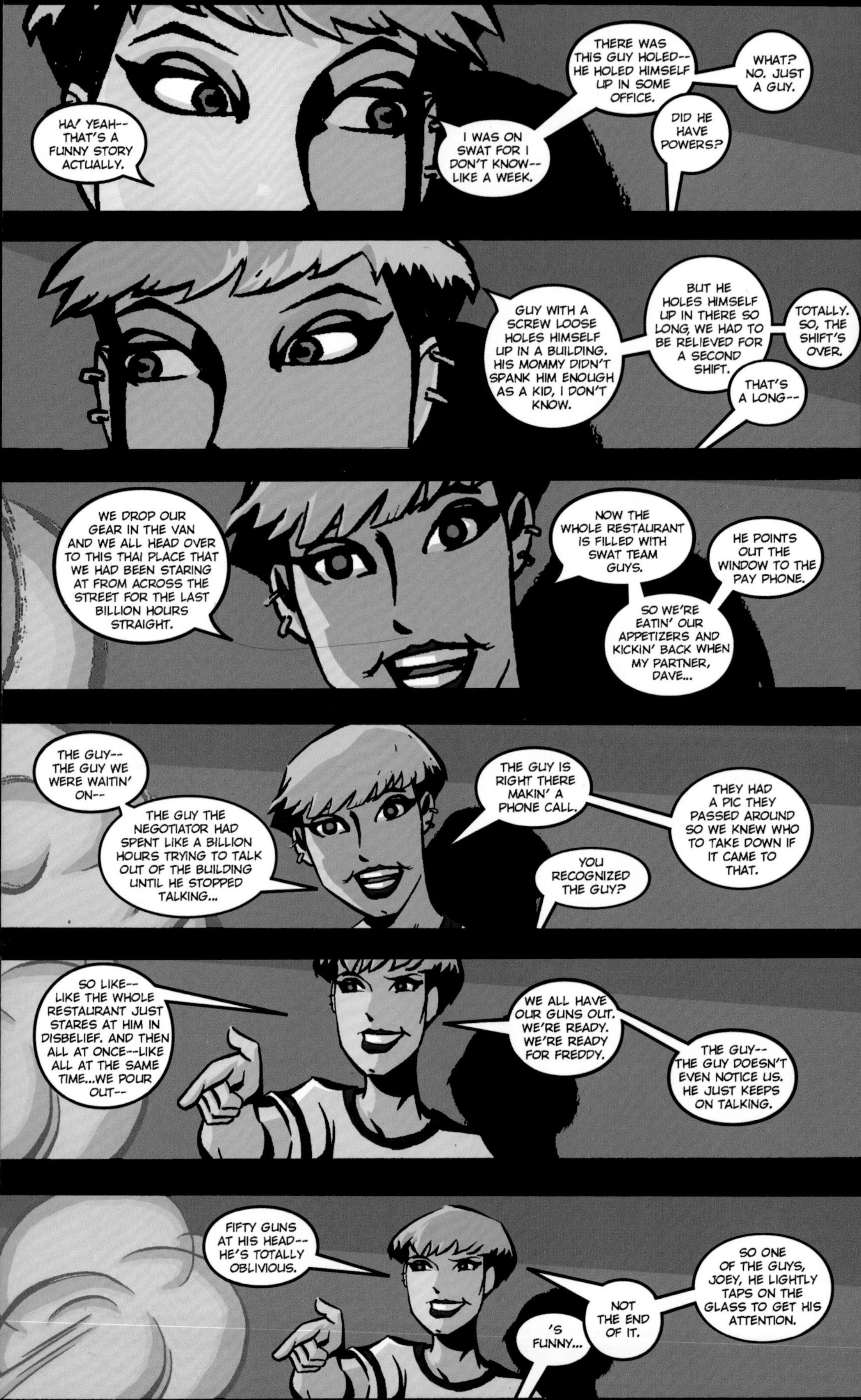
HA! YEAH--THAT'S A FUNNY STORY ACTUALLY.
I WAS ON SWAT FOR I DON'T KNOW--LIKE A WEEK.
THERE WAS THIS GUY HOLED--HE HOLED HIMSELF UP IN SOME OFFICE.
DID HE HAVE POWERS?
WHAT? NO. JUST A GUY.
GUY WITH A SCREW LOOSE HOLES HIMSELF UP IN A BUILDING. HIS MOMMY DIDN'T SPANK HIM ENOUGH AS A KID, I DON'T KNOW.
BUT HE HOLES HIMSELF UP IN THERE SO LONG, WE HAD TO BE RELIEVED FOR A SECOND SHIFT.
THAT'S A LONG--
TOTALLY. SO, THE SHIFT'S OVER.
WE DROP OUR GEAR IN THE VAN AND WE ALL HEAD OVER TO THIS THAI PLACE THAT WE HAD BEEN STARING AT FROM ACROSS THE STREET FOR THE LAST BILLION HOURS STRAIGHT.
NOW THE WHOLE RESTAURANT IS FILLED WITH SWAT TEAM GUYS.
SO WE'RE EATIN' OUR APPETIZERS AND KICKIN' BACK WHEN MY PARTNER, DAVE...
HE POINTS OUT THE WINDOW TO THE PAY PHONE.
THE GUY--THE GUY WE WERE WAITIN' ON--
THE GUY THE NEGOTIATOR HAD SPENT LIKE A BILLION HOURS TRYING TO TALK OUT OF THE BUILDING UNTIL HE STOPPED TALKING...
THE GUY IS RIGHT THERE MAKIN' A PHONE CALL.
YOU RECOGNIZED THE GUY?
THEY HAD A PIC THEY PASSED AROUND SO WE KNEW WHO TO TAKE DOWN IF IT CAME TO THAT.
SO LIKE--LIKE THE WHOLE RESTAURANT JUST STARES AT HIM IN DISBELIEF. AND THEN ALL AT ONCE--LIKE ALL AT THE SAME TIME...WE POUR OUT--
WE ALL HAVE OUR GUNS OUT. WE'RE READY. WE'RE READY FOR FREDDY.
THE GUY--THE GUY DOESN'T EVEN NOTICE US. HE JUST KEEPS ON TALKING.
FIFTY GUNS AT HIS HEAD--HE'S TOTALLY OBLIVIOUS.
'S FUNNY...
NOT THE END OF IT.
SO ONE OF THE GUYS, JOEY, HE LIGHTLY TAPS ON THE GLASS TO GET HIS ATTENTION.

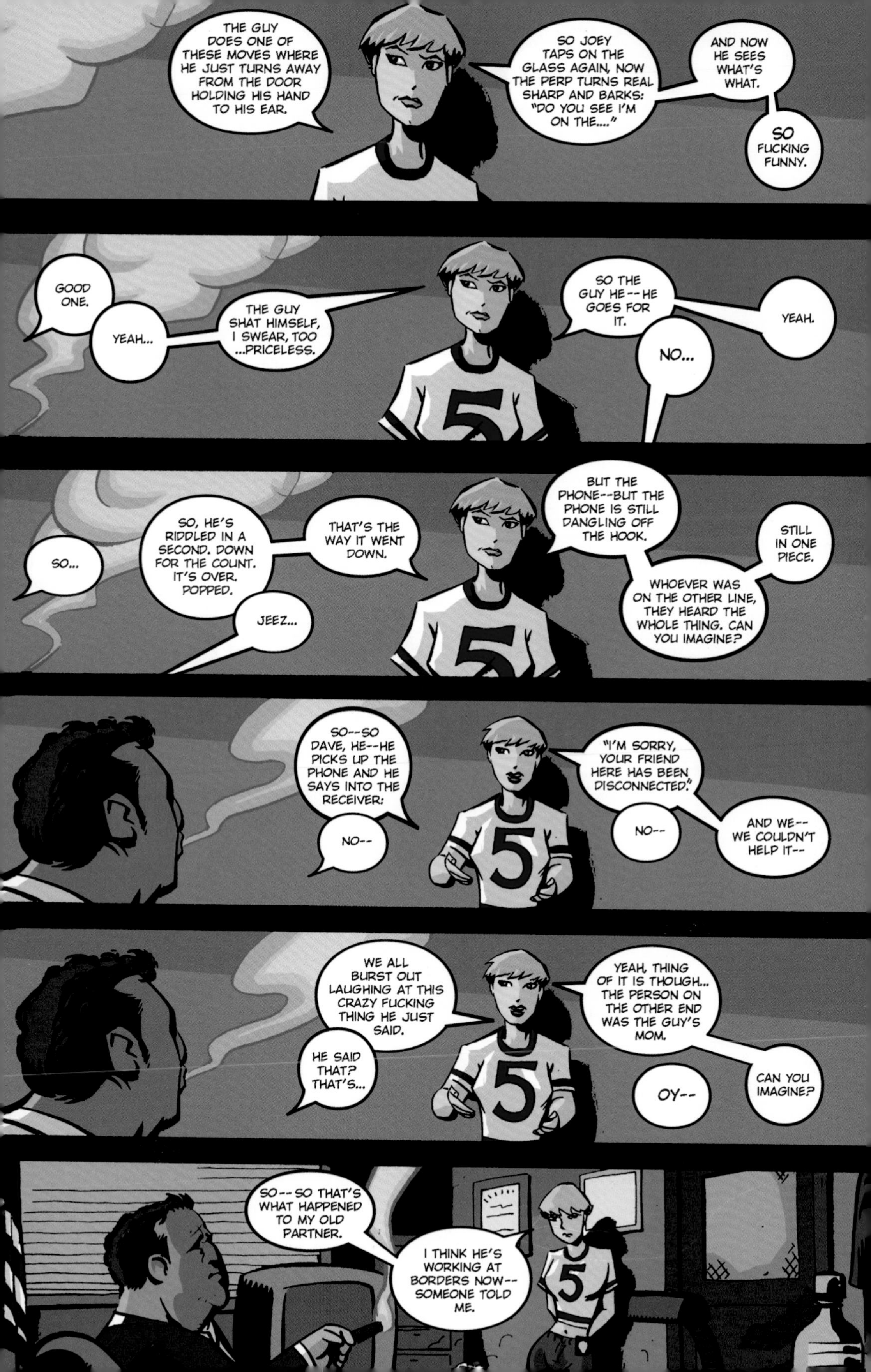

THE GUY DOES ONE OF THESE MOVES WHERE HE JUST TURNS AWAY FROM THE DOOR HOLDING HIS HAND TO HIS EAR.
SO JOEY TAPS ON THE GLASS AGAIN, NOW THE PERP TURNS REAL SHARP AND BARKS: "DO YOU SEE I'M ON THE...."
AND NOW HE SEES WHAT'S WHAT.
SO FUCKING FUNNY.
GOOD ONE.
YEAH...
THE GUY SHAT HIMSELF, I SWEAR, TOO ...PRICELESS.
SO THE GUY HE--HE GOES FOR IT.
YEAH.
NO...
SO...
SO, HE'S RIDDLED IN A SECOND. DOWN FOR THE COUNT. IT'S OVER. POPPED.
JEEZ...
THAT'S THE WAY IT WENT DOWN.
BUT THE PHONE--BUT THE PHONE IS STILL DANGLING OFF THE HOOK.
STILL IN ONE PIECE.
WHOEVER WAS ON THE OTHER LINE, THEY HEARD THE WHOLE THING. CAN YOU IMAGINE?
SO--SO DAVE, HE--HE PICKS UP THE PHONE AND HE SAYS INTO THE RECEIVER:
NO--
"I'M SORRY, YOUR FRIEND HERE HAS BEEN DISCONNECTED."
NO--
AND WE--WE COULDN'T HELP IT--
WE ALL BURST OUT LAUGHING AT THIS CRAZY FUCKING THING HE JUST SAID.
HE SAID THAT? THAT'S...
YEAH, THING OF IT IS THOUGH... THE PERSON ON THE OTHER END WAS THE GUY'S MOM.
OY--
CAN YOU IMAGINE?
SO--SO THAT'S WHAT HAPPENED TO MY OLD PARTNER.
I THINK HE'S WORKING AT BORDERS NOW--SOMEONE TOLD ME.

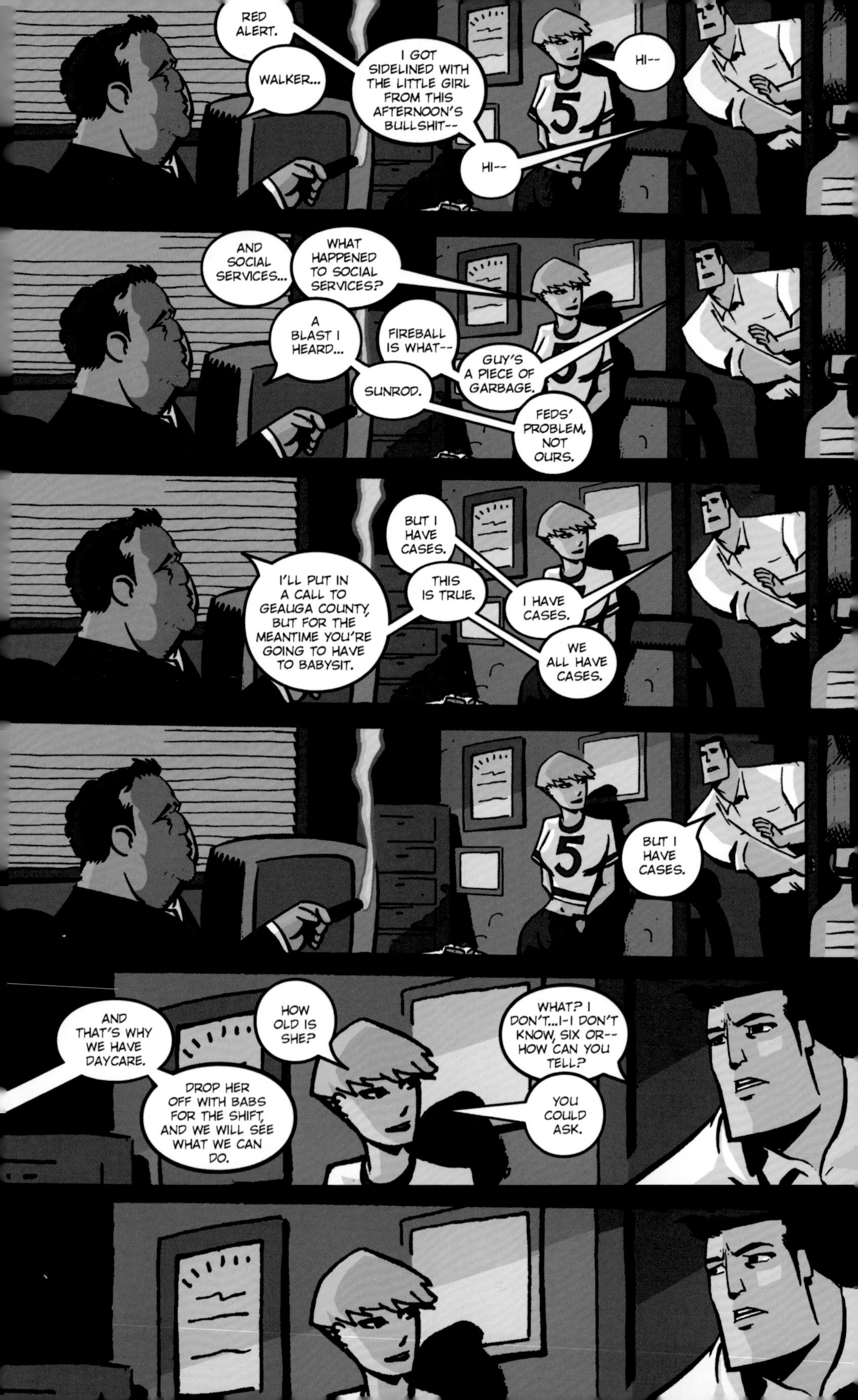
RED ALERT.
WALKER...
I GOT SIDELINED WITH THE LITTLE GIRL FROM THIS AFTERNOON'S BULLSHIT--
HI--
HI--
AND SOCIAL SERVICES...
WHAT HAPPENED TO SOCIAL SERVICES?
A BLAST I HEARD...
FIREBALL IS WHAT--
GUY'S A PIECE OF GARBAGE.
SUNROD.
FEDS' PROBLEM, NOT OURS.
I'LL PUT IN A CALL TO GEAUGA COUNTY, BUT FOR THE MEANTIME YOU'RE GOING TO HAVE TO BABYSIT.
BUT I HAVE CASES.
THIS IS TRUE.
I HAVE CASES.
WE ALL HAVE CASES.
BUT I HAVE CASES.
AND THAT'S WHY WE HAVE DAYCARE.
HOW OLD IS SHE?
WHAT? I DON'T...I-I DON'T KNOW, SIX OR-- HOW CAN YOU TELL?
DROP HER OFF WITH BABS FOR THE SHIFT, AND WE WILL SEE WHAT WE CAN DO.
YOU COULD ASK.

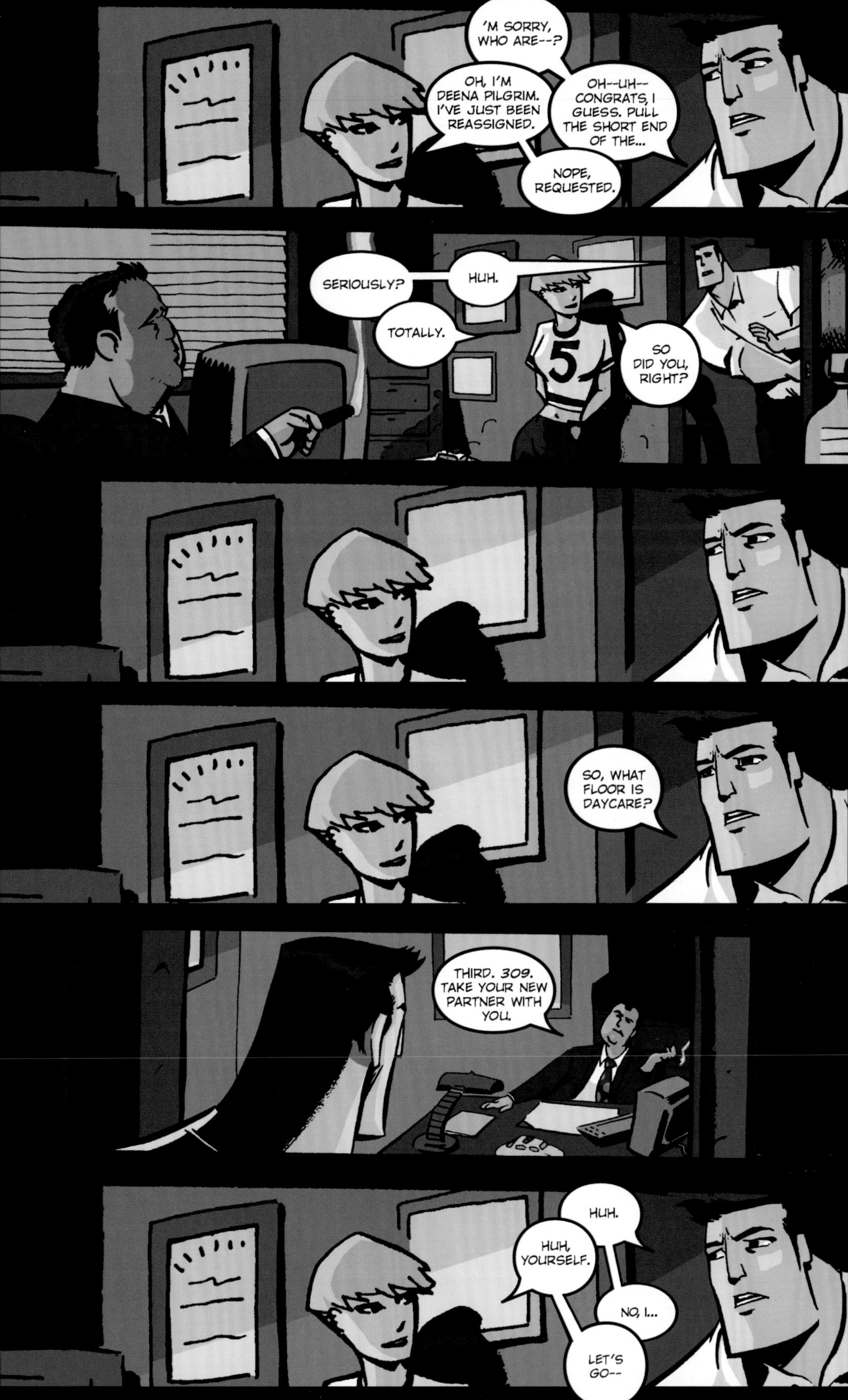
'M SORRY, WHO ARE--?
OH, I'M DEENA PILGRIM. I'VE JUST BEEN REASSIGNED.
OH--UH-- CONGRATS, I GUESS. PULL THE SHORT END OF THE...
NOPE, REQUESTED.
SERIOUSLY?
HUH.
TOTALLY.
SO DID YOU, RIGHT?
5
SO, WHAT FLOOR IS DAYCARE?
THIRD. 309. TAKE YOUR NEW PARTNER WITH YOU.
HUH.
HUH, YOURSELF.
NO, I...
LET'S GO--

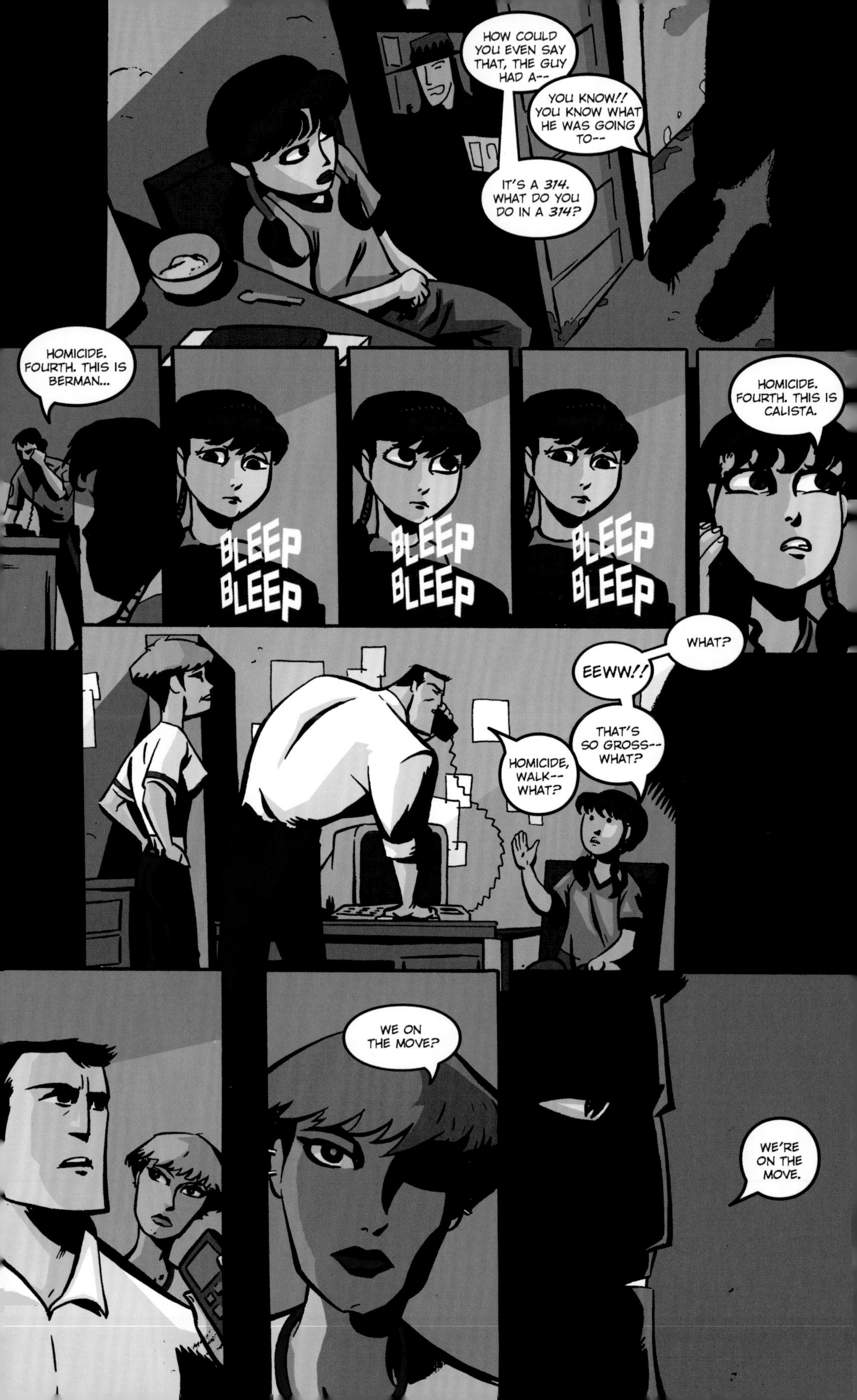
HOW COULD YOU EVEN SAY THAT, THE GUY HAD A--
YOU KNOW!! YOU KNOW WHAT HE WAS GOING TO--
IT'S A 314. WHAT DO YOU DO IN A 314?
HOMICIDE. FOURTH. THIS IS BERMAN...
BLEEP BLEEP
BLEEP BLEEP
BLEEP BLEEP
HOMICIDE. FOURTH. THIS IS CALISTA.
WHAT?
EEWW!!
THAT'S SO GROSS-- WHAT?
HOMICIDE, WALK-- WHAT?
WE ON THE MOVE?
WE'RE ON THE MOVE.

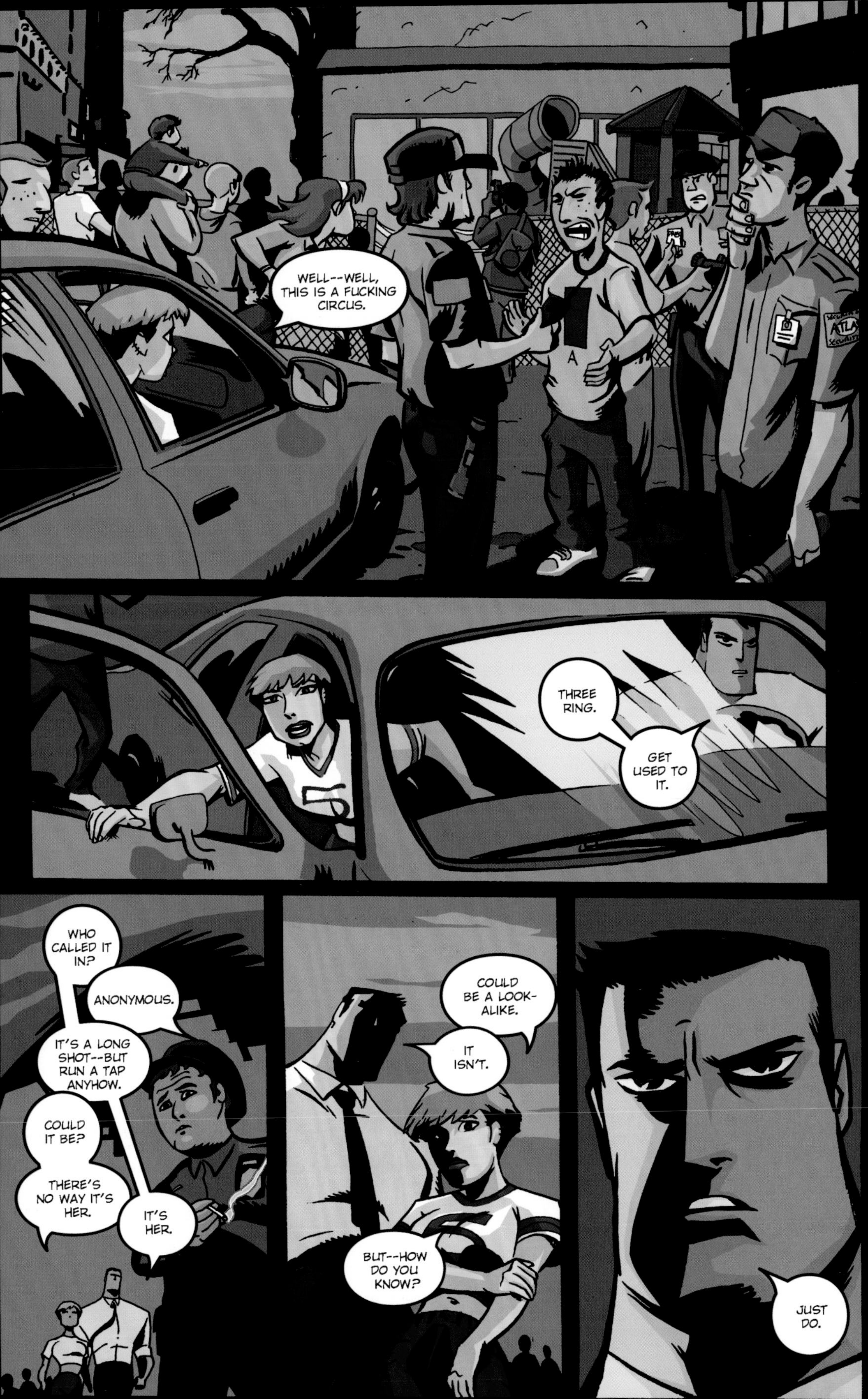
WELL--WELL, THIS IS A FUCKING CIRCUS.
THREE RING.
GET USED TO IT.
WHO CALLED IT IN?
ANONYMOUS.
IT'S A LONG SHOT--BUT RUN A TAP ANYHOW.
COULD IT BE?
THERE'S NO WAY IT'S HER.
IT'S HER.
COULD BE A LOOK-ALIKE.
IT ISN'T.
BUT--HOW DO YOU KNOW?
JUST DO.

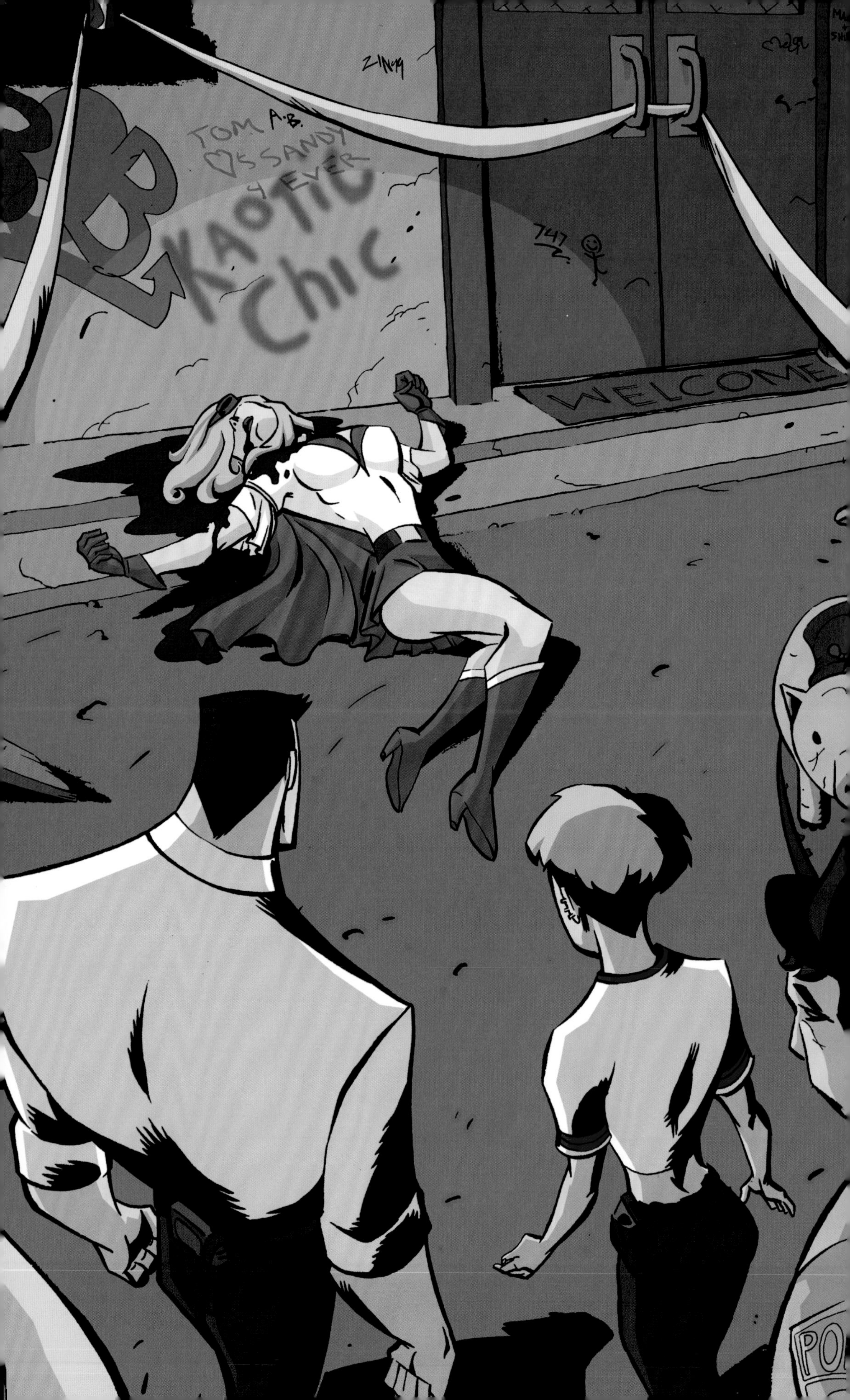
TOM A.B. ♡'S SANDY 4 EVER
KAOTIC Chic
747
WELCOME

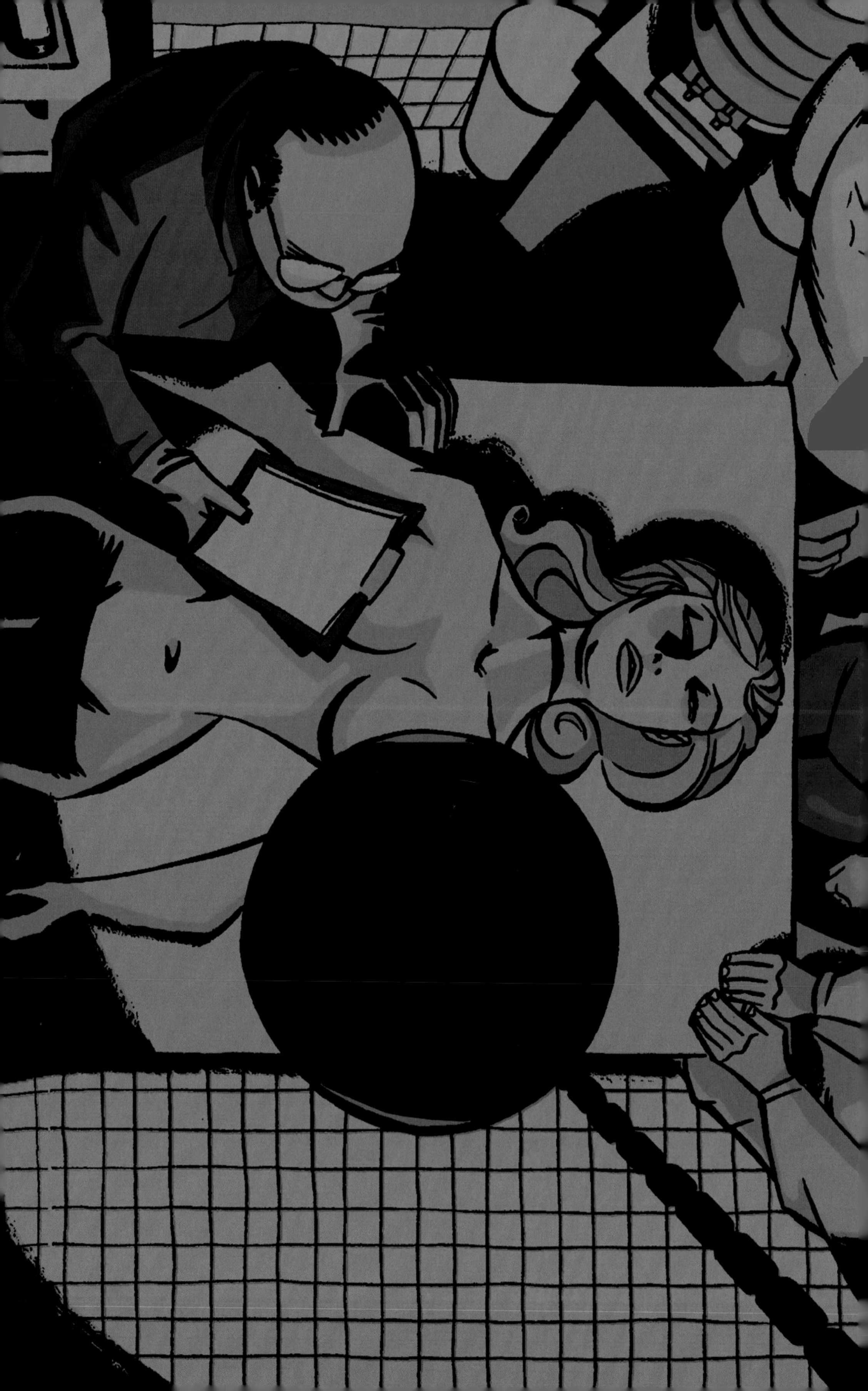

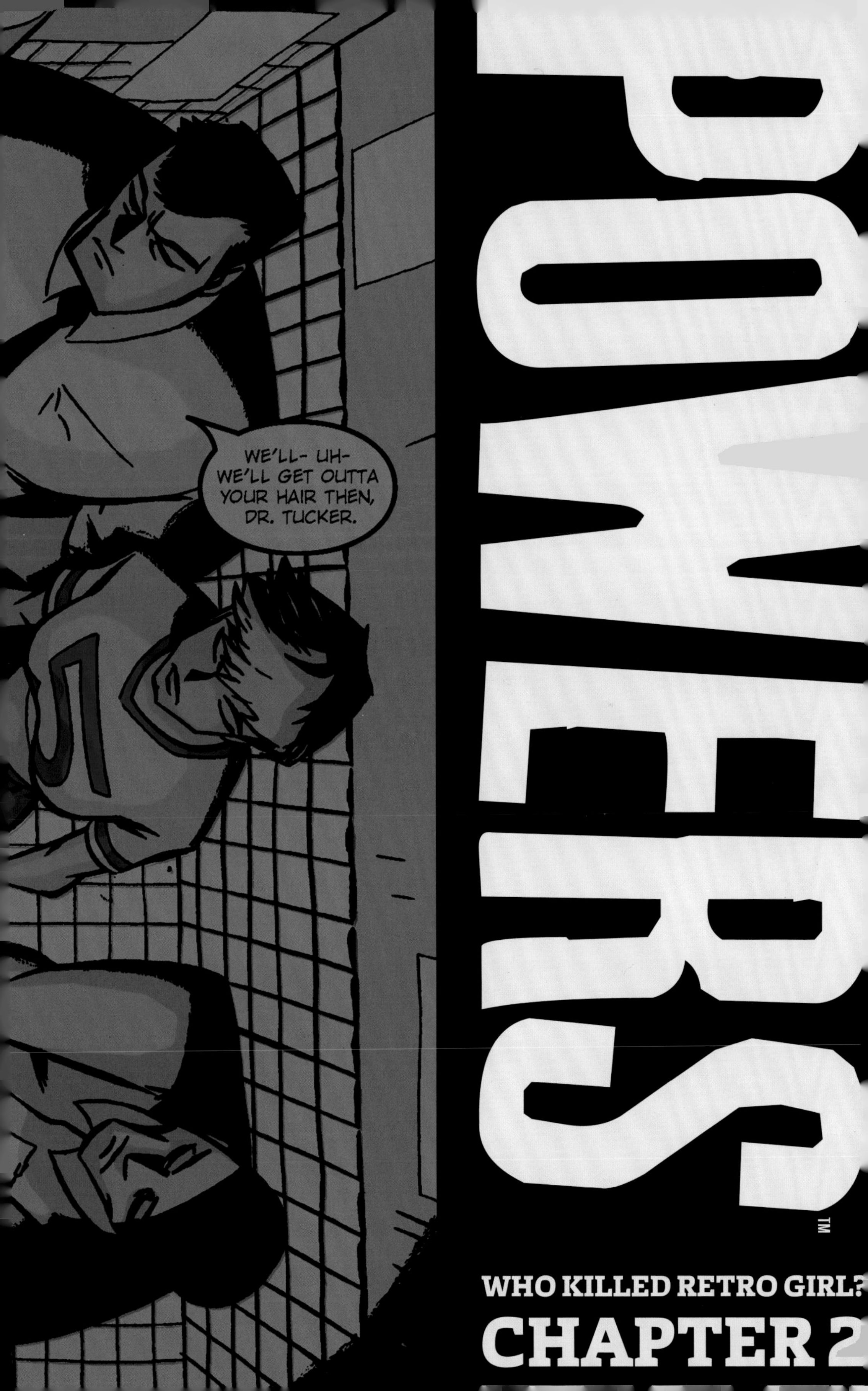
WE'LL- UH- WE'LL GET OUTTA YOUR HAIR THEN, DR. TUCKER.

POWERS™

WHO KILLED RETRO GIRL?

CHAPTER 2

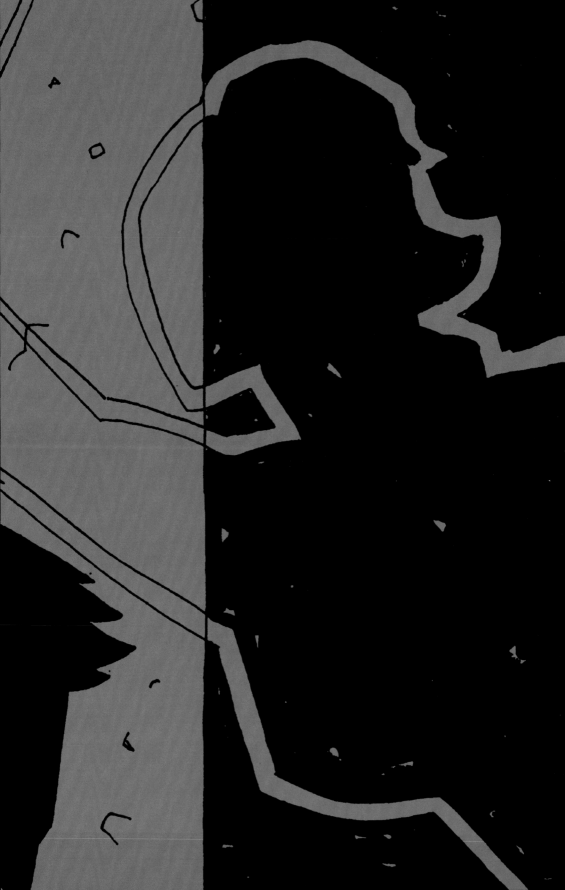

A PAIR OF RED LEATHER BOOTS. SIZE FOUR.

ITEM 476-99.

WHAT IS THIS? I GUESS IT'S HER CAPE.

ITEM 476-003.

IT'S HER CAPE.

HAD TO REMOVE THESE WITH A HACKSAW AND A BLOW-TORCH.

HAD TO GET THEM OFF.

TWO STEEL ARM-BANDS.

ITEM 476-000.

A BLOW-TORCH?

HER TUNIC...

SIGH...

OR COSTUME OR WHATEVER--

ITEM NUMBER 476-006.

THAT'S SO--SO SAD.

YEAH--

CAN YOU TELL US HOW YOU'RE FEELING?

SNIFF... I FEEL BAD.

SHE--SHE WAS SO BEAUTIFUL.

AS YOU CAN IMAGINE, DAVID, THE MOOD AT MORRISON ELEMENTARY IS GRIM INDEED.

IT IS HERE AND AT SCHOOLS ALL OVER THE WORLD THAT THIS TERRIBLE LOSS IS BEING FELT THE MOST.

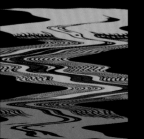

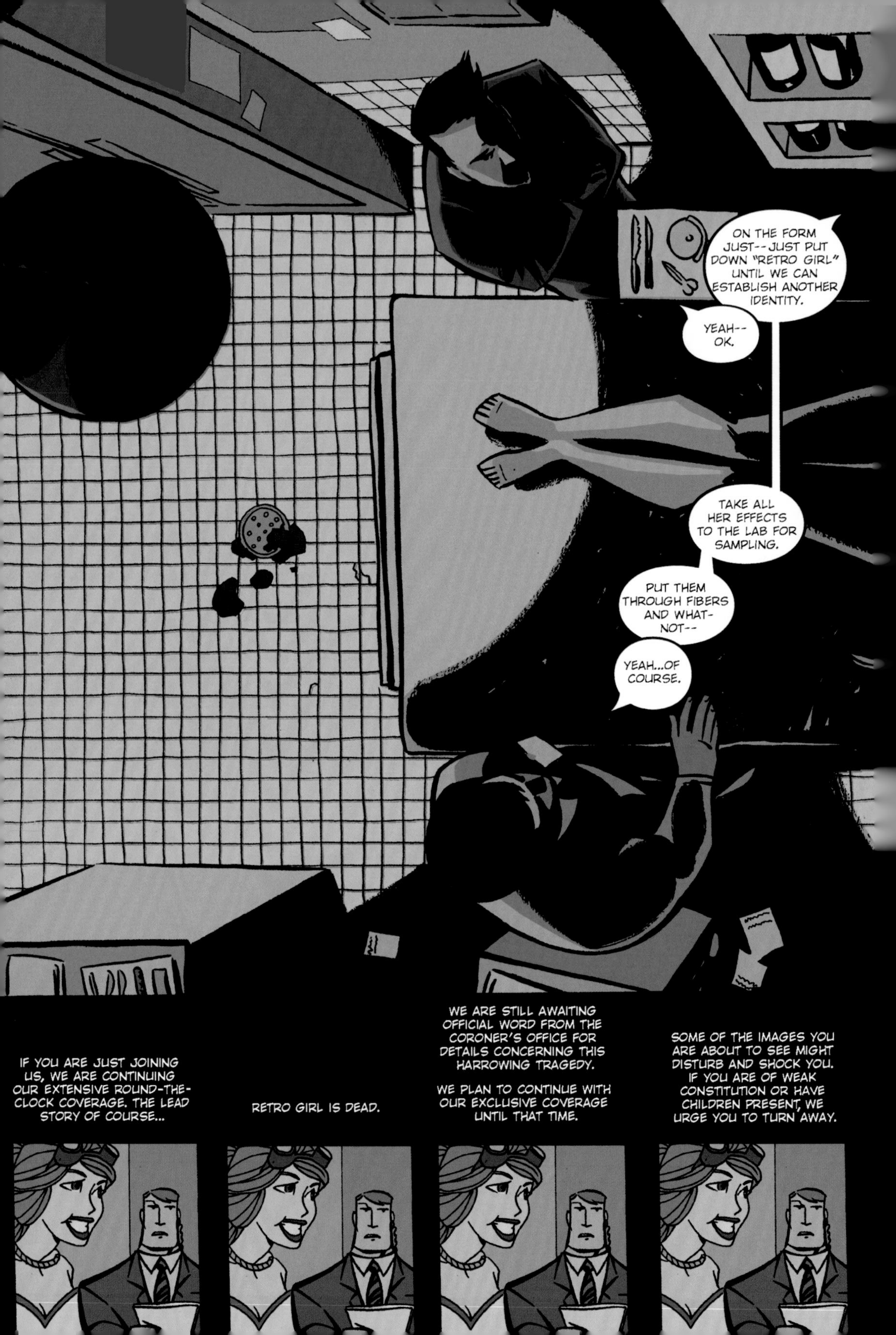
ON THE FORM JUST--JUST PUT DOWN "RETRO GIRL" UNTIL WE CAN ESTABLISH ANOTHER IDENTITY.
YEAH-- OK.
TAKE ALL HER EFFECTS TO THE LAB FOR SAMPLING.
PUT THEM THROUGH FIBERS AND WHAT-NOT--
YEAH...OF COURSE.
IF YOU ARE JUST JOINING US, WE ARE CONTINUING OUR EXTENSIVE ROUND-THE-CLOCK COVERAGE. THE LEAD STORY OF COURSE...
RETRO GIRL IS DEAD.
WE ARE STILL AWAITING OFFICIAL WORD FROM THE CORONER'S OFFICE FOR DETAILS CONCERNING THIS HARROWING TRAGEDY.
WE PLAN TO CONTINUE WITH OUR EXCLUSIVE COVERAGE UNTIL THAT TIME.
SOME OF THE IMAGES YOU ARE ABOUT TO SEE MIGHT DISTURB AND SHOCK YOU. IF YOU ARE OF WEAK CONSTITUTION OR HAVE CHILDREN PRESENT, WE URGE YOU TO TURN AWAY.

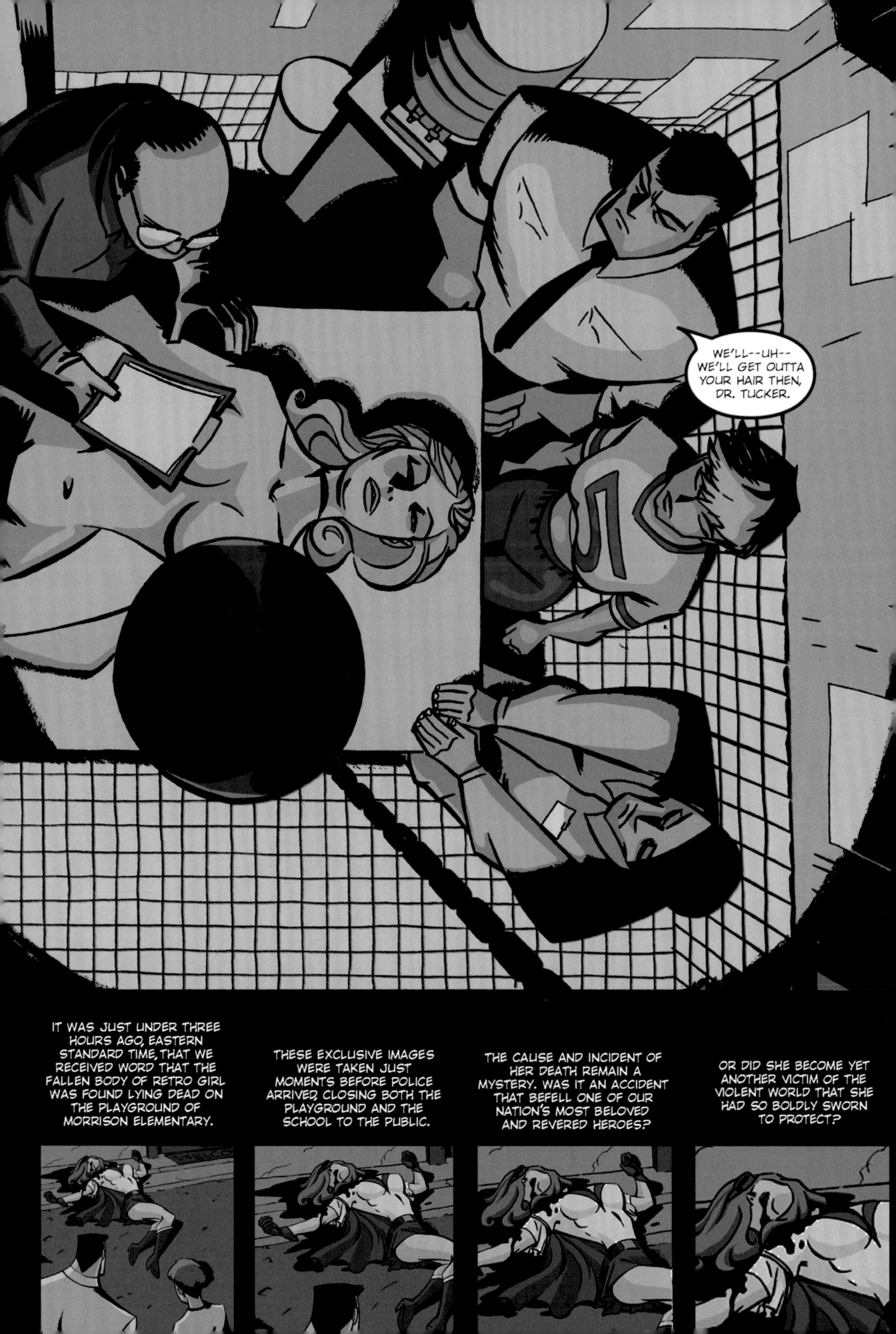
WE'LL--UH--
WE'LL GET OUTTA YOUR HAIR THEN, DR. TUCKER.
IT WAS JUST UNDER THREE HOURS AGO, EASTERN STANDARD TIME, THAT WE RECEIVED WORD THAT THE FALLEN BODY OF RETRO GIRL WAS FOUND LYING DEAD ON THE PLAYGROUND OF MORRISON ELEMENTARY.
THESE EXCLUSIVE IMAGES WERE TAKEN JUST MOMENTS BEFORE POLICE ARRIVED, CLOSING BOTH THE PLAYGROUND AND THE SCHOOL TO THE PUBLIC.
THE CAUSE AND INCIDENT OF HER DEATH REMAIN A MYSTERY. WAS IT AN ACCIDENT THAT BEFELL ONE OF OUR NATION'S MOST BELOVED AND REVERED HEROES?
OR DID SHE BECOME YET ANOTHER VICTIM OF THE VIOLENT WORLD THAT SHE HAD SO BOLDLY SWORN TO PROTECT?

I KNOW.

WHY'S THAT?

YOU KNOW HOW THESE THINGS GO--

I CAN'T-- THERE'S NO GUARANTEES.

WHY? WHY DO YOU THINK, DETECTIVE?

COULD IT BE THAT WE MIGHT NOT BE ABLE TO FIGURE OUT HOW TO BREAK HER SKIN TO PERFORM THE AUTOPSY?

COULD IT BE THAT WE DON'T EVEN KNOW IF SHE'S BIOLOGICALLY HUMAN--?

COME ON, WE KNOW SHE'S HUMAN--

WE DO?

HOW'S THAT EXACTLY?

CAN YOU FLY AROUND THE ROOM AND THROW CARS ACROSS A PARKING LOT?

TAKE MANY BULLETS, DO YA?

HERE IS CORRESPONDENT COLLETTE MCDANIEL WITH A SPECIAL REPORT ON THE LIFE OF A WOMAN KNOWN TO THE WORLD ONLY AS RETRO GIRL.

LIKE MANY OF HER PEERS ON BOTH SIDES OF THE LAW, VERY LITTLE IS KNOWN TO THE PUBLIC ABOUT THE LIFE AND LEGACY OF RETRO GIRL.

BUT IT WAS HERE, ON THE ROOF OF THE UNITY BUILDING DOWNTOWN, THAT RETRO GIRL ACHIEVED ONE OF HER MOST HEROIC MOMENTS IN HISTORY.

MY GRANDSON, HE WANTED TO COME UP TO THE TOP OF THE UNITY BUILDING, SEE THE SIGHTS AND ALL.

SO WE WAS UP HERE ON THE ROOF WITH A BUNCH OF THE OTHERS WHEN ALL KINDS OF CRAZINESS STARTED A-HAPPENING AROUND US.

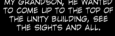

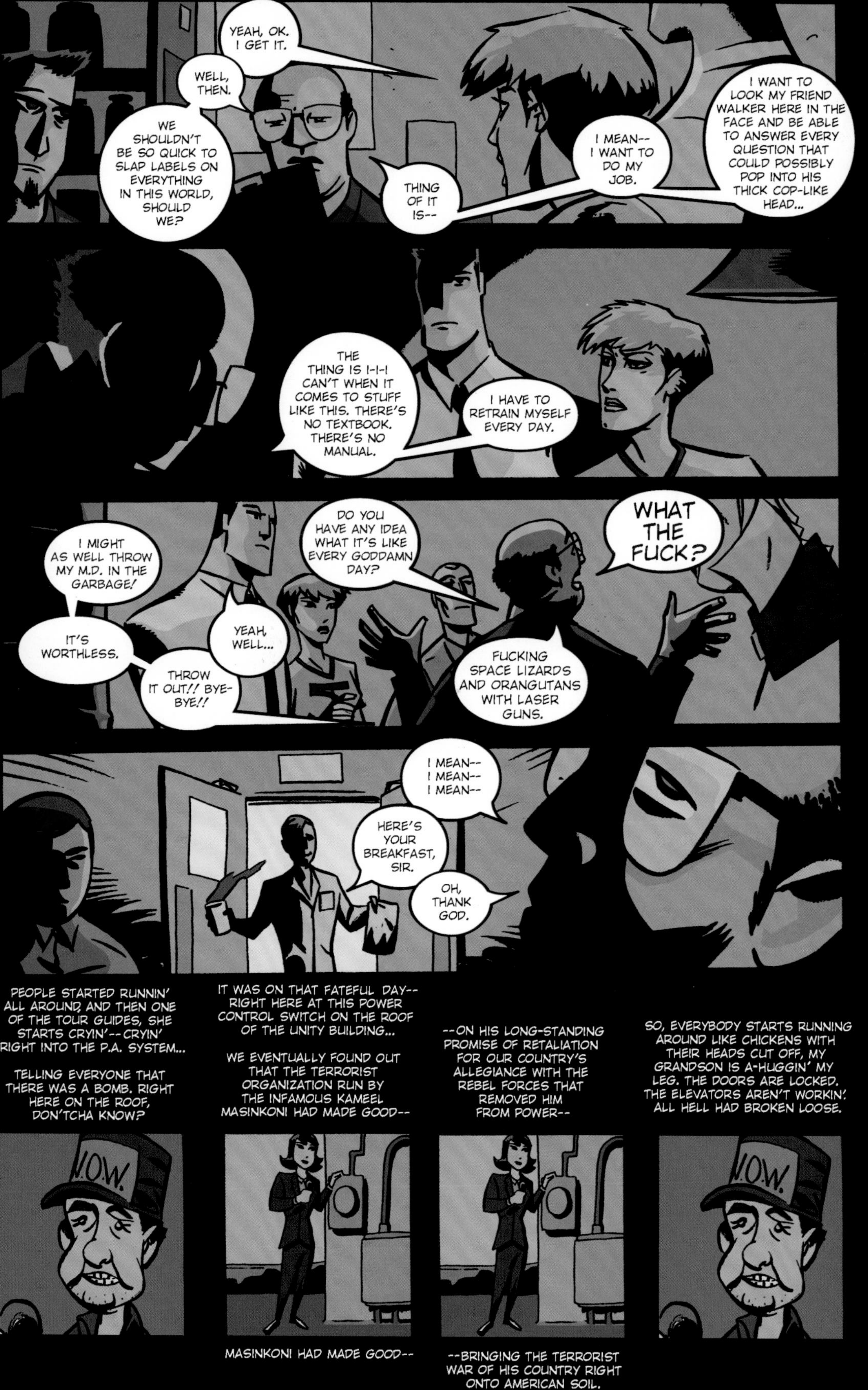
YEAH, OK. I GET IT.
WELL, THEN.
WE SHOULDN'T BE SO QUICK TO SLAP LABELS ON EVERYTHING IN THIS WORLD, SHOULD WE?
THING OF IT IS--
I MEAN-- I WANT TO DO MY JOB.
I WANT TO LOOK MY FRIEND WALKER HERE IN THE FACE AND BE ABLE TO ANSWER EVERY QUESTION THAT COULD POSSIBLY POP INTO HIS THICK COP-LIKE HEAD...
THE THING IS I-I-I CAN'T WHEN IT COMES TO STUFF LIKE THIS. THERE'S NO TEXTBOOK. THERE'S NO MANUAL.
I HAVE TO RETRAIN MYSELF EVERY DAY.
I MIGHT AS WELL THROW MY M.D. IN THE GARBAGE!
IT'S WORTHLESS.
THROW IT OUT!! BYE-BYE!!
YEAH, WELL...
DO YOU HAVE ANY IDEA WHAT IT'S LIKE EVERY GODDAMN DAY?
WHAT THE FUCK?
FUCKING SPACE LIZARDS AND ORANGUTANS WITH LASER GUNS.
I MEAN-- I MEAN-- I MEAN--
HERE'S YOUR BREAKFAST, SIR.
OH, THANK GOD.
PEOPLE STARTED RUNNIN' ALL AROUND, AND THEN ONE OF THE TOUR GUIDES, SHE STARTS CRYIN'--CRYIN' RIGHT INTO THE P.A. SYSTEM...
TELLING EVERYONE THAT THERE WAS A BOMB. RIGHT HERE ON THE ROOF, DON'TCHA KNOW?
V.O.W.
IT WAS ON THAT FATEFUL DAY-- RIGHT HERE AT THIS POWER CONTROL SWITCH ON THE ROOF OF THE UNITY BUILDING...
WE EVENTUALLY FOUND OUT THAT THE TERRORIST ORGANIZATION RUN BY THE INFAMOUS KAMEEL MASINKONI HAD MADE GOOD--
MASINKONI HAD MADE GOOD--
--ON HIS LONG-STANDING PROMISE OF RETALIATION FOR OUR COUNTRY'S ALLEGIANCE WITH THE REBEL FORCES THAT REMOVED HIM FROM POWER--
--BRINGING THE TERRORIST WAR OF HIS COUNTRY RIGHT ONTO AMERICAN SOIL.
SO, EVERYBODY STARTS RUNNING AROUND LIKE CHICKENS WITH THEIR HEADS CUT OFF, MY GRANDSON IS A-HUGGIN' MY LEG. THE DOORS ARE LOCKED. THE ELEVATORS AREN'T WORKIN'. ALL HELL HAD BROKEN LOOSE.
V.O.W.

AAAAHHH! MAMA LUCIOUSEN!

WHAT WAS I SAYING?

"ORANGUTANS WITH LASER GUNS"...

OH YEAH. OH--NEVER MIND ABOUT THAT--

I HAVE TO GET TO WORK.

I'LL SEE WHAT I CAN DO ABOUT OUR FALLEN HERO.

GREAT.

THIS IS DEENA PILGRIM. SHE'S WORKING WITH ME, IT SEEMS.

THIS IS HER FIRST--

I DIDN'T GET YOUR NAME--

WELL, VERY NICE TO MEET YOU. I GUESS WE'LL BE TALKING OFTEN.

GREAT.

O.T.R.

NO SHIT.

I MEAN, HAVE YOU EVER SEEN HER IN PERSON?

SHE'S-- SHE'S QUITE A HANDSOME LITTLE WOMAN. EVEN WITH ALL THE RUCKUS AND THE BOMB AND ALL. I COULDN'T HELP BUT NOTICE.

AND I MEAN, AS FAST AS YOU CAN SAY FANG DANG DOODLE-- SHE RIPPED THE GODDAMN CONTRAPTION OR WHATEVER IT WAS OFF THE WALL AND FLEW WAY UP INTO THE SKY WITH IT.

--AND THAT'S-- THAT'S WHEN I FIRST SAW HER.

AND THEN...BLOOEY!

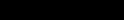

AMATUER VIDEO FOOTAGE

AMATUER VIDEO FOOTAGE

AMATUER VIDEO FOOTAGE

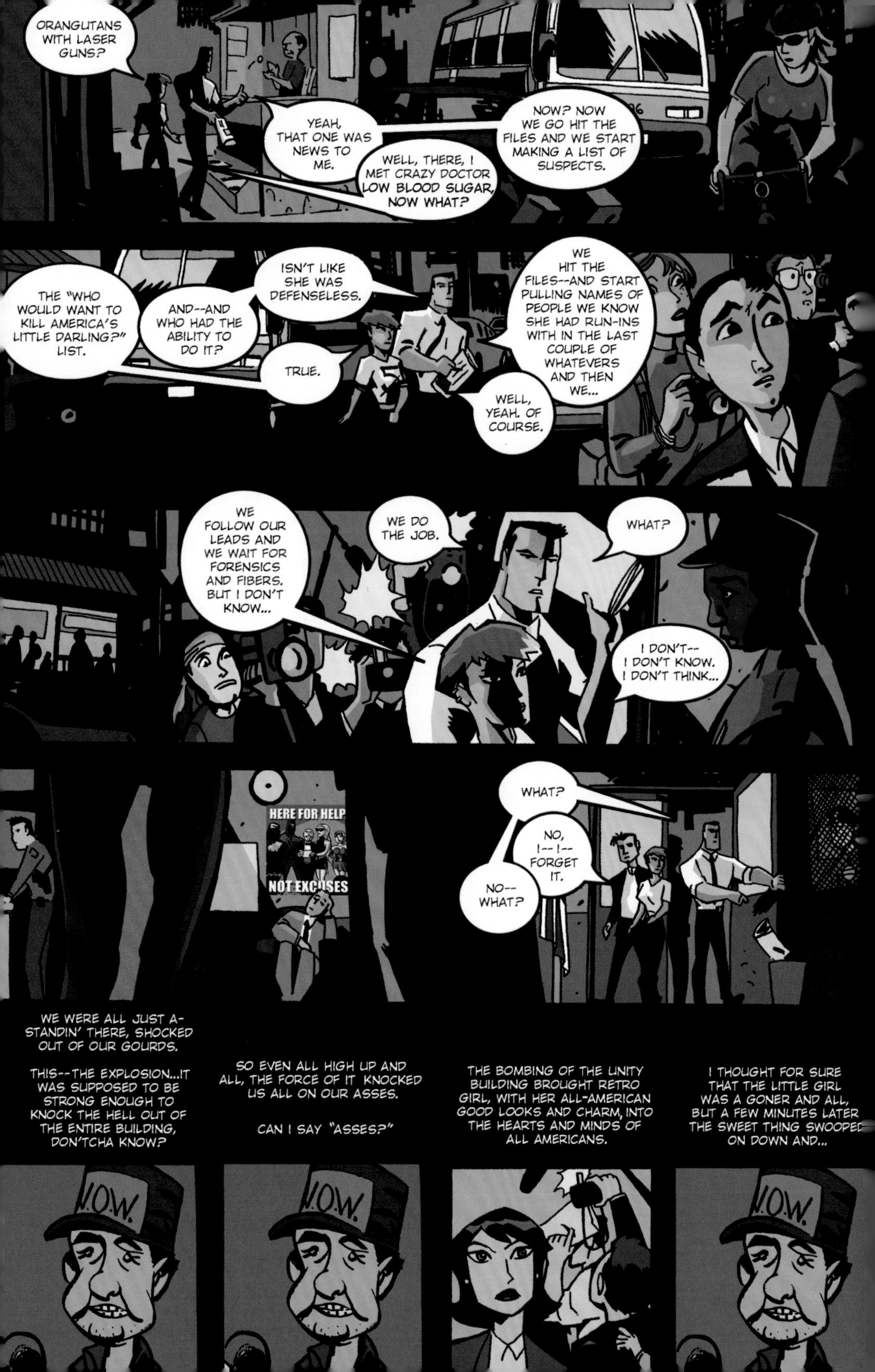
ORANGUTANS WITH LASER GUNS?
YEAH, THAT ONE WAS NEWS TO ME.
WELL, THERE, I MET CRAZY DOCTOR LOW BLOOD SUGAR, NOW WHAT?
NOW? NOW WE GO HIT THE FILES AND WE START MAKING A LIST OF SUSPECTS.
THE "WHO WOULD WANT TO KILL AMERICA'S LITTLE DARLING?" LIST.
AND--AND WHO HAD THE ABILITY TO DO IT?
ISN'T LIKE SHE WAS DEFENSELESS.
TRUE.
WE HIT THE FILES--AND START PULLING NAMES OF PEOPLE WE KNOW SHE HAD RUN-INS WITH IN THE LAST COUPLE OF WHATEVERS AND THEN WE...
WELL, YEAH. OF COURSE.
WE FOLLOW OUR LEADS AND WE WAIT FOR FORENSICS AND FIBERS. BUT I DON'T KNOW...
WE DO THE JOB.
WHAT?
I DON'T-- I DON'T KNOW. I DON'T THINK...
HERE FOR HELP
NOT EXCUSES
WHAT?
NO, I-- I-- FORGET IT.
NO-- WHAT?
WE WERE ALL JUST A-STANDIN' THERE, SHOCKED OUT OF OUR GOURDS.
THIS--THE EXPLOSION...IT WAS SUPPOSED TO BE STRONG ENOUGH TO KNOCK THE HELL OUT OF THE ENTIRE BUILDING, DON'TCHA KNOW?
SO EVEN ALL HIGH UP AND ALL, THE FORCE OF IT KNOCKED US ALL ON OUR ASSES.
CAN I SAY "ASSES?"
THE BOMBING OF THE UNITY BUILDING BROUGHT RETRO GIRL, WITH HER ALL-AMERICAN GOOD LOOKS AND CHARM, INTO THE HEARTS AND MINDS OF ALL AMERICANS.
I THOUGHT FOR SURE THAT THE LITTLE GIRL WAS A GONER AND ALL, BUT A FEW MINUTES LATER THE SWEET THING SWOOPED ON DOWN AND...
N.O.W.
N.O.W.
N.O.W.

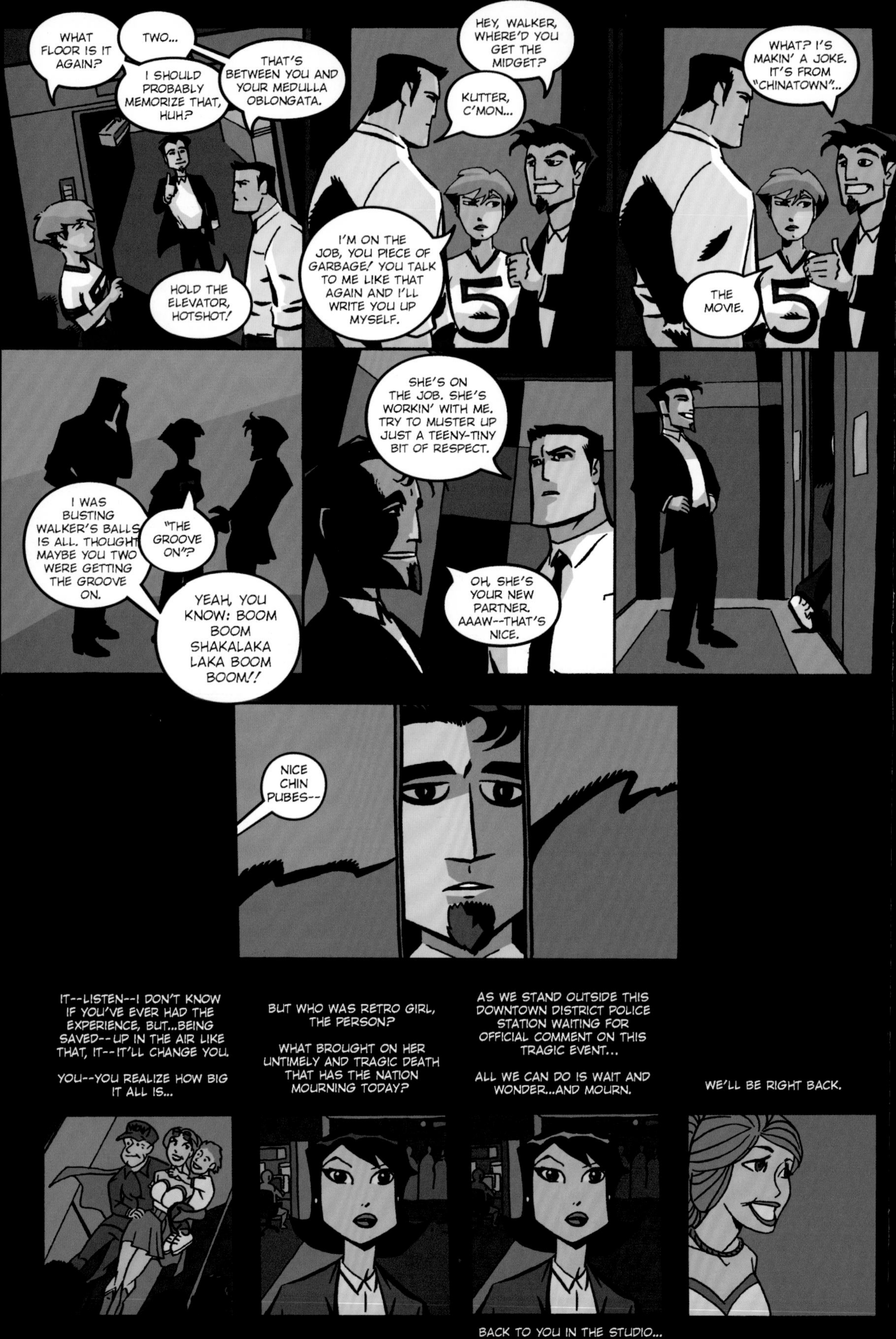
WHAT FLOOR IS IT AGAIN?
TWO...
I SHOULD PROBABLY MEMORIZE THAT, HUH?
THAT'S BETWEEN YOU AND YOUR MEDULLA OBLONGATA.
HOLD THE ELEVATOR, HOTSHOT!
HEY, WALKER, WHERE'D YOU GET THE MIDGET?
KUTTER, C'MON...
I'M ON THE JOB, YOU PIECE OF GARBAGE! YOU TALK TO ME LIKE THAT AGAIN AND I'LL WRITE YOU UP MYSELF.
WHAT? I'S MAKIN' A JOKE. IT'S FROM "CHINATOWN"...
THE MOVIE.
I WAS BUSTING WALKER'S BALLS IS ALL. THOUGHT MAYBE YOU TWO WERE GETTING THE GROOVE ON.
"THE GROOVE ON"?
YEAH, YOU KNOW: BOOM BOOM SHAKALAKA LAKA BOOM BOOM!!
SHE'S ON THE JOB. SHE'S WORKIN' WITH ME. TRY TO MUSTER UP JUST A TEENY-TINY BIT OF RESPECT.
OH, SHE'S YOUR NEW PARTNER. AAAW--THAT'S NICE.
NICE CHIN PUBES--
IT--LISTEN--I DON'T KNOW IF YOU'VE EVER HAD THE EXPERIENCE, BUT...BEING SAVED--UP IN THE AIR LIKE THAT, IT--IT'LL CHANGE YOU.
YOU--YOU REALIZE HOW BIG IT ALL IS...
BUT WHO WAS RETRO GIRL, THE PERSON?
WHAT BROUGHT ON HER UNTIMELY AND TRAGIC DEATH THAT HAS THE NATION MOURNING TODAY?
AS WE STAND OUTSIDE THIS DOWNTOWN DISTRICT POLICE STATION WAITING FOR OFFICIAL COMMENT ON THIS TRAGIC EVENT...
ALL WE CAN DO IS WAIT AND WONDER...AND MOURN.
WE'LL BE RIGHT BACK.
BACK TO YOU IN THE STUDIO...

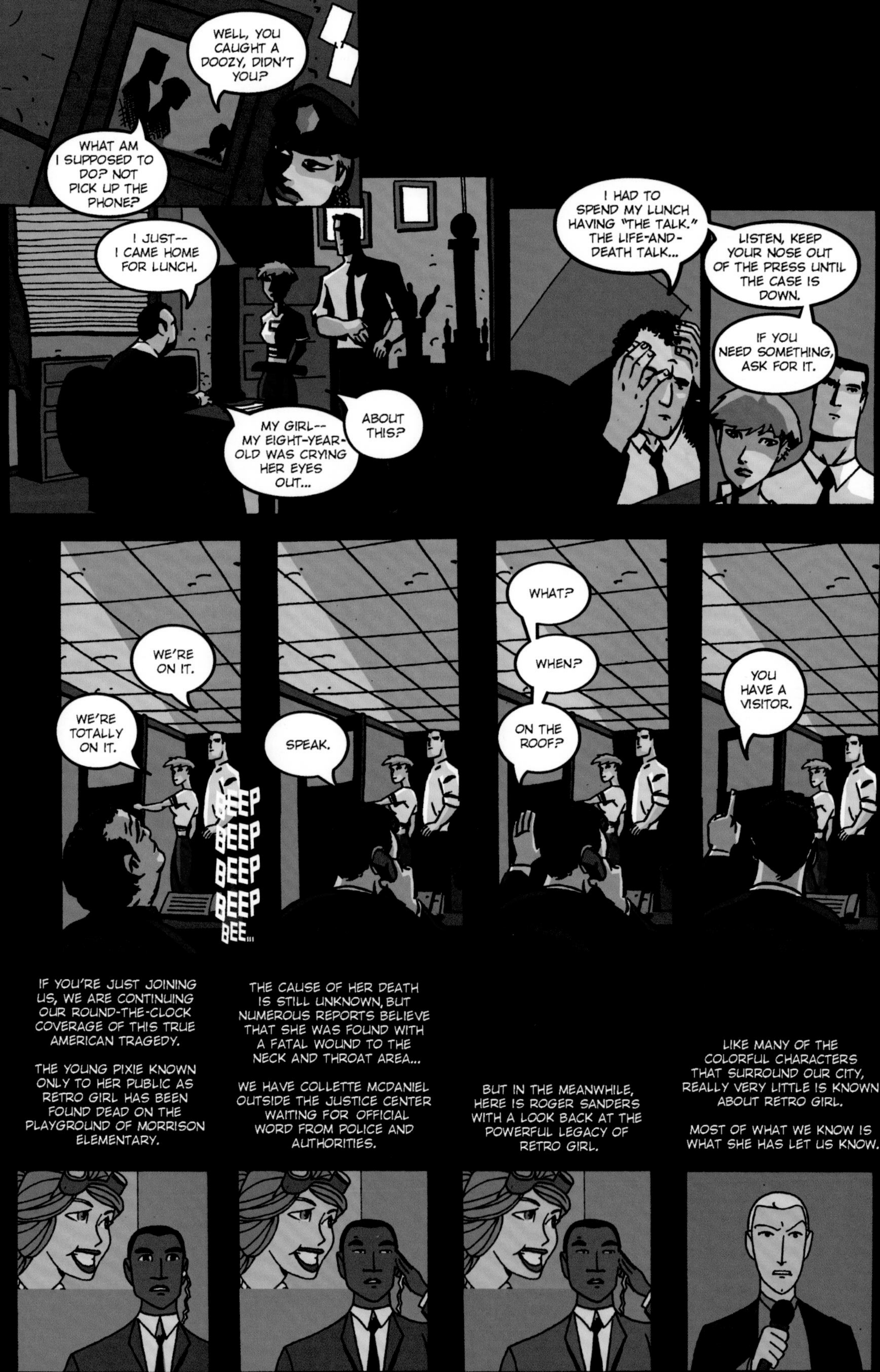
WELL, YOU CAUGHT A DOOZY, DIDN'T YOU?
WHAT AM I SUPPOSED TO DO? NOT PICK UP THE PHONE?
I JUST-- I CAME HOME FOR LUNCH.
MY GIRL-- MY EIGHT-YEAR-OLD WAS CRYING HER EYES OUT...
ABOUT THIS?
I HAD TO SPEND MY LUNCH HAVING "THE TALK." THE LIFE-AND-DEATH TALK...
LISTEN, KEEP YOUR NOSE OUT OF THE PRESS UNTIL THE CASE IS DOWN.
IF YOU NEED SOMETHING, ASK FOR IT.
WE'RE ON IT.
WE'RE TOTALLY ON IT.
BEEP BEEP BEEP BEEP BEE...
SPEAK.
WHAT?
WHEN?
ON THE ROOF?
YOU HAVE A VISITOR.
IF YOU'RE JUST JOINING US, WE ARE CONTINUING OUR ROUND-THE-CLOCK COVERAGE OF THIS TRUE AMERICAN TRAGEDY.
THE YOUNG PIXIE KNOWN ONLY TO HER PUBLIC AS RETRO GIRL HAS BEEN FOUND DEAD ON THE PLAYGROUND OF MORRISON ELEMENTARY.
THE CAUSE OF HER DEATH IS STILL UNKNOWN, BUT NUMEROUS REPORTS BELIEVE THAT SHE WAS FOUND WITH A FATAL WOUND TO THE NECK AND THROAT AREA...
WE HAVE COLLETTE MCDANIEL OUTSIDE THE JUSTICE CENTER WAITING FOR OFFICIAL WORD FROM POLICE AND AUTHORITIES.
BUT IN THE MEANWHILE, HERE IS ROGER SANDERS WITH A LOOK BACK AT THE POWERFUL LEGACY OF RETRO GIRL.
LIKE MANY OF THE COLORFUL CHARACTERS THAT SURROUND OUR CITY, REALLY VERY LITTLE IS KNOWN ABOUT RETRO GIRL.
MOST OF WHAT WE KNOW IS WHAT SHE HAS LET US KNOW.

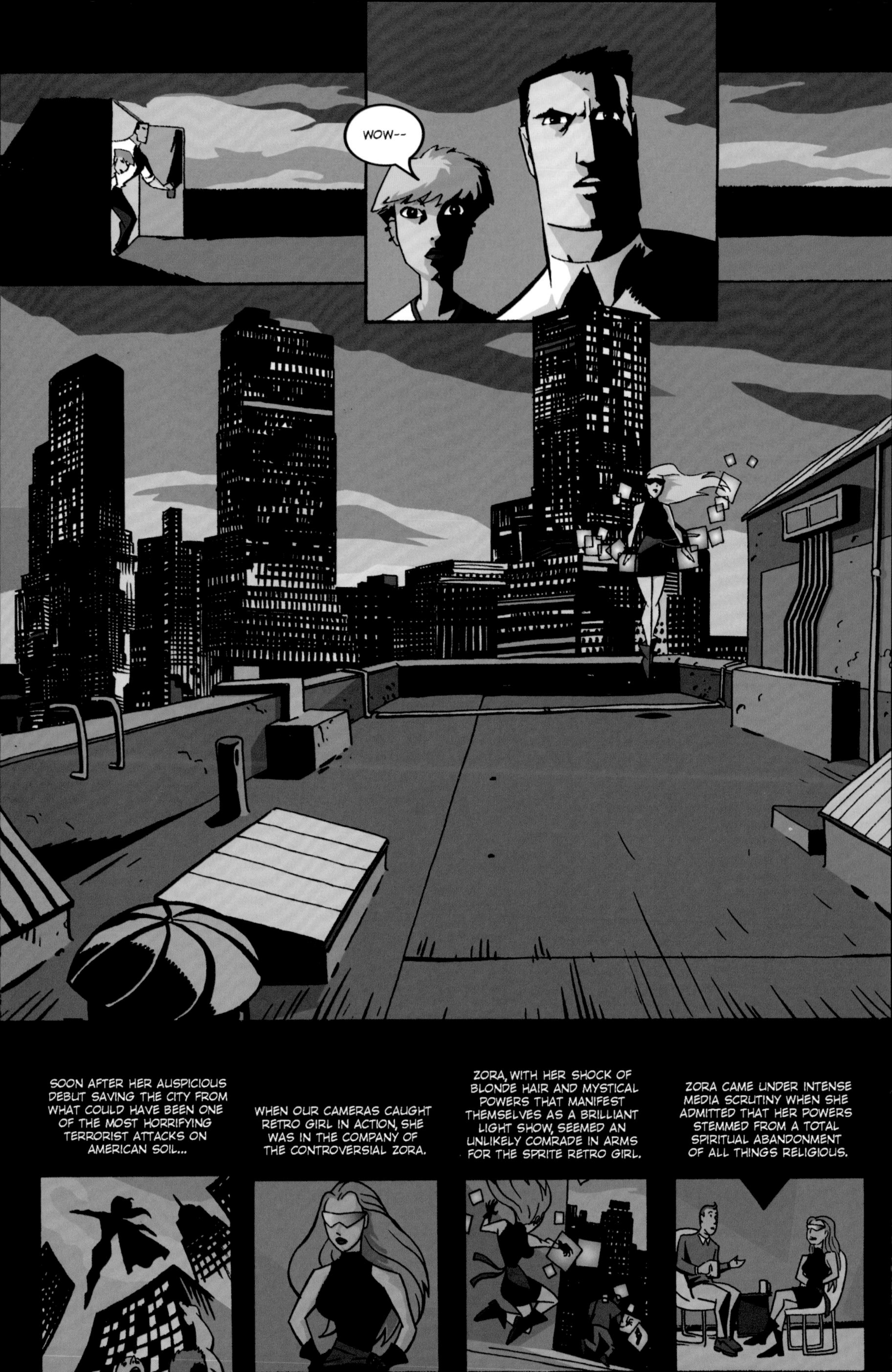
WOW--
SOON AFTER HER AUSPICIOUS DEBUT SAVING THE CITY FROM WHAT COULD HAVE BEEN ONE OF THE MOST HORRIFYING TERRORIST ATTACKS ON AMERICAN SOIL...
WHEN OUR CAMERAS CAUGHT RETRO GIRL IN ACTION, SHE WAS IN THE COMPANY OF THE CONTROVERSIAL ZORA.
ZORA, WITH HER SHOCK OF BLONDE HAIR AND MYSTICAL POWERS THAT MANIFEST THEMSELVES AS A BRILLIANT LIGHT SHOW, SEEMED AN UNLIKELY COMRADE IN ARMS FOR THE SPRITE RETRO GIRL.
ZORA CAME UNDER INTENSE MEDIA SCRUTINY WHEN SHE ADMITTED THAT HER POWERS STEMMED FROM A TOTAL SPIRITUAL ABANDONMENT OF ALL THINGS RELIGIOUS.

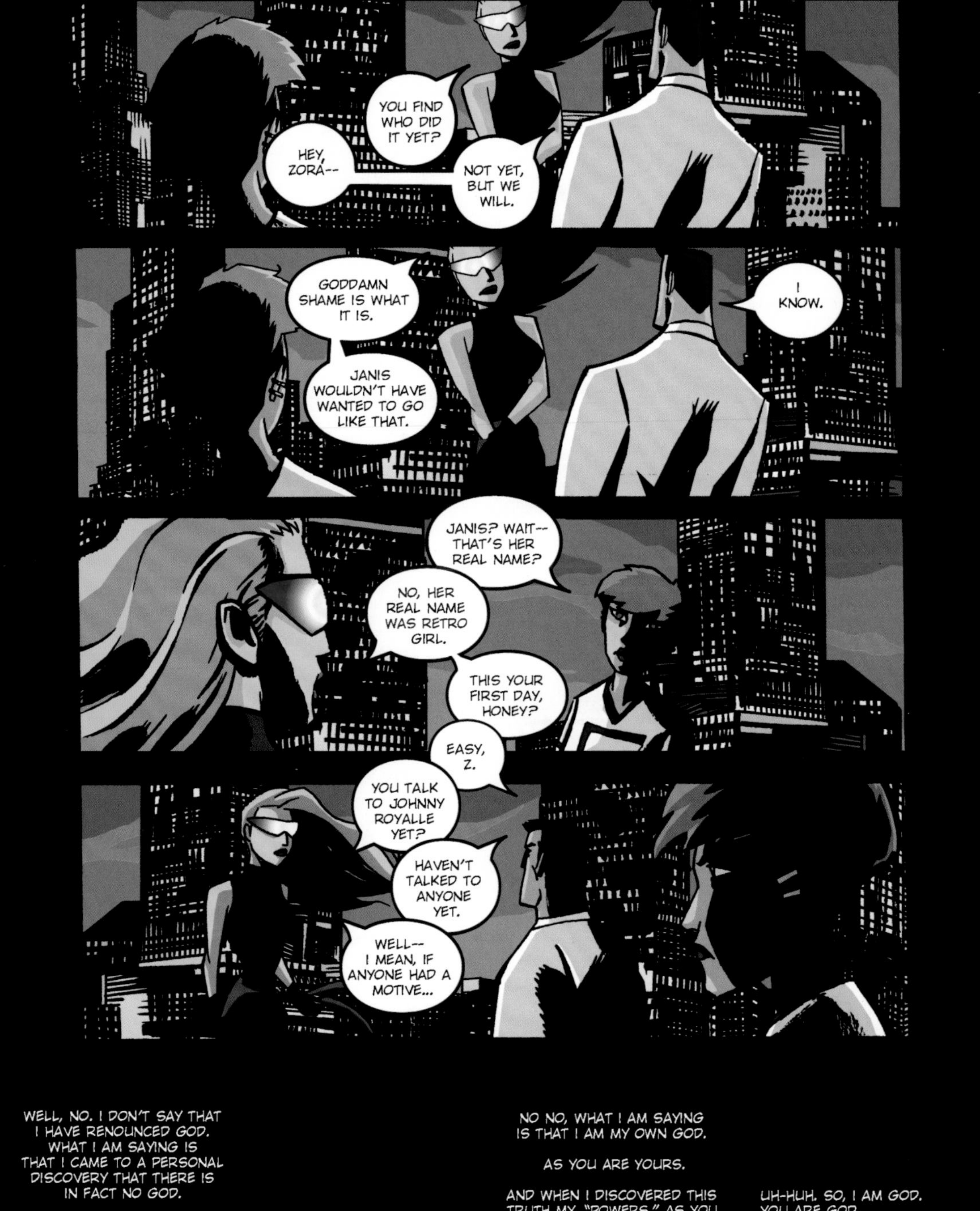

YOU FIND WHO DID IT YET?
HEY, ZORA--
NOT YET, BUT WE WILL.
GODDAMN SHAME IS WHAT IT IS.
JANIS WOULDN'T HAVE WANTED TO GO LIKE THAT.
I KNOW.
JANIS? WAIT-- THAT'S HER REAL NAME?
NO, HER REAL NAME WAS RETRO GIRL.
THIS YOUR FIRST DAY, HONEY?
EASY, Z.
YOU TALK TO JOHNNY ROYALLE YET?
HAVEN'T TALKED TO ANYONE YET.
WELL-- I MEAN, IF ANYONE HAD A MOTIVE...

WELL, NO. I DON'T SAY THAT I HAVE RENOUNCED GOD. WHAT I AM SAYING IS THAT I CAME TO A PERSONAL DISCOVERY THAT THERE IS IN FACT NO GOD.

AND IF THERE IS NO GOD, THEN BY DEFAULT I AM MY OWN GOD.

SO, YOU'RE SAYING THAT YOU ARE GOD?

NO NO, WHAT I AM SAYING IS THAT I AM MY OWN GOD.

AS YOU ARE YOURS.

AND WHEN I DISCOVERED THIS TRUTH, MY "POWERS," AS YOU CALL THEM--

THEY--THEY JUST WERE.

UH-HUH. SO, I AM GOD. YOU ARE GOD.

THAT'S RIGHT.

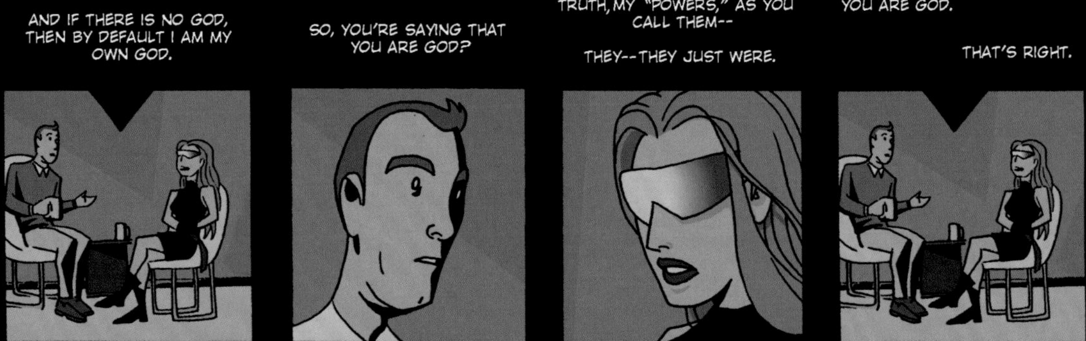

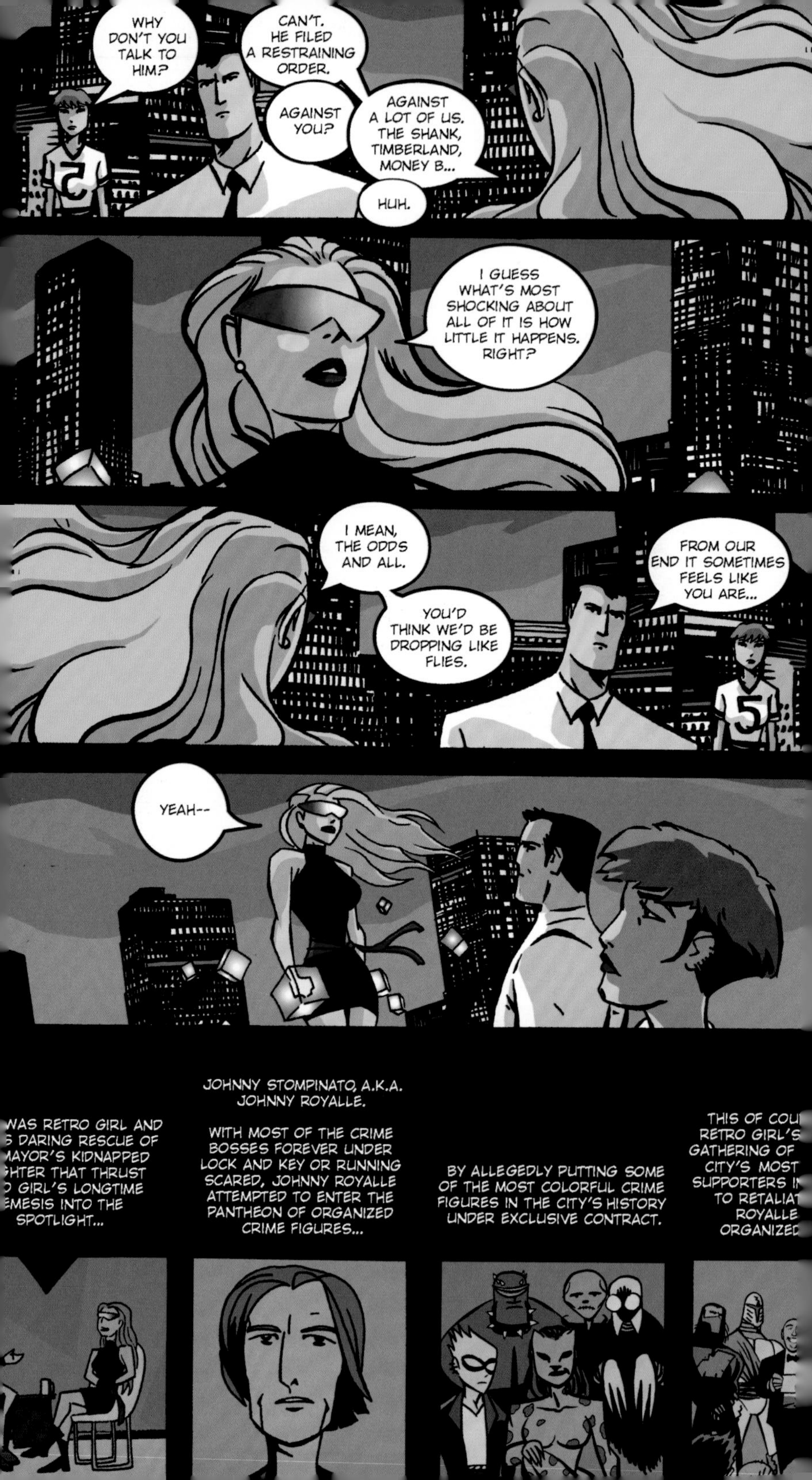
WHY DON'T YOU TALK TO HIM?
CAN'T. HE FILED A RESTRAINING ORDER.
AGAINST YOU?
AGAINST A LOT OF US. THE SHANK, TIMBERLAND, MONEY B...
HUH.
I GUESS WHAT'S MOST SHOCKING ABOUT ALL OF IT IS HOW LITTLE IT HAPPENS. RIGHT?
I MEAN, THE ODDS AND ALL.
YOU'D THINK WE'D BE DROPPING LIKE FLIES.
FROM OUR END IT SOMETIMES FEELS LIKE YOU ARE...
YEAH--
WAS RETRO GIRL AND DARING RESCUE OF MAYOR'S KIDNAPPED GHTER THAT THRUST GIRL'S LONGTIME EMESIS INTO THE SPOTLIGHT...
JOHNNY STOMPINATO, A.K.A. JOHNNY ROYALLE.
WITH MOST OF THE CRIME BOSSES FOREVER UNDER LOCK AND KEY OR RUNNING SCARED, JOHNNY ROYALLE ATTEMPTED TO ENTER THE PANTHEON OF ORGANIZED CRIME FIGURES...
BY ALLEGEDLY PUTTING SOME OF THE MOST COLORFUL CRIME FIGURES IN THE CITY'S HISTORY UNDER EXCLUSIVE CONTRACT.
THIS OF COU RETRO GIRL'S GATHERING OF CITY'S MOST SUPPORTERS IN TO RETALIAT ROYALLE ORGANIZED

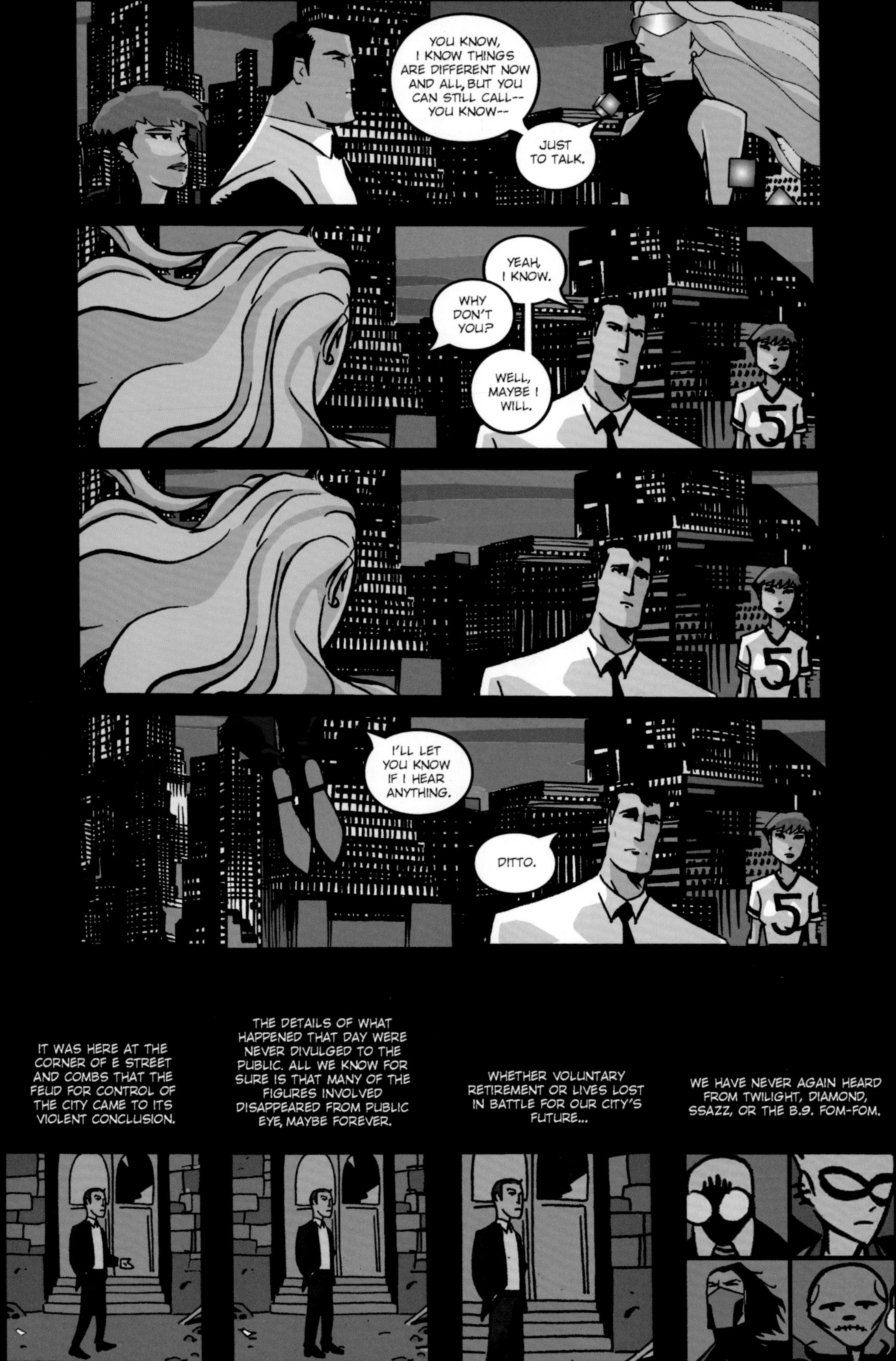
YOU KNOW, I KNOW THINGS ARE DIFFERENT NOW AND ALL, BUT YOU CAN STILL CALL-- YOU KNOW--
JUST TO TALK.
YEAH, I KNOW.
WHY DON'T YOU?
WELL, MAYBE I WILL.
I'LL LET YOU KNOW IF I HEAR ANYTHING.
DITTO.
IT WAS HERE AT THE CORNER OF E STREET AND COMBS THAT THE FEUD FOR CONTROL OF THE CITY CAME TO ITS VIOLENT CONCLUSION.
THE DETAILS OF WHAT HAPPENED THAT DAY WERE NEVER DIVULGED TO THE PUBLIC. ALL WE KNOW FOR SURE IS THAT MANY OF THE FIGURES INVOLVED DISAPPEARED FROM PUBLIC EYE, MAYBE FOREVER.
WHETHER VOLUNTARY RETIREMENT OR LIVES LOST IN BATTLE FOR OUR CITY'S FUTURE...
WE HAVE NEVER AGAIN HEARD FROM TWILIGHT, DIAMOND, SSAZZ, OR THE B.9. FOM-FOM.

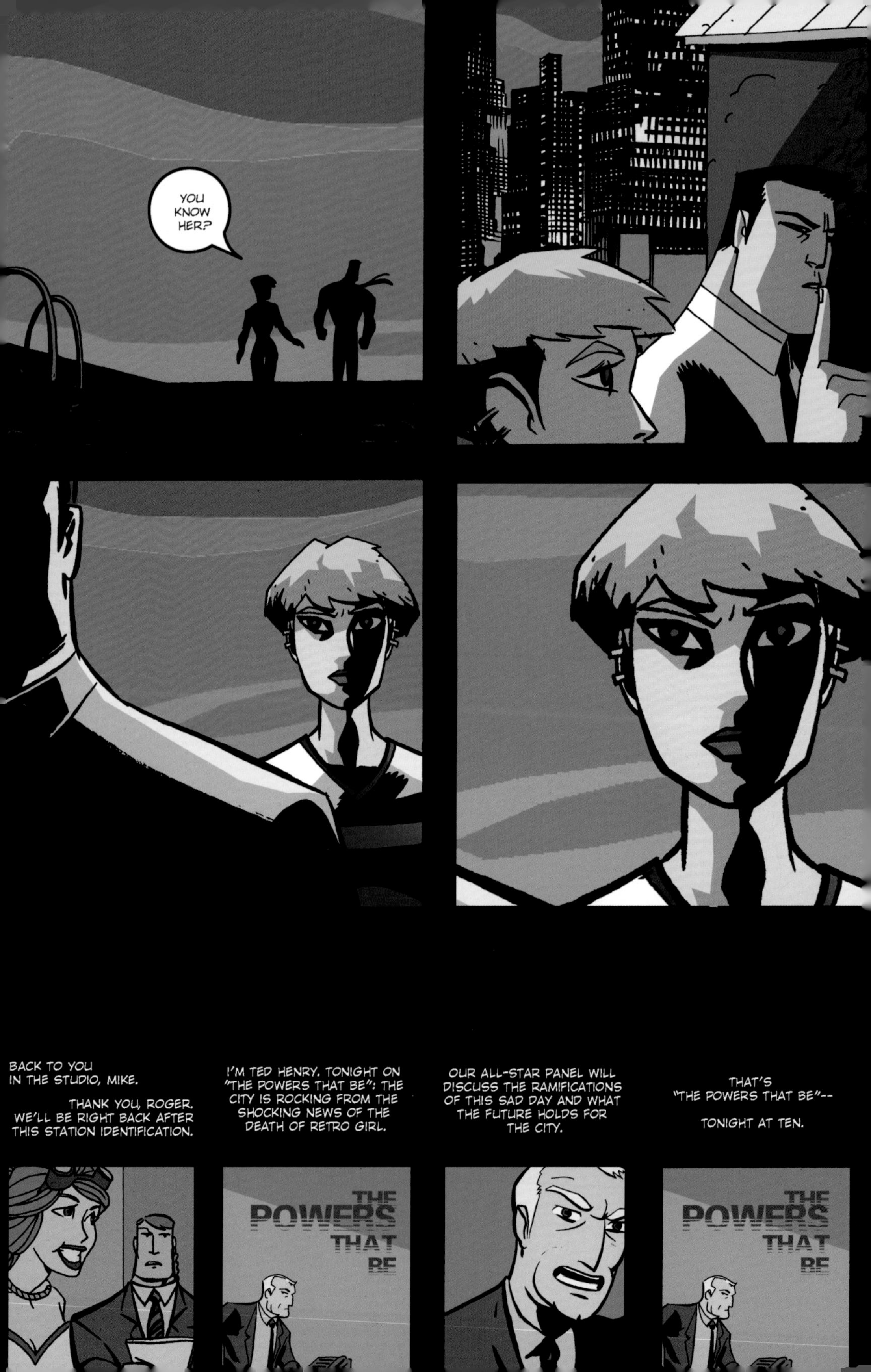
YOU KNOW HER?
BACK TO YOU IN THE STUDIO, MIKE.
THANK YOU, ROGER. WE'LL BE RIGHT BACK AFTER THIS STATION IDENTIFICATION.
THE POWERS THAT BE
I'M TED HENRY. TONIGHT ON "THE POWERS THAT BE": THE CITY IS ROCKING FROM THE SHOCKING NEWS OF THE DEATH OF RETRO GIRL.
OUR ALL-STAR PANEL WILL DISCUSS THE RAMIFICATIONS OF THIS SAD DAY AND WHAT THE FUTURE HOLDS FOR THE CITY.
THAT'S "THE POWERS THAT BE"--
TONIGHT AT TEN.
THE POWERS THAT BE

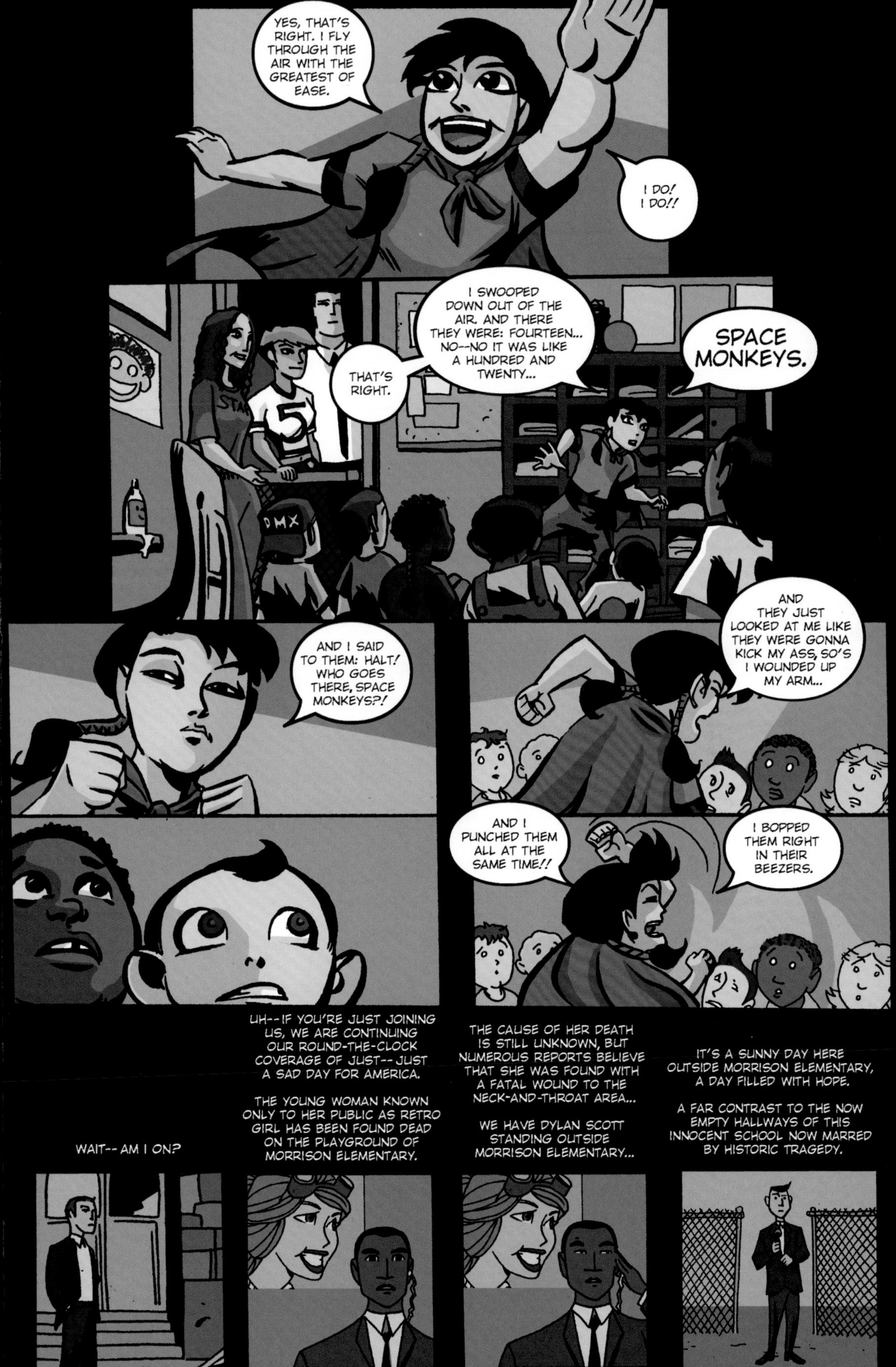

YES, THAT'S RIGHT. I FLY THROUGH THE AIR WITH THE GREATEST OF EASE.
I DO! I DO!!
THAT'S RIGHT.
I SWOOPED DOWN OUT OF THE AIR. AND THERE THEY WERE: FOURTEEN... NO--NO IT WAS LIKE A HUNDRED AND TWENTY...
SPACE MONKEYS.
DMX
AND I SAID TO THEM: HALT! WHO GOES THERE, SPACE MONKEYS?!
AND THEY JUST LOOKED AT ME LIKE THEY WERE GONNA KICK MY ASS, SO'S I WOUNDED UP MY ARM...
AND I PUNCHED THEM ALL AT THE SAME TIME!!
I BOPPED THEM RIGHT IN THEIR BEEZERS.
WAIT-- AM I ON?
UH-- IF YOU'RE JUST JOINING US, WE ARE CONTINUING OUR ROUND-THE-CLOCK COVERAGE OF JUST-- JUST A SAD DAY FOR AMERICA.
THE YOUNG WOMAN KNOWN ONLY TO HER PUBLIC AS RETRO GIRL HAS BEEN FOUND DEAD ON THE PLAYGROUND OF MORRISON ELEMENTARY.
THE CAUSE OF HER DEATH IS STILL UNKNOWN, BUT NUMEROUS REPORTS BELIEVE THAT SHE WAS FOUND WITH A FATAL WOUND TO THE NECK-AND-THROAT AREA...
WE HAVE DYLAN SCOTT STANDING OUTSIDE MORRISON ELEMENTARY...
IT'S A SUNNY DAY HERE OUTSIDE MORRISON ELEMENTARY, A DAY FILLED WITH HOPE.
A FAR CONTRAST TO THE NOW EMPTY HALLWAYS OF THIS INNOCENT SCHOOL NOW MARRED BY HISTORIC TRAGEDY.

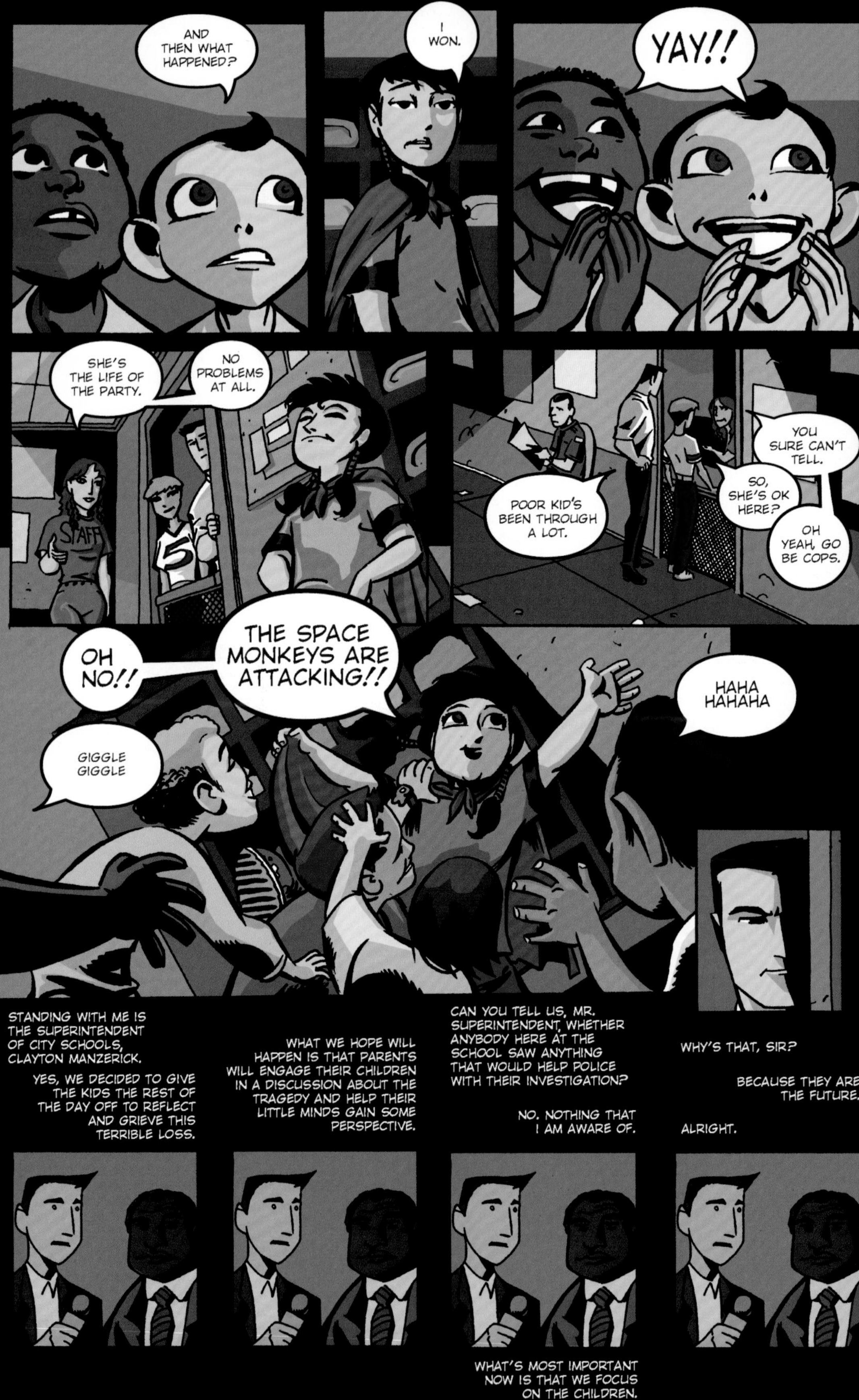
AND THEN WHAT HAPPENED?
I WON.
YAY!!
SHE'S THE LIFE OF THE PARTY.
NO PROBLEMS AT ALL.
STAFF
5
YOU SURE CAN'T TELL.
POOR KID'S BEEN THROUGH A LOT.
SO, SHE'S OK HERE?
OH YEAH, GO BE COPS.
OH NO!!
THE SPACE MONKEYS ARE ATTACKING!!
HAHA HAHAHA
GIGGLE GIGGLE
STANDING WITH ME IS THE SUPERINTENDENT OF CITY SCHOOLS, CLAYTON MANZERICK.
YES, WE DECIDED TO GIVE THE KIDS THE REST OF THE DAY OFF TO REFLECT AND GRIEVE THIS TERRIBLE LOSS.
WHAT WE HOPE WILL HAPPEN IS THAT PARENTS WILL ENGAGE THEIR CHILDREN IN A DISCUSSION ABOUT THE TRAGEDY AND HELP THEIR LITTLE MINDS GAIN SOME PERSPECTIVE.
CAN YOU TELL US, MR. SUPERINTENDENT, WHETHER ANYBODY HERE AT THE SCHOOL SAW ANYTHING THAT WOULD HELP POLICE WITH THEIR INVESTIGATION?
NO. NOTHING THAT I AM AWARE OF.
WHAT'S MOST IMPORTANT NOW IS THAT WE FOCUS ON THE CHILDREN.
WHY'S THAT, SIR?
BECAUSE THEY ARE THE FUTURE.
ALRIGHT.

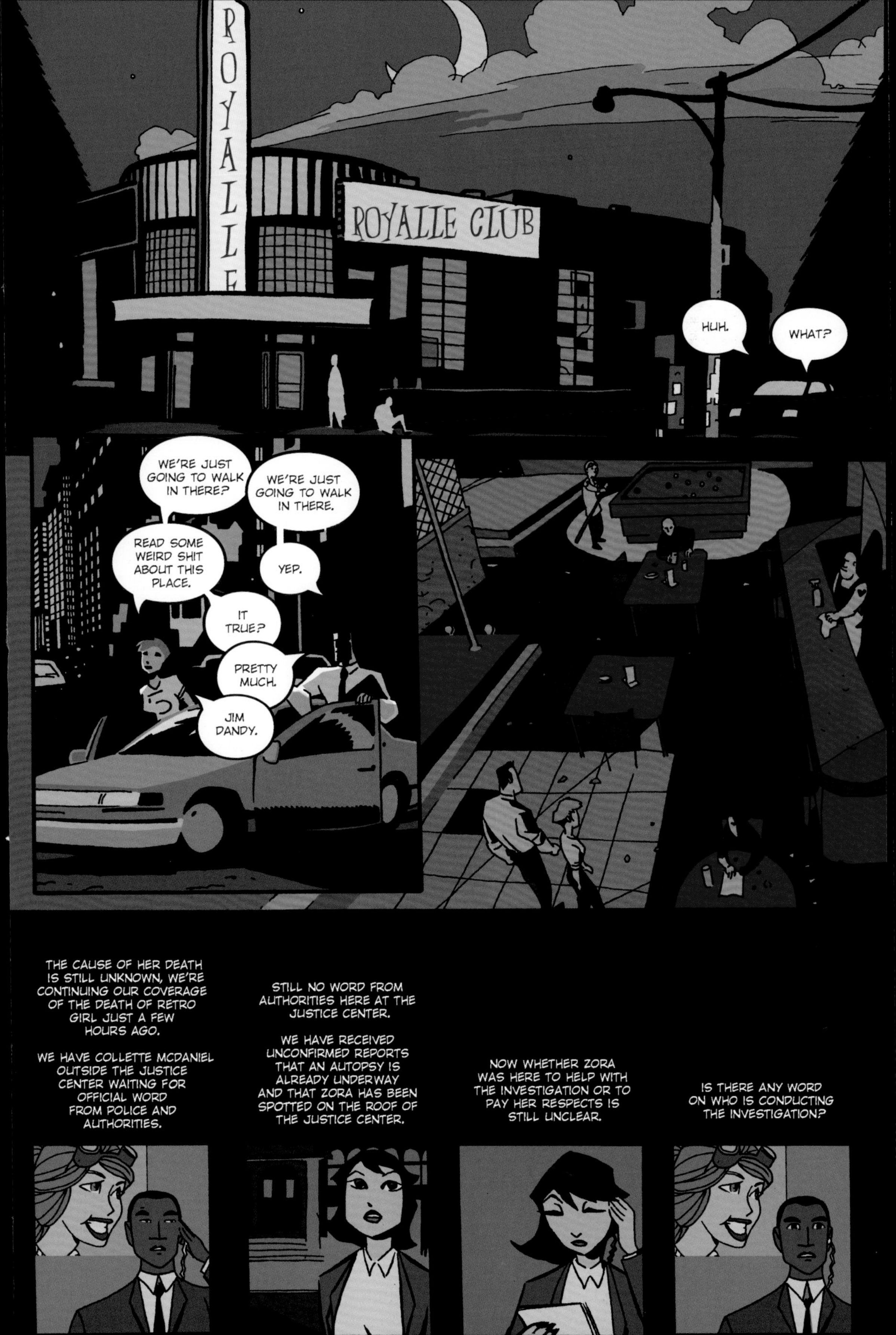
ROYALLE
ROYALLE CLUB
HUH.
WHAT?
WE'RE JUST GOING TO WALK IN THERE?
WE'RE JUST GOING TO WALK IN THERE.
READ SOME WEIRD SHIT ABOUT THIS PLACE.
YEP.
IT TRUE?
PRETTY MUCH.
JIM DANDY.
THE CAUSE OF HER DEATH IS STILL UNKNOWN, WE'RE CONTINUING OUR COVERAGE OF THE DEATH OF RETRO GIRL JUST A FEW HOURS AGO.
WE HAVE COLLETTE MCDANIEL OUTSIDE THE JUSTICE CENTER WAITING FOR OFFICIAL WORD FROM POLICE AND AUTHORITIES.
STILL NO WORD FROM AUTHORITIES HERE AT THE JUSTICE CENTER.
WE HAVE RECEIVED UNCONFIRMED REPORTS THAT AN AUTOPSY IS ALREADY UNDERWAY AND THAT ZORA HAS BEEN SPOTTED ON THE ROOF OF THE JUSTICE CENTER.
NOW WHETHER ZORA WAS HERE TO HELP WITH THE INVESTIGATION OR TO PAY HER RESPECTS IS STILL UNCLEAR.
IS THERE ANY WORD ON WHO IS CONDUCTING THE INVESTIGATION?

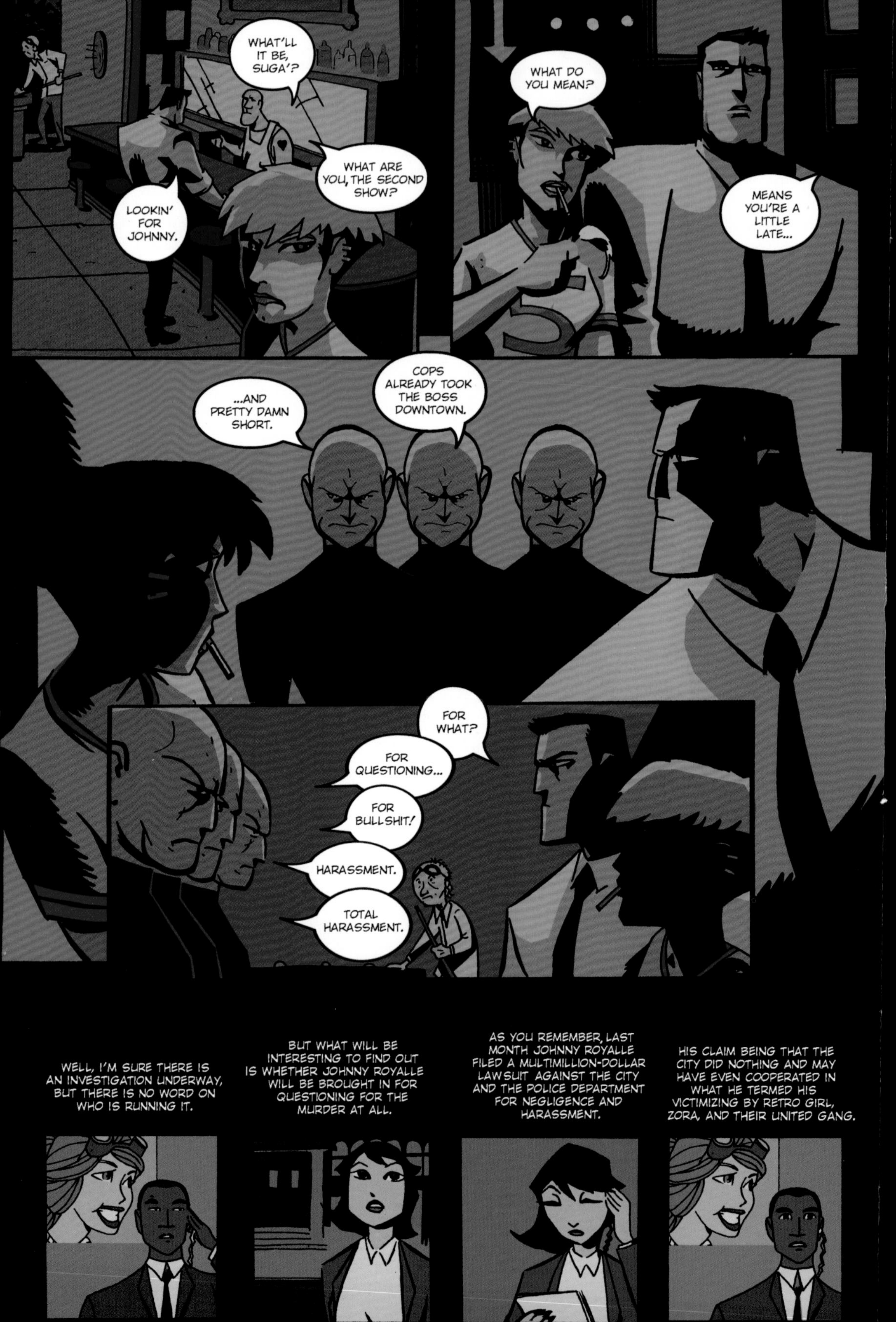
WHAT'LL IT BE, SUGA'?
LOOKIN' FOR JOHNNY.
WHAT ARE YOU, THE SECOND SHOW?
WHAT DO YOU MEAN?
MEANS YOU'RE A LITTLE LATE...
...AND PRETTY DAMN SHORT.
COPS ALREADY TOOK THE BOSS DOWNTOWN.
FOR WHAT?
FOR QUESTIONING...
FOR BULLSHIT!
HARASSMENT.
TOTAL HARASSMENT.
WELL, I'M SURE THERE IS AN INVESTIGATION UNDERWAY, BUT THERE IS NO WORD ON WHO IS RUNNING IT.
BUT WHAT WILL BE INTERESTING TO FIND OUT IS WHETHER JOHNNY ROYALLE WILL BE BROUGHT IN FOR QUESTIONING FOR THE MURDER AT ALL.
AS YOU REMEMBER, LAST MONTH JOHNNY ROYALLE FILED A MULTIMILLION-DOLLAR LAWSUIT AGAINST THE CITY AND THE POLICE DEPARTMENT FOR NEGLIGENCE AND HARASSMENT.
HIS CLAIM BEING THAT THE CITY DID NOTHING AND MAY HAVE EVEN COOPERATED IN WHAT HE TERMED HIS VICTIMIZING BY RETRO GIRL, ZORA, AND THEIR UNITED GANG.

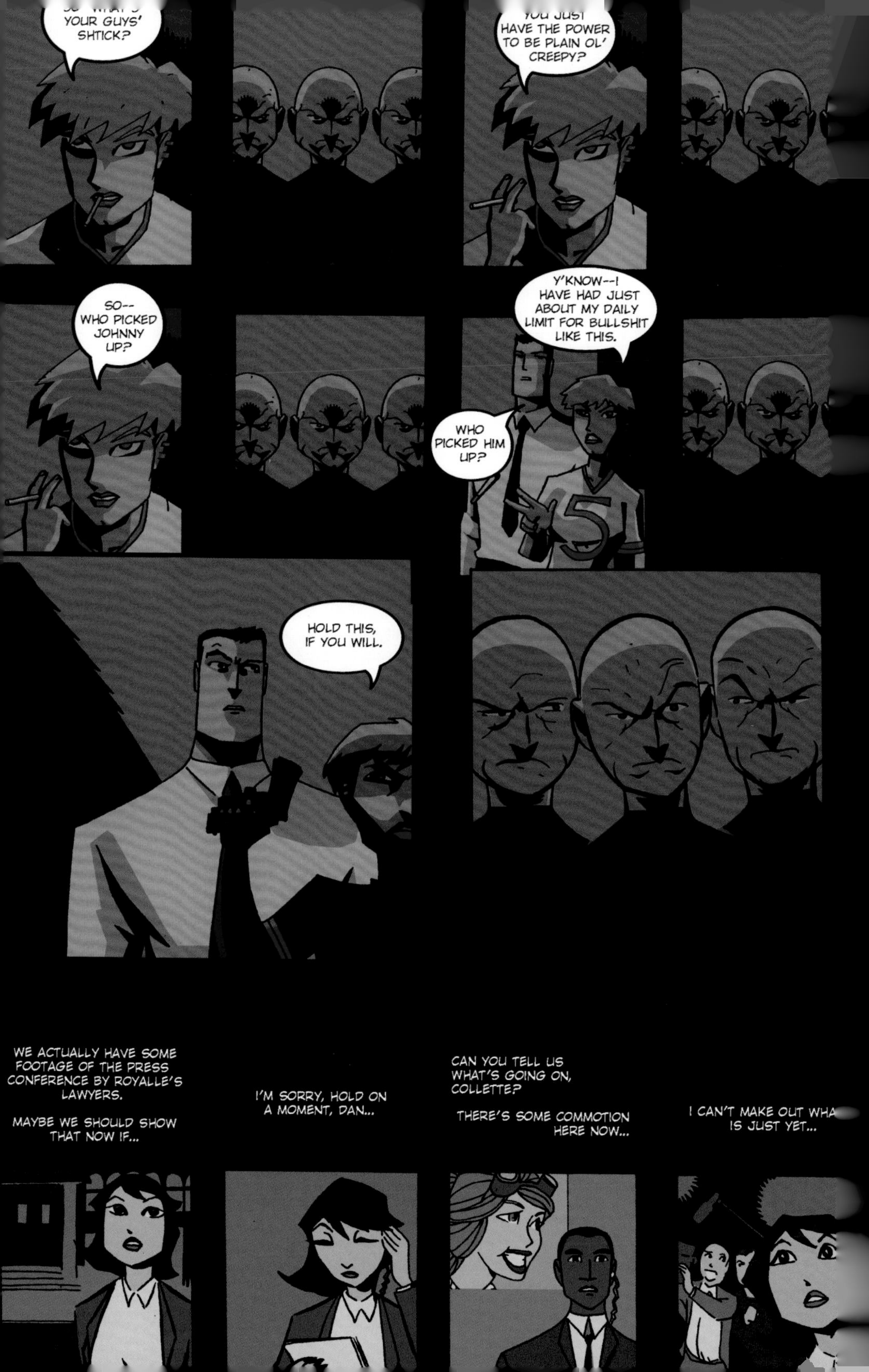
YOUR GUYS' SHTICK?
YOU JUST HAVE THE POWER TO BE PLAIN OL' CREEPY?
SO-- WHO PICKED JOHNNY UP?
Y'KNOW--I HAVE HAD JUST ABOUT MY DAILY LIMIT FOR BULLSHIT LIKE THIS.
WHO PICKED HIM UP?
HOLD THIS, IF YOU WILL.
WE ACTUALLY HAVE SOME FOOTAGE OF THE PRESS CONFERENCE BY ROYALLE'S LAWYERS.
MAYBE WE SHOULD SHOW THAT NOW IF...
I'M SORRY, HOLD ON A MOMENT, DAN...
CAN YOU TELL US WHAT'S GOING ON, COLLETTE?
THERE'S SOME COMMOTION HERE NOW...
I CAN'T MAKE OUT WHA IS JUST YET...

BOBBY, TURN THE
CAMERA AROUND.

HOLD ON.

NOT ON ME, AROUND.

WE'RE--WE'RE TRYING TO--
TO GET IN HERE--

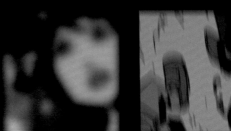

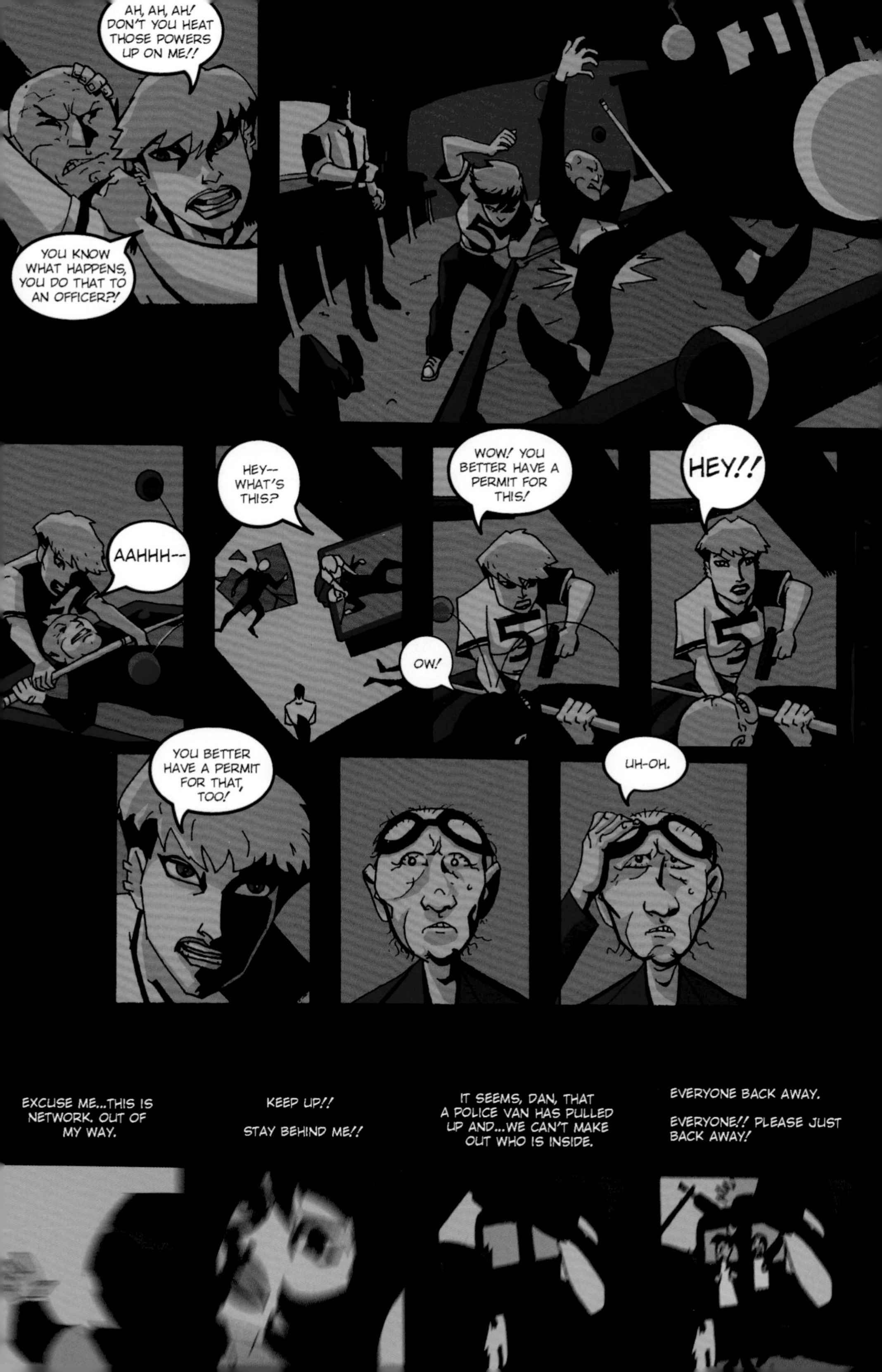
AH, AH, AH! DON'T YOU HEAT THOSE POWERS UP ON ME!!
YOU KNOW WHAT HAPPENS, YOU DO THAT TO AN OFFICER?!
AAHHH--
HEY-- WHAT'S THIS?
WOW! YOU BETTER HAVE A PERMIT FOR THIS!
OW!
HEY!!
YOU BETTER HAVE A PERMIT FOR THAT, TOO!
UH-OH.
EXCUSE ME...THIS IS NETWORK. OUT OF MY WAY.
KEEP UP!!
STAY BEHIND ME!!
IT SEEMS, DAN, THAT A POLICE VAN HAS PULLED UP AND...WE CAN'T MAKE OUT WHO IS INSIDE.
EVERYONE BACK AWAY.
EVERYONE!! PLEASE JUST BACK AWAY!

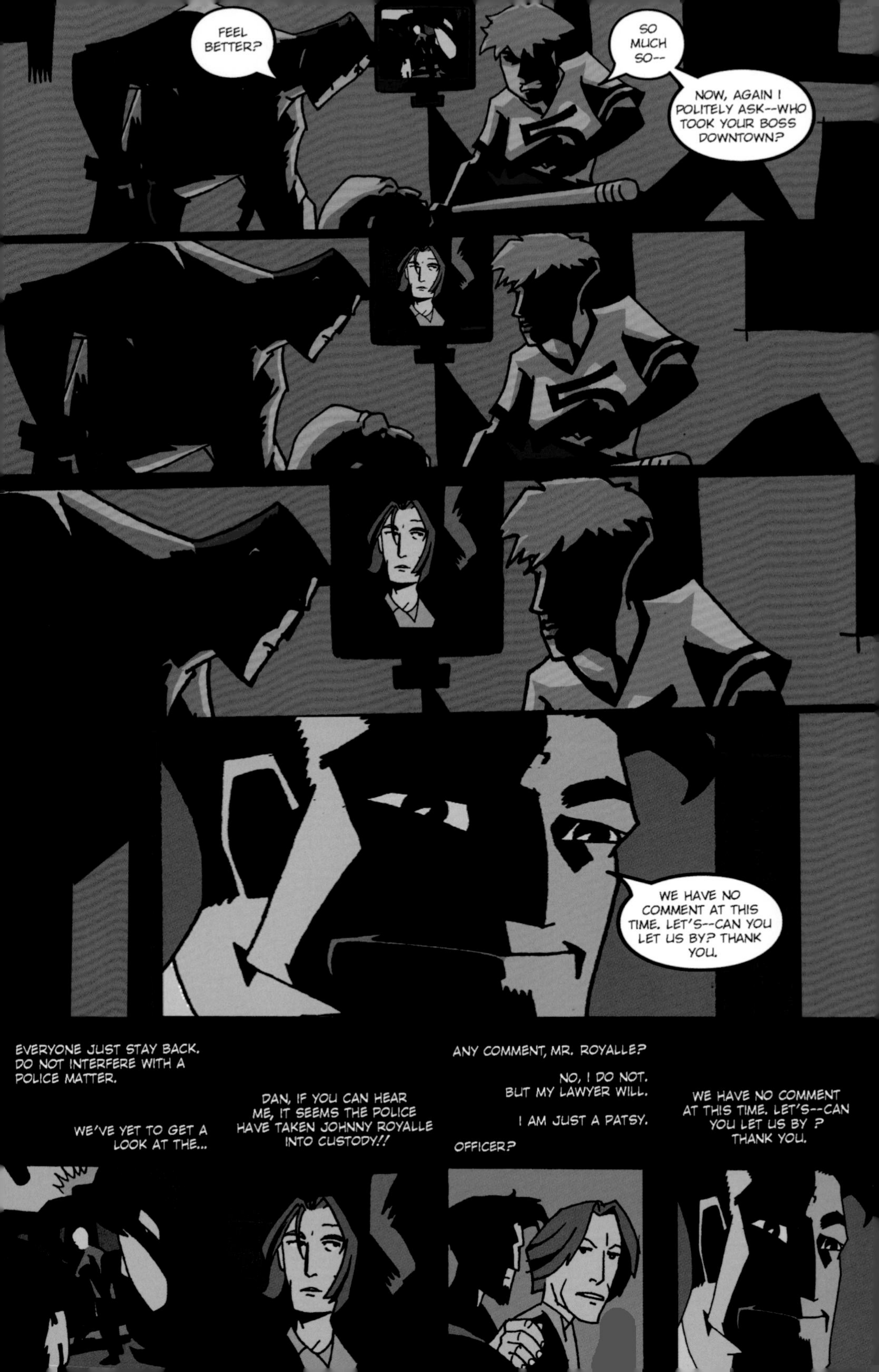

FEEL BETTER?
SO MUCH SO--
NOW, AGAIN I POLITELY ASK--WHO TOOK YOUR BOSS DOWNTOWN?
WE HAVE NO COMMENT AT THIS TIME. LET'S--CAN YOU LET US BY? THANK YOU.
EVERYONE JUST STAY BACK. DO NOT INTERFERE WITH A POLICE MATTER.
WE'VE YET TO GET A LOOK AT THE...
DAN, IF YOU CAN HEAR ME, IT SEEMS THE POLICE HAVE TAKEN JOHNNY ROYALLE INTO CUSTODY!!
ANY COMMENT, MR. ROYALLE?
NO, I DO NOT. BUT MY LAWYER WILL.
I AM JUST A PATSY.
OFFICER?
WE HAVE NO COMMENT AT THIS TIME. LET'S--CAN YOU LET US BY ? THANK YOU.

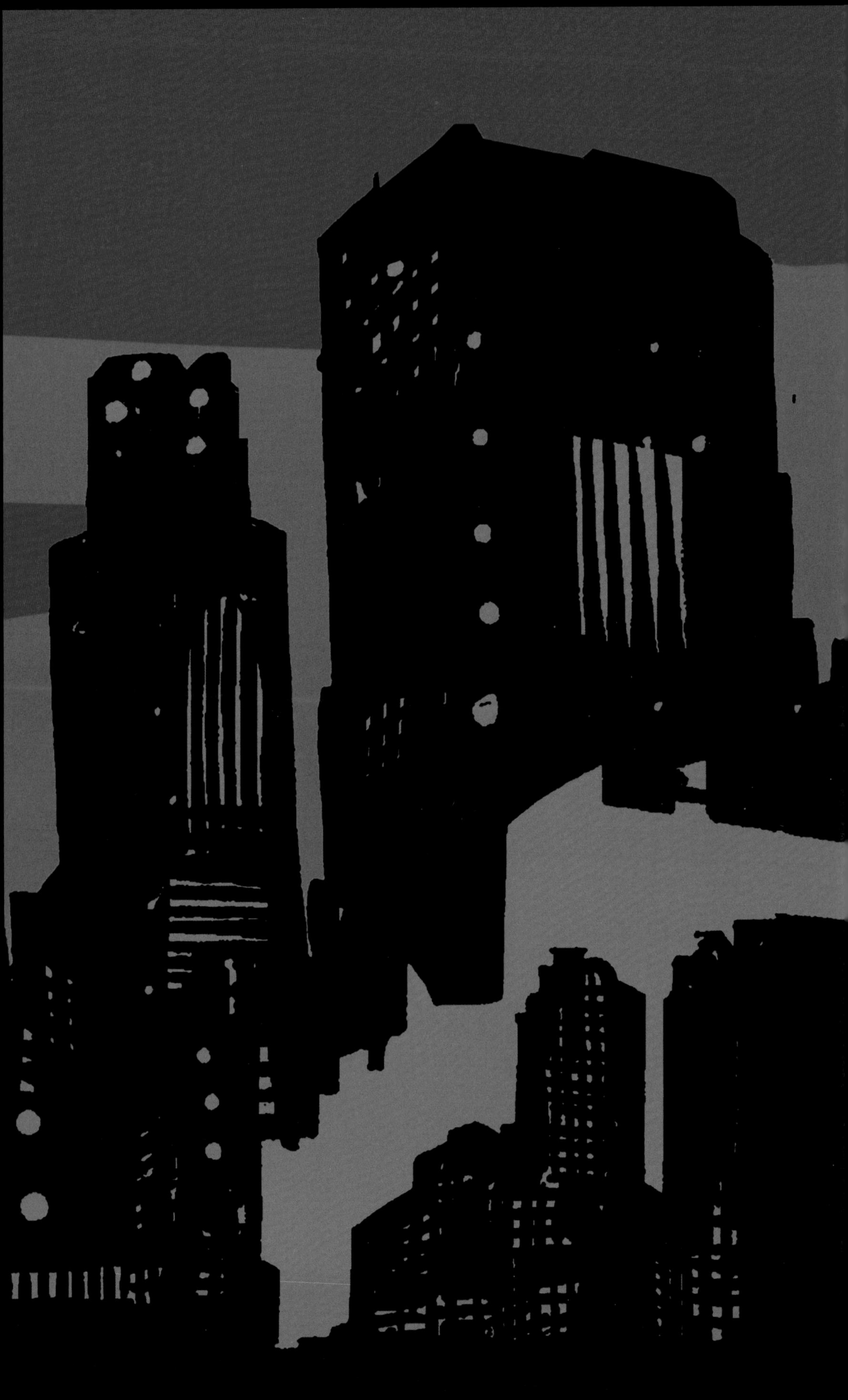

POWERS™

WHO KILLED RETRO GIRL?
CHAPTER 3

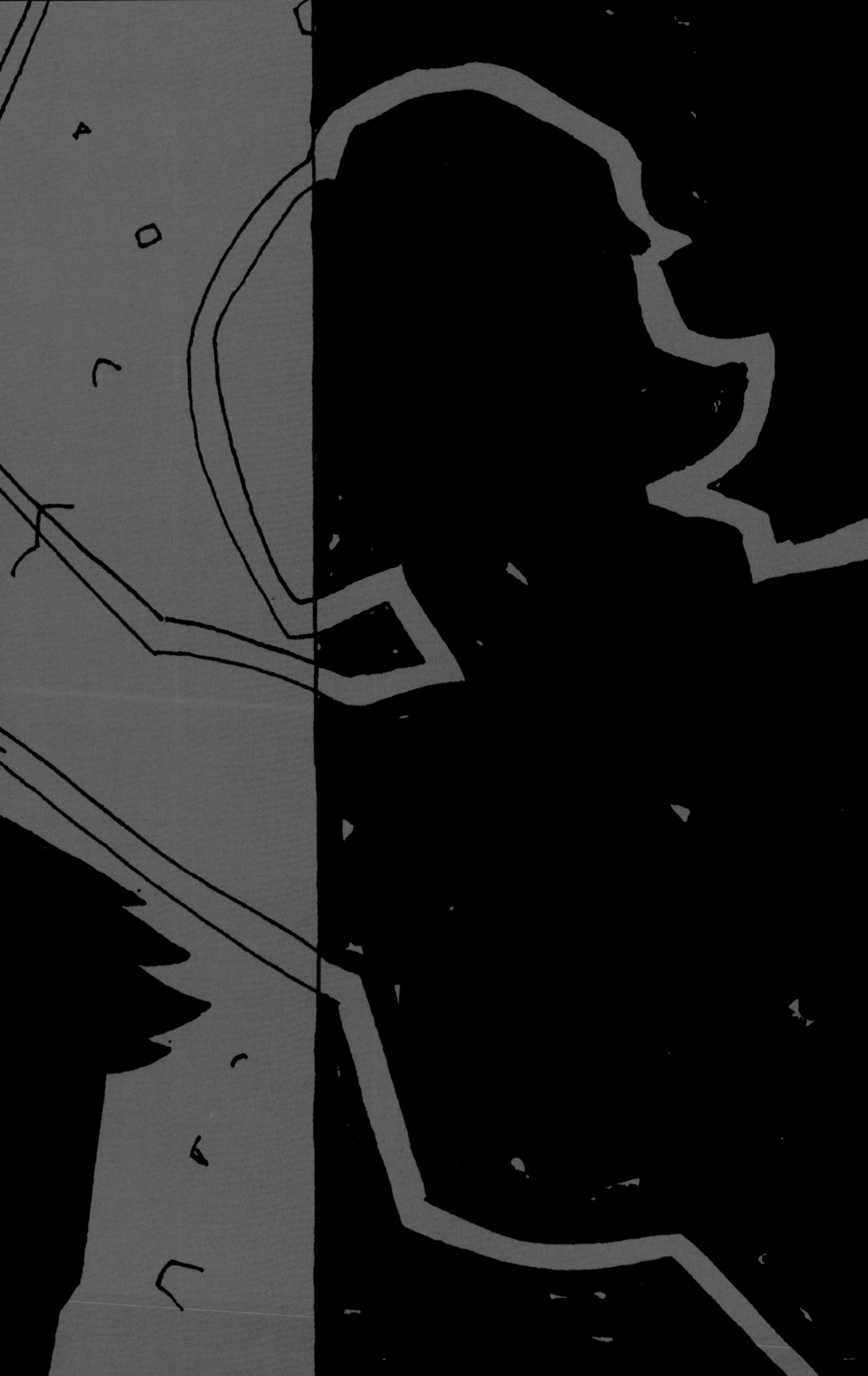

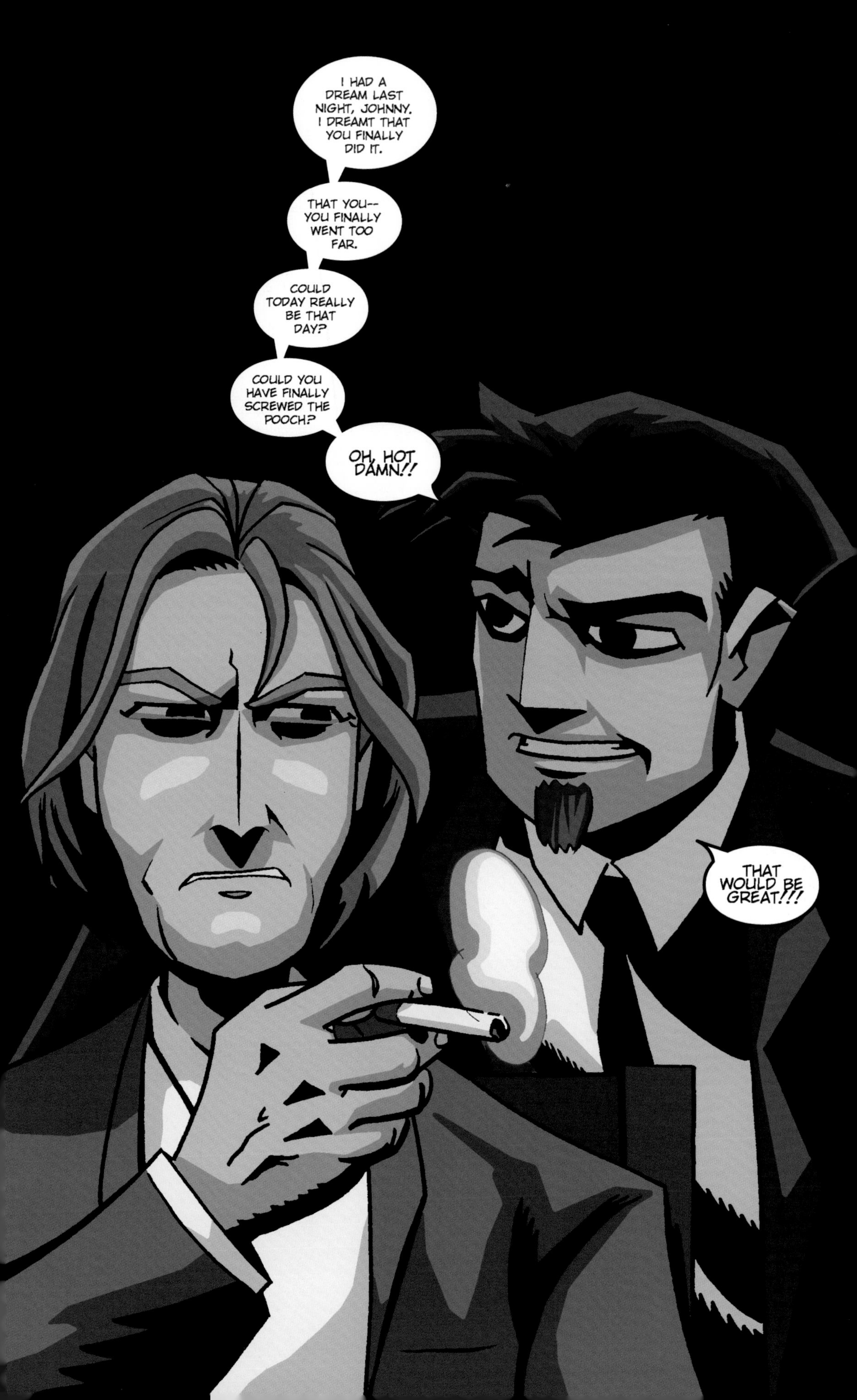
I HAD A DREAM LAST NIGHT, JOHNNY. I DREAMT THAT YOU FINALLY DID IT.
THAT YOU-- YOU FINALLY WENT TOO FAR.
COULD TODAY REALLY BE THAT DAY?
COULD YOU HAVE FINALLY SCREWED THE POOCH?
OH, HOT DAMN!!
THAT WOULD BE GREAT!!!

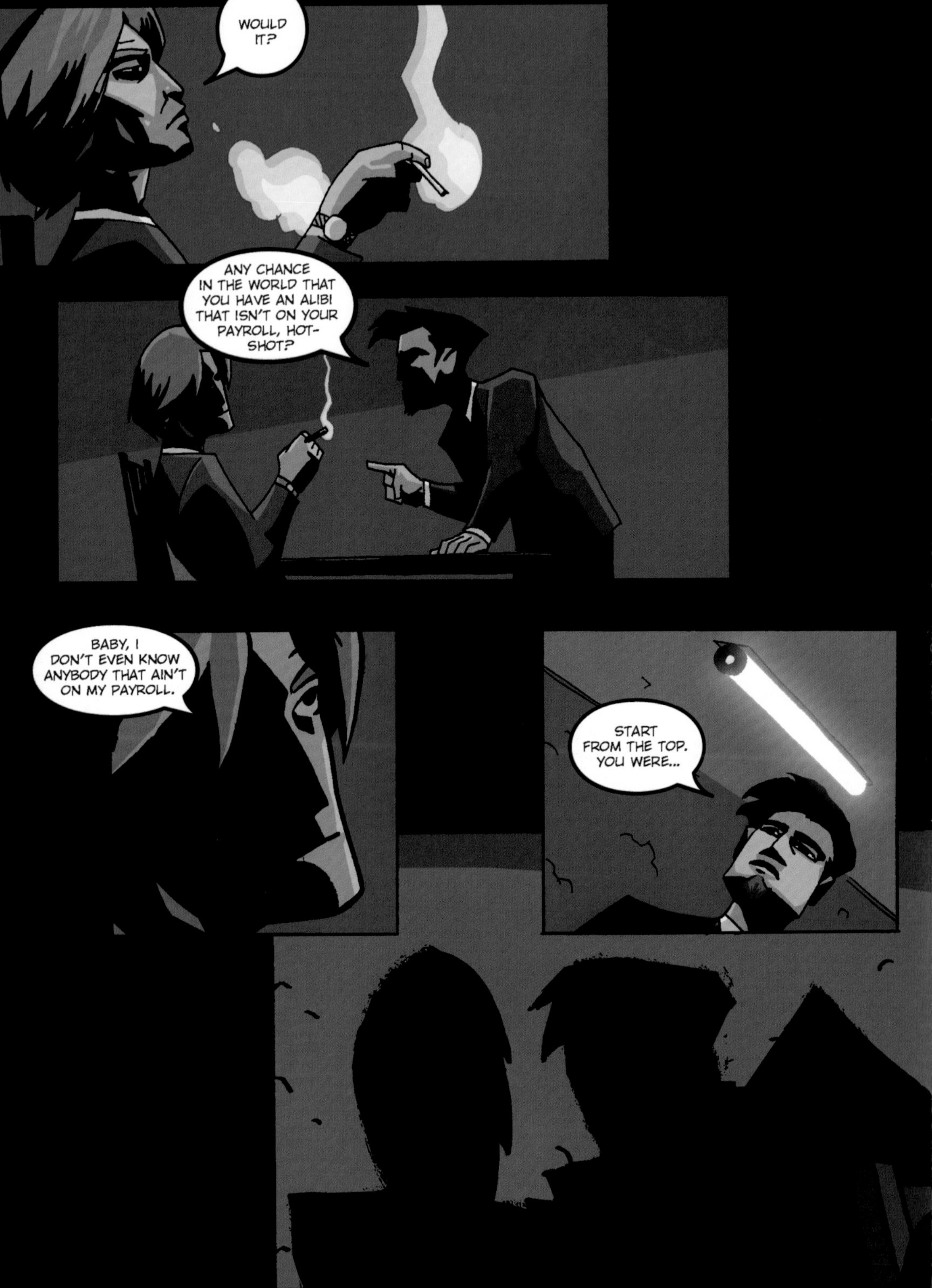
WOULD IT?
ANY CHANCE IN THE WORLD THAT YOU HAVE AN ALIBI THAT ISN'T ON YOUR PAYROLL, HOT-SHOT?
BABY, I DON'T EVEN KNOW ANYBODY THAT AIN'T ON MY PAYROLL.
START FROM THE TOP. YOU WERE...

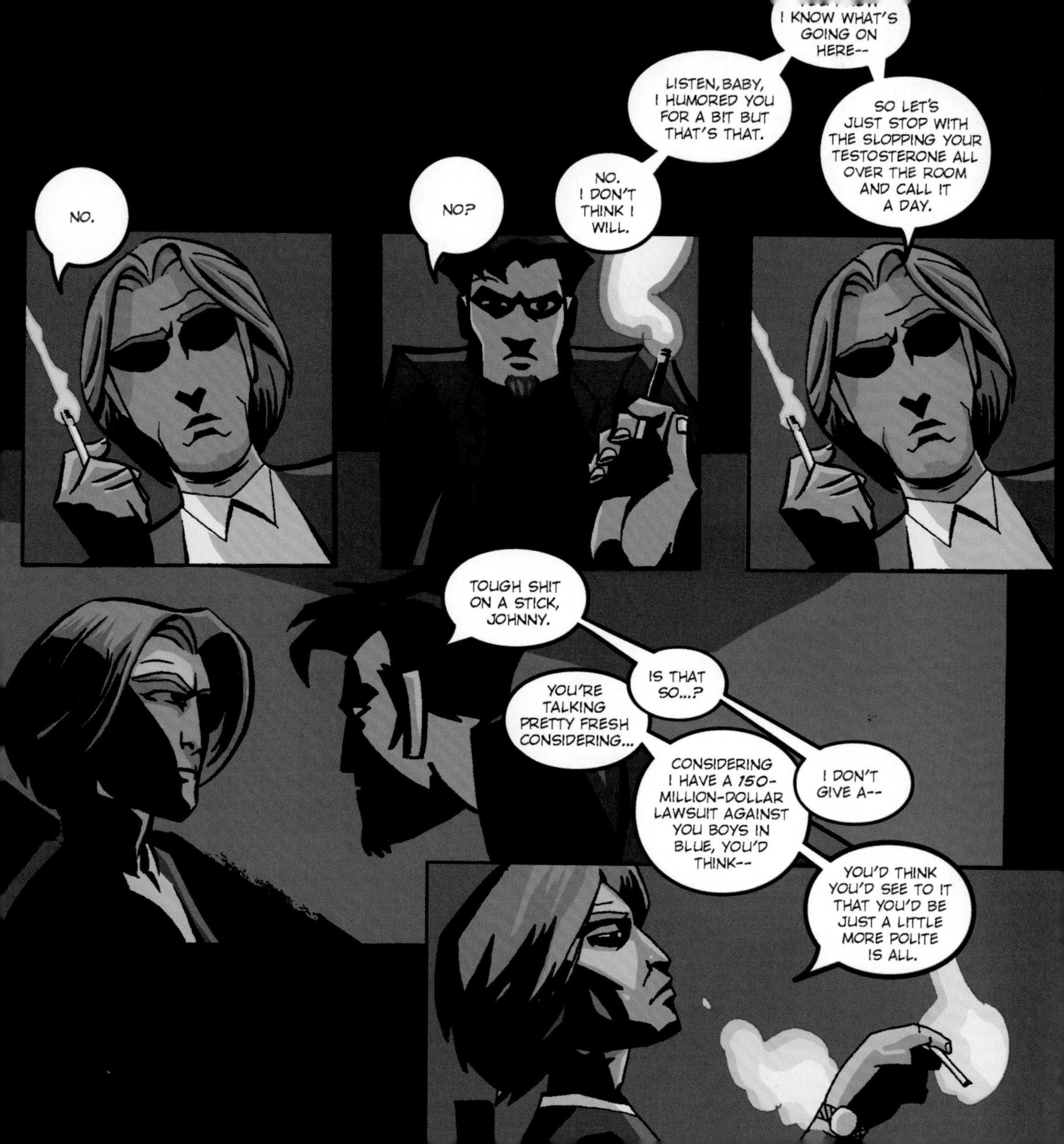
NO.
NO?
NO. I DON'T THINK I WILL.
LISTEN, BABY, I HUMORED YOU FOR A BIT BUT THAT'S THAT.
I KNOW WHAT'S GOING ON HERE--
SO LET'S JUST STOP WITH THE SLOPPING YOUR TESTOSTERONE ALL OVER THE ROOM AND CALL IT A DAY.
TOUGH SHIT ON A STICK, JOHNNY.
YOU'RE TALKING PRETTY FRESH CONSIDERING...
IS THAT SO...?
CONSIDERING I HAVE A 150-MILLION-DOLLAR LAWSUIT AGAINST YOU BOYS IN BLUE, YOU'D THINK--
I DON'T GIVE A--
YOU'D THINK YOU'D SEE TO IT THAT YOU'D BE JUST A LITTLE MORE POLITE IS ALL.

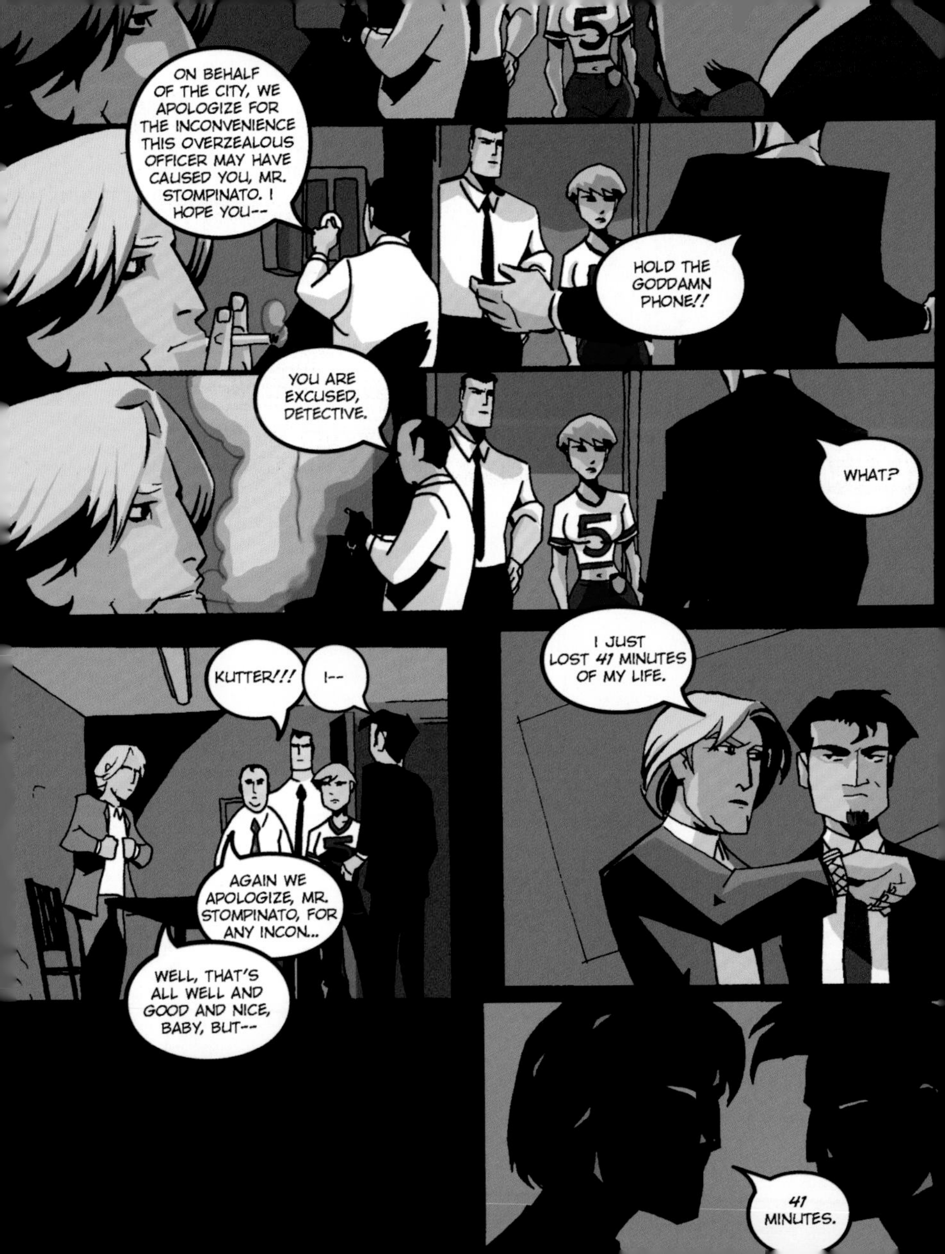
ON BEHALF OF THE CITY, WE APOLOGIZE FOR THE INCONVENIENCE THIS OVERZEALOUS OFFICER MAY HAVE CAUSED YOU, MR. STOMPINATO. I HOPE YOU--
HOLD THE GODDAMN PHONE!!
YOU ARE EXCUSED, DETECTIVE.
WHAT?
KUTTER!!!
I--
AGAIN WE APOLOGIZE, MR. STOMPINATO, FOR ANY INCON...
WELL, THAT'S ALL WELL AND GOOD AND NICE, BABY, BUT--
I JUST LOST 41 MINUTES OF MY LIFE.
41 MINUTES.

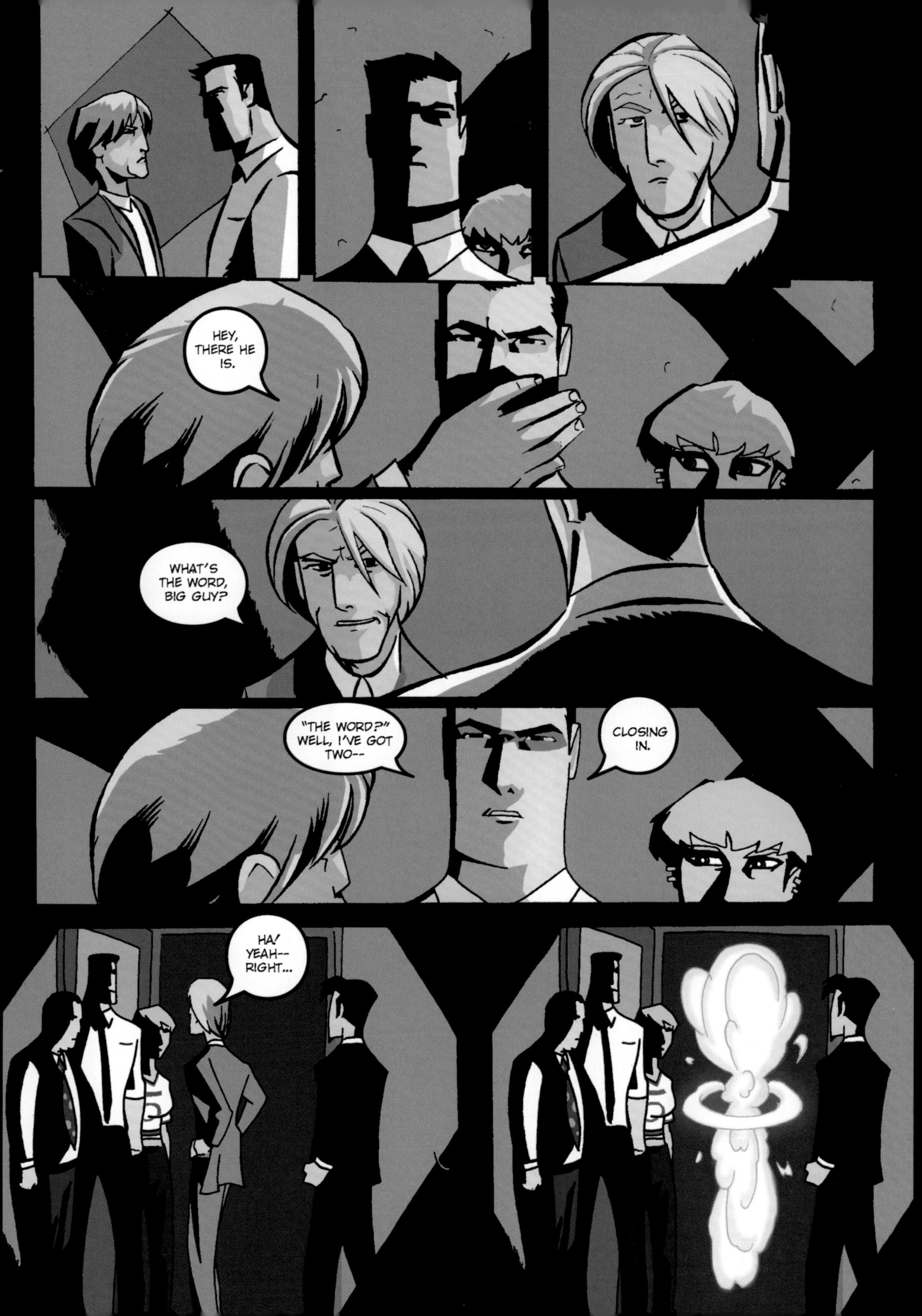
HEY, THERE HE IS.
WHAT'S THE WORD, BIG GUY?
"THE WORD?" WELL, I'VE GOT TWO--
CLOSING IN.
HA! YEAH-- RIGHT...

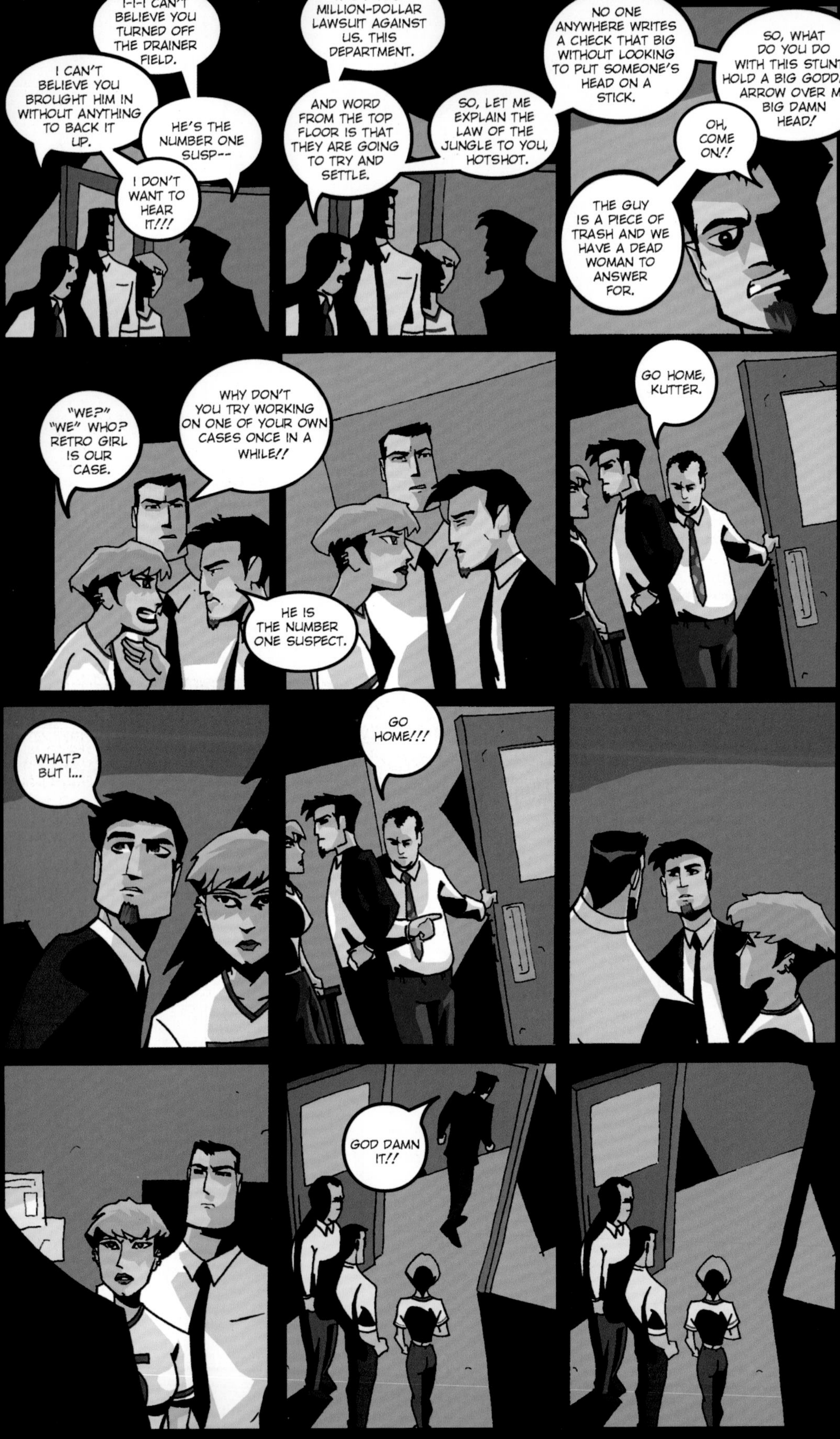
I-I-I CAN'T BELIEVE YOU TURNED OFF THE DRAINER FIELD.
I CAN'T BELIEVE YOU BROUGHT HIM IN WITHOUT ANYTHING TO BACK IT UP.
HE'S THE NUMBER ONE SUSP--
I DON'T WANT TO HEAR IT!!!
IT'S A 150-MILLION-DOLLAR LAWSUIT AGAINST US. THIS DEPARTMENT.
AND WORD FROM THE TOP FLOOR IS THAT THEY ARE GOING TO TRY AND SETTLE.
SO, LET ME EXPLAIN THE LAW OF THE JUNGLE TO YOU, HOTSHOT.
NO ONE ANYWHERE WRITES A CHECK THAT BIG WITHOUT LOOKING TO PUT SOMEONE'S HEAD ON A STICK.
SO, WHAT DO YOU DO WITH THIS STUNT? HOLD A BIG GODDAMN ARROW OVER MY BIG DAMN HEAD!
OH, COME ON!!
THE GUY IS A PIECE OF TRASH AND WE HAVE A DEAD WOMAN TO ANSWER FOR.
"WE?" "WE" WHO? RETRO GIRL IS OUR CASE.
WHY DON'T YOU TRY WORKING ON ONE OF YOUR OWN CASES ONCE IN A WHILE!!
HE IS THE NUMBER ONE SUSPECT.
GO HOME, KUTTER.
WHAT? BUT I...
GO HOME!!!
GOD DAMN IT!!

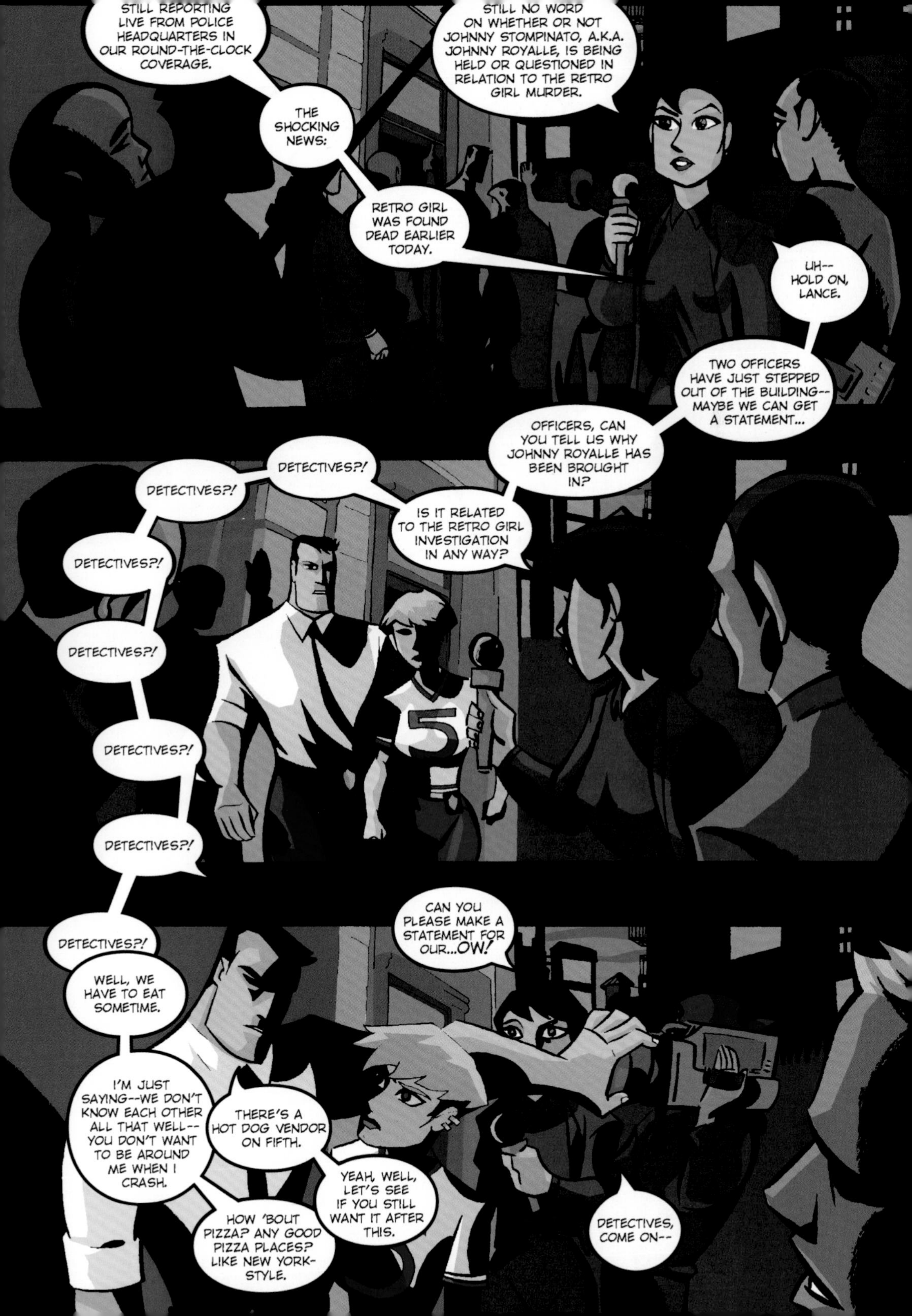
STILL REPORTING LIVE FROM POLICE HEADQUARTERS IN OUR ROUND-THE-CLOCK COVERAGE.
THE SHOCKING NEWS:
RETRO GIRL WAS FOUND DEAD EARLIER TODAY.
STILL NO WORD ON WHETHER OR NOT JOHNNY STOMPINATO, A.K.A. JOHNNY ROYALLE, IS BEING HELD OR QUESTIONED IN RELATION TO THE RETRO GIRL MURDER.
UH-- HOLD ON, LANCE.
TWO OFFICERS HAVE JUST STEPPED OUT OF THE BUILDING-- MAYBE WE CAN GET A STATEMENT...
OFFICERS, CAN YOU TELL US WHY JOHNNY ROYALLE HAS BEEN BROUGHT IN?
IS IT RELATED TO THE RETRO GIRL INVESTIGATION IN ANY WAY?
DETECTIVES?!
DETECTIVES?!
DETECTIVES?!
DETECTIVES?!
DETECTIVES?!
DETECTIVES?!
DETECTIVES?!
CAN YOU PLEASE MAKE A STATEMENT FOR OUR...OW!
WELL, WE HAVE TO EAT SOMETIME.
I'M JUST SAYING--WE DON'T KNOW EACH OTHER ALL THAT WELL-- YOU DON'T WANT TO BE AROUND ME WHEN I CRASH.
THERE'S A HOT DOG VENDOR ON FIFTH.
HOW 'BOUT PIZZA? ANY GOOD PIZZA PLACES? LIKE NEW YORK-STYLE.
YEAH, WELL, LET'S SEE IF YOU STILL WANT IT AFTER THIS.
DETECTIVES, COME ON--

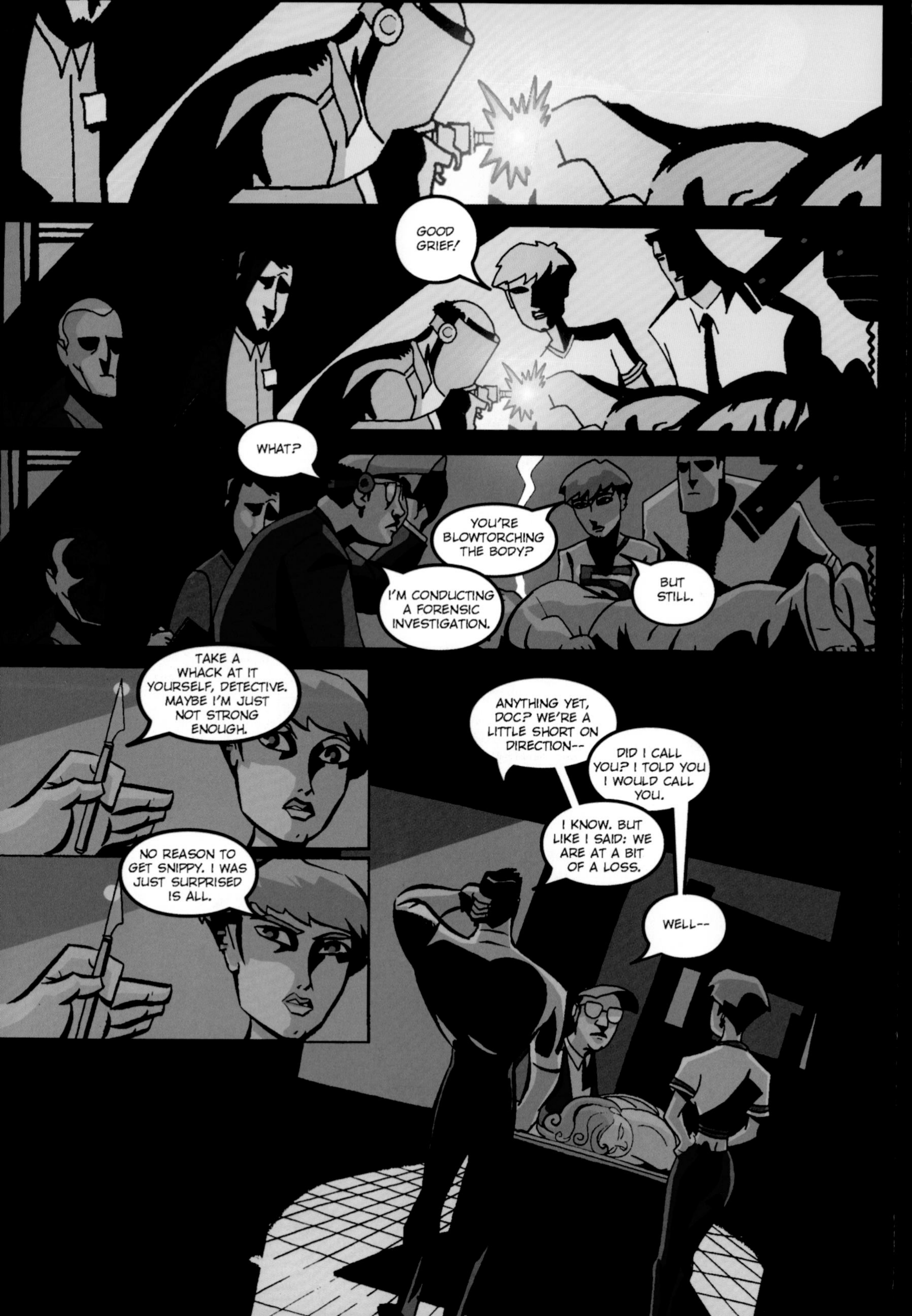
GOOD GRIEF!
WHAT?
YOU'RE BLOWTORCHING THE BODY?
I'M CONDUCTING A FORENSIC INVESTIGATION.
BUT STILL.
TAKE A WHACK AT IT YOURSELF, DETECTIVE. MAYBE I'M JUST NOT STRONG ENOUGH.
NO REASON TO GET SNIPPY. I WAS JUST SURPRISED IS ALL.
ANYTHING YET, DOC? WE'RE A LITTLE SHORT ON DIRECTION--
DID I CALL YOU? I TOLD YOU I WOULD CALL YOU.
I KNOW. BUT LIKE I SAID: WE ARE AT A BIT OF A LOSS.
WELL--

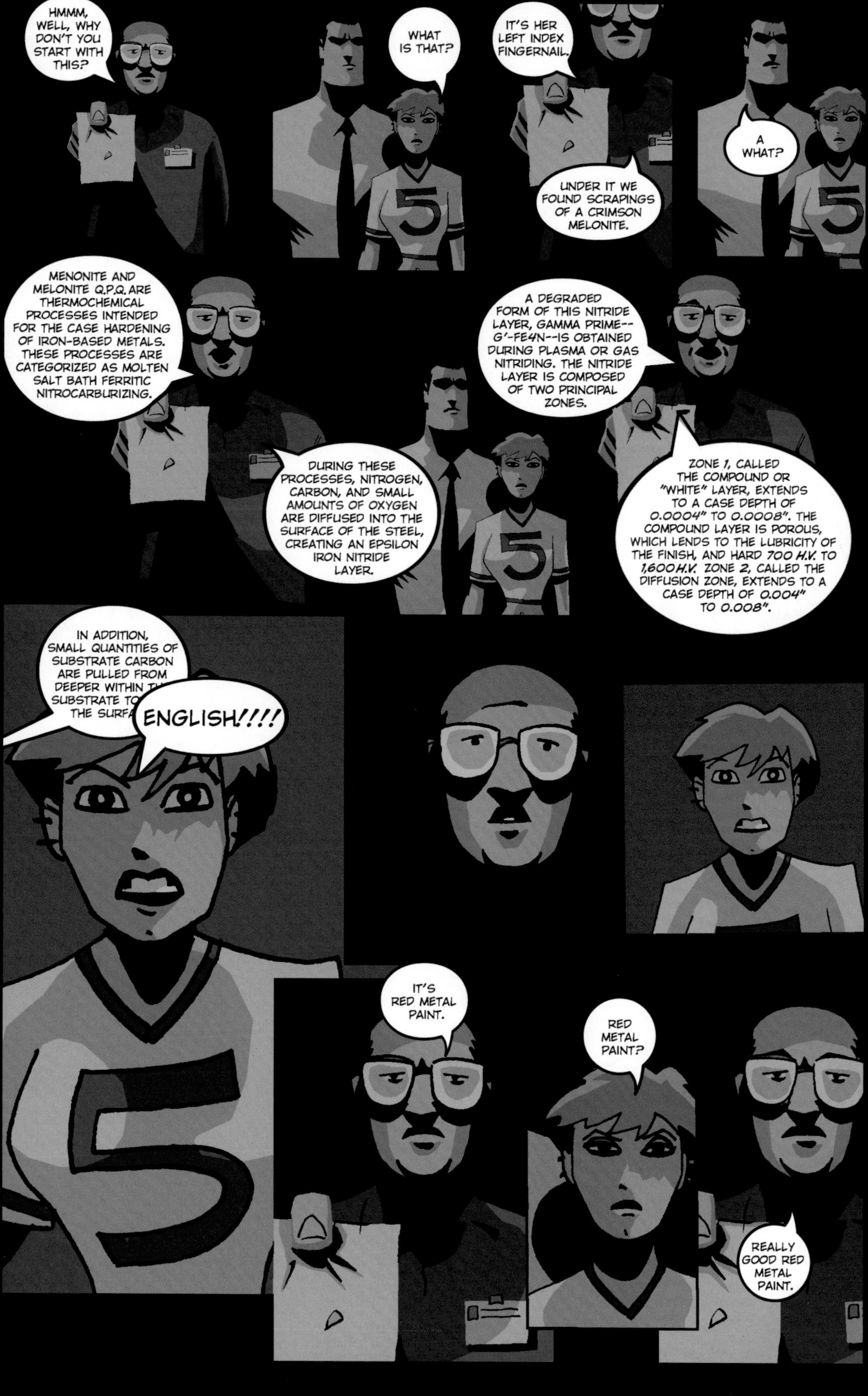
HMMM, WELL, WHY DON'T YOU START WITH THIS?
WHAT IS THAT?
IT'S HER LEFT INDEX FINGERNAIL.
UNDER IT WE FOUND SCRAPINGS OF A CRIMSON MELONITE.
A WHAT?
MENONITE AND MELONITE Q.P.Q. ARE THERMOCHEMICAL PROCESSES INTENDED FOR THE CASE HARDENING OF IRON-BASED METALS. THESE PROCESSES ARE CATEGORIZED AS MOLTEN SALT BATH FERRITIC NITROCARBURIZING.
DURING THESE PROCESSES, NITROGEN, CARBON, AND SMALL AMOUNTS OF OXYGEN ARE DIFFUSED INTO THE SURFACE OF THE STEEL, CREATING AN EPSILON IRON NITRIDE LAYER.
A DEGRADED FORM OF THIS NITRIDE LAYER, GAMMA PRIME--G'-FE4N--IS OBTAINED DURING PLASMA OR GAS NITRIDING. THE NITRIDE LAYER IS COMPOSED OF TWO PRINCIPAL ZONES.
ZONE 1, CALLED THE COMPOUND OR "WHITE" LAYER, EXTENDS TO A CASE DEPTH OF 0.0004" TO 0.0008". THE COMPOUND LAYER IS POROUS, WHICH LENDS TO THE LUBRICITY OF THE FINISH, AND HARD 700 H.V. TO 1,600 H.V. ZONE 2, CALLED THE DIFFUSION ZONE, EXTENDS TO A CASE DEPTH OF 0.004" TO 0.008".
IN ADDITION, SMALL QUANTITIES OF SUBSTRATE CARBON ARE PULLED FROM DEEPER WITHIN TH SUBSTRATE TO THE SURFA
ENGLISH!!!!
IT'S RED METAL PAINT.
RED METAL PAINT?
REALLY GOOD RED METAL PAINT.

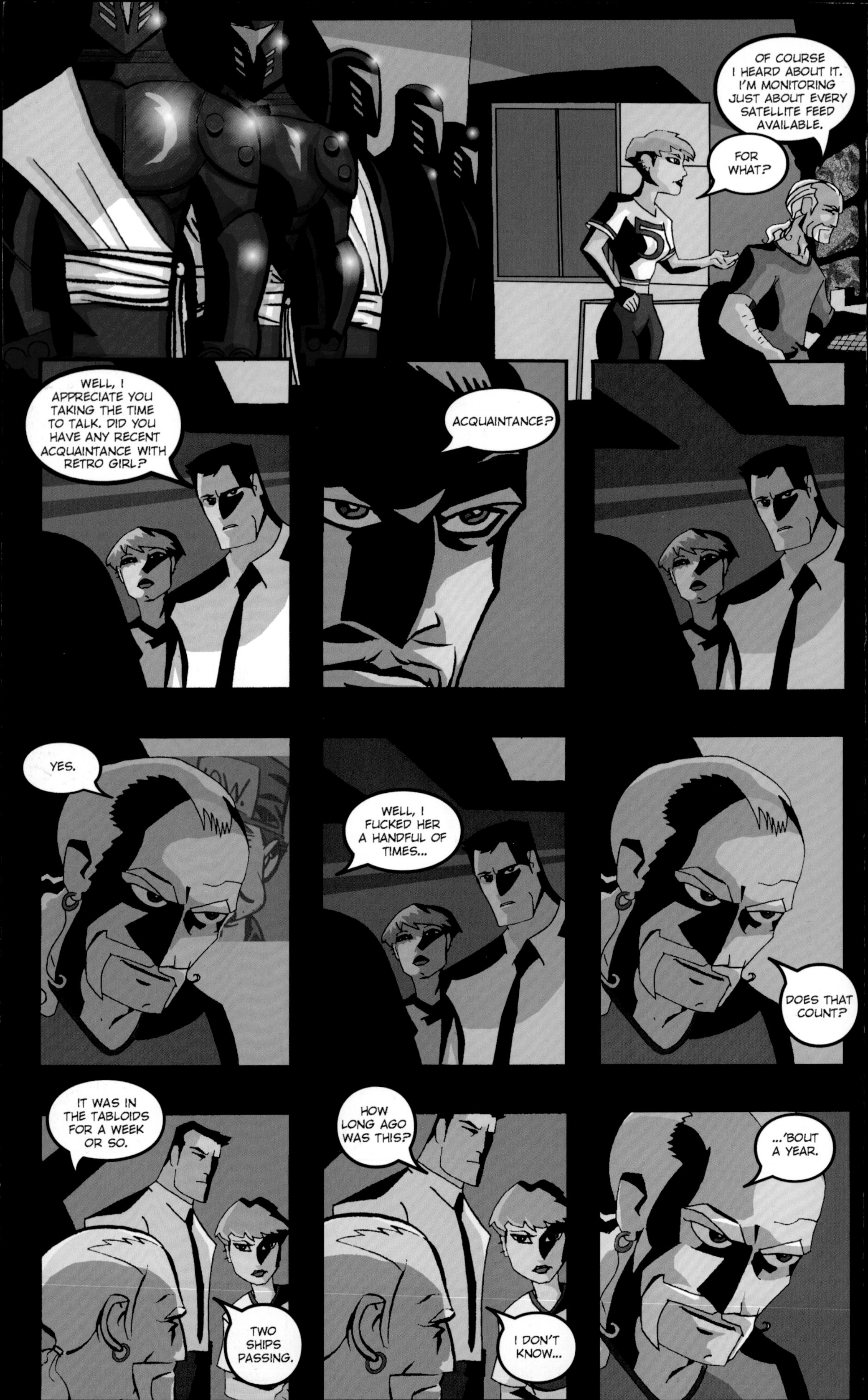
OF COURSE I HEARD ABOUT IT. I'M MONITORING JUST ABOUT EVERY SATELLITE FEED AVAILABLE.
FOR WHAT?
WELL, I APPRECIATE YOU TAKING THE TIME TO TALK. DID YOU HAVE ANY RECENT ACQUAINTANCE WITH RETRO GIRL?
ACQUAINTANCE?
YES.
WELL, I FUCKED HER A HANDFUL OF TIMES...
DOES THAT COUNT?
IT WAS IN THE TABLOIDS FOR A WEEK OR SO.
TWO SHIPS PASSING.
HOW LONG AGO WAS THIS?
I DON'T KNOW...
...'BOUT A YEAR.

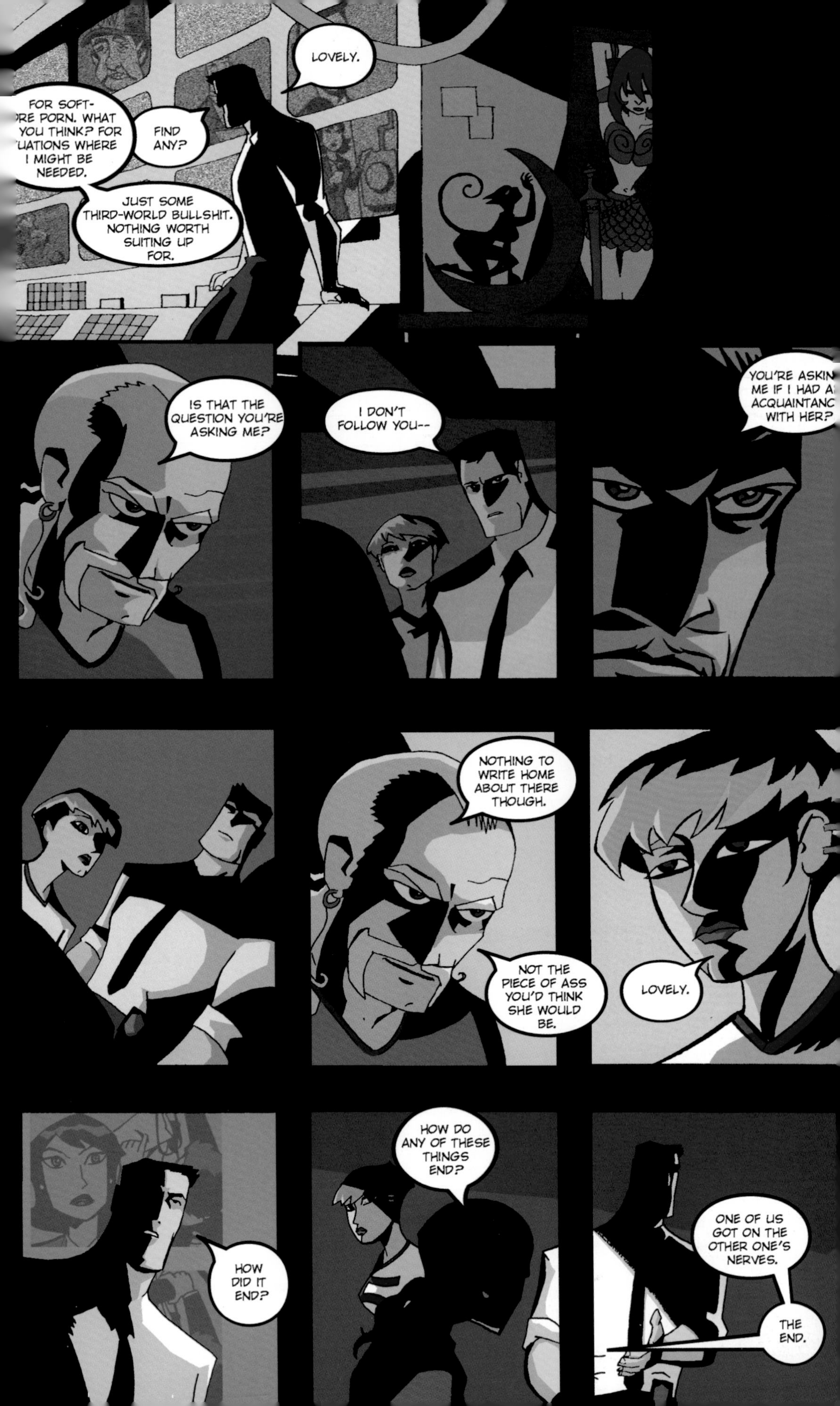

LOVELY.
FOR SOFT-
-ORE PORN. WHAT
YOU THINK? FOR
-UATIONS WHERE
I MIGHT BE
NEEDED.
FIND ANY?
JUST SOME THIRD-WORLD BULLSHIT. NOTHING WORTH SUITING UP FOR.
IS THAT THE QUESTION YOU'RE ASKING ME?
I DON'T FOLLOW YOU--
YOU'RE ASKIN
ME IF I HAD A
ACQUAINTANC
WITH HER?
NOTHING TO WRITE HOME ABOUT THERE THOUGH.
NOT THE PIECE OF ASS YOU'D THINK SHE WOULD BE.
LOVELY.
HOW DID IT END?
HOW DO ANY OF THESE THINGS END?
ONE OF US GOT ON THE OTHER ONE'S NERVES.
THE END.

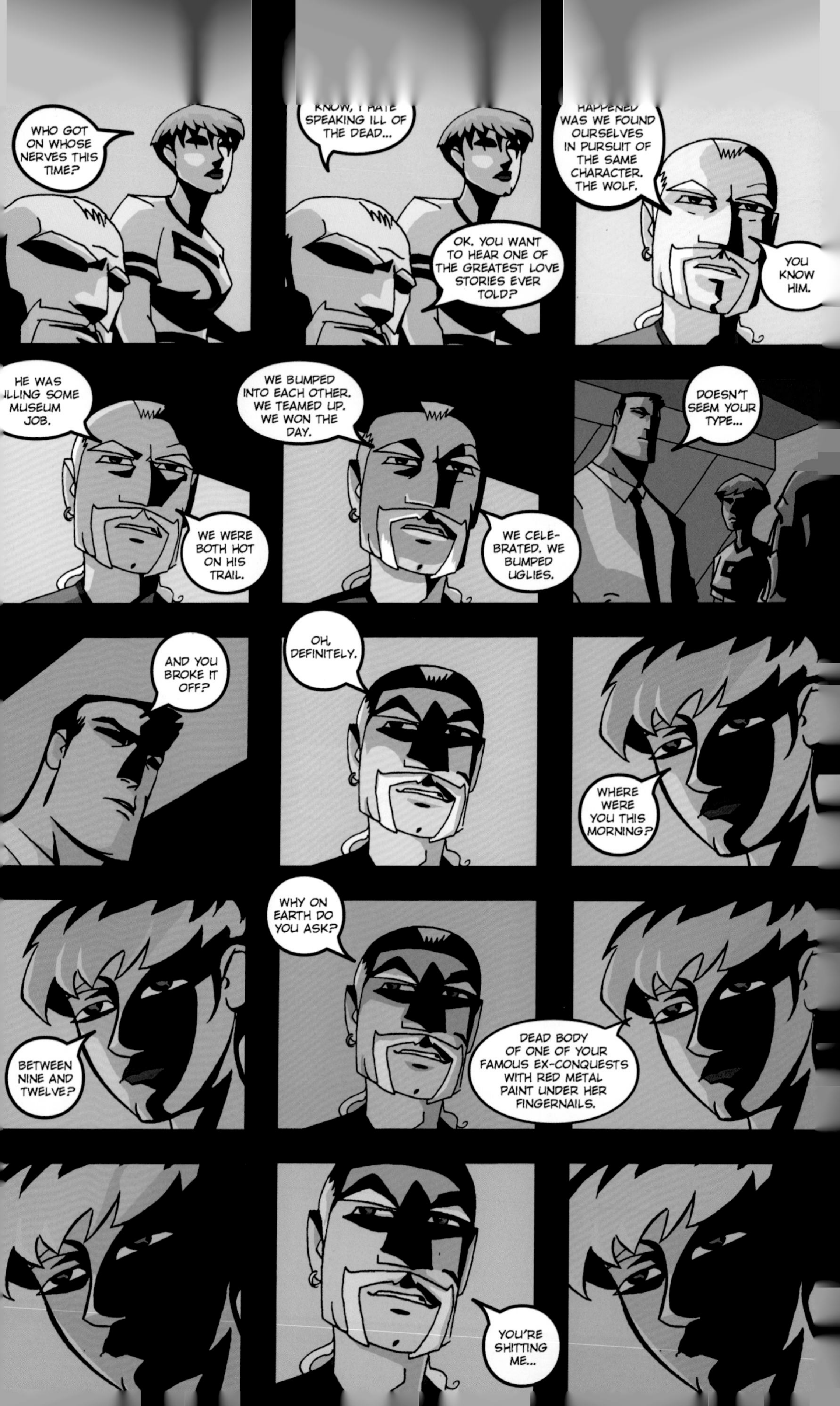
WHO GOT ON WHOSE NERVES THIS TIME?
KNOW, I HATE SPEAKING ILL OF THE DEAD...
OK. YOU WANT TO HEAR ONE OF THE GREATEST LOVE STORIES EVER TOLD?
HAPPENED WAS WE FOUND OURSELVES IN PURSUIT OF THE SAME CHARACTER. THE WOLF.
YOU KNOW HIM.
HE WAS ILLING SOME MUSEUM JOB.
WE WERE BOTH HOT ON HIS TRAIL.
WE BUMPED INTO EACH OTHER. WE TEAMED UP. WE WON THE DAY.
WE CELE-BRATED. WE BUMPED UGLIES.
DOESN'T SEEM YOUR TYPE...
AND YOU BROKE IT OFF?
OH, DEFINITELY.
WHERE WERE YOU THIS MORNING?
BETWEEN NINE AND TWELVE?
WHY ON EARTH DO YOU ASK?
DEAD BODY OF ONE OF YOUR FAMOUS EX-CONQUESTS WITH RED METAL PAINT UNDER HER FINGERNAILS.
YOU'RE SHITTING ME...

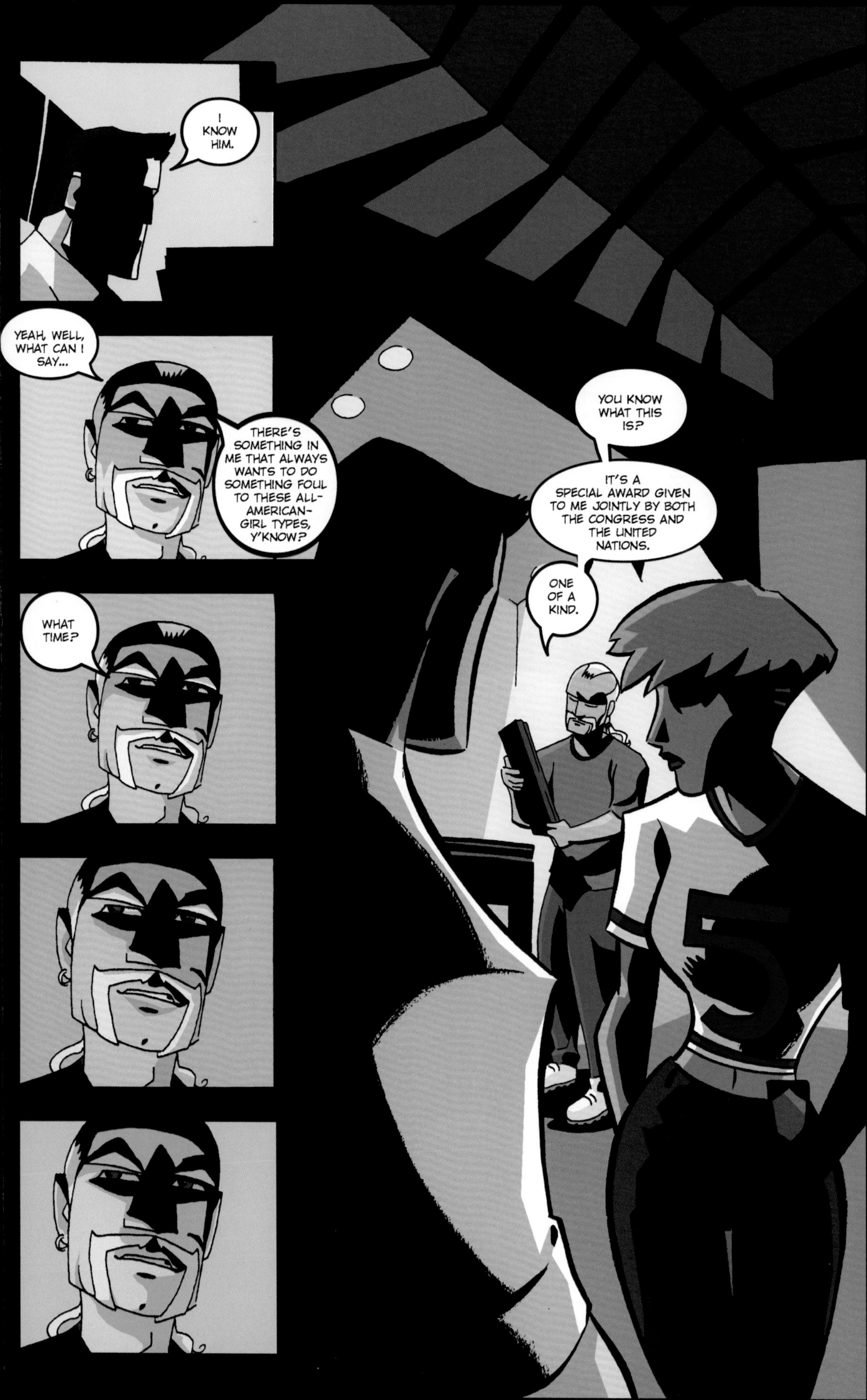
I KNOW HIM.
YEAH, WELL, WHAT CAN I SAY...
THERE'S SOMETHING IN ME THAT ALWAYS WANTS TO DO SOMETHING FOUL TO THESE ALL-AMERICAN-GIRL TYPES, Y'KNOW?
WHAT TIME?
YOU KNOW WHAT THIS IS?
IT'S A SPECIAL AWARD GIVEN TO ME JOINTLY BY BOTH THE CONGRESS AND THE UNITED NATIONS.
ONE OF A KIND.
5

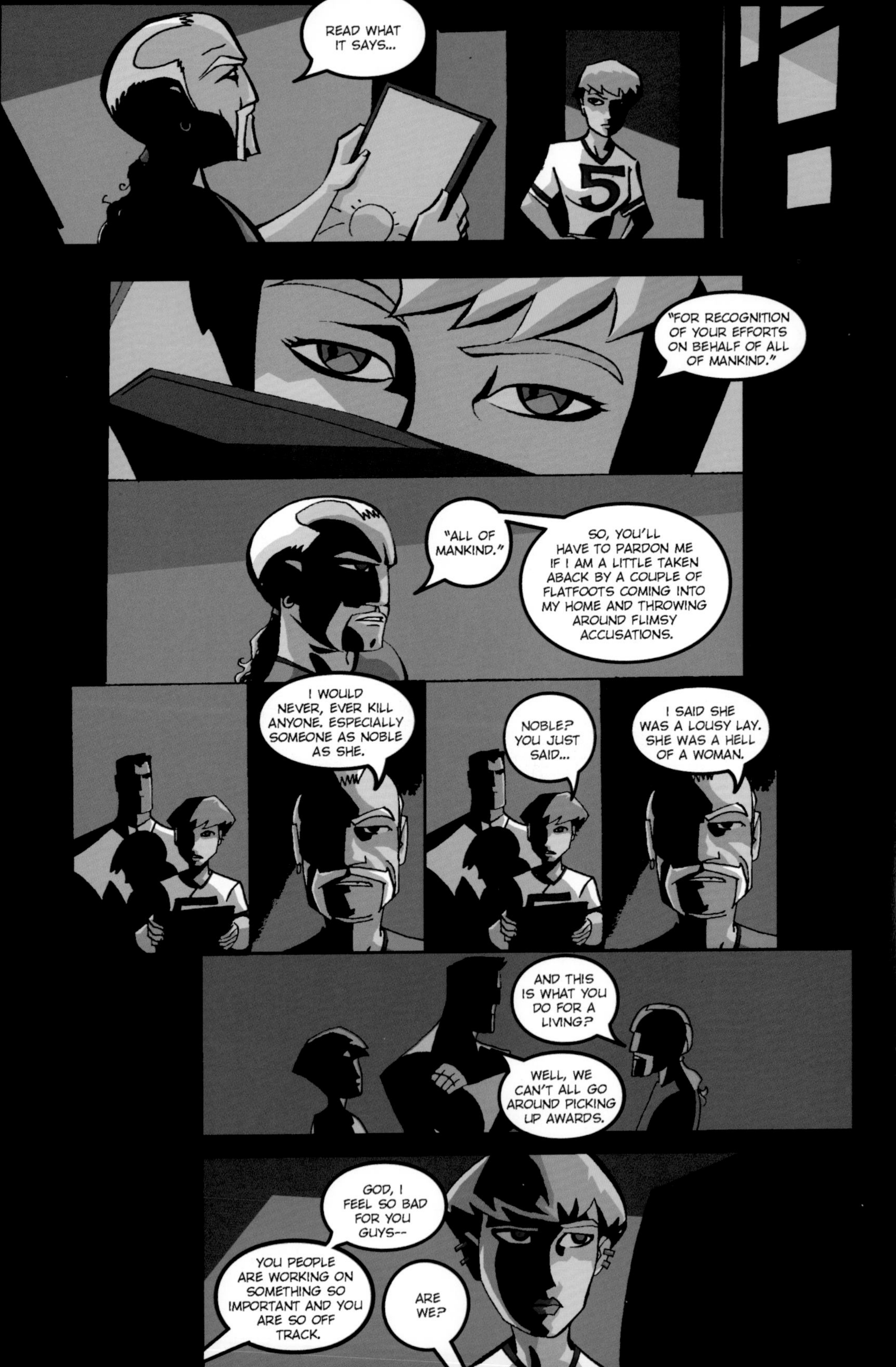

READ WHAT IT SAYS...
"FOR RECOGNITION OF YOUR EFFORTS ON BEHALF OF ALL OF MANKIND."
"ALL OF MANKIND."
SO, YOU'LL HAVE TO PARDON ME IF I AM A LITTLE TAKEN ABACK BY A COUPLE OF FLATFOOTS COMING INTO MY HOME AND THROWING AROUND FLIMSY ACCUSATIONS.
I WOULD NEVER, EVER KILL ANYONE. ESPECIALLY SOMEONE AS NOBLE AS SHE.
NOBLE? YOU JUST SAID...
I SAID SHE WAS A LOUSY LAY. SHE WAS A HELL OF A WOMAN.
AND THIS IS WHAT YOU DO FOR A LIVING?
WELL, WE CAN'T ALL GO AROUND PICKING UP AWARDS.
GOD, I FEEL SO BAD FOR YOU GUYS--
YOU PEOPLE ARE WORKING ON SOMETHING SO IMPORTANT AND YOU ARE SO OFF TRACK.
ARE WE?

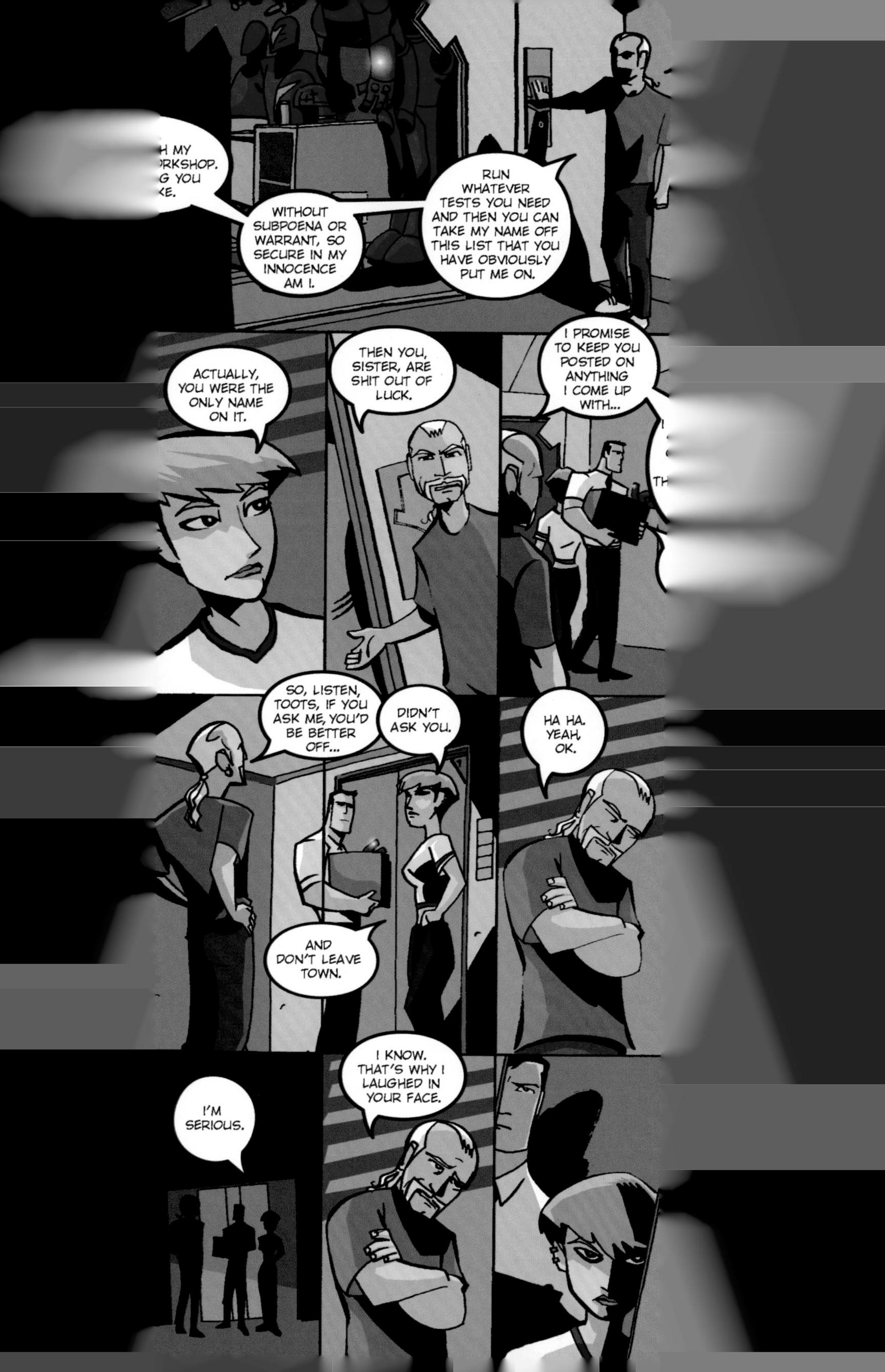
WITHOUT SUBPOENA OR WARRANT, SO SECURE IN MY INNOCENCE AM I.
RUN WHATEVER TESTS YOU NEED AND THEN YOU CAN TAKE MY NAME OFF THIS LIST THAT YOU HAVE OBVIOUSLY PUT ME ON.
ACTUALLY, YOU WERE THE ONLY NAME ON IT.
THEN YOU, SISTER, ARE SHIT OUT OF LUCK.
I PROMISE TO KEEP YOU POSTED ON ANYTHING I COME UP WITH...
SO, LISTEN, TOOTS, IF YOU ASK ME, YOU'D BE BETTER OFF...
DIDN'T ASK YOU.
AND DON'T LEAVE TOWN.
HA HA. YEAH, OK.
I'M SERIOUS.
I KNOW. THAT'S WHY I LAUGHED IN YOUR FACE.

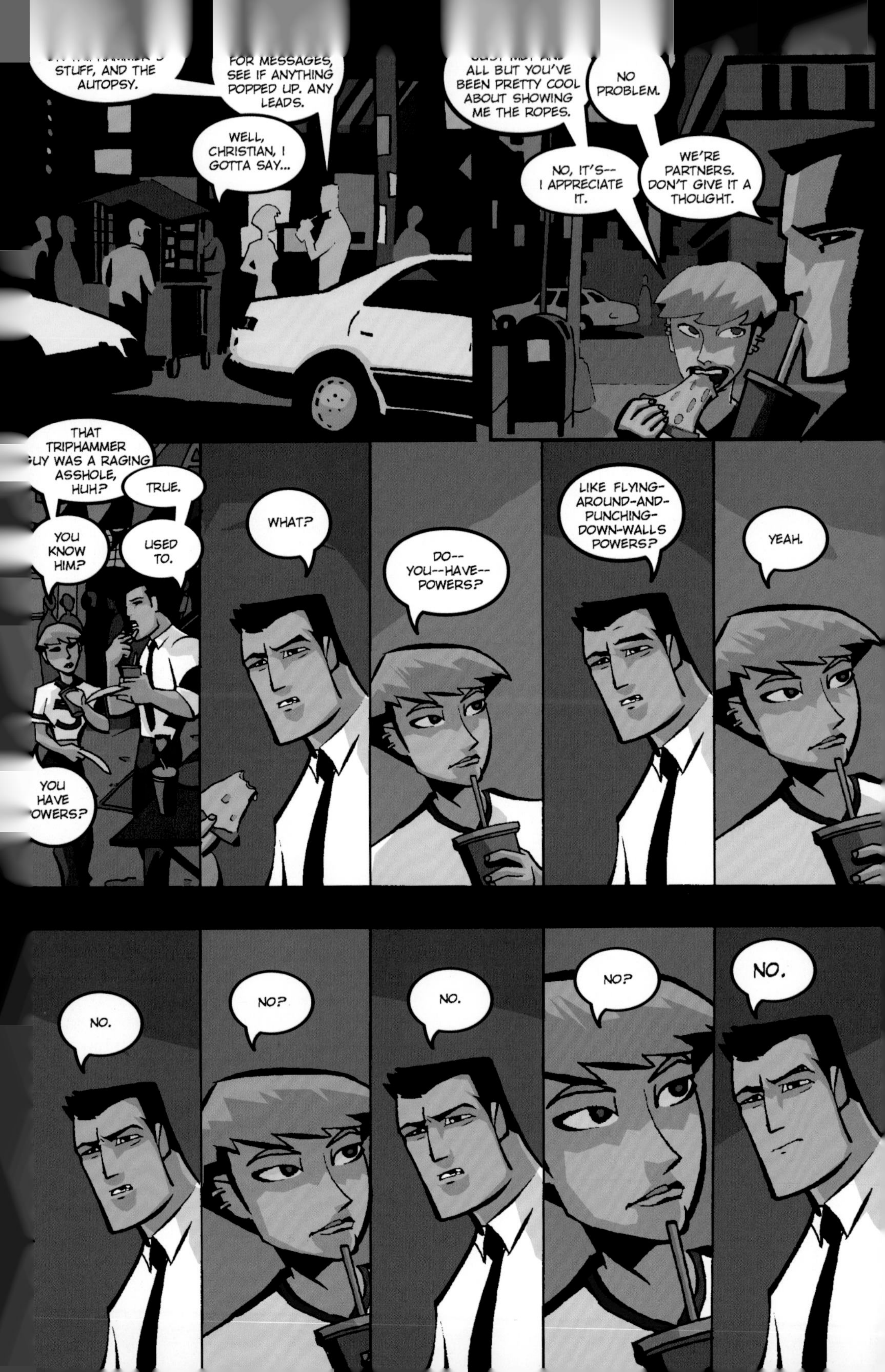

STUFF, AND THE AUTOPSY.
FOR MESSAGES, SEE IF ANYTHING POPPED UP. ANY LEADS.
WELL, CHRISTIAN, I GOTTA SAY...
ALL BUT YOU'VE BEEN PRETTY COOL ABOUT SHOWING ME THE ROPES.
NO PROBLEM.
NO, IT'S-- I APPRECIATE IT.
WE'RE PARTNERS. DON'T GIVE IT A THOUGHT.
THAT TRIPHAMMER UY WAS A RAGING ASSHOLE, HUH?
TRUE.
YOU KNOW HIM?
USED TO.
YOU HAVE OWERS?
WHAT?
DO-- YOU--HAVE-- POWERS?
LIKE FLYING-AROUND-AND-PUNCHING-DOWN-WALLS POWERS?
YEAH.
NO.
NO?
NO.
NO?
NO.

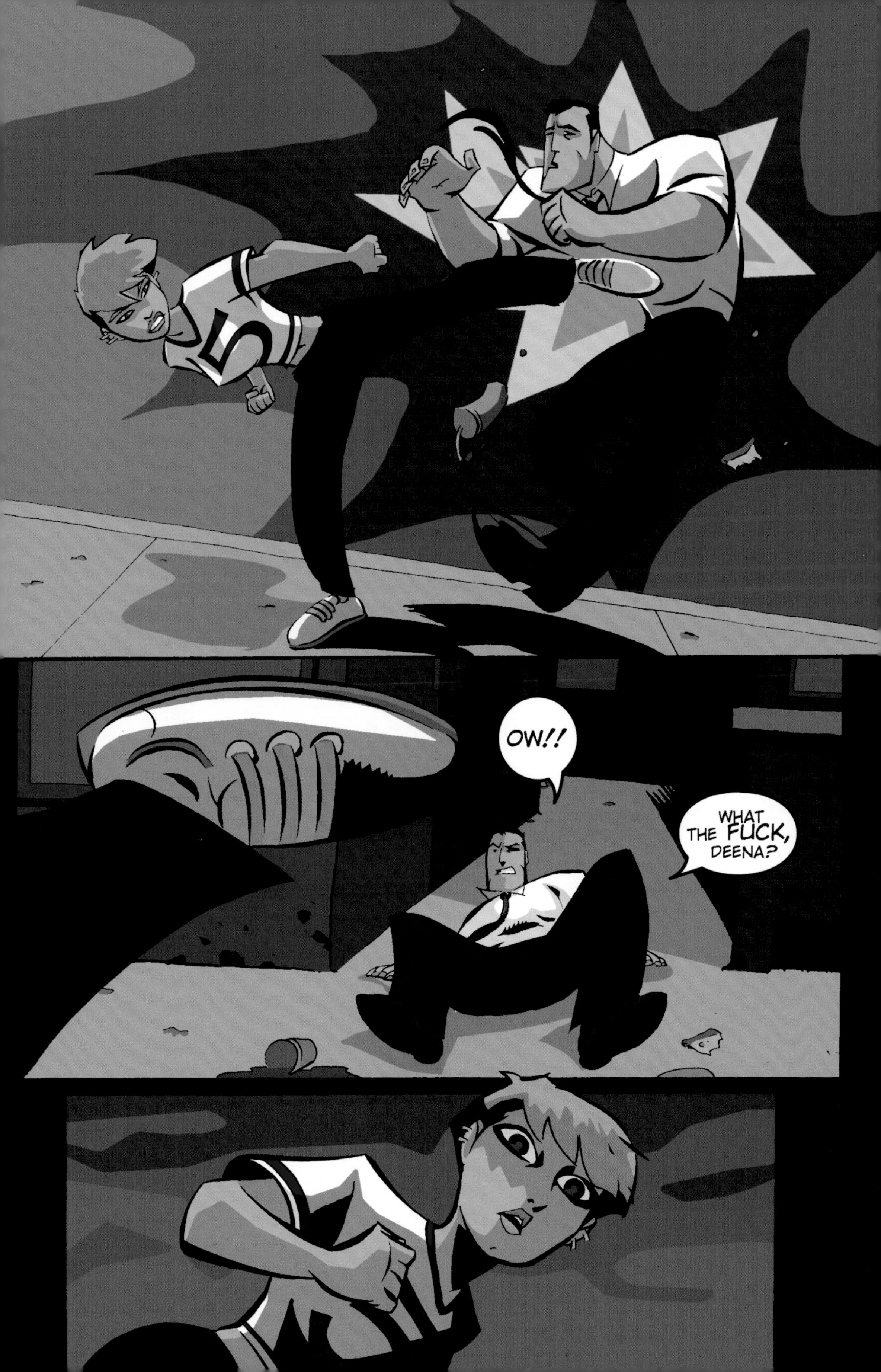
OW!!
WHAT THE FUCK, DEENA?

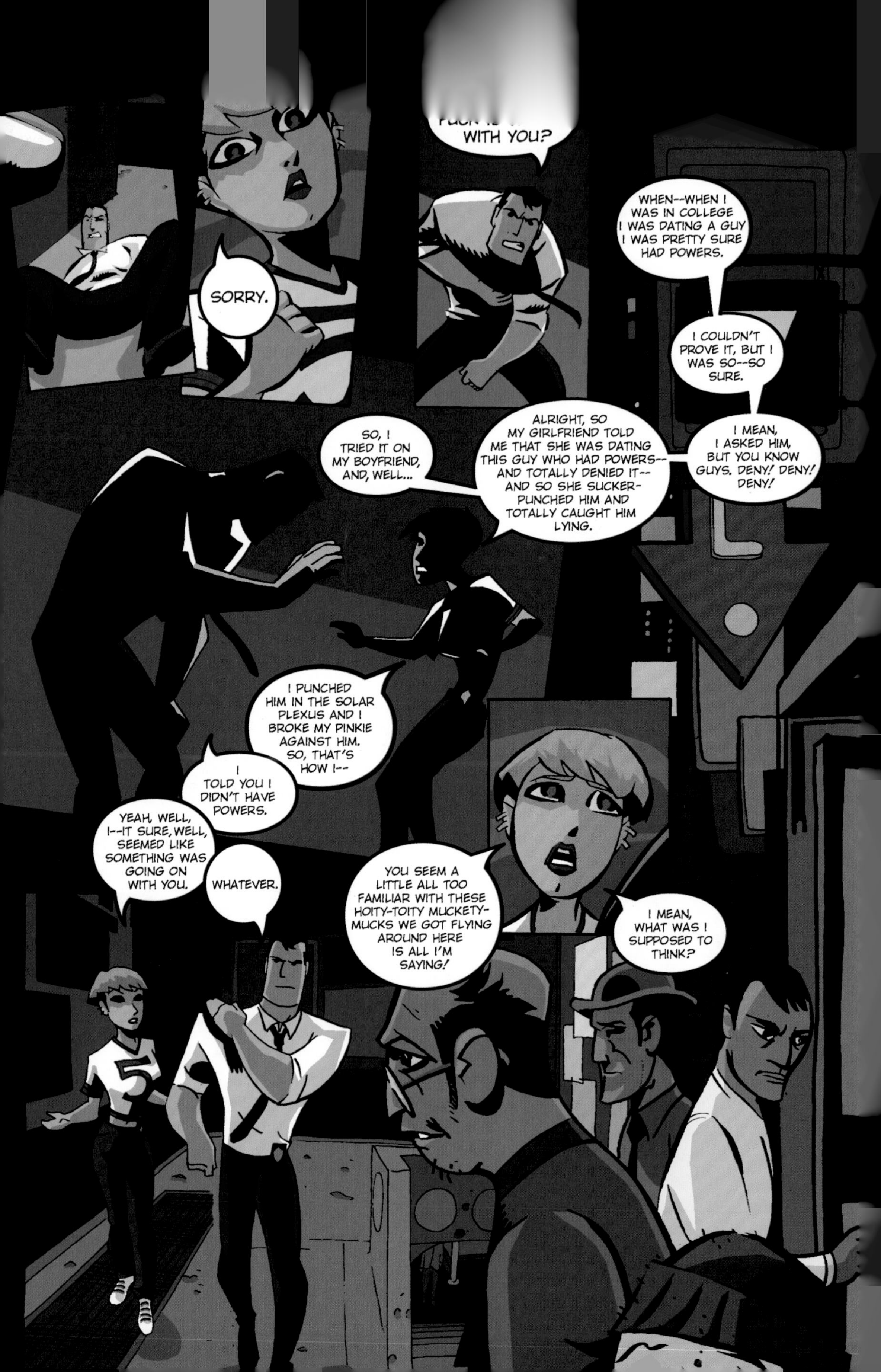
SORRY.
WITH YOU?
WHEN--WHEN I WAS IN COLLEGE I WAS DATING A GUY I WAS PRETTY SURE HAD POWERS.
I COULDN'T PROVE IT, BUT I WAS SO--SO SURE.
I MEAN, I ASKED HIM, BUT YOU KNOW GUYS. DENY! DENY! DENY!
ALRIGHT, SO MY GIRLFRIEND TOLD ME THAT SHE WAS DATING THIS GUY WHO HAD POWERS-- AND TOTALLY DENIED IT-- AND SO SHE SUCKER-PUNCHED HIM AND TOTALLY CAUGHT HIM LYING.
SO, I TRIED IT ON MY BOYFRIEND, AND, WELL...
I PUNCHED HIM IN THE SOLAR PLEXUS AND I BROKE MY PINKIE AGAINST HIM. SO, THAT'S HOW I--
I TOLD YOU I DIDN'T HAVE POWERS.
YEAH, WELL, I--IT SURE, WELL, SEEMED LIKE SOMETHING WAS GOING ON WITH YOU.
WHATEVER.
YOU SEEM A LITTLE ALL TOO FAMILIAR WITH THESE HOITY-TOITY MUCKETY-MUCKS WE GOT FLYING AROUND HERE IS ALL I'M SAYING!
I MEAN, WHAT WAS I SUPPOSED TO THINK?

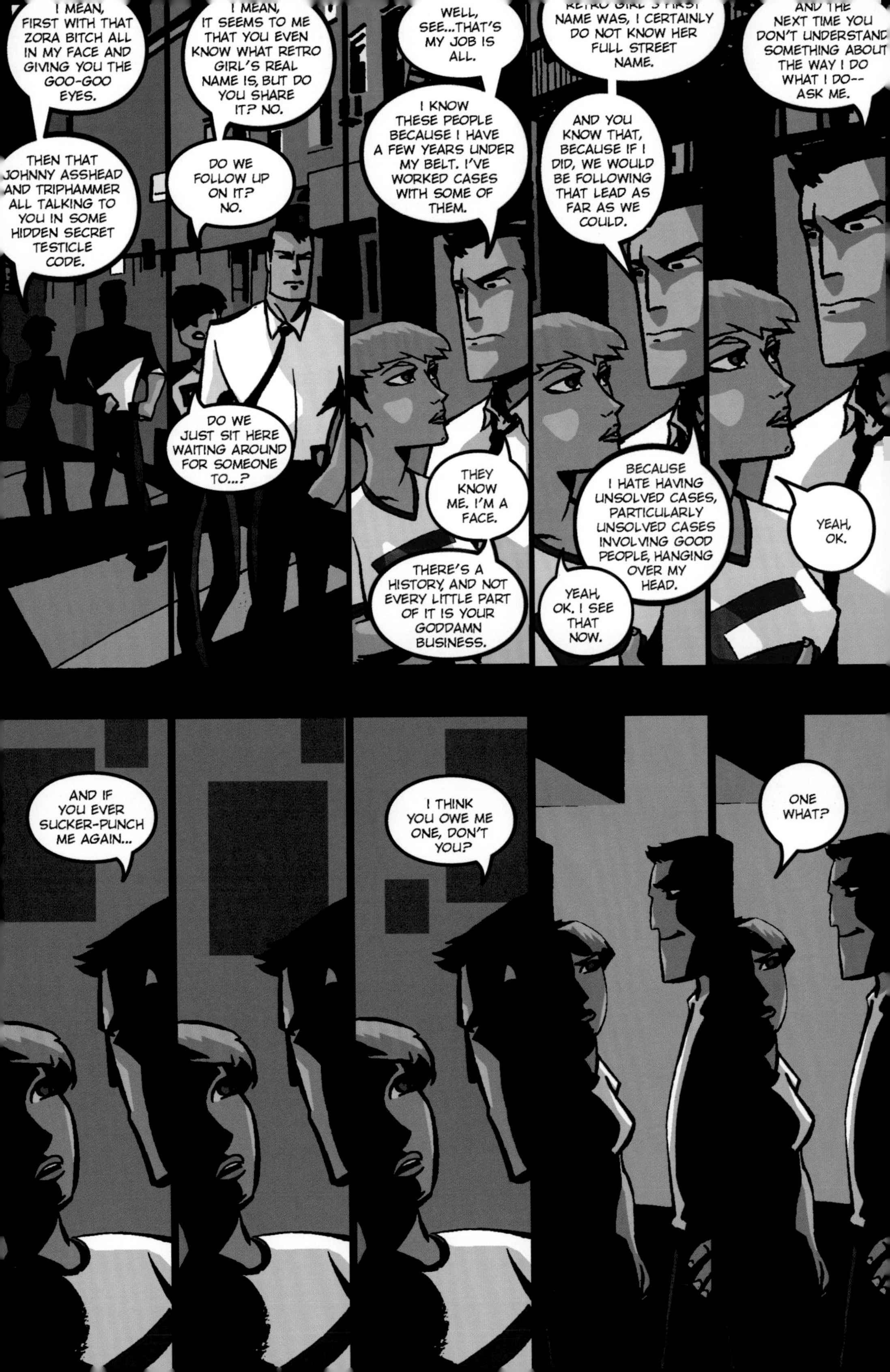
I MEAN, FIRST WITH THAT ZORA BITCH ALL IN MY FACE AND GIVING YOU THE GOO-GOO EYES.
THEN THAT JOHNNY ASSHEAD AND TRIPHAMMER ALL TALKING TO YOU IN SOME HIDDEN SECRET TESTICLE CODE.
I MEAN, IT SEEMS TO ME THAT YOU EVEN KNOW WHAT RETRO GIRL'S REAL NAME IS, BUT DO YOU SHARE IT? NO.
DO WE FOLLOW UP ON IT? NO.
DO WE JUST SIT HERE WAITING AROUND FOR SOMEONE TO...?
WELL, SEE...THAT'S MY JOB IS ALL.
I KNOW THESE PEOPLE BECAUSE I HAVE A FEW YEARS UNDER MY BELT. I'VE WORKED CASES WITH SOME OF THEM.
THEY KNOW ME. I'M A FACE.
THERE'S A HISTORY, AND NOT EVERY LITTLE PART OF IT IS YOUR GODDAMN BUSINESS.
NAME WAS, I CERTAINLY DO NOT KNOW HER FULL STREET NAME.
AND YOU KNOW THAT, BECAUSE IF I DID, WE WOULD BE FOLLOWING THAT LEAD AS FAR AS WE COULD.
BECAUSE I HATE HAVING UNSOLVED CASES, PARTICULARLY UNSOLVED CASES INVOLVING GOOD PEOPLE, HANGING OVER MY HEAD.
YEAH, OK. I SEE THAT NOW.
AND THE NEXT TIME YOU DON'T UNDERSTAND SOMETHING ABOUT THE WAY I DO WHAT I DO-- ASK ME.
YEAH, OK.
AND IF YOU EVER SUCKER-PUNCH ME AGAIN...
I THINK YOU OWE ME ONE, DON'T YOU?
ONE WHAT?

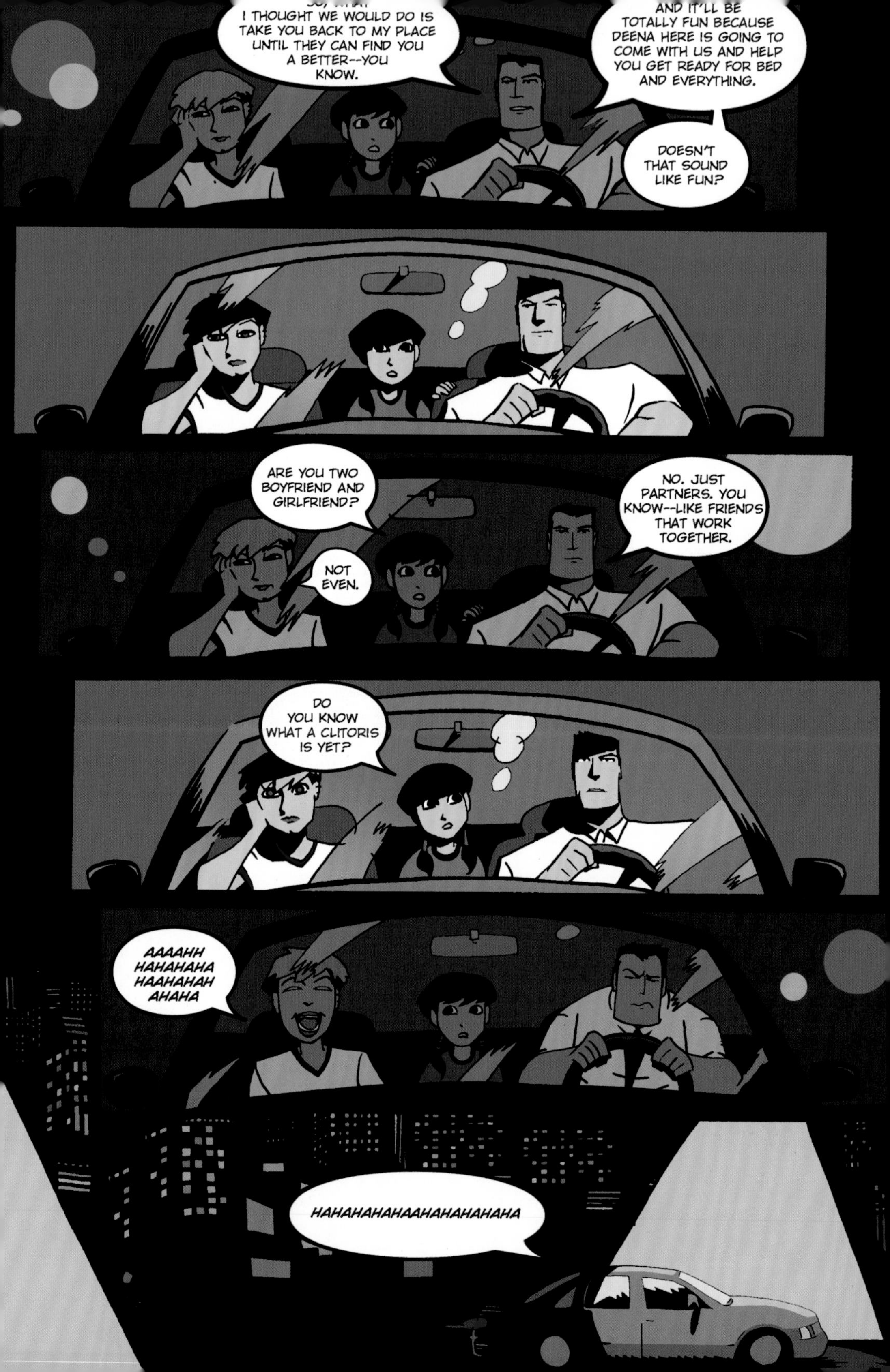
I THOUGHT WE WOULD DO IS TAKE YOU BACK TO MY PLACE UNTIL THEY CAN FIND YOU A BETTER--YOU KNOW.
AND IT'LL BE TOTALLY FUN BECAUSE DEENA HERE IS GOING TO COME WITH US AND HELP YOU GET READY FOR BED AND EVERYTHING.
DOESN'T THAT SOUND LIKE FUN?
ARE YOU TWO BOYFRIEND AND GIRLFRIEND?
NO. JUST PARTNERS. YOU KNOW--LIKE FRIENDS THAT WORK TOGETHER.
NOT EVEN.
DO YOU KNOW WHAT A CLITORIS IS YET?
AAAAHH HAHAHAHA HAAHAHAH AHAHA
HAHAHAHAHAAHAHAHAHAHA

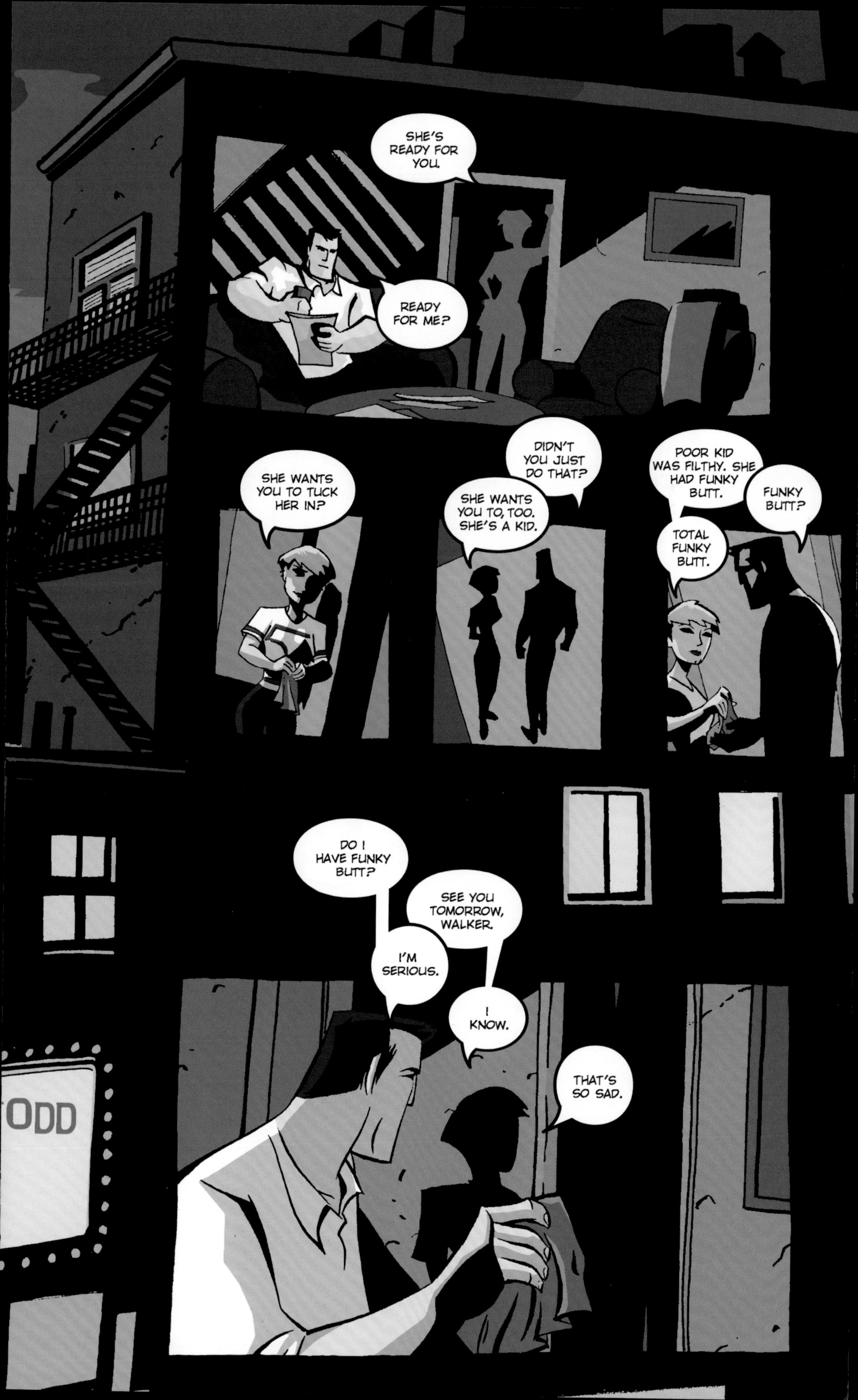
SHE'S READY FOR YOU.
READY FOR ME?
SHE WANTS YOU TO TUCK HER IN?
DIDN'T YOU JUST DO THAT?
SHE WANTS YOU TO, TOO. SHE'S A KID.
POOR KID WAS FILTHY. SHE HAD FUNKY BUTT.
FUNKY BUTT?
TOTAL FUNKY BUTT.
DO I HAVE FUNKY BUTT?
SEE YOU TOMORROW, WALKER.
I'M SERIOUS.
I KNOW.
THAT'S SO SAD.
ODD

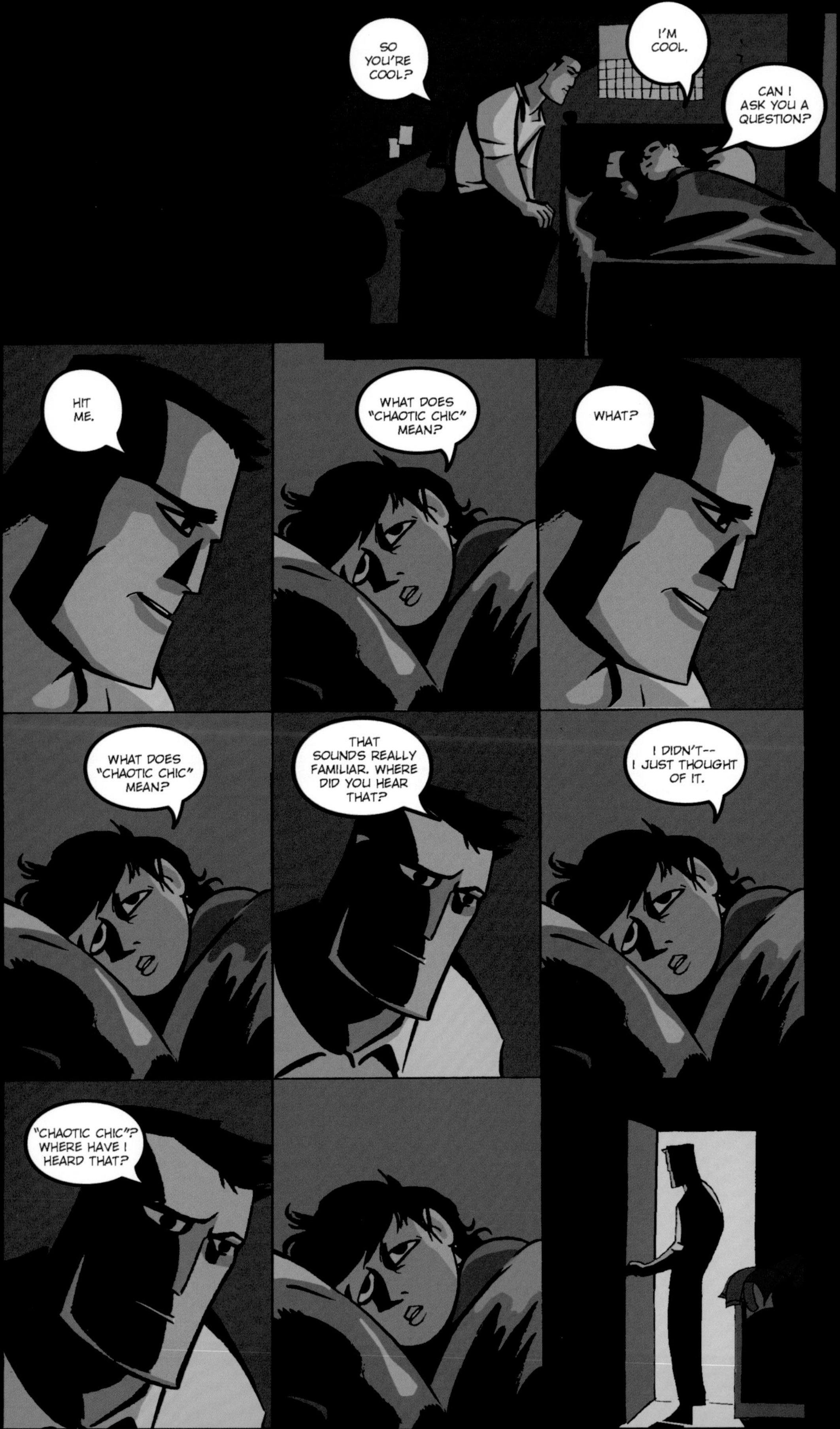
SO YOU'RE COOL?
I'M COOL.
CAN I ASK YOU A QUESTION?
HIT ME.
WHAT DOES "CHAOTIC CHIC" MEAN?
WHAT?
WHAT DOES "CHAOTIC CHIC" MEAN?
THAT SOUNDS REALLY FAMILIAR. WHERE DID YOU HEAR THAT?
I DIDN'T-- I JUST THOUGHT OF IT.
"CHAOTIC CHIC"? WHERE HAVE I HEARD THAT?

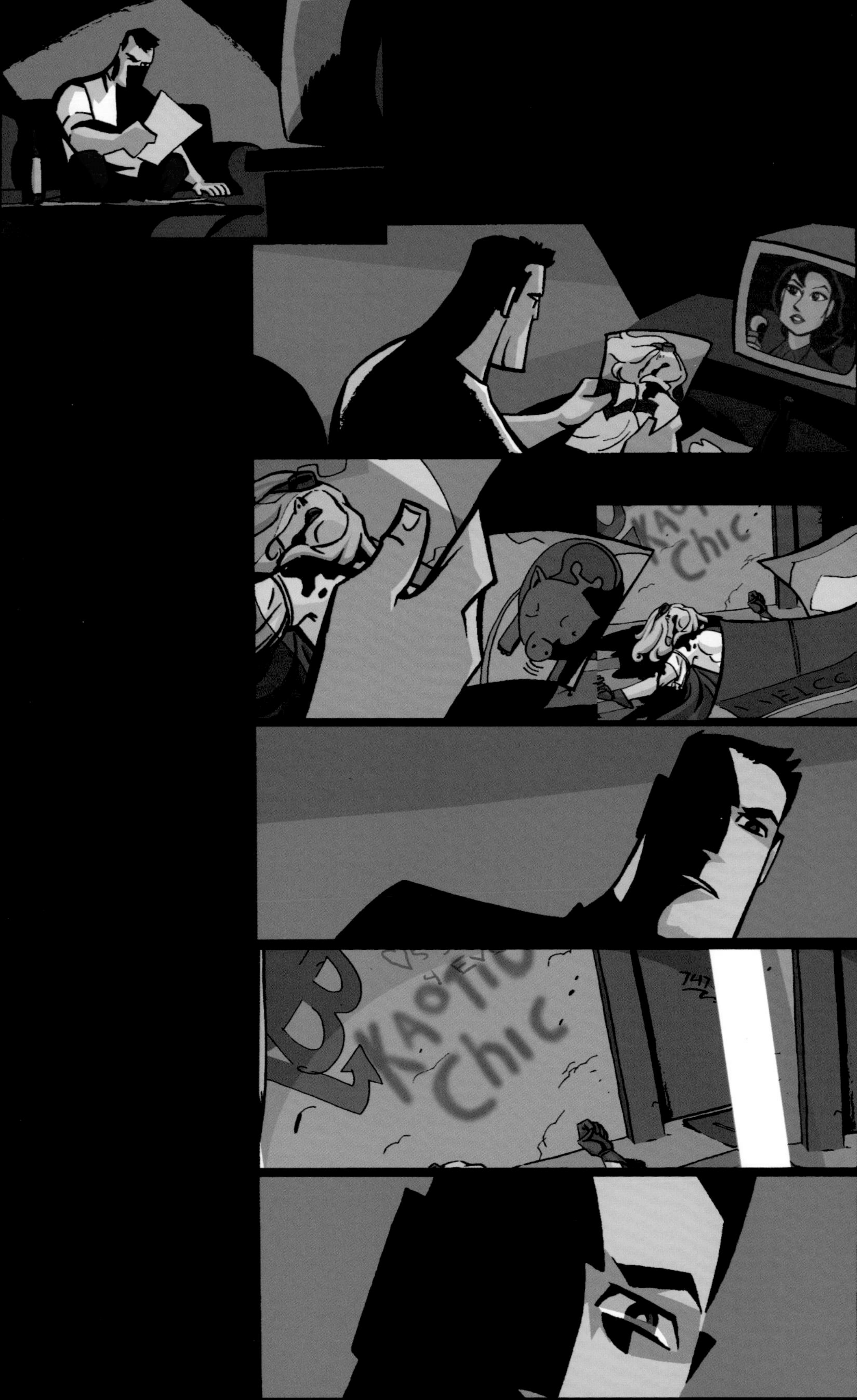
Chic

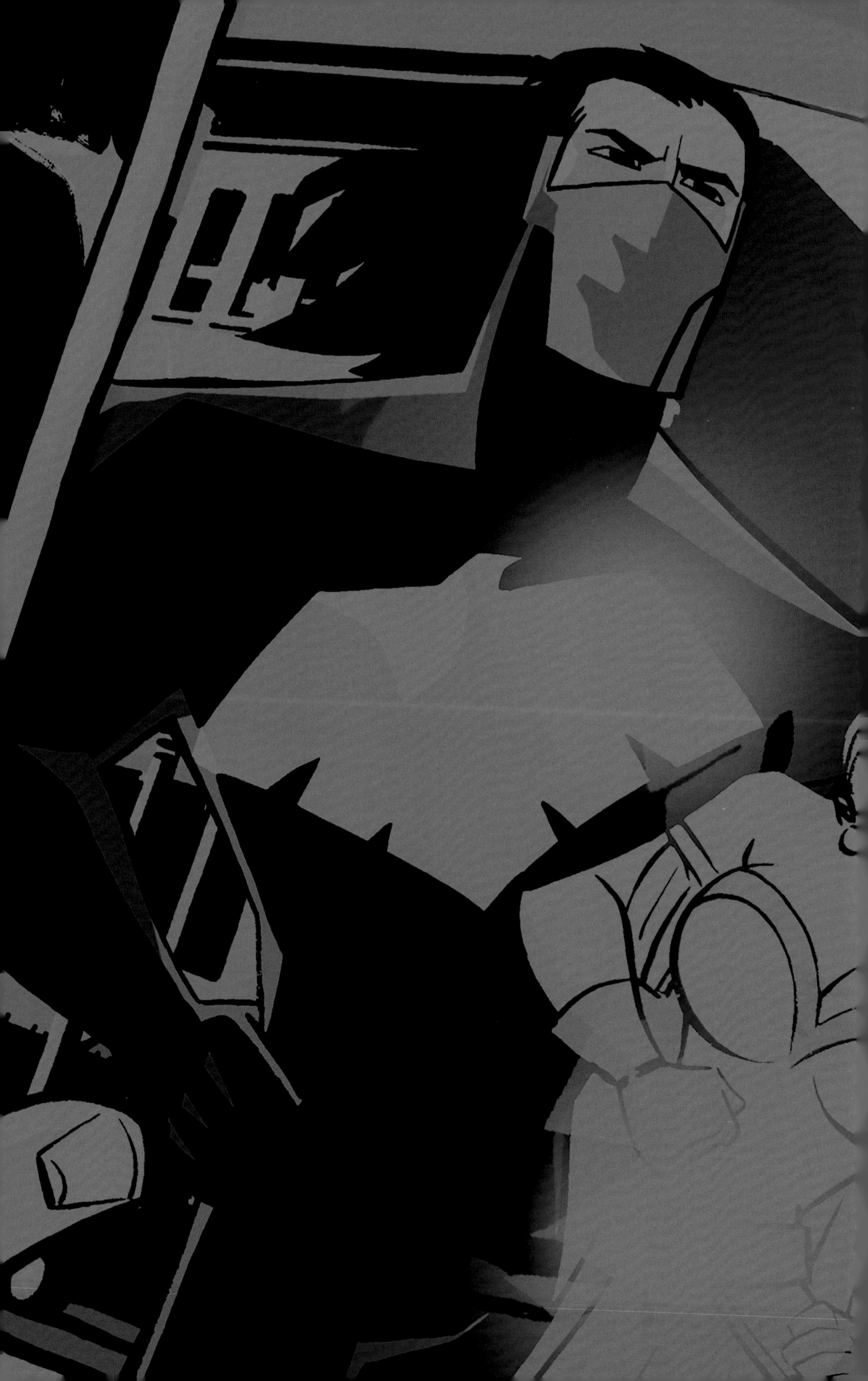

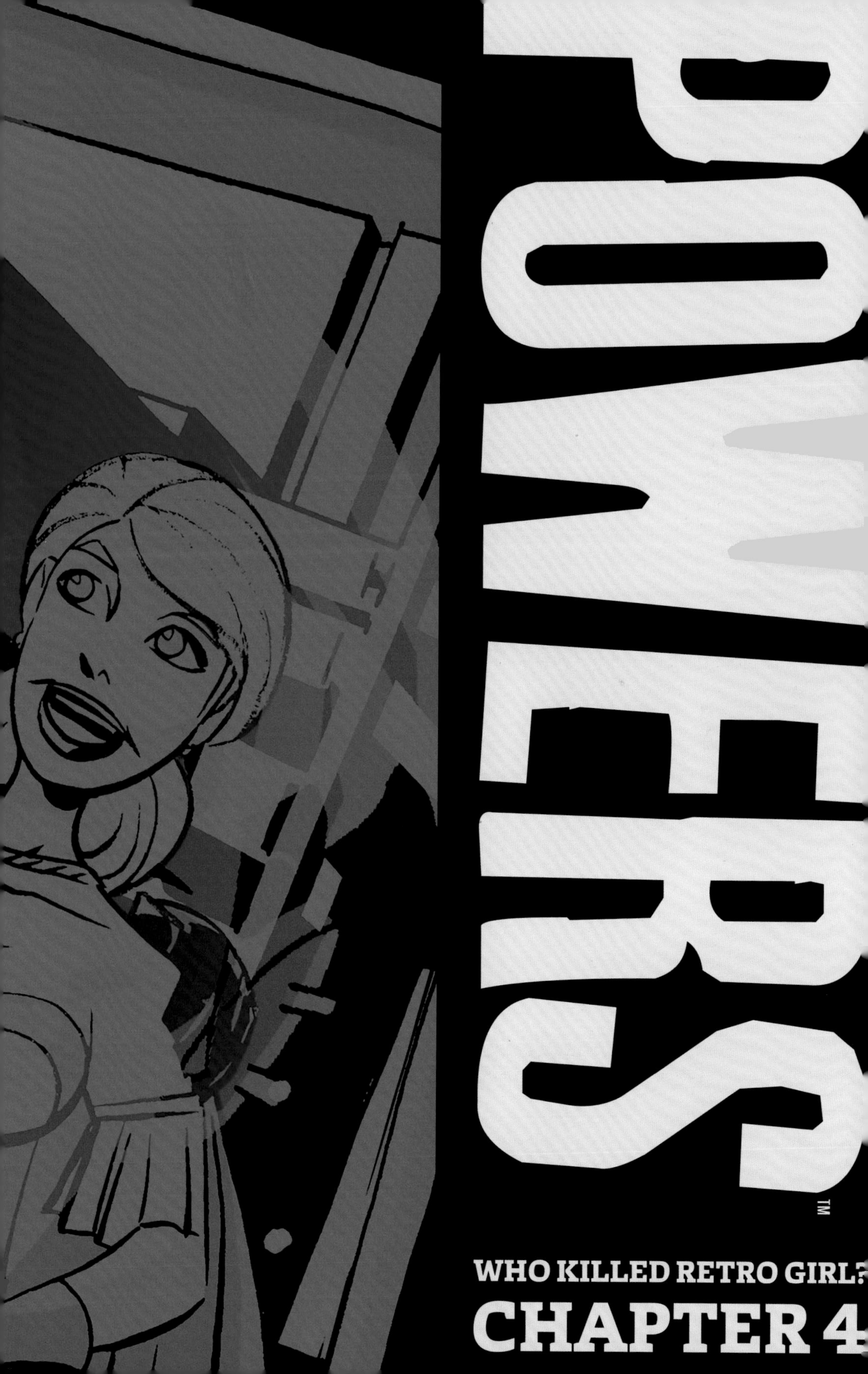

POWERS™

WHO KILLED RETRO GIRL?

CHAPTER 4

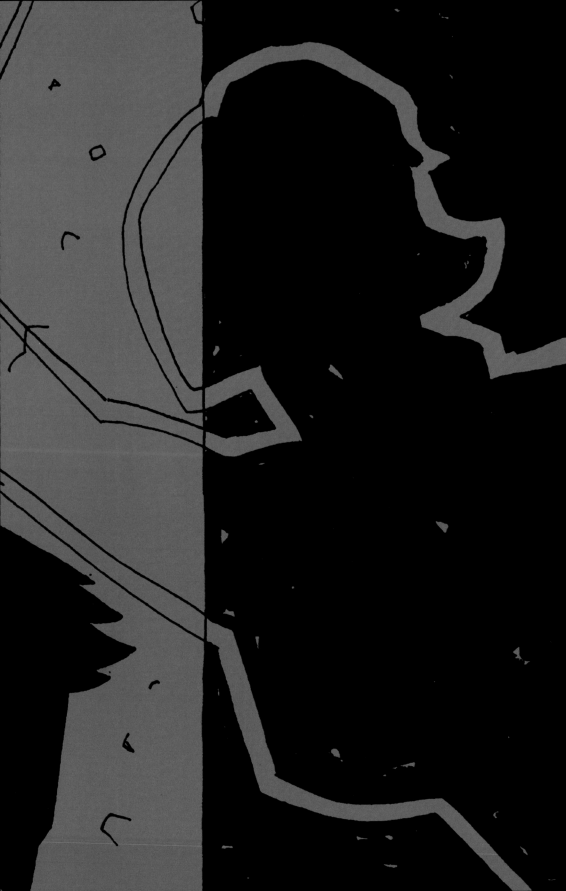

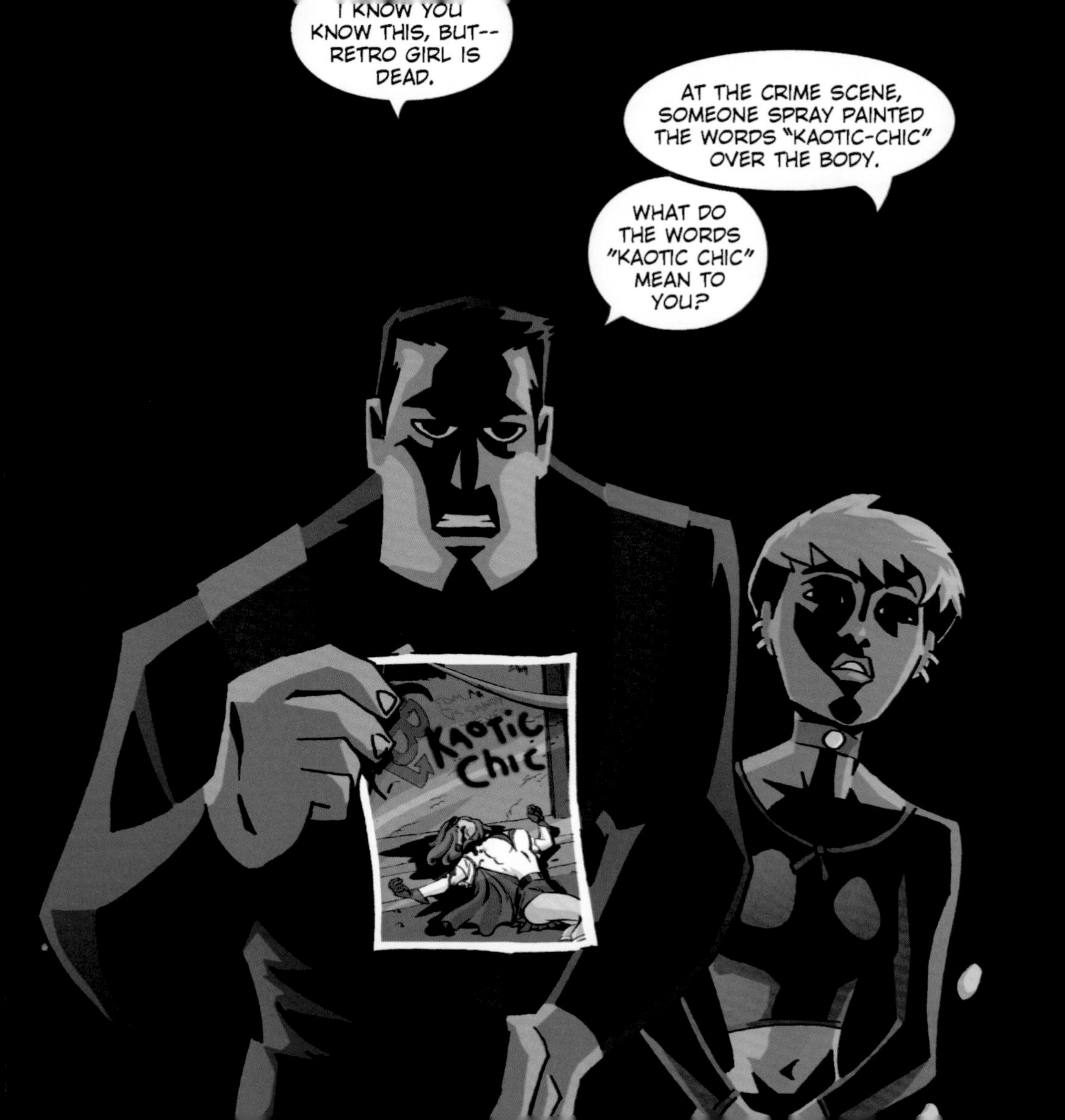
I KNOW YOU KNOW THIS, BUT-- RETRO GIRL IS DEAD.
AT THE CRIME SCENE, SOMEONE SPRAY PAINTED THE WORDS "KAOTIC-CHIC" OVER THE BODY.
WHAT DO THE WORDS "KAOTIC CHIC" MEAN TO YOU?
KAOTIC CHIC

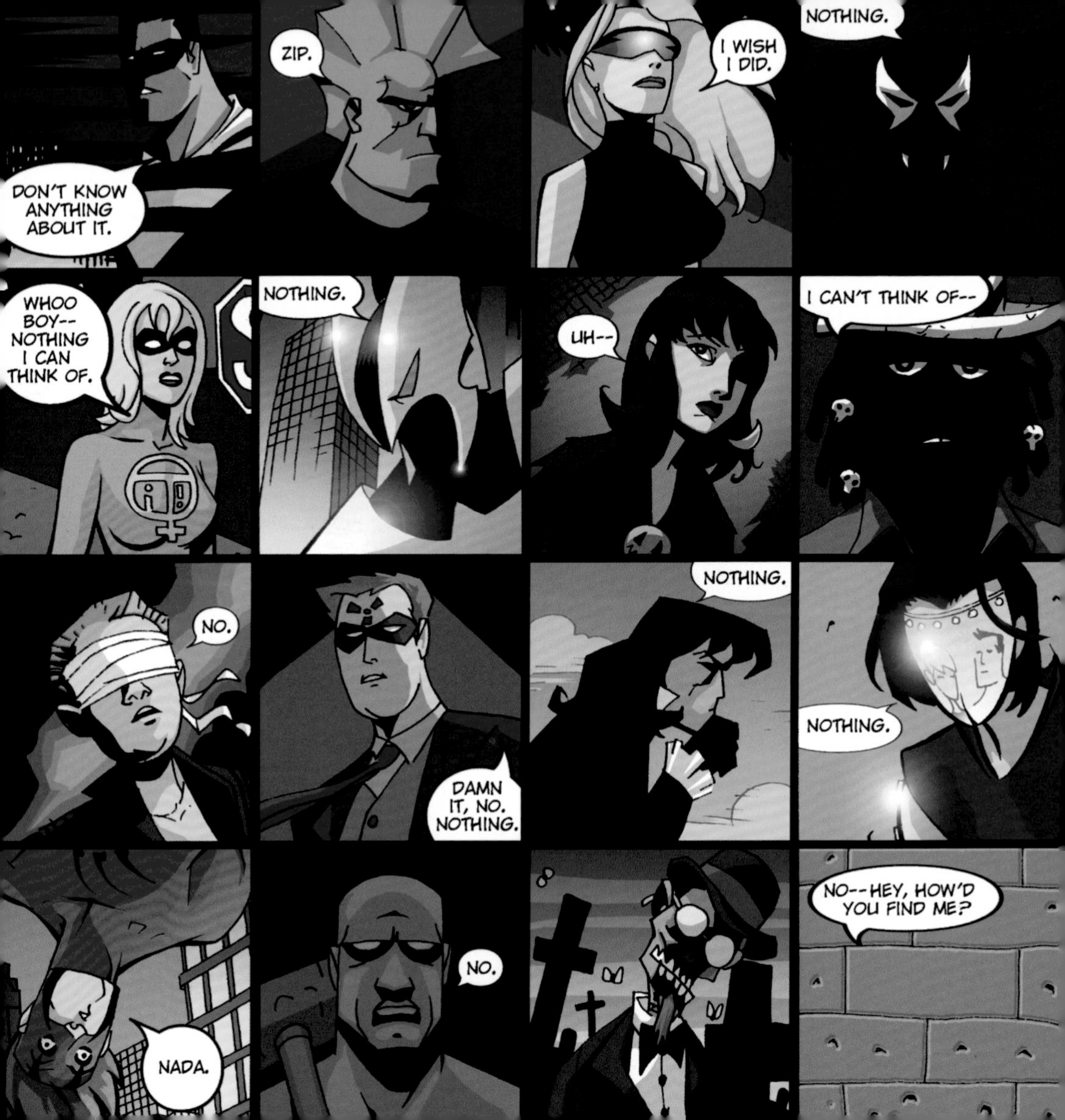
DON'T KNOW ANYTHING ABOUT IT.
ZIP.
I WISH I DID.
NOTHING.
WHOO BOY-- NOTHING I CAN THINK OF.
NOTHING.
UH--
I CAN'T THINK OF--
NO.
DAMN IT, NO. NOTHING.
NOTHING.
NOTHING.
NADA.
NO.
NO--HEY, HOW'D YOU FIND ME?

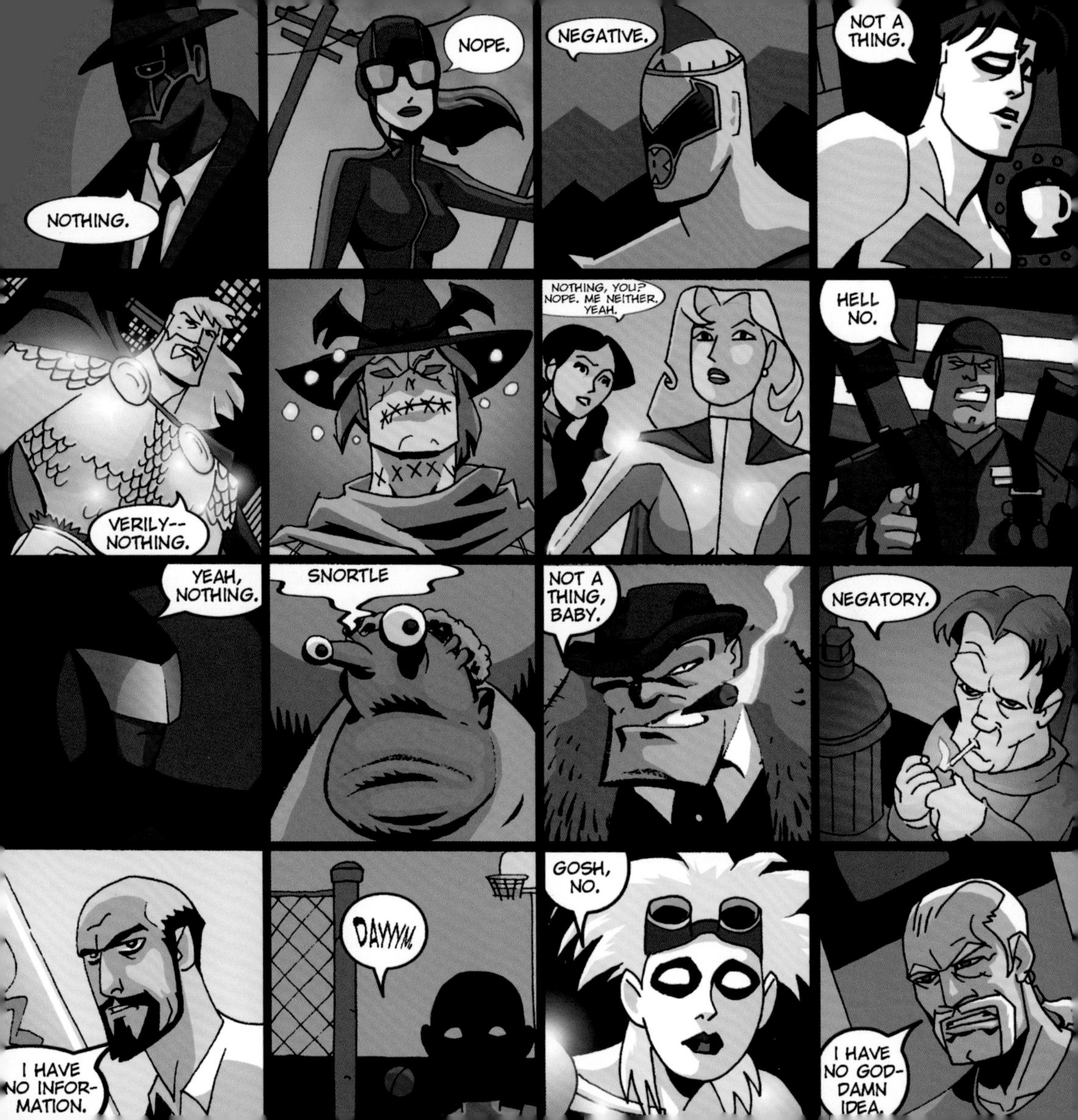
NOTHING.
NOPE.
NEGATIVE.
NOT A THING.
VERILY-- NOTHING.
NOTHING, YOU? NOPE. ME NEITHER. YEAH.
HELL NO.
YEAH, NOTHING.
SNORTLE
NOT A THING, BABY.
NEGATORY.
I HAVE NO INFOR-MATION.
DAYYYM.
GOSH, NO.
I HAVE NO GOD-DAMN IDEA.

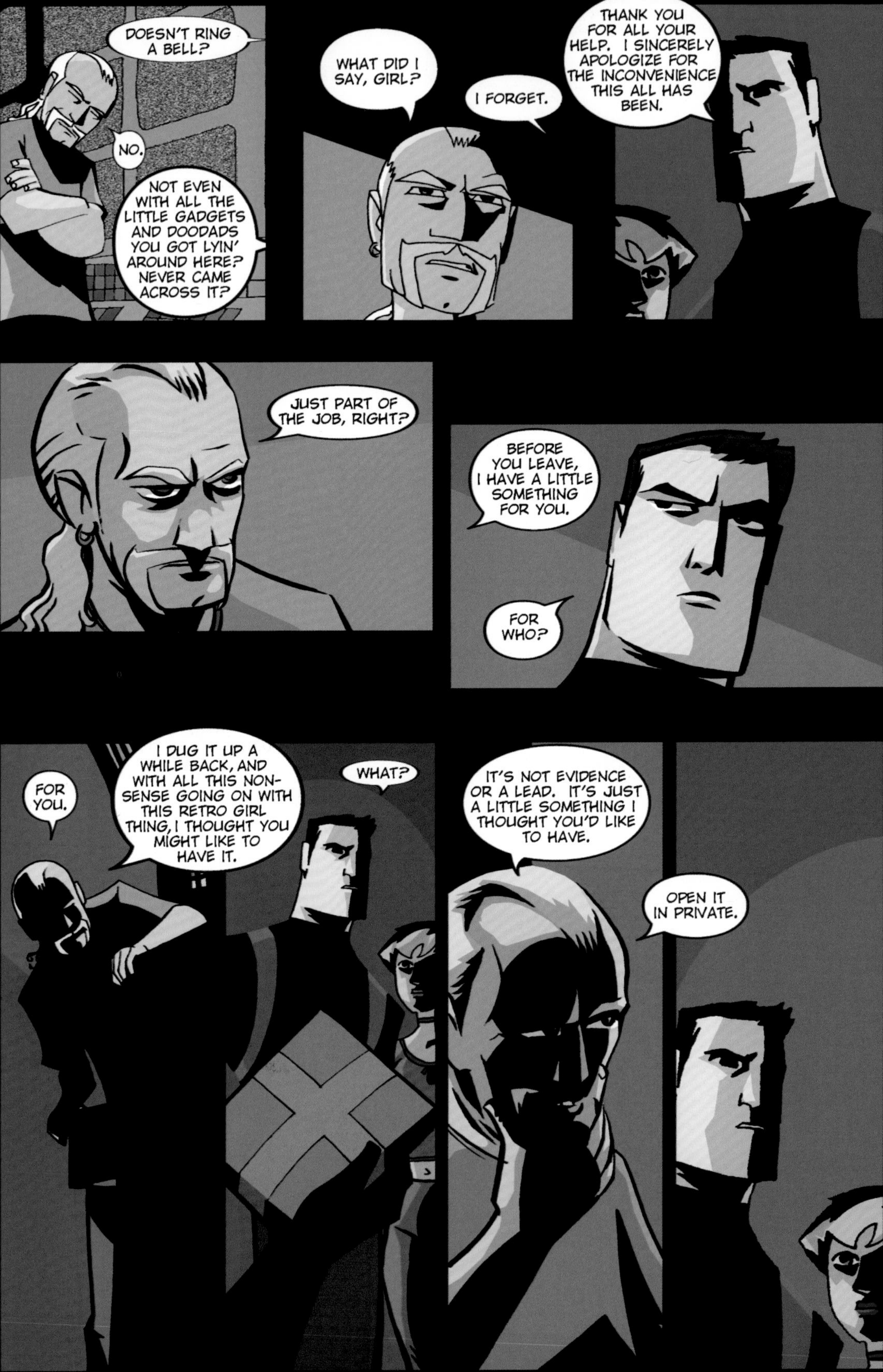
DOESN'T RING A BELL?
NO.
NOT EVEN WITH ALL THE LITTLE GADGETS AND DOODADS YOU GOT LYIN' AROUND HERE? NEVER CAME ACROSS IT?
WHAT DID I SAY, GIRL?
I FORGET.
THANK YOU FOR ALL YOUR HELP. I SINCERELY APOLOGIZE FOR THE INCONVENIENCE THIS ALL HAS BEEN.
JUST PART OF THE JOB, RIGHT?
BEFORE YOU LEAVE, I HAVE A LITTLE SOMETHING FOR YOU.
FOR WHO?
FOR YOU.
I DUG IT UP A WHILE BACK, AND WITH ALL THIS NON-SENSE GOING ON WITH THIS RETRO GIRL THING, I THOUGHT YOU MIGHT LIKE TO HAVE IT.
WHAT?
IT'S NOT EVIDENCE OR A LEAD. IT'S JUST A LITTLE SOMETHING I THOUGHT YOU'D LIKE TO HAVE.
OPEN IT IN PRIVATE.

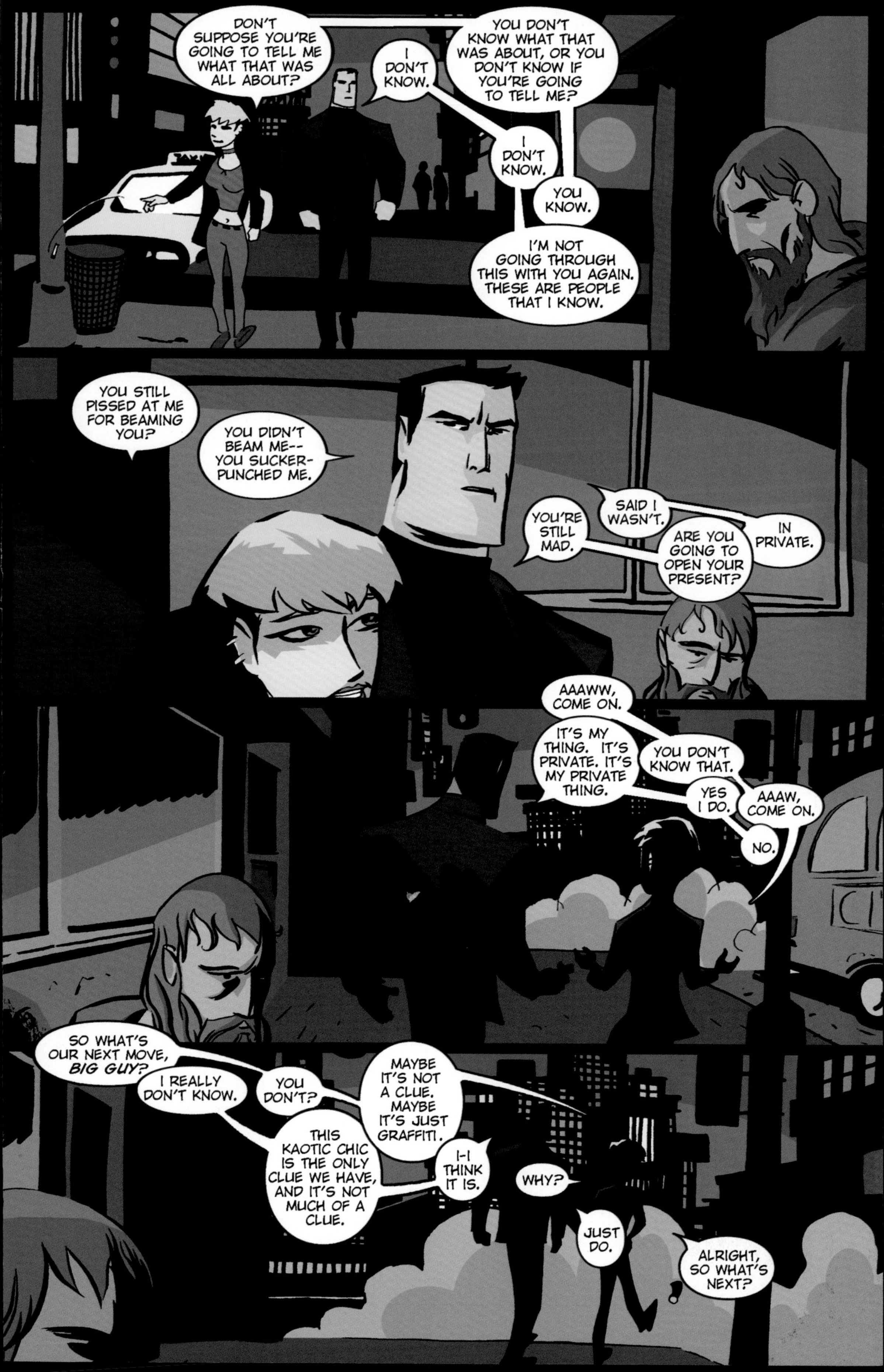
DON'T SUPPOSE YOU'RE GOING TO TELL ME WHAT THAT WAS ALL ABOUT?
I DON'T KNOW.
YOU DON'T KNOW WHAT THAT WAS ABOUT, OR YOU DON'T KNOW IF YOU'RE GOING TO TELL ME?
I DON'T KNOW.
YOU KNOW.
I'M NOT GOING THROUGH THIS WITH YOU AGAIN. THESE ARE PEOPLE THAT I KNOW.
YOU STILL PISSED AT ME FOR BEAMING YOU?
YOU DIDN'T BEAM ME-- YOU SUCKER-PUNCHED ME.
YOU'RE STILL MAD.
SAID I WASN'T.
ARE YOU GOING TO OPEN YOUR PRESENT?
IN PRIVATE.
AAAWW, COME ON.
IT'S MY THING. IT'S PRIVATE. IT'S MY PRIVATE THING.
YOU DON'T KNOW THAT.
YES I DO.
AAAW, COME ON.
NO.
SO WHAT'S OUR NEXT MOVE, *BIG GUY?*
I REALLY DON'T KNOW.
YOU DON'T?
THIS KAOTIC CHIC IS THE ONLY CLUE WE HAVE, AND IT'S NOT MUCH OF A CLUE.
MAYBE IT'S NOT A CLUE. MAYBE IT'S JUST GRAFFITI.
I-I THINK IT IS.
WHY?
JUST DO.
ALRIGHT, SO WHAT'S NEXT?

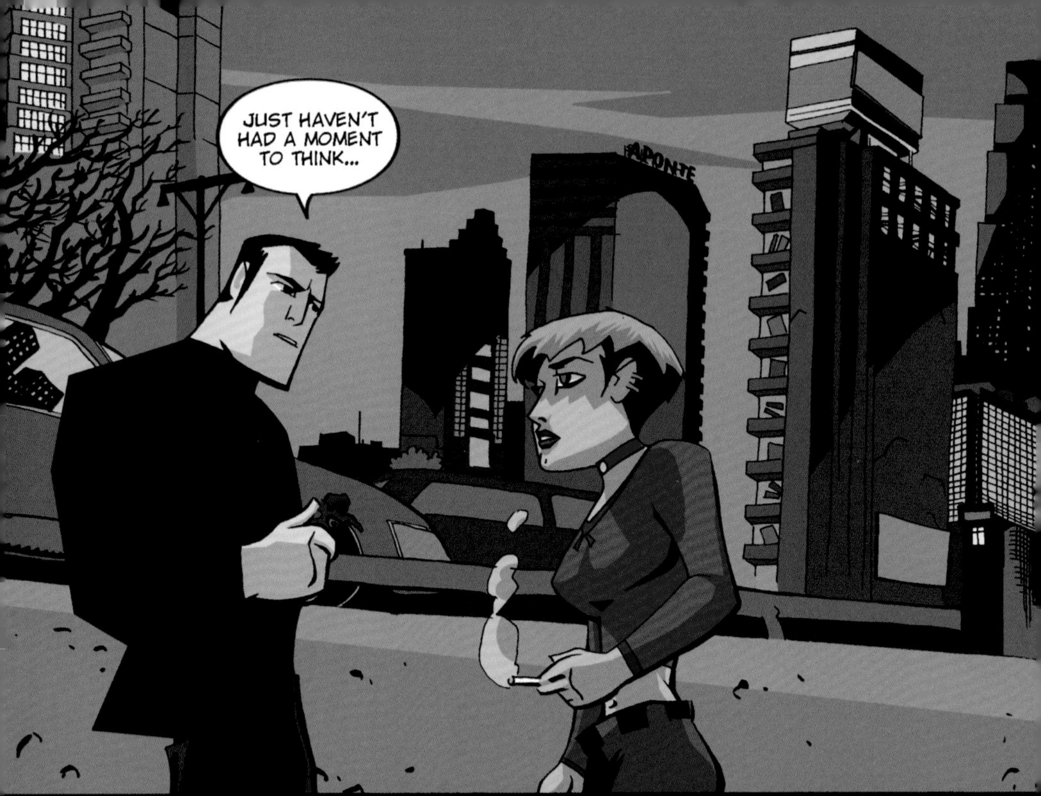
JUST HAVEN'T HAD A MOMENT TO THINK...
APONTE

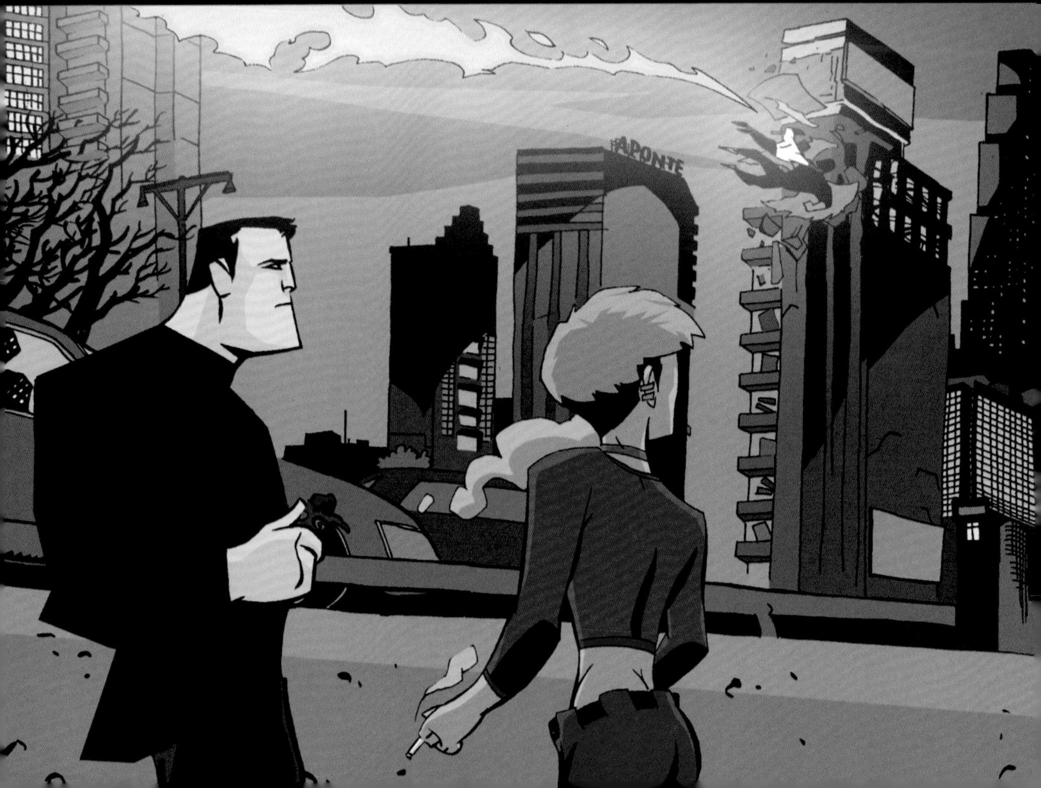
APONTE

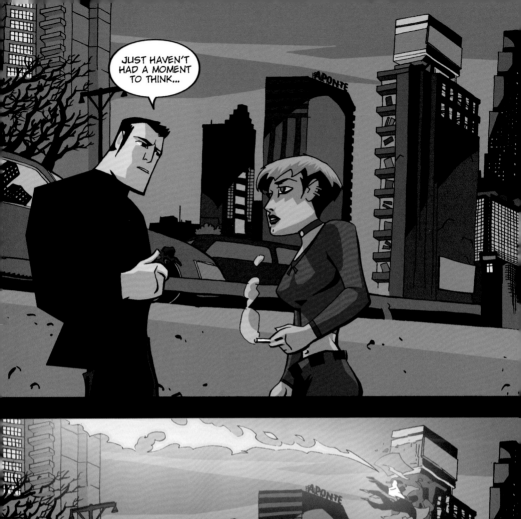

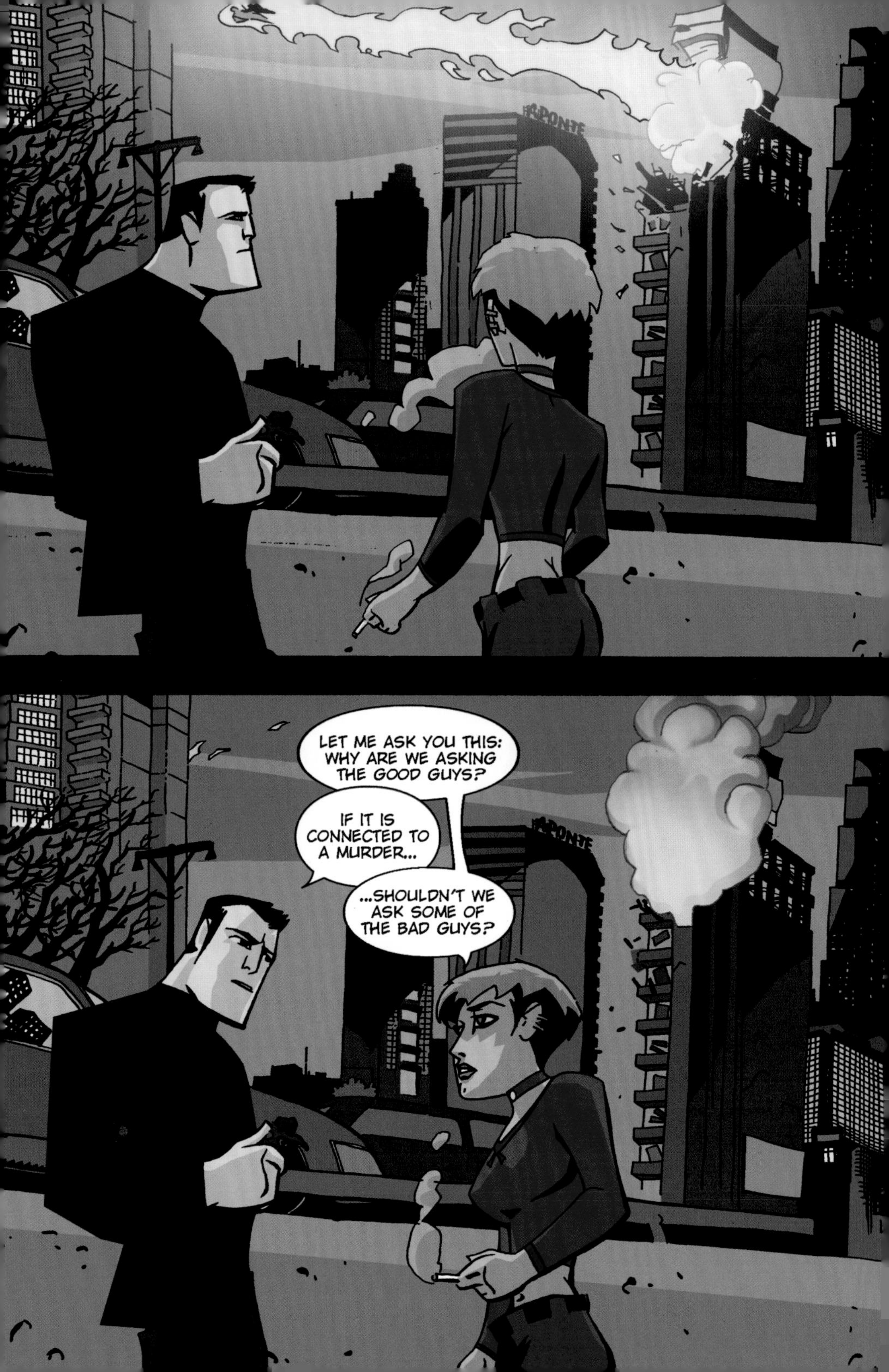
LET ME ASK YOU THIS: WHY ARE WE ASKING THE GOOD GUYS?
IF IT IS CONNECTED TO A MURDER...
...SHOULDN'T WE ASK SOME OF THE BAD GUYS?

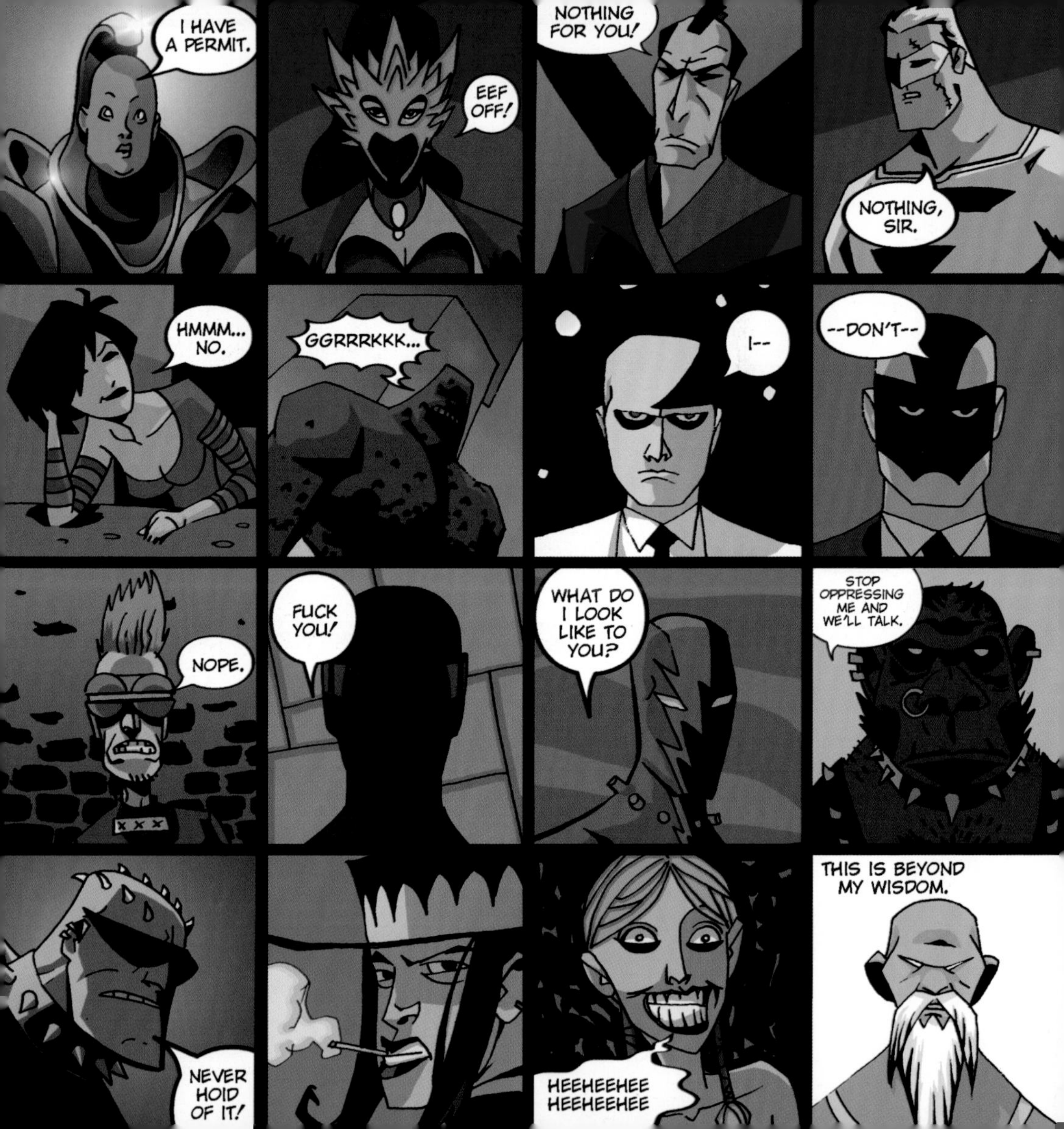
I HAVE A PERMIT.
EEF OFF!
NOTHING FOR YOU!
NOTHING, SIR.
HMMM... NO.
GGRRRKKK...
I--
--DON'T--
NOPE.
FUCK YOU!
WHAT DO I LOOK LIKE TO YOU?
STOP OPPRESSING ME AND WE'LL TALK.
NEVER HOID OF IT!
HEEHEEHEE HEEHEEHEE
THIS IS BEYOND MY WISDOM.

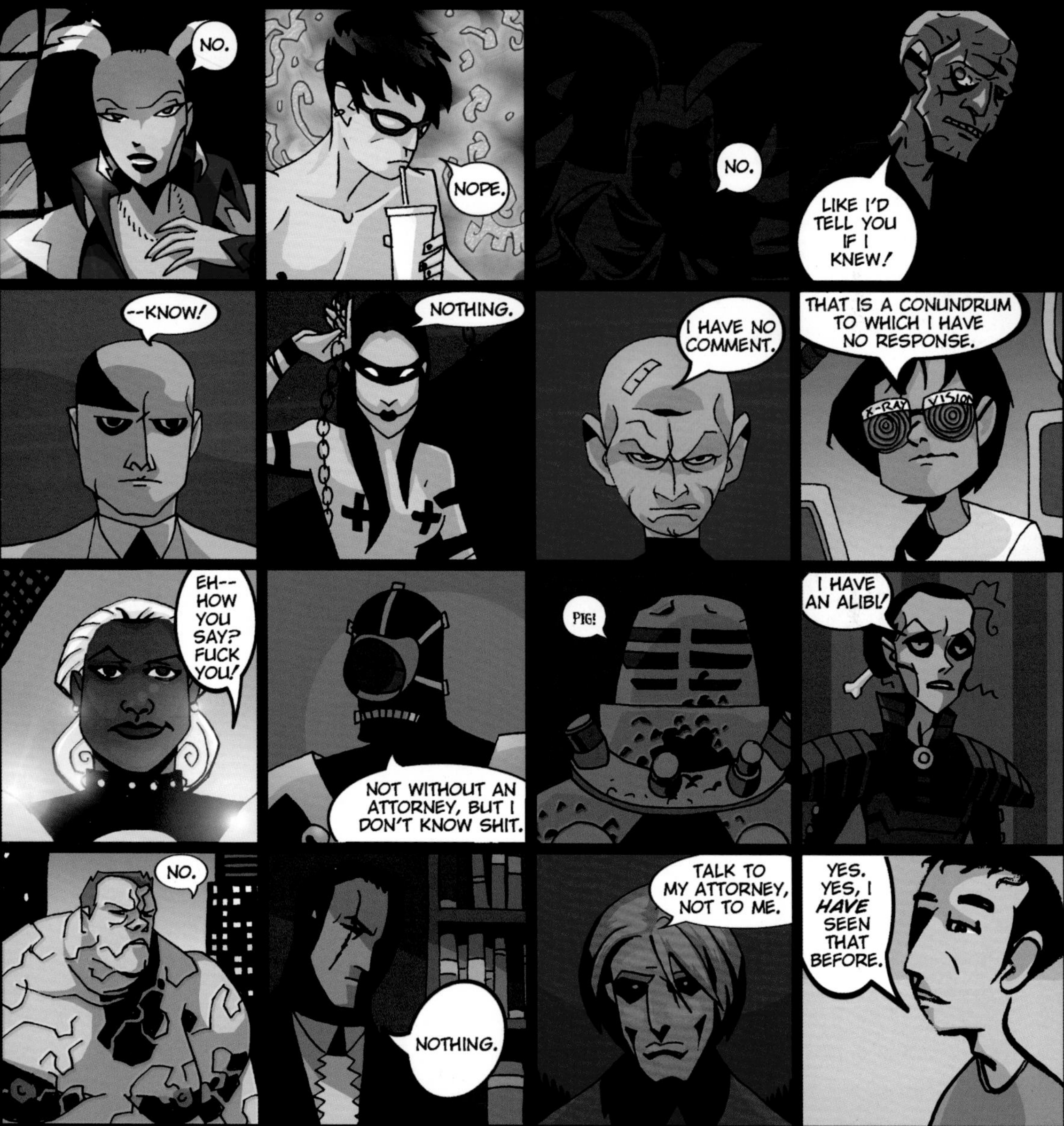
NO.
NOPE.
NO.
LIKE I'D TELL YOU IF I KNEW!
--KNOW!
NOTHING.
I HAVE NO COMMENT.
THAT IS A CONUNDRUM TO WHICH I HAVE NO RESPONSE.
X-RAY VISION
EH-- HOW YOU SAY? FUCK YOU!
NOT WITHOUT AN ATTORNEY, BUT I DON'T KNOW SHIT.
PIG!
I HAVE AN ALIBI!
NO.
NOTHING.
TALK TO MY ATTORNEY, NOT TO ME.
YES. YES, I HAVE SEEN THAT BEFORE.

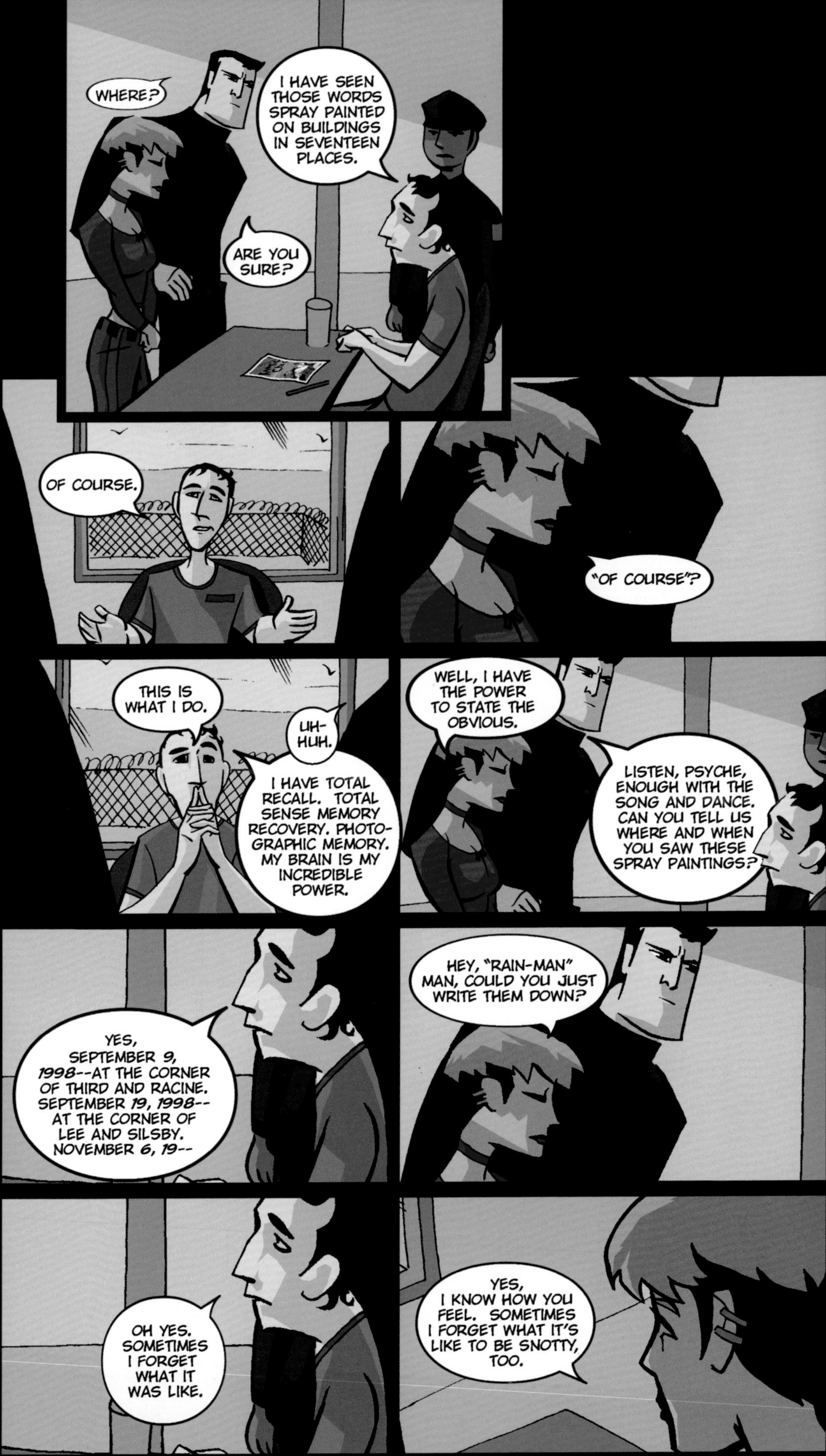
WHERE?
I HAVE SEEN THOSE WORDS SPRAY PAINTED ON BUILDINGS IN SEVENTEEN PLACES.
ARE YOU SURE?
OF COURSE.
"OF COURSE"?
THIS IS WHAT I DO.
UH-HUH.
I HAVE TOTAL RECALL. TOTAL SENSE MEMORY RECOVERY. PHOTO-GRAPHIC MEMORY. MY BRAIN IS MY INCREDIBLE POWER.
WELL, I HAVE THE POWER TO STATE THE OBVIOUS.
LISTEN, PSYCHE, ENOUGH WITH THE SONG AND DANCE. CAN YOU TELL US WHERE AND WHEN YOU SAW THESE SPRAY PAINTINGS?
YES, SEPTEMBER 9, 1998--AT THE CORNER OF THIRD AND RACINE. SEPTEMBER 19, 1998--AT THE CORNER OF LEE AND SILSBY. NOVEMBER 6, 19--
HEY, "RAIN-MAN" MAN, COULD YOU JUST WRITE THEM DOWN?
OH YES. SOMETIMES I FORGET WHAT IT WAS LIKE.
YES, I KNOW HOW YOU FEEL. SOMETIMES I FORGET WHAT IT'S LIKE TO BE SNOTTY, TOO.

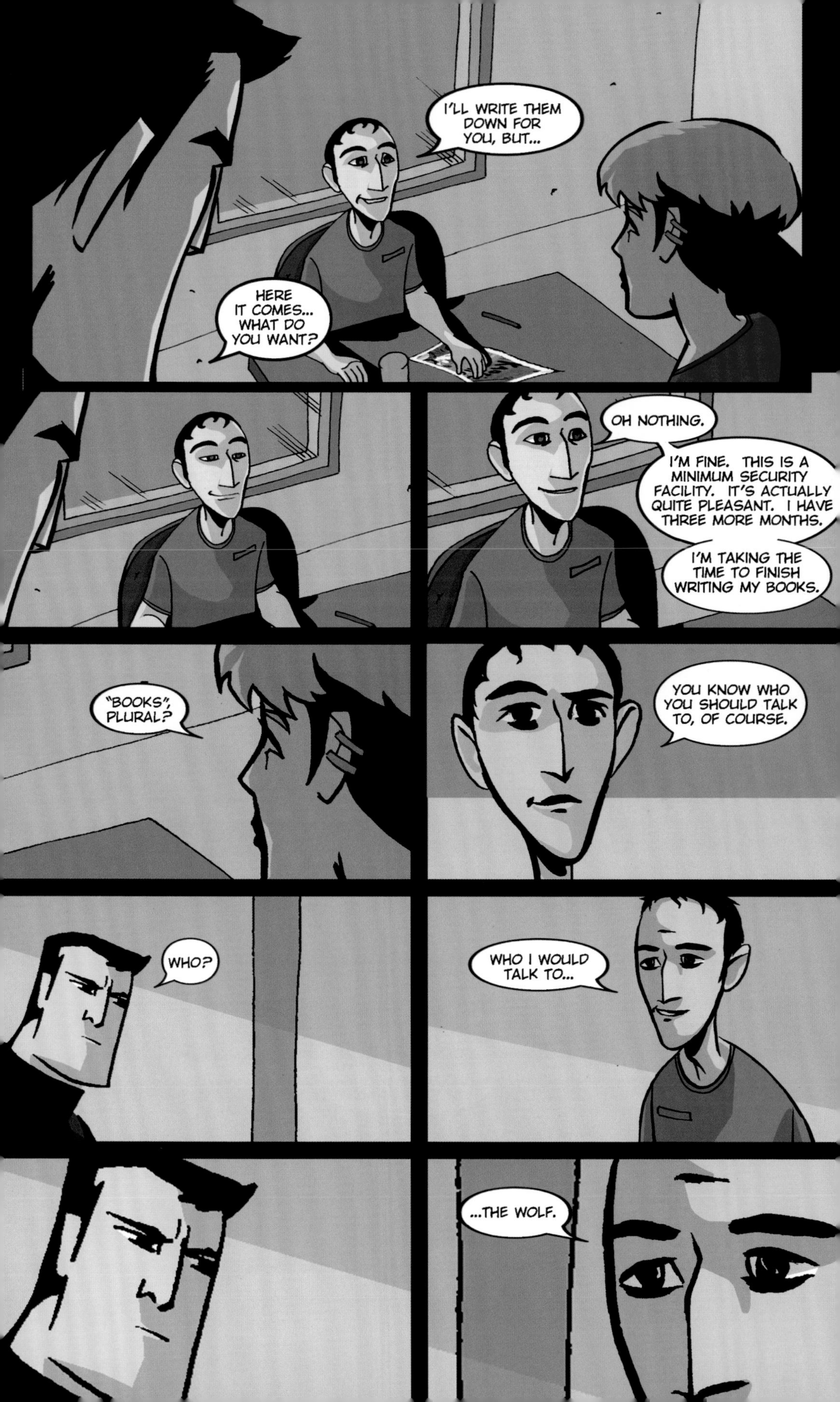
I'LL WRITE THEM DOWN FOR YOU, BUT...
HERE IT COMES... WHAT DO YOU WANT?
OH NOTHING.
I'M FINE. THIS IS A MINIMUM SECURITY FACILITY. IT'S ACTUALLY QUITE PLEASANT. I HAVE THREE MORE MONTHS.
I'M TAKING THE TIME TO FINISH WRITING MY BOOKS.
"BOOKS", PLURAL?
YOU KNOW WHO YOU SHOULD TALK TO, OF COURSE.
WHO?
WHO I WOULD TALK TO...
...THE WOLF.

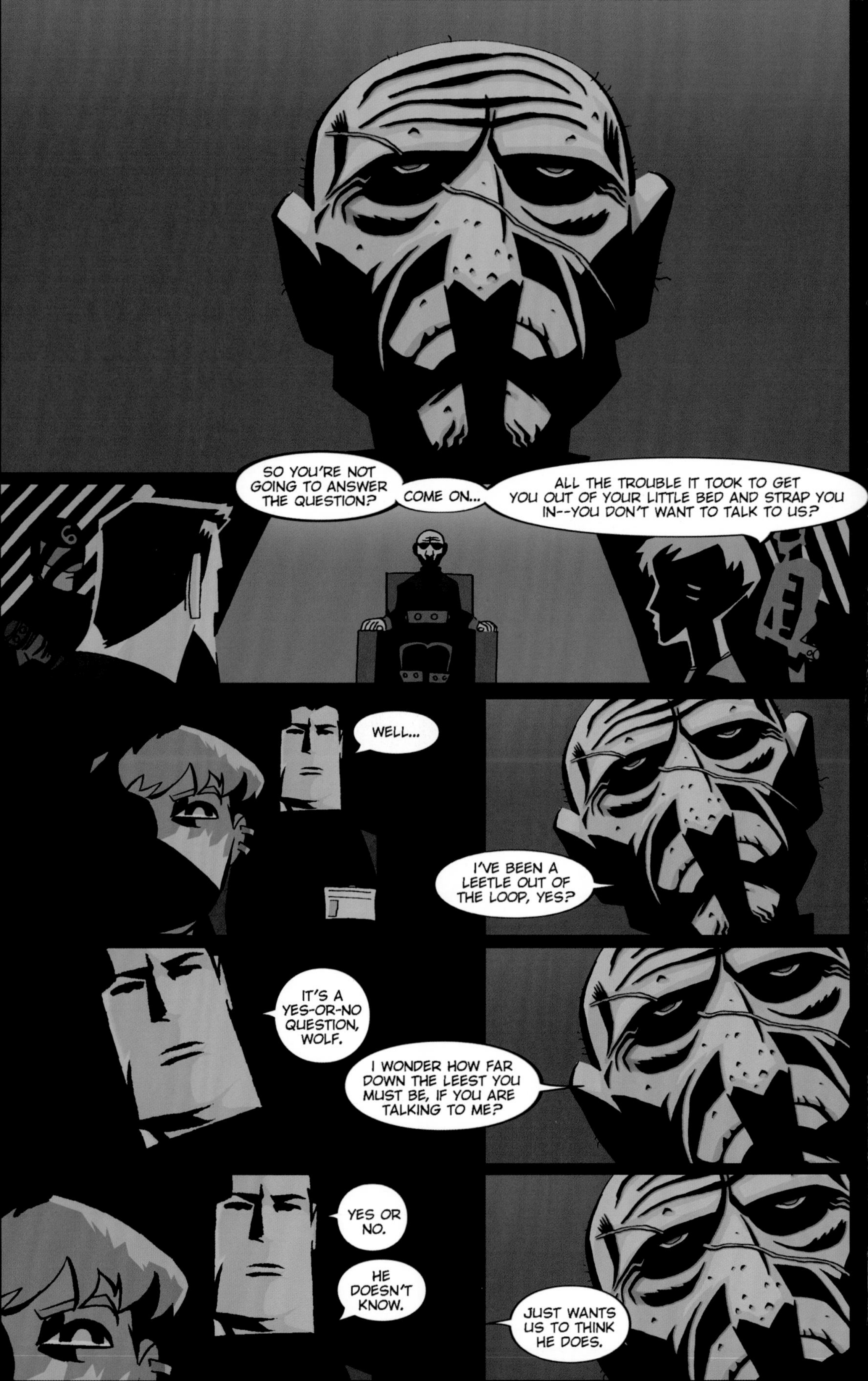
SO YOU'RE NOT GOING TO ANSWER THE QUESTION?
COME ON...
ALL THE TROUBLE IT TOOK TO GET YOU OUT OF YOUR LITTLE BED AND STRAP YOU IN--YOU DON'T WANT TO TALK TO US?
WELL...
I'VE BEEN A LEETLE OUT OF THE LOOP, YES?
IT'S A YES-OR-NO QUESTION, WOLF.
I WONDER HOW FAR DOWN THE LEEST YOU MUST BE, IF YOU ARE TALKING TO ME?
YES OR NO.
HE DOESN'T KNOW.
JUST WANTS US TO THINK HE DOES.

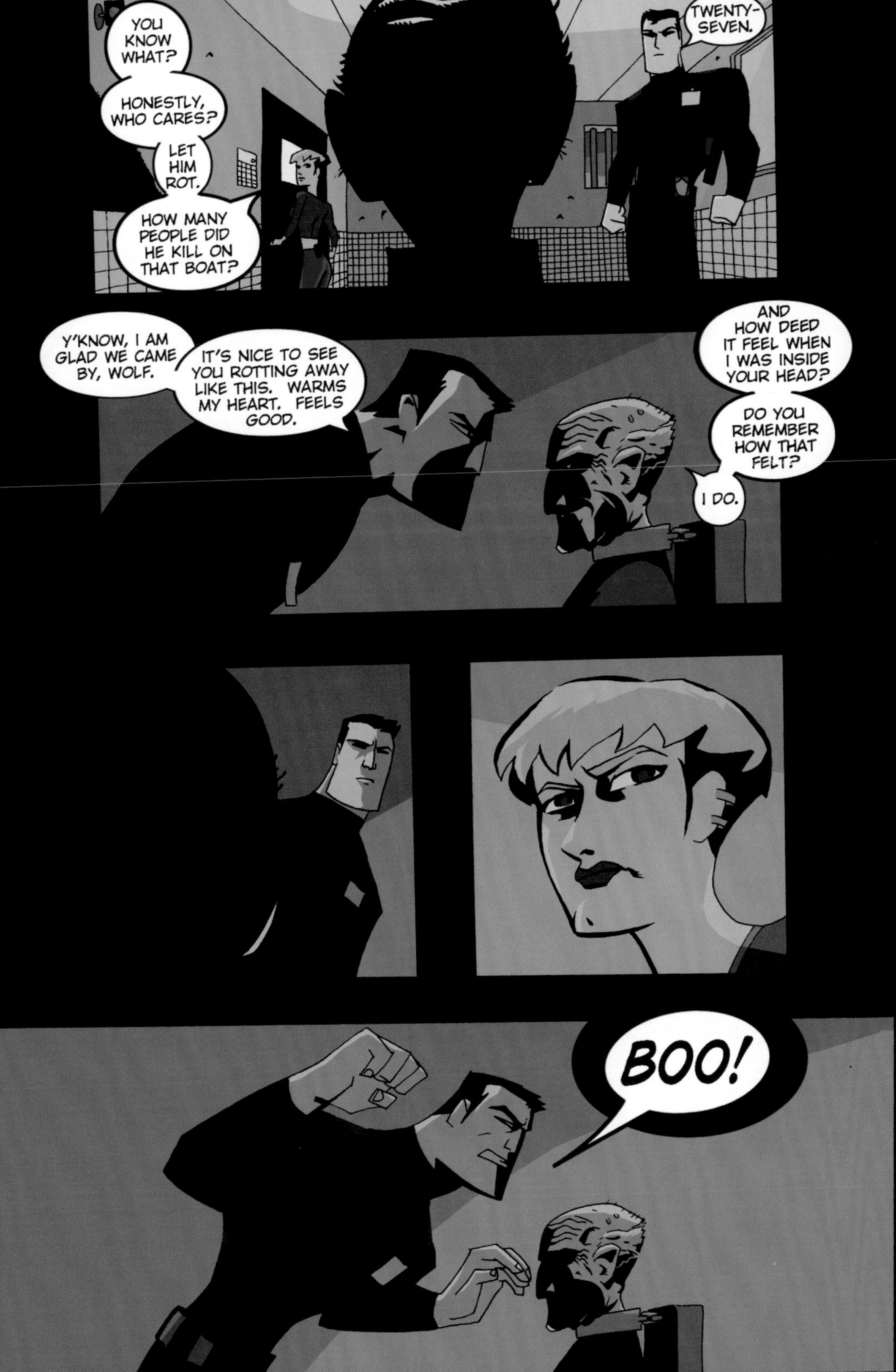
YOU KNOW WHAT?
HONESTLY, WHO CARES?
LET HIM ROT.
HOW MANY PEOPLE DID HE KILL ON THAT BOAT?
TWENTY-SEVEN.
Y'KNOW, I AM GLAD WE CAME BY, WOLF.
IT'S NICE TO SEE YOU ROTTING AWAY LIKE THIS. WARMS MY HEART. FEELS GOOD.
AND HOW DEED IT FEEL WHEN I WAS INSIDE YOUR HEAD?
DO YOU REMEMBER HOW THAT FELT?
I DO.
BOO!

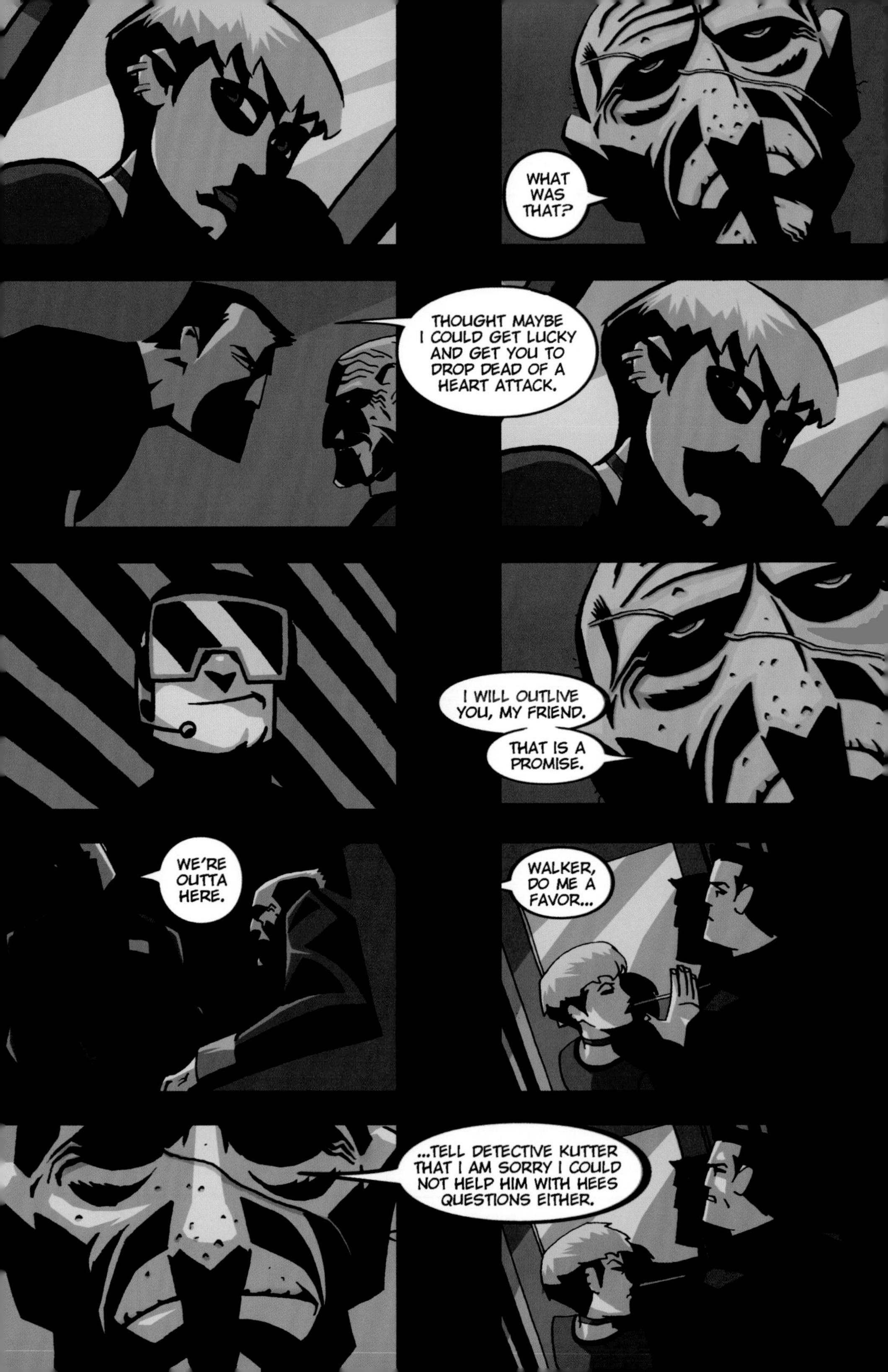
WHAT WAS THAT?
THOUGHT MAYBE I COULD GET LUCKY AND GET YOU TO DROP DEAD OF A HEART ATTACK.
I WILL OUTLIVE YOU, MY FRIEND.
THAT IS A PROMISE.
WE'RE OUTTA HERE.
WALKER, DO ME A FAVOR...
...TELL DETECTIVE KUTTER THAT I AM SORRY I COULD NOT HELP HIM WITH HEES QUESTIONS EITHER.

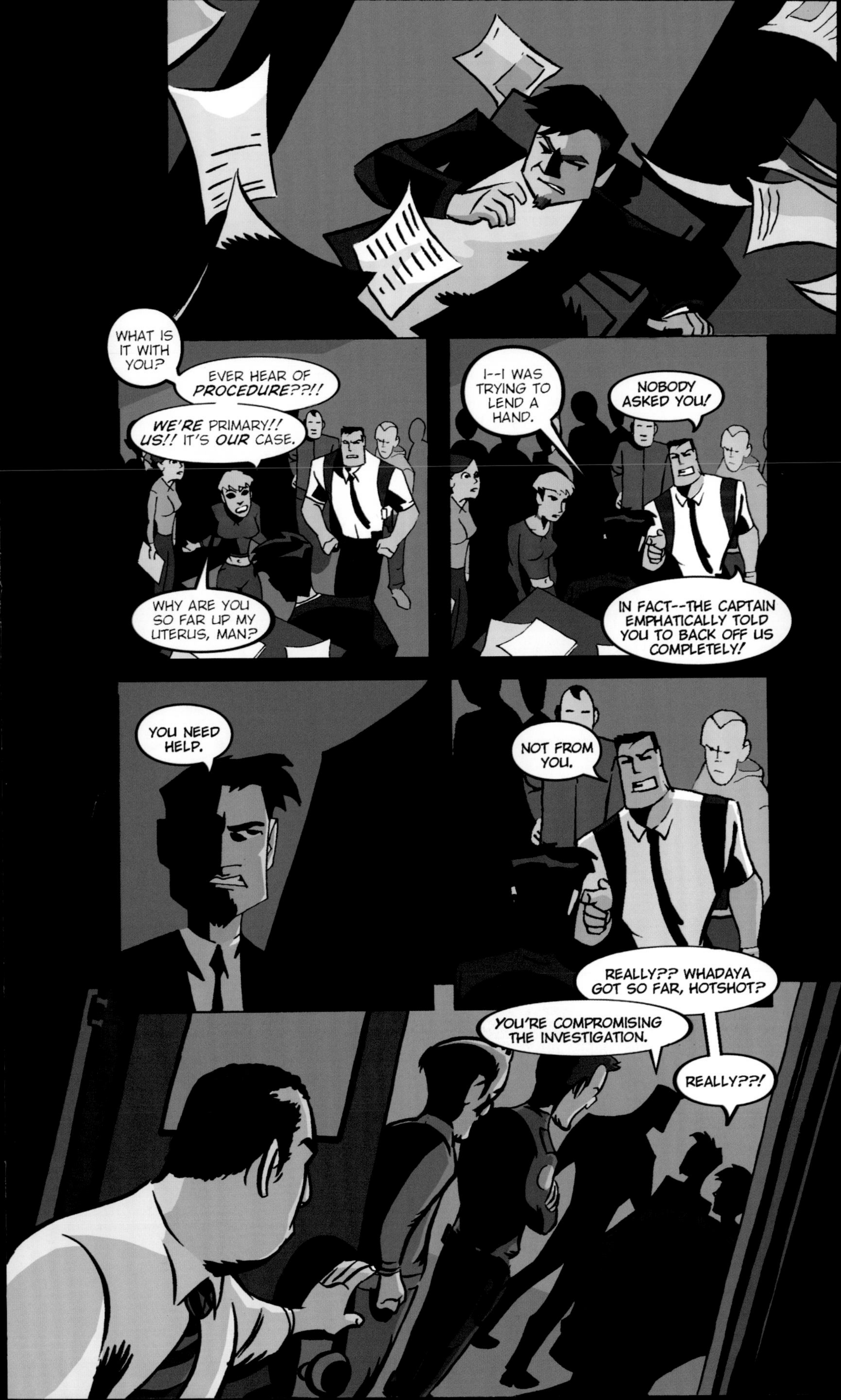
WHAT IS IT WITH YOU?
EVER HEAR OF PROCEDURE??!!
WE'RE PRIMARY!! US!! IT'S OUR CASE.
WHY ARE YOU SO FAR UP MY UTERUS, MAN?
I--I WAS TRYING TO LEND A HAND.
NOBODY ASKED YOU!
IN FACT--THE CAPTAIN EMPHATICALLY TOLD YOU TO BACK OFF US COMPLETELY!
YOU NEED HELP.
NOT FROM YOU.
REALLY?? WHADAYA GOT SO FAR, HOTSHOT?
YOU'RE COMPROMISING THE INVESTIGATION.
REALLY??!

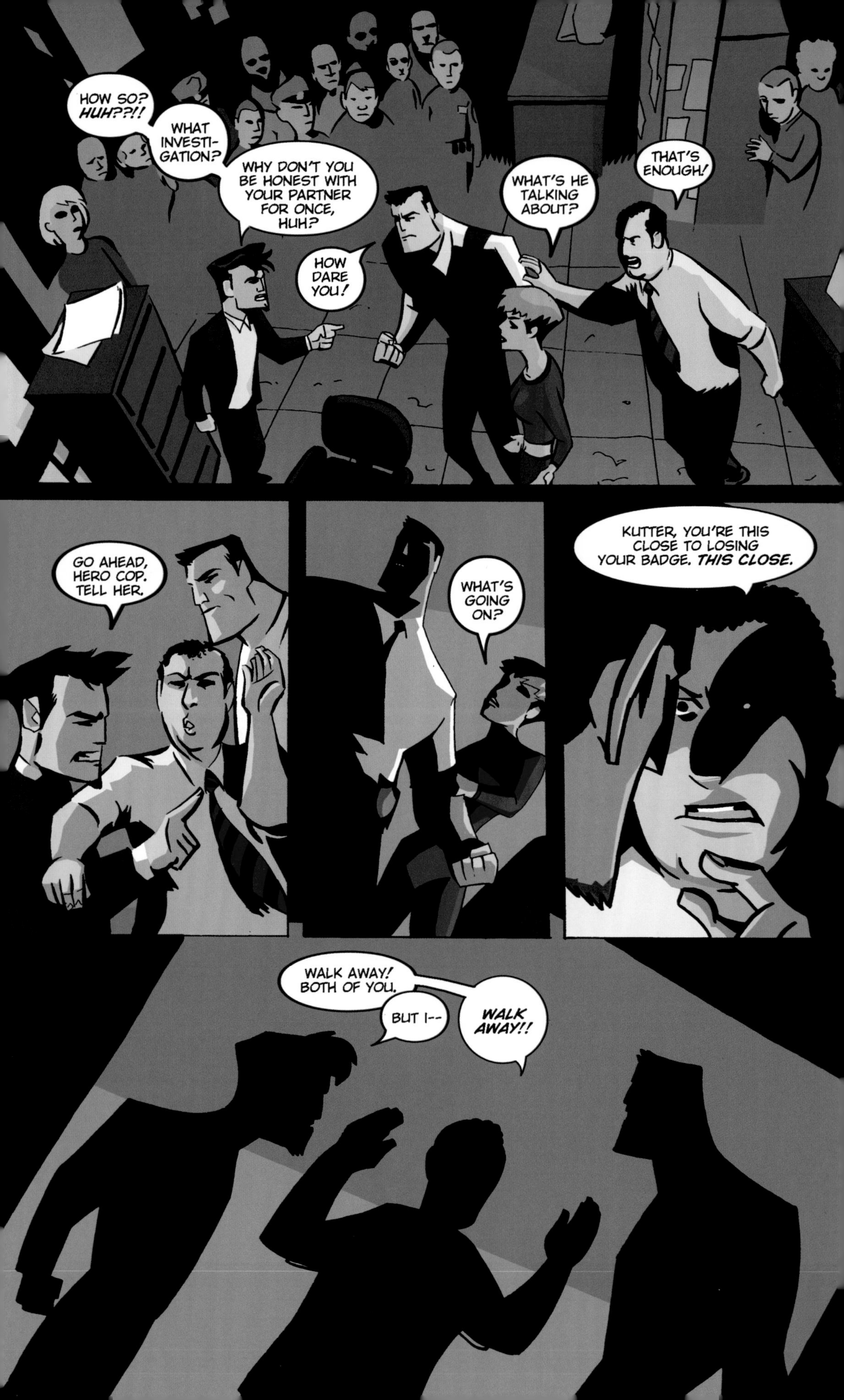
HOW SO? HUH??!!
WHAT INVESTI-GATION?
WHY DON'T YOU BE HONEST WITH YOUR PARTNER FOR ONCE, HUH?
HOW DARE YOU!
WHAT'S HE TALKING ABOUT?
THAT'S ENOUGH!
GO AHEAD, HERO COP. TELL HER.
WHAT'S GOING ON?
KUTTER, YOU'RE THIS CLOSE TO LOSING YOUR BADGE. THIS CLOSE.
WALK AWAY! BOTH OF YOU.
BUT I--
WALK AWAY!!

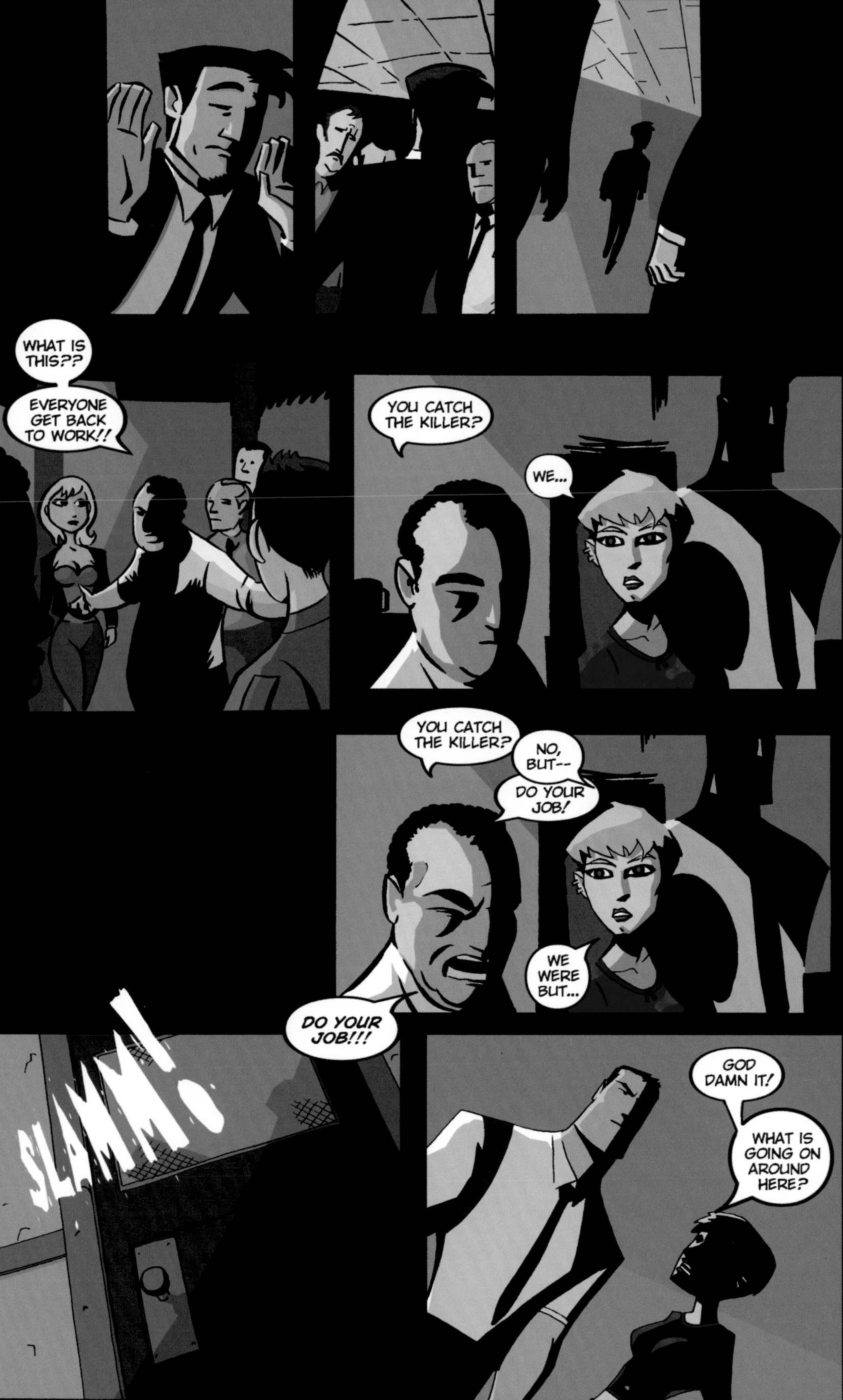
WHAT IS THIS??
EVERYONE GET BACK TO WORK!!
YOU CATCH THE KILLER?
WE...
YOU CATCH THE KILLER?
NO, BUT--
DO YOUR JOB!
WE WERE BUT...
DO YOUR JOB!!!
SLAM!
GOD DAMN IT!
WHAT IS GOING ON AROUND HERE?

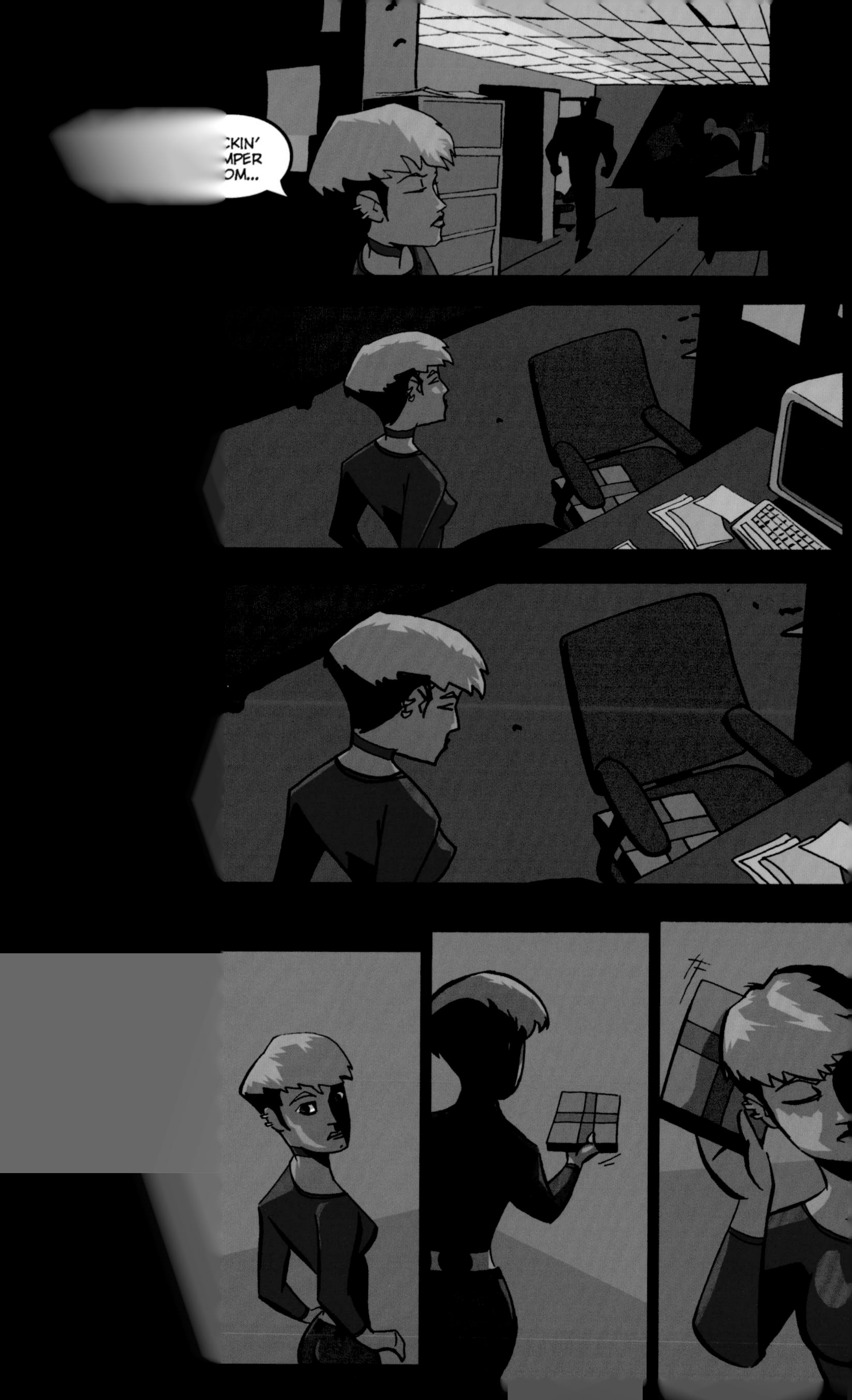
CKIN'
MPER
OM...

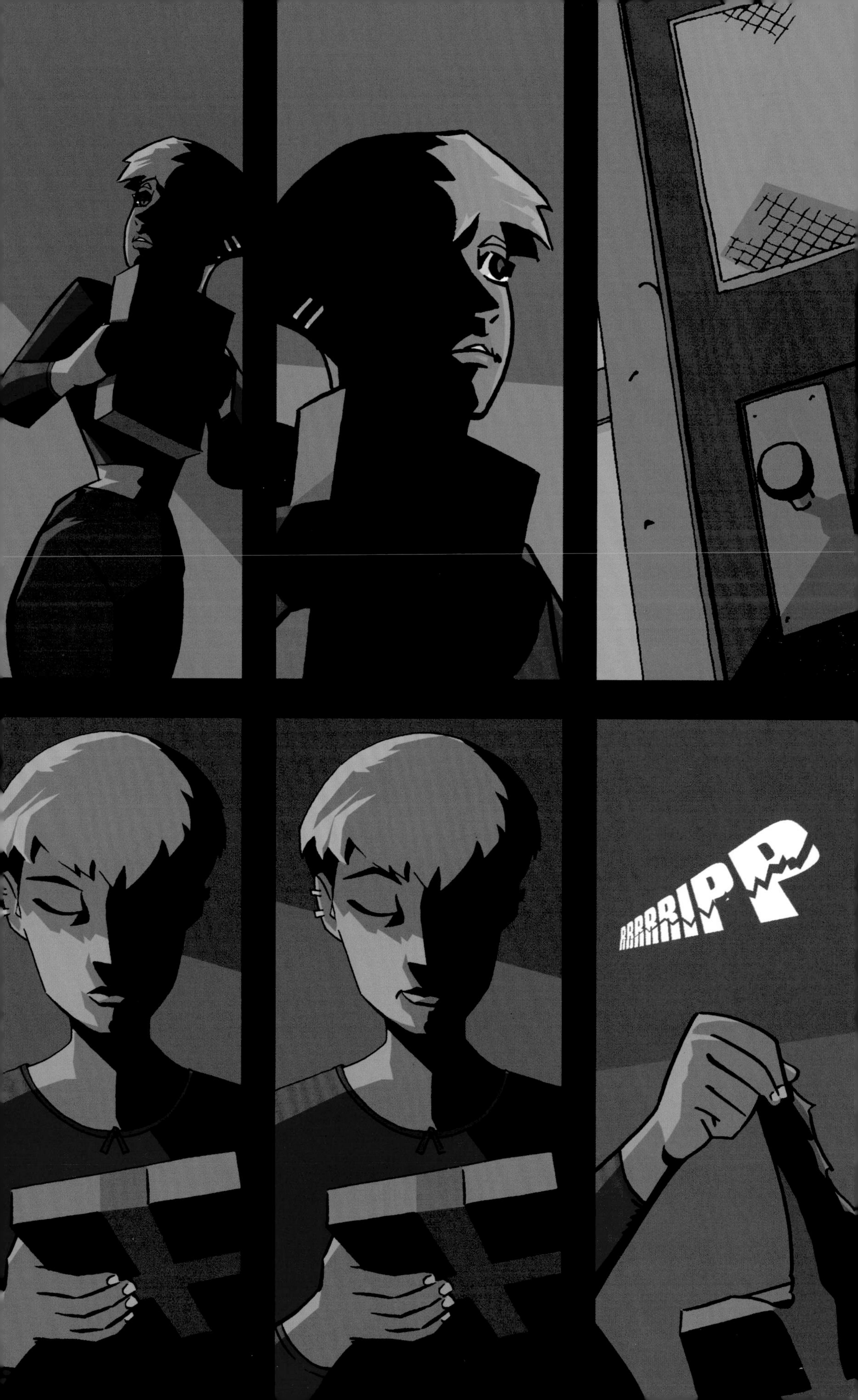
RRRRRIPP

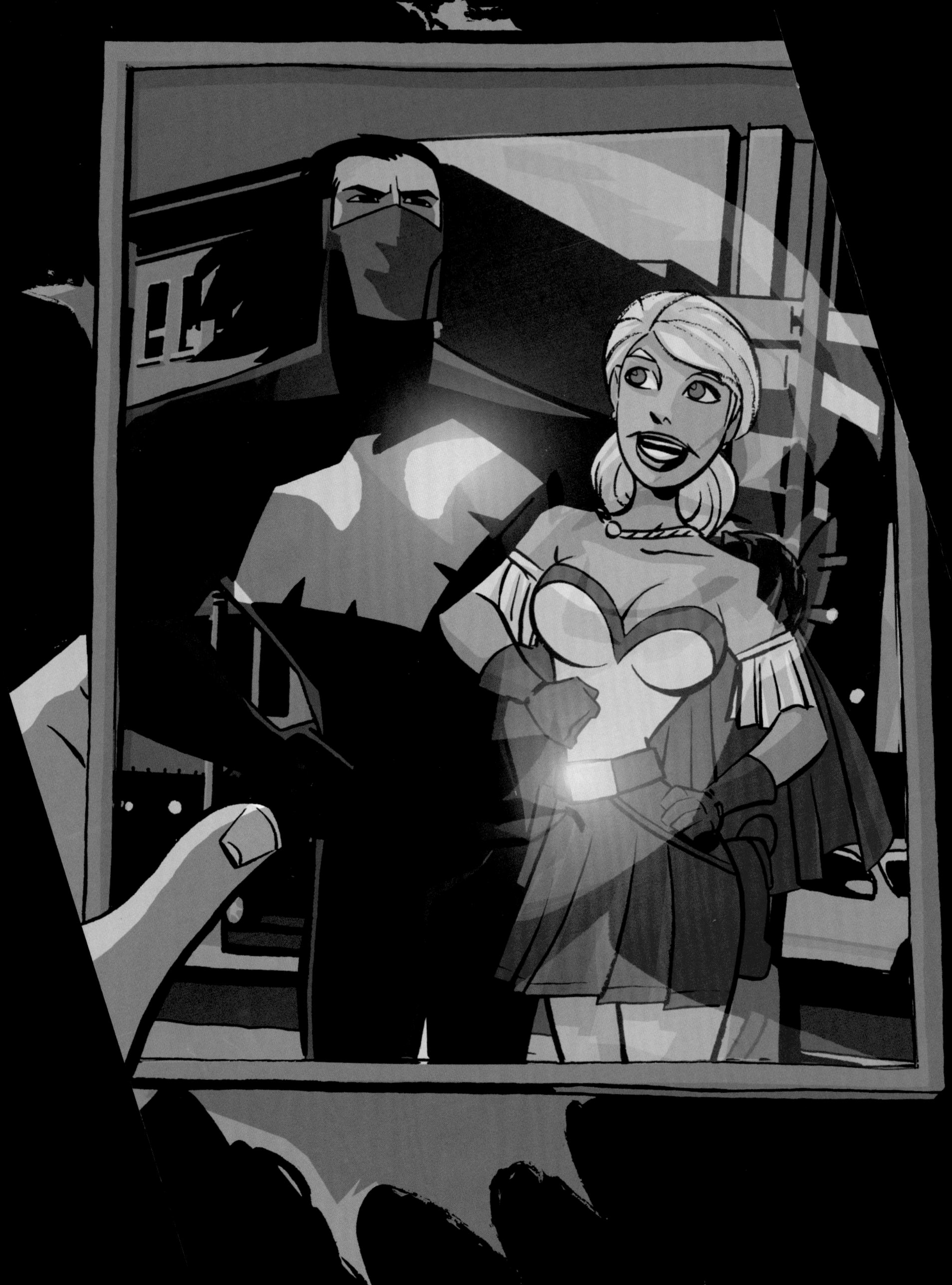

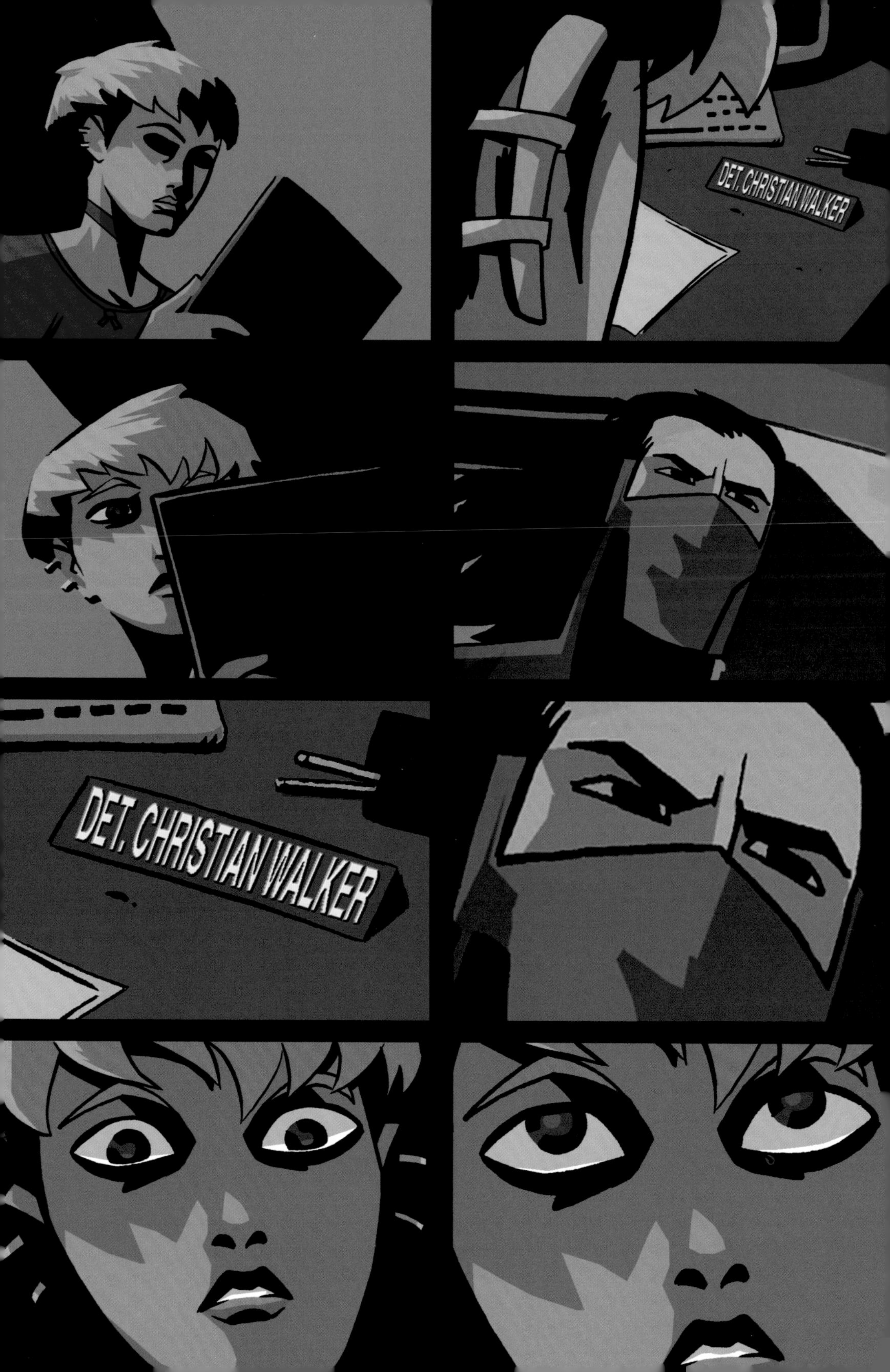
DET. CHRISTIAN WALKER
DET. CHRISTIAN WALKER

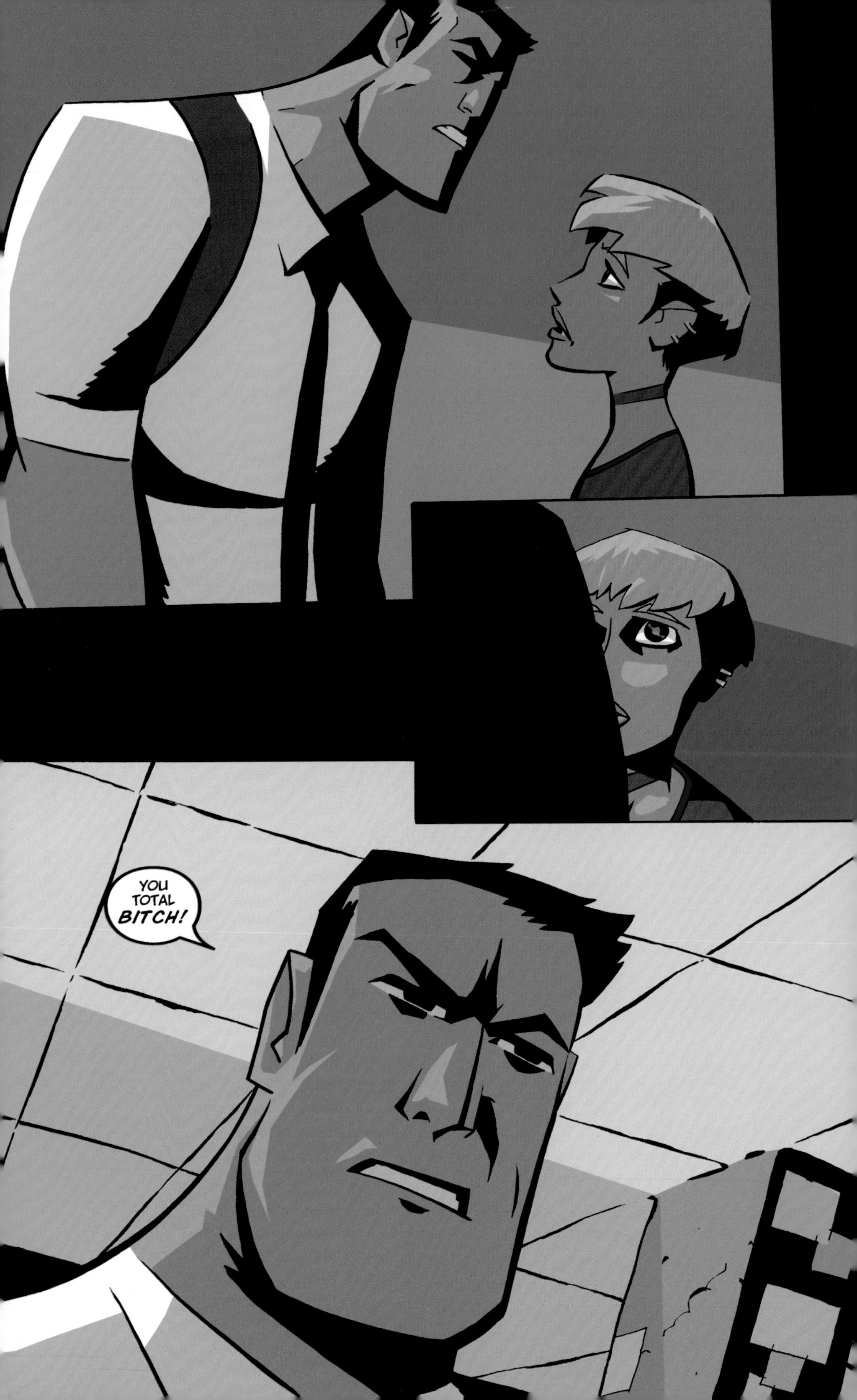
YOU TOTAL BITCH!

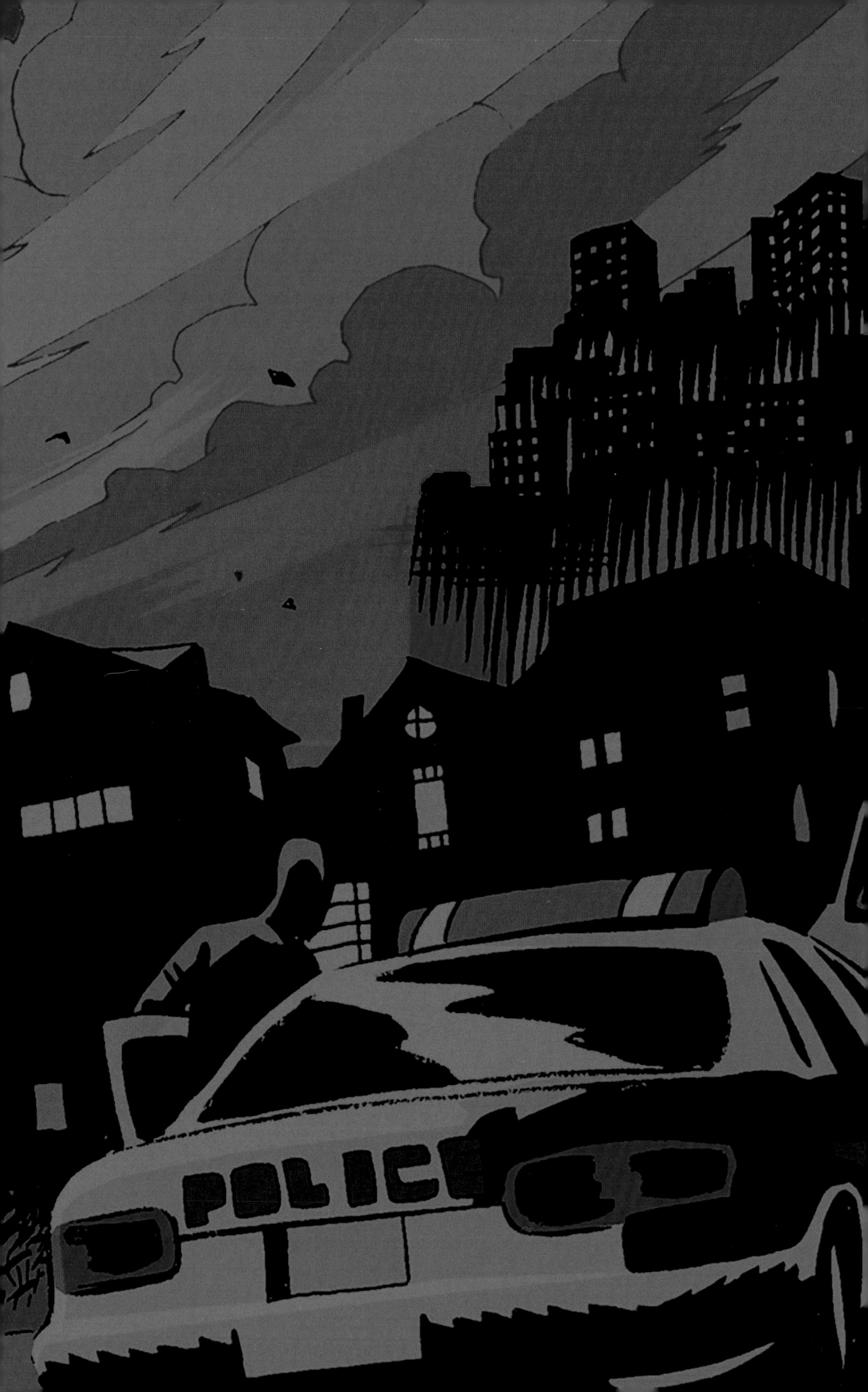
POLICE

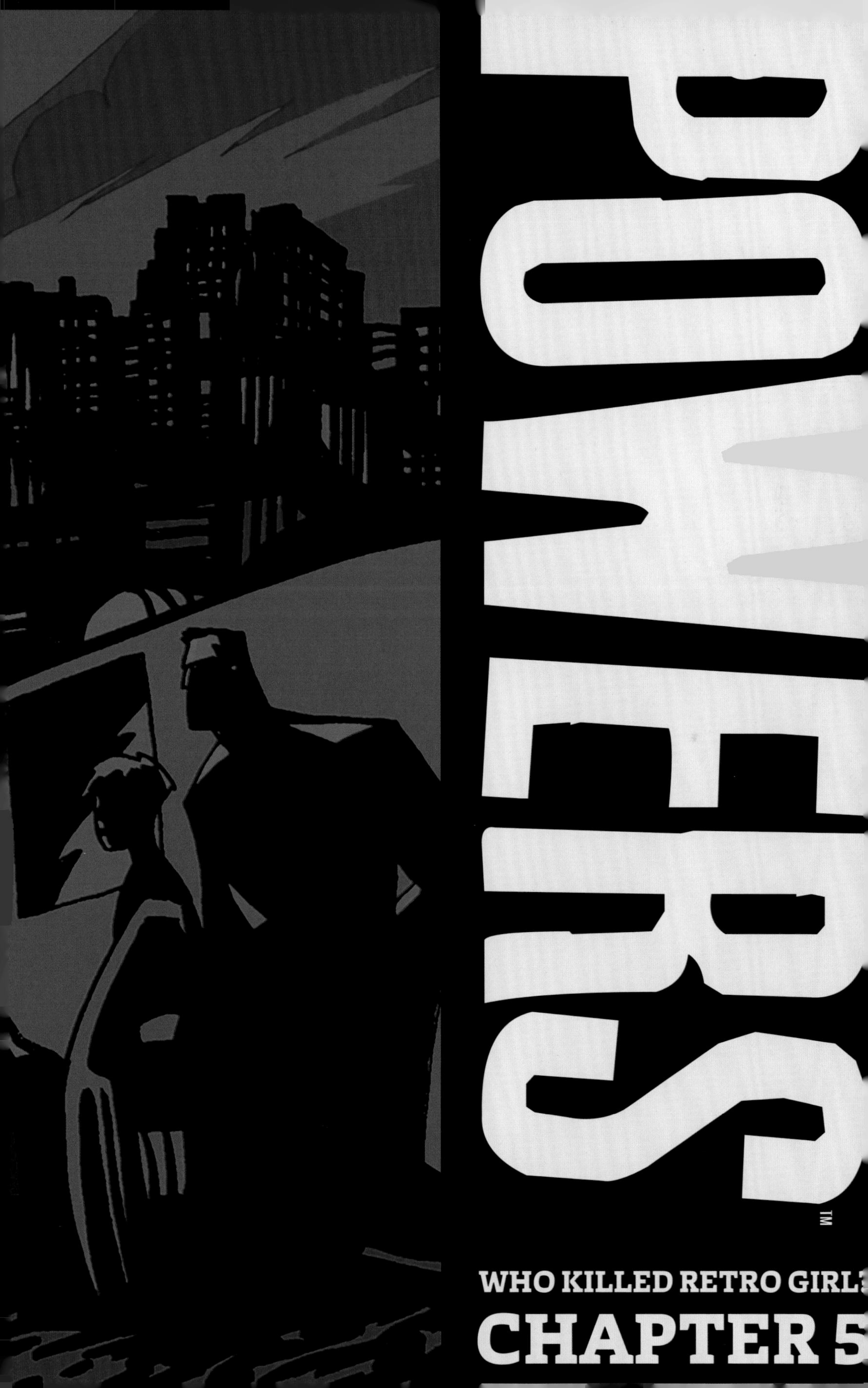

POWERS™

WHO KILLED RETRO GIRL?

CHAPTER 5

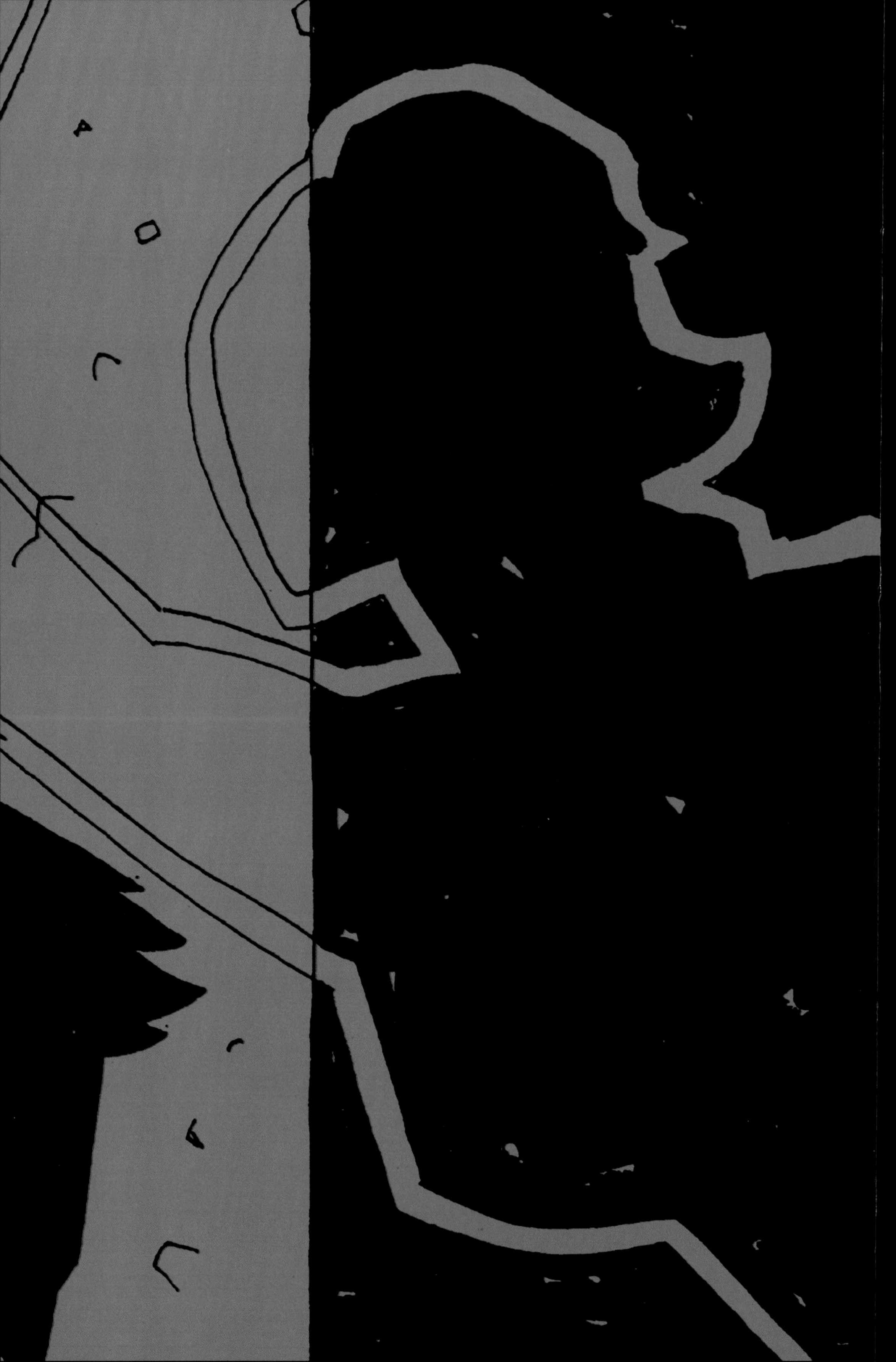

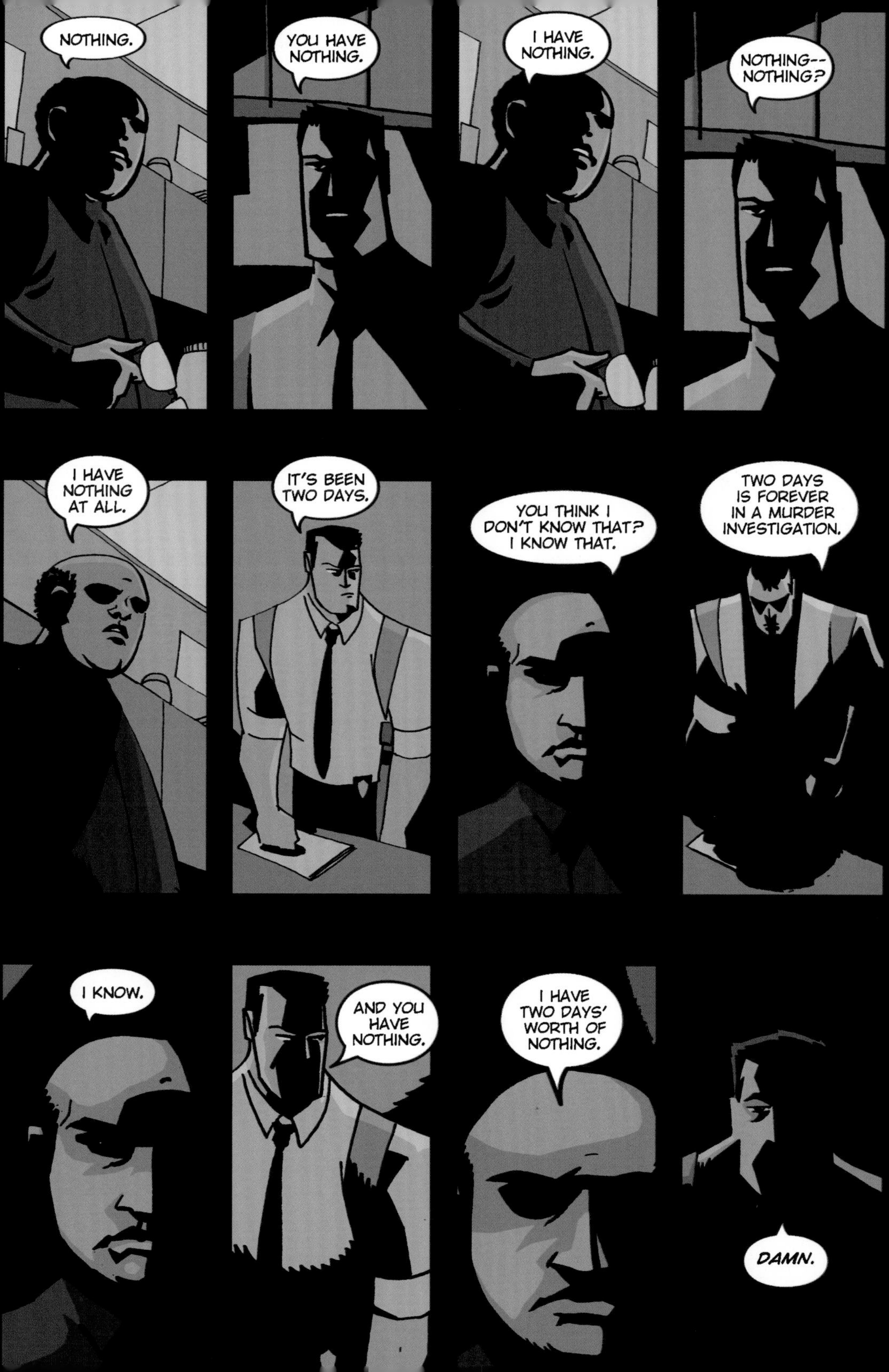
NOTHING.
YOU HAVE NOTHING.
I HAVE NOTHING.
NOTHING-- NOTHING?
I HAVE NOTHING AT ALL.
IT'S BEEN TWO DAYS.
YOU THINK I DON'T KNOW THAT? I KNOW THAT.
TWO DAYS IS FOREVER IN A MURDER INVESTIGATION.
I KNOW.
AND YOU HAVE NOTHING.
I HAVE TWO DAYS' WORTH OF NOTHING.
DAMN.

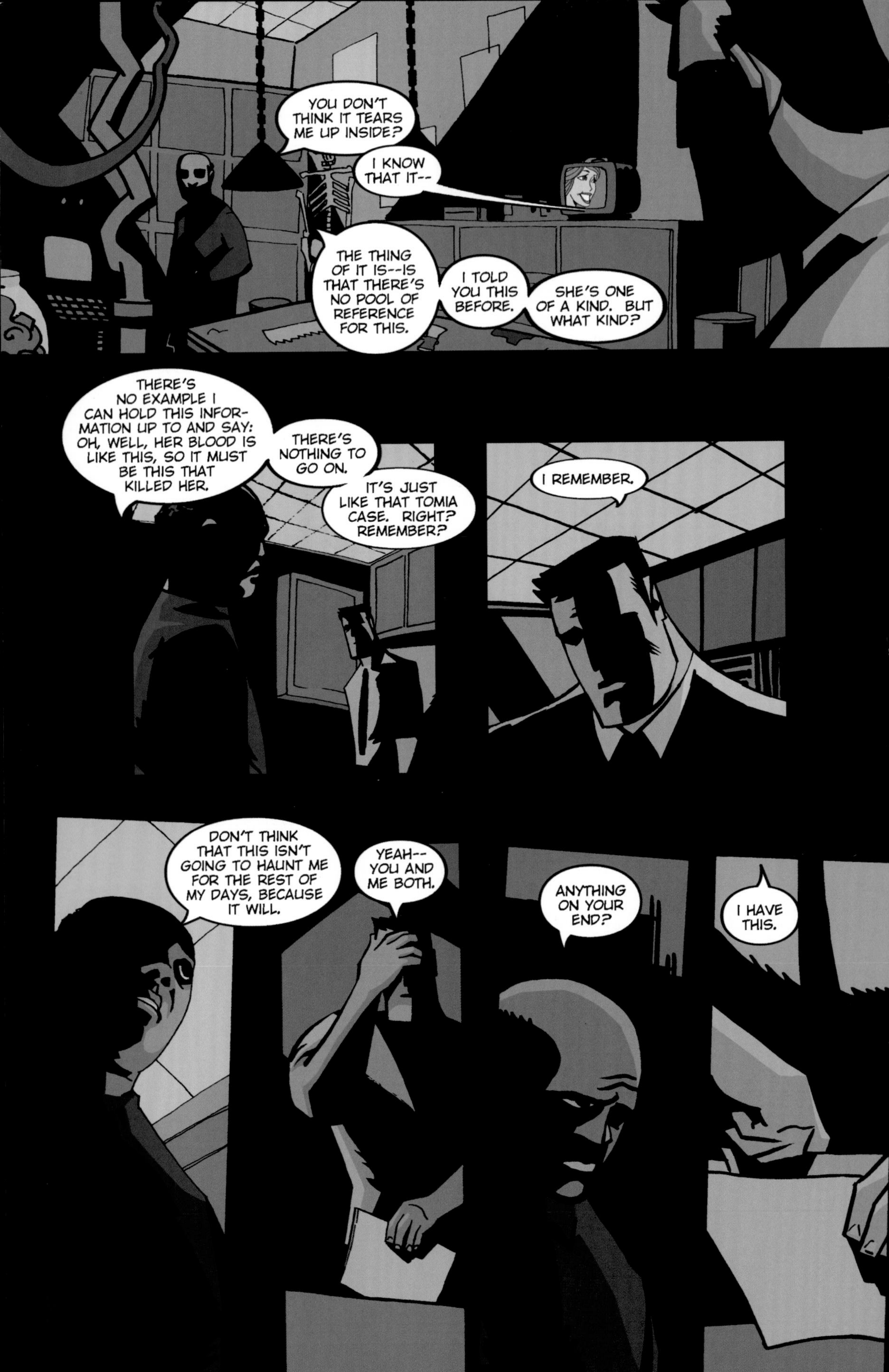
YOU DON'T THINK IT TEARS ME UP INSIDE?
I KNOW THAT IT--
THE THING OF IT IS--IS THAT THERE'S NO POOL OF REFERENCE FOR THIS.
I TOLD YOU THIS BEFORE.
SHE'S ONE OF A KIND. BUT WHAT KIND?
THERE'S NO EXAMPLE I CAN HOLD THIS INFORMATION UP TO AND SAY: OH, WELL, HER BLOOD IS LIKE THIS, SO IT MUST BE THIS THAT KILLED HER.
THERE'S NOTHING TO GO ON.
IT'S JUST LIKE THAT TOMIA CASE. RIGHT? REMEMBER?
I REMEMBER.
DON'T THINK THAT THIS ISN'T GOING TO HAUNT ME FOR THE REST OF MY DAYS, BECAUSE IT WILL.
YEAH-- YOU AND ME BOTH.
ANYTHING ON YOUR END?
I HAVE THIS.

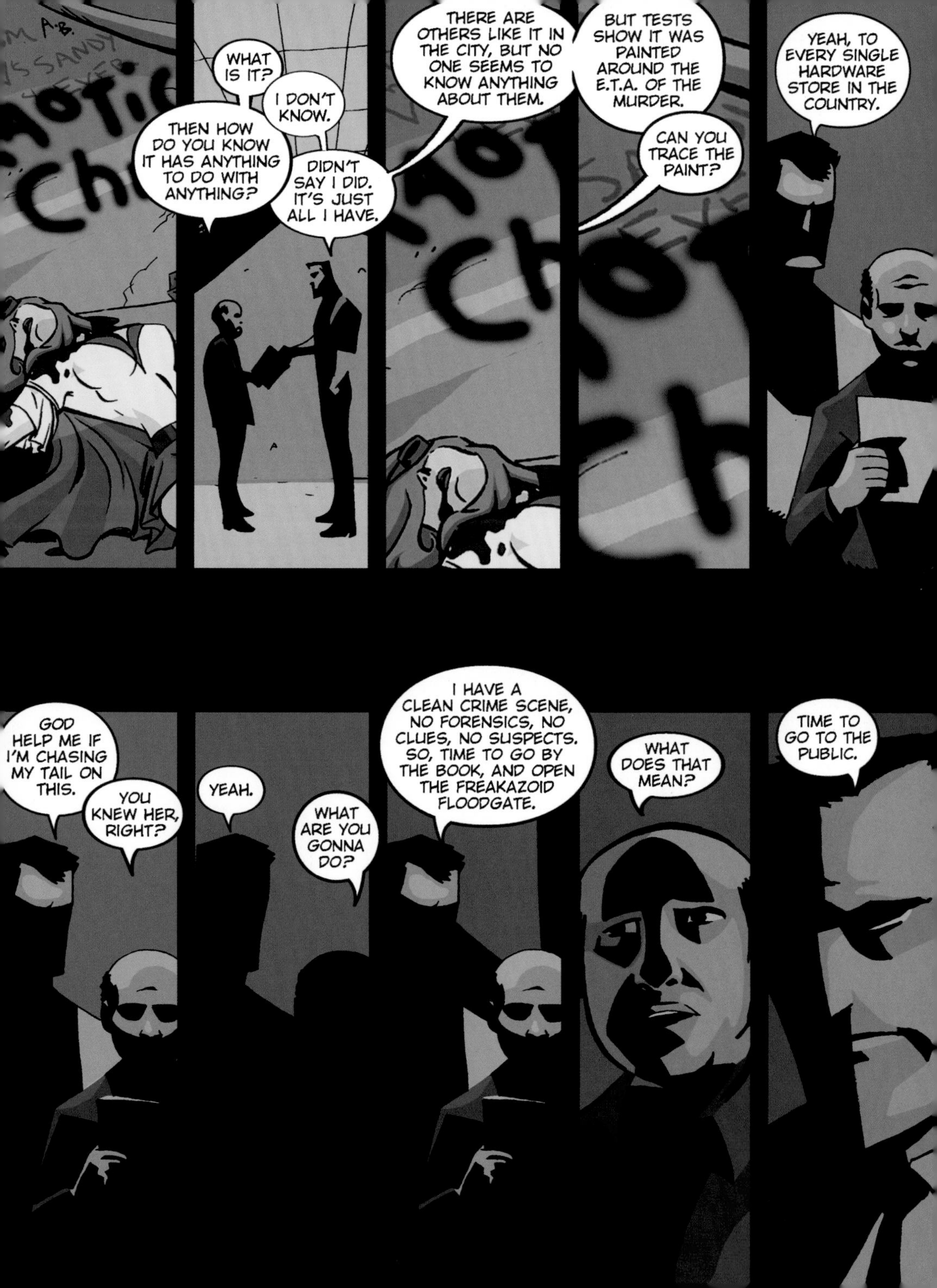
WHAT IS IT?
I DON'T KNOW.
THEN HOW DO YOU KNOW IT HAS ANYTHING TO DO WITH ANYTHING?
DIDN'T SAY I DID. IT'S JUST ALL I HAVE.
THERE ARE OTHERS LIKE IT IN THE CITY, BUT NO ONE SEEMS TO KNOW ANYTHING ABOUT THEM.
BUT TESTS SHOW IT WAS PAINTED AROUND THE E.T.A. OF THE MURDER.
CAN YOU TRACE THE PAINT?
YEAH, TO EVERY SINGLE HARDWARE STORE IN THE COUNTRY.
GOD HELP ME IF I'M CHASING MY TAIL ON THIS.
YOU KNEW HER, RIGHT?
YEAH.
WHAT ARE YOU GONNA DO?
I HAVE A CLEAN CRIME SCENE, NO FORENSICS, NO CLUES, NO SUSPECTS. SO, TIME TO GO BY THE BOOK, AND OPEN THE FREAKAZOID FLOODGATE.
WHAT DOES THAT MEAN?
TIME TO GO TO THE PUBLIC.

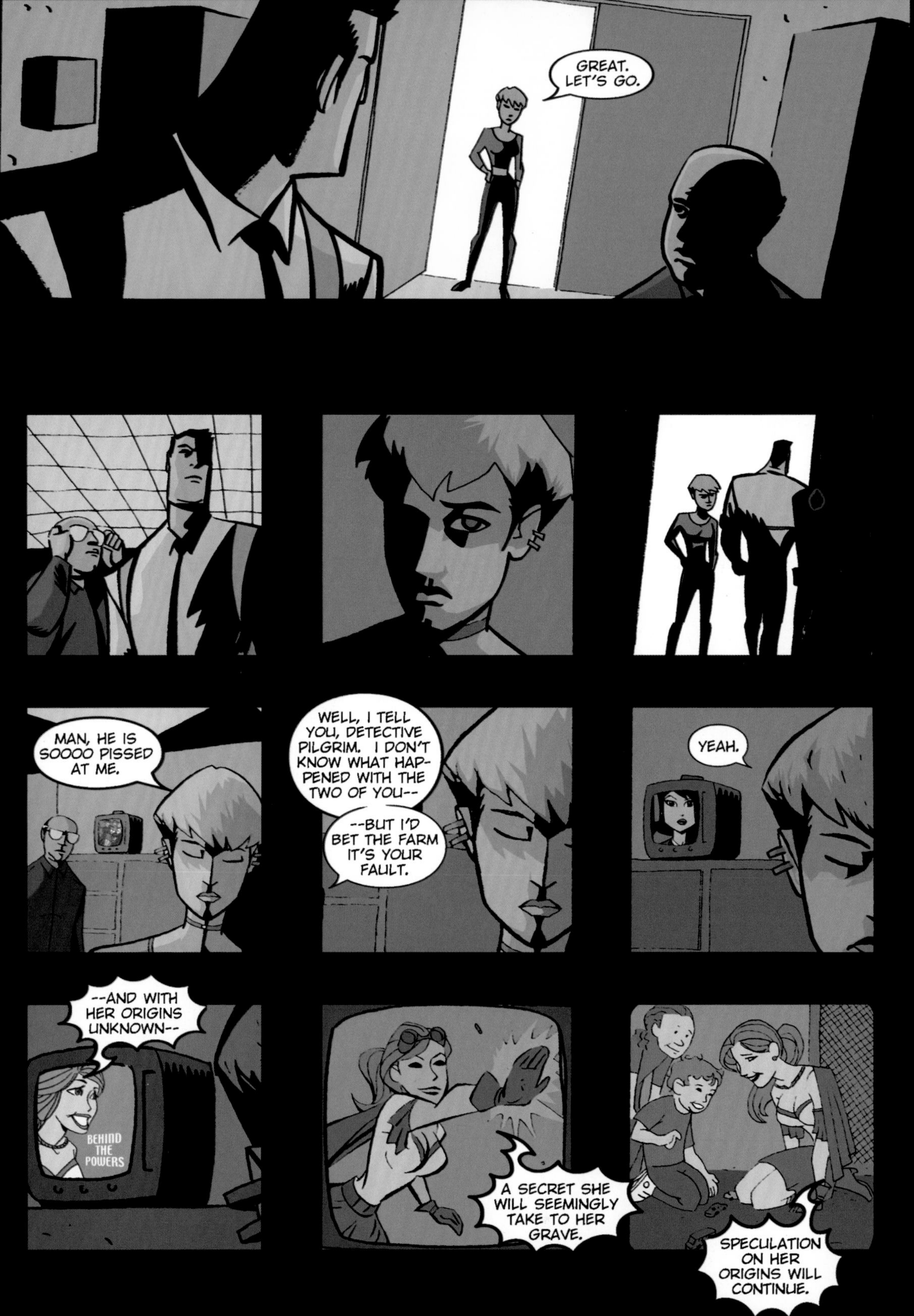
GREAT. LET'S GO.
MAN, HE IS SOOOO PISSED AT ME.
WELL, I TELL YOU, DETECTIVE PILGRIM. I DON'T KNOW WHAT HAP-PENED WITH THE TWO OF YOU--
--BUT I'D BET THE FARM IT'S YOUR FAULT.
YEAH.
--AND WITH HER ORIGINS UNKNOWN--
BEHIND THE POWERS
A SECRET SHE WILL SEEMINGLY TAKE TO HER GRAVE.
SPECULATION ON HER ORIGINS WILL CONTINUE.

WHAT I'M SAYING--

--WHAT I HAVE ALWAYS BEEN SAYING IS THAT IT IS MY THEORY THAT WE HAVE HAD A RETRO GIRL FIGURE IN OUR LIVES SINCE THE DAWN OF MAN.

OF COURSE WE DIDN'T CALL HER RETRO GIRL. BUT THAT IS WHERE THE NAME CAME FROM. SHE HARKS BACK TO ANOTHER TIME. A MORE INNOCENT TIME. RIGHT? SHE HAS A WORLDLY, TIMELESS BEAUTY.

BUT--BUT IF YOU LOOK AT THESE DOCUMENTS AND PICTORIALS IT'S ARGUABLE THAT THESE OTHER WOMEN HERE ARE HER SPITTING IMAGE. SEE HERE? JOAN OF ARC. CLEOPATRA.

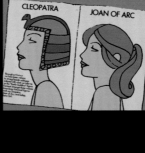

STRONG, WORLDLY, HEROIC WOMEN THAT WE NEEDED IN THAT TIME AND THAT PLACE. WOMEN THAT ENDED UP ONLY LIVING A SHORT LIFE.

AND THESE ARE JUST THE WOMEN WHO ROSE TO A MODICUM OF FAME THROUGH CIRCUM- STANCE. WHO KNOWS HOW MANY INCARNATIONS SHE HAD THAT LIVED LIVES OF QUIET AND UNASSUMING HEROISM?

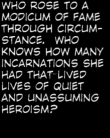

YES--YES--YES. I'VE HEARD THOSE THEORIES. IT'S-- PEOPLE LIKE TO CONCOCT THESE THEORIES ON EVERYTHING. YES?

ALL OF A SUDDEN, SHE'S MOTHER NATURE?

IN MY FINDINGS, THE SIMPLEST ANSWER IS ALWAYS THE ANSWER. SHE LIVED A GOOD LIFE, AND NOW, SADLY, SHE IS DEAD. LIKE ELVIS, MARILYN, JAMES DEAN--DEAD, DEAD, DEAD.

ACTION
5
Special
Report

WE INTERRUPT YOUR VIEWING OF *"BEHIND THE POWERS"* FOR AN ACTION FIVE SPECIAL REPORT

THIS IS AN ACTION
FIVE SPECIAL
REPORT.

WE NOW
BRING YOU
INSIDE THE CITY
JUSTICE CENTER,
WHERE COLLETTE
MCDANIEL IS
REPORTING LIVE.
COLLETTE?

ACTION
5
Special
Report

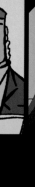

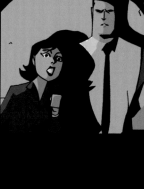

THIS IS COLLETTE
MCDANIEL. I AM
HERE INSIDE THE
HOMICIDE UNIT OF
DISTRICT 55.

STANDING WITH
ME IS DETECTIVE
CHRISTIAN
WALKER.

DETECTIVE WALKER
IS THE PRIMARY
DETECTIVE FOR THE
RETRO GIRL
MURDER INVESTI-
GATION--THE
HORRIBLE RETRO
GIRL TRAGEDY
THAT HAS GRIPPED
OUR CITY IN
MOURNING.

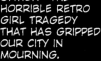

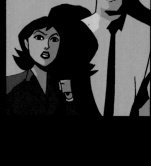

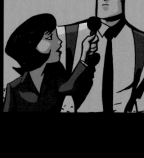

DETECTIVE, WHAT
CAN YOU TELL US
ABOUT YOUR
PROGRESS
ON THE
INVESTIGATION
SO FAR?

WELL, MA'AM,
MOST OF THAT
INFORMATION IS
CLASSIFIED UNTIL
THE CASE IS
OFFICIALLY
CLOSED, WHICH
AT THIS TIME IS
NOT THE CASE.

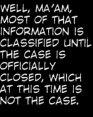

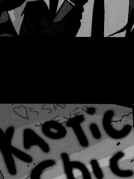

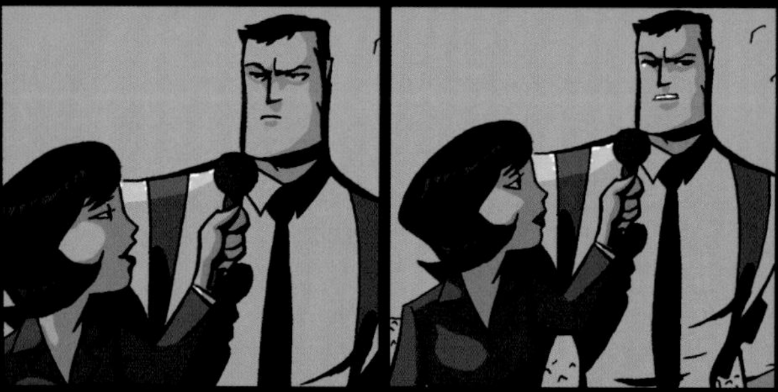

WE ARE ASKING
THE PUBLIC'S HELP
WITH INFORMATION
IN REGARD TO
THE MURDER,
SPECIFICALLY TO A
PIECE OF GRAFFITI
THAT WE HAVE AT
THE CRIME SCENE.
I BELIEVE WE HA--

YES, IT'S UP NOW.

ANY INFORMATION
THAT ANYONE
HAS ABOUT THIS
OR ANYTHING THAT
CAN HELP US IN
OUR INVESTIGATION
--ANY INFORMATION
ABOUT THE MEANING
OF THE WORDS OF
THE PERSON OR
PERSONS RESPON-
SIBLE FOR THE
GRAFFITI--
PLEASE CALL
OUR HOTLINE AT
1-888-333-6665.

KAOTIC
CHIC

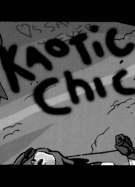

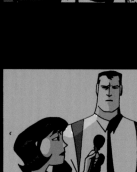

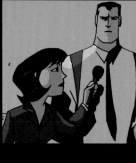

OBVIOUSLY THIS
MATTER IS OF THE
HIGHEST IMPOR-
TANCE--ANYONE
CALLING WITH
PURPOSELY FALSE
OR PRANK INFOR-
MATION WILL BE
TRACED AND
PROSECUTED FOR
OBSTRUCTION OF
JUSTICE.

DETECTIVE, ANY
WORD ON WHY
JOHNNY ROYALLE

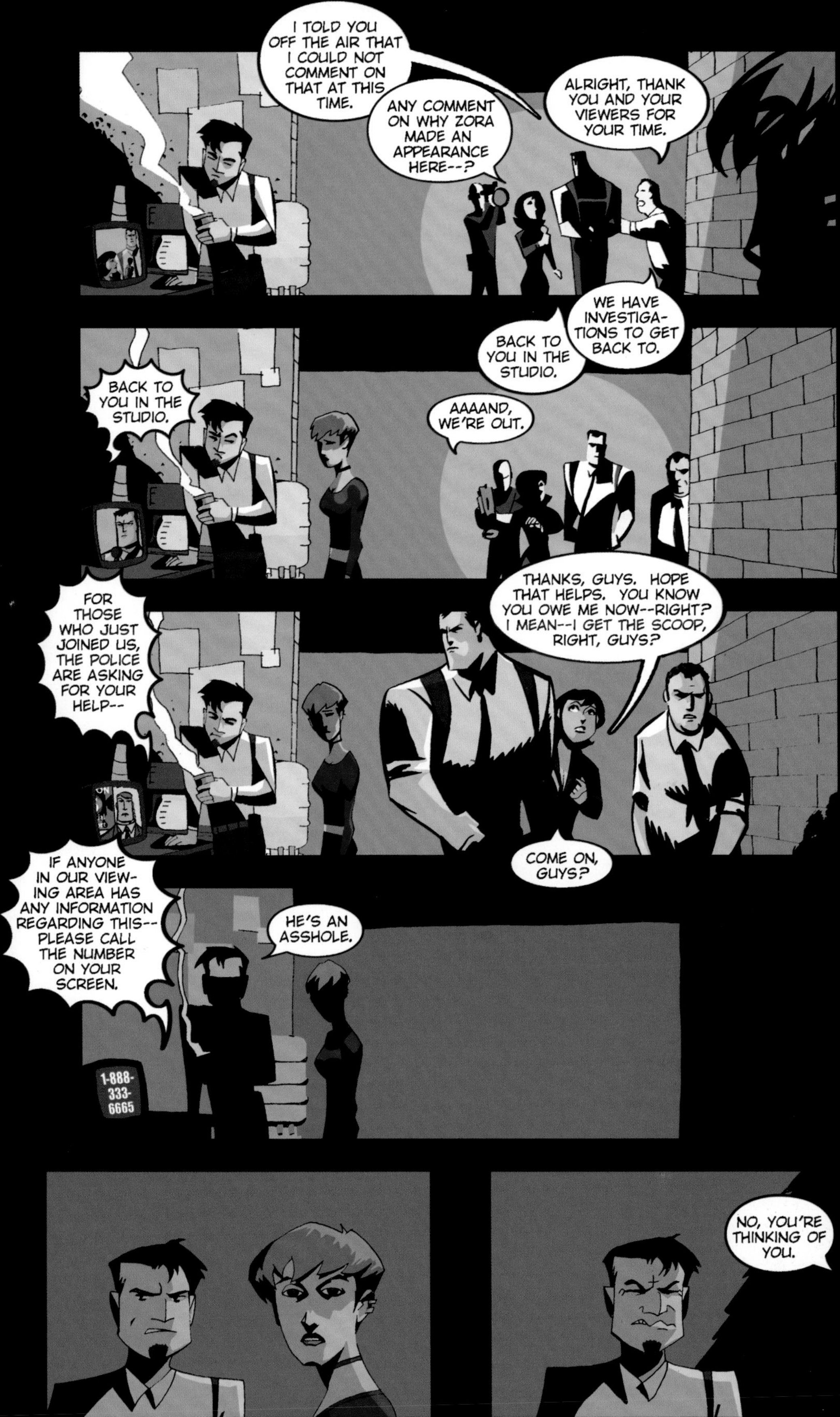

I TOLD YOU OFF THE AIR THAT I COULD NOT COMMENT ON THAT AT THIS TIME.
ANY COMMENT ON WHY ZORA MADE AN APPEARANCE HERE--?
ALRIGHT, THANK YOU AND YOUR VIEWERS FOR YOUR TIME.
WE HAVE INVESTIGA-TIONS TO GET BACK TO.
BACK TO YOU IN THE STUDIO.
BACK TO YOU IN THE STUDIO.
AAAAND, WE'RE OUT.
FOR THOSE WHO JUST JOINED US, THE POLICE ARE ASKING FOR YOUR HELP--
THANKS, GUYS. HOPE THAT HELPS. YOU KNOW YOU OWE ME NOW--RIGHT? I MEAN--I GET THE SCOOP, RIGHT, GUYS?
COME ON, GUYS?
IF ANYONE IN OUR VIEW-ING AREA HAS ANY INFORMATION REGARDING THIS--PLEASE CALL THE NUMBER ON YOUR SCREEN.
1-888-333-6665
HE'S AN ASSHOLE.
NO, YOU'RE THINKING OF YOU.

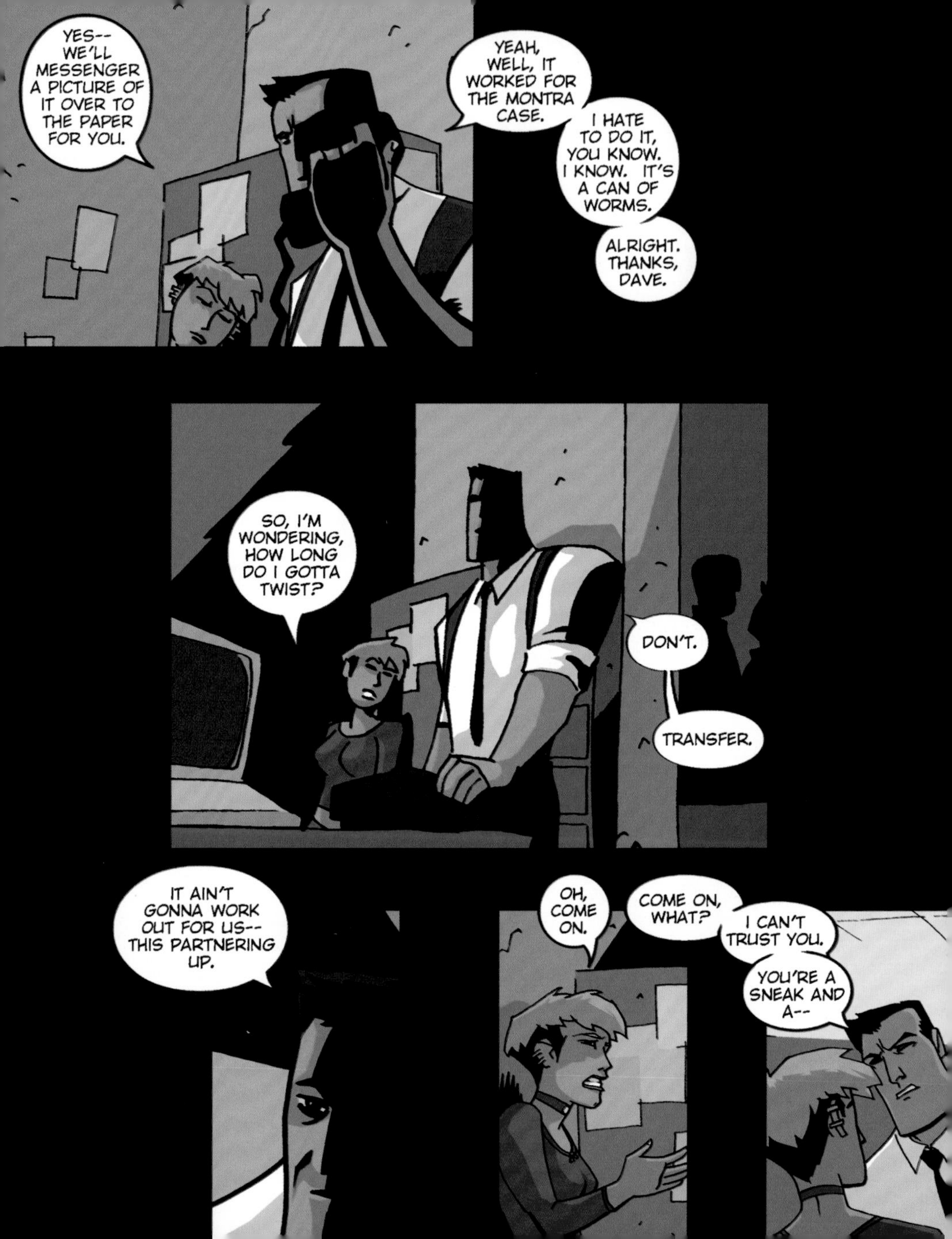
YES-- WE'LL MESSENGER A PICTURE OF IT OVER TO THE PAPER FOR YOU.
YEAH, WELL, IT WORKED FOR THE MONTRA CASE.
I HATE TO DO IT, YOU KNOW. I KNOW. IT'S A CAN OF WORMS.
ALRIGHT. THANKS, DAVE.
SO, I'M WONDERING, HOW LONG DO I GOTTA TWIST?
DON'T.
TRANSFER.
IT AIN'T GONNA WORK OUT FOR US-- THIS PARTNERING UP.
OH, COME ON.
COME ON, WHAT?
I CAN'T TRUST YOU.
YOU'RE A SNEAK AND A--

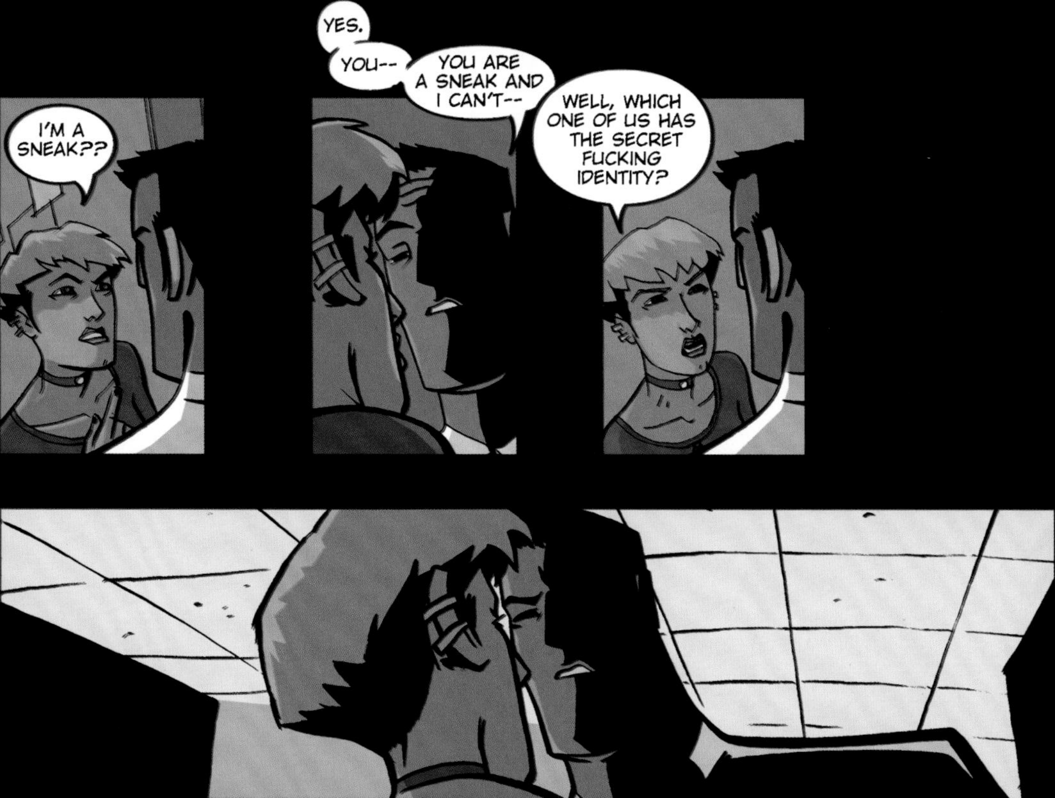
I'M A SNEAK??
YES.
YOU--
YOU ARE A SNEAK AND I CAN'T--
WELL, WHICH ONE OF US HAS THE SECRET FUCKING IDENTITY?

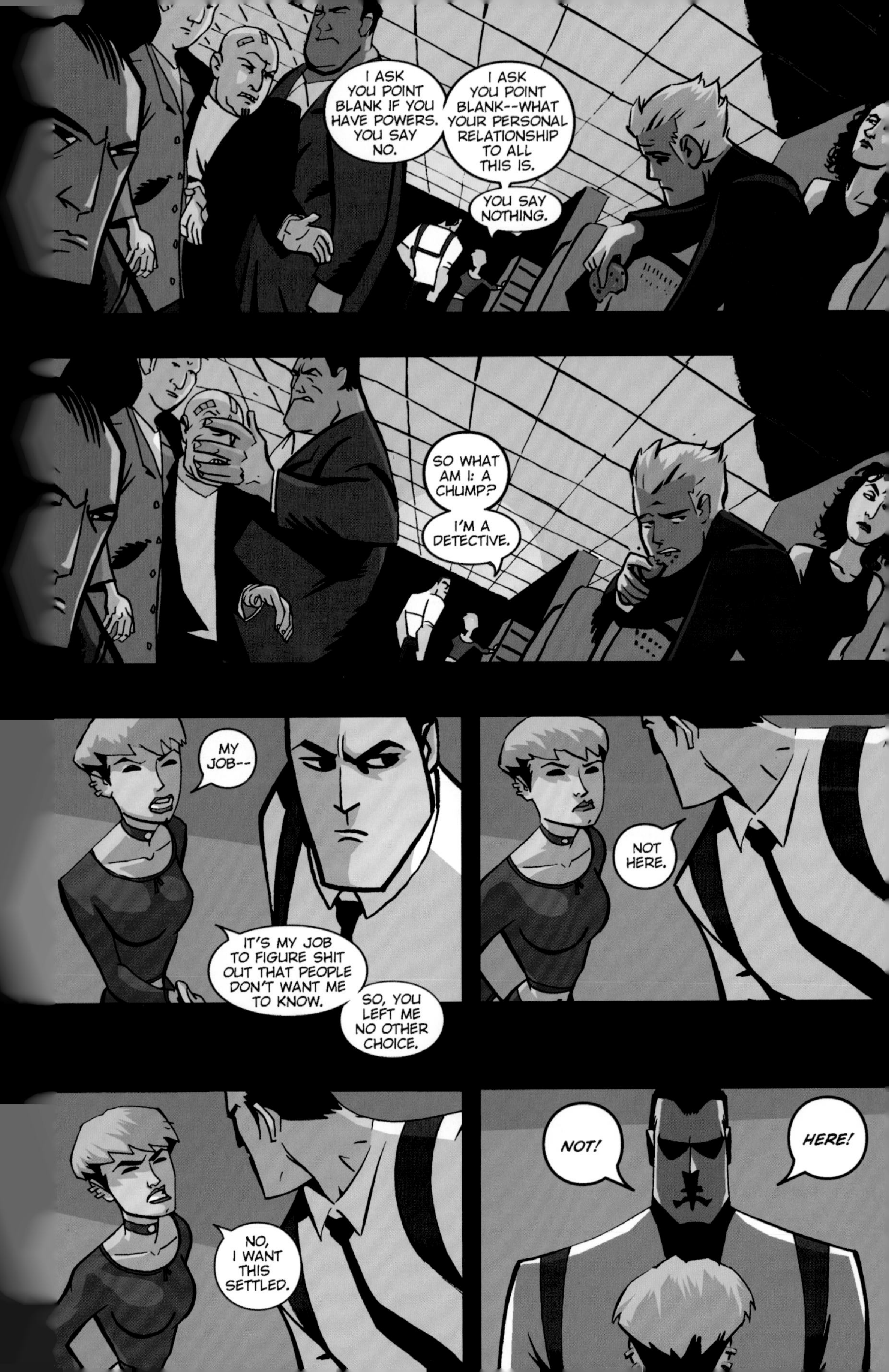
I ASK YOU POINT BLANK IF YOU HAVE POWERS. YOU SAY NO.
I ASK YOU POINT BLANK--WHAT YOUR PERSONAL RELATIONSHIP TO ALL THIS IS.
YOU SAY NOTHING.
SO WHAT AM I: A CHUMP?
I'M A DETECTIVE.
MY JOB--
IT'S MY JOB TO FIGURE SHIT OUT THAT PEOPLE DON'T WANT ME TO KNOW.
SO, YOU LEFT ME NO OTHER CHOICE.
NOT HERE.
NO, I WANT THIS SETTLED.
NOT!
HERE!

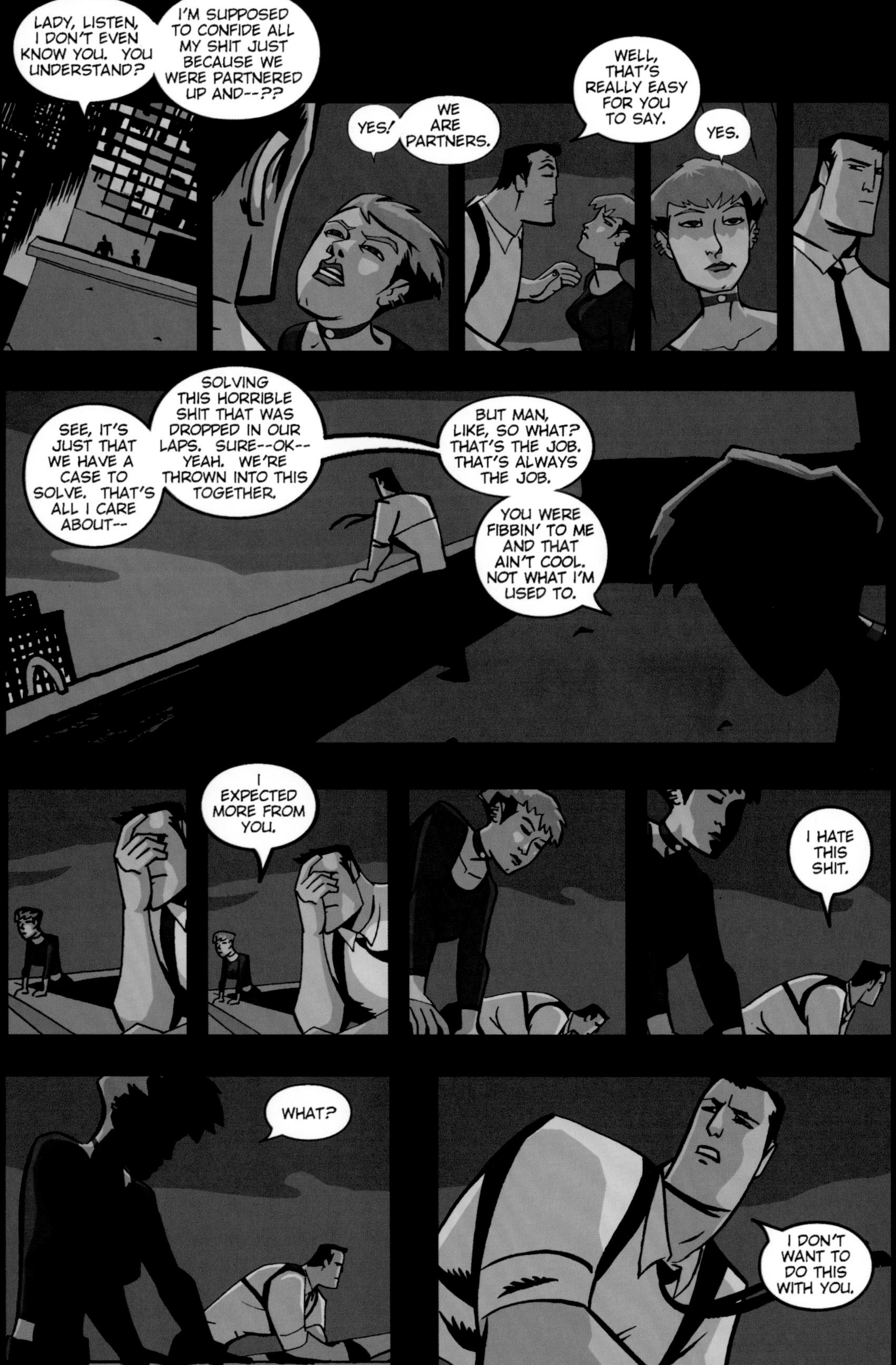
LADY, LISTEN, I DON'T EVEN KNOW YOU. YOU UNDERSTAND?
I'M SUPPOSED TO CONFIDE ALL MY SHIT JUST BECAUSE WE WERE PARTNERED UP AND--??
YES!
WE ARE PARTNERS.
WELL, THAT'S REALLY EASY FOR YOU TO SAY.
YES.
SEE, IT'S JUST THAT WE HAVE A CASE TO SOLVE. THAT'S ALL I CARE ABOUT--
SOLVING THIS HORRIBLE SHIT THAT WAS DROPPED IN OUR LAPS. SURE--OK--YEAH. WE'RE THROWN INTO THIS TOGETHER.
BUT MAN, LIKE, SO WHAT? THAT'S THE JOB. THAT'S ALWAYS THE JOB.
YOU WERE FIBBIN' TO ME AND THAT AIN'T COOL. NOT WHAT I'M USED TO.
I EXPECTED MORE FROM YOU.
I HATE THIS SHIT.
WHAT?
I DON'T WANT TO DO THIS WITH YOU.

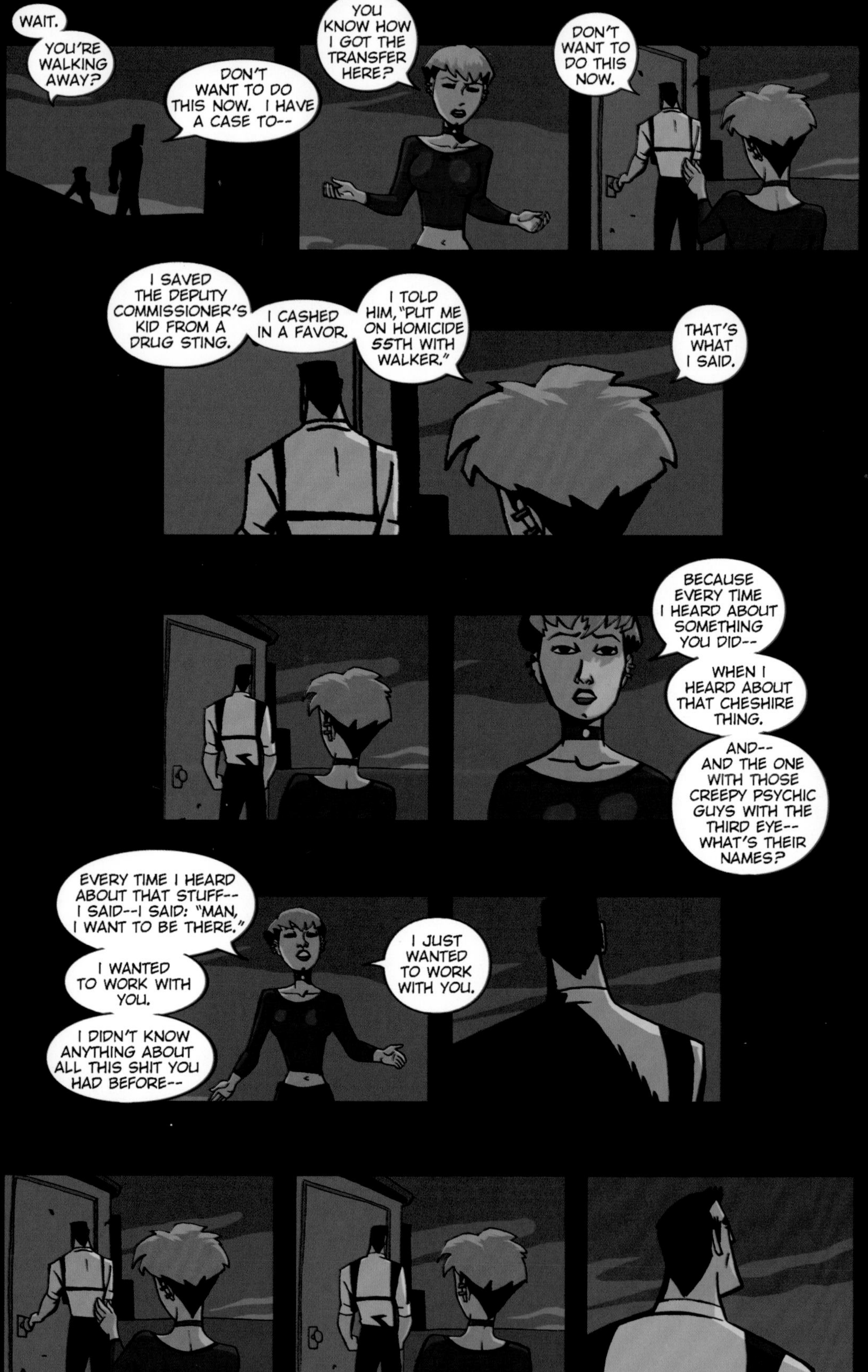
WAIT.
YOU'RE WALKING AWAY?
DON'T WANT TO DO THIS NOW. I HAVE A CASE TO--
YOU KNOW HOW I GOT THE TRANSFER HERE?
DON'T WANT TO DO THIS NOW.
I SAVED THE DEPUTY COMMISSIONER'S KID FROM A DRUG STING.
I CASHED IN A FAVOR.
I TOLD HIM, "PUT ME ON HOMICIDE 55TH WITH WALKER."
THAT'S WHAT I SAID.
BECAUSE EVERY TIME I HEARD ABOUT SOMETHING YOU DID--
WHEN I HEARD ABOUT THAT CHESHIRE THING.
AND-- AND THE ONE WITH THOSE CREEPY PSYCHIC GUYS WITH THE THIRD EYE-- WHAT'S THEIR NAMES?
EVERY TIME I HEARD ABOUT THAT STUFF-- I SAID--I SAID: "MAN, I WANT TO BE THERE."
I WANTED TO WORK WITH YOU.
I DIDN'T KNOW ANYTHING ABOUT ALL THIS SHIT YOU HAD BEFORE--
I JUST WANTED TO WORK WITH YOU.

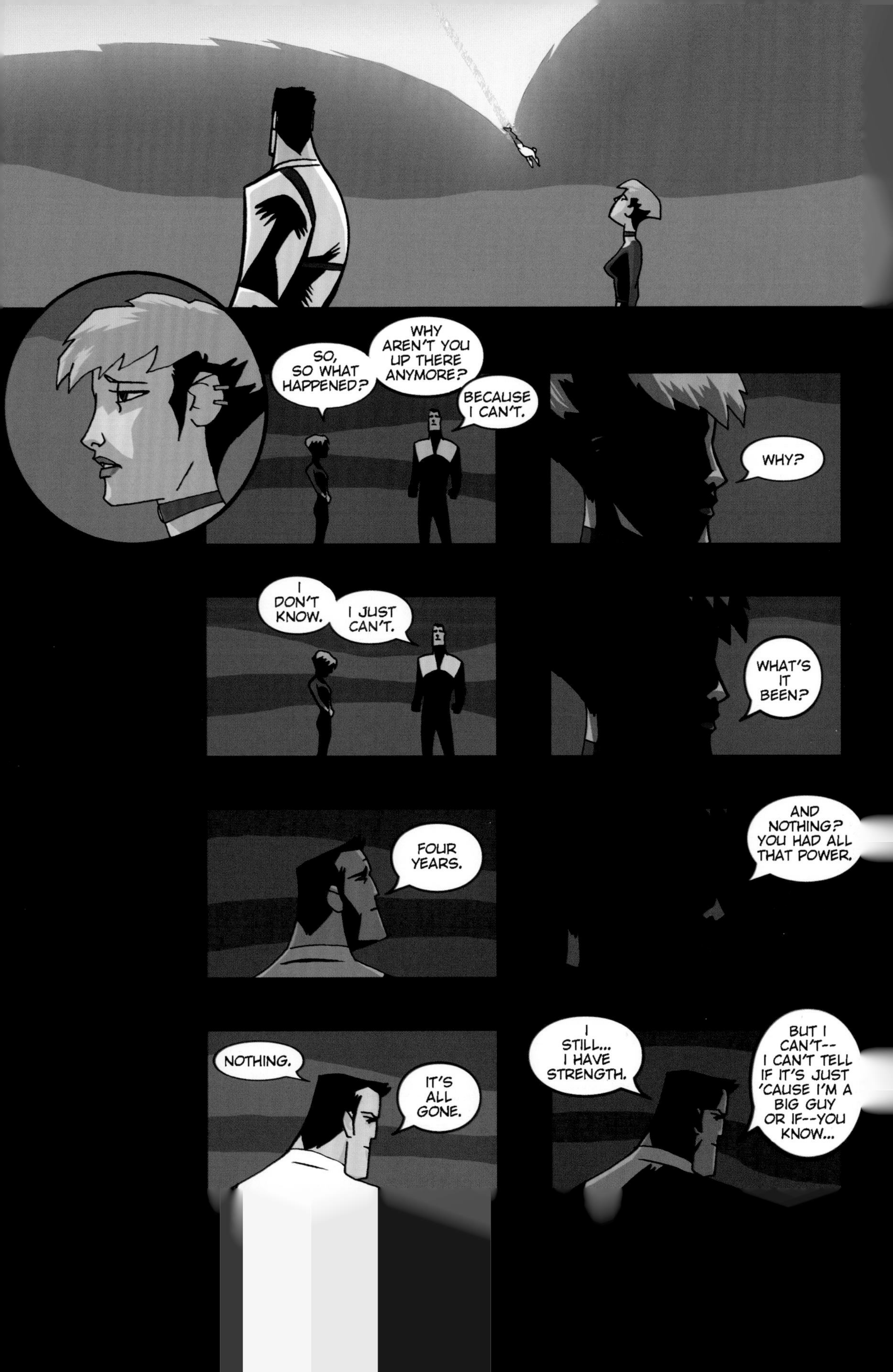
SO, SO WHAT HAPPENED?
WHY AREN'T YOU UP THERE ANYMORE?
BECAUSE I CAN'T.
WHY?
I DON'T KNOW.
I JUST CAN'T.
WHAT'S IT BEEN?
FOUR YEARS.
AND NOTHING? YOU HAD ALL THAT POWER.
NOTHING.
IT'S ALL GONE.
I STILL... I HAVE STRENGTH.
BUT I CAN'T-- I CAN'T TELL IF IT'S JUST 'CAUSE I'M A BIG GUY OR IF--YOU KNOW...

WELL Y'SEE, I--I REALLY HAVE NO DAMN IDEA WHAT HAPPENED. JUST WHEN--IT WAS DURING THE WHOLE TERRIBLE INCIDENT WITH THE JOHNNY ROYALLE GANG.

OH YEAH--THAT'S THE LAST ANYONE EVER SAW OR HEARD FROM YOU--LIKE THAT. AS DIAMOND.

YEAH. WE WERE--WE WERE GOING AT IT PRETTY TOUGH, YOU KNOW. I MEAN--ALL THE FIGHTS ARE TOUGH--BUT THIS ONE--THIS ONE--THERE WAS SOMETHING JUST OFF ABOUT IT. IT WAS VERY CARNAL. VERY ANIMAL-LIKE. IT WAS ME AND TRIPHAMMER, WHO YOU'VE MET, AND ZORA AND RETRO GIRL AGAINST ALL THESE WACKOS. I MEAN, I DON'T EVEN REMEMBER HOW IT STARTED. SOME STUPID SCHEME OR SOMETHING.

SHIT! THAT FREAKY B.9. FOM-FOM DUDE WAS THERE.

YEAH--YEAH THAT'S RIGHT. AND CHESHIRE, AND TWILIGHT, BUT I WAS FIGHTING SSAZZ. AGAIN! HE'S SOME KIND OF MUTATION OR SOMETHING. ONE OF THOSE GENETIC MISHAPS WITH A HARD-ON FOR EVERY-THING. AND HE SMELLS SO--SO BAD. WE HAD FOUGHT BEFORE, Y'SEE, AND OF COURSE I BEAT THE HOLY CRAP OUT OF HIM. BUT THIS TIME HE HAD SOME KIND OF--SOME KIND OF ENHANCEMENT ON HIM OR SOMETHING.

LIKE A POWER ENHANCER?

YEAH.

I READ ABOUT THOSE IN "SCIENTIFIC AMERI"--

AND--AND I'M DOING EVERY-THING I CAN JUST TO END THE FIGHT. JUST END THE FIGHTING. JUST STOP IT. I GET, LIKE, THIS SUDDEN BURST OF ADRENALINE OR WHATNOT, LIKE A BURST OF ENERGY. NEVER HAPPENED BEFORE. BUT, WHAM! AND I WAS WINNING THE DAY. AND THEN--AND THEN--*POOF!*

POOF?

POOF.

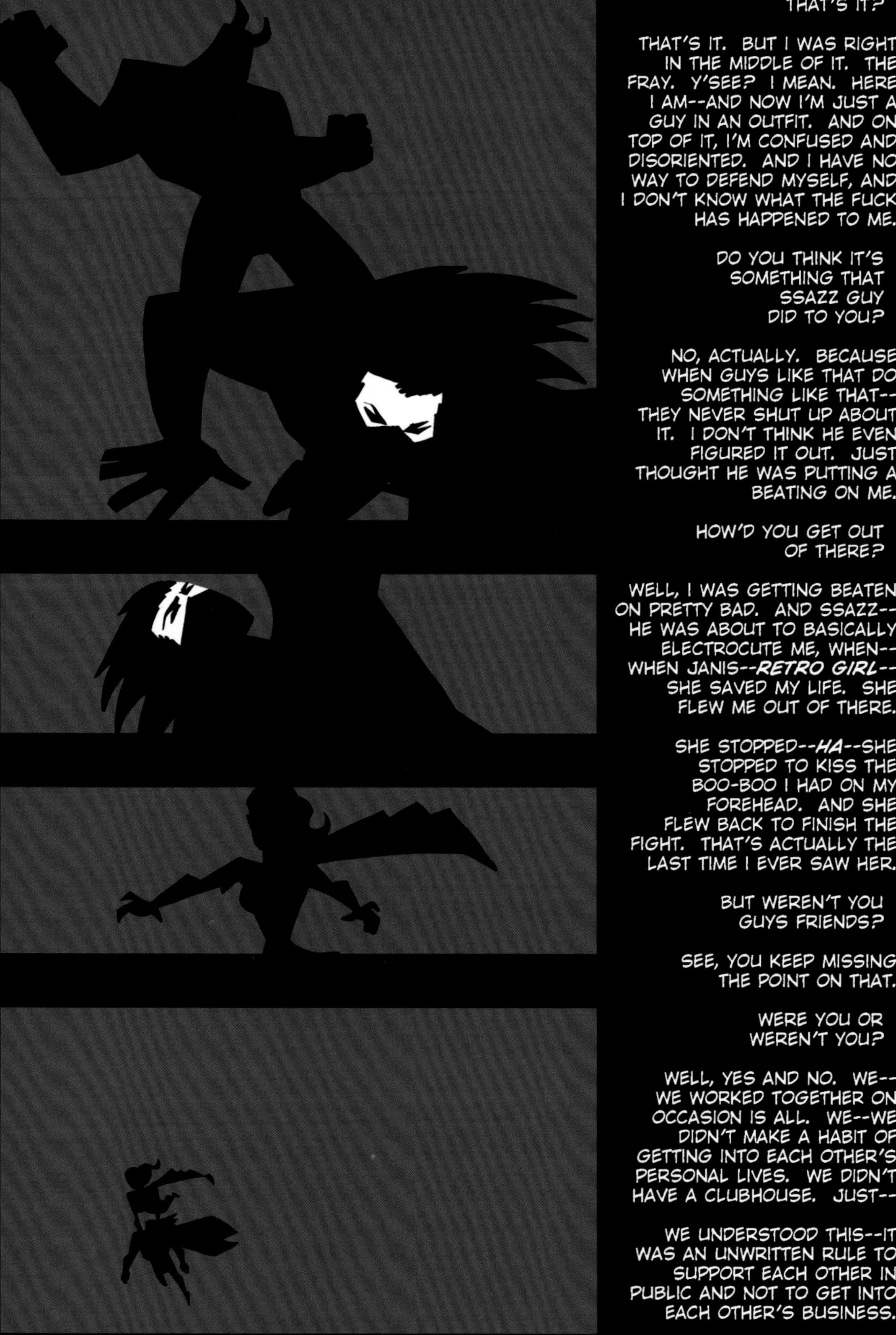
THAT'S IT?
THAT'S IT. BUT I WAS RIGHT IN THE MIDDLE OF IT. THE FRAY. Y'SEE? I MEAN. HERE I AM--AND NOW I'M JUST A GUY IN AN OUTFIT. AND ON TOP OF IT, I'M CONFUSED AND DISORIENTED. AND I HAVE NO WAY TO DEFEND MYSELF, AND I DON'T KNOW WHAT THE FUCK HAS HAPPENED TO ME.
DO YOU THINK IT'S SOMETHING THAT SSAZZ GUY DID TO YOU?
NO, ACTUALLY. BECAUSE WHEN GUYS LIKE THAT DO SOMETHING LIKE THAT--THEY NEVER SHUT UP ABOUT IT. I DON'T THINK HE EVEN FIGURED IT OUT. JUST THOUGHT HE WAS PUTTING A BEATING ON ME.
HOW'D YOU GET OUT OF THERE?
WELL, I WAS GETTING BEATEN ON PRETTY BAD. AND SSAZZ--HE WAS ABOUT TO BASICALLY ELECTROCUTE ME, WHEN--WHEN JANIS--***RETRO GIRL***--SHE SAVED MY LIFE. SHE FLEW ME OUT OF THERE.
SHE STOPPED--***HA***--SHE STOPPED TO KISS THE BOO-BOO I HAD ON MY FOREHEAD. AND SHE FLEW BACK TO FINISH THE FIGHT. THAT'S ACTUALLY THE LAST TIME I EVER SAW HER.
BUT WEREN'T YOU GUYS FRIENDS?
SEE, YOU KEEP MISSING THE POINT ON THAT.
WERE YOU OR WEREN'T YOU?
WELL, YES AND NO. WE--WE WORKED TOGETHER ON OCCASION IS ALL. WE--WE DIDN'T MAKE A HABIT OF GETTING INTO EACH OTHER'S PERSONAL LIVES. WE DIDN'T HAVE A CLUBHOUSE. JUST--
WE UNDERSTOOD THIS--IT WAS AN UNWRITTEN RULE TO SUPPORT EACH OTHER IN PUBLIC AND NOT TO GET INTO EACH OTHER'S BUSINESS.

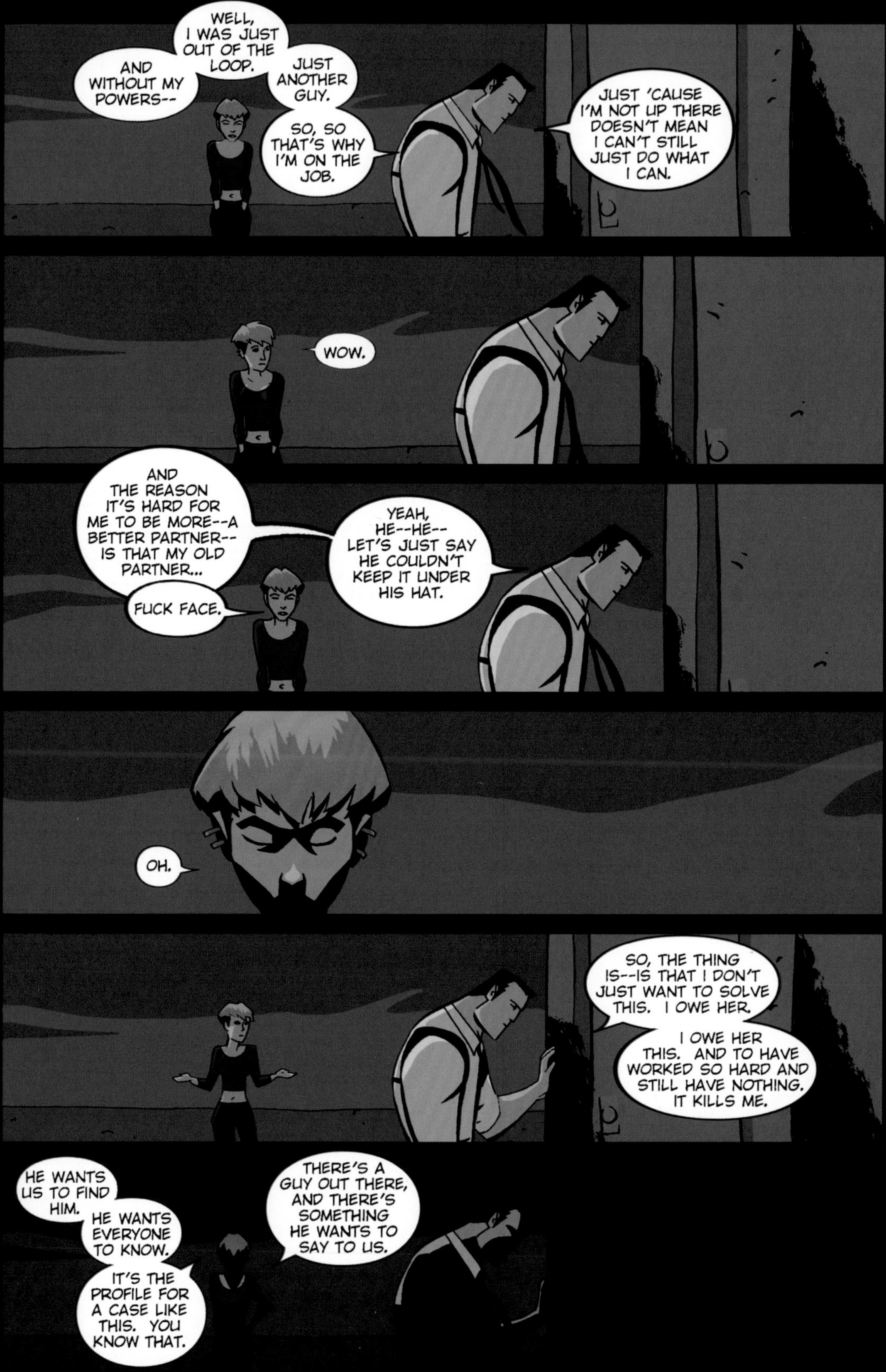
AND WITHOUT MY POWERS--
WELL, I WAS JUST OUT OF THE LOOP.
JUST ANOTHER GUY.
SO, SO THAT'S WHY I'M ON THE JOB.
JUST 'CAUSE I'M NOT UP THERE DOESN'T MEAN I CAN'T STILL JUST DO WHAT I CAN.
WOW.
AND THE REASON IT'S HARD FOR ME TO BE MORE--A BETTER PARTNER--IS THAT MY OLD PARTNER...
FUCK FACE.
YEAH, HE--HE--LET'S JUST SAY HE COULDN'T KEEP IT UNDER HIS HAT.
OH.
SO, THE THING IS--IS THAT I DON'T JUST WANT TO SOLVE THIS. I OWE HER.
I OWE HER THIS. AND TO HAVE WORKED SO HARD AND STILL HAVE NOTHING. IT KILLS ME.
HE WANTS US TO FIND HIM.
HE WANTS EVERYONE TO KNOW.
IT'S THE PROFILE FOR A CASE LIKE THIS. YOU KNOW THAT.
THERE'S A GUY OUT THERE, AND THERE'S SOMETHING HE WANTS TO SAY TO US.

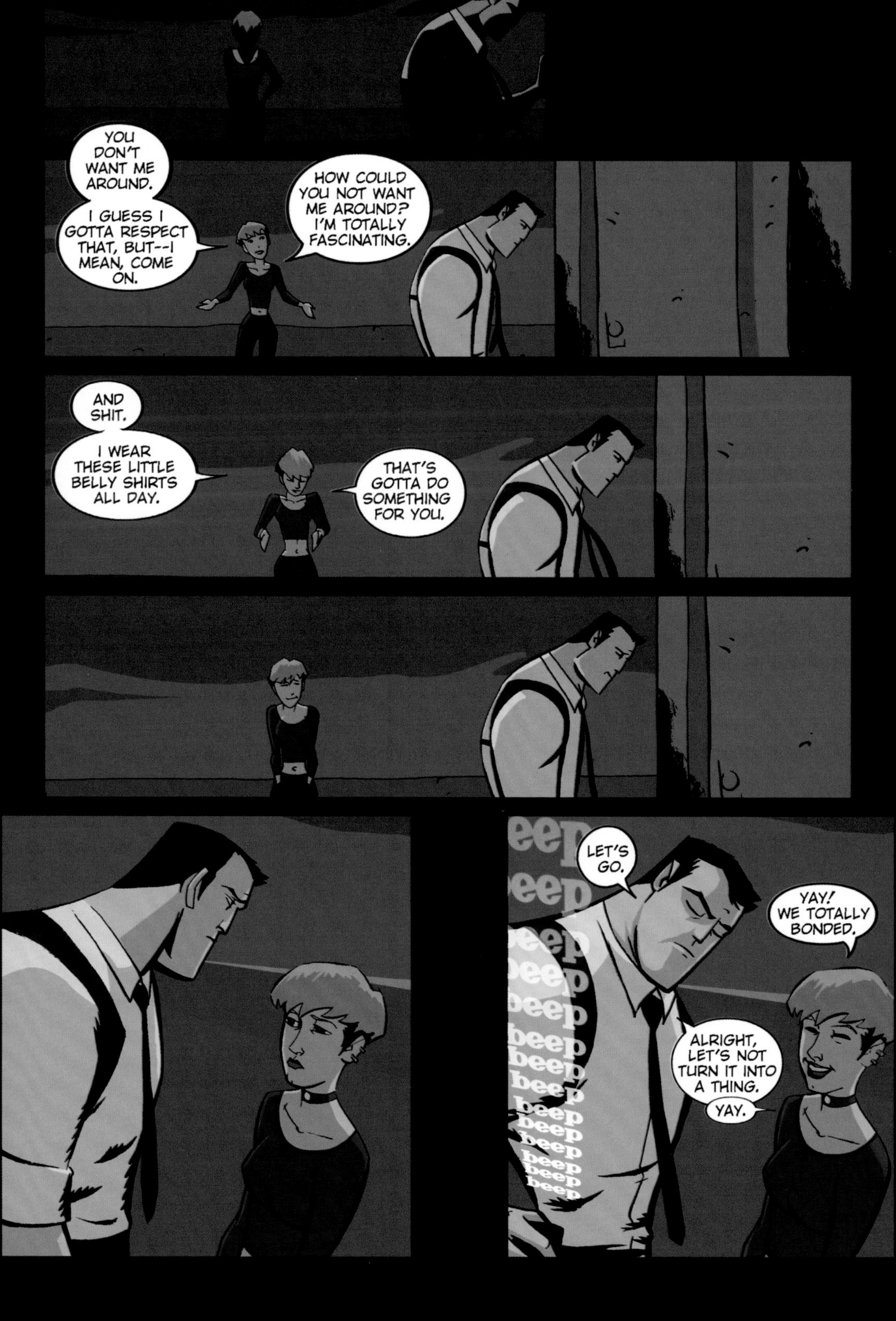
YOU DON'T WANT ME AROUND.
I GUESS I GOTTA RESPECT THAT, BUT--I MEAN, COME ON.
HOW COULD YOU NOT WANT ME AROUND? I'M TOTALLY FASCINATING.
AND SHIT.
I WEAR THESE LITTLE BELLY SHIRTS ALL DAY.
THAT'S GOTTA DO SOMETHING FOR YOU.
beep beep beep beep beep beep beep beep beep beep beep beep beep beep
LET'S GO.
YAY! WE TOTALLY BONDED.
ALRIGHT, LET'S NOT TURN IT INTO A THING.
YAY.

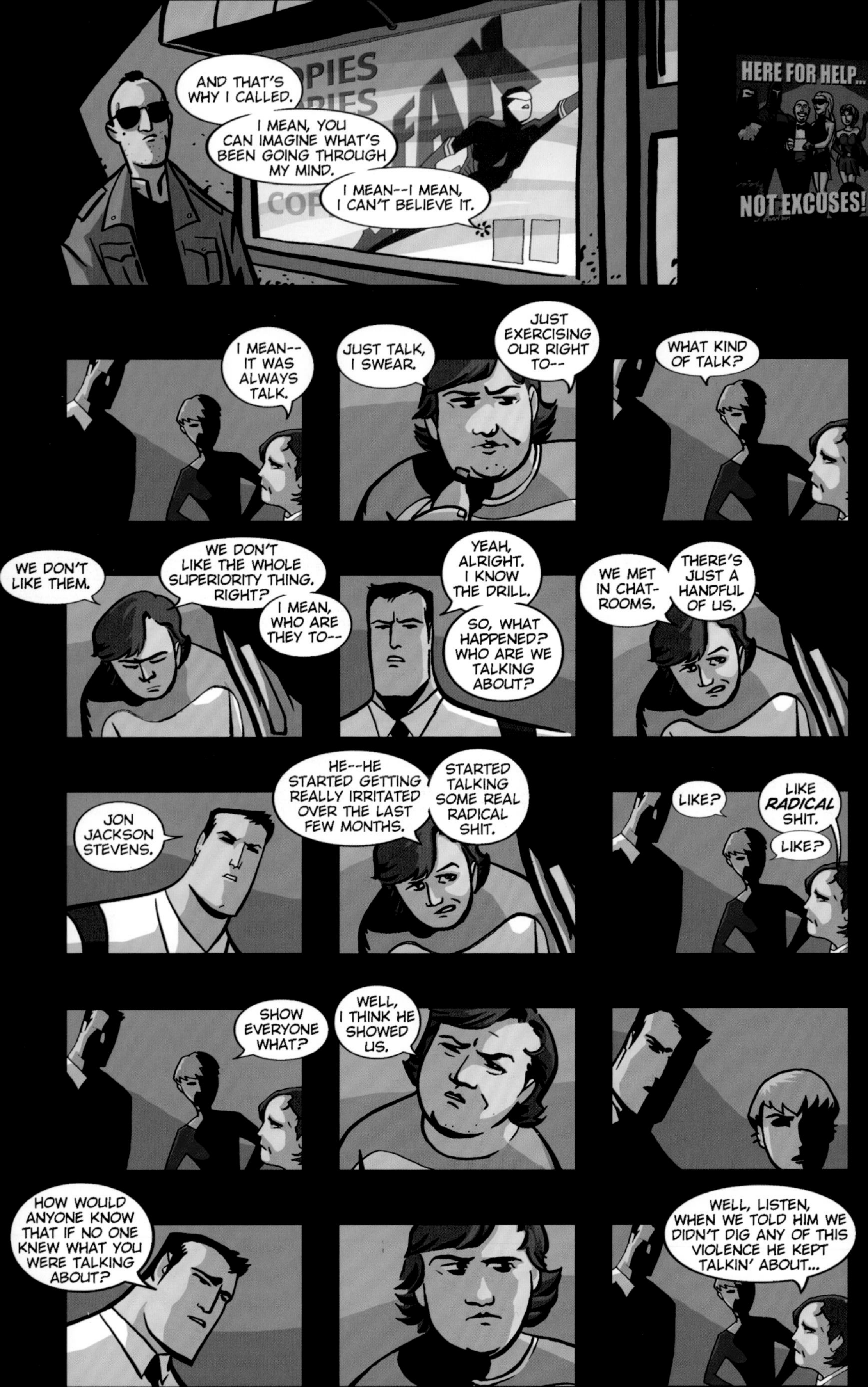
COPIES
FAX
COP
AND THAT'S WHY I CALLED.
I MEAN, YOU CAN IMAGINE WHAT'S BEEN GOING THROUGH MY MIND.
I MEAN--I MEAN, I CAN'T BELIEVE IT.
HERE FOR HELP...
NOT EXCUSES!
I MEAN-- IT WAS ALWAYS TALK.
JUST TALK, I SWEAR.
JUST EXERCISING OUR RIGHT TO--
WHAT KIND OF TALK?
WE DON'T LIKE THEM.
WE DON'T LIKE THE WHOLE SUPERIORITY THING. RIGHT?
I MEAN, WHO ARE THEY TO--
YEAH, ALRIGHT. I KNOW THE DRILL.
SO, WHAT HAPPENED? WHO ARE WE TALKING ABOUT?
WE MET IN CHAT-ROOMS.
THERE'S JUST A HANDFUL OF US.
JON JACKSON STEVENS.
HE--HE STARTED GETTING REALLY IRRITATED OVER THE LAST FEW MONTHS.
STARTED TALKING SOME REAL RADICAL SHIT.
LIKE?
LIKE *RADICAL* SHIT.
LIKE?
SHOW EVERYONE WHAT?
WELL, I THINK HE SHOWED US.
HOW WOULD ANYONE KNOW THAT IF NO ONE KNEW WHAT YOU WERE TALKING ABOUT?
WELL, LISTEN, WHEN WE TOLD HIM WE DIDN'T DIG ANY OF THIS VIOLENCE HE KEPT TALKIN' ABOUT...

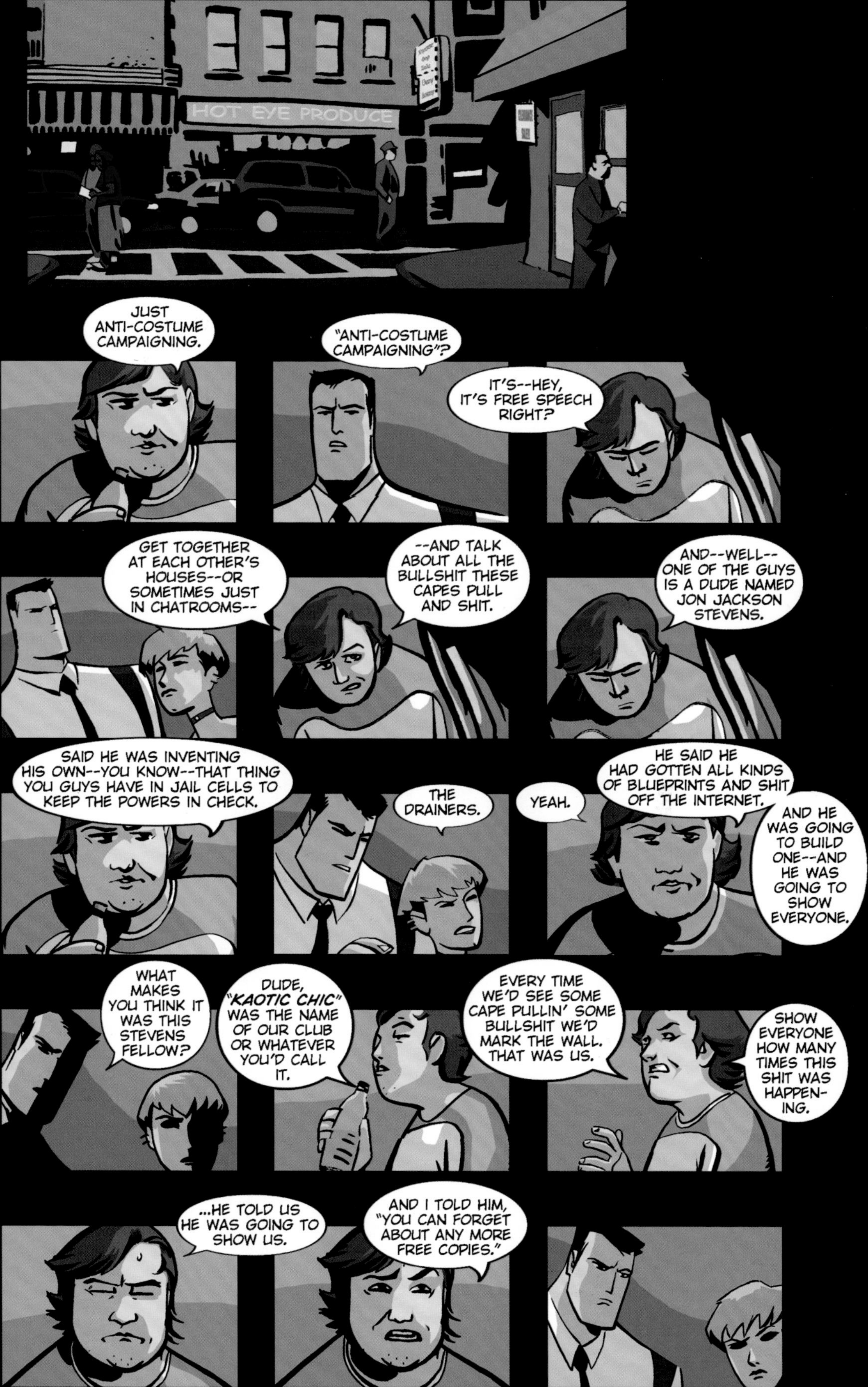
HOT EYE PRODUCE
JUST ANTI-COSTUME CAMPAIGNING.
"ANTI-COSTUME CAMPAIGNING"?
IT'S--HEY, IT'S FREE SPEECH RIGHT?
GET TOGETHER AT EACH OTHER'S HOUSES--OR SOMETIMES JUST IN CHATROOMS--
--AND TALK ABOUT ALL THE BULLSHIT THESE CAPES PULL AND SHIT.
AND--WELL--ONE OF THE GUYS IS A DUDE NAMED JON JACKSON STEVENS.
SAID HE WAS INVENTING HIS OWN--YOU KNOW--THAT THING YOU GUYS HAVE IN JAIL CELLS TO KEEP THE POWERS IN CHECK.
THE DRAINERS.
YEAH.
HE SAID HE HAD GOTTEN ALL KINDS OF BLUEPRINTS AND SHIT OFF THE INTERNET.
AND HE WAS GOING TO BUILD ONE--AND HE WAS GOING TO SHOW EVERYONE.
WHAT MAKES YOU THINK IT WAS THIS STEVENS FELLOW?
DUDE, "KAOTIC CHIC" WAS THE NAME OF OUR CLUB OR WHATEVER YOU'D CALL IT.
EVERY TIME WE'D SEE SOME CAPE PULLIN' SOME BULLSHIT WE'D MARK THE WALL. THAT WAS US.
SHOW EVERYONE HOW MANY TIMES THIS SHIT WAS HAPPEN-ING.
...HE TOLD US HE WAS GOING TO SHOW US.
AND I TOLD HIM, "YOU CAN FORGET ABOUT ANY MORE FREE COPIES."

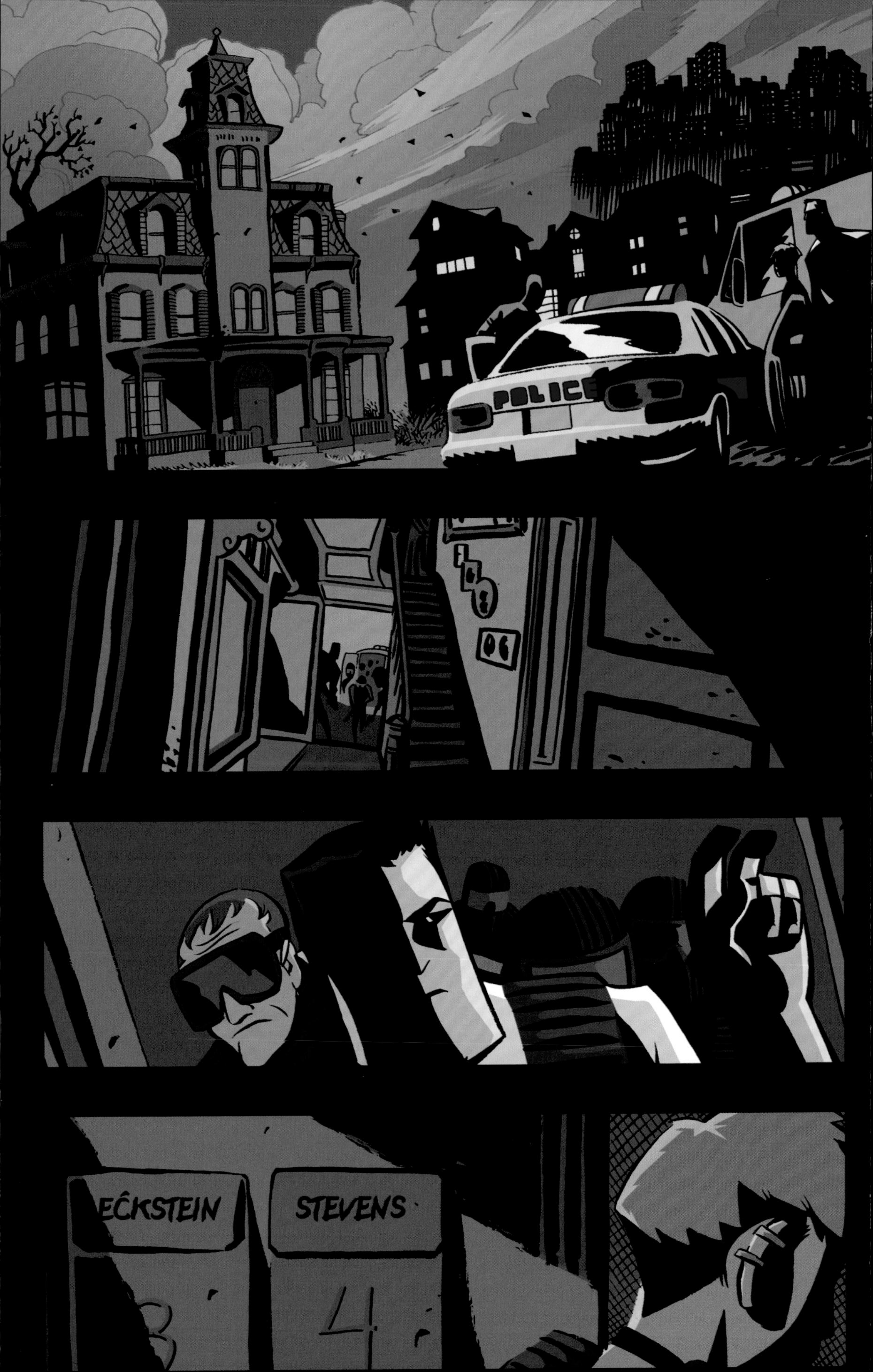

POLICE
ECKSTEIN
STEVENS
4

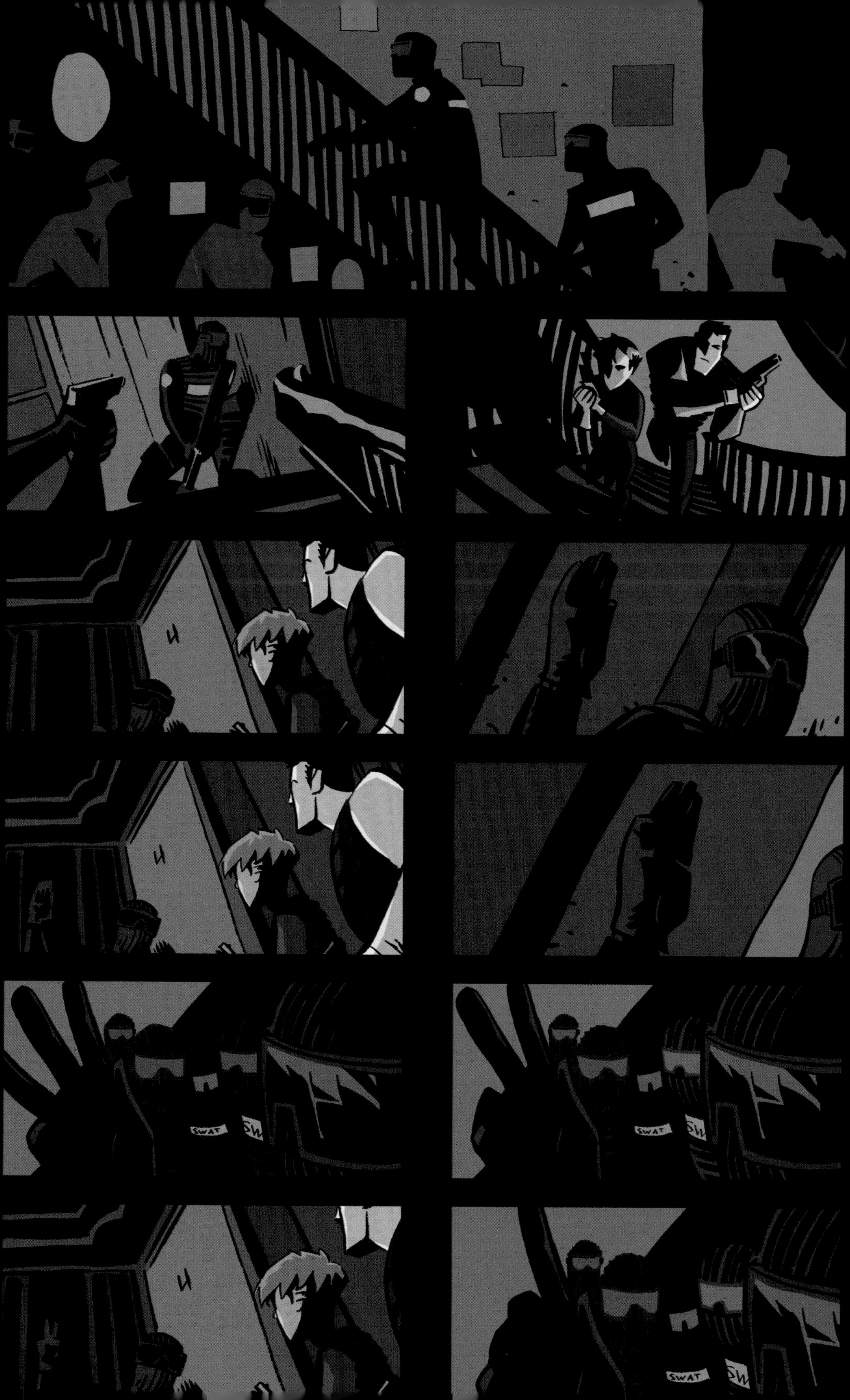
SWAT
SWAT
SWAT

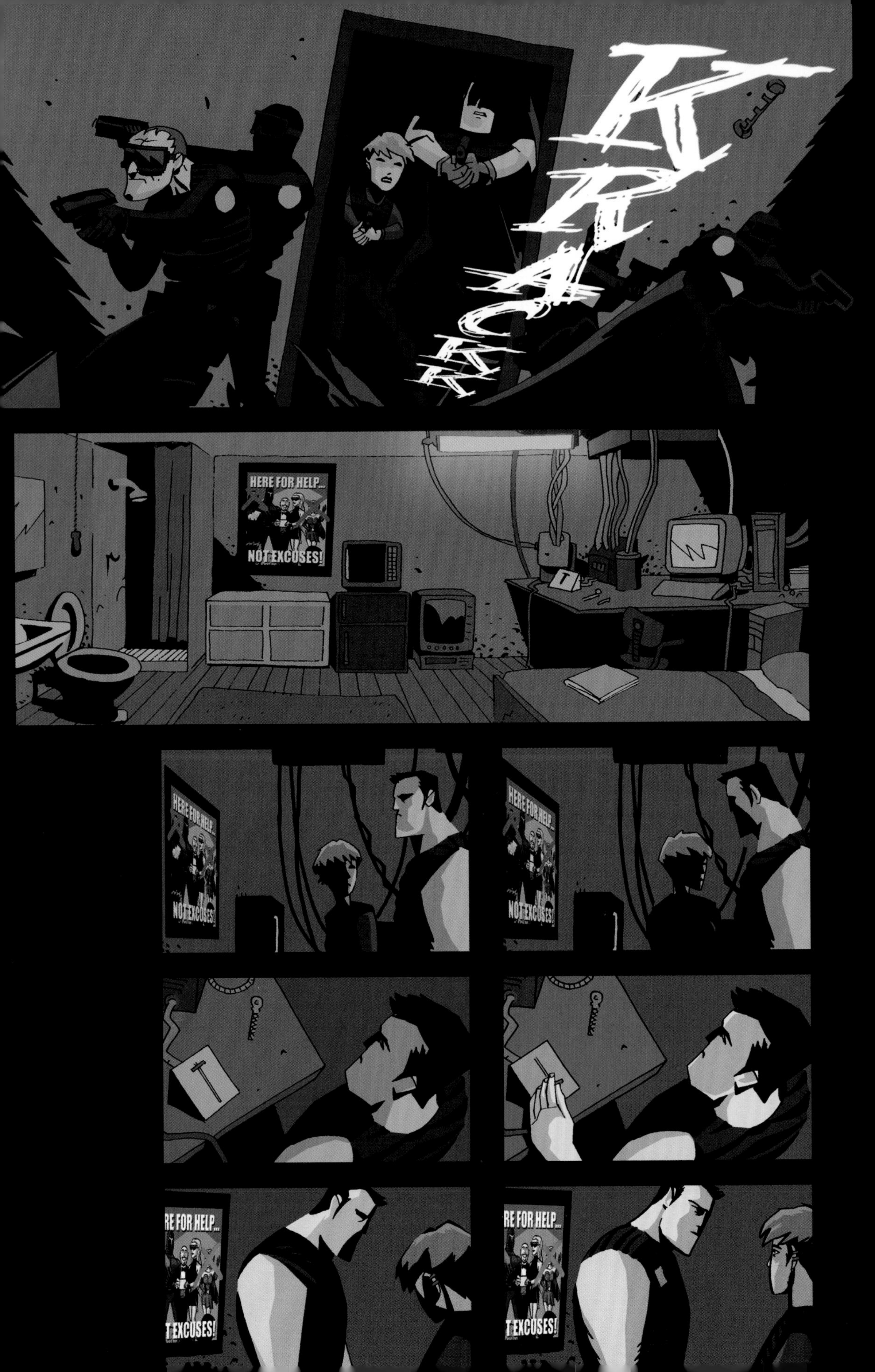
KRRACK
HERE FOR HELP...
NOT EXCUSES!

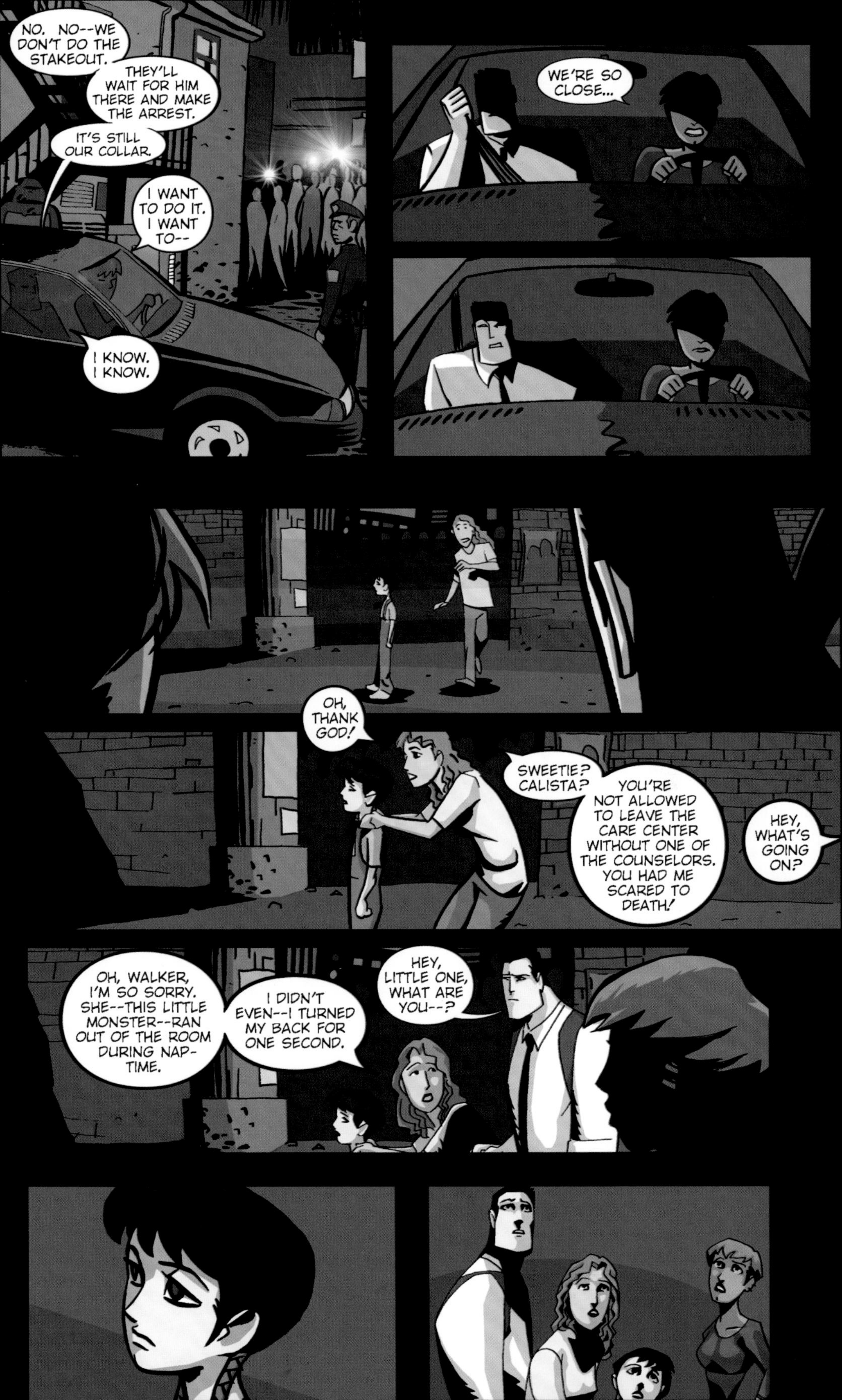
NO. NO--WE DON'T DO THE STAKEOUT.
THEY'LL WAIT FOR HIM THERE AND MAKE THE ARREST.
IT'S STILL OUR COLLAR.
I WANT TO DO IT. I WANT TO--
I KNOW. I KNOW.
WE'RE SO CLOSE...
OH, THANK GOD!
SWEETIE? CALISTA?
YOU'RE NOT ALLOWED TO LEAVE THE CARE CENTER WITHOUT ONE OF THE COUNSELORS. YOU HAD ME SCARED TO DEATH!
HEY, WHAT'S GOING ON?
OH, WALKER, I'M SO SORRY. SHE--THIS LITTLE MONSTER--RAN OUT OF THE ROOM DURING NAP-TIME.
I DIDN'T EVEN--I TURNED MY BACK FOR ONE SECOND.
HEY, LITTLE ONE, WHAT ARE YOU--?

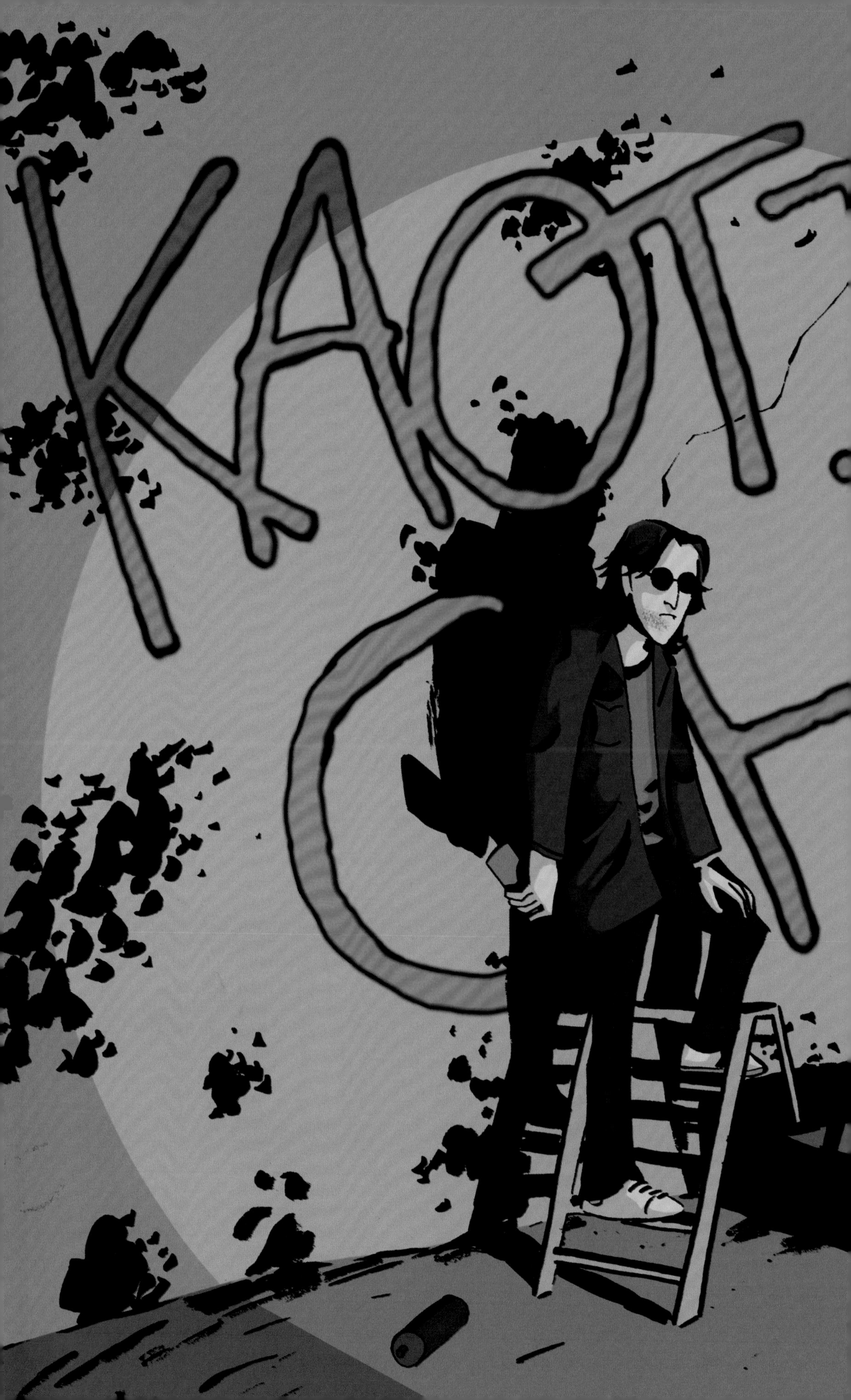

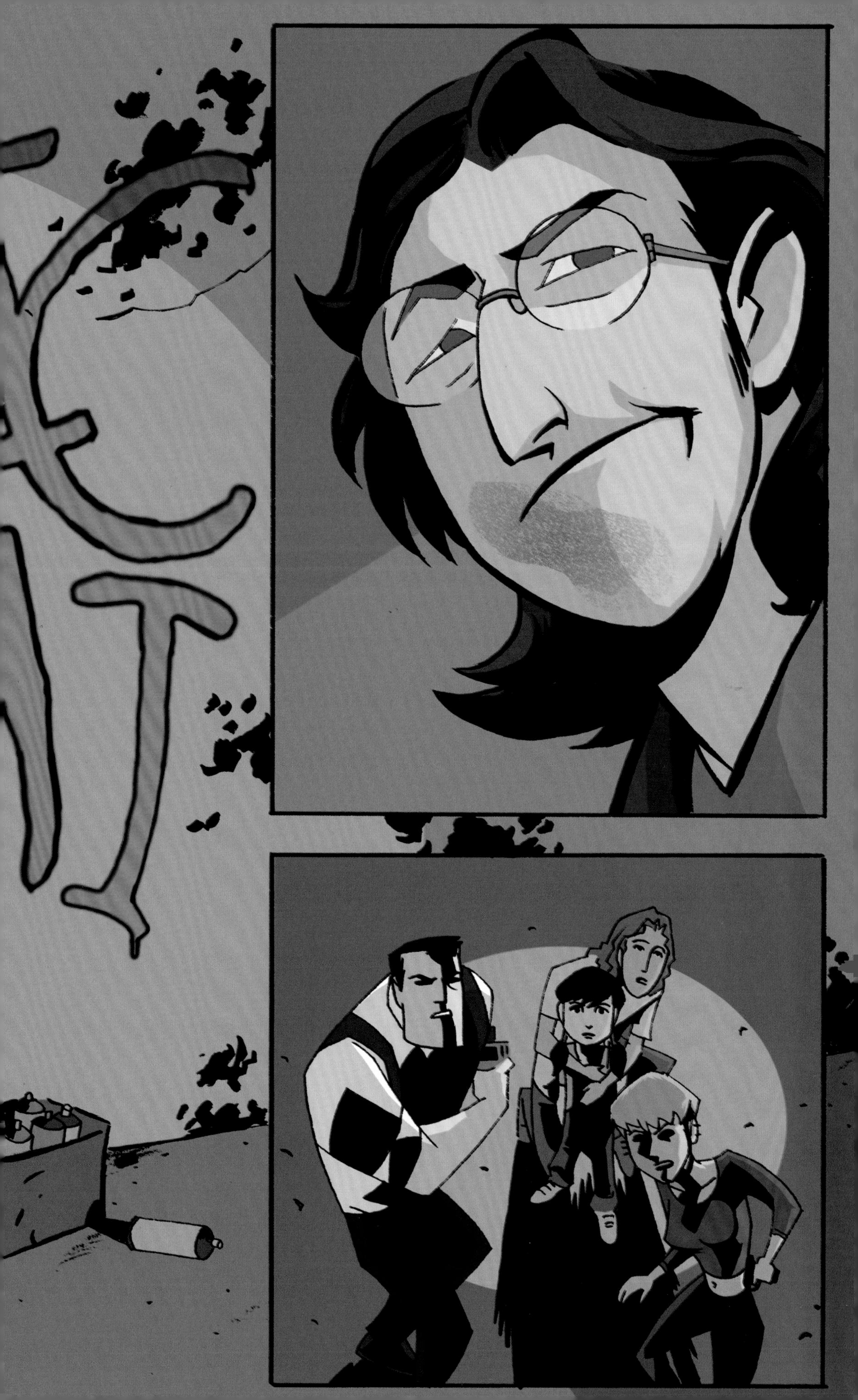

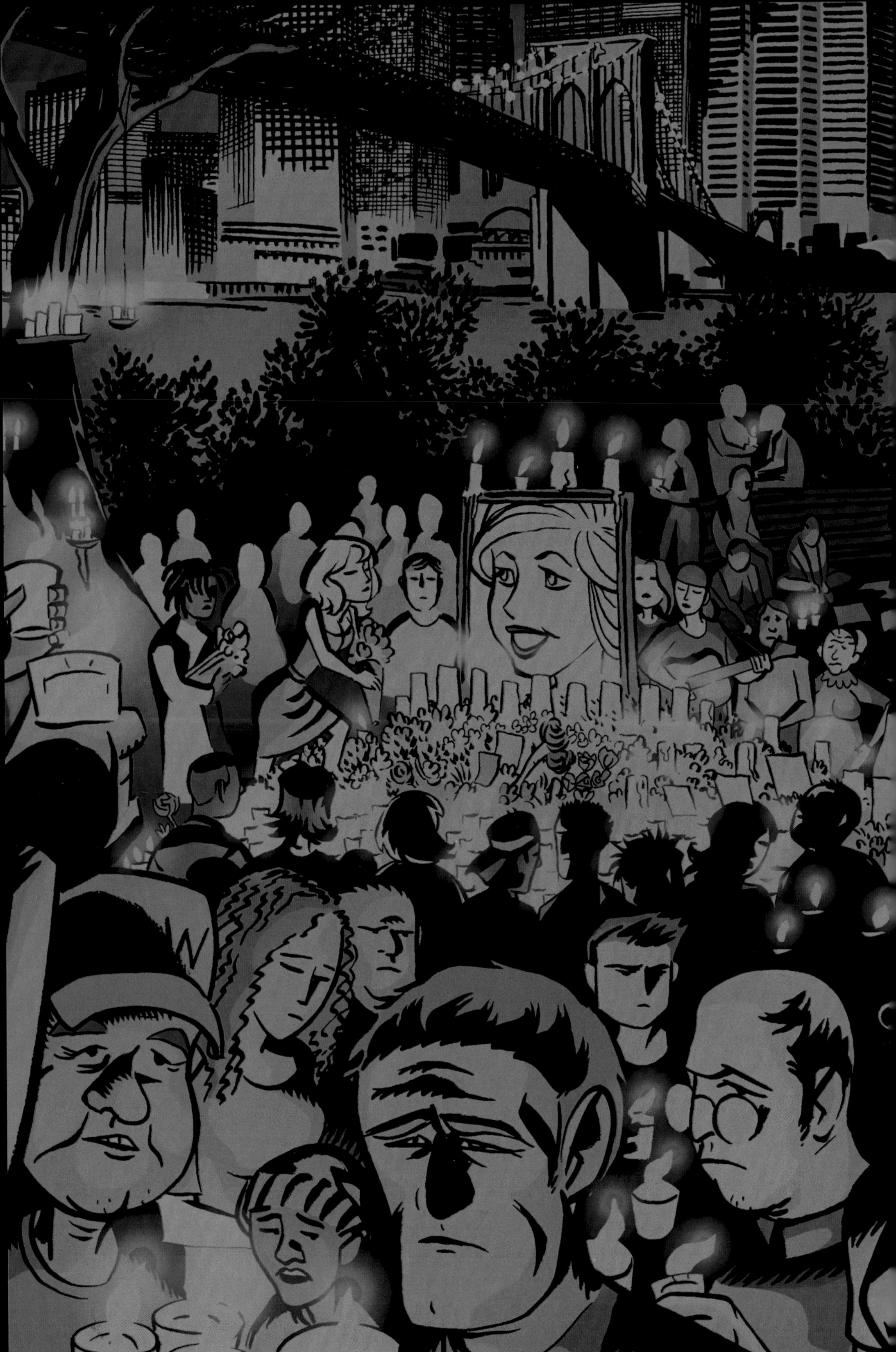

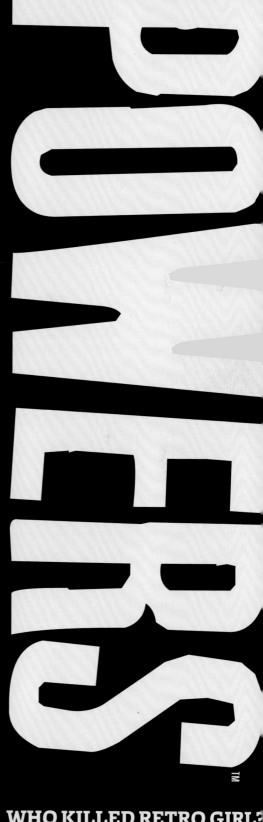

POWERS™

WHO KILLED RETRO GIRL?

CHAPTER 6

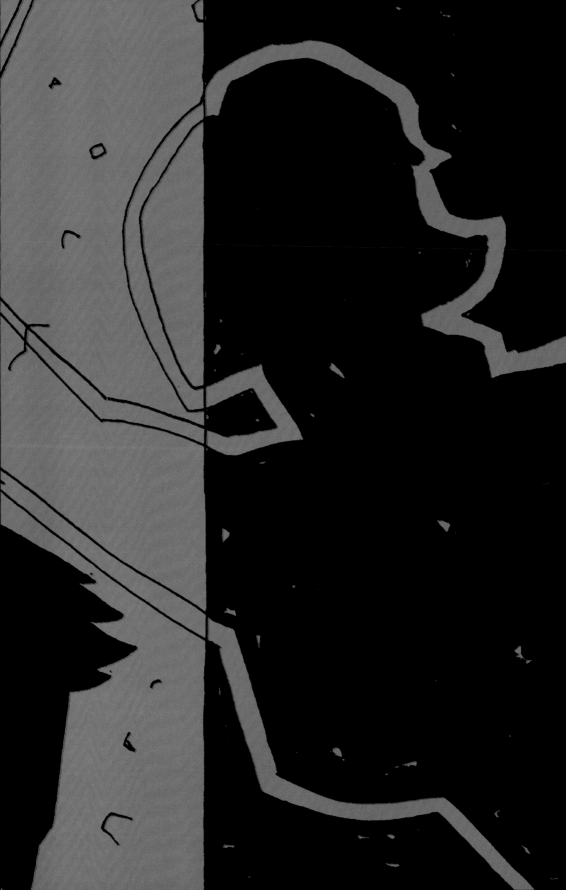

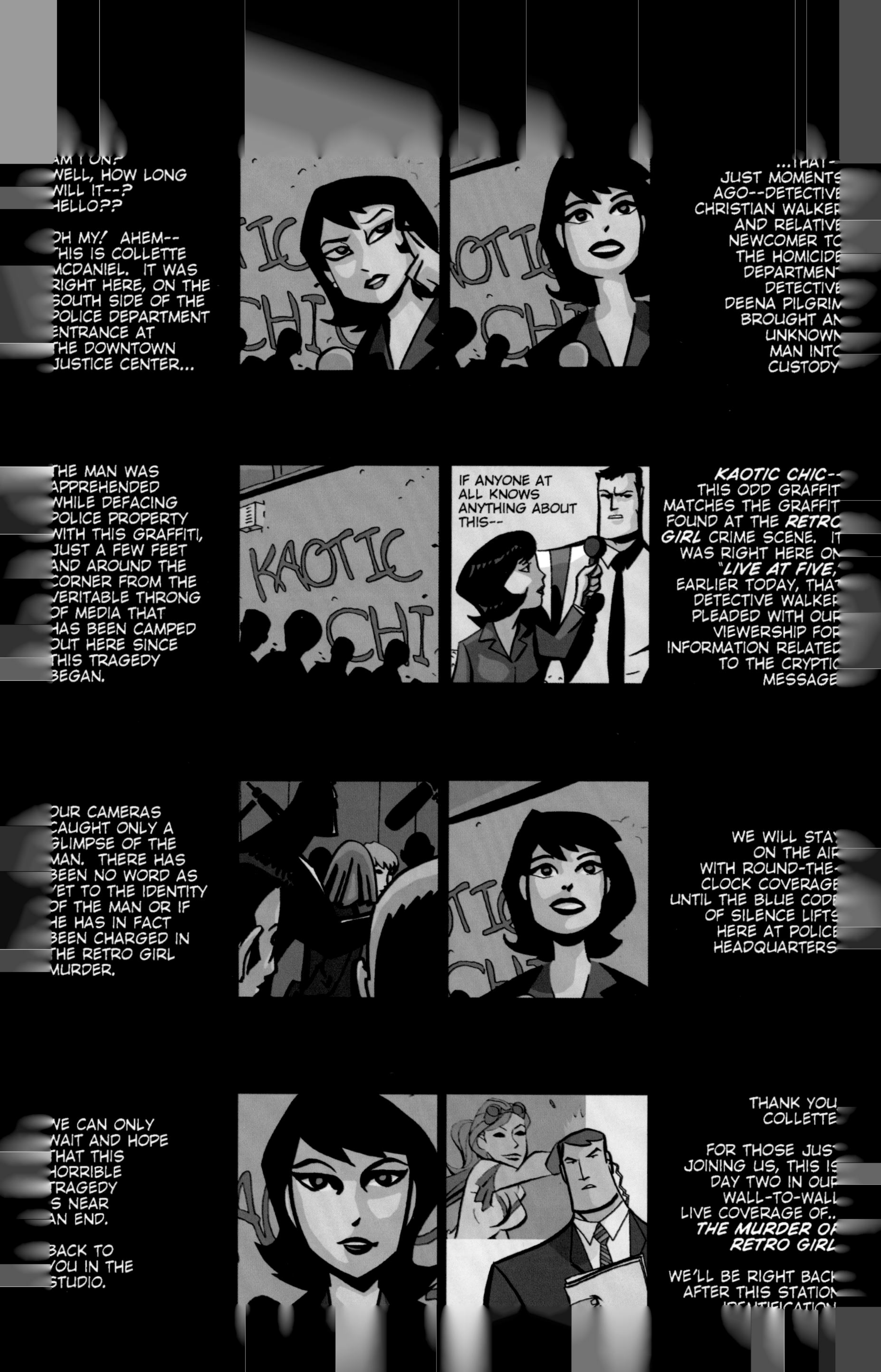
AM I ON? WELL, HOW LONG WILL IT--? HELLO??
OH MY! AHEM-- THIS IS COLLETTE MCDANIEL. IT WAS RIGHT HERE, ON THE SOUTH SIDE OF THE POLICE DEPARTMENT ENTRANCE AT THE DOWNTOWN JUSTICE CENTER...
...THAT-- JUST MOMENTS AGO--DETECTIVE CHRISTIAN WALKER AND RELATIVE NEWCOMER TO THE HOMICIDE DEPARTMENT DETECTIVE DEENA PILGRIM BROUGHT AN UNKNOWN MAN INTO CUSTODY
THE MAN WAS APPREHENDED WHILE DEFACING POLICE PROPERTY WITH THIS GRAFFITI, JUST A FEW FEET AND AROUND THE CORNER FROM THE VERITABLE THRONG OF MEDIA THAT HAS BEEN CAMPED OUT HERE SINCE THIS TRAGEDY BEGAN.
KAOTIC CHI
IF ANYONE AT ALL KNOWS ANYTHING ABOUT THIS--
KAOTIC CHIC-- THIS ODD GRAFFIT MATCHES THE GRAFFIT FOUND AT THE RETRO GIRL CRIME SCENE. IT WAS RIGHT HERE ON "LIVE AT FIVE," EARLIER TODAY, THAT DETECTIVE WALKER PLEADED WITH OUR VIEWERSHIP FOR INFORMATION RELATED TO THE CRYPTIC MESSAGE
OUR CAMERAS CAUGHT ONLY A GLIMPSE OF THE MAN. THERE HAS BEEN NO WORD AS YET TO THE IDENTITY OF THE MAN OR IF HE HAS IN FACT BEEN CHARGED IN THE RETRO GIRL MURDER.
WE WILL STAY ON THE AIR WITH ROUND-THE-CLOCK COVERAGE UNTIL THE BLUE CODE OF SILENCE LIFTS HERE AT POLICE HEADQUARTERS
WE CAN ONLY WAIT AND HOPE THAT THIS HORRIBLE TRAGEDY IS NEAR AN END.
BACK TO YOU IN THE STUDIO.
THANK YOU, COLLETTE
FOR THOSE JUST JOINING US, THIS IS DAY TWO IN OUR WALL-TO-WALL LIVE COVERAGE OF... THE MURDER OF RETRO GIRL
WE'LL BE RIGHT BACK AFTER THIS STATION

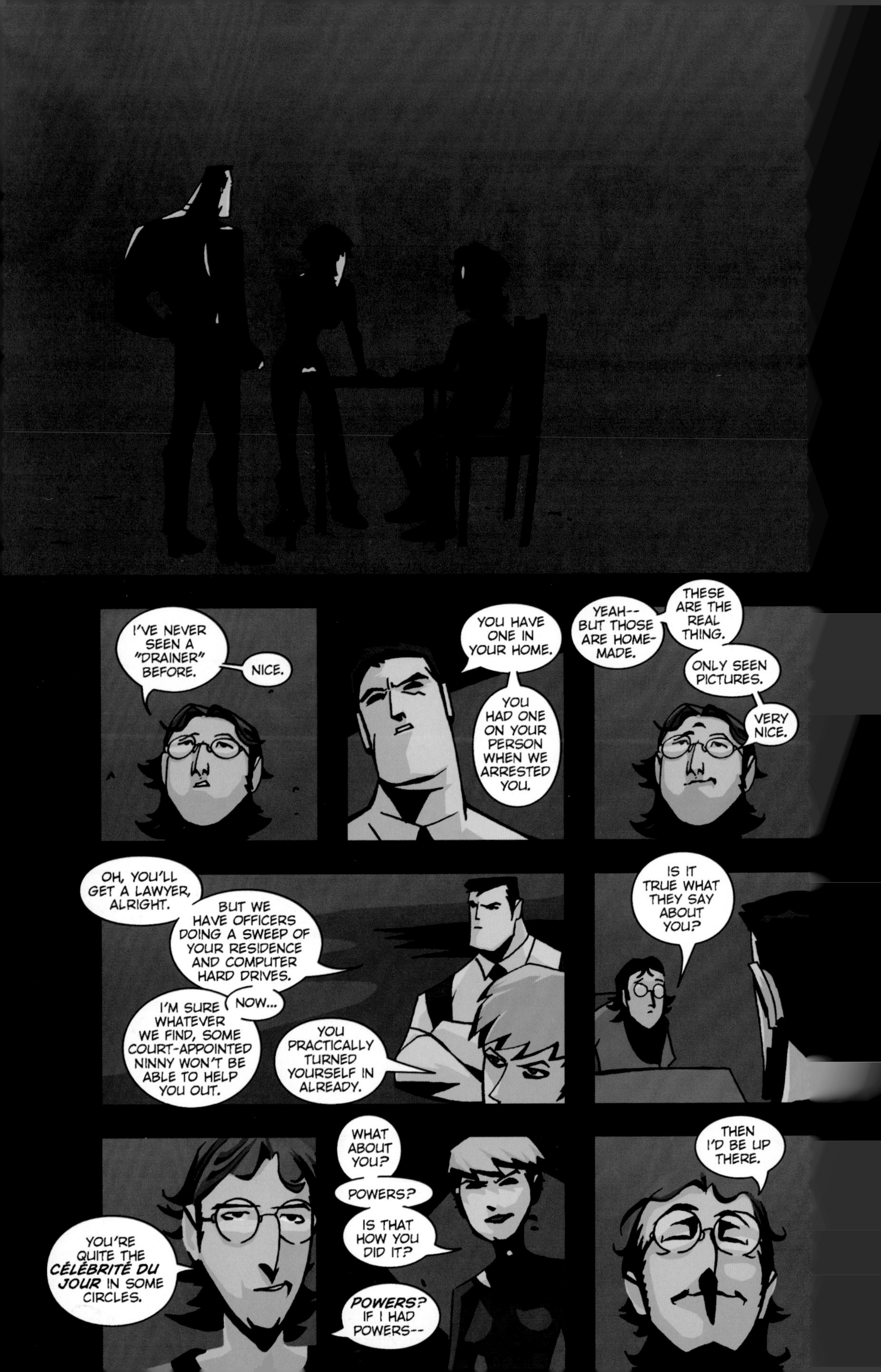
I'VE NEVER SEEN A "DRAINER" BEFORE.
NICE.
YOU HAVE ONE IN YOUR HOME.
YOU HAD ONE ON YOUR PERSON WHEN WE ARRESTED YOU.
YEAH-- BUT THOSE ARE HOME-MADE.
THESE ARE THE REAL THING.
ONLY SEEN PICTURES.
VERY NICE.
OH, YOU'LL GET A LAWYER, ALRIGHT.
BUT WE HAVE OFFICERS DOING A SWEEP OF YOUR RESIDENCE AND COMPUTER HARD DRIVES.
NOW...
I'M SURE WHATEVER WE FIND, SOME COURT-APPOINTED NINNY WON'T BE ABLE TO HELP YOU OUT.
YOU PRACTICALLY TURNED YOURSELF IN ALREADY.
IS IT TRUE WHAT THEY SAY ABOUT YOU?
YOU'RE QUITE THE CÉLÈBRITÉ DU JOUR IN SOME CIRCLES.
WHAT ABOUT YOU?
POWERS?
IS THAT HOW YOU DID IT?
POWERS? IF I HAD POWERS--
THEN I'D BE UP THERE.

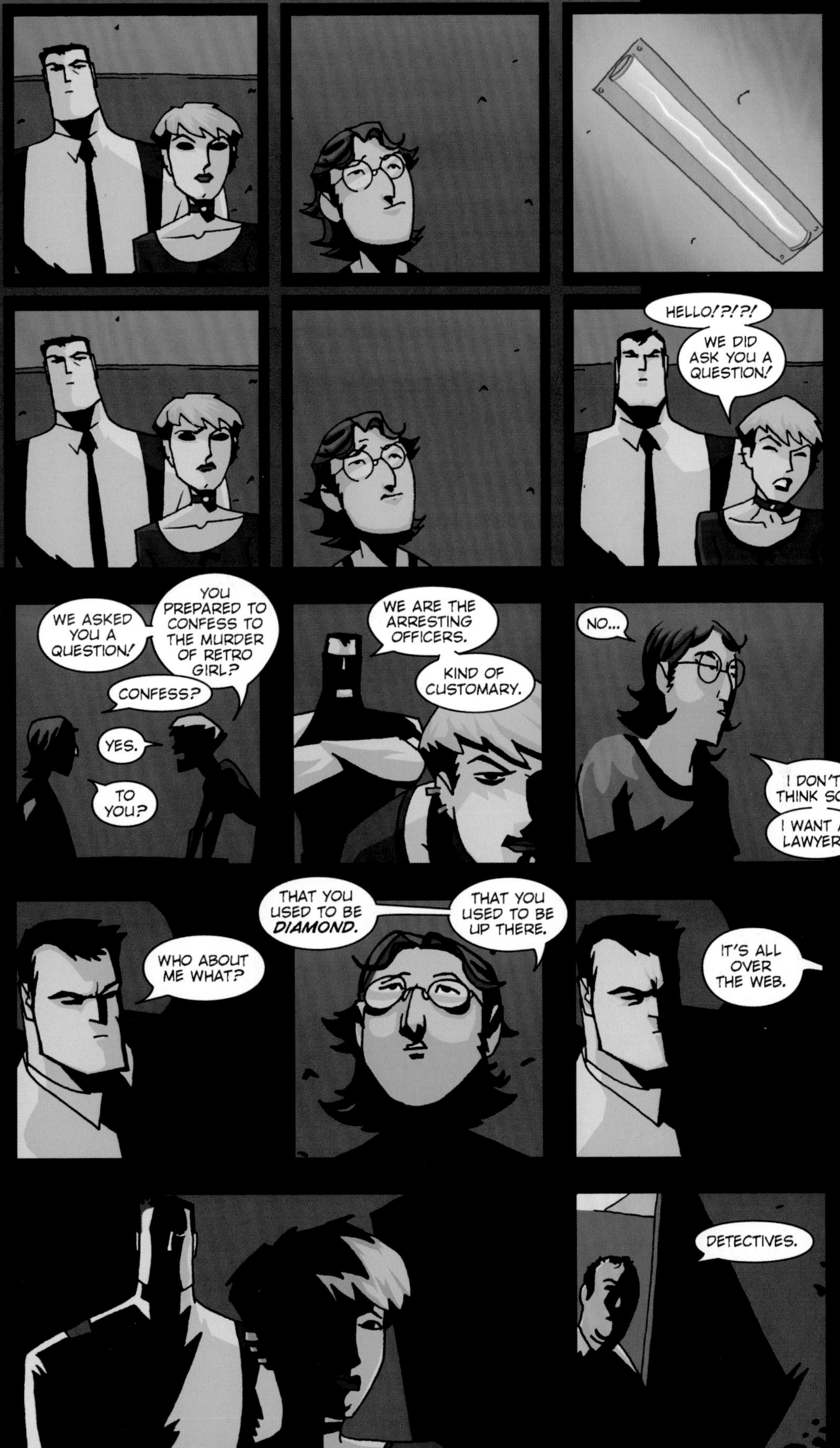
HELLO!?!?!
WE DID ASK YOU A QUESTION!
WE ASKED YOU A QUESTION!
YOU PREPARED TO CONFESS TO THE MURDER OF RETRO GIRL?
CONFESS?
YES.
TO YOU?
WE ARE THE ARRESTING OFFICERS.
KIND OF CUSTOMARY.
NO...
I DON'T THINK SO.
I WANT A LAWYER.
WHO ABOUT ME WHAT?
THAT YOU USED TO BE DIAMOND.
THAT YOU USED TO BE UP THERE.
IT'S ALL OVER THE WEB.
DETECTIVES.

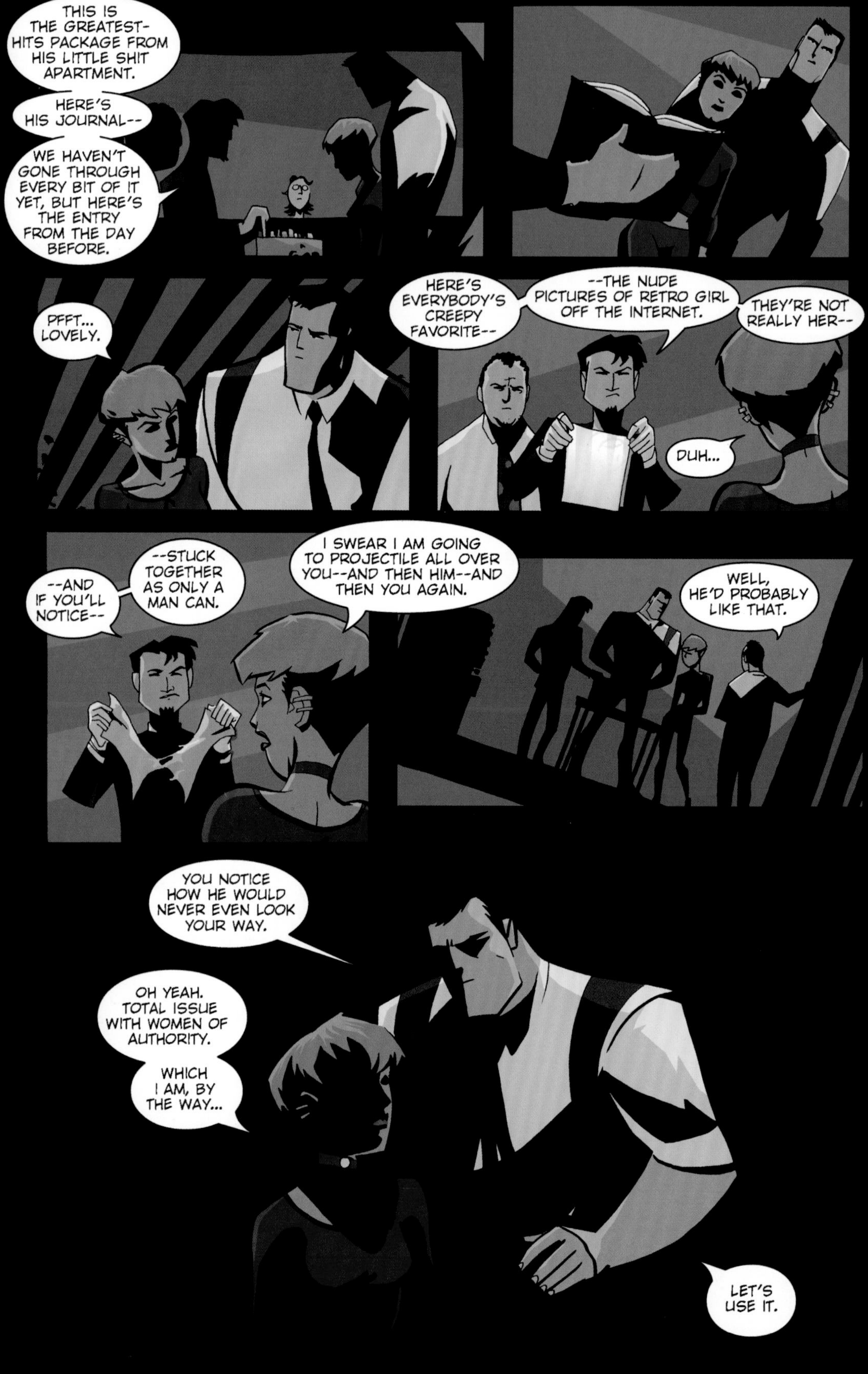
THIS IS THE GREATEST-HITS PACKAGE FROM HIS LITTLE SHIT APARTMENT.
HERE'S HIS JOURNAL--
WE HAVEN'T GONE THROUGH EVERY BIT OF IT YET, BUT HERE'S THE ENTRY FROM THE DAY BEFORE.
PFFT... LOVELY.
HERE'S EVERYBODY'S CREEPY FAVORITE--
--THE NUDE PICTURES OF RETRO GIRL OFF THE INTERNET.
THEY'RE NOT REALLY HER--
DUH...
--AND IF YOU'LL NOTICE--
--STUCK TOGETHER AS ONLY A MAN CAN.
I SWEAR I AM GOING TO PROJECTILE ALL OVER YOU--AND THEN HIM--AND THEN YOU AGAIN.
WELL, HE'D PROBABLY LIKE THAT.
YOU NOTICE HOW HE WOULD NEVER EVEN LOOK YOUR WAY.
OH YEAH. TOTAL ISSUE WITH WOMEN OF AUTHORITY.
WHICH I AM, BY THE WAY...
LET'S USE IT.

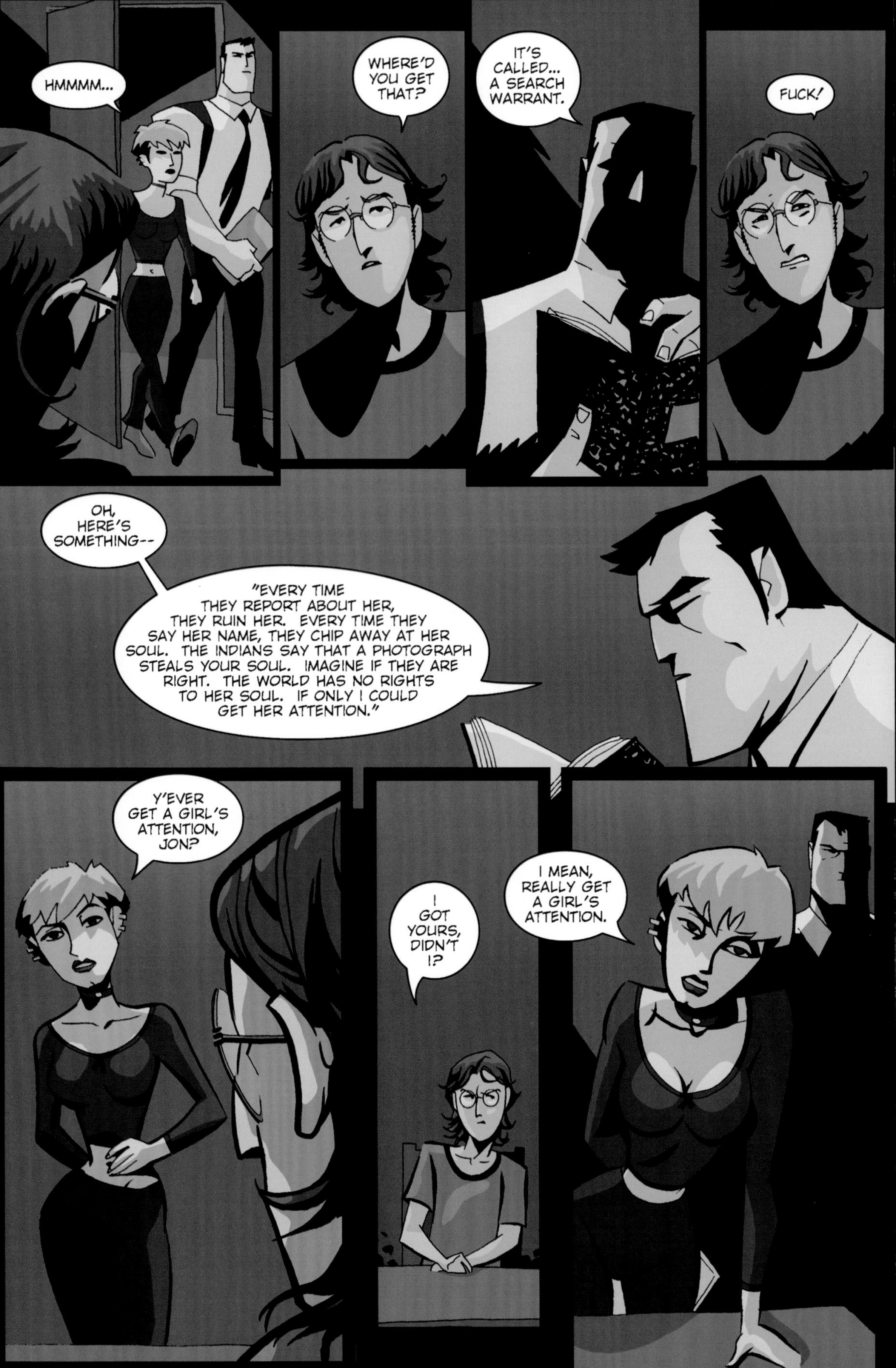
HMMMM...
WHERE'D YOU GET THAT?
IT'S CALLED... A SEARCH WARRANT.
FUCK!
OH, HERE'S SOMETHING--
"EVERY TIME THEY REPORT ABOUT HER, THEY RUIN HER. EVERY TIME THEY SAY HER NAME, THEY CHIP AWAY AT HER SOUL. THE INDIANS SAY THAT A PHOTOGRAPH STEALS YOUR SOUL. IMAGINE IF THEY ARE RIGHT. THE WORLD HAS NO RIGHTS TO HER SOUL. IF ONLY I COULD GET HER ATTENTION."
Y'EVER GET A GIRL'S ATTENTION, JON?
I GOT YOURS, DIDN'T I?
I MEAN, REALLY GET A GIRL'S ATTENTION.

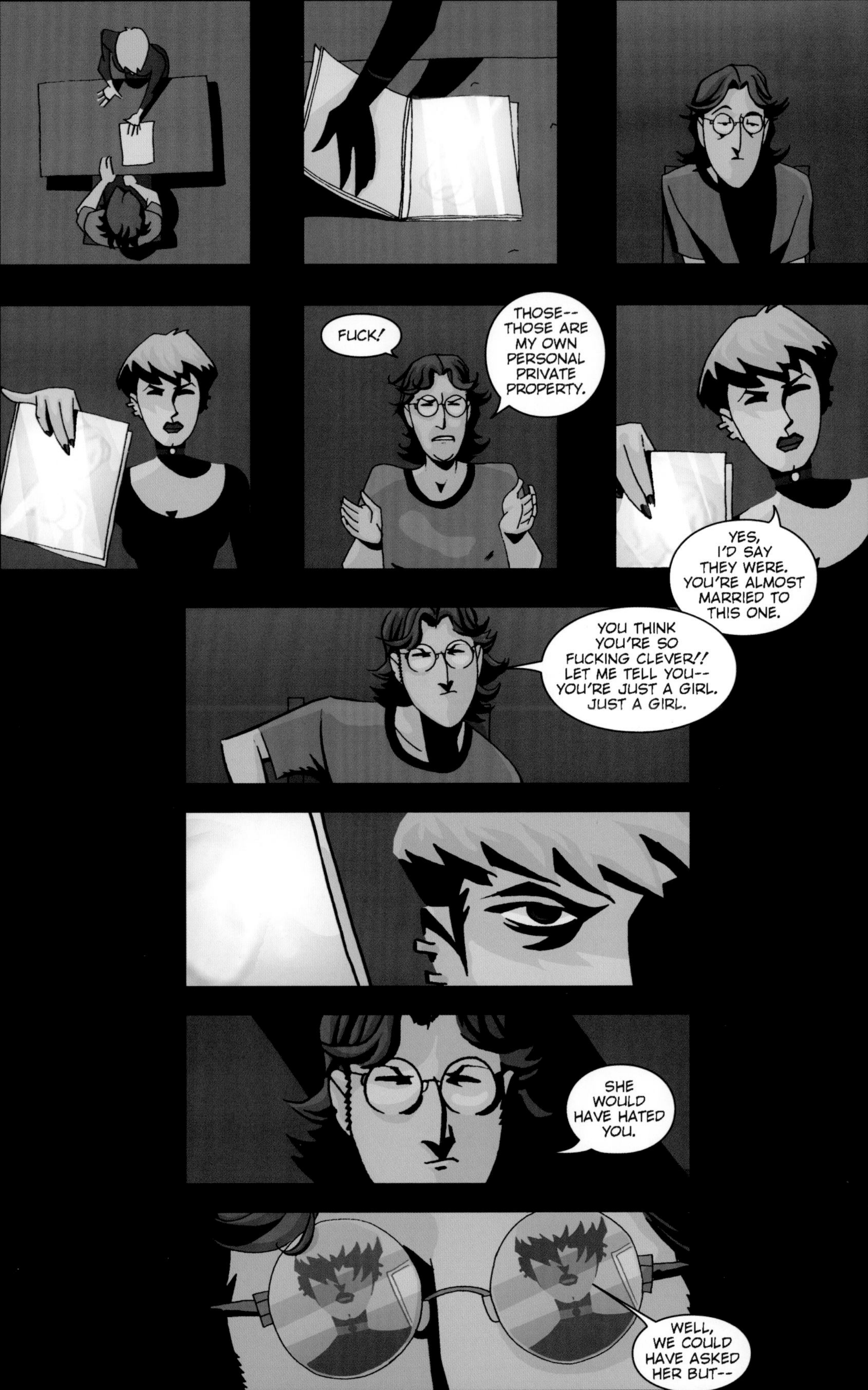
FUCK!
THOSE-- THOSE ARE MY OWN PERSONAL PRIVATE PROPERTY.
YES, I'D SAY THEY WERE. YOU'RE ALMOST MARRIED TO THIS ONE.
YOU THINK YOU'RE SO FUCKING CLEVER!! LET ME TELL YOU-- YOU'RE JUST A GIRL. JUST A GIRL.
SHE WOULD HAVE HATED YOU.
WELL, WE COULD HAVE ASKED HER BUT--

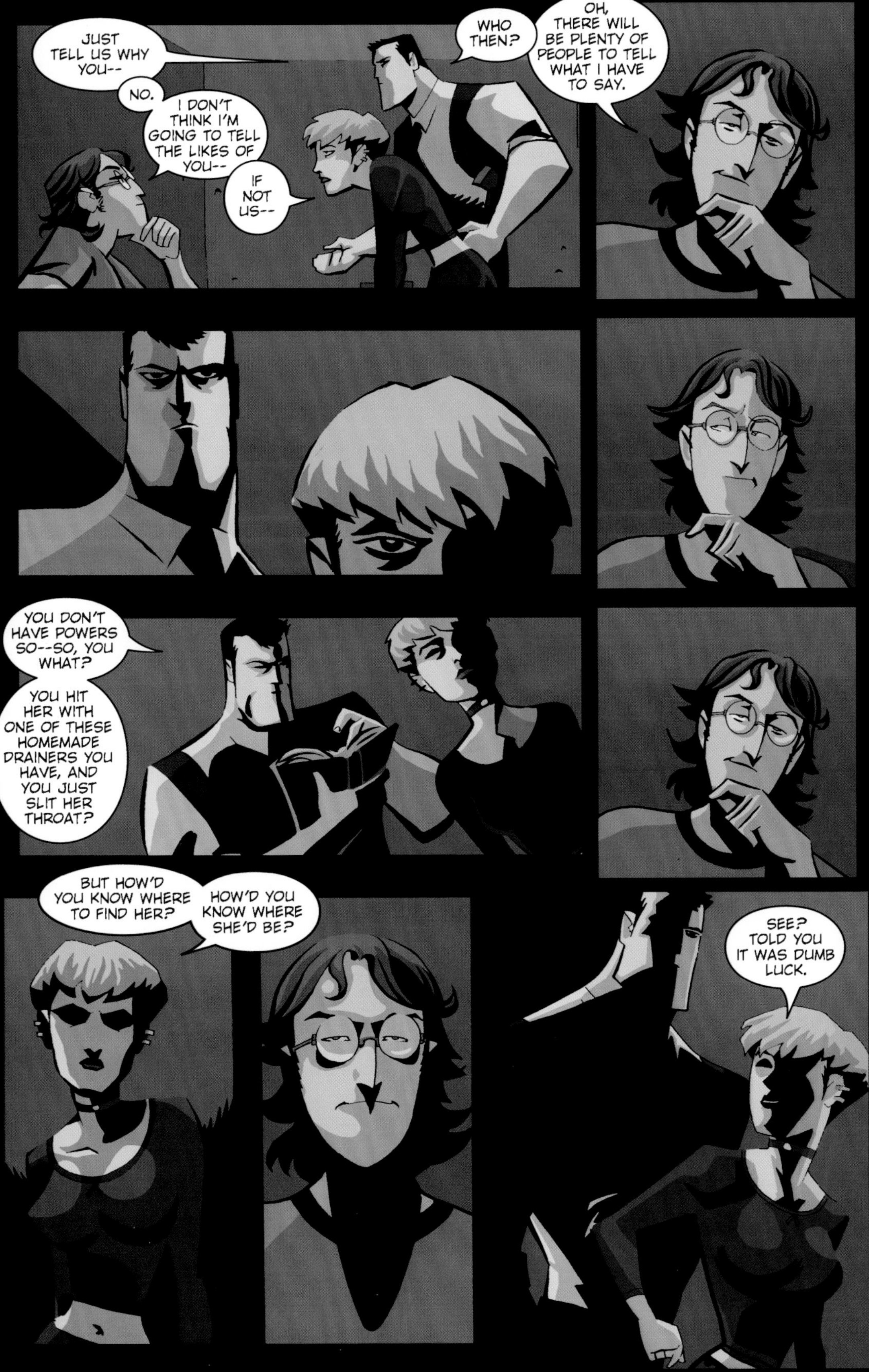
JUST TELL US WHY YOU--
NO.
I DON'T THINK I'M GOING TO TELL THE LIKES OF YOU--
IF NOT US--
WHO THEN?
OH, THERE WILL BE PLENTY OF PEOPLE TO TELL WHAT I HAVE TO SAY.
YOU DON'T HAVE POWERS SO--SO, YOU WHAT?
YOU HIT HER WITH ONE OF THESE HOMEMADE DRAINERS YOU HAVE, AND YOU JUST SLIT HER THROAT?
BUT HOW'D YOU KNOW WHERE TO FIND HER?
HOW'D YOU KNOW WHERE SHE'D BE?
SEE? TOLD YOU IT WAS DUMB LUCK.

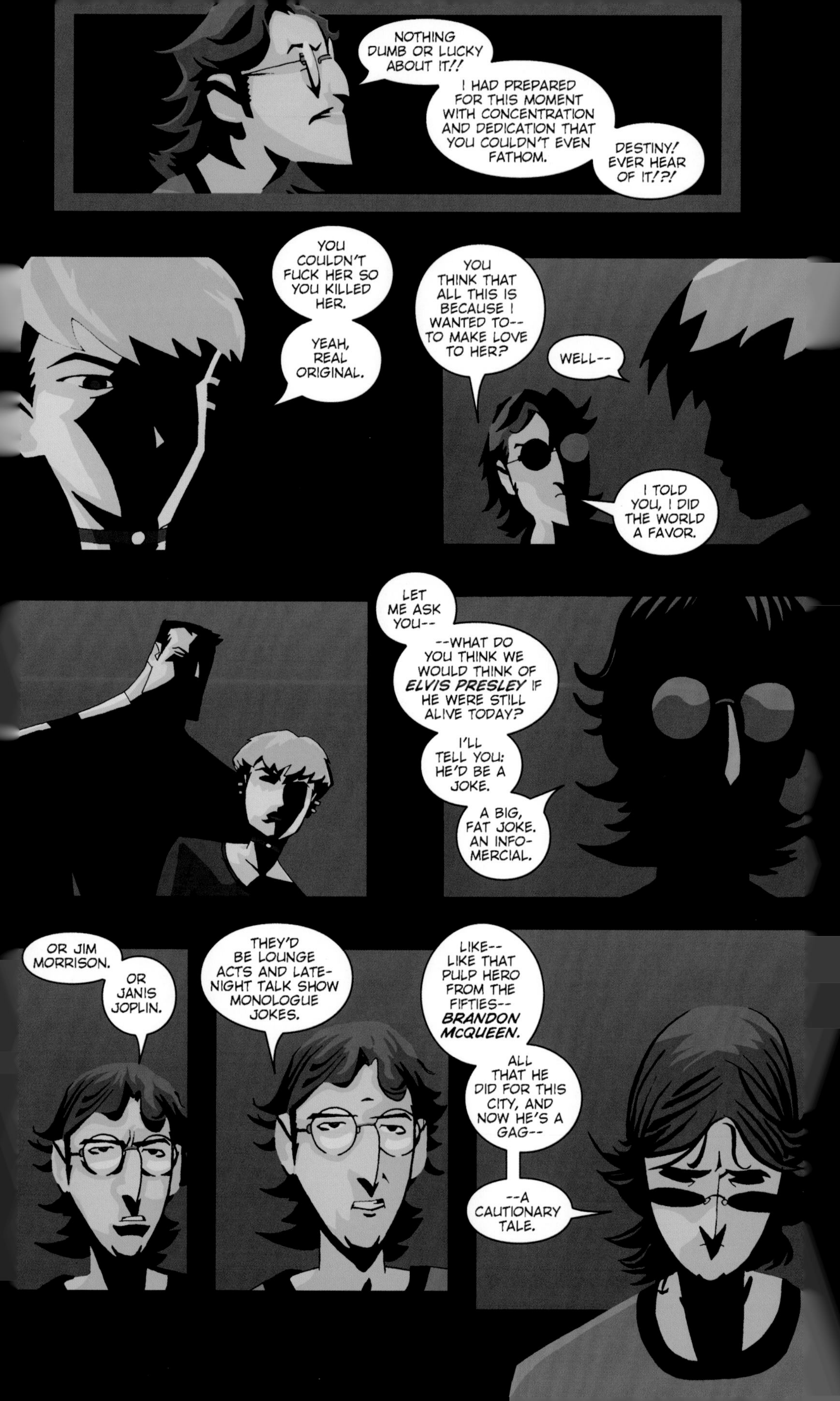
NOTHING DUMB OR LUCKY ABOUT IT!!
I HAD PREPARED FOR THIS MOMENT WITH CONCENTRATION AND DEDICATION THAT YOU COULDN'T EVEN FATHOM.
DESTINY! EVER HEAR OF IT!?!
YOU COULDN'T FUCK HER SO YOU KILLED HER.
YEAH, REAL ORIGINAL.
YOU THINK THAT ALL THIS IS BECAUSE I WANTED TO-- TO MAKE LOVE TO HER?
WELL--
I TOLD YOU, I DID THE WORLD A FAVOR.
LET ME ASK YOU--
--WHAT DO YOU THINK WE WOULD THINK OF ELVIS PRESLEY IF HE WERE STILL ALIVE TODAY?
I'LL TELL YOU: HE'D BE A JOKE.
A BIG, FAT JOKE. AN INFO-MERCIAL.
OR JIM MORRISON.
OR JANIS JOPLIN.
THEY'D BE LOUNGE ACTS AND LATE-NIGHT TALK SHOW MONOLOGUE JOKES.
LIKE-- LIKE THAT PULP HERO FROM THE FIFTIES-- BRANDON McQUEEN.
ALL THAT HE DID FOR THIS CITY, AND NOW HE'S A GAG--
--A CAUTIONARY TALE.

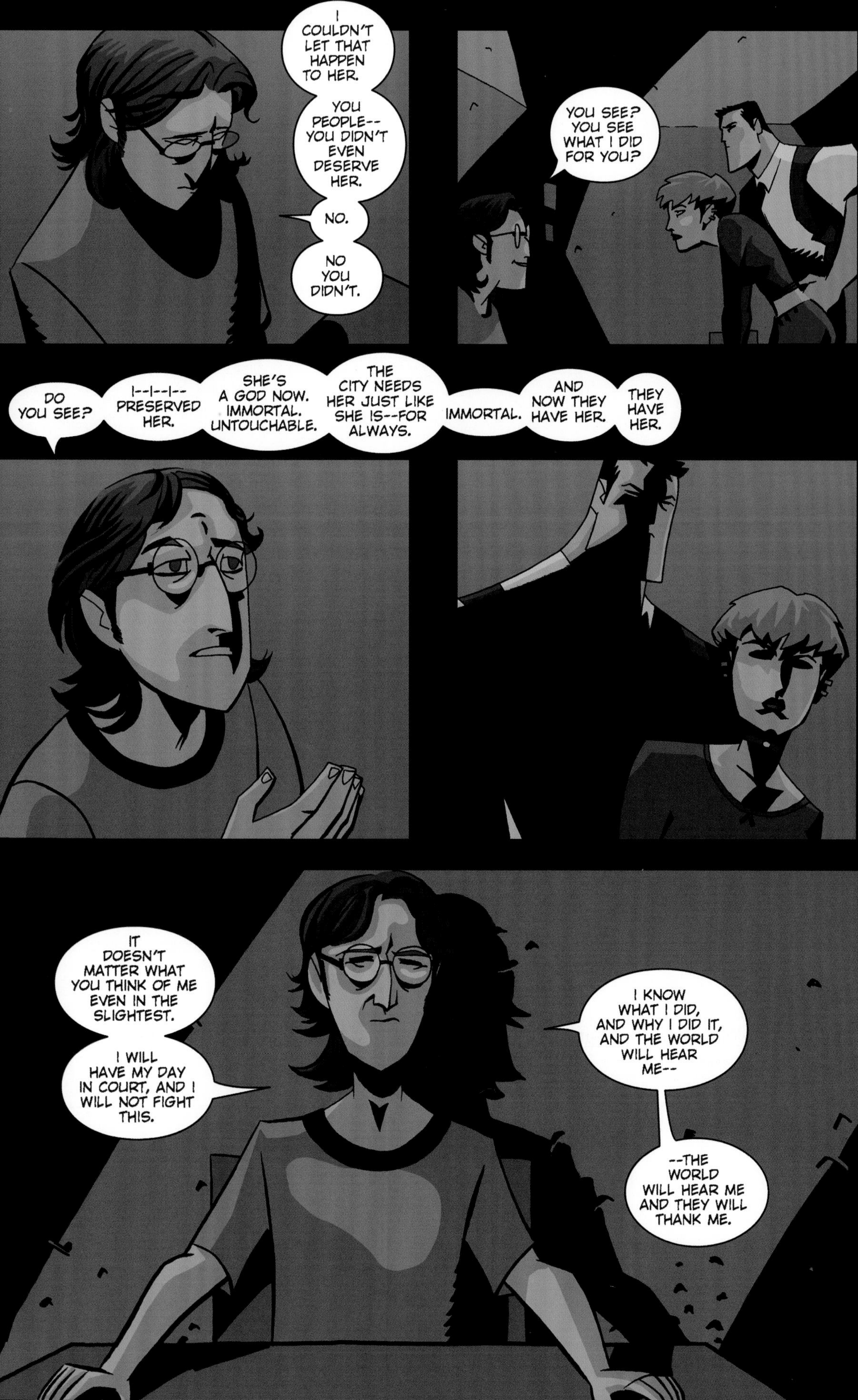
I COULDN'T LET THAT HAPPEN TO HER.
YOU PEOPLE-- YOU DIDN'T EVEN DESERVE HER.
NO.
NO YOU DIDN'T.
YOU SEE? YOU SEE WHAT I DID FOR YOU?
DO YOU SEE?
I--I--I-- PRESERVED HER.
SHE'S A GOD NOW. IMMORTAL. UNTOUCHABLE.
THE CITY NEEDS HER JUST LIKE SHE IS--FOR ALWAYS.
IMMORTAL.
AND NOW THEY HAVE HER.
THEY HAVE HER.
IT DOESN'T MATTER WHAT YOU THINK OF ME EVEN IN THE SLIGHTEST.
I WILL HAVE MY DAY IN COURT, AND I WILL NOT FIGHT THIS.
I KNOW WHAT I DID, AND WHY I DID IT, AND THE WORLD WILL HEAR ME--
--THE WORLD WILL HEAR ME AND THEY WILL THANK ME.

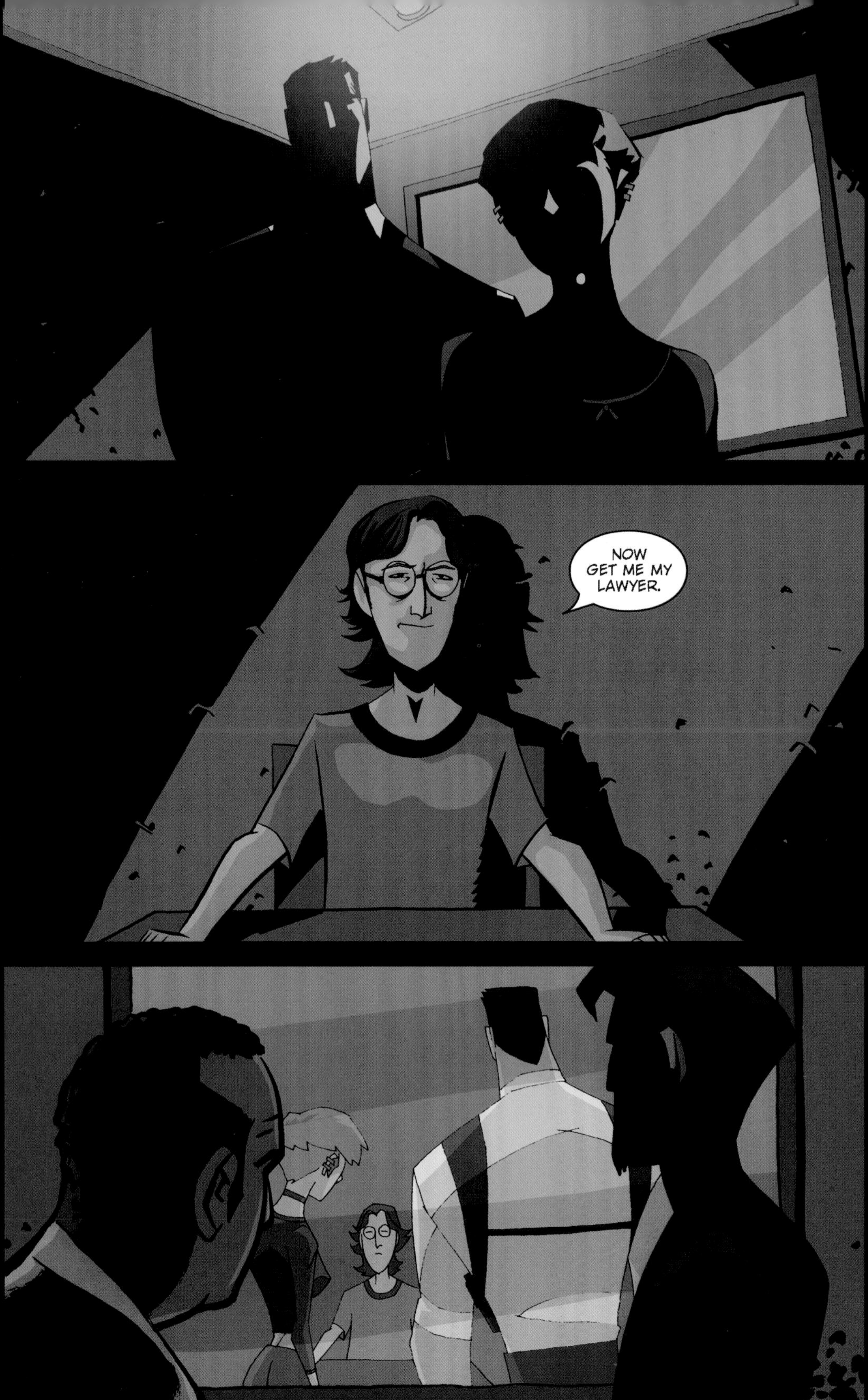
NOW GET ME MY LAWYER.

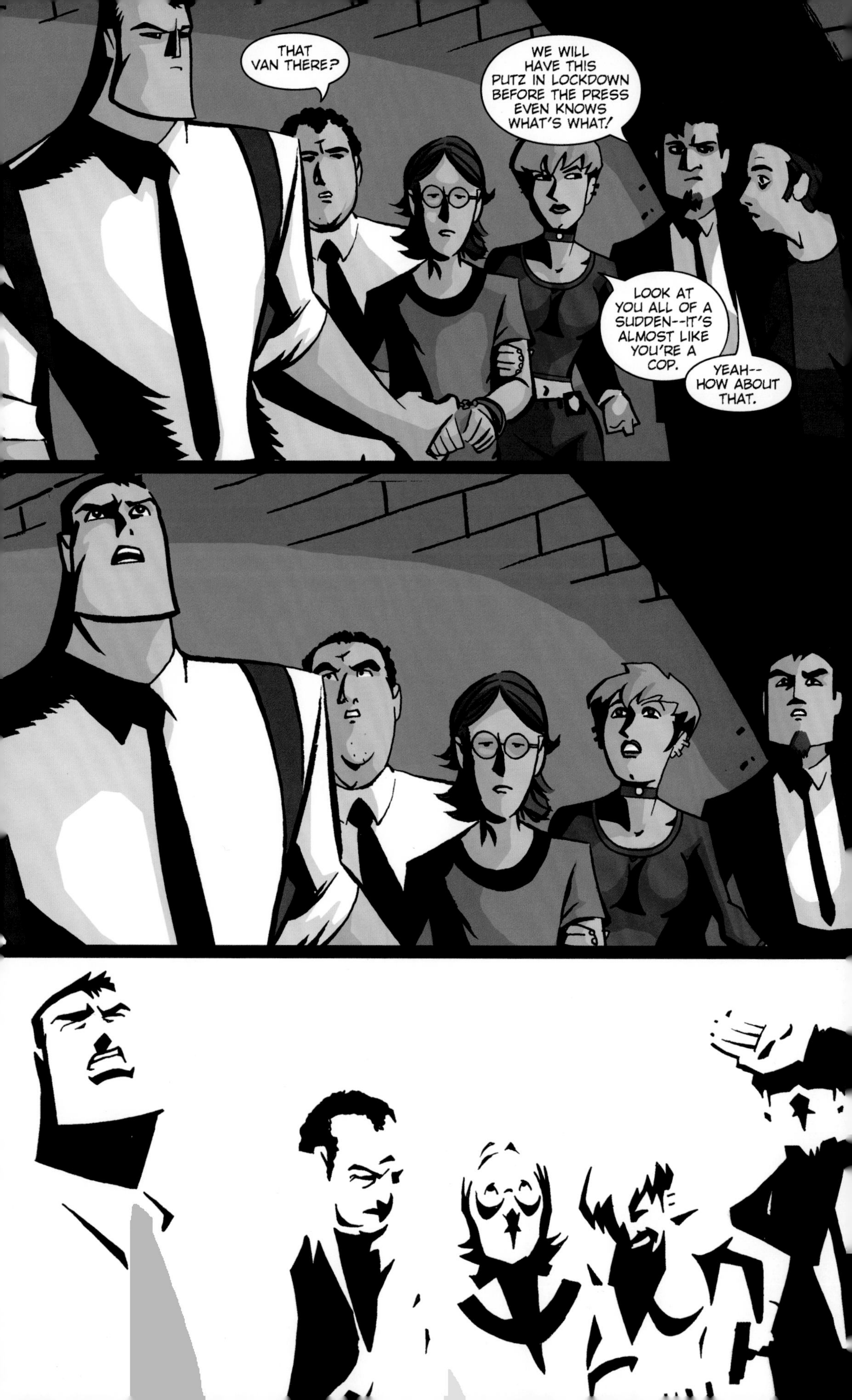
THAT VAN THERE?
WE WILL HAVE THIS PUTZ IN LOCKDOWN BEFORE THE PRESS EVEN KNOWS WHAT'S WHAT!
LOOK AT YOU ALL OF A SUDDEN--IT'S ALMOST LIKE YOU'RE A COP.
YEAH-- HOW ABOUT THAT.

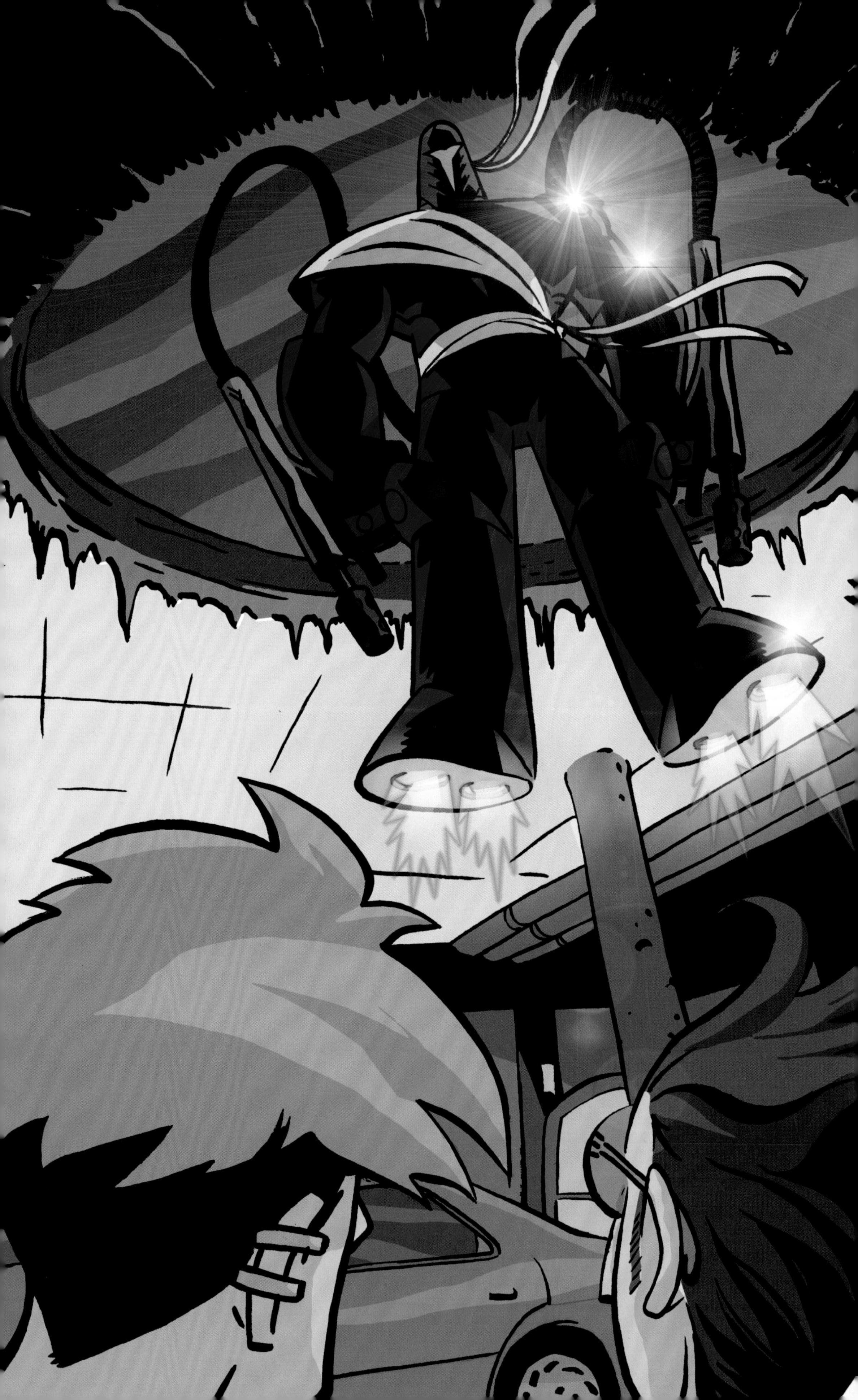

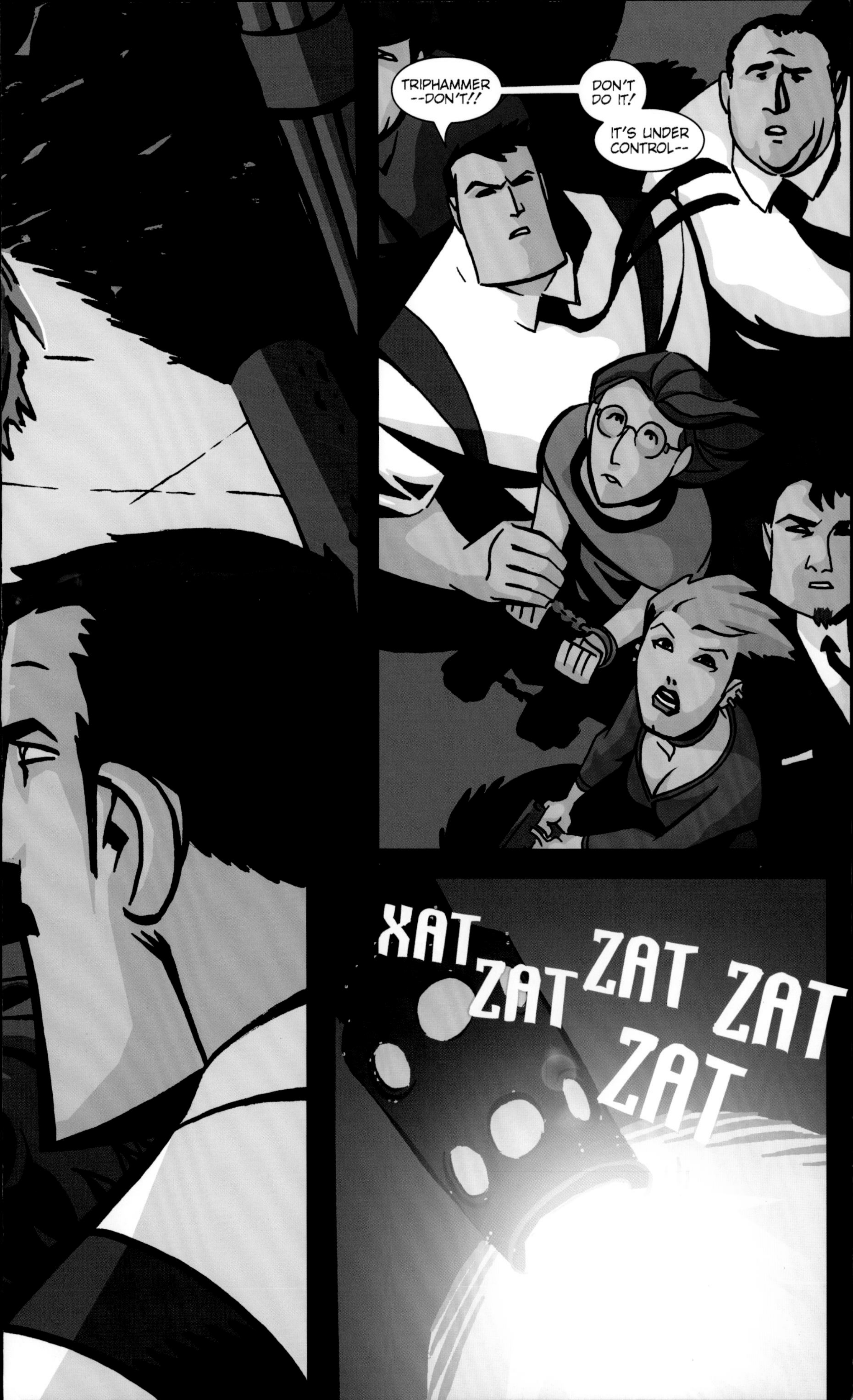
TRIPHAMMER --DON'T!!
DON'T DO IT!
IT'S UNDER CONTROL--
XAT
ZAT
ZAT ZAT
ZAT

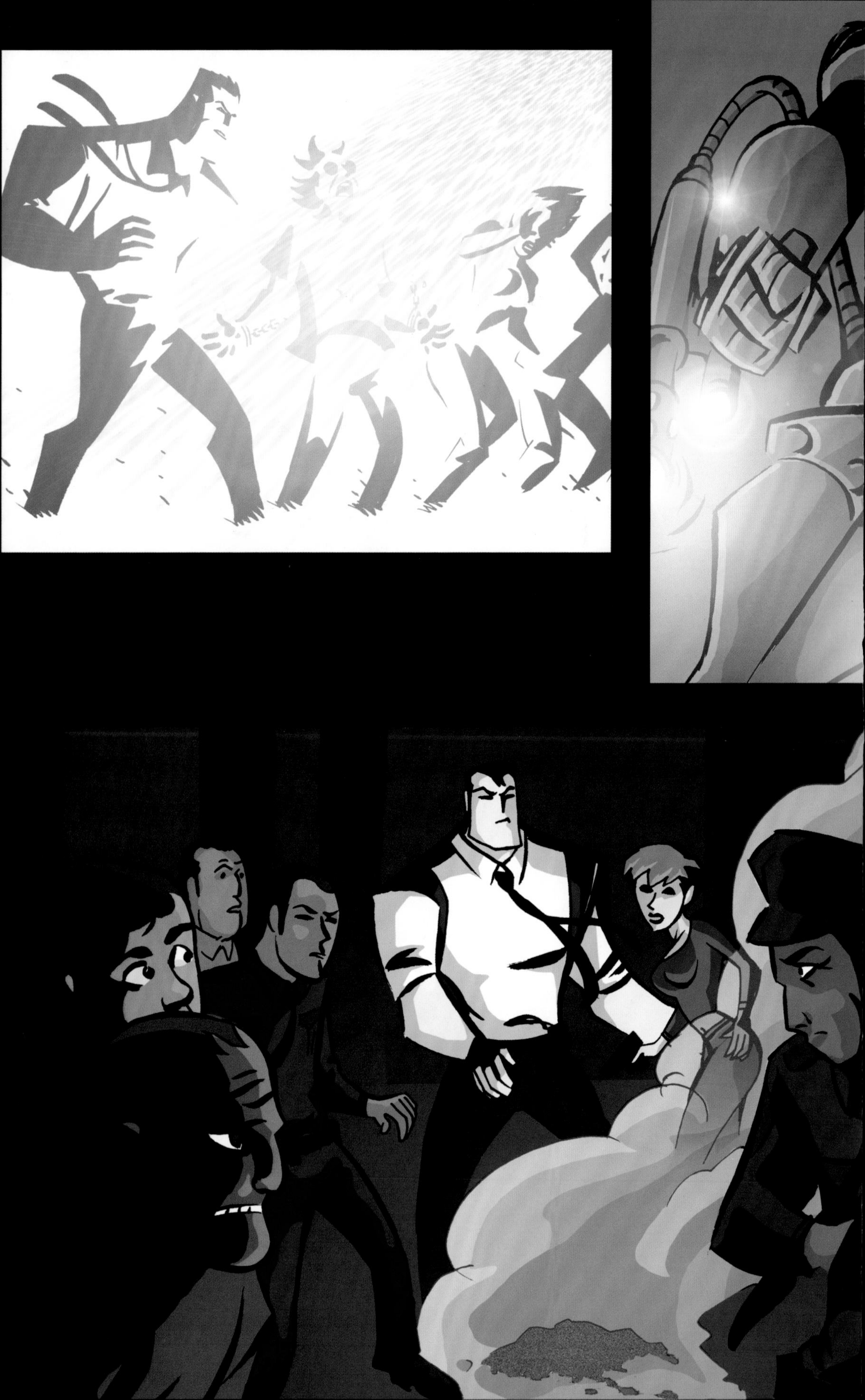

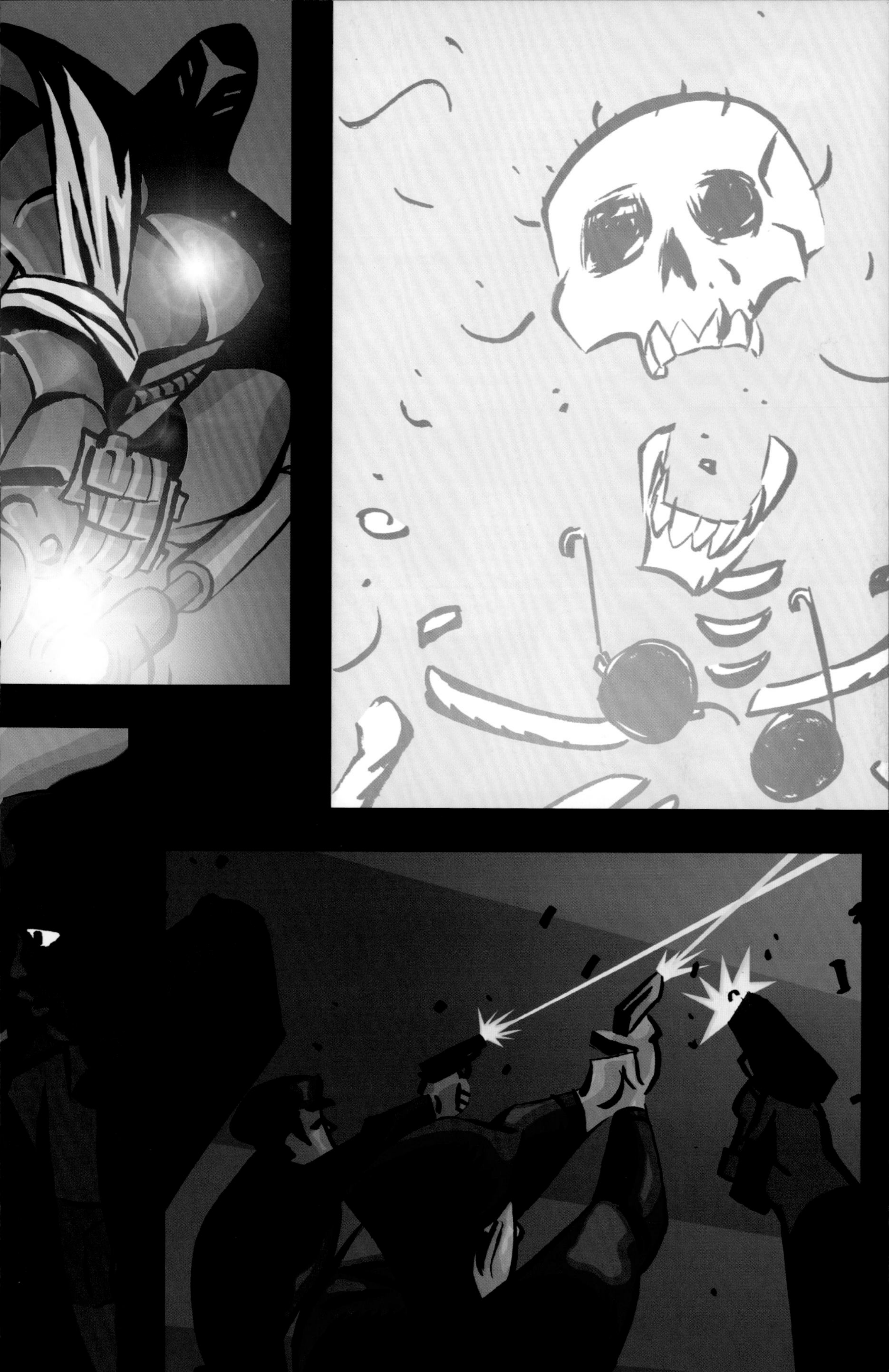

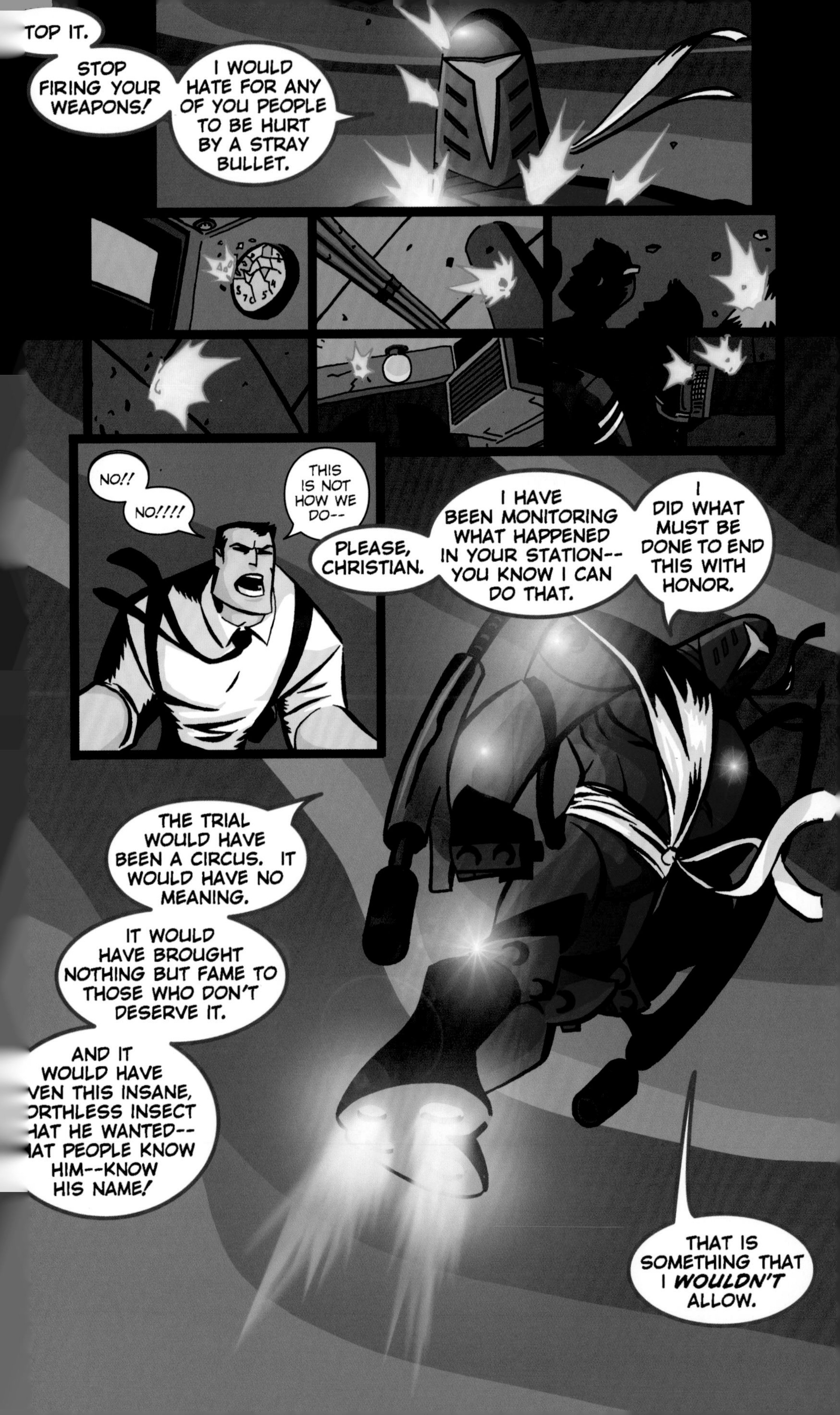
TOP IT.
STOP FIRING YOUR WEAPONS!
I WOULD HATE FOR ANY OF YOU PEOPLE TO BE HURT BY A STRAY BULLET.
NO!!
NO!!!!
THIS IS NOT HOW WE DO--
PLEASE, CHRISTIAN.
I HAVE BEEN MONITORING WHAT HAPPENED IN YOUR STATION-- YOU KNOW I CAN DO THAT.
I DID WHAT MUST BE DONE TO END THIS WITH HONOR.
THE TRIAL WOULD HAVE BEEN A CIRCUS. IT WOULD HAVE NO MEANING.
IT WOULD HAVE BROUGHT NOTHING BUT FAME TO THOSE WHO DON'T DESERVE IT.
AND IT WOULD HAVE
VEN THIS INSANE,
ORTHLESS INSECT
HAT HE WANTED--
HAT PEOPLE KNOW
HIM--KNOW
HIS NAME!
THAT IS SOMETHING THAT I *WOULDN'T* ALLOW.

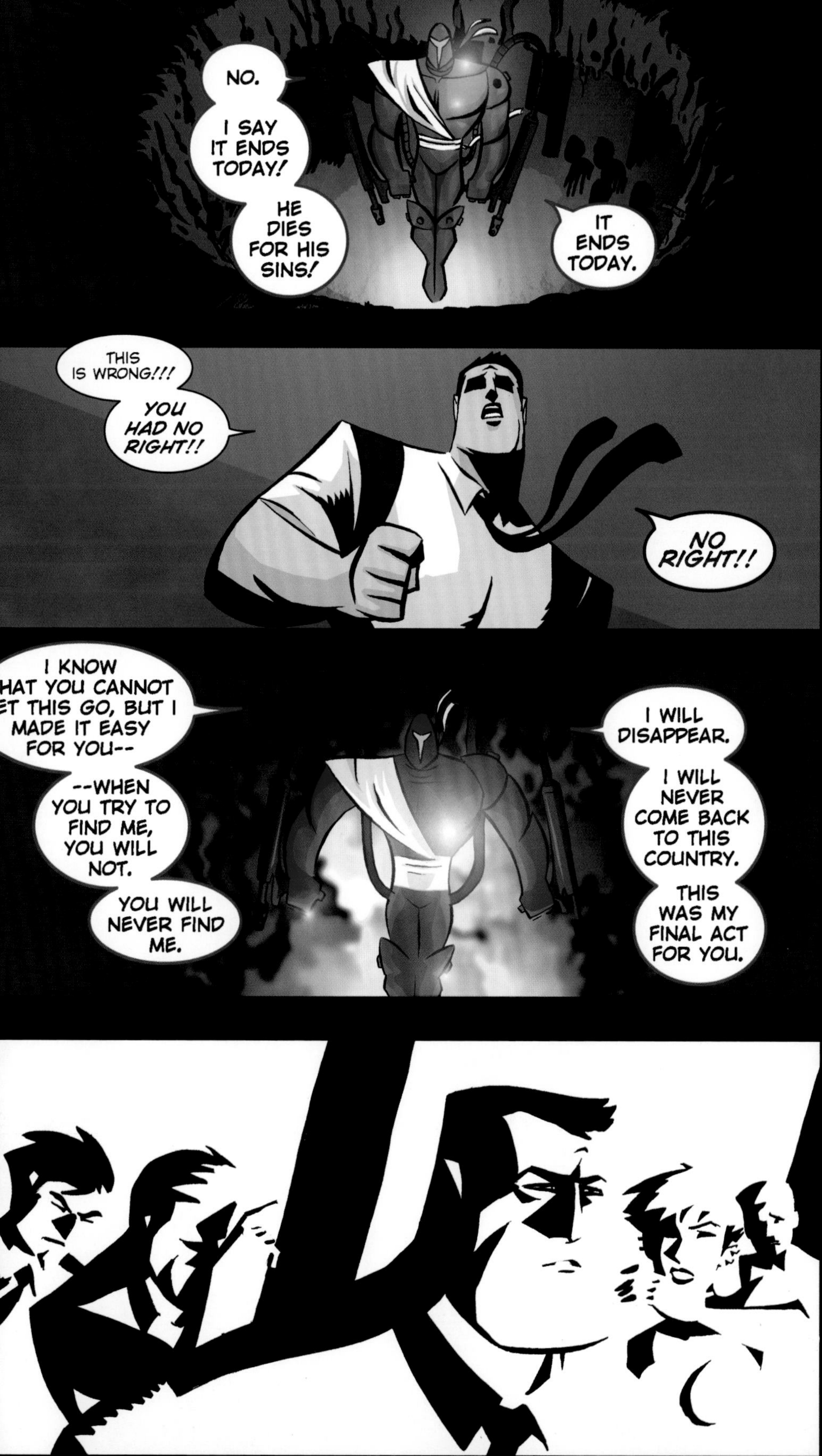
NO.
I SAY IT ENDS TODAY!
HE DIES FOR HIS SINS!
IT ENDS TODAY.
THIS IS WRONG!!!
YOU HAD NO RIGHT!!
NO RIGHT!!
I KNOW HAT YOU CANNOT ET THIS GO, BUT I MADE IT EASY FOR YOU--
--WHEN YOU TRY TO FIND ME, YOU WILL NOT.
YOU WILL NEVER FIND ME.
I WILL DISAPPEAR.
I WILL NEVER COME BACK TO THIS COUNTRY.
THIS WAS MY FINAL ACT FOR YOU.

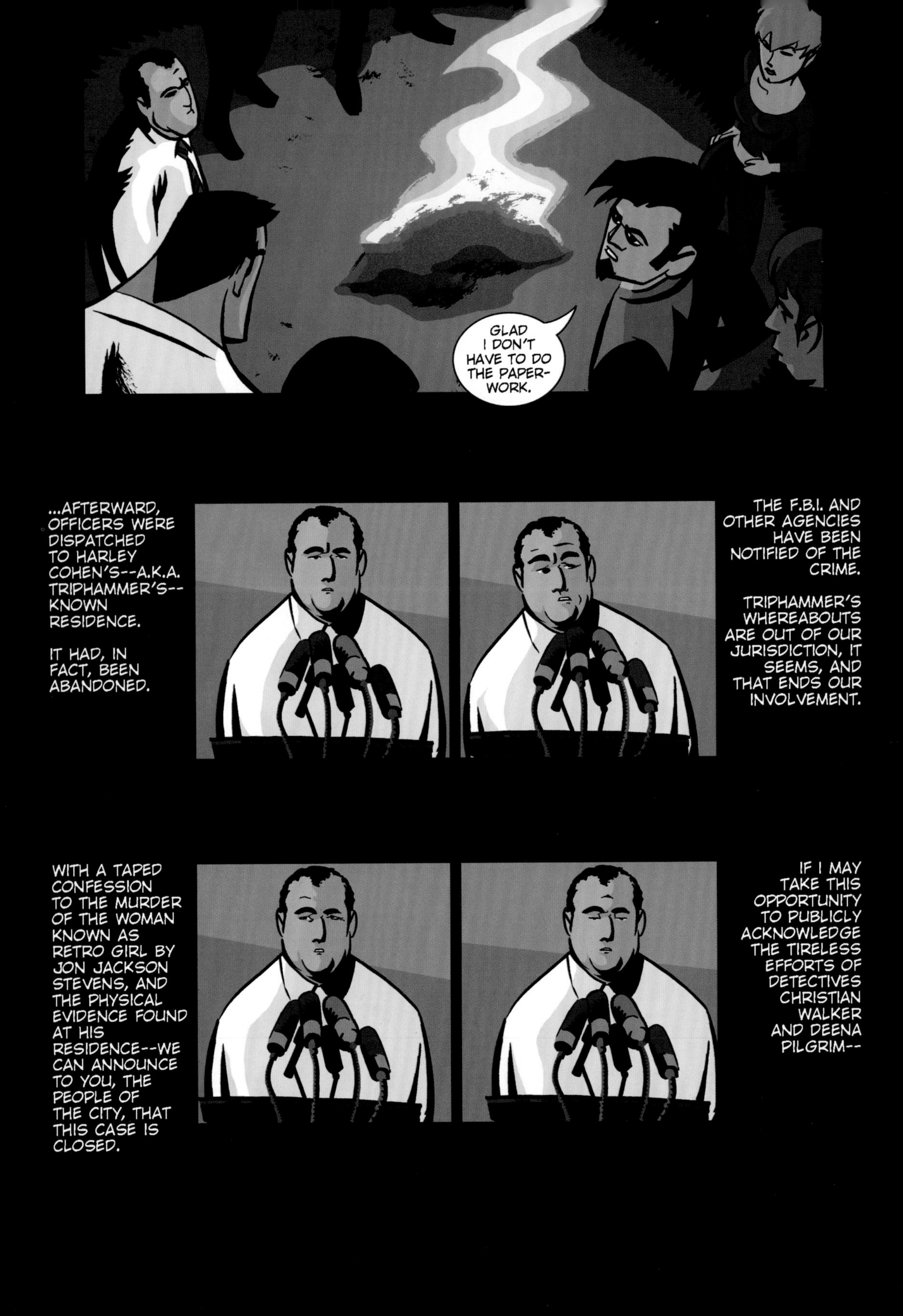
GLAD I DON'T HAVE TO DO THE PAPER-WORK.
...AFTERWARD, OFFICERS WERE DISPATCHED TO HARLEY COHEN'S--A.K.A. TRIPHAMMER'S--KNOWN RESIDENCE.
IT HAD, IN FACT, BEEN ABANDONED.
THE F.B.I. AND OTHER AGENCIES HAVE BEEN NOTIFIED OF THE CRIME.
TRIPHAMMER'S WHEREABOUTS ARE OUT OF OUR JURISDICTION, IT SEEMS, AND THAT ENDS OUR INVOLVEMENT.
WITH A TAPED CONFESSION TO THE MURDER OF THE WOMAN KNOWN AS RETRO GIRL BY JON JACKSON STEVENS, AND THE PHYSICAL EVIDENCE FOUND AT HIS RESIDENCE--WE CAN ANNOUNCE TO YOU, THE PEOPLE OF THE CITY, THAT THIS CASE IS CLOSED.
IF I MAY TAKE THIS OPPORTUNITY TO PUBLICLY ACKNOWLEDGE THE TIRELESS EFFORTS OF DETECTIVES CHRISTIAN WALKER AND DEENA PILGRIM--

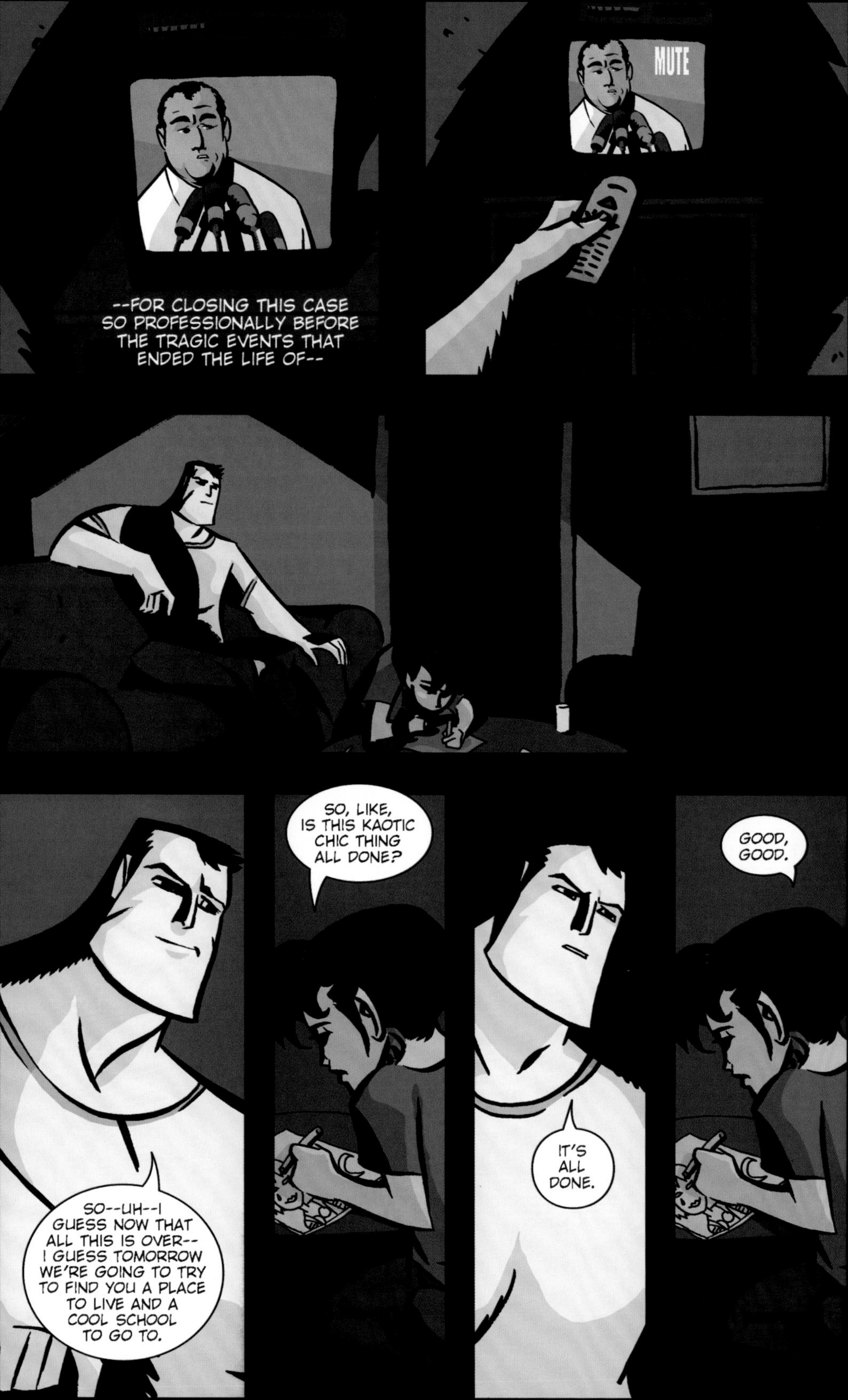
--FOR CLOSING THIS CASE SO PROFESSIONALLY BEFORE THE TRAGIC EVENTS THAT ENDED THE LIFE OF--
MUTE
SO--UH--I GUESS NOW THAT ALL THIS IS OVER--I GUESS TOMORROW WE'RE GOING TO TRY TO FIND YOU A PLACE TO LIVE AND A COOL SCHOOL TO GO TO.
SO, LIKE, IS THIS KAOTIC CHIC THING ALL DONE?
IT'S ALL DONE.
GOOD, GOOD.

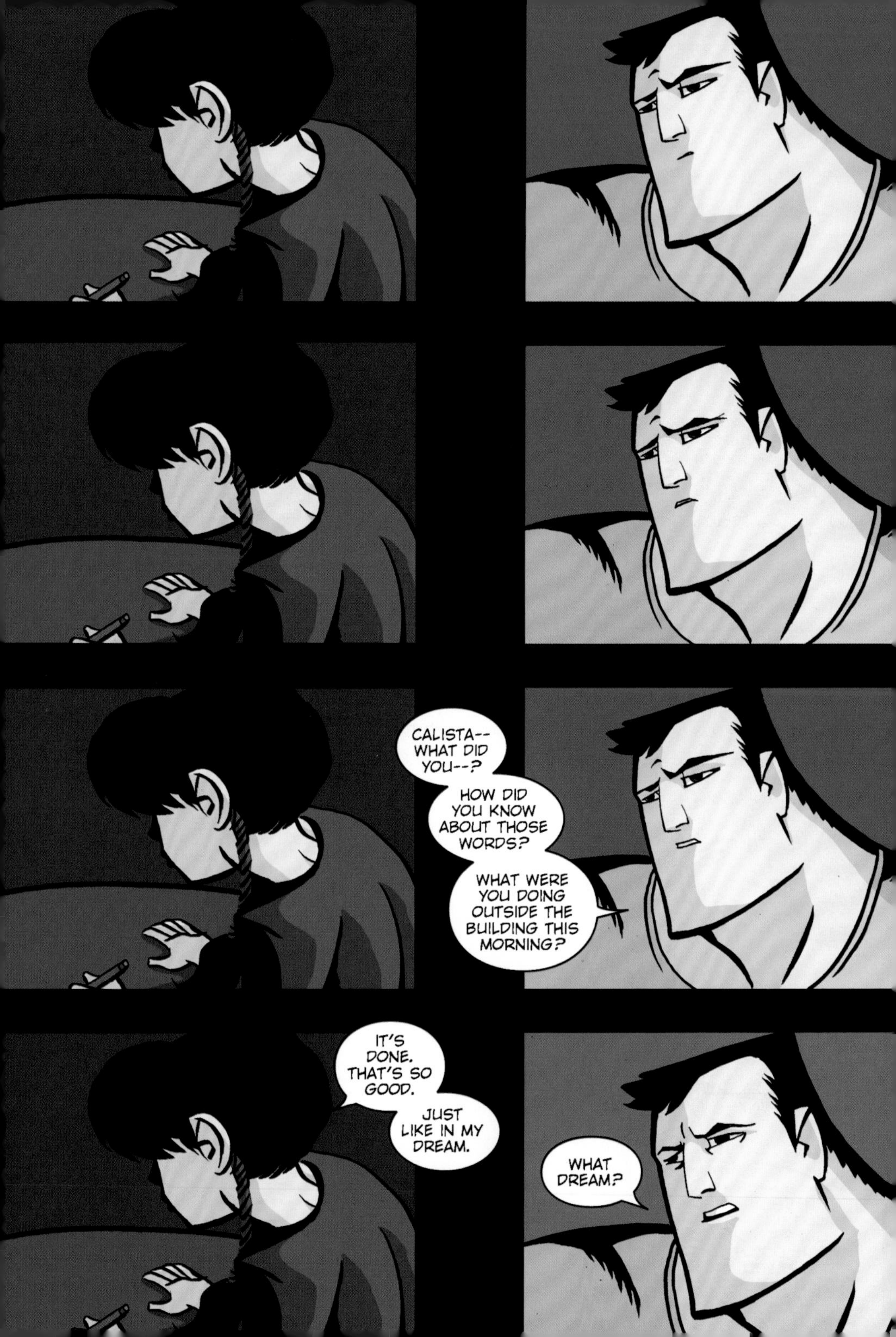
CALISTA-- WHAT DID YOU--?
HOW DID YOU KNOW ABOUT THOSE WORDS?
WHAT WERE YOU DOING OUTSIDE THE BUILDING THIS MORNING?
IT'S DONE. THAT'S SO GOOD.
JUST LIKE IN MY DREAM.
WHAT DREAM?

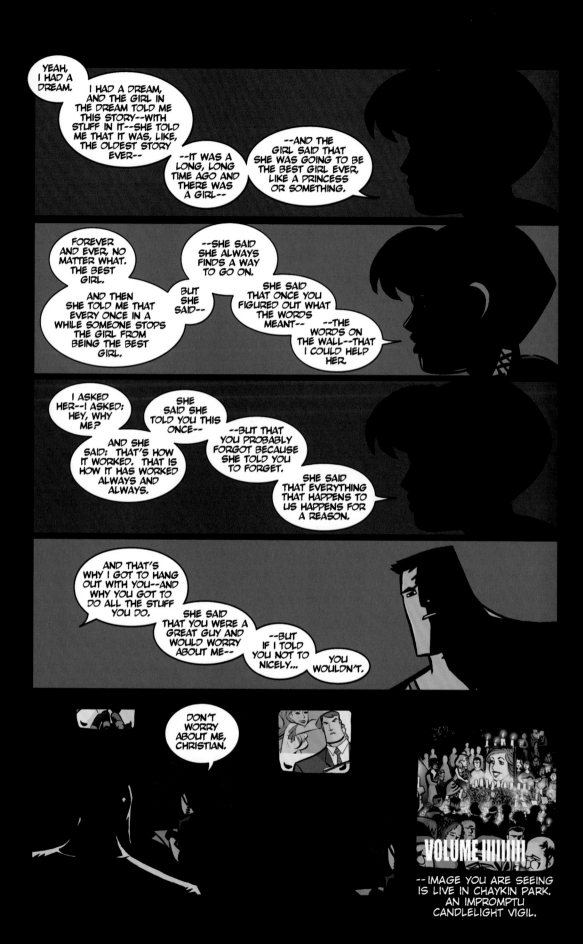

YEAH, I HAD A DREAM.

I HAD A DREAM, AND THE GIRL IN THE DREAM TOLD ME THIS STORY--WITH STUFF IN IT--SHE TOLD ME THAT IT WAS, LIKE, THE OLDEST STORY EVER--

--IT WAS A LONG, LONG TIME AGO AND THERE WAS A GIRL--

--AND THE GIRL SAID THAT SHE WAS GOING TO BE THE BEST GIRL EVER, LIKE A PRINCESS OR SOMETHING.

FOREVER AND EVER, NO MATTER WHAT. THE BEST GIRL.

AND THEN SHE TOLD ME THAT EVERY ONCE IN A WHILE SOMEONE STOPS THE GIRL FROM BEING THE BEST GIRL.

BUT SHE SAID--

--SHE SAID SHE ALWAYS FINDS A WAY TO GO ON.

SHE SAID THAT ONCE YOU FIGURED OUT WHAT THE WORDS MEANT--

--THE WORDS ON THE WALL--THAT I COULD HELP HER.

I ASKED HER--I ASKED: HEY, WHY ME?

SHE SAID SHE TOLD YOU THIS ONCE--

AND SHE SAID: THAT'S HOW IT WORKED. THAT IS HOW IT HAS WORKED ALWAYS AND ALWAYS.

--BUT THAT YOU PROBABLY FORGOT BECAUSE SHE TOLD YOU TO FORGET.

SHE SAID THAT EVERYTHING THAT HAPPENS TO US HAPPENS FOR A REASON.

AND THAT'S WHY I GOT TO HANG OUT WITH YOU--AND WHY YOU GOT TO DO ALL THE STUFF YOU DO.

SHE SAID THAT YOU WERE A GREAT GUY AND WOULD WORRY ABOUT ME--

--BUT IF I TOLD YOU NOT TO NICELY...

YOU WOULDN'T.

DON'T WORRY ABOUT ME, CHRISTIAN.

VOLUME IIIIIIIII

--IMAGE YOU ARE SEEING IS LIVE IN CHAYKIN PARK. AN IMPROMPTU CANDLELIGHT VIGIL.

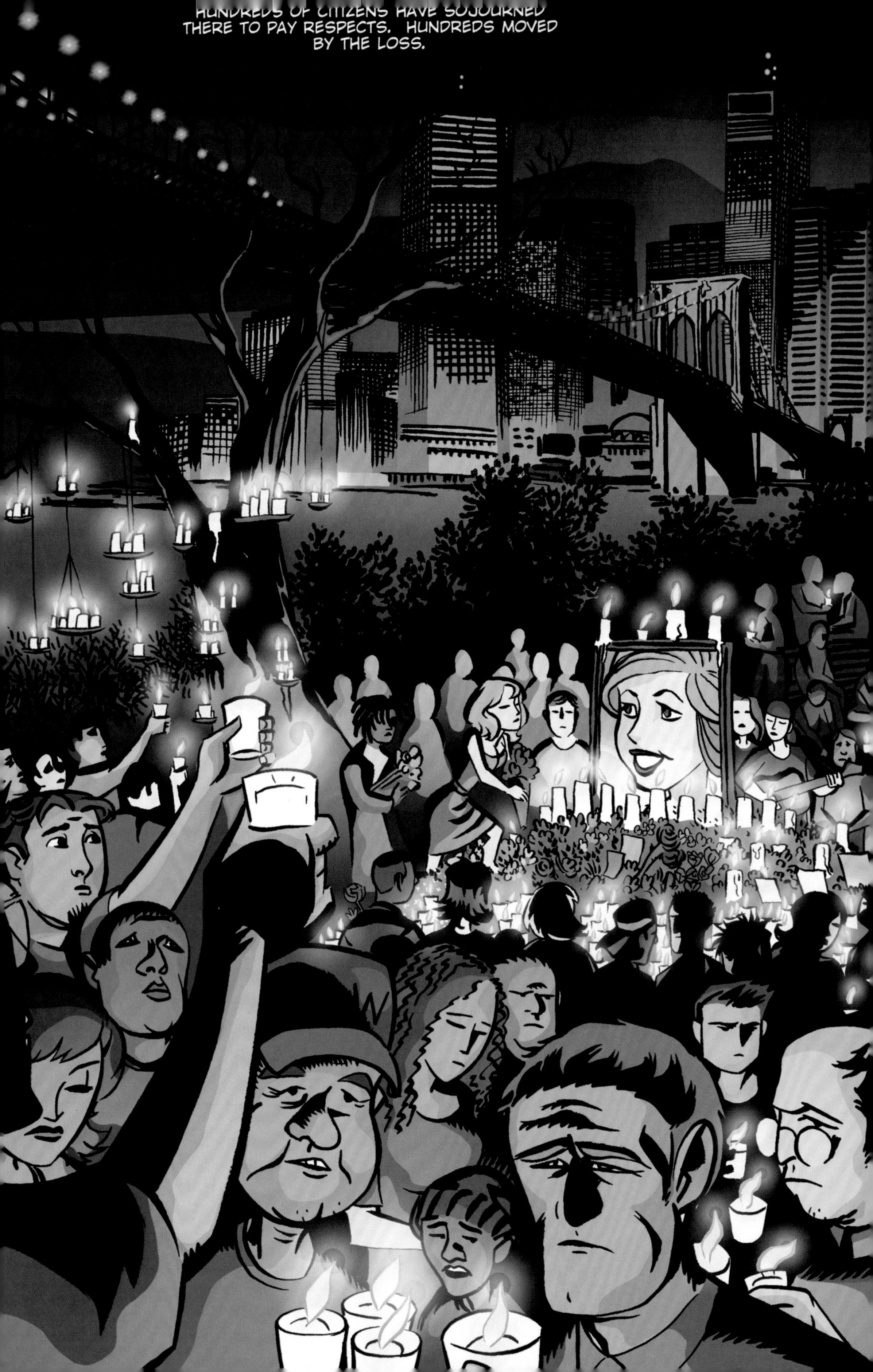
HUNDREDS OF CITIZENS HAVE SOJOURNED THERE TO PAY RESPECTS. HUNDREDS MOVED BY THE LOSS.

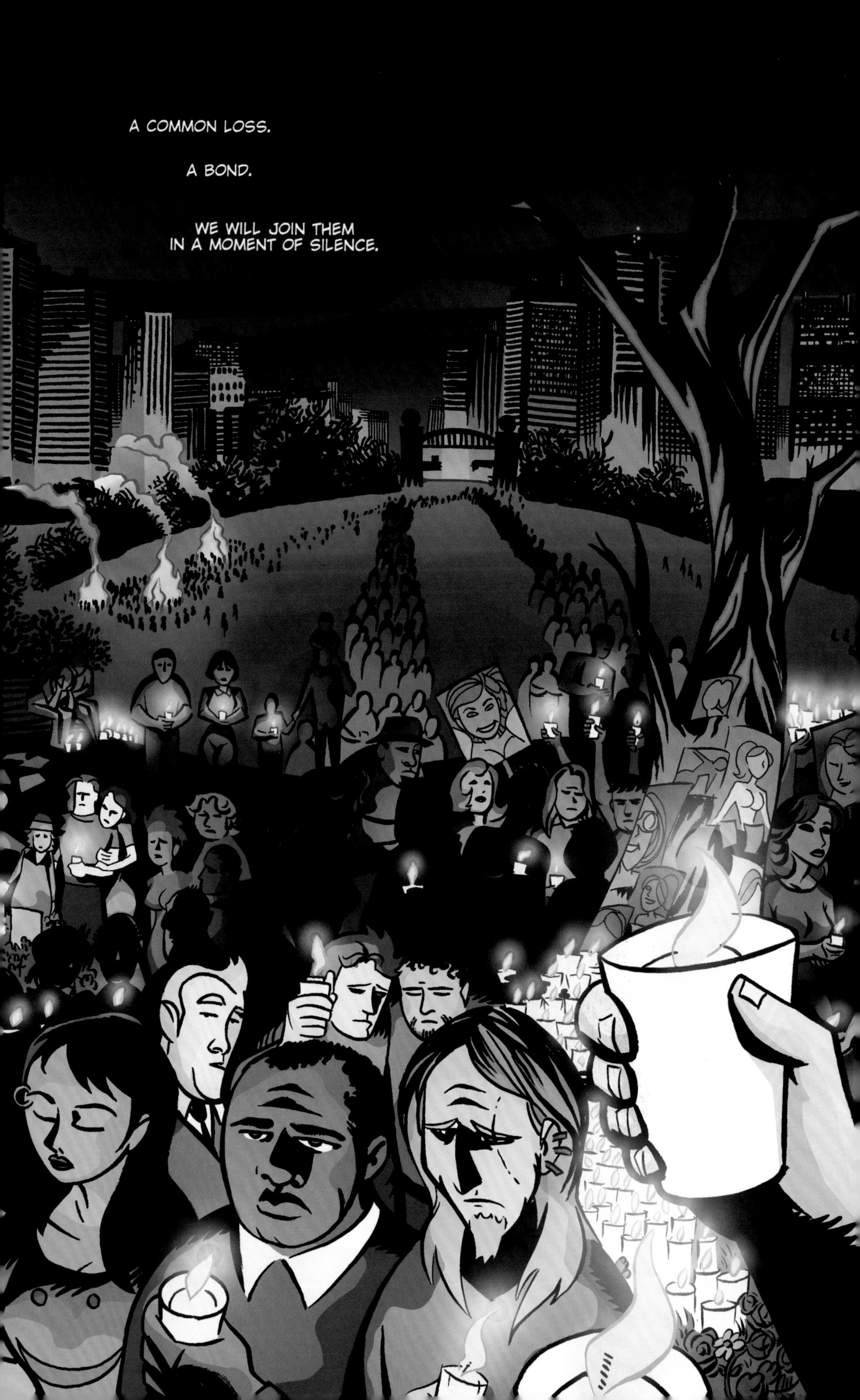
A COMMON LOSS.
A BOND.
WE WILL JOIN THEM IN A MOMENT OF SILENCE.

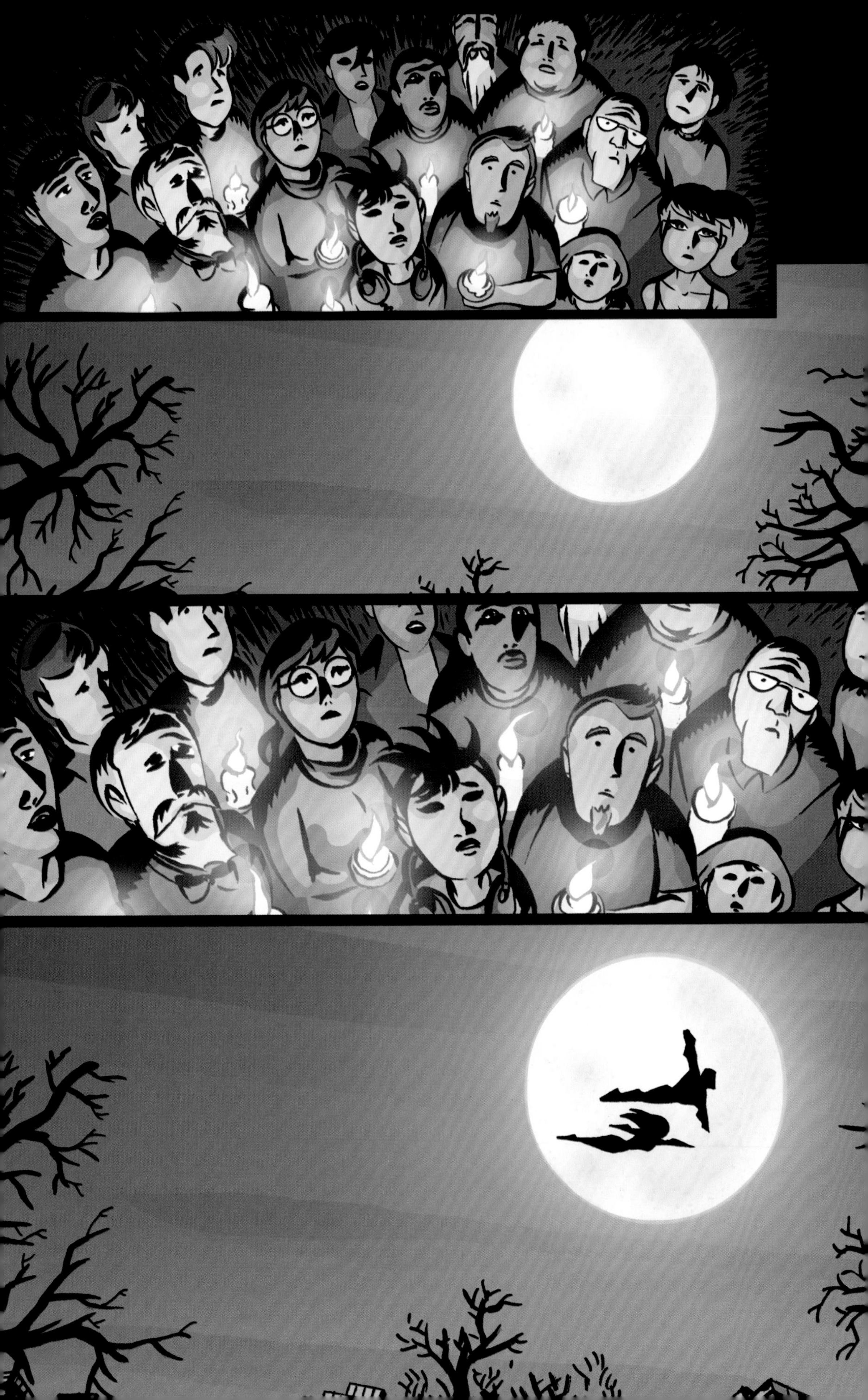

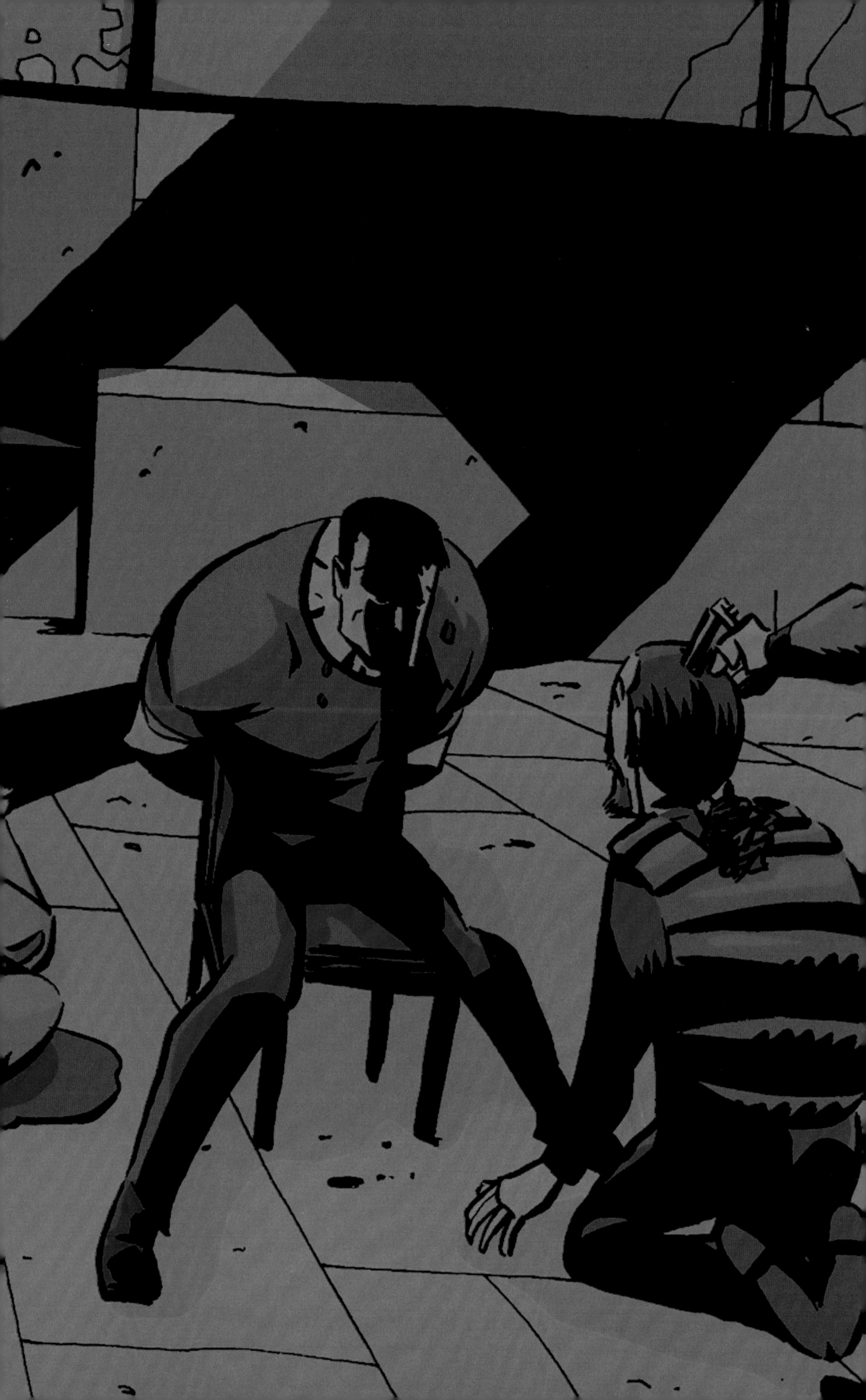

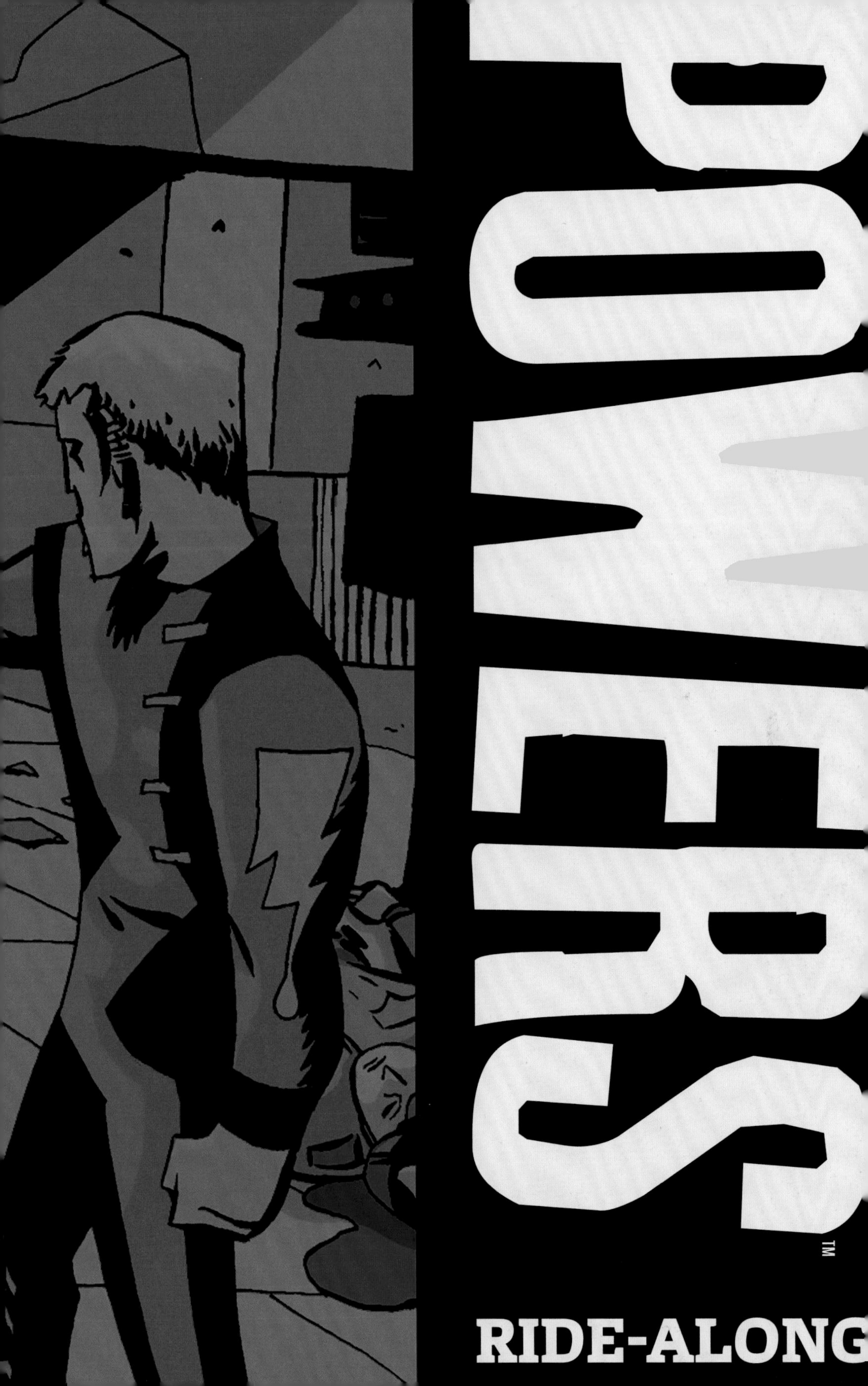

POWERS™

RIDE-ALONG

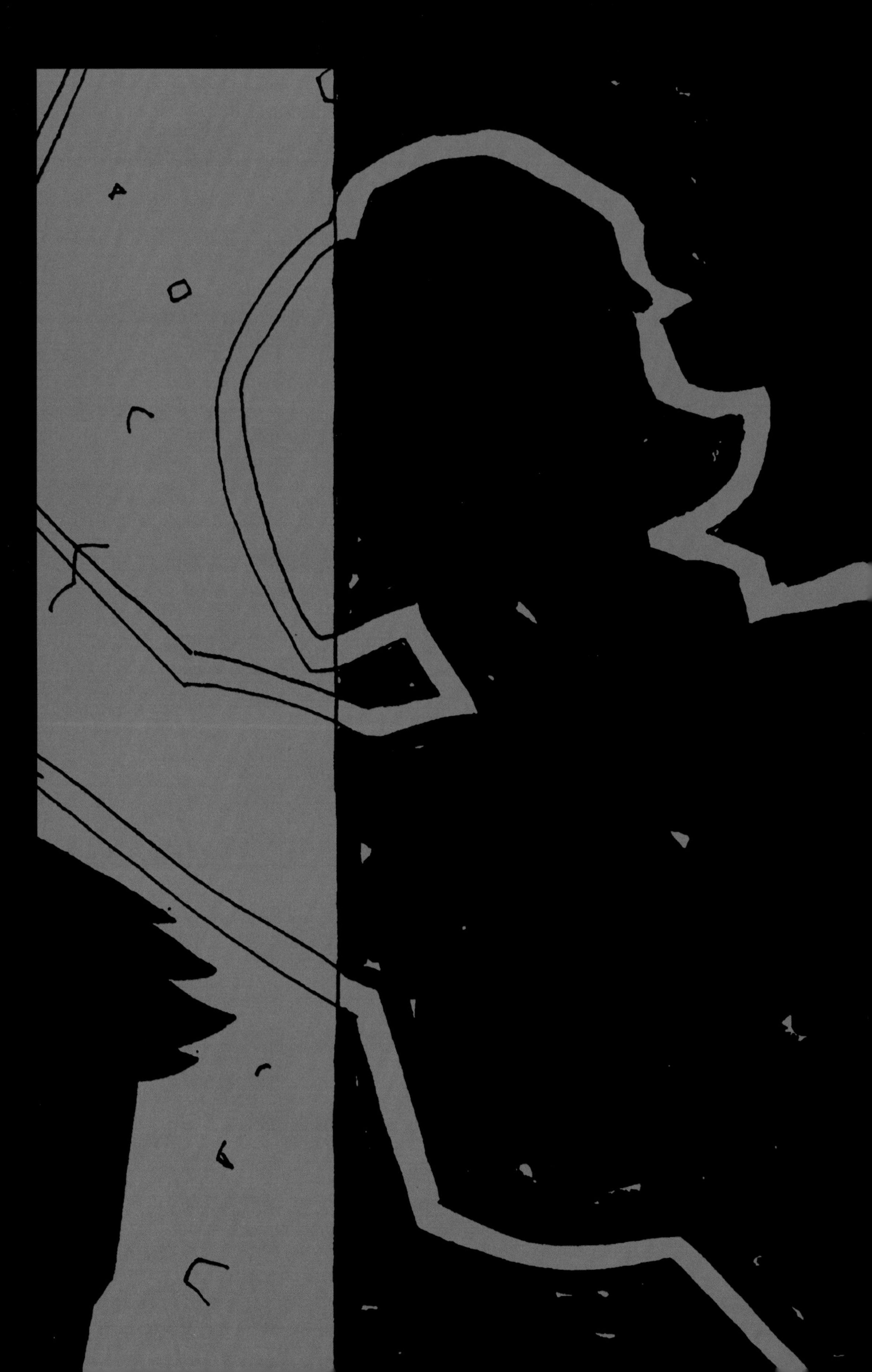

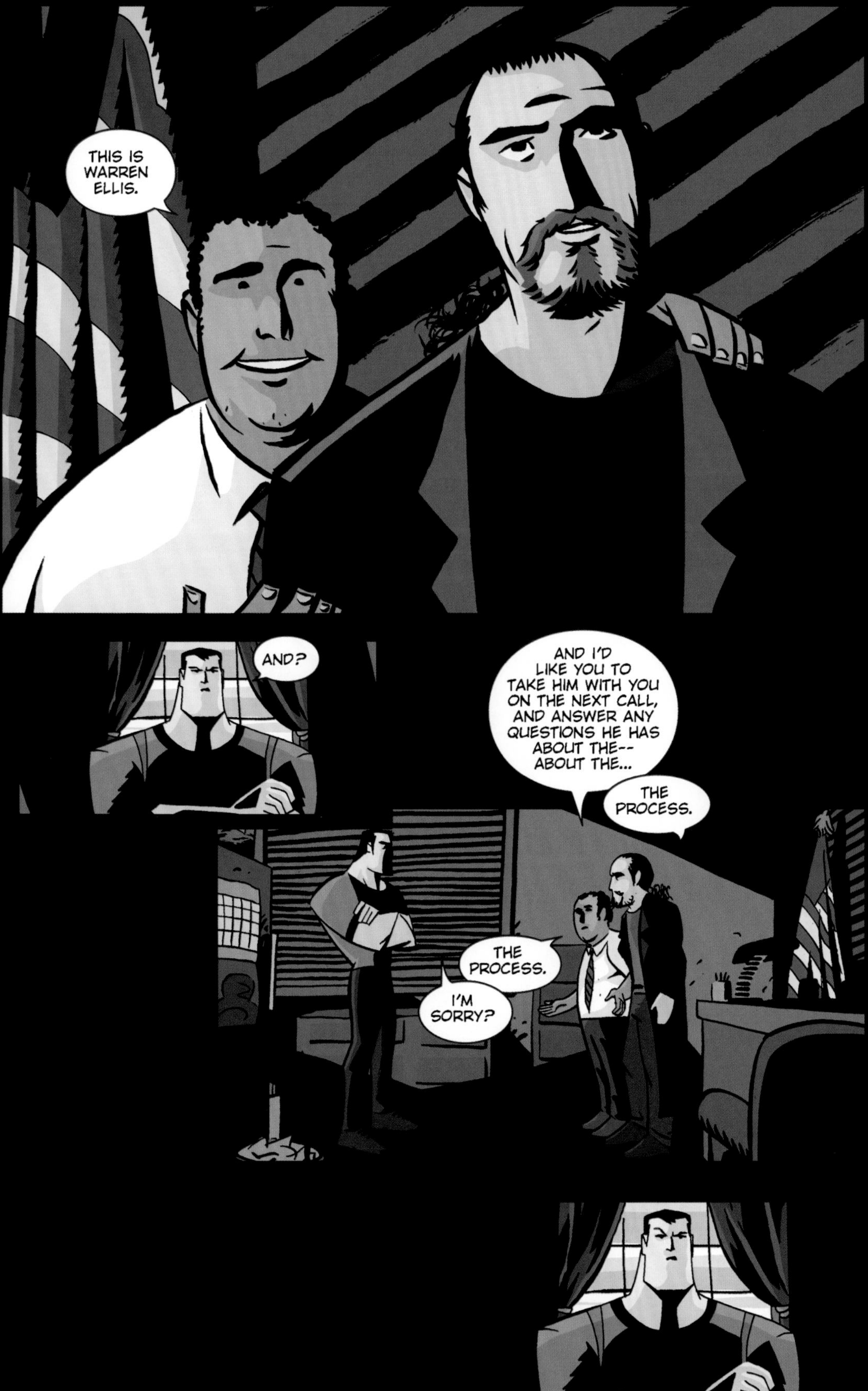
THIS IS WARREN ELLIS.
AND?
AND I'D LIKE YOU TO TAKE HIM WITH YOU ON THE NEXT CALL, AND ANSWER ANY QUESTIONS HE HAS ABOUT THE-- ABOUT THE...
THE PROCESS.
THE PROCESS.
I'M SORRY?

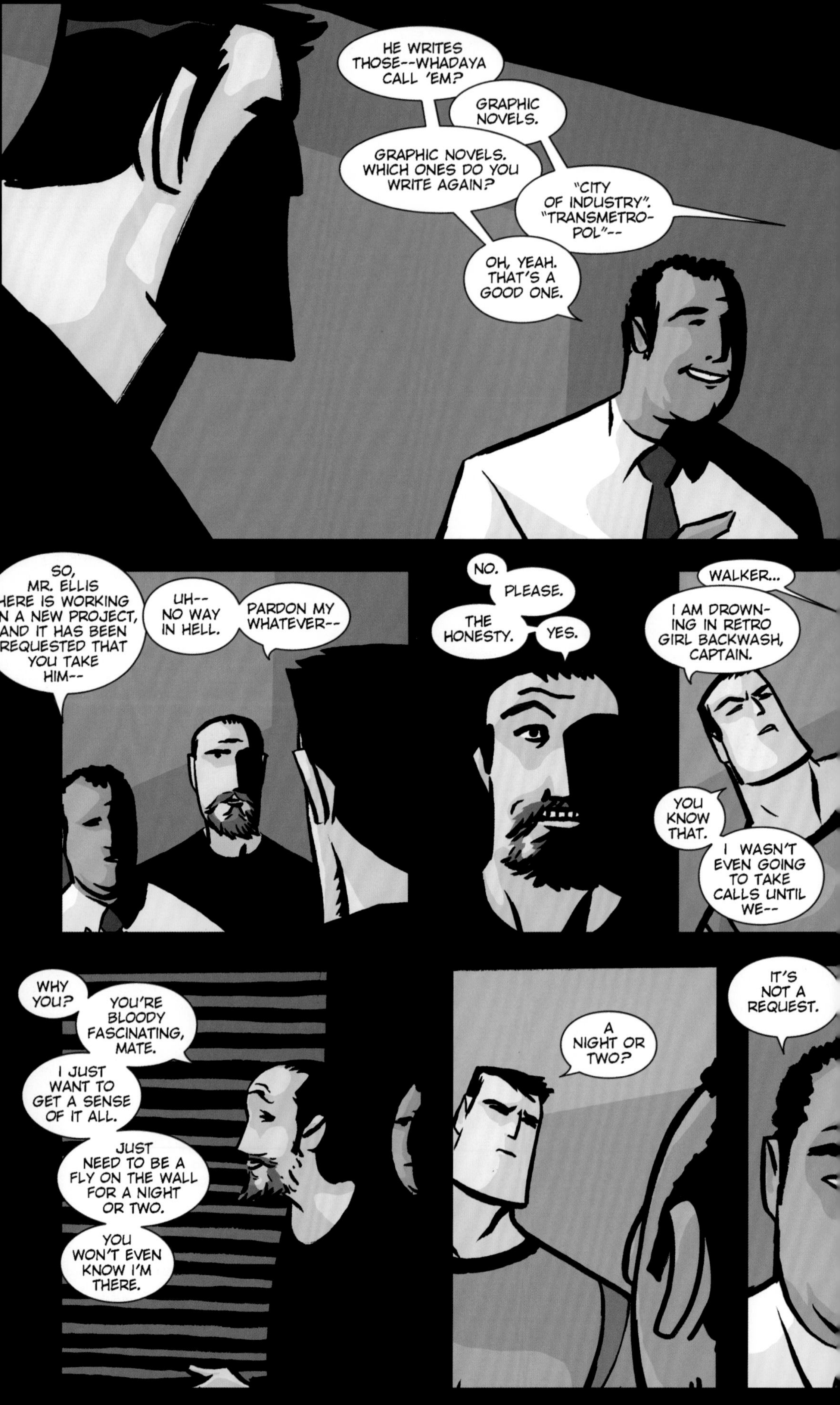
HE WRITES THOSE--WHADAYA CALL 'EM?
GRAPHIC NOVELS.
GRAPHIC NOVELS. WHICH ONES DO YOU WRITE AGAIN?
"CITY OF INDUSTRY". "TRANSMETROPOL"--
OH, YEAH. THAT'S A GOOD ONE.
SO, MR. ELLIS HERE IS WORKING ON A NEW PROJECT, AND IT HAS BEEN REQUESTED THAT YOU TAKE HIM--
UH-- NO WAY IN HELL.
PARDON MY WHATEVER--
NO.
PLEASE.
THE HONESTY.
YES.
WALKER...
I AM DROWNING IN RETRO GIRL BACKWASH, CAPTAIN.
YOU KNOW THAT.
I WASN'T EVEN GOING TO TAKE CALLS UNTIL WE--
WHY YOU?
YOU'RE BLOODY FASCINATING, MATE.
I JUST WANT TO GET A SENSE OF IT ALL.
JUST NEED TO BE A FLY ON THE WALL FOR A NIGHT OR TWO.
YOU WON'T EVEN KNOW I'M THERE.
A NIGHT OR TWO?
IT'S NOT A REQUEST.

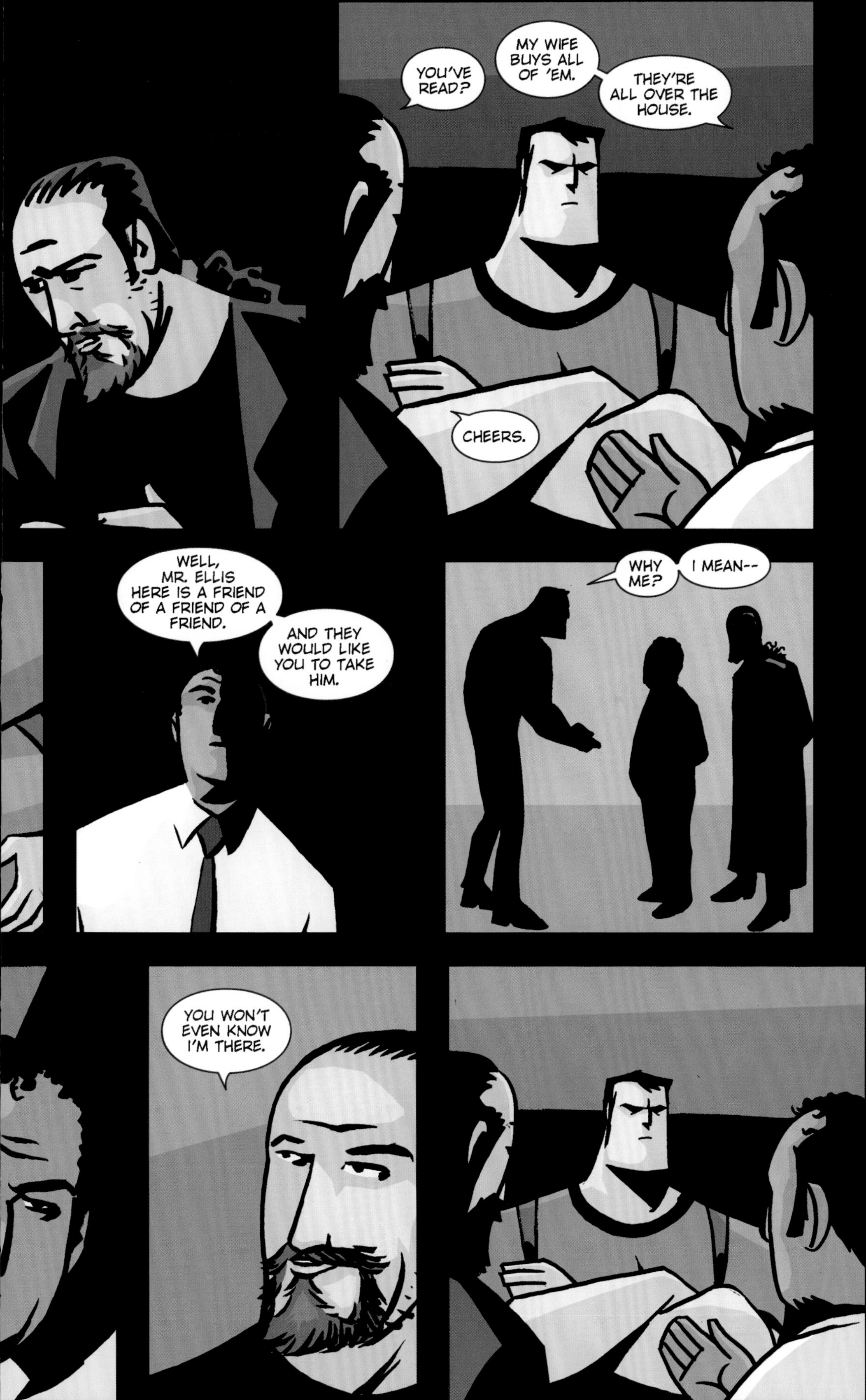
YOU'VE READ?
MY WIFE BUYS ALL OF 'EM.
THEY'RE ALL OVER THE HOUSE.
CHEERS.
WELL, MR. ELLIS HERE IS A FRIEND OF A FRIEND OF A FRIEND.
AND THEY WOULD LIKE YOU TO TAKE HIM.
WHY ME?
I MEAN--
YOU WON'T EVEN KNOW I'M THERE.

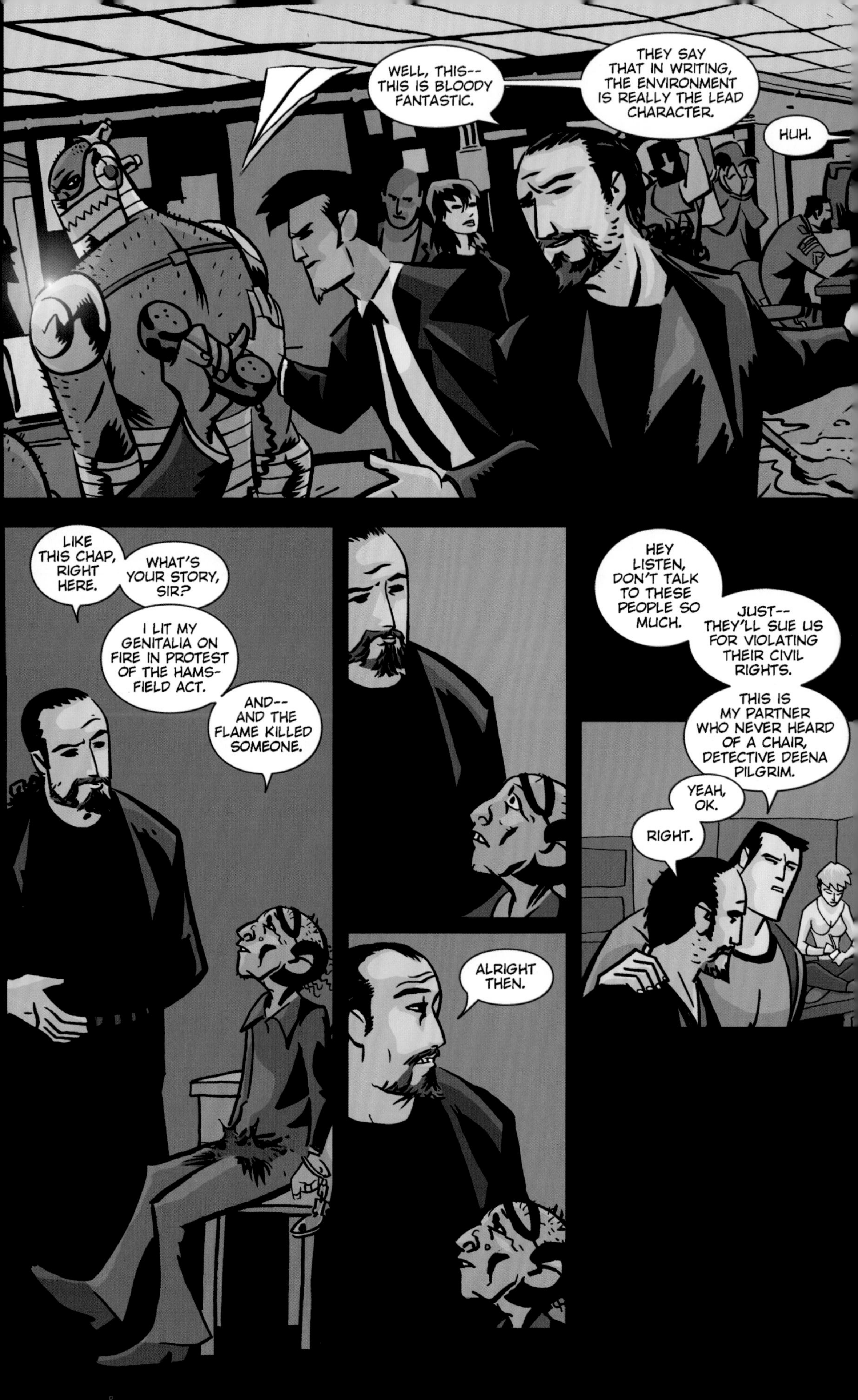
WELL, THIS-- THIS IS BLOODY FANTASTIC.
THEY SAY THAT IN WRITING, THE ENVIRONMENT IS REALLY THE LEAD CHARACTER.
HUH.
LIKE THIS CHAP, RIGHT HERE.
WHAT'S YOUR STORY, SIR?
I LIT MY GENITALIA ON FIRE IN PROTEST OF THE HAMS-FIELD ACT.
AND-- AND THE FLAME KILLED SOMEONE.
ALRIGHT THEN.
HEY LISTEN, DON'T TALK TO THESE PEOPLE SO MUCH.
JUST-- THEY'LL SUE US FOR VIOLATING THEIR CIVIL RIGHTS.
THIS IS MY PARTNER WHO NEVER HEARD OF A CHAIR, DETECTIVE DEENA PILGRIM.
YEAH, OK.
RIGHT.

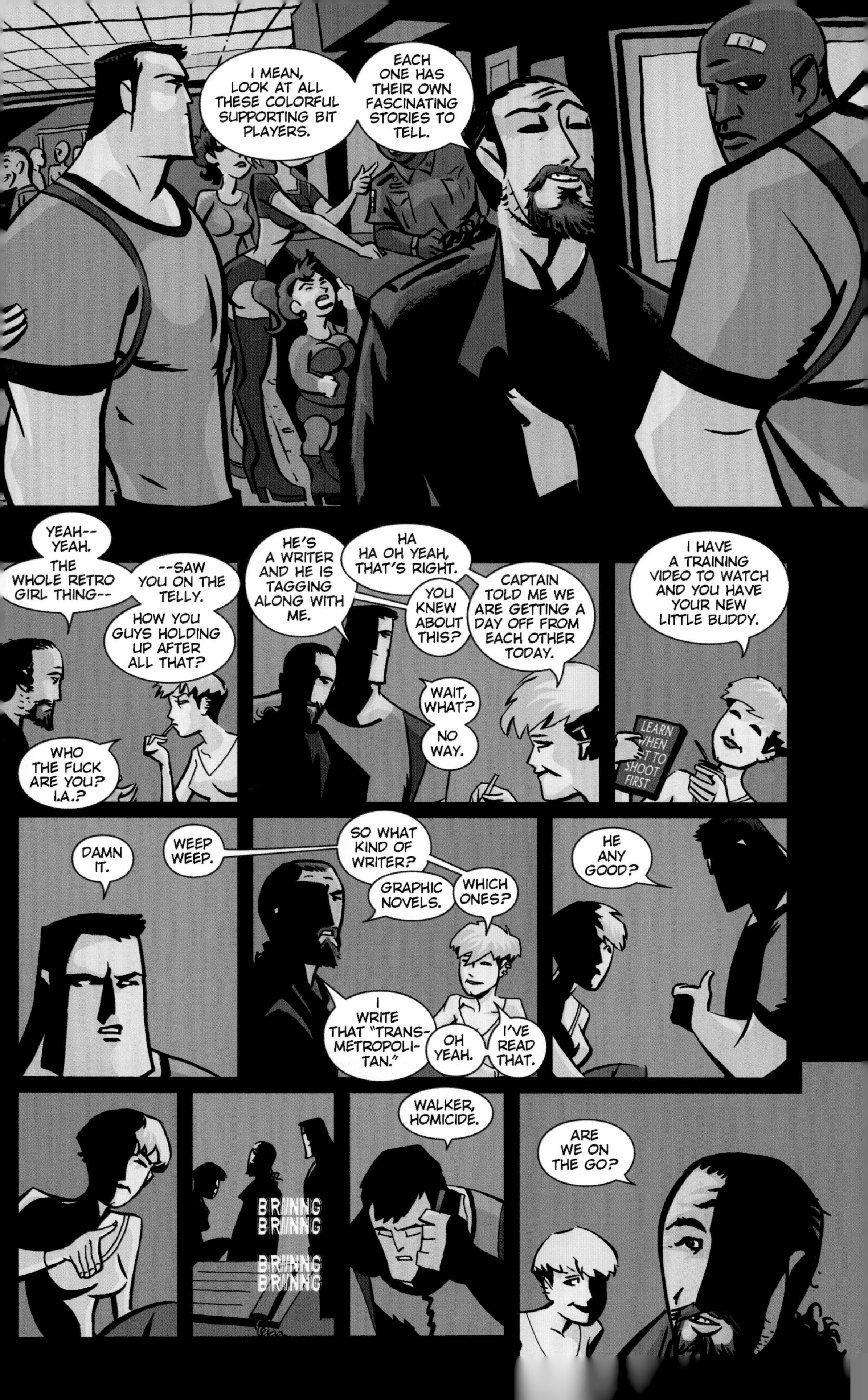
I MEAN, LOOK AT ALL THESE COLORFUL SUPPORTING BIT PLAYERS.
EACH ONE HAS THEIR OWN FASCINATING STORIES TO TELL.
YEAH-- YEAH.
THE WHOLE RETRO GIRL THING--
--SAW YOU ON THE TELLY.
HOW YOU GUYS HOLDING UP AFTER ALL THAT?
WHO THE FUCK ARE YOU? I.A.?
HE'S A WRITER AND HE IS TAGGING ALONG WITH ME.
HA HA OH YEAH, THAT'S RIGHT.
YOU KNEW ABOUT THIS?
CAPTAIN TOLD ME WE ARE GETTING A DAY OFF FROM EACH OTHER TODAY.
WAIT, WHAT?
NO WAY.
I HAVE A TRAINING VIDEO TO WATCH AND YOU HAVE YOUR NEW LITTLE BUDDY.
LEARN WHEN T TO SHOOT FIRST
DAMN IT.
WEEP WEEP.
SO WHAT KIND OF WRITER?
GRAPHIC NOVELS.
WHICH ONES?
I WRITE THAT "TRANS-METROPOLI-TAN."
OH YEAH.
I'VE READ THAT.
HE ANY GOOD?
BRIINNG BRIINNG
BRIINNG BRIINNG
WALKER, HOMICIDE.
ARE WE ON THE GO?

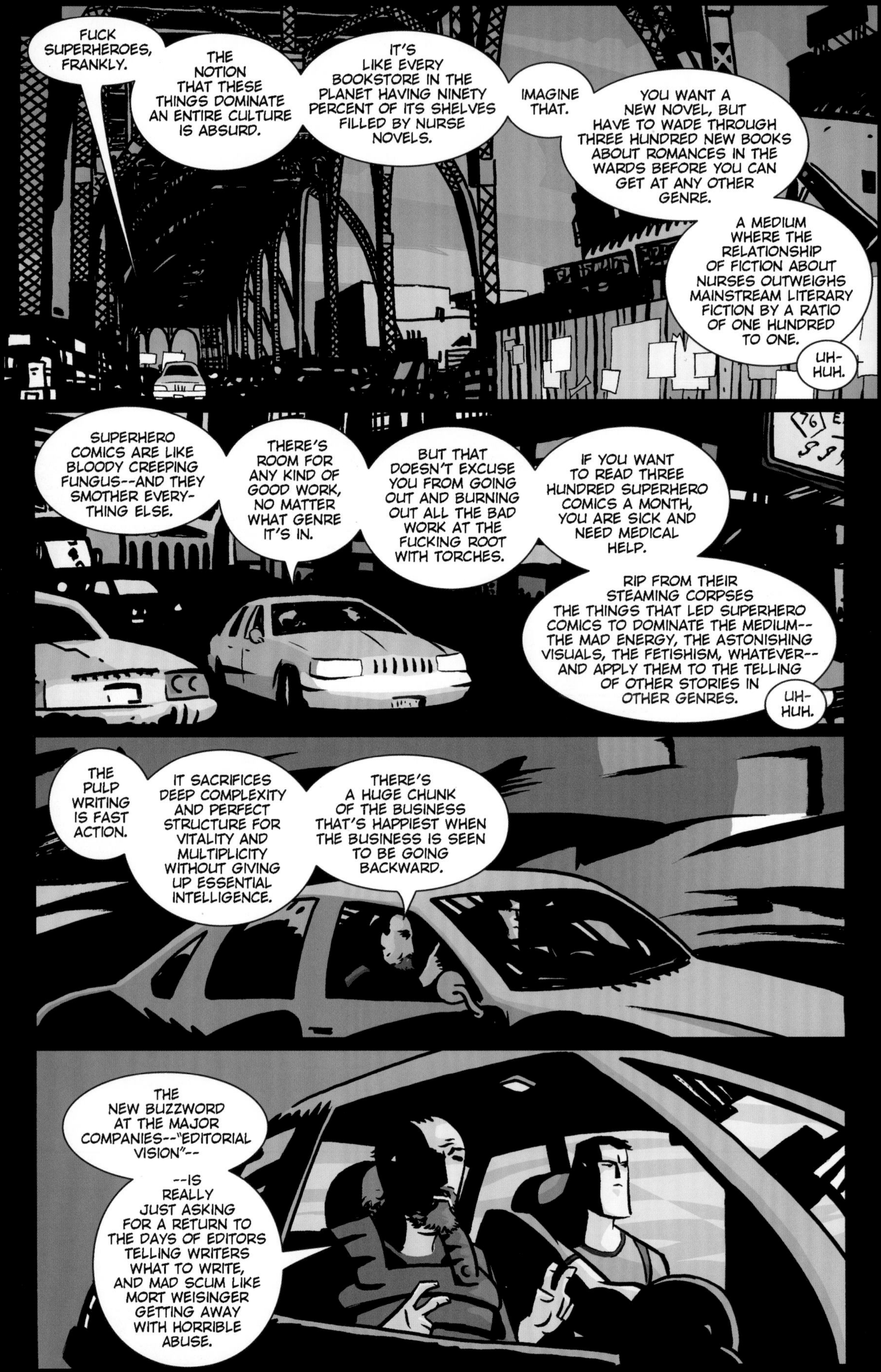
FUCK SUPERHEROES, FRANKLY.
THE NOTION THAT THESE THINGS DOMINATE AN ENTIRE CULTURE IS ABSURD.
IT'S LIKE EVERY BOOKSTORE IN THE PLANET HAVING NINETY PERCENT OF ITS SHELVES FILLED BY NURSE NOVELS.
IMAGINE THAT.
YOU WANT A NEW NOVEL, BUT HAVE TO WADE THROUGH THREE HUNDRED NEW BOOKS ABOUT ROMANCES IN THE WARDS BEFORE YOU CAN GET AT ANY OTHER GENRE.
A MEDIUM WHERE THE RELATIONSHIP OF FICTION ABOUT NURSES OUTWEIGHS MAINSTREAM LITERARY FICTION BY A RATIO OF ONE HUNDRED TO ONE.
UH-HUH.
SUPERHERO COMICS ARE LIKE BLOODY CREEPING FUNGUS--AND THEY SMOTHER EVERY-THING ELSE.
THERE'S ROOM FOR ANY KIND OF GOOD WORK, NO MATTER WHAT GENRE IT'S IN.
BUT THAT DOESN'T EXCUSE YOU FROM GOING OUT AND BURNING OUT ALL THE BAD WORK AT THE FUCKING ROOT WITH TORCHES.
IF YOU WANT TO READ THREE HUNDRED SUPERHERO COMICS A MONTH, YOU ARE SICK AND NEED MEDICAL HELP.
RIP FROM THEIR STEAMING CORPSES THE THINGS THAT LED SUPERHERO COMICS TO DOMINATE THE MEDIUM--THE MAD ENERGY, THE ASTONISHING VISUALS, THE FETISHISM, WHATEVER--AND APPLY THEM TO THE TELLING OF OTHER STORIES IN OTHER GENRES.
UH-HUH.
THE PULP WRITING IS FAST ACTION.
IT SACRIFICES DEEP COMPLEXITY AND PERFECT STRUCTURE FOR VITALITY AND MULTIPLICITY WITHOUT GIVING UP ESSENTIAL INTELLIGENCE.
THERE'S A HUGE CHUNK OF THE BUSINESS THAT'S HAPPIEST WHEN THE BUSINESS IS SEEN TO BE GOING BACKWARD.
THE NEW BUZZWORD AT THE MAJOR COMPANIES--"EDITORIAL VISION"--
--IS REALLY JUST ASKING FOR A RETURN TO THE DAYS OF EDITORS TELLING WRITERS WHAT TO WRITE, AND MAD SCUM LIKE MORT WEISINGER GETTING AWAY WITH HORRIBLE ABUSE.

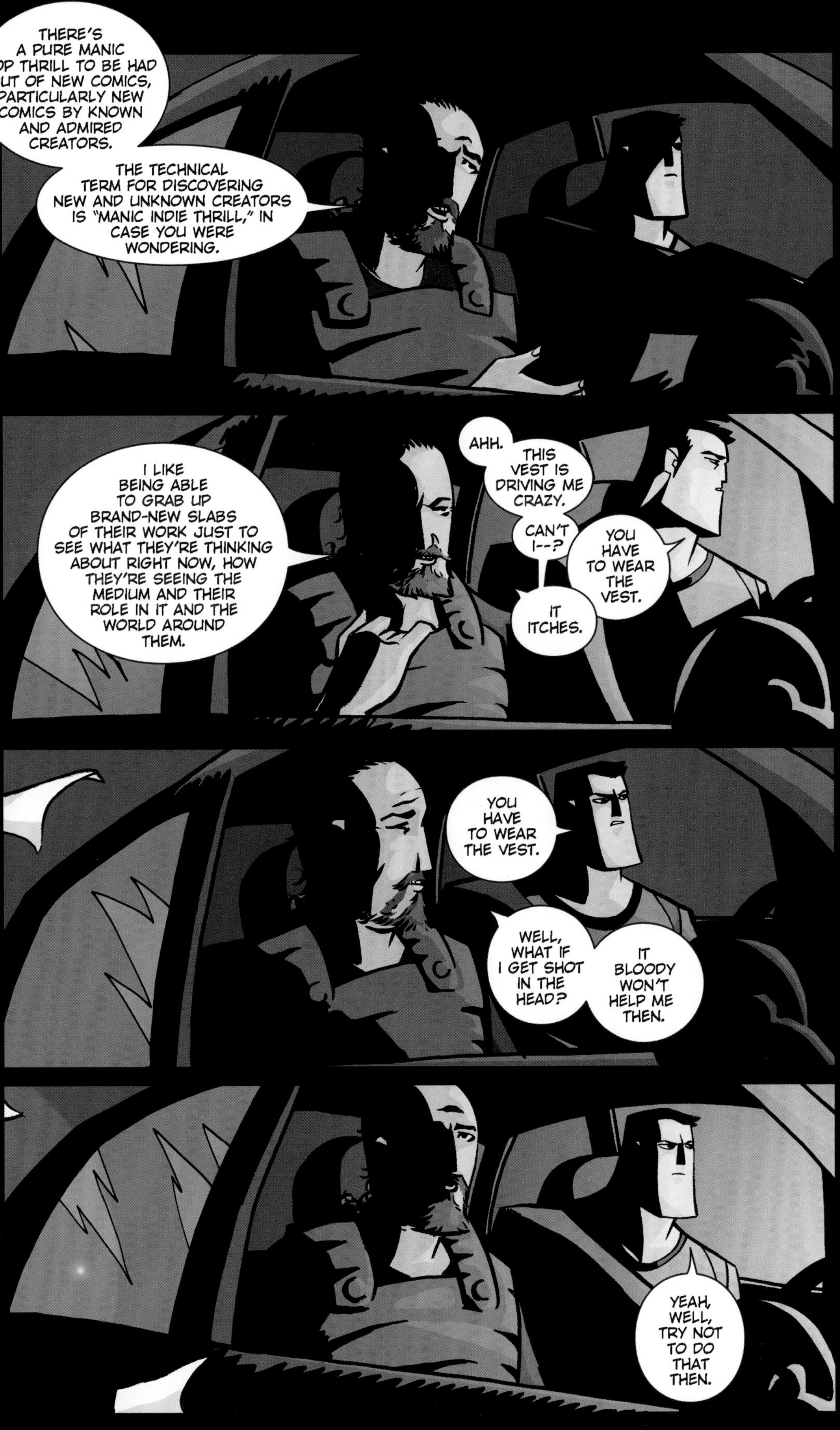
THERE'S A PURE MANIC POP THRILL TO BE HAD OUT OF NEW COMICS, PARTICULARLY NEW COMICS BY KNOWN AND ADMIRED CREATORS.
THE TECHNICAL TERM FOR DISCOVERING NEW AND UNKNOWN CREATORS IS "MANIC INDIE THRILL," IN CASE YOU WERE WONDERING.
I LIKE BEING ABLE TO GRAB UP BRAND-NEW SLABS OF THEIR WORK JUST TO SEE WHAT THEY'RE THINKING ABOUT RIGHT NOW, HOW THEY'RE SEEING THE MEDIUM AND THEIR ROLE IN IT AND THE WORLD AROUND THEM.
AHH.
THIS VEST IS DRIVING ME CRAZY.
CAN'T I--?
IT ITCHES.
YOU HAVE TO WEAR THE VEST.
YOU HAVE TO WEAR THE VEST.
WELL, WHAT IF I GET SHOT IN THE HEAD?
IT BLOODY WON'T HELP ME THEN.
YEAH, WELL, TRY NOT TO DO THAT THEN.

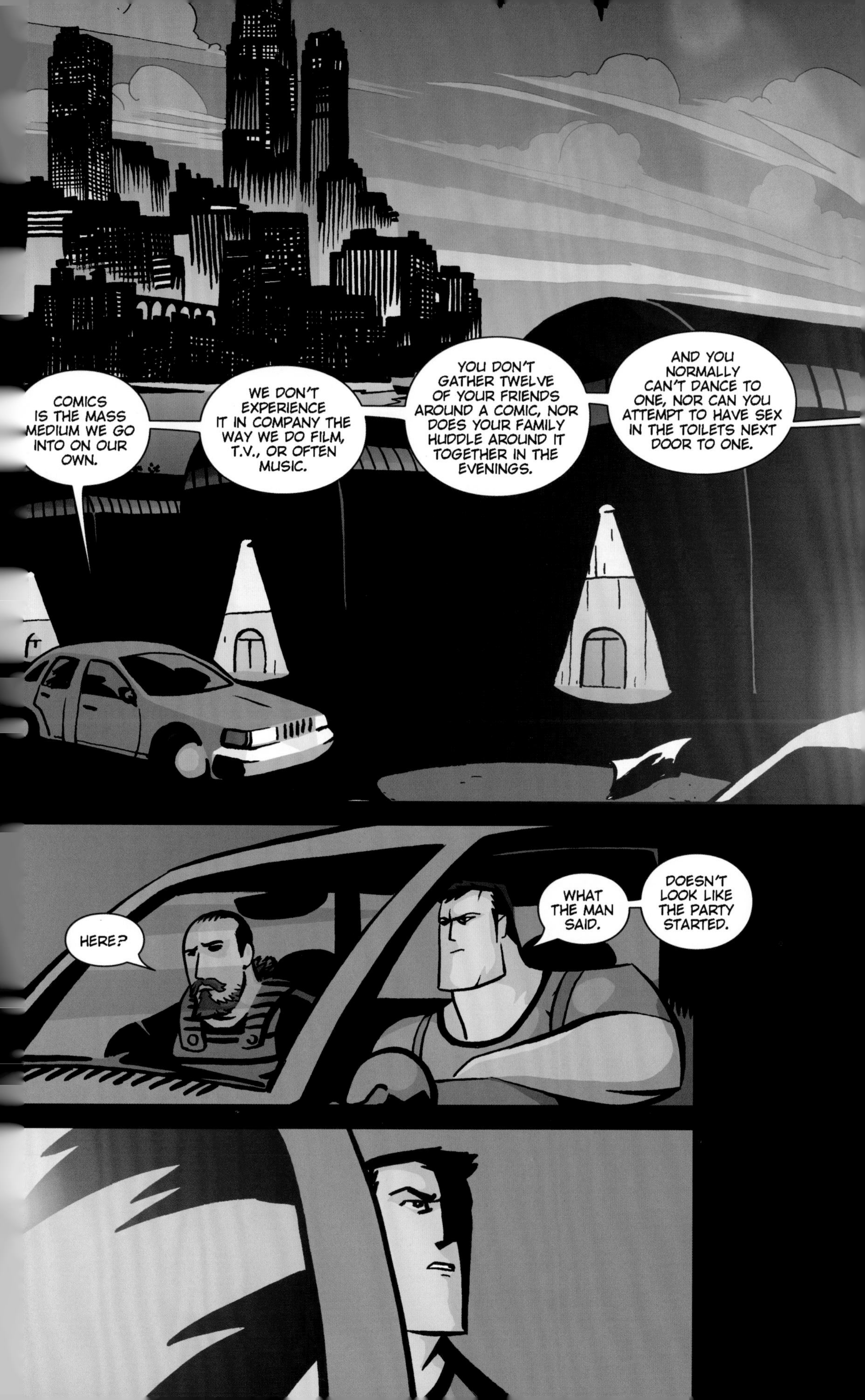
COMICS IS THE MASS MEDIUM WE GO INTO ON OUR OWN.
WE DON'T EXPERIENCE IT IN COMPANY THE WAY WE DO FILM, T.V., OR OFTEN MUSIC.
YOU DON'T GATHER TWELVE OF YOUR FRIENDS AROUND A COMIC, NOR DOES YOUR FAMILY HUDDLE AROUND IT TOGETHER IN THE EVENINGS.
AND YOU NORMALLY CAN'T DANCE TO ONE, NOR CAN YOU ATTEMPT TO HAVE SEX IN THE TOILETS NEXT DOOR TO ONE.
HERE?
WHAT THE MAN SAID.
DOESN'T LOOK LIKE THE PARTY STARTED.

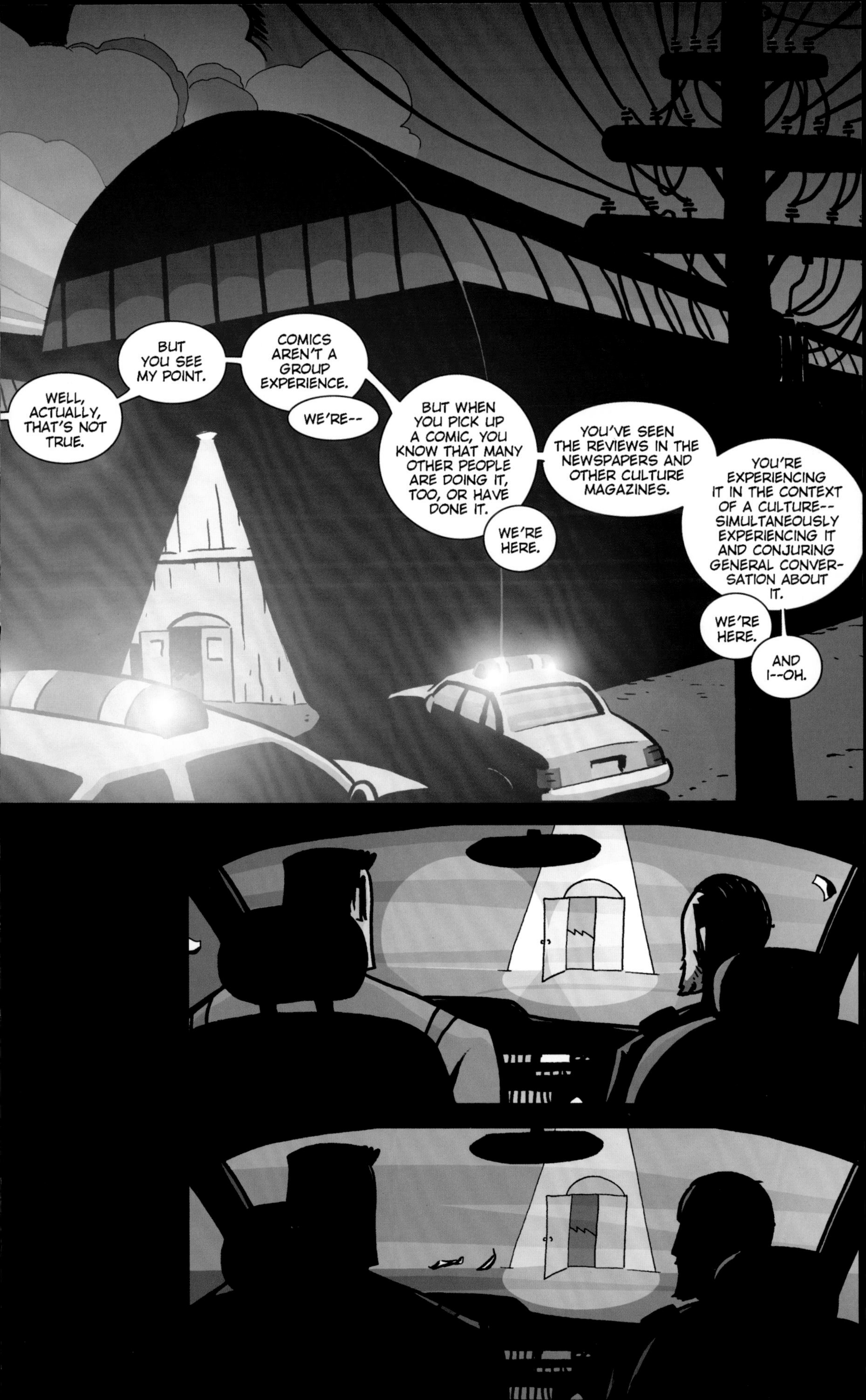
WELL, ACTUALLY, THAT'S NOT TRUE.
BUT YOU SEE MY POINT.
COMICS AREN'T A GROUP EXPERIENCE.
WE'RE--
BUT WHEN YOU PICK UP A COMIC, YOU KNOW THAT MANY OTHER PEOPLE ARE DOING IT, TOO, OR HAVE DONE IT.
WE'RE HERE.
YOU'VE SEEN THE REVIEWS IN THE NEWSPAPERS AND OTHER CULTURE MAGAZINES.
YOU'RE EXPERIENCING IT IN THE CONTEXT OF A CULTURE-- SIMULTANEOUSLY EXPERIENCING IT AND CONJURING GENERAL CONVERSATION ABOUT IT.
WE'RE HERE.
AND I--OH.

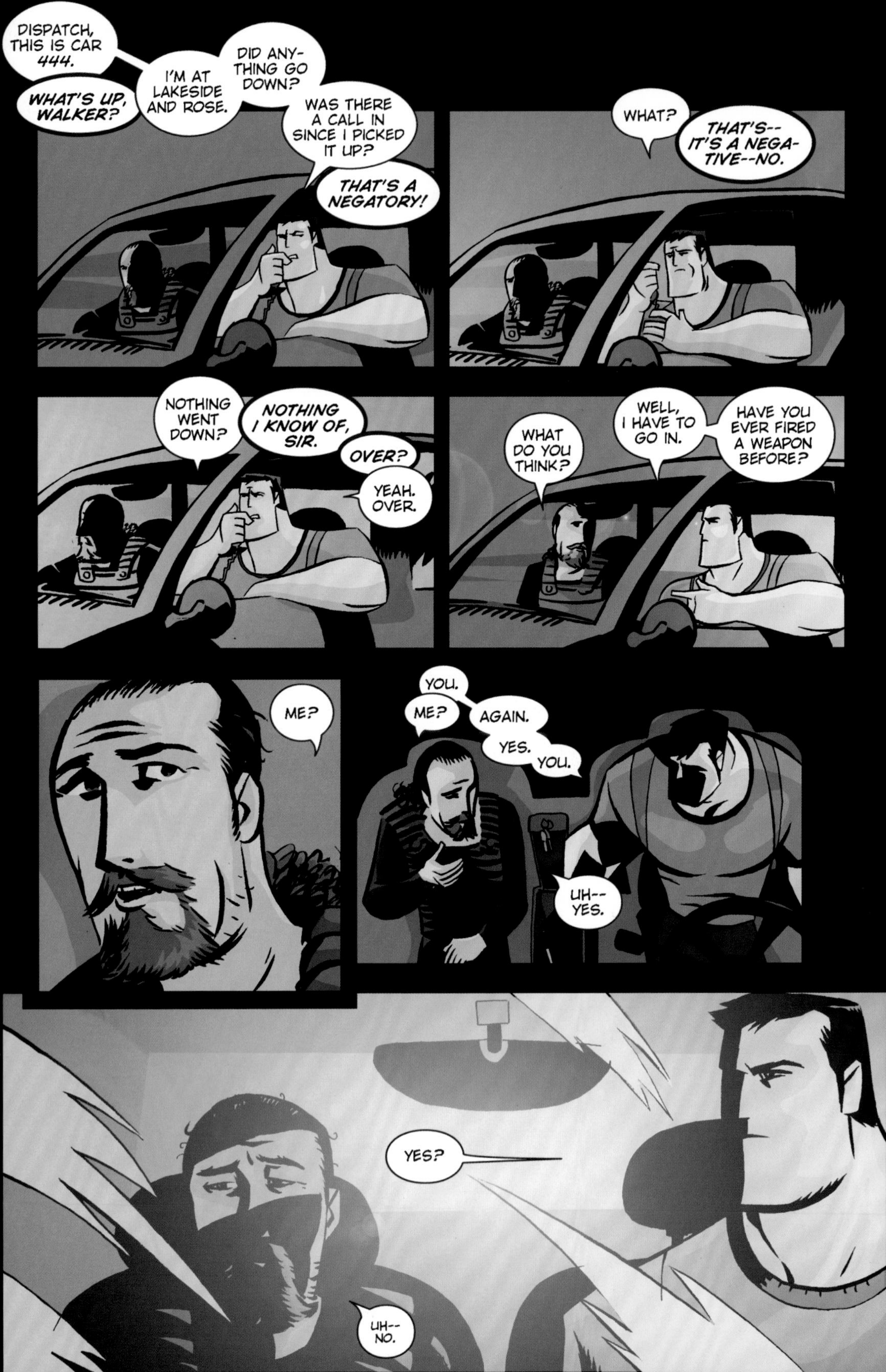
DISPATCH, THIS IS CAR 444.
WHAT'S UP, WALKER?
I'M AT LAKESIDE AND ROSE.
DID ANY-THING GO DOWN?
WAS THERE A CALL IN SINCE I PICKED IT UP?
THAT'S A NEGATORY!
WHAT?
THAT'S-- IT'S A NEGA-TIVE--NO.
NOTHING WENT DOWN?
NOTHING I KNOW OF, SIR.
OVER?
YEAH. OVER.
WHAT DO YOU THINK?
WELL, I HAVE TO GO IN.
HAVE YOU EVER FIRED A WEAPON BEFORE?
ME?
YOU.
ME?
AGAIN.
YES.
YOU.
UH-- YES.
YES?
UH-- NO.

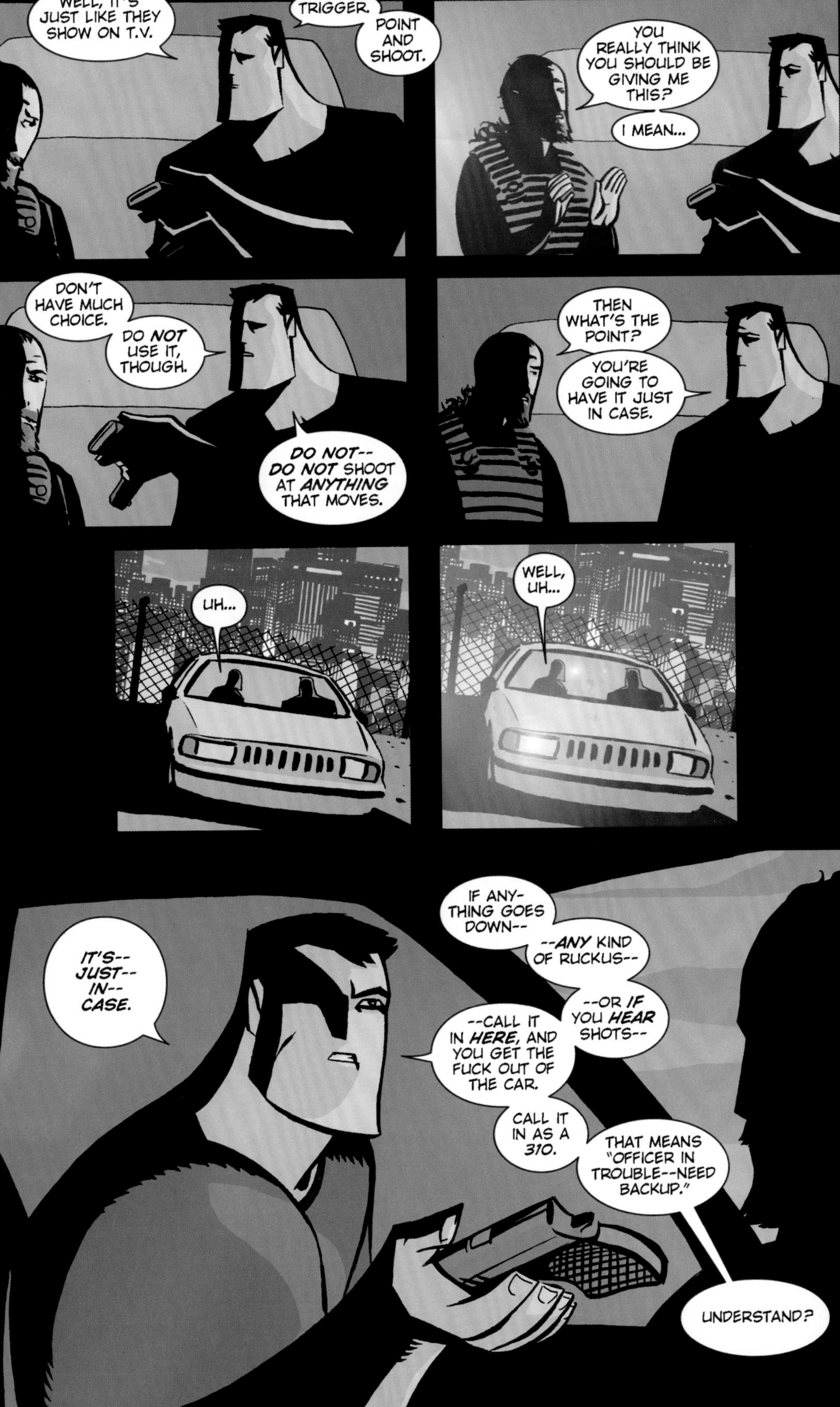

WELL, IT'S JUST LIKE THEY SHOW ON T.V.
TRIGGER.
POINT AND SHOOT.
YOU REALLY THINK YOU SHOULD BE GIVING ME THIS?
I MEAN...
DON'T HAVE MUCH CHOICE.
DO *NOT* USE IT, THOUGH.
DO NOT-- DO NOT SHOOT AT *ANYTHING* THAT MOVES.
THEN WHAT'S THE POINT?
YOU'RE GOING TO HAVE IT JUST IN CASE.
UH...
WELL, UH...
IF ANY-THING GOES DOWN--
--*ANY* KIND OF RUCKUS--
--OR *IF* YOU *HEAR* SHOTS--
--CALL IT IN *HERE,* AND YOU GET THE FUCK OUT OF THE CAR.
CALL IT IN AS A *310.*
THAT MEANS "OFFICER IN TROUBLE--NEED BACKUP."
UNDERSTAND?
IT'S-- JUST-- IN-- CASE.

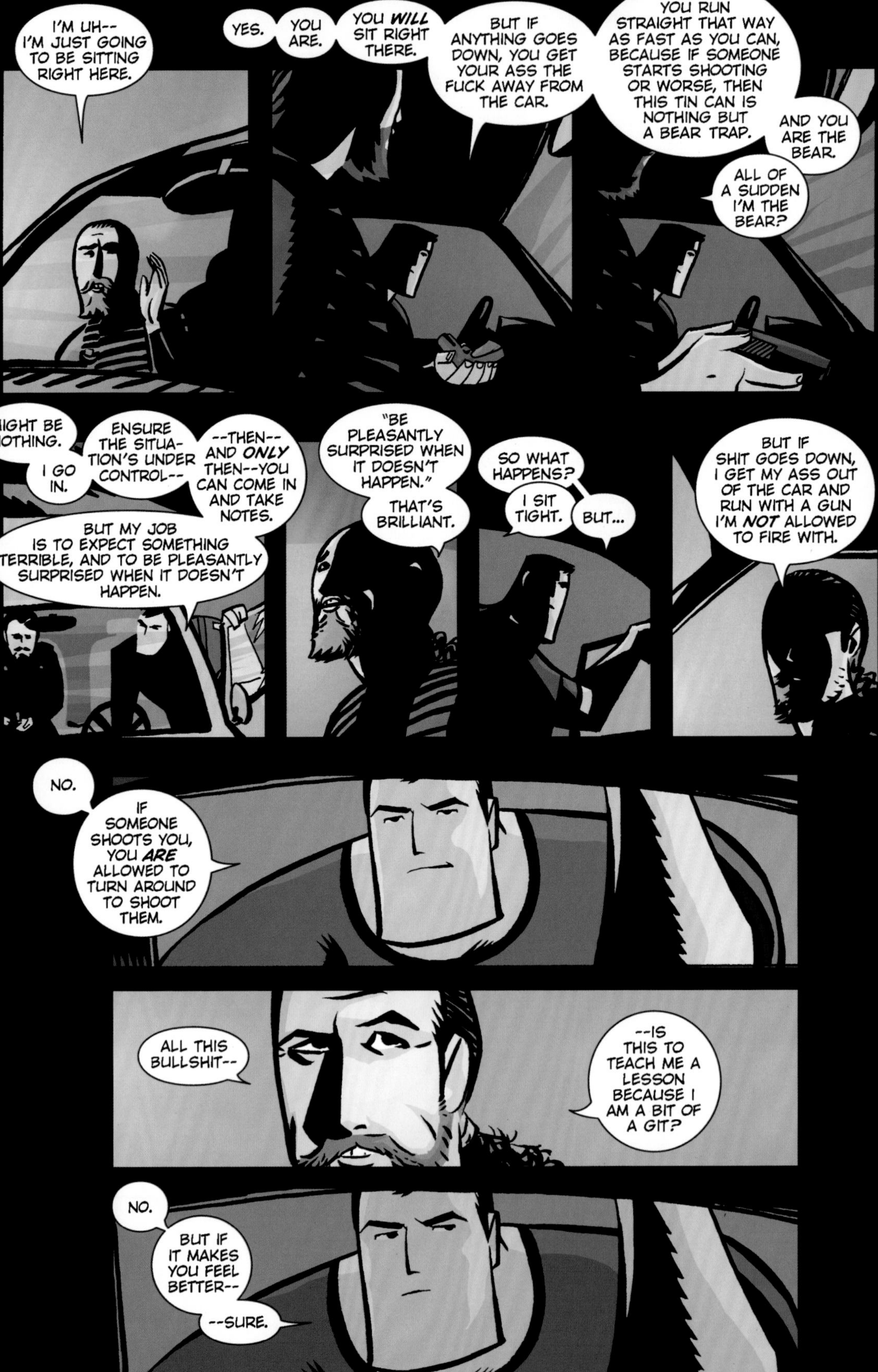
I'M UH-- I'M JUST GOING TO BE SITTING RIGHT HERE.
YES.
YOU ARE.
YOU WILL SIT RIGHT THERE.
BUT IF ANYTHING GOES DOWN, YOU GET YOUR ASS THE FUCK AWAY FROM THE CAR.
YOU RUN STRAIGHT THAT WAY AS FAST AS YOU CAN, BECAUSE IF SOMEONE STARTS SHOOTING OR WORSE, THEN THIS TIN CAN IS NOTHING BUT A BEAR TRAP.
AND YOU ARE THE BEAR.
ALL OF A SUDDEN I'M THE BEAR?
MIGHT BE NOTHING.
I GO IN.
ENSURE THE SITUATION'S UNDER CONTROL--
--THEN--AND ONLY THEN--YOU CAN COME IN AND TAKE NOTES.
BUT MY JOB IS TO EXPECT SOMETHING TERRIBLE, AND TO BE PLEASANTLY SURPRISED WHEN IT DOESN'T HAPPEN.
"BE PLEASANTLY SURPRISED WHEN IT DOESN'T HAPPEN."
THAT'S BRILLIANT.
SO WHAT HAPPENS?
I SIT TIGHT.
BUT...
BUT IF SHIT GOES DOWN, I GET MY ASS OUT OF THE CAR AND RUN WITH A GUN I'M NOT ALLOWED TO FIRE WITH.
NO.
IF SOMEONE SHOOTS YOU, YOU ARE ALLOWED TO TURN AROUND TO SHOOT THEM.
ALL THIS BULLSHIT--
--IS THIS TO TEACH ME A LESSON BECAUSE I AM A BIT OF A GIT?
NO.
BUT IF IT MAKES YOU FEEL BETTER--
--SURE.

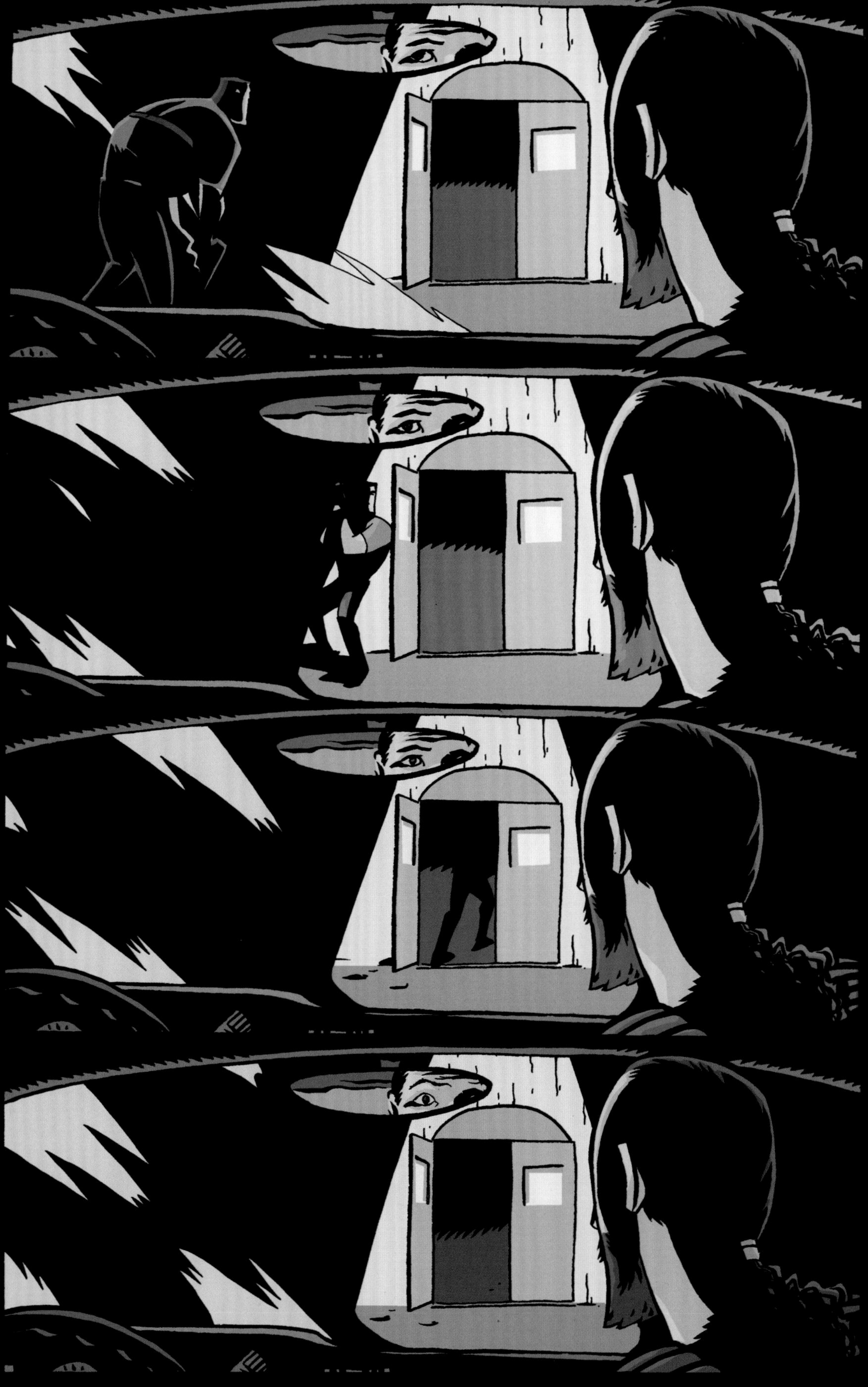

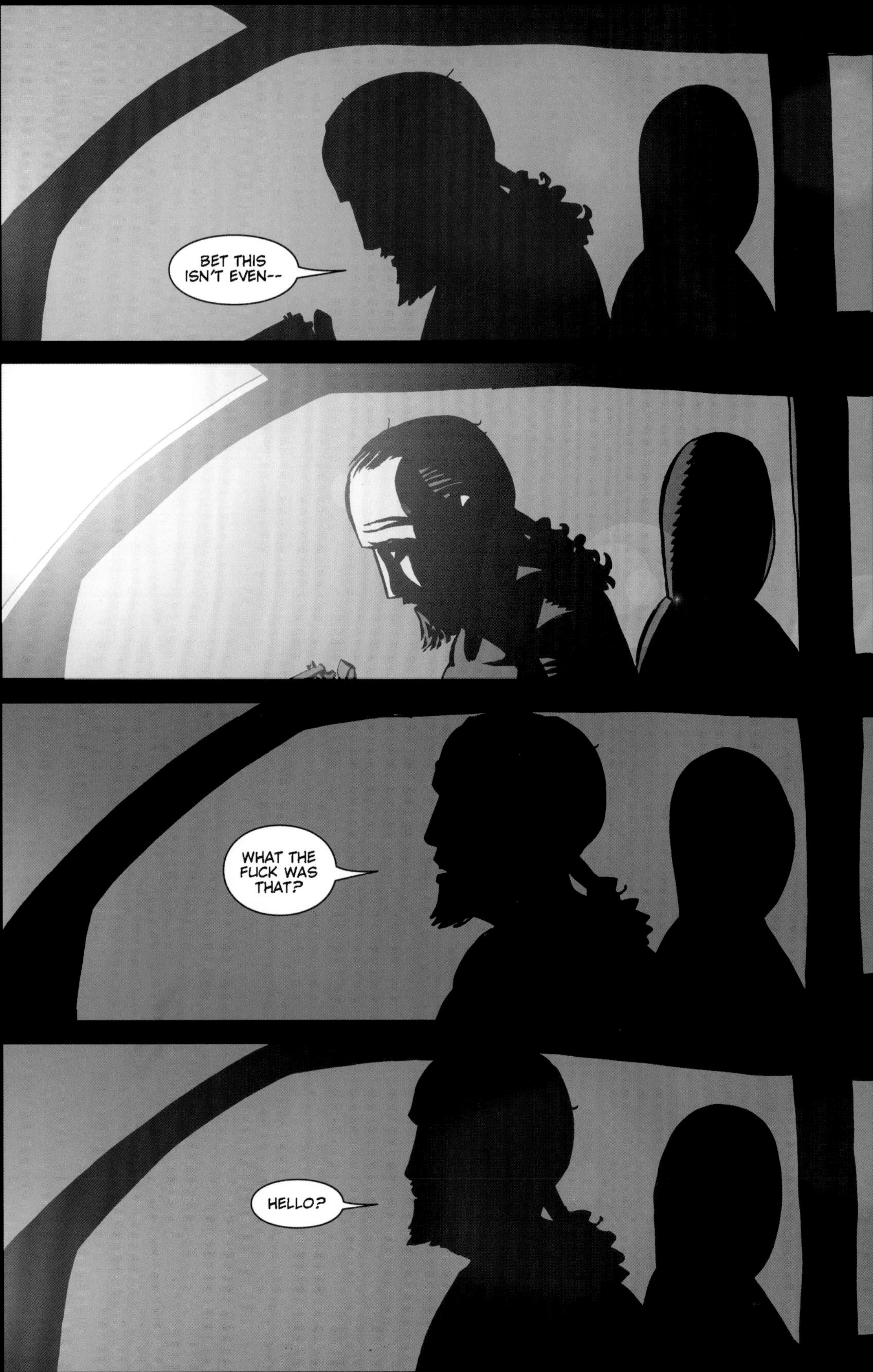
BET THIS ISN'T EVEN--
WHAT THE FUCK WAS THAT?
HELLO?

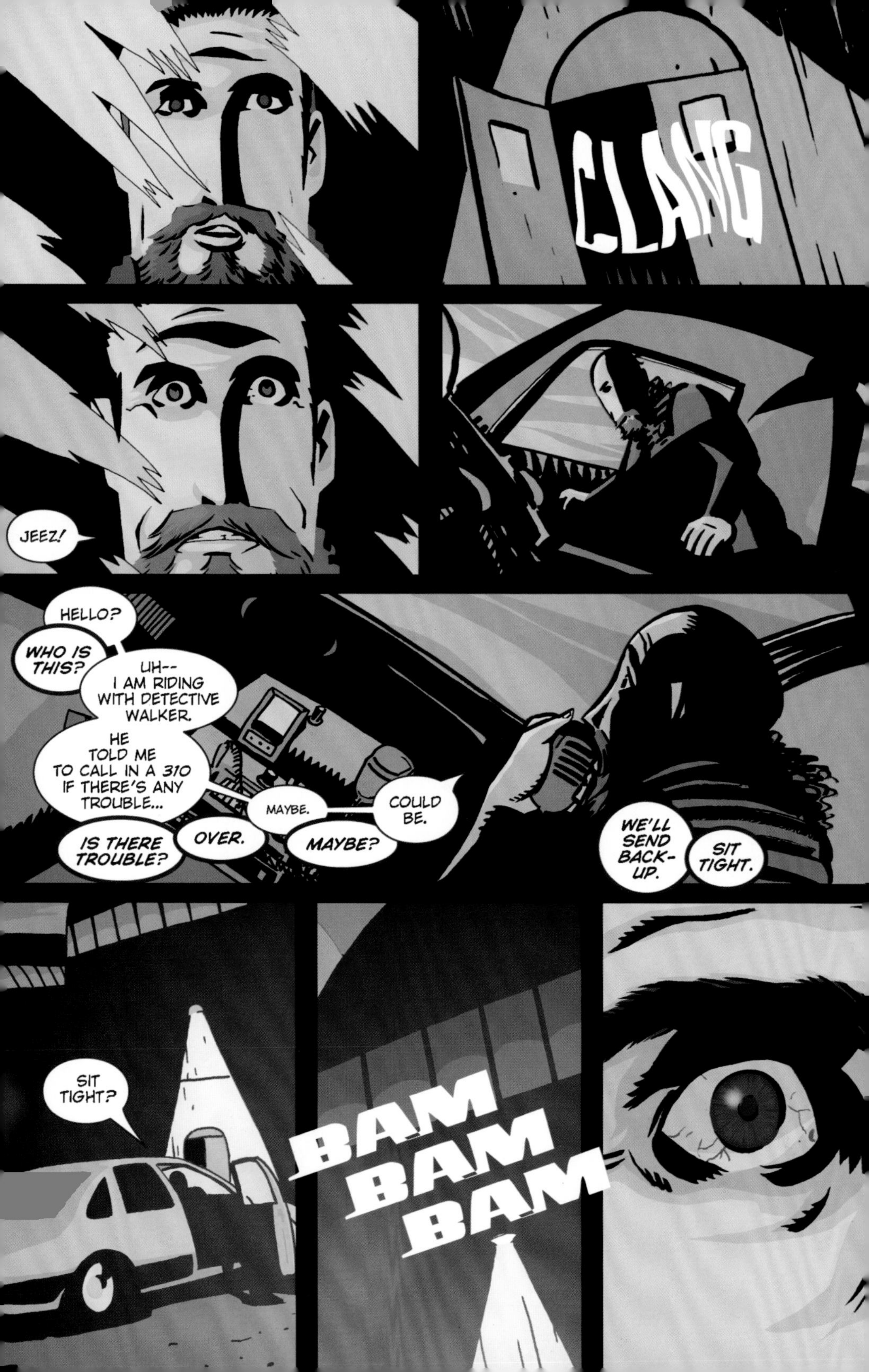
CLANG
JEEZ!
HELLO?
WHO IS THIS?
UH-- I AM RIDING WITH DETECTIVE WALKER.
HE TOLD ME TO CALL IN A 310 IF THERE'S ANY TROUBLE...
MAYBE.
COULD BE.
IS THERE TROUBLE?
OVER.
MAYBE?
WE'LL SEND BACK-UP.
SIT TIGHT.
SIT TIGHT?
BAM BAM BAM

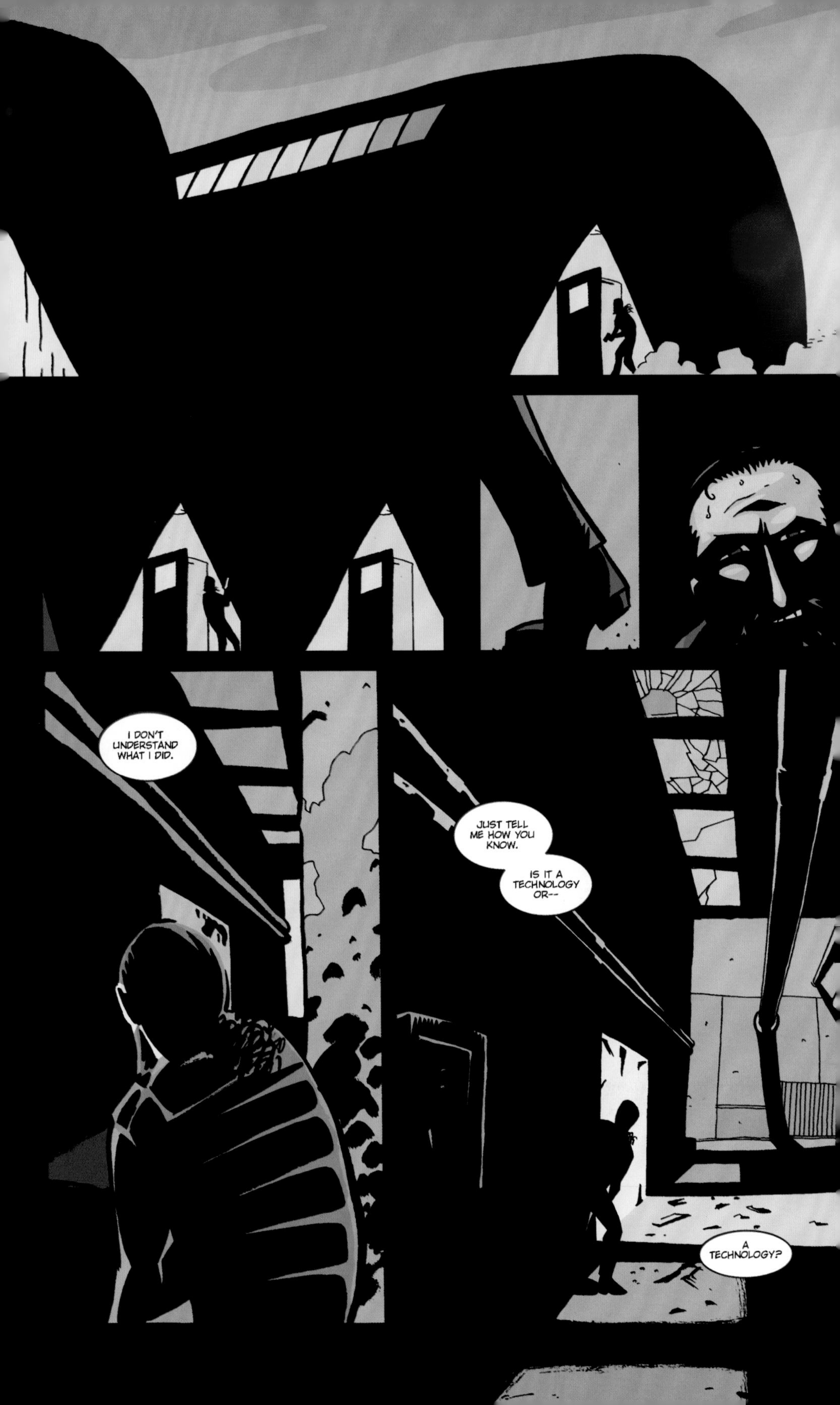
I DON'T UNDERSTAND WHAT I DID.
JUST TELL ME HOW YOU KNOW.
IS IT A TECHNOLOGY OR--
A TECHNOLOGY?

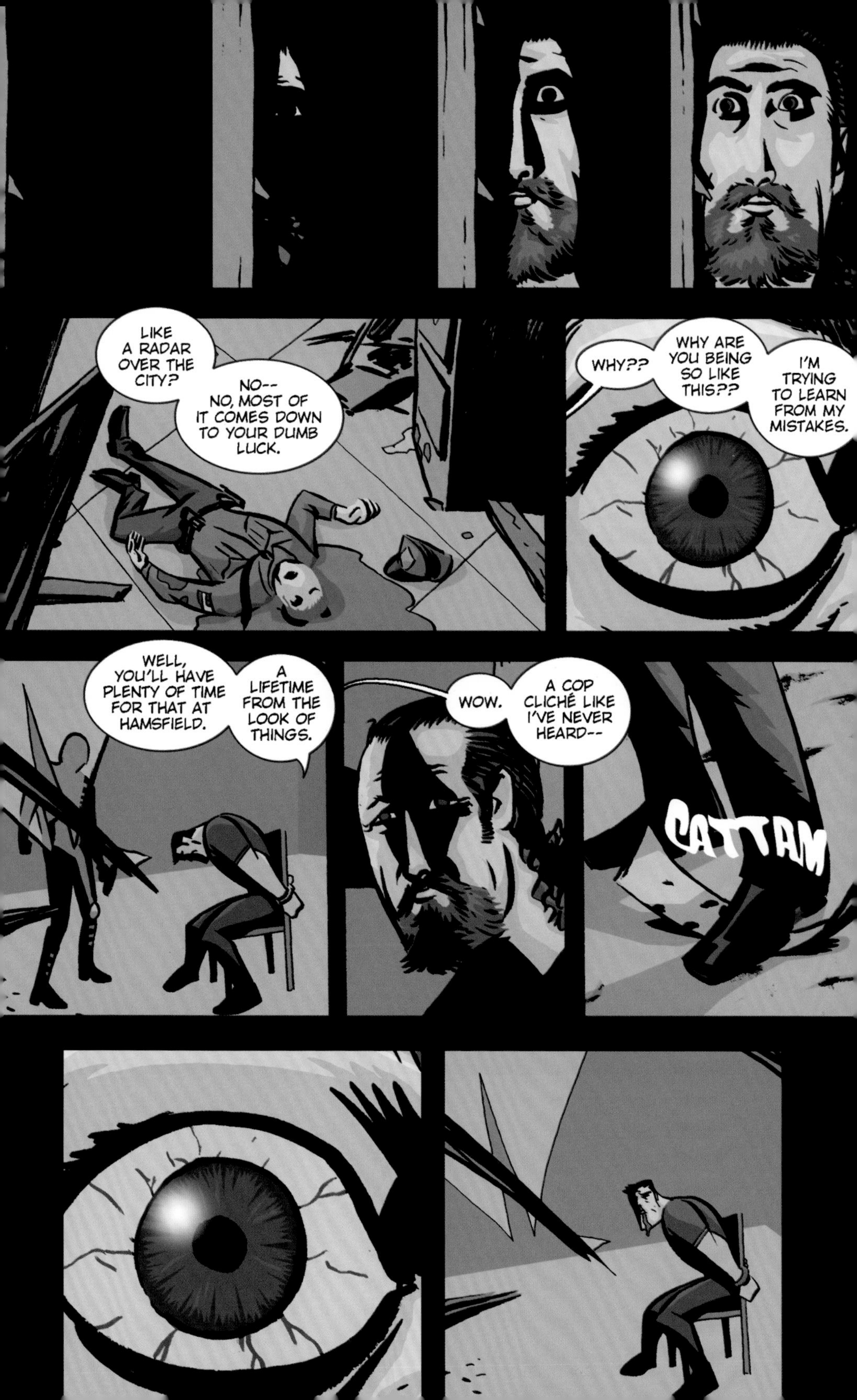
LIKE A RADAR OVER THE CITY?
NO-- NO, MOST OF IT COMES DOWN TO YOUR DUMB LUCK.
WHY??
WHY ARE YOU BEING SO LIKE THIS??
I'M TRYING TO LEARN FROM MY MISTAKES.
WELL, YOU'LL HAVE PLENTY OF TIME FOR THAT AT HAMSFIELD.
A LIFETIME FROM THE LOOK OF THINGS.
WOW.
A COP CLICHÉ LIKE I'VE NEVER HEARD--
CATTAM

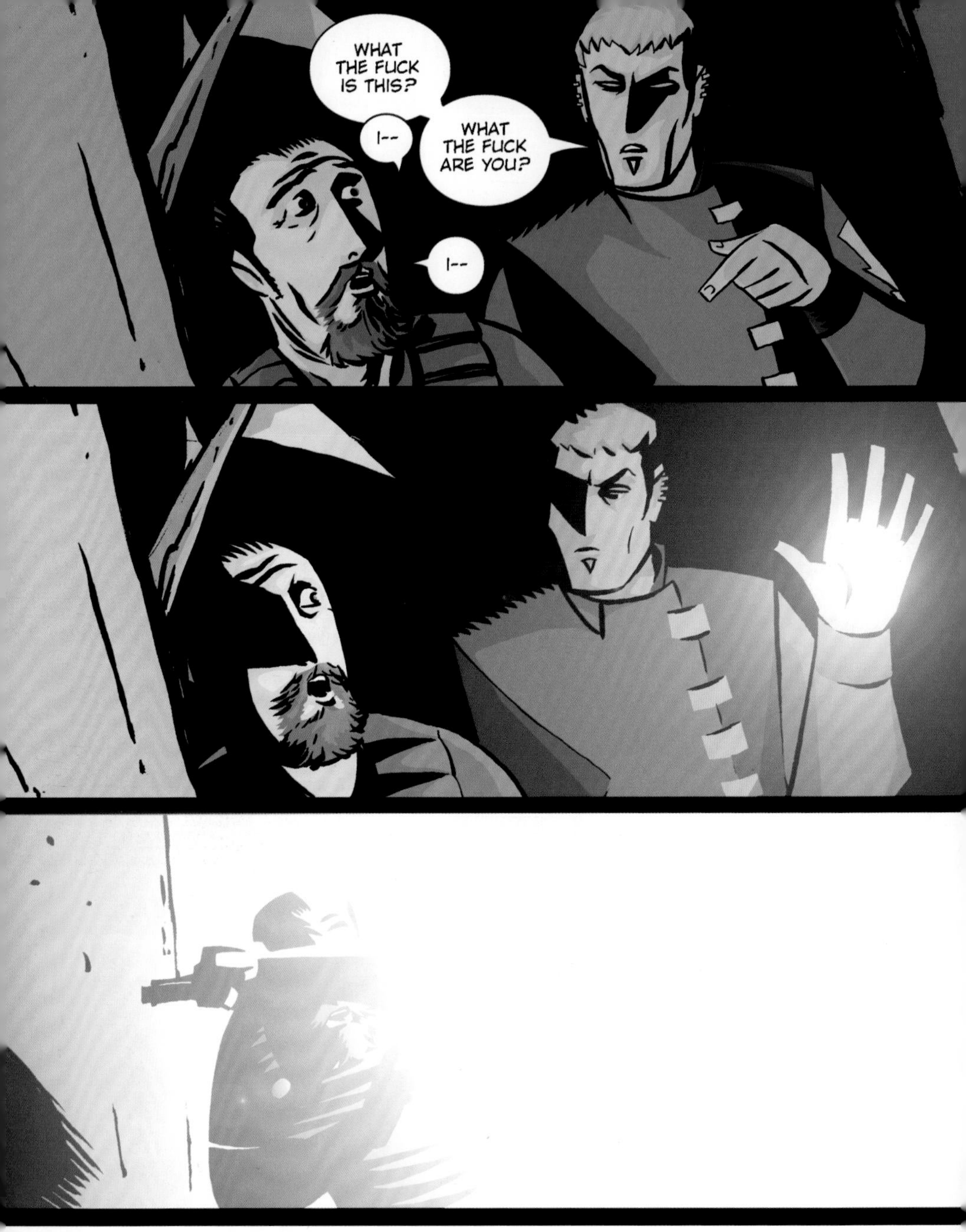
WHAT THE FUCK IS THIS?
I--
WHAT THE FUCK ARE YOU?
I--

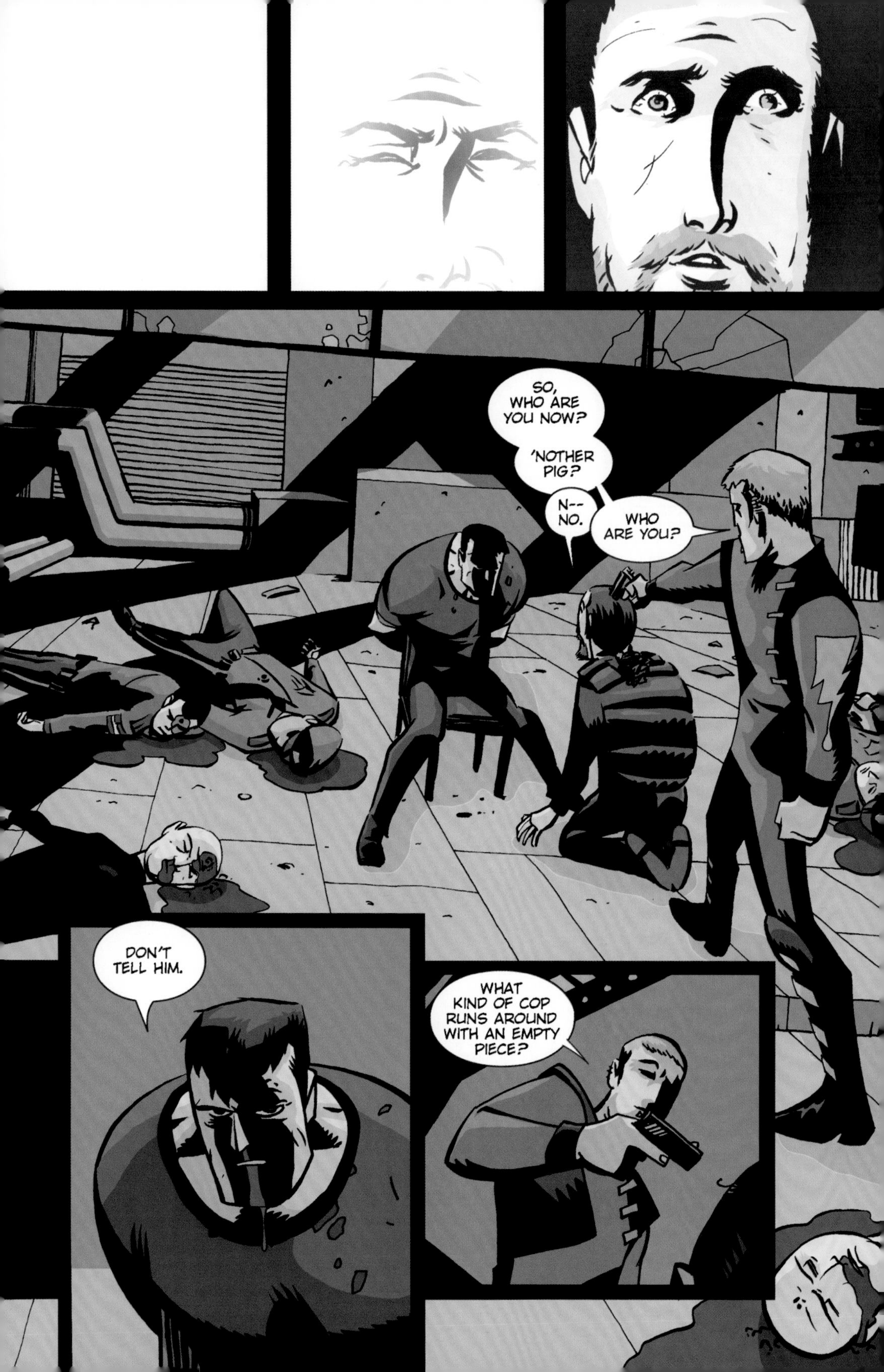
SO, WHO ARE YOU NOW?
'NOTHER PIG?
N-- NO.
WHO ARE YOU?
DON'T TELL HIM.
WHAT KIND OF COP RUNS AROUND WITH AN EMPTY PIECE?

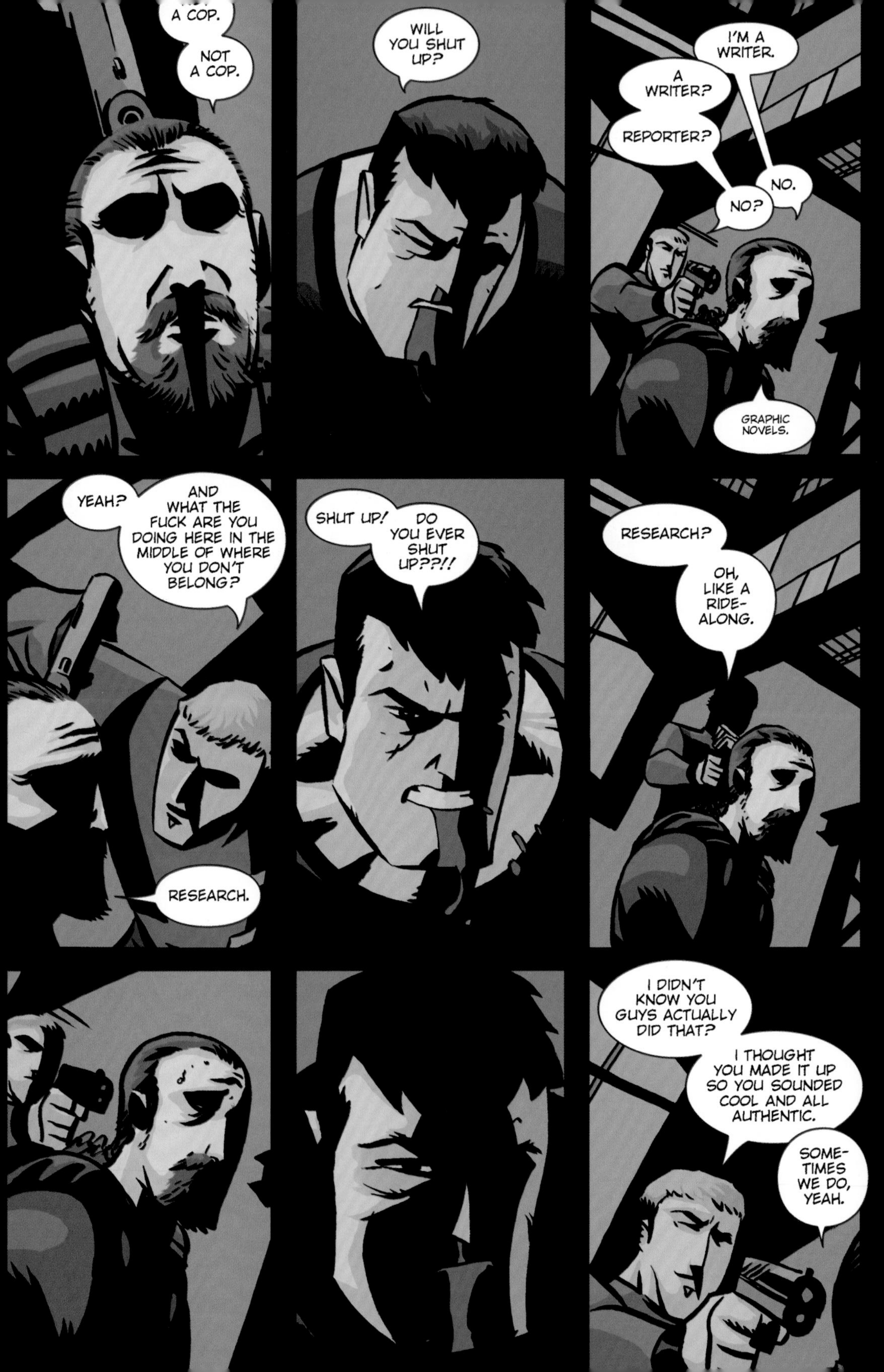
A COP.
NOT A COP.
WILL YOU SHUT UP?
I'M A WRITER.
A WRITER?
REPORTER?
NO?
NO.
GRAPHIC NOVELS.
YEAH?
AND WHAT THE FUCK ARE YOU DOING HERE IN THE MIDDLE OF WHERE YOU DON'T BELONG?
RESEARCH.
SHUT UP!
DO YOU EVER SHUT UP??!!
RESEARCH?
OH, LIKE A RIDE-ALONG.
I DIDN'T KNOW YOU GUYS ACTUALLY DID THAT?
I THOUGHT YOU MADE IT UP SO YOU SOUNDED COOL AND ALL AUTHENTIC.
SOME-TIMES WE DO, YEAH.

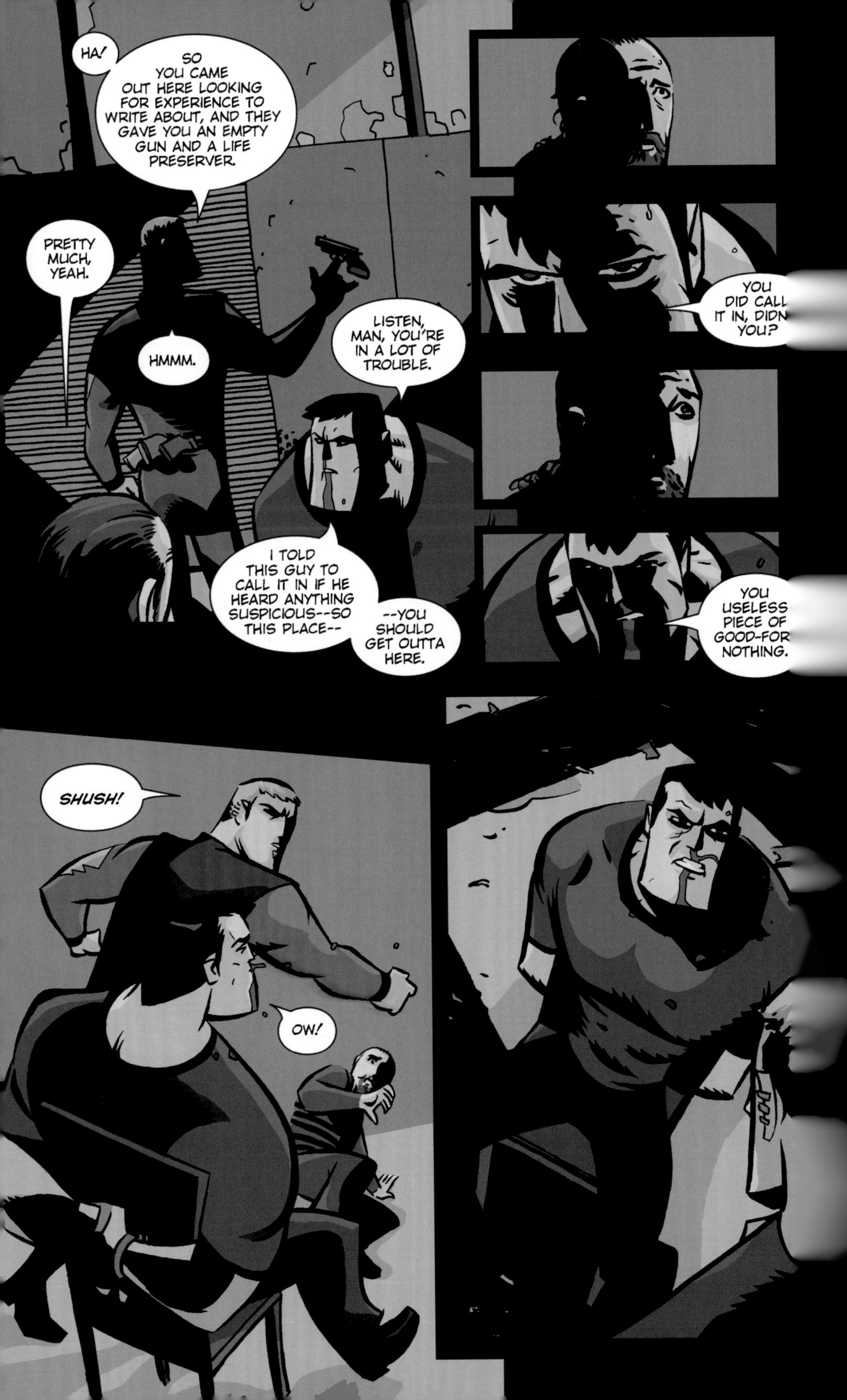
HA!
SO YOU CAME OUT HERE LOOKING FOR EXPERIENCE TO WRITE ABOUT, AND THEY GAVE YOU AN EMPTY GUN AND A LIFE PRESERVER.
PRETTY MUCH, YEAH.
HMMM.
LISTEN, MAN, YOU'RE IN A LOT OF TROUBLE.
I TOLD THIS GUY TO CALL IT IN IF HE HEARD ANYTHING SUSPICIOUS--SO THIS PLACE--
--YOU SHOULD GET OUTTA HERE.
YOU DID CALL IT IN, DIDN YOU?
YOU USELESS PIECE OF GOOD-FOR NOTHING.
SHUSH!
OW!

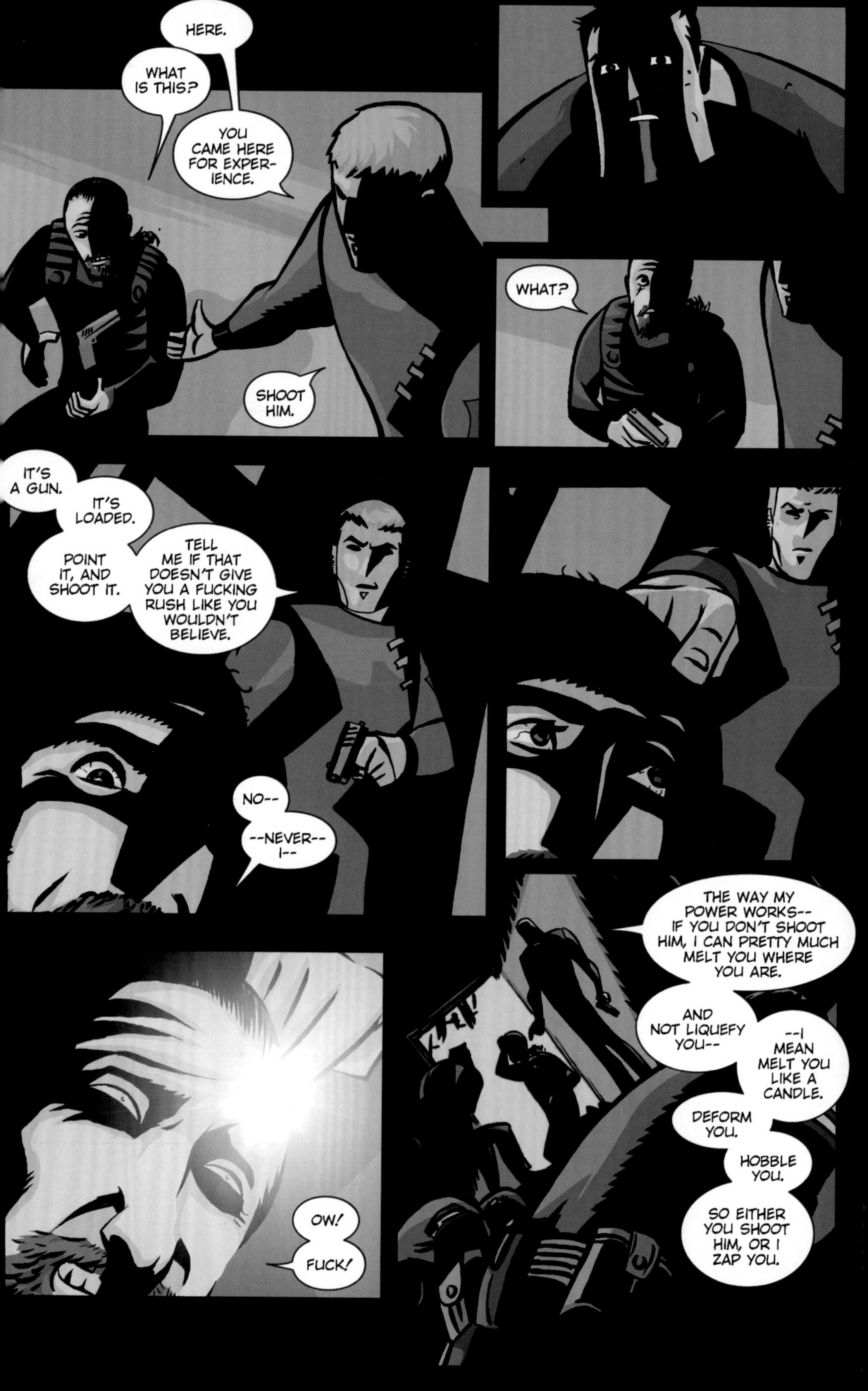
HERE.
WHAT IS THIS?
YOU CAME HERE FOR EXPER-IENCE.
SHOOT HIM.
WHAT?
IT'S A GUN.
IT'S LOADED.
POINT IT, AND SHOOT IT.
TELL ME IF THAT DOESN'T GIVE YOU A FUCKING RUSH LIKE YOU WOULDN'T BELIEVE.
NO--
--NEVER--
I--
THE WAY MY POWER WORKS-- IF YOU DON'T SHOOT HIM, I CAN PRETTY MUCH MELT YOU WHERE YOU ARE.
AND NOT LIQUEFY YOU--
--I MEAN MELT YOU LIKE A CANDLE.
DEFORM YOU.
HOBBLE YOU.
SO EITHER YOU SHOOT HIM, OR I ZAP YOU.
OW!
FUCK!

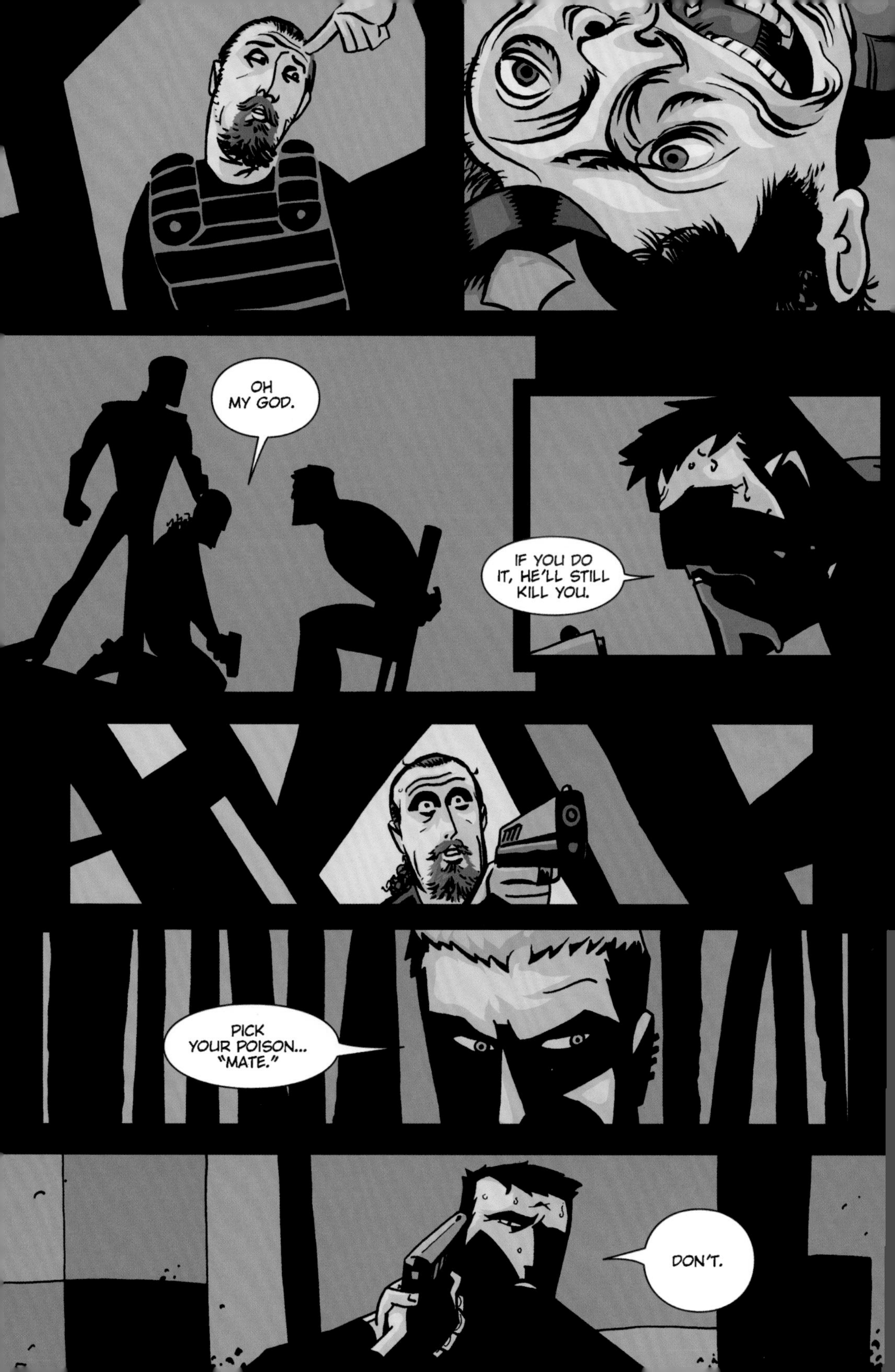
OH MY GOD.
IF YOU DO IT, HE'LL STILL KILL YOU.
PICK YOUR POISON... "MATE."
DON'T.

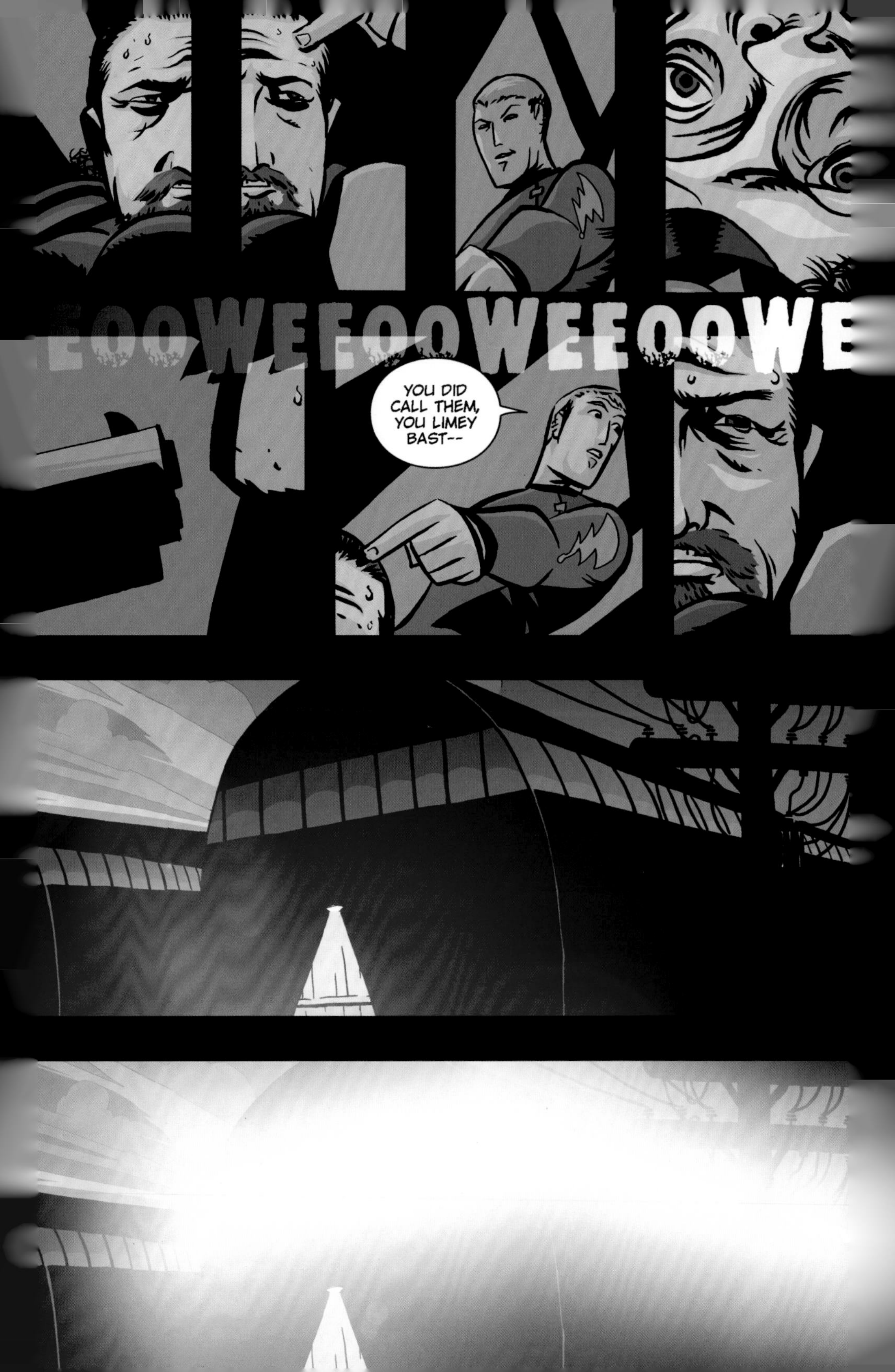
EOOWEEOOWEEOOWEEOOWE
YOU DID CALL THEM, YOU LIMEY BAST--

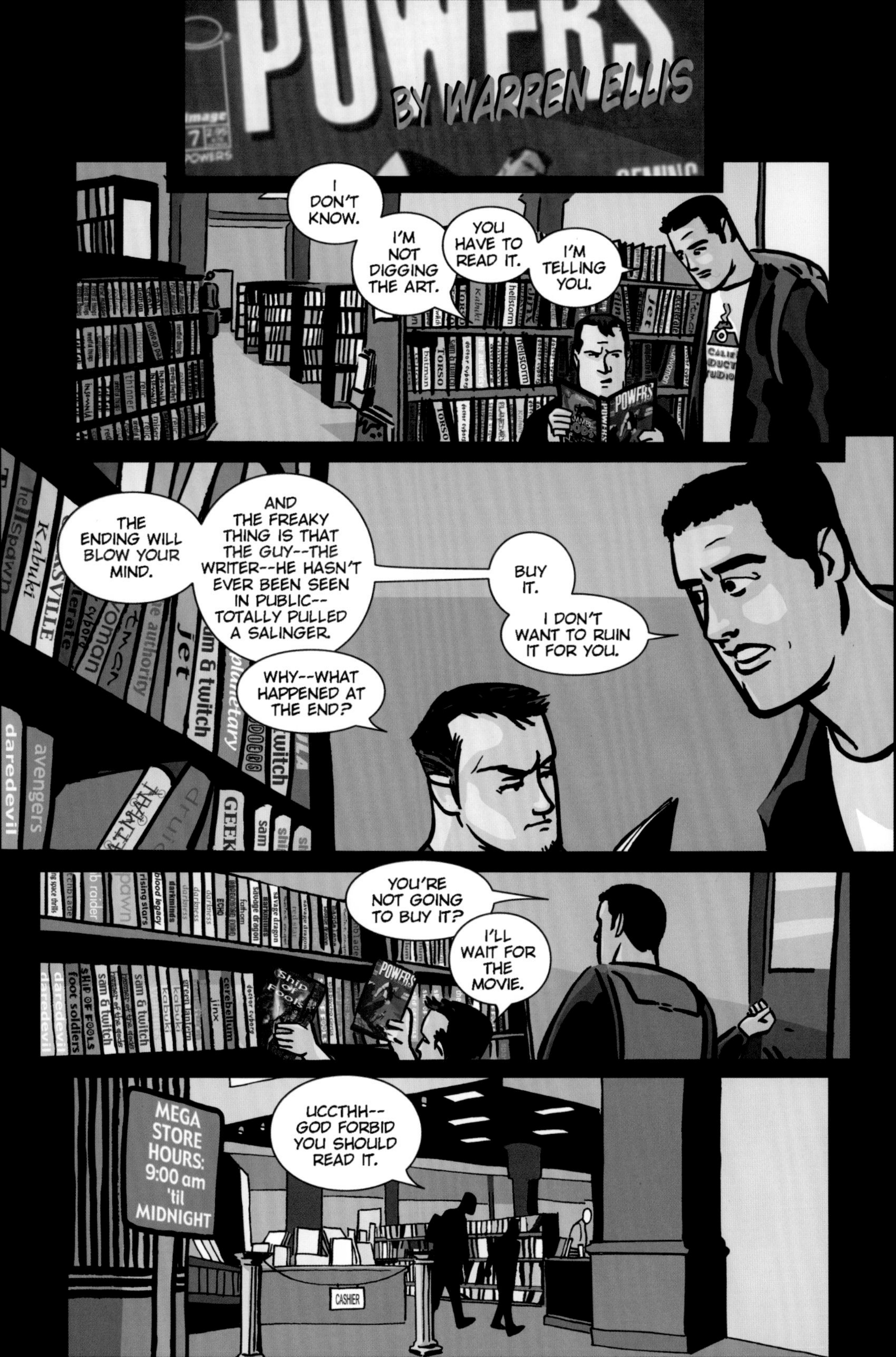
POWERS
BY WARREN ELLIS
I DON'T KNOW.
I'M NOT DIGGING THE ART.
YOU HAVE TO READ IT.
I'M TELLING YOU.
THE ENDING WILL BLOW YOUR MIND.
AND THE FREAKY THING IS THAT THE GUY--THE WRITER--HE HASN'T EVER BEEN SEEN IN PUBLIC--TOTALLY PULLED A SALINGER.
BUY IT.
I DON'T WANT TO RUIN IT FOR YOU.
WHY--WHAT HAPPENED AT THE END?
YOU'RE NOT GOING TO BUY IT?
I'LL WAIT FOR THE MOVIE.
MEGA STORE HOURS: 9:00 am 'til MIDNIGHT
UCCTHH--GOD FORBID YOU SHOULD READ IT.
CASHIER

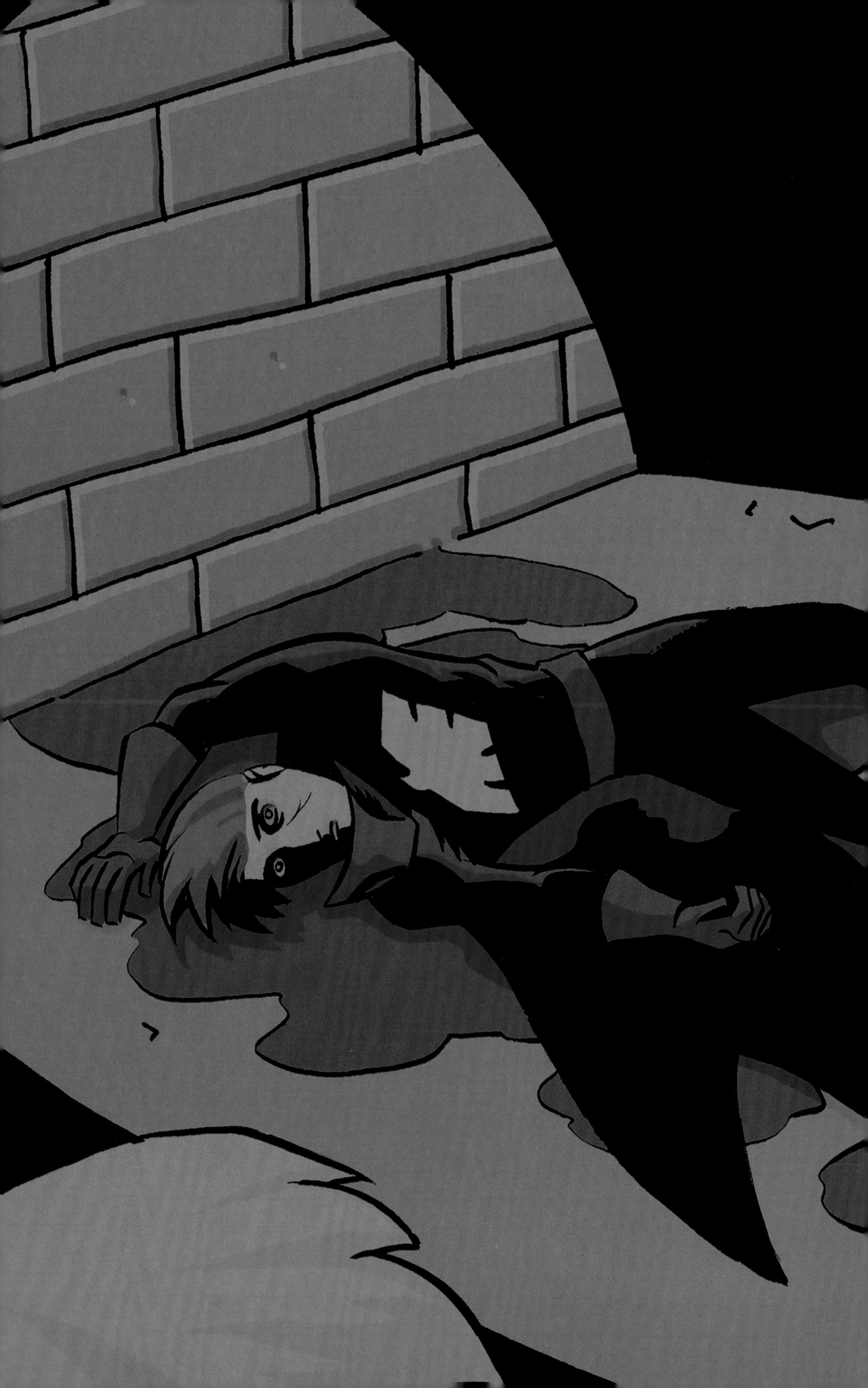

POWERS

ROLEPLAY
CHAPTER 1

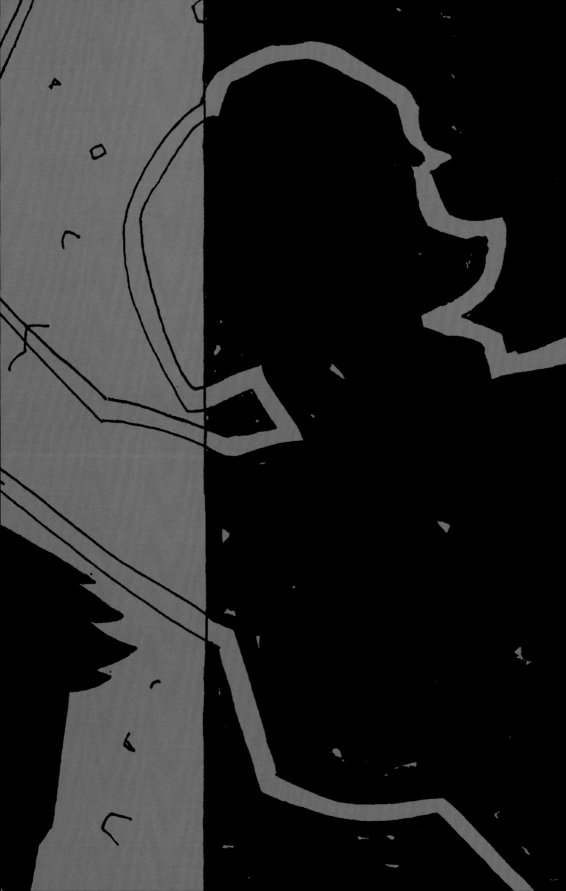

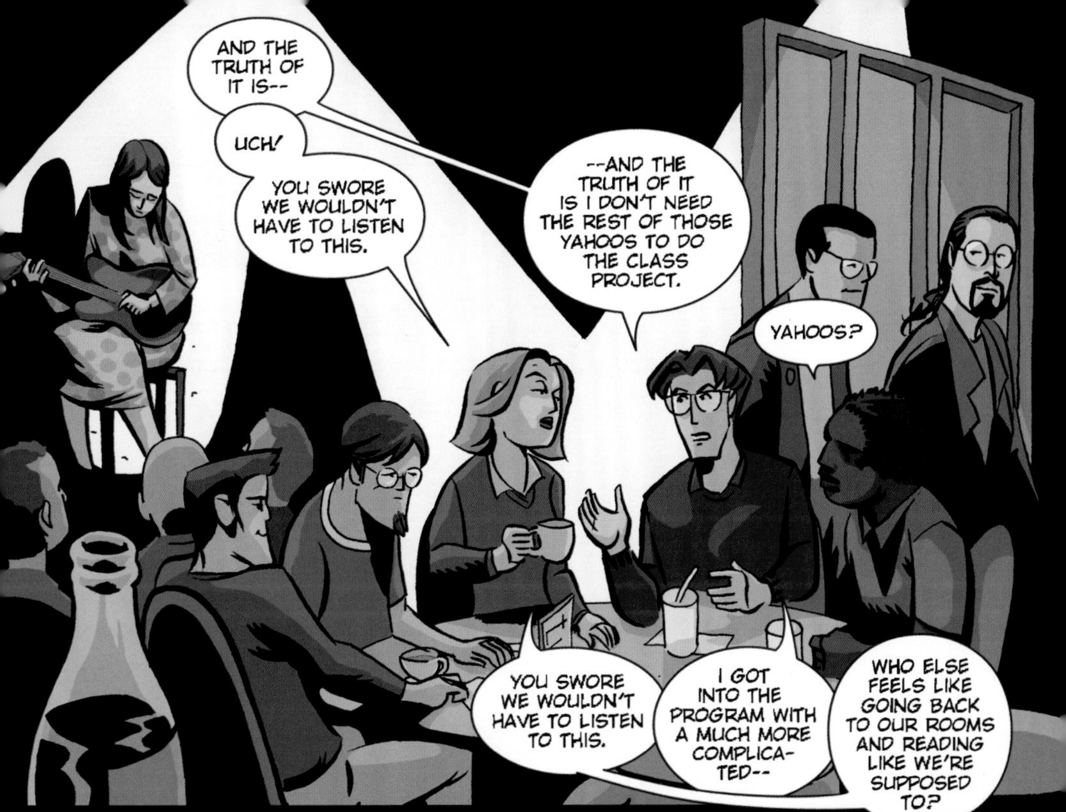
AND THE TRUTH OF IT IS--
UCH!
YOU SWORE WE WOULDN'T HAVE TO LISTEN TO THIS.
--AND THE TRUTH OF IT IS I DON'T NEED THE REST OF THOSE YAHOOS TO DO THE CLASS PROJECT.
YAHOOS?
YOU SWORE WE WOULDN'T HAVE TO LISTEN TO THIS.
I GOT INTO THE PROGRAM WITH A MUCH MORE COMPLICA-TED--
WHO ELSE FEELS LIKE GOING BACK TO OUR ROOMS AND READING LIKE WE'RE SUPPOSED TO?
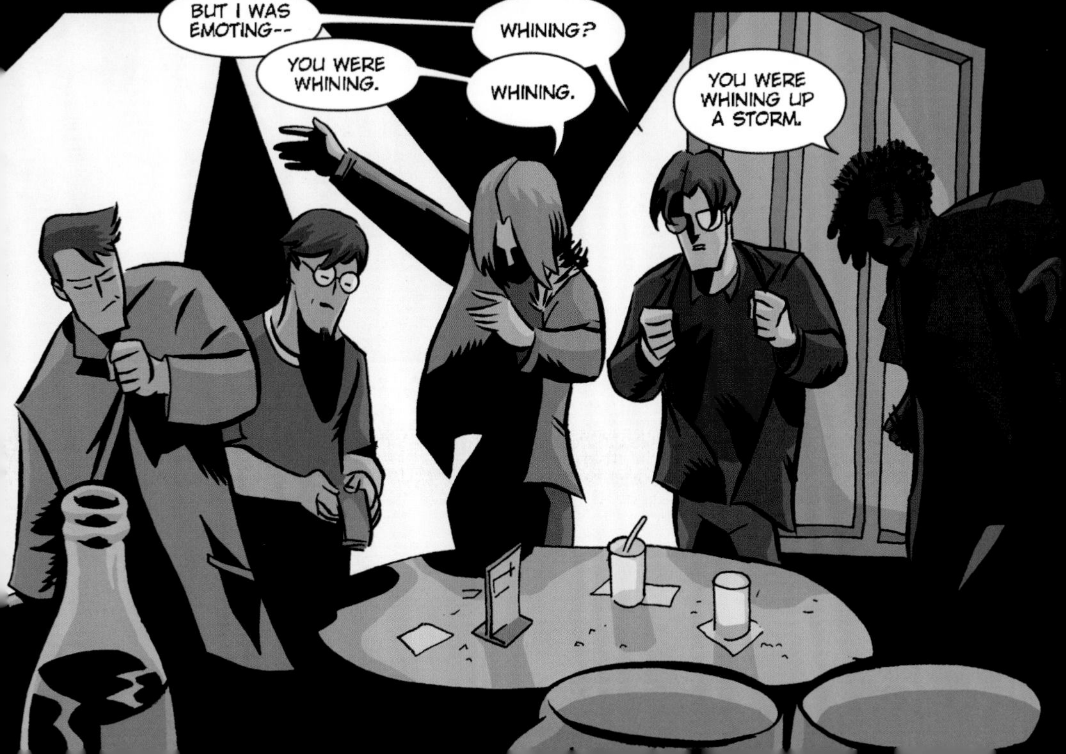
BUT I WAS EMOTING--
WHINING?
YOU WERE WHINING.
WHINING.
YOU WERE WHINING UP A STORM.

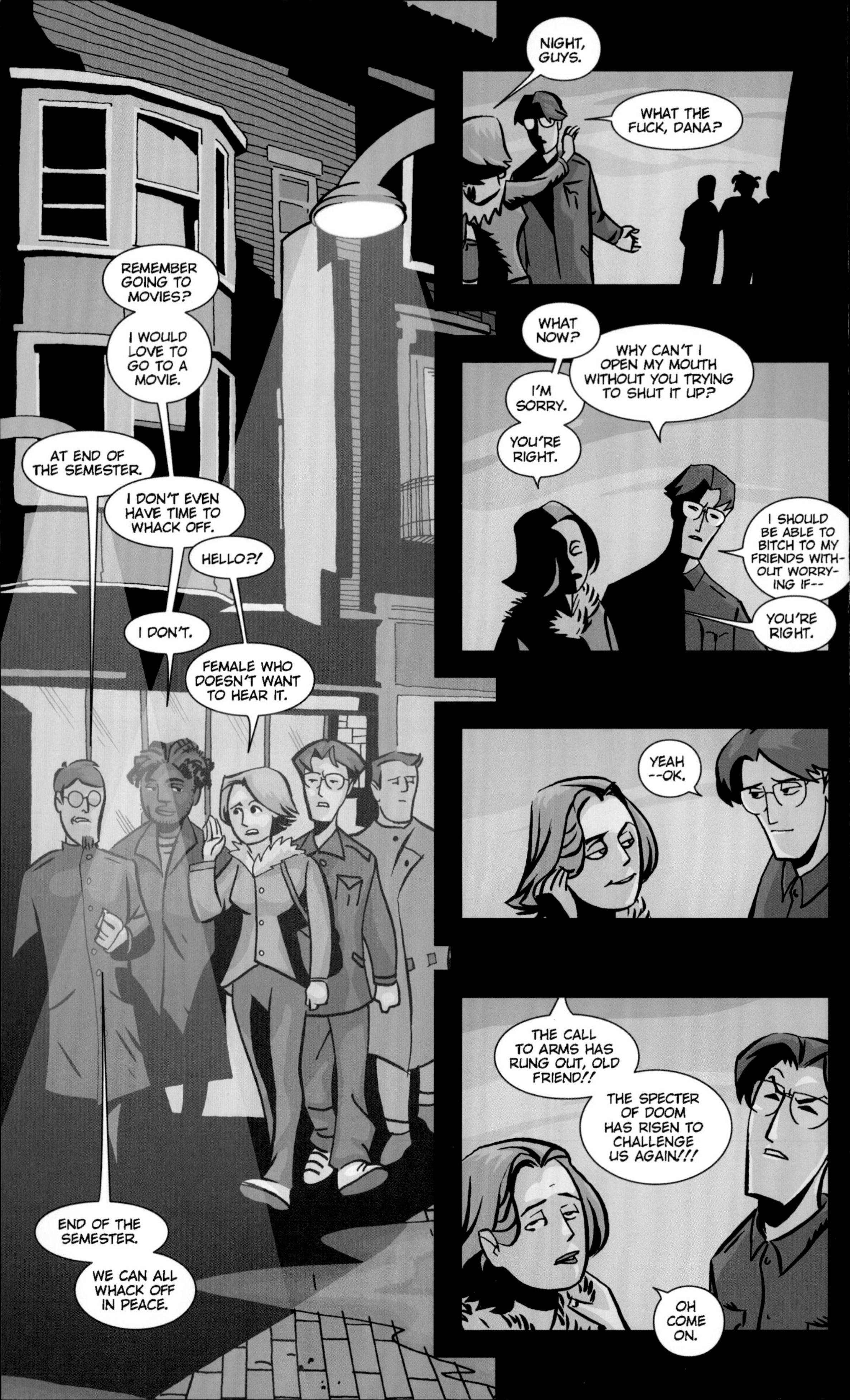
REMEMBER GOING TO MOVIES?
I WOULD LOVE TO GO TO A MOVIE.
AT END OF THE SEMESTER.
I DON'T EVEN HAVE TIME TO WHACK OFF.
HELLO?!
I DON'T.
FEMALE WHO DOESN'T WANT TO HEAR IT.
END OF THE SEMESTER.
WE CAN ALL WHACK OFF IN PEACE.
NIGHT, GUYS.
WHAT THE FUCK, DANA?
WHAT NOW?
WHY CAN'T I OPEN MY MOUTH WITHOUT YOU TRYING TO SHUT IT UP?
I'M SORRY.
YOU'RE RIGHT.
I SHOULD BE ABLE TO BITCH TO MY FRIENDS WITH-OUT WORRY-ING IF--
YOU'RE RIGHT.
YEAH --OK.
THE CALL TO ARMS HAS RUNG OUT, OLD FRIEND!!
THE SPECTER OF DOOM HAS RISEN TO CHALLENGE US AGAIN!!!
OH COME ON.

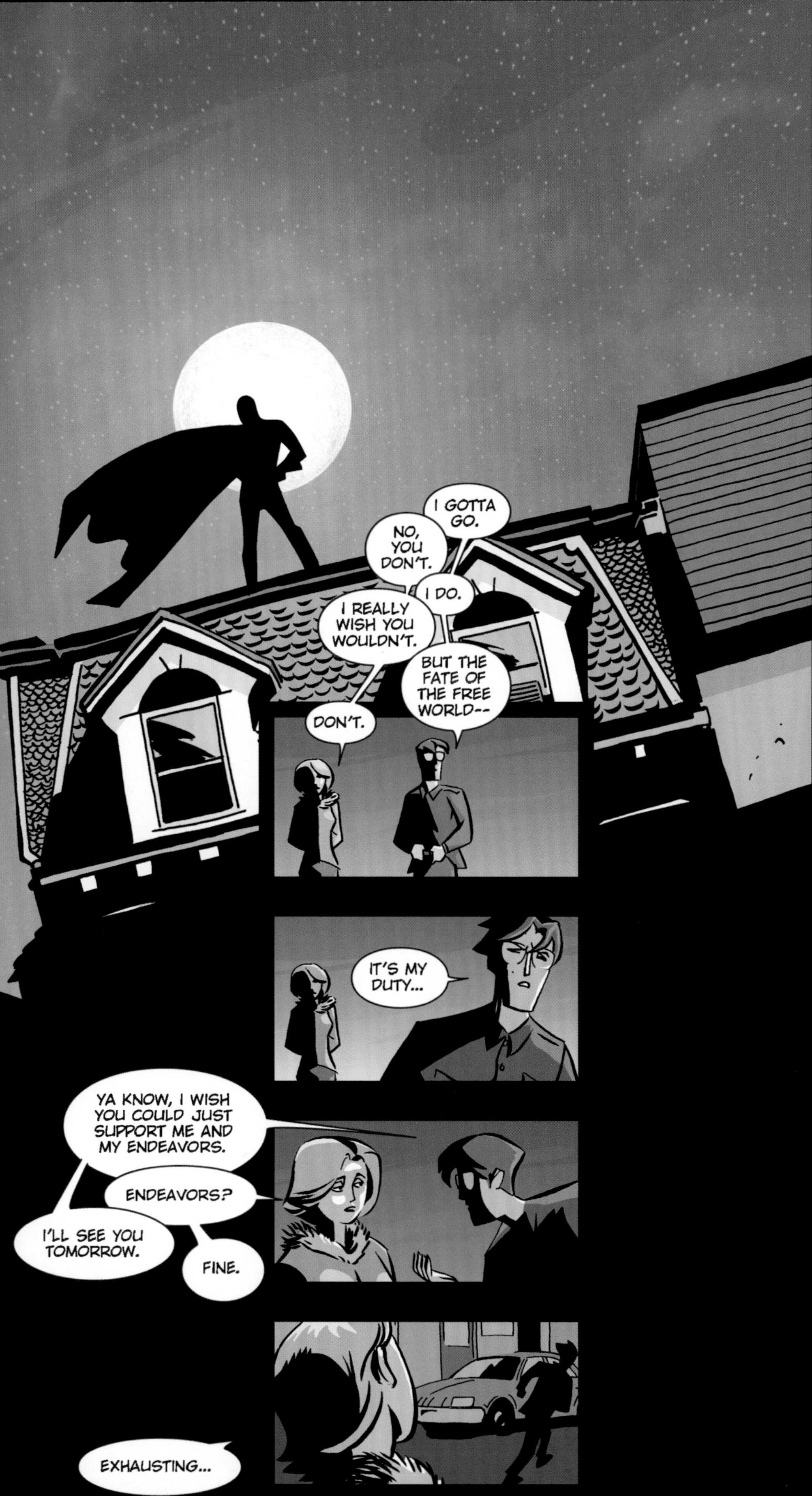
I GOTTA GO.
NO, YOU DON'T.
I DO.
I REALLY WISH YOU WOULDN'T.
BUT THE FATE OF THE FREE WORLD--
DON'T.
IT'S MY DUTY...
YA KNOW, I WISH YOU COULD JUST SUPPORT ME AND MY ENDEAVORS.
ENDEAVORS?
I'LL SEE YOU TOMORROW.
FINE.
EXHAUSTING...

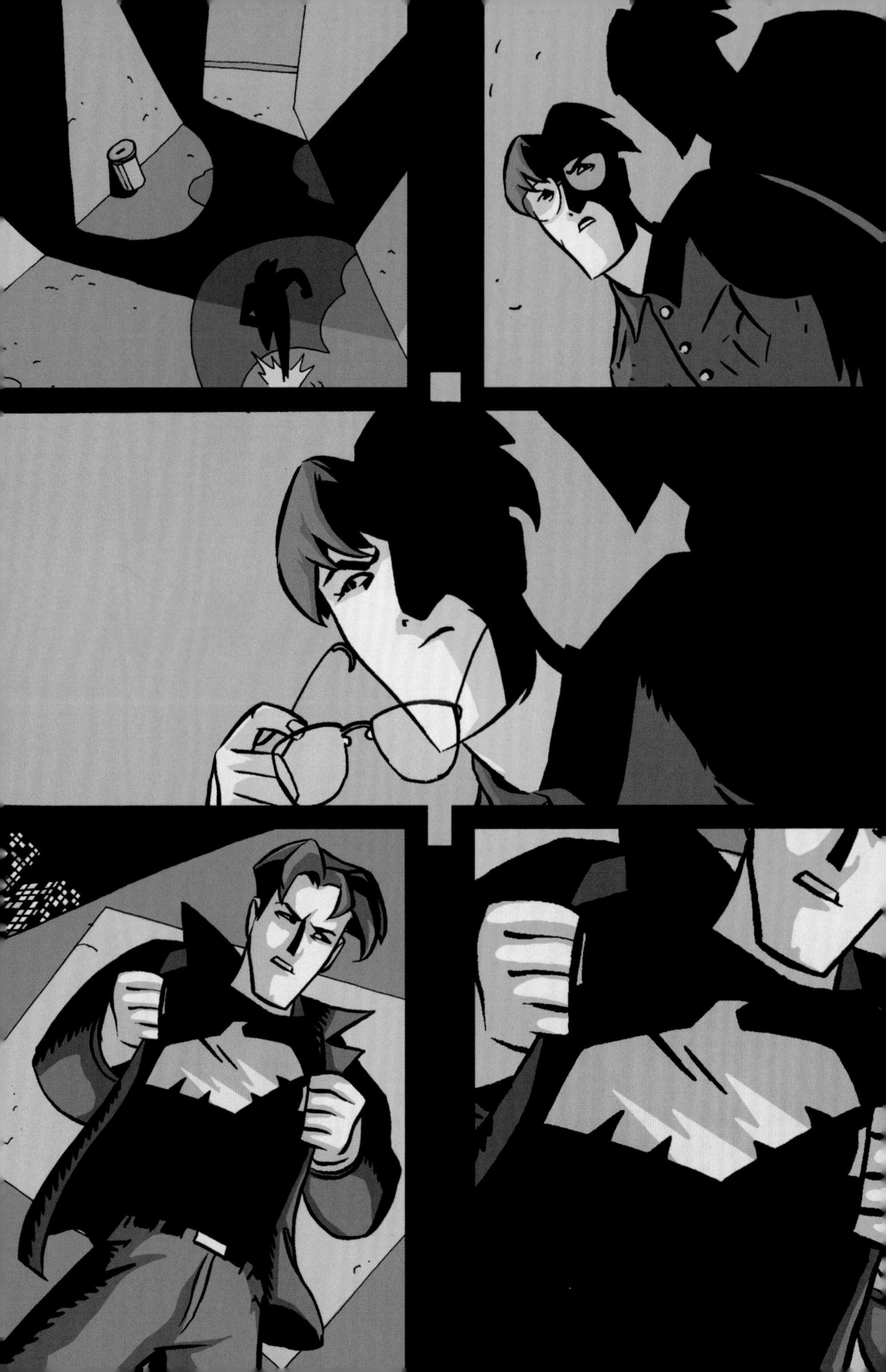

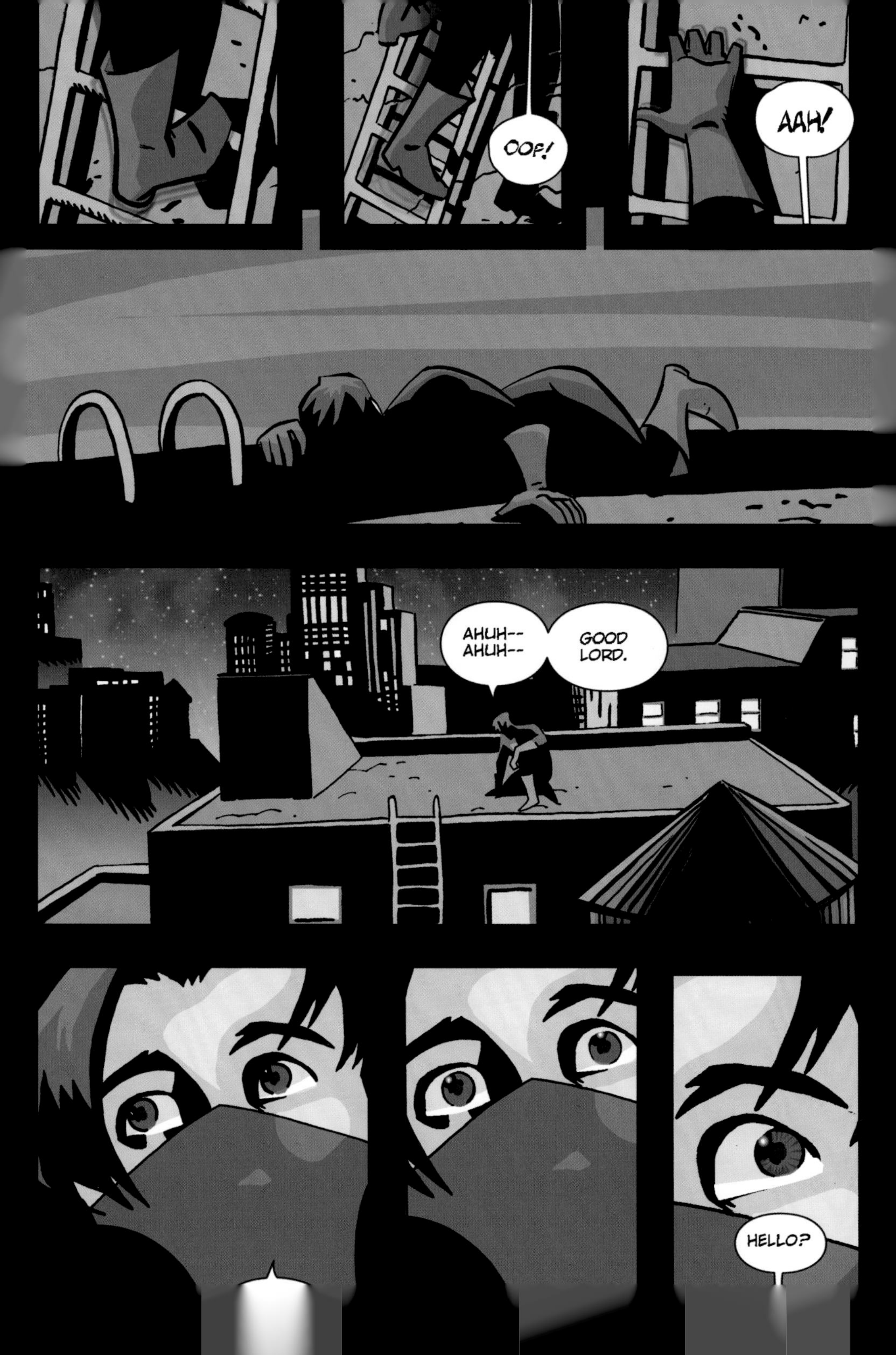
OOF!
AAH!
AHUH-- AHUH--
GOOD LORD.
HELLO?

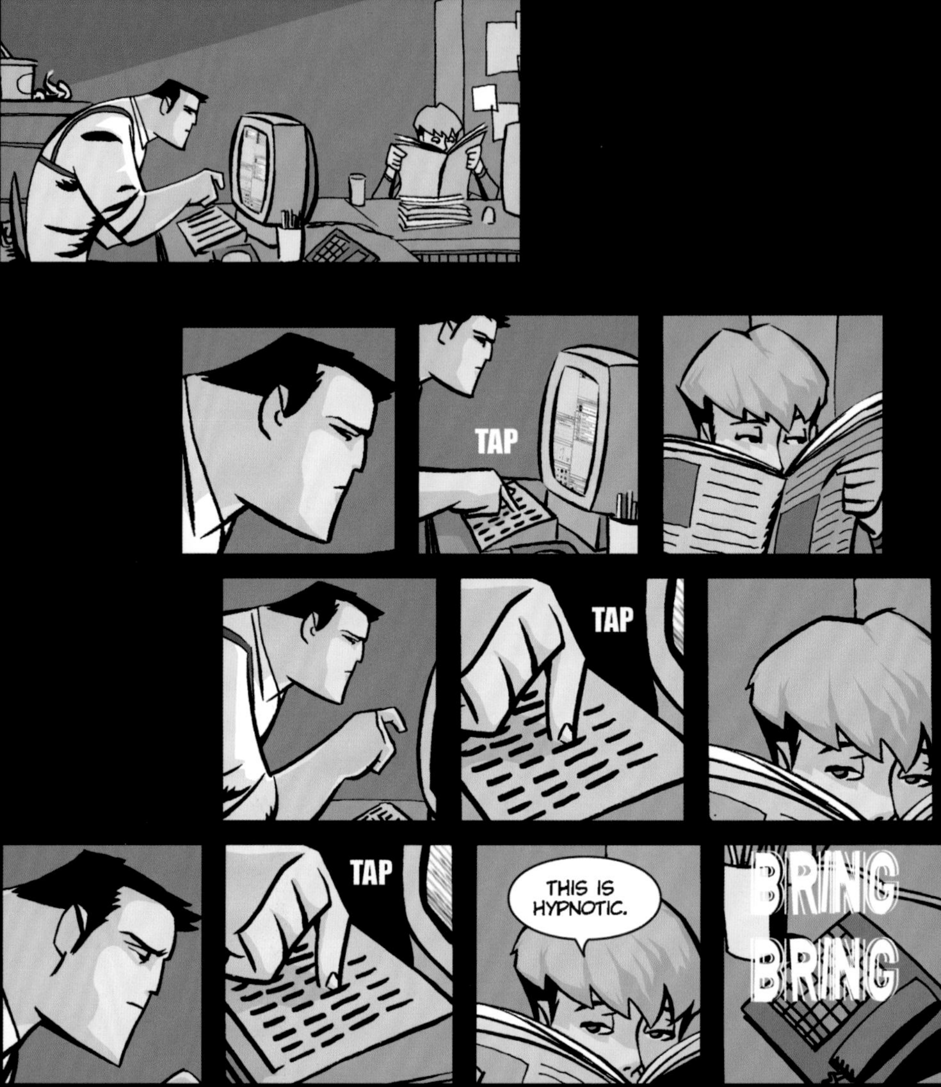
TAP
TAP
TAP
THIS IS HYPNOTIC.
BRING BRING

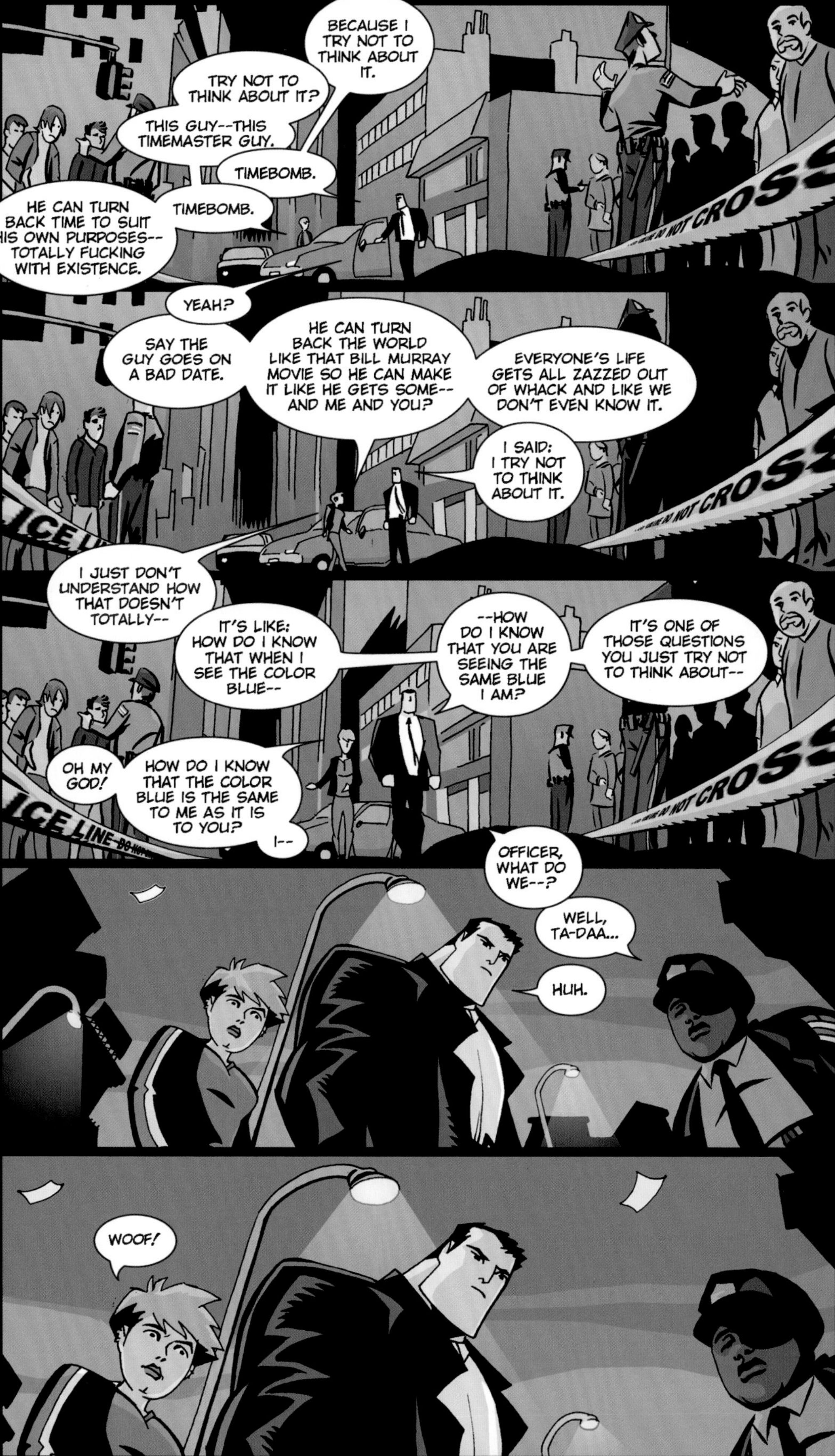
HE CAN TURN BACK TIME TO SUIT HIS OWN PURPOSES-- TOTALLY FUCKING WITH EXISTENCE.
THIS GUY--THIS TIMEMASTER GUY.
TIMEBOMB.
TIMEBOMB.
TRY NOT TO THINK ABOUT IT?
BECAUSE I TRY NOT TO THINK ABOUT IT.
DO NOT CROSS
YEAH?
SAY THE GUY GOES ON A BAD DATE.
HE CAN TURN BACK THE WORLD LIKE THAT BILL MURRAY MOVIE SO HE CAN MAKE IT LIKE HE GETS SOME-- AND ME AND YOU?
EVERYONE'S LIFE GETS ALL ZAZZED OUT OF WHACK AND LIKE WE DON'T EVEN KNOW IT.
I SAID: I TRY NOT TO THINK ABOUT IT.
DO NOT CROSS
I JUST DON'T UNDERSTAND HOW THAT DOESN'T TOTALLY--
IT'S LIKE: HOW DO I KNOW THAT WHEN I SEE THE COLOR BLUE--
--HOW DO I KNOW THAT YOU ARE SEEING THE SAME BLUE I AM?
IT'S ONE OF THOSE QUESTIONS YOU JUST TRY NOT TO THINK ABOUT--
OH MY GOD!
HOW DO I KNOW THAT THE COLOR BLUE IS THE SAME TO ME AS IT IS TO YOU?
I--
DO NOT CROSS
OFFICER, WHAT DO WE--?
WELL, TA-DAA...
HUH.
WOOF!

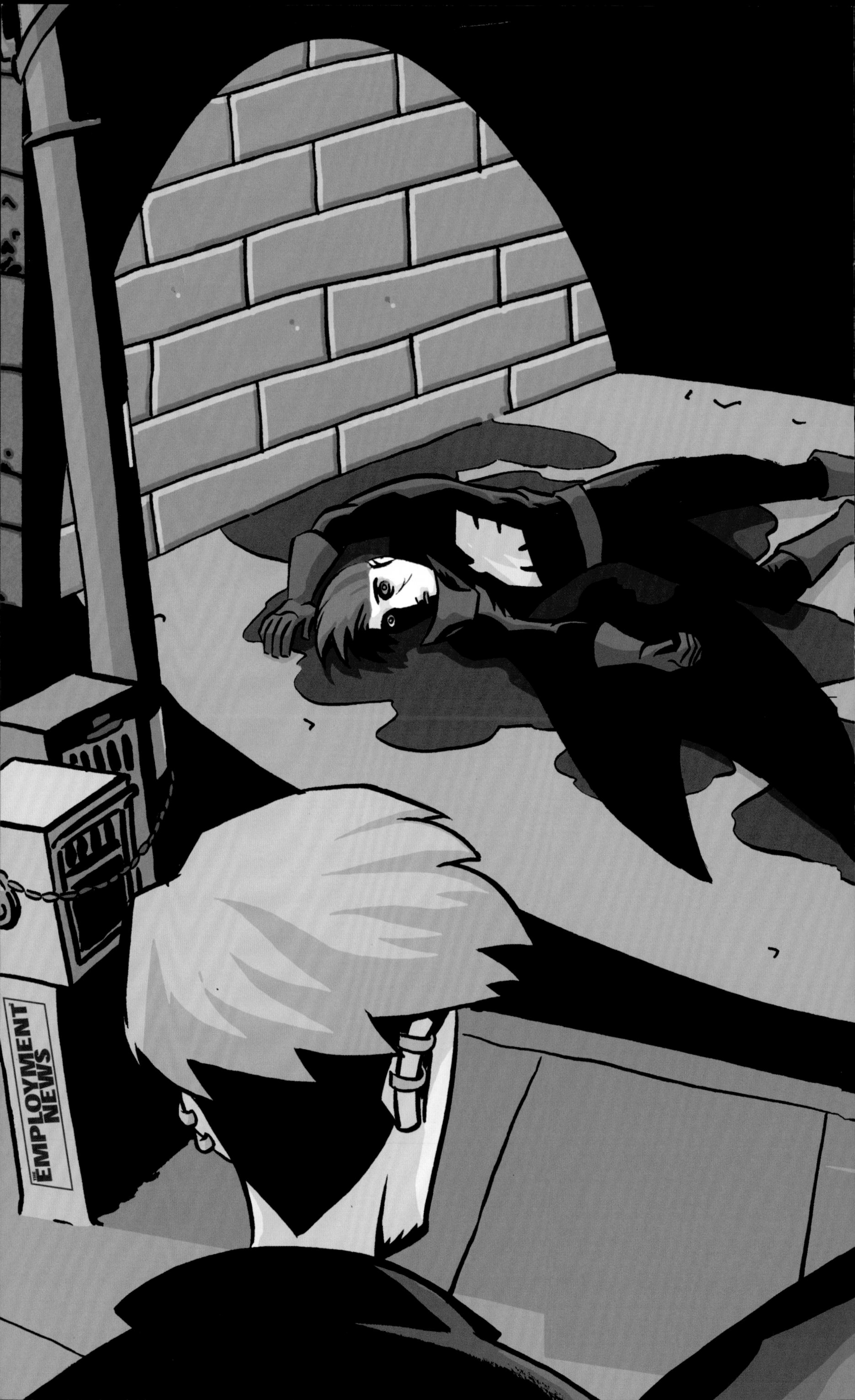
THE EMPLOYMENT NEWS

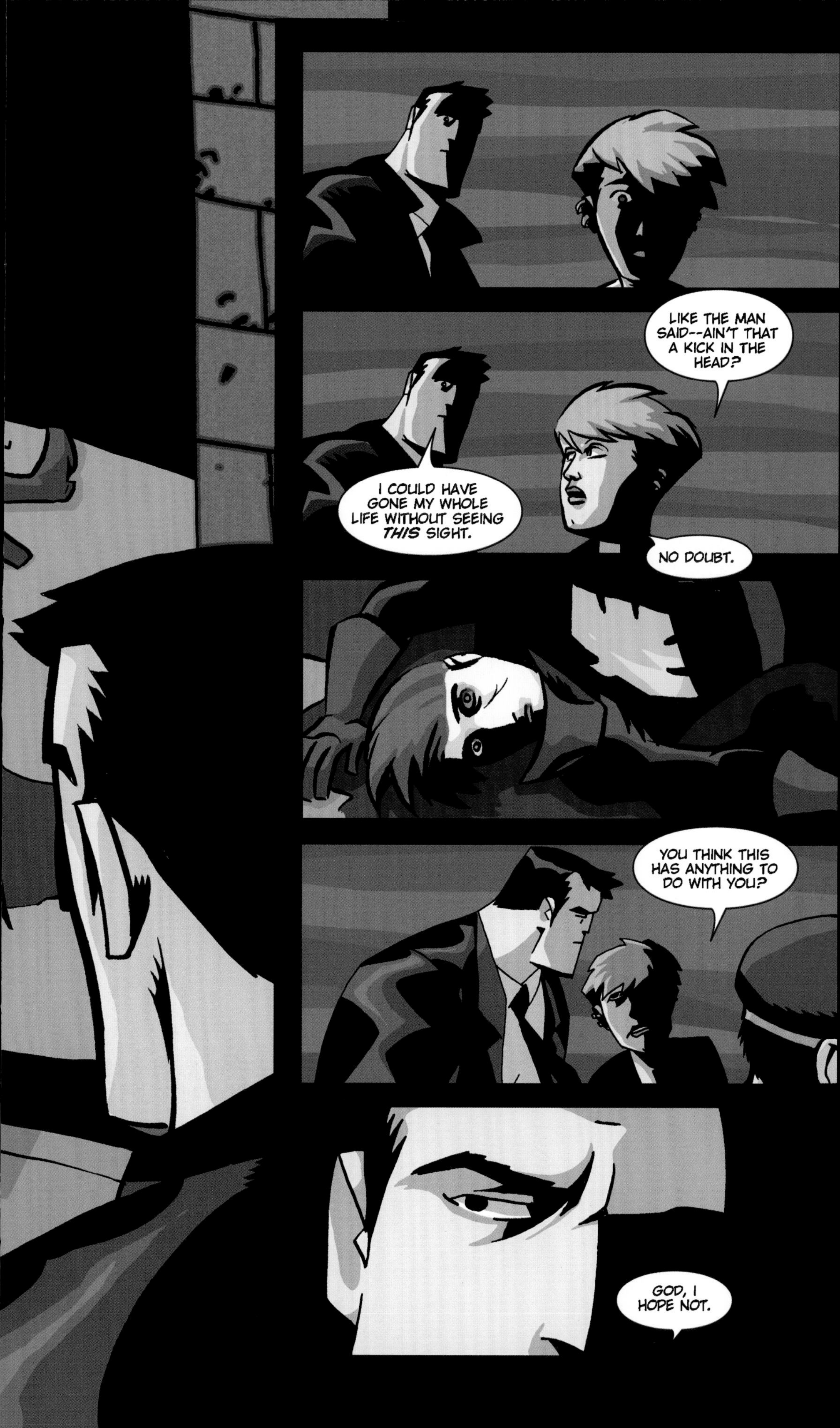
LIKE THE MAN SAID--AIN'T THAT A KICK IN THE HEAD?
I COULD HAVE GONE MY WHOLE LIFE WITHOUT SEEING *THIS* SIGHT.
NO DOUBT.
YOU THINK THIS HAS ANYTHING TO DO WITH YOU?
GOD, I HOPE NOT.

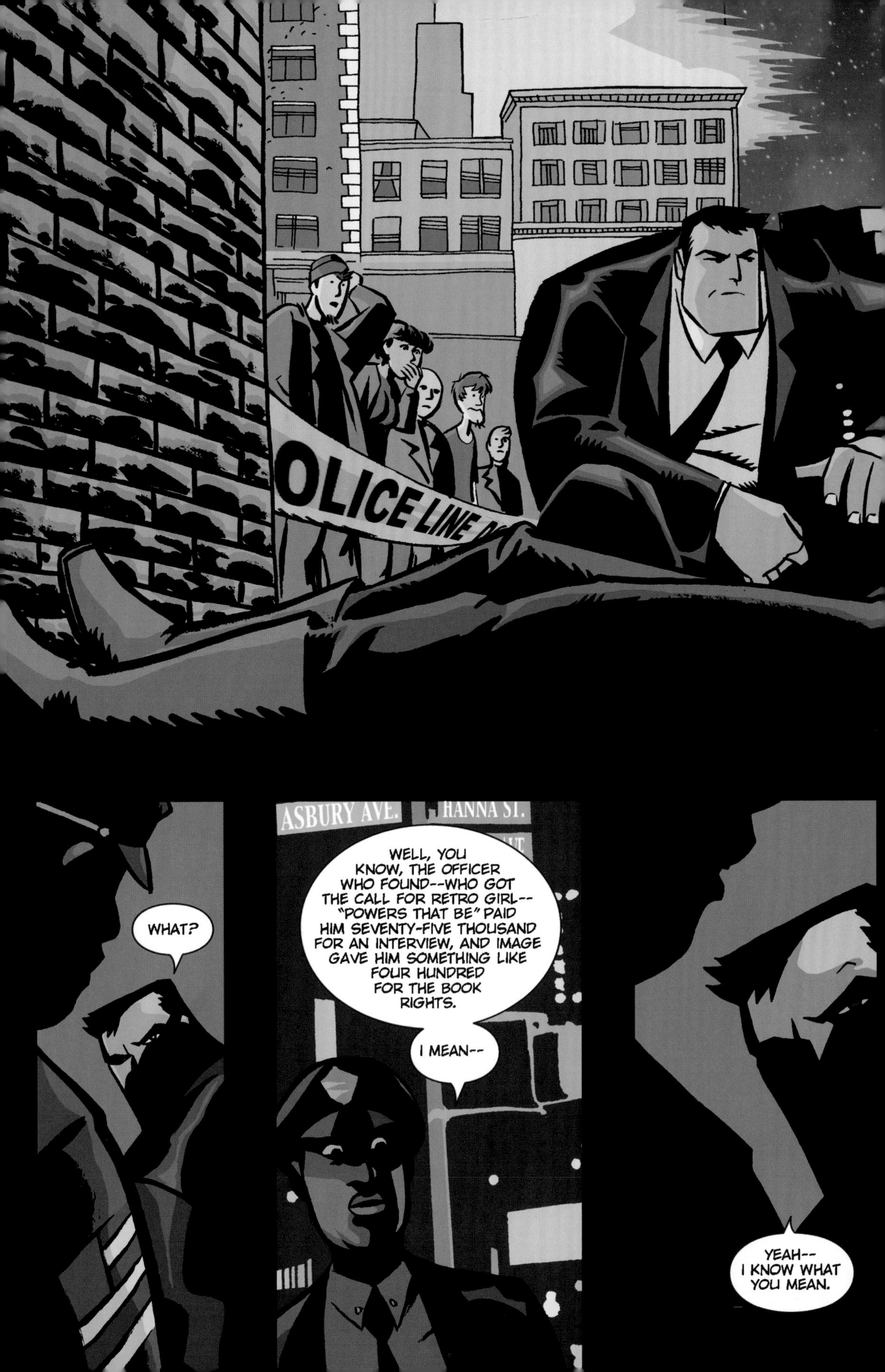
OLICE LINE D
ASBURY AVE.
HANNA ST.
WHAT?
WELL, YOU KNOW, THE OFFICER WHO FOUND--WHO GOT THE CALL FOR RETRO GIRL-- "POWERS THAT BE" PAID HIM SEVENTY-FIVE THOUSAND FOR AN INTERVIEW, AND IMAGE GAVE HIM SOMETHING LIKE FOUR HUNDRED FOR THE BOOK RIGHTS.
I MEAN--
YEAH-- I KNOW WHAT YOU MEAN.

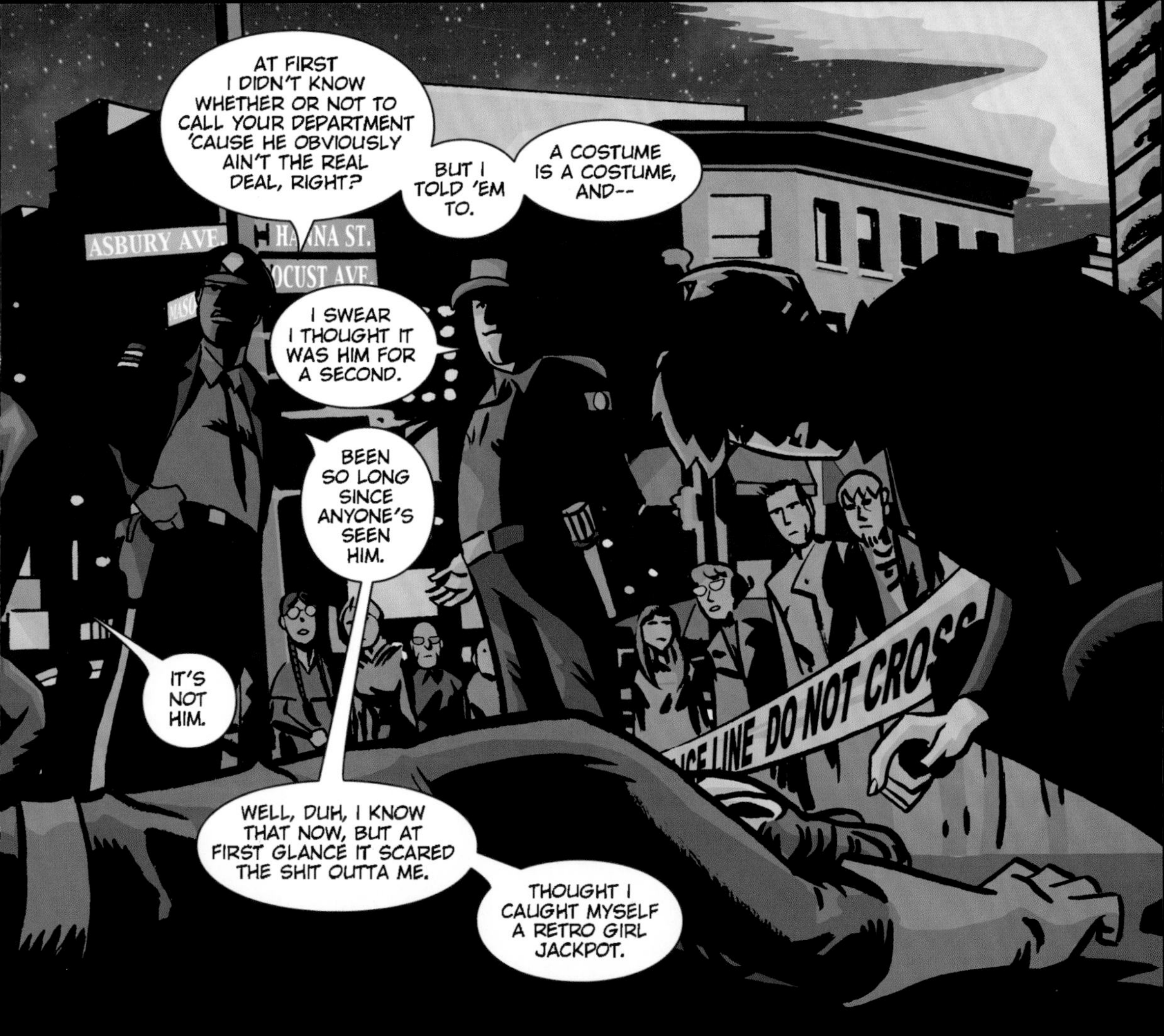
AT FIRST I DIDN'T KNOW WHETHER OR NOT TO CALL YOUR DEPARTMENT 'CAUSE HE OBVIOUSLY AIN'T THE REAL DEAL, RIGHT?
BUT I TOLD 'EM TO.
A COSTUME IS A COSTUME, AND--
ASBURY AVE.
HANNA ST.
LOCUST AVE.
I SWEAR I THOUGHT IT WAS HIM FOR A SECOND.
BEEN SO LONG SINCE ANYONE'S SEEN HIM.
IT'S NOT HIM.
DO NOT CROSS
WELL, DUH, I KNOW THAT NOW, BUT AT FIRST GLANCE IT SCARED THE SHIT OUTTA ME.
THOUGHT I CAUGHT MYSELF A RETRO GIRL JACKPOT.

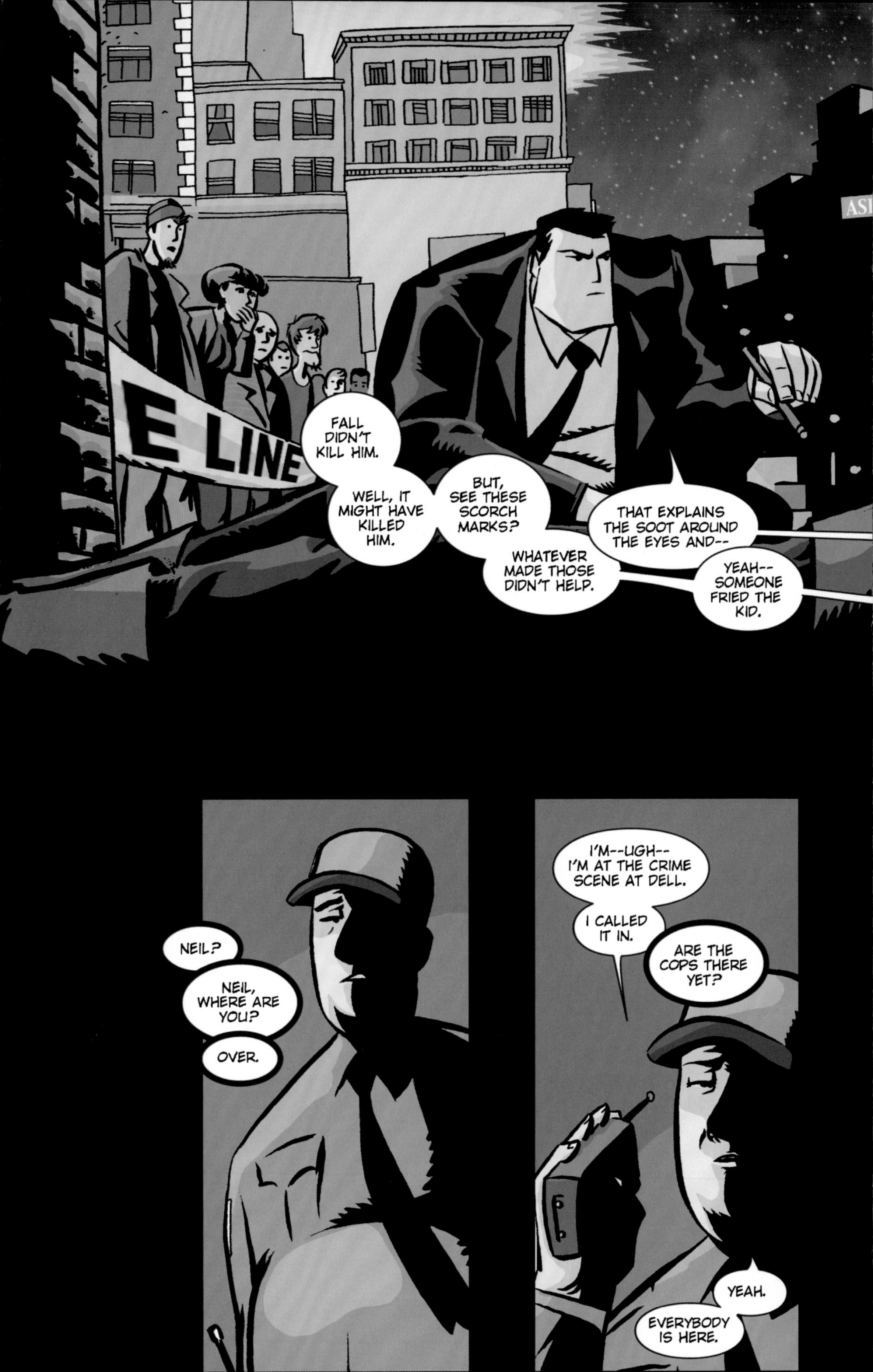
E LINE
ASI
FALL DIDN'T KILL HIM.
WELL, IT MIGHT HAVE KILLED HIM.
BUT, SEE THESE SCORCH MARKS?
WHATEVER MADE THOSE DIDN'T HELP.
THAT EXPLAINS THE SOOT AROUND THE EYES AND--
YEAH-- SOMEONE FRIED THE KID.
NEIL?
NEIL, WHERE ARE YOU?
OVER.
I'M--UGH-- I'M AT THE CRIME SCENE AT DELL.
I CALLED IT IN.
ARE THE COPS THERE YET?
YEAH.
EVERYBODY IS HERE.

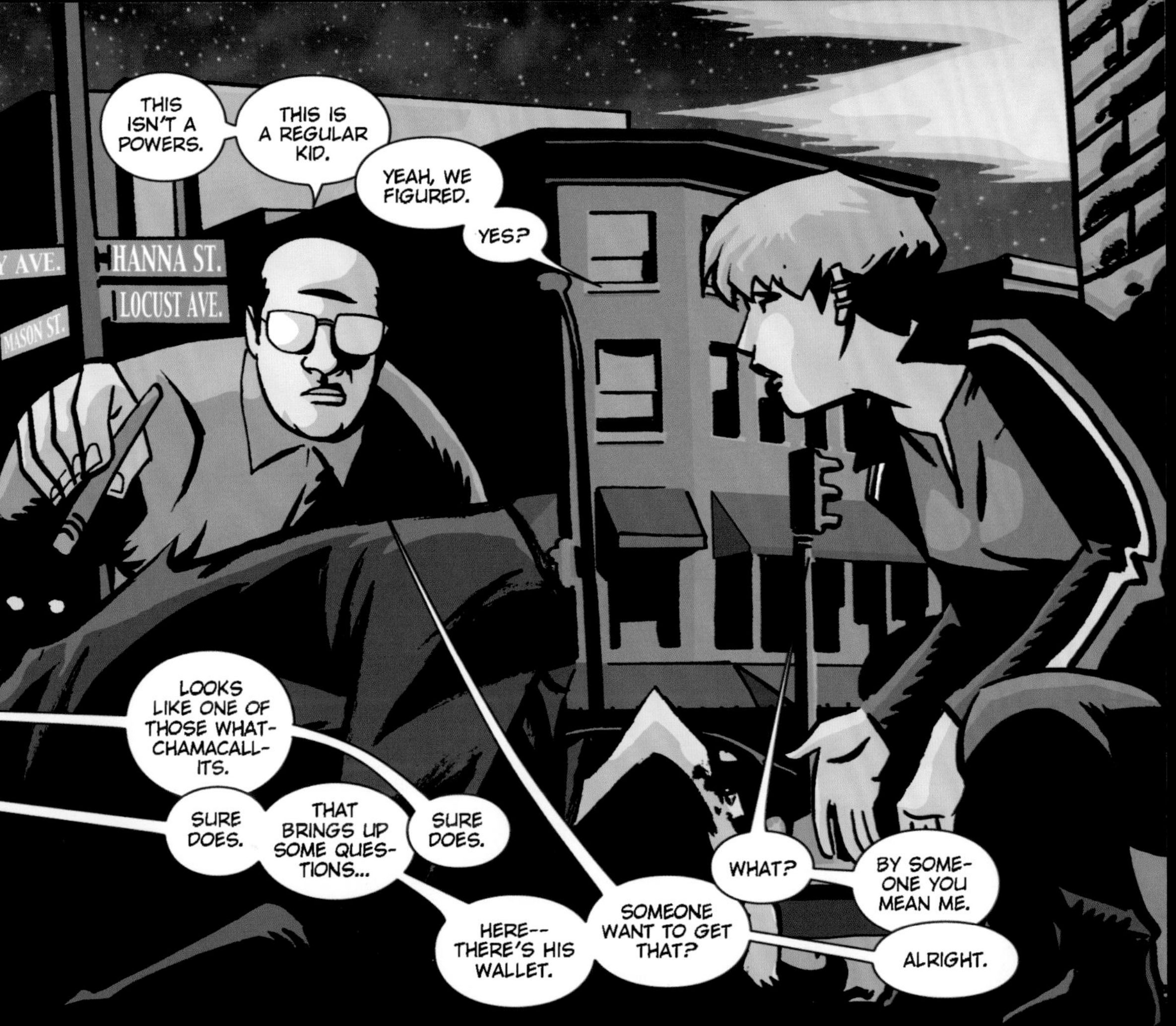

HANNA ST.
LOCUST AVE.
MASON ST.
THIS ISN'T A POWERS.
THIS IS A REGULAR KID.
YEAH, WE FIGURED.
YES?
LOOKS LIKE ONE OF THOSE WHAT-CHAMACALL-ITS.
SURE DOES.
THAT BRINGS UP SOME QUES-TIONS...
SURE DOES.
HERE-- THERE'S HIS WALLET.
SOMEONE WANT TO GET THAT?
WHAT?
BY SOME-ONE YOU MEAN ME.
ALRIGHT.

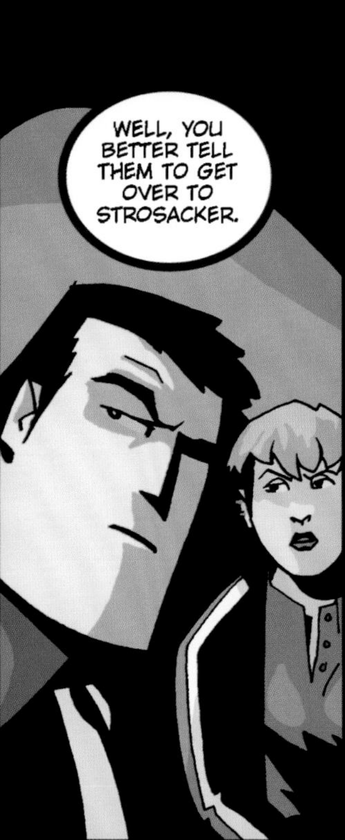

WELL, YOU BETTER TELL THEM TO GET OVER TO STROSACKER.

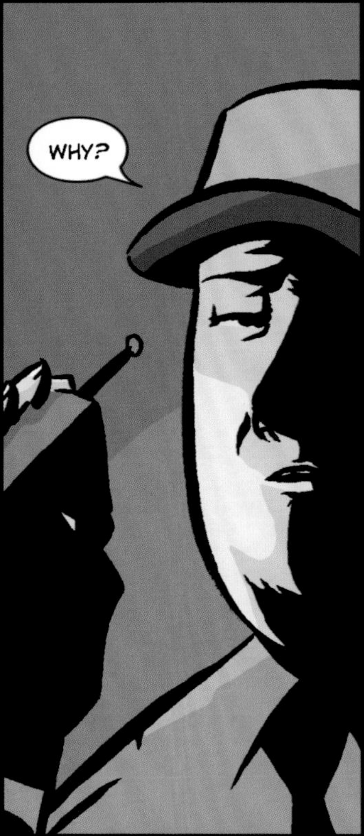

WHY?

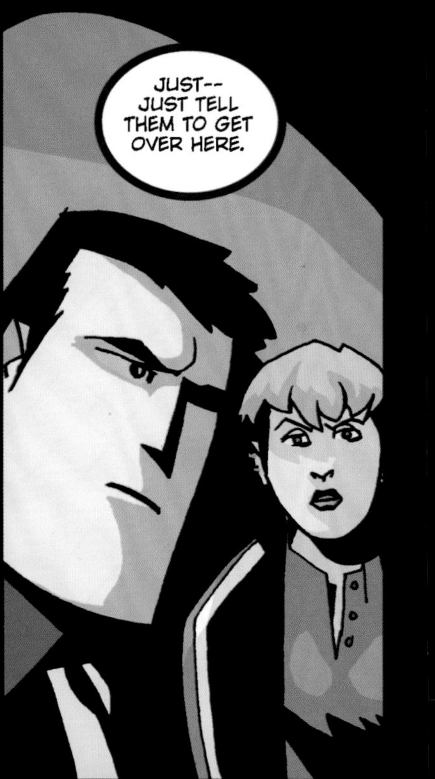

JUST-- JUST TELL THEM TO GET OVER HERE.

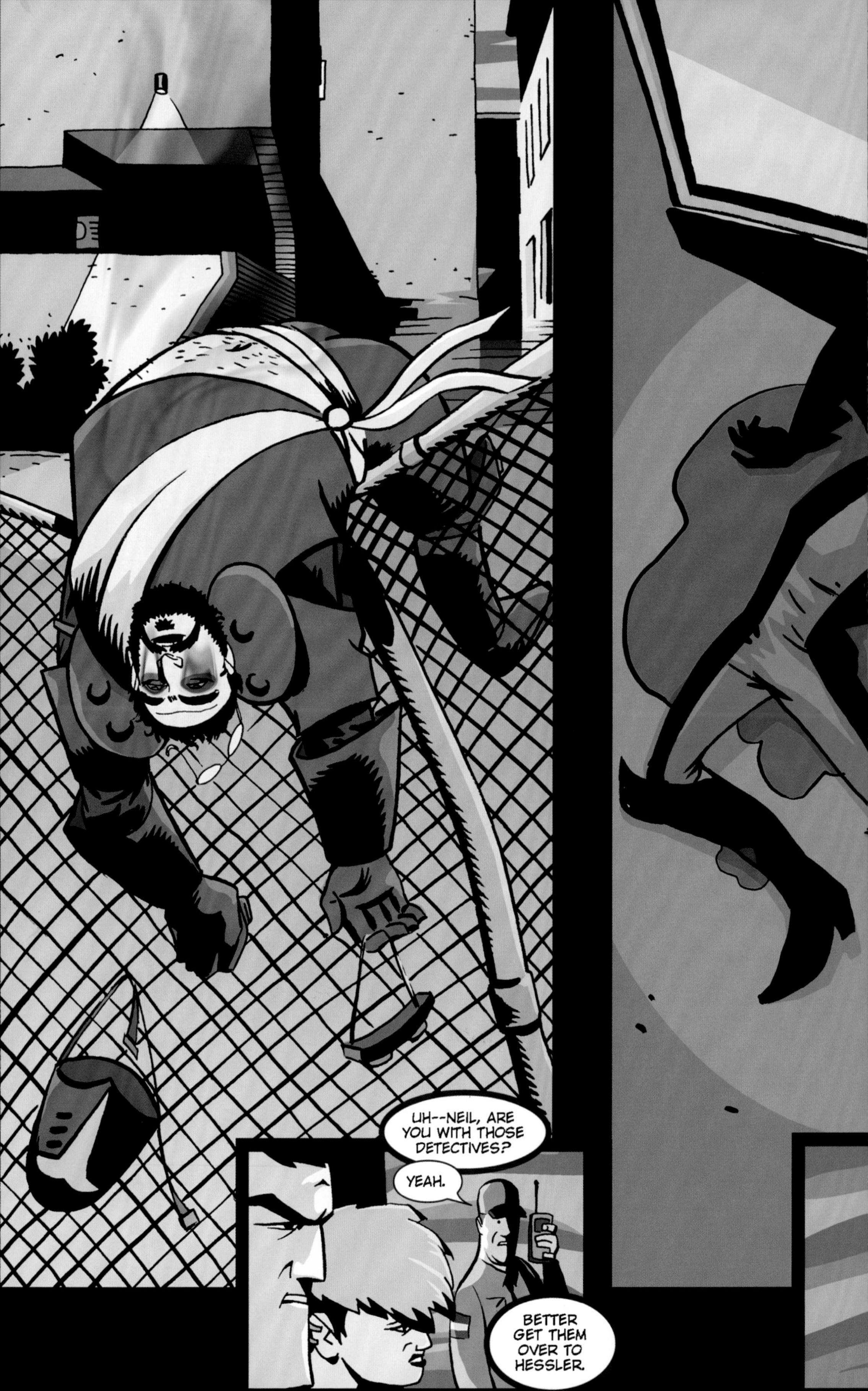
UH--NEIL, ARE YOU WITH THOSE DETECTIVES?
YEAH.
BETTER GET THEM OVER TO HESSLER.

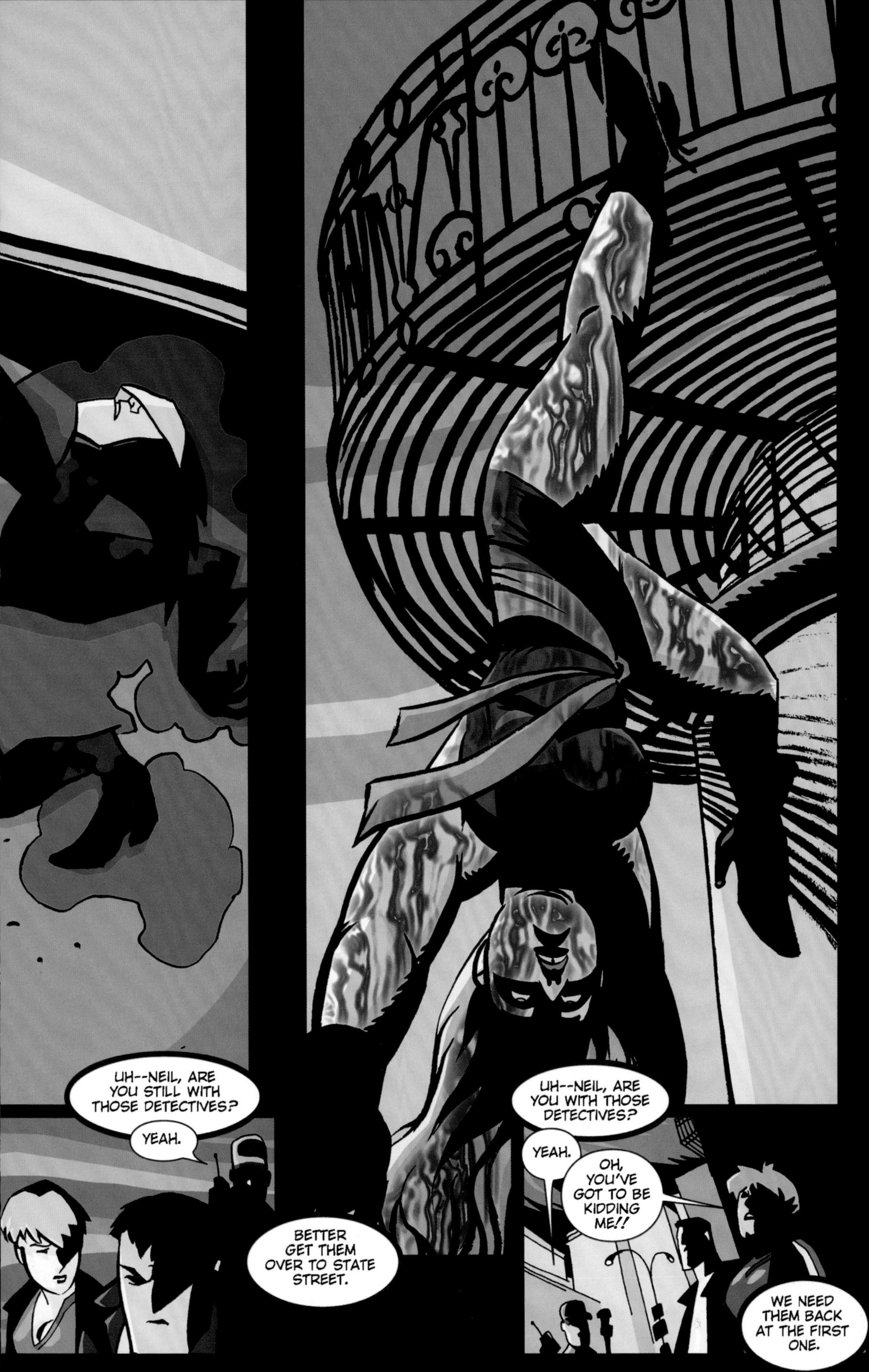
UH--NEIL, ARE YOU STILL WITH THOSE DETECTIVES?
YEAH.
BETTER GET THEM OVER TO STATE STREET.
UH--NEIL, ARE YOU WITH THOSE DETECTIVES?
YEAH.
OH, YOU'VE GOT TO BE KIDDING ME!!
WE NEED THEM BACK AT THE FIRST ONE.

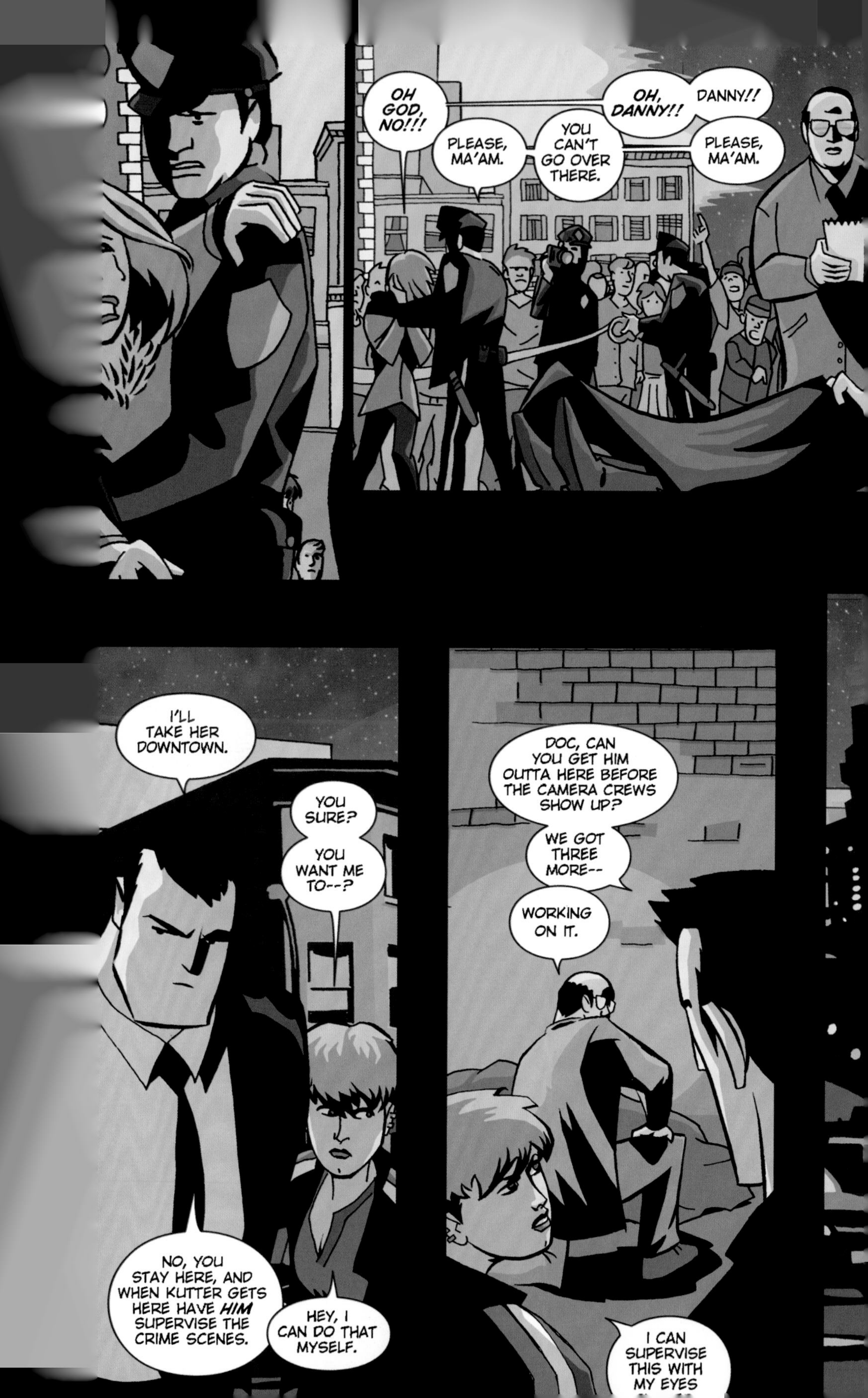
OH GOD, NO!!!
PLEASE, MA'AM.
YOU CAN'T GO OVER THERE.
OH, DANNY!!
DANNY!!
PLEASE, MA'AM.
I'LL TAKE HER DOWNTOWN.
YOU SURE?
YOU WANT ME TO--?
NO, YOU STAY HERE, AND WHEN KUTTER GETS HERE HAVE *HIM* SUPERVISE THE CRIME SCENES.
HEY, I CAN DO THAT MYSELF.
DOC, CAN YOU GET HIM OUTTA HERE BEFORE THE CAMERA CREWS SHOW UP?
WE GOT THREE MORE--
WORKING ON IT.
I CAN SUPERVISE THIS WITH MY EYES

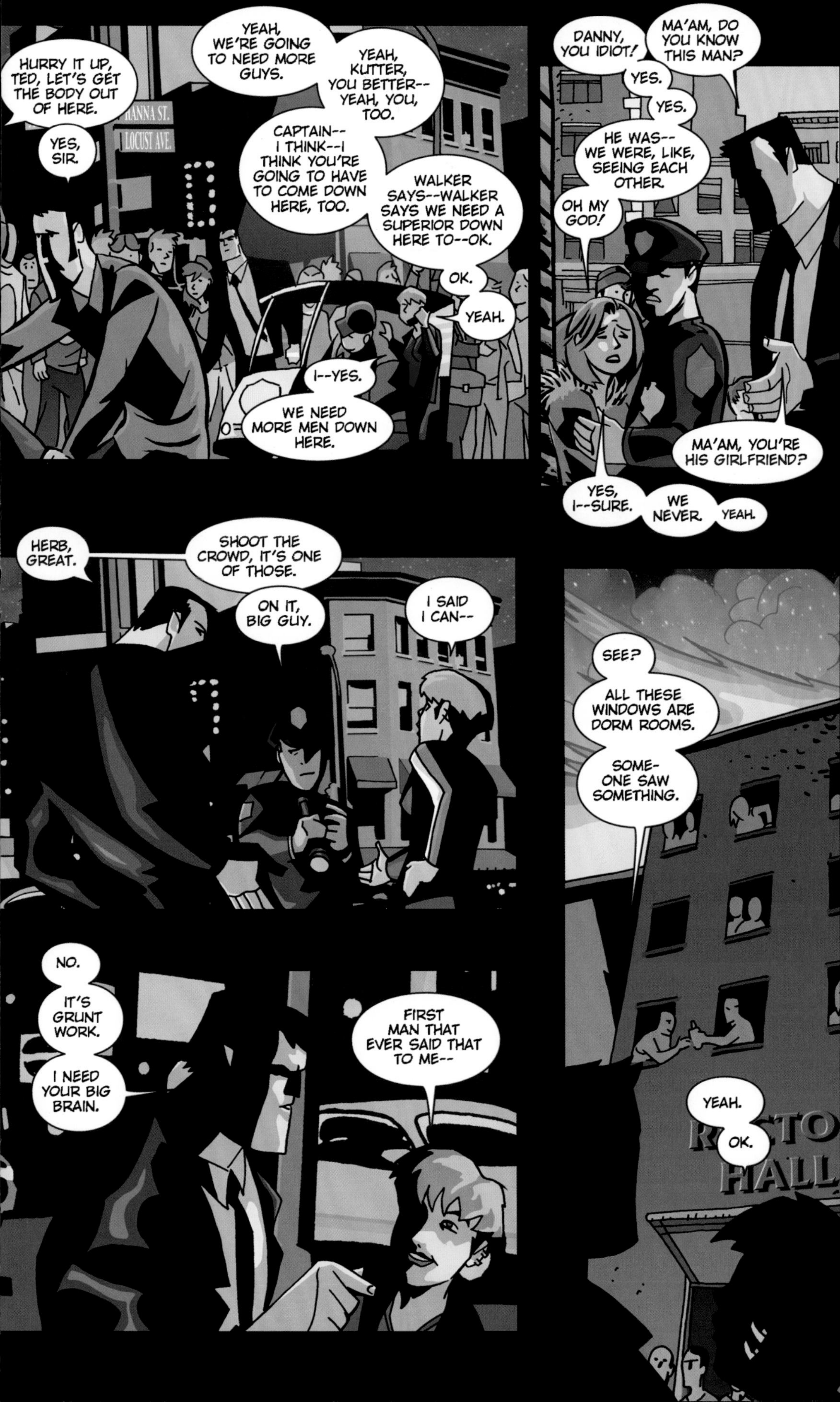
HURRY IT UP, TED, LET'S GET THE BODY OUT OF HERE.
YES, SIR.
HANNA ST.
LOCUST AVE.
YEAH, WE'RE GOING TO NEED MORE GUYS.
YEAH, KUTTER, YOU BETTER-- YEAH, YOU, TOO.
CAPTAIN-- I THINK--I THINK YOU'RE GOING TO HAVE TO COME DOWN HERE, TOO.
WALKER SAYS--WALKER SAYS WE NEED A SUPERIOR DOWN HERE TO--OK.
OK.
YEAH.
I--YES.
WE NEED MORE MEN DOWN HERE.
DANNY, YOU IDIOT!
MA'AM, DO YOU KNOW THIS MAN?
YES.
YES.
HE WAS-- WE WERE, LIKE, SEEING EACH OTHER.
OH MY GOD!
MA'AM, YOU'RE HIS GIRLFRIEND?
YES, I--SURE.
WE NEVER.
YEAH.
HERB, GREAT.
SHOOT THE CROWD, IT'S ONE OF THOSE.
ON IT, BIG GUY.
I SAID I CAN--
SEE?
ALL THESE WINDOWS ARE DORM ROOMS.
SOME-ONE SAW SOMETHING.
NO.
IT'S GRUNT WORK.
I NEED YOUR BIG BRAIN.
FIRST MAN THAT EVER SAID THAT TO ME--
YEAH.
OK.

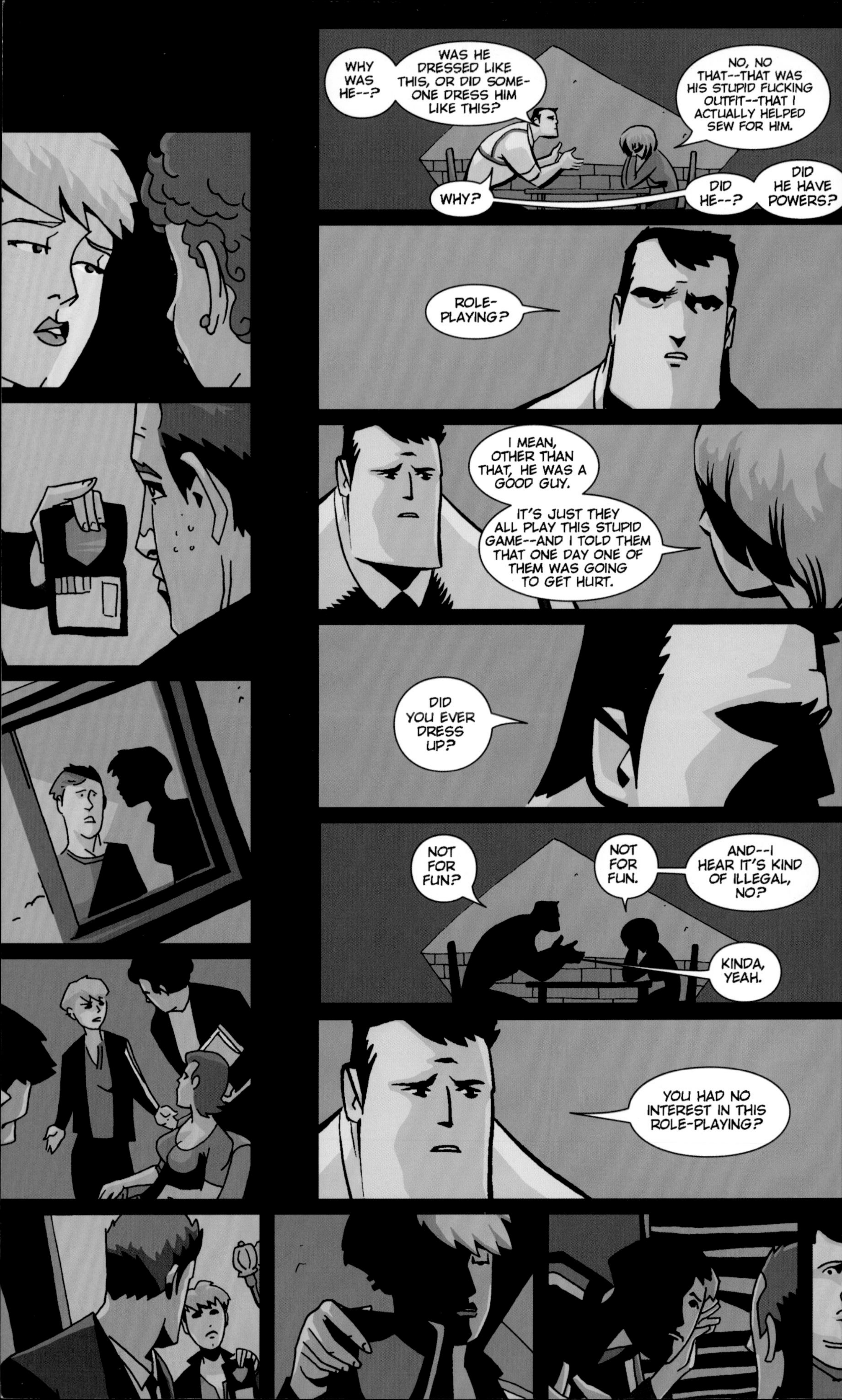
WHY WAS HE--?
WAS HE DRESSED LIKE THIS, OR DID SOME-ONE DRESS HIM LIKE THIS?
NO, NO THAT--THAT WAS HIS STUPID FUCKING OUTFIT--THAT I ACTUALLY HELPED SEW FOR HIM.
WHY?
DID HE--?
DID HE HAVE POWERS?
ROLE-PLAYING?
I MEAN, OTHER THAN THAT, HE WAS A GOOD GUY.
IT'S JUST THEY ALL PLAY THIS STUPID GAME--AND I TOLD THEM THAT ONE DAY ONE OF THEM WAS GOING TO GET HURT.
DID YOU EVER DRESS UP?
NOT FOR FUN?
NOT FOR FUN.
AND--I HEAR IT'S KIND OF ILLEGAL, NO?
KINDA, YEAH.
YOU HAD NO INTEREST IN THIS ROLE-PLAYING?

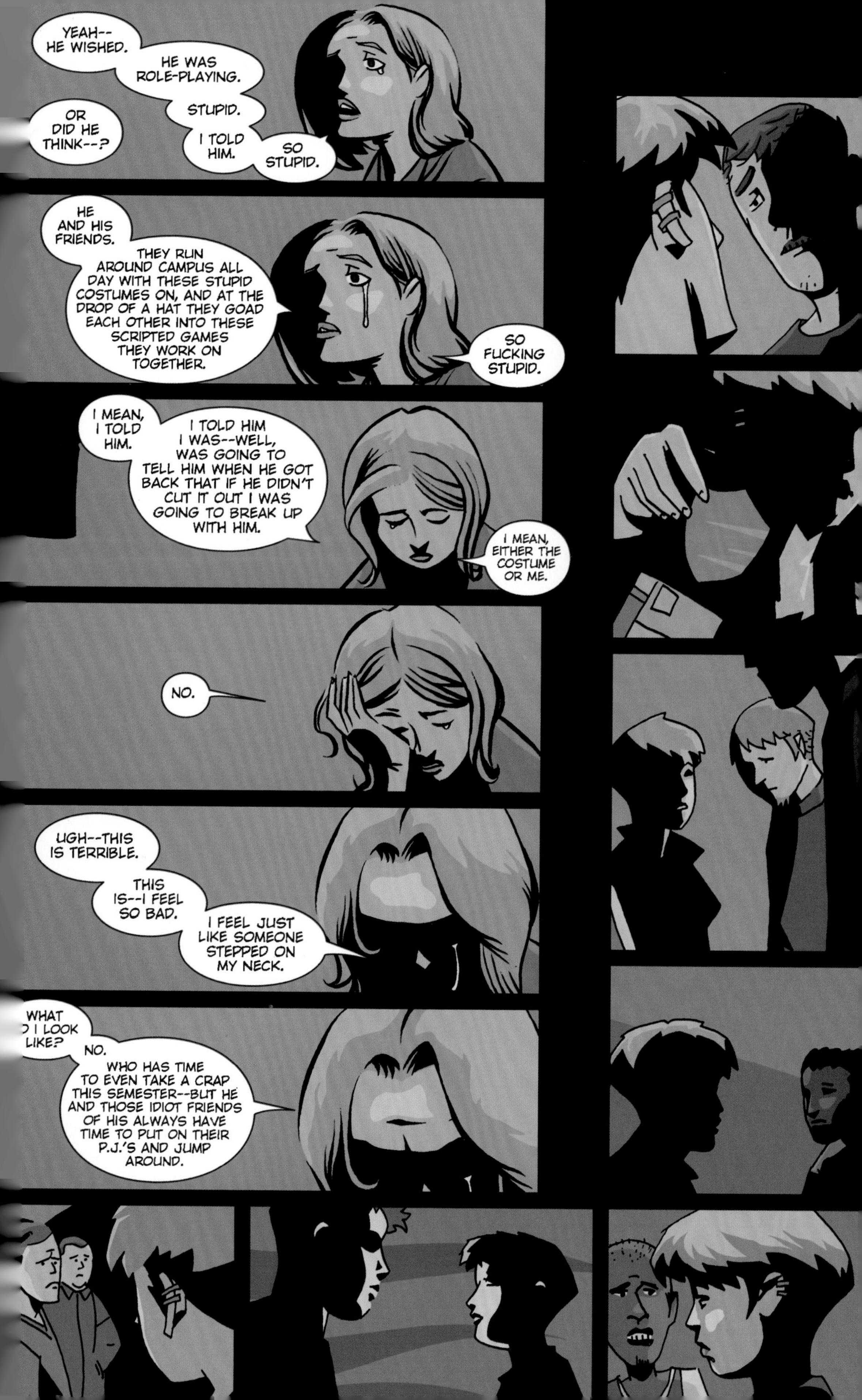

YEAH-- HE WISHED.
HE WAS ROLE-PLAYING.
STUPID.
OR DID HE THINK--?
I TOLD HIM.
SO STUPID.
HE AND HIS FRIENDS.
THEY RUN AROUND CAMPUS ALL DAY WITH THESE STUPID COSTUMES ON, AND AT THE DROP OF A HAT THEY GOAD EACH OTHER INTO THESE SCRIPTED GAMES THEY WORK ON TOGETHER.
SO FUCKING STUPID.
I MEAN, I TOLD HIM.
I TOLD HIM I WAS--WELL, WAS GOING TO TELL HIM WHEN HE GOT BACK THAT IF HE DIDN'T CUT IT OUT I WAS GOING TO BREAK UP WITH HIM.
I MEAN, EITHER THE COSTUME OR ME.
NO.
UGH--THIS IS TERRIBLE.
THIS IS--I FEEL SO BAD.
I FEEL JUST LIKE SOMEONE STEPPED ON MY NECK.
WHAT I LOOK LIKE?
NO.
WHO HAS TIME TO EVEN TAKE A CRAP THIS SEMESTER--BUT HE AND THOSE IDIOT FRIENDS OF HIS ALWAYS HAVE TIME TO PUT ON THEIR P.J.'S AND JUMP AROUND.

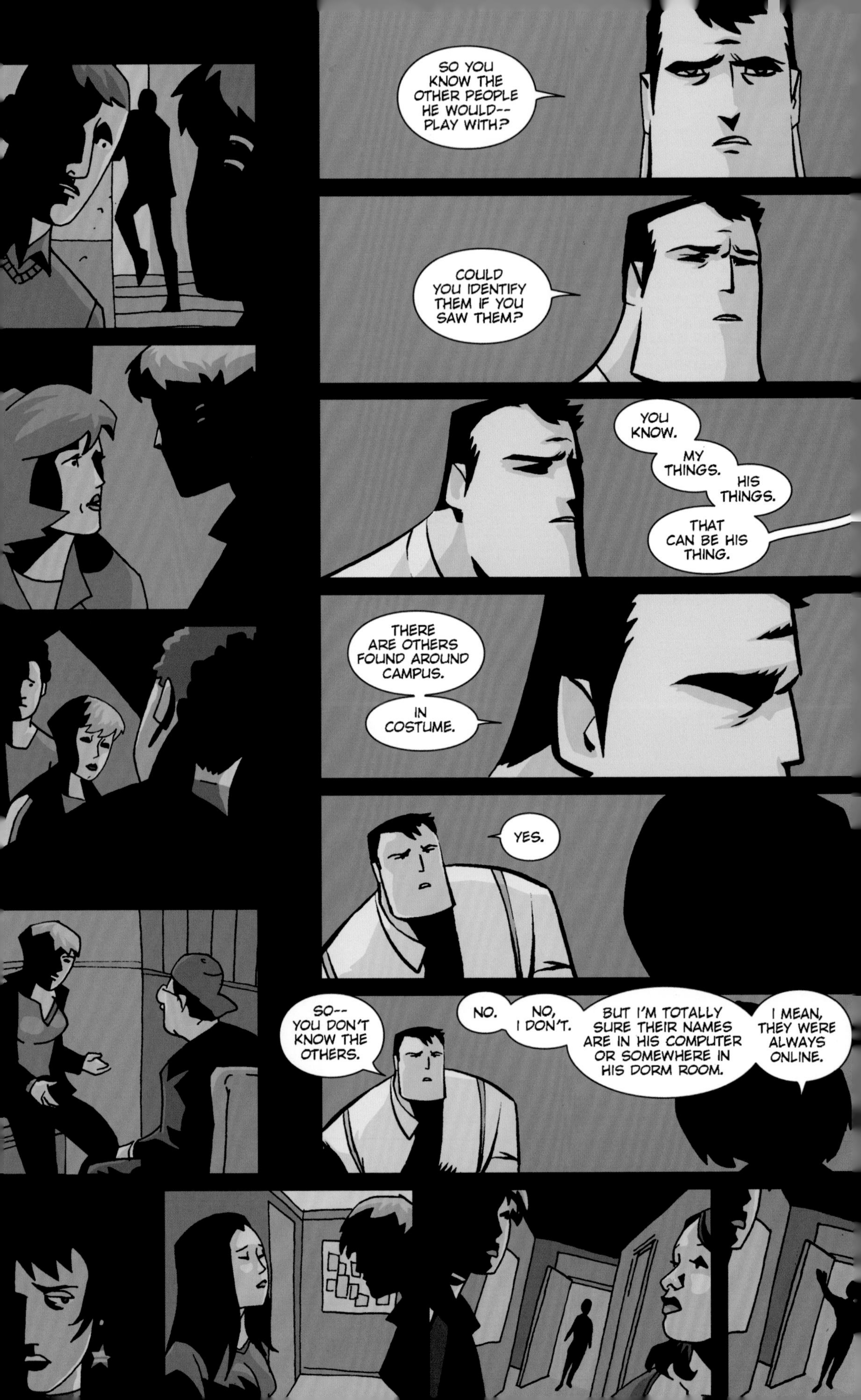
SO YOU KNOW THE OTHER PEOPLE HE WOULD-- PLAY WITH?
COULD YOU IDENTIFY THEM IF YOU SAW THEM?
YOU KNOW.
MY THINGS.
HIS THINGS.
THAT CAN BE HIS THING.
THERE ARE OTHERS FOUND AROUND CAMPUS.
IN COSTUME.
YES.
SO-- YOU DON'T KNOW THE OTHERS.
NO.
NO, I DON'T.
BUT I'M TOTALLY SURE THEIR NAMES ARE IN HIS COMPUTER OR SOMEWHERE IN HIS DORM ROOM.
I MEAN, THEY WERE ALWAYS ONLINE.

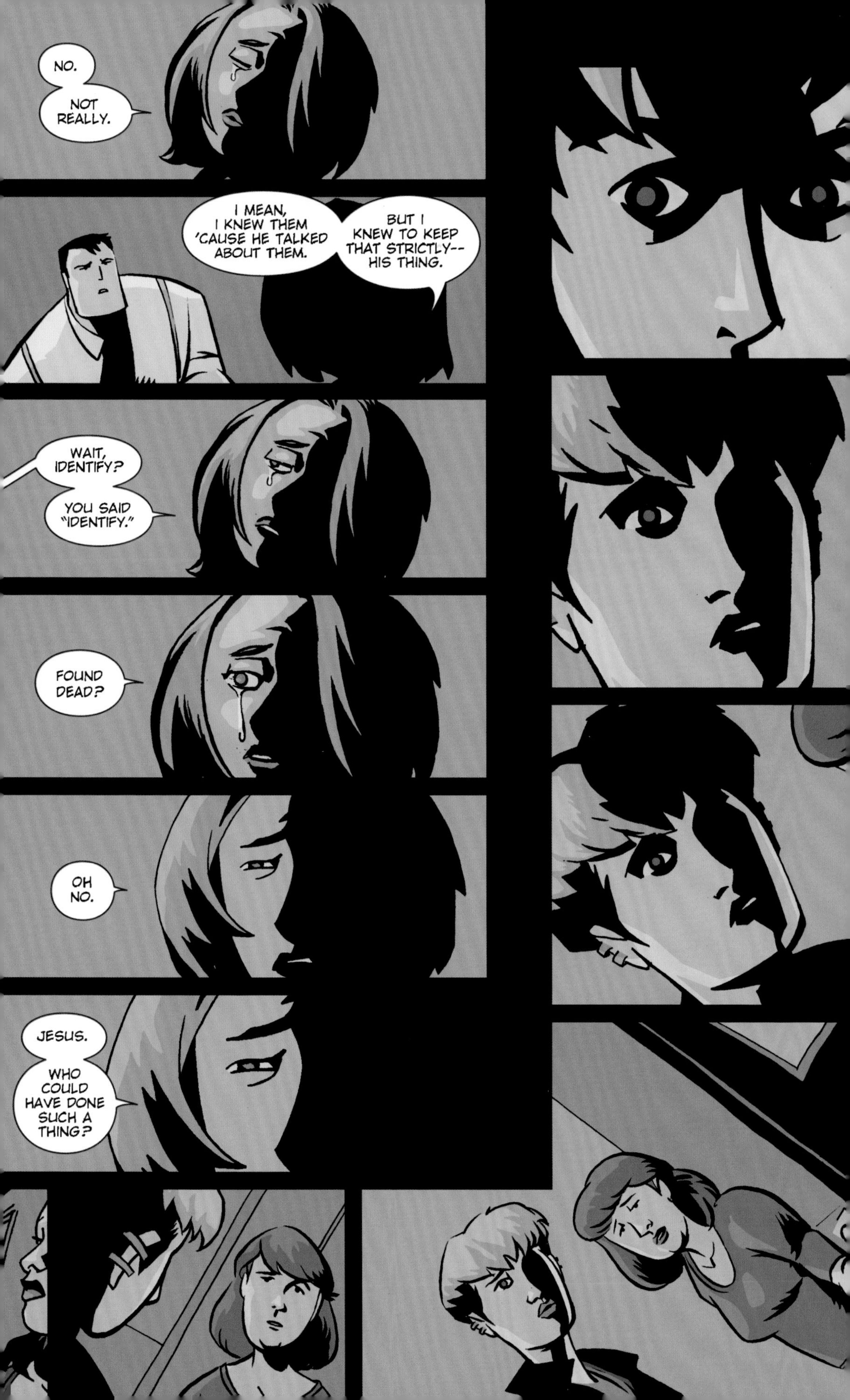
NO.
NOT REALLY.
I MEAN, I KNEW THEM 'CAUSE HE TALKED ABOUT THEM.
BUT I KNEW TO KEEP THAT STRICTLY-- HIS THING.
WAIT, IDENTIFY?
YOU SAID "IDENTIFY."
FOUND DEAD?
OH NO.
JESUS.
WHO COULD HAVE DONE SUCH A THING?

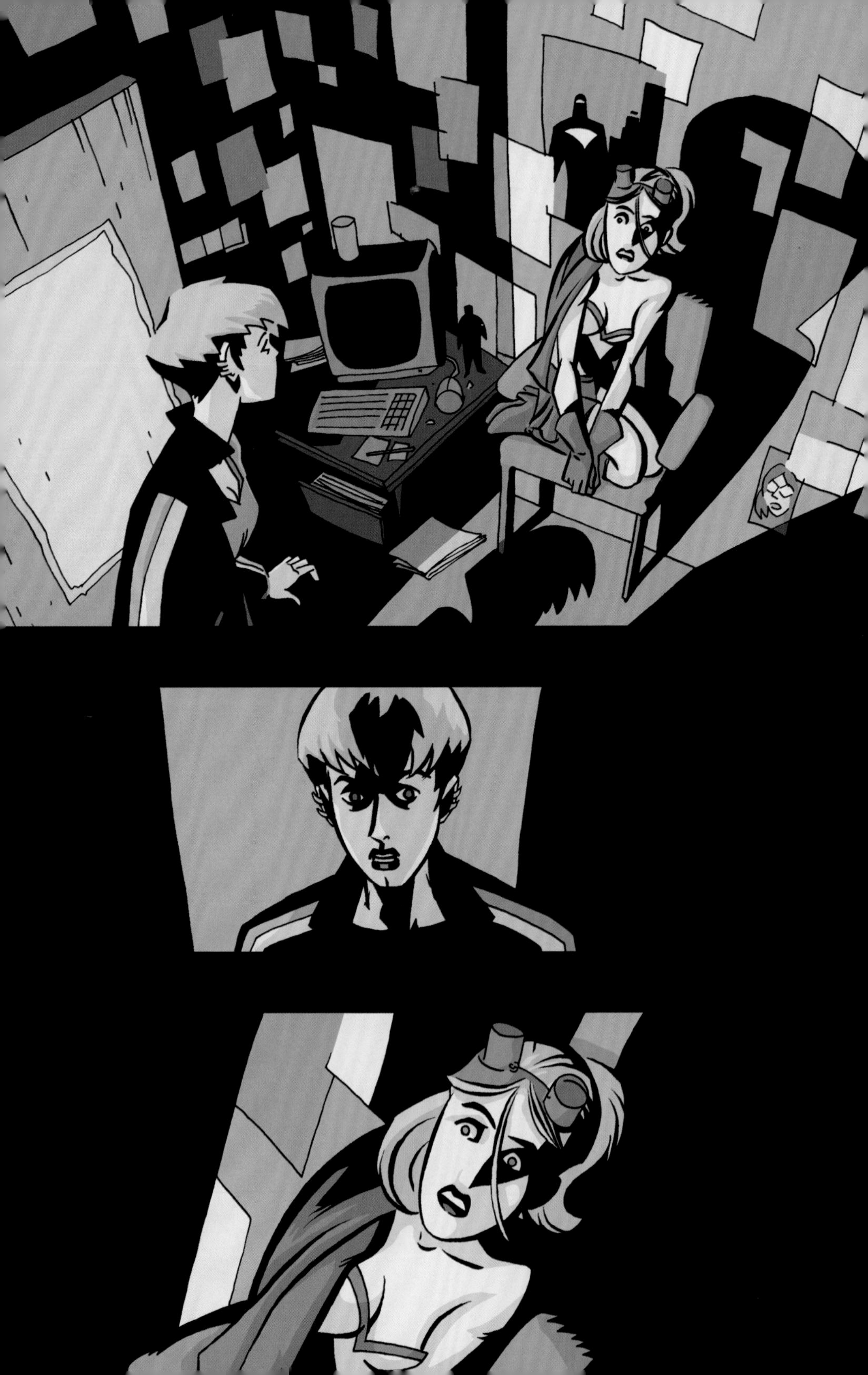

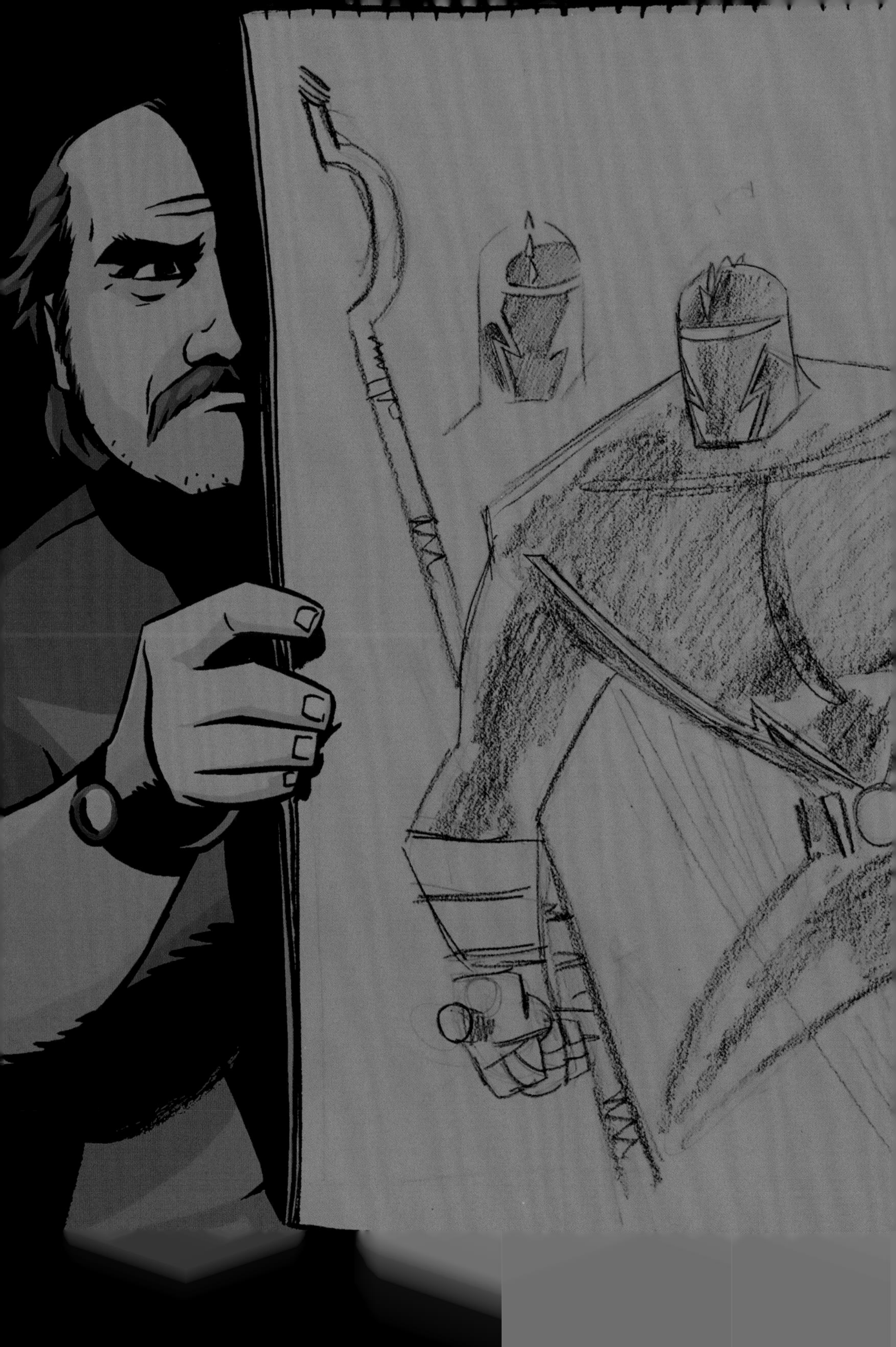

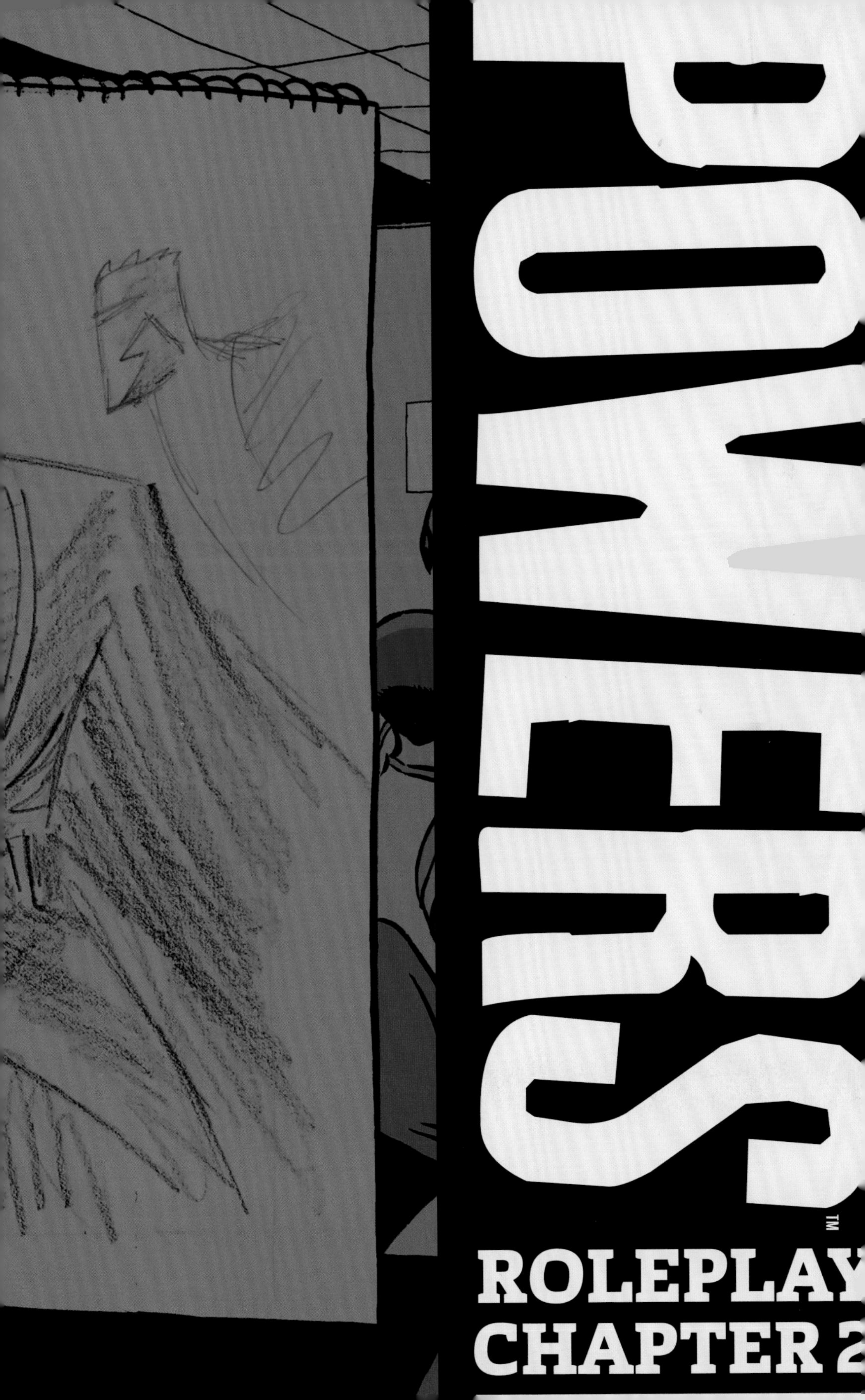

POWERS™

ROLEPLAY
CHAPTER 2

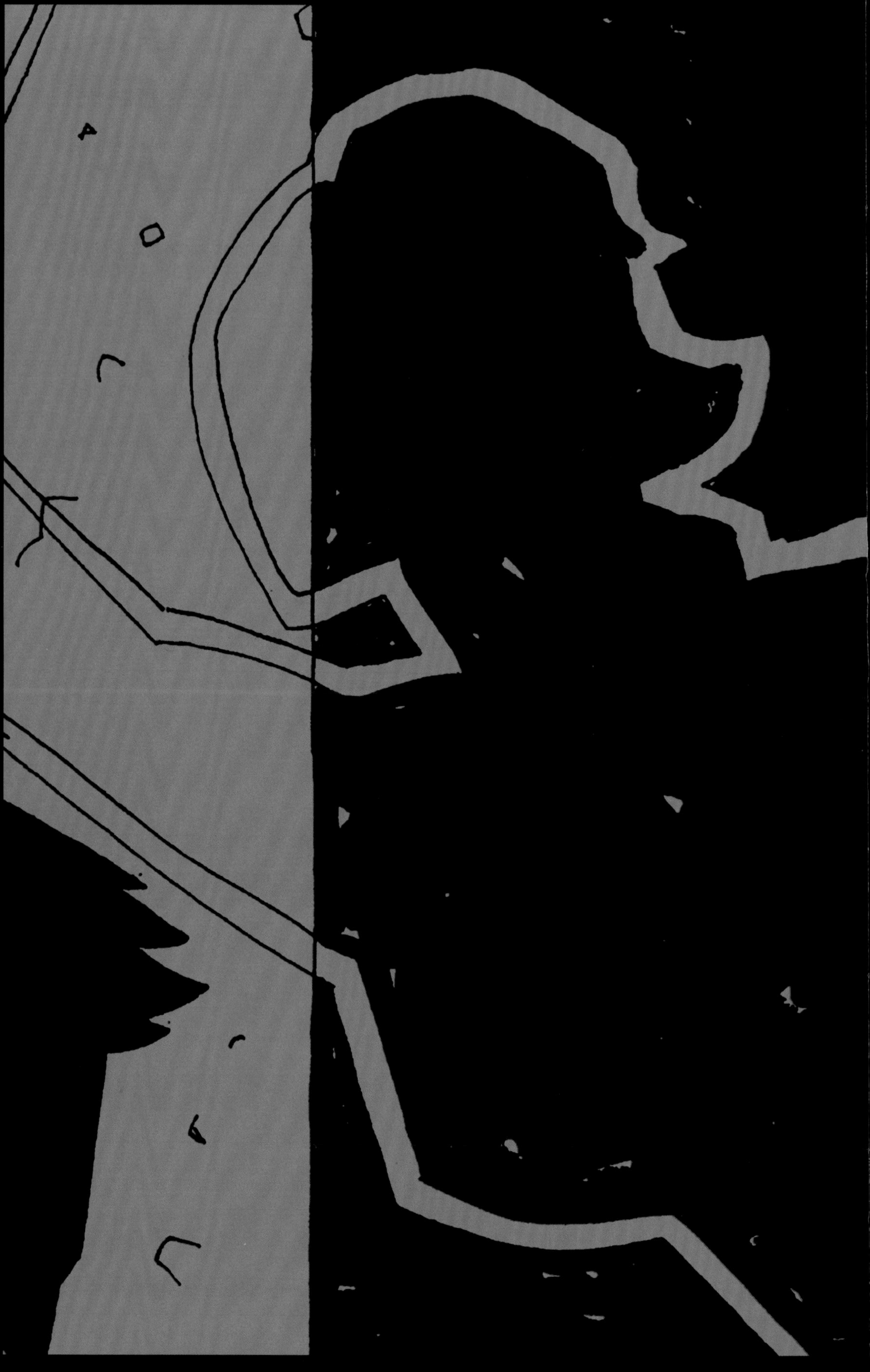

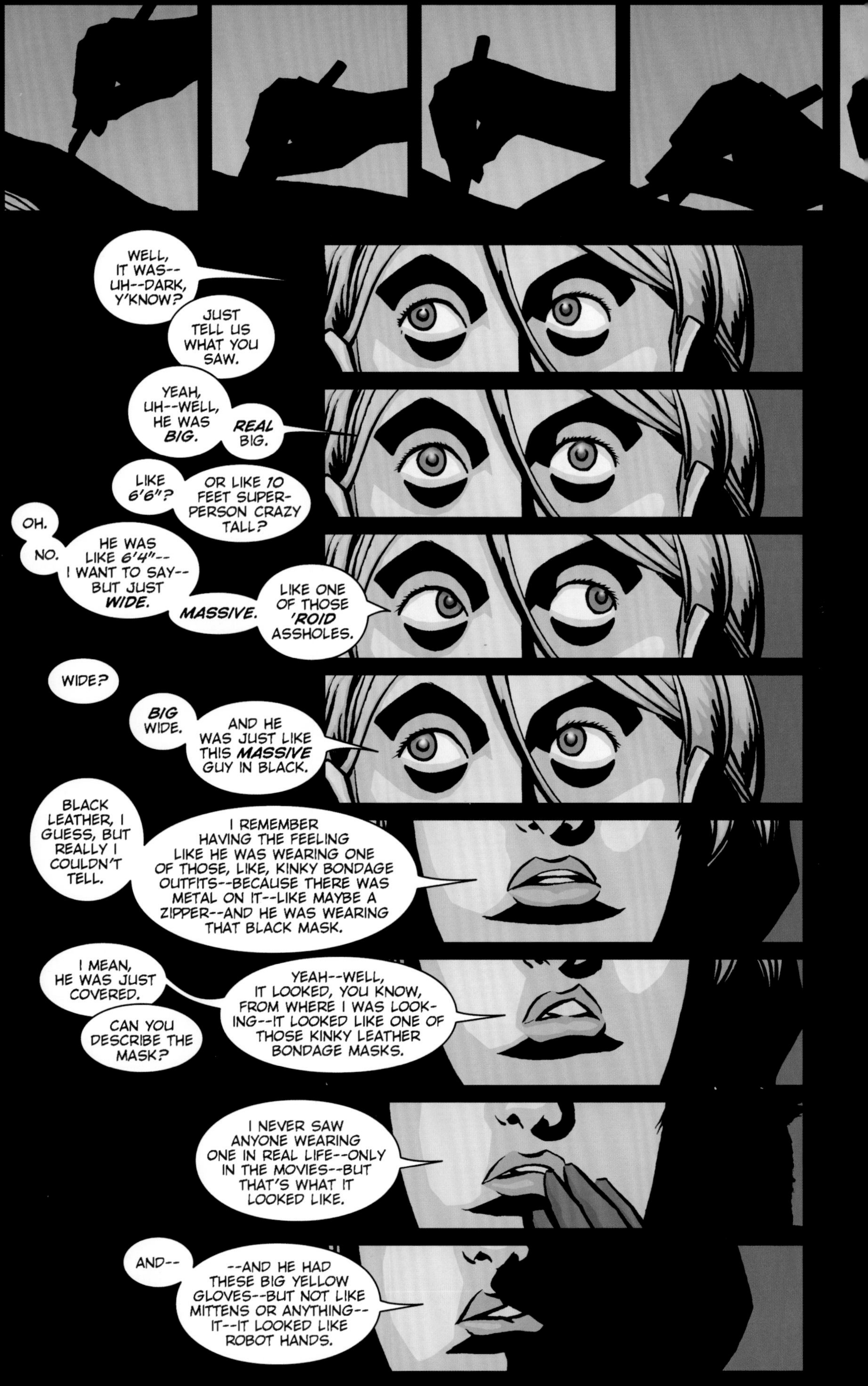
WELL, IT WAS-- UH--DARK, Y'KNOW?
JUST TELL US WHAT YOU SAW.
YEAH, UH--WELL, HE WAS BIG.
REAL BIG.
LIKE 6'6"?
OR LIKE 10 FEET SUPER-PERSON CRAZY TALL?
OH.
NO.
HE WAS LIKE 6'4"-- I WANT TO SAY-- BUT JUST WIDE.
MASSIVE.
LIKE ONE OF THOSE 'ROID ASSHOLES.
WIDE?
BIG WIDE.
AND HE WAS JUST LIKE THIS MASSIVE GUY IN BLACK.
BLACK LEATHER, I GUESS, BUT REALLY I COULDN'T TELL.
I REMEMBER HAVING THE FEELING LIKE HE WAS WEARING ONE OF THOSE, LIKE, KINKY BONDAGE OUTFITS--BECAUSE THERE WAS METAL ON IT--LIKE MAYBE A ZIPPER--AND HE WAS WEARING THAT BLACK MASK.
I MEAN, HE WAS JUST COVERED.
CAN YOU DESCRIBE THE MASK?
YEAH--WELL, IT LOOKED, YOU KNOW, FROM WHERE I WAS LOOK-ING--IT LOOKED LIKE ONE OF THOSE KINKY LEATHER BONDAGE MASKS.
I NEVER SAW ANYONE WEARING ONE IN REAL LIFE--ONLY IN THE MOVIES--BUT THAT'S WHAT IT LOOKED LIKE.
AND--
--AND HE HAD THESE BIG YELLOW GLOVES--BUT NOT LIKE MITTENS OR ANYTHING-- IT--IT LOOKED LIKE ROBOT HANDS.

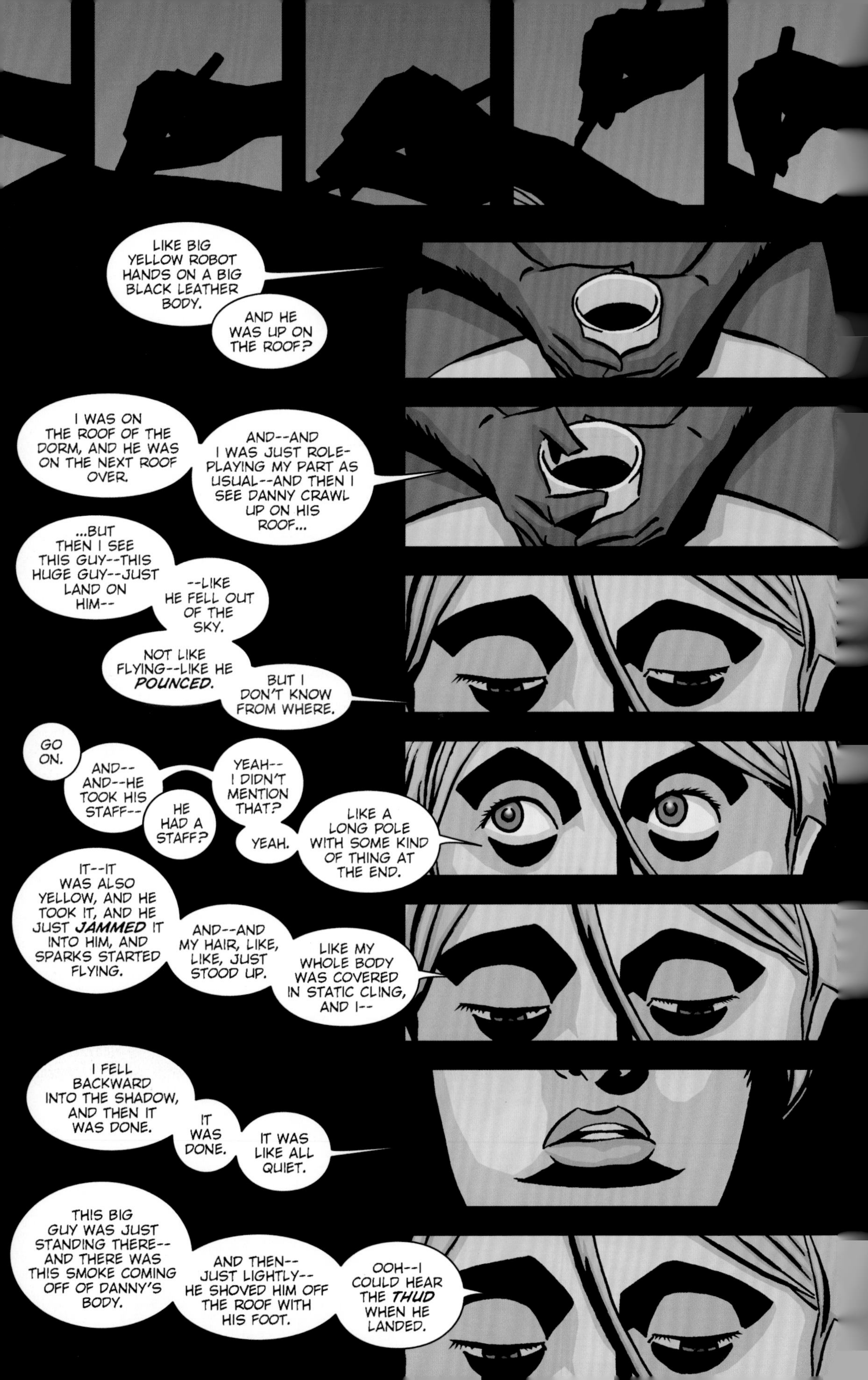

LIKE BIG YELLOW ROBOT HANDS ON A BIG BLACK LEATHER BODY.
AND HE WAS UP ON THE ROOF?
I WAS ON THE ROOF OF THE DORM, AND HE WAS ON THE NEXT ROOF OVER.
AND--AND I WAS JUST ROLE-PLAYING MY PART AS USUAL--AND THEN I SEE DANNY CRAWL UP ON HIS ROOF...
...BUT THEN I SEE THIS GUY--THIS HUGE GUY--JUST LAND ON HIM--
--LIKE HE FELL OUT OF THE SKY.
NOT LIKE FLYING--LIKE HE POUNCED.
BUT I DON'T KNOW FROM WHERE.
GO ON.
AND--AND--HE TOOK HIS STAFF--
HE HAD A STAFF?
YEAH--I DIDN'T MENTION THAT?
YEAH.
LIKE A LONG POLE WITH SOME KIND OF THING AT THE END.
IT--IT WAS ALSO YELLOW, AND HE TOOK IT, AND HE JUST JAMMED IT INTO HIM, AND SPARKS STARTED FLYING.
AND--AND MY HAIR, LIKE, LIKE, JUST STOOD UP.
LIKE MY WHOLE BODY WAS COVERED IN STATIC CLING, AND I--
I FELL BACKWARD INTO THE SHADOW, AND THEN IT WAS DONE.
IT WAS DONE.
IT WAS LIKE ALL QUIET.
THIS BIG GUY WAS JUST STANDING THERE--AND THERE WAS THIS SMOKE COMING OFF OF DANNY'S BODY.
AND THEN--JUST LIGHTLY--HE SHOVED HIM OFF THE ROOF WITH HIS FOOT.
OOH--I COULD HEAR THE THUD WHEN HE LANDED.

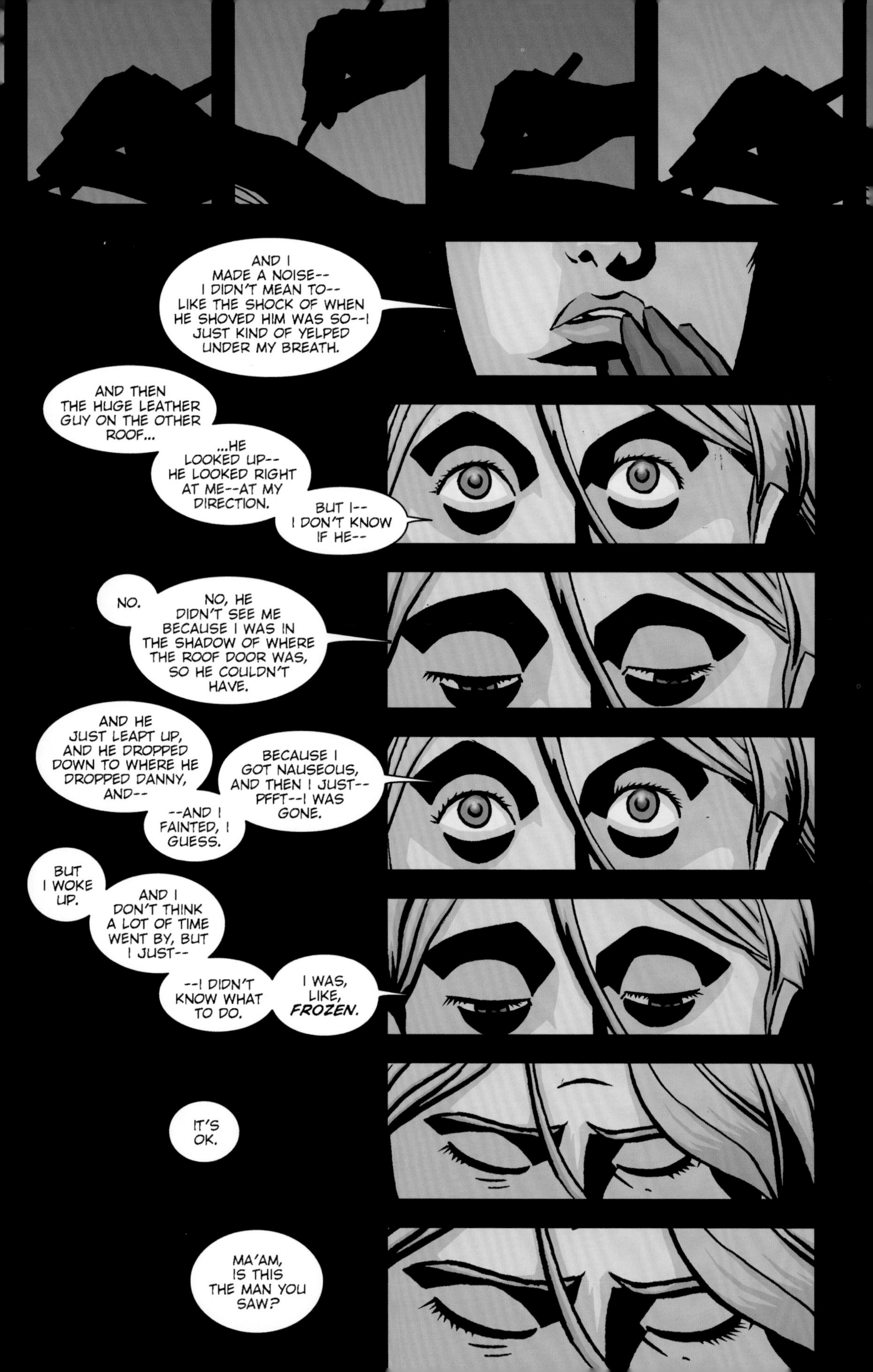
AND I MADE A NOISE-- I DIDN'T MEAN TO-- LIKE THE SHOCK OF WHEN HE SHOVED HIM WAS SO--I JUST KIND OF YELPED UNDER MY BREATH.
AND THEN THE HUGE LEATHER GUY ON THE OTHER ROOF...
...HE LOOKED UP-- HE LOOKED RIGHT AT ME--AT MY DIRECTION.
BUT I-- I DON'T KNOW IF HE--
NO.
NO, HE DIDN'T SEE ME BECAUSE I WAS IN THE SHADOW OF WHERE THE ROOF DOOR WAS, SO HE COULDN'T HAVE.
AND HE JUST LEAPT UP, AND HE DROPPED DOWN TO WHERE HE DROPPED DANNY, AND--
--AND I FAINTED, I GUESS.
BECAUSE I GOT NAUSEOUS, AND THEN I JUST-- PFFT--I WAS GONE.
BUT I WOKE UP.
AND I DON'T THINK A LOT OF TIME WENT BY, BUT I JUST--
--I DIDN'T KNOW WHAT TO DO.
I WAS, LIKE, *FROZEN*.
IT'S OK.
MA'AM, IS THIS THE MAN YOU SAW?

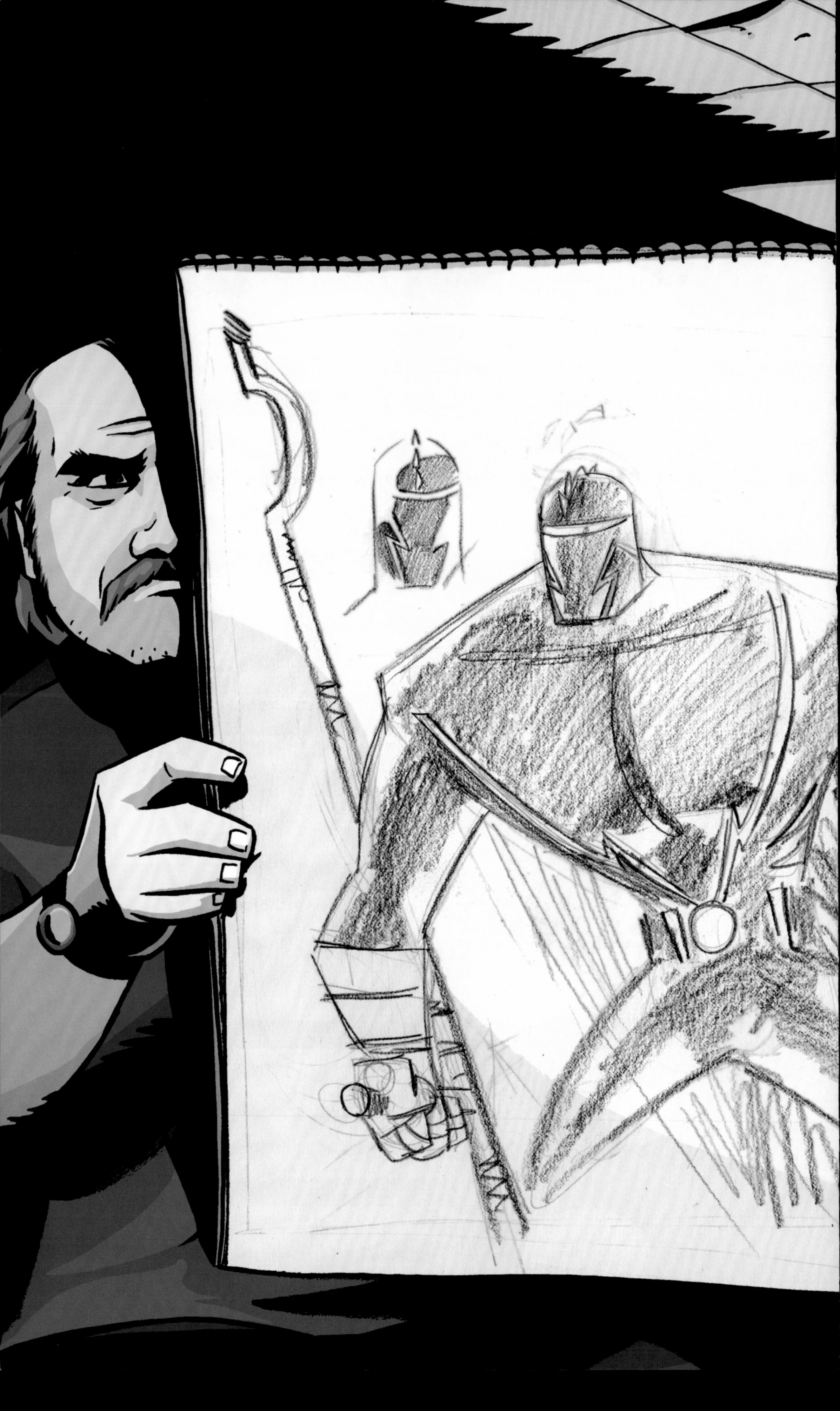

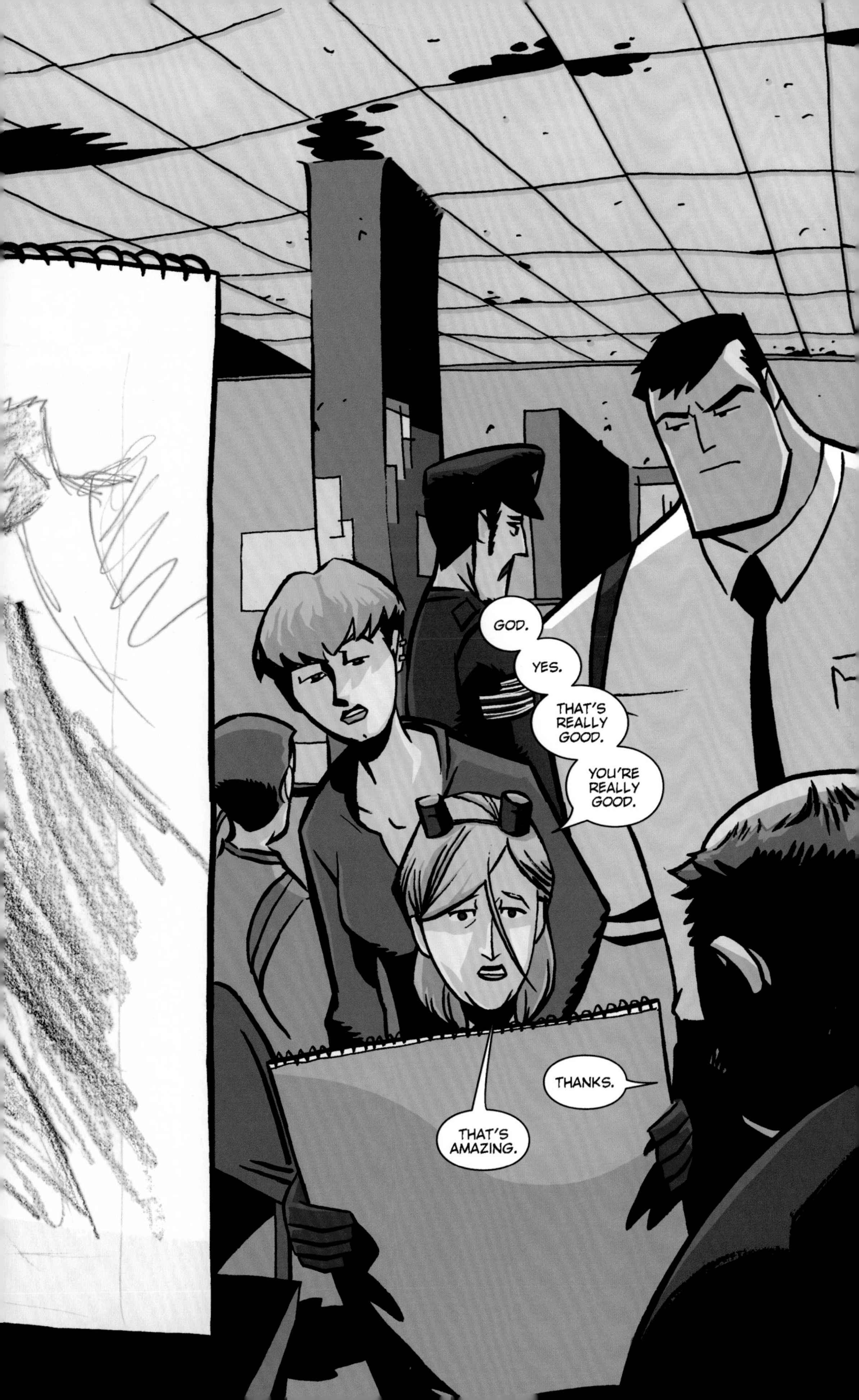
GOD.
YES.
THAT'S REALLY GOOD.
YOU'RE REALLY GOOD.
THAT'S AMAZING.
THANKS.

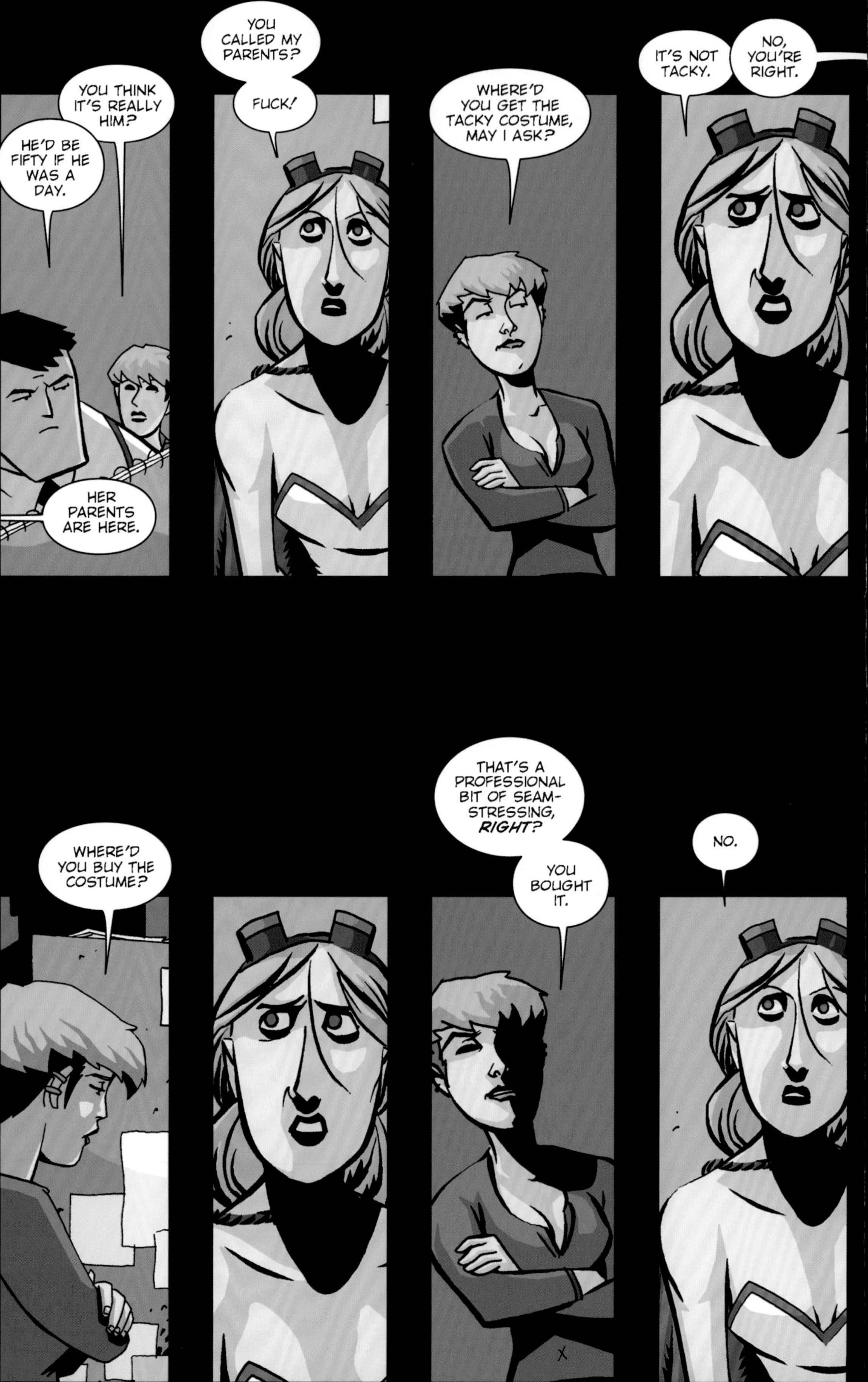
YOU THINK IT'S REALLY HIM?
HE'D BE FIFTY IF HE WAS A DAY.
HER PARENTS ARE HERE.
YOU CALLED MY PARENTS?
FUCK!
WHERE'D YOU GET THE TACKY COSTUME, MAY I ASK?
IT'S NOT TACKY.
NO, YOU'RE RIGHT.
WHERE'D YOU BUY THE COSTUME?
THAT'S A PROFESSIONAL BIT OF SEAM-STRESSING, *RIGHT?*
YOU BOUGHT IT.
NO.

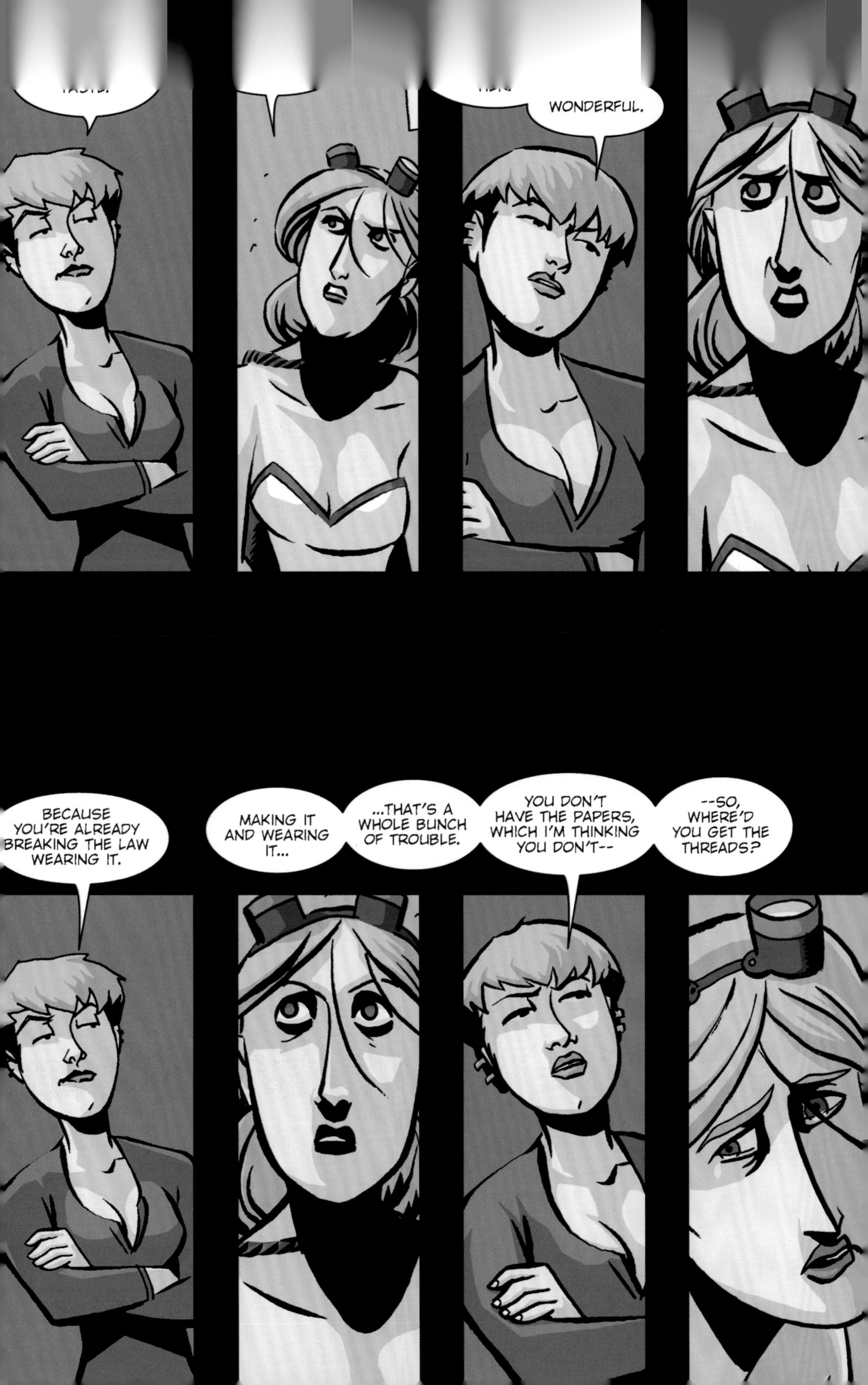
WONDERFUL.
BECAUSE YOU'RE ALREADY BREAKING THE LAW WEARING IT.
MAKING IT AND WEARING IT...
...THAT'S A WHOLE BUNCH OF TROUBLE.
YOU DON'T HAVE THE PAPERS, WHICH I'M THINKING YOU DON'T--
--SO, WHERE'D YOU GET THE THREADS?

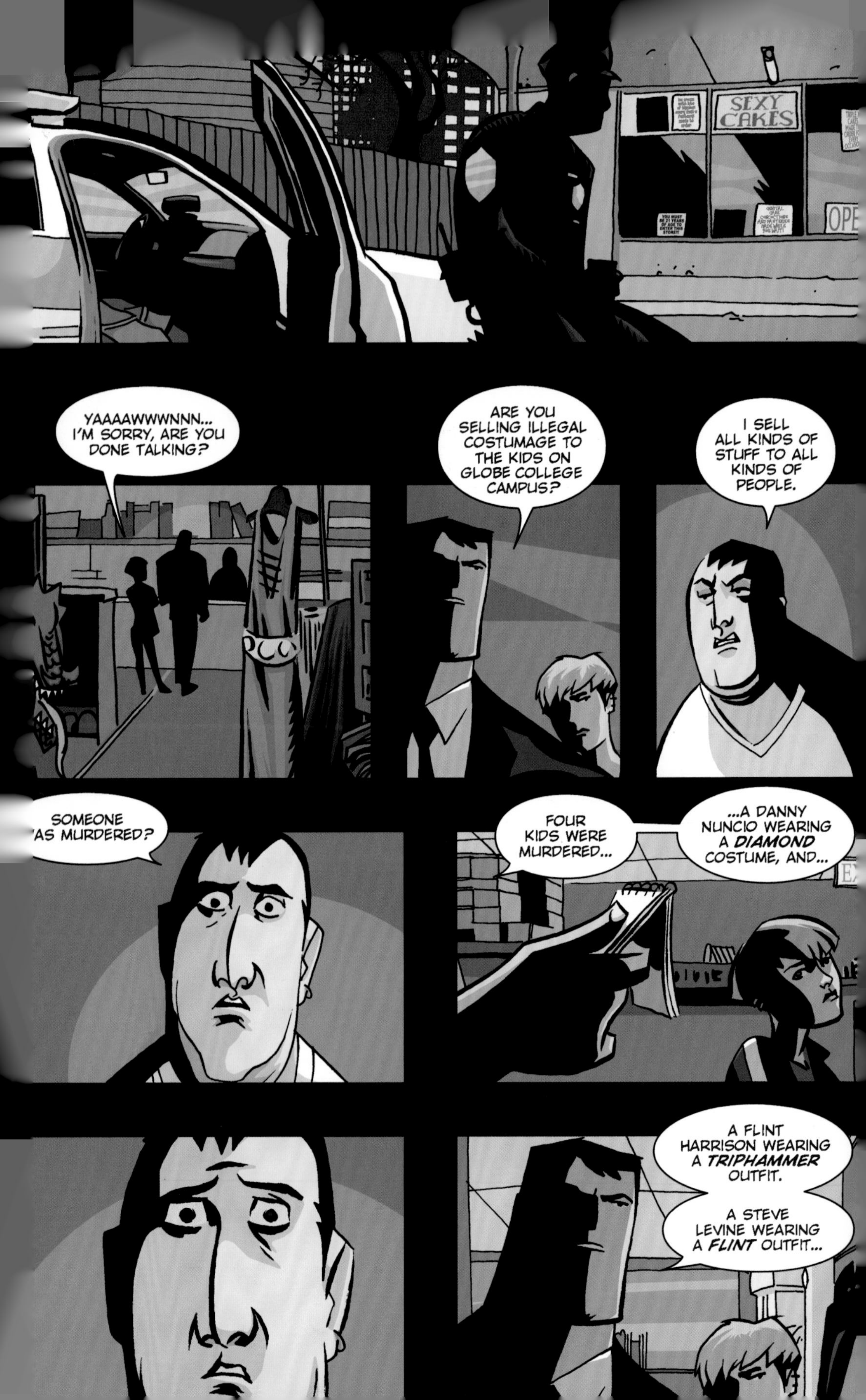
SEXY CAKES
YAAAAWWNNN... I'M SORRY, ARE YOU DONE TALKING?
ARE YOU SELLING ILLEGAL COSTUMAGE TO THE KIDS ON GLOBE COLLEGE CAMPUS?
I SELL ALL KINDS OF STUFF TO ALL KINDS OF PEOPLE.
SOMEONE AS MURDERED?
FOUR KIDS WERE MURDERED...
...A DANNY NUNCIO WEARING A *DIAMOND* COSTUME, AND...
A FLINT HARRISON WEARING A *TRIPHAMMER* OUTFIT.
A STEVE LEVINE WEARING A *FLINT* OUTFIT...

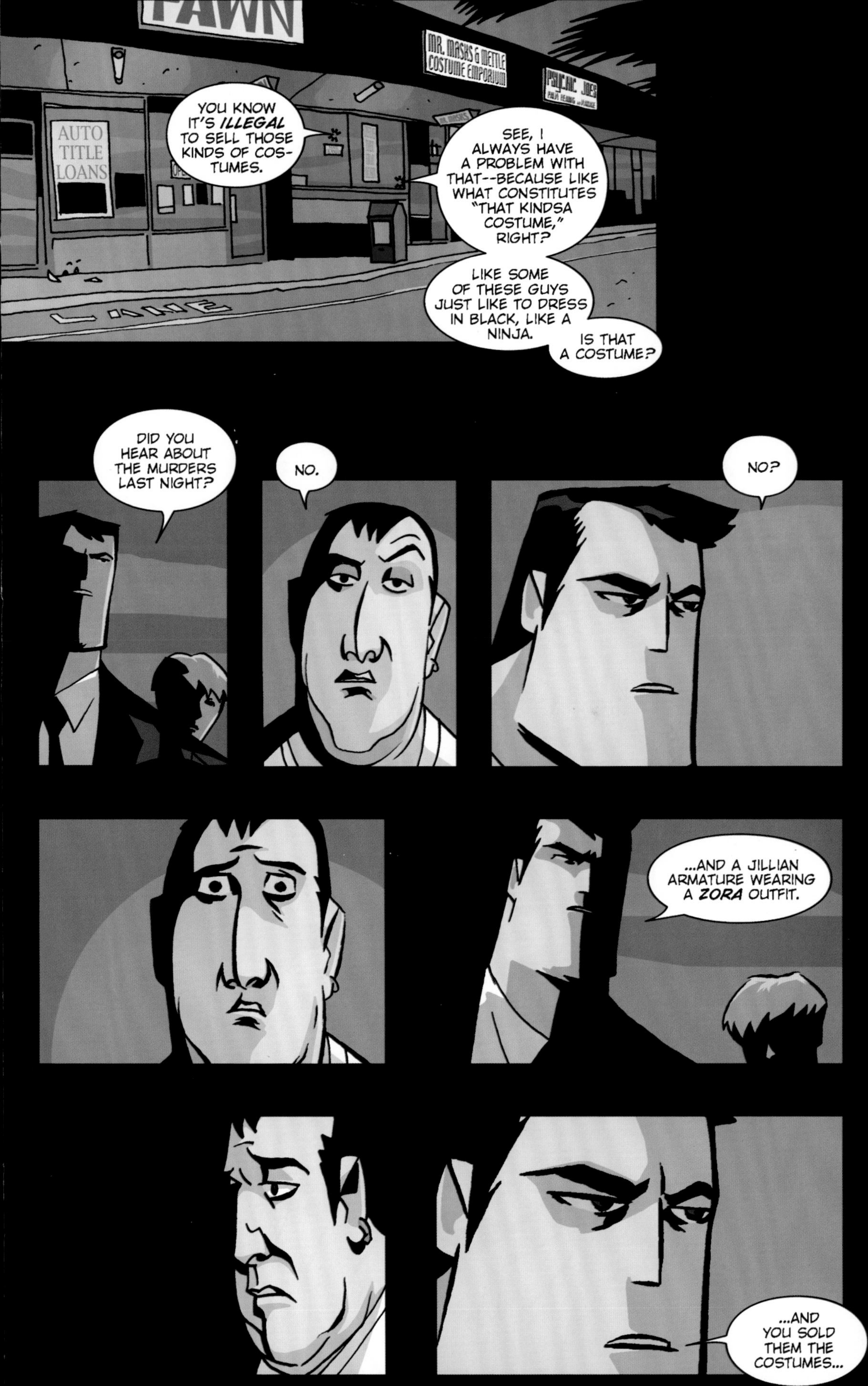
PAWN
MR. MASKS & METTLE COSTUME EMPORIUM
AUTO TITLE LOANS
YOU KNOW IT'S *ILLEGAL* TO SELL THOSE KINDS OF COS-TUMES.
SEE, I ALWAYS HAVE A PROBLEM WITH THAT--BECAUSE LIKE WHAT CONSTITUTES "THAT KINDSA COSTUME," RIGHT?
LIKE SOME OF THESE GUYS JUST LIKE TO DRESS IN BLACK, LIKE A NINJA.
IS THAT A COSTUME?
DID YOU HEAR ABOUT THE MURDERS LAST NIGHT?
NO.
NO?
...AND A JILLIAN ARMATURE WEARING A *ZORA* OUTFIT.
...AND YOU SOLD THEM THE COSTUMES...

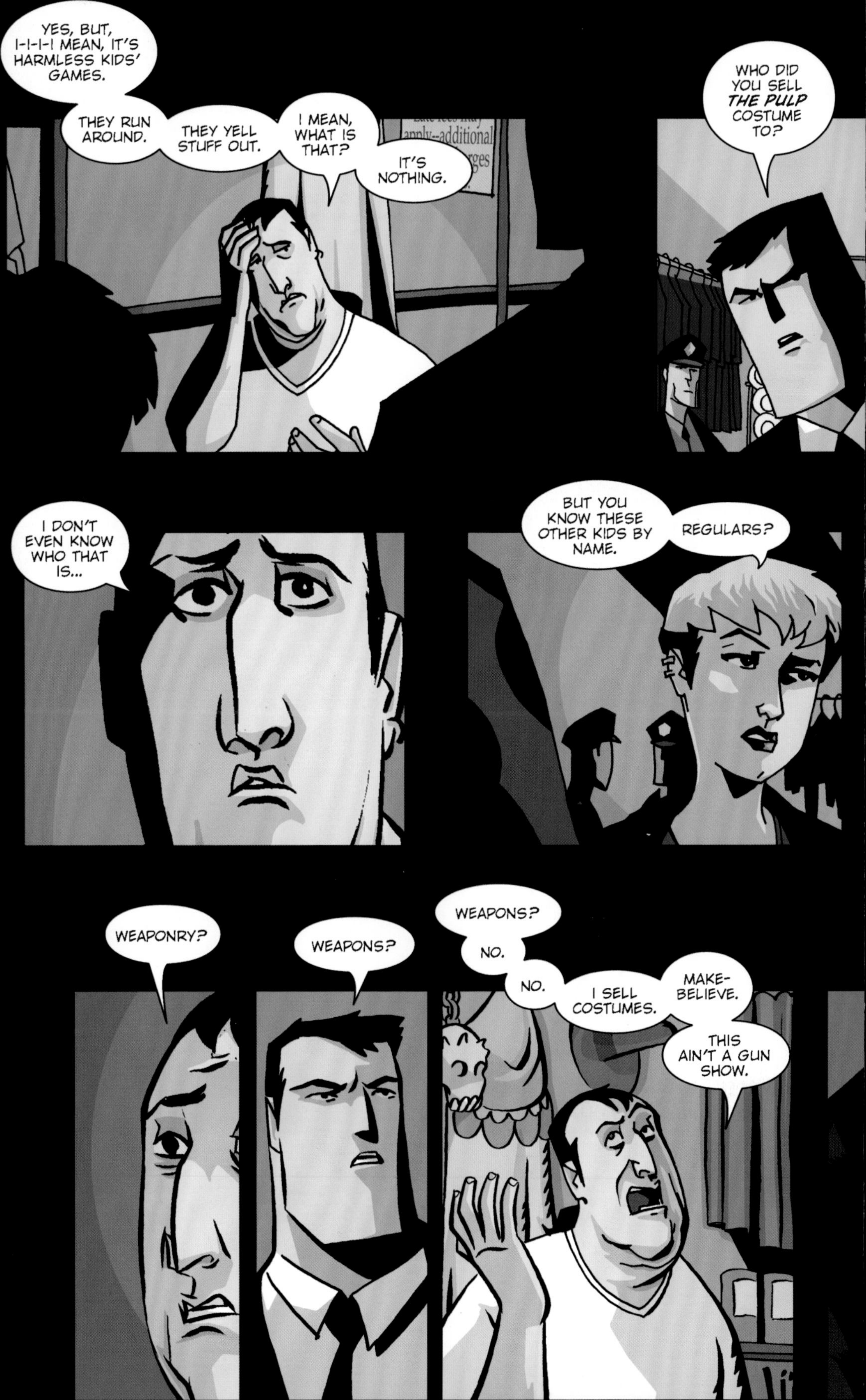

YES, BUT, I-I-I-I MEAN, IT'S HARMLESS KIDS' GAMES.
THEY RUN AROUND.
THEY YELL STUFF OUT.
I MEAN, WHAT IS THAT?
IT'S NOTHING.
WHO DID YOU SELL *THE PULP* COSTUME TO?
I DON'T EVEN KNOW WHO THAT IS...
BUT YOU KNOW THESE OTHER KIDS BY NAME.
REGULARS?
WEAPONRY?
WEAPONS?
WEAPONS?
NO.
NO.
I SELL COSTUMES.
MAKE-BELIEVE.
THIS AIN'T A GUN SHOW.

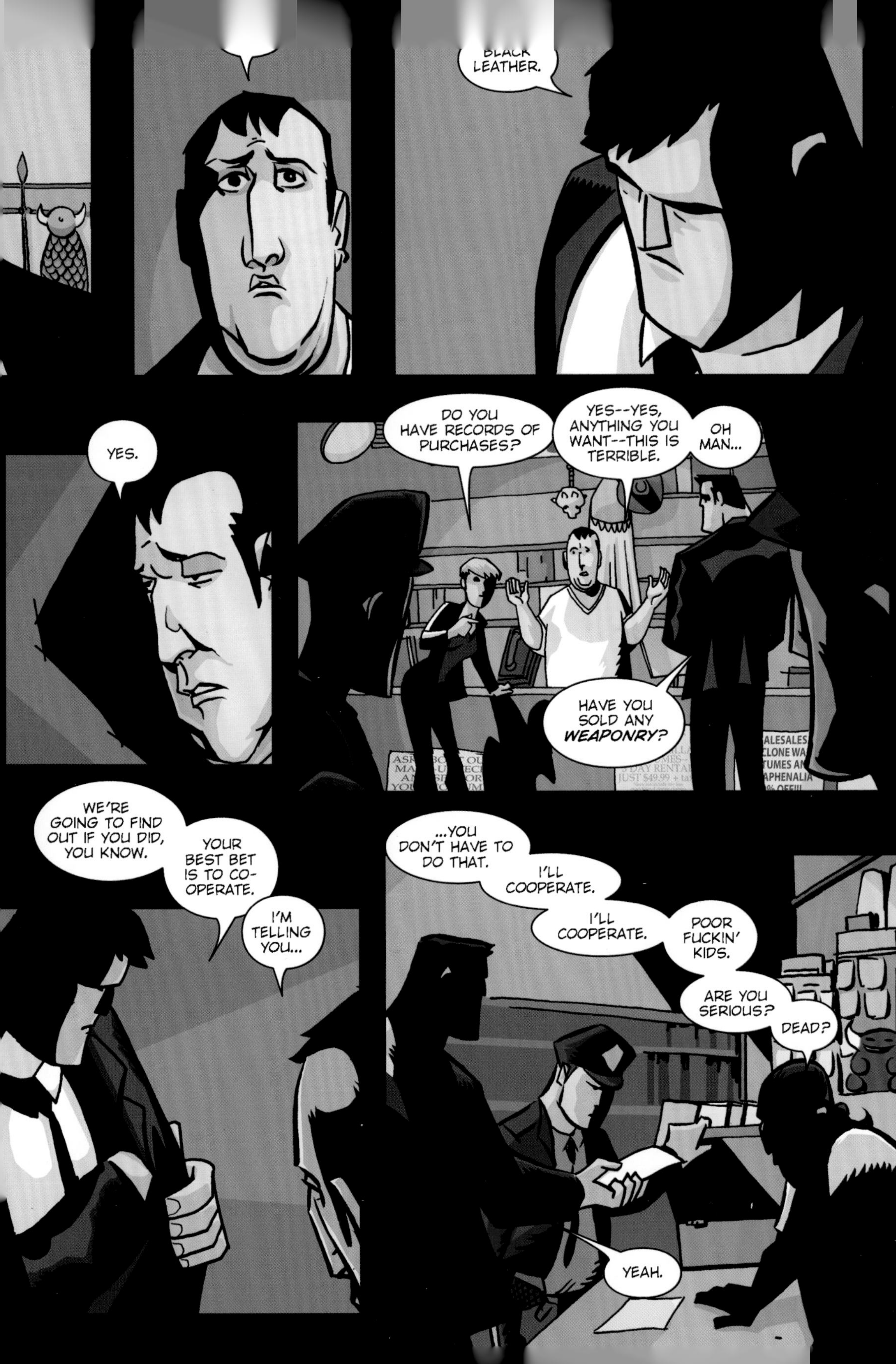
LEATHER.
YES.
DO YOU HAVE RECORDS OF PURCHASES?
YES--YES, ANYTHING YOU WANT--THIS IS TERRIBLE.
OH MAN...
HAVE YOU SOLD ANY WEAPONRY?
WE'RE GOING TO FIND OUT IF YOU DID, YOU KNOW.
YOUR BEST BET IS TO CO-OPERATE.
I'M TELLING YOU...
...YOU DON'T HAVE TO DO THAT.
I'LL COOPERATE.
I'LL COOPERATE.
POOR FUCKIN' KIDS.
ARE YOU SERIOUS?
DEAD?
YEAH.

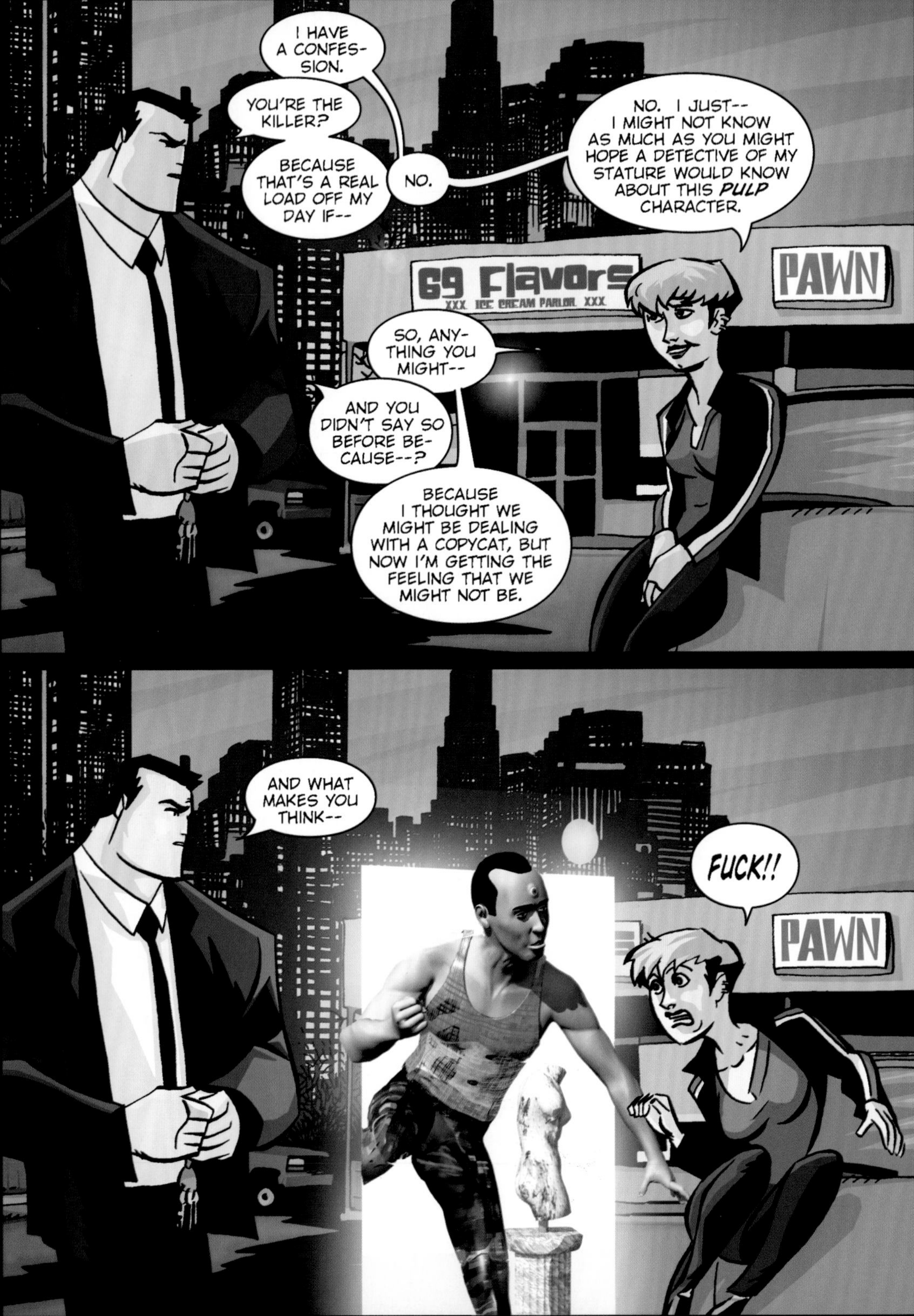
I HAVE A CONFESSION.
YOU'RE THE KILLER?
BECAUSE THAT'S A REAL LOAD OFF MY DAY IF--
NO.
NO. I JUST-- I MIGHT NOT KNOW AS MUCH AS YOU MIGHT HOPE A DETECTIVE OF MY STATURE WOULD KNOW ABOUT THIS *PULP* CHARACTER.
69 Flavors
XXX ICE CREAM PARLOR XXX
PAWN
SO, ANYTHING YOU MIGHT--
AND YOU DIDN'T SAY SO BEFORE BECAUSE--?
BECAUSE I THOUGHT WE MIGHT BE DEALING WITH A COPYCAT, BUT NOW I'M GETTING THE FEELING THAT WE MIGHT NOT BE.
AND WHAT MAKES YOU THINK--
FUCK!!
PAWN

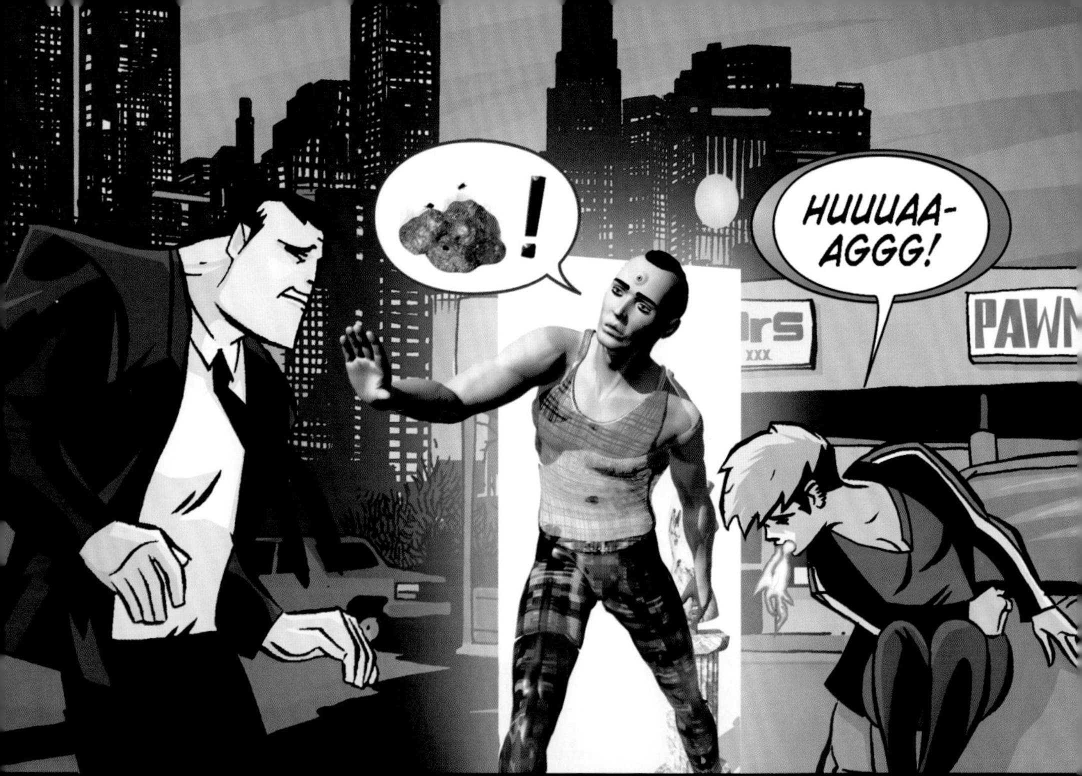
!
HUUUAA-AGGG!
PAWN

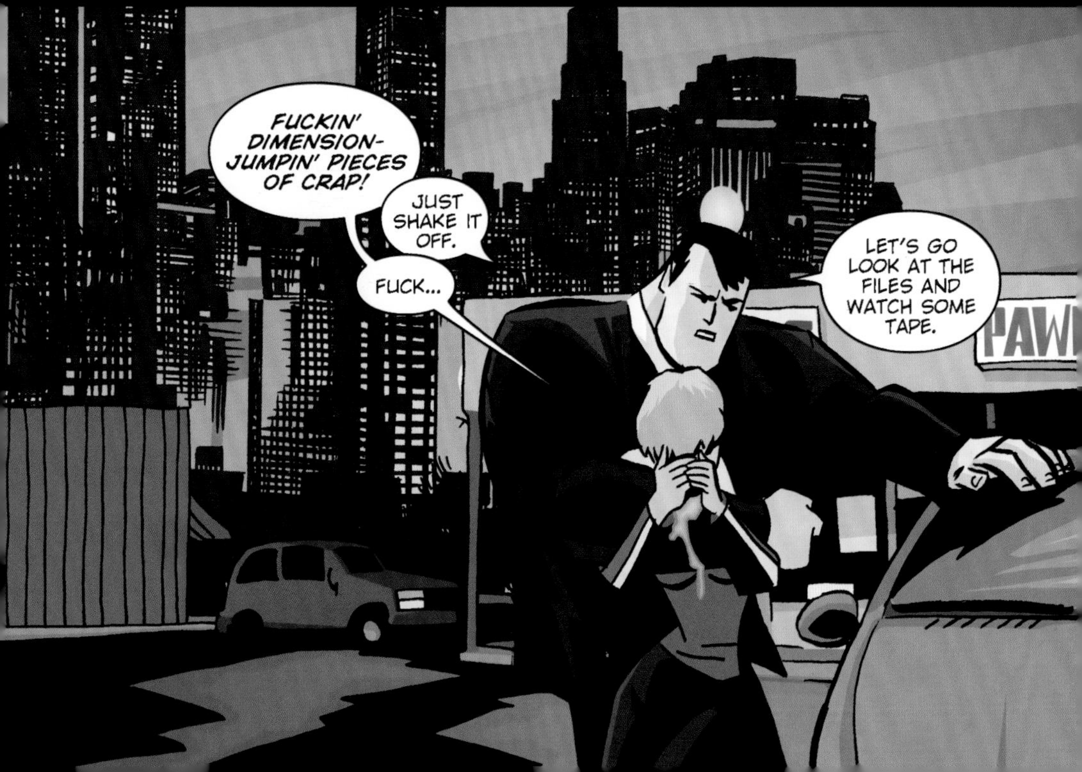
FUCKIN' DIMENSION-JUMPIN' PIECES OF CRAP!
JUST SHAKE IT OFF.
FUCK...
LET'S GO LOOK AT THE FILES AND WATCH SOME TAPE.
PAWN

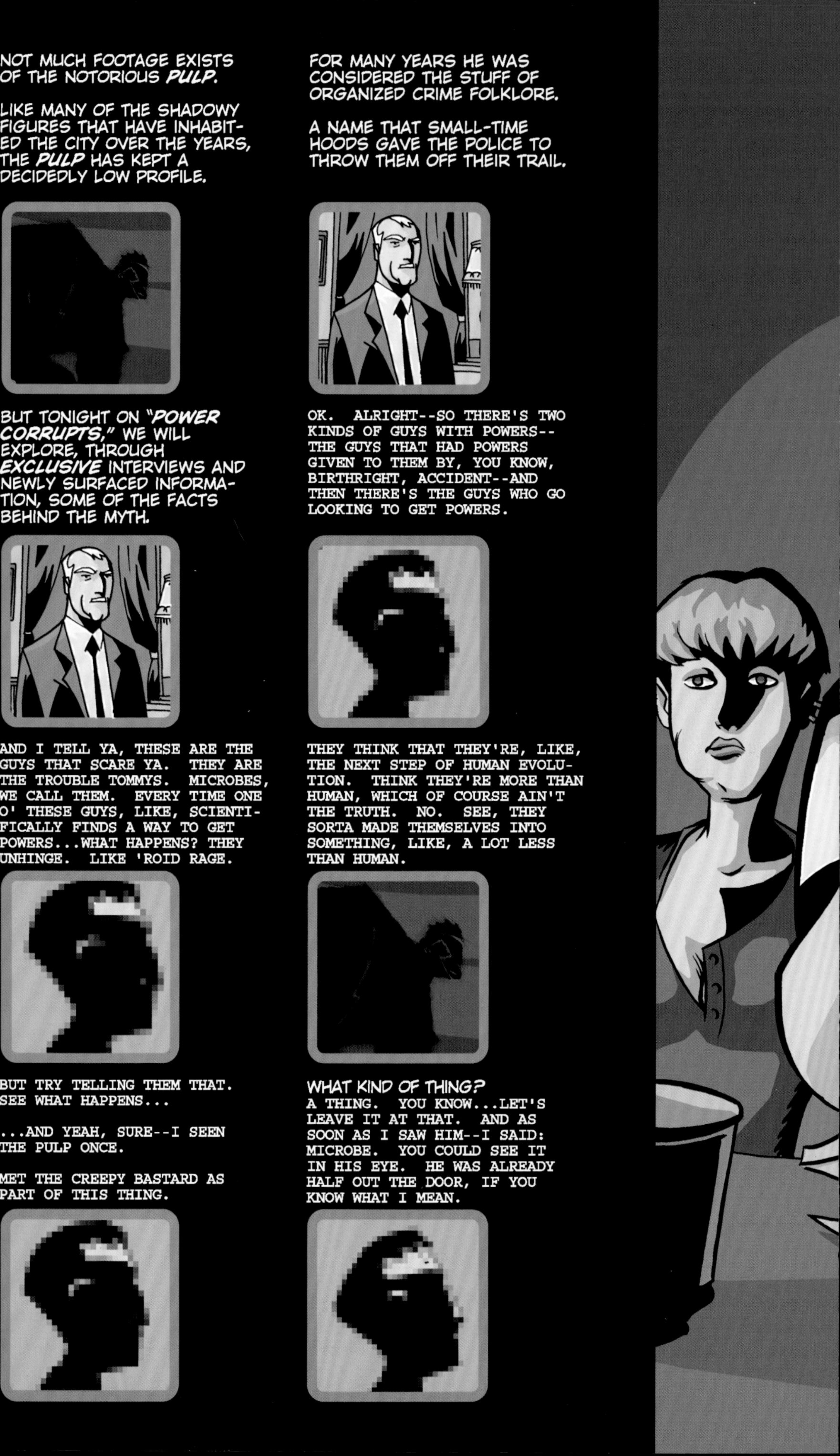
NOT MUCH FOOTAGE EXISTS OF THE NOTORIOUS *PULP*.
LIKE MANY OF THE SHADOWY FIGURES THAT HAVE INHABITED THE CITY OVER THE YEARS, THE *PULP* HAS KEPT A DECIDEDLY LOW PROFILE.
FOR MANY YEARS HE WAS CONSIDERED THE STUFF OF ORGANIZED CRIME FOLKLORE.
A NAME THAT SMALL-TIME HOODS GAVE THE POLICE TO THROW THEM OFF THEIR TRAIL.
BUT TONIGHT ON *"POWER CORRUPTS,"* WE WILL EXPLORE, THROUGH *EXCLUSIVE* INTERVIEWS AND NEWLY SURFACED INFORMATION, SOME OF THE FACTS BEHIND THE MYTH.
OK. ALRIGHT--SO THERE'S TWO KINDS OF GUYS WITH POWERS--THE GUYS THAT HAD POWERS GIVEN TO THEM BY, YOU KNOW, BIRTHRIGHT, ACCIDENT--AND THEN THERE'S THE GUYS WHO GO LOOKING TO GET POWERS.
AND I TELL YA, THESE ARE THE GUYS THAT SCARE YA. THEY ARE THE TROUBLE TOMMYS. MICROBES, WE CALL THEM. EVERY TIME ONE O' THESE GUYS, LIKE, SCIENTIFICALLY FINDS A WAY TO GET POWERS...WHAT HAPPENS? THEY UNHINGE. LIKE 'ROID RAGE.
THEY THINK THAT THEY'RE, LIKE, THE NEXT STEP OF HUMAN EVOLUTION. THINK THEY'RE MORE THAN HUMAN, WHICH OF COURSE AIN'T THE TRUTH. NO. SEE, THEY SORTA MADE THEMSELVES INTO SOMETHING, LIKE, A LOT LESS THAN HUMAN.
BUT TRY TELLING THEM THAT. SEE WHAT HAPPENS...
...AND YEAH, SURE--I SEEN THE PULP ONCE.
MET THE CREEPY BASTARD AS PART OF THIS THING.
WHAT KIND OF THING?
A THING. YOU KNOW...LET'S LEAVE IT AT THAT. AND AS SOON AS I SAW HIM--I SAID: MICROBE. YOU COULD SEE IT IN HIS EYE. HE WAS ALREADY HALF OUT THE DOOR, IF YOU KNOW WHAT I MEAN.

HMM?

NO. NO I COULDN'T PICK HIM OUT OF A LINEUP IF YOU PAID ME. NO, SEE, WITH THESE GUYS, THERE'S USUALLY TWO PEOPLE WHO KNOW THE "BEFORE" PART OF THE PICTURE. THE SECRET IDENTITY.

HEY! 99% OF THE TIME A MICROBE'S FIRST ORDER OF BUSINESS IS TO PULL THE PLUG ON THE DOC WHO GAVE HIM THE POWERS IN THE FIRST PLACE. SO YOU KNOW: POWERS, AND NO PAPER TRAIL.

--WHO IS BEST KNOWN AS *JOHNNY ROYALE.*

LEGALLY WE HERE AT *"POWER CORRUPTS"* ARE FORBIDDEN FROM DISCUSSING THIS MATTER DIRECTLY.

BUT MUCH OF THIS SUPPOSED RELATIONSHIP BETWEEN THE PULP AND JOHNNY ROYALLE IS DETAILED IN THE BOOK *"SHADOWS,"* BY THE LATE *EDWIN BRUBAKER.*

THE GUY AND THE SCIENTIST.

THE SCIENTIST GUY THAT WAS EITHER PAID, BLACKMAILED, OR THREATENED TO JACK HIM UP INTO WHAT HE BECAME...

MUCH MYSTERY ENCOMPASSES THE CONNECTIONS BETWEEN SOME OF THE PULP'S VICTIMS AND THEIR BUSINESS DEALINGS WITH JOHNNY STOMPINATO--

THE PRODUCERS OF THIS SHOW HAVE BEEN NAMED IN A MULTI-MILLION-DOLLAR LAWSUIT BY MR. STOMPINATO RELATED TO SUCH CLAIMS IN THE PAST-- AND A GAG ORDER HAS BEEN HANDED TO US BY THE COURT.

WHEN *"POWER CORRUPTS"* RETURNS...A WITNESS TO ONE OF THE PULP'S MOST NOTORIOUS CRIME SCENES SPEAKS OUT FOR THE FIRST TIME. AND LATER... YOUR ANSWERS TO OUR ONLINE POLL.

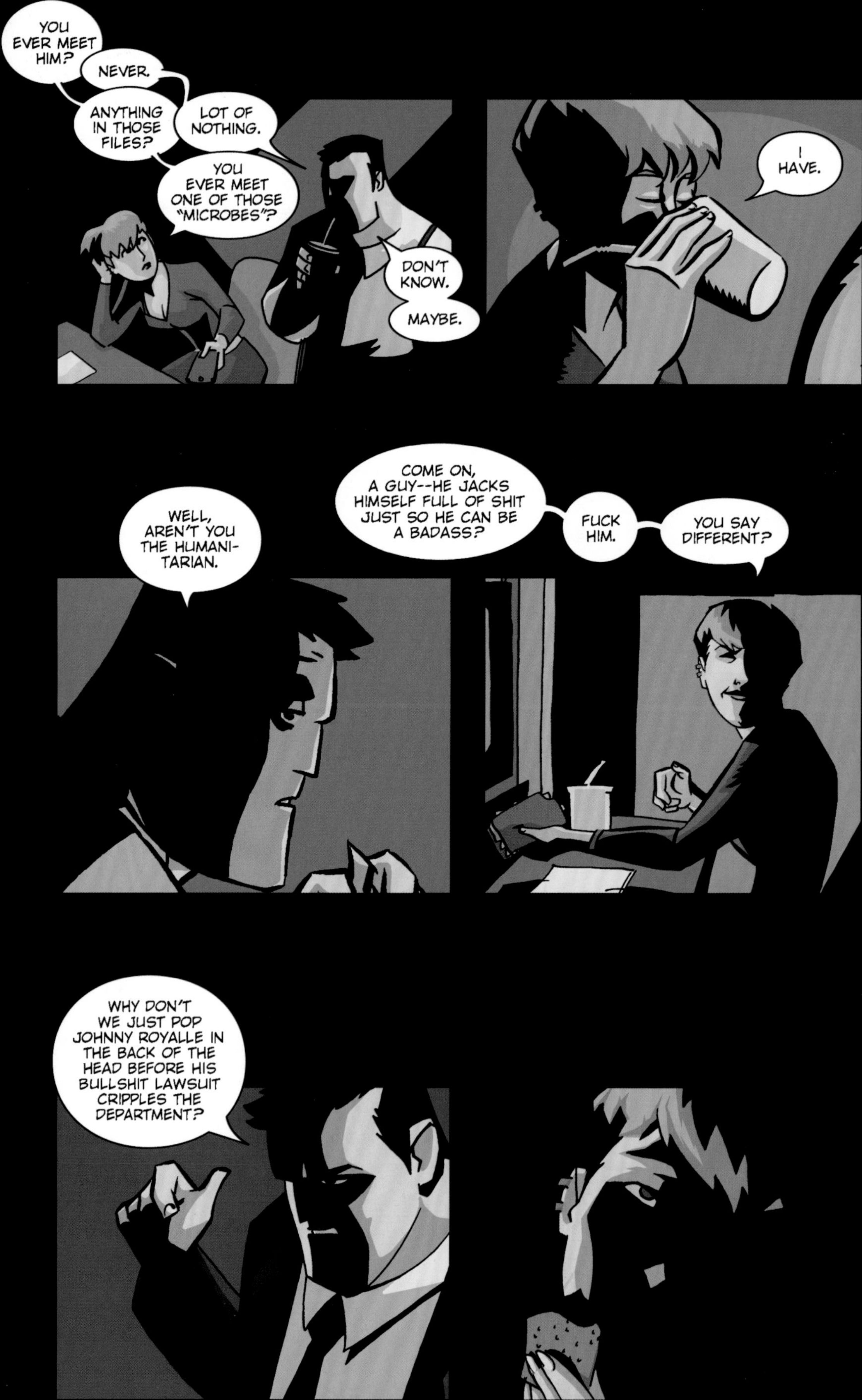
YOU EVER MEET HIM?
NEVER.
ANYTHING IN THOSE FILES?
LOT OF NOTHING.
YOU EVER MEET ONE OF THOSE "MICROBES"?
DON'T KNOW.
MAYBE.
I HAVE.
WELL, AREN'T YOU THE HUMANI-TARIAN.
COME ON, A GUY--HE JACKS HIMSELF FULL OF SHIT JUST SO HE CAN BE A BADASS?
FUCK HIM.
YOU SAY DIFFERENT?
WHY DON'T WE JUST POP JOHNNY ROYALLE IN THE BACK OF THE HEAD BEFORE HIS BULLSHIT LAWSUIT CRIPPLES THE DEPARTMENT?

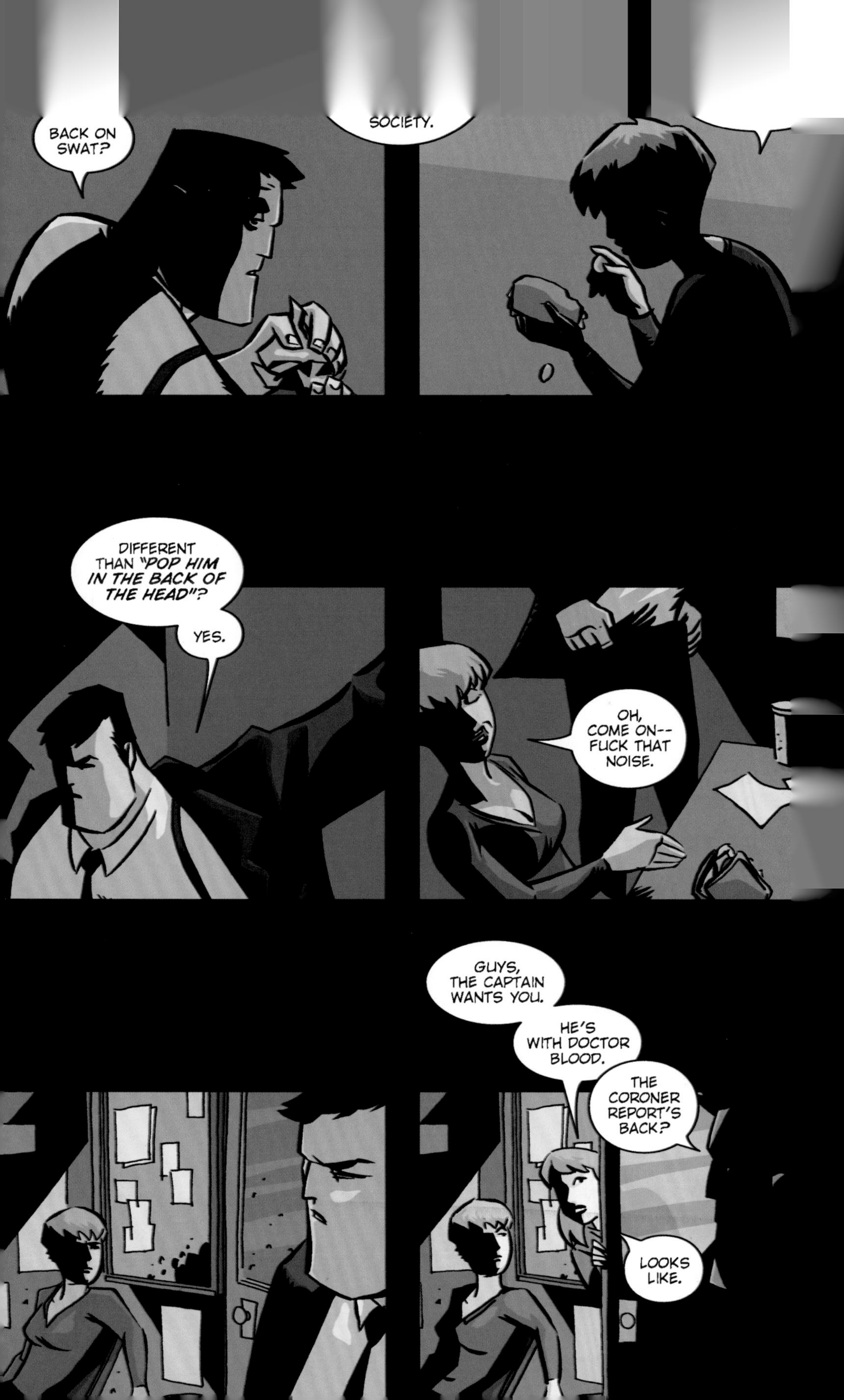
BACK ON SWAT?
SOCIETY.
DIFFERENT THAN *"POP HIM IN THE BACK OF THE HEAD"*?
YES.
OH, COME ON-- FUCK THAT NOISE.
GUYS, THE CAPTAIN WANTS YOU.
HE'S WITH DOCTOR BLOOD.
THE CORONER REPORT'S BACK?
LOOKS LIKE.

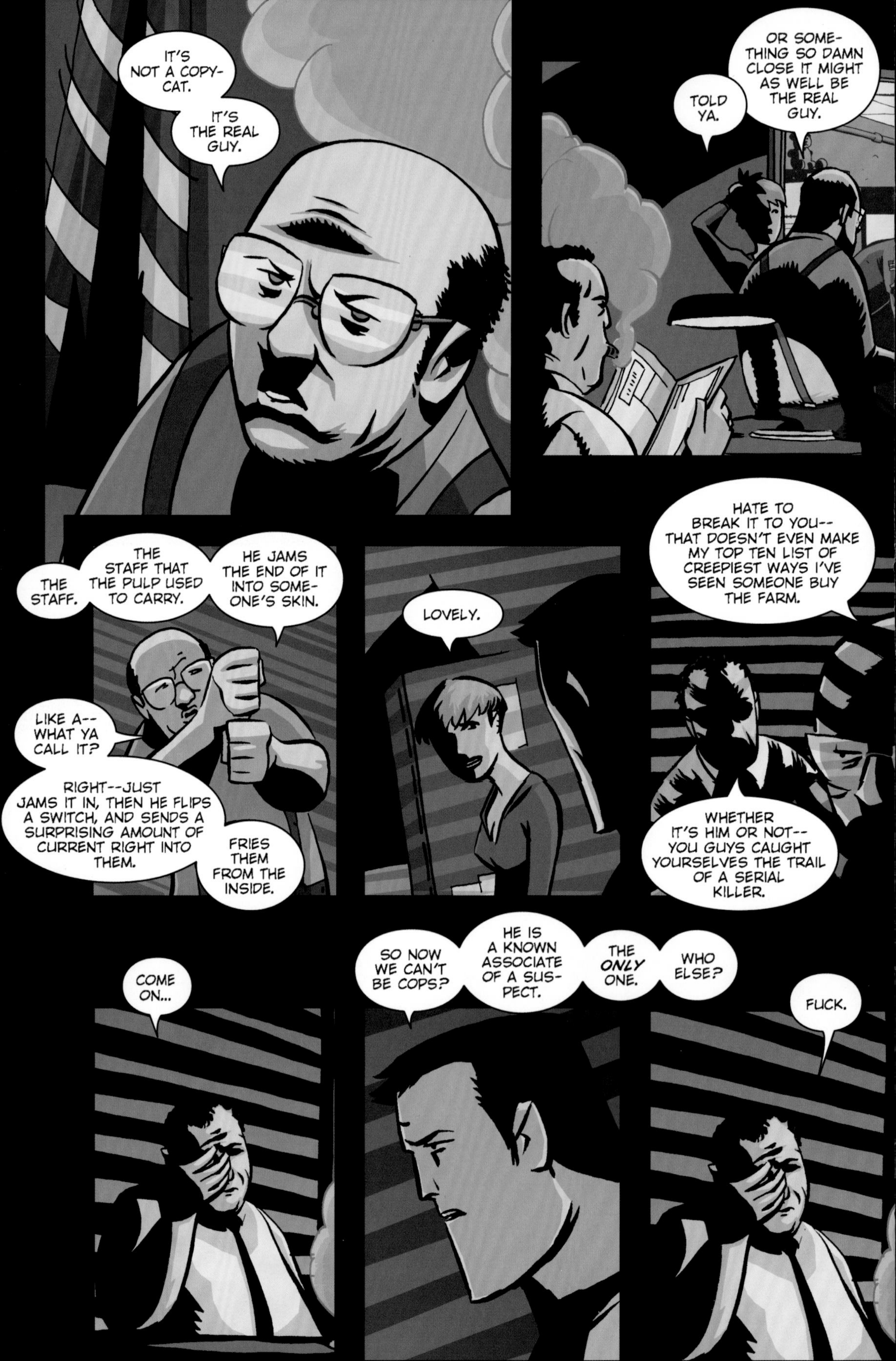
IT'S NOT A COPY-CAT.
IT'S THE REAL GUY.
TOLD YA.
OR SOME-THING SO DAMN CLOSE IT MIGHT AS WELL BE THE REAL GUY.
THE STAFF.
THE STAFF THAT THE PULP USED TO CARRY.
HE JAMS THE END OF IT INTO SOME-ONE'S SKIN.
LIKE A-- WHAT YA CALL IT?
RIGHT--JUST JAMS IT IN, THEN HE FLIPS A SWITCH, AND SENDS A SURPRISING AMOUNT OF CURRENT RIGHT INTO THEM.
FRIES THEM FROM THE INSIDE.
LOVELY.
HATE TO BREAK IT TO YOU-- THAT DOESN'T EVEN MAKE MY TOP TEN LIST OF CREEPIEST WAYS I'VE SEEN SOMEONE BUY THE FARM.
WHETHER IT'S HIM OR NOT-- YOU GUYS CAUGHT YOURSELVES THE TRAIL OF A SERIAL KILLER.
COME ON...
SO NOW WE CAN'T BE COPS?
HE IS A KNOWN ASSOCIATE OF A SUS-PECT.
THE ONLY ONE.
WHO ELSE?
FUCK.

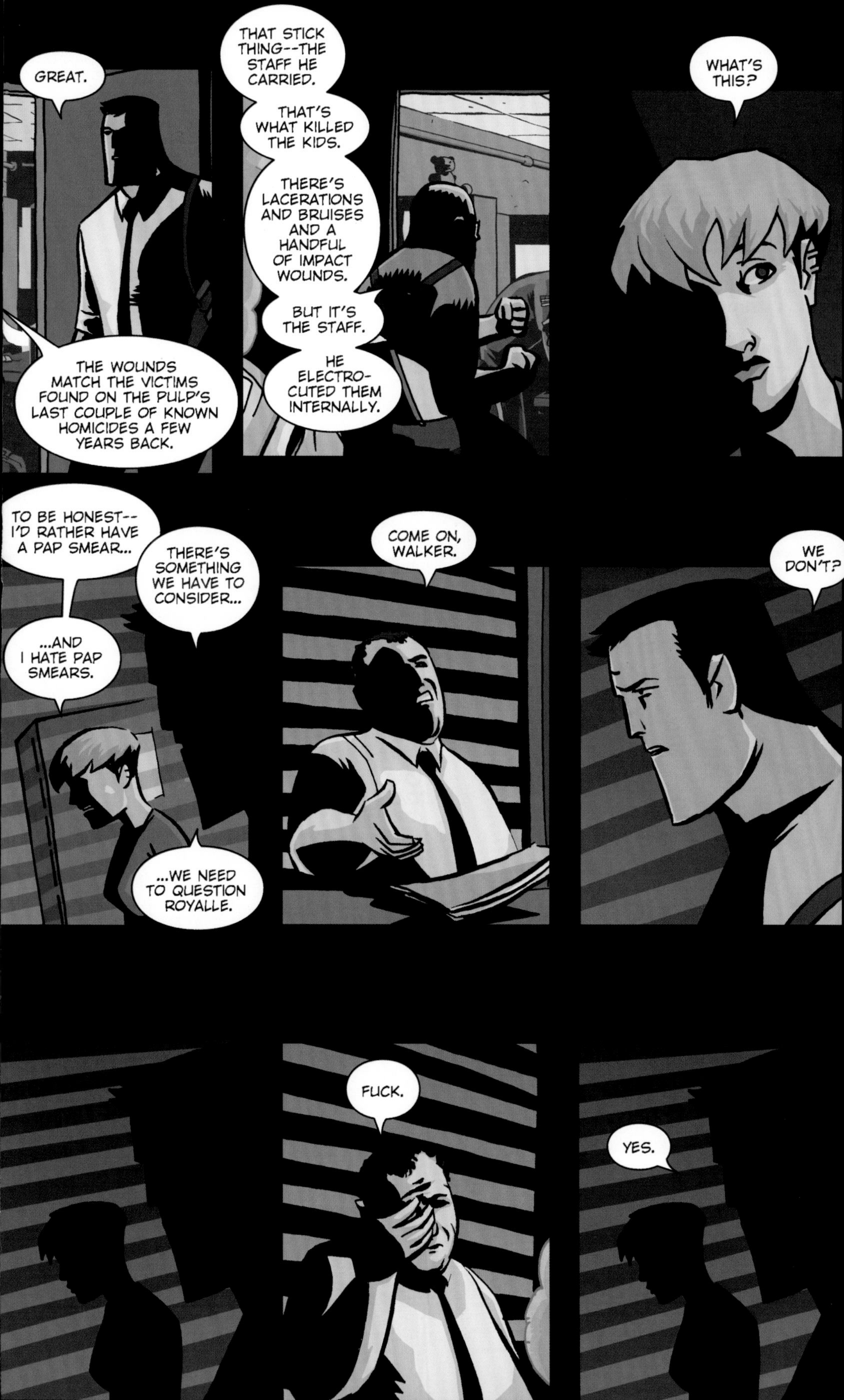
GREAT.
THE WOUNDS MATCH THE VICTIMS FOUND ON THE PULP'S LAST COUPLE OF KNOWN HOMICIDES A FEW YEARS BACK.
THAT STICK THING--THE STAFF HE CARRIED.
THAT'S WHAT KILLED THE KIDS.
THERE'S LACERATIONS AND BRUISES AND A HANDFUL OF IMPACT WOUNDS.
BUT IT'S THE STAFF.
HE ELECTROCUTED THEM INTERNALLY.
WHAT'S THIS?
TO BE HONEST-- I'D RATHER HAVE A PAP SMEAR...
...AND I HATE PAP SMEARS.
THERE'S SOMETHING WE HAVE TO CONSIDER...
...WE NEED TO QUESTION ROYALLE.
COME ON, WALKER.
WE DON'T?
FUCK.
YES.

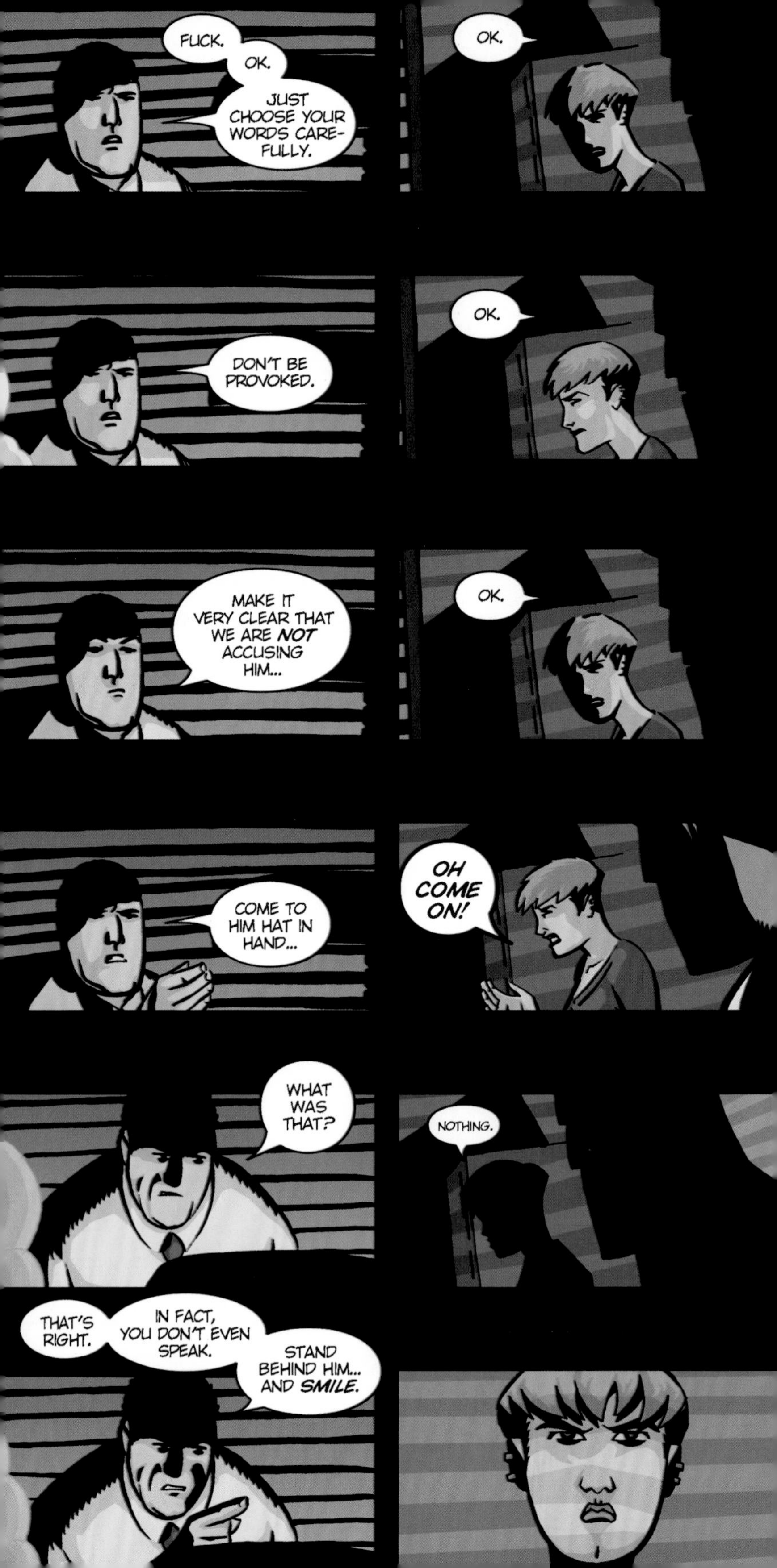
FUCK.
OK.
JUST CHOOSE YOUR WORDS CARE-FULLY.
OK.
DON'T BE PROVOKED.
OK.
MAKE IT VERY CLEAR THAT WE ARE ***NOT*** ACCUSING HIM...
OK.
COME TO HIM HAT IN HAND...
OH COME ON!
WHAT WAS THAT?
NOTHING.
THAT'S RIGHT.
IN FACT, YOU DON'T EVEN SPEAK.
STAND BEHIND HIM... AND ***SMILE.***

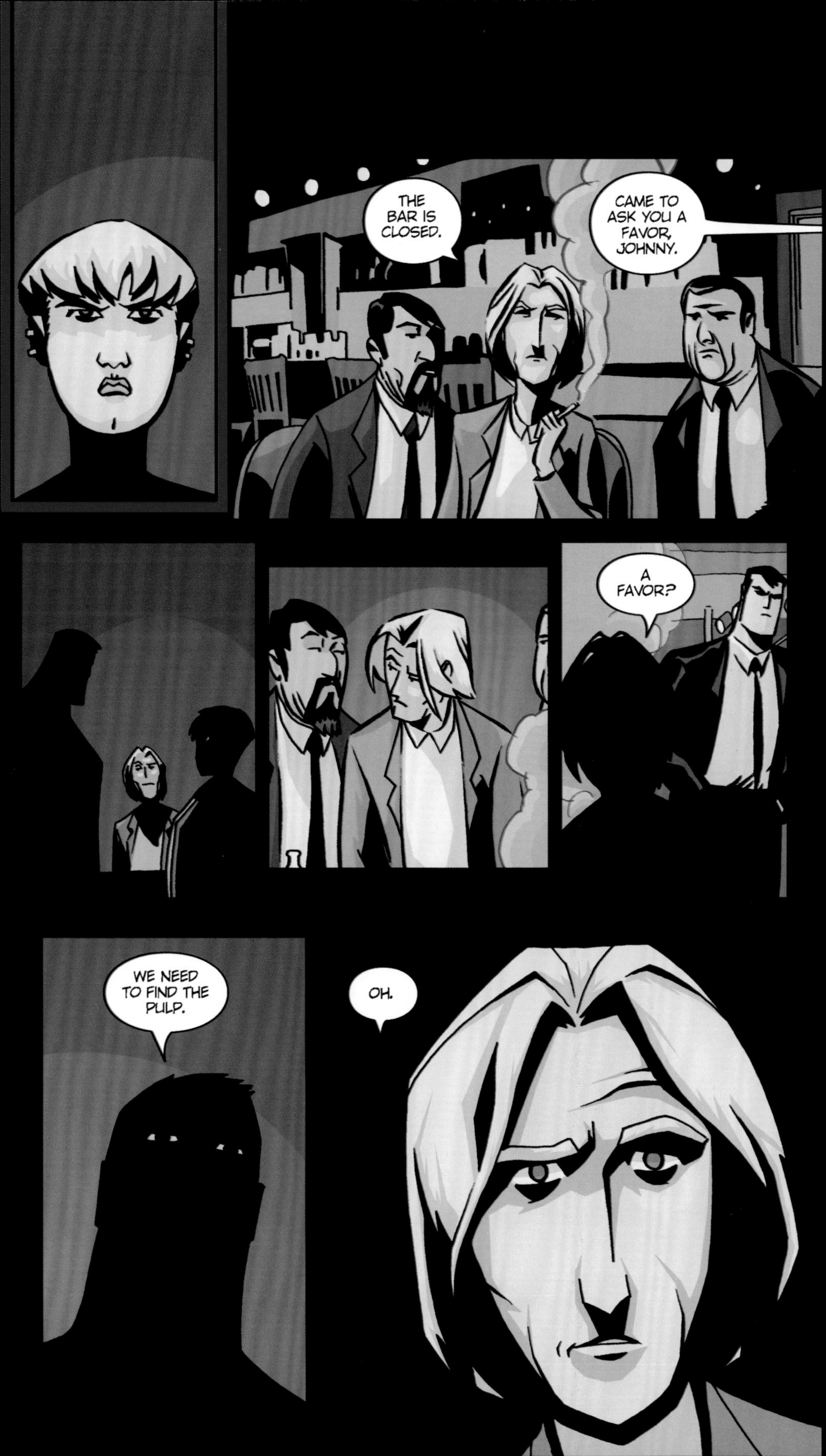
THE BAR IS CLOSED.
CAME TO ASK YOU A FAVOR, JOHNNY.
A FAVOR?
WE NEED TO FIND THE PULP.
OH.

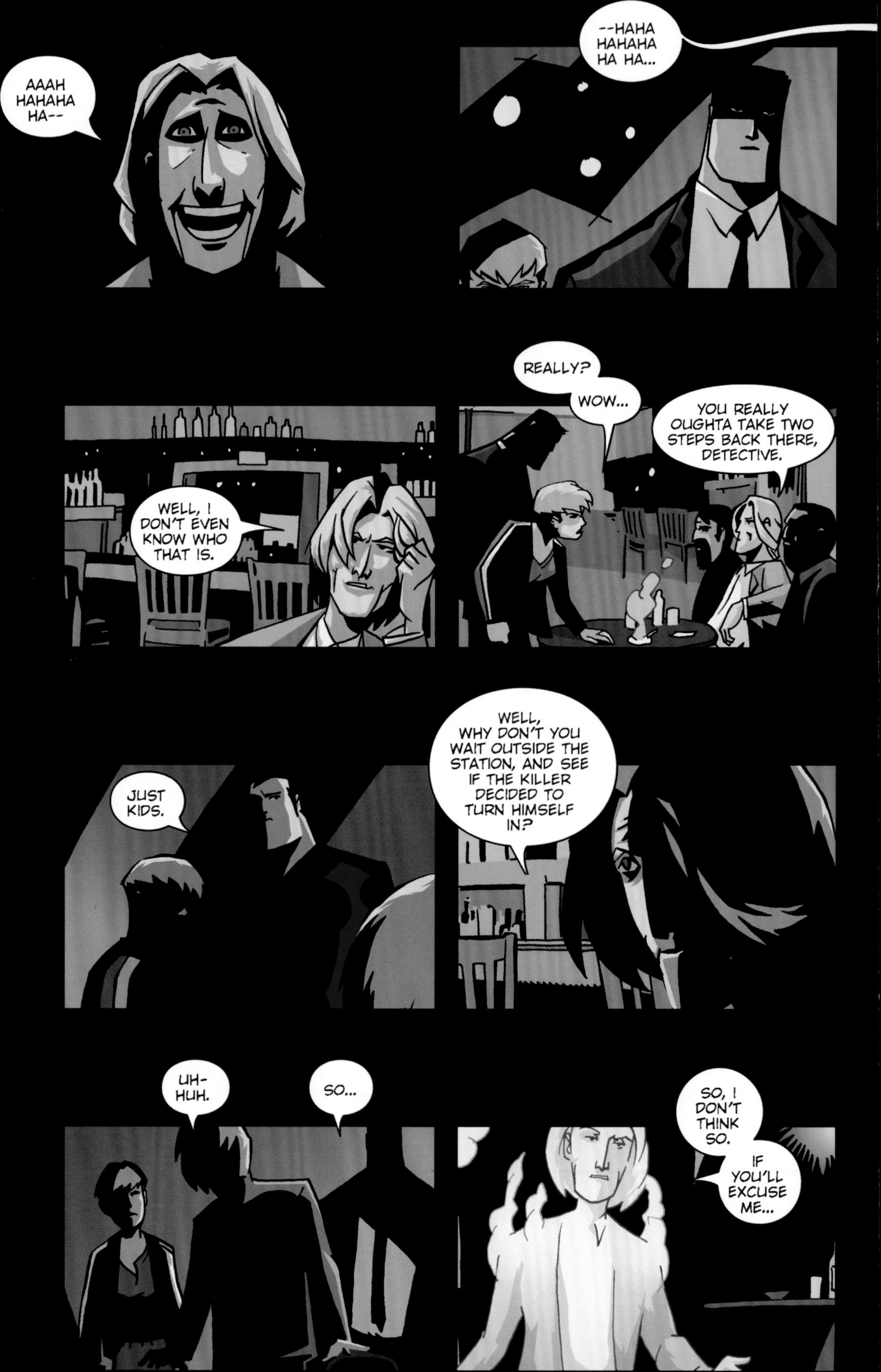
AAAH HAHAHA HA--
--HAHA HAHAHA HA HA...
WELL, I DON'T EVEN KNOW WHO THAT IS.
REALLY?
WOW...
YOU REALLY OUGHTA TAKE TWO STEPS BACK THERE, DETECTIVE.
JUST KIDS.
WELL, WHY DON'T YOU WAIT OUTSIDE THE STATION, AND SEE IF THE KILLER DECIDED TO TURN HIMSELF IN?
UH-HUH.
SO...
SO, I DON'T THINK SO.
IF YOU'LL EXCUSE ME...

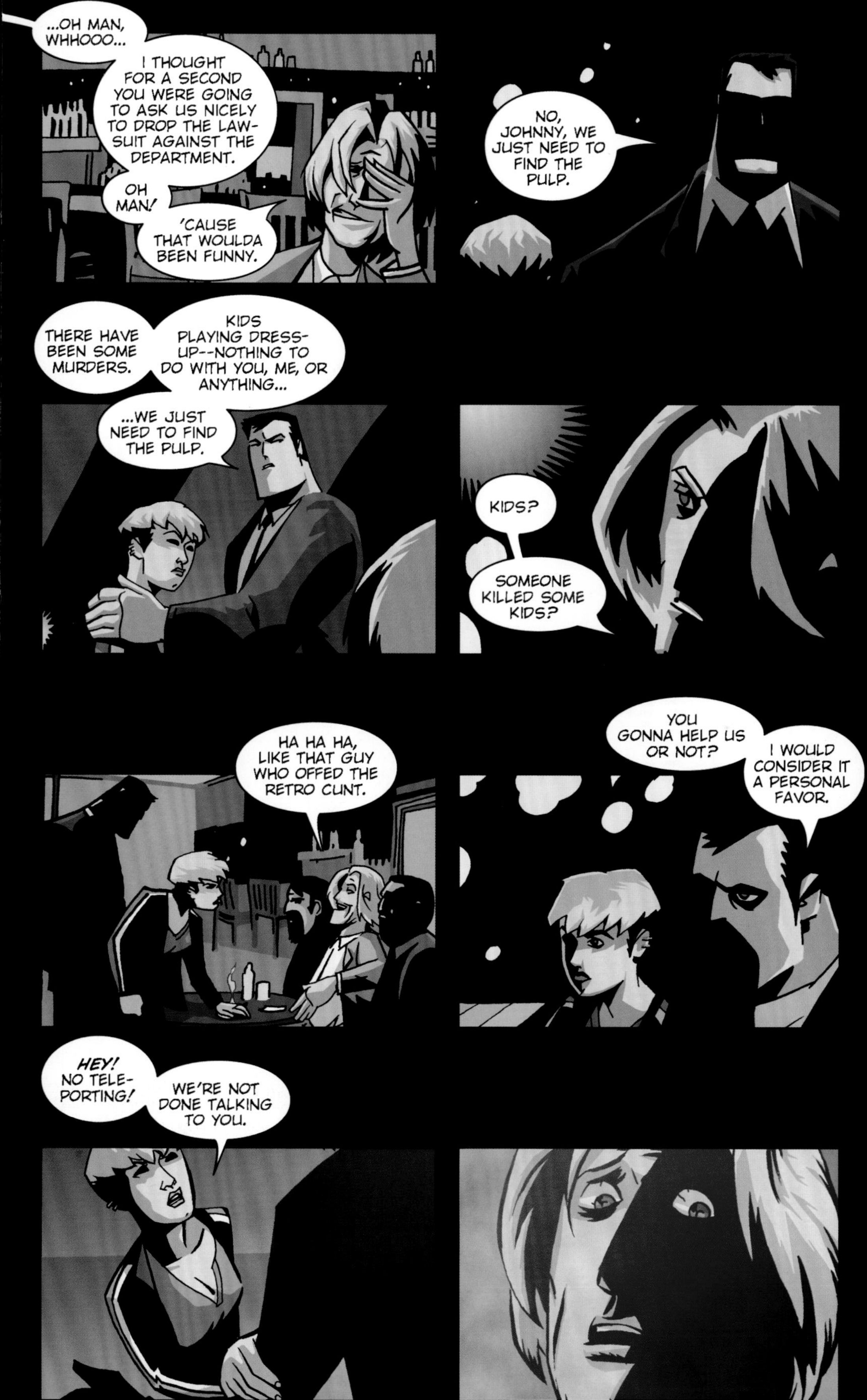
...OH MAN, WHHOOO...
I THOUGHT FOR A SECOND YOU WERE GOING TO ASK US NICELY TO DROP THE LAW-SUIT AGAINST THE DEPARTMENT.
OH MAN!
'CAUSE THAT WOULDA BEEN FUNNY.
NO, JOHNNY, WE JUST NEED TO FIND THE PULP.
THERE HAVE BEEN SOME MURDERS.
KIDS PLAYING DRESS-UP--NOTHING TO DO WITH YOU, ME, OR ANYTHING...
...WE JUST NEED TO FIND THE PULP.
KIDS?
SOMEONE KILLED SOME KIDS?
HA HA HA, LIKE THAT GUY WHO OFFED THE RETRO CUNT.
YOU GONNA HELP US OR NOT?
I WOULD CONSIDER IT A PERSONAL FAVOR.
HEY! NO TELE-PORTING!
WE'RE NOT DONE TALKING TO YOU.

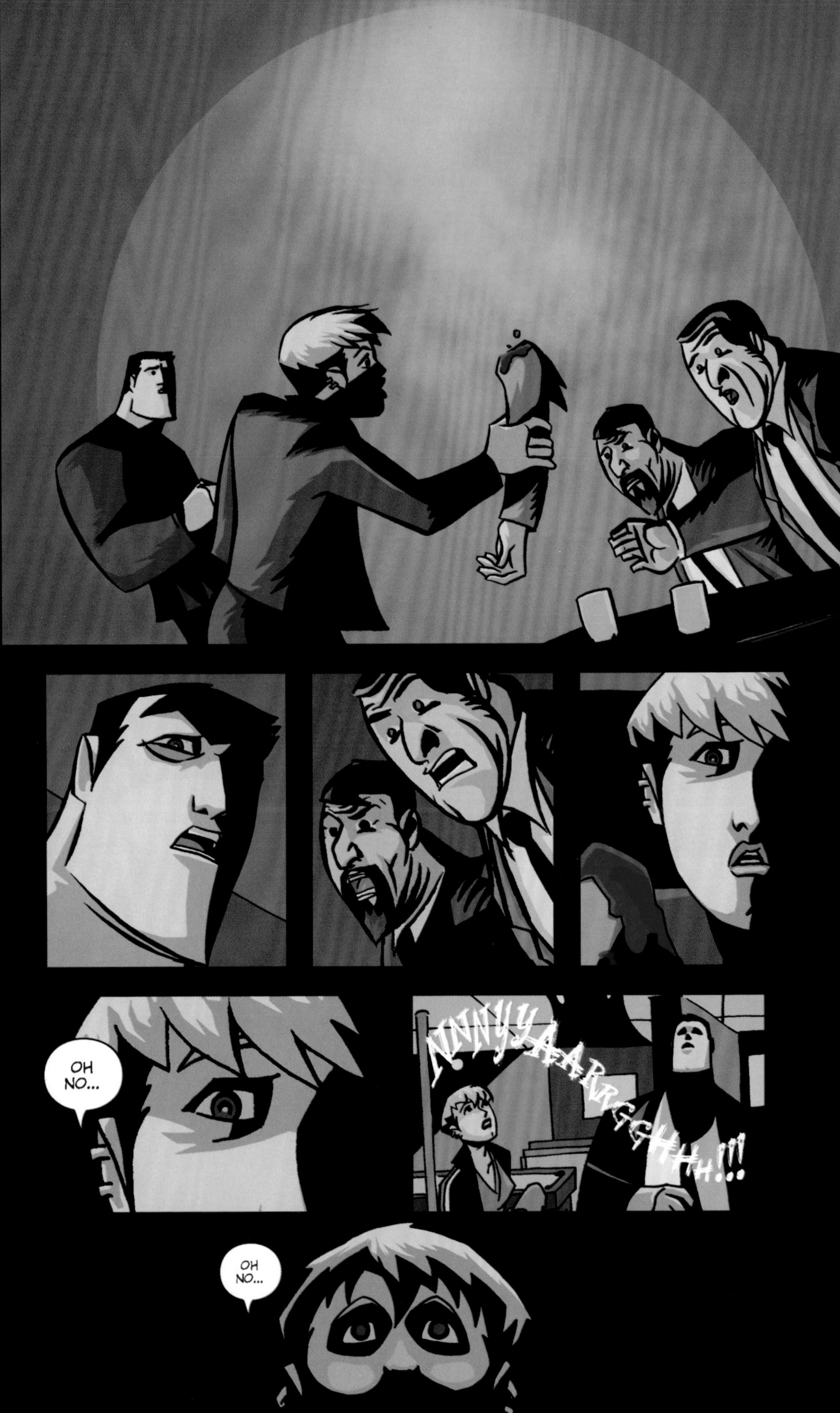
OH NO...
NNNYYAARRGGHHH!!!
OH NO...

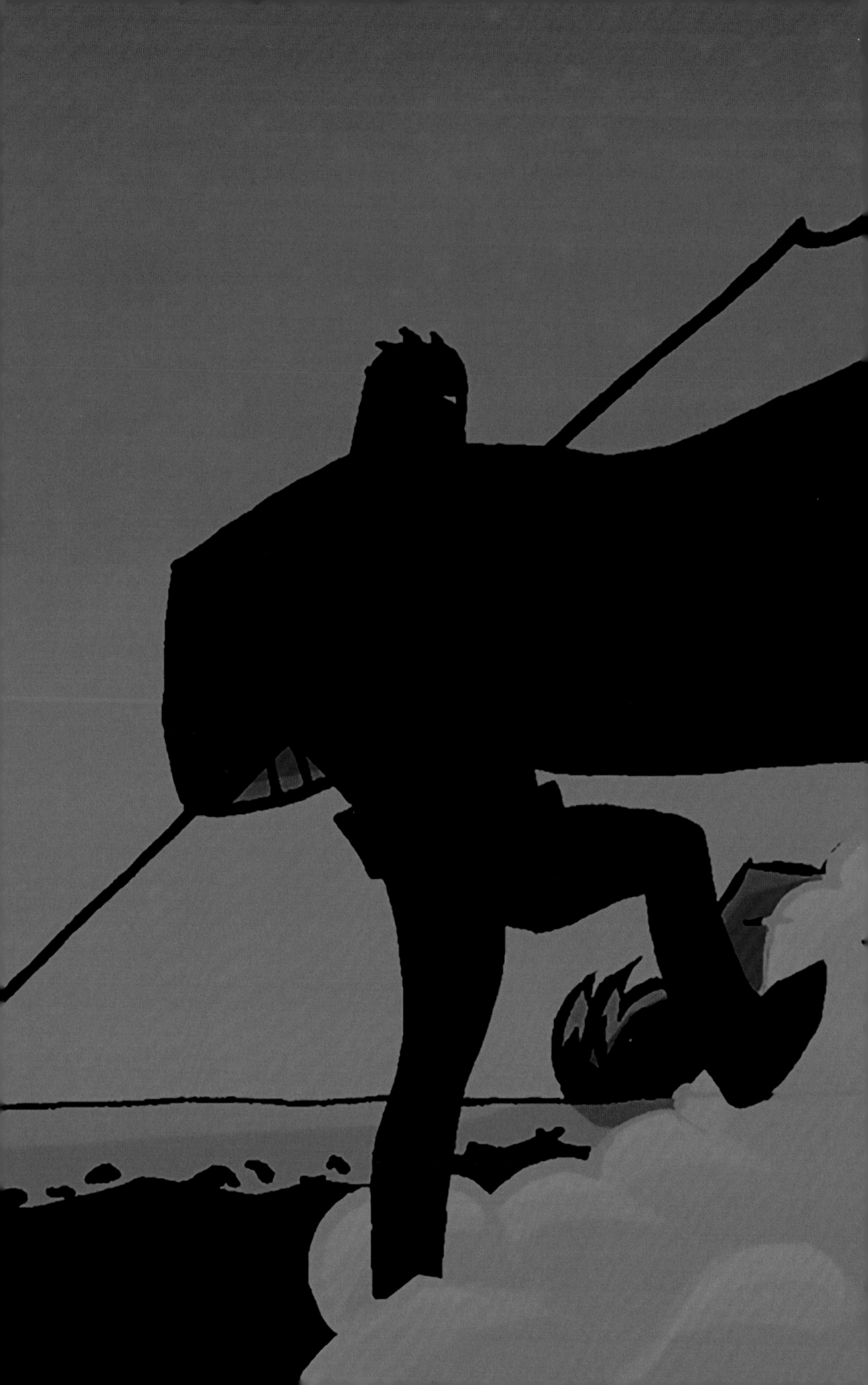

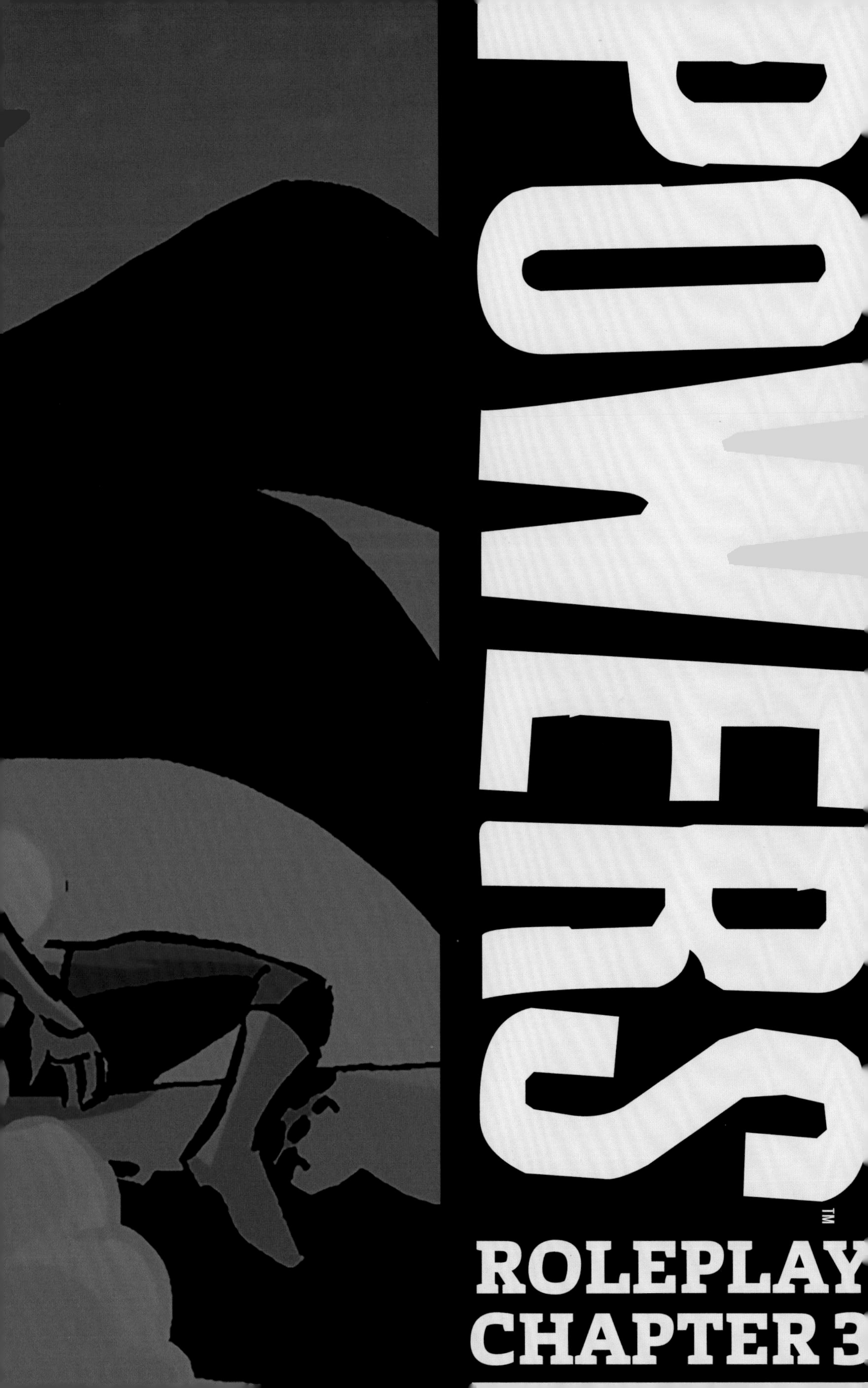

POWERS™

ROLEPLAY
CHAPTER 3

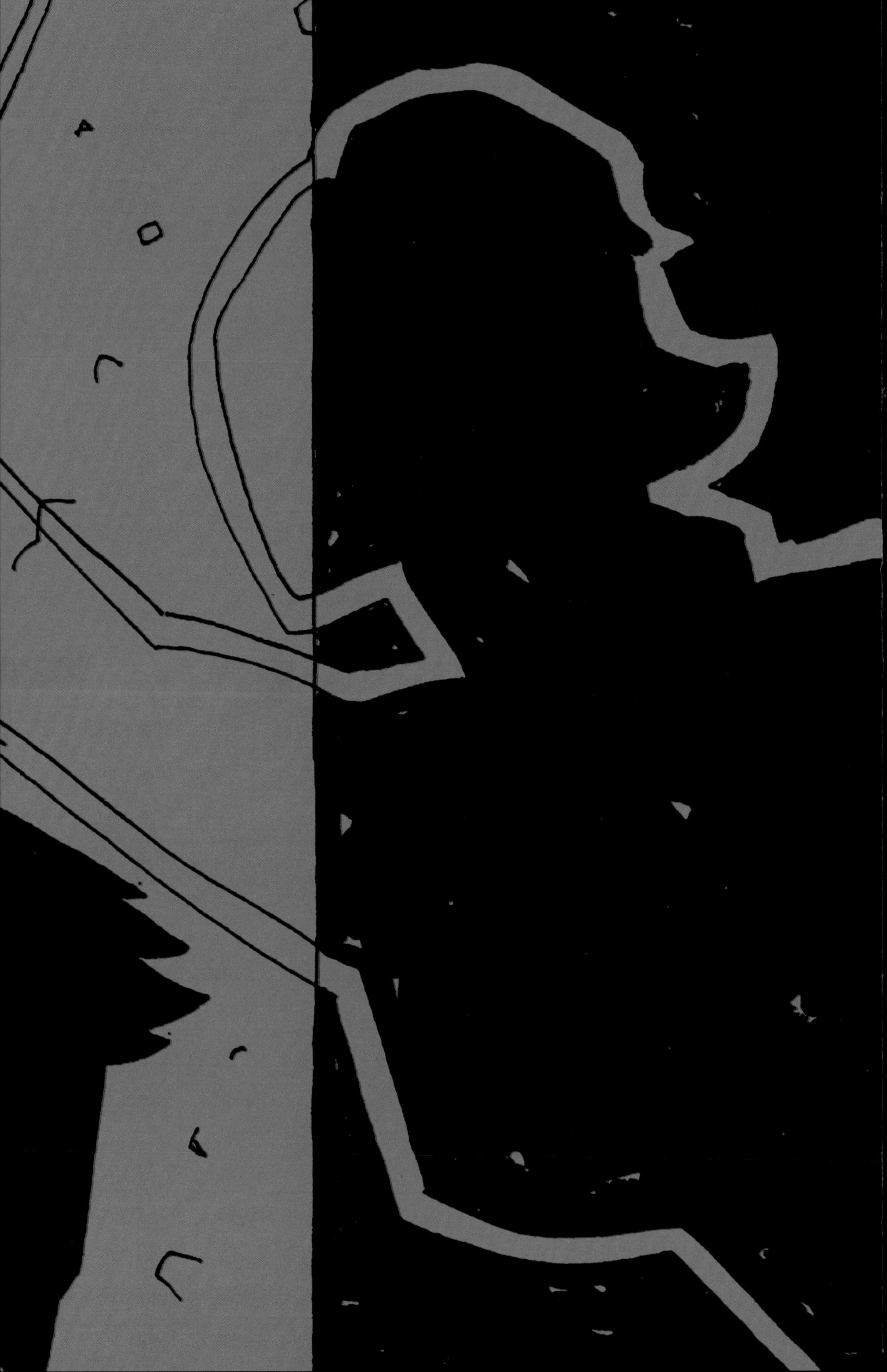

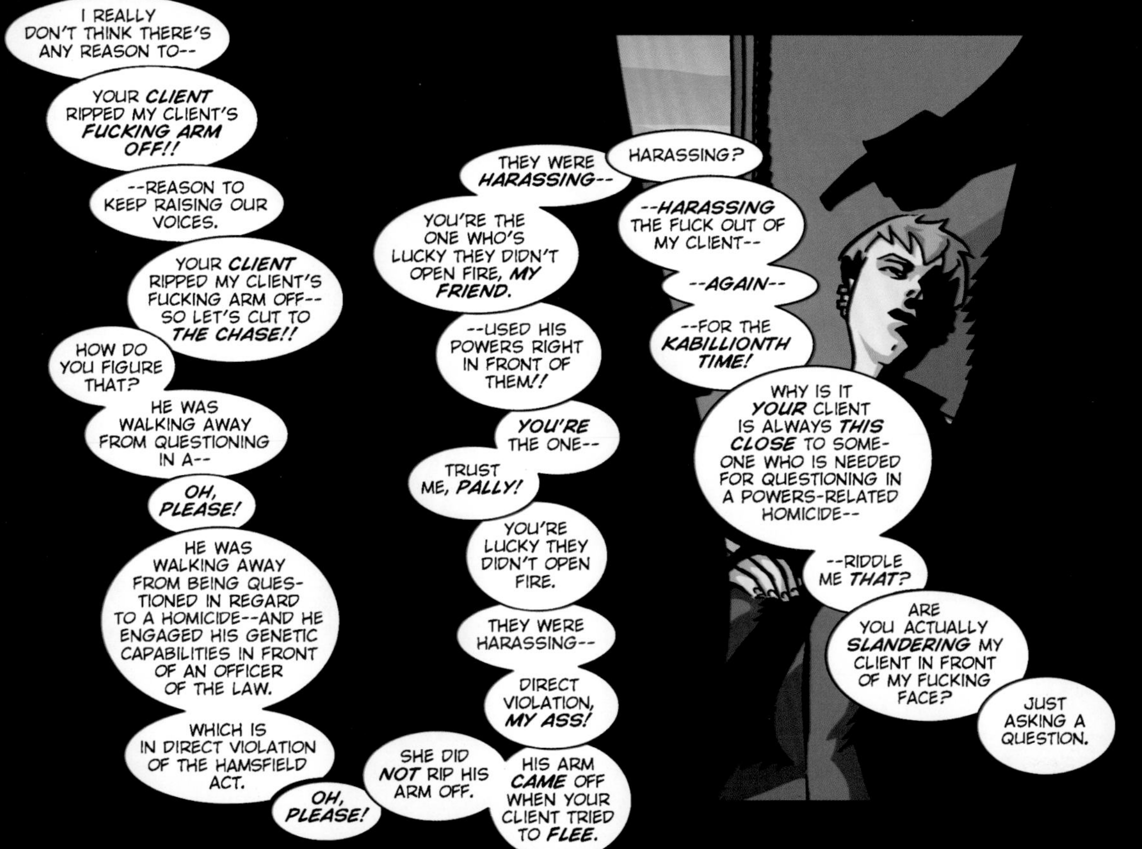
I REALLY DON'T THINK THERE'S ANY REASON TO--
YOUR *CLIENT* RIPPED MY CLIENT'S *FUCKING ARM OFF!!*
--REASON TO KEEP RAISING OUR VOICES.
YOUR *CLIENT* RIPPED MY CLIENT'S FUCKING ARM OFF-- SO LET'S CUT TO *THE CHASE!!*
HOW DO YOU FIGURE THAT?
HE WAS WALKING AWAY FROM QUESTIONING IN A--
OH, PLEASE!
HE WAS WALKING AWAY FROM BEING QUESTIONED IN REGARD TO A HOMICIDE--AND HE ENGAGED HIS GENETIC CAPABILITIES IN FRONT OF AN OFFICER OF THE LAW.
WHICH IS IN DIRECT VIOLATION OF THE HAMSFIELD ACT.
OH, PLEASE!
THEY WERE *HARASSING--*
HARASSING?
YOU'RE THE ONE WHO'S LUCKY THEY DIDN'T OPEN FIRE, *MY FRIEND.*
--USED HIS POWERS RIGHT IN FRONT OF THEM*!!*
YOU'RE THE ONE--
TRUST ME, *PALLY!*
YOU'RE LUCKY THEY DIDN'T OPEN FIRE.
THEY WERE HARASSING--
DIRECT VIOLATION, *MY ASS!*
SHE DID *NOT* RIP HIS ARM OFF.
HIS ARM *CAME* OFF WHEN YOUR CLIENT TRIED TO *FLEE.*
--HARASSING THE FUCK OUT OF MY CLIENT--
--AGAIN--
--FOR THE *KABILLIONTH TIME!*
WHY IS IT *YOUR* CLIENT IS ALWAYS *THIS CLOSE* TO SOME-ONE WHO IS NEEDED FOR QUESTIONING IN A POWERS-RELATED HOMICIDE--
--RIDDLE ME *THAT?*
ARE YOU ACTUALLY *SLANDERING* MY CLIENT IN FRONT OF MY FUCKING FACE?
JUST ASKING A QUESTION.

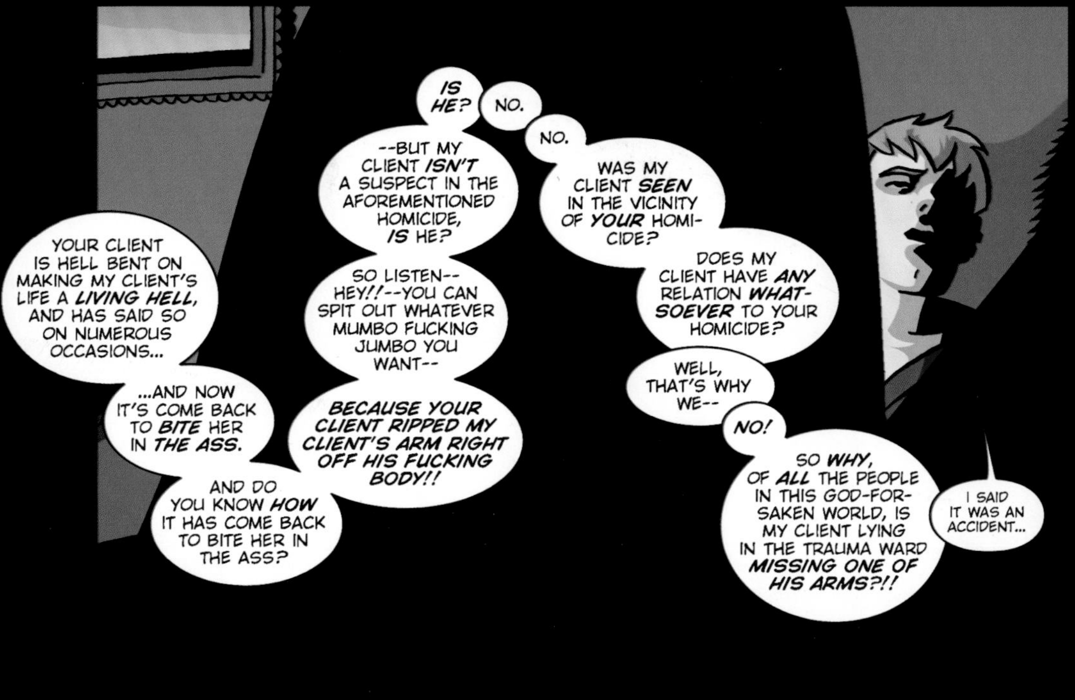
YOUR CLIENT IS HELL BENT ON MAKING MY CLIENT'S LIFE A *LIVING HELL,* AND HAS SAID SO ON NUMEROUS OCCASIONS...
...AND NOW IT'S COME BACK TO *BITE* HER IN *THE ASS.*
AND DO YOU KNOW *HOW* IT HAS COME BACK TO BITE HER IN THE ASS?
IS HE?
NO.
NO.
--BUT MY CLIENT *ISN'T* A SUSPECT IN THE AFOREMENTIONED HOMICIDE, *IS* HE?
SO LISTEN-- HEY*!!*--YOU CAN SPIT OUT WHATEVER MUMBO FUCKING JUMBO YOU WANT--
BECAUSE YOUR CLIENT RIPPED MY CLIENT'S ARM RIGHT OFF HIS FUCKING BODY!!
WAS MY CLIENT *SEEN* IN THE VICINITY OF *YOUR* HOMI-CIDE?
DOES MY CLIENT HAVE *ANY* RELATION *WHAT-SOEVER* TO YOUR HOMICIDE?
WELL, THAT'S WHY WE--
NO!
SO *WHY,* OF *ALL* THE PEOPLE IN THIS GOD-FOR-SAKEN WORLD, IS MY CLIENT LYING IN THE TRAUMA WARD *MISSING ONE OF HIS ARMS?!!*
I SAID IT WAS AN ACCIDENT...

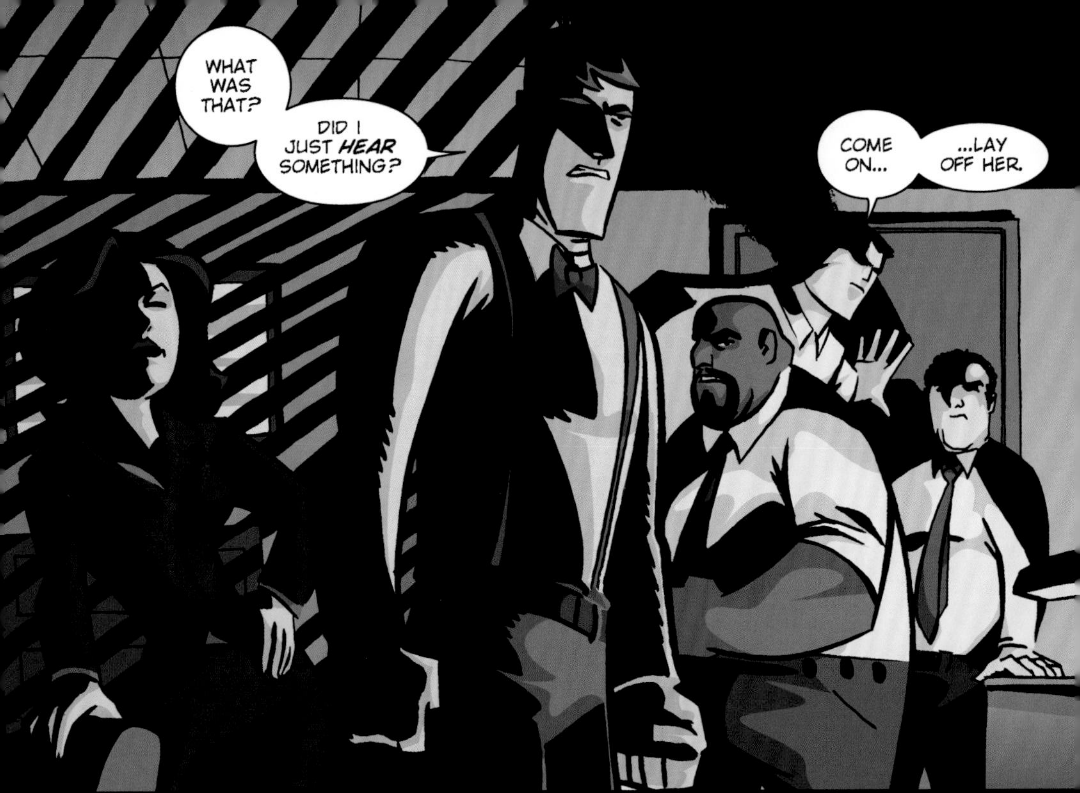
WHAT WAS THAT?
DID I JUST HEAR SOMETHING?
COME ON...
...LAY OFF HER.

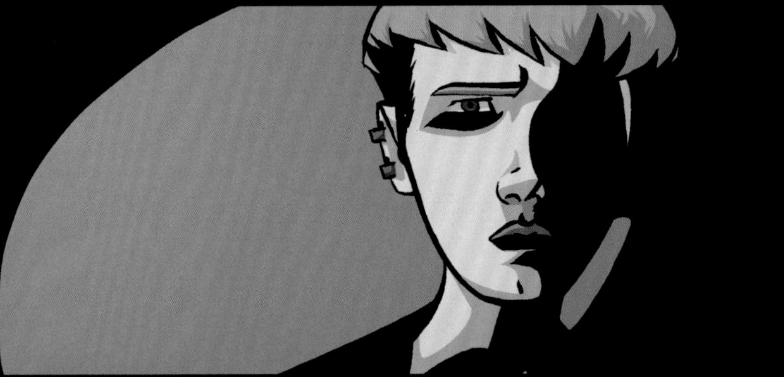

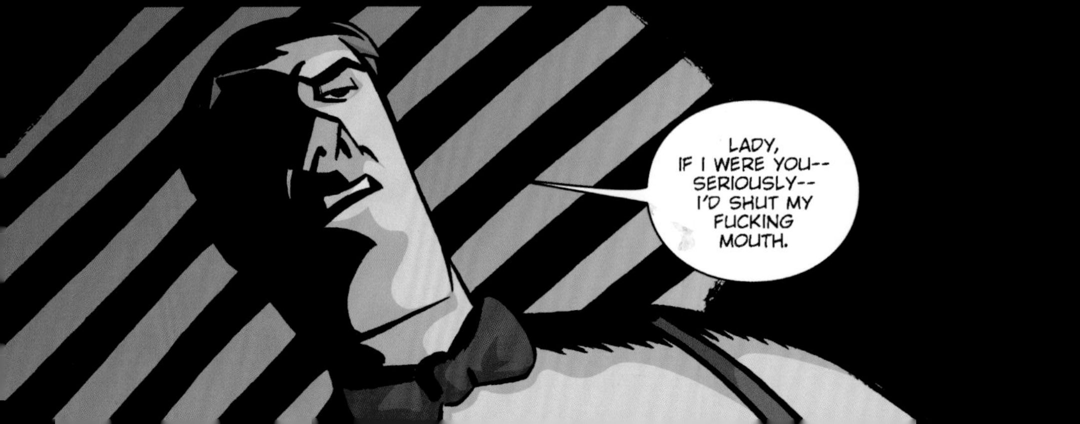
LADY, IF I WERE YOU-- SERIOUSLY-- I'D SHUT MY FUCKING MOUTH.

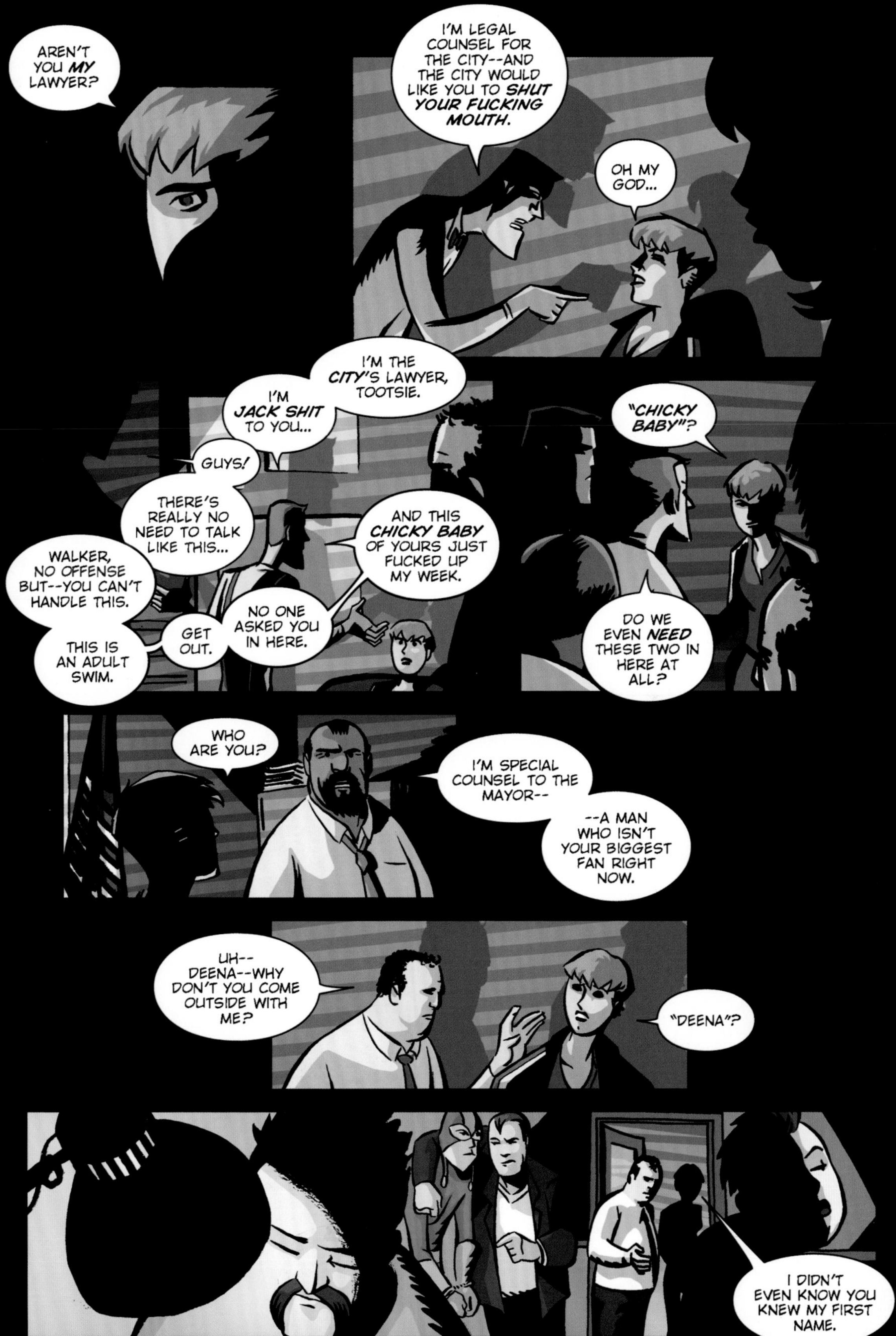

AREN'T YOU *MY* LAWYER?
I'M LEGAL COUNSEL FOR THE CITY--AND THE CITY WOULD LIKE YOU TO ***SHUT YOUR FUCKING MOUTH.***
OH MY GOD...
I'M ***JACK SHIT*** TO YOU...
I'M THE ***CITY***'S LAWYER, TOOTSIE.
"***CHICKY BABY***"?
GUYS!
THERE'S REALLY NO NEED TO TALK LIKE THIS...
AND THIS ***CHICKY BABY*** OF YOURS JUST FUCKED UP MY WEEK.
WALKER, NO OFFENSE BUT--YOU CAN'T HANDLE THIS.
NO ONE ASKED YOU IN HERE.
GET OUT.
THIS IS AN ADULT SWIM.
DO WE EVEN ***NEED*** THESE TWO IN HERE AT ALL?
WHO ARE YOU?
I'M SPECIAL COUNSEL TO THE MAYOR--
--A MAN WHO ISN'T YOUR BIGGEST FAN RIGHT NOW.
UH--DEENA--WHY DON'T YOU COME OUTSIDE WITH ME?
"DEENA"?
I DIDN'T EVEN KNOW YOU KNEW MY FIRST NAME.

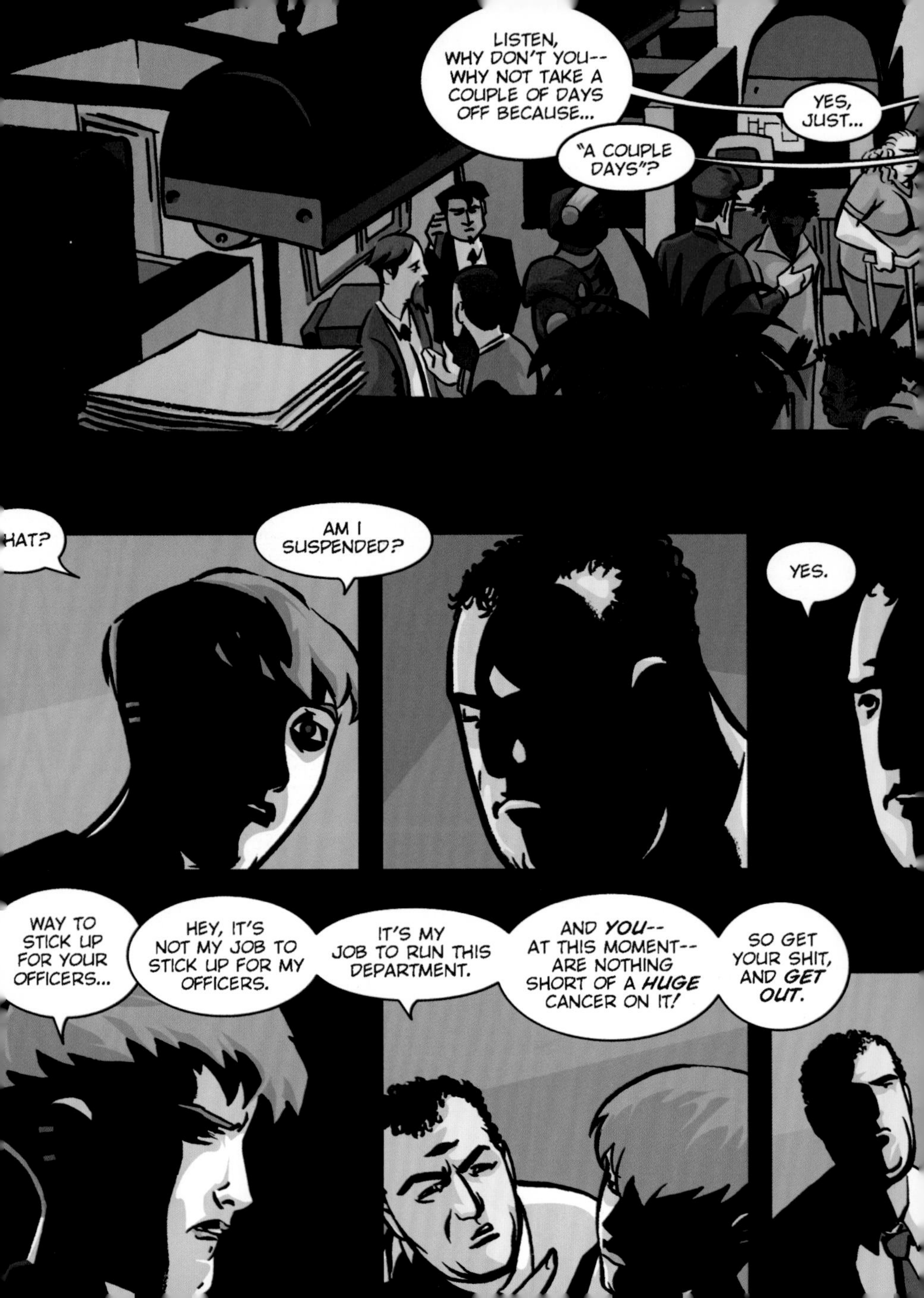
LISTEN, WHY DON'T YOU-- WHY NOT TAKE A COUPLE OF DAYS OFF BECAUSE...
"A COUPLE DAYS"?
YES, JUST...
HAT?
AM I SUSPENDED?
YES.
WAY TO STICK UP FOR YOUR OFFICERS...
HEY, IT'S NOT MY JOB TO STICK UP FOR MY OFFICERS.
IT'S MY JOB TO RUN THIS DEPARTMENT.
AND *YOU*-- AT THIS MOMENT-- ARE NOTHING SHORT OF A *HUGE* CANCER ON IT!
SO GET YOUR SHIT, AND *GET OUT*.

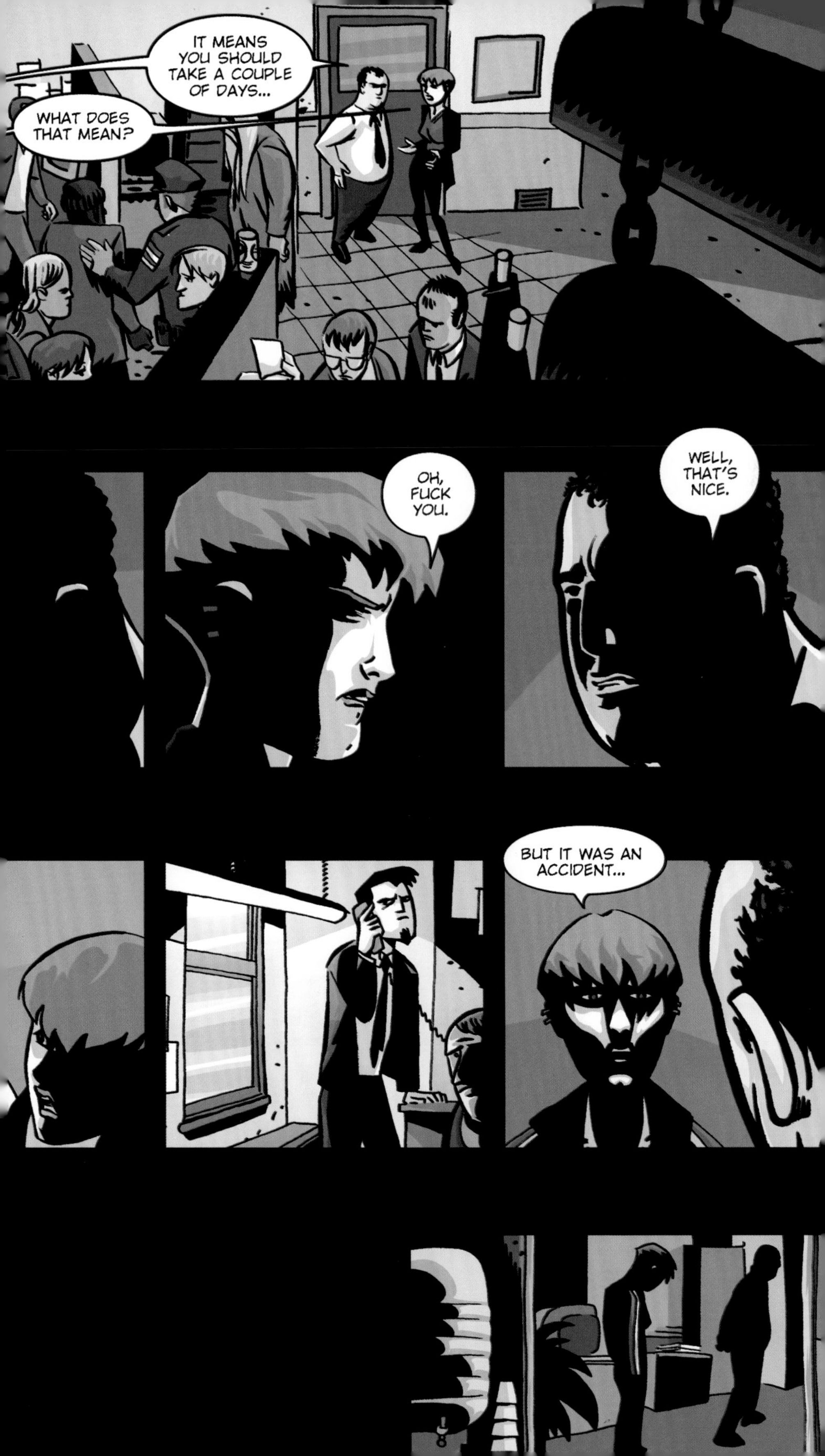
WHAT DOES THAT MEAN?
IT MEANS YOU SHOULD TAKE A COUPLE OF DAYS...
OH, FUCK YOU.
WELL, THAT'S NICE.
BUT IT WAS AN ACCIDENT...

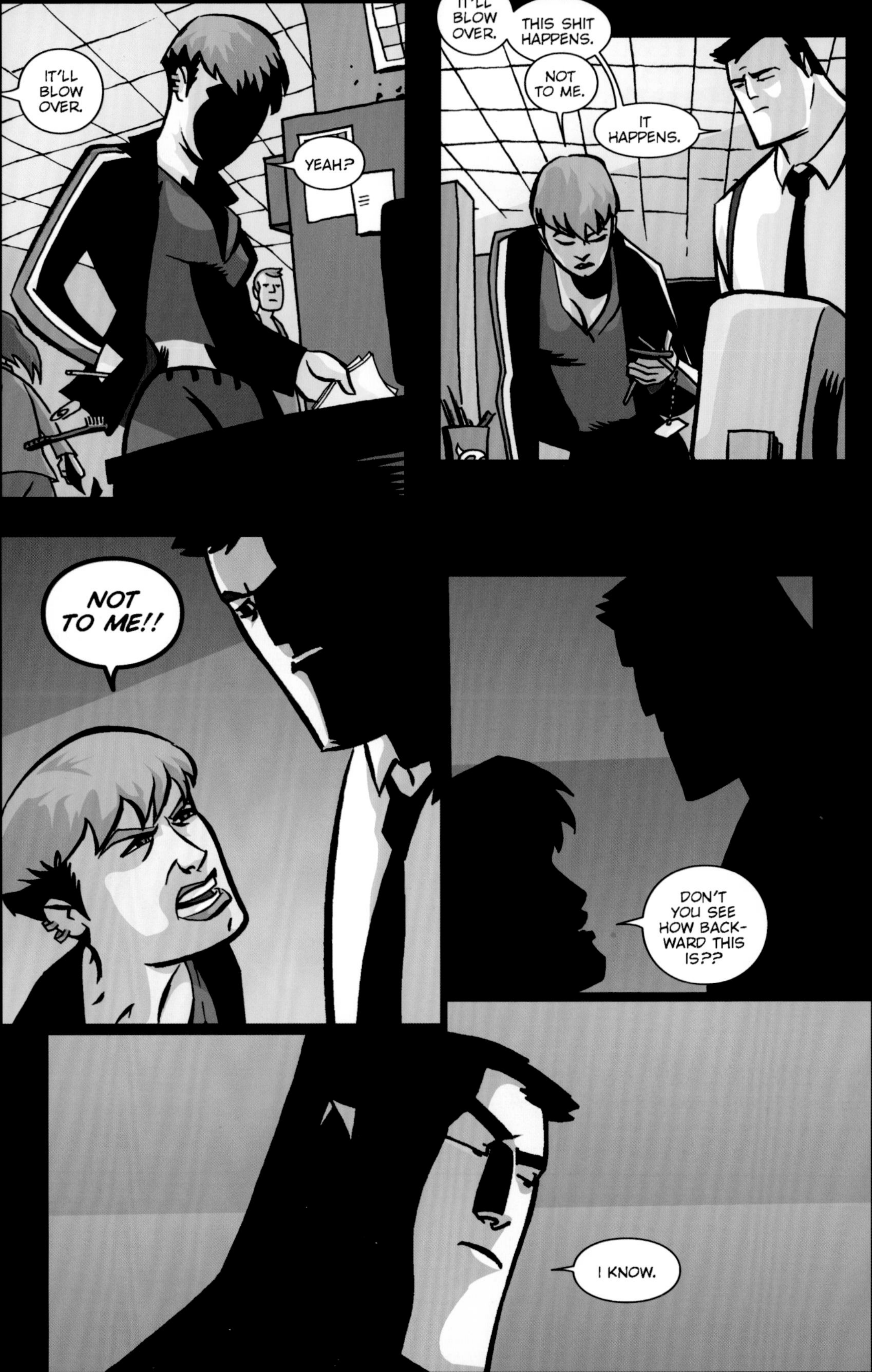
IT'LL BLOW OVER.
YEAH?
IT'LL BLOW OVER.
THIS SHIT HAPPENS.
NOT TO ME.
IT HAPPENS.
NOT TO ME!!
DON'T YOU SEE HOW BACK-WARD THIS IS??
I KNOW.

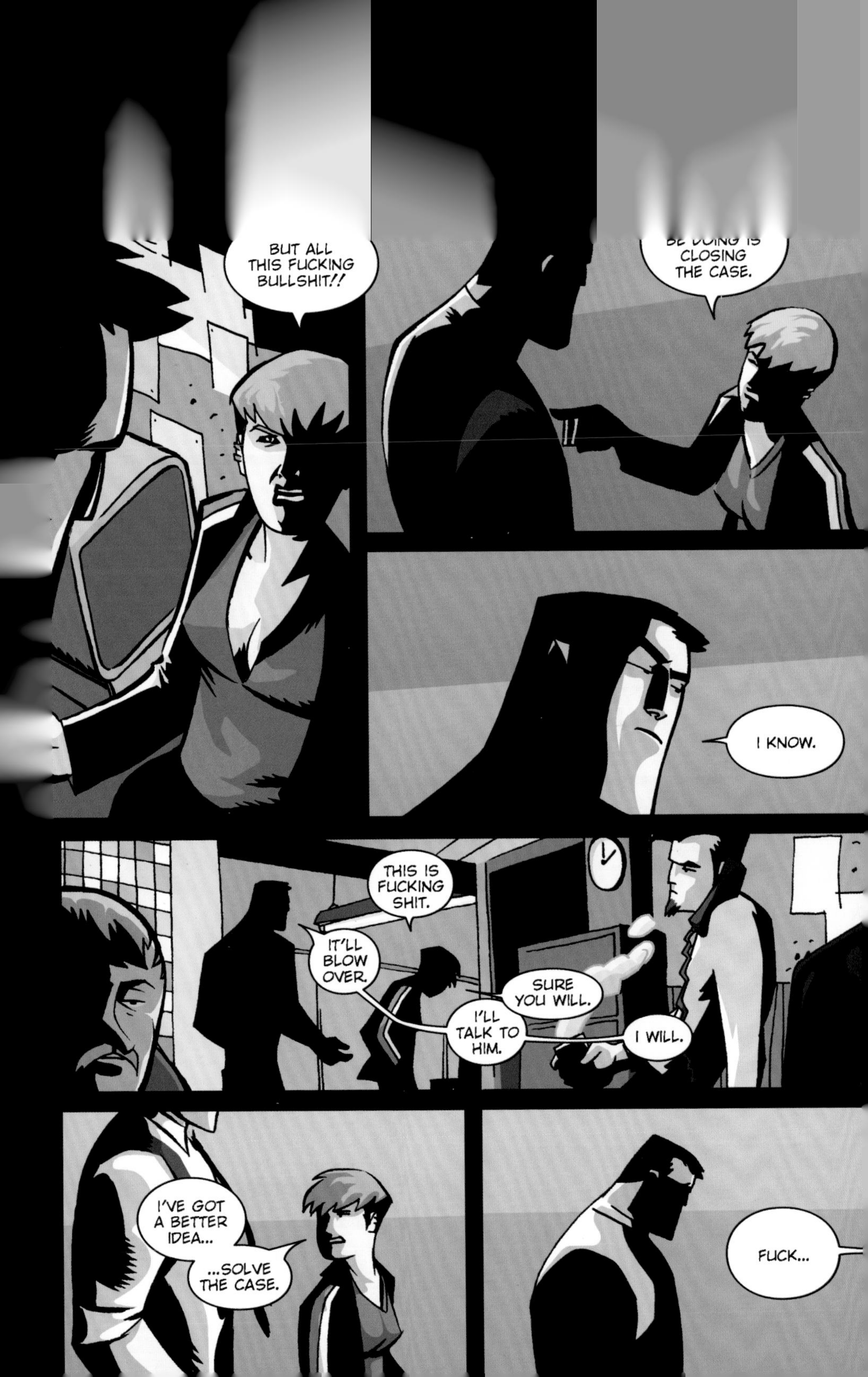
BUT ALL THIS FUCKING BULLSHIT!!
CLOSING THE CASE.
I KNOW.
THIS IS FUCKING SHIT.
IT'LL BLOW OVER.
SURE YOU WILL.
I'LL TALK TO HIM.
I WILL.
I'VE GOT A BETTER IDEA...
...SOLVE THE CASE.
FUCK...

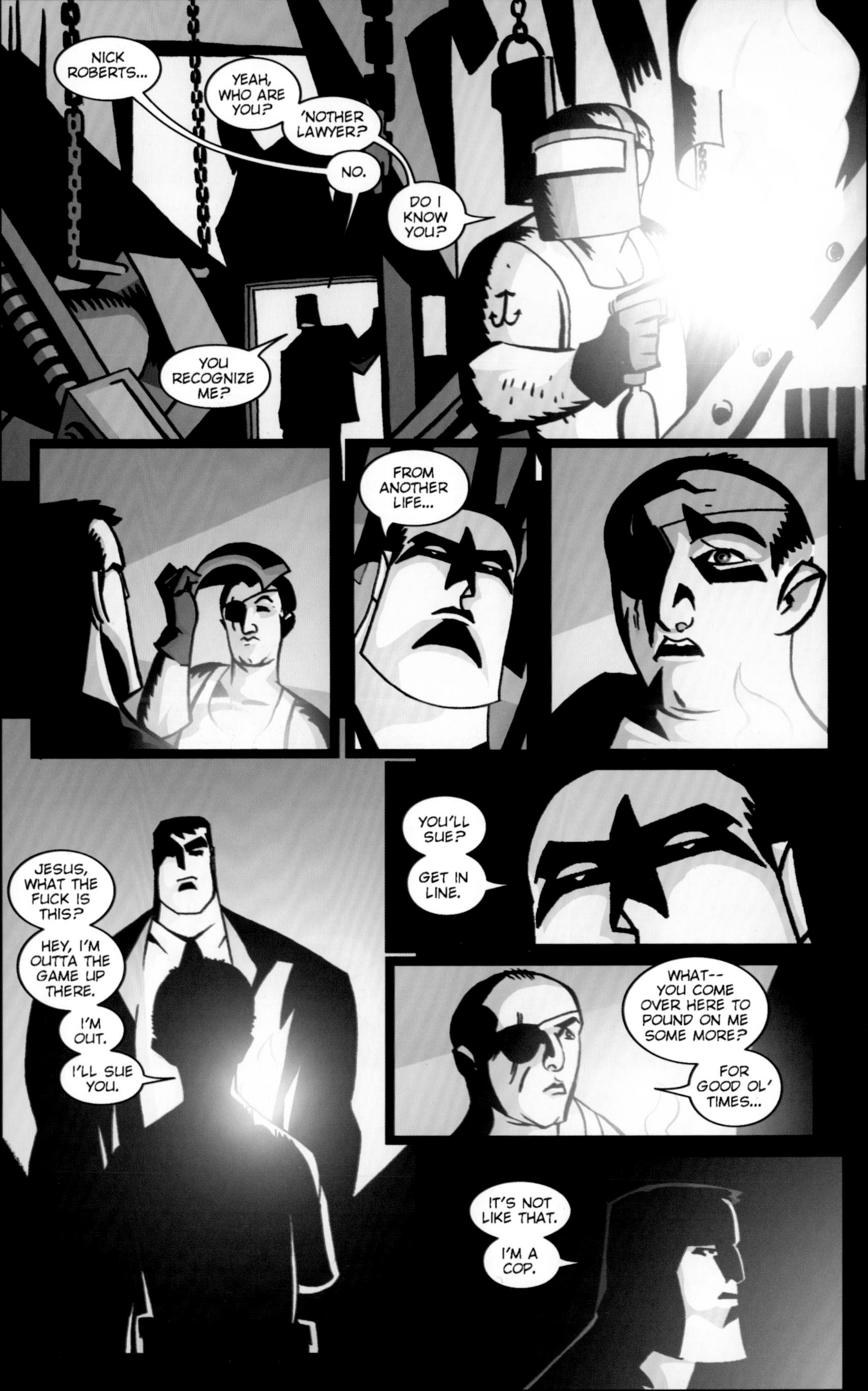
NICK ROBERTS...
YEAH, WHO ARE YOU?
'NOTHER LAWYER?
NO.
DO I KNOW YOU?
YOU RECOGNIZE ME?
FROM ANOTHER LIFE...
JESUS, WHAT THE FUCK IS THIS?
HEY, I'M OUTTA THE GAME UP THERE.
I'M OUT.
I'LL SUE YOU.
YOU'LL SUE?
GET IN LINE.
WHAT-- YOU COME OVER HERE TO POUND ON ME SOME MORE?
FOR GOOD OL' TIMES...
IT'S NOT LIKE THAT.
I'M A COP.

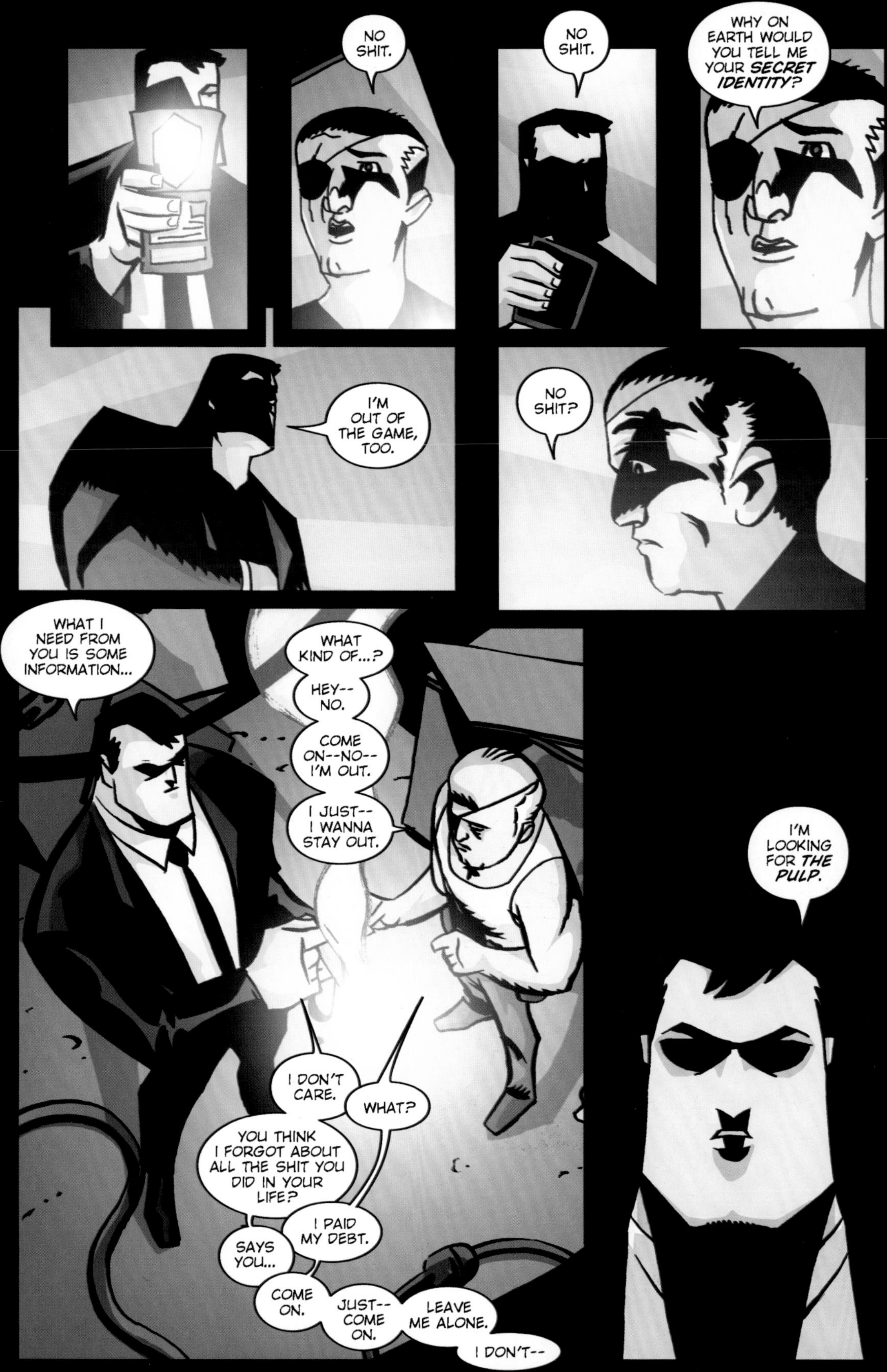
NO SHIT.
NO SHIT.
WHY ON EARTH WOULD YOU TELL ME YOUR SECRET IDENTITY?
I'M OUT OF THE GAME, TOO.
NO SHIT?
WHAT I NEED FROM YOU IS SOME INFORMATION...
WHAT KIND OF...?
HEY-- NO.
COME ON--NO-- I'M OUT.
I JUST-- I WANNA STAY OUT.
I'M LOOKING FOR THE PULP.
I DON'T CARE.
WHAT?
YOU THINK I FORGOT ABOUT ALL THE SHIT YOU DID IN YOUR LIFE?
I PAID MY DEBT.
SAYS YOU...
COME ON.
JUST-- COME ON.
LEAVE ME ALONE.
I DON'T--

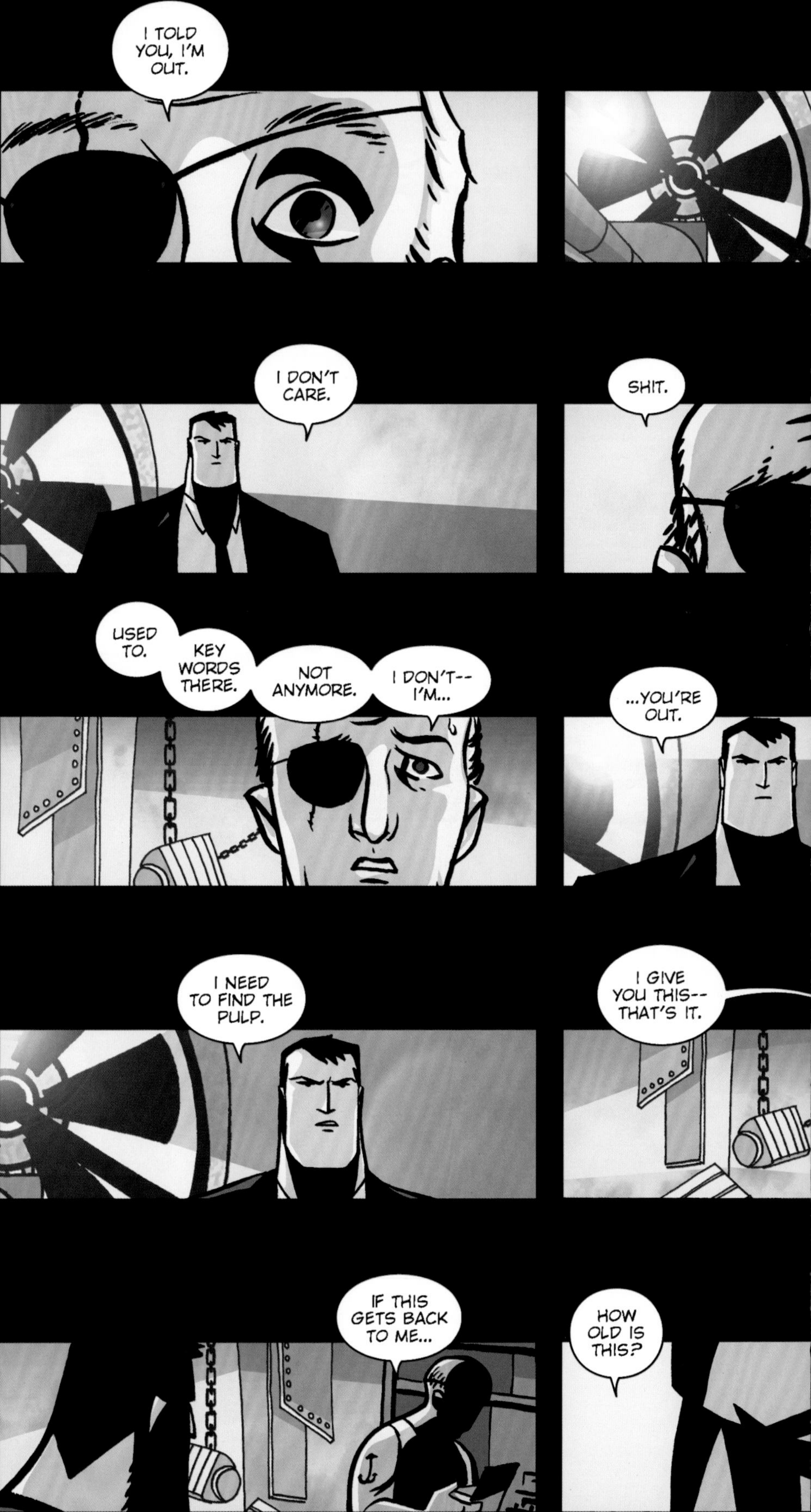
I TOLD YOU, I'M OUT.
I DON'T CARE.
SHIT.
USED TO.
KEY WORDS THERE.
NOT ANYMORE.
I DON'T-- I'M...
...YOU'RE OUT.
I NEED TO FIND THE PULP.
I GIVE YOU THIS-- THAT'S IT.
IF THIS GETS BACK TO ME...
HOW OLD IS THIS?

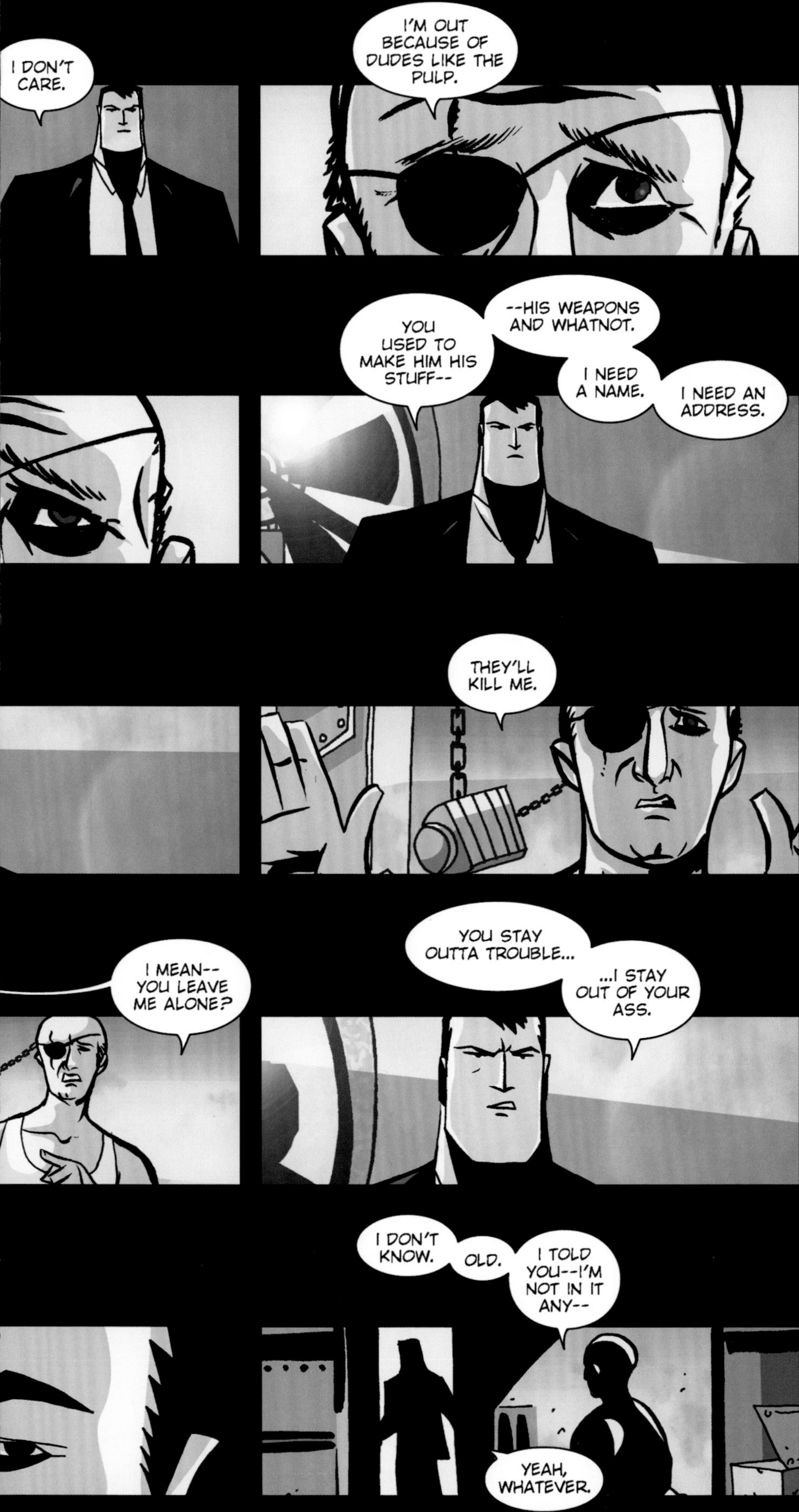
I DON'T CARE.
I'M OUT BECAUSE OF DUDES LIKE THE PULP.
YOU USED TO MAKE HIM HIS STUFF--
--HIS WEAPONS AND WHATNOT.
I NEED A NAME.
I NEED AN ADDRESS.
THEY'LL KILL ME.
I MEAN-- YOU LEAVE ME ALONE?
YOU STAY OUTTA TROUBLE...
...I STAY OUT OF YOUR ASS.
I DON'T KNOW.
OLD.
I TOLD YOU--I'M NOT IN IT ANY--
YEAH, WHATEVER.

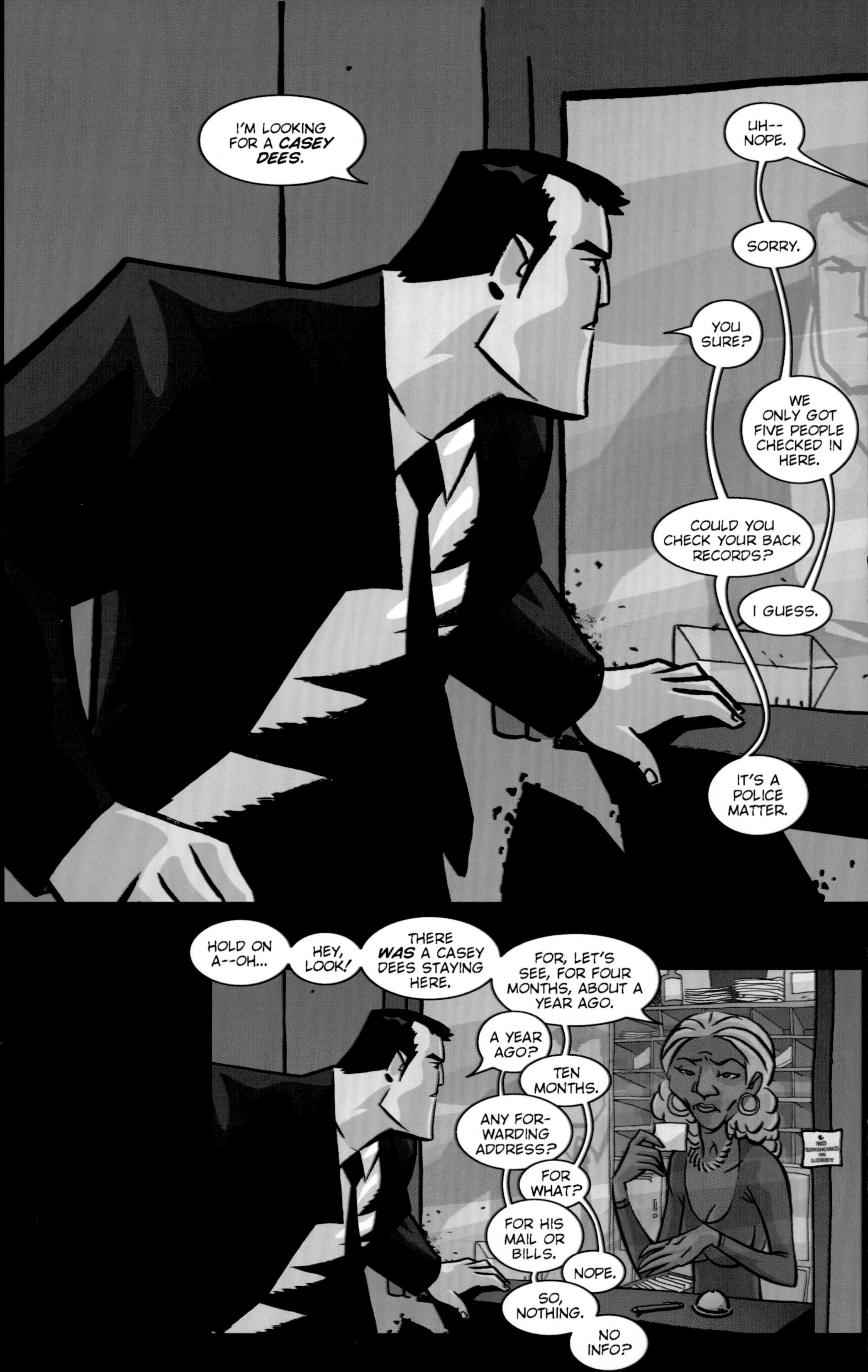
I'M LOOKING FOR A *CASEY DEES.*
UH-- NOPE.
SORRY.
YOU SURE?
WE ONLY GOT FIVE PEOPLE CHECKED IN HERE.
COULD YOU CHECK YOUR BACK RECORDS?
I GUESS.
IT'S A POLICE MATTER.
HOLD ON A--OH...
HEY, LOOK!
THERE *WAS* A CASEY DEES STAYING HERE.
FOR, LET'S SEE, FOR FOUR MONTHS, ABOUT A YEAR AGO.
A YEAR AGO?
TEN MONTHS.
ANY FOR-WARDING ADDRESS?
FOR WHAT?
FOR HIS MAIL OR BILLS.
NOPE.
SO, NOTHING.
NO INFO?

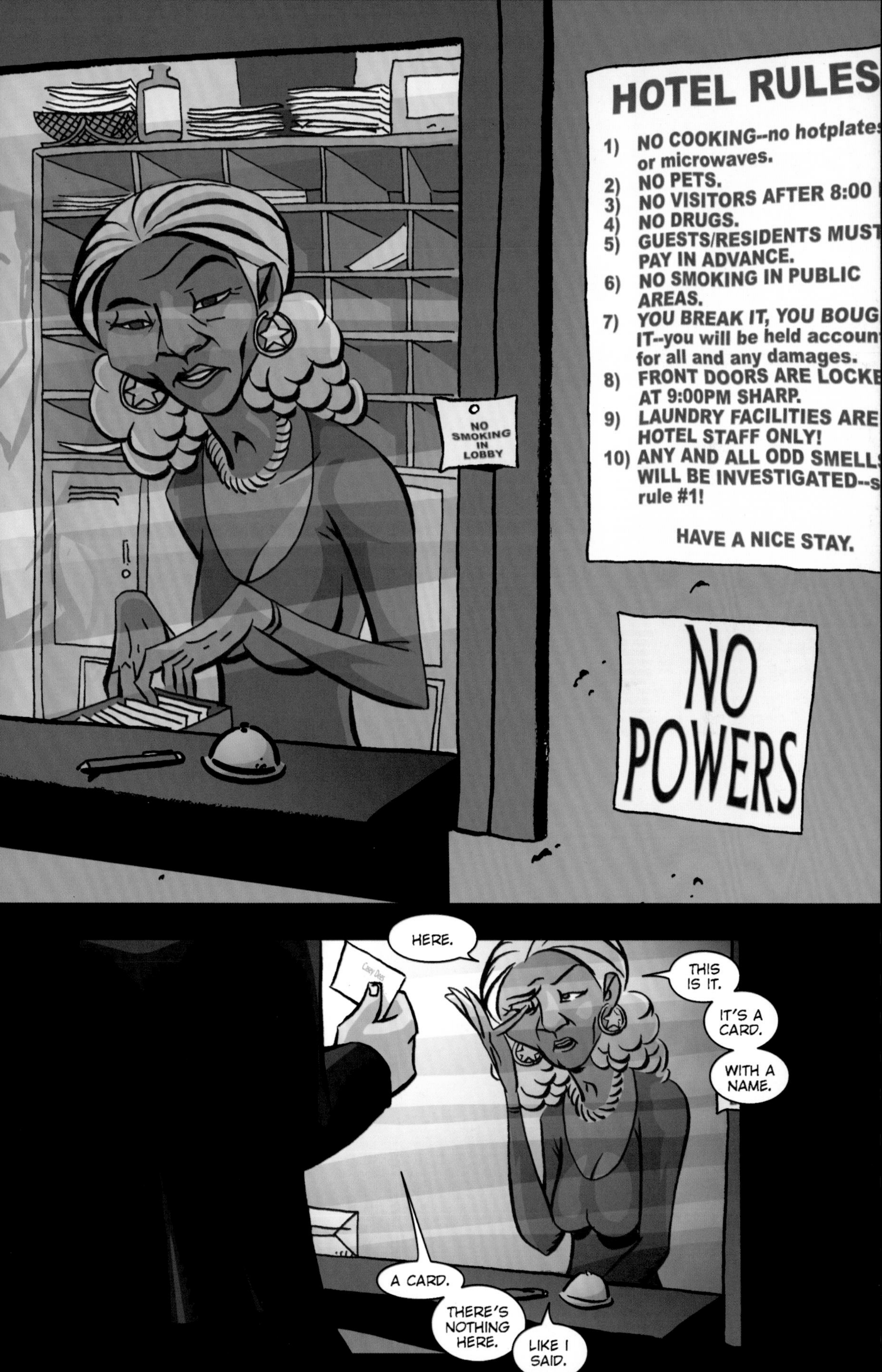

NO SMOKING IN LOBBY
HOTEL RULES
1) NO COOKING--no hotplates or microwaves.
2) NO PETS.
3) NO VISITORS AFTER 8:00
4) NO DRUGS.
5) GUESTS/RESIDENTS MUST PAY IN ADVANCE.
6) NO SMOKING IN PUBLIC AREAS.
7) YOU BREAK IT, YOU BOUG IT--you will be held accoun for all and any damages.
8) FRONT DOORS ARE LOCKE AT 9:00PM SHARP.
9) LAUNDRY FACILITIES ARE HOTEL STAFF ONLY!
10) ANY AND ALL ODD SMELL WILL BE INVESTIGATED--s rule #1!
HAVE A NICE STAY.
NO POWERS
HERE.
THIS IS IT.
IT'S A CARD.
WITH A NAME.
A CARD.
THERE'S NOTHING HERE.
LIKE I SAID.

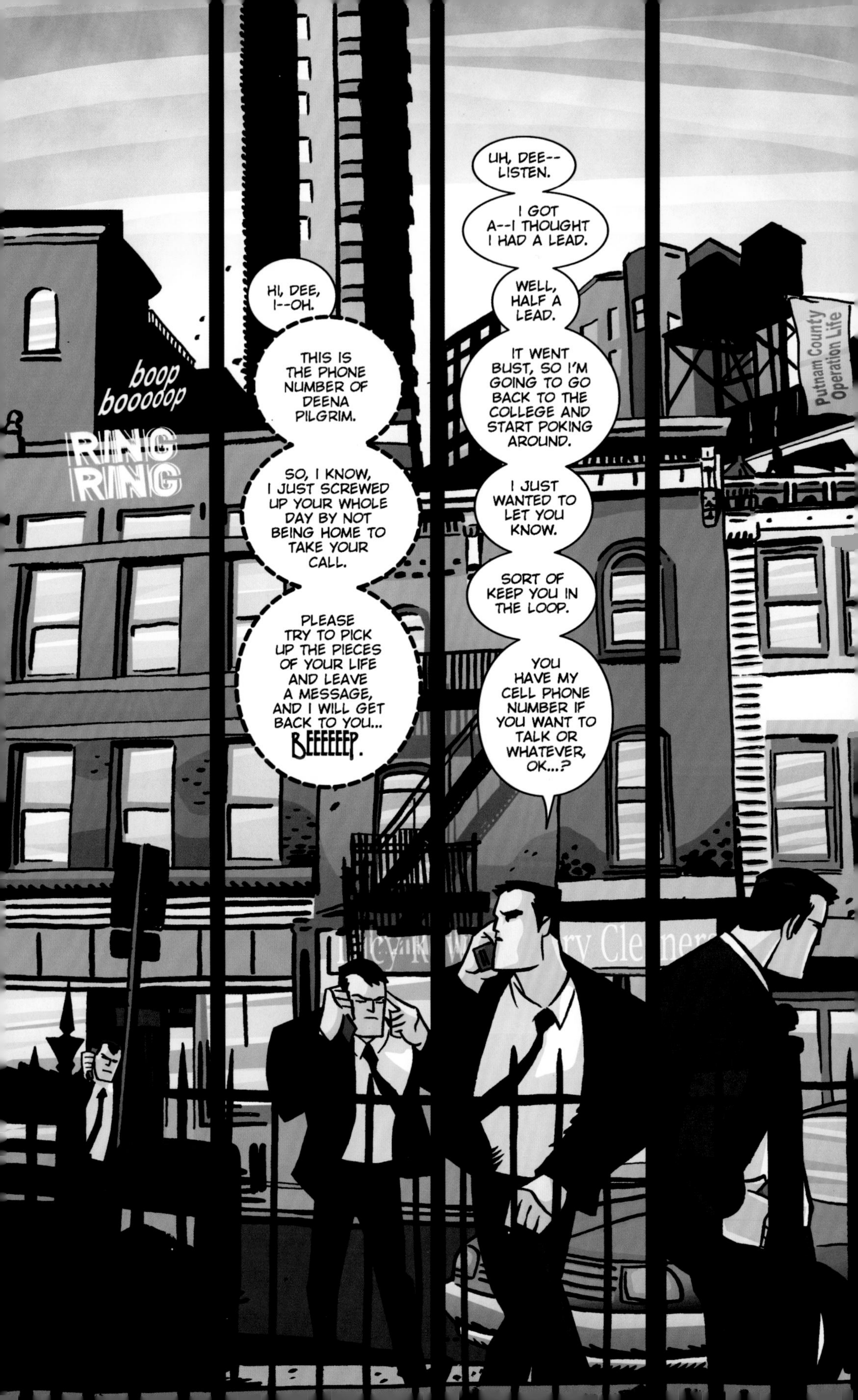
boop booooop
RING RING
HI, DEE, I--OH.
THIS IS THE PHONE NUMBER OF DEENA PILGRIM.
SO, I KNOW, I JUST SCREWED UP YOUR WHOLE DAY BY NOT BEING HOME TO TAKE YOUR CALL.
PLEASE TRY TO PICK UP THE PIECES OF YOUR LIFE AND LEAVE A MESSAGE, AND I WILL GET BACK TO YOU... BEEEEEEP.
UH, DEE-- LISTEN.
I GOT A--I THOUGHT I HAD A LEAD.
WELL, HALF A LEAD.
IT WENT BUST, SO I'M GOING TO GO BACK TO THE COLLEGE AND START POKING AROUND.
I JUST WANTED TO LET YOU KNOW.
SORT OF KEEP YOU IN THE LOOP.
YOU HAVE MY CELL PHONE NUMBER IF YOU WANT TO TALK OR WHATEVER, OK...?
Putnam County Operation Life

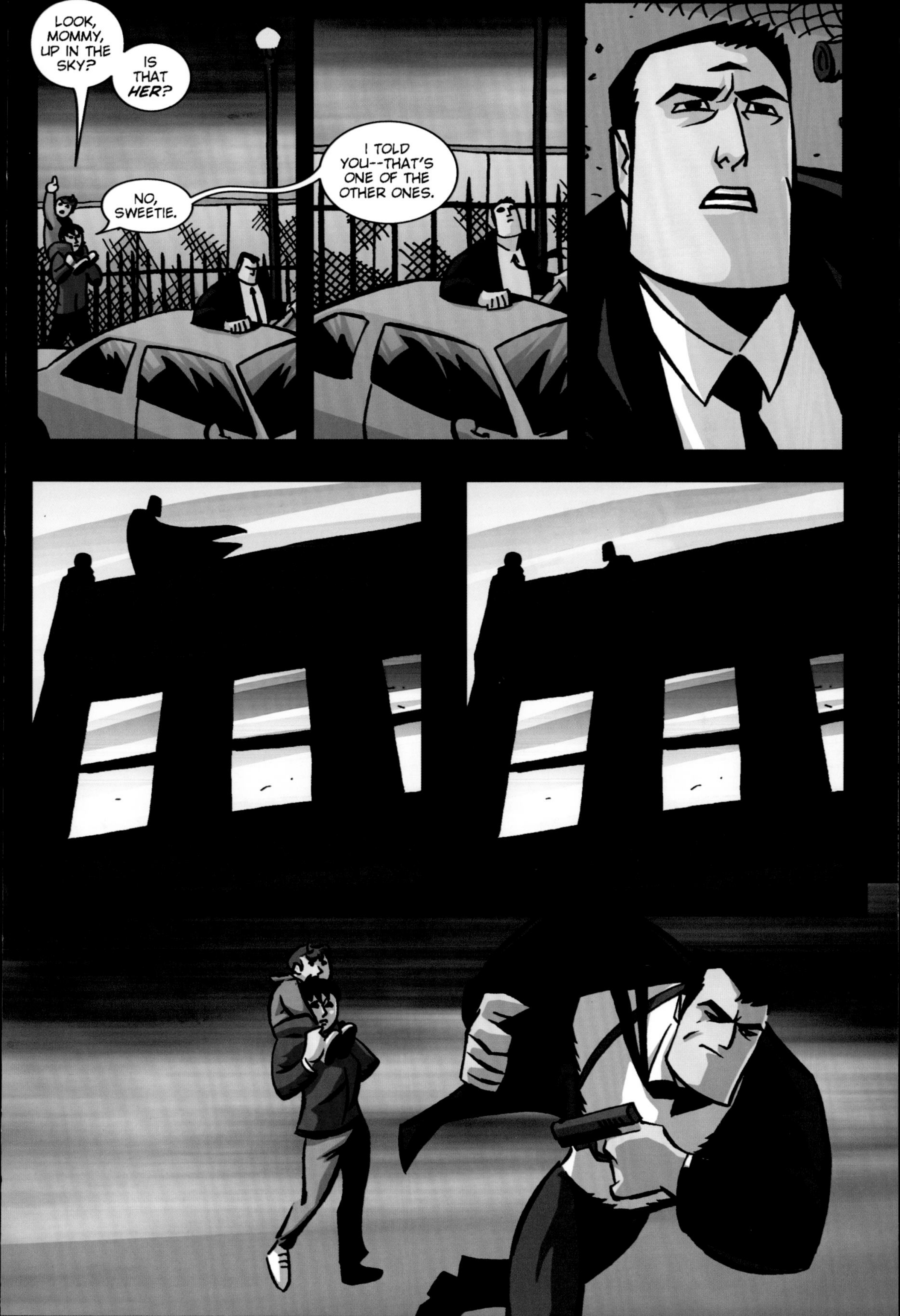
LOOK, MOMMY, UP IN THE SKY?
IS THAT HER?
NO, SWEETIE.
I TOLD YOU--THAT'S ONE OF THE OTHER ONES.

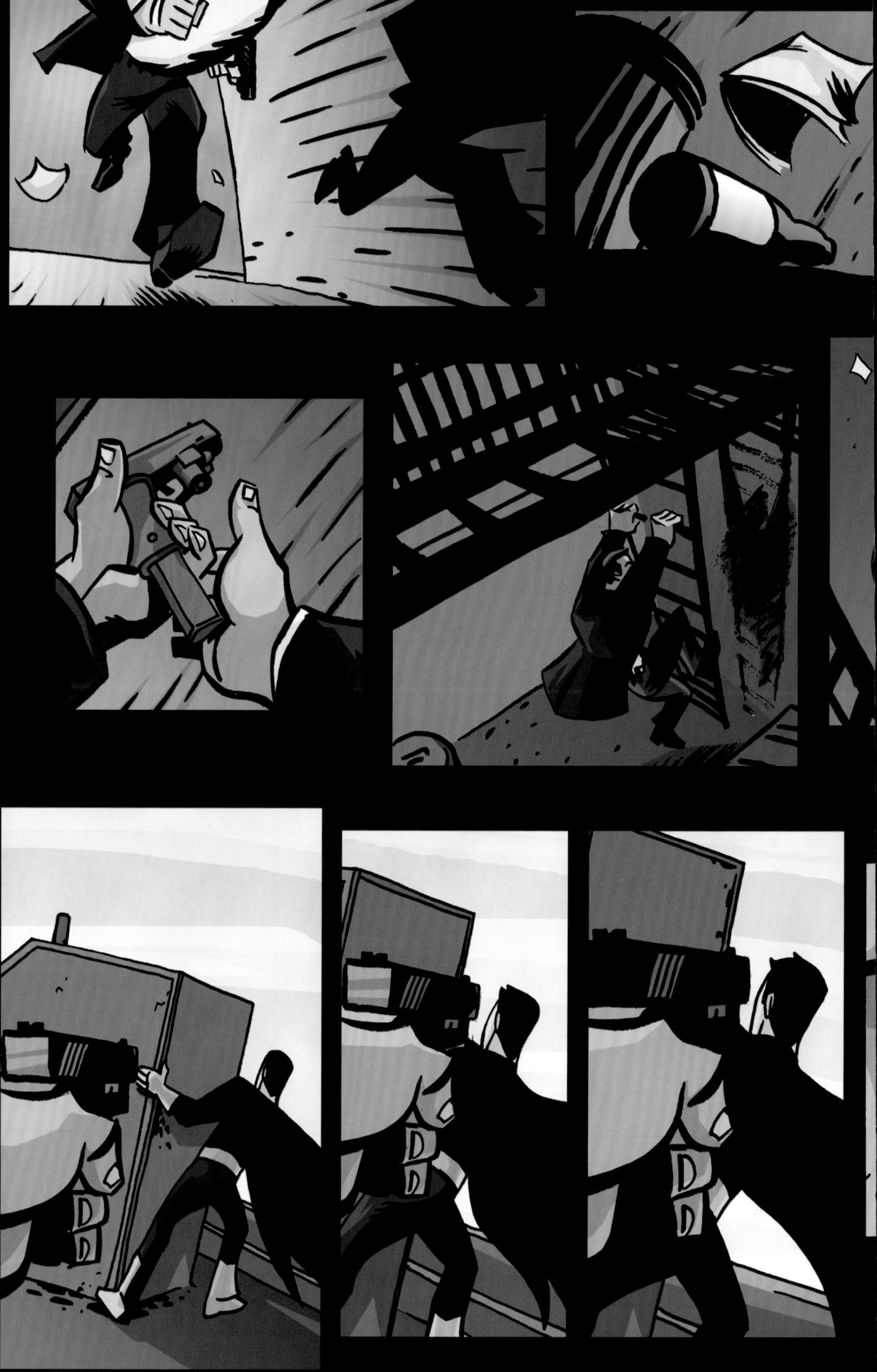

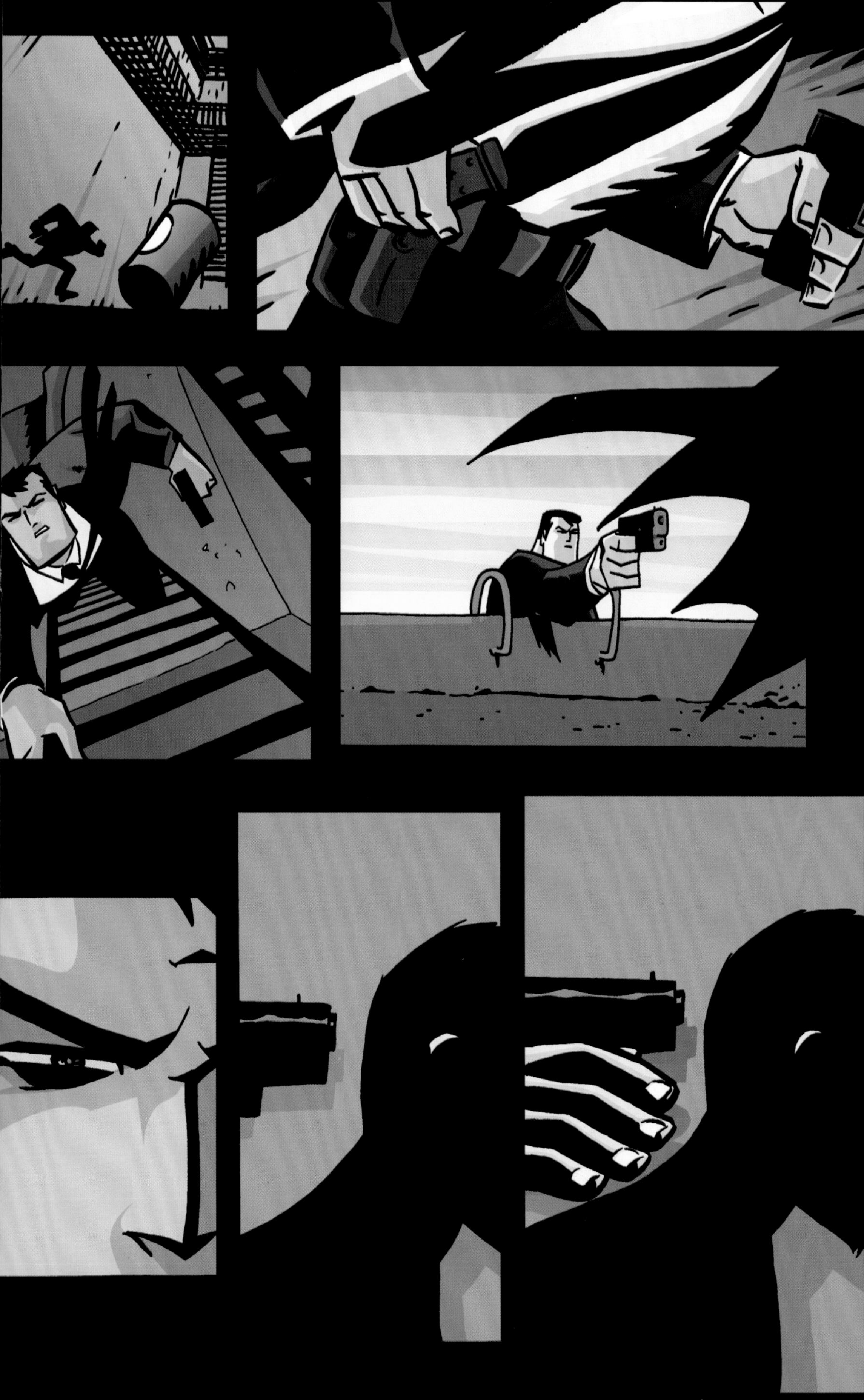

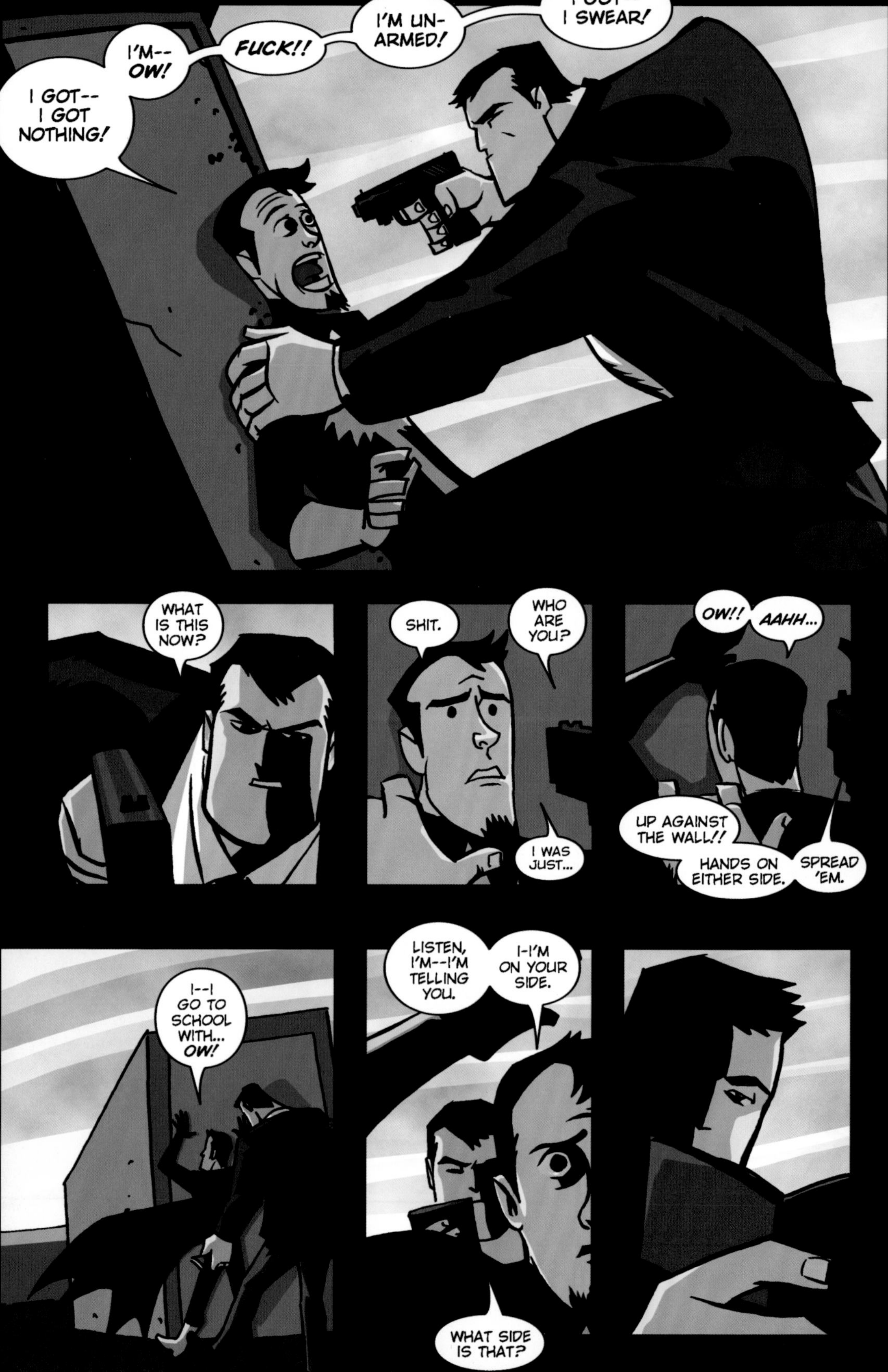
I GOT-- I GOT NOTHING!
I'M-- OW!
FUCK!!
I'M UN-ARMED!
I GOT-- I SWEAR!
WHAT IS THIS NOW?
SHIT.
WHO ARE YOU?
I WAS JUST...
OW!!
AAHH...
UP AGAINST THE WALL!!
HANDS ON EITHER SIDE.
SPREAD 'EM.
I--I GO TO SCHOOL WITH... OW!
LISTEN, I'M--I'M TELLING YOU.
I-I'M ON YOUR SIDE.
WHAT SIDE IS THAT?

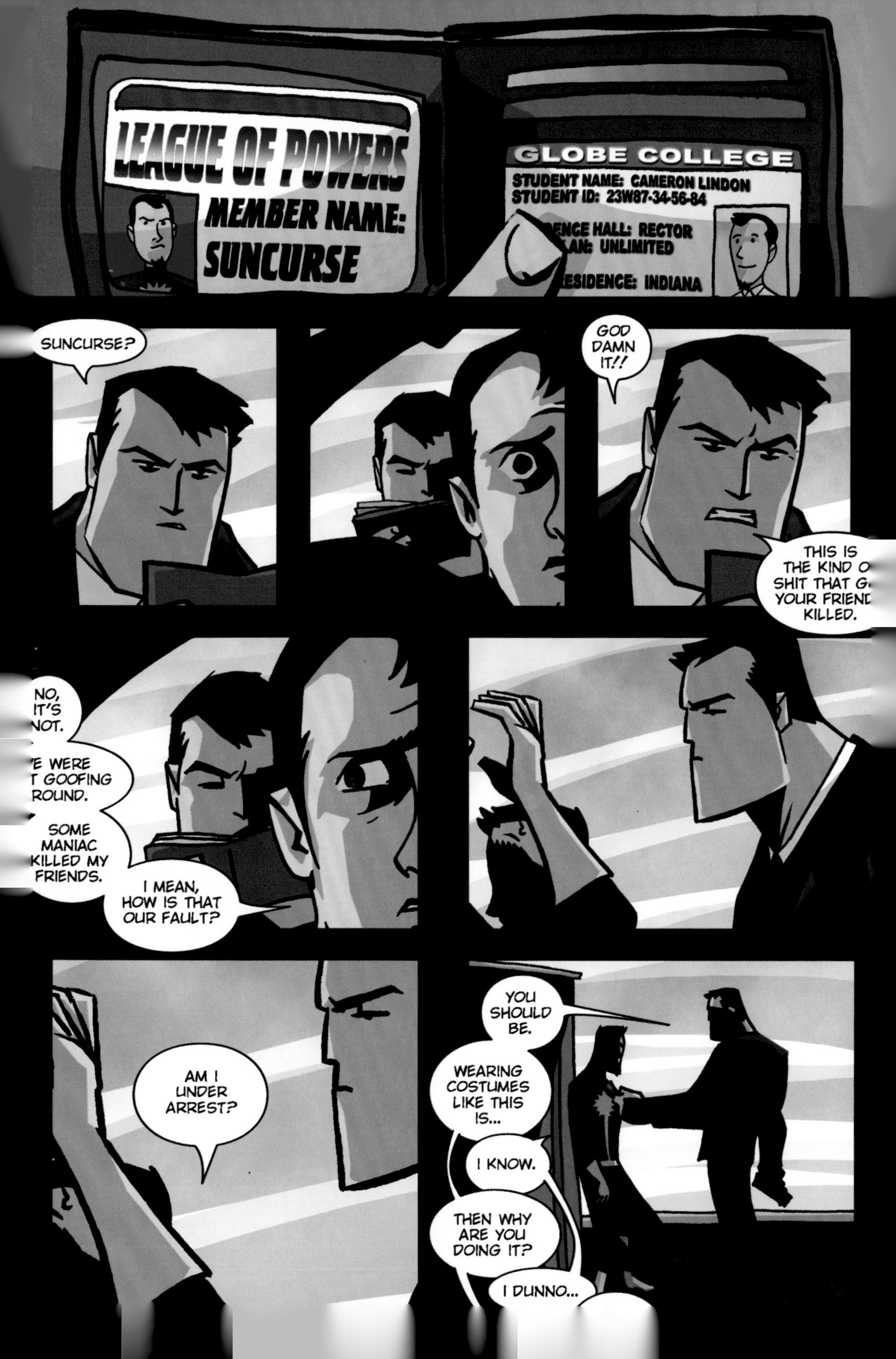
LEAGUE OF POWERS
MEMBER NAME:
SUNCURSE
GLOBE COLLEGE
STUDENT NAME: CAMERON LINDON
STUDENT ID: 23W87-34-56-84
ENCE HALL: RECTOR
AN: UNLIMITED
ESIDENCE: INDIANA
SUNCURSE?
GOD DAMN IT!!
THIS IS THE KIND O SHIT THAT G YOUR FRIEND KILLED.
NO, IT'S NOT.
E WERE T GOOFING ROUND.
SOME MANIAC KILLED MY FRIENDS.
I MEAN, HOW IS THAT OUR FAULT?
AM I UNDER ARREST?
YOU SHOULD BE.
WEARING COSTUMES LIKE THIS IS...
I KNOW.
THEN WHY ARE YOU DOING IT?
I DUNNO...

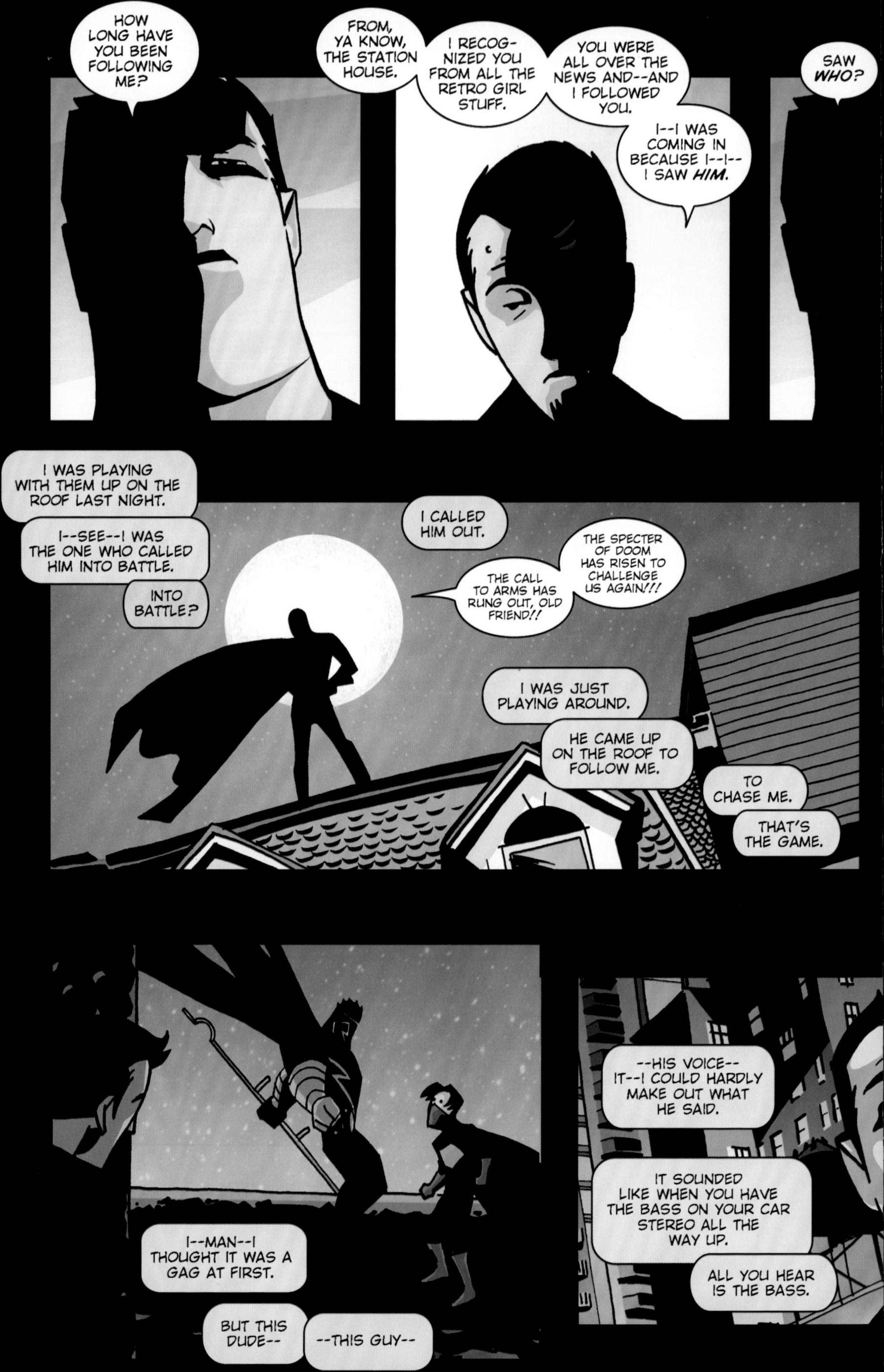
HOW LONG HAVE YOU BEEN FOLLOWING ME?
FROM, YA KNOW, THE STATION HOUSE.
I RECOG-NIZED YOU FROM ALL THE RETRO GIRL STUFF.
YOU WERE ALL OVER THE NEWS AND--AND I FOLLOWED YOU.
I--I WAS COMING IN BECAUSE I--I--I SAW *HIM.*
SAW *WHO?*
I WAS PLAYING WITH THEM UP ON THE ROOF LAST NIGHT.
I--SEE--I WAS THE ONE WHO CALLED HIM INTO BATTLE.
INTO BATTLE?
I CALLED HIM OUT.
THE CALL TO ARMS HAS RUNG OUT, OLD FRIEND!!
THE SPECTER OF DOOM HAS RISEN TO CHALLENGE US AGAIN!!!
I WAS JUST PLAYING AROUND.
HE CAME UP ON THE ROOF TO FOLLOW ME.
TO CHASE ME.
THAT'S THE GAME.
I--MAN--I THOUGHT IT WAS A GAG AT FIRST.
BUT THIS DUDE--
--THIS GUY--
--HIS VOICE--IT--I COULD HARDLY MAKE OUT WHAT HE SAID.
IT SOUNDED LIKE WHEN YOU HAVE THE BASS ON YOUR CAR STEREO ALL THE WAY UP.
ALL YOU HEAR IS THE BASS.

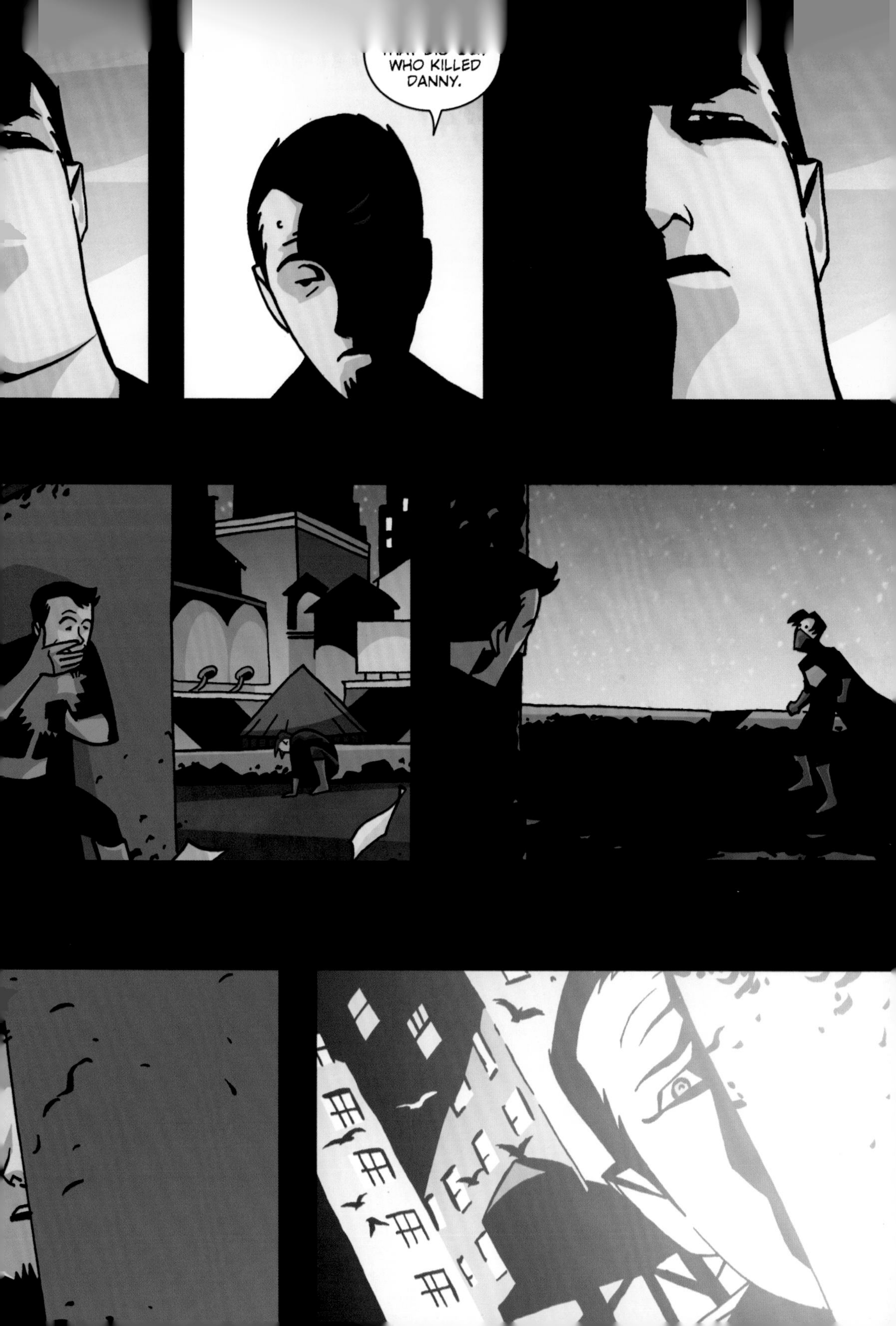
WHO KILLED DANNY.

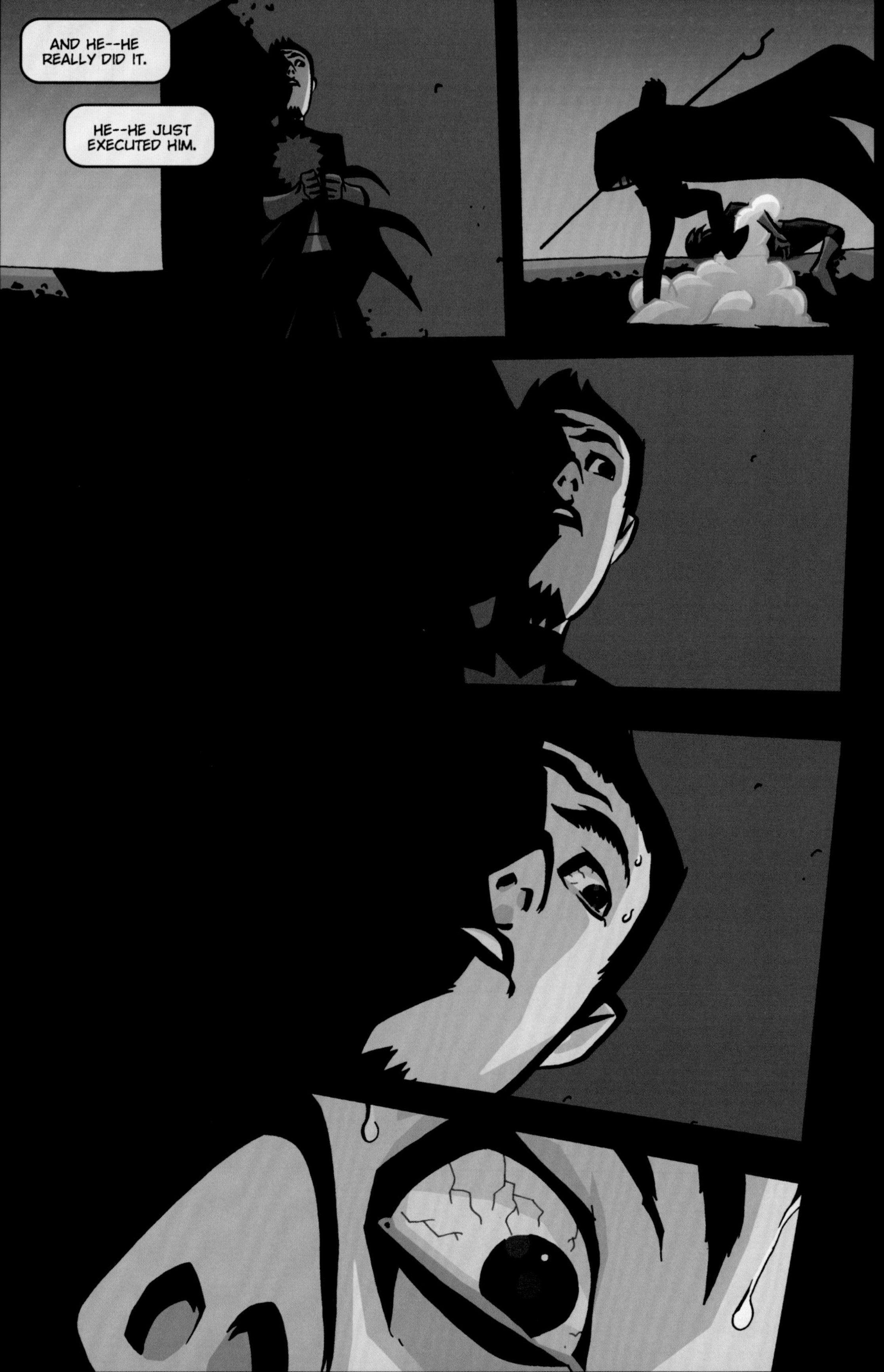
AND HE--HE REALLY DID IT.
HE--HE JUST EXECUTED HIM.

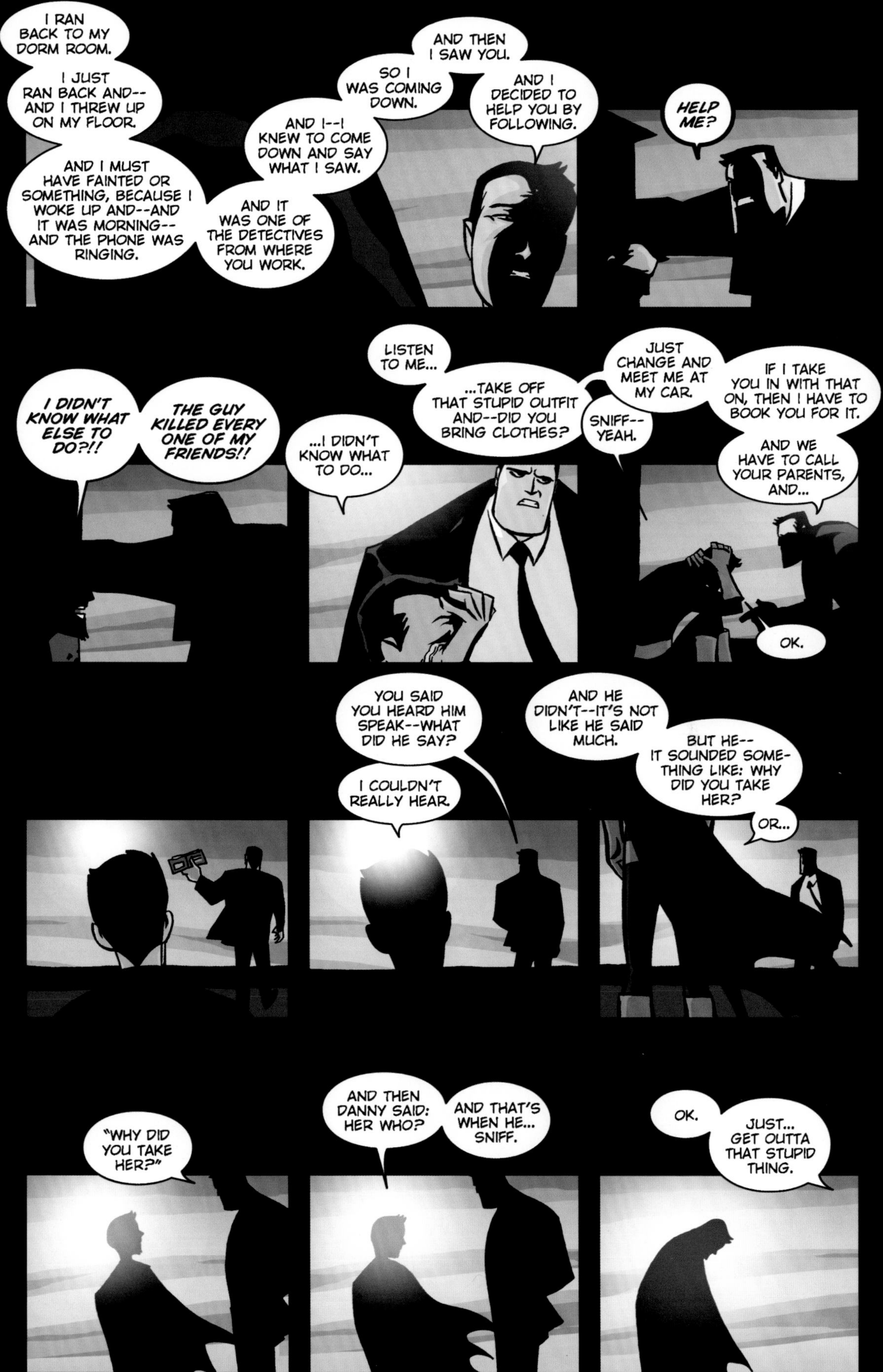
I RAN BACK TO MY DORM ROOM.
I JUST RAN BACK AND-- AND I THREW UP ON MY FLOOR.
AND I MUST HAVE FAINTED OR SOMETHING, BECAUSE I WOKE UP AND--AND IT WAS MORNING-- AND THE PHONE WAS RINGING.
AND IT WAS ONE OF THE DETECTIVES FROM WHERE YOU WORK.
AND I--I KNEW TO COME DOWN AND SAY WHAT I SAW.
SO I WAS COMING DOWN.
AND THEN I SAW YOU.
AND I DECIDED TO HELP YOU BY FOLLOWING.
HELP ME?
I DIDN'T KNOW WHAT ELSE TO DO?!!
THE GUY KILLED EVERY ONE OF MY FRIENDS!!
...I DIDN'T KNOW WHAT TO DO...
LISTEN TO ME...
...TAKE OFF THAT STUPID OUTFIT AND--DID YOU BRING CLOTHES?
SNIFF-- YEAH.
JUST CHANGE AND MEET ME AT MY CAR.
IF I TAKE YOU IN WITH THAT ON, THEN I HAVE TO BOOK YOU FOR IT.
AND WE HAVE TO CALL YOUR PARENTS, AND...
OK.
YOU SAID YOU HEARD HIM SPEAK--WHAT DID HE SAY?
I COULDN'T REALLY HEAR.
AND HE DIDN'T--IT'S NOT LIKE HE SAID MUCH.
BUT HE-- IT SOUNDED SOMETHING LIKE: WHY DID YOU TAKE HER?
OR...
"WHY DID YOU TAKE HER?"
AND THEN DANNY SAID: HER WHO?
AND THAT'S WHEN HE... SNIFF.
OK.
JUST... GET OUTTA THAT STUPID THING.

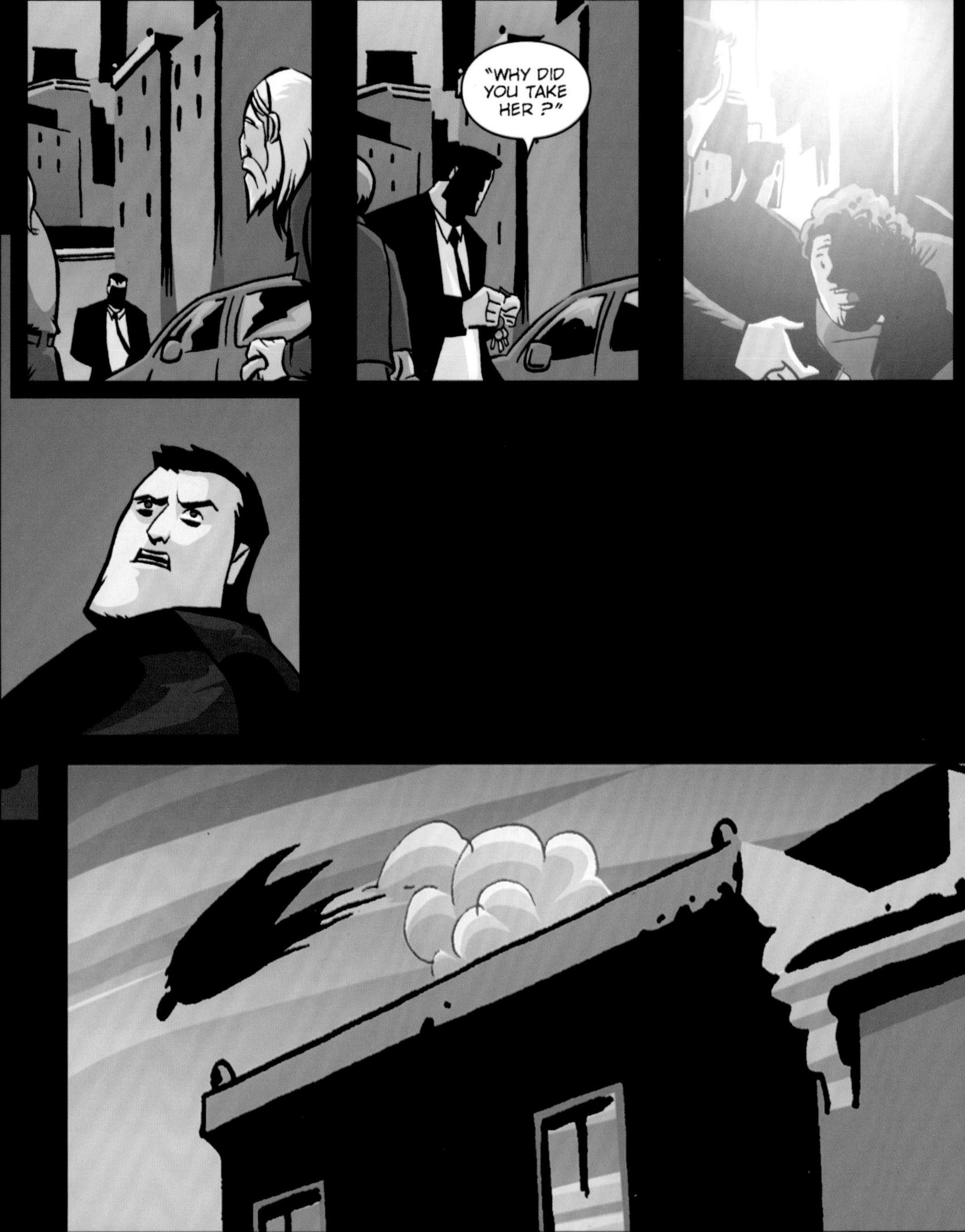
"WHY DID YOU TAKE HER ?"

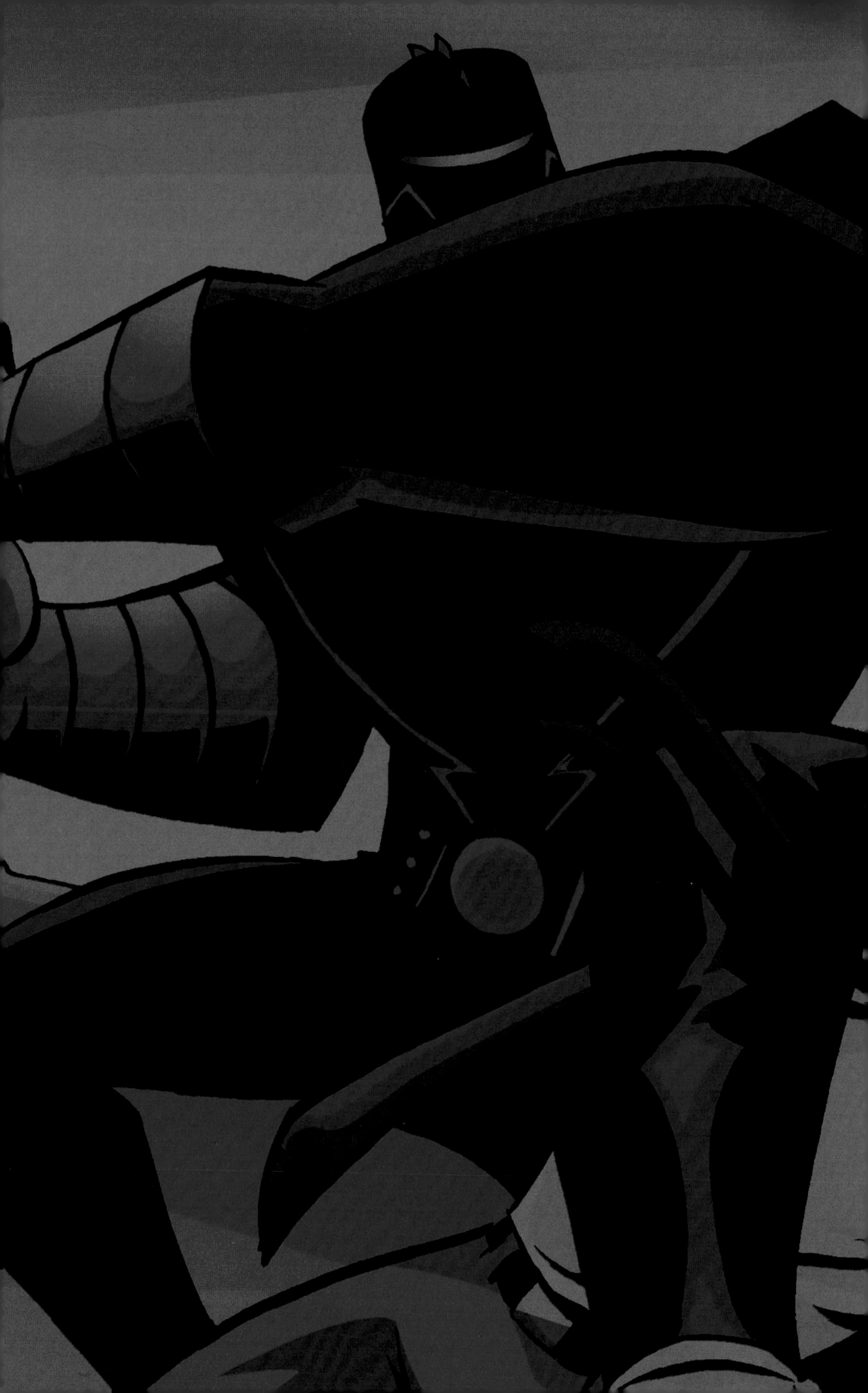

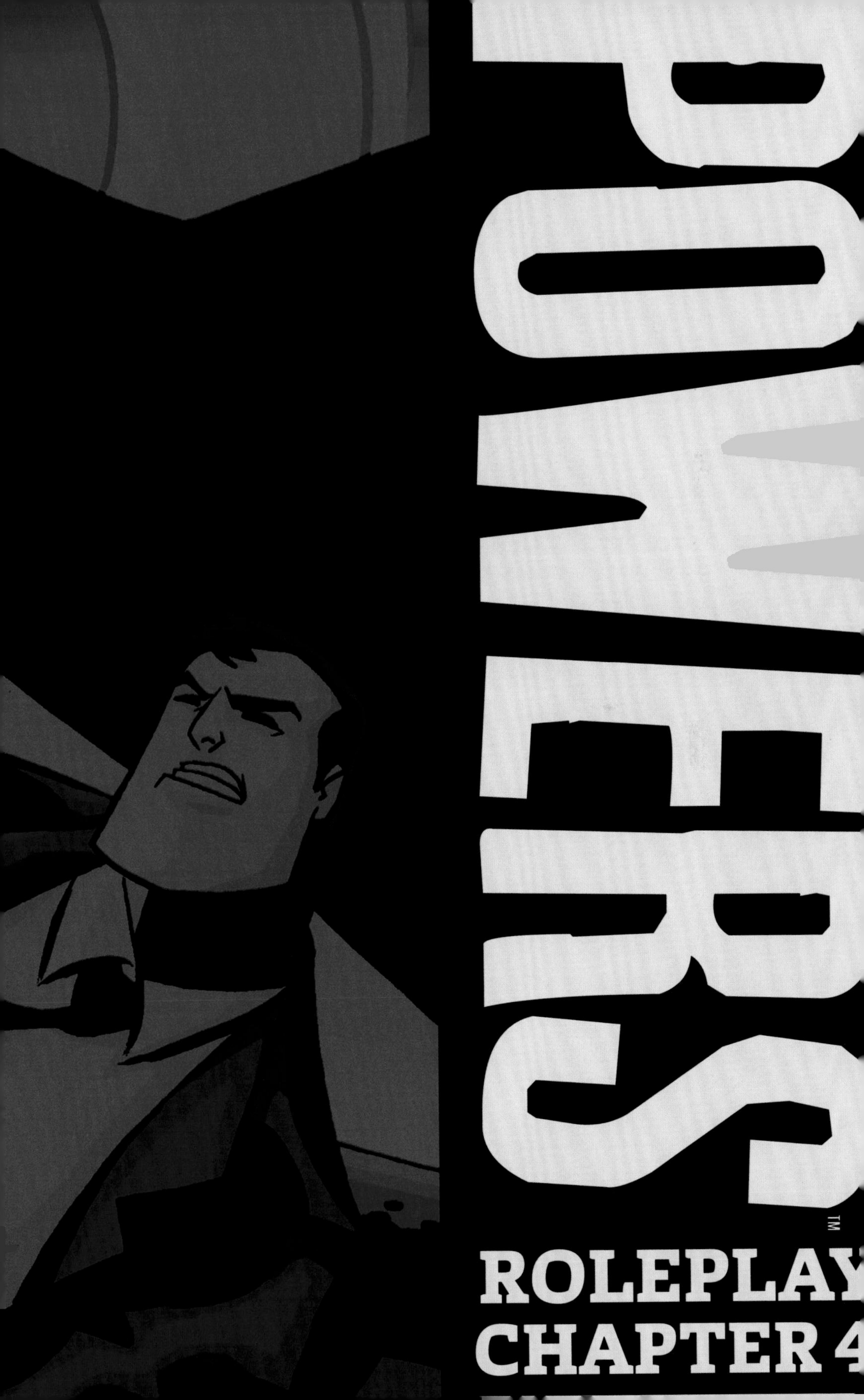

POWERS™

ROLEPLAY CHAPTER 4

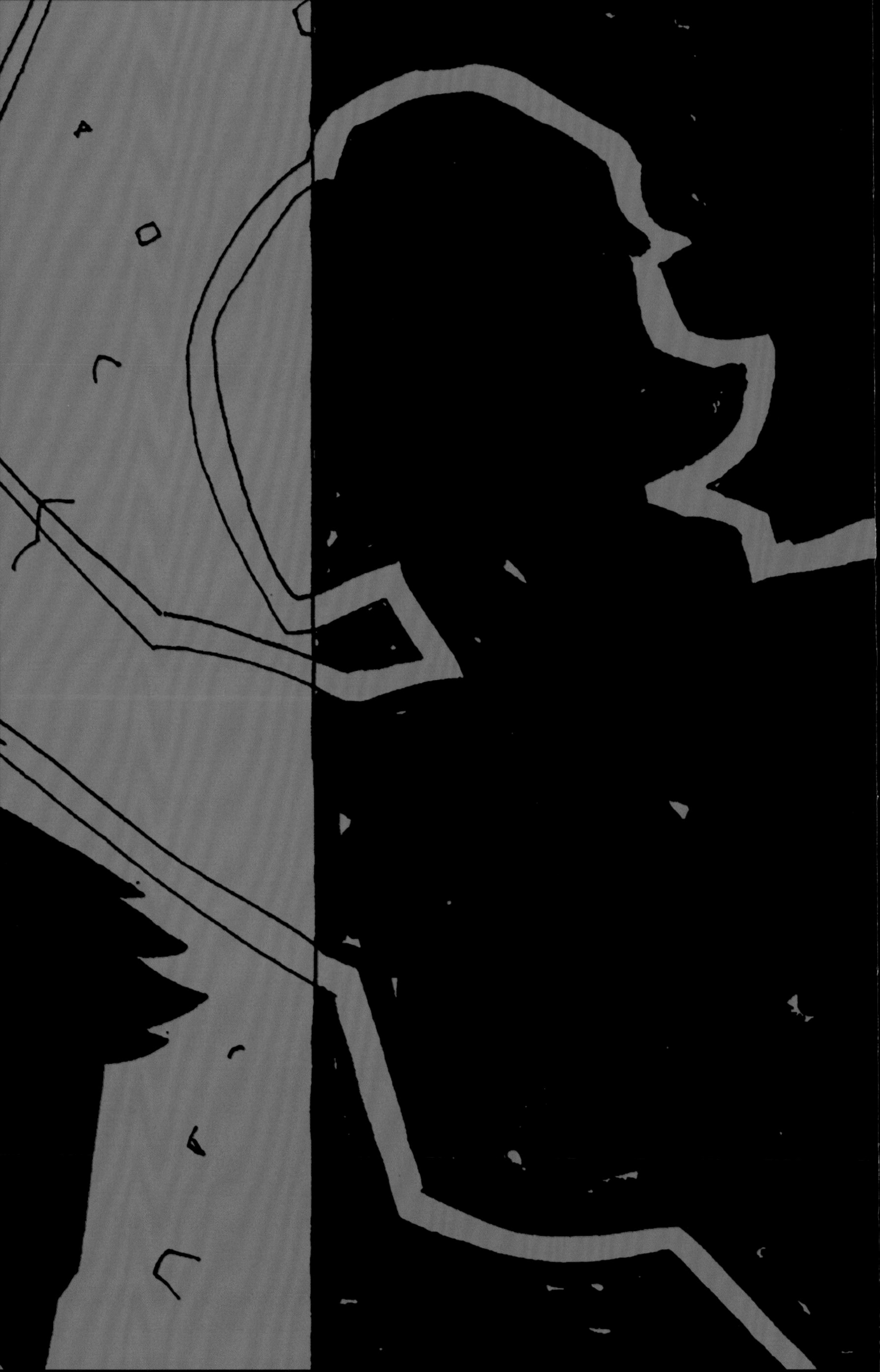

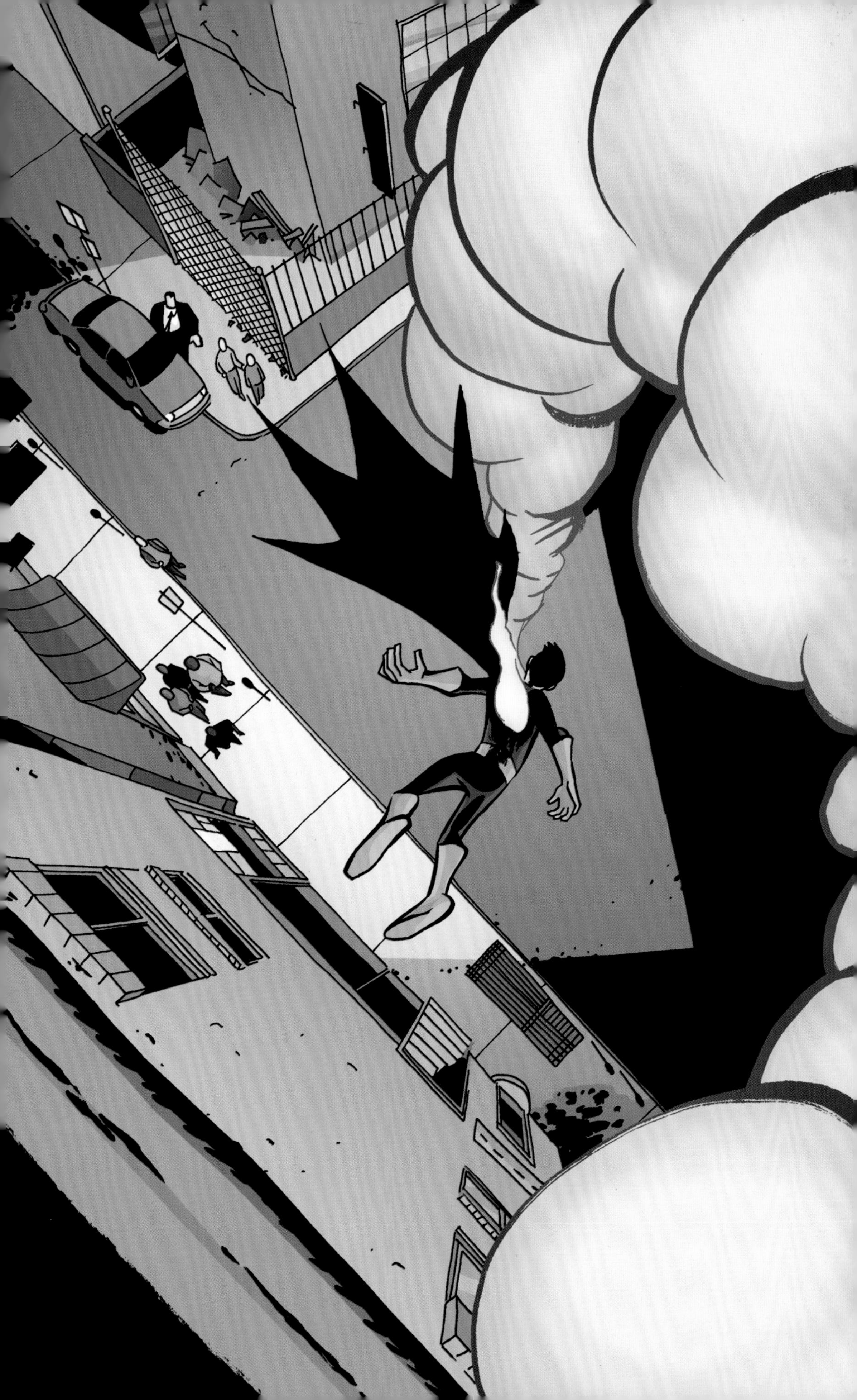

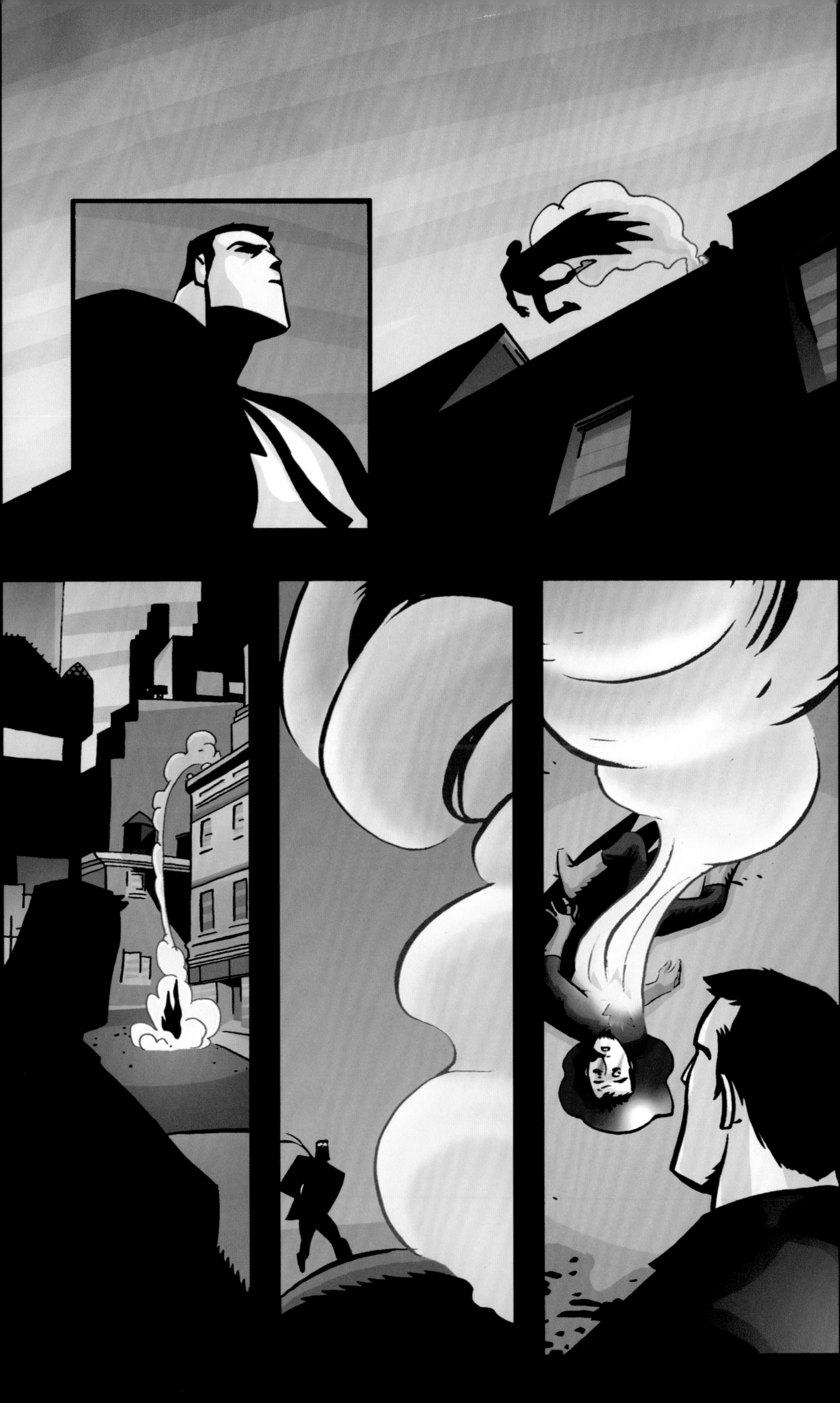

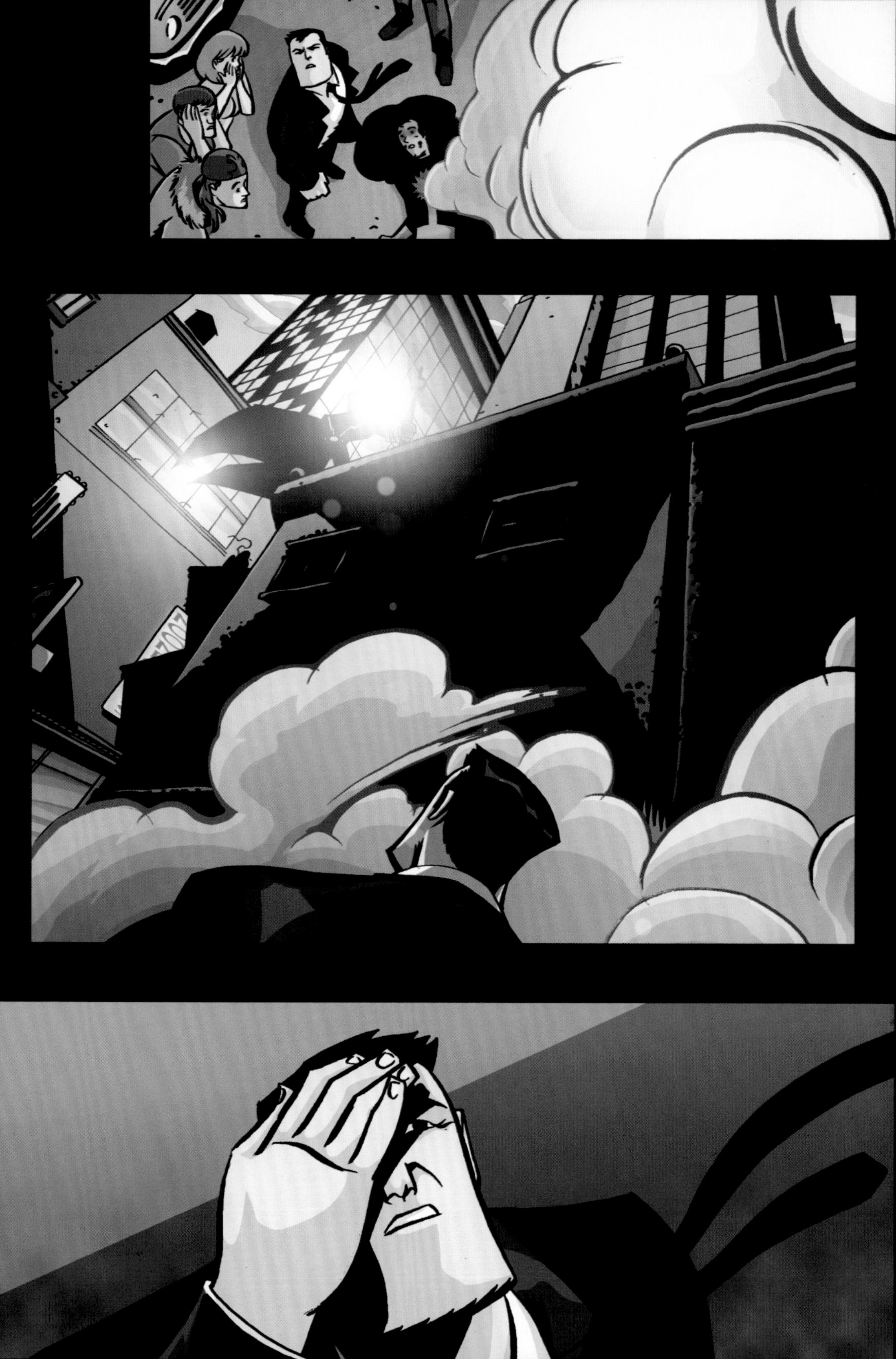

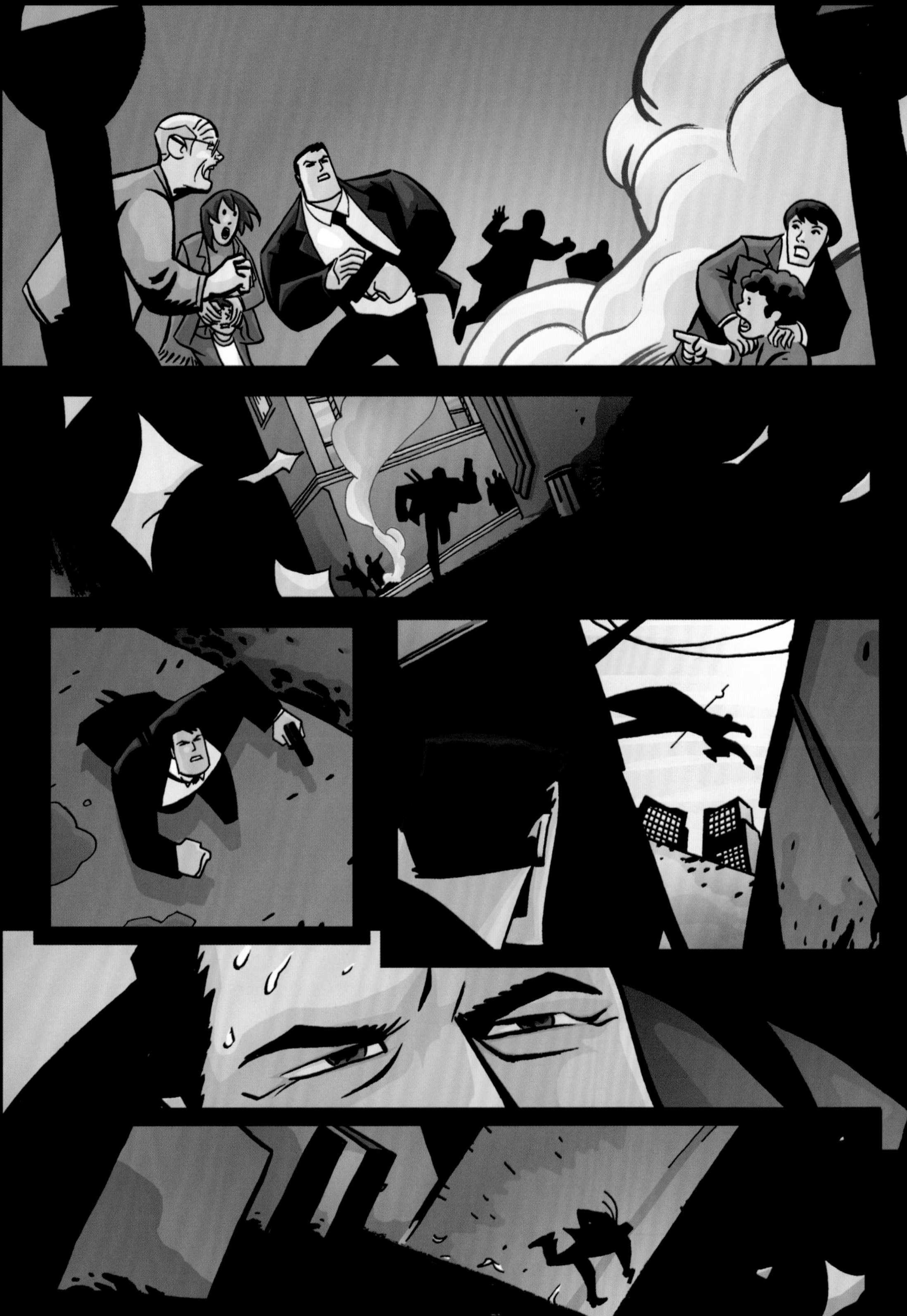

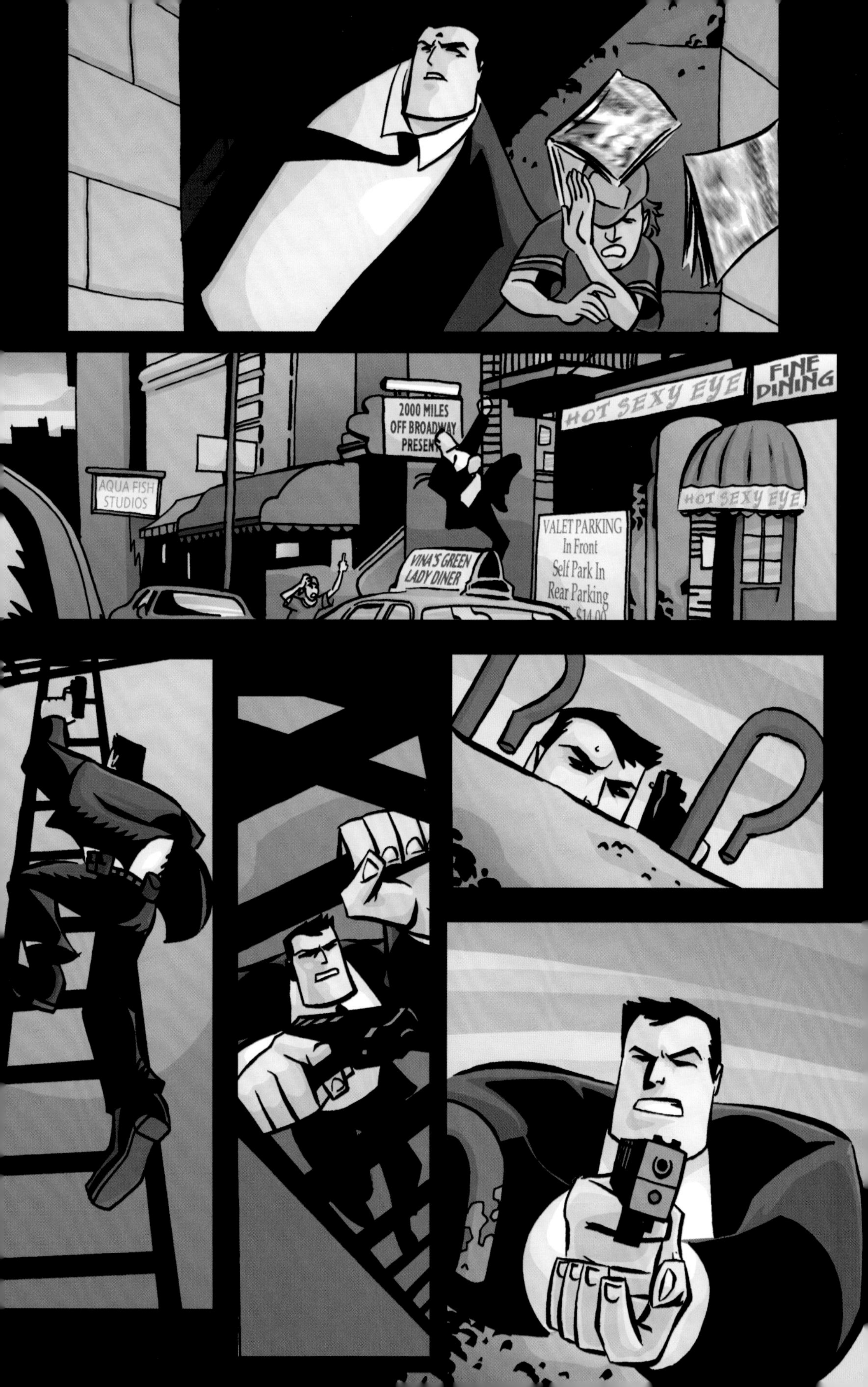
2000 MILES
OFF BROADWAY
HOT SEXY EYE
FINE DINING
AQUA FISH STUDIOS
HOT SEXY EYE
VALET PARKING
In Front
Self Park In
Rear Parking
VINA'S GREEN LADY DINER

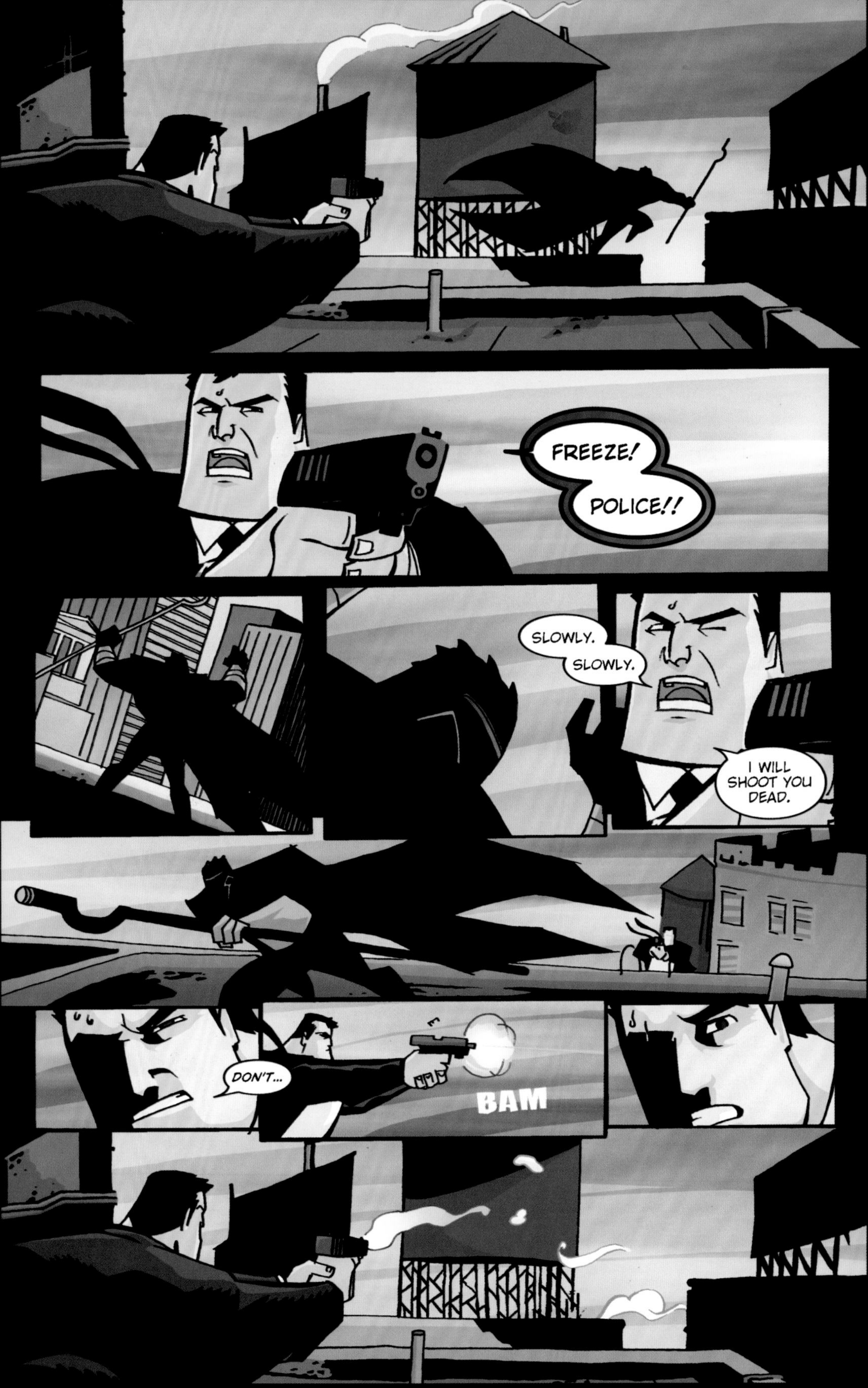
FREEZE!
POLICE!!
SLOWLY.
SLOWLY.
I WILL SHOOT YOU DEAD.
DON'T...
BAM

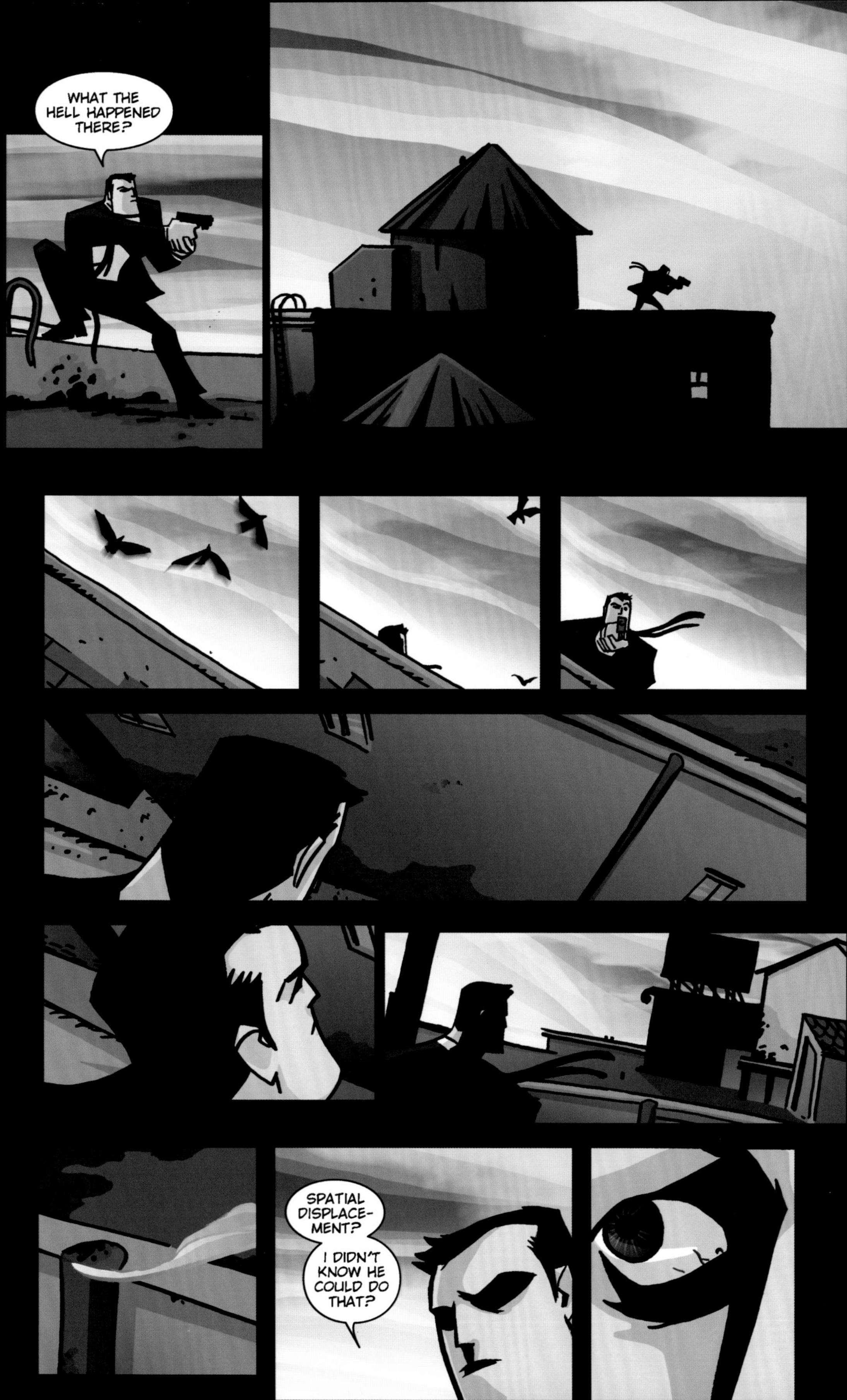
WHAT THE HELL HAPPENED THERE?
SPATIAL DISPLACE- MENT?
I DIDN'T KNOW HE COULD DO THAT?

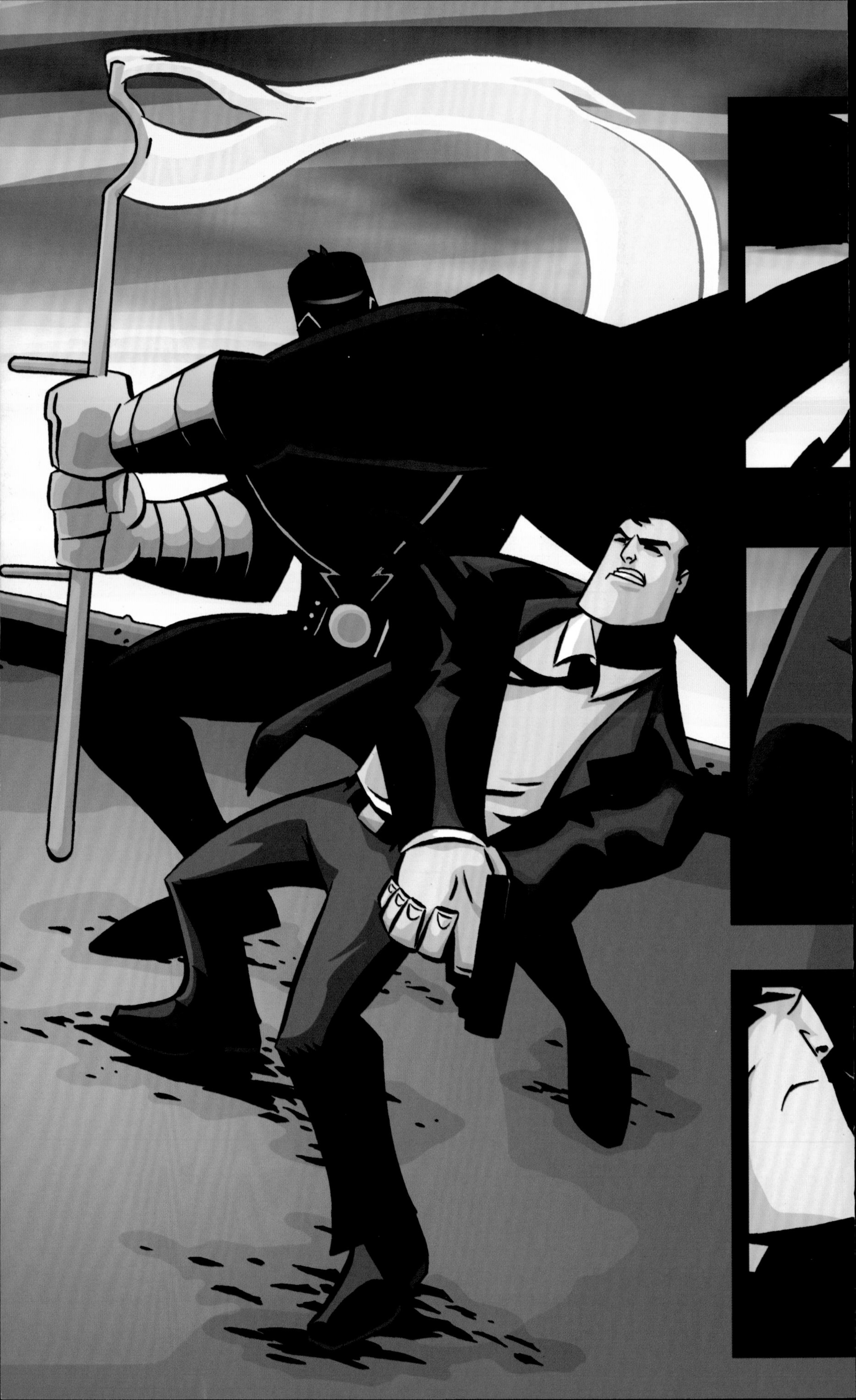

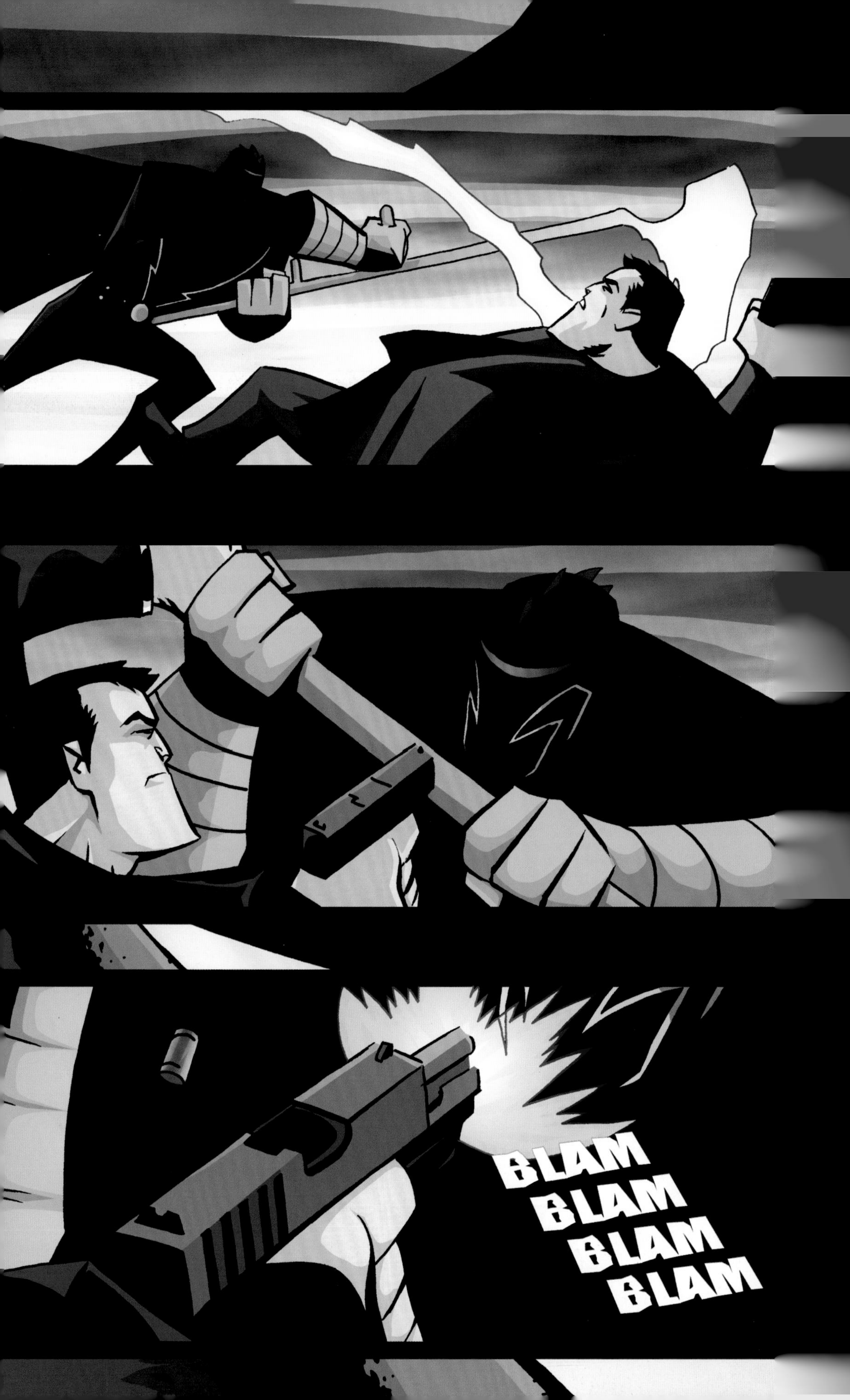
BLAM
BLAM
BLAM
BLAM

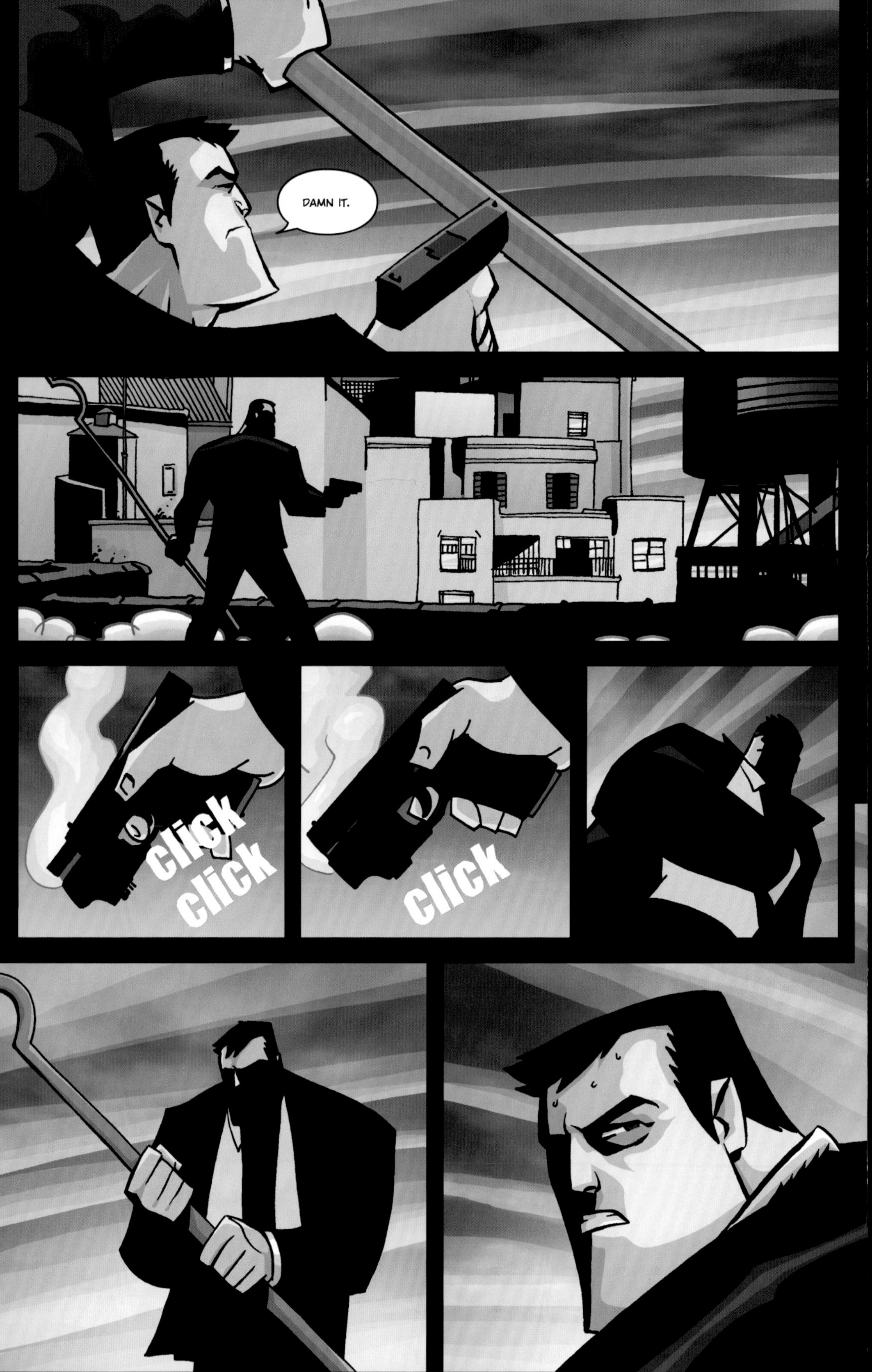
DAMN IT.
click
click
click

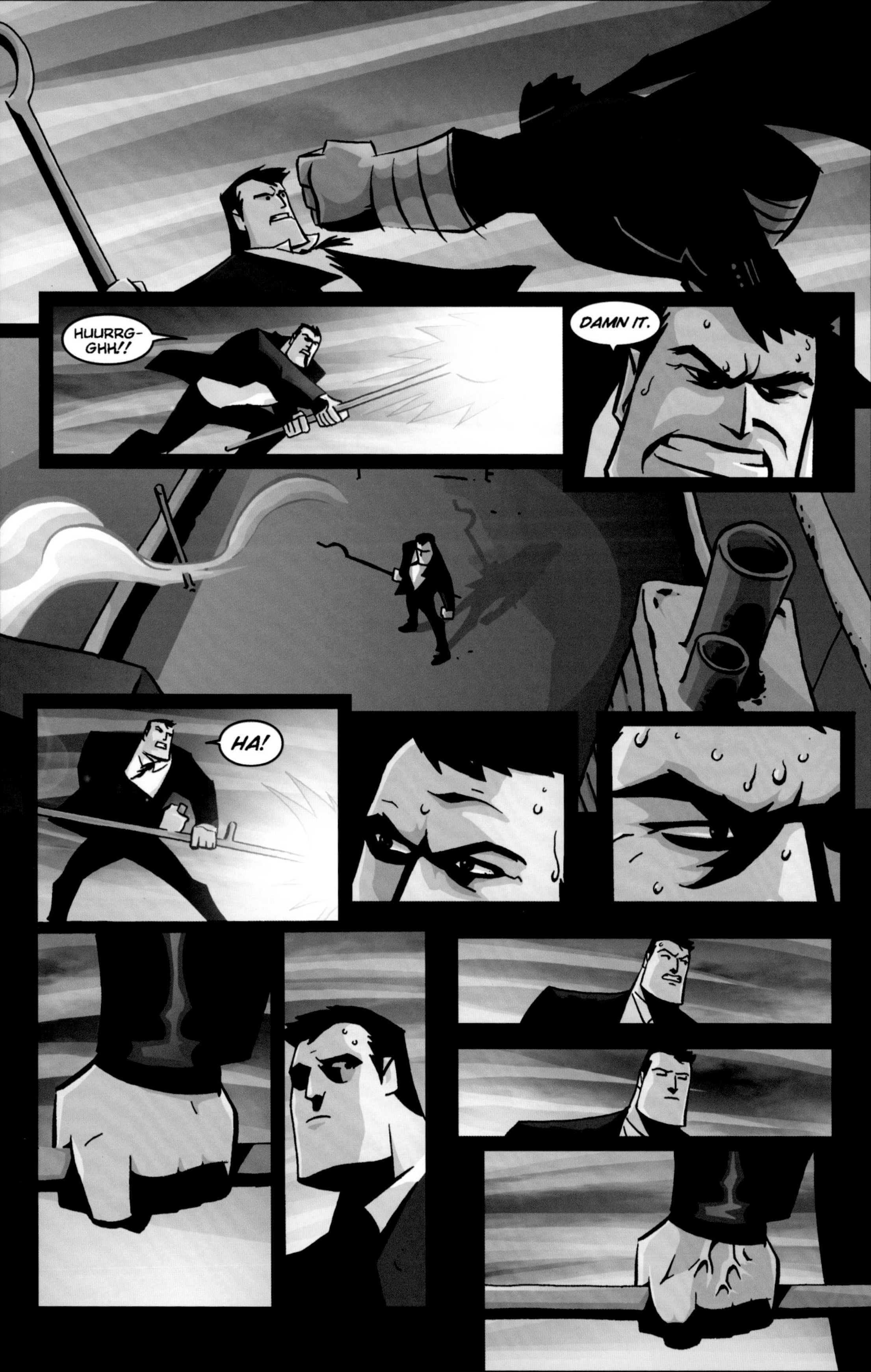
HUURRG-GHH!!
DAMN IT.
HA!

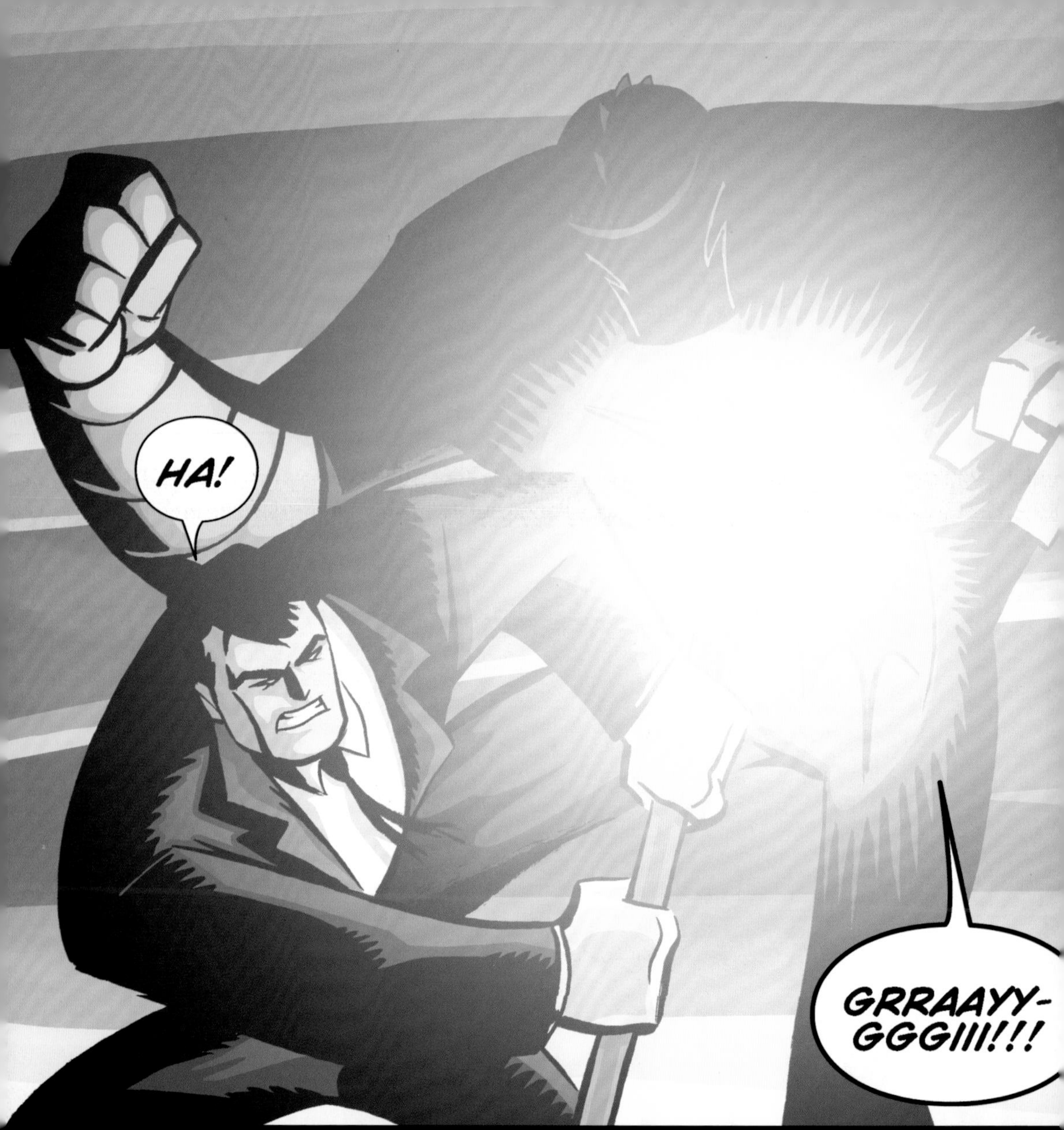
HA!
GRRAAYY-
GGGIII!!!
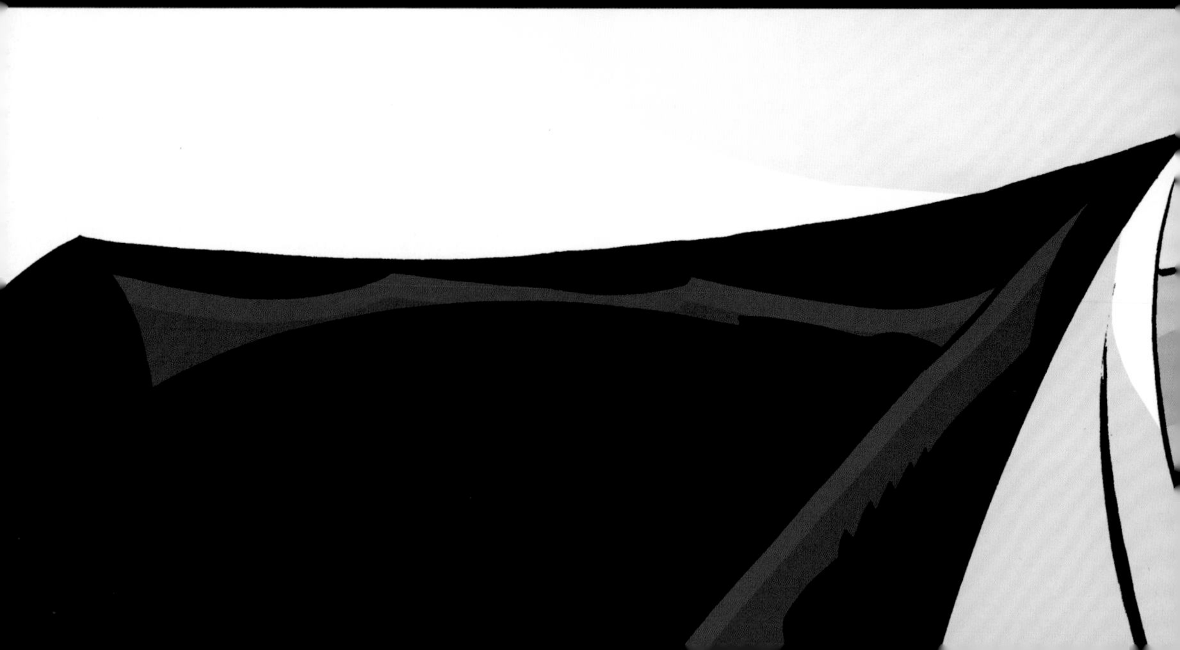

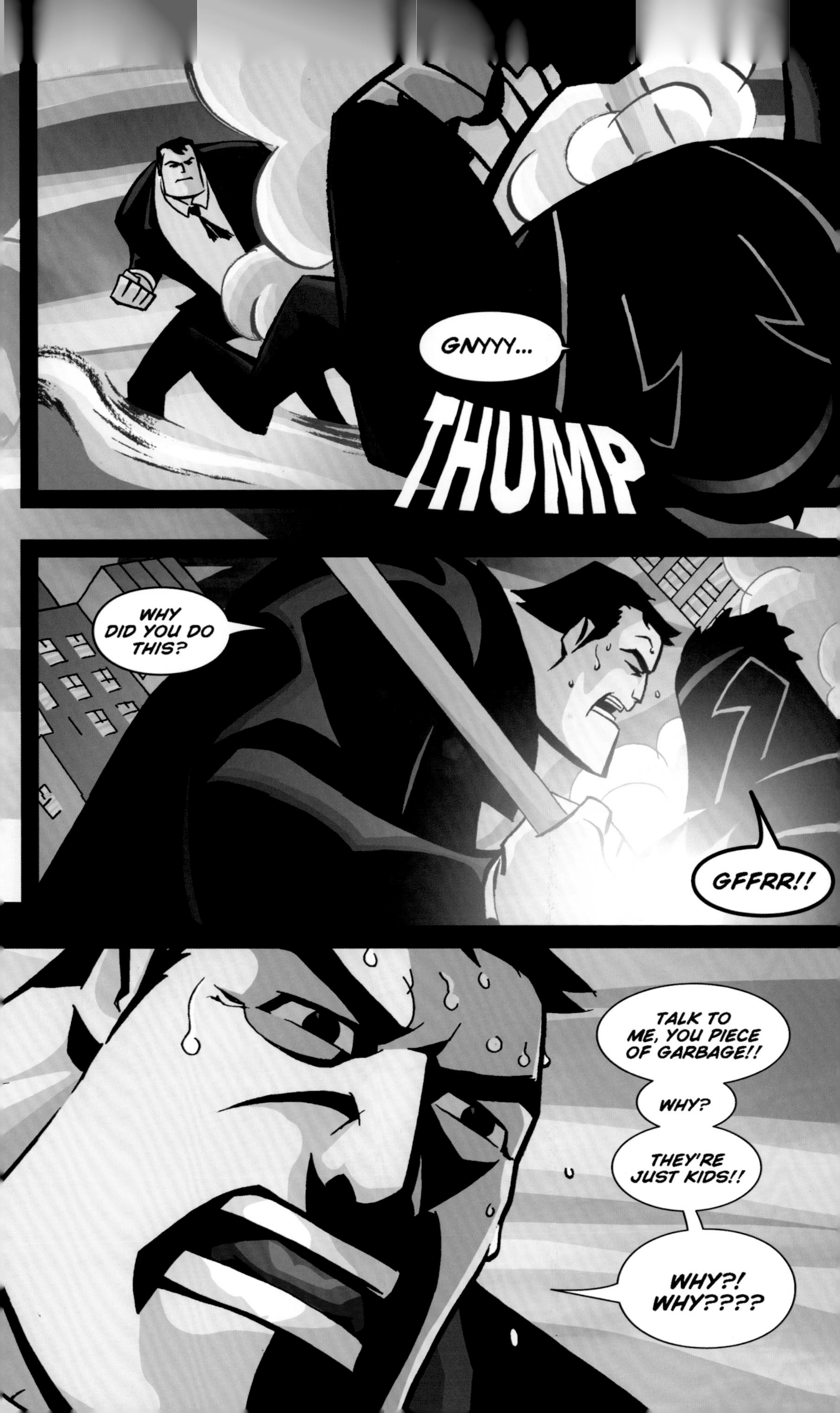
GNYYY...
THUMP
WHY DID YOU DO THIS?
GFFRR!!
TALK TO ME, YOU PIECE OF GARBAGE!!
WHY?
THEY'RE JUST KIDS!!
WHY?! WHY????

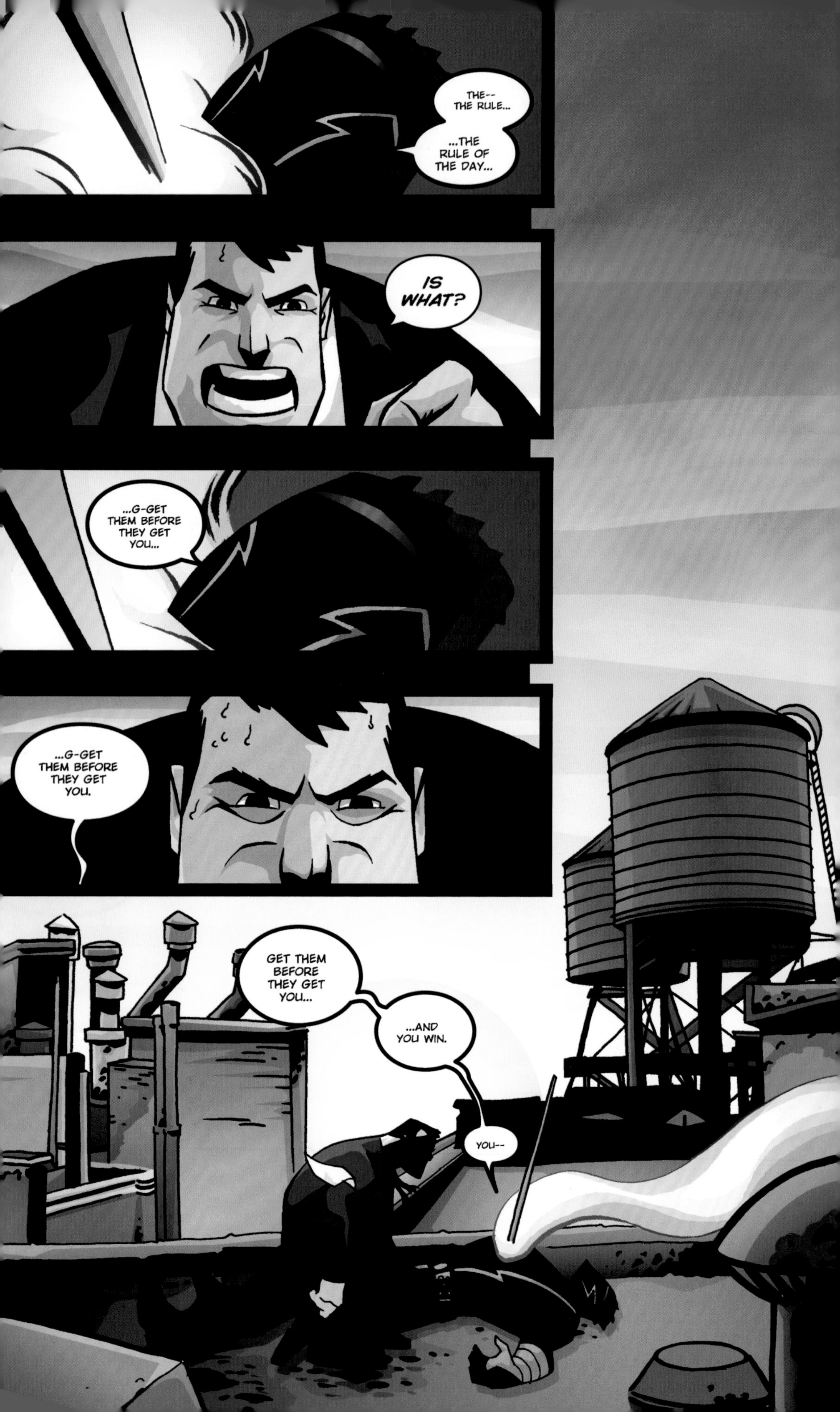
THE-- THE RULE...
...THE RULE OF THE DAY...
IS WHAT?
...G-GET THEM BEFORE THEY GET YOU...
...G-GET THEM BEFORE THEY GET YOU.
GET THEM BEFORE THEY GET YOU...
...AND YOU WIN.
YOU--

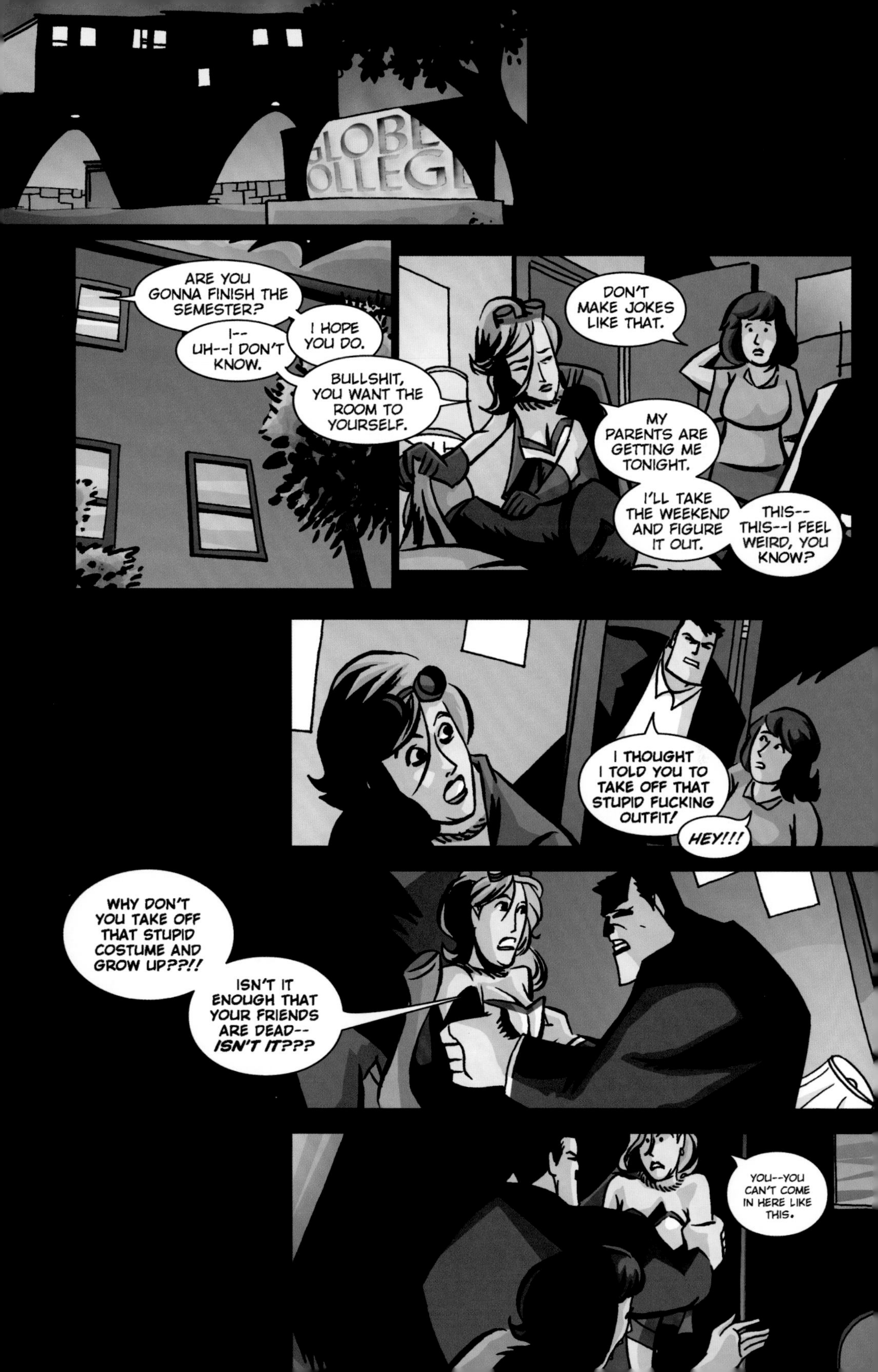
GLOBE COLLEGE
ARE YOU GONNA FINISH THE SEMESTER?
I-- UH--I DON'T KNOW.
I HOPE YOU DO.
BULLSHIT, YOU WANT THE ROOM TO YOURSELF.
DON'T MAKE JOKES LIKE THAT.
MY PARENTS ARE GETTING ME TONIGHT.
I'LL TAKE THE WEEKEND AND FIGURE IT OUT.
THIS--THIS--I FEEL WEIRD, YOU KNOW?
I THOUGHT I TOLD YOU TO TAKE OFF THAT STUPID FUCKING OUTFIT!
HEY!!!
WHY DON'T YOU TAKE OFF THAT STUPID COSTUME AND GROW UP??!!
ISN'T IT ENOUGH THAT YOUR FRIENDS ARE DEAD-- ISN'T IT???
YOU--YOU CAN'T COME IN HERE LIKE THIS.

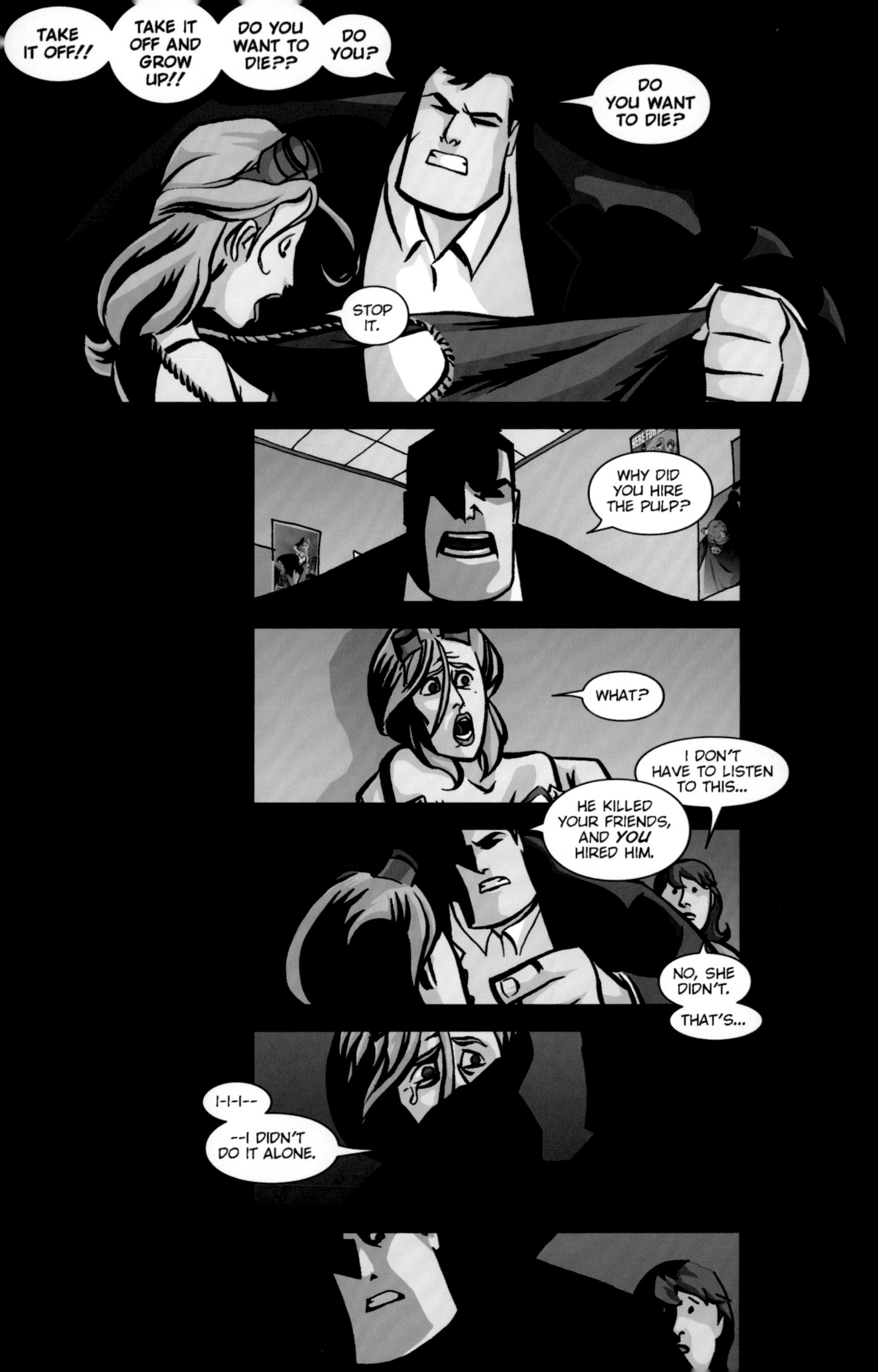
TAKE IT OFF!!
TAKE IT OFF AND GROW UP!!
DO YOU WANT TO DIE??
DO YOU?
DO YOU WANT TO DIE?
STOP IT.
WHY DID YOU HIRE THE PULP?
WHAT?
I DON'T HAVE TO LISTEN TO THIS...
HE KILLED YOUR FRIENDS, AND YOU HIRED HIM.
NO, SHE DIDN'T.
THAT'S...
I-I-I--
--I DIDN'T DO IT ALONE.

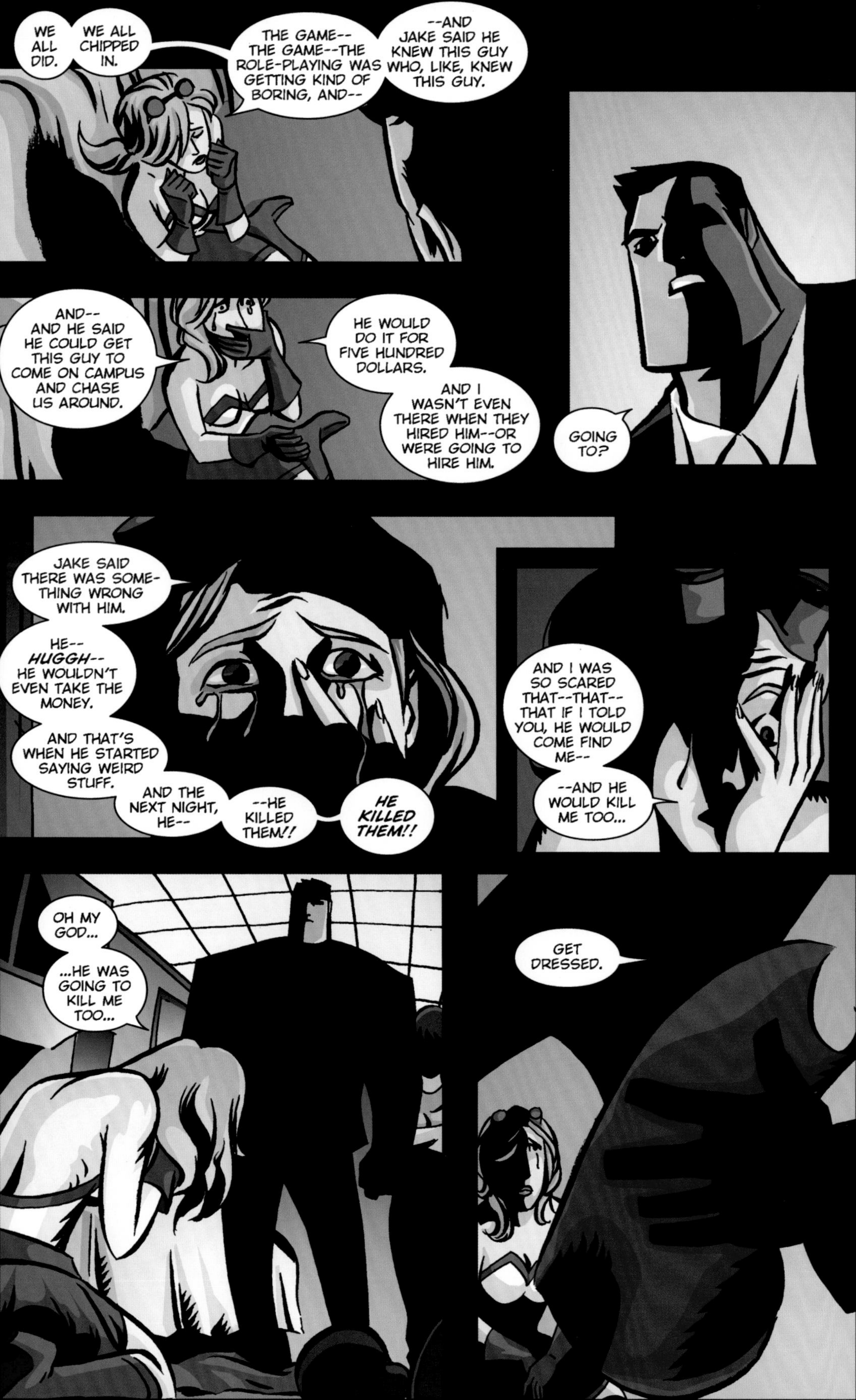
WE ALL DID.
WE ALL CHIPPED IN.
THE GAME-- THE GAME--THE ROLE-PLAYING WAS GETTING KIND OF BORING, AND--
--AND JAKE SAID HE KNEW THIS GUY WHO, LIKE, KNEW THIS GUY.
AND-- AND HE SAID HE COULD GET THIS GUY TO COME ON CAMPUS AND CHASE US AROUND.
HE WOULD DO IT FOR FIVE HUNDRED DOLLARS.
AND I WASN'T EVEN THERE WHEN THEY HIRED HIM--OR WERE GOING TO HIRE HIM.
GOING TO?
JAKE SAID THERE WAS SOME-THING WRONG WITH HIM.
HE-- *HUGGH*-- HE WOULDN'T EVEN TAKE THE MONEY.
AND THAT'S WHEN HE STARTED SAYING WEIRD STUFF.
AND THE NEXT NIGHT, HE--
--HE KILLED THEM!!
HE KILLED THEM!!
AND I WAS SO SCARED THAT--THAT-- THAT IF I TOLD YOU, HE WOULD COME FIND ME--
--AND HE WOULD KILL ME TOO...
OH MY GOD...
...HE WAS GOING TO KILL ME TOO...
GET DRESSED.

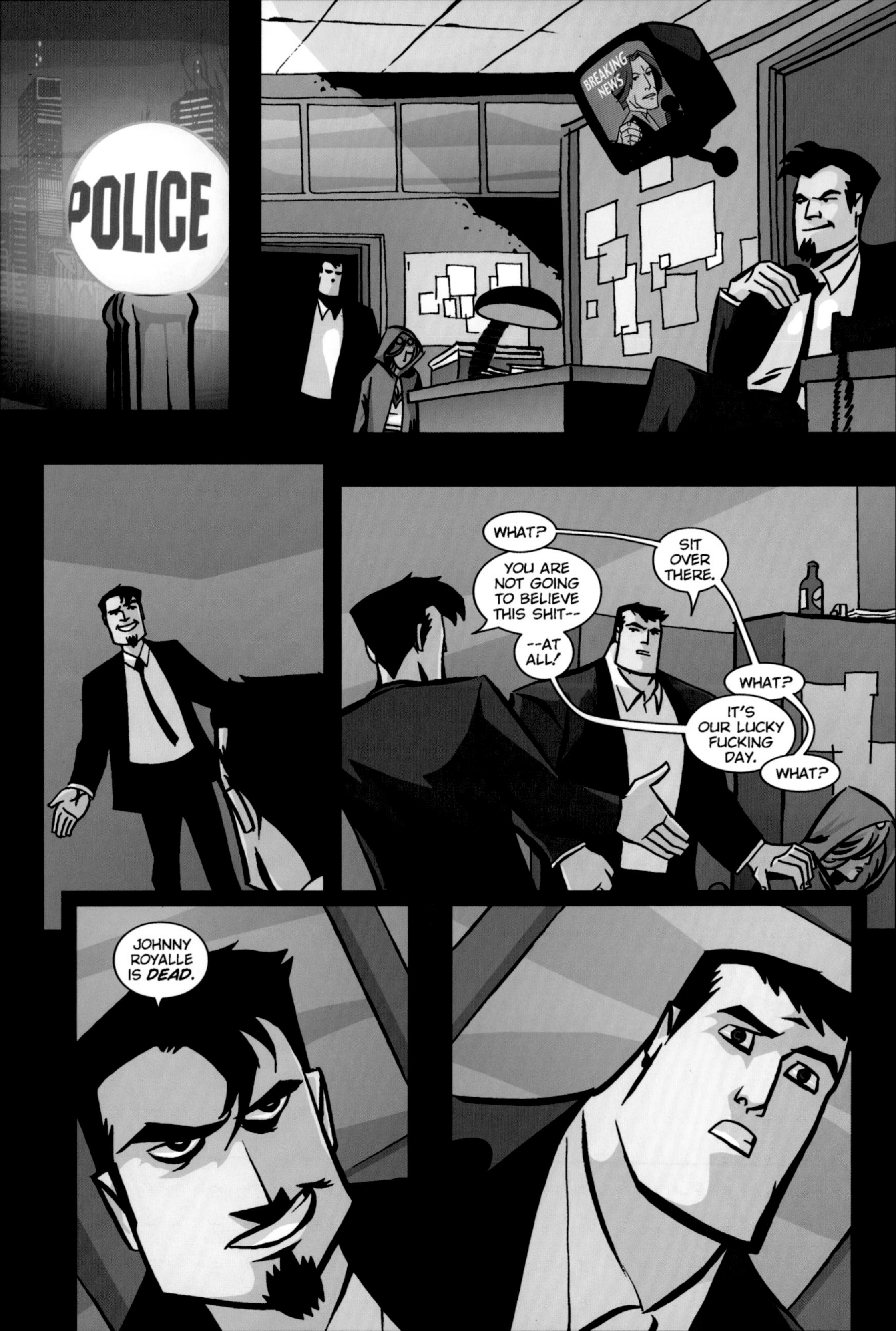
POLICE
BREAKING NEWS
WHAT?
SIT OVER THERE.
YOU ARE NOT GOING TO BELIEVE THIS SHIT--
--AT ALL!
WHAT?
IT'S OUR LUCKY FUCKING DAY.
WHAT?
JOHNNY ROYALLE IS *DEAD*.

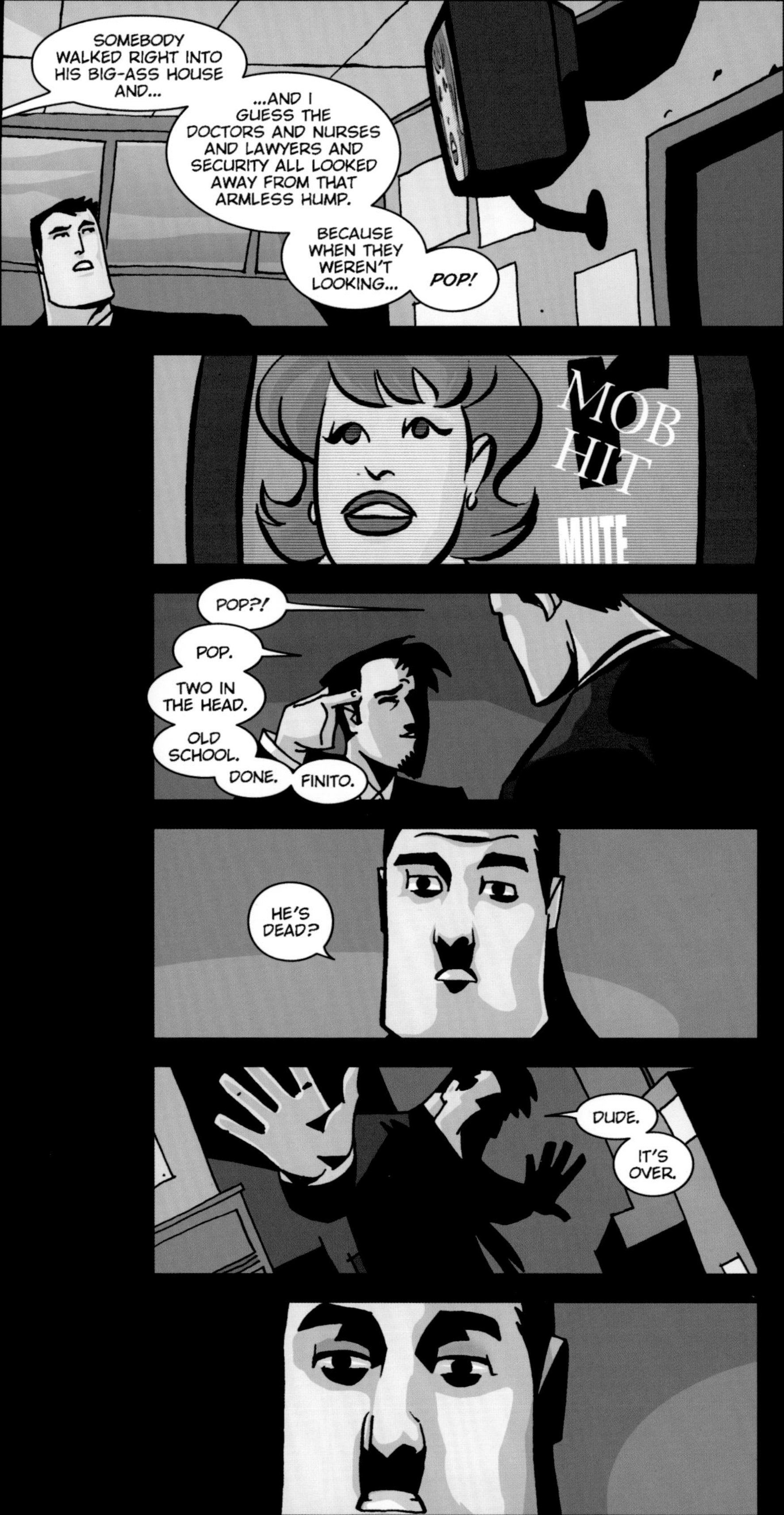
SOMEBODY WALKED RIGHT INTO HIS BIG-ASS HOUSE AND...
...AND I GUESS THE DOCTORS AND NURSES AND LAWYERS AND SECURITY ALL LOOKED AWAY FROM THAT ARMLESS HUMP.
BECAUSE WHEN THEY WEREN'T LOOKING...
POP!
MOB HIT
MUTE
POP?!
POP.
TWO IN THE HEAD.
OLD SCHOOL.
DONE.
FINITO.
HE'S DEAD?
DUDE.
IT'S OVER.

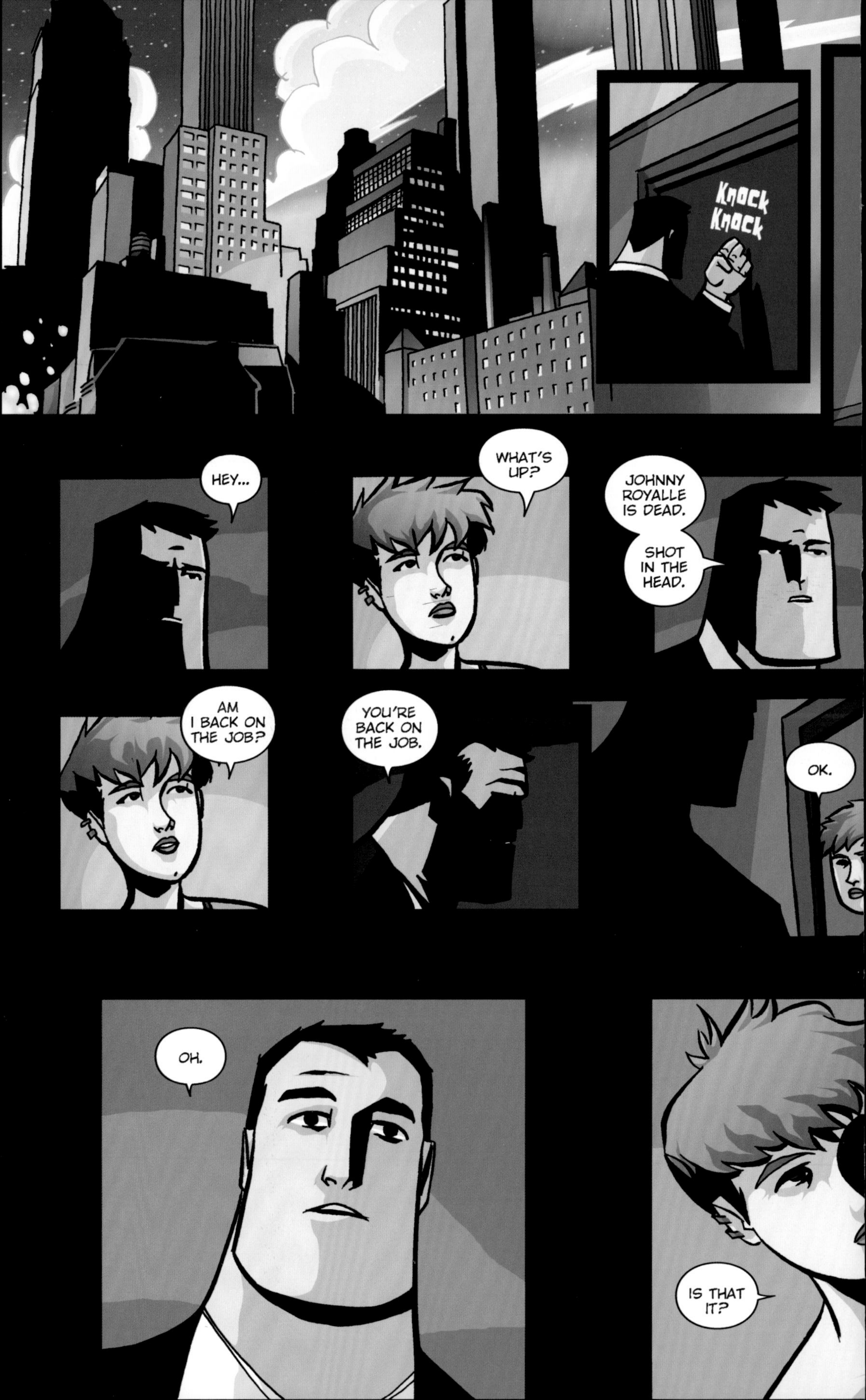
Knock
Knock
HEY...
WHAT'S UP?
JOHNNY ROYALLE IS DEAD.
SHOT IN THE HEAD.
AM I BACK ON THE JOB?
YOU'RE BACK ON THE JOB.
OK.
OH.
IS THAT IT?

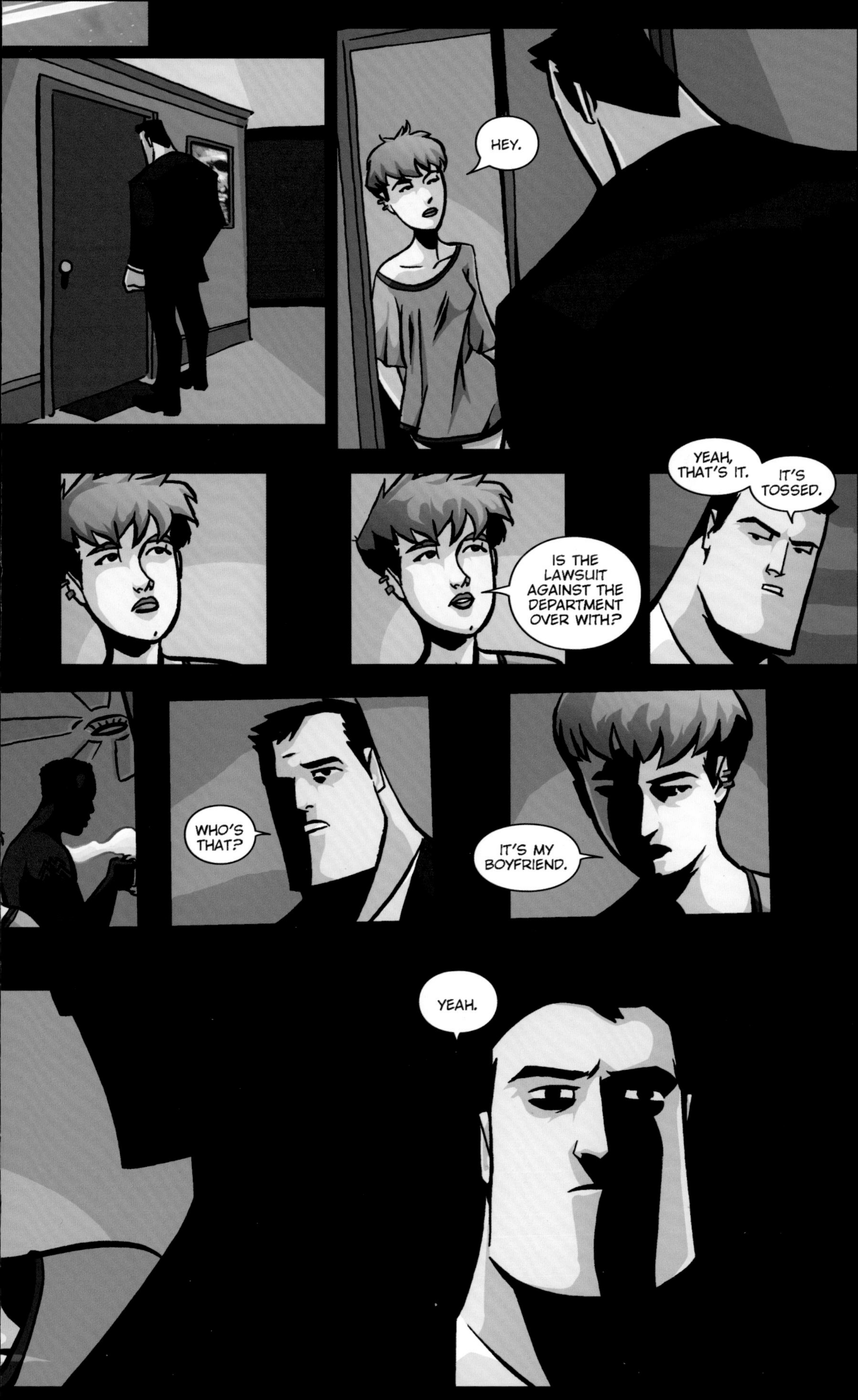
HEY.
IS THE LAWSUIT AGAINST THE DEPARTMENT OVER WITH?
YEAH, THAT'S IT.
IT'S TOSSED.
WHO'S THAT?
IT'S MY BOYFRIEND.
YEAH.

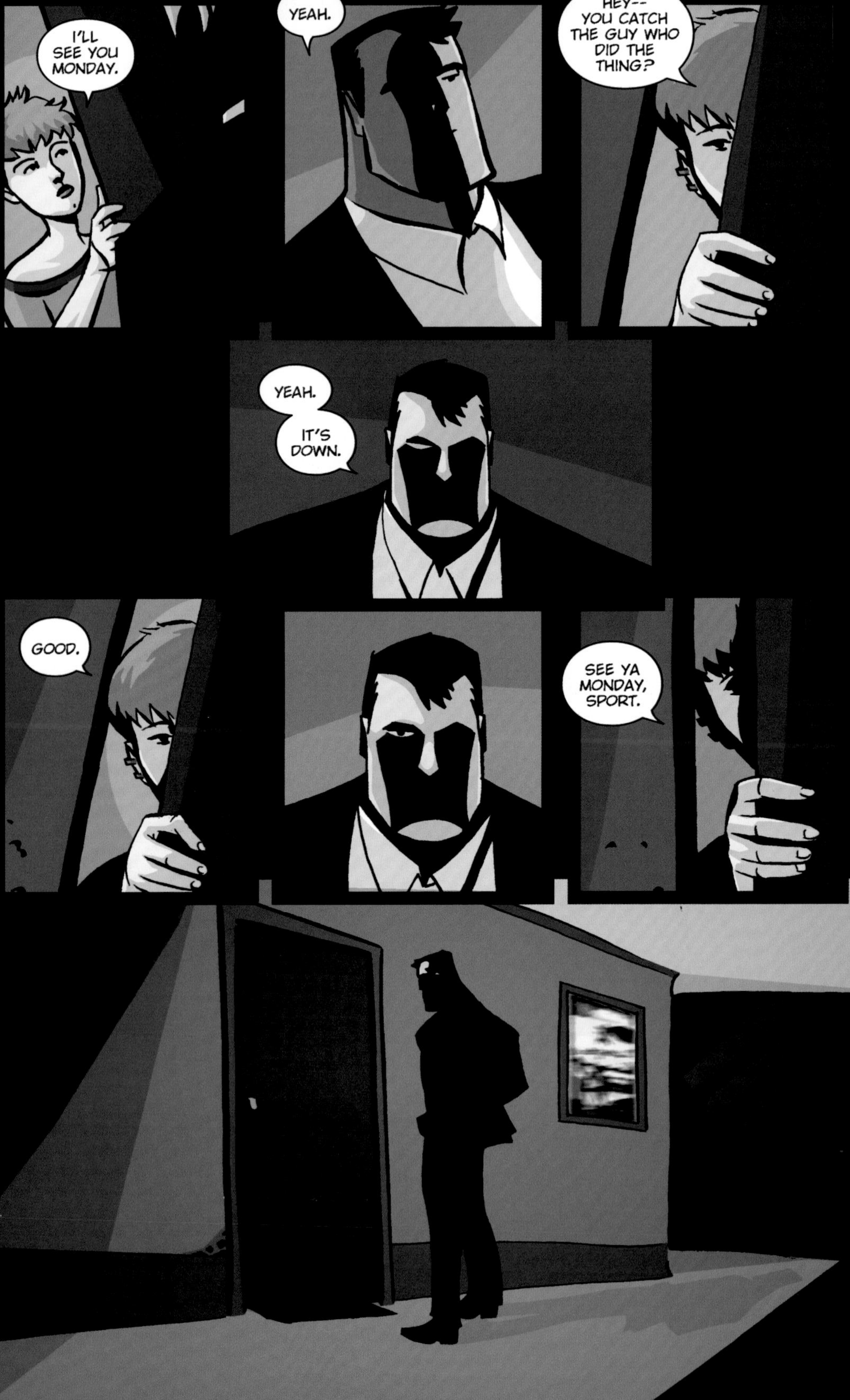
I'LL SEE YOU MONDAY.
YEAH.
HEY-- YOU CATCH THE GUY WHO DID THE THING?
YEAH.
IT'S DOWN.
GOOD.
SEE YA MONDAY, SPORT.

POWERS™

SUPPLEMENTAL MATERIAL

Hi! *Powers* writer Brian Michael Bendis here, serving as your tour guide through this bonus section.

Developing this work became one of the most creatively vibrant projects of our lives, and you may view this section as a sort of diary of the experience.

POWERS™

THE *COMIC SHOP NEWS* STRIPS

Cliff Biggers and Ward Batty, longtime supporters of my career, were kind enough to offer a preview of our new series as strips in their excellent periodical *Comic Shop News*. Because Pat hadn't yet joined our team, I did the coloring and lettering

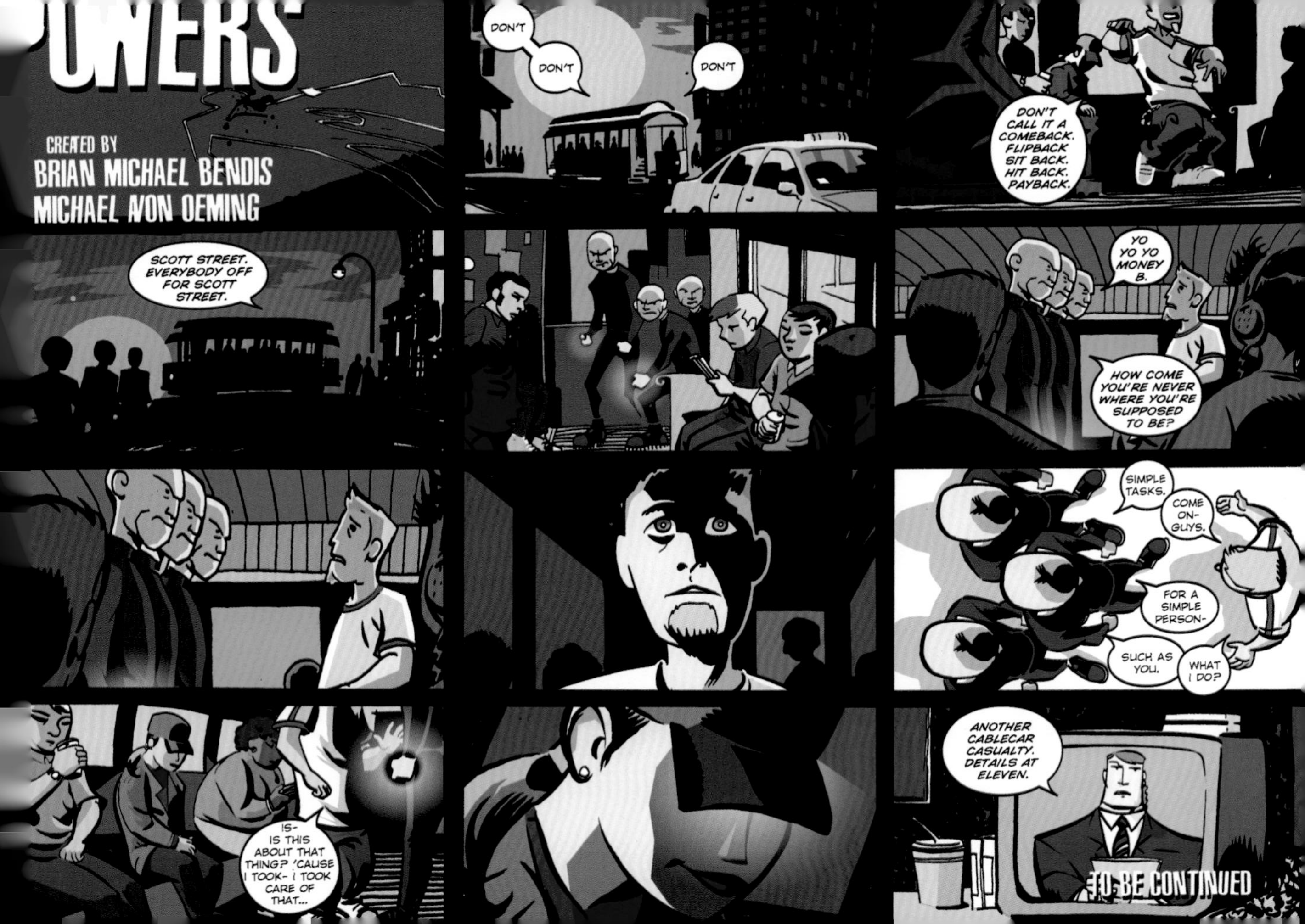
OWERS
CREATED BY
BRIAN MICHAEL BENDIS
MICHAEL AVON OEMING
DON'T
DON'T
DON'T
DON'T CALL IT A COMEBACK. FLIPBACK SIT BACK. HIT BACK. PAYBACK.
SCOTT STREET. EVERYBODY OFF FOR SCOTT STREET.
YO YO YO MONEY B.
HOW COME YOU'RE NEVER WHERE YOU'RE SUPPOSED TO BE?
SIMPLE TASKS.
COME ON-GUYS.
FOR A SIMPLE PERSON-
SUCH AS YOU.
WHAT I DO?
IS-IS THIS ABOUT THAT THING? 'CAUSE I TOOK- I TOOK CARE OF THAT...
ANOTHER CABLECAR CASUALTY. DETAILS AT ELEVEN.
TO BE CONTINUED

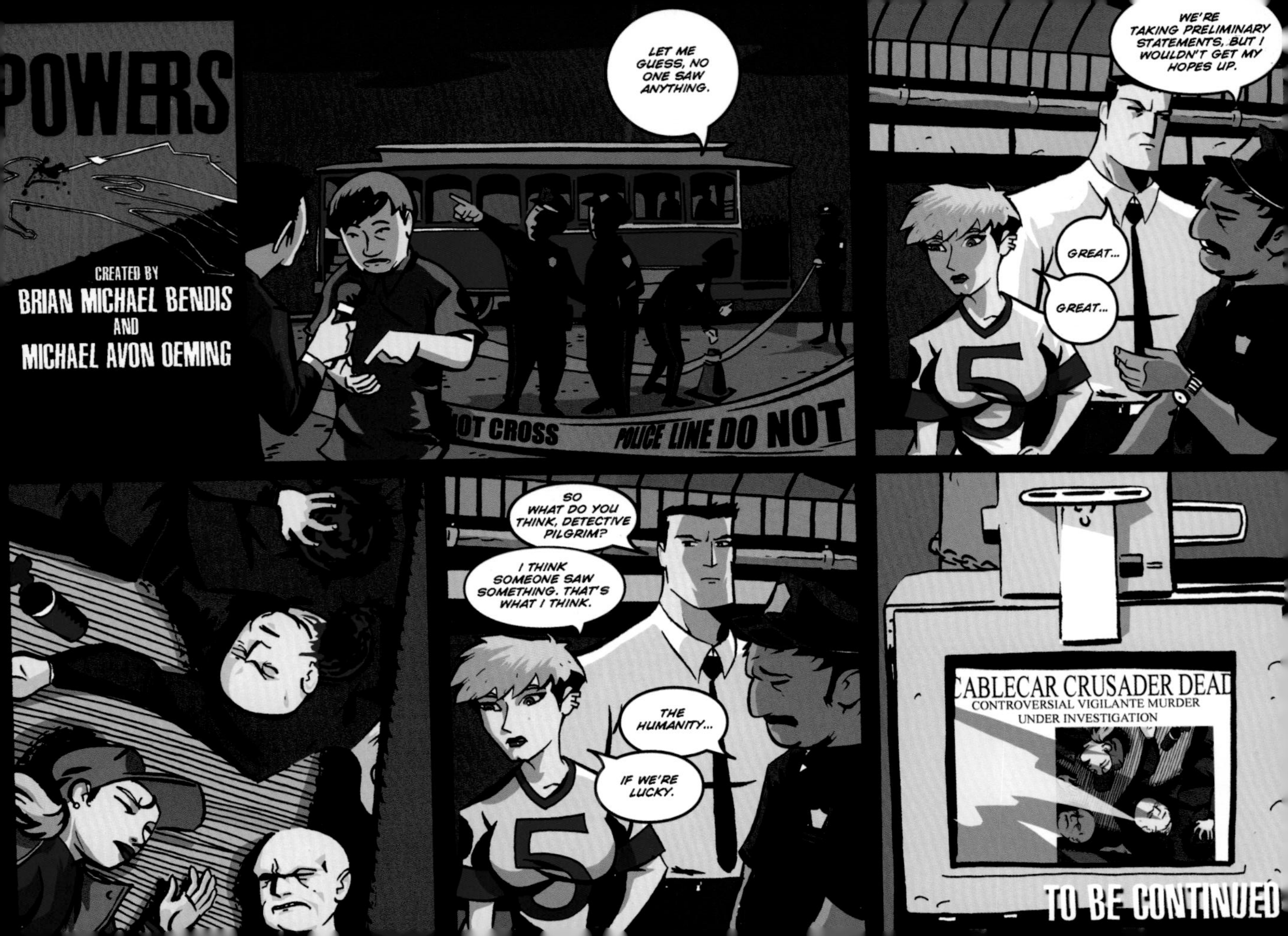
POWERS
CREATED BY
BRIAN MICHAEL BENDIS
AND
MICHAEL AVON OEMING
LET ME GUESS, NO ONE SAW ANYTHING.
OT CROSS
POLICE LINE DO NOT
WE'RE TAKING PRELIMINARY STATEMENTS, BUT I WOULDN'T GET MY HOPES UP.
GREAT...
GREAT...
SO WHAT DO YOU THINK, DETECTIVE PILGRIM?
I THINK SOMEONE SAW SOMETHING. THAT'S WHAT I THINK.
THE HUMANITY...
IF WE'RE LUCKY.
CABLECAR CRUSADER DEAD
CONTROVERSIAL VIGILANTE MURDER
UNDER INVESTIGATION
TO BE CONTINUED

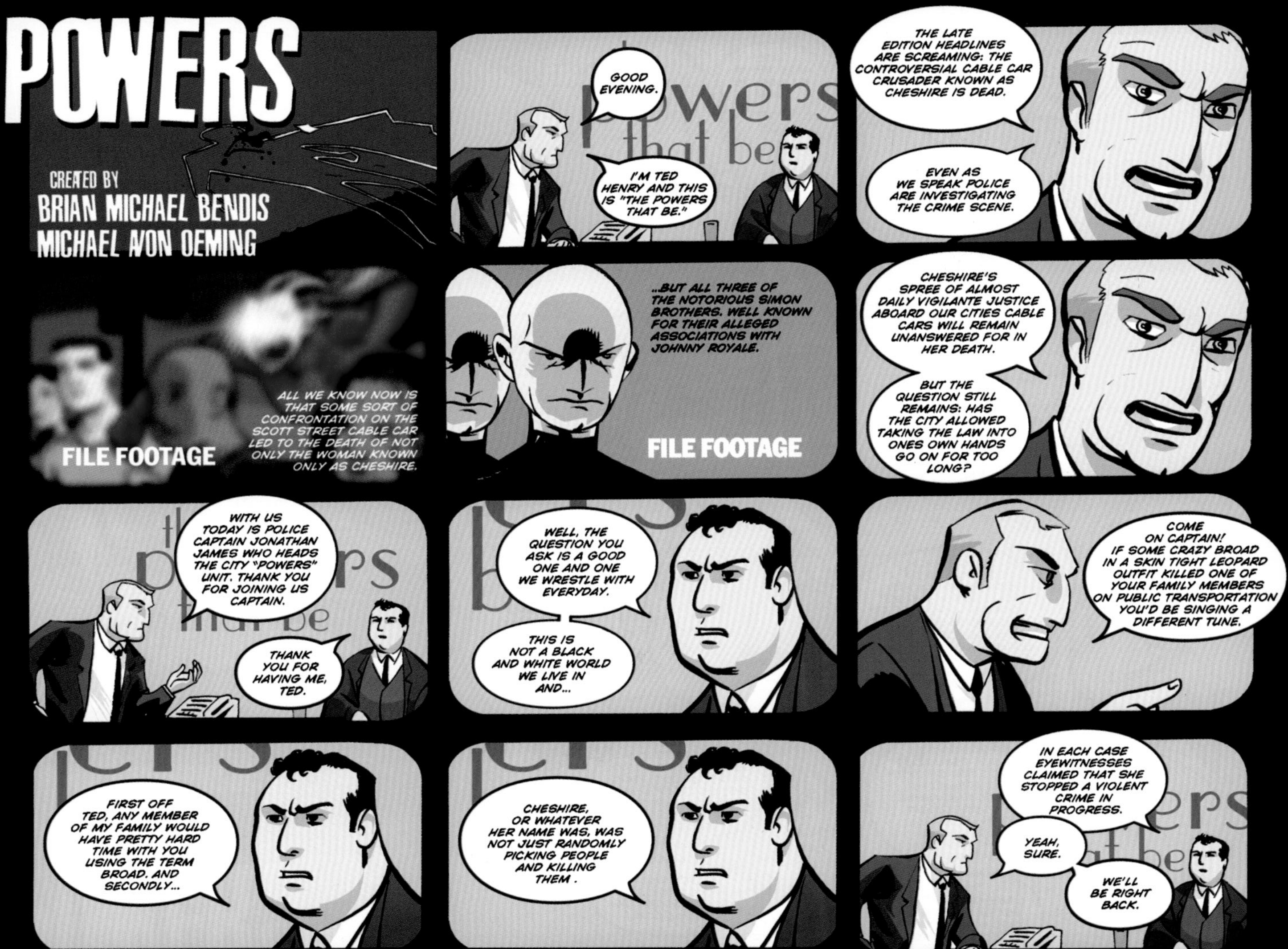
POWERS
CREATED BY
BRIAN MICHAEL BENDIS
MICHAEL AVON OEMING
GOOD EVENING.
I'M TED HENRY AND THIS IS "THE POWERS THAT BE."
powers that be
THE LATE EDITION HEADLINES ARE SCREAMING: THE CONTROVERSIAL CABLE CAR CRUSADER KNOWN AS CHESHIRE IS DEAD.
EVEN AS WE SPEAK POLICE ARE INVESTIGATING THE CRIME SCENE.
ALL WE KNOW NOW IS THAT SOME SORT OF CONFRONTATION ON THE SCOTT STREET CABLE CAR LED TO THE DEATH OF NOT ONLY THE WOMAN KNOWN ONLY AS CHESHIRE.
FILE FOOTAGE
...BUT ALL THREE OF THE NOTORIOUS SIMON BROTHERS. WELL KNOWN FOR THEIR ALLEGED ASSOCIATIONS WITH JOHNNY ROYALE.
FILE FOOTAGE
CHESHIRE'S SPREE OF ALMOST DAILY VIGILANTE JUSTICE ABOARD OUR CITIES CABLE CARS WILL REMAIN UNANSWERED FOR IN HER DEATH.
BUT THE QUESTION STILL REMAINS: HAS THE CITY ALLOWED TAKING THE LAW INTO ONES OWN HANDS GO ON FOR TOO LONG?
WITH US TODAY IS POLICE CAPTAIN JONATHAN JAMES WHO HEADS THE CITY "POWERS" UNIT. THANK YOU FOR JOINING US CAPTAIN.
THANK YOU FOR HAVING ME, TED.
WELL, THE QUESTION YOU ASK IS A GOOD ONE AND ONE WE WRESTLE WITH EVERYDAY.
THIS IS NOT A BLACK AND WHITE WORLD WE LIVE IN AND...
COME ON CAPTAIN! IF SOME CRAZY BROAD IN A SKIN TIGHT LEOPARD OUTFIT KILLED ONE OF YOUR FAMILY MEMBERS ON PUBLIC TRANSPORTATION YOU'D BE SINGING A DIFFERENT TUNE.
FIRST OFF TED, ANY MEMBER OF MY FAMILY WOULD HAVE PRETTY HARD TIME WITH YOU USING THE TERM BROAD. AND SECONDLY...
CHESHIRE, OR WHATEVER HER NAME WAS, WAS NOT JUST RANDOMLY PICKING PEOPLE AND KILLING THEM .
IN EACH CASE EYEWITNESSES CLAIMED THAT SHE STOPPED A VIOLENT CRIME IN PROGRESS.
YEAH, SURE.
WE'LL BE RIGHT BACK.

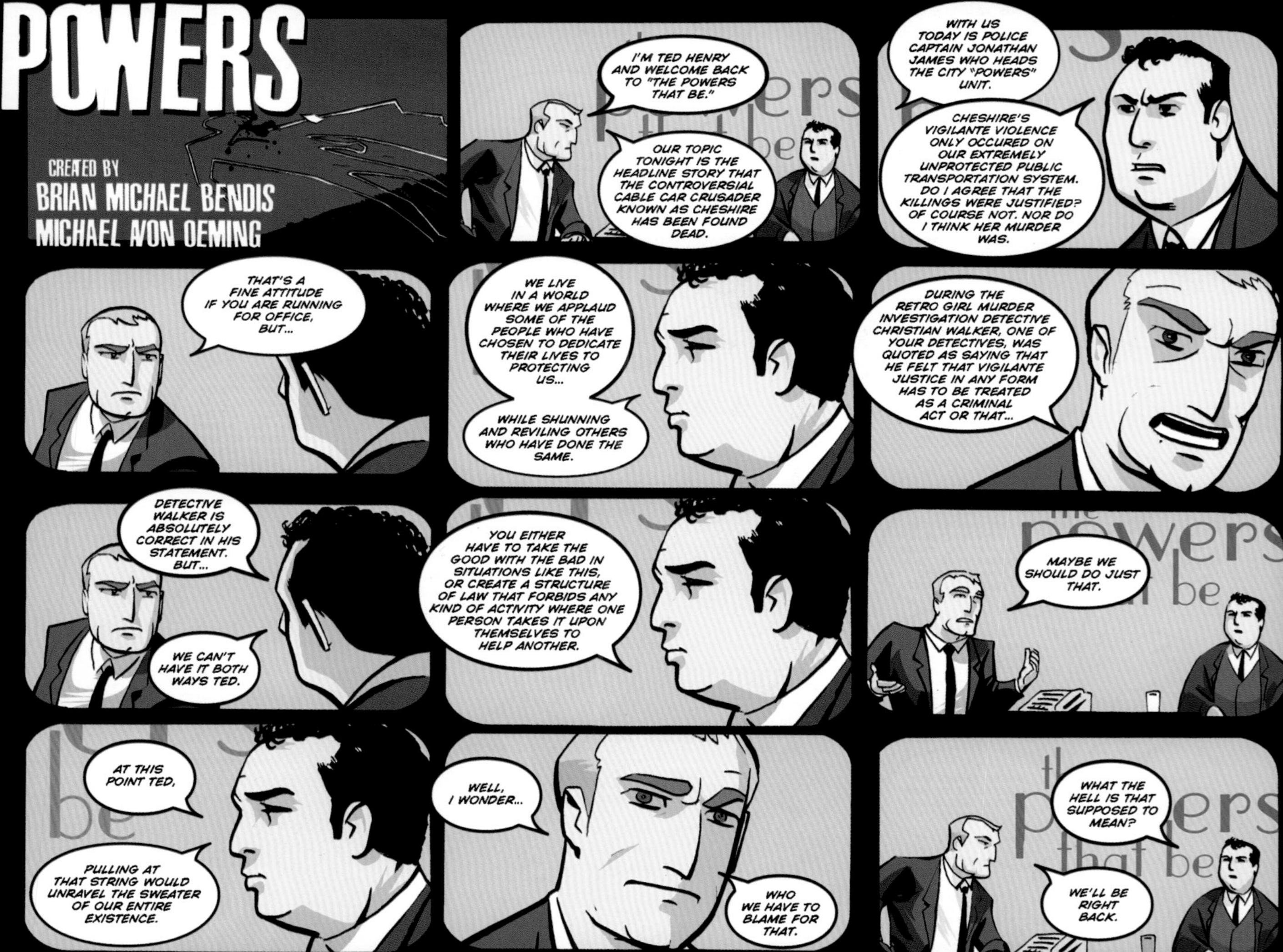
POWERS
CREATED BY
BRIAN MICHAEL BENDIS
MICHAEL AVON OEMING
I'M TED HENRY AND WELCOME BACK TO "THE POWERS THAT BE."
OUR TOPIC TONIGHT IS THE HEADLINE STORY THAT THE CONTROVERSIAL CABLE CAR CRUSADER KNOWN AS CHESHIRE HAS BEEN FOUND DEAD.
WITH US TODAY IS POLICE CAPTAIN JONATHAN JAMES WHO HEADS THE CITY "POWERS" UNIT.
CHESHIRE'S VIGILANTE VIOLENCE ONLY OCCURED ON OUR EXTREMELY UNPROTECTED PUBLIC TRANSPORTATION SYSTEM. DO I AGREE THAT THE KILLINGS WERE JUSTIFIED? OF COURSE NOT. NOR DO I THINK HER MURDER WAS.
THAT'S A FINE ATTITUDE IF YOU ARE RUNNING FOR OFFICE, BUT...
WE LIVE IN A WORLD WHERE WE APPLAUD SOME OF THE PEOPLE WHO HAVE CHOSEN TO DEDICATE THEIR LIVES TO PROTECTING US...
WHILE SHUNNING AND REVILING OTHERS WHO HAVE DONE THE SAME.
DURING THE RETRO GIRL MURDER INVESTIGATION DETECTIVE CHRISTIAN WALKER, ONE OF YOUR DETECTIVES, WAS QUOTED AS SAYING THAT HE FELT THAT VIGILANTE JUSTICE IN ANY FORM HAS TO BE TREATED AS A CRIMINAL ACT OR THAT...
DETECTIVE WALKER IS ABSOLUTELY CORRECT IN HIS STATEMENT. BUT...
WE CAN'T HAVE IT BOTH WAYS TED.
YOU EITHER HAVE TO TAKE THE GOOD WITH THE BAD IN SITUATIONS LIKE THIS, OR CREATE A STRUCTURE OF LAW THAT FORBIDS ANY KIND OF ACTIVITY WHERE ONE PERSON TAKES IT UPON THEMSELVES TO HELP ANOTHER.
MAYBE WE SHOULD DO JUST THAT.
AT THIS POINT TED,
PULLING AT THAT STRING WOULD UNRAVEL THE SWEATER OF OUR ENTIRE EXISTENCE.
WELL, I WONDER...
WHO WE HAVE TO BLAME FOR THAT.
WHAT THE HELL IS THAT SUPPOSED TO MEAN?
WE'LL BE RIGHT BACK.

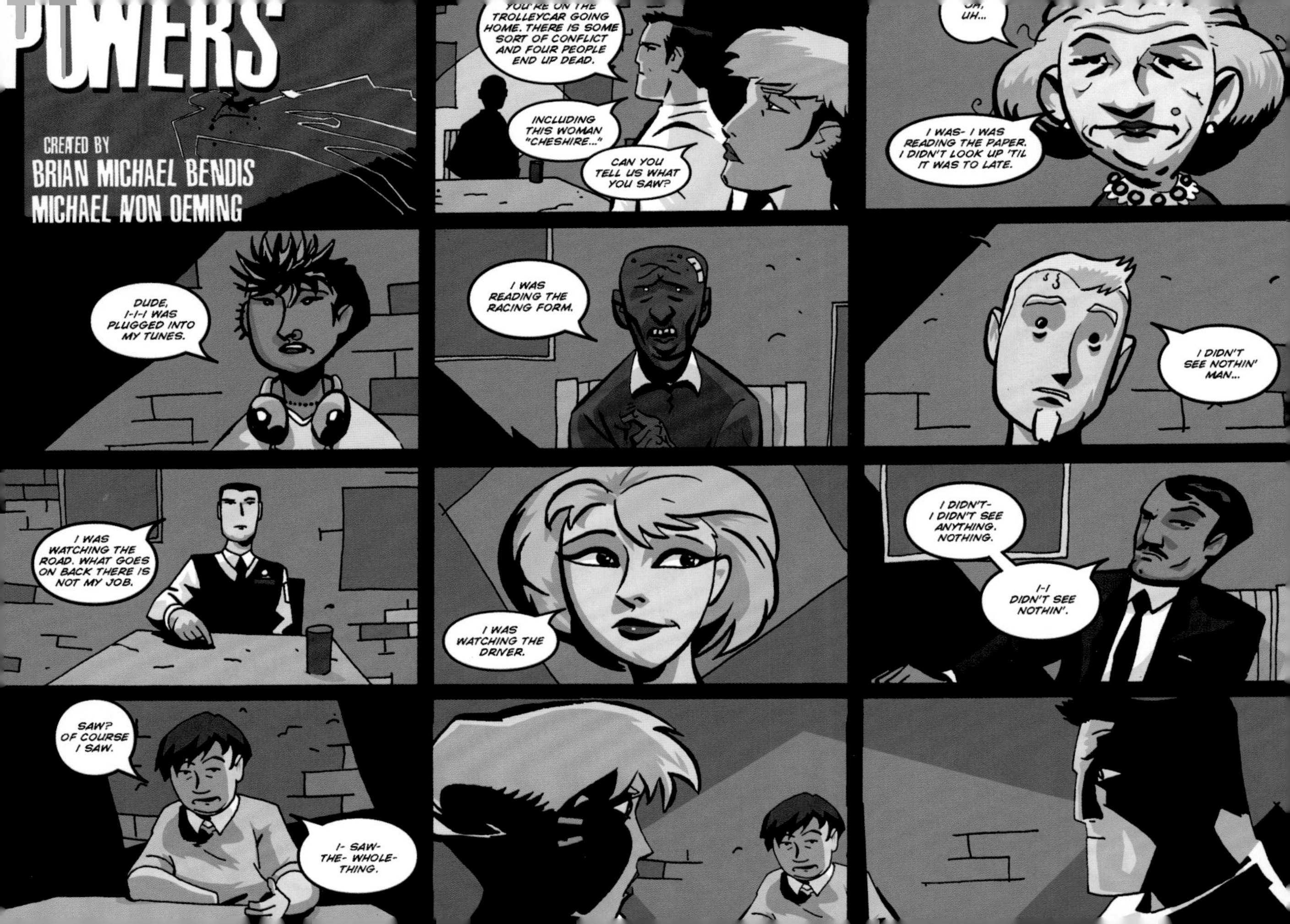
POWERS
CREATED BY
BRIAN MICHAEL BENDIS
MICHAEL AVON OEMING
YOU'RE ON THE TROLLEYCAR GOING HOME. THERE IS SOME SORT OF CONFLICT AND FOUR PEOPLE END UP DEAD.
INCLUDING THIS WOMAN "CHESHIRE..."
CAN YOU TELL US WHAT YOU SAW?
UH, UH...
I WAS- I WAS READING THE PAPER. I DIDN'T LOOK UP 'TIL IT WAS TO LATE.
DUDE, I-I-I WAS PLUGGED INTO MY TUNES.
I WAS READING THE RACING FORM.
I DIDN'T SEE NOTHIN' MAN...
I WAS WATCHING THE ROAD. WHAT GOES ON BACK THERE IS NOT MY JOB.
I WAS WATCHING THE DRIVER.
I DIDN'T- I DIDN'T SEE ANYTHING. NOTHING.
I-I DIDN'T SEE NOTHIN'.
SAW? OF COURSE I SAW.
I- SAW- THE- WHOLE- THING.

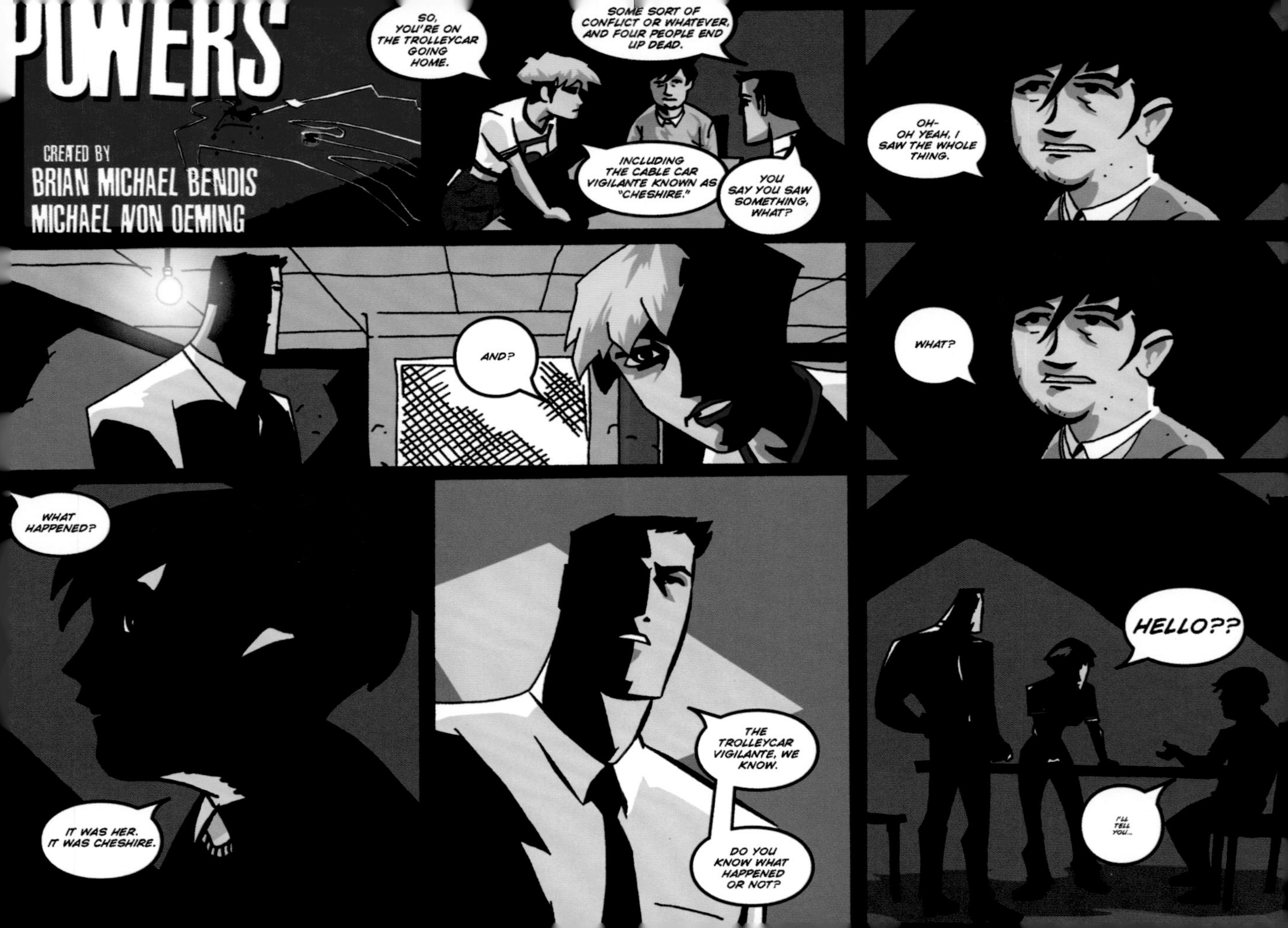
POWERS
CREATED BY
BRIAN MICHAEL BENDIS
MICHAEL AVON OEMING
SO, YOU'RE ON THE TROLLEYCAR GOING HOME.
SOME SORT OF CONFLICT OR WHATEVER, AND FOUR PEOPLE END UP DEAD.
INCLUDING THE CABLE CAR VIGILANTE KNOWN AS "CHESHIRE."
YOU SAY YOU SAW SOMETHING, WHAT?
OH- OH YEAH, I SAW THE WHOLE THING.
AND?
WHAT?
WHAT HAPPENED?
IT WAS HER. IT WAS CHESHIRE.
THE TROLLEYCAR VIGILANTE, WE KNOW.
DO YOU KNOW WHAT HAPPENED OR NOT?
HELLO??
I'LL TELL YOU...

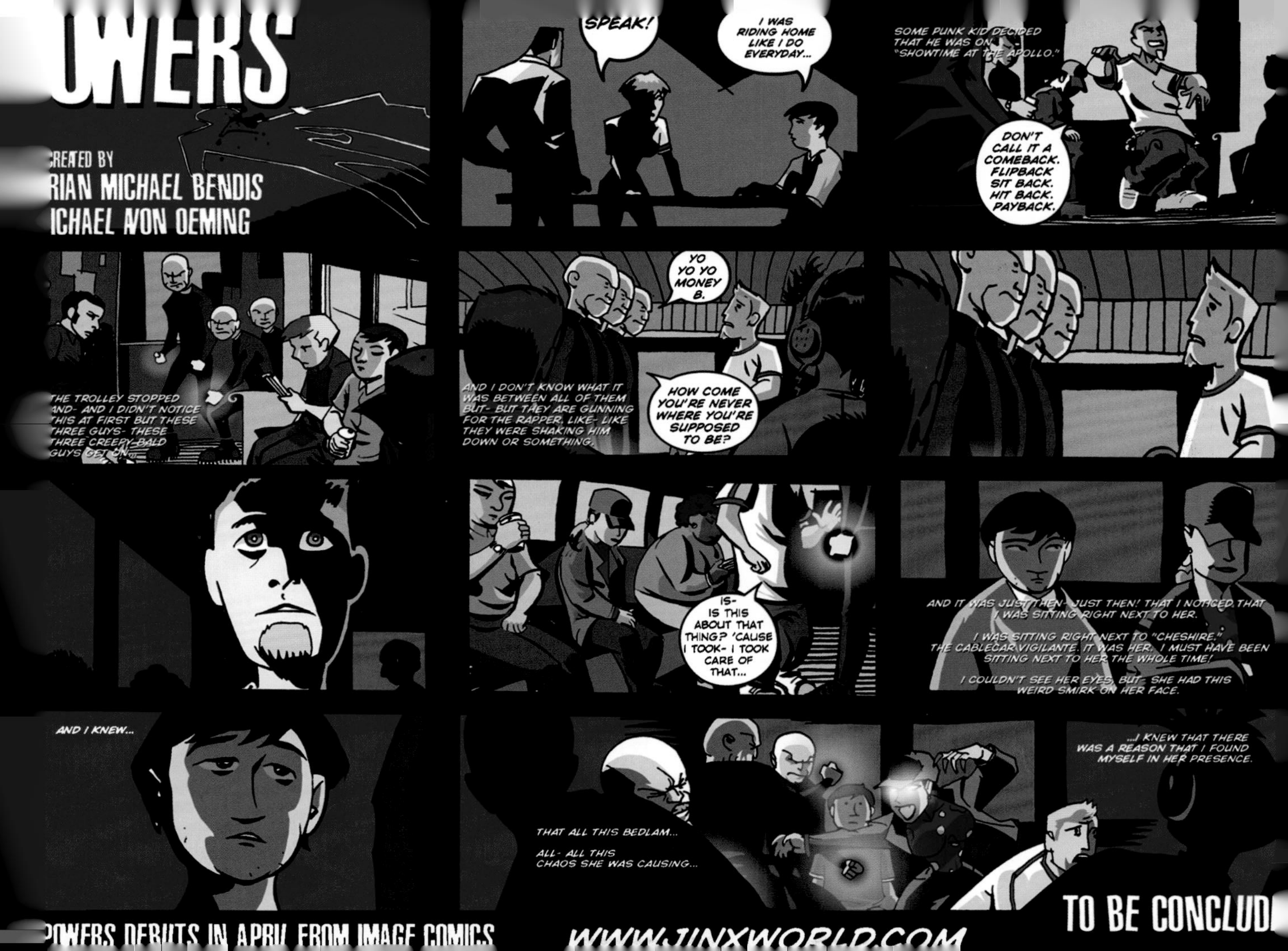
OWERS
CREATED BY
RIAN MICHAEL BENDIS
ICHAEL AVON OEMING
SPEAK!
I WAS RIDING HOME LIKE I DO EVERYDAY...
SOME PUNK KID DECIDED THAT HE WAS ON "SHOWTIME AT THE APOLLO."
DON'T CALL IT A COMEBACK. FLIPBACK SIT BACK. HIT BACK. PAYBACK.
THE TROLLEY STOPPED AND- AND I DIDN'T NOTICE THIS AT FIRST BUT THESE THREE GUYS- THESE THREE CREEPY BALD GUYS GET ON...
AND I DON'T KNOW WHAT IT WAS BETWEEN ALL OF THEM BUT- BUT THEY ARE GUNNING FOR THE RAPPER, LIKE- LIKE THEY WERE SHAKING HIM DOWN OR SOMETHING.
YO YO YO MONEY B.
HOW COME YOU'RE NEVER WHERE YOU'RE SUPPOSED TO BE?
IS- IS THIS ABOUT THAT THING? 'CAUSE I TOOK- I TOOK CARE OF THAT...
AND IT WAS JUST THEN- JUST THEN! THAT I NOTICED THAT I WAS SITTING RIGHT NEXT TO HER.
I WAS SITTING RIGHT NEXT TO "CHESHIRE." THE CABLECAR VIGILANTE. IT WAS HER. I MUST HAVE BEEN SITTING NEXT TO HER THE WHOLE TIME!
I COULDN'T SEE HER EYES, BUT- SHE HAD THIS WEIRD SMIRK ON HER FACE.
AND I KNEW...
THAT ALL THIS BEDLAM...
ALL- ALL THIS CHAOS SHE WAS CAUSING...
...I KNEW THAT THERE WAS A REASON THAT I FOUND MYSELF IN HER PRESENCE.
TO BE CONCLUD
POWERS DEBUTS IN APRIL FROM IMAGE COMICS
WWW.JINXWORLD.COM

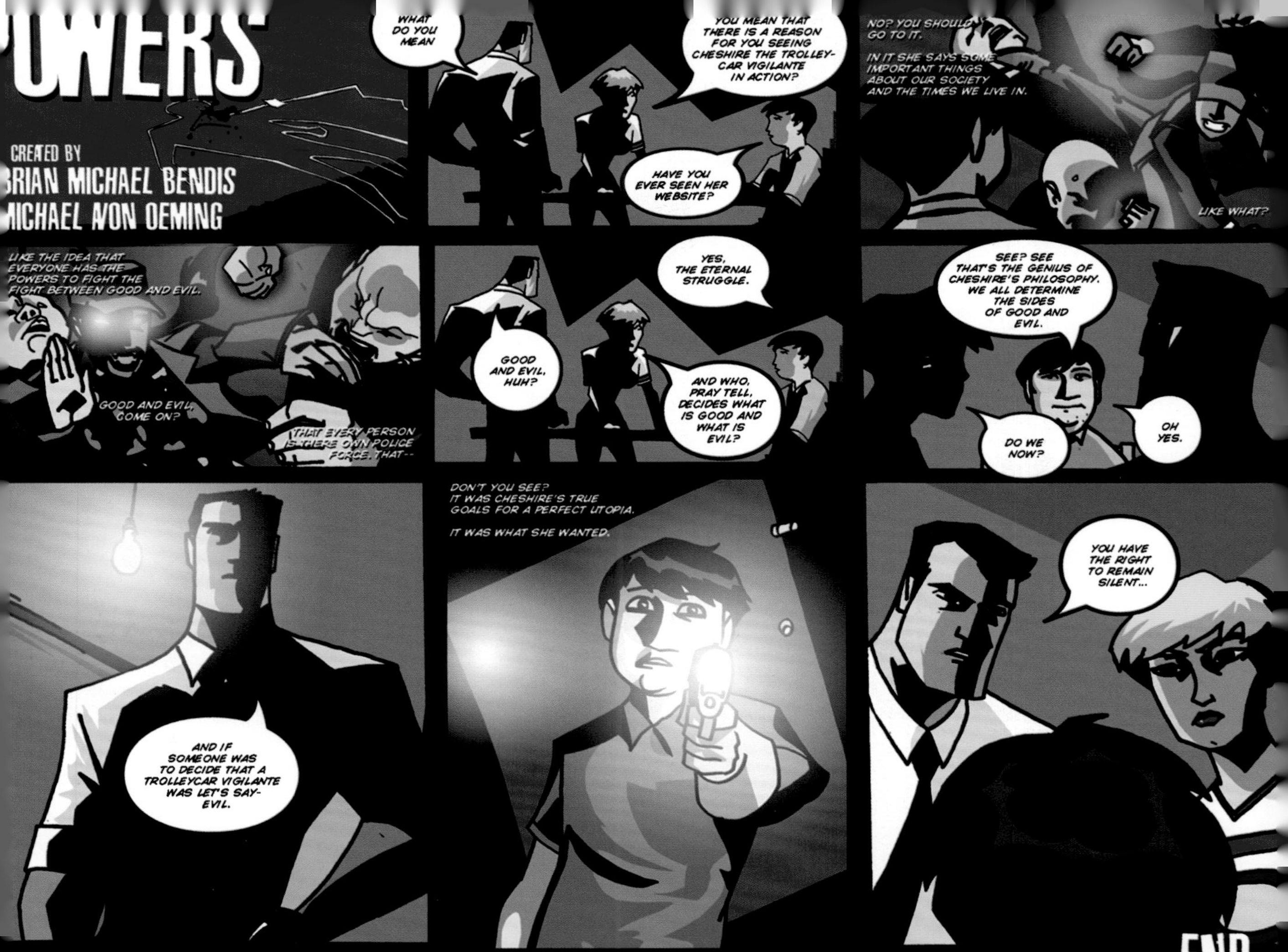
CREATED BY
MICHAEL BENDIS
MICHAEL AVON OEMING
WHAT DO YOU MEAN
YOU MEAN THAT THERE IS A REASON FOR YOU SEEING CHESHIRE THE TROLLEY-CAR VIGILANTE IN ACTION?
HAVE YOU EVER SEEN HER WEBSITE?
NO? YOU SHOULD GO TO IT.
IN IT SHE SAYS SOME IMPORTANT THINGS ABOUT OUR SOCIETY AND THE TIMES WE LIVE IN.
LIKE WHAT?
LIKE THE IDEA THAT EVERYONE HAS THE POWERS TO FIGHT THE FIGHT BETWEEN GOOD AND EVIL.
GOOD AND EVIL, COME ON?
THAT EVERY PERSON IS THERE OWN POLICE FORCE. THAT--
YES, THE ETERNAL STRUGGLE.
GOOD AND EVIL, HUH?
AND WHO, PRAY TELL, DECIDES WHAT IS GOOD AND WHAT IS EVIL?
SEE? SEE THAT'S THE GENIUS OF CHESHIRE'S PHILOSOPHY. WE ALL DETERMINE THE SIDES OF GOOD AND EVIL.
DO WE NOW?
OH YES.
AND IF SOMEONE WAS TO DECIDE THAT A TROLLEYCAR VIGILANTE WAS LET'S SAY- EVIL.
DON'T YOU SEE? IT WAS CHESHIRE'S TRUE GOALS FOR A PERFECT UTOPIA.
IT WAS WHAT SHE WANTED.
YOU HAVE THE RIGHT TO REMAIN SILENT...
END

POWERS

™

THAT BE

FIVE MINUTES WITH MIKE OEMING

One of the hottest, most intriguing comics out there right now is *Powers*, a book that's taken the industry by storm. Following the best of two human detectives investigating "powers-related" crimes in their superhuman world, *Powers* escaped from the minds of writer Brian Michael Bendis, who has had his own success as writer/artist with *A.K.A. Goldfish* and *Jinx*, and artist Michael Avon Oeming, whose work on *Ship of Fools* caught him even more attention after his work on books like *Judge Dredd* and his superhero work.

The stylistic approach to *Powers* is very specific; in fact, Mike Oeming notes it was the impetus behind getting together with Brian Michael Bendis and specifically creating a crime comic.

"I met Brian Bendis years ago when he was doing store signings for *A.K.A. Goldfish*. We just clicked right away," Oeming relates. "We stayed in touch and talked about working together. After different

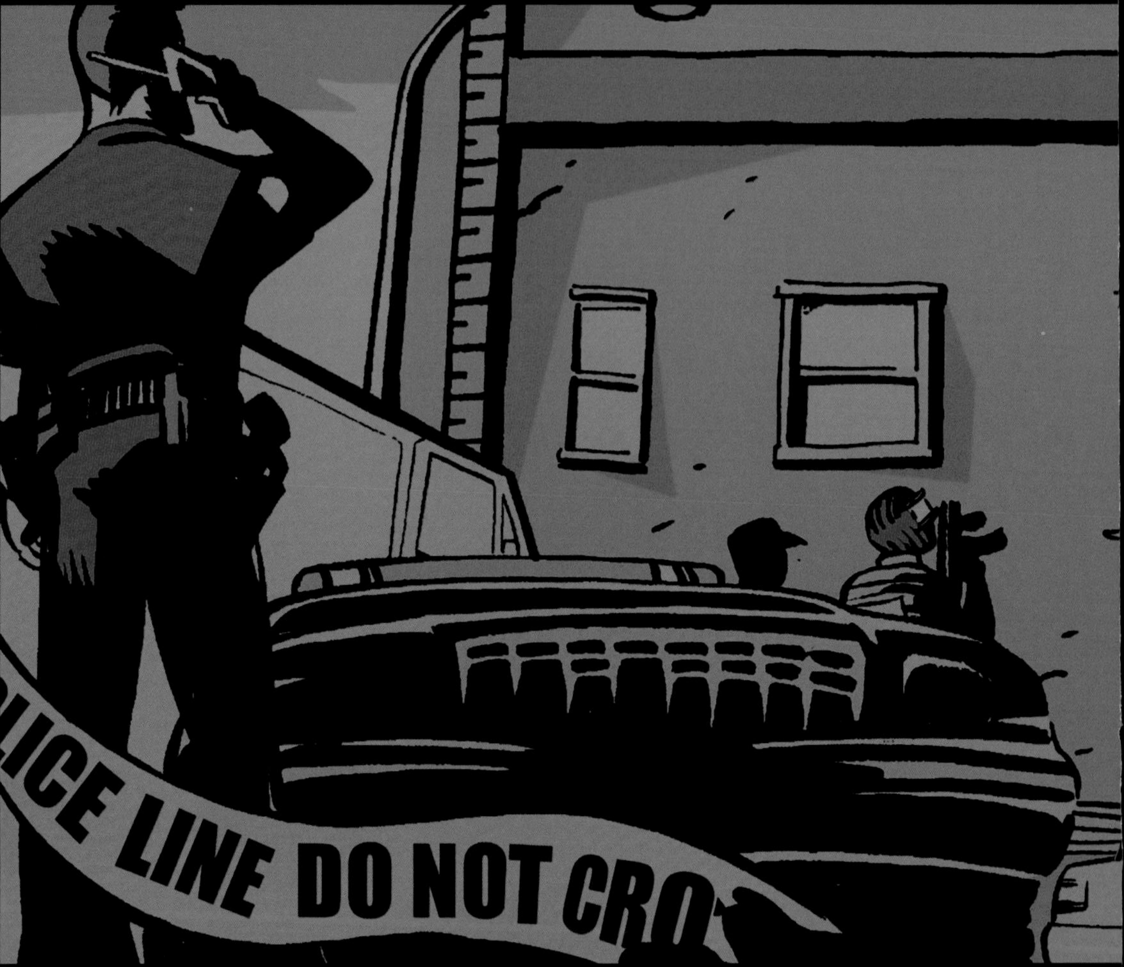
LICE LINE DO NOT CRO

projects came and went, I was looking for something new to do. I called Brian and was like, 'I want to do a crime book and I want to use this particular kind of style'—this Bruce Timm-ish / Alex Toth kind of animated stuff. And I really wanted to use it in a crime thing."

The artist explains the development of the realistic animated look of *Powers*. "The style developed from my trying to get work on the *Batman Adventures* stuff. I liked that style, but I couldn't stay on model, because I saw other things it had potential for that the series wasn't quite allowing. I really like stuff that Timm was influenced by, specifically Alex Toth, who was a huge influence on me. I just wanted to do some crime stuff using a combination of their two styles.

"That's basically what I told Brian." Oeming affects a begging tone to his voice and says, " 'I want to do a crime book with you 'cause you're a good writer.' And he was like, 'Absolutely!' We mulled over things. I faxed him some ideas. I didn't care what it was; I knew that we would just have fun on it. When it started out, all we were looking to do was a black-and-white crime book. I assumed that it would be one issue or a couple of issues that would be released through Image central as a black and white. At the time, I had just been doing *Ship of Fools* with Bryan Glass, and he was still doing *Torso*. So that's all we thought: little, tiny black-and-white book.

"It just kind of blossomed from there," Oeming explains. "Brian basically had *Powers* in its nutshell. He showed me the thing, and I was hesitant at first. I wanted to do a straightforward crime thing. And I was like, 'What's this?' And he said, 'No, no, it's not about the heroes!' So even I took some convincing and thank God I saw his way!"

Of course, as everyone is well aware—or if you're not, you are now—that little, tiny black-and-white book is a bit bigger. Oeming for one is taken by surprise by the success.

"I'm not sure why it happened," Oeming admits of the sudden hit. "I think a lot of it had to do with Bendis's fans. He's been doing these crime books

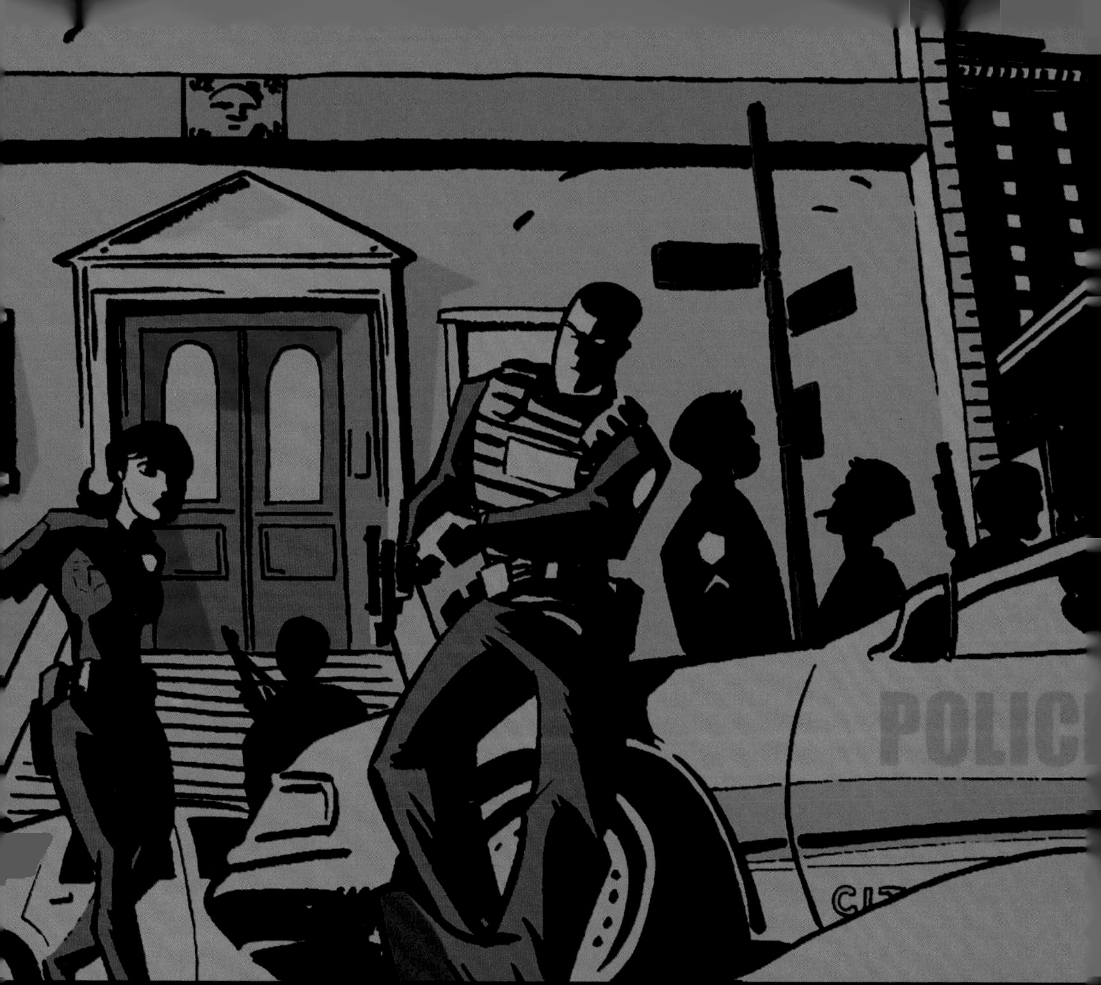

for many years now. First it was *A.K.A. Goldfish*, which ran into *Jinx*, which ran into *Torso*, and then he started getting picked up for other companies to do books, like *Sam and Twitch*. So he really started building this fan base. So that and the commerciality of my artwork—it was what people were looking for, or at least people who hadn't read his stuff before. I think that's what I brought into the fold, really, was a certain amount of commerciality. My work's very iconic, you look at it and immediately know what it is; it's so simple. That's what I like about it. Brian's artwork is more realistic, but both show the same elements of noir—the use of blacks and lighting. Even though physically the artwork looks very different, if you look at the pacing, the lighting, we're working the same way, just in slightly different elements."

Bendis as a writer/artist has a unique way of telling his stories for Oeming, and that system works out very well. "His scripts are completely visual, which works because we're on the same page, no pun intended," the artist says. "We know exactly what the other is thinking. Originally, for the first issue, he supplied me with layouts, with the grids and stuff because he had a specific way, a very cinematic way, of presenting the panel-to-panel work. Once I got ahold of that, we've come up with our own secret language where he'll just call me up and say, 'Change the so-and-so with blah-blah-blah' and I'll know what he means! And I'll change the so-and-so and blah-blah-blah so we're definitely on the same wavelength. His sense of visuals comes through very clearly."

The newest news in regard to *Powers* is the recently announced movie deal at Sony with Mace Neufeld. Oeming is excited by it all but keeps calm about it, because no matter how cool a *Powers* movie could be, "I haven't seen it yet," so he's withholding a certain level of enthusiasm. "What really happens when you make a deal—and we have a really good deal, and when I say 'good deal' I mean we're well respected by the company. We're being treated very fairly, but the movie is out of our hands, so we just sit back and hope they make a good film. They have a good track record. Mace Neufeld is just widely known for doing quality stuff, so that's on our side."

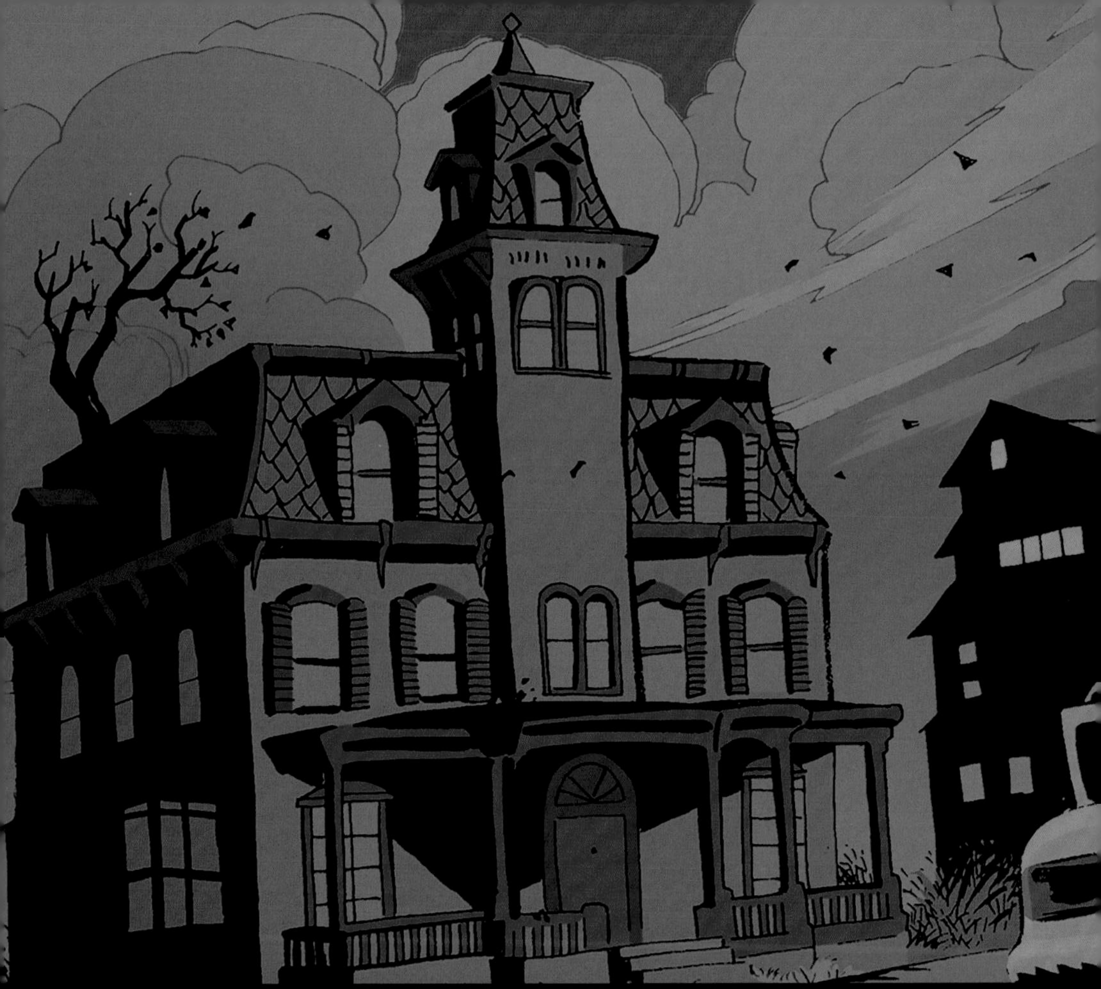

But while the comic awaits Hollywood treatment, the book itself continues to work its magic on the public. In fact, in most outlets, issues can't be found. Oeming explains that "the reason we're going to trade paperback so quickly is because we're basically sold out of the book. We way overprinted, but the reorders were so high, there's not enough to go around anymore!"

In fact, something completely new will be coming out in the near future. As Oeming describes: "Brian and I do a lot of research for our projects, and before I actually started *Powers* I went to the local police station and introduced myself. I got to do ride-alongs, I met with the captain, I took extensive photo reference of all their equipment, they let me shoot a couple of rounds off at some criminals . . . wait, what was the original question? I got distracted and all excited about shooting people." He laughs.

Back on topic, Oeming tells the origin of what will be the *Powers Coloring/Activity Book*. "So, hanging around at the police station, you start noticing all the little knickknacks they have lying around. And one of those things is something for kids . . . safety coloring books! Big cartoony cops saying, 'Hey kids, if you see power lines down, don't touch them!' I sent Brian some as kind of a joke and he said, 'This is a great idea!' So, the *Powers* coloring book will be a variation of this. You'll have safety tips like 'If you're walking down the street and you see two superhero beings fighting this guy and fire is blasting out of their eyes, immediately duck and cover.' 'Do not touch flame-retardant superheroes' . . . It's safety tips for the *Powers* universe. Kind of like kids during the A-bomb scare, but there's superheroes flying out of the sky! We're going to be making some pretty good jokes about ourselves and the process of doing the book. It'll be fun."

A big jump from what they normally do, when you think about it. And Oeming laughs and agrees: "In between dead people, we get to do a coloring book!"

—Maureen McTigue

POWERS™

COLORING/ACTIVITY BOOK

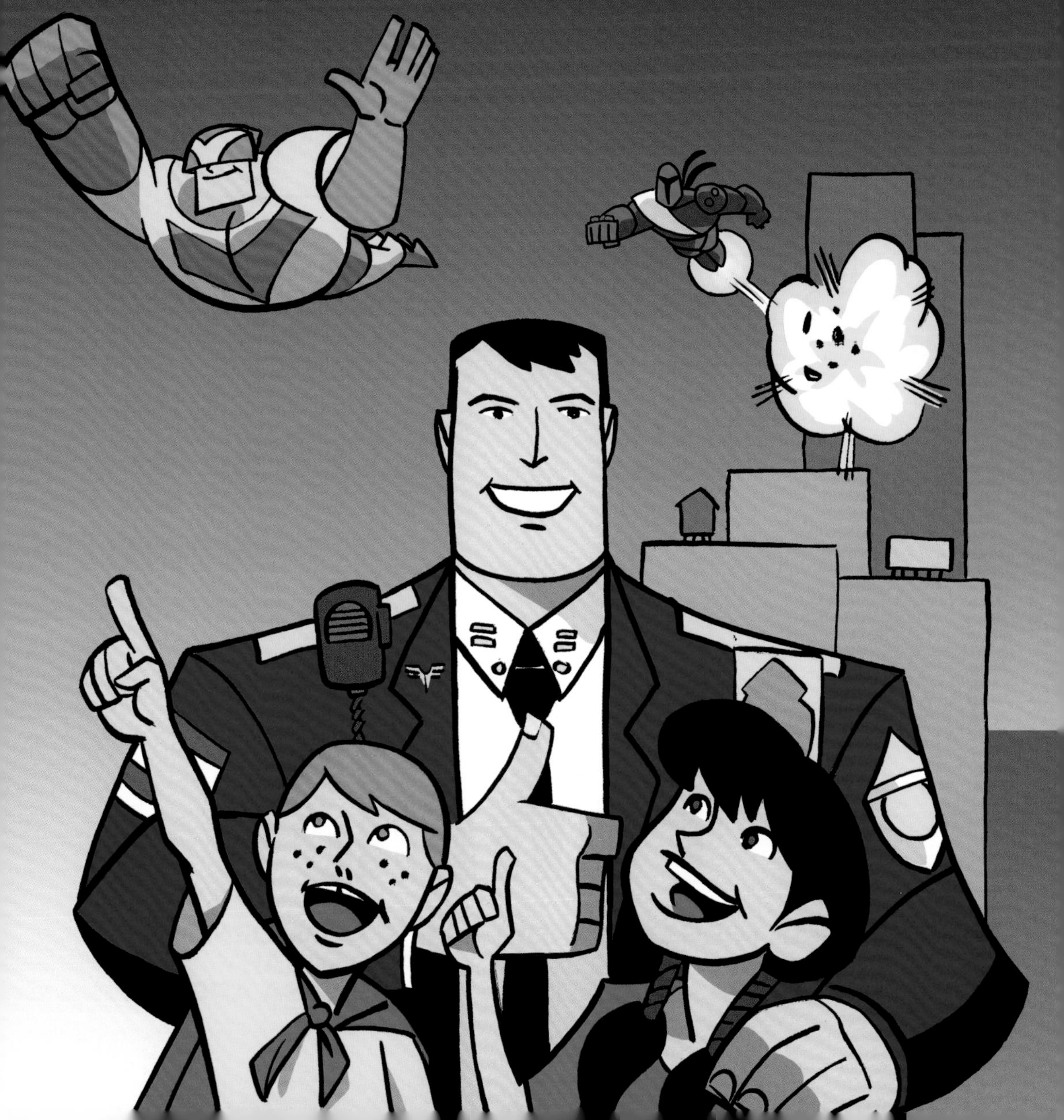

SAFETY KID

I, _____ , promise to use caution and safety everywhere I go. I will remind my relatives and friends how important it is to use safety all day long because this world is filled with super-powered maniacs and assorted radioactive menaces hellbent on destroying the Universe. So I will look both ways before I cross the street, always use a safety belt, and never touch anything in my house that has the word 'NULLIFIER' written on it.

_____
WRITE YOUR NAME HERE

_____   _____
DATE   AGE

POWERS™

Created by
BRIAN MICHAEL BENDIS and **MIKE AVON OEMING**
Color, Art, Lettering, and Production by **PAT GARRAHY**
Business Affairs **ALISA BENDIS** Word Search **MELISSA APONTE**

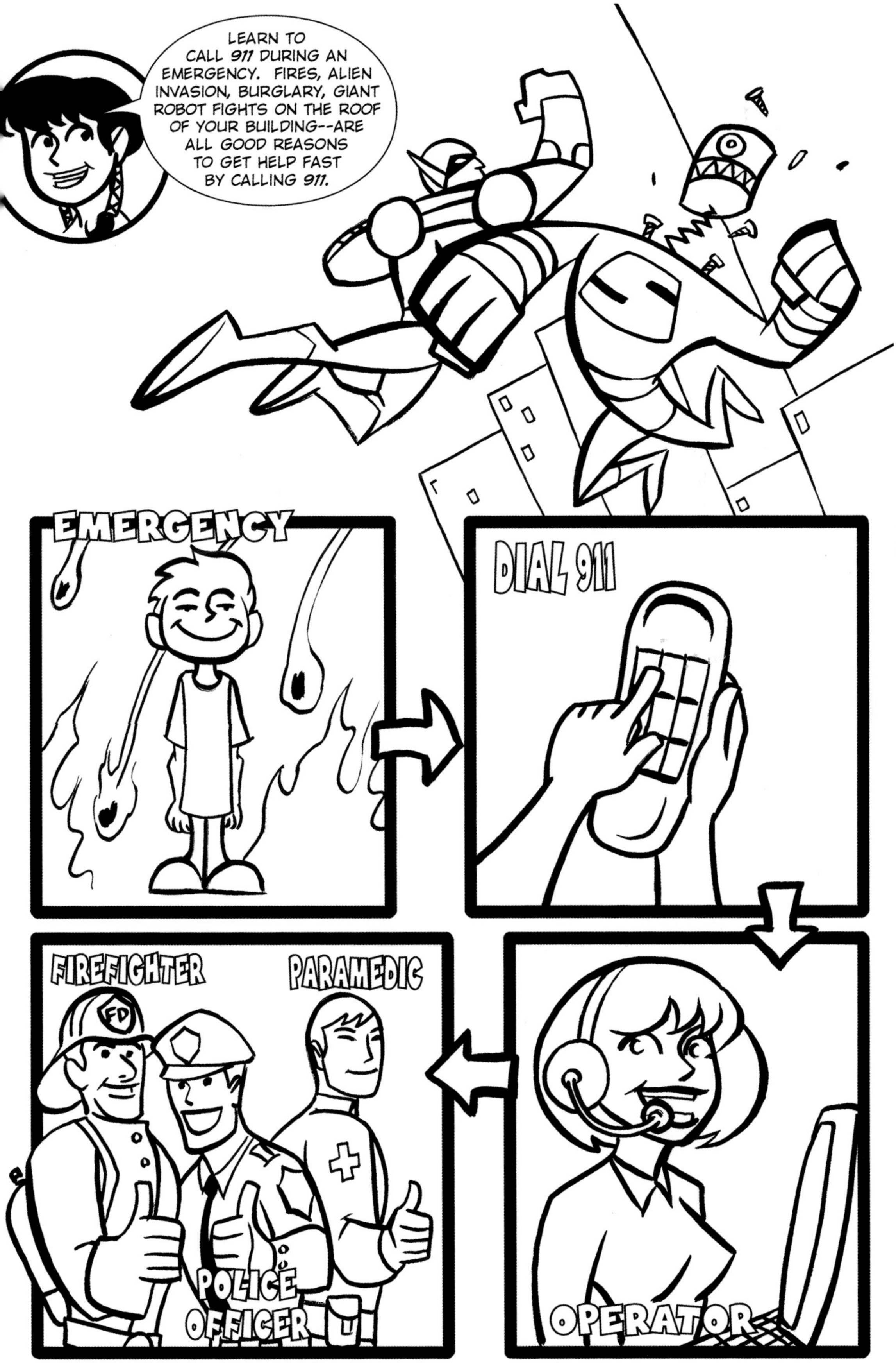
LEARN TO CALL 911 DURING AN EMERGENCY. FIRES, ALIEN INVASION, BURGLARY, GIANT ROBOT FIGHTS ON THE ROOF OF YOUR BUILDING--ARE ALL GOOD REASONS TO GET HELP FAST BY CALLING 911.
EMERGENCY
DIAL 911
OPERATOR
FIREFIGHTER
PARAMEDIC
FD
POLICE OFFICER

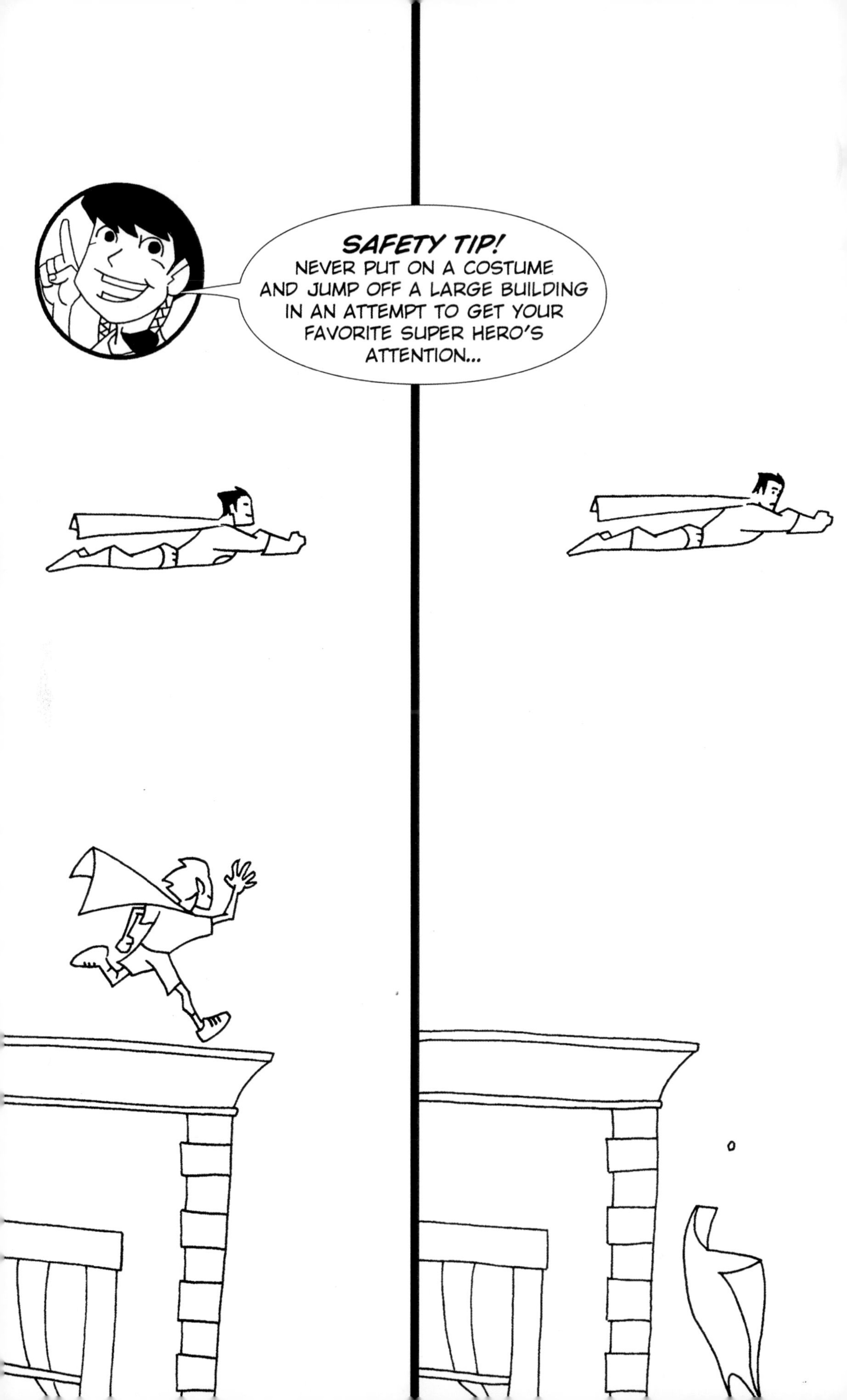
SAFETY TIP!
NEVER PUT ON A COSTUME AND JUMP OFF A LARGE BUILDING IN AN ATTEMPT TO GET YOUR FAVORITE SUPER HERO'S ATTENTION...

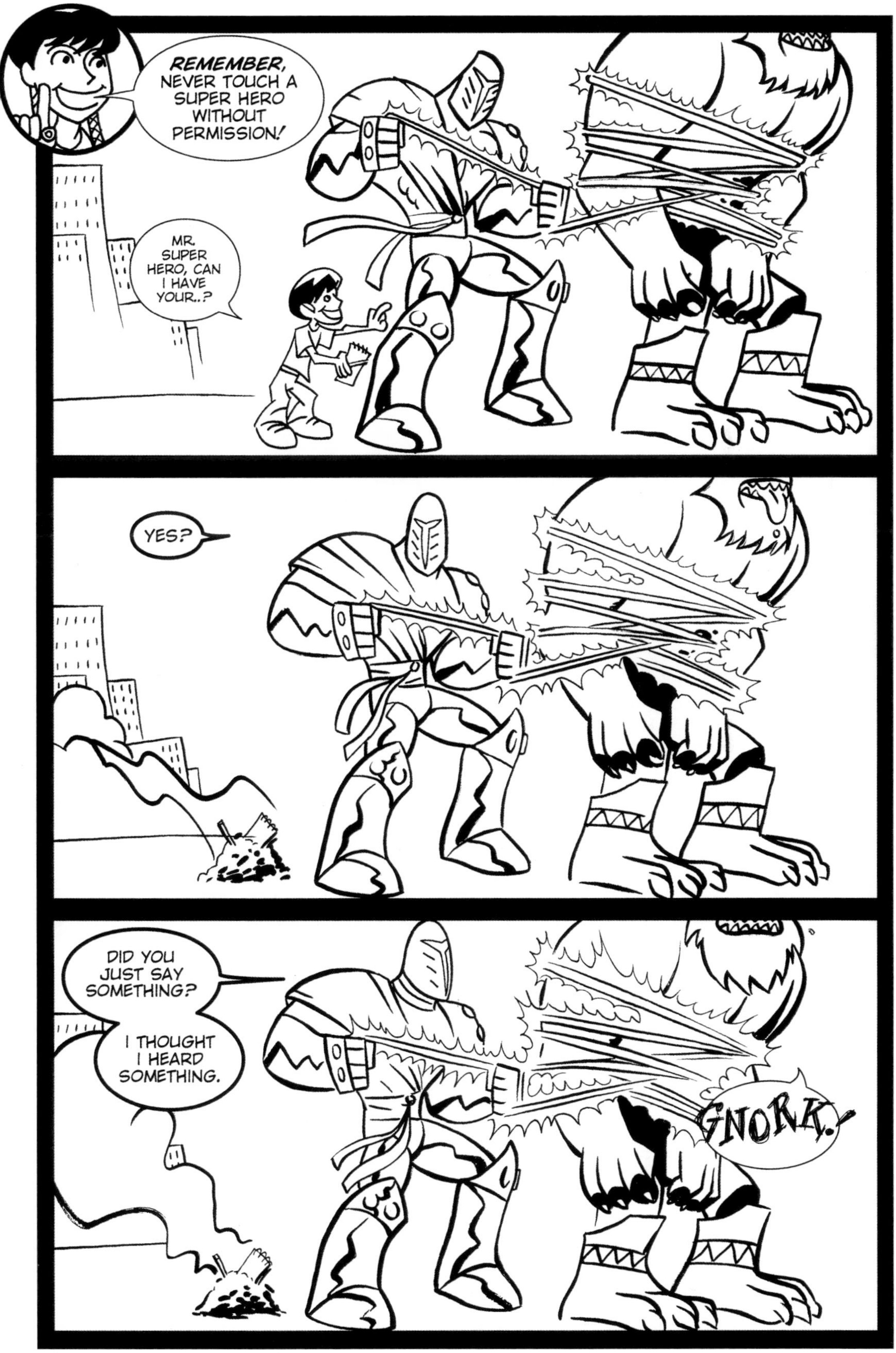
REMEMBER, NEVER TOUCH A SUPER HERO WITHOUT PERMISSION!
MR. SUPER HERO, CAN I HAVE YOUR..?
YES?
DID YOU JUST SAY SOMETHING?
I THOUGHT I HEARD SOMETHING.
GNORK!

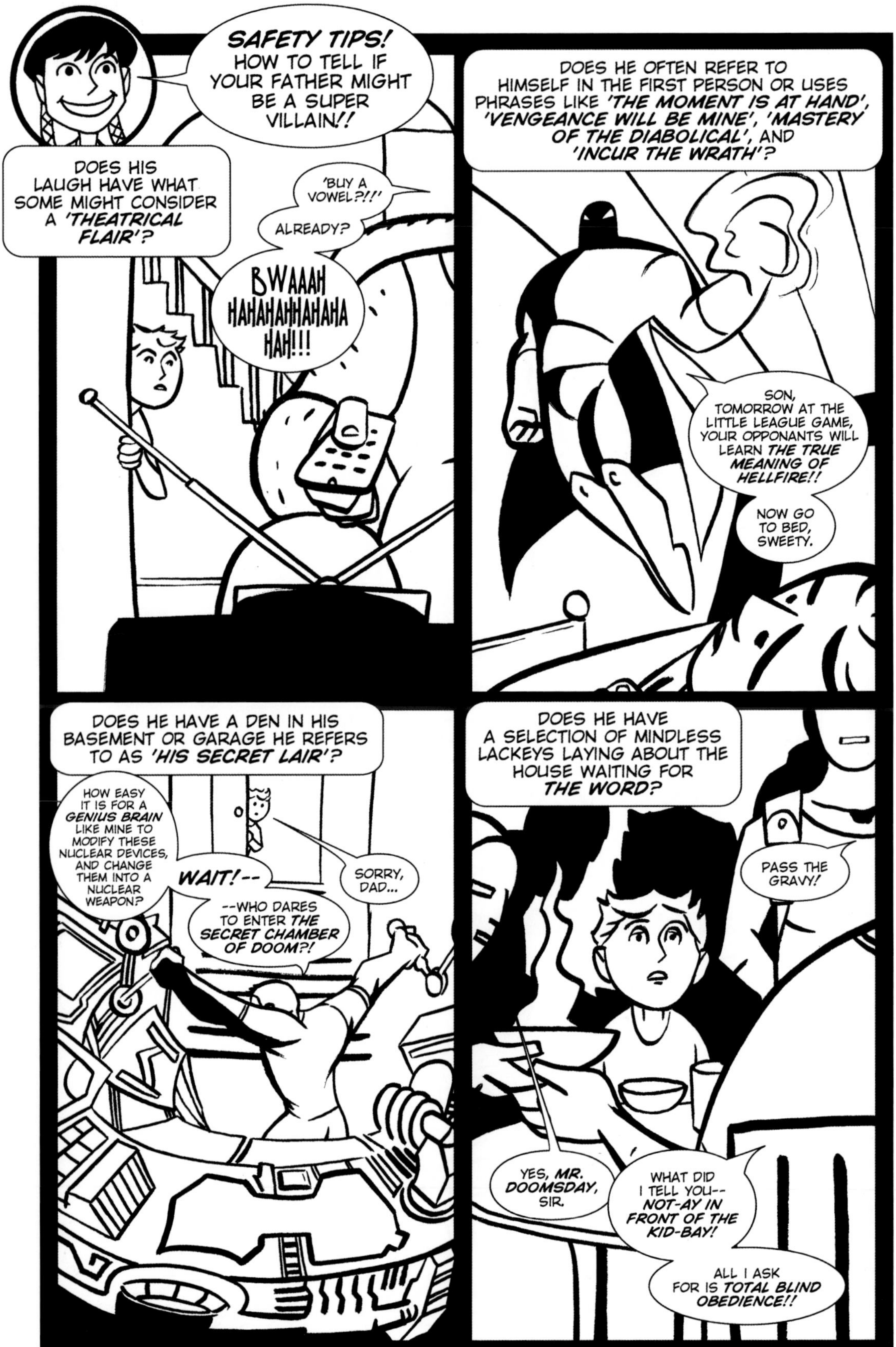
SAFETY TIPS!
HOW TO TELL IF YOUR FATHER MIGHT BE A SUPER VILLAIN!!
DOES HIS LAUGH HAVE WHAT SOME MIGHT CONSIDER A 'THEATRICAL FLAIR'?
'BUY A VOWEL?!!'
ALREADY?
BWAAAH HAHAHAHHAHAHA HAH!!!
DOES HE OFTEN REFER TO HIMSELF IN THE FIRST PERSON OR USES PHRASES LIKE 'THE MOMENT IS AT HAND', 'VENGEANCE WILL BE MINE', 'MASTERY OF THE DIABOLICAL', AND 'INCUR THE WRATH'?
SON, TOMORROW AT THE LITTLE LEAGUE GAME, YOUR OPPONANTS WILL LEARN THE TRUE MEANING OF HELLFIRE!!
NOW GO TO BED, SWEETY.
DOES HE HAVE A DEN IN HIS BASEMENT OR GARAGE HE REFERS TO AS 'HIS SECRET LAIR'?
HOW EASY IT IS FOR A GENIUS BRAIN LIKE MINE TO MODIFY THESE NUCLEAR DEVICES, AND CHANGE THEM INTO A NUCLEAR WEAPON?
WAIT!--
--WHO DARES TO ENTER THE SECRET CHAMBER OF DOOM?!
SORRY, DAD...
DOES HE HAVE A SELECTION OF MINDLESS LACKEYS LAYING ABOUT THE HOUSE WAITING FOR THE WORD?
PASS THE GRAVY!
YES, MR. DOOMSDAY, SIR.
WHAT DID I TELL YOU--NOT-AY IN FRONT OF THE KID-BAY!
ALL I ASK FOR IS TOTAL BLIND OBEDIENCE!!

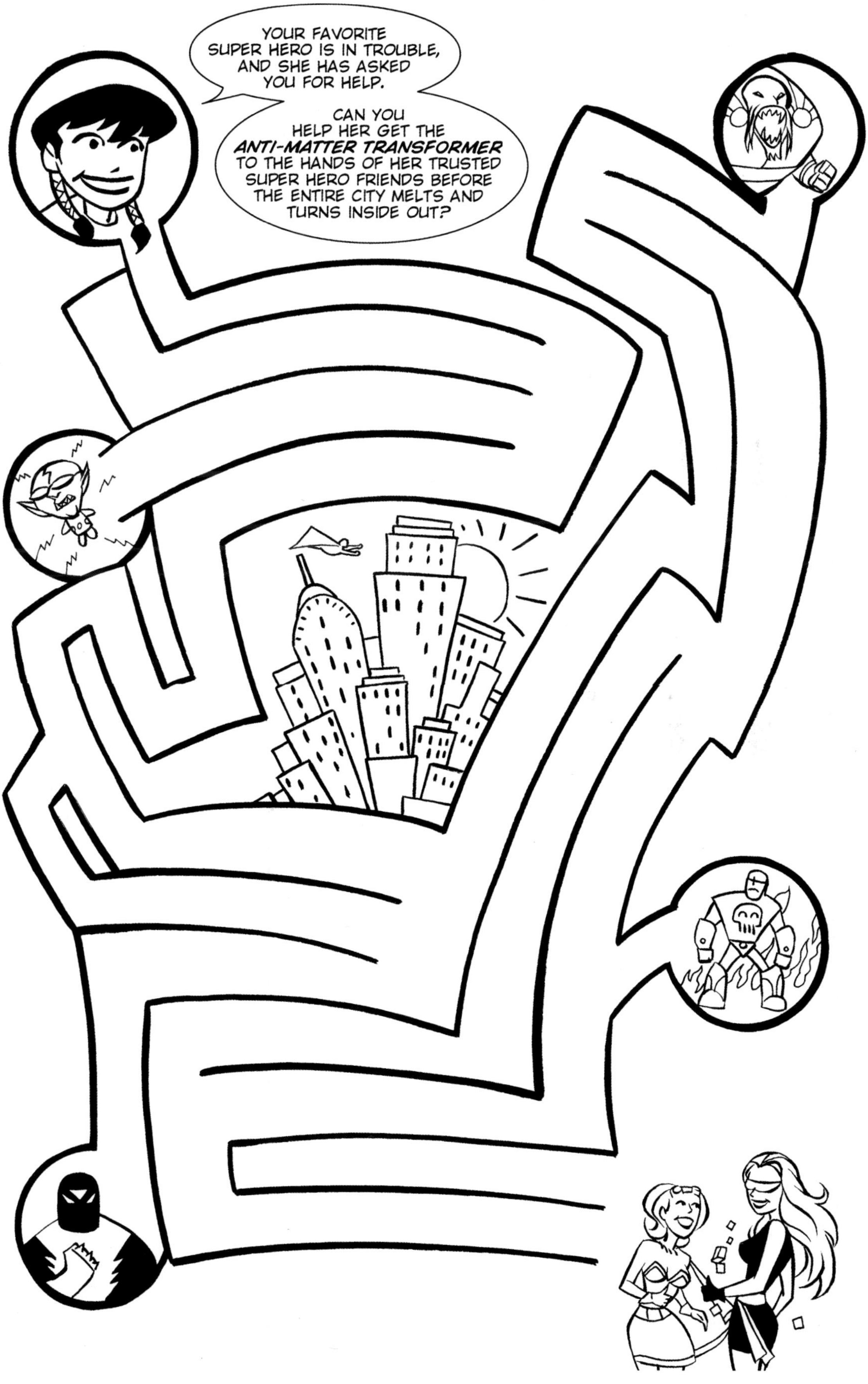

YOUR FAVORITE SUPER HERO IS IN TROUBLE, AND SHE HAS ASKED YOU FOR HELP.
CAN YOU HELP HER GET THE ***ANTI-MATTER TRANSFORMER*** TO THE HANDS OF HER TRUSTED SUPER HERO FRIENDS BEFORE THE ENTIRE CITY MELTS AND TURNS INSIDE OUT?

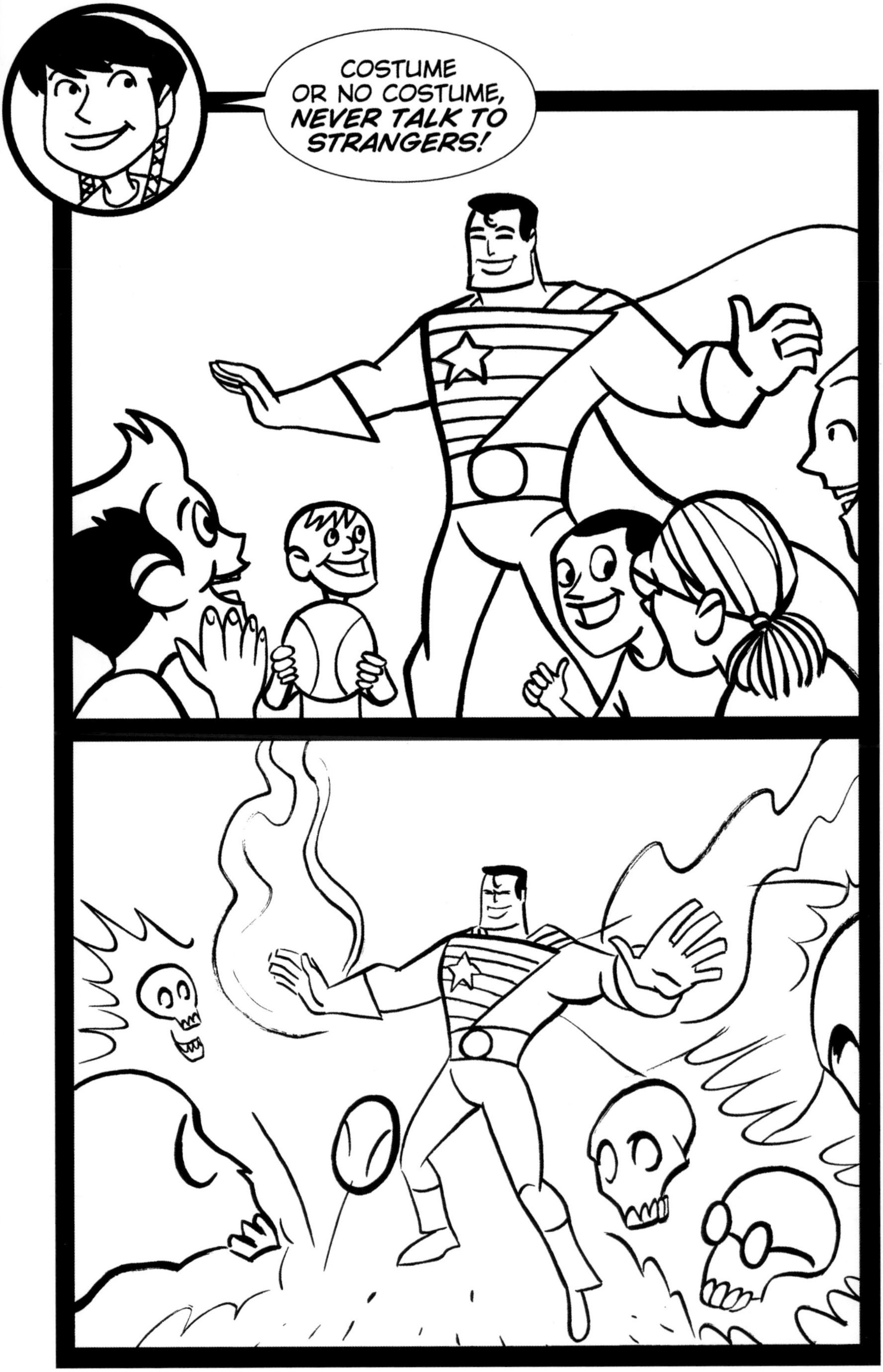
COSTUME OR NO COSTUME, NEVER TALK TO STRANGERS!

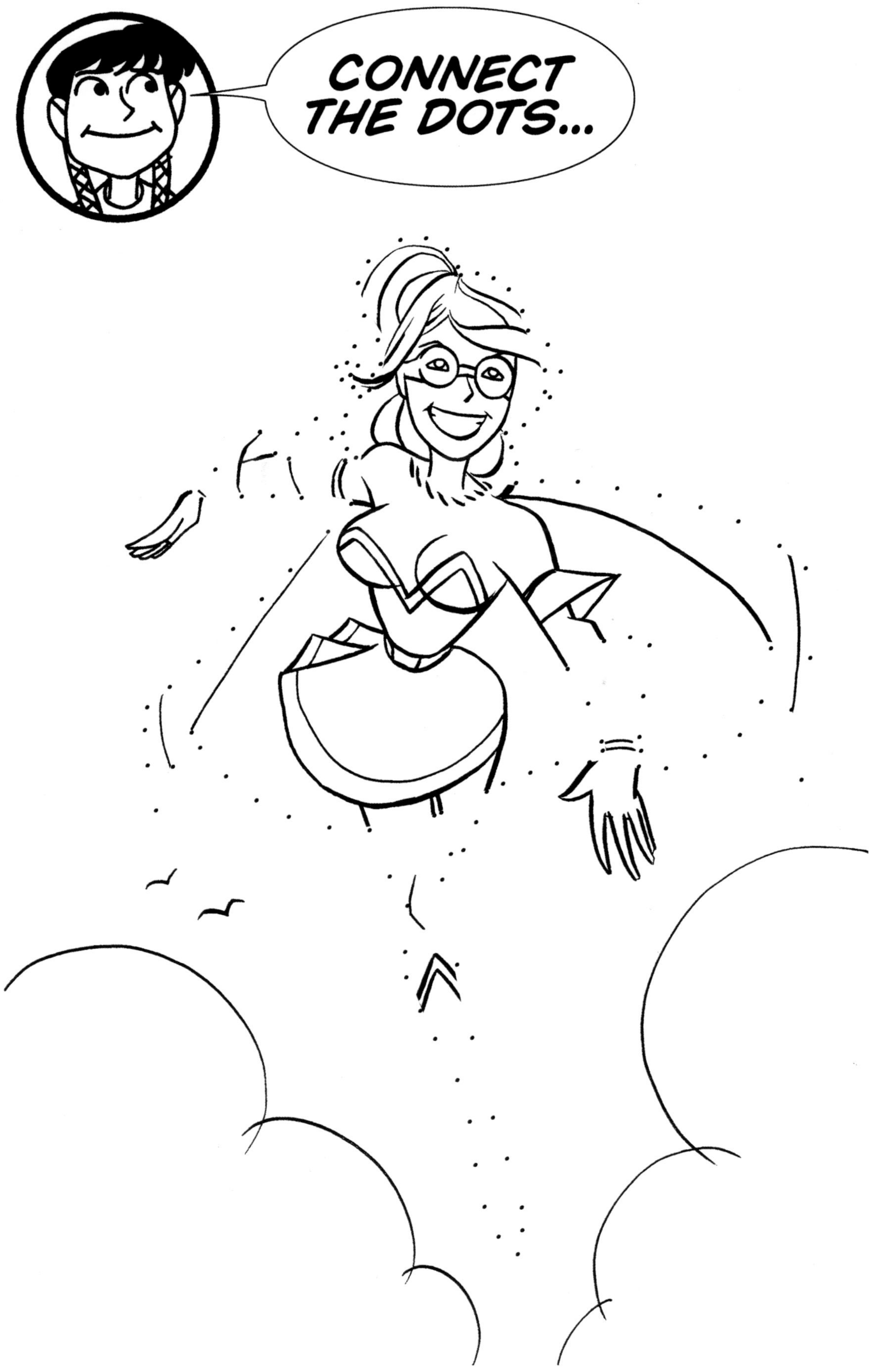
CONNECT THE DOTS...

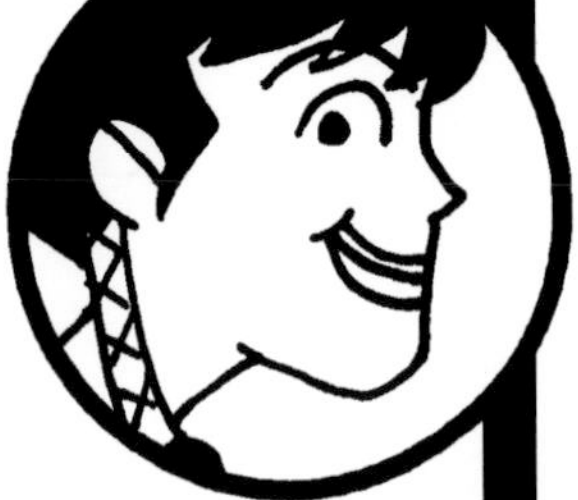

IT'S TIME TO PLAY...

FIND THE SUPER VILLAIN!

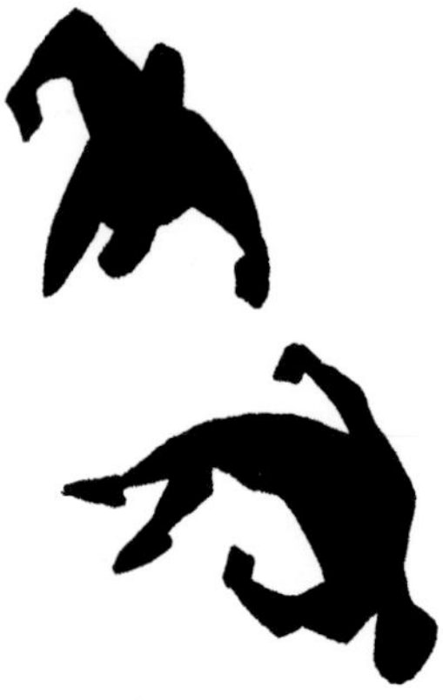

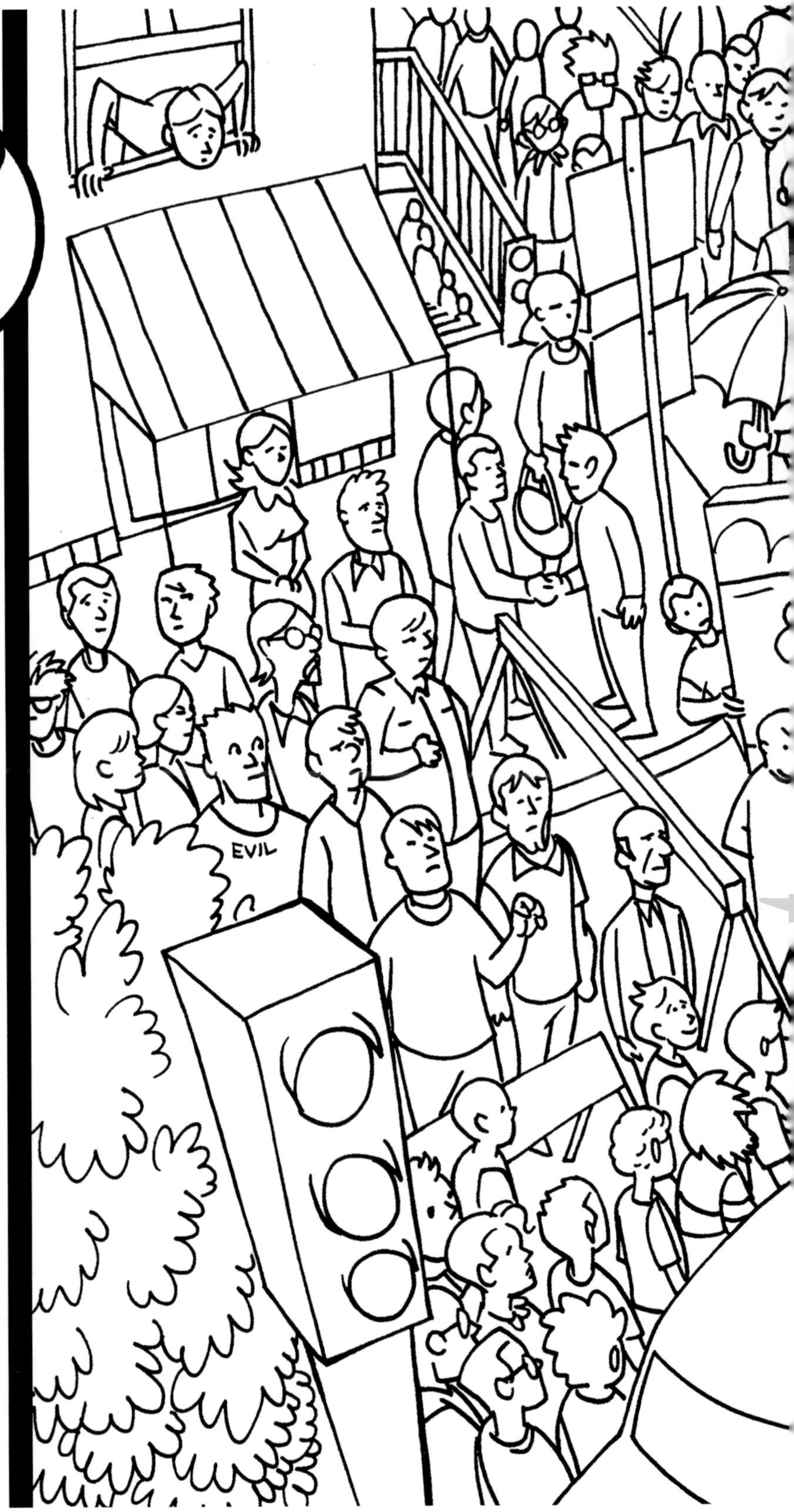
EVIL

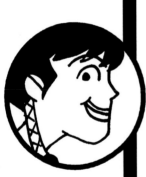

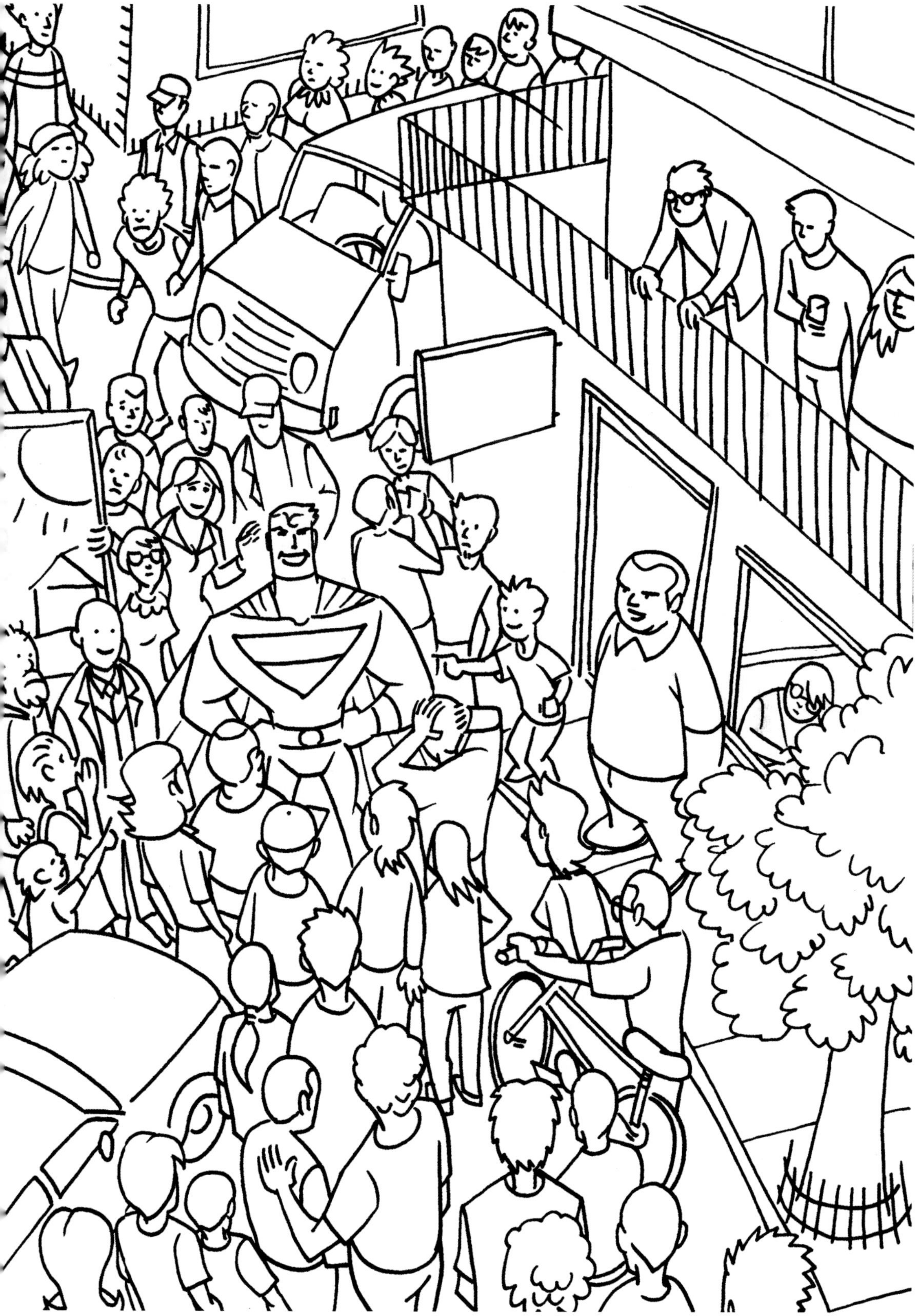

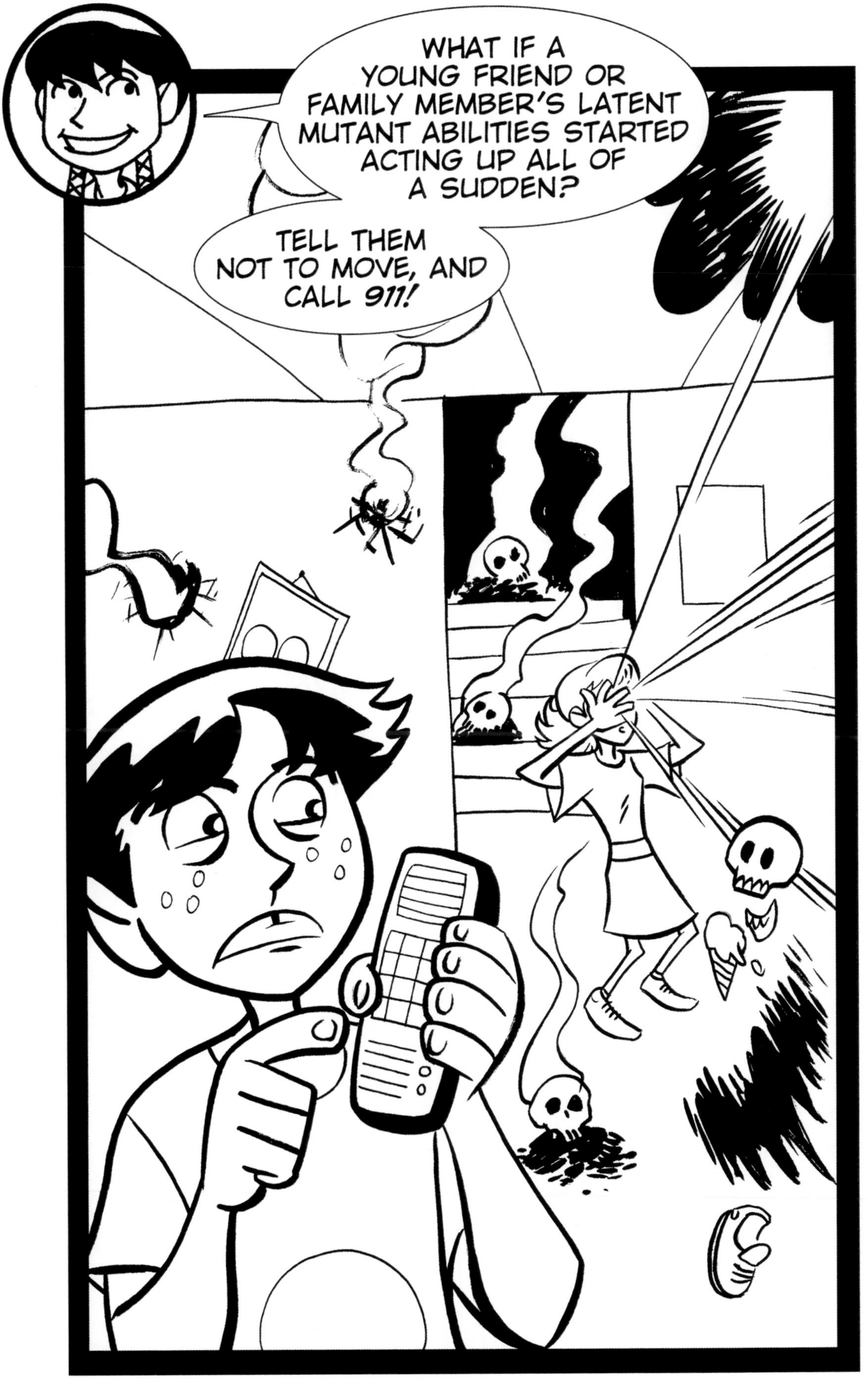
WHAT IF A YOUNG FRIEND OR FAMILY MEMBER'S LATENT MUTANT ABILITIES STARTED ACTING UP ALL OF A SUDDEN?
TELL THEM NOT TO MOVE, AND CALL 911!

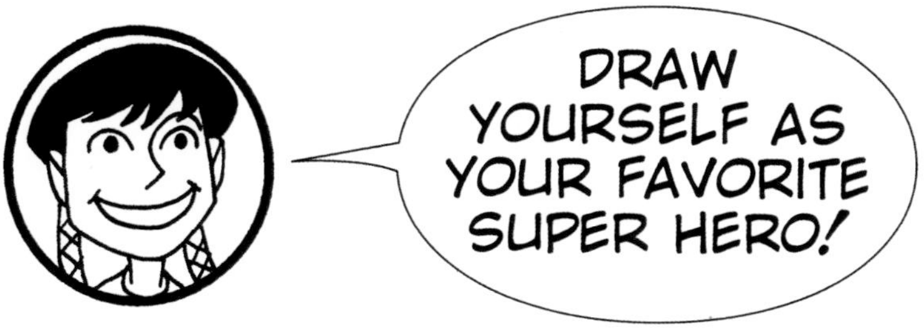
DRAW YOURSELF AS YOUR FAVORITE SUPER HERO!

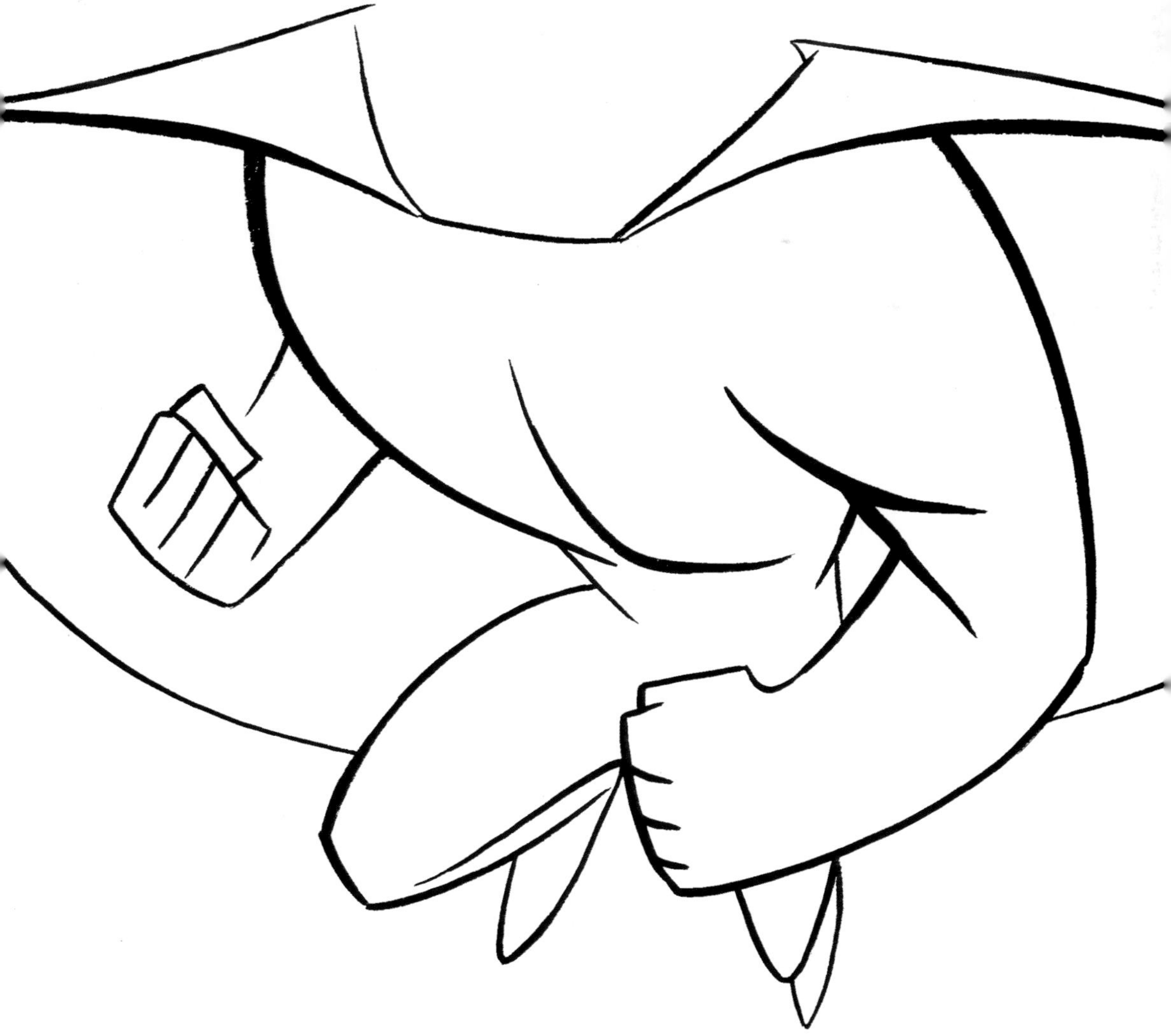

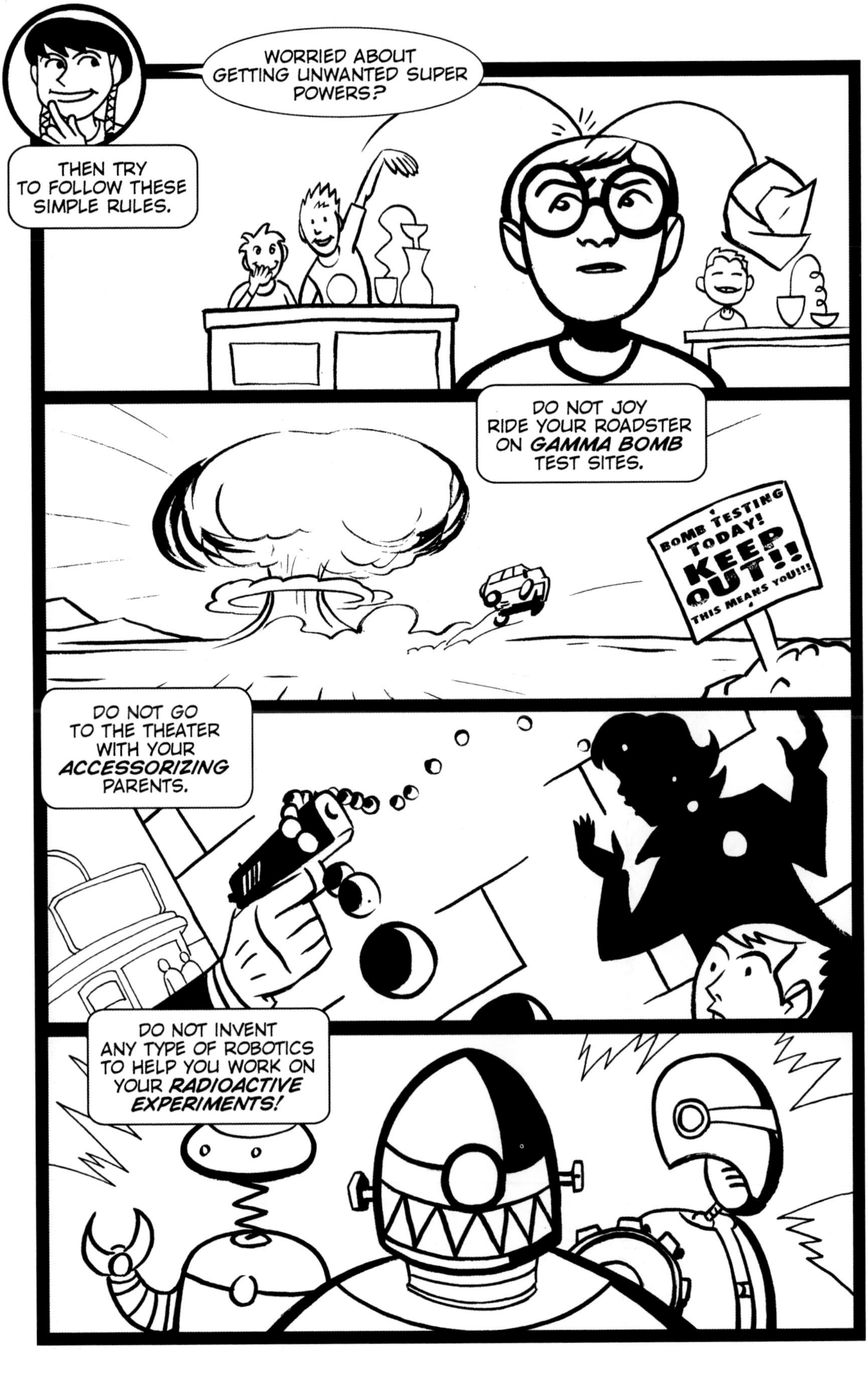
WORRIED ABOUT GETTING UNWANTED SUPER POWERS?
THEN TRY TO FOLLOW THESE SIMPLE RULES.
DO NOT JOY RIDE YOUR ROADSTER ON GAMMA BOMB TEST SITES.
BOMB TESTING TODAY! KEEP OUT!! THIS MEANS YOU!!!
DO NOT GO TO THE THEATER WITH YOUR ACCESSORIZING PARENTS.
DO NOT INVENT ANY TYPE OF ROBOTICS TO HELP YOU WORK ON YOUR RADIOACTIVE EXPERIMENTS!

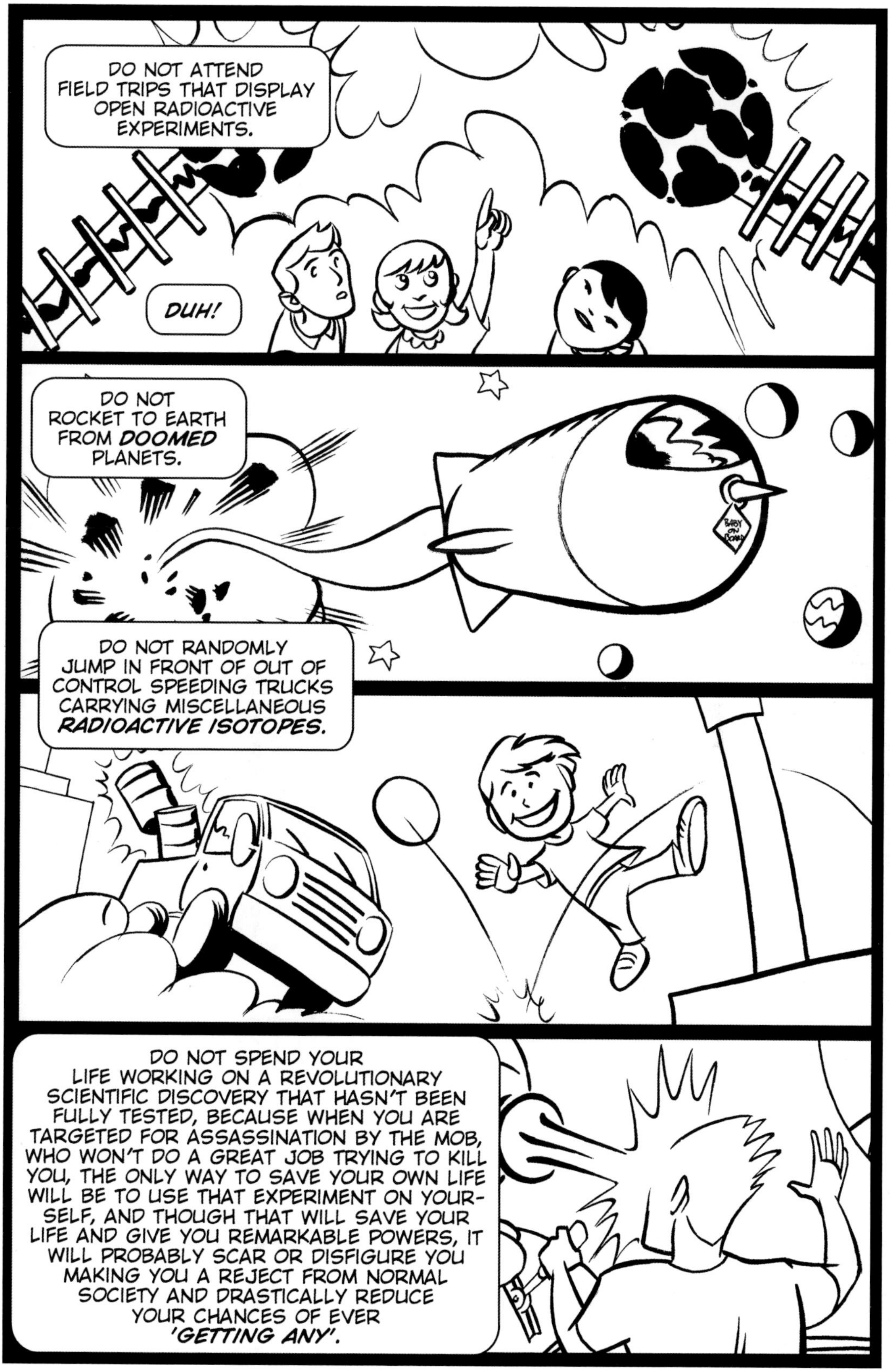
DO NOT ATTEND FIELD TRIPS THAT DISPLAY OPEN RADIOACTIVE EXPERIMENTS.
DUH!
DO NOT ROCKET TO EARTH FROM ***DOOMED*** PLANETS.
BABY ON BOARD
DO NOT RANDOMLY JUMP IN FRONT OF OUT OF CONTROL SPEEDING TRUCKS CARRYING MISCELLANEOUS ***RADIOACTIVE ISOTOPES.***
DO NOT SPEND YOUR LIFE WORKING ON A REVOLUTIONARY SCIENTIFIC DISCOVERY THAT HASN'T BEEN FULLY TESTED, BECAUSE WHEN YOU ARE TARGETED FOR ASSASSINATION BY THE MOB, WHO WON'T DO A GREAT JOB TRYING TO KILL YOU, THE ONLY WAY TO SAVE YOUR OWN LIFE WILL BE TO USE THAT EXPERIMENT ON YOURSELF, AND THOUGH THAT WILL SAVE YOUR LIFE AND GIVE YOU REMARKABLE POWERS, IT WILL PROBABLY SCAR OR DISFIGURE YOU MAKING YOU A REJECT FROM NORMAL SOCIETY AND DRASTICALLY REDUCE YOUR CHANCES OF EVER ***'GETTING ANY'.***

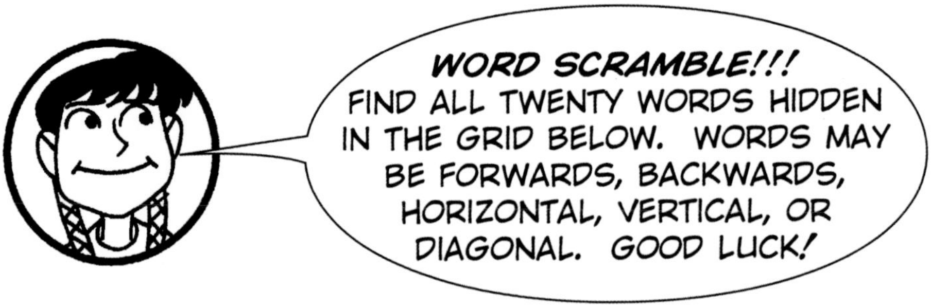

WORD SCRAMBLE!!!
FIND ALL TWENTY WORDS HIDDEN
IN THE GRID BELOW. WORDS MAY
BE FORWARDS, BACKWARDS,
HORIZONTAL, VERTICAL, OR
DIAGONAL. GOOD LUCK!

WORDS TO FIND:

1. HERO
2. VILLAIN
3. HEMPSTEAD ACT
4. DRAINERS
5. TRIPHAMMER
6. ZORA
7. COSTUME
8. REWARD
9. RETRO GIRL
10. DIAMOND
11. REPORT
12. MANIAC
13. SAFETY
14. STRANGER
15. ALTER EGO
16. SECRET IDENTITY
17. POWERS
18. CHESHIRE
19. POLICE
20. DANGER

L	I	V	E	R	D	E	G	G	B	S	W	Q	X	Z	K	A	C	Y	U
R	C	O	P	A	D	S	H	T	R	O	P	E	R	L	U	M	B	J	S
I	M	Z	X	C	A	Q	I	F	D	O	E	N	I	T	B	I	T	D	J
G	N	V	O	W	A	D	C	R	E	G	N	A	D	R	V	D	D	O	B
O	A	V	X	W	E	I	U	Y	F	R	W	E	C	I	L	O	P	S	C
R	Q	B	N	N	O	R	E	D	E	C	I	V	Q	P	U	L	P	B	M
T	U	E	T	R	E	T	I	Y	N	U	I	O	A	H	P	A	S	D	G
E	A	I	S	P	X	P	B	H	D	T	D	L	J	A	N	E	T	N	R
R	T	S	O	Q	A	W	C	V	S	Z	T	O	R	M	V	N	G	E	A
Y	R	R	C	R	I	M	E	H	E	E	R	M	R	M	A	P	W	V	H
T	I	E	R	O	D	I	R	T	R	B	H	O	U	E	B	A	B	I	L
H	P	N	C	U	M	E	R	E	K	R	P	C	C	R	R	C	U	T	F
G	L	I	F	U	G	C	G	D	W	E	E	R	K	D	E	P	M	C	B
I	L	A	M	N	P	O	W	E	R	S	J	G	E	P	L	N	S	A	I
F	G	R	A	F	T	T	R	H	O	W	D	D	N	O	M	A	I	D	W
I	T	D	N	H	O	E	N	F	A	B	I	A	T	A	F	G	A	A	I
N	S	T	I	I	R	N	R	L	I	C	E	S	T	E	R	W	O	E	F
N	W	E	A	R	B	T	W	C	E	N	I	N	T	D	E	T	C	T	I
R	E	D	C	O	U	R	A	G	E	O	U	Y	B	R	S	U	S	S	P
E	E	R	C	A	L	I	F	R	M	S	L	I	E	S	T	I	C	P	E
X	P	V	I	L	L	A	I	N	U	I	A	P	W	L	I	D	C	M	I
O	U	S	I	D	O	E	L	I	T	C	O	U	A	S	T	H	G	E	Q
U	I	K	R	R	E	D	F	O	S	R	X	J	R	U	M	P	E	H	D
O	V	E	E	R	T	H	L	A	O	Z	Y	B	E	R	O	W	N	S	D
O	G	H	G	P	A	O	C	P	C	S	A	R	O	Z	S	D	I	O	S

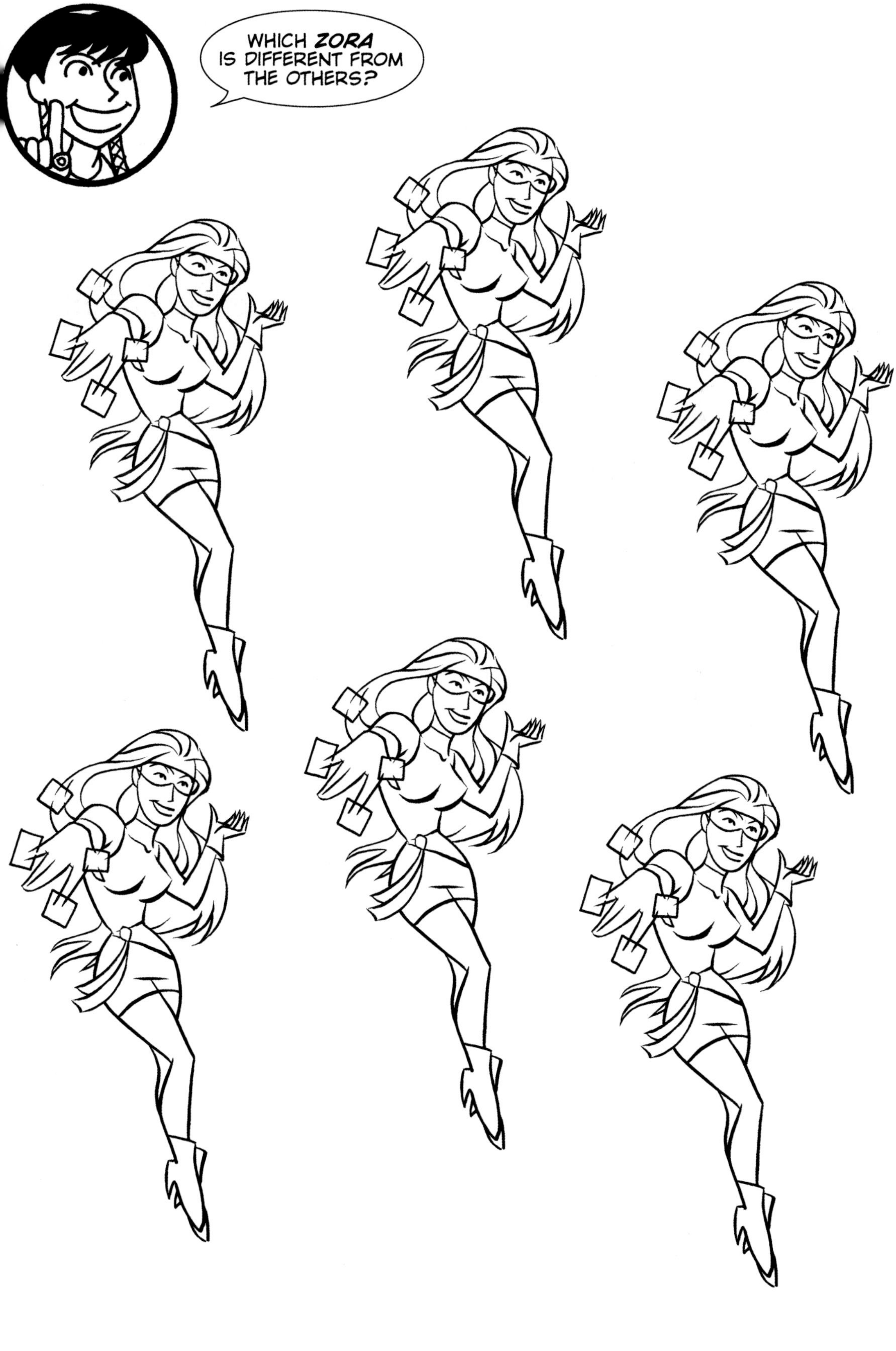
WHICH ***ZORA*** IS DIFFERENT FROM THE OTHERS?

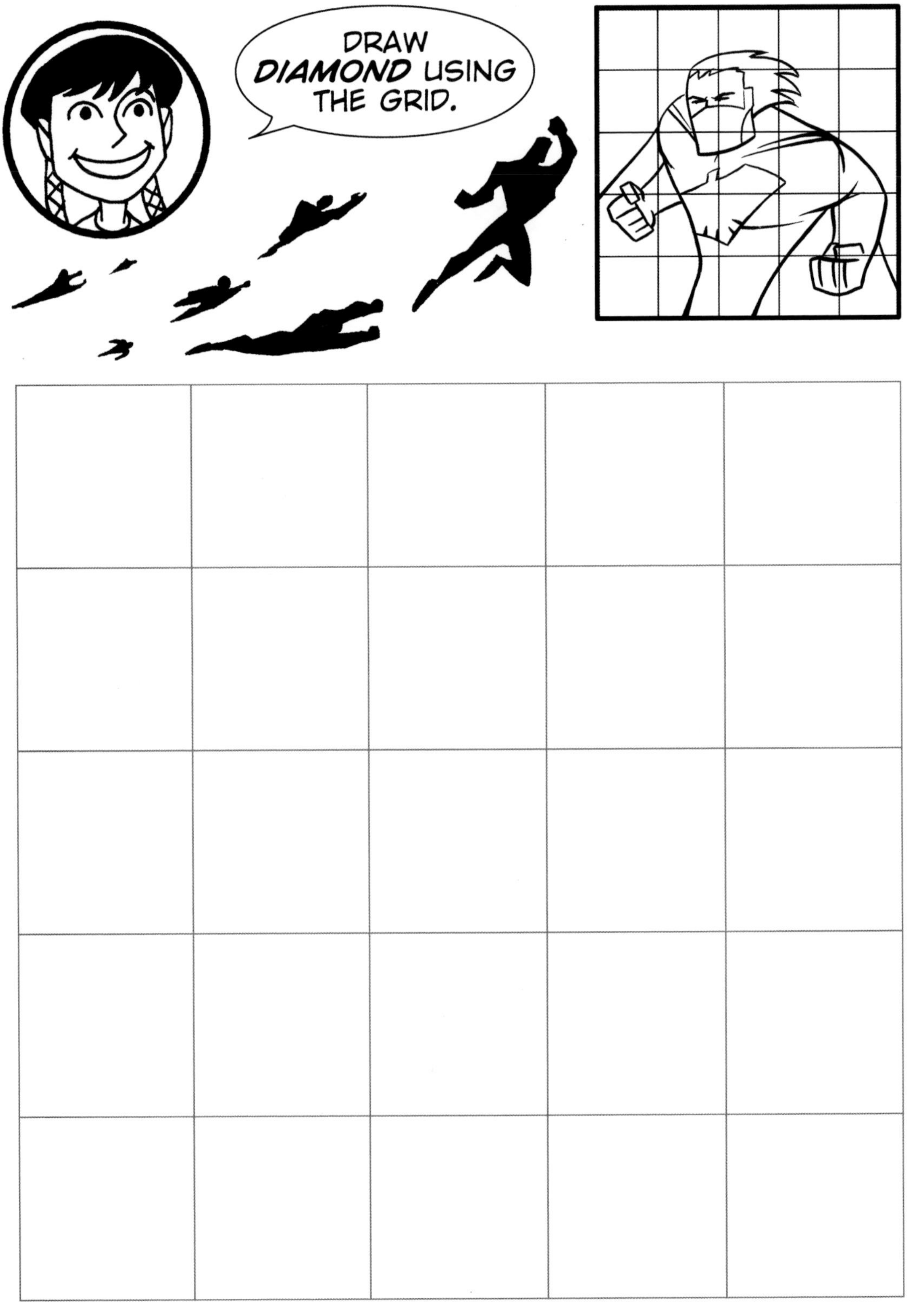
DRAW DIAMOND USING THE GRID.

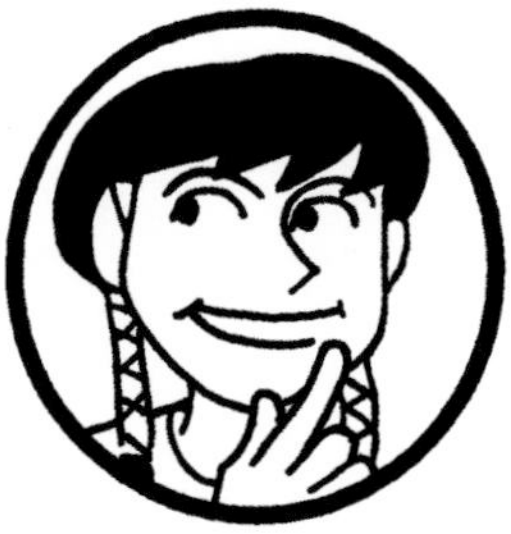

USE COMMON SENSE AND BE CAREFUL IN AN EMERGENCY. SOMETIMES, SCARY THINGS HAPPEN. IF YOU KNOW WHAT TO DO, HELP IS JUST A PHONE CALL AWAY!

- TRY TO STAY VERY CALM.
- PICK UP THE PHONE AND DIAL 9-1-1.
- WHEN THE OPERATOR ANSWERS, SPEAK CLEARLY AND LOUD ENOUGH SO HE OR SHE CAN UNDERSTAND YOU.
- TELL THE OPERATOR THE NATURE OF THE EMERGENCY.
- ANSWER QUESTIONS, AND DON'T HANG UP UNTIL YOU ARE TOLD TO BY THE OPERATOR!

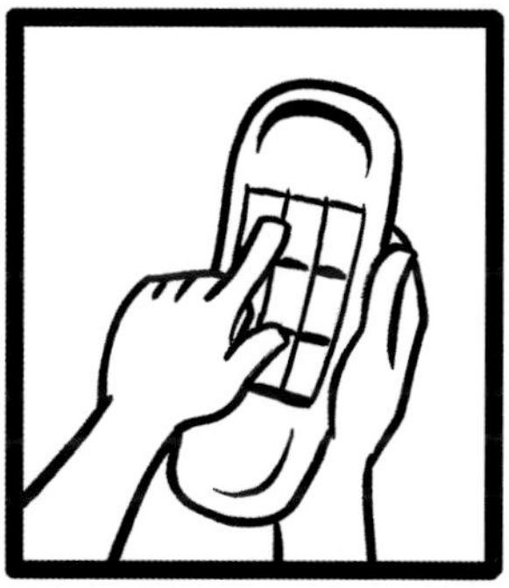

DIAL 911

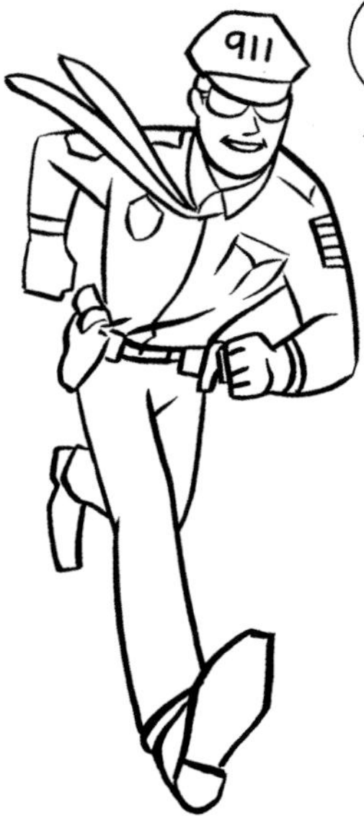
911
BE READY TO GIVE THE OPERATOR THE FOLLOWING INFORMATION.
YOU CAN FILL THIS OUT AND KEEP IT HANDY IN CASE OF A REAL EMERGENCY!

MY NAME: ____________________

MY ADDRESS: ____________________

____

MY PHONE: ____________________

MY AGE: ____________________

WHAT'S THE NATURE OF THE EMERGENCY: ____________________

____

ARE SUPER-POWERED BEINGS INVOLVED: ____________________

____

911 MEANS **HELP** IS ON THE WAY!

SUPER HEROES
and what they do!
An EDUCATIONAL COLORING and ACTIVITY BOOK!!

image® comics presents:

Compliments of the
POLICE DEPARTMENT!!!

BRIAN MICHAEL BENDIS
director of public wording

MICHAEL AVON OEMING
chief of ink

PAT GARRAHY
sanitation supervisor

www.jinxworld.com

POWERS

By popular demand (well, someone asked me at a convention once), we present to you the full script of the very first issue of *Powers*. I have not copy edited or corrected this in any way in an attempt to show it to you exactly the way Mike first saw it.

For aspiring writers: this is not the proper script format. This is the format I use when writing books I own.

This was prepared using the Final Draft screen writing program.

Enjoy!

ISSUE ONE
SCRIPT

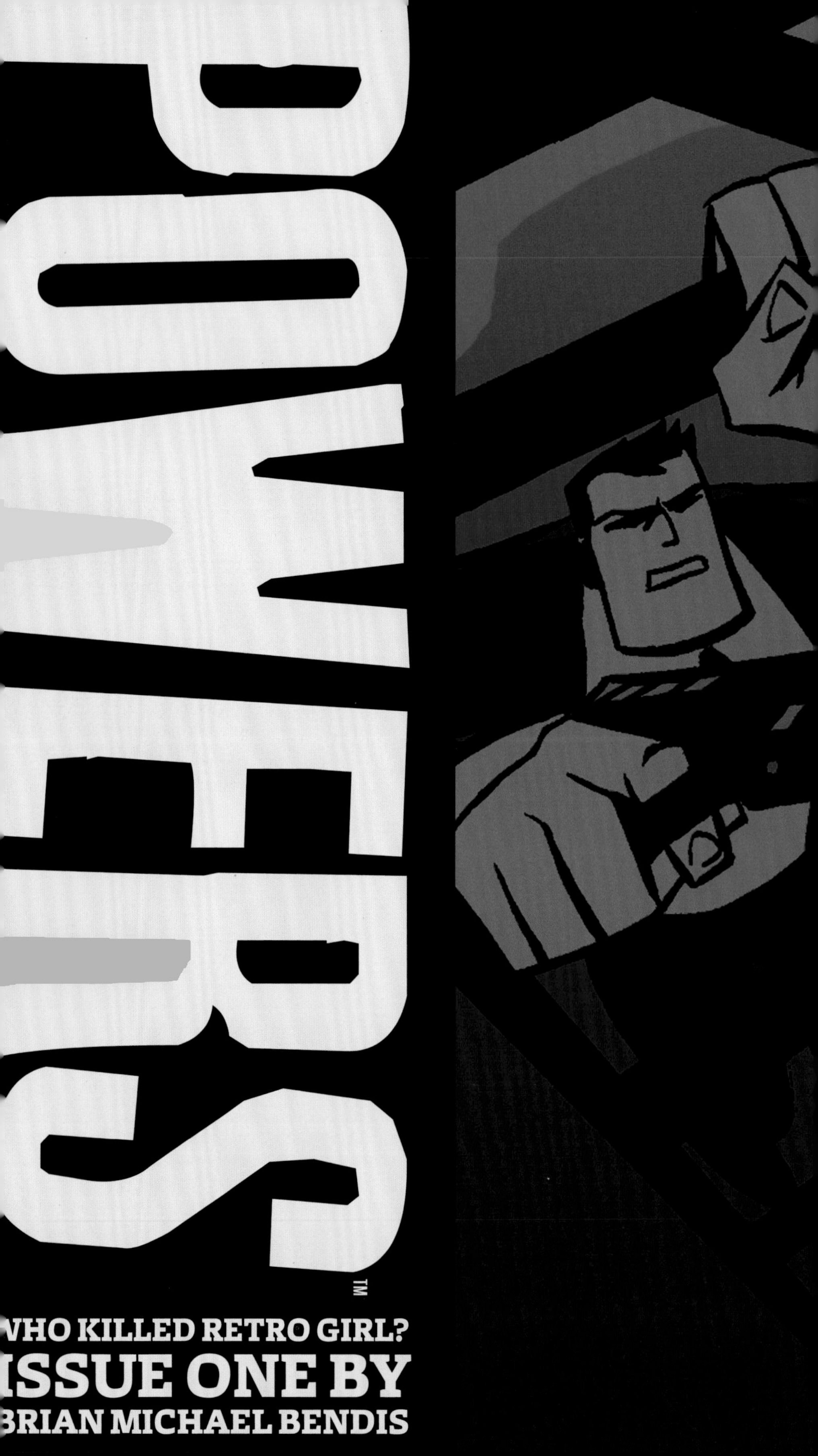
POWERS™
WHO KILLED RETRO GIRL?
ISSUE ONE BY
BRIAN MICHAEL BENDIS

POWERS

WHO KILLED RETRO GIRL?

ISSUE ONE

BY BRIAN MICHAEL BENDIS FOR MIKE AVON OEMING

PAGE IFC & 1 ~

THREE EQUAL SIZED PAGE LONG PANELS.

PANEL 1 ~ THE SKY LINE OF OUR NAMELESS CITY. SILHOUETTE TOWERS PIERCE A GRAY BLUE NIGHT SKY.

MIKE: THIS IS OUR WORLD AND WE MAKE THE RULES, BUT WHATEVER RULES WE MAKE HERE WE HAVE TO STICK TO.

THIS CITY IS AN EQUAL CHARACTER TO EVERY LEAD IN THE BOOK. IT HAS TO SMELL AND BREATHE AND TASTE LIKE IT.

2 ~ TIGHTER ON A INDISCRIMINATE BLOCK OF BUILDINGS. EACH HAS ITS OWN DISTINCT CHARACTERS.

3 ~ A SLIGHT WORM'S EYE OF A CITY STREET CORNER BELOW. IT'S A HOSTAGE CRIME SCENE OUTSIDE A SEMI-RUNDOWN APARTMENT BUILDING. GO AHEAD AND FIND PHOTO REFERENCE FOR IT.

POLICE CARS, EMERGENCY VEHICLES. YELLOW POLICE TAPE IS UP KEEPING THE CASUAL SMATTERING OF A CROWD AT BAY.

A COUPLE OF NEWS VANS ARE PARKED AS CLOSE AS THEY CAN GET.

COPS MILL ABOUT. THIS HAS BEEN GOING ON FOR QUITE A WHILE.

A NONDESCRIPT WHITE CAR HAS MADE ITS WAY TO THE FRONT OF THE SCENE.

PAGE 2 ~

FIVE EQUAL SIZED PAGE LONG PANELS.

EACH PANEL IS THE SAME SHOT ~ IT'S THE SAME CRIME SCENE THE SAME MOMENT AS THE LAST PANEL, BUT FROM THE TOP OF THE STAIRS OF THE APARTMENT BUILDING LOOKING DOWN ONTO THE STREET.

1 ~ THE WHITE CAR HAS STOPPED DEAD-CENTER OF THE PANEL. GETTING OUT OF THE CAR IS DETECTIVE CHRISTIAN WALKER WHO IS IMMEDIATELY SURROUNDED BY THE TOP COPS WHO WERE ALREADY ON THE SCENE.

THEY FOLLOW HIM AS THEY TALK.

CAPTAIN

WALKER.

WALKER

CAPTAIN...

CAPTAIN

WE BEEN CALLING...

(CONTINUED)

WALKER
I WAS AT THE MOVIES.

CAPTAIN
WE BEEN CALLING IS ALL...

WALKER
YEAH, WELL--WHAT IS THIS? I'M HOMICIDE.

CAPTAIN
YOU'RE A COP, AND THE GUY INSIDE WANTS YOU.

WALKER
WHO? WILLIAMS?

WILLIAMS
(THE NEGOTIATOR)
NO - HEY WALKER - NO, I SCREWED THE POOCH.

CAPTAIN
YOU COULDN'T NEGOTIATE SUPER-SIZING A HAPPY MEAL, YOU PIECE OF--!!!

WILLIAMS
COME ON CAPTAIN! I -
CAPTAIN
I'M GOING TO DEAL WITH YOUR INCOMPETENT ASS LATER. NO, THE GUY HOLDING
THE PLACE, HE ASKED FOR YOU.

WALKER
THE GUY INSIDE?
HE ASKED FOR ME?

CAPTAIN
AND YOU ONLY?

WALKER
HE ASKED FOR ME? WHO IS IT?
CAPTAIN
SOME SCHMUCK GOES BY THE NAME OF - OF FINCH.

WALKER
FINCH?

CAPTAIN

FINCH. WEARS A GREEN THING WITH A THING ON HIS BACK.

WALKER

FINCH?

CAPTAIN

HE'S GOT A LITTLE GIRL IN THERE. USED TO DATE THE MOM.

CAPTAIN

HE CAME OVER THEY GOT INTO A DOMESTIC...HE THREW HER OUT THE SECOND STORY
WINDOW AND BOARDED HIMSELF UP IN THERE.

WALKER

THE WOMAN? THE MOM?

CAPTAIN

TOOK HER DOWN TO MERCY? SHE WAS ALERT ENOUGH TO CALL US.

WALKER

FINCH? I DON'T KNOW A FINCH.

CAPTAIN

THEN THE DOCTORS AT THE HOSPITAL LEFT HER ALONE FOR SOMETHING LIKE TWO
SECONDS AND SHE VANISHED.

WALKER

VANISHED?

CAPTAIN

THE GUY INSIDE- THEY GUYS GOT ONE OF THOSE BACK PACK THINGS. GOT PINCHED
ON A COUPLE OF DEPARMENT STORE HOLD UPS...

WALKER

DOESN'T HELP ME...

CAPTAIN

WELL, HE KNOWS YOU AND HE'S GOT A GOD DAMN SEVEN YEAR OLD IN THERE. GUYS
BEEN CRYING LIKE A BABY FOR OVER AND HOUR.

WALKER

THE GIRL OR THE GUY?

CAPTAIN

THE GUY.

AND I'M NOT GOING TO HAVE THIS LOSER PSYCHO POP A GIRL ON THE SIX
O'CLOCK!! NOT TODAY. NOT ANY DAY.

WALKER

YEAH...WELL, COULD YA-

LET'S TRY TO MODULATE THE VOLUME, OK?

PAGE 3 -

1 - WALKER IS AT THE DOOR TO THE APARTMENT WITH HIS GUN OUT OF THE
HOLSTER. THERE ARE SWAT GUYS ALL AROUND. ONE IN PARTICULAR IS HUGGING
THE OTHER SIDE OF THE DOOR.

VARIANTS OF THIS SHOT IS REPEATED OVER AND OVER UNTIL THE SCENE IS OVER.

SETZER

HEY WALKER...

WALKER

HEY, OH HEY SETZER. WHAT'S GOING ON?

SETZER

WHERE YOU BEEN?

WALKER

MOVIES.

SETZER

WHAT YOU SEE?

WALKER

THE TRAILERS.

SETZER

WELL, THIS SUCKS, THIS GUY IN HERE SUCKS. FUCK THIS GUY.

GUY'S GOING TO DO THE DUTCH IS ALL.

THE KID'S WATCHING CARTOONS. HE KEEPS CRYIN' LIKE A...

WALKER

--LIKE A BABY. I HEARD.

2 - PAUSE AS THEY LISTEN TO THE GUYS FAINT RAMBLING.

3 -

WALKER (CONT'D)

(TO THE DOOR)

FINCH. IT'S DETECTIVE WALKER.

(CONTINUED)

4 - PAUSE.

5 -

WALKER (CONT'D)

FINCH? WHAT DID YOU CALL ME DOWN HERE FOR?

FLINCH

OOOOOH!!! EFF YOU WEAR YOU LIVE, WALKER!! YOU SHITHEEL!!!

WALKER

DO I KNOW YOU?

FLINCH

ITS FLINCH!! NOT FINCH, FLINCH!!! YOU EFFIN' ASSHOLES!!!

WALKER

OH!!! FLINCH!!! DUDE!! I'M SORRY MAN. THESE ASSHOLES DON'T KNOW ANYTHING OUT HERE.

PAGE 4 -

1 - SETZER LOOKS TO HIM AS IF TO SAY: "YOU KNOW THIS GUY."

WALKER LOOKS BACK AS IF TO SAY: "I HAVE NO FUCKING IDEA WHO THIS IS."

FLINCH

YEAH, WELL. I'VE HAD TO LISTEN TO THEIR BULLSHIT ALL DAY!!! STUPID, STUPID BULLSHIT!!

WALKER

YEAH, WELL, EVERYONE'S SORTA OUTTA SORTS TODAY-- SEEING AS YOU GOT A KID IN THERE.

2 - PAUSE.

3 -

WALKER (CONT'D)

NO MORE BULLSHIT, FLINCH. THIS IS THE GOODS-- IF YOU SEND THE KID OUT OF THERE WE CAN HAVE A TALK.

FLINCH

MOTHER'S A BITCH!!!

WALKER

PROBABLY IS, FLINCH, DOESN'T HAVE A THING TO DO WITH THE KID.

(CONTINUED)

4 - PAUSE.

5 -

WALKER (CONT'D)
RIGHT?

FLINCH
BITCH TOOK ALL MY MONEY!!

WALKER
SHE DID?

FLINCH
I WAS SAVING THAT MONEY TO FINISH MY GOD DAMN PROJECT AND NOW I'M GOING
TO...AAAARRGGHH!!!
IT'S ALL RUINED. DO YOU KNOW WALKER? DO YOU KNOW? YOU DON'T KNOW.

WALKER
I KNOW THAT THE GIRL IN THERE IS NOT THE ANSWER TO YOUR PROBLEMS.
AND I CAN'T EVEN THINK ABOUT HELPING YOU UNTIL YOU GIVE ME THE GIRL AND
START TALKING TO ME MAN TO MAN.
FACE TO FACE.

PAGE 5 -

1 - PAUSE

2 - SAME SHOT, BUT IT IS GETTING SLIGHTLY TIGHTER ON WALKER

WALKER
TODAY'S A SHIT DAY, FLINCH.
I SWEAR TO YOU - I SWEAR TO YOU I KNOW THAT KIND OF DAY.
BUT YOU GOTTA LOOK AT IT ANOTHER WAY. A DAY LIKE THIS - A DAY LIKE THIS IS
WHEN YOU
FIND OUT WHAT YOUR MADE OF. RIGHT?
ANY ASSHOLE CAN KEEP THEIR SHIT TOGETHER ON THE GOOD DAYS.
BUT THE SHIT DAY?
THAT'S WHEN YOU SHOW YOUR CHARACTER. TODAY'S THE DAY YOU SHOW EVERYONE
WHAT YOU'RE REALLY MADE OF.

3 - SAME BUT EVEN TIGHTER.

WALKER

AND I DAMN WELL KNOW YOU'RE MADE OF BETTER THAN THIS, RIGHT FLINCH?

YOU'RE GONNA LET A GIRL DRIVE YOU NUTS LIKE THIS?

ROLL IT OFF AND BE A MAN.

ALL YOU DONE IN YOUR LIFE - ALL THE STUFF THAT MADE YOU, YOU--

--AND YOU WANNA BE REMEMBERED AS SOME SHMUCK HELD A LITTLE GIRL?

HELL, NO. AM I RIGHT? THIS IS SILLY SHIT.

I SAY--I SAY WE FORGET THIS SILLY SHIT TODAY, YOU OPEN THE DOOR, THEN ME AND YOU, WHAT ARE WE GONNA DO?

WE'LL FIND THAT BITCH AND GET YOUR MONEY BACK IS WHAT.

4 - PAUSE. SAME EVEN TIGHTER

5 - SAME EVEN TIGHTER. THIS IS NOW A CLOSE UP ON WALKERS DETERMINED FACE. JUST ONE BEAD OF SWEAT.

FLINCH

AH DAMN IT...THIS IS JUST...

WALKER

YEAH, LET'S JUST OPEN THE DOOR AND...

PAGE 6 -

1 - BIG PANEL- HALF A PAGE

SPX: BOOM!!

WIDER SHOT OF HALLWAY. THE NOISE KNOCKS WALKER AND THE SWAT TEAM OFF THEIR FEET FOR A SECOND.

2 - IN A FURY OF ACTIVITY, LIKE A WELL OILED MACHINE, POWERS DIVES OUT OF THE WAY SO THE SWAT TEAM CAN BURST THE DOOR DOWN.

SPX: CRACK!!

3 - FROM POWERS P.O.V. POWER'S GUN IS OUT IN THE FOREGROUND. IN THE LIVING ROOM OF A TYPICAL CHEAP APARTMENT. RUBBLE IS FALLING DOWN IN THE CENTER OF THE ROOM. SWAT TEAM IS RUNNING ALL OVER THE APARTMENT.

4 - HE POINTS HIS GUN TO A GIANT HOLE IN THE CEILING.

5 - THEN POINTS DOWN TO THE FLOOR WHERE THE FALLING RUBBLE LANDS.

6 - THEN POINTS TO THE RIGHT, NOTHING BUT HALLWAY AND SWAT.

7 - THEN TO THE LEFT, A CUTE SEVEN-YEAR-OLD GIRL, CALISTA IS EATING
PEANUT BUTTER OUT OF A JAR AND WATCHING A CARTOON TAPE. SHE IS JUST NOW,
BROKEN FROM HER INTENSE TELEVISION WATCHING TO SEE THE LARGE GROUP OF
MEN COMING INTO THE ROOM.

8 - SAME. TIGHT ON WALKER LOOKING AT THE GIRL. SHES OK.

PAGE 7 -

2 EQUAL HALF PAGE PANELS

1 - WALKER AND A COUPLE OF SWAT LOOK UP THROUGH THE HOLE IN THE CEILING.
ALL WE CAN SEE IS A DOT WITH A SMOKE TRAIL.

2 - A HIGH BIRD'S EYE LOOK DOWN AT WALKER AND A COUPLE OF SWAT STARING UP
AT THE SKY. THEY LOOK LIKE LITTLE KIDS LOOKING UP AT A KITE.

SETZER

TOTAL ASSHOLE!

WALKER

WELL, HE FOUND ANOTHER WAY OUT.

SETZER

HE COULDN'T DO THAT THREE HOURS AGO? I MISSED THE GAME.

PAGES 8 - 9

DOUBLE PAGE SPREAD

PANELS 1-3 ARE PAGE LONG SLANTED SHOTS.

A STREET LEVEL WORM'S EYE VIEW OF WALKER AND SOME OF THE SWAT TEAM
COMING OUT THE FRONT DOOR OF THE APARTMENT BUILDING. THEY ARE LOOKING
UP TOWARDS THE DOT AND SMOKE TRAIL THAT POPPED OUT OF THE ROOF OF THE
APARTMENT. IT IS A LITTLE BIGGER NOW.

3 - SAME. WE ARE FOLLOWING WALKER AND THE COPS AS THEY FOLLOW FLINCH LIKE
HE IS A KITE IN THE AIR. THEY ARE NOW DOWN THE STAIRS IN THE MIDDLE OF THE
STREET.

THERE ARE MANY GUNS TRAINED ON THE DOT AND TRAIL AS IT IS NOW COMING
TOWARDS THEM. WALKER HAS TURNED TOWARDS THE READER BUT IS LOOKING
ANNOYED AT THE OTHER COPS.

WALKER

WHOAH WHOAH WHOAH!

DO NOT SHOOT!!

SETZER

WHAT?

WALKER

WHO KNOWS WHAT HE- HE COULD HAVE A NUCLEAR DEVISE STRAPPED TO HIS BACK FOR ALL WE KNOW!! CHRIST SAKE!!

4 - SAME. THE GUNS ARE STILL TRAINED ON FLINCH, WHO WE CAN CLEARLY SEE. HE IS HEADING TOWARDS THE GROUND. FEET FIRST.

FLINCH IS A SKINNY LOSER IN A GREEN JUMP SUIT WITH A CRAPPY VERSION OF THE ROCKETEER BACK PACK STRAPPED TO HIS BACK.

HIS BACK PACK IS PUTTING...

SPX: PUT PUT PUT

THIS IS SLOWING FLINCH'S DESCENT DOWN, BUT HE ISN'T IN CONTROL OF HIS LANDING.

FLINCH

OW...OW...OW...HO NO...

5 - WORM'S EYE VIEW OF WALKER, THE COPS AND THE PRESS. THEY ALL FLINCH AS FLINCH HITS THE GROUND WITH A THUD.

SPX: THUD.

6 - THE BILL MURRAY I HAVE BEEN SLIMED SHOT FROM GHOSTBUSTERS. FLINCH IS LAYING ON HIS BACK PACK, IN PAIN

FLINCH

SERIOUSLY...OW!

PAGE 10 -

1 - THE EDDIE MURPHY "IS THERE A PROBLEM OFFICER'S?" SHOT FROM TRADING PLACES. TIGHT ON FLINCH'S FACE WHICH NOW HAS EIGHT GUNS TO IT.

2 - WIDE SHOT. THE STREET IS A CHAOS OF ACTIVITY. IN THE FOREGROUND FLINCH IS BEING PUT INTO AN AMBULANCE. WALKER HAS CAUGHT UP JUST BEFORE THEY SLIDE HIM IN. IN THE BACKGROUND WE CAN SEE A COUPLE OF SPECIAL SWAT TEAM MEMBERS PUTTING HIS BACK PACT INTO A TRANSPARENT HIGH TECH CONTAINER. THE PRESS IS EATING IT ALL UP.

WALKER

HOLD ON A SEC, GUYS.

3 - TWO SHOT OF WALKER. HE IS IN FLINCH'S FACE.

WALKER

HEY! YOU ASSHOLE, WHAT'S WITH YOU, MAN?

FLINCH

WHAT?

WALKER

I'VE NEVER SEEN YOU BEFORE IN MY LIFE? WHAT IS WITH YOU CALLING ME DOWN
HERE TO DEAL WITH ALL YOUR BULLSHIT?

4 - TIGHT ON FLINCH, IN PAIN AND A LITTLE SCARED. WALKER IS CASTING A
SHADOW OVER HIM.

FLINCH

IT WAS- IT WAS WOLFE...HE...

5 - WALKER FREOM FLINCH'S P.O.V.

WALKER

WHAT?

6 - SAME AS FOUR.

FLINCH

IT WAS WOLFE!! HE - HE SAID...WHEN I WAS HOLD UP IN BLAIR GREEN WITH WOLFE
AND THOSE GUYS...

HE SAID - HE SAID IF THE SHIT EVER GOT TO THICK WE SHOULD ALWAYS ASK FOR YOU
- D-D-D-DETECTIVE CHRISTIAN WALKER...

7 - SAME AS FIVE.

WALKER

WHY?

8 - SAME AS FOUR.

FLINCH

HE SAID YOU WERE SOFT - SOFT ON GUYS WITH POWERS.

9 - SAME AS FIVE. WALKER IS REALLY MIFFED AT THIS.

PAGE 11 -

1 - SAME AS PANEL 2 OF LAST PAGE. A TWO SHOT OF FLINCH AND WALKER. BUT
WALKER IS GRABBING FLINCH BY THE COLLAR AND IS READY TO HIT HIM. THE
OTHER PEOPLE REACT, TRYING TO STOP HIM.

WALKER

WELL, YOU TELL WOLFE THAT WHEN HE'S UP FOR PAROLE IN 4 YEARS AND 3
MONTHS!!

WALKER

YOU TELL HIM THAT I'LL BE THERE AT THE HEARING AND HE'LL SEE HOW SOFT I
AM!!

FLINCH

PLEASE - NO, DON'T.

AMBULANCE DRIVER

DETECTIVE, PLEASE!!

CAPTAIN

WHAT'S GOING ON HERE?

2 - MID SHOT OF WALKER. HE HAS COMPOSED HIMSELF AND NOW HE IS A LITTLE
ASHAMED OF HIMSELF. HIS CAPTAIN IS STANDING BEHIND HIM.

CAPTAIN

WALKER, WHAT'S WRONG WITH YOU?

THE PRESS IS ALL OVER THIS.

WALKER

IT'S DONE. LET'S NOT MAKE A THING OF IT.

CAPTAIN

A THING? I'LL SEE YOU BACK AT THE STATION.

3 - WALKER IS WATCHING HIS CAPTAIN KISS THE MEDIA'S ASS AS HE GOES TO
LEAVE THE OTHER COPS CLEAN UP THE MESS.

IN THE BACKGROUND IS THE FRONT OF THE APARTMENT BUILDING. A SWAT TEAM
MEMBER IS HOLDING THE GIRL.

SWAT 1

WALKER...

4 - THE SWAT TEAM MEMBER HOLDING THE GIRL COMES UP TO WALKER.

SWAT 1 (CONT'D)

HAPPY BIRTHDAY!

WALKER

WHAT IS THIS?

SWAT 1

LIEUTENANT SAYS SHE'S YOURS...

WALKER

HOW SO?

SWAT 1

YOUR COLLAR. DEM'S THE RULES...

5 - TIGHT ON CALISTA'S ADORABLE FACE. SHE IS SAD AND CONFUSED.

6 - HER POINT OF VIEW, WALKER LOOKS DOWN AT HER.

PAGE 12 -

1 - EXTERIOR SHOT OF THE POLICE STATION. AN OLD FASHIONED BUILDING ON
THE OUTSIDE. SOMETHING OUT OF A 50'S CRIME MOVIE. THE LIT BALL LIGHT
OUTSIDE THAT SAYS POLICE STATION.

WALKER

YES HELLO? I'VE BEEN ON HOLD FOR--

LISTEN THIS IS DETECTIVE CHRISTIAN WALKER...HOMI-HOMICIDE. YES.

WHAT? NO, I NEED YOUR HELP. I - WHAT? NO. IS THIS SOCIAL SERVICES? WELL,
I HAVE A YOUNG--WHAT?

NO. NO I DIDN'T HEAR. NO.

2 - THE INSIDE OF THE HOMICIDE SQUAD ROOM. IT'S A HUSTLE AND A BUSTLE.
IT'S A TYPICAL STATION HOUSE, GO GET YOUR PHOTO REFERENCE YOU LAZY
FUCKER.

PEOPLE HUSTLE ABOUT, BUT...

BIG BUT.

THERE IS SOMETHING A LITTLE OFF ABOUT IT. WE CAN TELL THAT PEOPLE WITH
SUPERPOWERS EFFECT EVERY PART OF THE STATION.

THERE ARE BULLETPROOF GLASS CAGES AND SOME PEOPLE HAVE WEIRD ARMOR
ON. THERE ARE POSTERS ON THE WALL. ONE OF THEM IS RETRO GIRL SAYING TO
BUCKLY YOUR SEAT BELT. THIS BROUGHT TO YOU BY RETRO GIRL INC. AND CITY
COUNCIL FOR A BETTER TOMORROW.

WALKER (CONT'D)

WHEN DID THIS HAPPEN? NO, I HAVEN'T SEEN THE NEWS. NO, I DIDN'T--WERE PEOPLE HURT?

GONE, GONE?

THE BUILDING IS JUST - IT'S GONE?

FIREBALL? FIREBALL - GOOD LORD! YEAH, I THOUGHT THAT GUY WAS...NO.

OK. WELL, I AM REALLY SORRY TO - THAT'S HORRIBLE. IT...

WELL, I HAVE THIS LITTLE GIRL AND...

HOW IS THAT GOING TO? WELL, I CAN'T. I UNDERSTAND THERE'S NOBODY THERE.

YES, I UNDERSTAND THAT THERE IS NO THERE ANYMORE.

HEY, I SAID I - YES I DO.

I AM A HOMICIDE DETECTIVE AND I AM IN THE MIDDLE OF FIFTEEN OPEN - NO I CAN'T.

3 - TIGHTER ON WALKER. HE IS LOSING HIS BATTLE ON THE PHONE.

WALKER (CONT'D)

NO - NO I CAN'T.

'CAUSE YOU'RE SUPPOSED TO - CAN'T YOU SEE I AM TRYING TO DO THE BEST THING FOR THE--

DAMN.

4 - THE CONVERSATION HAS OBVIOUSLY ENDED.

5 - RUBBING HIS FACE IN FRUSTRATION WITH ONE HAND, WALKER DANGLES THE PHONE OVER THE RECEIVER.

6 - THEN HANGS IT UP.

7 - TIGHT ON THE GIRL LOOKING AT THE PHONE

8 - THEN AT WALKER.

9 - WALKER IS INTERNALLY CONFUSED AS TO WHAT TO DO NOW.

PAGE 13 -

1 - HE LOOKS AT THE GIRL.

2 - SHE LOOKS BACK. INNOCENT EYES. CHILDLIKE EXPRESSION OF CURIOSITY.

CALISTA

WHAT'S A CLITORIS?

3 - WALKER JUST STARES AT HER BLANKLY.

4 - SAME.

WALKER
UH - I DON'T KNOW.

5 - CALISTA LOOKING AT THE FLOOR. TALKING TO HERSELF.

CALISTA
HOW COME NOBODY KNOWS THAT?
I ASK EVERYONE AND NOBODY HAS A CLUE.

PAGE 14 - 15
DOUBLE PAGE SPREAD.

A ROW OF LITTLE PANELS ON TOP. A LONG DOUBLE PAGE SPREAD OF THE ROOM IN THE MIDDLE AND ANOTHER ROW OF LITTLE PANELS ON THE BOTTOM.

1 - WALKER.

WALKER
YOU HUNGRY?

2 - WALKER REACHES INTO HIS DESK AND PULLS OUT A BOWL.

CALISTA
TOTALLY. LAST NIGHT MY MOM MADE THESE PORK CHOPS LIKE SHE SAW ON THE FOOD CHANNEL,

3 - THEN ANOTHER. THEN SILVERWARE.

CALISTA (CONT'D)
BUT SHE LIKE TOTALLY BURNED THE SHIT OUT OF THEM. AND I HATE PEAS. YOU LIKE PEAS?

4 - THEN A BIG BOX OF FRUITY CHOCO CRUNCHIES SERIAL.

WALKER
I DO NOT LIKE PEAS.

5 - CALISTA AMAZED.

CALISTA

YOU KEEP CEREAL IN YOUR DESK?

6 - WALKER OPENS THE BOX AND POURS THE DRY CEREAL IN.

WALKER

YEP.

7 - CALISTA IMPRESSED.

CALISTA

THAT IS THE COOLEST THING I'VE EVER SEEN IN MY LIFE.

8 - WALKER HANDS HER BOWL OF DRY CEREAL AND HOLDS HIS.

WALKER

WELL, YOU'RE YOUNG.

9 - BIG PANEL!! - WALKER AND THE GIRL WALK THROUGH HOMICIDE
DEPARTMENT. A WAIST LEVEL LOOK AROUND THIS UNIQUE DEPARMENT.

CALISTA

HEY, YOU WHAT?

WALKER

WHAT?

CALISTA

MY MOMMY SAYS THAT I CAN EXPRENTIATE MYSELF ANY WAY I WANT.

WALKER

EXPRENTIATE?

CALISTA

SHE SAYS HER DADDY - HE USED TO LIKE SMACK HER EVERYTIME SHE TALKED
AND THAT I CAN TALK ABOUT WHATEVER I WANT BECAUSE SHE SAID HE WAS AN
ASSHOLE.

WALKER

YOU DON'T SAY?

CALISTA

DO YOU KNOW HIM?

WALKER
WHO?

LITTLE PANELS.
10 - WALKER AND CALISTA AT THE VENDING MACHINES.

CALISTA
MY MOM'S DAD?

WALKER
DO I KNOW HIM? NO.

CALISTA
OH. I THINK HE KILLED SOMEBODY OR SOMETHING, THAT'S WHY I ASKED IS ALL.

11 - WALKER LOOKS DOWN PUZZLED AT HER. HE HAS A MILK.

WALKER
HE DID?

CALISTA
I THINK. OR SOMEBODY KILLED HIM OR
SOMETHING, I DON'T KNOW.

WALKER
YOU'RE TOO LITTLE TO BE THINKING ABOUT THINGS LIKE THAT.

12 - CALISTA LOOKS AT HER BOWL OF DRY CEREAL.

CALISTA
YOU WATCH CARTOONS?

WALKER
USED TO.

13 - CALISTA LOOKS UP.

CALISTA
DO YOU SEE THIS THING THAT SOMETIMES THE BACKGROUNDS AND THE PEOPLE
DON'T LOOK RIGHT?

14 - WALKER IS LOOKING ACROSS THE STATION HOUSE. THERE IS COMMOTION.

PAGE 16 ~

ALL THE KUTTER SHOTS ARE WIDE. FROM WALKERS POV.

KUTTER, 20'S, IS A YOUNG SEVERELY AMBITIOUS ROOKIE DETECTIVE WHOSE IDEALS AND ALLEGIANCES MAY OR MAY NOT BE ON THE UP AND UP.

HE LOOKS JUST LIKE BENJAMIN BRATT FROM LAW AND ORDER

1 ~ HE HAS BROUGHT IN A VILLAIN...YOUR CHOICE MIKE.

VILLAIN

YOU ONLY THINK YOU CAN HOLD ME!! DO YOU UNDERSTAND? DO YOU? YOUR PLANE OF EXISTENCE IS ONLY ONE OF...

KUTTER

OH, CALM DOWN, BIG TIME!

IT'S OVER. YOU KNOW IT'S OVER. I KNOW IT'S OVER. SUCK IT UP.

2 ~ WALKER IS WATCHING.

WALKER

HOW SO?

CALISTA

SOMETIMES THE BACKGROUNDS ARE ALL COOL LOOKING AND NICELY COLORED IN OR SOMETHING. BUT THE PEOPLE AREN'T. THEY ~ THEY ARE JUST FLAT LOOKING. SUCKY.

3 ~ THE VILLAIN TRIES TO ESCAPE AND THEY HIT HIM WITH SOMETHING THAT IS SIMILAR TO A CATTLEPROD.

VILLAIN

YOU WILL NEVER LEARN!! YOU WILL NEVER...!!

4 ~ WALKER IS WATCHING THIS AND NOT THE GIRL.

WALKER

NEVER NOTICED.

5 ~ THEY THROW HIM IN THE TANK.

CALISTA

NEVER NOTICED? IT DRIVES ME UP THE DAMN WALL IS ALL. WHY DO THEY DO THAT?? WHY CAN'T THEY PAINT THE PEOPLE AS NICE AS THEY PAINT THE SKY?

COP

KUTTER, CAN YOU KEEP IT UNDER CONTROL OVER THERE? I'M TRYING TO READ!!

KUTTER

GOOD LUCK, HOT SHOT.

6 - KUTTER SEE THAT WALKER IS WATCHING HIM.

WALKER

YEAH, I DON'T - I DON'T KNOW.

7 - KUTTER SMILES THERE IS SOMETHING BAD BETWEEN THE TWO.

PAGE 17 -

1 - WALKER IS FOCUSED BACK ON THE GIRL. THEY ARE WALKING BACK TO THE DESK.

WALKER (CONT'D)

HEY, WHY DO YOU HAVE TO SWEAR EVERY THIRTY SECONDS?

CALISTA

SWEAR?

WALKER

YOU KNOW...

CALISTA

I TOLD YOU, MY MOM...

WALKER

YOUR MOM DOESN'T LET YOU TALK THAT WAY, YOU AIN'T FOOLING ME.

2 - THEY ARE BACK AT THE DESK. CALISTA SITTING IN HER LITTLE CHAIR.

CALISTA

SHE AIN'T COMIN' BACK TO GET ME IS SHE?

3 - WALKER IN HIS SEAT. SERIOUS.

WALKER

I DON'T KNOW.

4 - SHE LOOKS AT HER CEREAL.

CALISTA

DAMN SUCKY CARTOONS.

5 - TIGHT ON THE BOWL FULL OF LITTLE 'R'S FLOATING IN MILK.

PAGE 18 -

SIX PAGE LONG PANELS

A VERY TIGHT CLOSE UP OF DEENA PILGRIM. SHE IS TELLING AN ANECDOTE.

THE SHOT EVENTUALLY PULLS OUT TO A WIDE SHOT OF THE CAPTAIN'S OFFICE. HE LISTENS INTENTLY.

1 -

DEENA

HA! YEAH--THAT'S A FUNNY STORY ACTUALLY.

I WAS ON SWAT FOR I DON'T KNOW - LIKE A WEEK.

THERE WAS THIS GUY HOLD - HE HOLD HIMSELF UP IN SOME GOVERNMENT OFFICE.

CAPTAIN

DID HE HAVE...?

DEENA

WHAT? NO. JUST A GUY.

GUY WITH A BEEF. GUY WITH A SCREW LOOSE HOLDS HIMSELF UP IN A BUILDING. HIS MOMMY DIDN'T SPANK HIM ENOUGH AS A KID, I DON'T KNOW.

BUT HE HOLDS HIMSELF UP IN THERE SO LONG

WE HAD TO BE RELIEVED FOR A SECOND SHIFT.

CAPTAIN

THAT'S A LONG...

DEENA

TOTALLY. SO, THE SHIFTS OVER. WE DROP OUR GEAR IN THE VAN AND WE ALL HEAD OVER TO THIS THAI PLACE THAT WE HAD BEEN STARING AT FROM ACROSS THE STREET FOR THE LAST BILLION HOURS STRAIGHT.

2 -

NOW THE WHOLE RESTAURANT IS FILLED WITH SWAT TEAM GUYS. SO WE'RE EATIN' OUR APPETIZERS AND KICKIN' BACK WHEN MY PARTNER DAVE...

HE POINTS OUT THE WINDOW TO THE PAYPHONE.

THE GUY - THE GUY WE WERE WAITIN' ON THE GUY THE NEGOTIATOR HAD SPENT LIKE A BILLION HOURS TRYING TO TALK OUT OF THE BUILDING UNTIL HE STOPPED TALKING...

THE GUY IS RIGHT THERE MAKIN' A PHONE CALL.

CAPTAIN

YOU RECOGNIZED THE GUY?

DEENA

WELL, WE ALL DID ONCE WE SEEN HIM.

THEY HAD A PIC THEY PASSED AROUND SO WE KNEW WHO TO TAKE DOWN IF IT
CAME TO THAT.

SO LIKE - LIKE THE WHOLE RESTAURANT JUST STARES AT HIM IN DISBELIEF.
AND THEN ALL AT ONCE - LIKE ALL AT THE SAME TIME...WE POUR OUT--

THE WHOLE RESTAURANT POURS OUT ONTO THE STREET AND CIRCLES THE PHONE
BOOTH.

3 -

DEENA (CONT'D)

WE ALL HAVE OUR GUNS OUT. WE'RE READY. WE'RE READY FOR FREDDY.

THE GUY - THE GUY DOESN'T EVEN NOTICE US. HE JUST KEEPS ON TALKING.

FIFTY GUNS AT HIS HEAD HE'S TOTALLY OBLIVIOUS.

CAPTAIN

'S FUNNY...

DEENA

NOT THE END OF IT.

SO ONE OF THE GUYS, JOEY, HE LIGHTLY TAPS ON THE GLASS TO GET HIS
ATTENTION.

THE GUY DOES ONE OF THESE MOVES WHERE HE JUST TURNS AWAY FROM THE DOOR
HOLDING HIS HAND TO HIS EAR.

SO JOEY TAPS ON THE GLASS AGAIN, NOW THE PERP TURNS REAL SHARP AND
BARKS: "DO YOU

SEE I'M ON THE..."

AND NOW HE SEES WHAT'S WHAT. SO FUCKING FUNNY. THE GUY SHAT HIMSELF I
SWEAR

TOO...PRICELESS.

CAPTAIN

GOOD ONE.

4 -

DEENA

YEAH...

SO THE GUY HE - HE GOES FOR IT.

CAPTAIN

NO...

DEENA

YEAH.

CAPTAIN

SO...

DEENA

SO, HE'S RIDDLED IN A SECOND. DOWN FOR THE COUNT. IT'S OVER. POPPED.

CAPTAIN

JEEZ...

DEENA

THAT'S THE WAY IT WENT DOWN.

BUT THE PHONE - BUT THE PHONE IS STILL

DANGLING OFF THE HOOK.

STILL IN ONE PIECE.

WHOEVER WAS ON THE OTHER LINE, THEY HEARD THE WHOLE THING. CAN YOU IMAGINE?

SO - SO DAVE HE - HE PICKS UP THE PHONE AND HE SAYS INTO THE RECEIVER:

"I'M SORRY, YOUR FRIEND HERE HAS BEEN

DISCONNECTED."

AND WE-WE COULDN'T HELP IT, WE ALL BURST OUT LAUGHING AT THIS CRAZY FUCKING THING

HE JUST SAID.

5 -

CAPTAIN

HE SAID THAT? THAT'S...

DEENA

YEAH, THING OF IT IS THOUGH...THE PERSON ON THE OTHER END WAS THE GUY'S MOM.

CAPTAIN

OY...

DEENA

CAN YOU IMAGINE?

SO - SO THAT'S WHAT HAPPENED TO MY OLD PARTNER.

I THINK HE'S WORKING AT BORDERS NOW SOMEONE TOLD ME.

PAGE 19 -

1 - SAME AS SIX FROM LAST PAGE. WALKER BARGES IN.

WALKER
RED ALERT.

CAPTAIN
WALKER...

WALKER
I GOT SIDELINED WITH THE LITTLE GIRL FROM THIS AFTERNOON'S BULLSHIT--
(TO DEENA)
HI -
(TO CAPTAIN)
AND SOCIAL SERVICES...

CAPTAIN
IS NO MORE. I KNOW.

WALKER
I DIDN'T. I CAN'T - I DON'T KNOW WHAT TO DO WITH...

2 - SAME BUT TIGHTER. WALKER IS A LITTLE FRAZZED COMPARED TO THE OTHER
TWO'S LAID BACK MEETING.

DEENA
WHAT HAPPENED TO SOCIAL SERVICES?

CAPTAIN
A BLAST I HEARD...

WALKER
FIREBALL IS WHAT...

CAPTAIN
I'LL PUT IN A CALL TO GEAUGA COUNTY BUT FOR THE MEANTIME YOU'RE GOING TO
HAVE TO BABY-SIT, I...

WALKER
BUT I HAVE CASES.

CAPTAIN
THIS IS TRUE.

WALKER
I HAVE CASES.

CAPTAIN
WE ALL HAVE CASES.

WALKER
BUT I HAVE CASES.

CAPTAIN
AND THAT'S WHY WE HAVE DAY CARE.
DROP HER OFF WITH BABS FOR THE SHIFT, AND WE WILL SEE WHAT WE CAN DO.

3 - SAME BUT TIGHTER ONTO DEENA AND WALKER.

DEENA
HOW OLD IS SHE?

WALKER
WHAT? I DON'T I - I DON'T KNOW, SIX OR - HOW CAN YOU TELL?

DEENA
YOU COULD ASK.

WALKER
YEAH, WELL IT'S A - I'M SORRY, WHO ARE...?
DEENA
OH, I'M DEENA PILGRIM. I'VE JUST BEEN REASSIGNED.
WALKER
OH - UH - CONGRATS I GUESS. PULL THE SHORT END OF THE...

DEENA
NOPE, REQUESTED.

WALKER
SERIOUSLY?

DEENA
TOTALLY.

WALKER
HUH.

(CONTINUED)

DEENA

SO DID YOU, RIGHT?

4 - WALKER JUST STARES AT HER.

5 - WALKER BACK TO THE CAPTAIN

WALKER

(TO CAPTAIN)

SO, WHAT FLOOR IS DAY CARE?

CAPTAIN

THIRD. 309. TAKE YOUR NEW PARTNER WITH YOU.

6 - WALKER JUST STARES AT HER AGAIN.

WALKER

HUH.

DEENA

HUH, YOURSELF.

WALKER

NO I...

DEENA

COME ON.

PAGE 20 -

1 - CALISTA LOOKING AROUND THE SQUAD ROOM. SHE SEES A COUPLE OF COPS
ARGUING.

COP 1

HOW COULD YOU EVEN SAY THAT, THE GUY HAD A...

COP 2

YOU KNOW!! YOU KNOW WHAT HE WAS GOING TO...

COP 1

IT'S A 314. WHAT DO YOU DO IN A 314?

2 - CALISTA WATCHES A COP PICK UP THE PHONE.

COP 3

HOMICIDE. 4TH. THIS IS BERMAN.

3 - CALISTA LOOKS TO THE PHONE ON WALKER'S DESK AS IT RINGS.

4 - AND RINGS.

5 - AND RINGS, CALISTA IS LOOKING TO SEE IF SOMEONE IS GOING TO PICK IT UP.

6 - CALISTA PICKS IT UP.

CALISTA

HOMICIDE. 4TH. THIS IS CALISTA.

WHAT?

EEWW!!

THAT'S SO GROSS - WHAT?

7 - BIGGER PANEL. WALKER, PILGRIM BEHIND HIM, GRABS THE PHONE AWAY FROM HER.

WALKER

HOMICIDE, WAL - WHAT?

8 - WALKER LOOKS LIKE HE SAW A GHOST.

9 - DEENA LOOKS AT HIS REACTION.

DEENA

WE ON THE MOVE?

10 - SAME AS 8

WALKER

WE'RE ON THE MOVE.

PAGE 21 -

1 - BIG PANEL. WALKER AND PILGRIM PULL UP TO A CRIME SCENE.

THIS ONE IS A BARRICADED ALLY. THE COPS ARE FENDING OFF AN EXTREMELY LARGE GATHERING CROWD.

THE PRESS BEAT THEM TO IT BUT CAN'T GET NEAR THE SCENE.

2 - DEENA AND WALKER IN THE CAR.

DEENA

WELL - WELL, THIS IS A FUCKING CIRCUS.

WALKER

THREE RING. GET USED TO IT.

3 - THESE SHOTS ARE FROM THE P.O.V. OF THE CORPSE WE ARE LOOKING UP AT
WALKER AND PILGRIM AND A UNIFORM YOUNG POLICEMAN.

WALKER (CONT'D)

WHO CALLED IT IN?

COP

ANONYMOUS.

WALKER

IT'S A LONG SHOT - BUT RUN A TAP ANYHOW.

DEENA

COULD IT BE? THERE'S NO WAY IT'S HER.

WALKER

IT'S HER.

DEENA

COULD BE A LOOK-A-LIKE.

5 - SAME, WALKER IS VERY SERIOUS.

WALKER

COULD BE. BUT IT ISN'T.

DEENA

BUT - HOW DO YOU KNOW?

WALKER

MET HER.

DEENA

STILL...

WALKER

TRUST ME.

SHES NOT -

6 - WALKER

WALKER (CONT'D)

YOU DON'T FORGET HER.

IT'S HER.

PAGE 22 -

BIG PAGE SHOT OVER THEIR SHOULDERS DOWN TO THE GROUND OF THE ALLEY.

IT IS A DEAD GIRL IN A HIP AND TASTEFUL WONDER GIRL STYLE SUPERHERO
OUTFIT AND SHORT SKIRT AND GO-GO BOOTS.

ITS RETRO GIRL.

AND SHE IS DEAD. HER THROAT CUT. A POOL OF ALMOST BLACK BLOOD.

ON THE ALLEY WALL. MORE GRAFFITI LIKE IN THE FIRST SCENE.

THE PHRASE KAOTIC CHIC IS SPRAY PAINTED ON THE WALL WITH SOME OTHER
STUFF.

DEENA

BUT SHE'S - SHE'S...

WALKER

WHO COULD HAVE KILLED RETRO GIRL?

DEENA

SHIT OL' MIGHTY, CAN I PICK EM.

NEXT ISSUE: WHO KILLED RETRO GIRL?

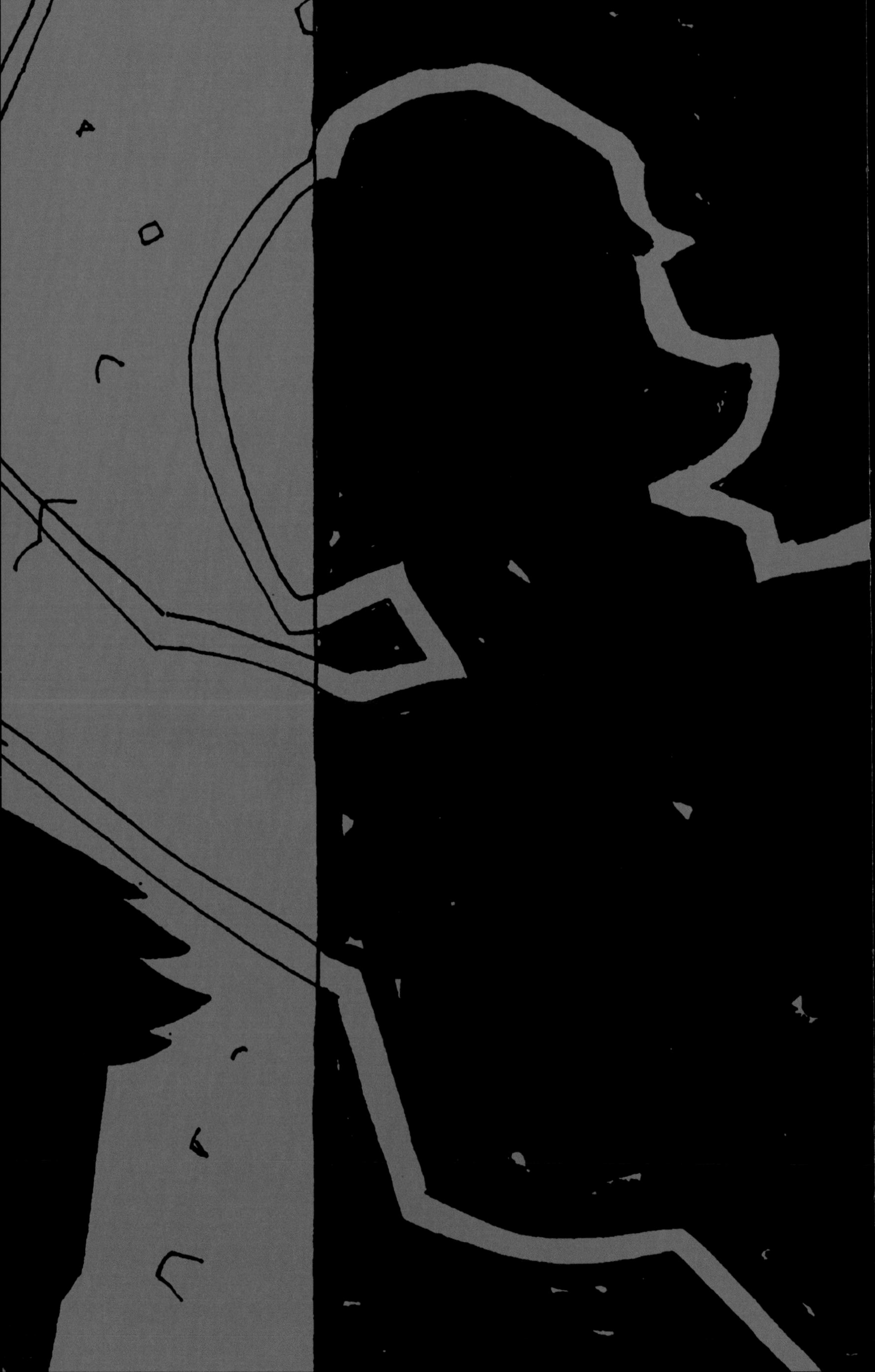

Ever notice how there are about five basic mainstream comic book cover designs? You know them:

→ **The hero leaping at you, ready for battle.**

→ **The close-up of the hero grimacing at you, with the shadow of whatever villain he is facing cast over half his face.**

→ **The logo of the comic smashing from the force of the great battle raging beneath it.**

→ **The close-up of the big villain laughing maniacally.**

→ **And the ever-popular giant boobs smushed together in the middle of the cover, with a couple spots of blood on them that somewhat resemble nipplage.**

These are what we in the business call "Comic Book Clichés." And if ever I am responsible for purposefully executing one here in *Powers*, I will kill myself but make it look like Mike Oeming did it.

Mike and I decided very early to create themed covers for each story arc. For example, for the *Roleplay* story line, we mimicked cover designs from albums you might find in a college dorm room.

But the road to good ideas is not always smooth. A lot of really bad ideas are pursued. Or, as Mike likes to say, they're forced down artists' throats by know-it-all writers. Or they're conceived by artists hopped up on paint fumes.

Here we have included original sketch work or ink work that Mike sent for discussion before he committed to the final art. The colors on many of these covers were done by yours truly for completely selfish purposes—I just wanted to be part of the process.

Also included here is a smattering of unused covers and promotional images. Among these rejects are some of our favorites that we felt just did not suit the respective issues.

Join us now on a trip through the cover gallery, then on to abandoned cover concepts and sketches. We hope that you will find it interesting . . . and by that, I mean I hope it gets us nominated for something.

POWERS™

ANATOMY
OF A COVER CONCEPT

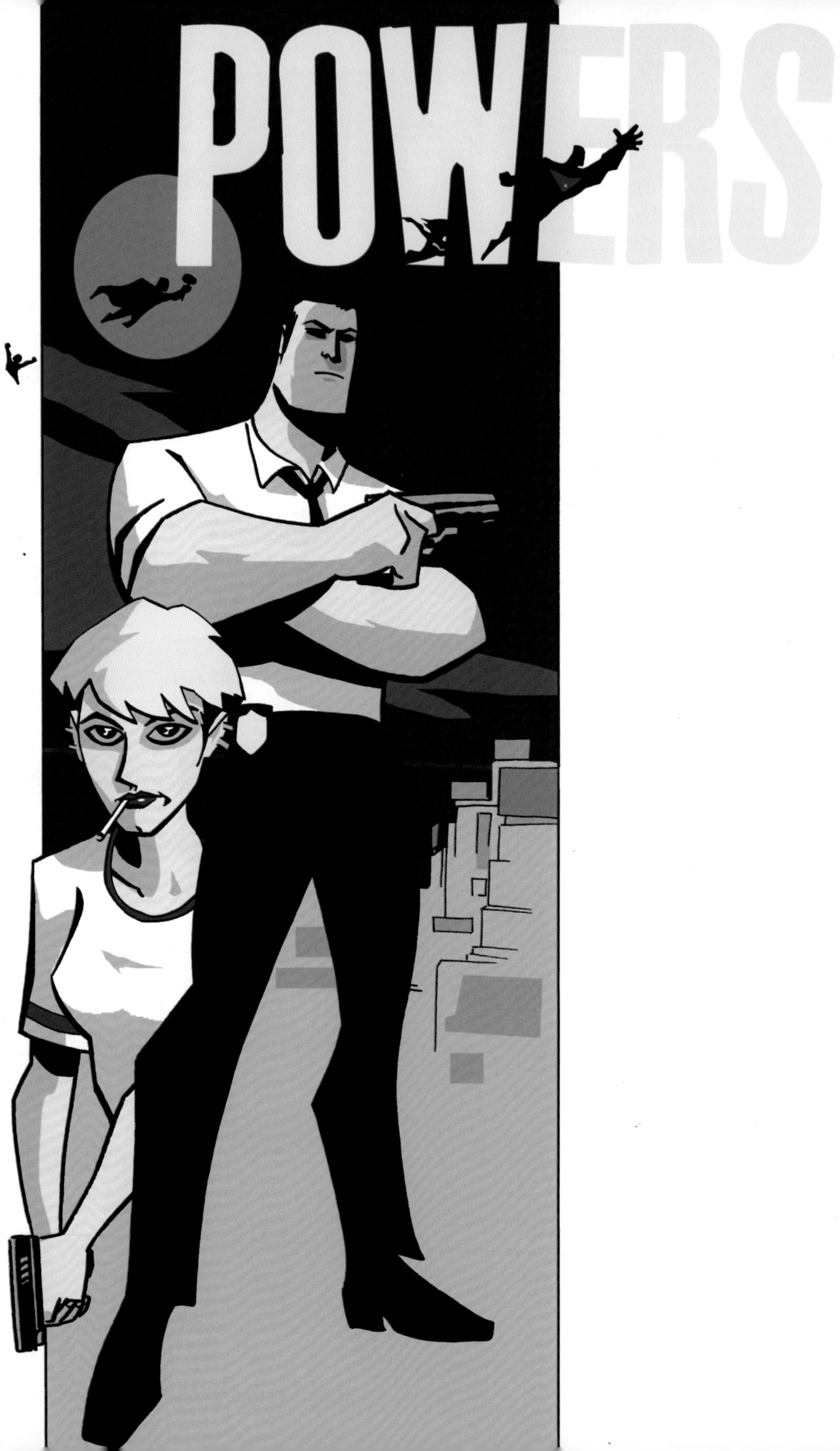
POWERS

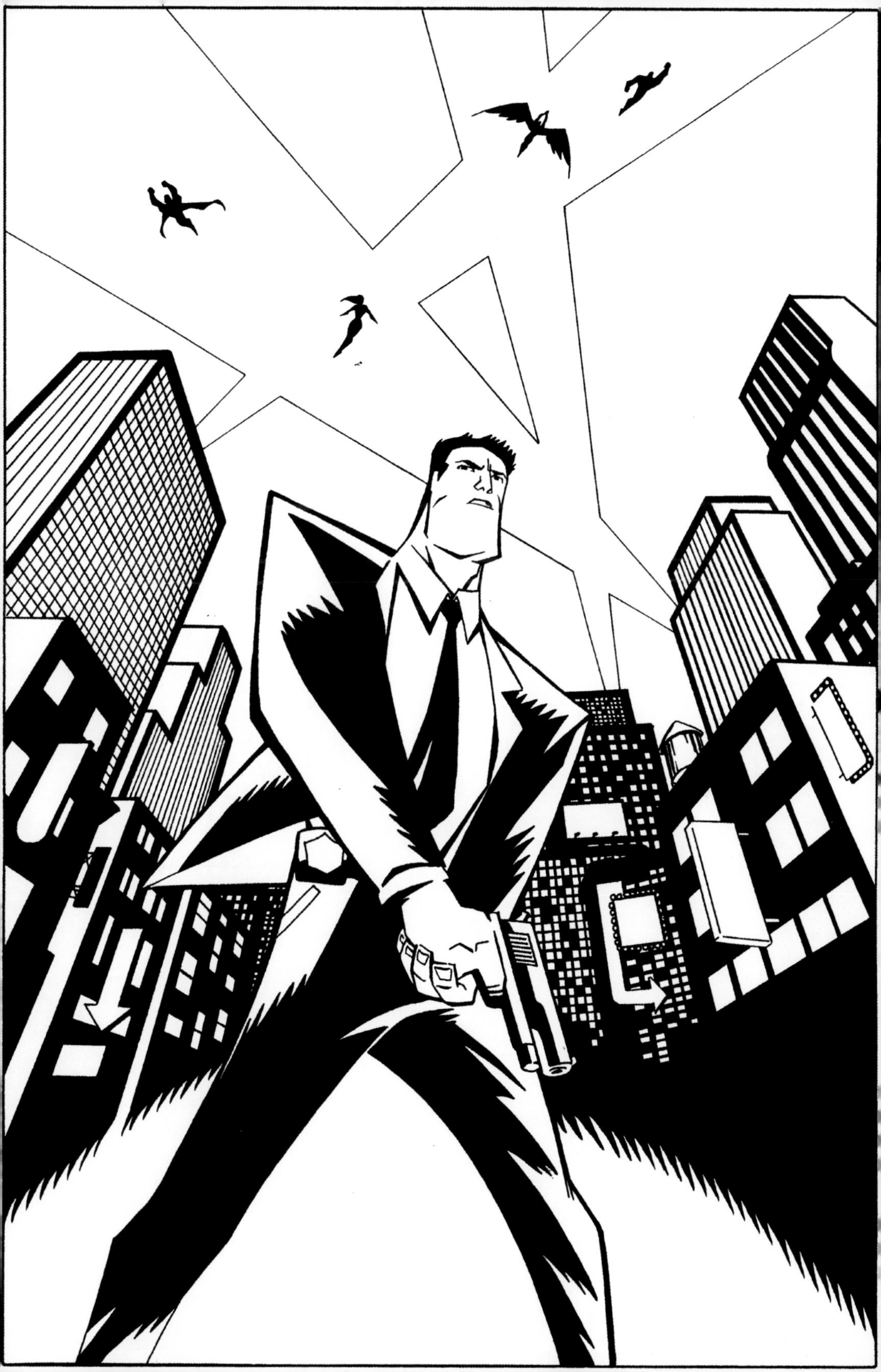

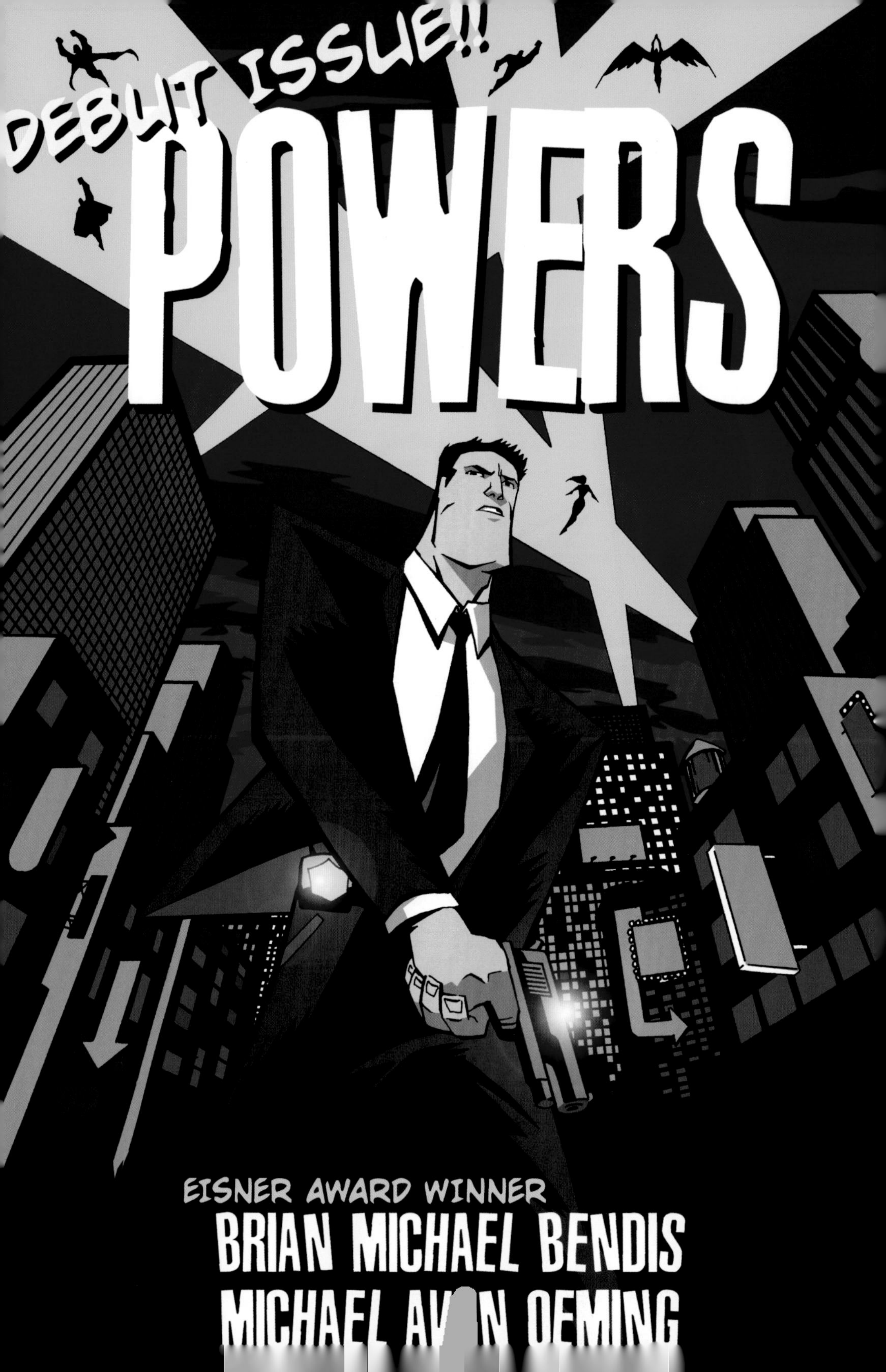
DEBUT ISSUE!!
POWERS
EISNER AWARD WINNER
BRIAN MICHAEL BENDIS
MICHAEL AV N OEMING

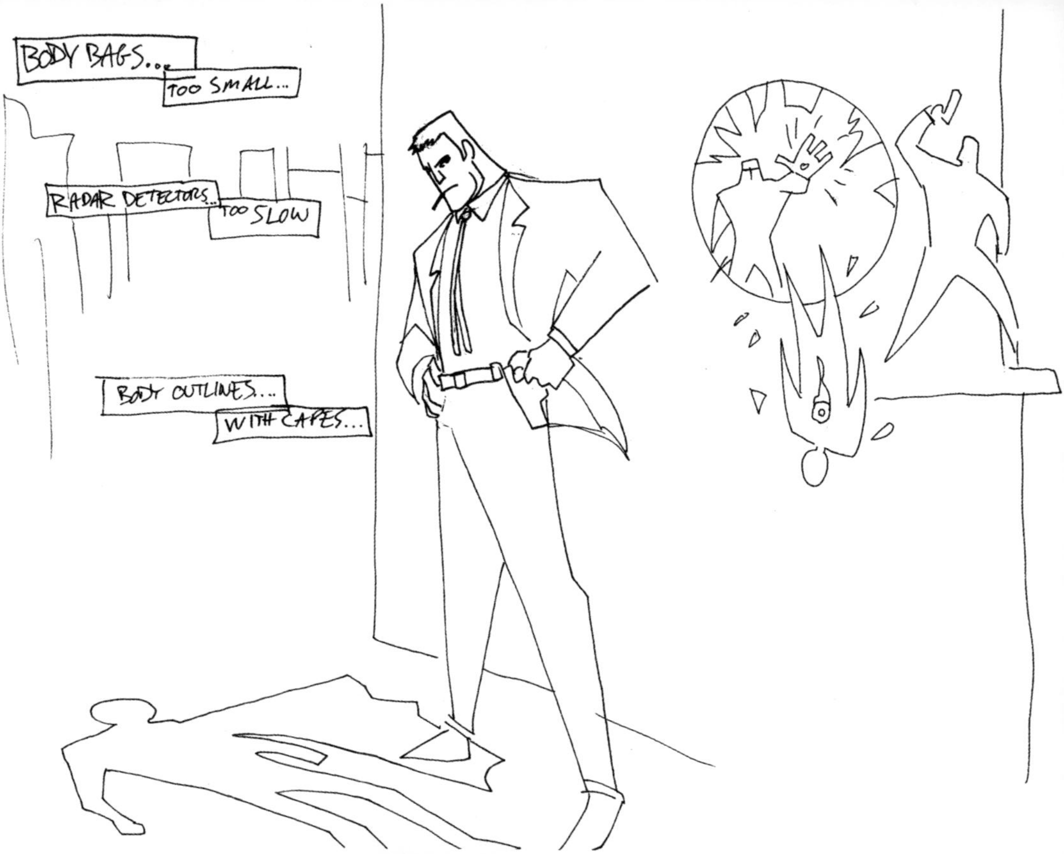
BODY BAGS...
TOO SMALL...
RADAR DETECTORS...
TOO SLOW
BODY OUTLINES...
WITH CAPES...

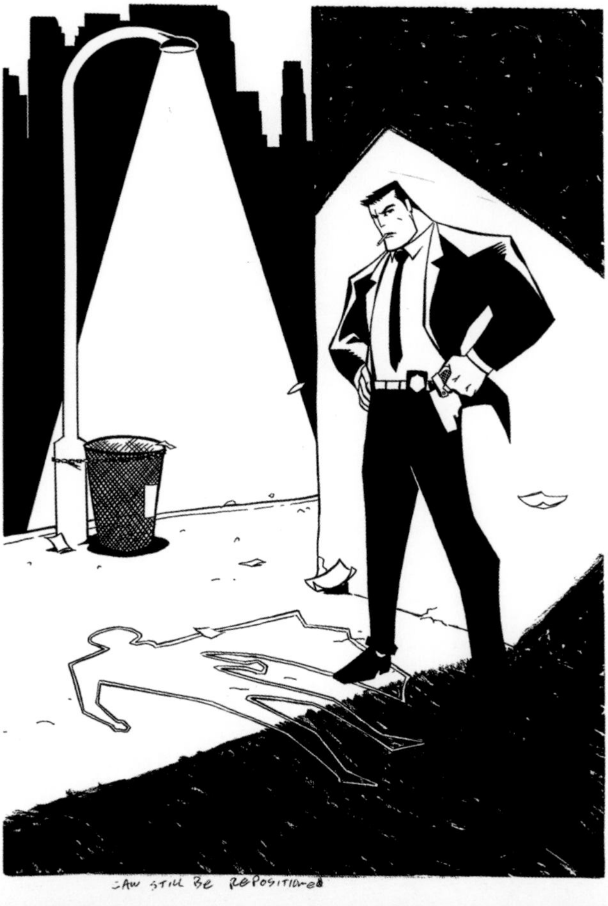
CAN STILL BE REPOSITIONED

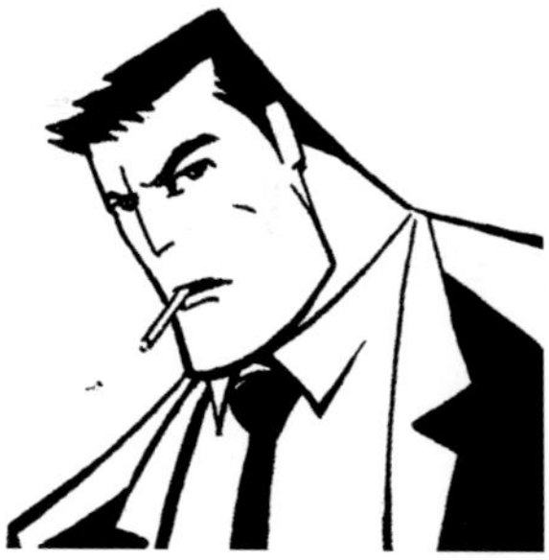

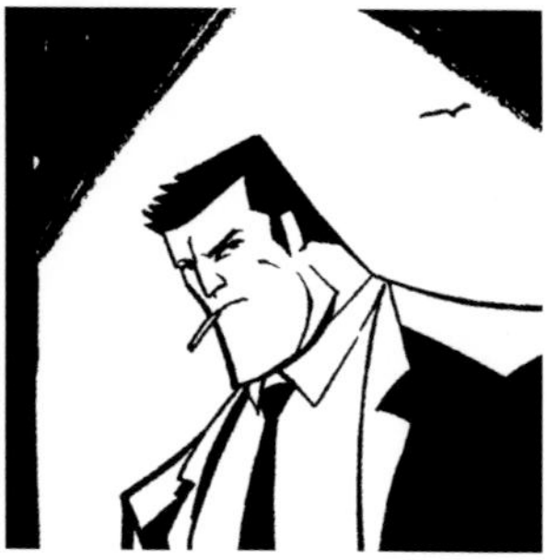

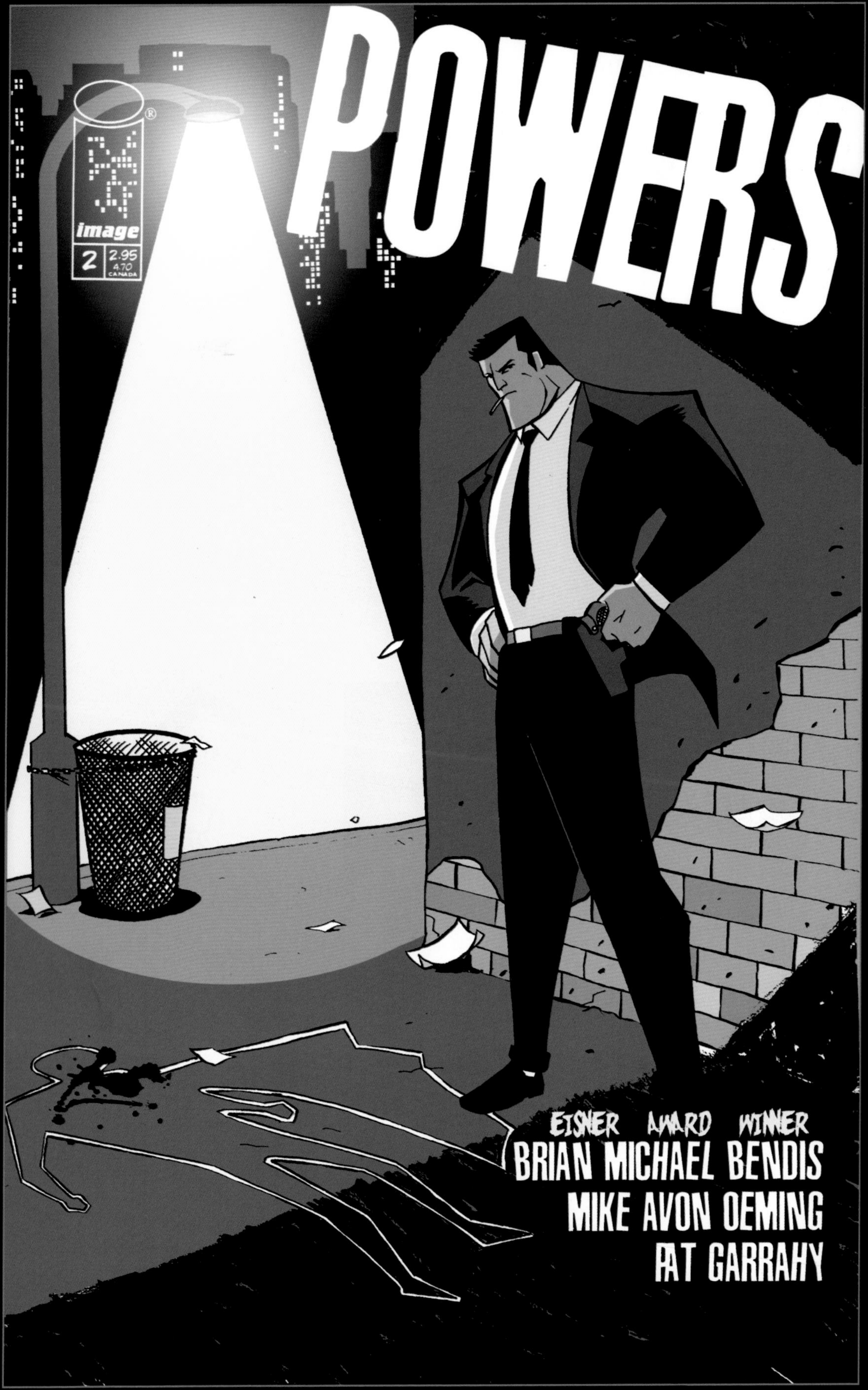
POWERS
image
2
2.95
4.70
CANADA
EISNER AWARD WINNER
BRIAN MICHAEL BENDIS
MIKE AVON OEMING
PAT GARRAHY

Powers #2 cover

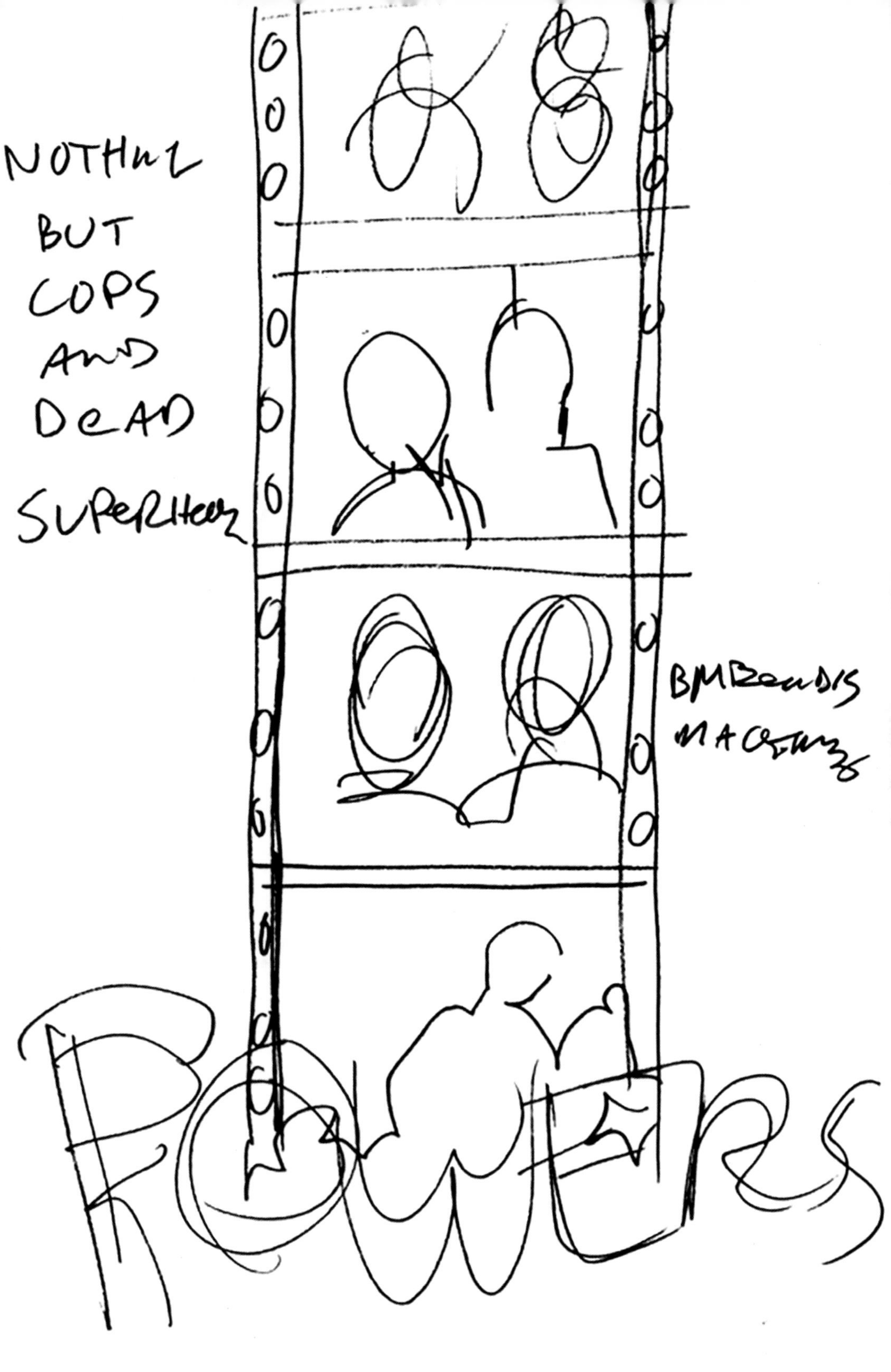
NOTHING
BUT
COPS
AND
DEAD
SUPERHEROES
BMBendis
POWERS

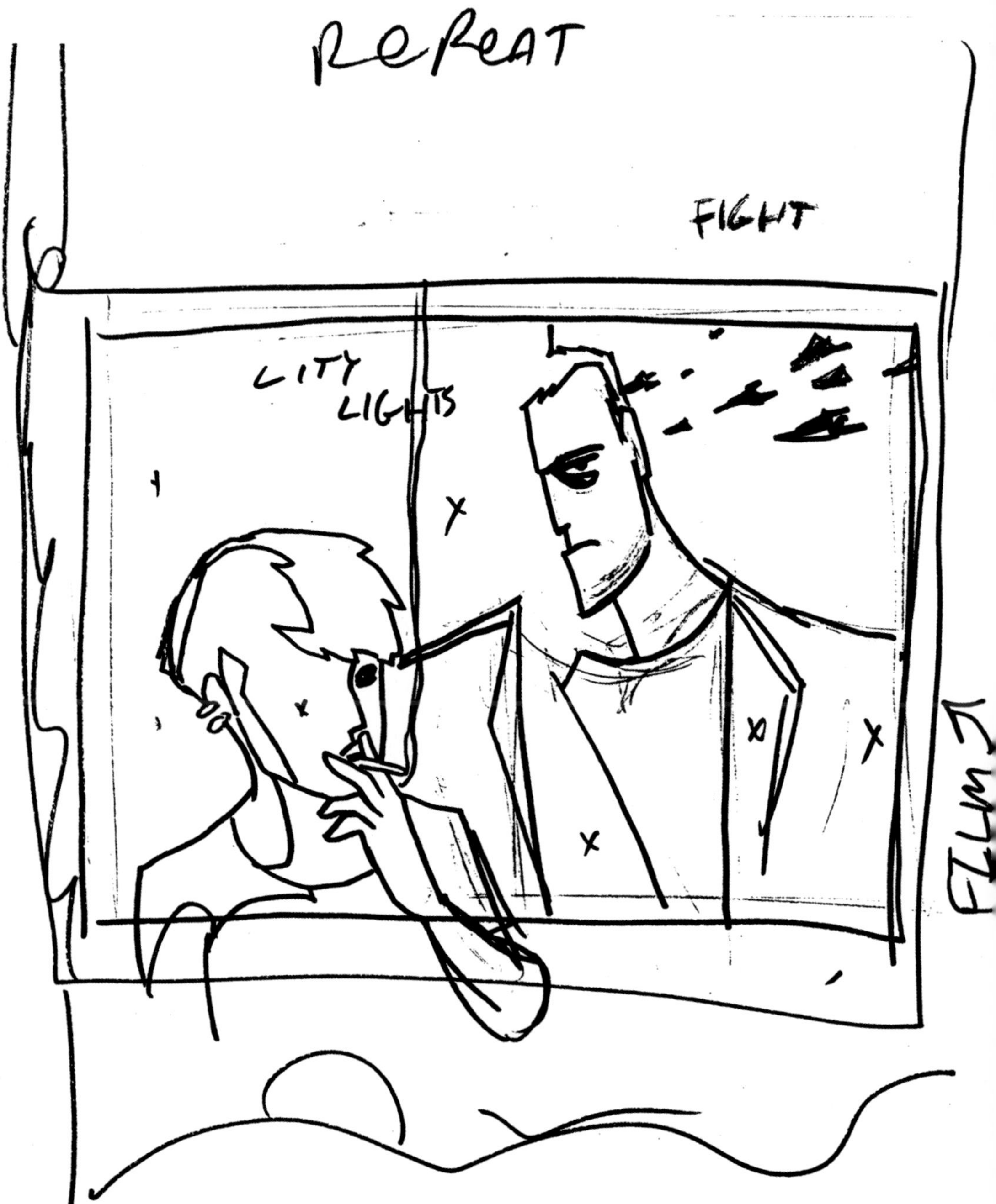

-B - I THINK THIS HAS LOTS OF POTENTIAL AD-WISE

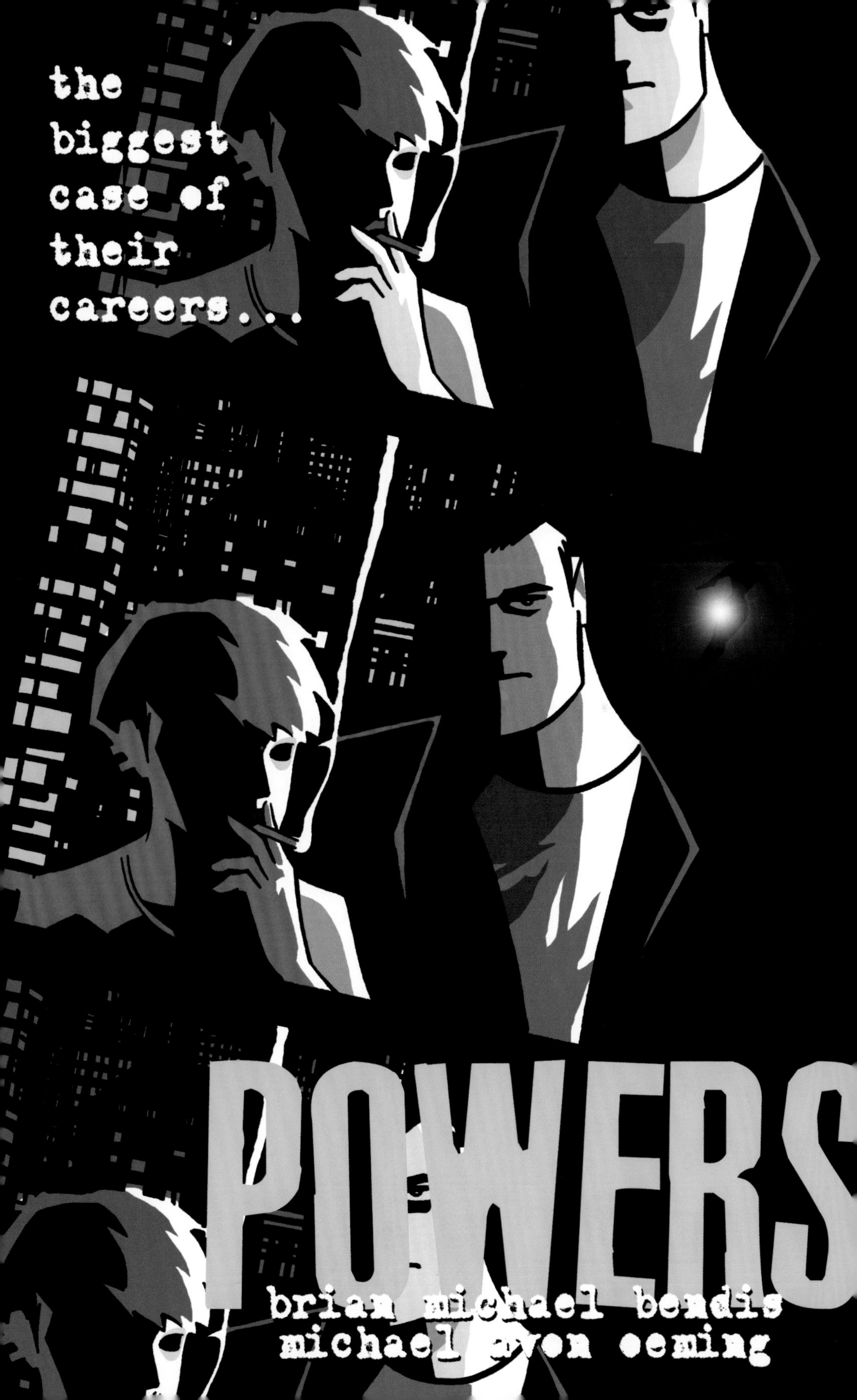
the biggest case of their careers...
POWERS
brian michael bendis
michael avon oeming

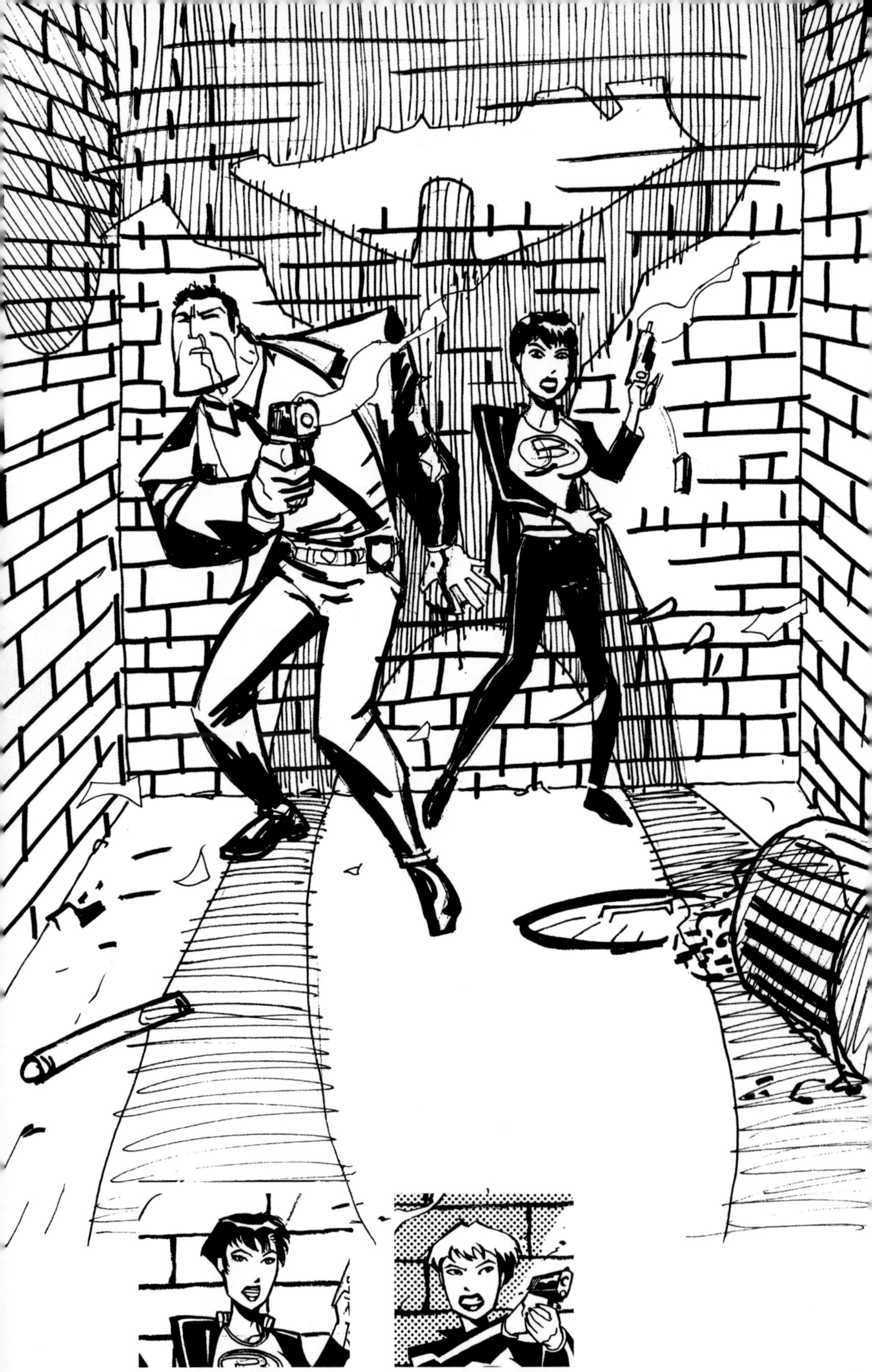

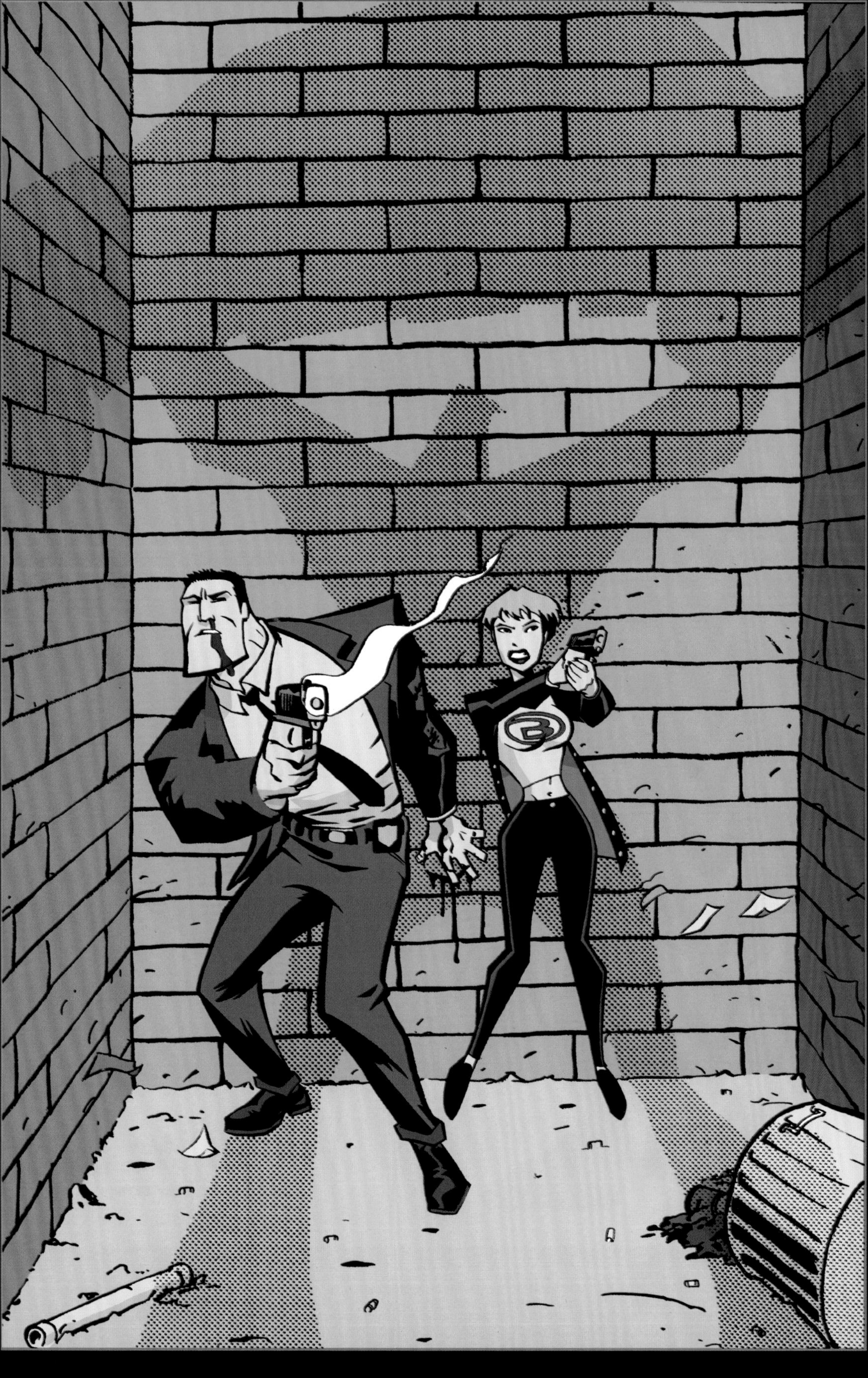

Unused *Powers* #3 cover
BENDIS: It ended up being the cover to the Mid-Ohio-Con program book. The ongoing saga of Deena's hair.

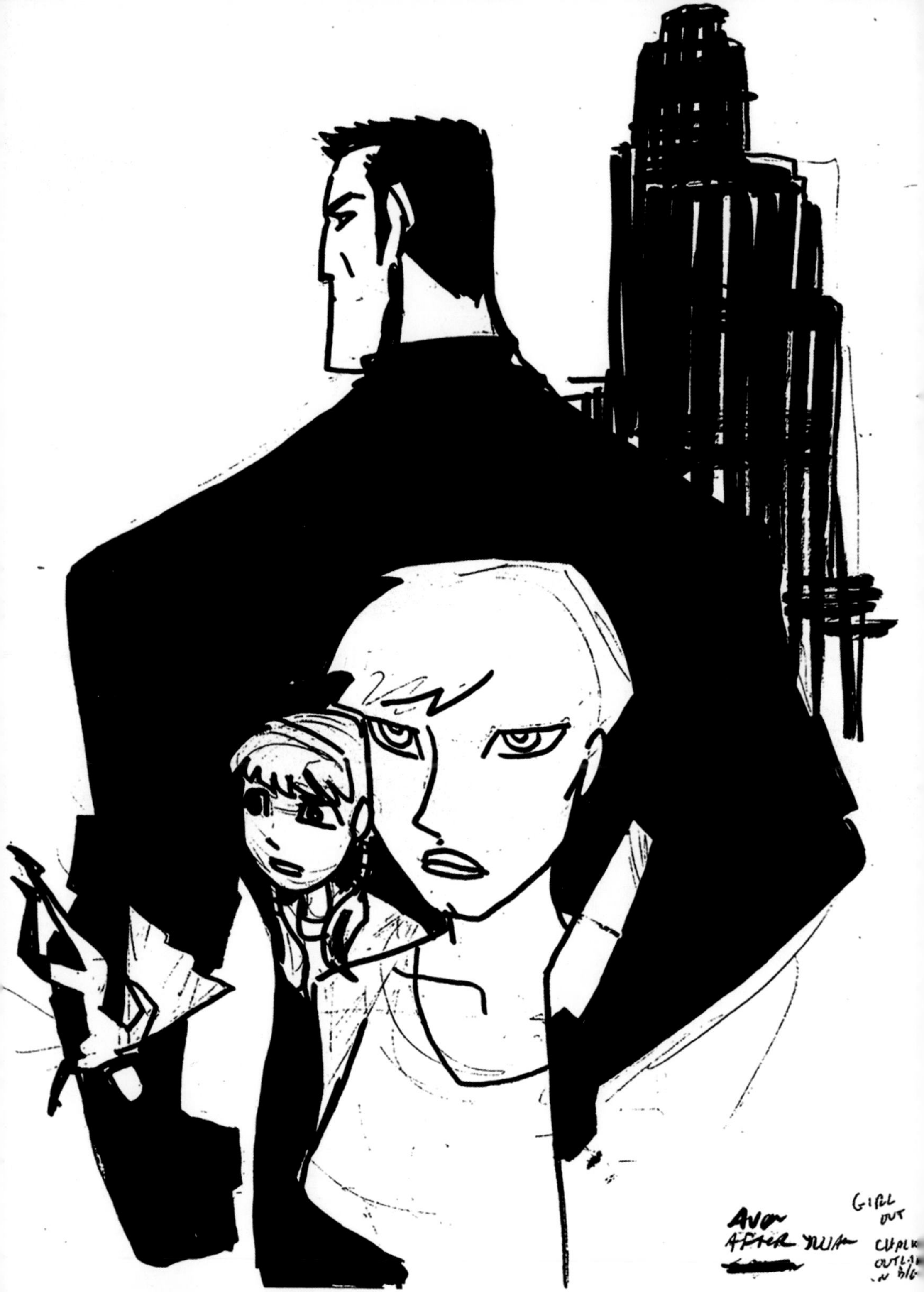

GIRL OUT

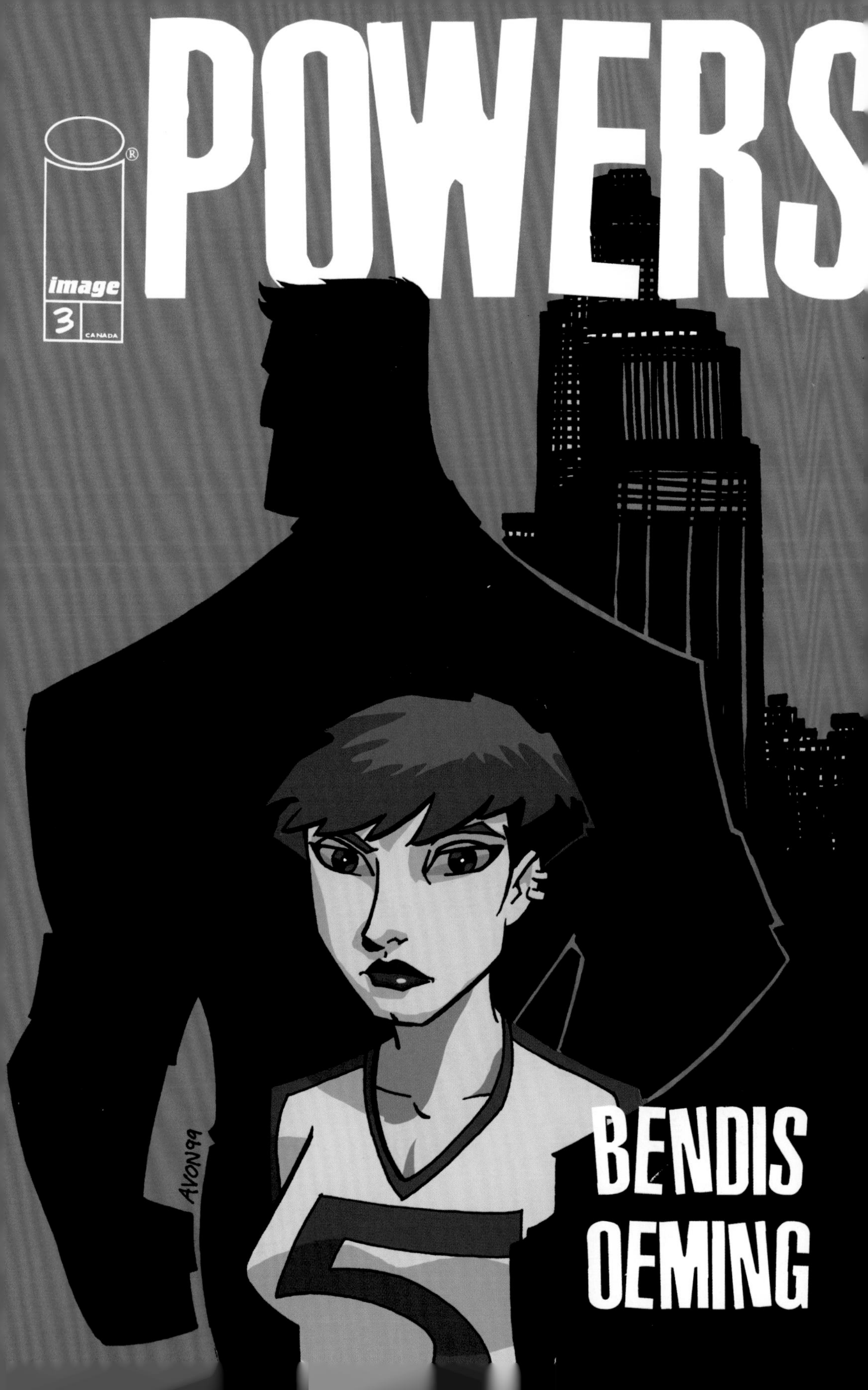
POWERS
image
3
CANADA
AVON99
BENDIS
OEMING

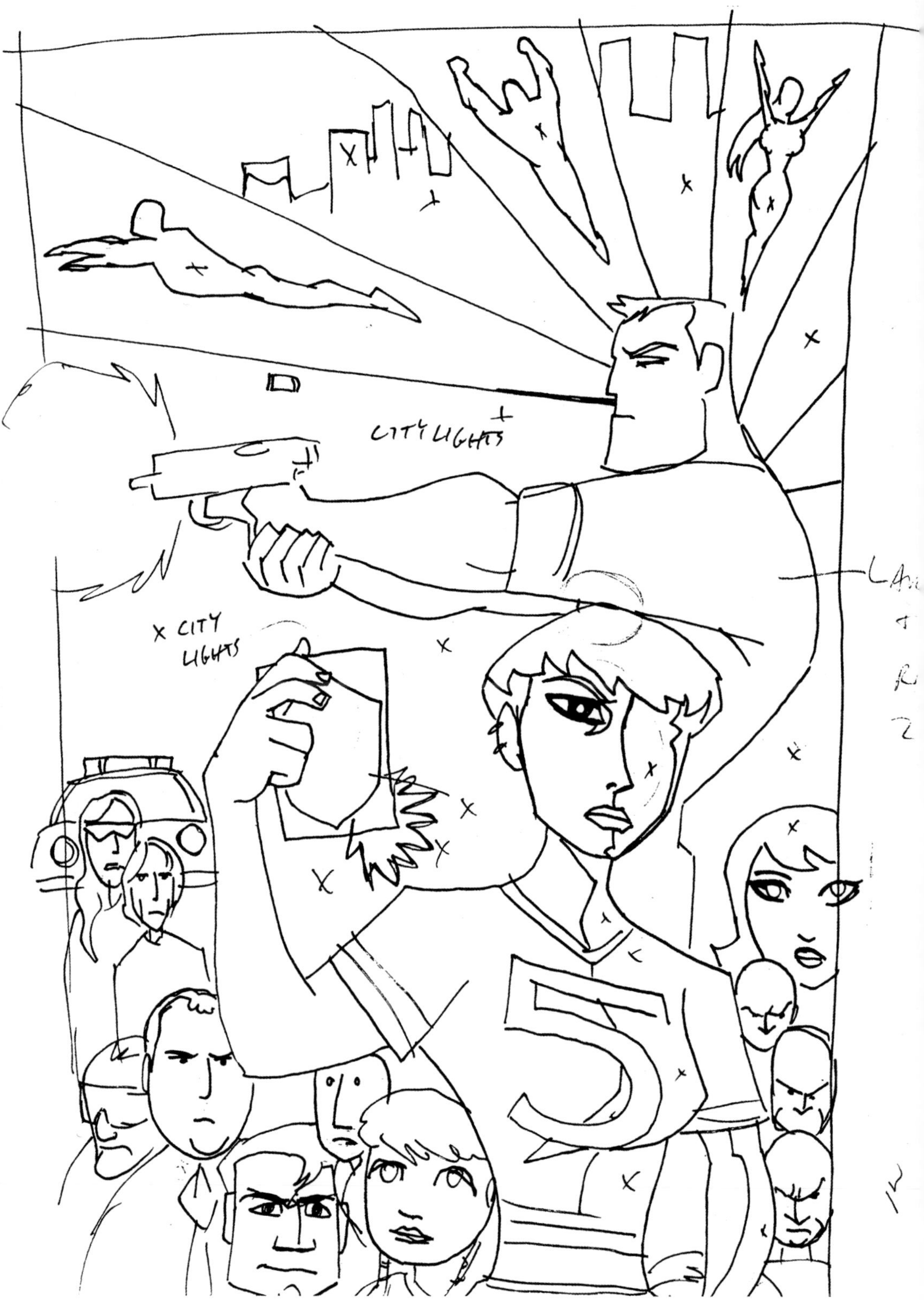
CITY LIGHTS
x CITY LIGHTS

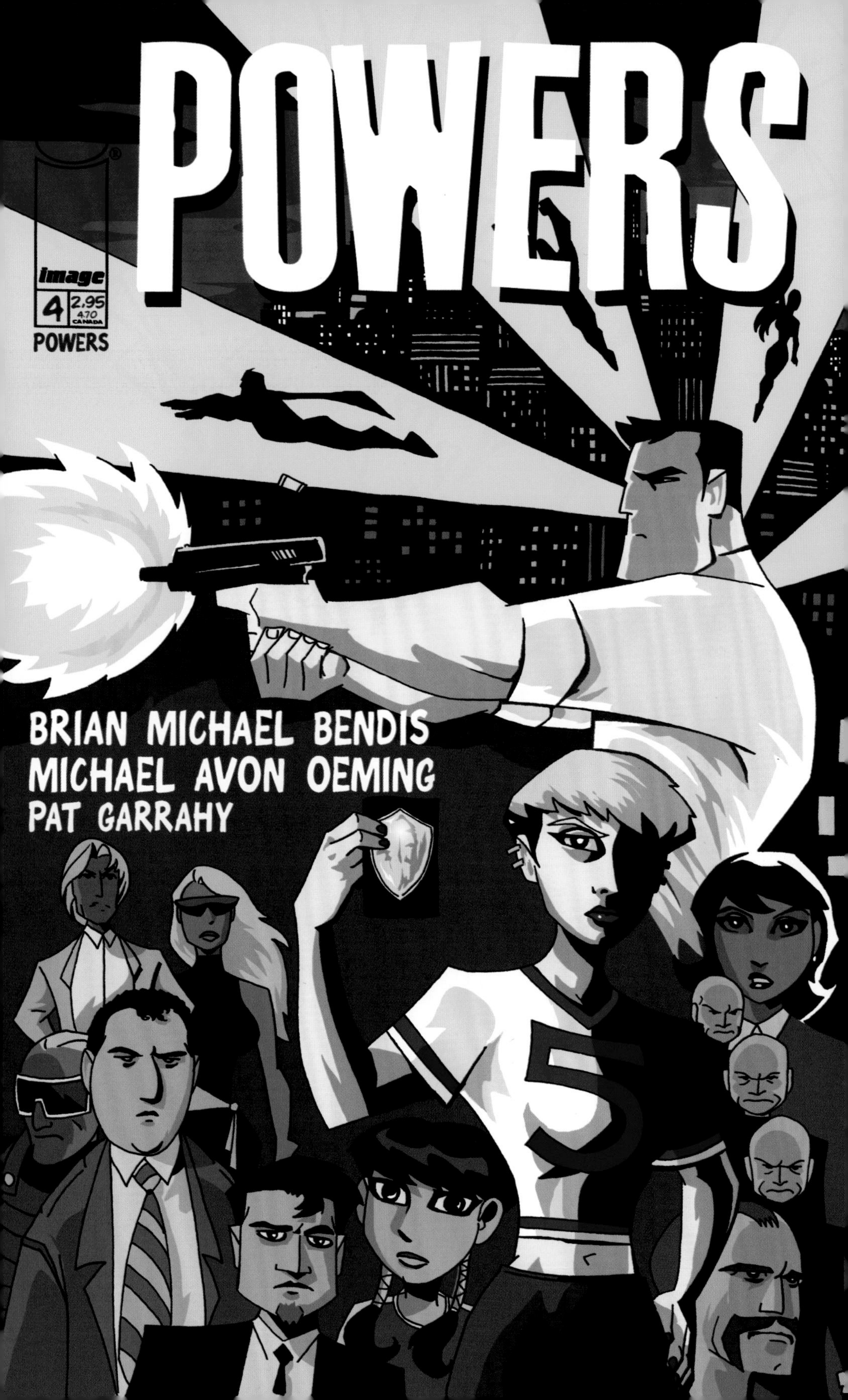
POWERS
image
4
2.95
4.70 CANADA
POWERS
BRIAN MICHAEL BENDIS
MICHAEL AVON OEMING
PAT GARRAHY

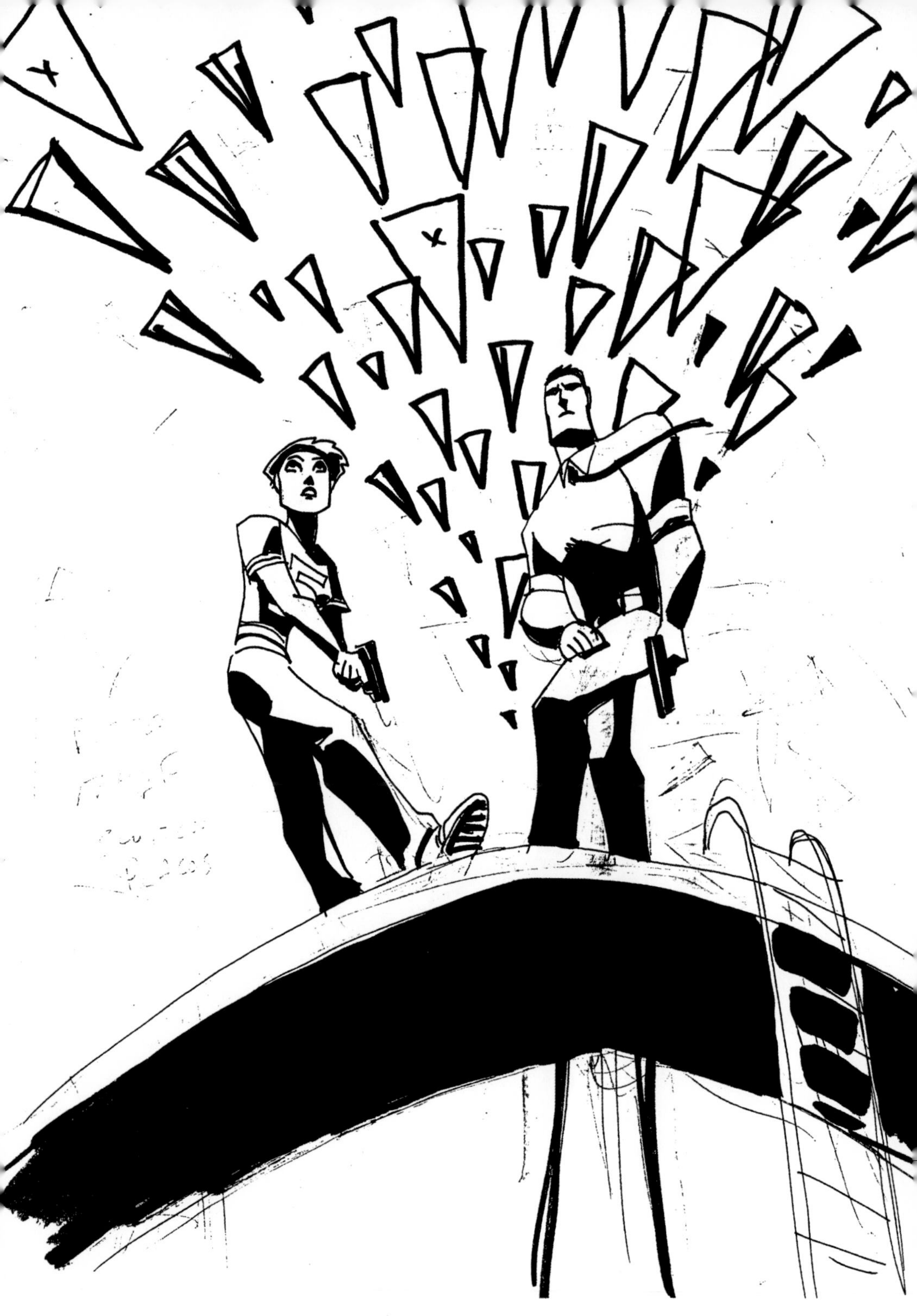

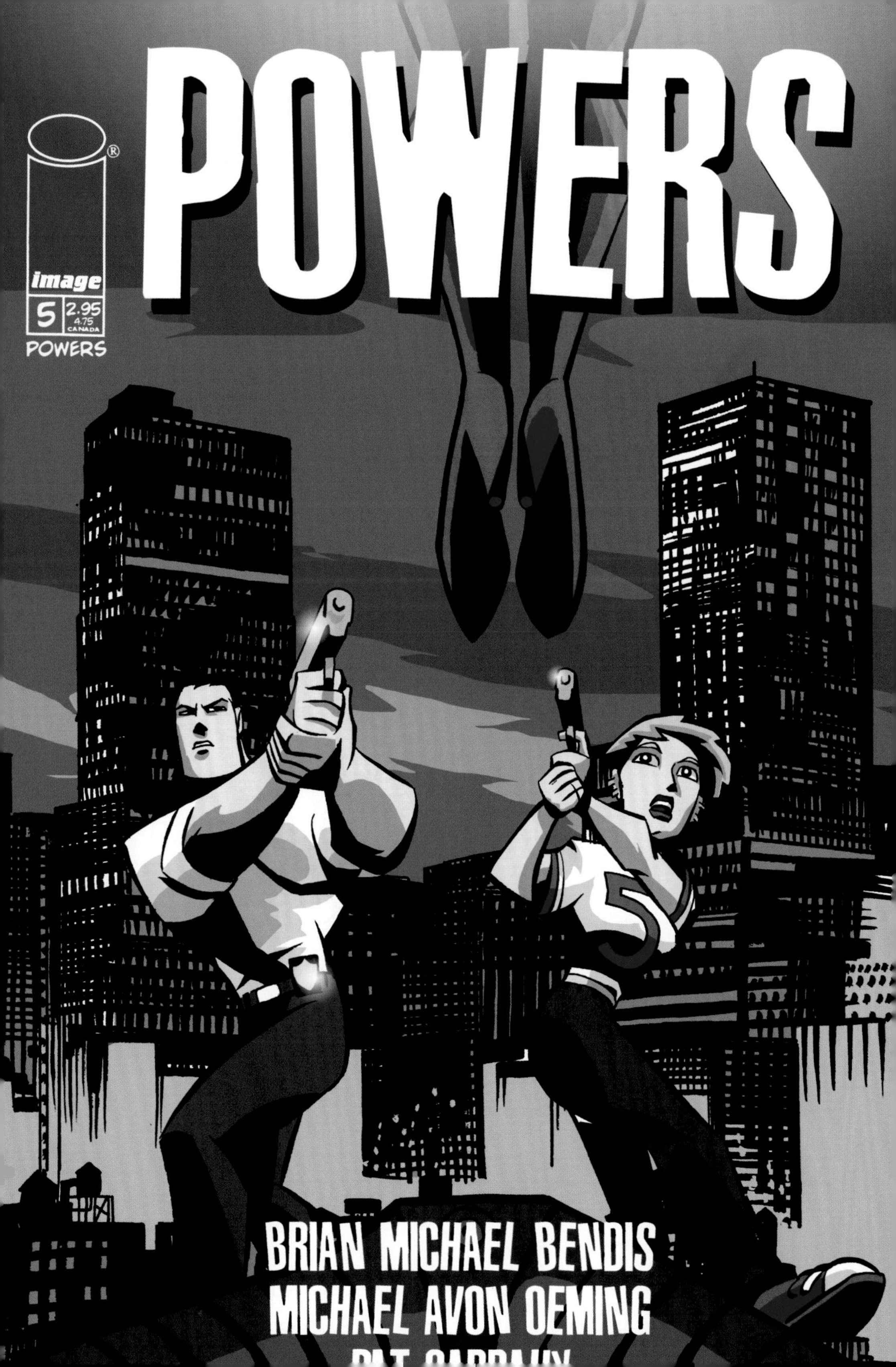
POWERS
image
5
2.95
4.75 CANADA
POWERS
BRIAN MICHAEL BENDIS
MICHAEL AVON OEMING

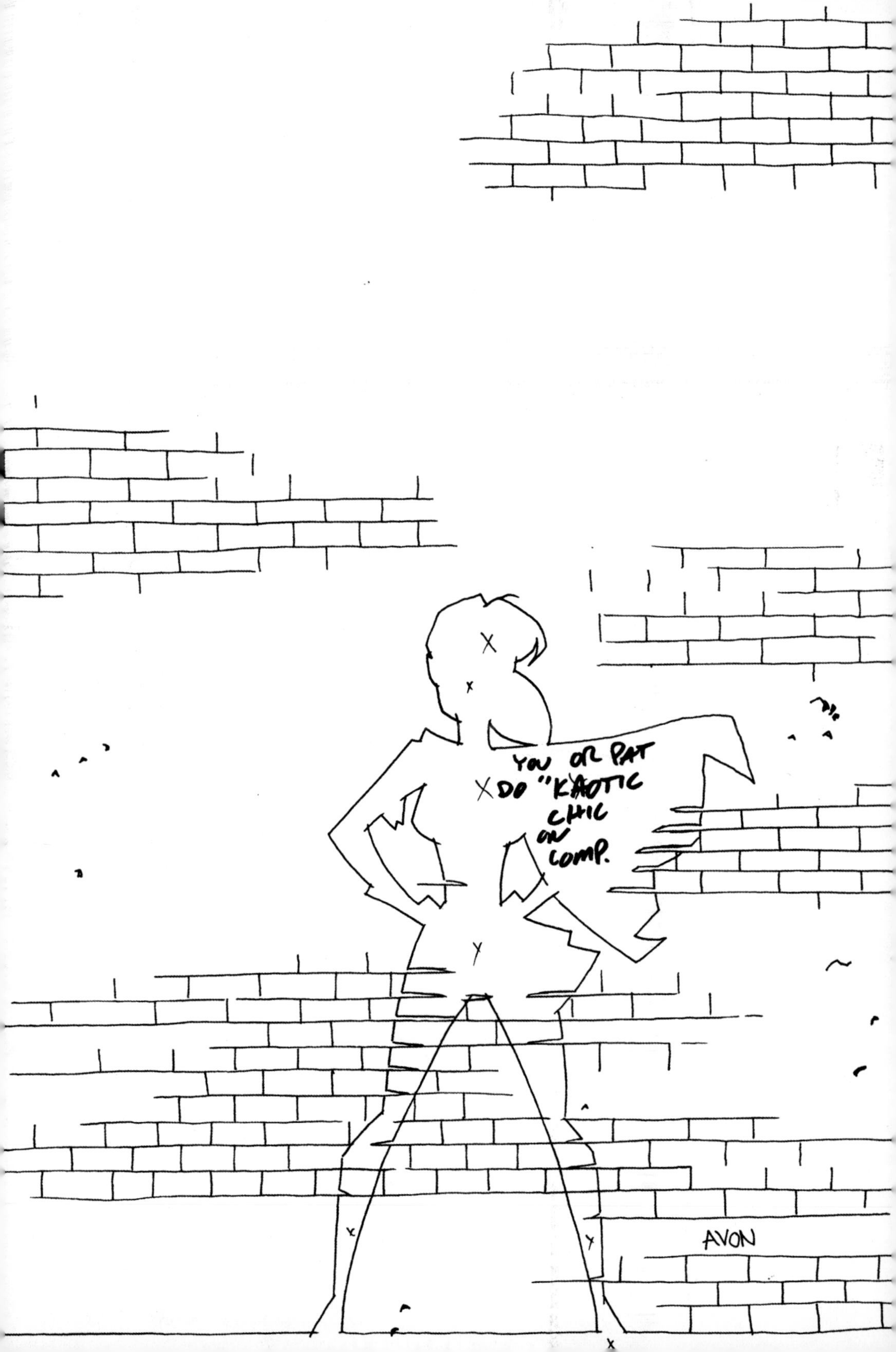
YOU OR PAT DO "KAOTIC CHIC ON COMP.
AVON

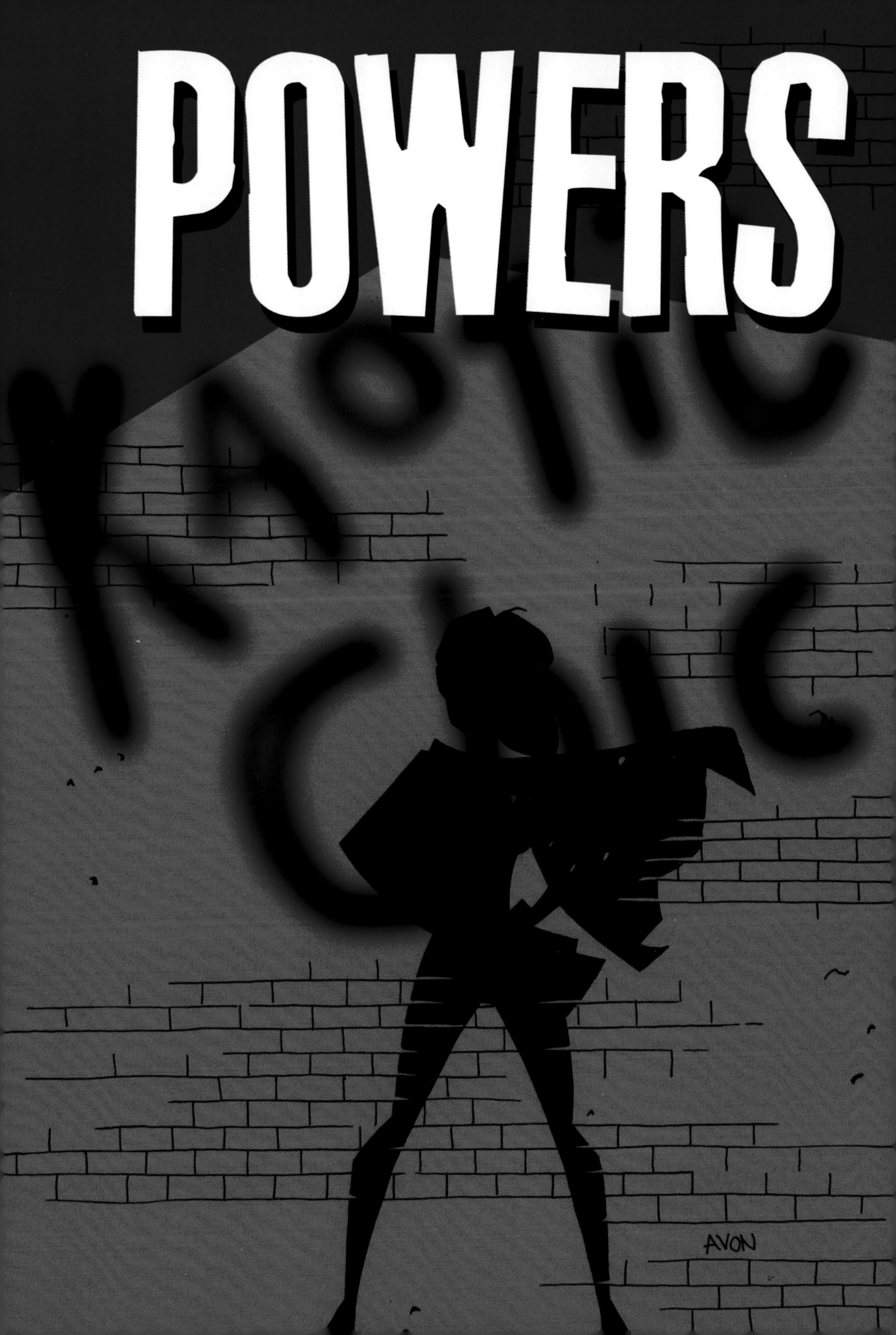
POWERS
KAOTIC CHIC
AVON

I don't care what you say...

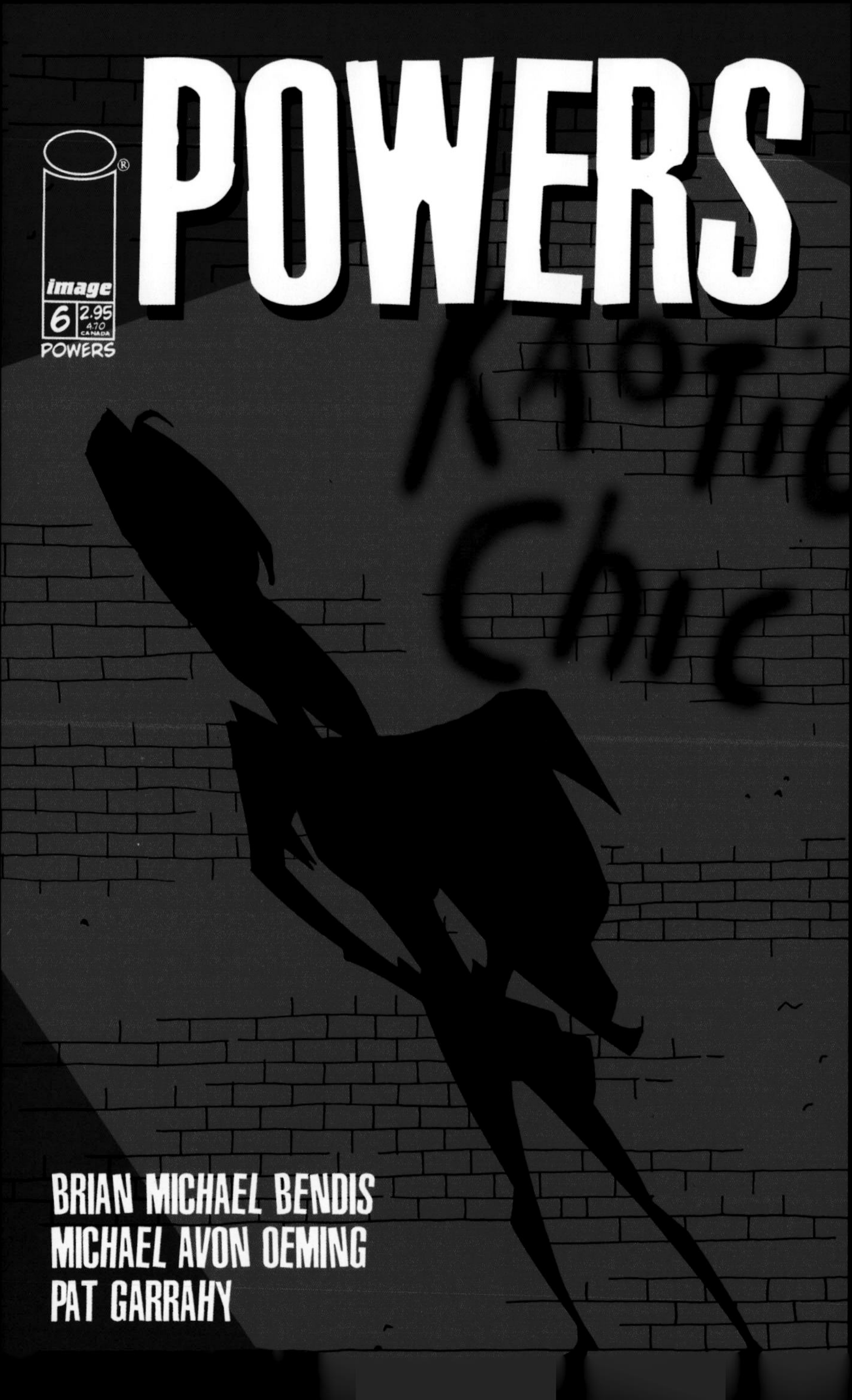
POWERS
image
6 2.95
4.70 CANADA
POWERS
KAOTIC
CHIC
BRIAN MICHAEL BENDIS
MICHAEL AVON OEMING
PAT GARRAHY

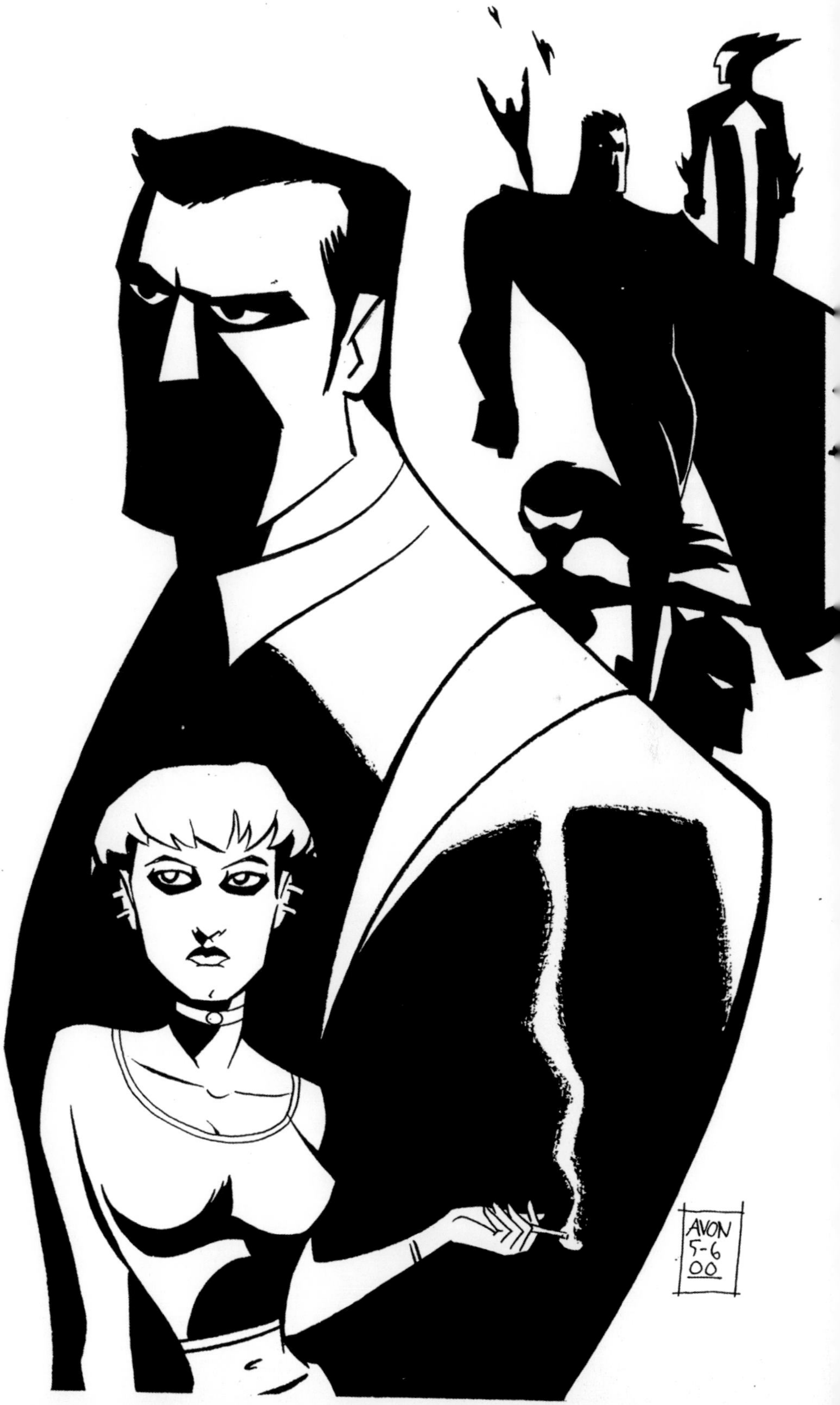
AVON
5-6
00

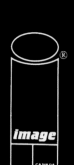

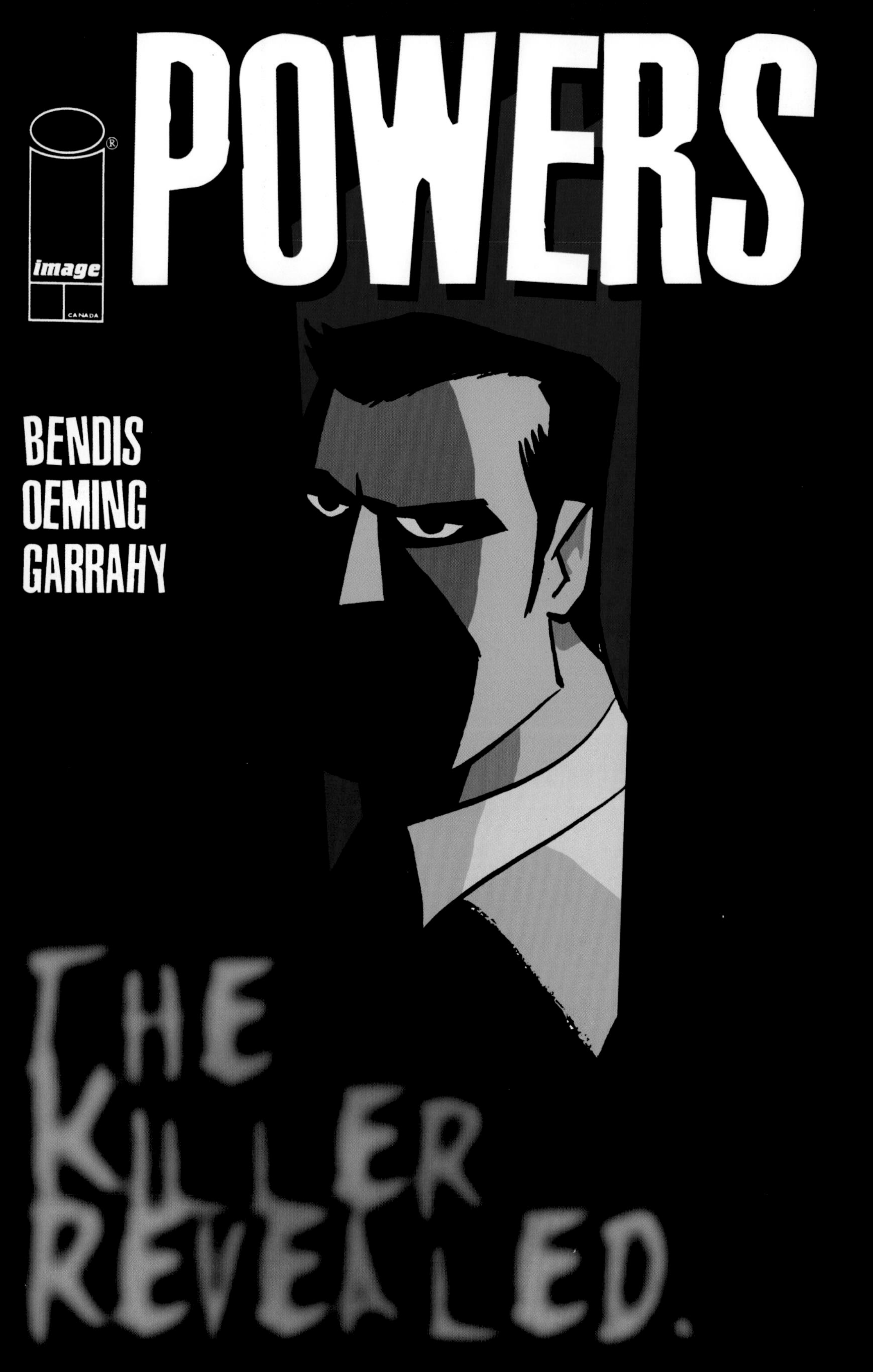

POWERS

BENDIS
OEMING
GARRAHY

THE KILLER REVEALED.

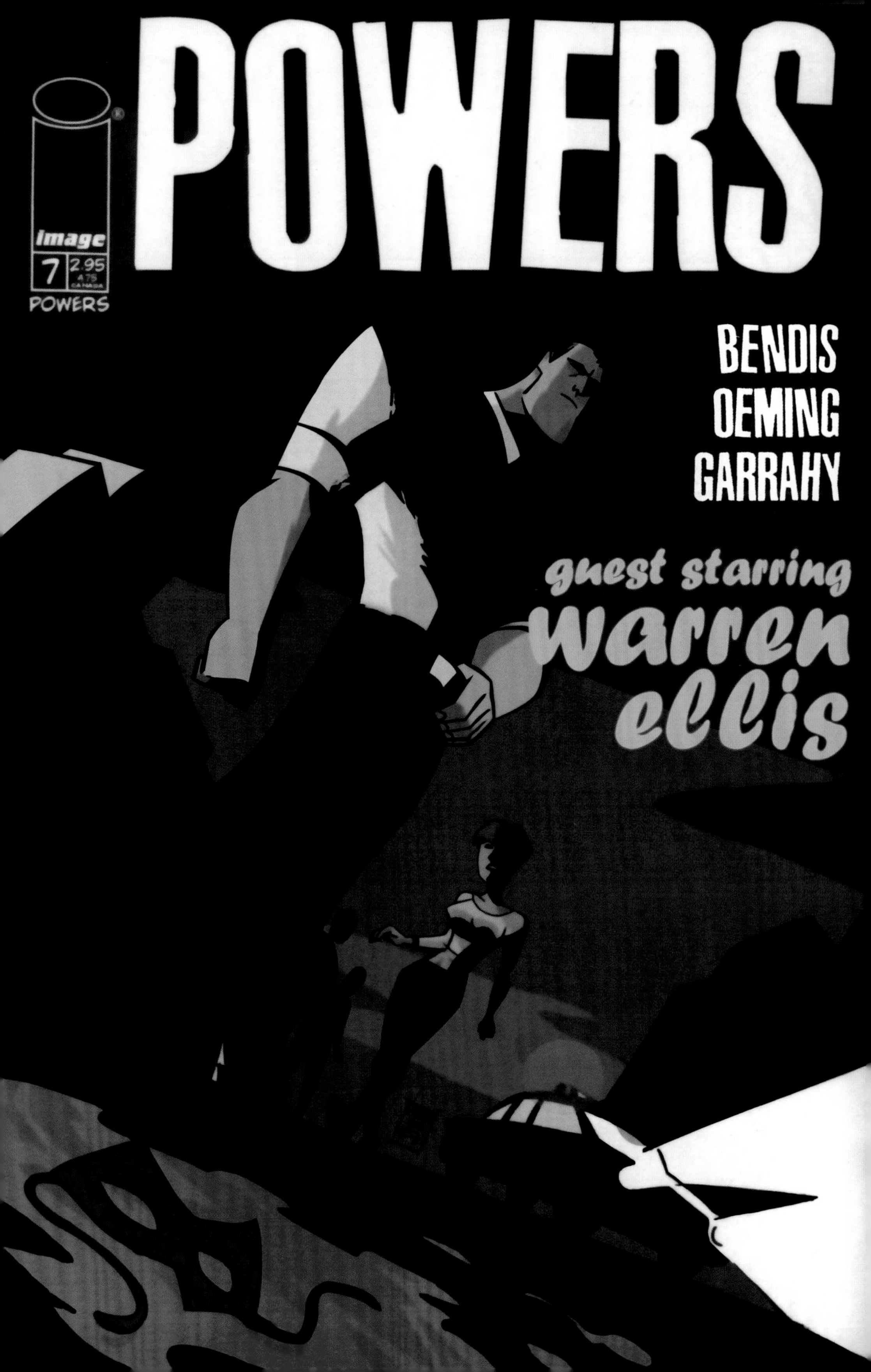
POWERS
image
7
2.95
4.75 CANADA
POWERS
BENDIS
OEMING
GARRAHY
guest starring
warren
ellis

image
8 2.95 4.75 CANADA
POWERS

POWERS

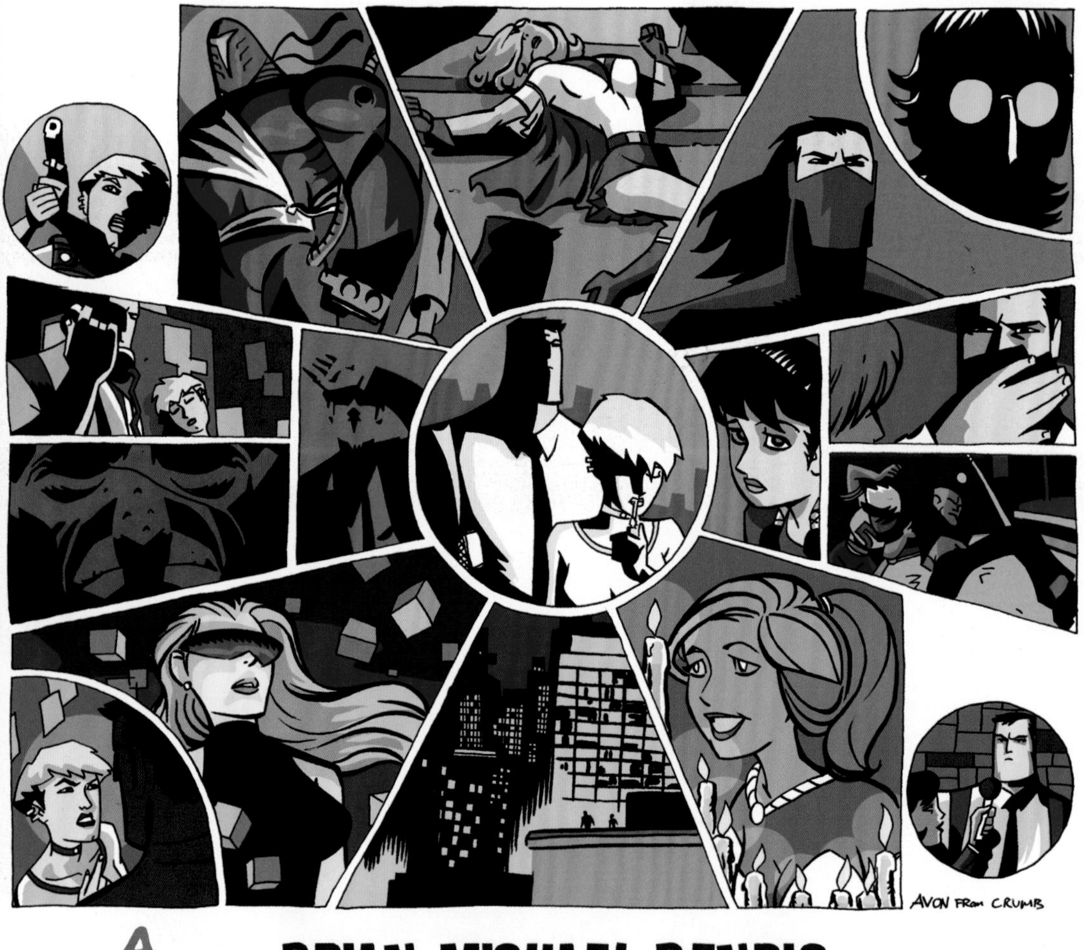
AVON FROM CRUMB

A BRAND NEW STORY ARC!

BRIAN MICHAEL BENDIS
MICHAEL AVON OEMING
PAT GARRAHY

ROLE PLAY PART ONE

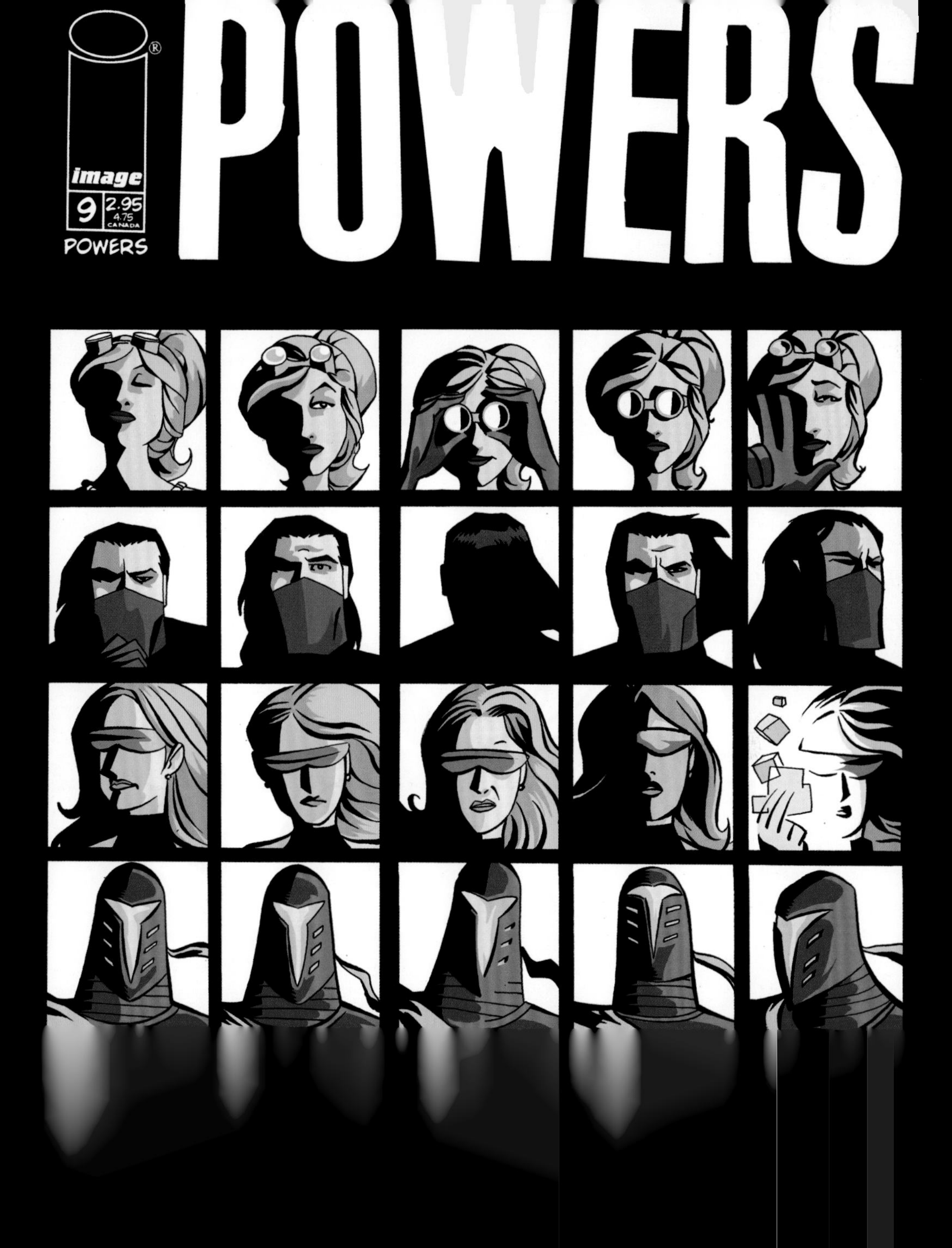
POWERS
image
9
2.95
4.75
CANADA
POWERS

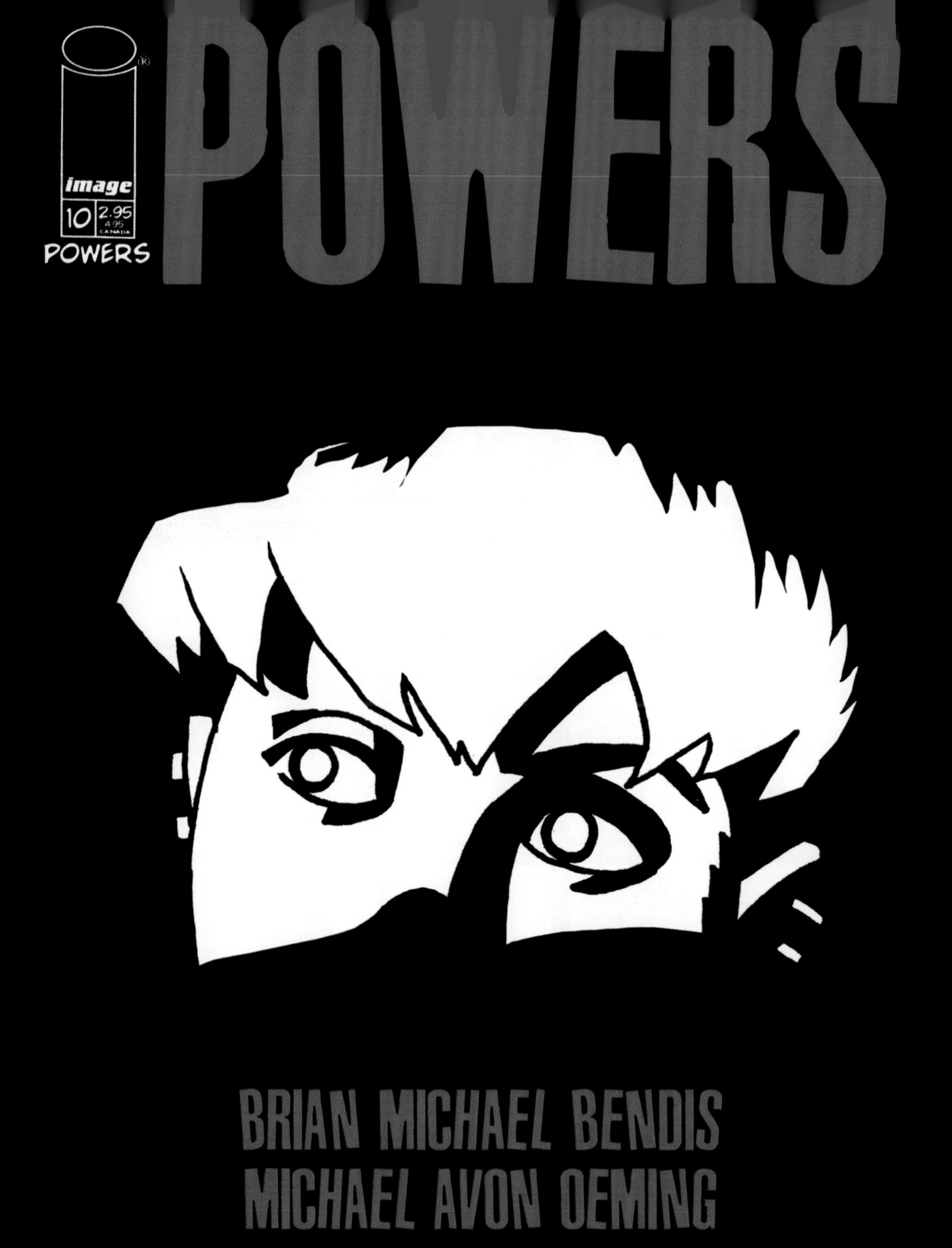
image
10
2.95
4.95 CANADA
POWERS
POWERS
BRIAN MICHAEL BENDIS
MICHAEL AVON OEMING

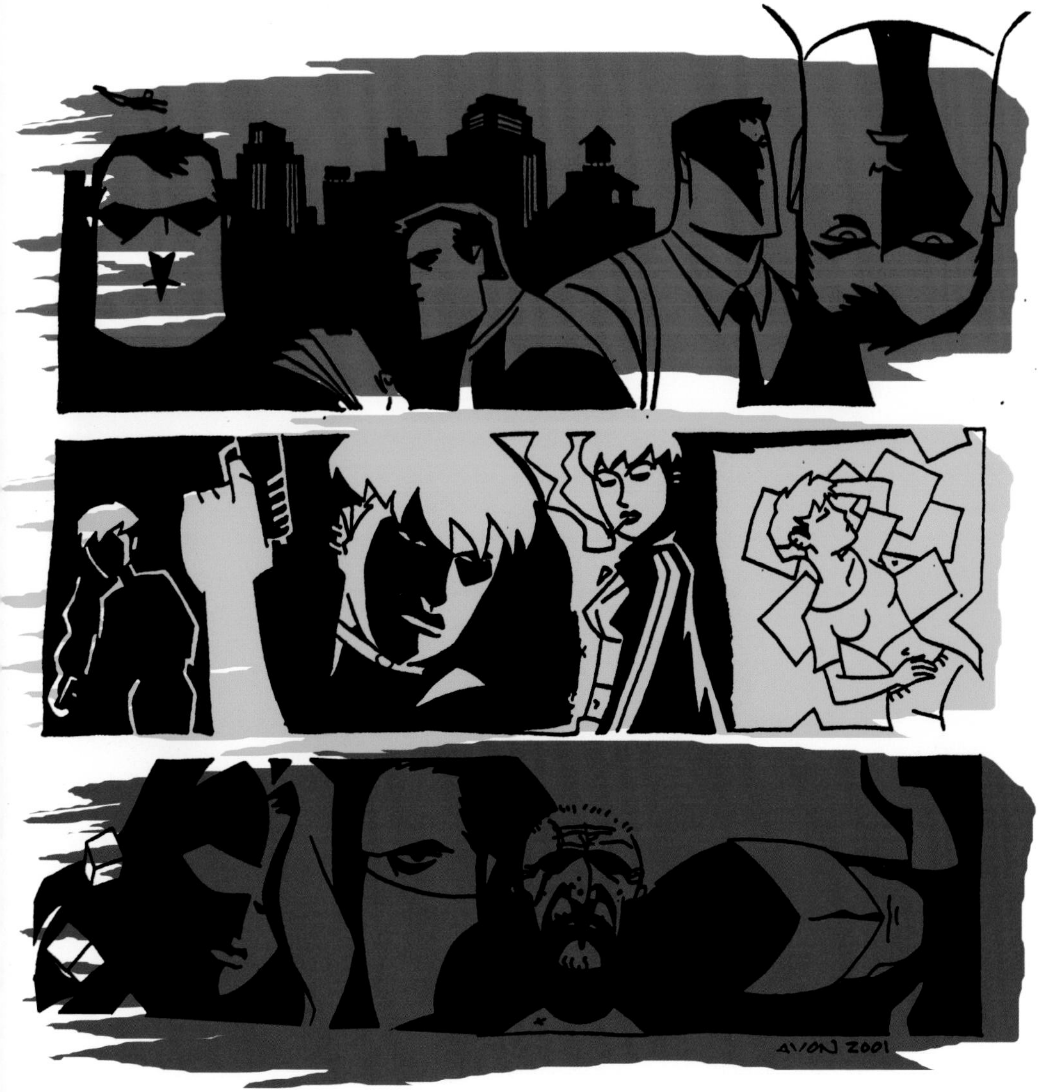
AVON 2001

image

11 | 2.95
4.75
CANADA

POWERS

BRIAN MICHAEL BENDIS
MICHAEL AVON OEMING

POWERS

brian michael bendis
michael avon oeming
image comics
2.95 usa

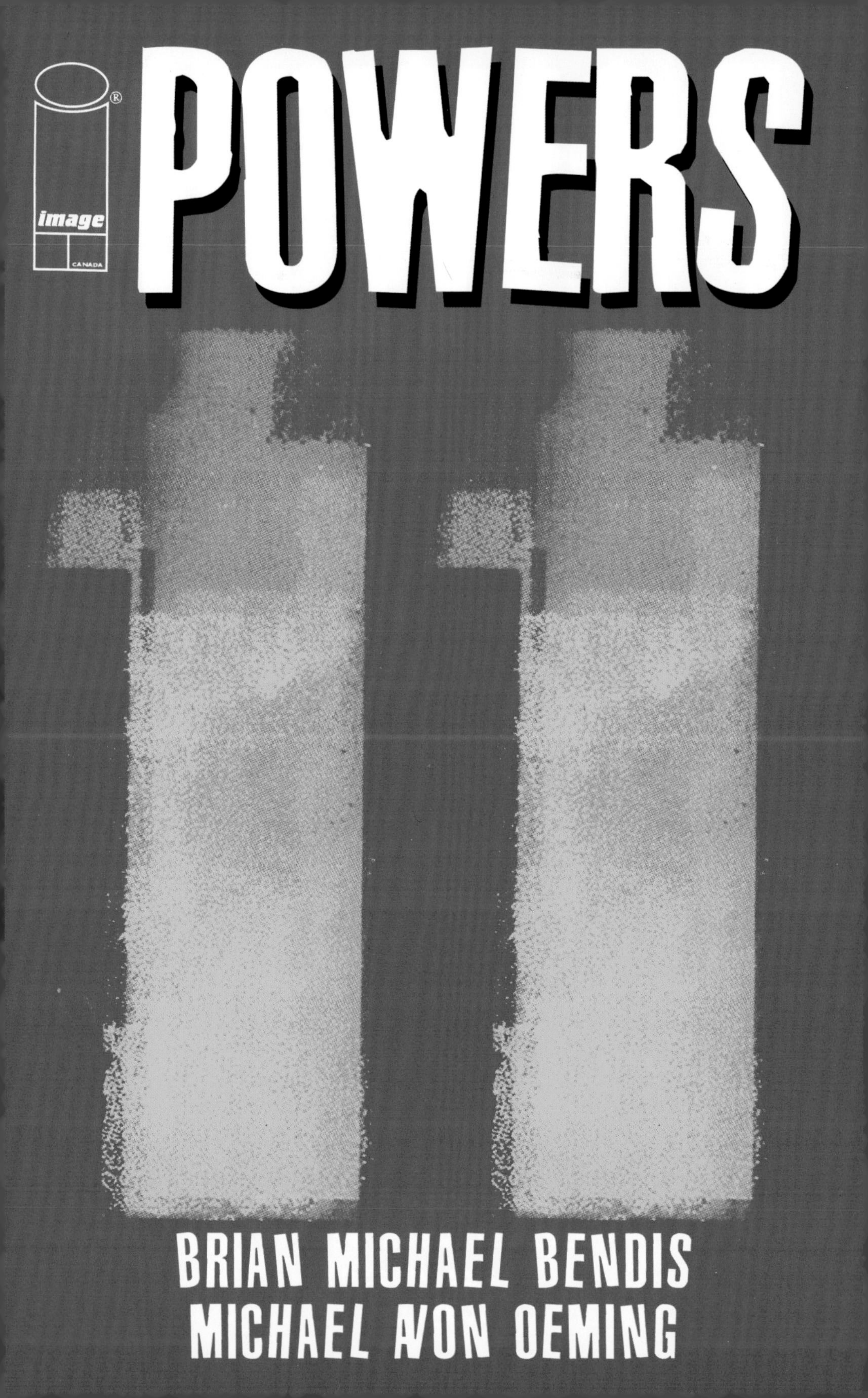
image
CANADA
POWERS
BRIAN MICHAEL BENDIS
MICHAEL AVON OEMING

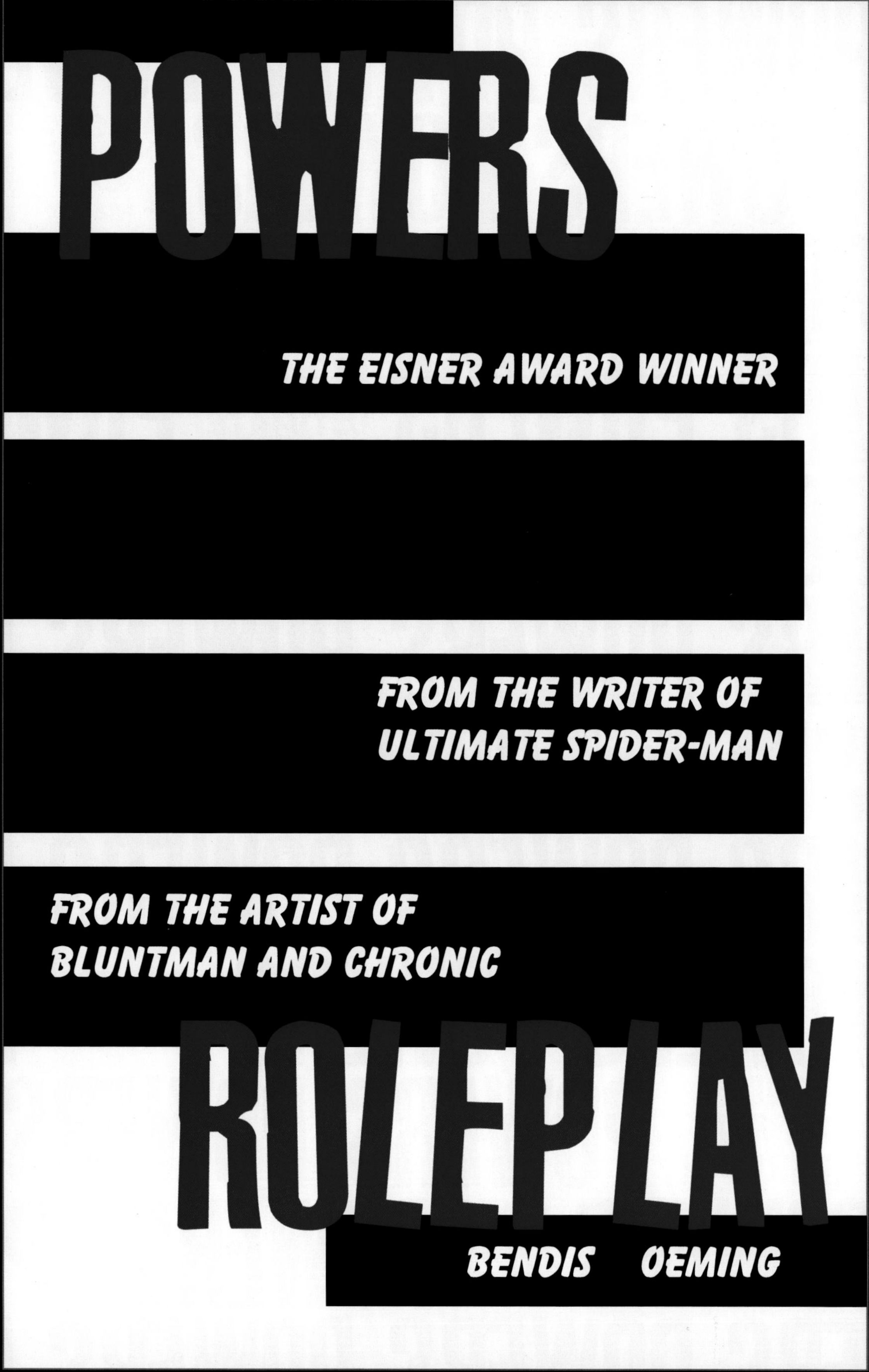
POWERS
THE EISNER AWARD WINNER
FROM THE WRITER OF
ULTIMATE SPIDER-MAN
FROM THE ARTIST OF
BLUNTMAN AND CHRONIC
ROLEPLAY
BENDIS OEMING

Unused *Powers* cover design using graphics instead of an image

POWERS POWERS POW
POWERS POWERS
A BOOK
YOU MUST
READ!
- WIZARD
POWERS POWERS POWE
ERS POWERS
FROM THE
WRITER OF
ULTIMATE
SPIDER-MAN
POW
POWERS POWERS POWE
ERS POWERS POWERS
S
RECOMMENDED
TO ANYONE
WHO BREATHES!
-COMICS INTERNATIONAL
POWERS POWE
ERS POWERS POWERS
POWERS POWERS
A PERFECT
COMIC BOOK!!
-FANDOM.COM
BENDIS
OEMING
GARRAHY
POWERS POWERS
POWERS
WWW.
JINX
WORLD.
COM
POWERS
P

image

ERS POWERS POWERS

Unused *Powers* cover design using graphics instead of an image

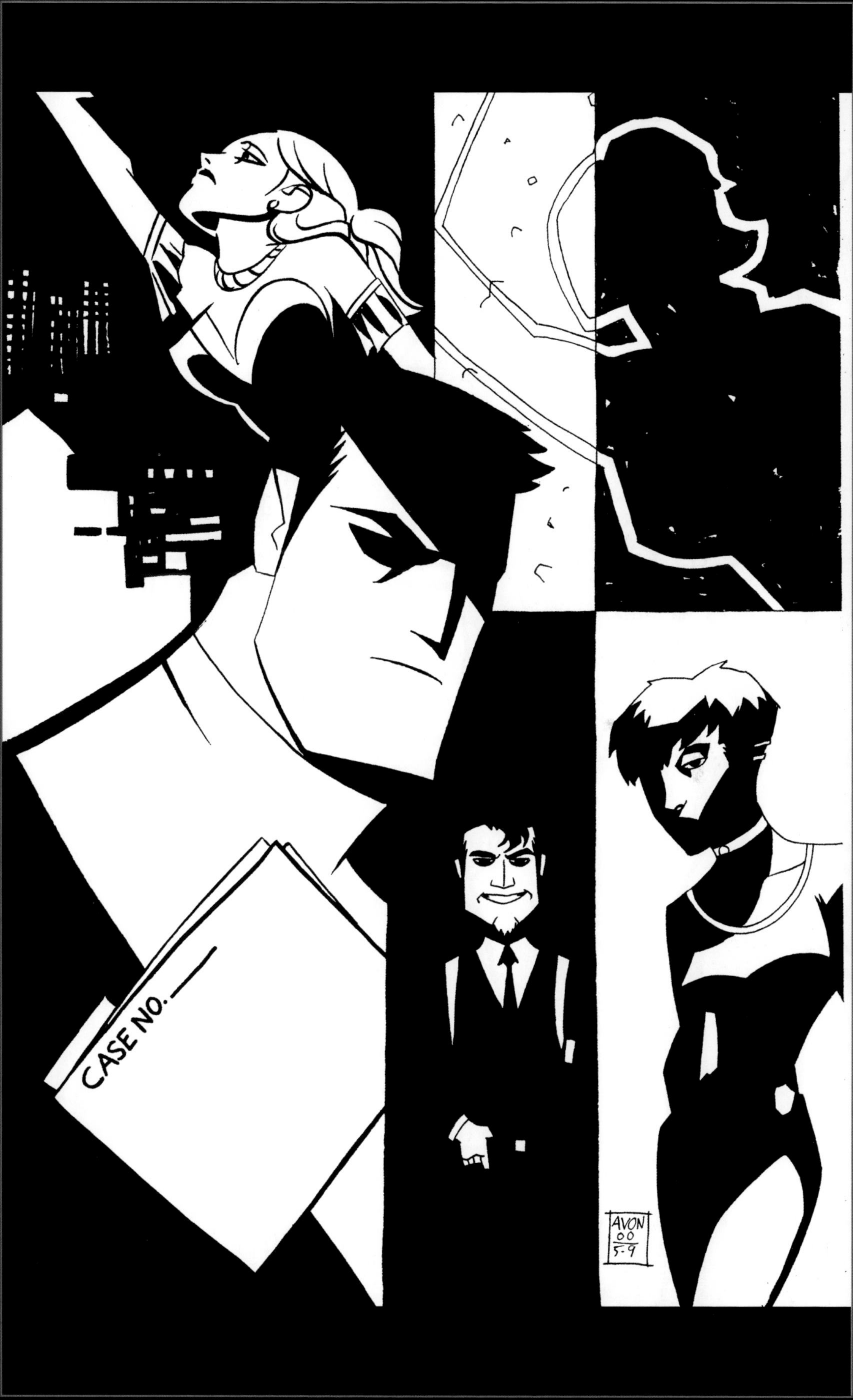
CASE NO.
AVON
00
5-9

Unused *Powers* cover inks

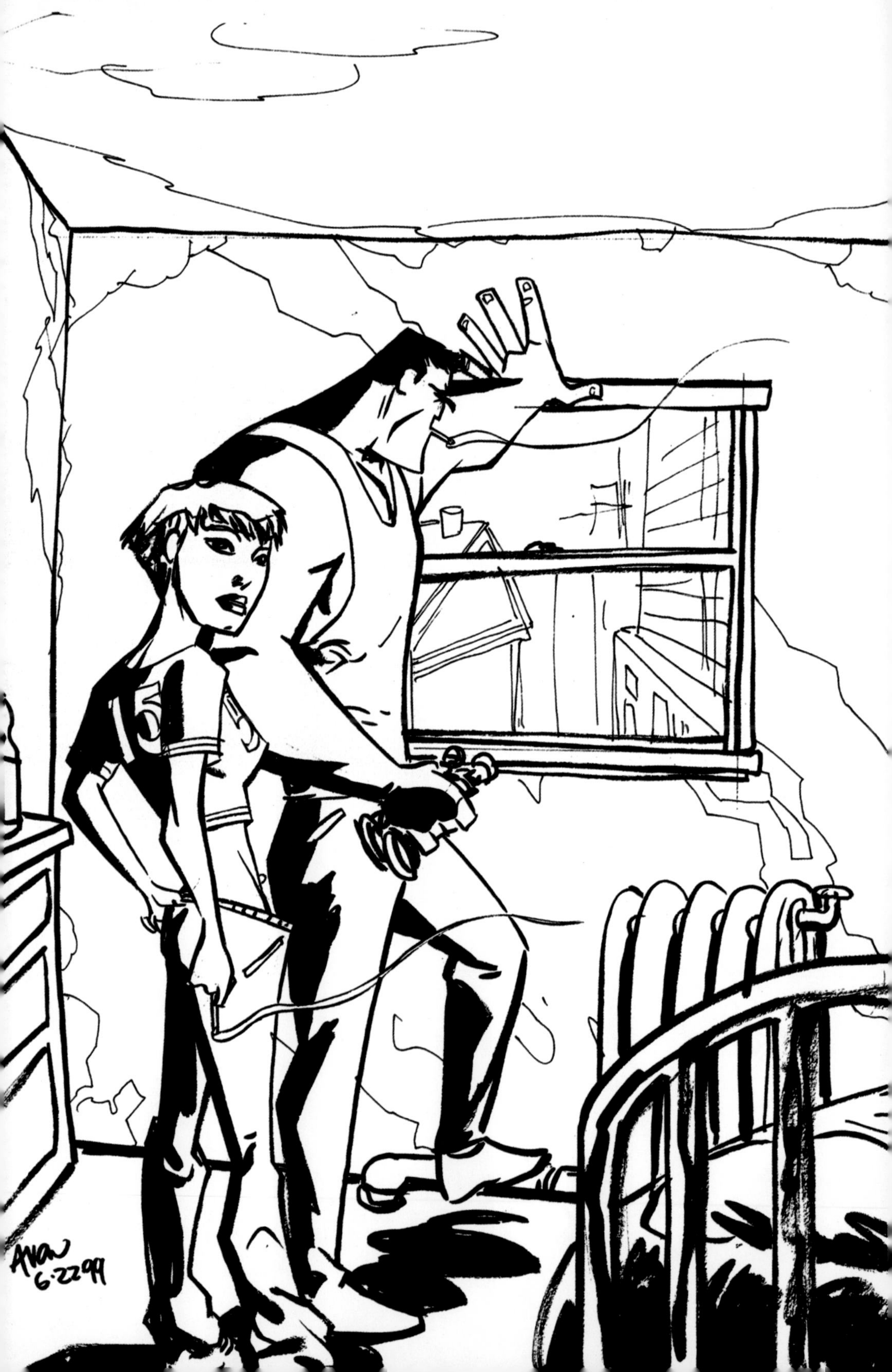

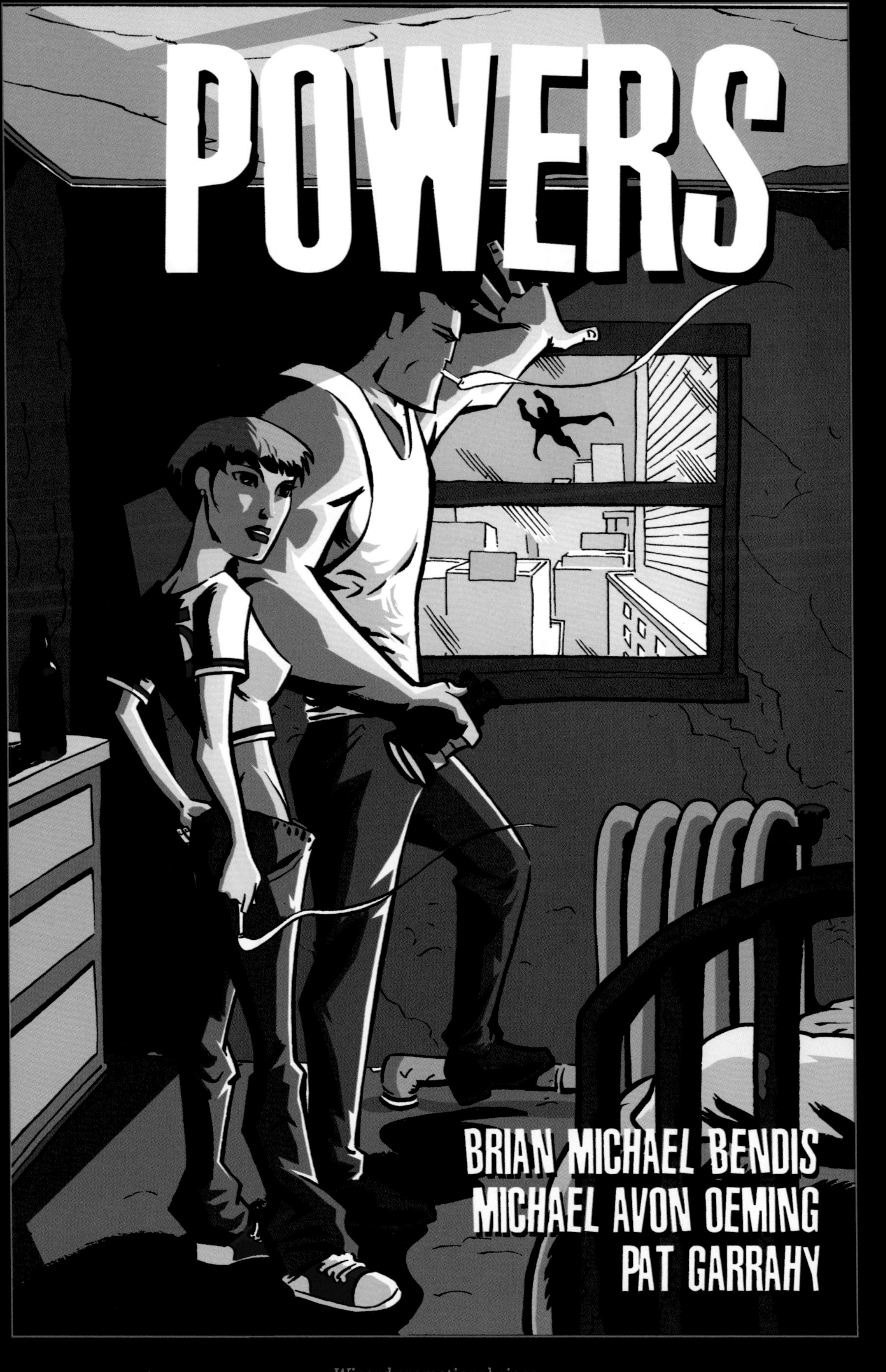
POWERS
BRIAN MICHAEL BENDIS
MICHAEL AVON OEMING
PAT GARRAHY

Wizard promotional piece

BENDIS: Unused cover idea, but one of my faves.

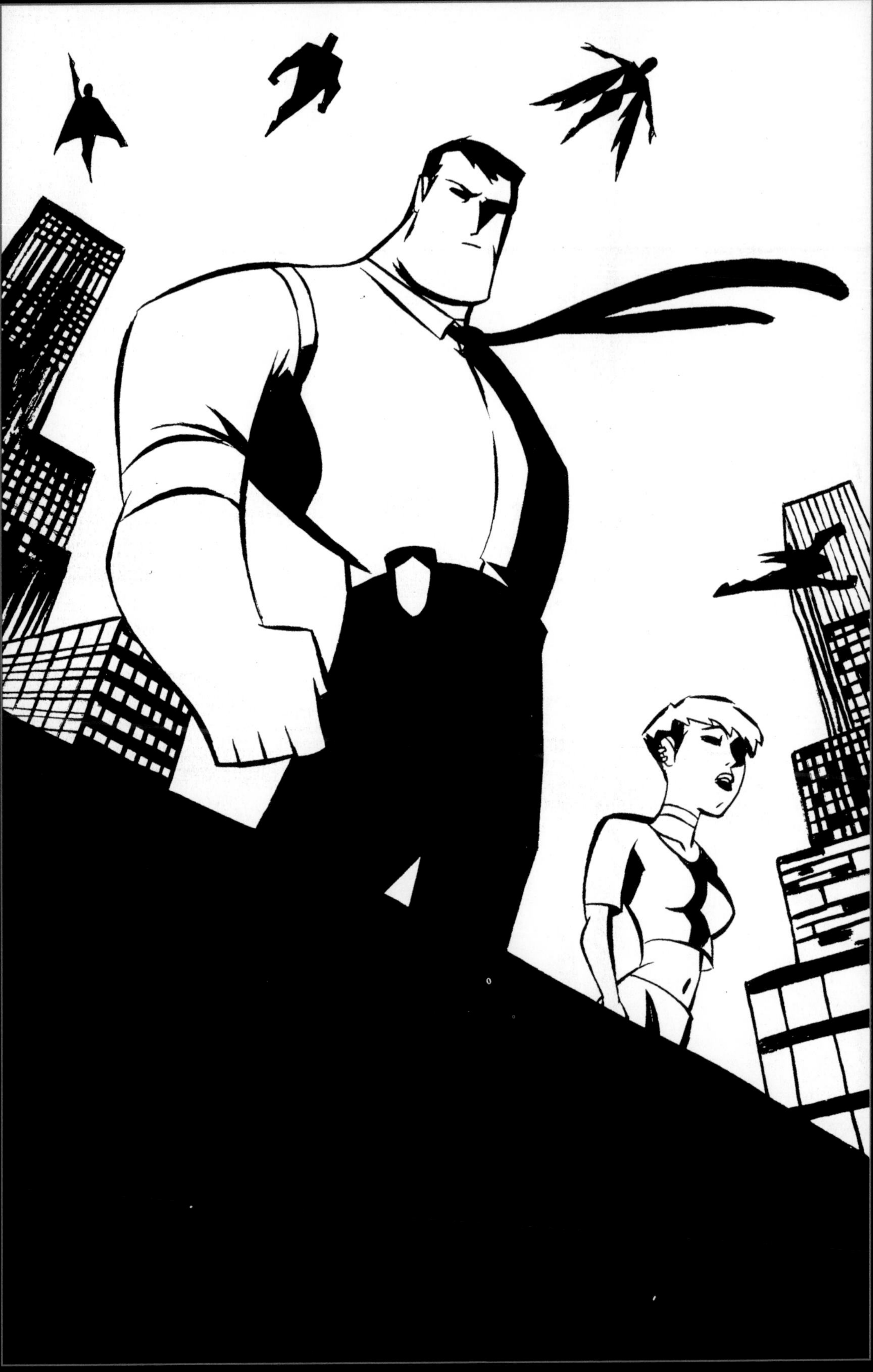

Unused *Powers* cover concept

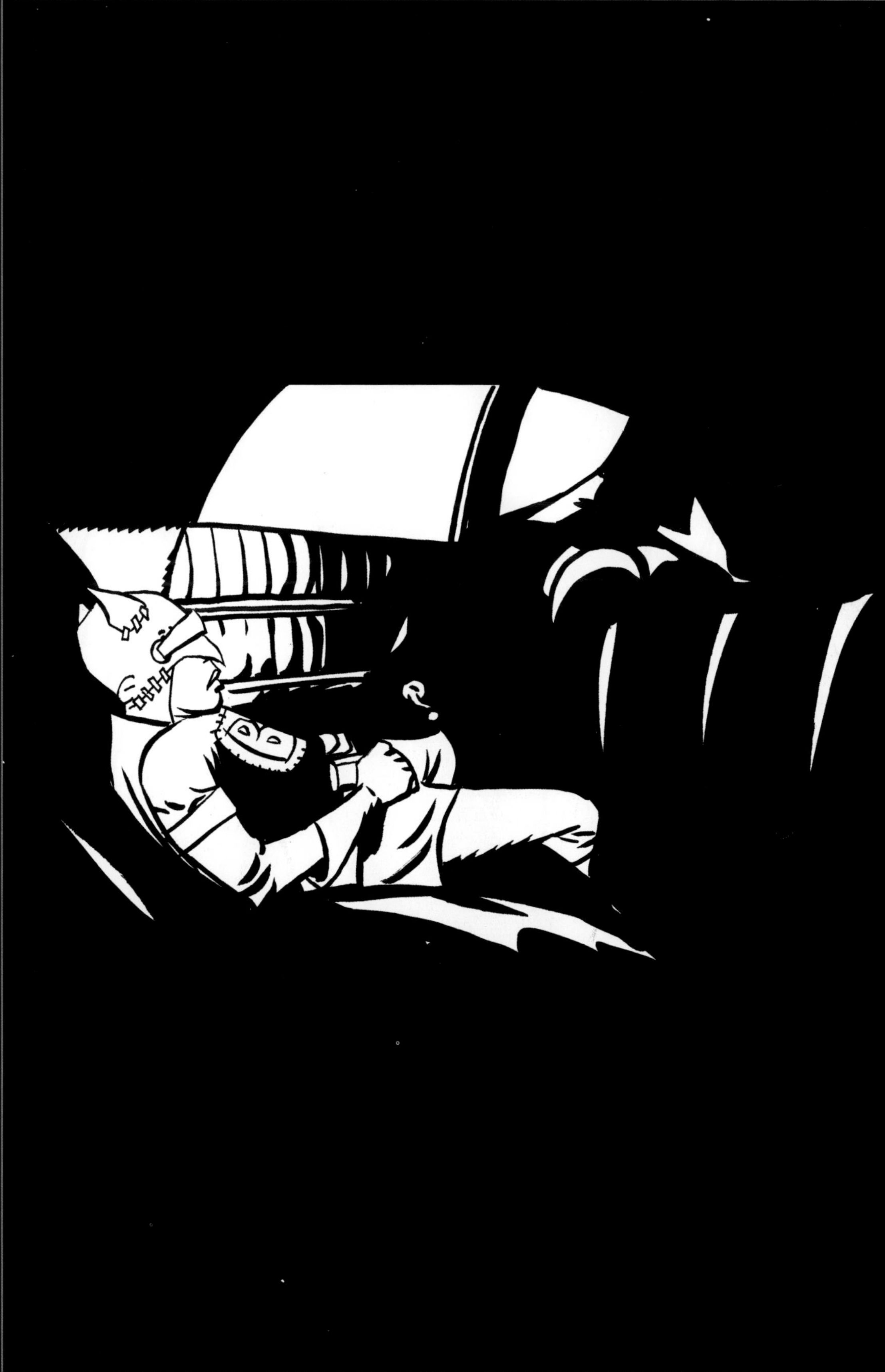

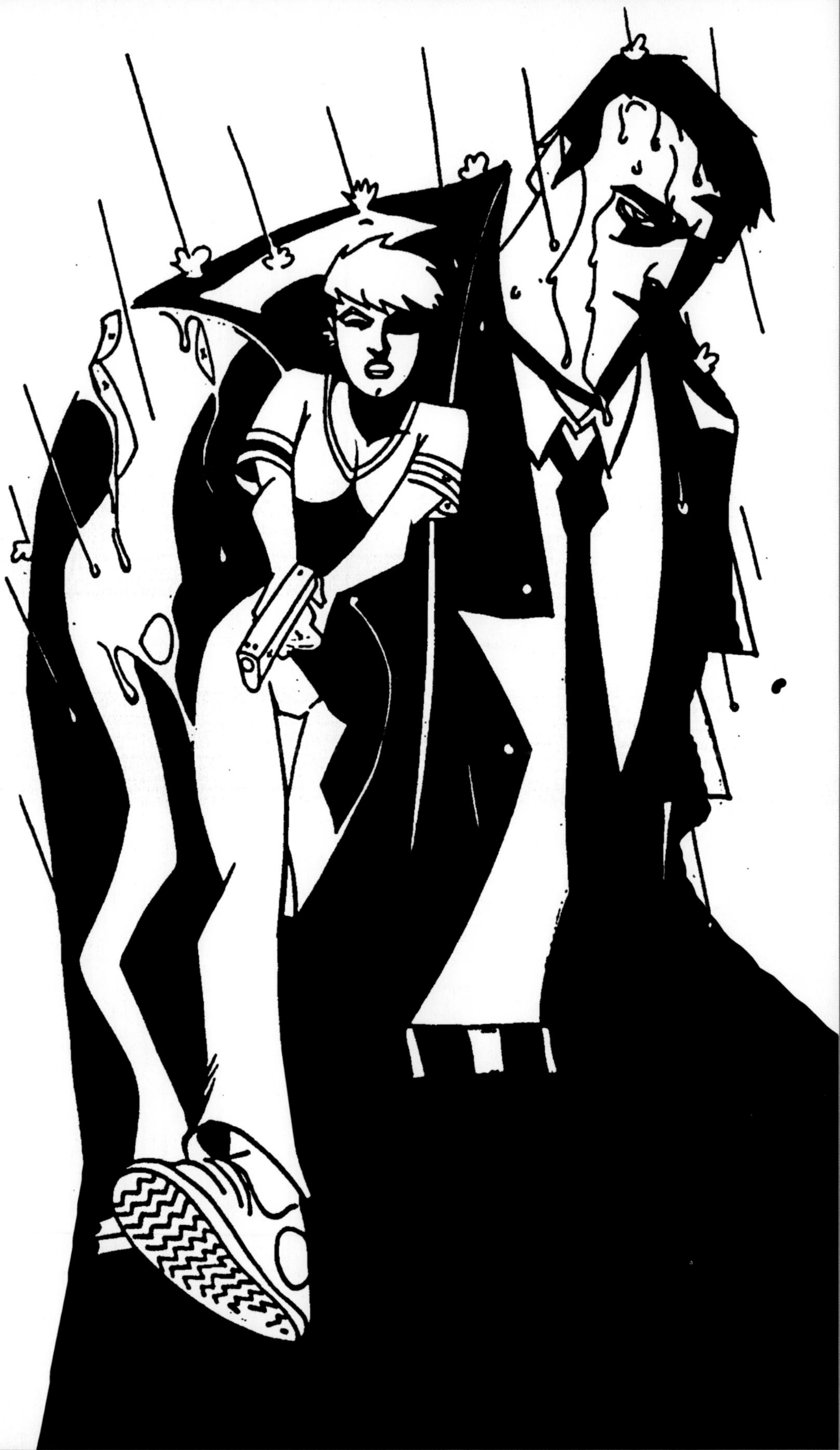

Unused *Powers* cover inks

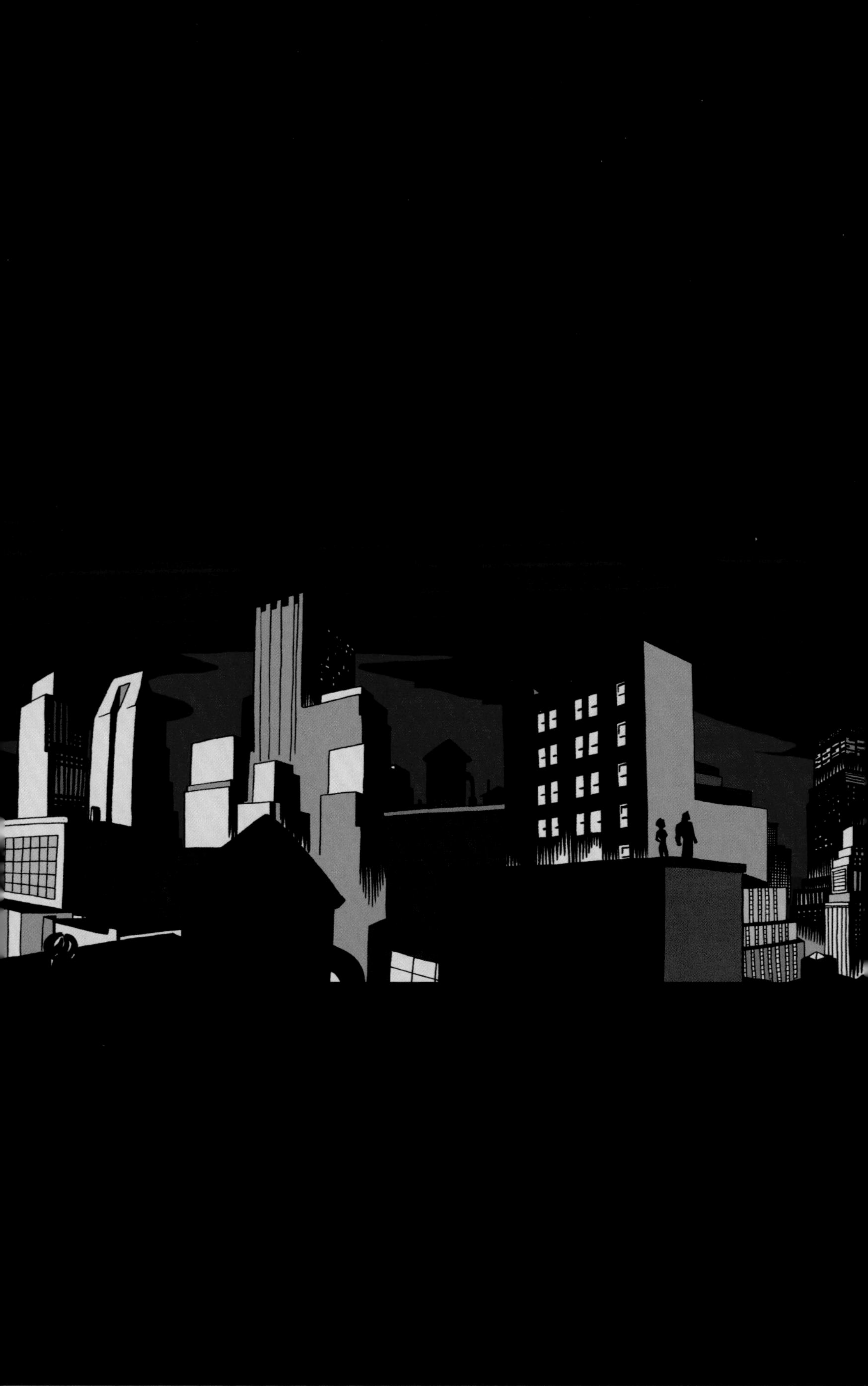

Powers Volume 1: *Who Killed Retro Girl?* cover, first printing

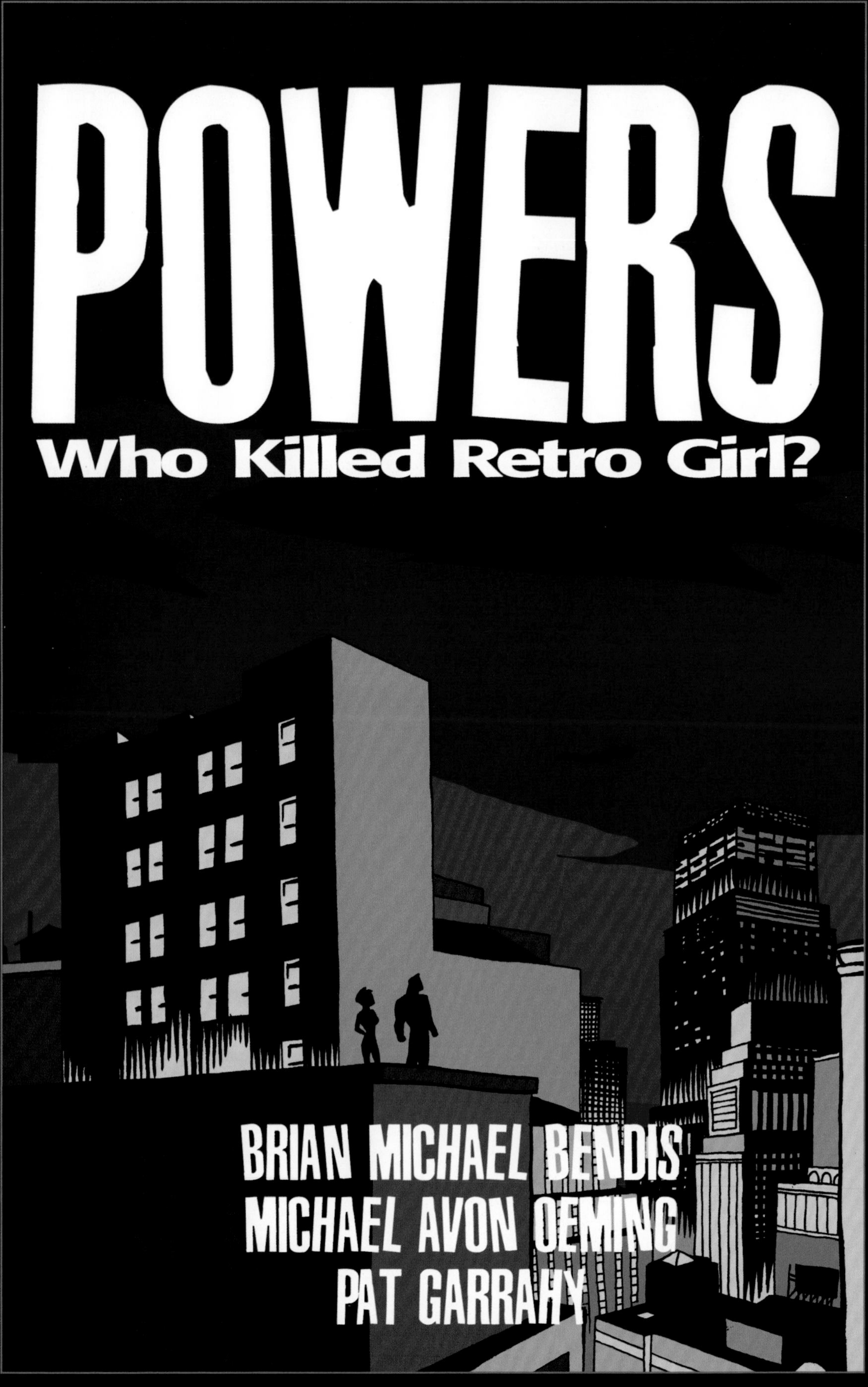
POWERS
Who Killed Retro Girl?
BRIAN MICHAEL BENDIS
MICHAEL AVON OEMING
PAT GARRAHY

Powers Volume 1: *Who Killed Retro Girl?* cover, second printing

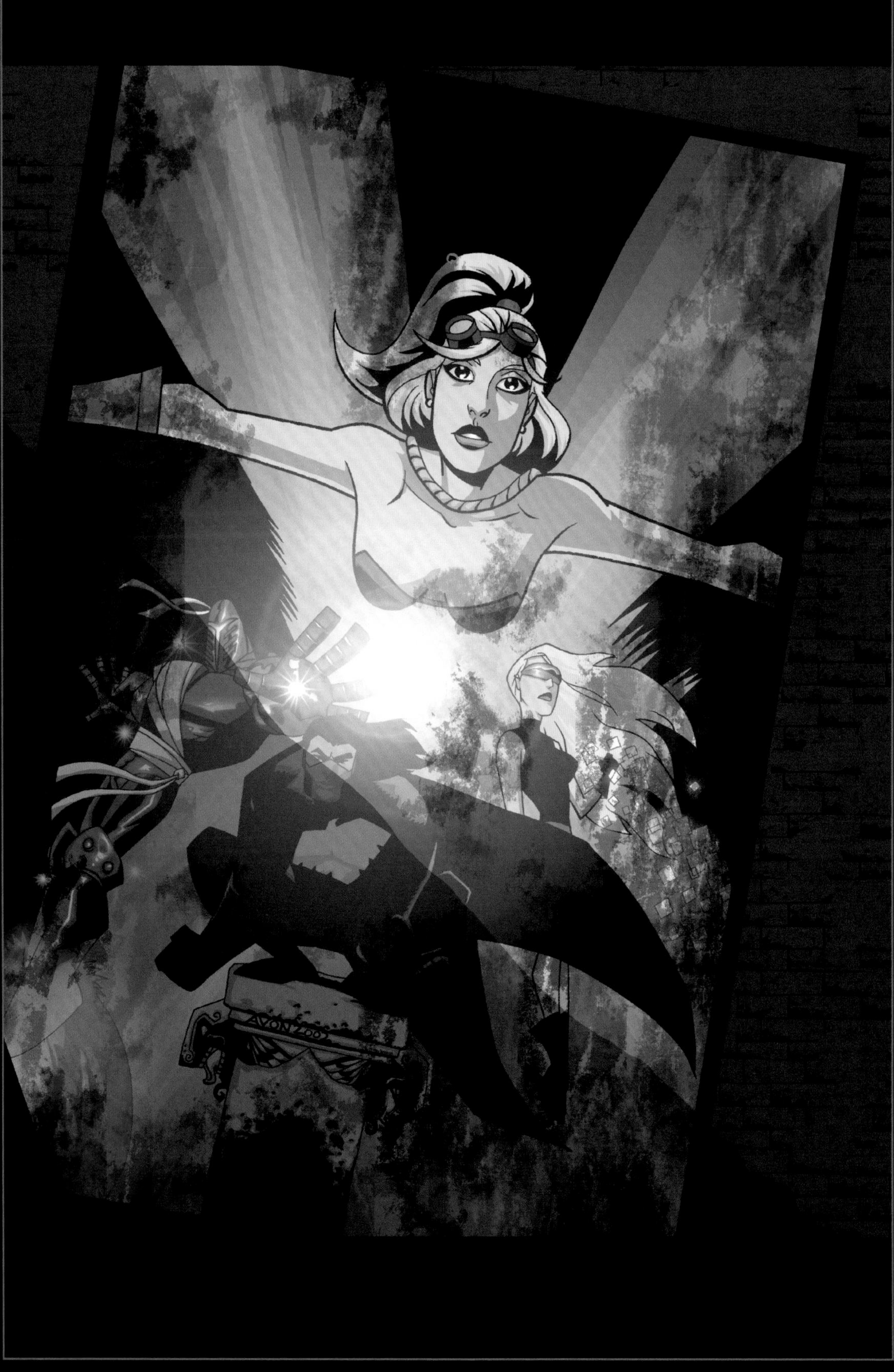

Powers Volume 1: *Who Killed Retro Girl?* cover, fifth printing

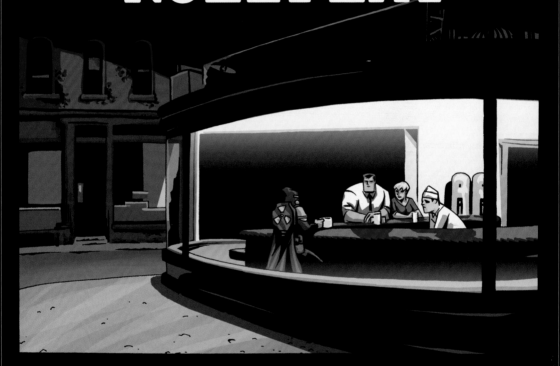

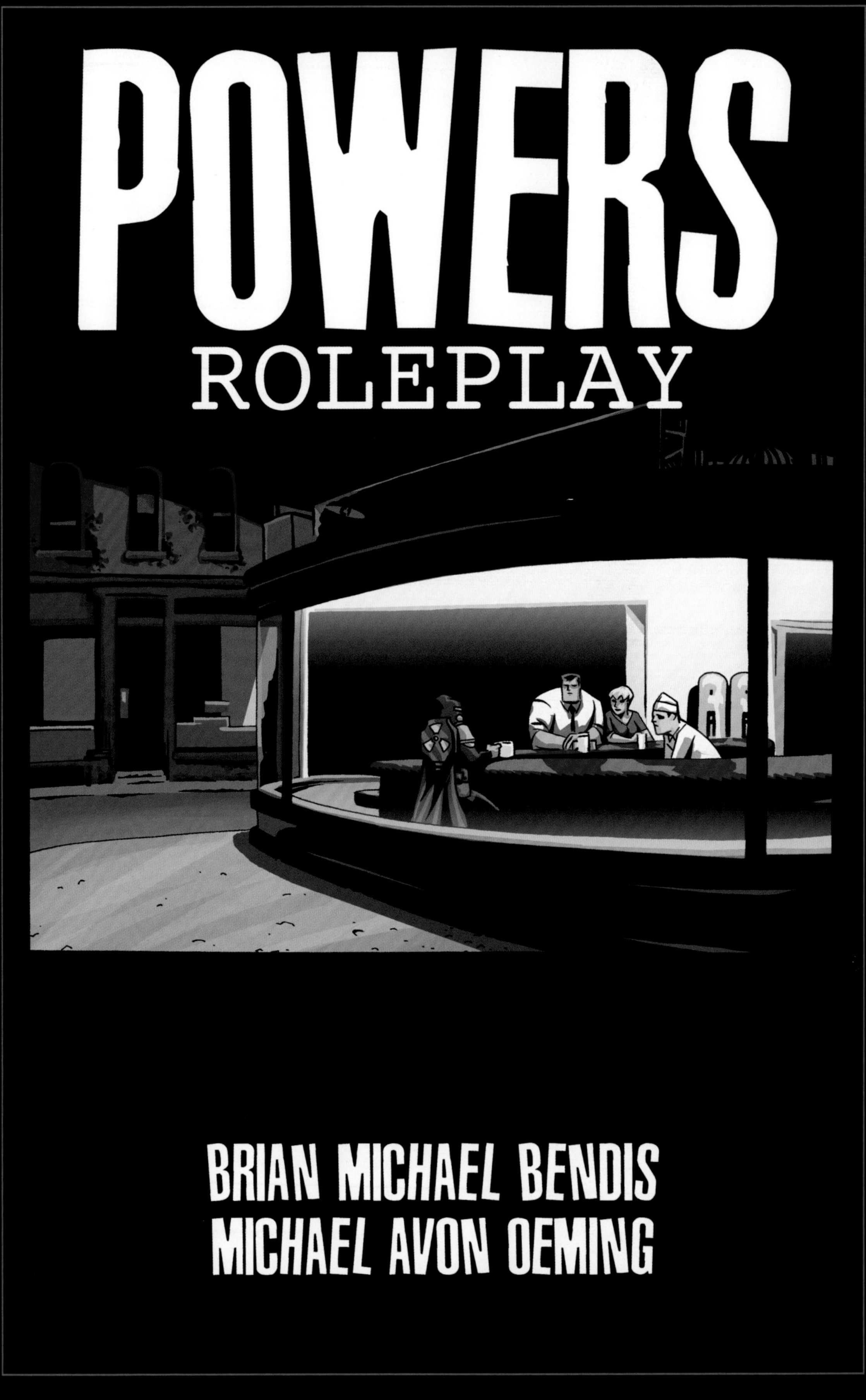

POWERS
ROLEPLAY

BRIAN MICHAEL BENDIS
MICHAEL AVON OEMING

Powers Volume 2: *Roleplay* cover, first printing

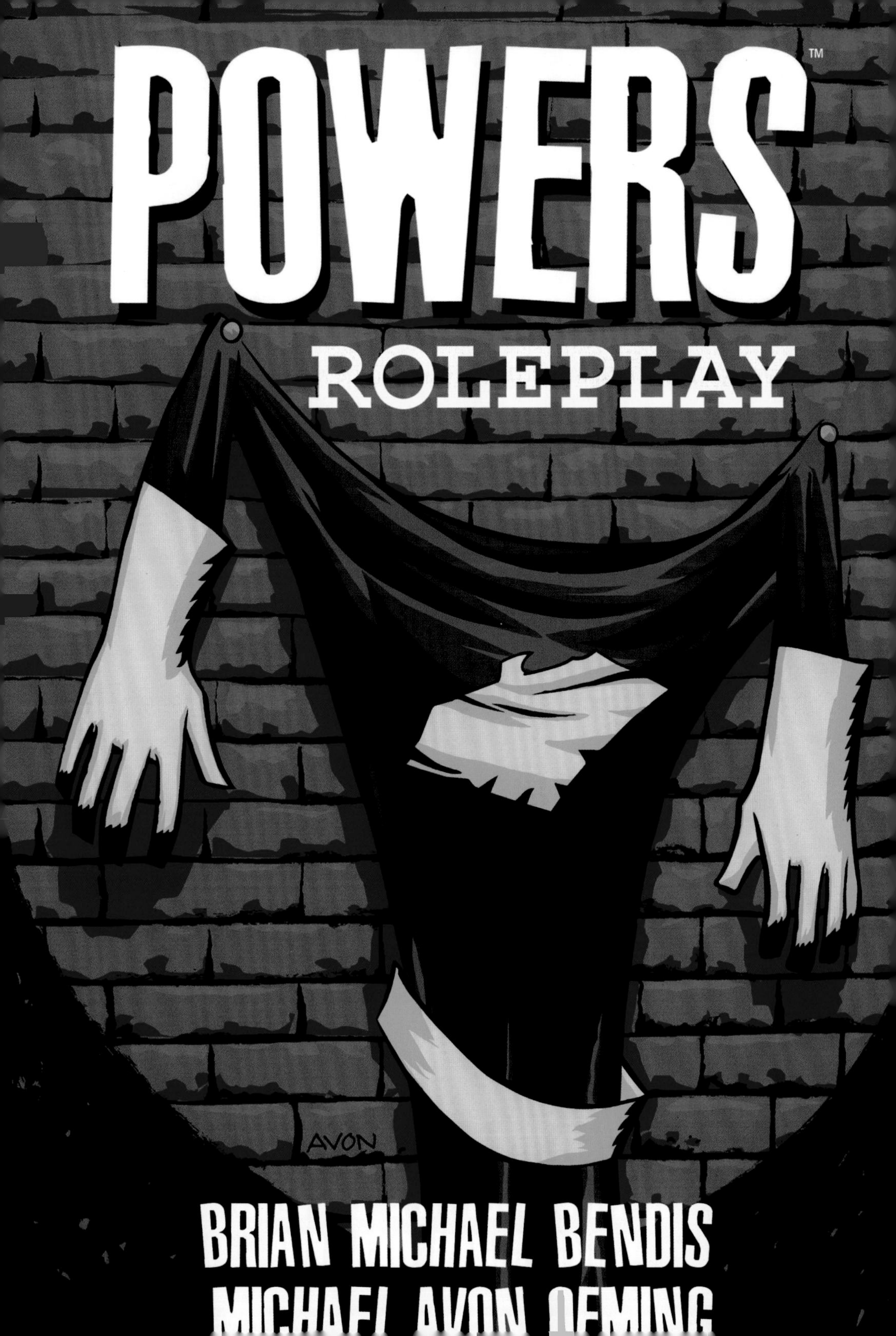
POWERS™
ROLEPLAY
AVON
BRIAN MICHAEL BENDIS
MICHAEL AVON OEMING

POWERS™

The Definitive Hardcover Collection

Volume One

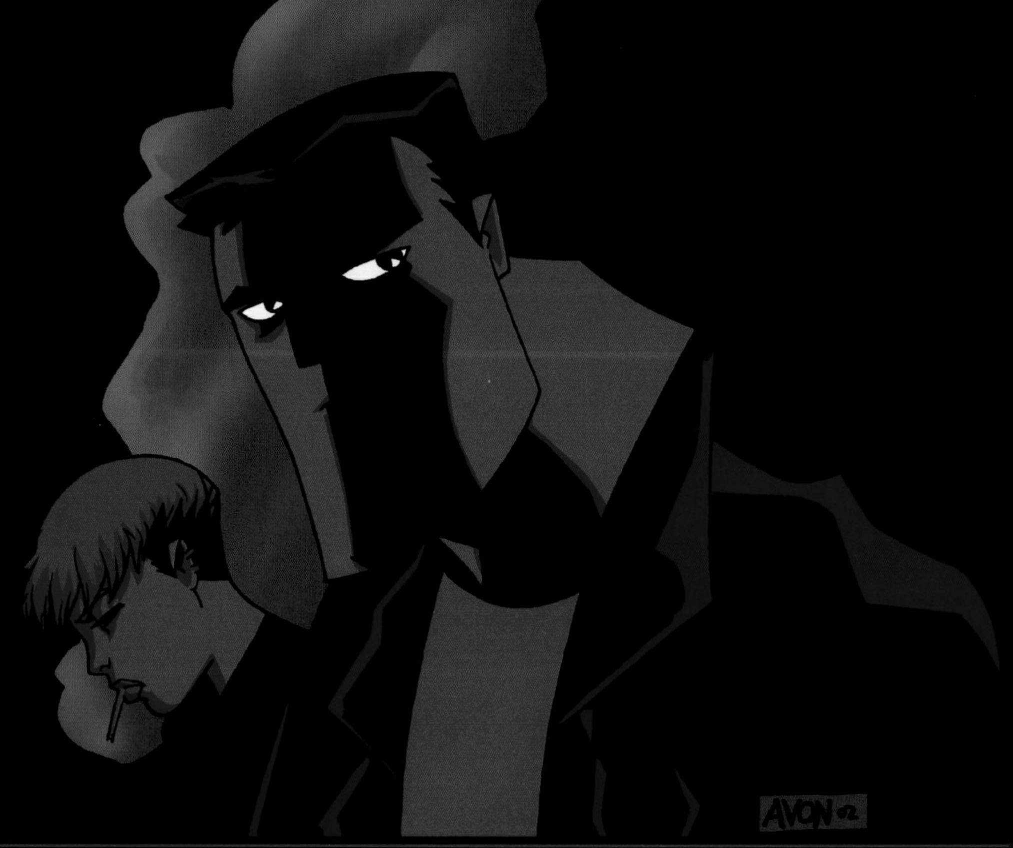
AVON '02

BRIAN MICHAEL BENDIS
MIKE AVON OEMING

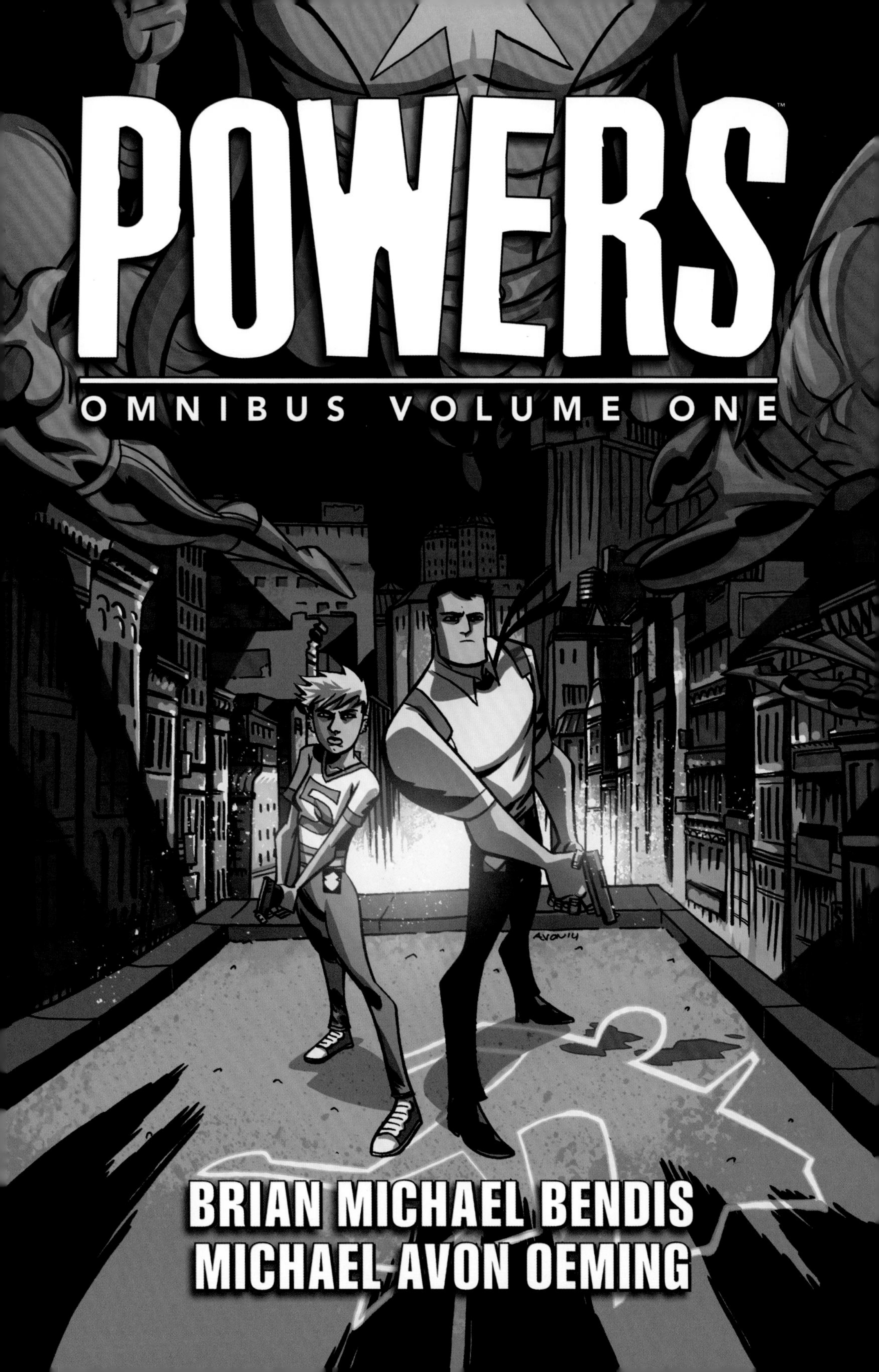
POWERS™
OMNIBUS VOLUME ONE
BRIAN MICHAEL BENDIS
MICHAEL AVON OEMING

POWERS™

SKETCHBOOK

In this section, you will see one of Michael Avon Oeming's true strengths as an artist. Every gesture, every character design, every brush-stroke looks so simple, so effortless, but in reality it is a laborious process. This is an intense decision-making process that defines everything about the book.

For every sketch revealed here, there are literally dozens more. Mike is a fountain of ideas and images. For months prior to working on the actual pages, I would receive daily faxes of these ideas and images. What a rush.

I hope you get even half the thrill from these that I do.

POWERS™

CHARACTERS

Here is a smattering of images that explore how many ways any of the characters could have gone.

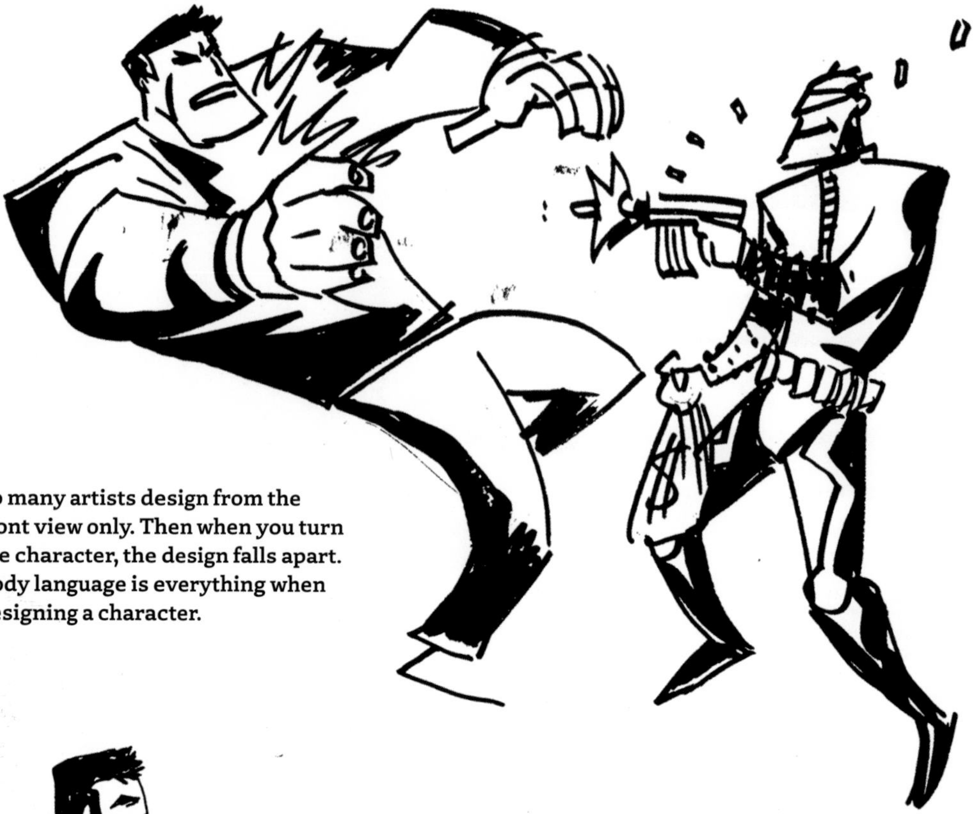

So many artists design from the front view only. Then when you turn the character, the design falls apart. Body language is everything when designing a character.

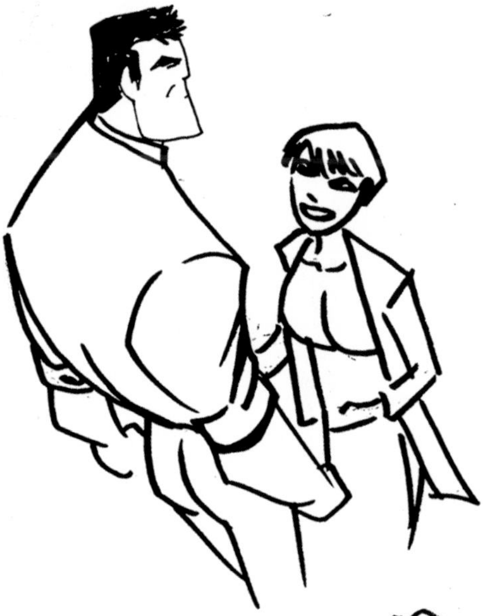

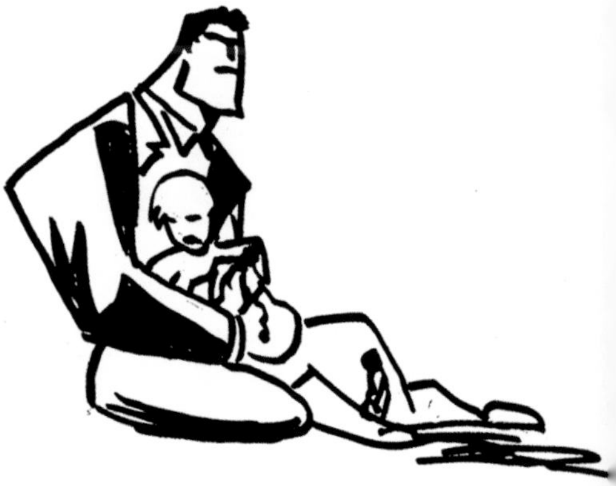

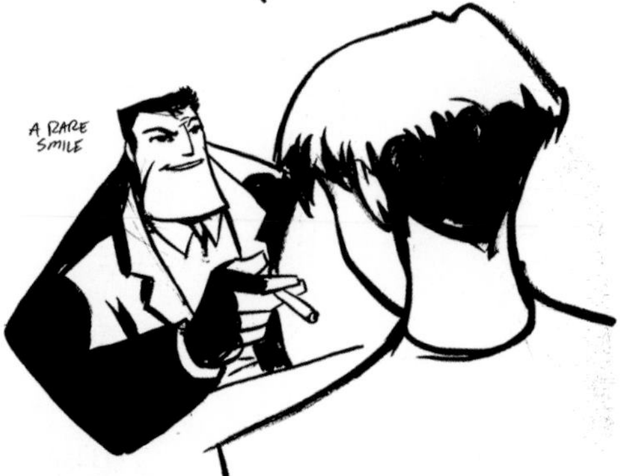
A RARE SMILE

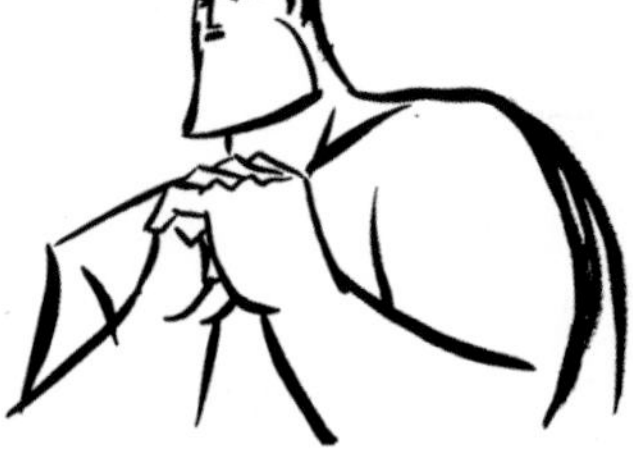

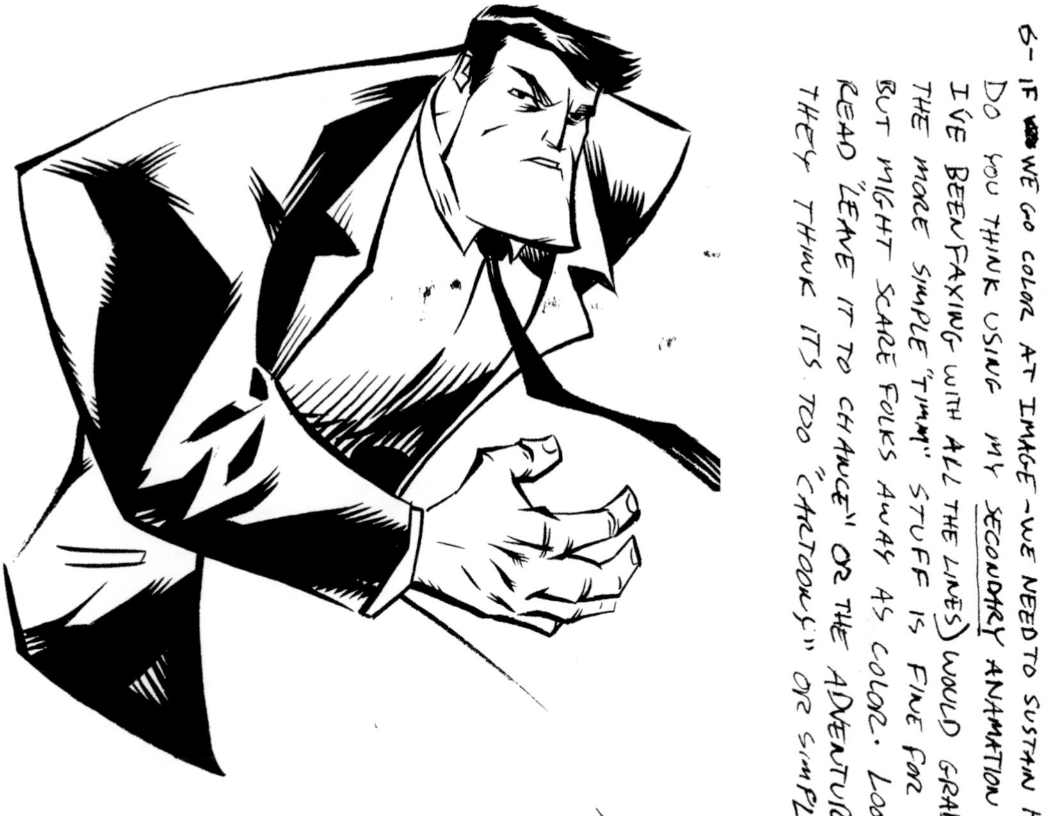

6- IF WE GO COLOR AT IMAGE - WE NEED TO SUSTAIN HIGHER NUMBERS -
DO YOU THINK USING MY SECONDARY ANAMATION STYLE (THE NEWER STUFF
I'VE BEEN FAXING WITH ALL THE LINES) WOULD GRAB US LARGER NUMBERS?
THE MORE SIMPLE "TIMM" STUFF IS FINE FOR A 2-3,000 B+W AUDIENCE,
BUT MIGHT SCARE FOLKS AWAY AS COLOR. LOOK AT HOW MANY DON'T
READ "LEAVE IT TO CHANCE" OR THE ADVENTURES BOOKS BECAUSE
THEY THINK ITS TOO "CARTOONS" OR SIMPLE. - WHAT ARE YOUR THOUGHTS

This is an extremely early stab at Walker that came with a hilarious note from Mike (which is being reprinted with his permission).

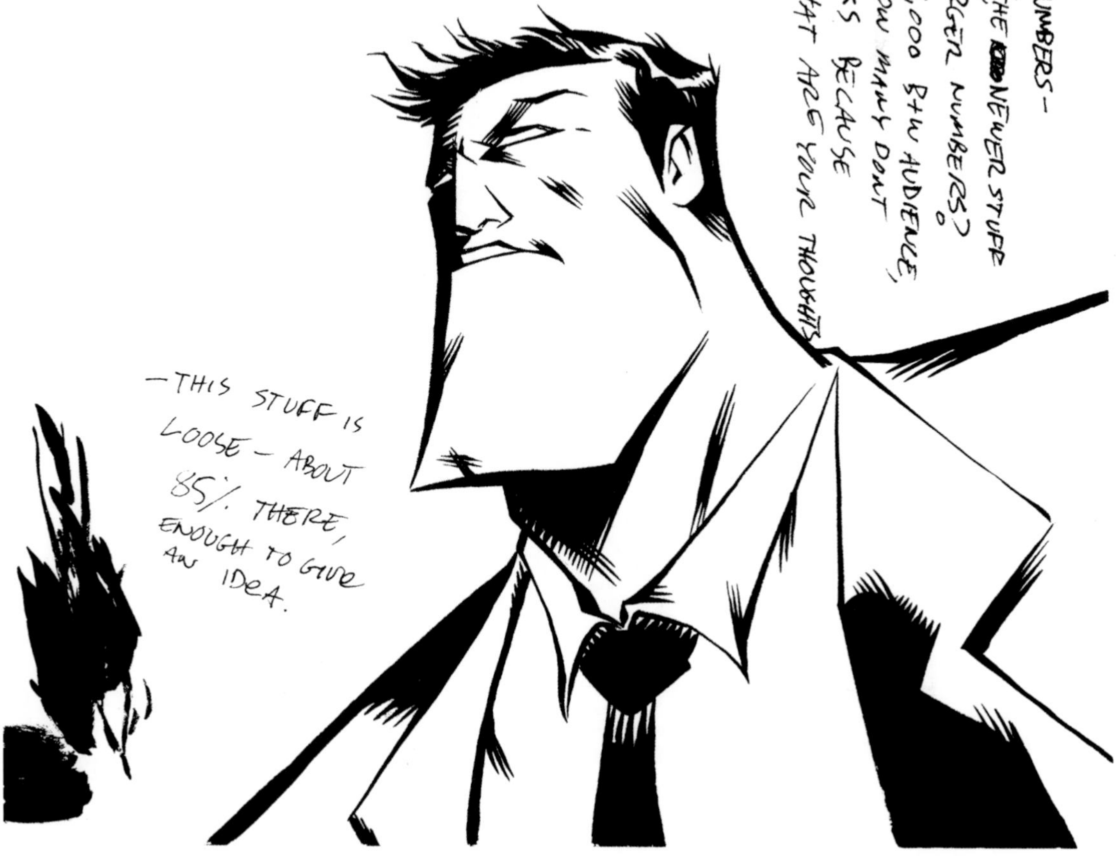

-THIS STUFF IS LOOSE - ABOUT 85% THERE, ENOUGH TO GIVE AN IDEA.

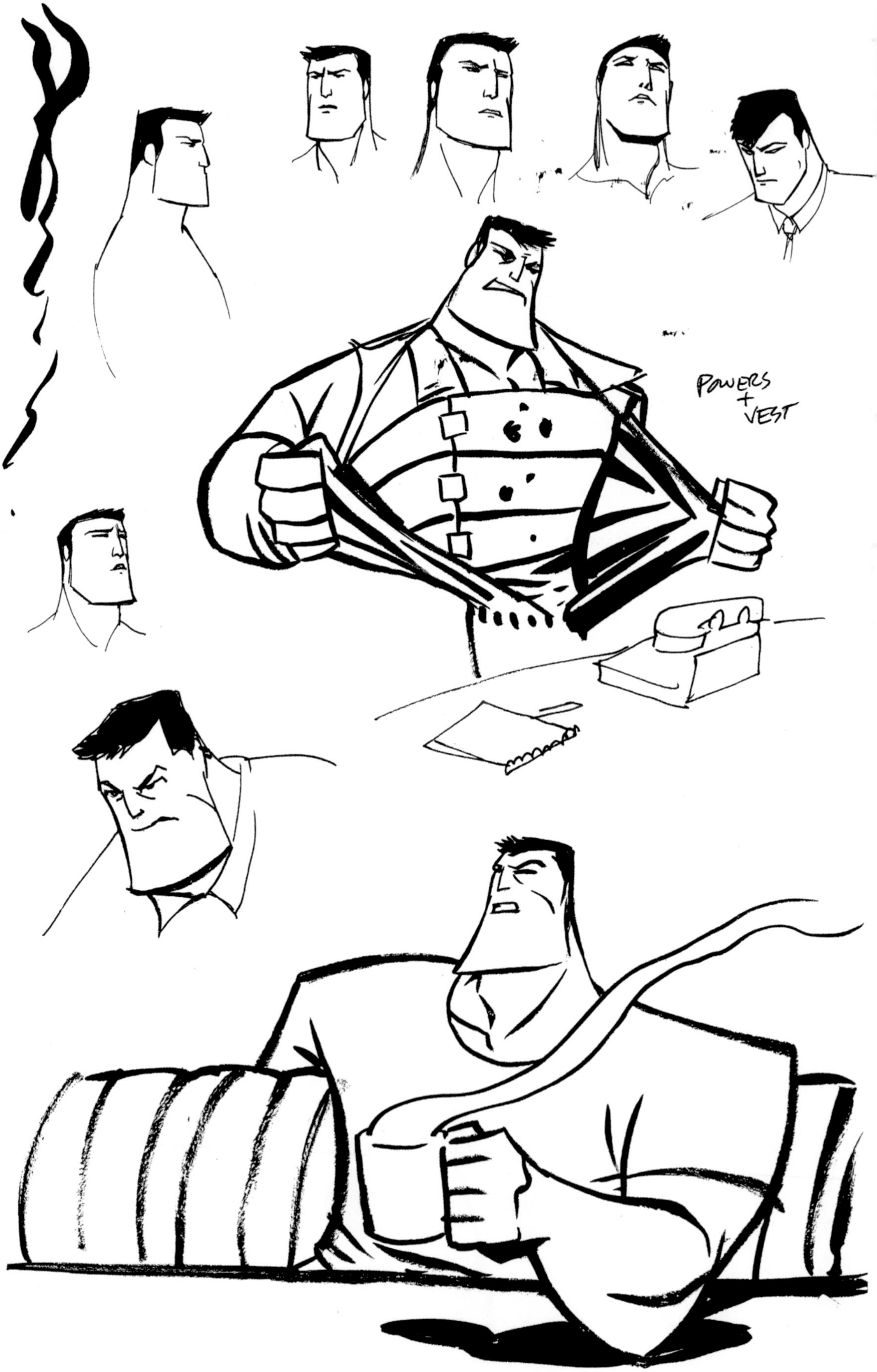
POWERS
+
VEST

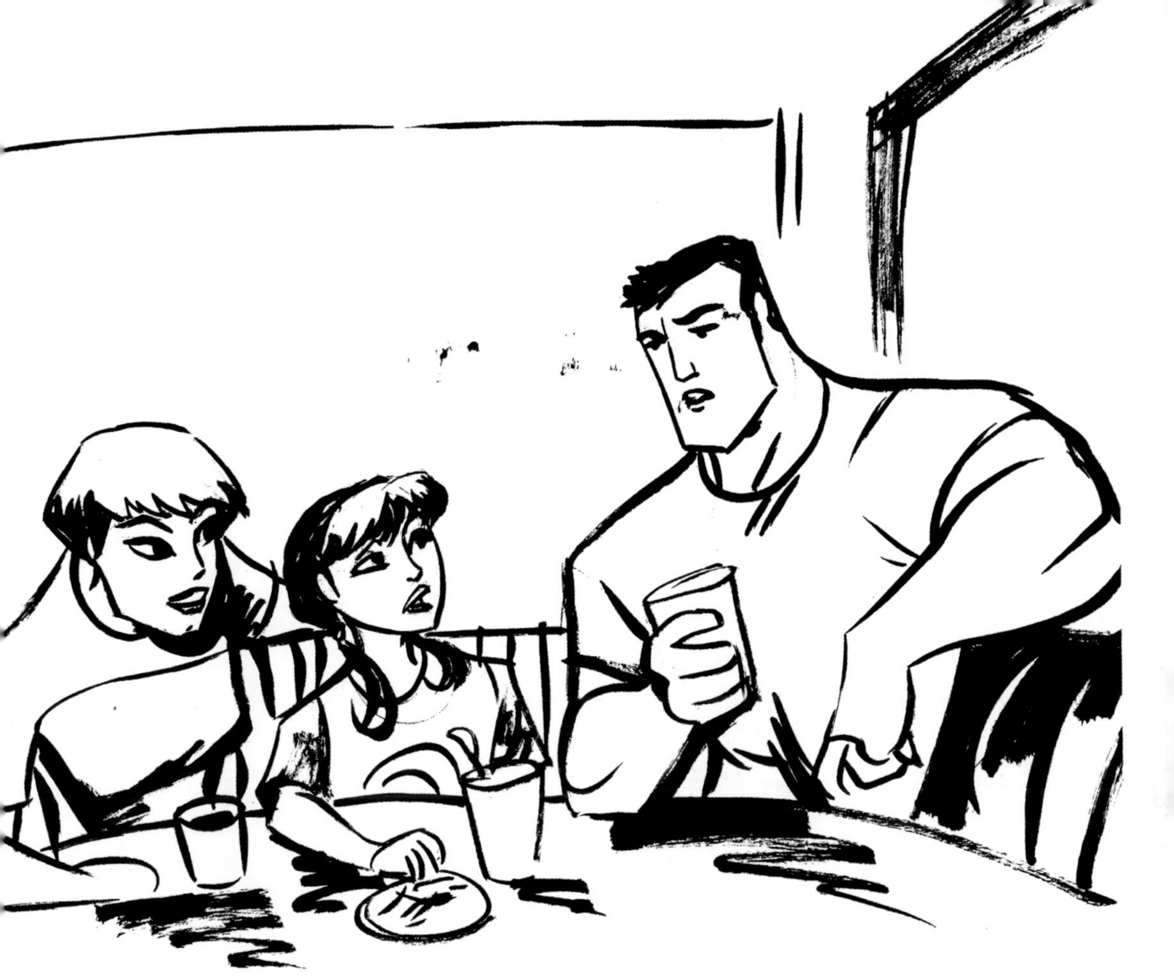

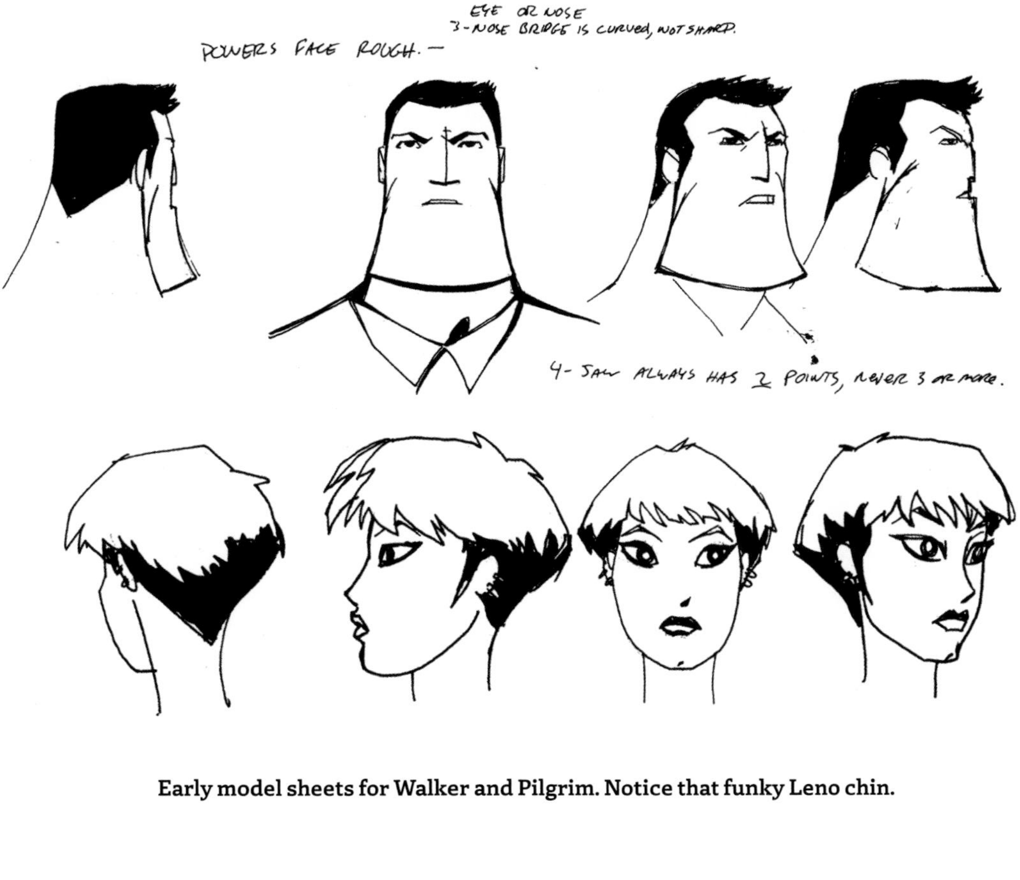
EYE OR NOSE
3- NOSE BRIDGE IS CURVED, NOT SHARP.
POWERS FACE ROUGH. —
4- JAW ALWAYS HAS 2 POINTS, NEVER 3 OR MORE.

Early model sheets for Walker and Pilgrim. Notice that funky Leno chin.

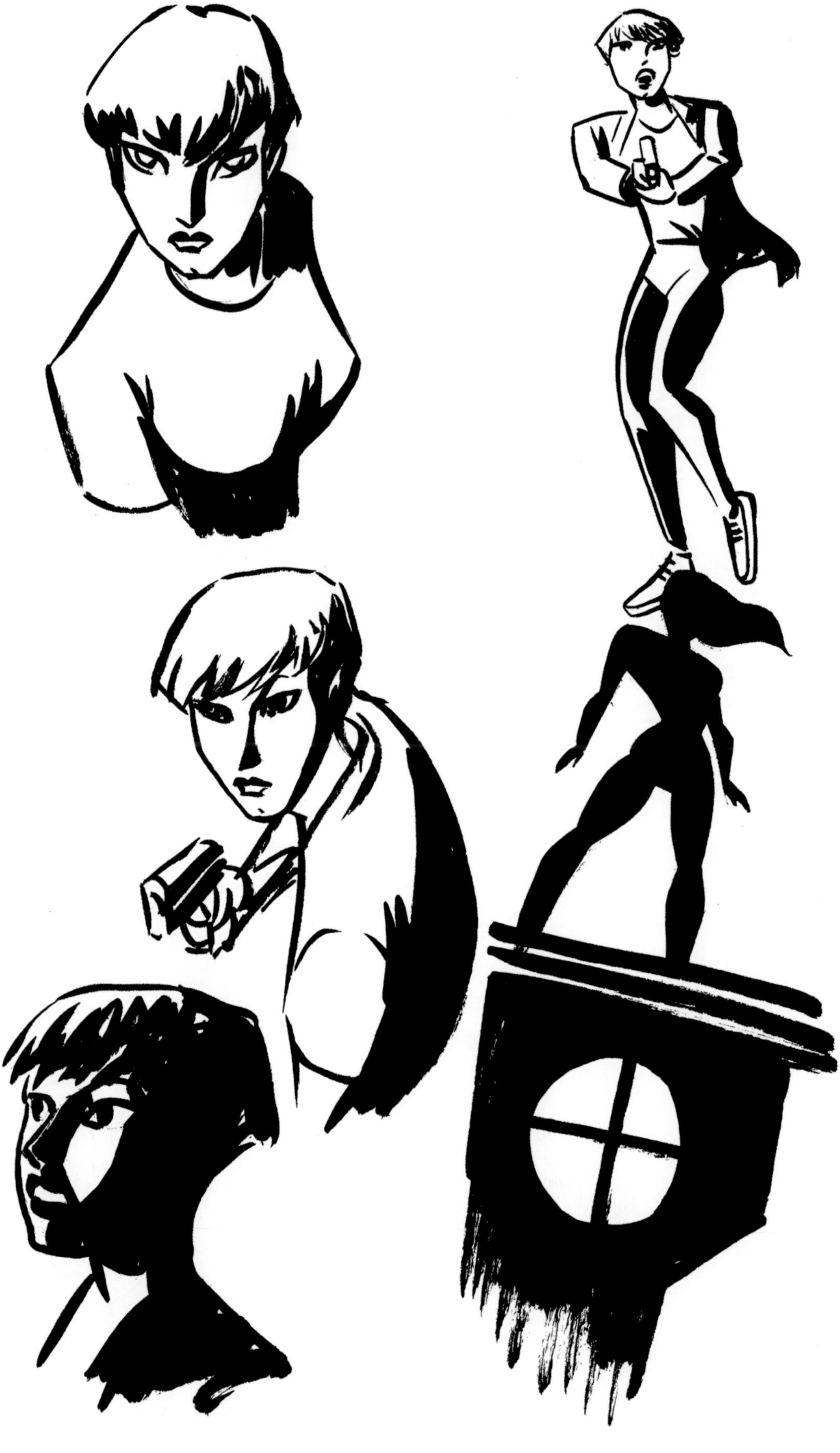

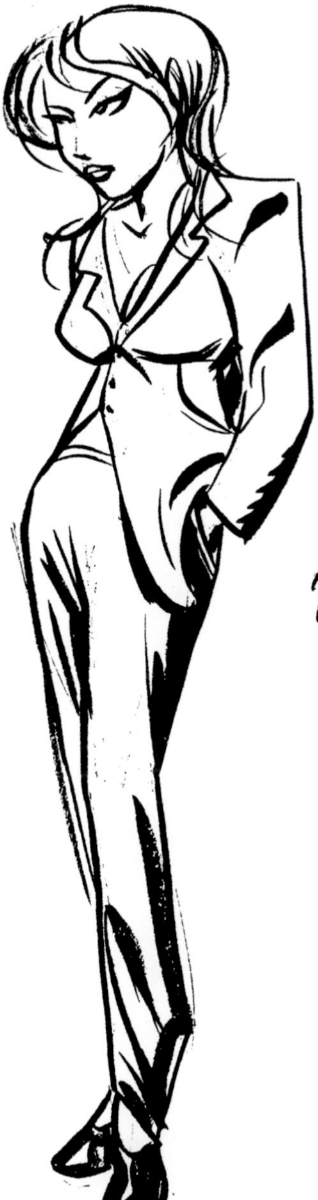

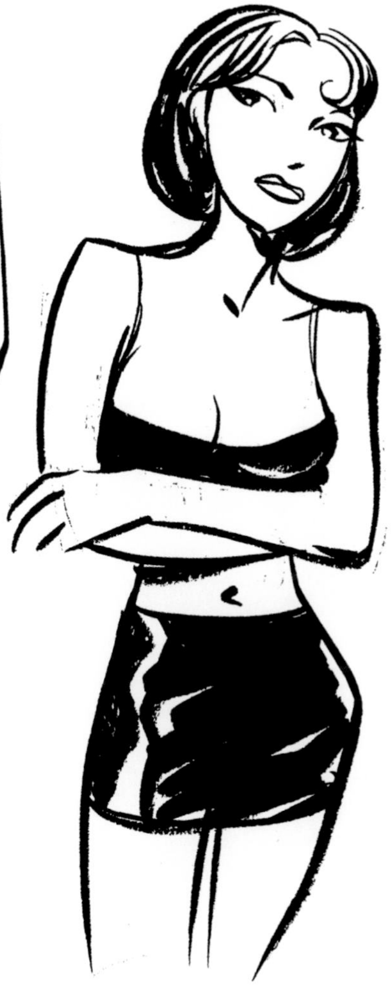

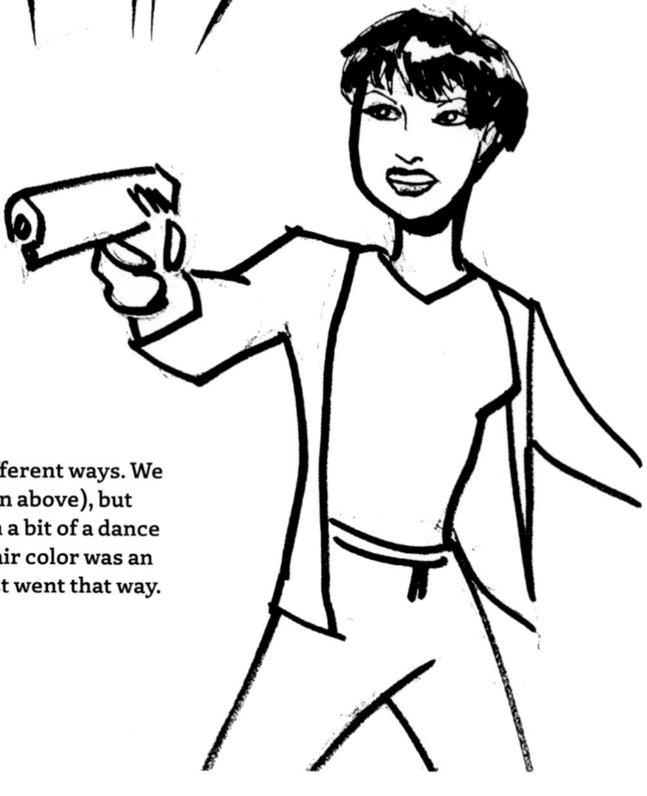

Deena could have gone so many different ways. We almost went with a Scully look (seen above), but pulling back from that put Deena in a bit of a dance club look (see above right). Even hair color was an issue. A brunette Deena? We almost went that way.

Little Calista. What age do we make Calista? We resisted the "cute little kid" look, but really, when it comes down to it . . . she's a cute little kid.

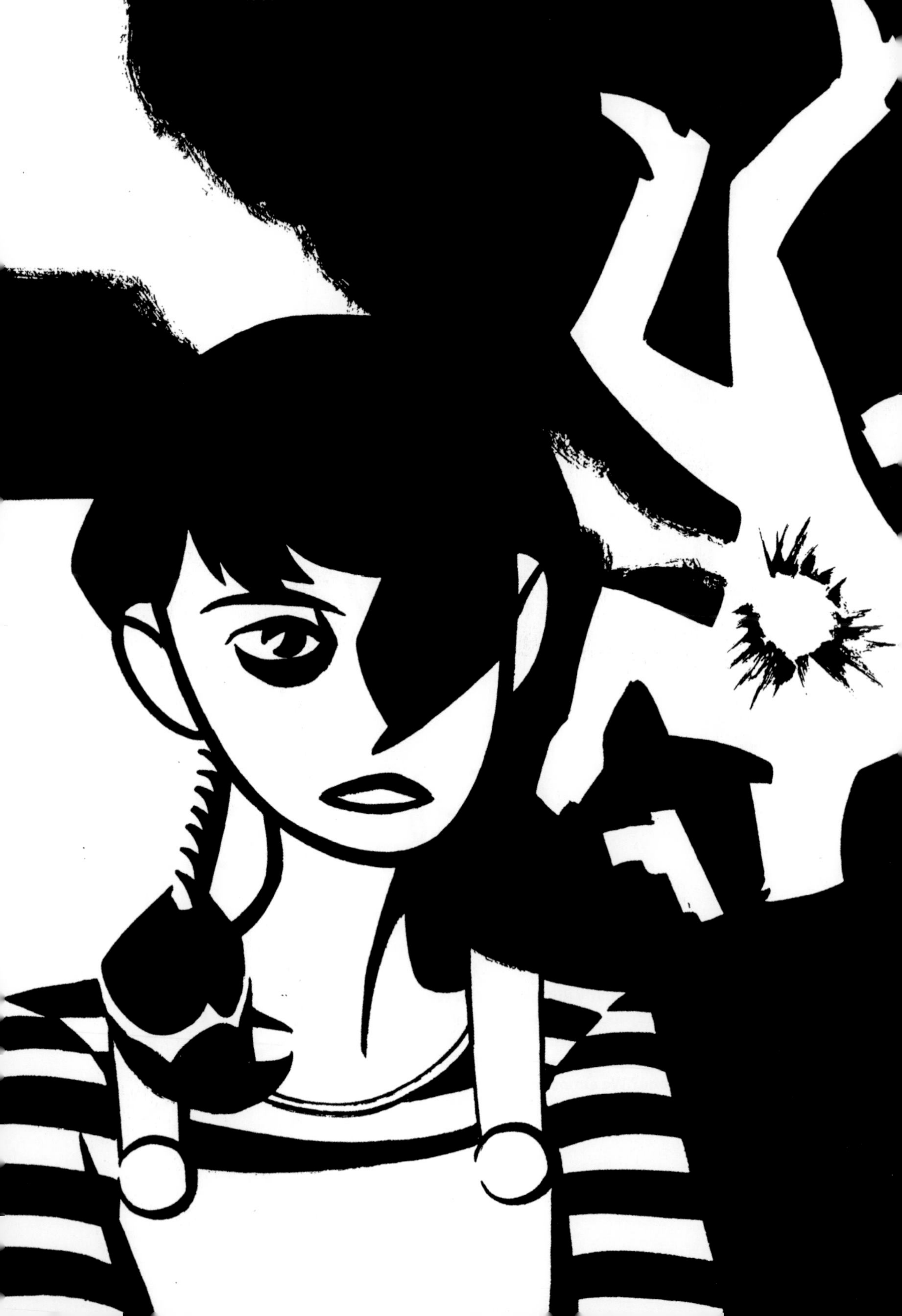

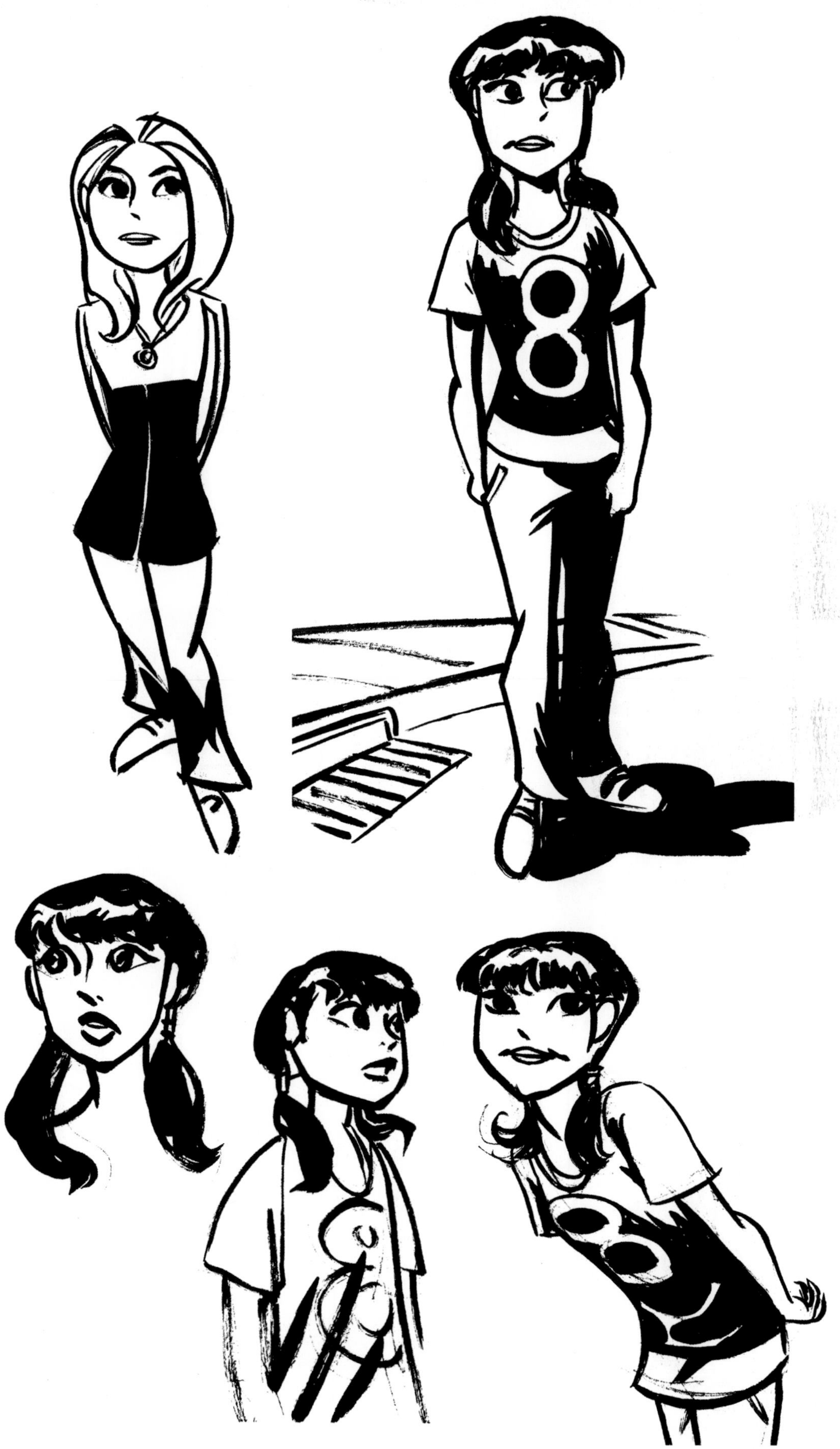

The sketch on the right is by far my all-time favorite. I just adore it.

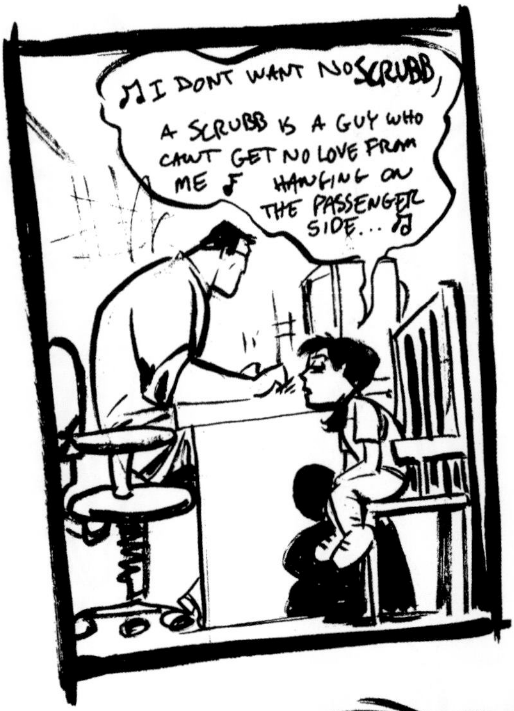
I DONT WANT NO SCRUBB, A SCRUBB IS A GUY WHO CAN'T GET NO LOVE FROM ME HANGING ON THE PASSENGER SIDE...

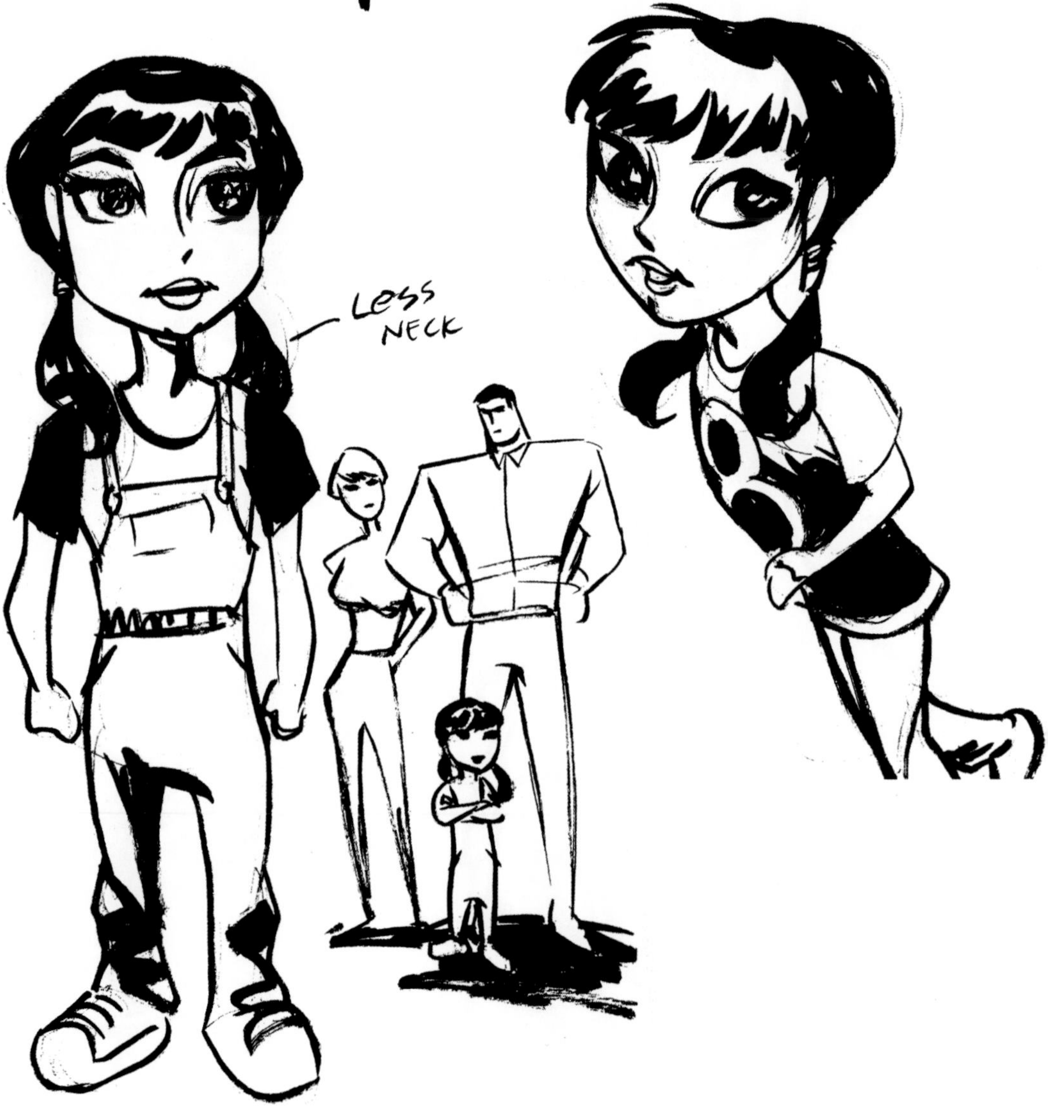
LESS NECK

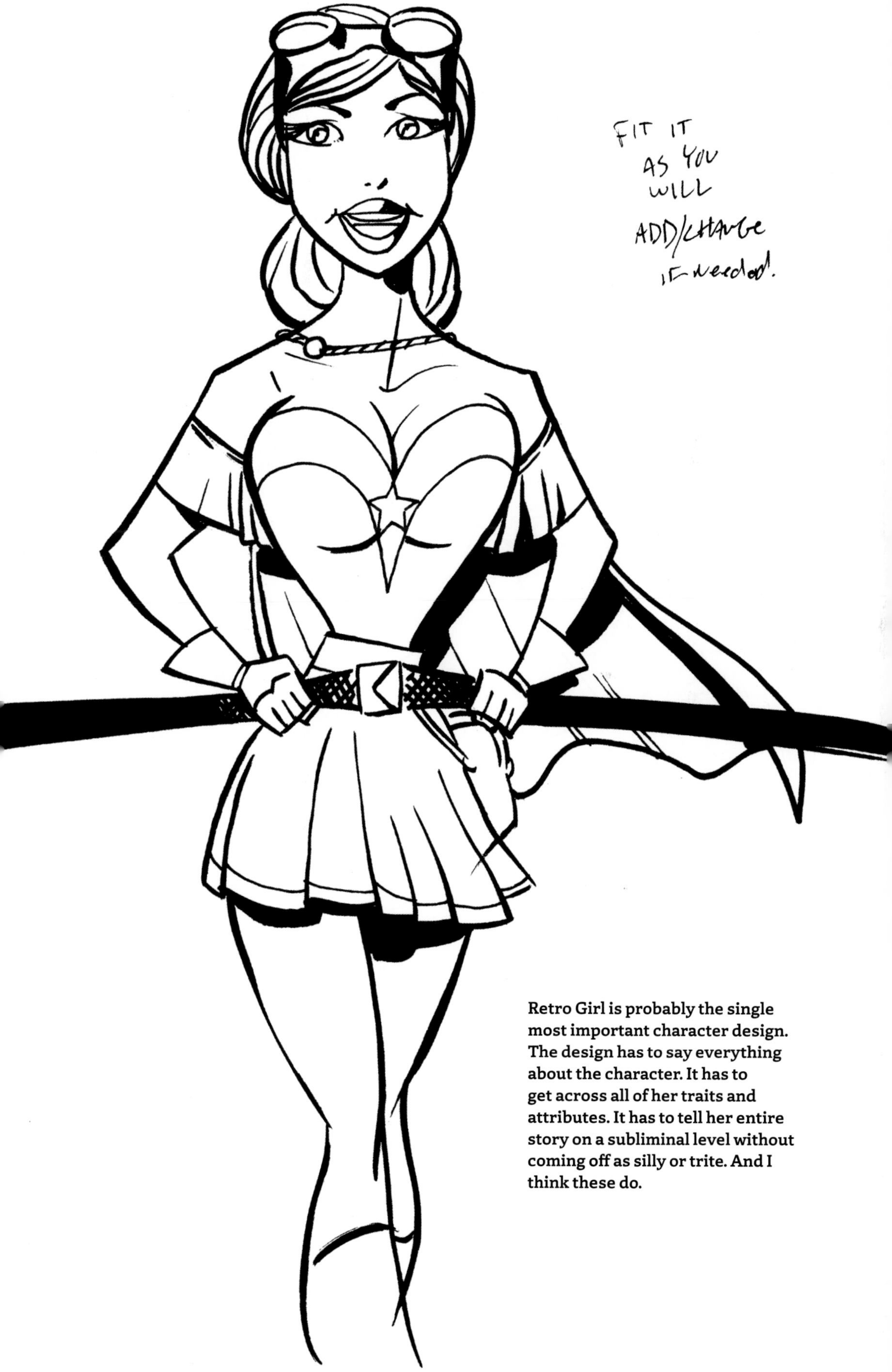
FIT IT AS YOU WILL ADD/CHANGE IF needed!

Retro Girl is probably the single most important character design. The design has to say everything about the character. It has to get across all of her traits and attributes. It has to tell her entire story on a subliminal level without coming off as silly or trite. And I think these do.

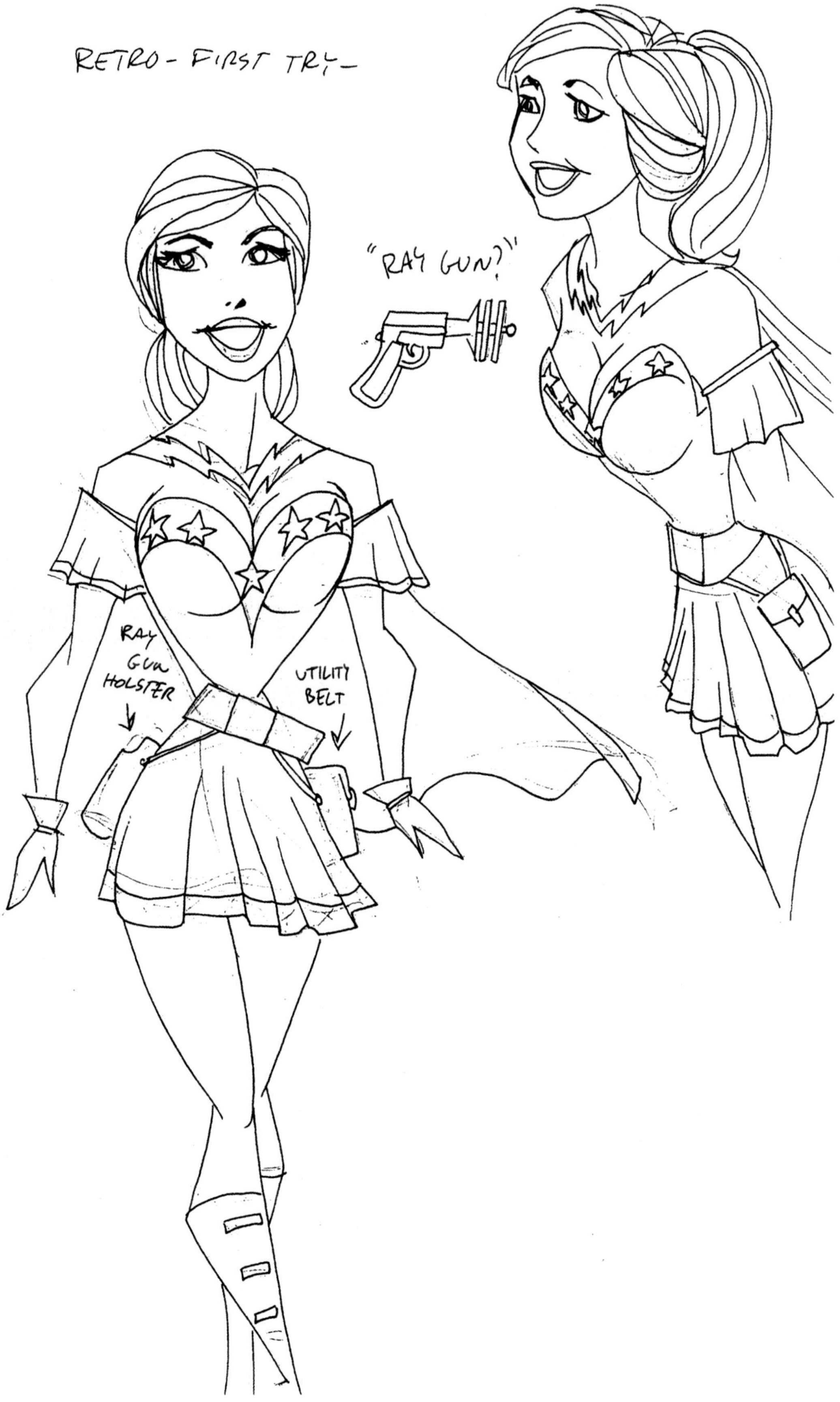
RETRO- FIRST TRY-
"RAY GUN?"
RAY GUN HOLSTER
UTILITY BELT

Retro Girl is Mike's most requested commission sketch. The following two pages are reproductions of a couple of my favorite pieces that Mike has done for a couple of lucky readers of the monthly book.

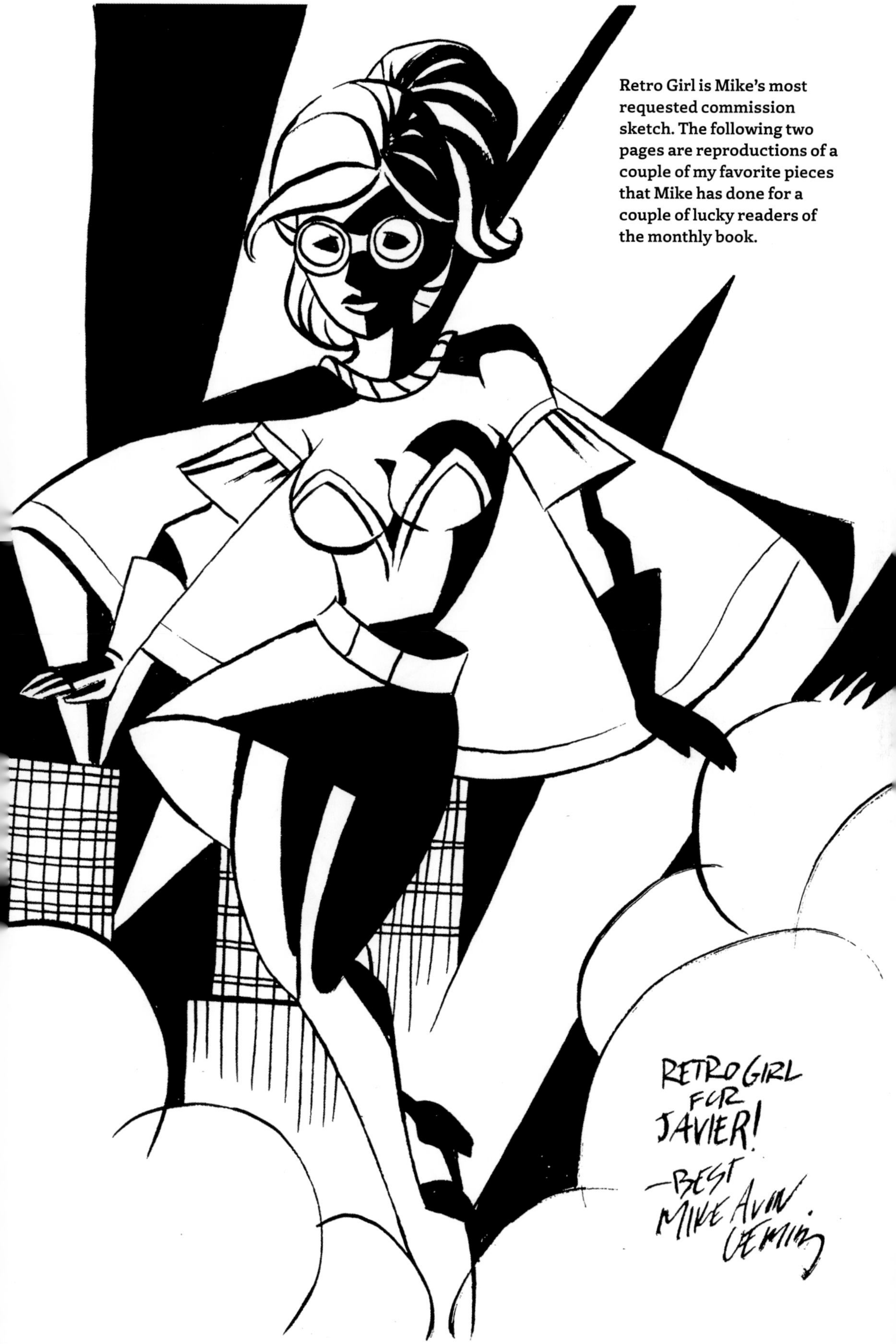
RETRO GIRL
FOR
JAVIER!
—BEST
MIKE AVON
OEMING

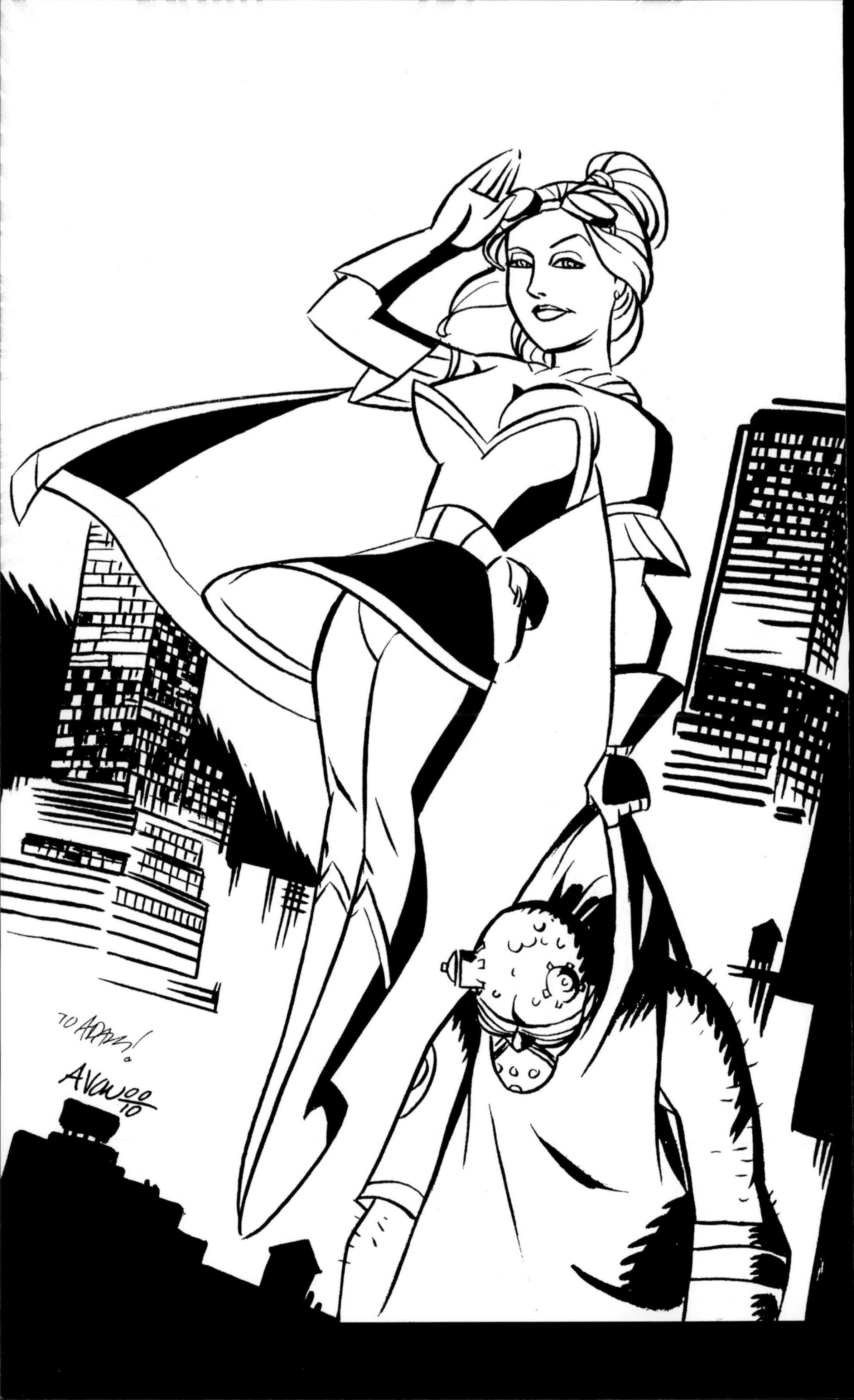
TO ADAM!

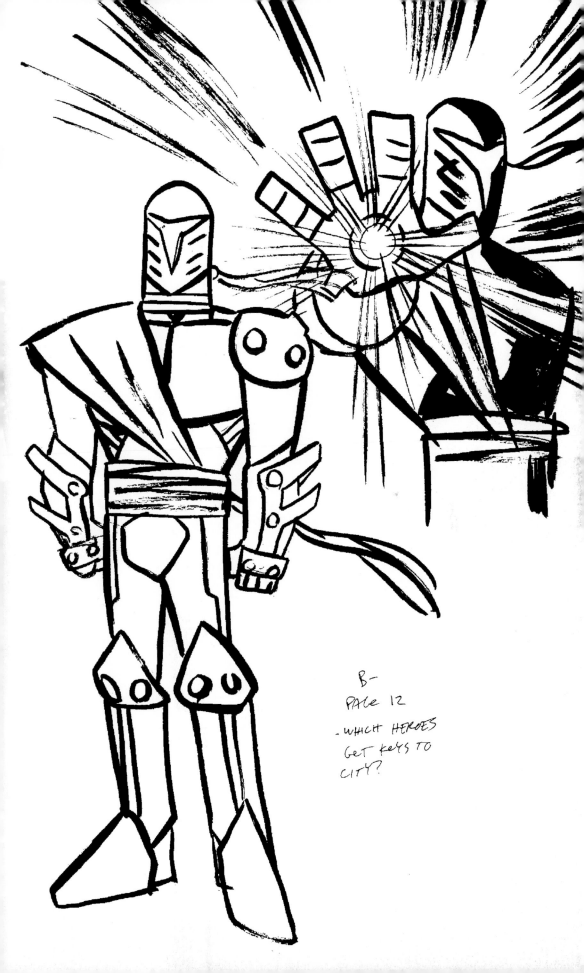

B—
PAGE 12
— WHICH HEROES
GET KEYS TO
CITY?

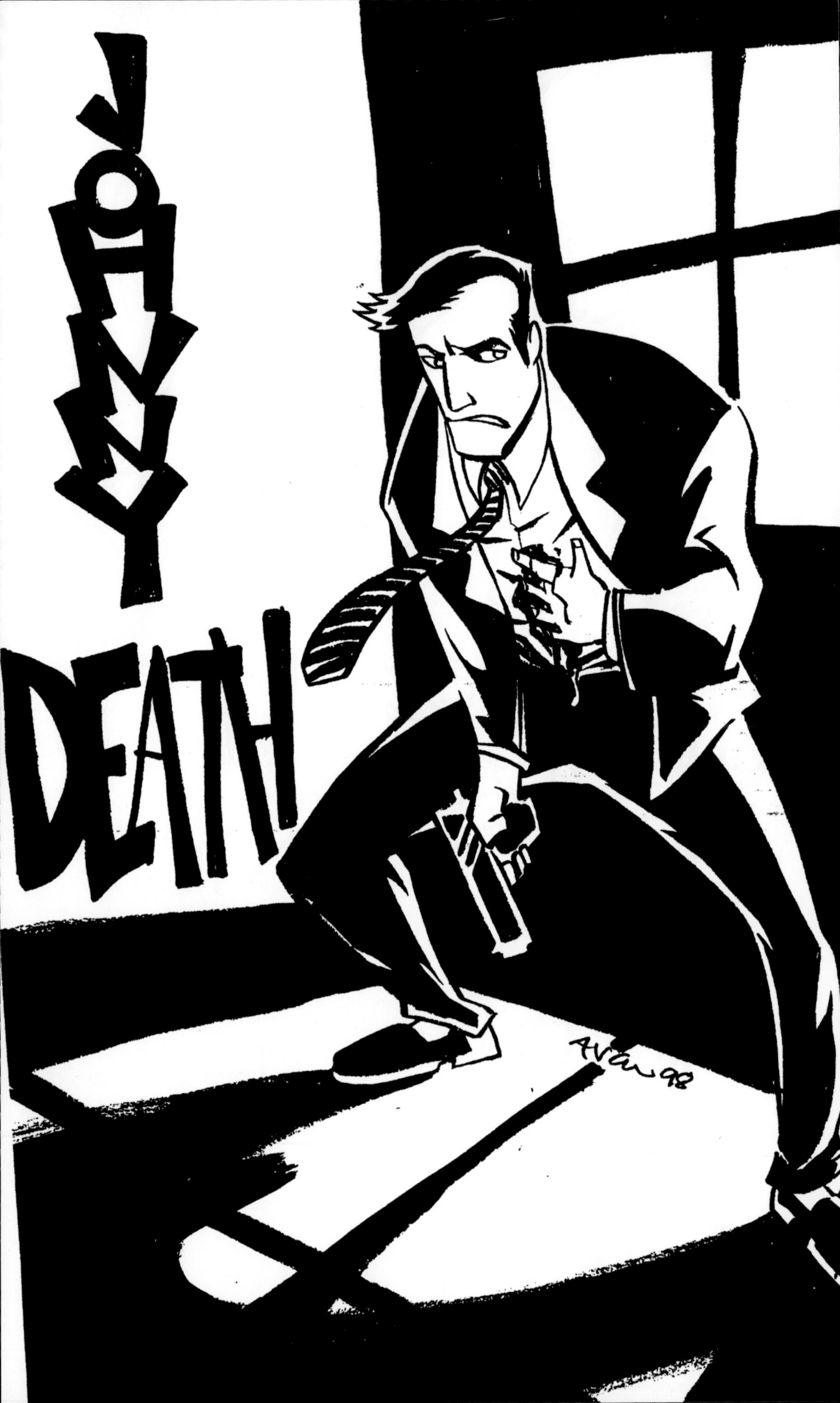
JOHNNY
DEATH

A.

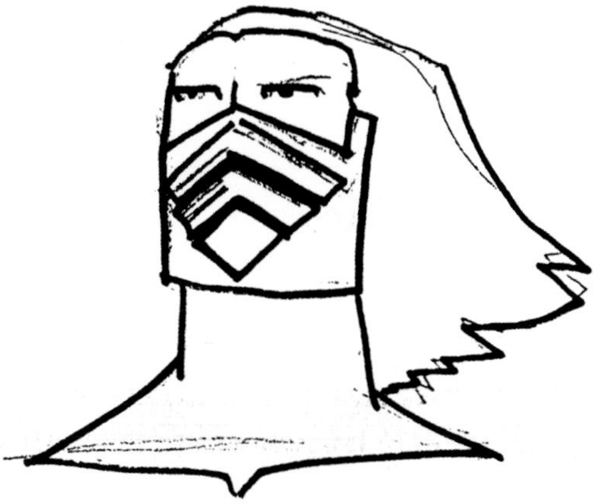

B.

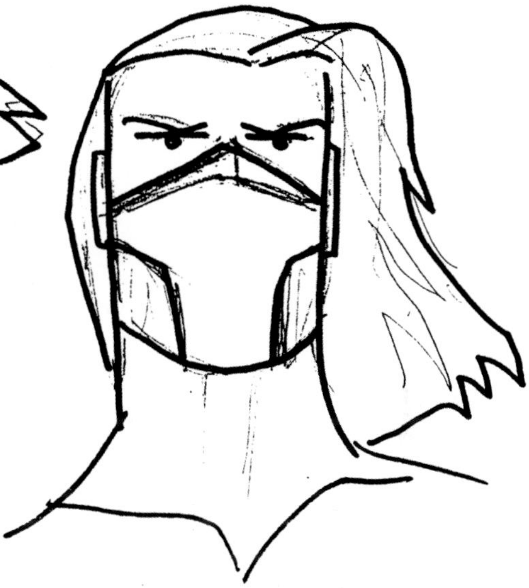

ALL BLACK OUTFIT?

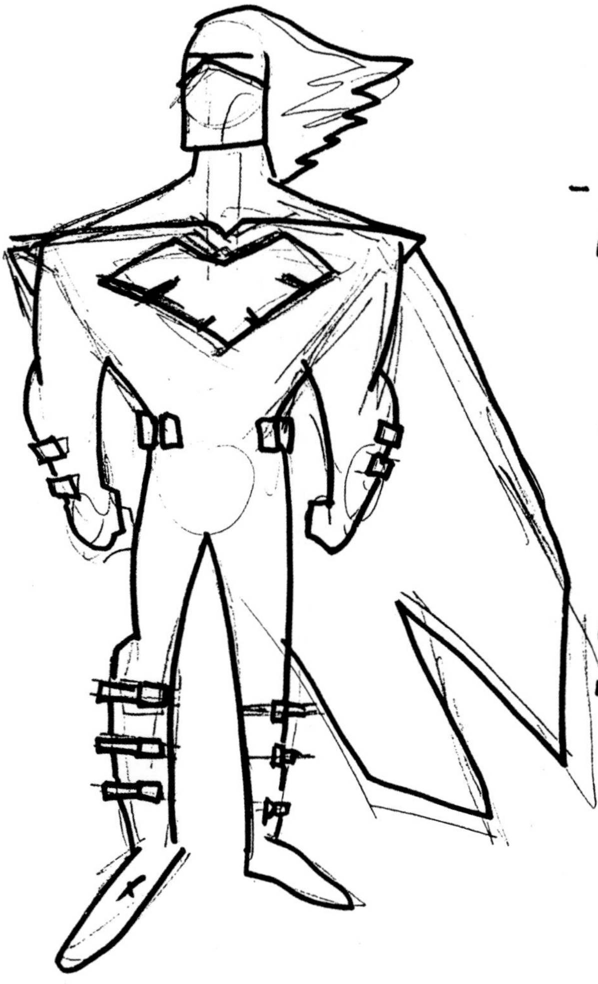

- IM SURE YOU HAVE HIS WHOLE "SCHTICK" DOWN - BUT I HAVE SOME IDEAS IF YOUR NOT SETTLED.

OTHER HEROES/VILLAINS NEED TO BE SETTLED TOO

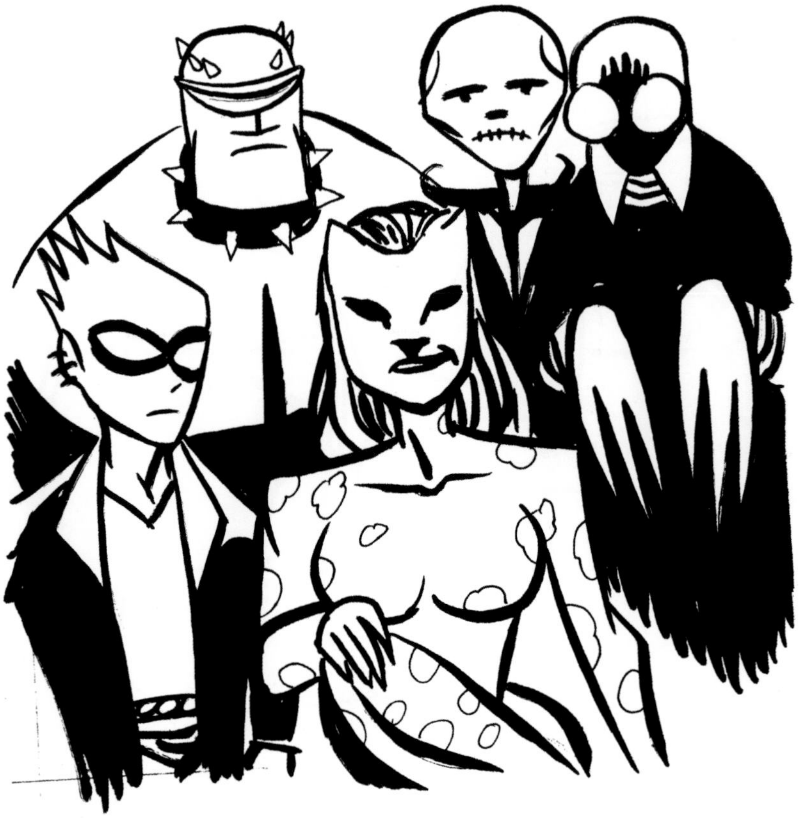

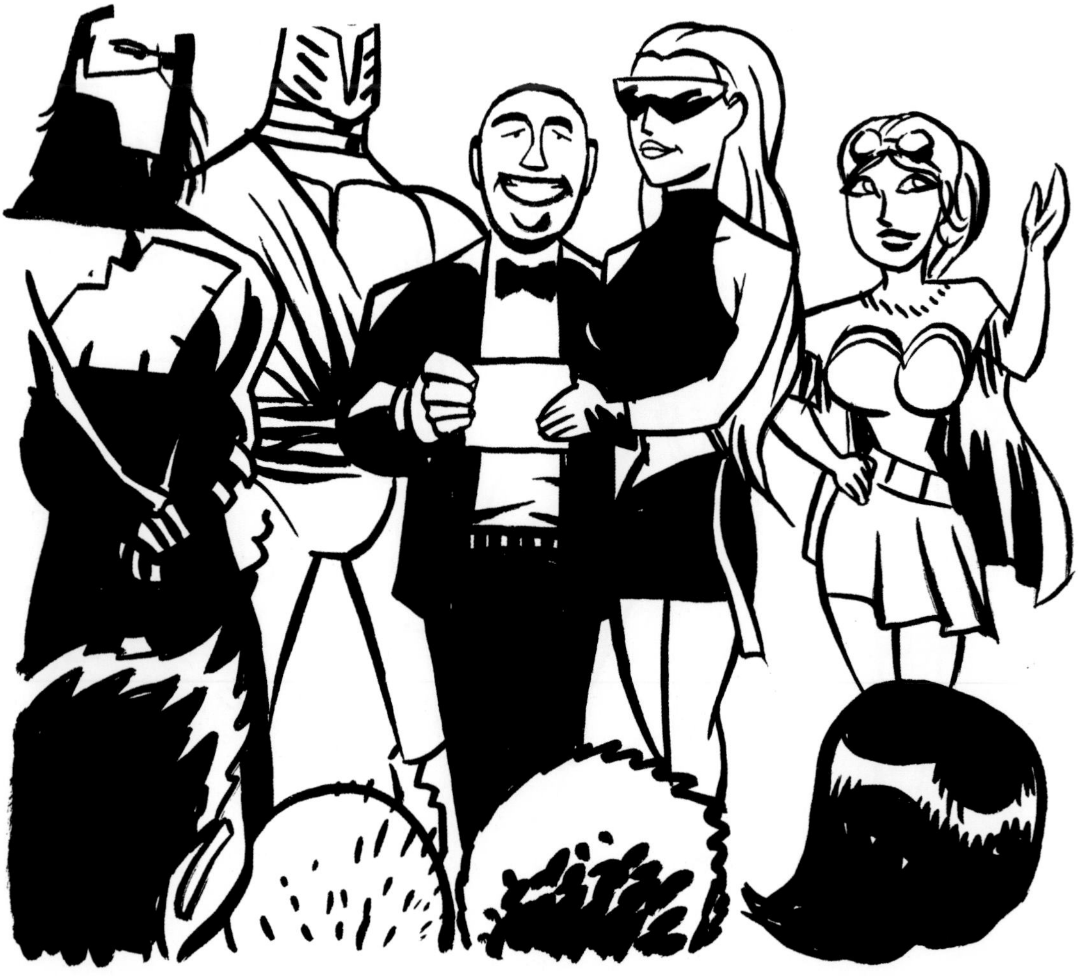

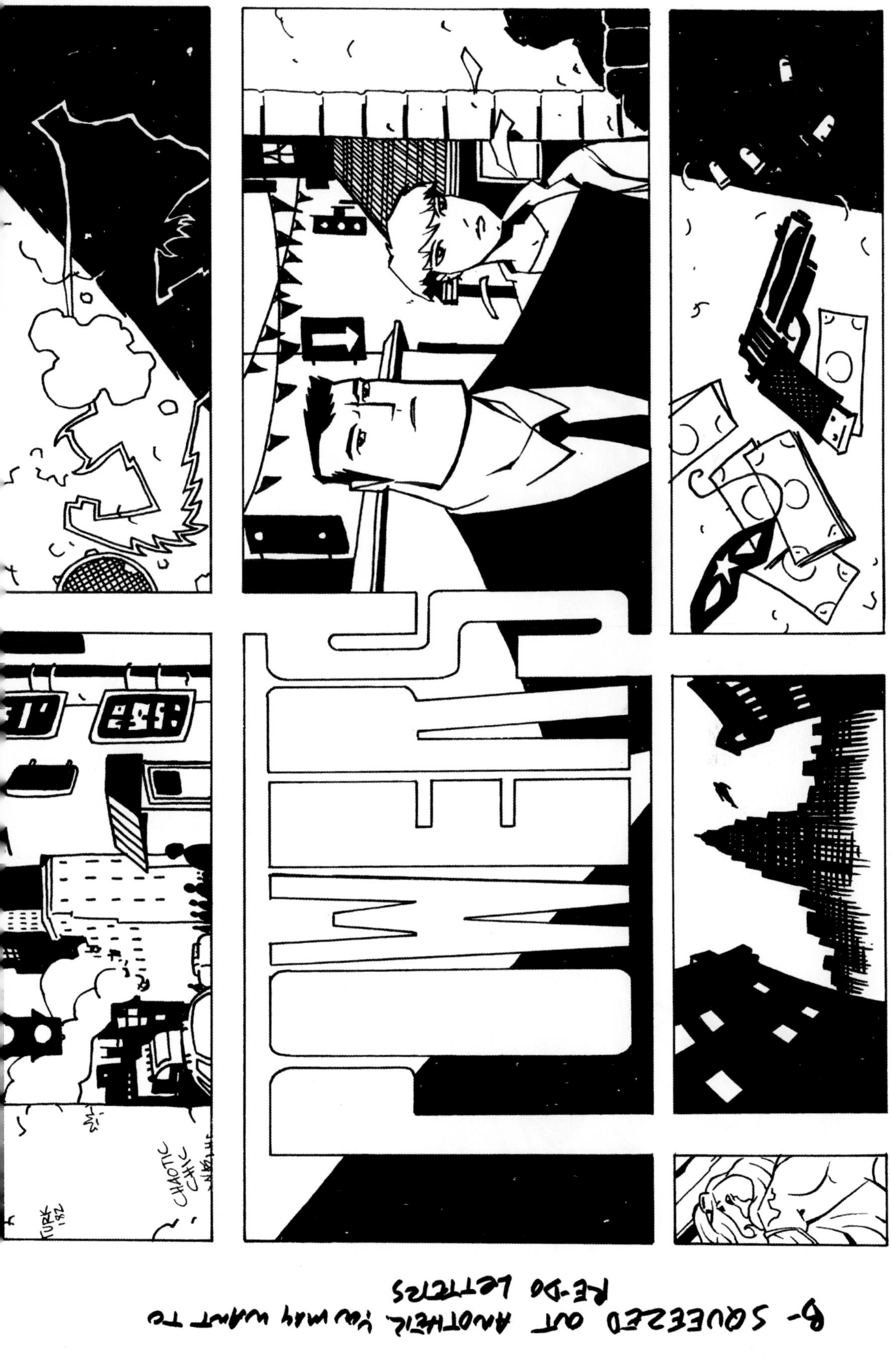
8- SQUEEZED OUT ANOTHER! YOU MAY WANT TO RE-DO LETTERS
CHAOTIC CHIC
TURK 182

Unused advertisement idea.

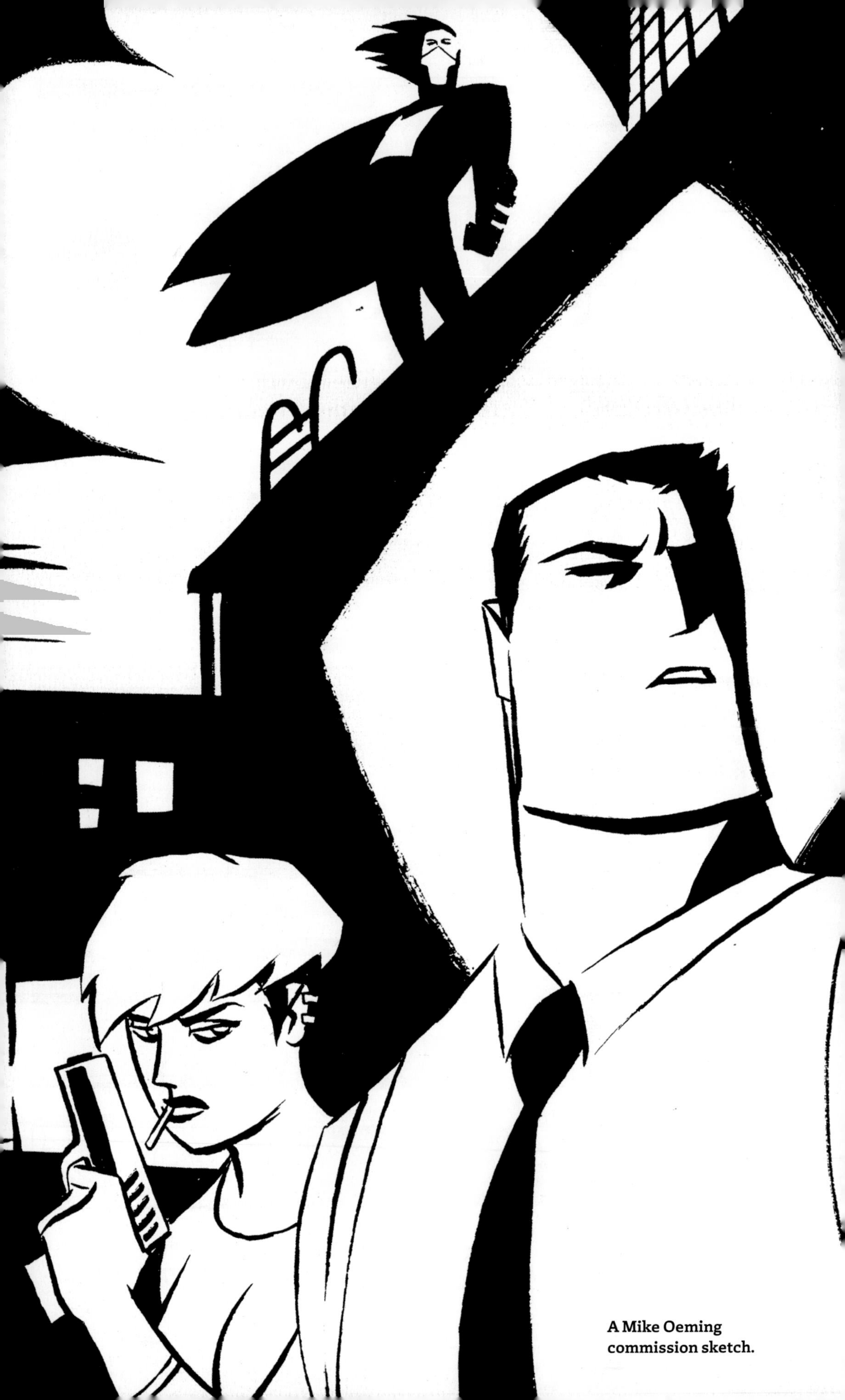

A Mike Oeming
commission sketch.

THE WORLD

They say that one of the rules of film noir is that the city itself should be considered a lead character. The look, the smells, the taste should all be distinct. The following drawings were the direct results of my and Mike's conversations on this subject.

I made Mike watch the documentary *Visions of Light*. This is an amazing documentary about cinematography and the art of lighting in film. In my opinion, it is also a great guide for the art of lighting in comic books.

Using this documentary as a guide, along with other sources, these images started just pouring out of Mike.

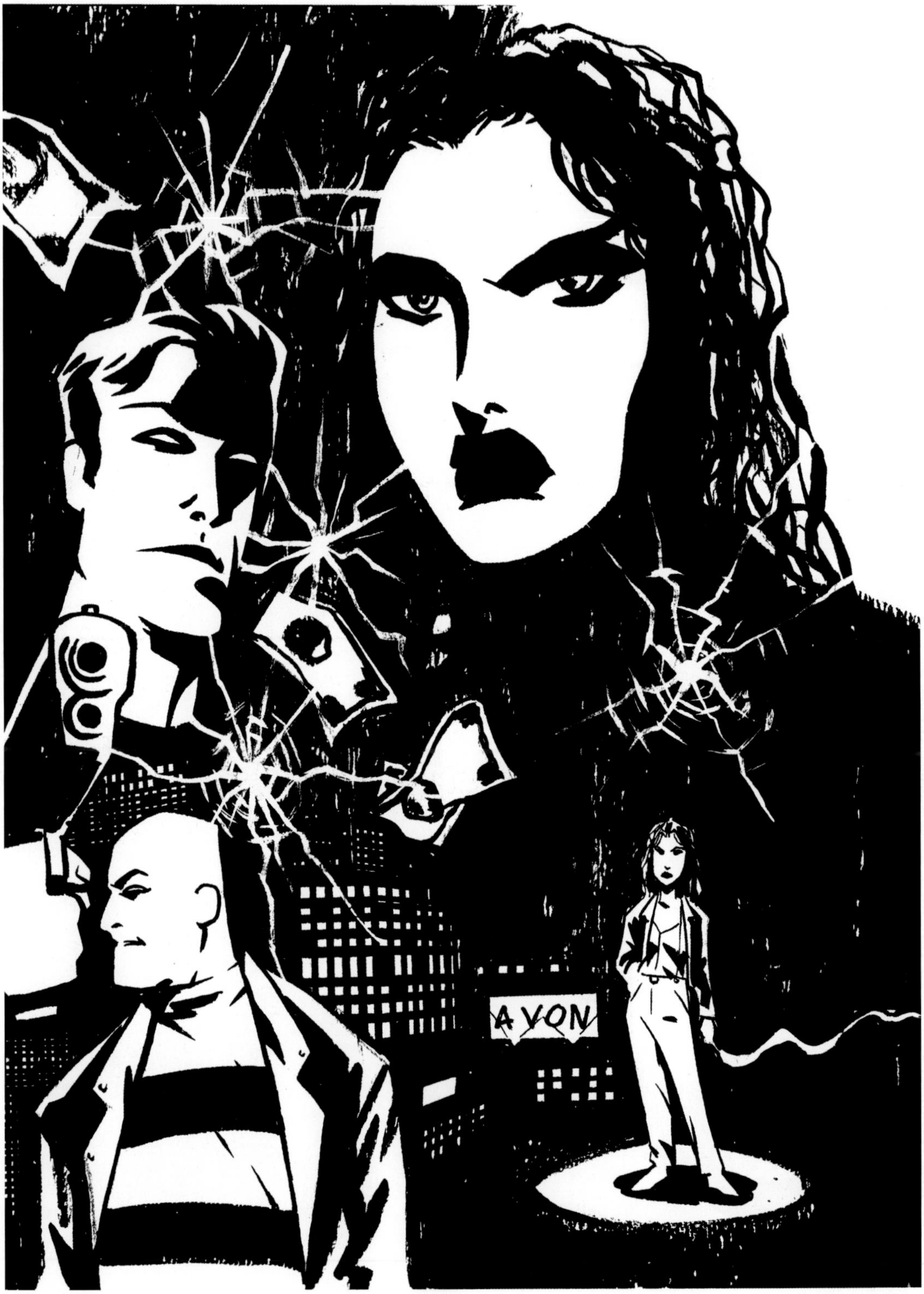
AVON

The image that started it all.

Years ago, Mike did a pinup (above) of my comic book series *Jinx*, and one of David Mack's comic book series, *Kabuki*, in a style he was trying out . . . just for fun. It's now referred to as his "*Powers* style." This single image inspired everything in this book.

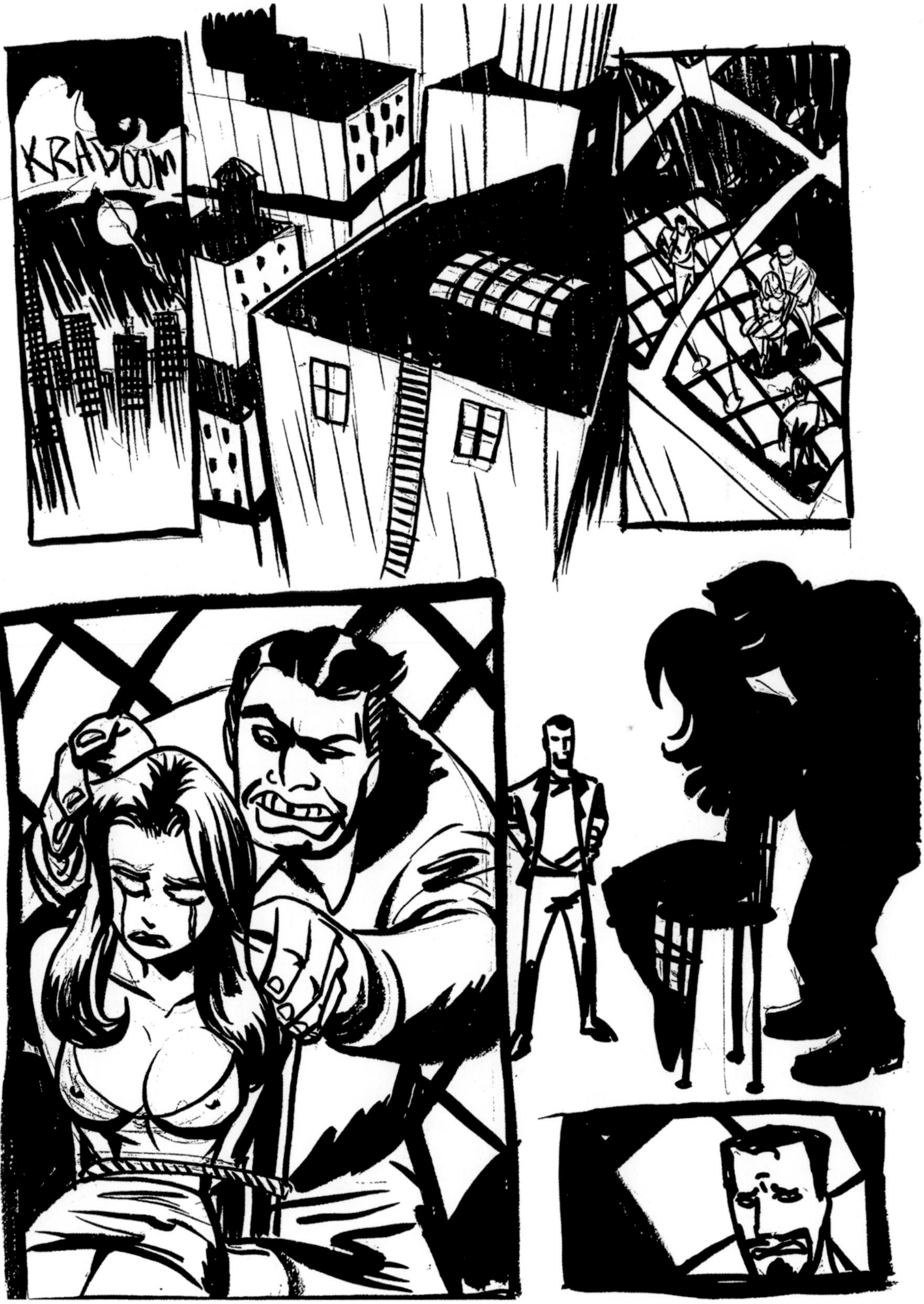
KRADOOM

Even before there was a script, Mike started doing practice pages so he could get a handle on how this style would feel "in use."

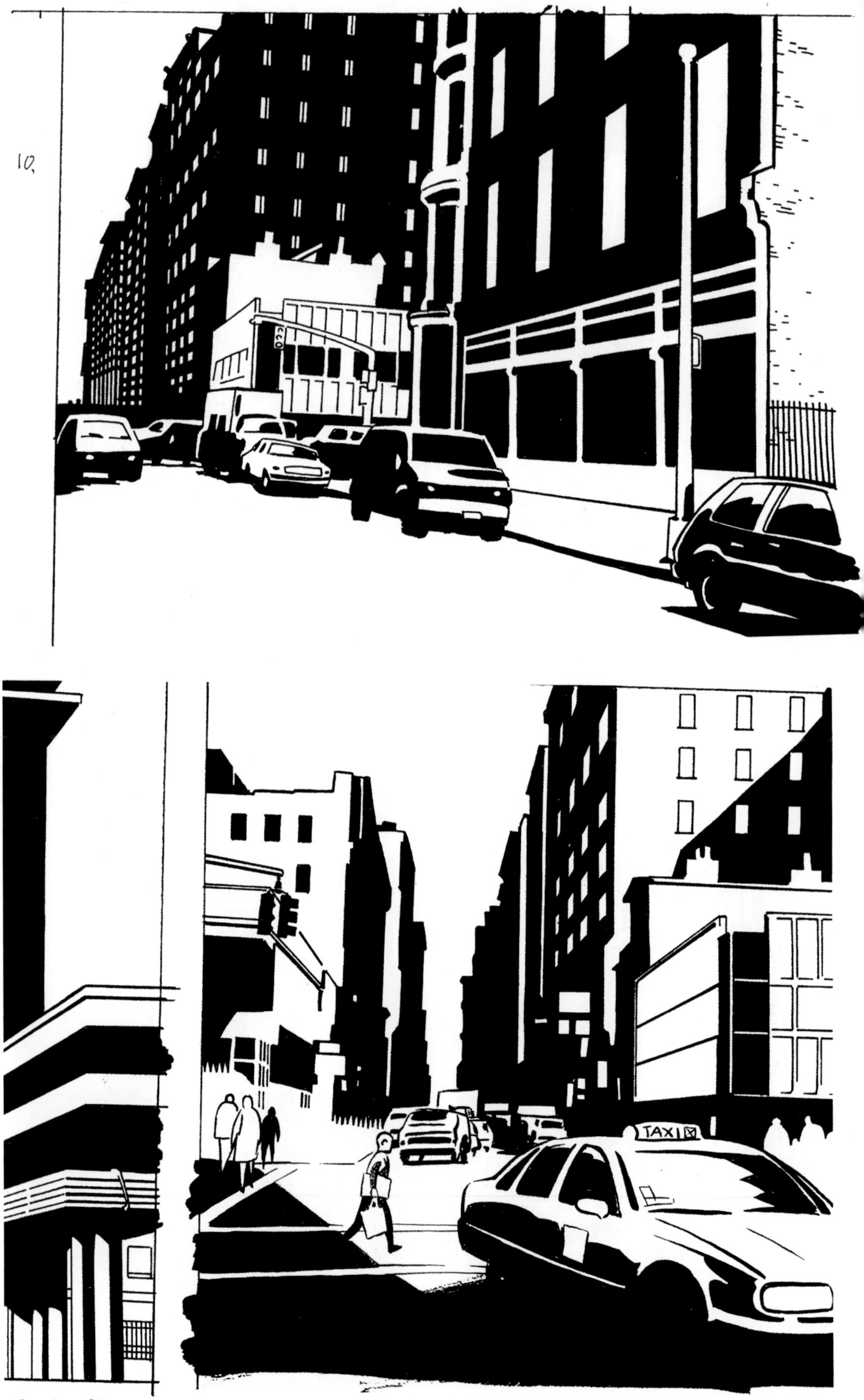
TAXI

The city of *Powers*.

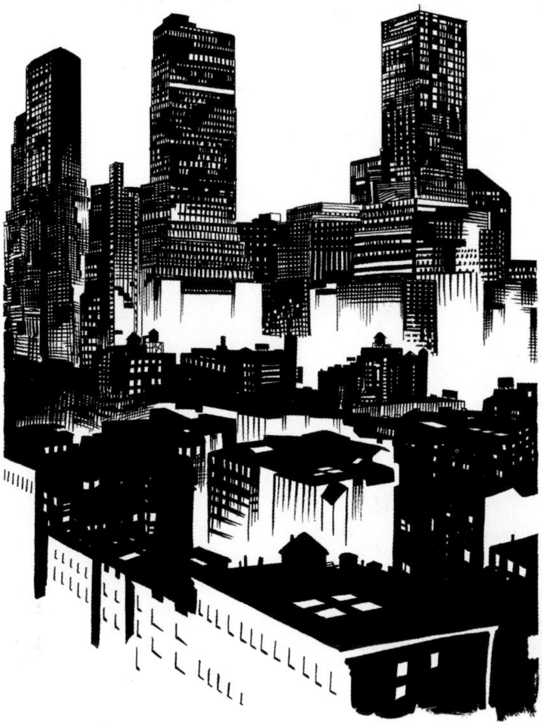
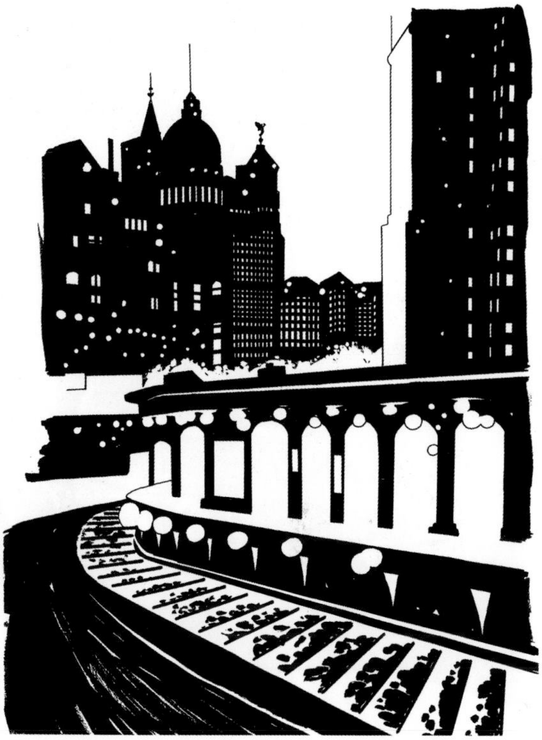
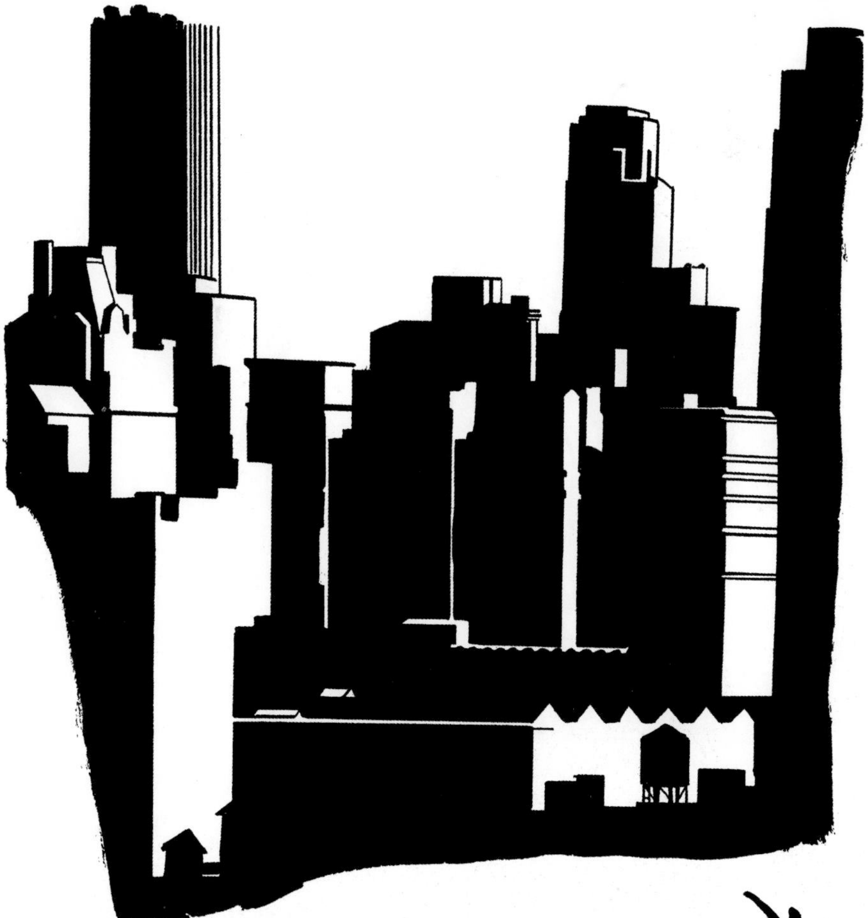

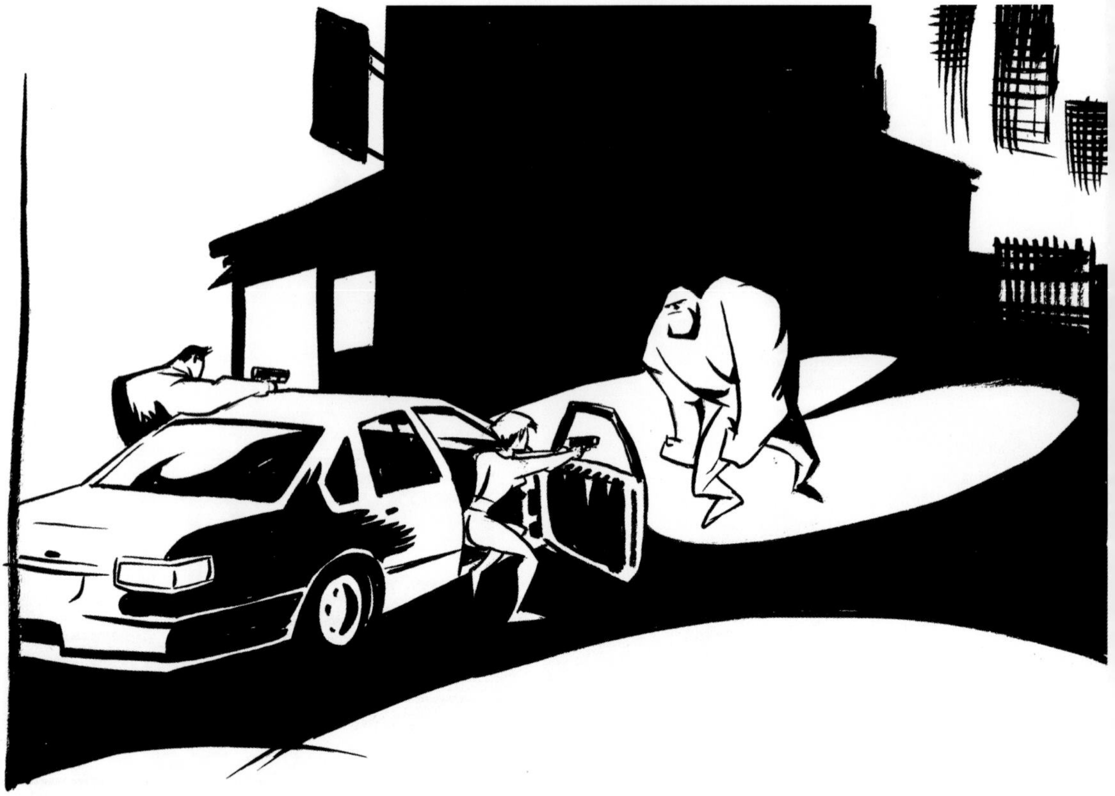

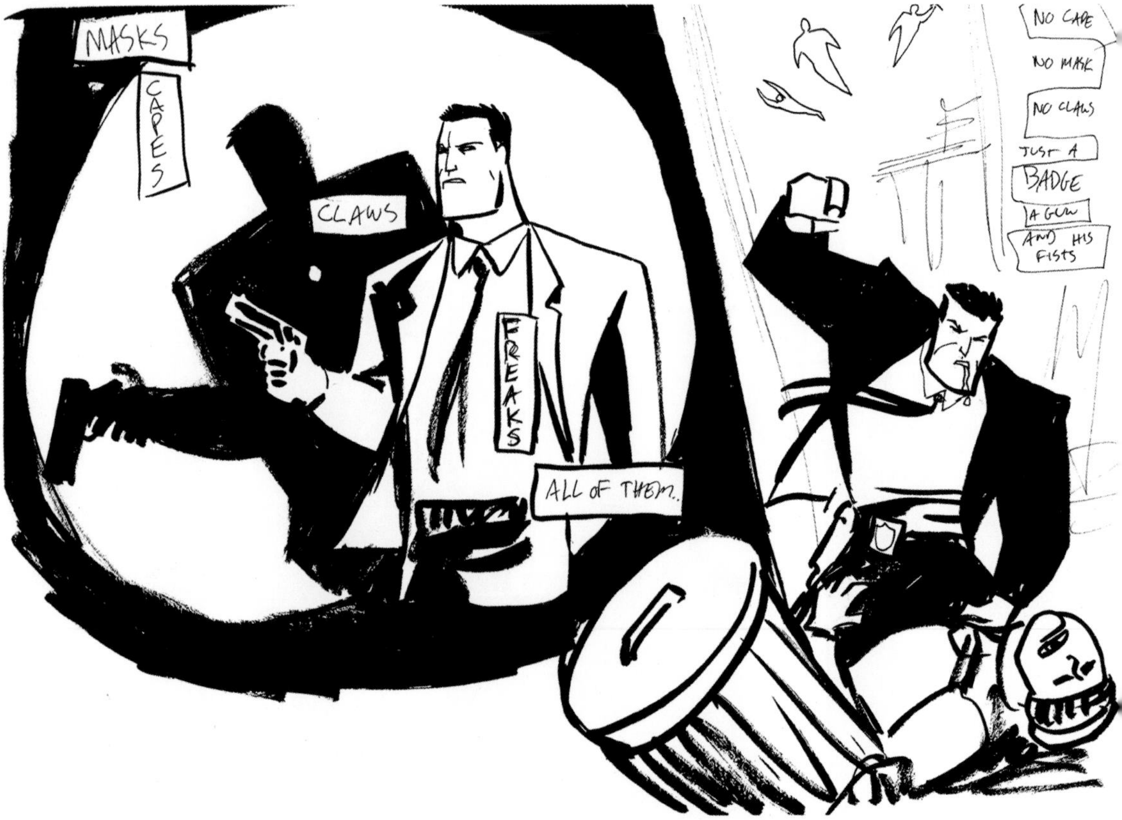
MASKS
CAPES
CLAWS
FREAKS
ALL OF THEM.
NO CAPE
NO MASK
NO CLAWS
JUST A
BADGE
A GUN
AND HIS FISTS

One of the key elements of the visuals of *Powers* is the juxtaposition of noir and superhero images. These are some of the ideas Mike was toying with while considering this juxtaposition.

POWERS™

NOTHING.
THIS IS BEYOND MY WISDOM.
GOSH, NO.
YEAH, NOTHING.
NOT A THING.
NO.

THE CAMEOS

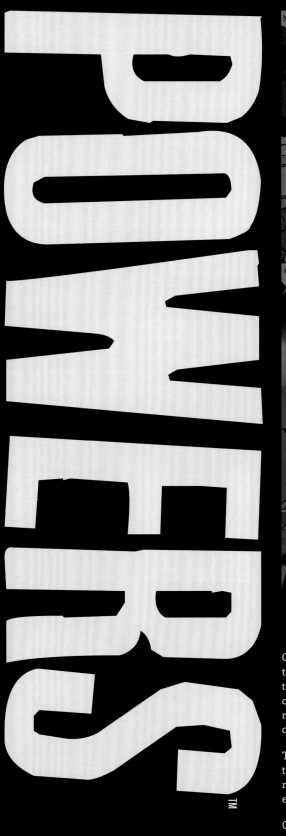

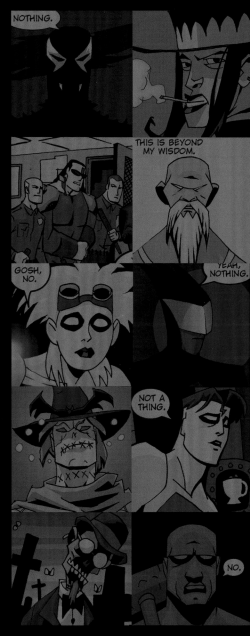

One of the best ideas we came up with for this book (and by "best ideas" I mean "logistical nightmares") was to ask our well-known comic book–creator friends to lend us brand-new superhero and villain creations to fill our cityscape.

This added an extra layer of fun to the whole thing. Many big-name talents—including some not usually associated with this genre—were extremely generous in lending us their babies.

On the following pages is a key to the identities of all the characters and their creators. Each character is the copyright of the creator named here. If no name is listed, that character is owned by Mike and me.

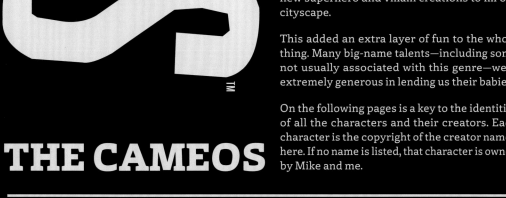

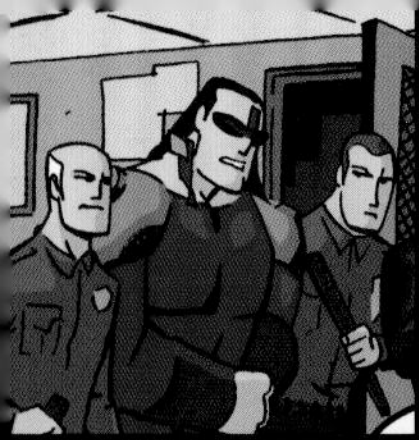

DREI
Dave Johnson

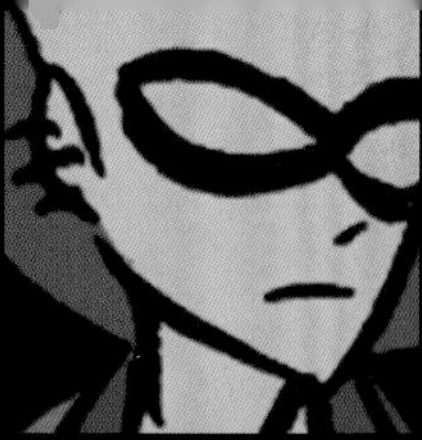

TWILIGHT
David Mack

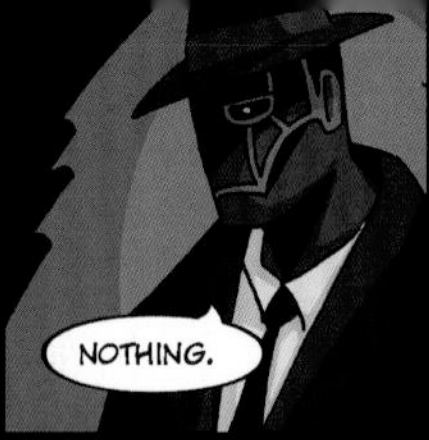
NOTHING.

DETECTIVE X
Eddy Newell

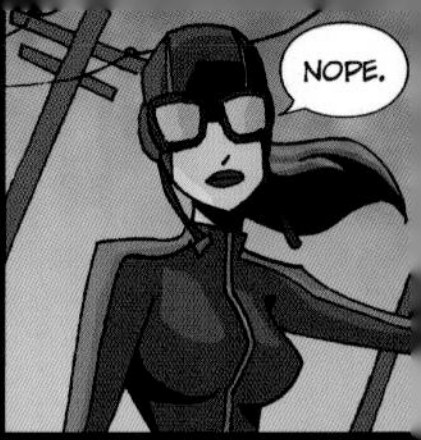
NOPE.

SQUIRREL GIRL
Mike Oeming

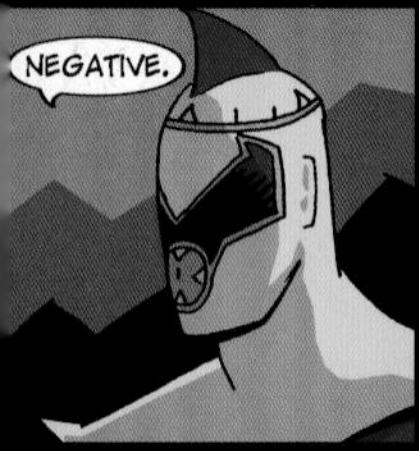
NEGATIVE.

F.L.U.X.
Angel Medina

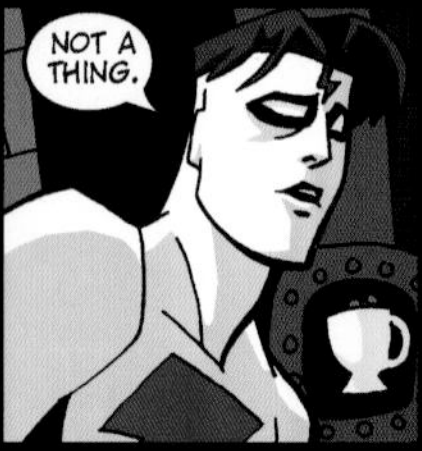
NOT A THING.

MADMAN
Mike Allred

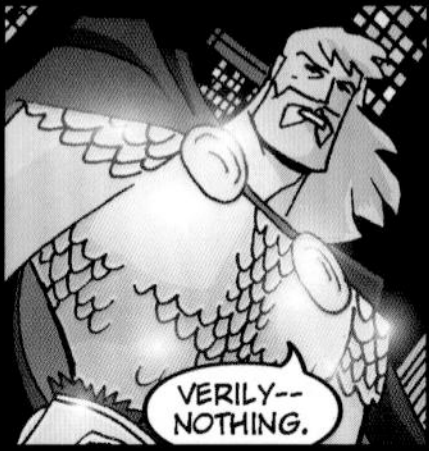
VERILY-- NOTHING.

MODI
Mike Oeming

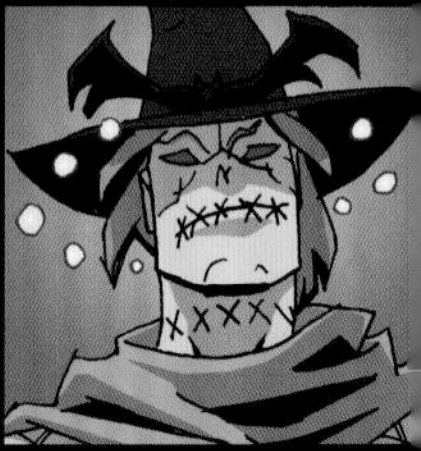

GUNWITCH
Dan Brereton

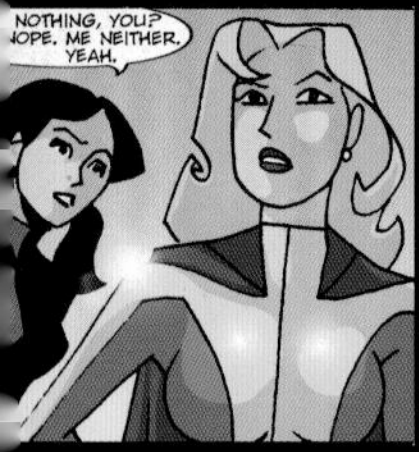
NOTHING, YOU?
ME NEITHER.
YEAH.

FLEX WOMAN
Bryan Glass

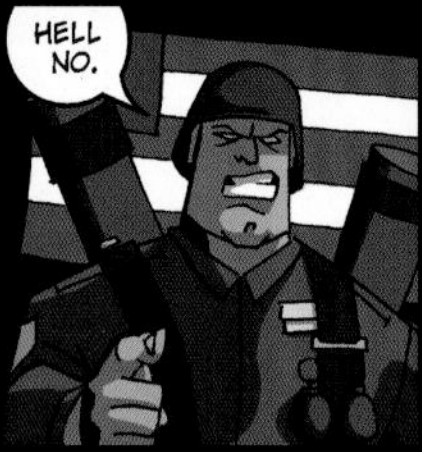
HELL NO.

ARTILLERY MAN
Paul Jenkins

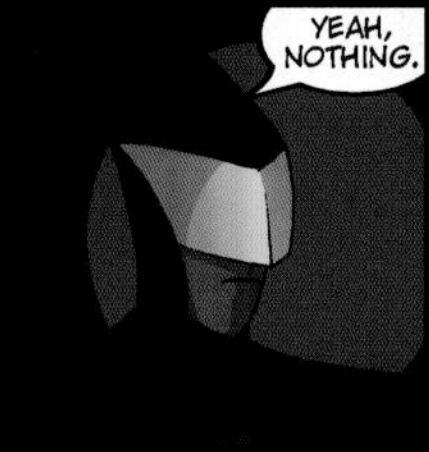
YEAH, NOTHING.

[redacted]

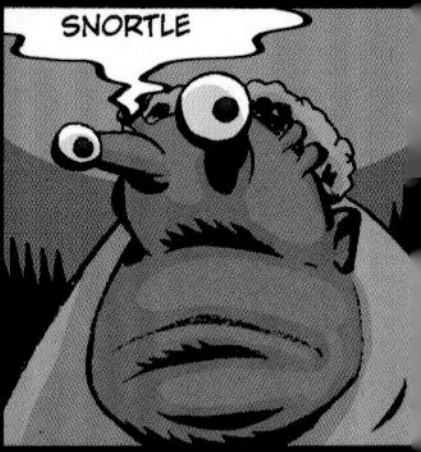
SNORTLE

THE SLUG
Mike Allred

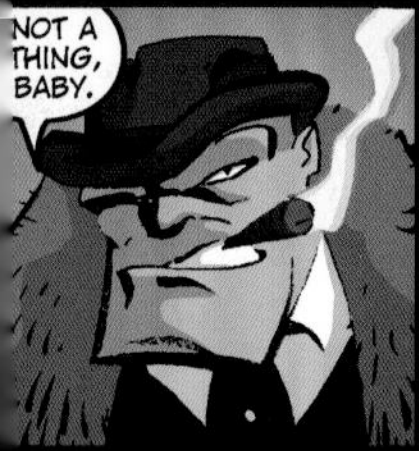
NOT A THING, BABY.

DEVLIN
Neil Vokes

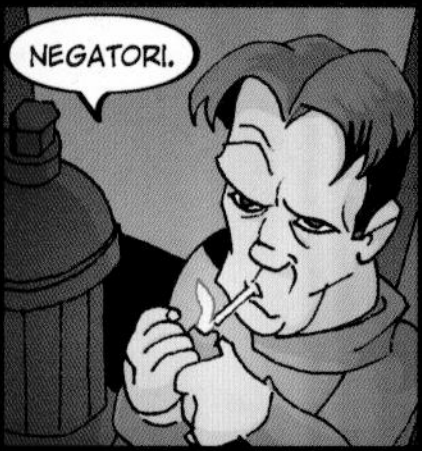
NEGATORI.

ORSON BEEKS
Judd Winick

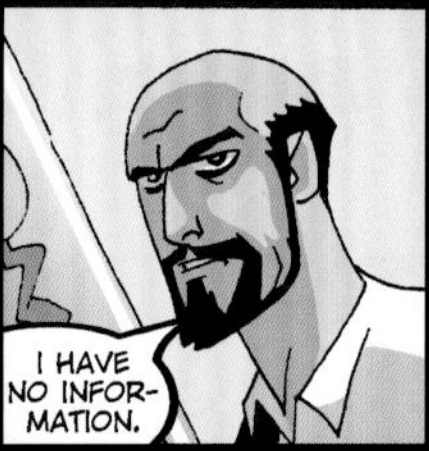
I HAVE NO INFORMATION.

DOC CYBORG
Allan Gross

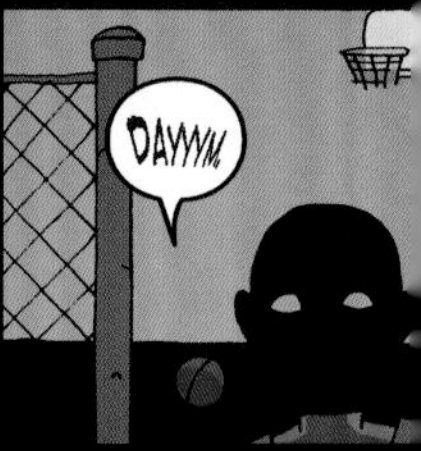
DAYYYM

[redacted]

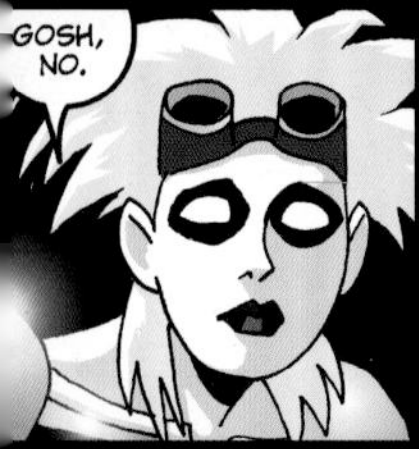
GOSH, NO.

86 VOLTS
Mike Oeming

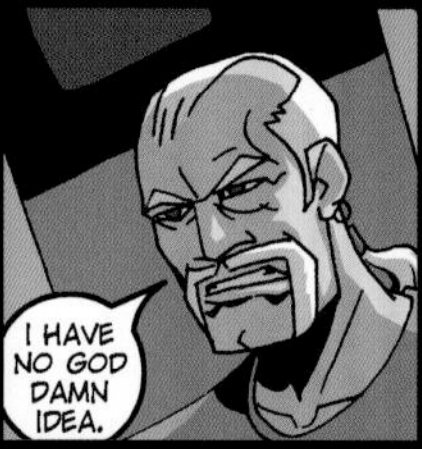
I HAVE NO GOD DAMN IDEA.

[redacted]

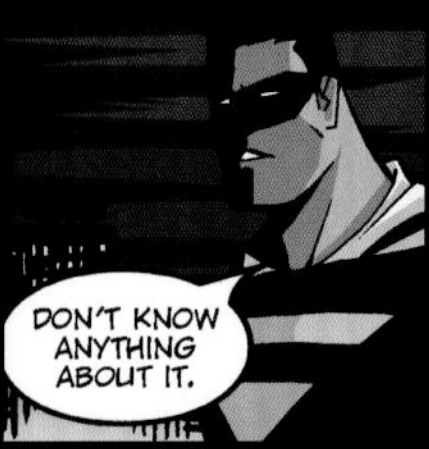
DON'T KNOW ANYTHING ABOUT IT.

[redacted]

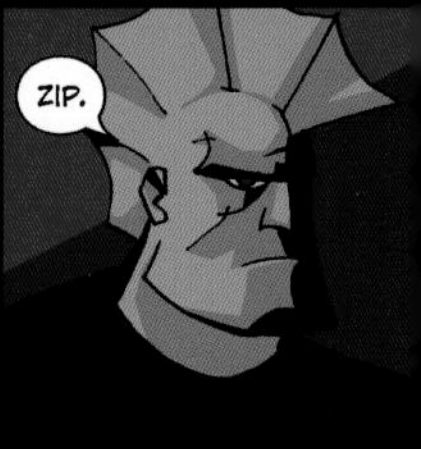
ZIP.

SAVAGE DRAGON
Eric Larsen

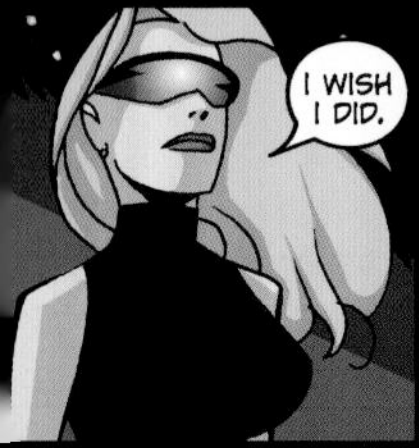
I WISH I DID.

[redacted]

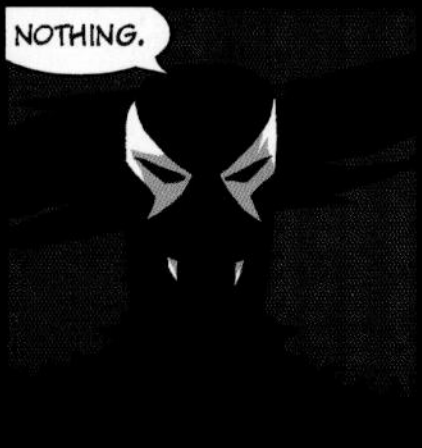
NOTHING.

THUNDERDOG
Mike Oeming

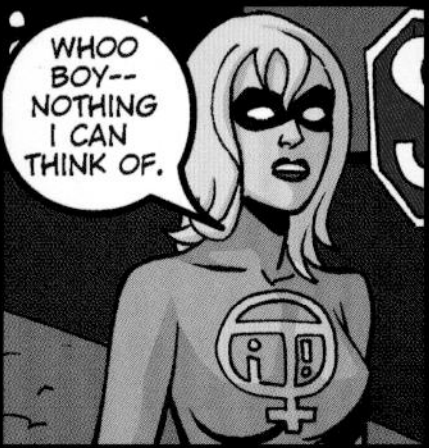
WHOO BOY-- NOTHING I CAN THINK OF.

IT GIRL
Mike Allred

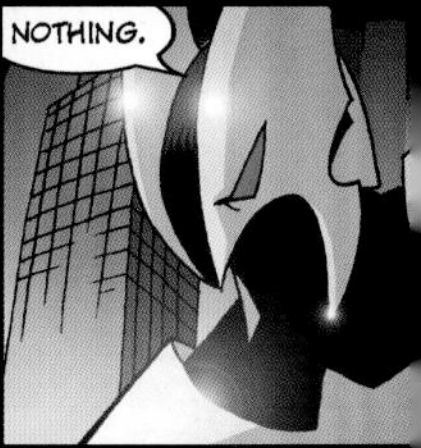
NOTHING.

SHADOWHAWK
Jim Valentino

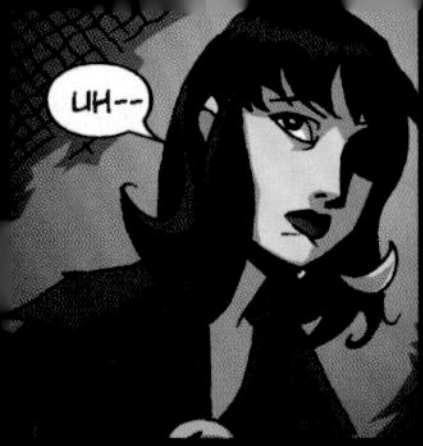
UH--

HALLOWEEN GIRL
Dan Brereton

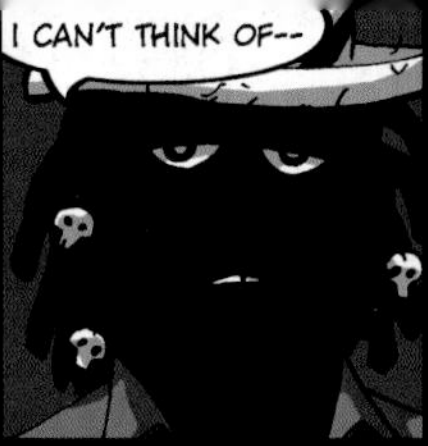
I CAN'T THINK OF--

STEVE LIEBER
[redacted]

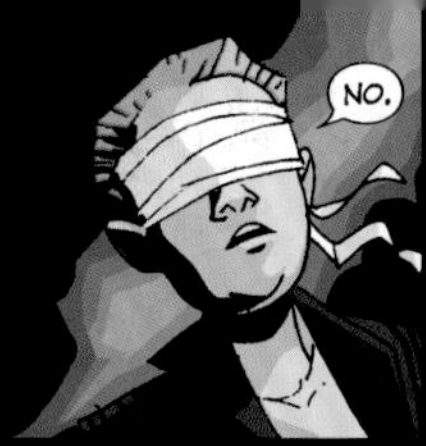
NO.

RAGS MURPHY
Jim Krueger

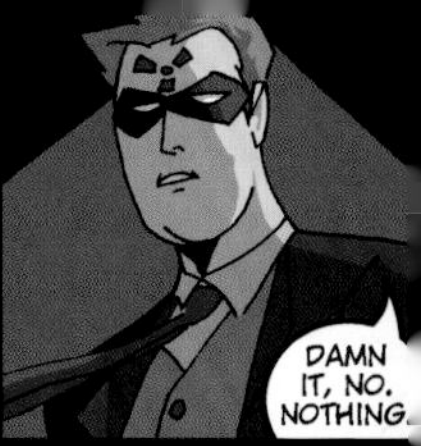
DAMN IT, NO. NOTHING.

MATT HAZARD
Mike Oeming

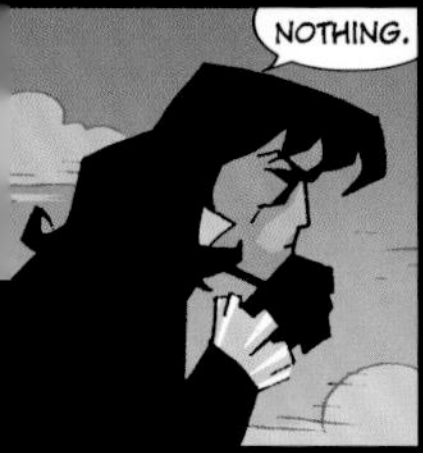
NOTHING.

EAGLE
Neil Vokes

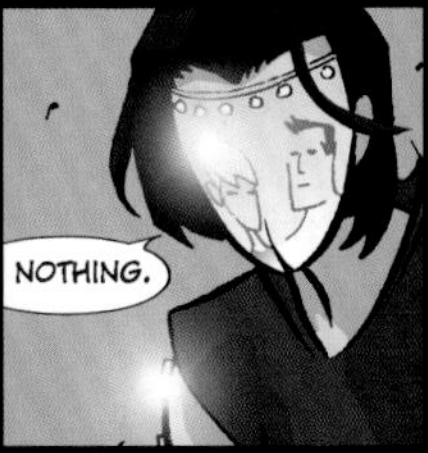
NOTHING.

WALLFLOWER
Jim Krueger

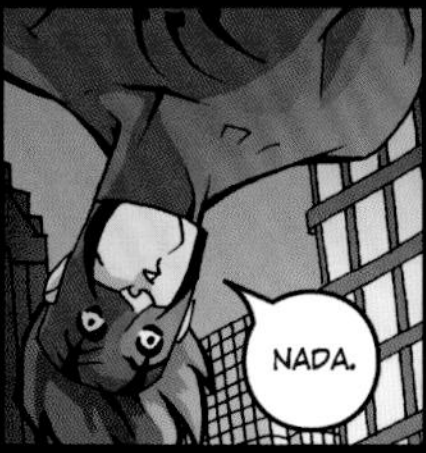
NADA.

THE BADGER
Mike Baron

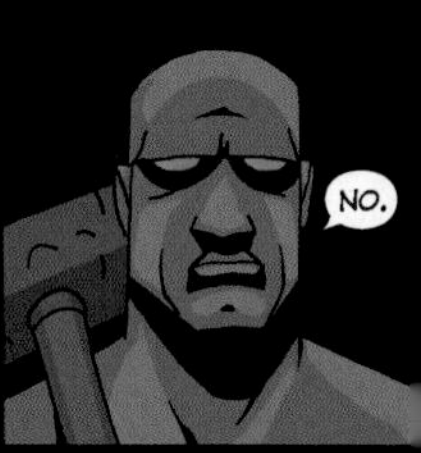
NO.

OL' JOHN HENRY
Mike Oeming

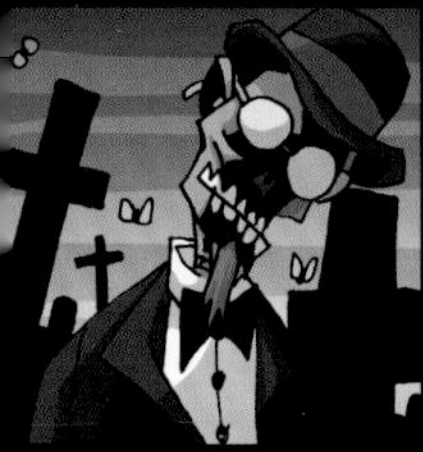

VON HELLSING
Mike Oeming

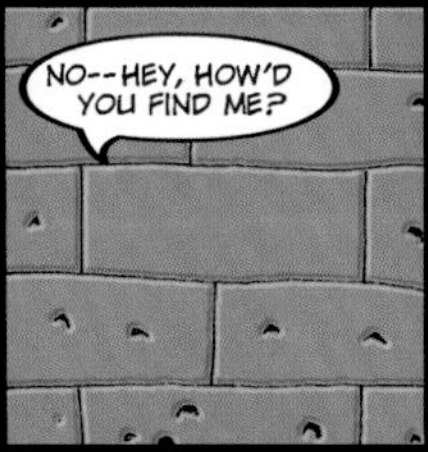
NO--HEY, HOW'D YOU FIND ME?

[redacted]

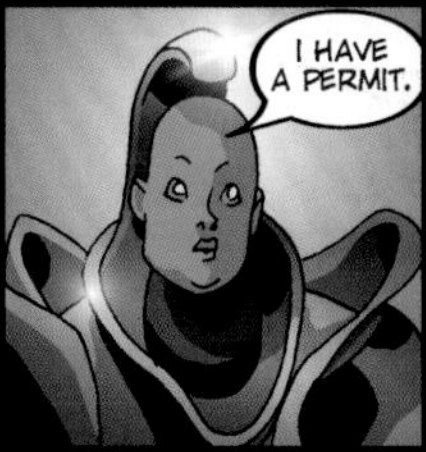
I HAVE A PERMIT.

DR. SOLOMON WEISS
Pat Garrahy

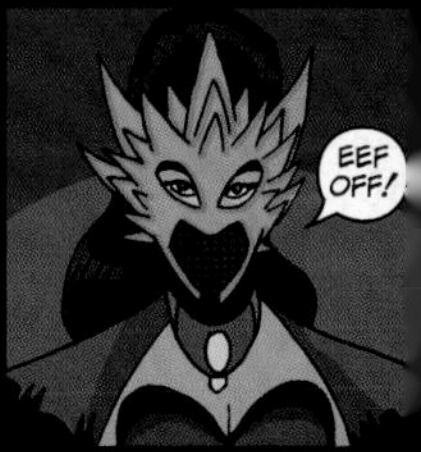
EEF OFF!

FETISH
Phil Jimenez

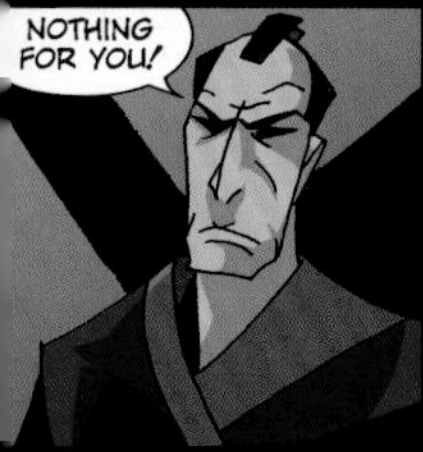
NOTHING FOR YOU!

[redacted]

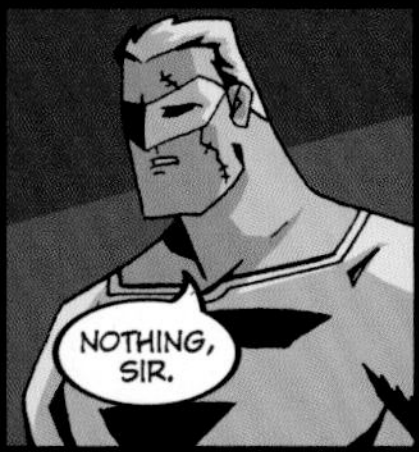
NOTHING, SIR.

[redacted]

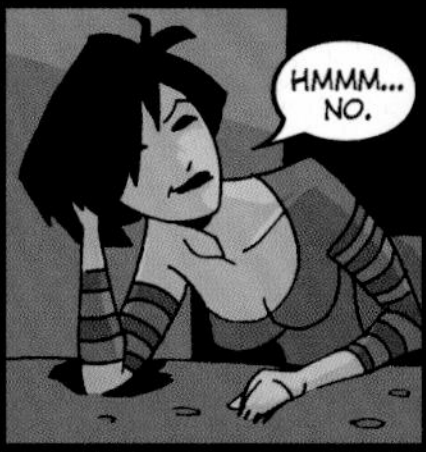
HMMM... NO.

PARTY GIRL
Mike Oeming

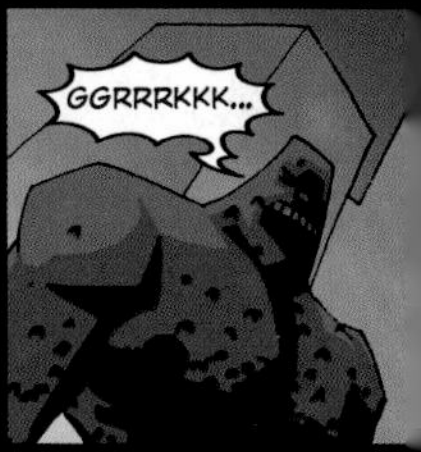
GGRRRKKK...

[redacted]

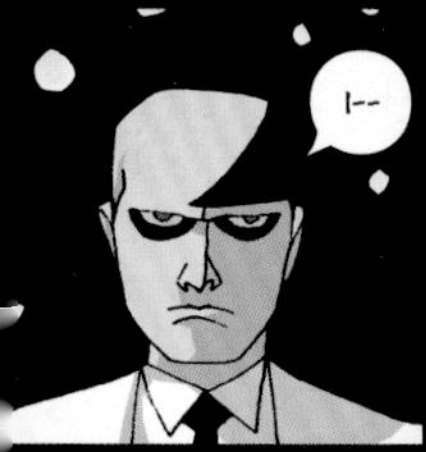
I--

MERGER
Scott Morse

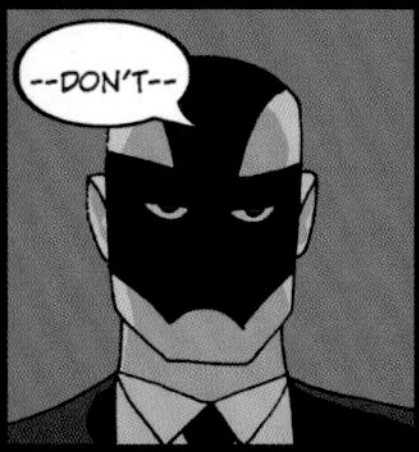
--DON'T--

CUTBACK
Scott Morse

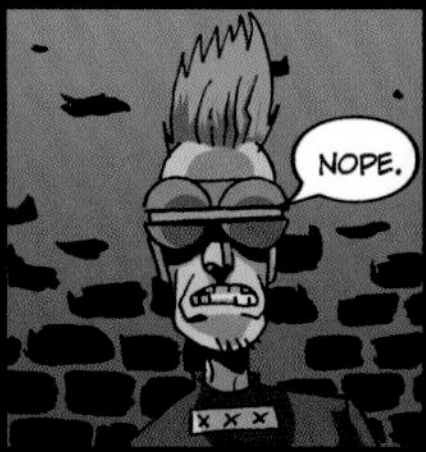
NOPE.

XXX RAY
Ed Brubaker

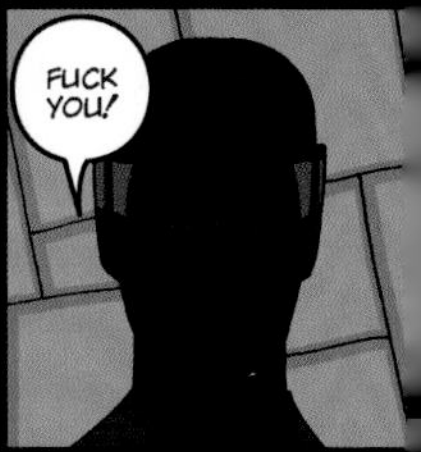
FUCK YOU!

[redacted]

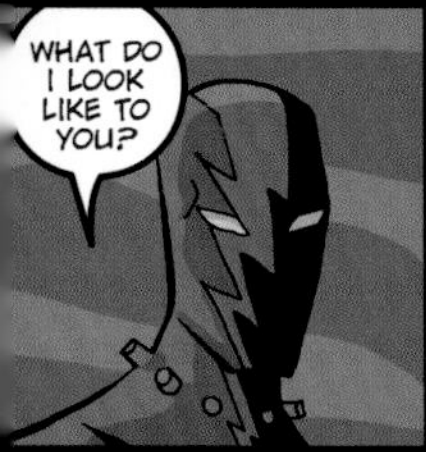
WHAT DO I LOOK LIKE TO YOU?

LIGHTNING ROD
Marc Andreyko

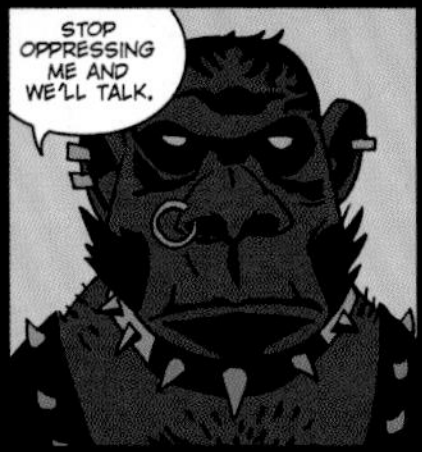
STOP OPPRESSING ME AND WE'LL TALK.

CASSIUS
Mike Oeming

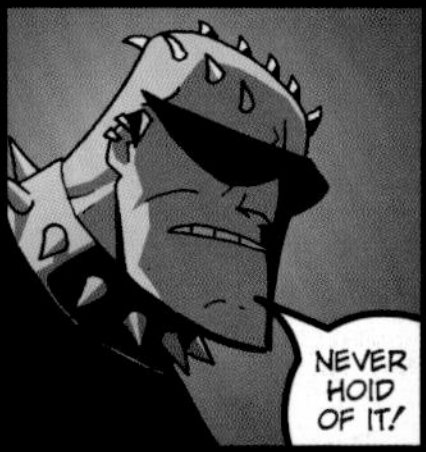
NEVER HOID OF IT!

THOMAS PAYNE
Mike Oeming

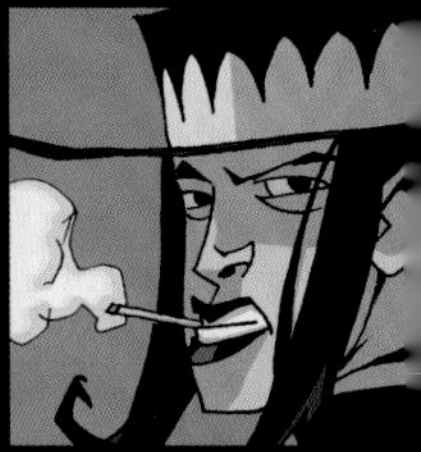

DUSTY STARR
Andrew Robinson

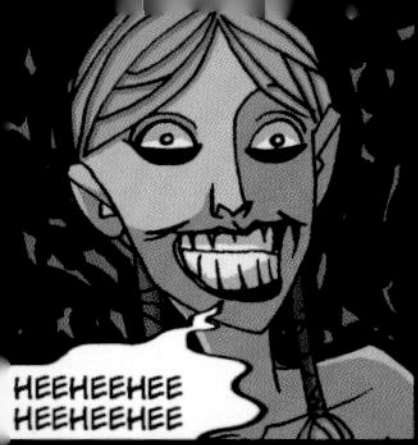
HEEHEEHEE
HEEHEEHEE

[redacted]

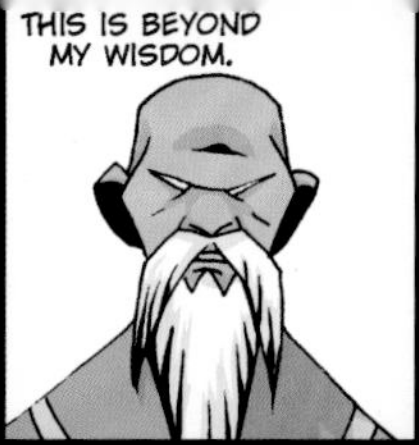
THIS IS BEYOND MY WISDOM.

[redacted]

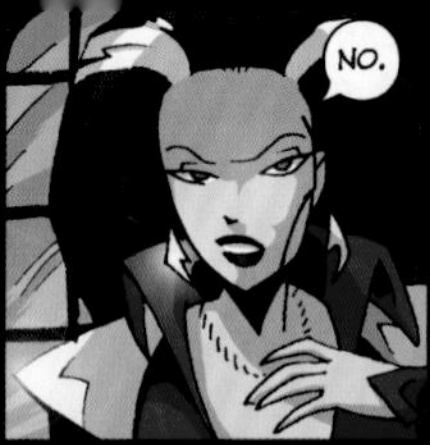
NO.

ACACIA
Neil Vokes

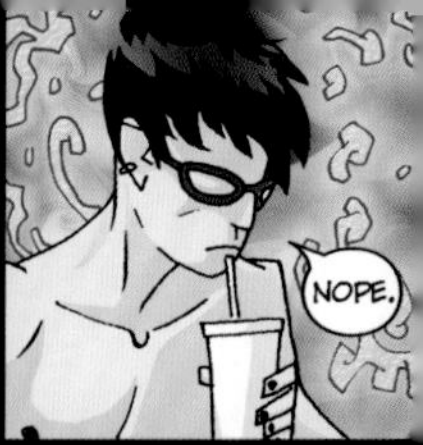
NOPE.

ACID LAD
Mike Oeming

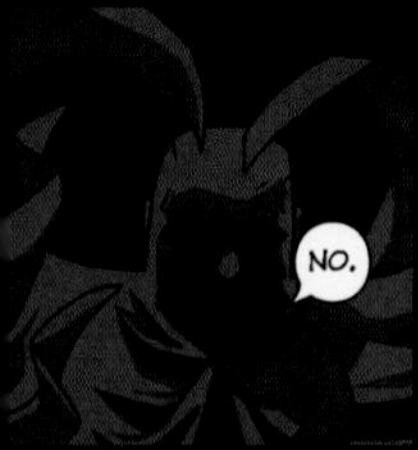
NO.

THE CAPE
Joe Quesada

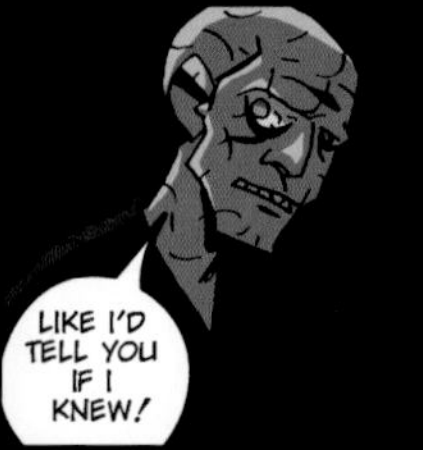
LIKE I'D TELL YOU IF I KNEW!

SCARMAN
Allan Gross

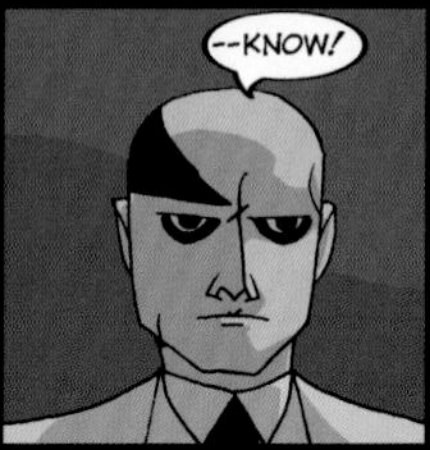
--KNOW!

HOSTILE TAKE OVER
Scott Morse

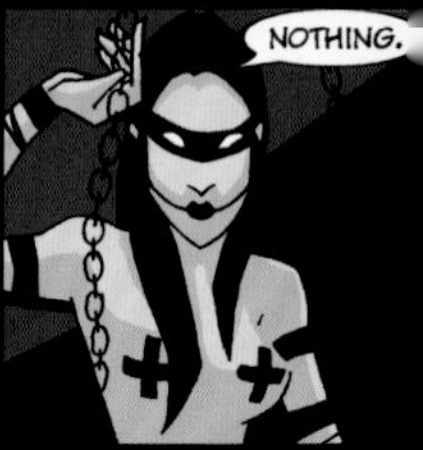
NOTHING.

SNAPDRAGON
David Mack

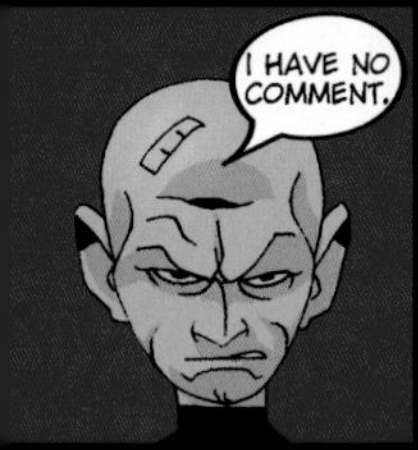
I HAVE NO COMMENT.

[redacted]

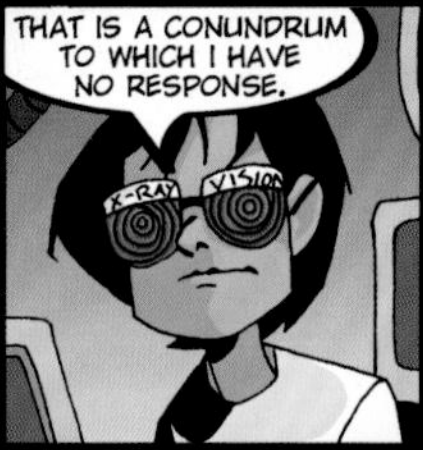
THAT IS A CONUNDRUM TO WHICH I HAVE NO RESPONSE.
X-RAY VISION

LINK
David Mack

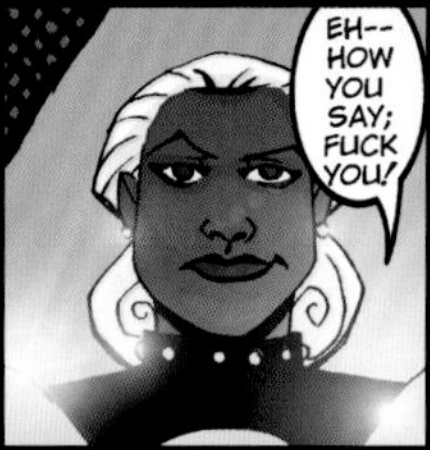
EH--HOW YOU SAY; FUCK YOU!

MAMA HADES
Mike Oeming

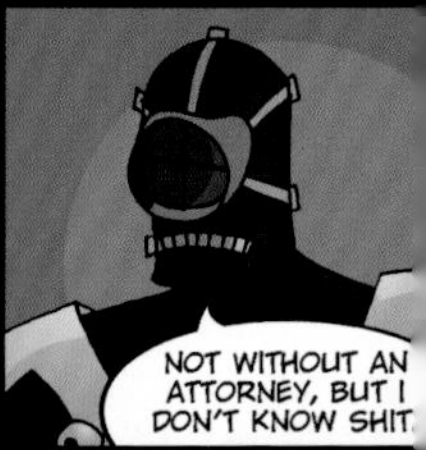
NOT WITHOUT AN ATTORNEY, BUT I DON'T KNOW SHIT.

JET BLACK ILLUMINAT
Mike Oeming

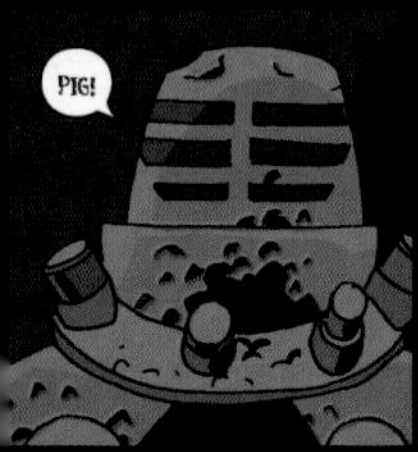
PIG!

BLACK LUNG
Mike Oeming

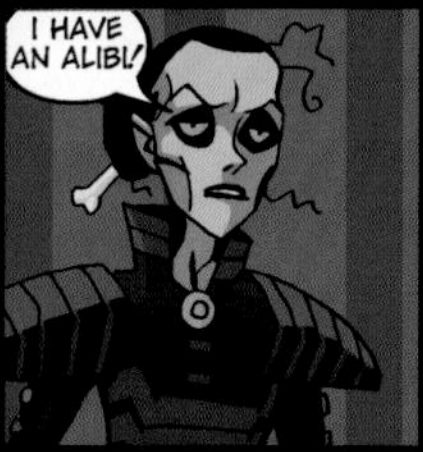
I HAVE AN ALIBI!

ANNIE REXIC
Mike Oeming

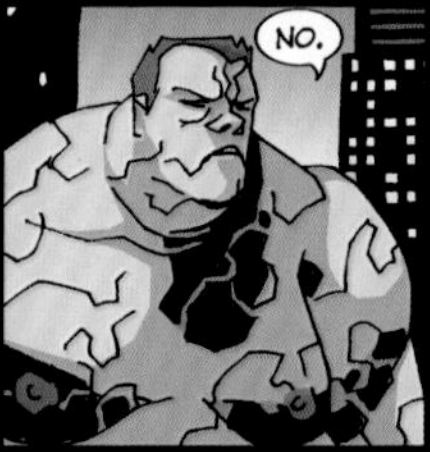
NO.

THORSLAND
Pat Garrahy

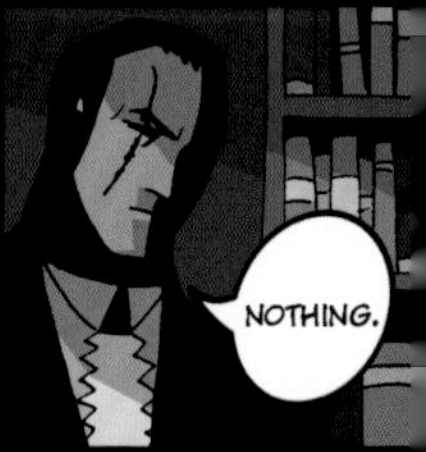
NOTHING.

KAI
David Mack

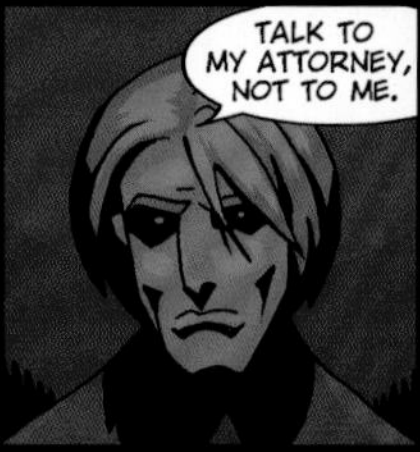
TALK TO MY ATTORNEY, NOT TO ME.

[redacted]

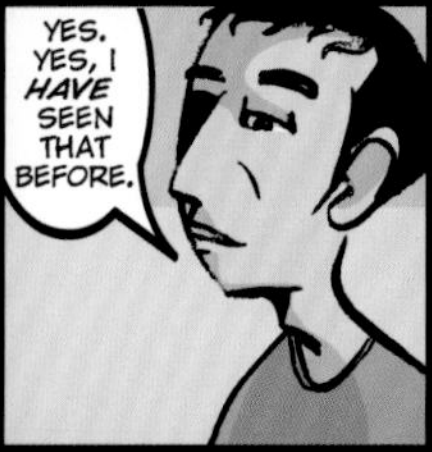
YES. YES, I HAVE SEEN THAT BEFORE.

[redacted]

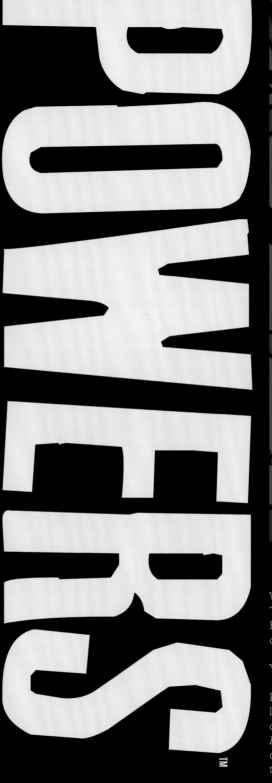

POWERS™

BEST OF LETTERS COLUMN

What the fuck is this exactly? The best of what? The best of clit jokes? The best of snotty digs at Bill Tucci? Could this actually be the most requested bonus extra we've ever had? This shit?

Yes.

Please enjoy this—my handpicked best-of-the-letters-column roundup. This is a smattering of letters and responses from the first year of *Powers*. We're also including little sidebars of our greatest media moments. Little bits about the book. It's sort of a time capsule.

And yes, nothing makes a joke funnier than being many years old . . .

Editor's note: Email addresses and last names have been redacted.

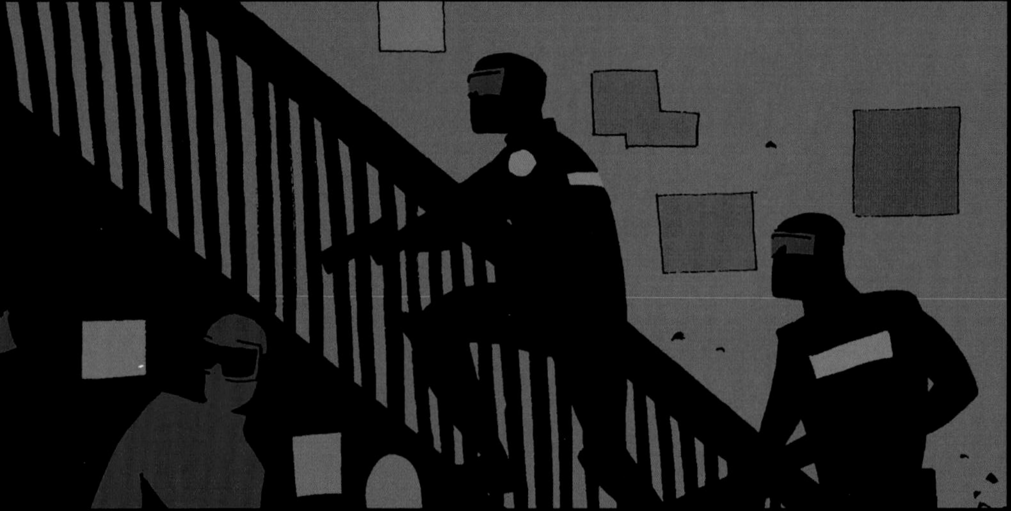

[redacted] Bendisyoubastard,

Do you ever have a bad day of writing, you sorry fucker? Does everything you write have to be near-perfect and entertaining? Have you never "fumbled the ball" and written something that was so bad it humiliated you? And do all your friends give you shit for using AOL like mine do? What's their problem, anyway?

Let me tell you something—you've gotta get new friends. They are sucking the life out of you. Can't you see that? If they are goofing on you for using AOL, imagine what they say about you when you're not around. I mean, first they goof on you for "selling out" by moving your book to full color, and now this. Oh wait—that's me. I'm sorry.

[redacted] Yo, B?!?! What's shakin'? First off let me tell ya, you are #1 baby! Your work is both diverse and creative. I use to read comics and have recently started again at the age of 25. My question to you is, what brought you to write/create comics?

The same thing that brought every one of us to create comics: total antisocial paranoid hysteria. Oh, and I get high off the markers.

[redacted] THE FOLLOWING IS A PAID ADVERTISEMENT BASED ON A TRUE STORY. (Well not really but it sounds official and shit)

So there I was a couple weeks ago at this Jewish Deli downtown. For some strange FUCKING reason they wouldn't serve me a ham and cheese sandwich like I was craving for. So instead I ordered the corned beef. Little did I know that this eatery was infamous for their RUBENS AS BIG AS YOUR FUCKING HEAD. Ignoring the fact that I have somewhat of a unstable digestive system I consumed all 13 pounds or so of this massive heart attack in the making. It was so delicious I hardly even noticed feeling my arteries clogging right then and there. Oh well, I was in bliss . . .

This is where things went wrong or in other words, the shit hit the bowl. I woke up the next day with a funny feeling in my gut and realized my worst nightmare had come true. I immediately hopped out of bed and stumbled into the bathroom depositing my ass on the mighty porcelain throne. Ah . . . Salvation . . . Then all of a sudden it hit me like a sonic boom. I had a case of the runny funnies. A real bad case. Right then I knew this was going to be a long day in the bathroom . . .

Now I was faced with a dilemma. What was going to help me pass the time during my daylong stay at Hotel Head? Sing along to the new N-Sync album? Read the articles in the latest issue of *Playboy*? Play connect the dots with my odd looking linoleum floor? No . . . I don't think so. There had to be something that would titillate my sense's in my greatest time of need. Something that'll give me that feeling you get after seeing *The Limey*, *Pulp Fiction* and *The Spanish Prisoner* for the first time. Something that isn't a product by the man and instead a creative vision by individuals. Something that . . . Then it hit me like a bullet to the temple. I didn't even bother pulling up my pants as I scurried into my bedroom. In my haste I stumbled to my knees in front of my dresser. I looked up and there it was . . . Glowing just like the Holy Mother Fucking Grail. I rose to my feet and picked it up in my hands, gently caressing the cover. What was it you ask? Issue #1 of Brian Michael Bendis and Mike Oeming's *POWERS*.

My prayers had been answered as I made my way back to the bathroom dragging toilet paper still stuck to my ass. I plopped back onto mighty whitey

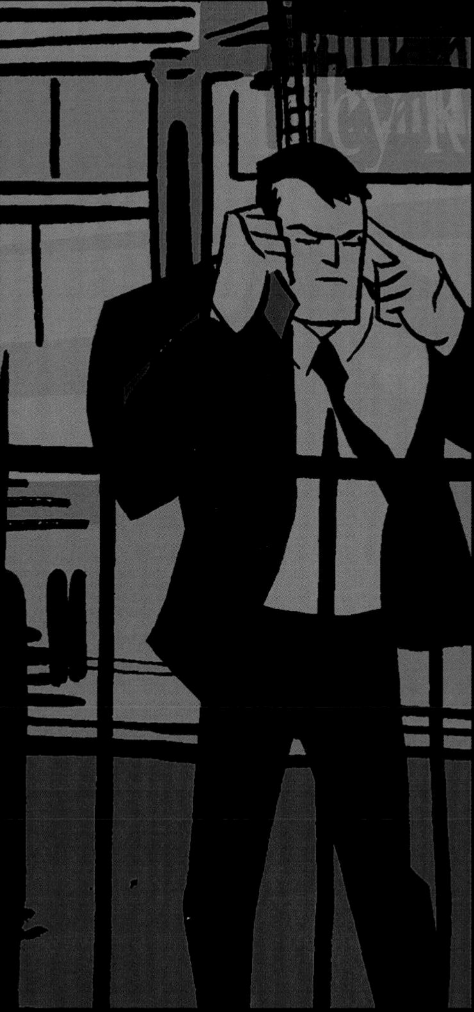

and my troubles went away. *Powers* from Cleveland had saved the day. Before me in my hands was not just any book. It was a open rebellion against all those shitty T&A books out there dominating the market today. A stand against all those tight wearing, ray shooting, claw bearing bitches that we've grown so sick of (not that there's anything wrong with that). What I held in my hands was *Powers*. A unique noir crime vision by these two talented cats named Bendis and Oeming. Not to mention all the other great writers and artists who'll be contributing characters along the way. And I for one hope this goes a long way, because I don't want to get off this ride.

THANKS *POWERS*!!!

That's a great letter. I love poop stories.

[redacted] The following are a few questions concerning the relationships between editors, writers, and artists. If you have the time, please answer them and e-mail them back to me. Thank you for any and all help.

1. Are ideas usually sparked by the writer or do publishers and editors seek out writers for projects they already have in mind?

I don't know where others get their ideas from—I buy mine from Ed Brubaker.

2. Once, the idea has been discussed, does the work then fall on the shoulders of the writer or does the writer get together and brainstorm with the editor and/or the artist?

I hire neighborhood kids to do most of the typing and stuff.

3. How much contact do you have with your artist?

As little as possible. Have you ever talked to an artist? I mean, how many heroin anecdotes can you listen to?

Do you have any hand in the selection of the artist? How does that work?

Best hand job wins. Isn't it the same in every business?

4. Once a first draft is completed, what process and revisions does it normally go through before the artist begins work?

Revisions?

5. How does an artist's involvement change the original concept of the story?

Usually cheapens it beyond recognition. But that's okay. It's just comics.

6. Please describe what you believe would be the ideal relationship between the writer and editor . . .

I don't know, uh . . . doggie style is fun, but really it depends on my mood.

I realize the answers will be different from project to project, but a rough idea is all that is needed. Thank you for your time.

Well, I can't imagine giving it to you any rougher than that.

[redacted]

To Mr. Brian Michael Bendis, and all who work on this fabulous comic. I am astounded by your work. I picked up this book on the chance that I might find a new interest. I happened to walk into the local comic book store yesterday, Collector's Corner, and I was feelin' a bit experimental. I picked up *Powers* and two others. I must say, *Powers* has wormed its way into my heart and is now one of my regular buys. The combination of Film Noir art and fantastic story that's realistic. Well, more realistic than most. Making Walker a detective instead of the usual "I'm a SUPERHERO!! Look at ME!" is great. I loved the little girl (you never mentioned her name). "What's a clitoris?" That caught me completely by surprise and left me laughing for a good five minutes!! Michael Avon Oeming's art is fantastic. Reminds me of the art style of the *Batman Animated* Series (before the new animation team and crappy stories). I love it. Does he pencil his art or does he just go straight to ink? Being a fellow artist I know how hard that is.

Mike says that he usually drinks himself unconscious, only to wake up to finished pages every morning. So hey, whatever works?

[redacted] Good God damn, man! I just read POWERS #1, and I loved it! I checked it out after reading *Fortune and Glory* and I gotta tell you, you've completely ruined me because now I have to go and buy *Powers*, *Sam and Twitch*, and whatever else you write. I am considering either becoming a drug lord or a pimp to pay for my newly increased comics fix, and I figured since you got me in this mess you could help me decide. Uh, anyways, back to making sense, you are one talented motherfucker and I hope you'll be doing lots of comics down the road.

P.S. Your head is shiny and I like it!
P.S.S. I am a dumbass.
P.S.P.P.S.P. Really.

Well, if I may . . . I recommend pimping. I saw a fascinating documentary on HBO on the subject, and it looks like a lot of fun.

[redacted]

Just wanted to drop you a line about *POWERS* #1. It's a cup of coffee in a greasy spoon diner, the only cop you can trust, the sounds of sirens lulling you to sleep. I enjoyed it.

[redacted]

Wow, that's great. And I am sorry about your last name. That's too bad.

[redacted] I'm sitting here eating a Subway sandwich, and they didn't have the good old Lays regular chips . . . so got these "naturally baked original potato crisps." Man, they suck!

POWERS PLAYS AT COLUMBIA PICTURES
Mon., September 11, 2000
By Cathy Dunkley

Columbia Pictures has optioned the feature film rights to Image Comics' popular comic book "Powers," created by writer-artist Brian Michael Bendis and Michael Avon Oeming, for producer Mace Neufeld and his Sony-based production company Mace Neufeld Prods ("Clear and Present Danger").

"Powers" focuses on Christian Walker and Deena Pilgrim, two homicide detectives who are anything but average. The city in which they work is unique: It has superheroes, villains and the like. Walker and Pilgrim take care of special cases—the "powers" cases—and are charged with solving "powers"-related murders.

No screenwriter has yet been hired to pen the adaptation.

Bendis—best known for writing and drawing Image Comics' graphic crime novels "Jinx," "Goldfish" and "Fire"—will receive a credit for co-producing the "Powers" project. His comic book "Fortune and Glory" tells of his adventures in setting up his first two comic books. He is also penning "The Ultimate Spiderman" and, separately, "Daredevil" for Marvel.

Neufeld Prods. Director of development David Engel brought the project to the studio. Overseeing the project will be Columbia Pictures exec VP Doug Belgrad and Neufeld Prods. VP development Kel Symons.

Subway. Barf!! I got an idea—why don't you take five dollars, toss it in the toilet, and shove the plunger handle up your ass. It will save ten minutes and create the same effect.

[redacted] What's up ultimate Bendis?

Lately I've been having problems shitting so maybe I should get me one of those SUPER REUBENS. Because I've been having these problems I haven't visited the toilet for my weekly comic reading. Consequently I've been reduced to reading your comics on couches and recliners. Thanks for the great books my man.

It's cute that you called me "ultimate Bendis," but seriously, when you see me at a con or email me, I only answer to "Mr. Marvel."

[redacted] Hello Mr. Bendis, quick comment about your guys' *Powers* book . . . I just finished reading the newest issue . . . the basic premise of *Powers* comic book seems to me basically *Watchmen*/*Marvels* through the point of view of a police detective??? I know the outcome and the storylines will be different and original. Also I know it's nothing like those two stories. But I'm asking about the basic premise . . . Yes, no . . . just curious . . .

We see it as more of an *It! The Living Colossus / Giant-Size Man-Thing* with a pinch of *Night Nurse*.

[redacted] Keep up the good work you multi-talented freak—what is it, like 30 books a month now, and all on time? What are you, a giant idea-filled head attached to a scrawny little body, with hands just big enough to type on a keyboard?

Yeah, so?

Neufeld's most recent project—the thriller "Bless the Child," starring Kim Basinger, Jimmy Smits and Christina Ricci—was released by Paramount Pictures last month.

Chris Silbermann and Justin Silvera at Broder Kurland Webb Uffner brokered the deal for Bendis. In December 1997, Dimension Films acquired film rights to his comic book series "AKA Goldfish."

So, for the record . . .

***Powers* the comic remains in production and on schedule. We own the publishing rights and will continue to put the book out for as long as you will have us.**

The *Jinx* animated web project remains in active production. We have about ten to twelve minutes done already. The holdup is the music rights.

I am not leaving comics! I love comics and I love all the opportunities I have. I will continue my runs on all the titles I am involved in. I am not one of those dudes looking for a way out of comics. I love comics.

I am not writing the script for the movie because of the pending Hollywood strike deadlines.

They don't have time to give me a crack at it—they need to get going with a more proven name in the area of summer-blockbuster-type stuff. I am a producer and am involved. The most recent story outline is pretty relevant to the comic.

So, Retro Girl is laid to rest but . . . IS *POWERS* OVER?

Hell no!

[redacted] You, sir, are absolutely fucking cool. Seriously, I never thought anything cool could come out of Cleveland, but you have certainly proved me wrong. Great stories, great characters, great dialogue, what's not to love about a man like you? Except that you're a man. I try not to love men. Nothing personal. It's more like a general rule. Plus you're married.

This is true—I am off the market. But Mike Oeming wants you all to know he has no problem with the occasional fan hand job, so . . .

[redacted] Mucho, Mucho thanx for *Powers*! Fantastic book, the best I've read this year, my other fave being . . . *Sam & Twitch* . . . coincidental, non? I may have to go and check out all your

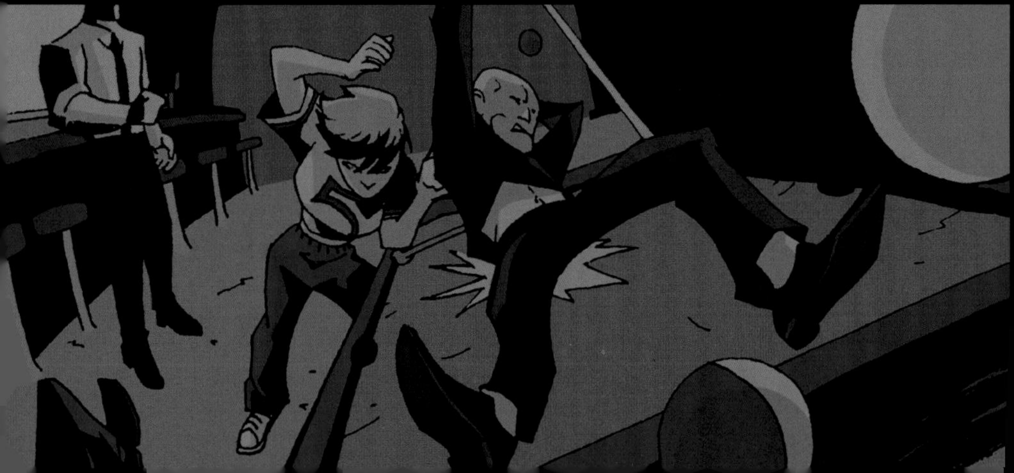

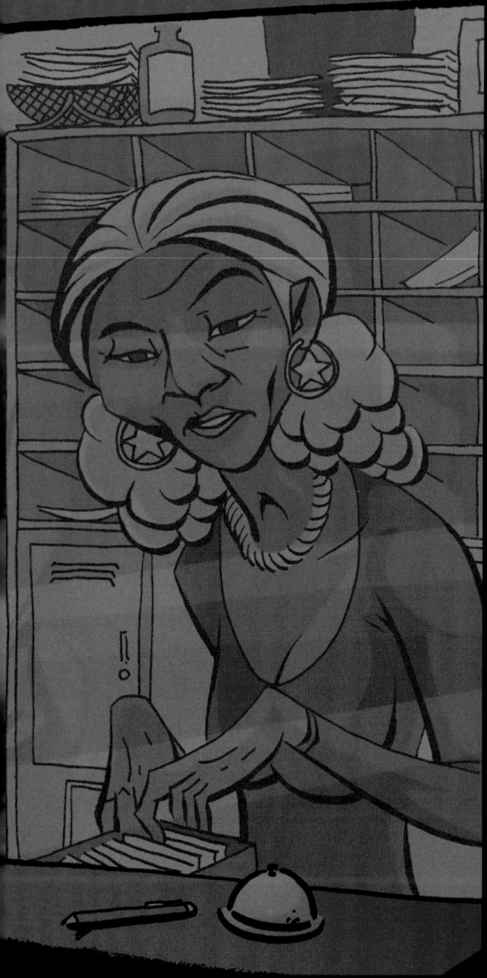

other work now . . . My bank manager curses you already.

Anyway, I am writing for one reason . . . to applaud you for one line! In the lift (elevator to non-Brits) when Kutter is talking to Walker, and utters "Boom Boom Shakalaka Laka Boom Boom!!"

Strike another Was (Not Was) fan on the board!!! First usage of "Walk the Dinosaur" that I've ever seen in comics . . . Hopefully not the last??

Well, there was a pretty good one in *Maus* Volume 2.

[redacted] A few days ago I was looking over the shelves at my local comic shop. I was feeling fairly frisky to try something new and saw *Powers* #2 sitting there and it just sort of whispered, "Psst, hey you . . . yeah you read me." Startled that the voices were back, I glanced thru a couple pages. The moment I laid eyes on Mike Oeming's art I decided to pick it up. As luck would have it, the last copy of issue #1 was sitting on another shelf. I was so happy I did a little happy dance right there in the store. Then immediately paid for my book and ran home as fast as I could.

Once home, I read both issues first thing. The way you tell a story man, its brilliant. I was hooked from page 2. "What's a clitoris?" BAHAHAH! I nearly messed myself that was so funny. The telephone booth story had me rolling for 20 minutes also. Anyway, I've bored you long enough and I know you're quite the busy guy. I just wanted to say keep up the great work and I am now a devoted Bendis fan or "Bendhead" if you will.

Okay—a fan who not only *hears* voices but *listens* to them, and who messes his pants when reading comic books. Okay. No sudden moves. Everything is . . . is . . . it's going to be all right.

[redacted] These first two issues of *Powers* are awesome!!! I'm the type of reader that loves a "hard-edge" type comic, and this definitely fits the bill. This is NOT your kiddie comic. After reading the second issue I felt I had to e-mail you some praises. Sometimes a comic can have just that first great issue to lure you in, but you know how to make us come back for more!

I did have two questions though: 1.) What does O.T.R. stand for? (Issue 2) And 2.) Will you guys (the creative team) be around for awhile? Nothings worse than picking up your favorite book and the creative teams have changed!!!

1) "O.T.R." stands for "on the rag," which means on her period, which means swimming against the crimson tide, which means bitchy as fuck, which means my ex-girlfriend the entire year I was dating her, which means you'll never hear the phrase "vagina envy."

2) Mike and I own the book, so no one is going anywhere. If we don't do it, it doesn't get done. Except for the next seven issues, which are going to be by Scott Lobdell and Chap Yaep. But I don't think you'll even notice the difference.

[redacted] Bendis –

In the great tradition of my casting for *Sam & Twitch: The Movie*, I present the cast of *Powers: The Movie*.

POWERS:
Directed by David O. Russell (*Three Kings*)
Detective Christian Walker .... George Clooney
Detective Deena Pilgrim .... Angelina Jolie
Detective Kutter .... Loren Dean
Johnny Stade .... Johnny Depp

Police Captian .... Dennis Franz
Retro Girl .... Reese Witherspoon
Triphammer .... Clint Eastwood
Flinch .... Grant Heslov
The Doctor .... James Woods
Zora .... Natasha Henstridge
The Little Girl .... The Pepsi Girl

I can feel the slap for that last one a million miles away.

[redacted] *Via France*

Hello, you self-loving bald bastard (I have to be rude . . . makes me sounds cool and all . . .).

Here I am writing you a brown-nosing mail from your site (print it out and wipe your ass with it, thinking about me, that'll do it). Enough of that nothing to say shit, let's get to the nasty ass-sucking part: *POWERS* IS SO GOOD I DON'T NEED MY DAILY NETPORN ANYMORE. Yep, we French dig bald Americans, especially if they write good comics!!)

Ben voila, encore bravo, a bientot et vive les slips! (I had to say that . . .)

Listen, *Powers* is good and all, but nothing—*NOTHING!*—replaces *daily netporn*!

[redacted] My name is Samuel [redacted] and I am a senior at Penn State University majoring in media studies. Recently I was speaking with my advisor and friend Pat [redacted] about entering the comic book industry as a writer. And while he was very helpful in terms of telling me how to prepare myself to enter the industry he admitted little knowledge of how to actually get into it. It was then that he advised me to get into contact with you, as you two have talked in the past, and hope that you have some advise for an aspiring comic book writer. As of right now, I have my stories, artist friends who are also willing to put in the time and effort, but have no idea where to go from there.

Thank you very much for your time and any advice you can give me.

My advice is to get away from any teacher who tells you to write comic books for advice. Wow!! That is tuition well spent.

[redacted]

POWERS:
Directed by Roger Corman
Detective Christian Walker .... Dolph Lundgren
Detective Deena Pilgrim .... Kathy Ireland
Detective Kutter .... Andrew Stevens
Johnny Suade .... Michael Dudikoff
Police Captian .... Robbie Coltrane
Retro Girl .... Helen Slater
Triphammer .... Richard Harris
Flinch .... David Caruso
The Doctor .... Eric Roberts
Zora .... Sybil Danning
The Little Girl .... Lourdes Ciccone

[redacted] I'm writing an article for Britain's '*What DVD?*' magazine about comic-book adaptations for the big screen and I was hoping you might be able to help me out by answering a few questions.

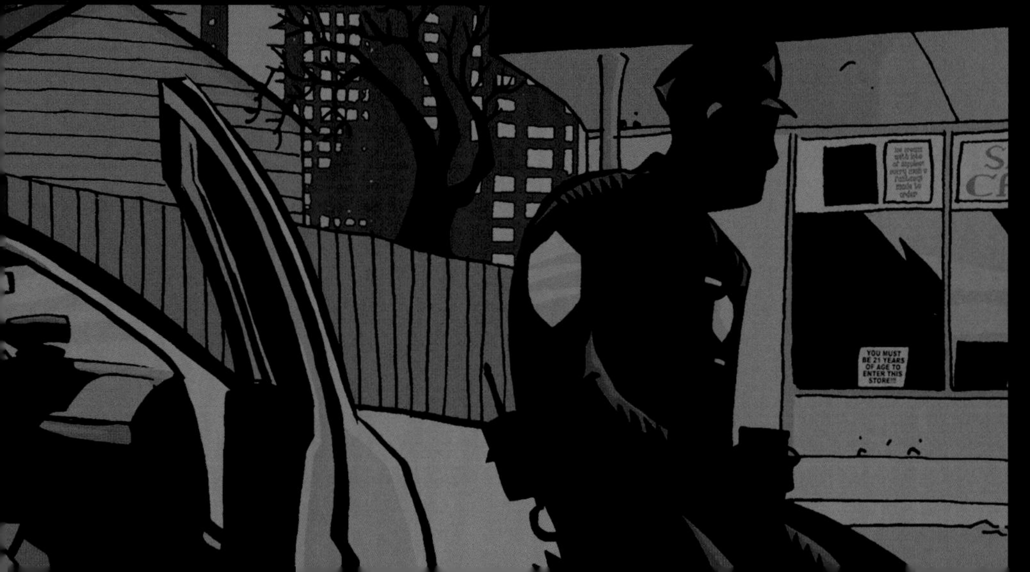
YOU MUST BE 21 YEARS OF AGE TO ENTER THIS STORE!!!

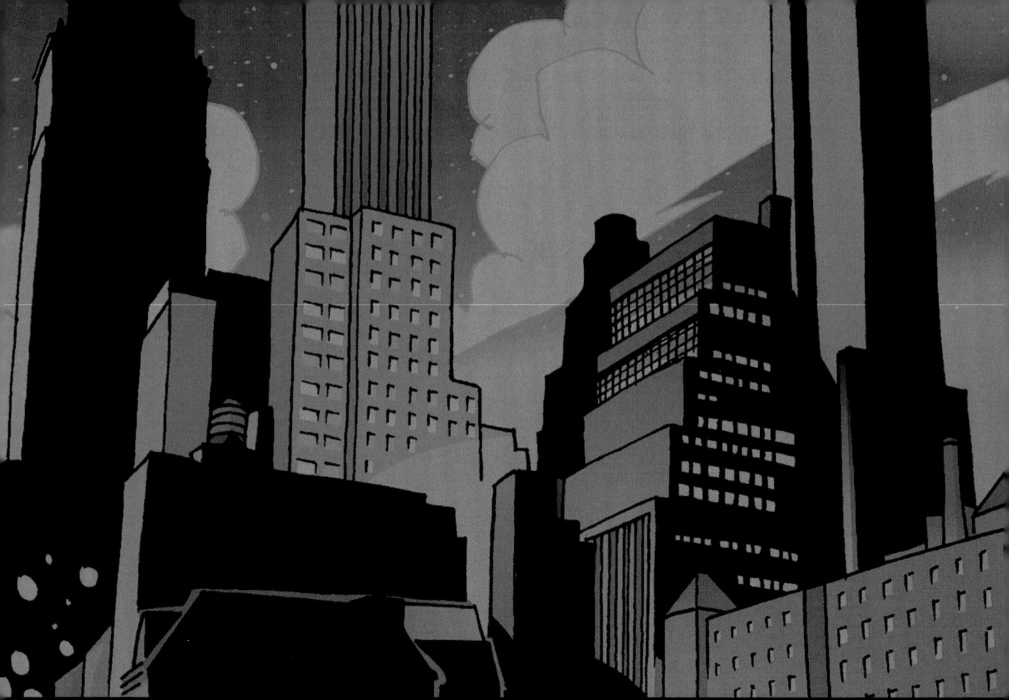

Firstly, what effect do you believe the *X-MEN* movie will have on future comic-book adaptations?

I think the next film adaptations of *Judge Dredd* and *Tank Girl* will still suck ass!

You've spent a lot of time in Hollywood. What is the movie industry's reaction to comics as a source of material?

Did you ever see that *Star Trek* episode with the woman who sucked the salt out of a guy using her suction-cup fingertips?

How do they treat 'comics people' out there?

The way they treat each other. Like Ike treated Tina.

Why do you think comics are such a popular resource for filmmakers?

They like the shiny colors.

What do you believe are the secrets of a successful comics-to-film adaptation?

Keep Schumacher the hell away from them.

What are the greatest challenges an adapter faces?

AC or DC.

Which films do you think have been the most faithful or effective adaptations?

***Gone with the Wind* was pretty good.**

Which future projects (yours or other peoples') are you most excited about?

The direct-to-video sequel to *Mimic*. The story had to be told.

Thanks very much for taking the time to go through these questions. I hope you'll be able to answer them. On a personal note, I'd like to say how much I love *POWERS*. It is without a doubt the book of the year.

Gee, I should have emailed this to him directly then. Shit.

[redacted] My name's John [redacted], and I work with a fellow at Lone Star Comics you might know by the name of Chris [redacted]. Our comic shop was the one that set out two copies of *Powers* and let customers read them all day. If you have no clue what I'm talking about feel free to disregard the first part of my email.

I will. Thanks.

No, seriously, I love my buds at Lone Star Comics. If you live anywhere within a three-hour radius of these fine folks, support them with your almighty dollar.

[redacted]

The best compliment I can pay you is that your book

were some of the first I steered my wife (girlfriend at the time . . . I was trying to impress her!) towards to prove that comic books are not all crap for juvenile illiterates. Of course, I had to guide her around the stacks of "*Breastula, Dark Queen of the Naked Underworld*" and variations thereof to get there . . . taking some of the steam out of my argument.

Breastula, Dark Queen of the Naked Underworld **. . . Man, don't you wish Danzig was still publishing? :)**

[redacted] Dear Brain (or is it Michael)

(or should I just call you Bendis?),

I have just finished reading both the *Jinx* and *Goldfish* Trade-Paper-Backs (There has to be a better word for them) and I was wondering if you could tell me where the two relate in a timeline. My guess is that the *Goldfish* story took place after he left with Jinx at the end of her story (Hence he was calling from Colorado). Am I totally off base here or not please tell me! I have a History degree and these things drive me crazy!

Wow, that must suck for you.

[redacted] Thank you for stealing my cash. I walked into my comic shop last Wednesday to get my week's worth of super-heroes and other some such things. Knowing it was the week for the purchase of a new trade I was torn between two as I drove to the store. Marvel's *Infinity Gauntlet* or Bendis' *Jinx*.

Jinx won. Volume and price. Volume and price.

One last thing: I finished it while making my sacrifice to the Great Porcelain God of the Bathroom. Ever take something in with you that is so good, you sit there for like twenty minutes on the can and just read it after your done with the Major Download because it REALLY is that good? *Jinx* was.

That is so sweet. I know what you're talking about. I had the same experience with *Wendy Whitebread, Undercover Slut*.

[redacted] Hello,

My name is Gerald [redacted]. I am writing in the hopes that there would be some way for me to fit on to the *Jinx* team. I have been a freelance illustrator for ten year, I've worked for a TV producer drawing storyboards for a local Spanish channel here in Miami, and I spent some time drawing comics for a small unknown here. I have also taught myself Photoshop. I hope there is something I can do.

[redacted]

Even though I am intrigued by your three French names, and I do have a soft spot for the total narcissism that you use all three names, we have no openings right now for a cowardly Frenchman.

[redacted] God, I want Boyd Matson's job!

And I wish I could pleasure myself orally. What's your point?

[redacted] Yo Bendis, I love your work.

I read comics about four years now. You must understand I am but a 14 year old. I started buying at the right time and, much to my dismay, I only bought Marvel comics. I was so pathetic that I didn't even think you could curse in comics. My favorite hero is Spider-Man. You know how fuckin' happy I am that you're going to write a comic with him in it? I thank you from the bottom of my heart. Thank you!! THANK YOU!!!!

I need your help on something: old works of yours. I'm a bit confused about these trade paperbacks that are coming out. Please help me:

1. I need you to tell me if every issue of *Jinx*, including the Caliber and Image comics, is going to be printed in one, unified trade paperback or in separate trade paperbacks, and when the paperback(s) is coming out.

2. Is the trade paperback of *Goldfish* going to collect every *Goldfish* comic produced? And when is the paperback coming out?

3. *Torso*'s trade paperback . . . is it collecting every issue of *Torso*? How many issues were there? Two? When is it coming out?

4. *Fortune & Glory*. I know that there's going to be a trade paperback, but when is it coming out and does it collect all the comics in that series?

5. *Fire*. The trade paperback is out? Good, good. Does it collect every issue of that title ever made?

6. What other comics, besides *Powers* and *Sam & Twitch*, are you going to write?

7. What comics are you writing now and are on newsstands (again, besides *Powers* and *S & T*)? And are they going to be ongoing?

So I'm breaking form here and not printing the original obnoxious answers to this letter. Instead I want to ponder what happened to this fine young gentleman.

My hope is he ended up getting that blowjob he so desperately needed and instantly realized, "WHO CARES?" Or he was committed to an asylum about a month or two after DC brought back the alt-cover programs.

Okay—back to the dated jokes. (Did you catch that Chap Yaep reference earlier? I had to Google the reference, and I wrote the joke.)

[redacted] I was looking through some of my comics the other night and came across a comic called *Angels of Destruction* by Malibu after they had been bought by Marvel. When I looked in the credits, I saw "Brian Michael Bendis–story." Is this one of your first pieces of work? It's dated October '96 and I have no clue how long you've been doing comics.

I don't know what you are talking about. I have no recollection of working on any such comic or even of the existence of the aforementioned comic.

(Hey—shut the fuck up before someone hears you, okay?)

[redacted] My friend Reggie is always preaching how he can take a dump and eat his dinner at the same time. Is that considered a super power?

If it were, my family would be the Justice League of America.

[redacted] Hello there, Mr. Bendis,

My name is Brett [redacted] and I'm a Film and English major at Chapman University. I am currently enrolled in an "Overview of Producing" class where aside from having to cram more information into my skull than humanly possible, we've been given an assignment to "investigate" a project currently in development, etc. Last night I read the *Hollywood Reporter* article in the letters page of *Powers* #6. I was wondering if I might ask you a few questions regarding Columbia's opting of the film rights and your co-producing credit.

Wow, an "Overview of Producing" class. For midterms, do you have to *find* a writer to fuck over, or do they *assign* you one?

GREAT EISNER

NOMINATIONS NEWS . . .

We were just informed that we received the following nominations . . .

Best New Series: *Powers*

Best Writer: Bendis, for *Powers*, *Fortune and Glory*, and *Ultimate Spider-Man*

Best Penciller/Inker: Michael Avon Oeming

Best Limited Series: *Fortune and Glory*

Best Humor Publication: *Fortune and Glory*

Thanks to anyone who thinks they deserve it.

[redacted] I need a Bendis Halloween mask. The reason would be 2-fold.

1. I would get all sorts of poon cuz I'd look like you and

2. I could take a pic of myself wearing it so you could look at it and remember what it was like to have a full head of hair, which would be good for you.

From the sound of it, I may have hair again before you get some, as you say, "poon." Take it from a wise and powerful member of the media—you calling it "poon" is probably the single biggest obstacle in the way of you actually getting any.

[redacted]

Bendis, I just wanted to send you one of the hundred million e-mails a day you must get that tell you how wonderful you are and basically give you the verbal equivalent to a blow job.

No offense, pal, but I can get that at home. Talk is cheap! I need an actual blowjob. A whole blowjob! You understand what I'm saying? From the very beginning to the sickening end. Oh, and from a girl would be preferable.

[redacted] Brian, could you answer the following for our web site www.npo.com? Thanks.

Rob Liefeld.

6. What is the worst comic you've ever worked on?

I can only pick one?

7. Pick three things you couldn't live without.

My brain stem.

8. Have you ever been mistaken for someone else?

Every bald lead singer of every rock band on MTV2.

9. Have you ever wanted to be someone else?

Every bald lead singer of every rock band on MTV2.

10. How many hours do you sleep each night?

Sleep is for pussies.

11. Do you sing in the shower?

No. I don't sing. But did you see *American Beauty*?

12. What is the strangest thing you have in your house?

Well, this house was built on an old Indian burial ground, so you'll have to be more specific . . .

13. Who is the last person you hung up on?

Actually, I've got a pretty good answer to that, but I will pass.

14. Is there a recent catchphrase you wish you'd never hear again?

Pretty much all of them. I like "Where's the beef?" though. That rocks.

15. What music are you listening to right now?

Oscar De La Hoya's kick-ass new album. All sports figures are great musicians.

16. What was the last good movie you saw?

When did *Chinatown* come out?

17. What is the name of the last book you couldn't finish reading?

The Bible. It just goes on and on—blah, blah, blah. It needs some polishing.

18. Who is your best friend?

1. What are you working on right now?

A twenty-piece Chicken McNuggets.

2. What is the best part of your job?

THE CONVENTION WHORES. Wait, no—that's computer software technicians. The best part of my job is dreaming about convention whores at computer software conventions.

3. What was the first comic book you ever bought?

I want to say *Wendy Whitebread, Undercover Slut*. But that's not the first—just the best.

4. If you weren't working in comics what would you be doing?

Convention whore.

5. What is the strangest thing you've ever seen at a comic convention?

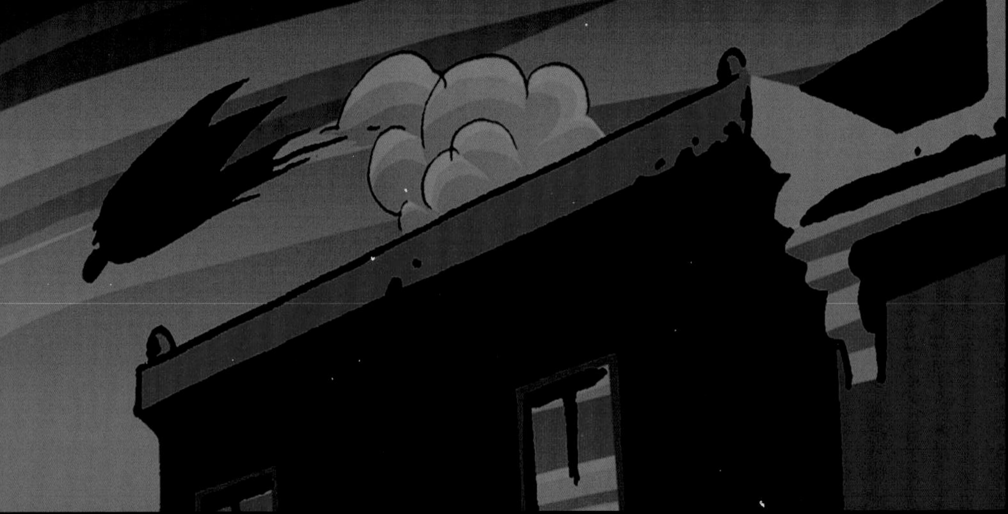

Jesus . . . or my dog. It's hard to choose.

9. What is the worst advice you've ever received?

'Hey, Brian—fill out this interview."

20. When was the last time you were truly fright-ened?

When I saw the trailer for *Charlie's Angels*. Shudder . . .

21. Have you ever thought the whole world was against you?

Not until this very second . . .

22. Life: grand design or cosmic joke?

I think of it as a grandly designed cosmic joke.

23. What the world needs now is . . .

. . . a new Frank Sinatra like I need a hole in my head.

[redacted] What does one say when they contact the single greatest writer none to man kind? Do they play it off as those it were not such the momentous occasion it was/Do they force small talk in hopes of fostering a friendship? Do they brown nose and kiss ass to the point of bleeding?

I would say to him that *Watchmen* rocked, and I love the black-and-white *Swamp Thing* reprints.

(Aaaww—see what I did there? I pretended I'm all humble, while in reality I whacked off to this letter three times. That's right! Three times. Oh yeah—I still got it . . .)

[redacted] Dear Brian Michael Bendis,

My name is Kyle [redacted] and I have been reading comic books since I was four years old. I am almost 15 now, and I am still reading more and more comics, and writing more and more stories that would do great in comic book format. *Powers*, *Hellspawn*, *Ultimate Spider-Man*, whatever you write is comic gold and apparently with the workload you handle you're writing all the time.

I have a few questions for you so that I can get my career in writing comics started, and hey, once I'm in maybe we could collaborate on something:

Oh no—it's another questionnaire where I get to rattle off cheap gags about shit and *Wendy Whitebread, Undercover Slut*.

1. How did you get into comics?

My wife drove me.

2. What is the address (if any) for submitting stories to Marvel? DC? Image?

It's all the same place actually:

Submissions Editor
13 Boone St.
Bromley, KY

3. What type of stories does each company like to get? Ex. Futuristic, action packed, super-hero?

Do you have anything along the lines of *Penthouse Variations*? Most editors I know read those.

4. Who was the first artist you ever worked with and who is your favorite current artist?

First guy I worked with was Brian Bendis, but all he cares about now is being in *Wizard* because he turned into a total fucking asshole. My new favorite artist is that guy on PBS with the 'fro who paints the landscapes. He wipes his ass with Alex Ross . . . and he's dead!!

5. How many titles do you currently write and what are they?

All of them! Just go down the *CSN* checklist—it's all mine.

That's a joke. I don't write *Shi*—no one does.

Hank you Bendis, you're a stud!

Sincerely,

Kyle [redacted]

p.s. If you ever want to chat comics or anything, drop me a line ([redacted])

Uh-oh—I smell cop . . .

[redacted] As a young aspiring comic writer, I feel overwhelmingly inclined to write you a somewhat alcohol-induced letter of invidious praise.

Aspiring comics writer? Alcohol? Get yourself a British accent and you're *there*, buddy!

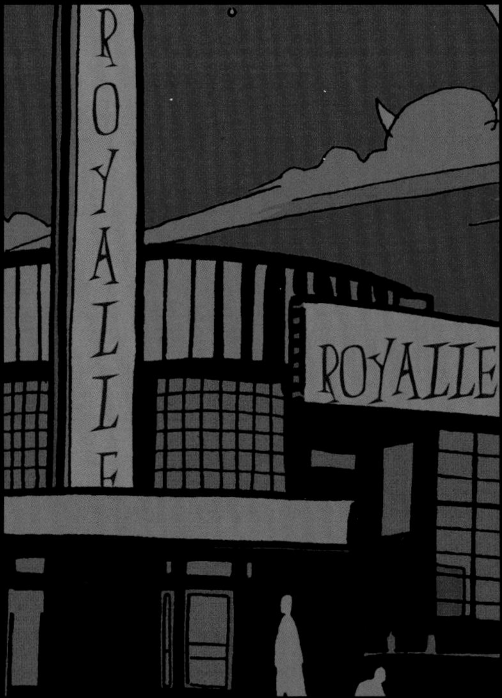

ROYALL
ROYALLE

[redacted] THE MEMORY

I walked up to your table at a Chicago Comicon some years ago and started looking at the wares you had laid out. You and Mack were chatting it up behind the table, and, as all fans (that have social skills) do, I felt intrusive. I paged through your huge stack of original artwork and, after a lull in your chat, was greeted cheerfully by the bald guy I already knew was Bendis. After an exchange of pleasantries I asked how much the art was. As I recall, I think 20 bucks was the answer.

I proceeded to pick out the 'Social Catastrophe' chapter and bought the whole damn thing. After an exchange of cash (and me thinking I had just made the steal of the show) I asked you to look at my colors. Amidst an honest appraisal of my work by you and Mack as being "not bad" (you really liked the Mignola Sin City Pin-Up) you looked at me and said something that I will never forget:

"Don't ever quit trying to break in, cause most of those other guys carrying around portfolios will."

I'd like to think I remembered the quote exactly, but I'm not a fucking savant. Even so, the spirit of what you said rings in my ear weekly. It really hit home.

THE SUMMATION

Everyone has moments in their life where things happen, things are said that help them understand their place in the world and truly "affects" them. I just wanted to thank you for one of those moments.

Oh yeah—I remember that like it was yesterday. After you walked away, I turned to David and said, "Wow—he's asking guys who do black-and-white comics at Caliber for career advice!! On coloring!! And he thought we were serious!"

Yeah . . . David laughed so hard he peed himself. That was great.

[redacted] Dear Mr. Bendis

Allow me to introduce myself, my name is Danny [redacted]. I am currently studying for my BA in graphic design and illustration, at Demontfort University, Lincoln England.

I am currently on my final year of said course and at the moment am in the process of compiling research for my final dissertation/essay, which I have chosen to do on comic book/sequential art, as this subject is very dear to me as well as of great interest to me also.

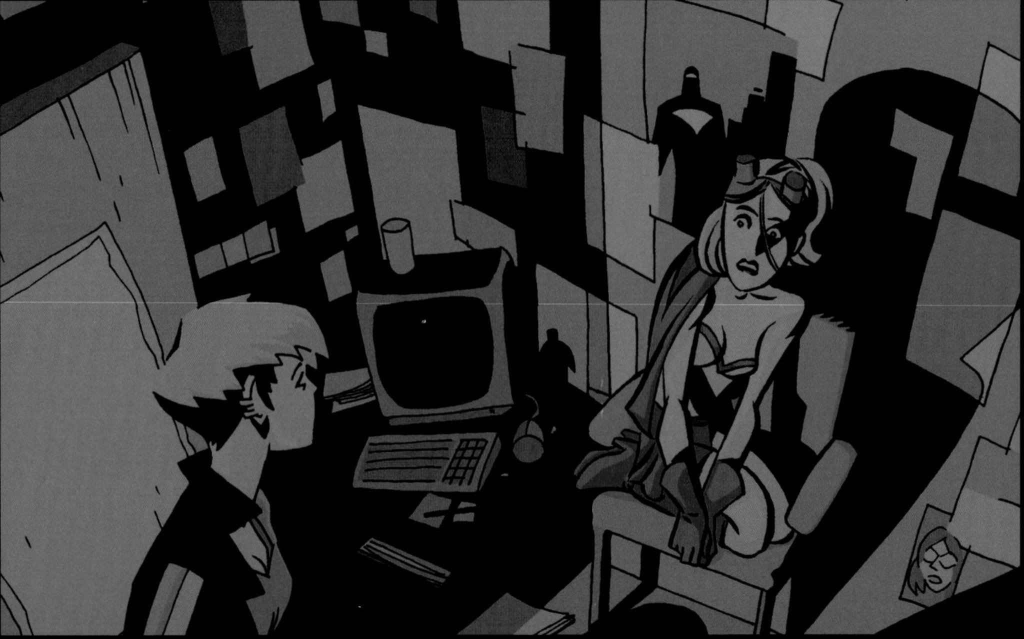

WARREN ELLIS GUEST STARS IN *POWERS* #7

"Something Incredibly Awful"
Happens to Brit Scribe
By Jim McLauchlin

After eight years in the comic business, Warren Ellis has finally achieved the same level as his creations—he is a comic character.

The popular writer of *Planetary* and Marvel's "Counter X" books will be the surprise guest star in Image Comics' *Powers* #7 in November. "I did it 'cause it made me laugh, basically," said Ellis. "No more than that."

Powers writer Brian Michael Bendis has frequent character guest stars, and thought adding Ellis would be a nice touch for the book that deals with cops who investigate superhero murders. "Writers go for ride-alongs with cops," Bendis said. "At least good writers do. You just need to soak up the flavor of it all."

Ellis will be one such rider. "I thought, 'How about a pompous British writer who just won't shut up?' Then I thought it could be really funny if it was someone we all know instead of a made-up character."

Enter Ellis. "I've known Warren a long time," Bendis said. "He's got a persona as a feisty, cantankerous, opinionated writer, a real pain in the ass. I mean, I don't think he's a pain in the ass, but I just thought the idea would be neat."

Ellis liked the idea, and Bendis's style. "I only asked him to change just a few lines of dialogue to make me sound a bit more English," Ellis said. "He took a lot from my published columns and interviews, so in many cases I'm speaking verbatim."

While Ellis liked the script, he may not be fond of what happens in the story. "Something incredibly awful happens to him," Bendis said. "I won't spoil it, but I think it's a first."

So who's next on Bendis's guest list? Will Chris Claremont be dropping by *Powers*?

"Nah," Bendis concluded. "I'm not going to repeat myself. I don't want to turn this into the running joke. Warren gets to be a one-time deal."

Therefore, I would like to ask, if it would be at all possible for you to give me a short response to the accompanying question, as it would be a great help to me, in completing a major part of this projects criteria.

I understand that you are a very busy individual.

Q: What are you views/opinions on comics as an artistic medium?

Artistic medium—that's hilarious! No, seriously . . . what's your question?

[redacted] And Brian do you think you could put my site, World of Bendis!, in the links section of your site?

World of Bendis!

http://hometown.aol.com/manwitoutfear/worldofbendis.html

Thanks bro—you da man!

Wow, my first-ever fan site! That is so flattering—wow.

I'm a little uncomfortable with the nudes, though. Goddamn roofies . . .

(Psst . . . I just checked to see if the site was still up, because I wanted to run this letter in the best-of roundup, and it's not there. The guy bailed on me. Guy's probably running a "Give Kirkman a Taintbath" site. Okay, so you didn't like *Ultimate Six*! It reads better collected, I swear!)

Okay—now for something from a guy I STILL get email from . . . but this bulk was from issue nine . . .

[redacted] Heya Brian,

I know there is a *Madman/Powers* crossover in the works.

So I'm just taking this opportunity to hint to you some crossovers that I would pay money to see.

1. *Powers/Strange Kisses: 3000 Inches To Graceland*

A well-connected politician is found murdered. The only suspect, an Elvis impersonator with 500 penises . . .

2. *Powers/100 Bullets: The Diamond That Dizzy Blew*

Agent Graves offers Walker a briefcase filled with a Glock, 100 bullets, and undeniable proof that his captain was behind him losing his powers. Walker kneecaps the old man and tells him to speak in straight lines and to stop being such an annoying pain in the ass. Then he shoots the captain and scores with that Dizzy Cordova hottie.

3. *Powers/Wendy Whitebread: Come Along*

Brian's dream project. Walker & Pilgrim try to bust Wendy for soliciting, only to discover that she's on the job. 46 pages of sex ensue.

4. *Powers/The Authority*

Walker and Pilgrim are ordered to bring in The Authority for crimes against humanity. Walker and Pilgrim turn in their badges because absolutely nobody fucks with The Authority. Ever. Then Pilgrim sleeps with Swift and Walker moves to New Indonesia to become a senior partner in Delgado's

Suckers Inc., a vacuum cleaner manufacturer. Royale is raped with a power tool when he calls The Midnighter a fag.

5. *Powers/Ultimate Spider-Man: The Bendis Clone Saga*

Convinced that the world can't get enough of him, a powerful egomaniac makes millions of copies of himself. Spidey and Walker and Pilgrim team up to stop him. Parker asks Pilgrim what a clitoris is.

That's all I've got right now. Don't blame me. I had to find something to do with all that free time which, for other people, would have been spent on sex. Oh, and that *Powers* book? Keep it good dammit. Don't make me have to go around yonder and smack ya!

En Ami,

[redacted]

Man, looks like everybody brought the funny themselves this month. Keep it comin'. Who's next?

[redacted] Dear Brian or Mr. Bendis, if you don't want to get too informal, *The Powers Coloring Book and Activity Special* was and is a very cool concept. I have to say the only way I got it was by ordering it through my local comic shop. I went to other comic book stores in the neighborhood and nowhere on the rack did I see the *Powers Coloring Book and Activity Special*. I was the only one who got the special in my store. Even to get *Powers* the comic one has to order it through their comic book store but the people who get *Powers* didn't get the activity book. I just don't get that, although I would guess that they might have not known about it. Maybe they don't study *Previews* like I do.

The good news is that I did get three issues of the activity book. I always get two issues of a comic because I also get comics for my friend. The third copy of the activity book was for me because I liked the concept of it. My comic guy even made fun of me for getting the activity book, in that jokey way. I get the *Powers* comic, then I should get the *Powers Activity Book*. Why is that so hard to understand? It is not like it is a statue.

I then took my comic guy by the collar and pushed him close to my face and through gritted teeth I said "NO ONE INSULTS *POWERS*!!" Then I pushed him against the wall and left the store. Okay this whole last part about me grabbing my comic book guy and the gritted teeth and pushing him didn't really happen, but I felt I had to spice up the story a bit. I actually just told him that people would be asking about the special when they come in the store. I would guess people didn't ask about the special, but hey maybe they did. *Powers* fans will be sorry if they missed this. Well that is the end of my first letter to you. I didn't curse yet. Buy I might in the future. I need a reason to curse not because I can.

Sincerely,

Mike . . . *Powers* Fan and that includes the *Powers Coloring Book and Activity Special.*

Tune in next month for the continuing story of this guy and his homoerotic relationship with his retailer!!

[redacted] I am sorry to bother you but I just couldn't help saying hello. I think your work is great and my favorites of yours are *Torso*, *Powers*, and *Ultimate Spider-man*. I bet you hear this all the time for geeky fan boys but your work seems to stand out more then most writers in the business and out. I am just a teenager but hope oneday to make a career in the filmmaking business and your monthly inspirations I read in comics give me some will power to set out and try to become something. By the way, the names Alan and I live in Miami Beach, FL. If you are ever not busy (which I know you are), reply back and we can chat some.

I'm not falling for that one again, you stinkin' feds.

[redacted]

Hey Brian. I'm a 48 year old mamma's boy with a healthy obsession with Deena cos she's my dream girl. I also wanna break into the comic business. Could you answer these questions in order to speed my entry into the big leagues and I'll make it worth yr while (I hear you like kids . . . so I can help)

1. The Spice Girls split - how would you deal with it?

Don't even joke about that!! Don't even joke . . . (Oh my god—that joke is so old, it has a yeast infection!)

2. How far are you willing to stoop in order to write for the majors?

Pretty far, it appears.

3. How far did you go with Joe Quesada in order to get all those Marvel titles?

Pretty far, it appears.

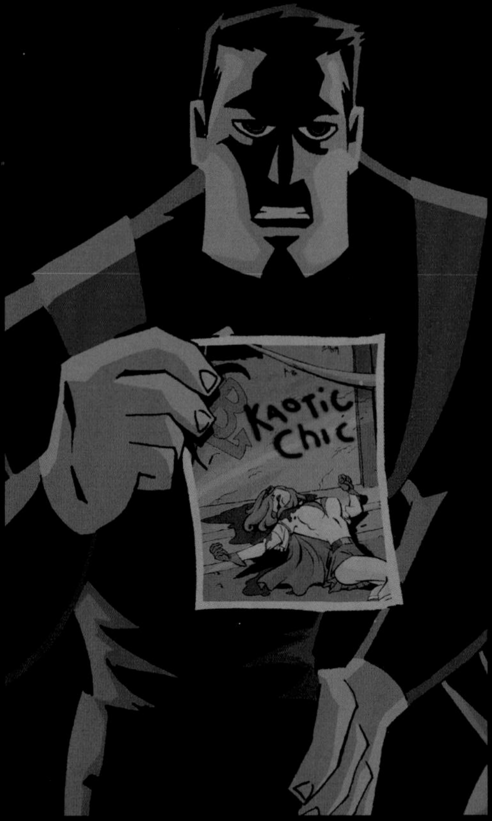
KAOTIC CHIC

3. –Part 2. Is being called a sellout by some of yr indie fanbase the funniest thing about being a writer?

No—counting my money while you do it is the funniest part. :)

4. Is it true what they say about bald men?

Yes, we are insecure and crave the sight of our names in print.

5. How many fibers are intertwined in a shredded wheat biscuit?

I'm Jewish—I don't know.

(I don't know what that means either.)

6. Ol' Dirty Bastard or Flava Flav? Who is funnier?

ODB. "Big Baby JeSUUUSS!!"

7. Will you draw comparison to Peter Parker's web fluid and his time alone with tissues and the female cast of *Saved By The Bell*?

No, but Paul Jenkins will.

8. Will you make Detective Walker gay? Or at least have him join a retired superhero version of the Village People?

No, but you can still whack off to him if you want to.

(God, I'm turning into Evan Dorkin here . . .)

9. I have to go now my mum is calling me. Will you go out with her?

I already did, my friend—I already did.

graeme [redacted]

ps. What do I do if I write joke letters to people but can't use a pseudonym?

Get published.

pps. Is that how you spell pseudonym?

You're asking *me*?!

[redacted] Hey man,

Hey dude . . .

I have been sick with strep throat lately, so I haven't been on the board and the post count was insane, but I got some questions for you (some of which I couldn't post on the board because they may not be public knowledge yet):

I just want to know how to get strep throat. Too many viewings of *Postcards from the Edge*?

1. You and your crime background aren't going to be doing a *Sopranos* book are you? My friend I work with, his parents live 2 stories above the butcher shop in the shows.

They had an artist come by a few weeks ago to take pictures of the building, the street and butcher shop from different angles. He used their apartment to take pictures of the street from an above view. I love getting scoops like this . . .

No, but we are doing a *G-String Divas* book.

2. Speaking of *Sopranos* and the new series, in the second episode, did you see Pussy's image in the mirror when Tony and others were standing in the hallway, prior to everyone saying a few words about his mom? What is up with that?

Dude, I see pussy everywhere, so don't ask me.

3. *The Art of the Matrix* book rocks, doesn't it?

Yes, it does.

They are supposedly going to do books for each of the sequels that Skroce and Darrow do. Do Mike or you have any involvement in the movie character designs/storyboards, etc?

Yes. We invented *The Invisibles*.

(Okay, that joke might be a little too inside.)

[redacted] Hello,

I was wondering if the *Storm* mini does well, could it become an ongoing?? I think that would be just really great.

Lord, what has my life become?? (Yes, this is an actual letter to me.)

[redacted] Dear herr Bendis,

I'm sorry to be disturbing you yet again. I was just

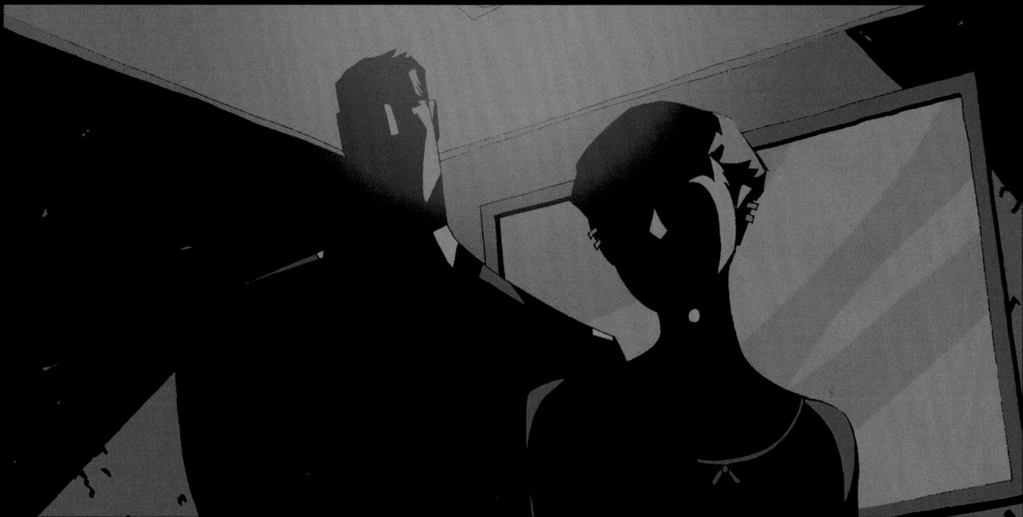

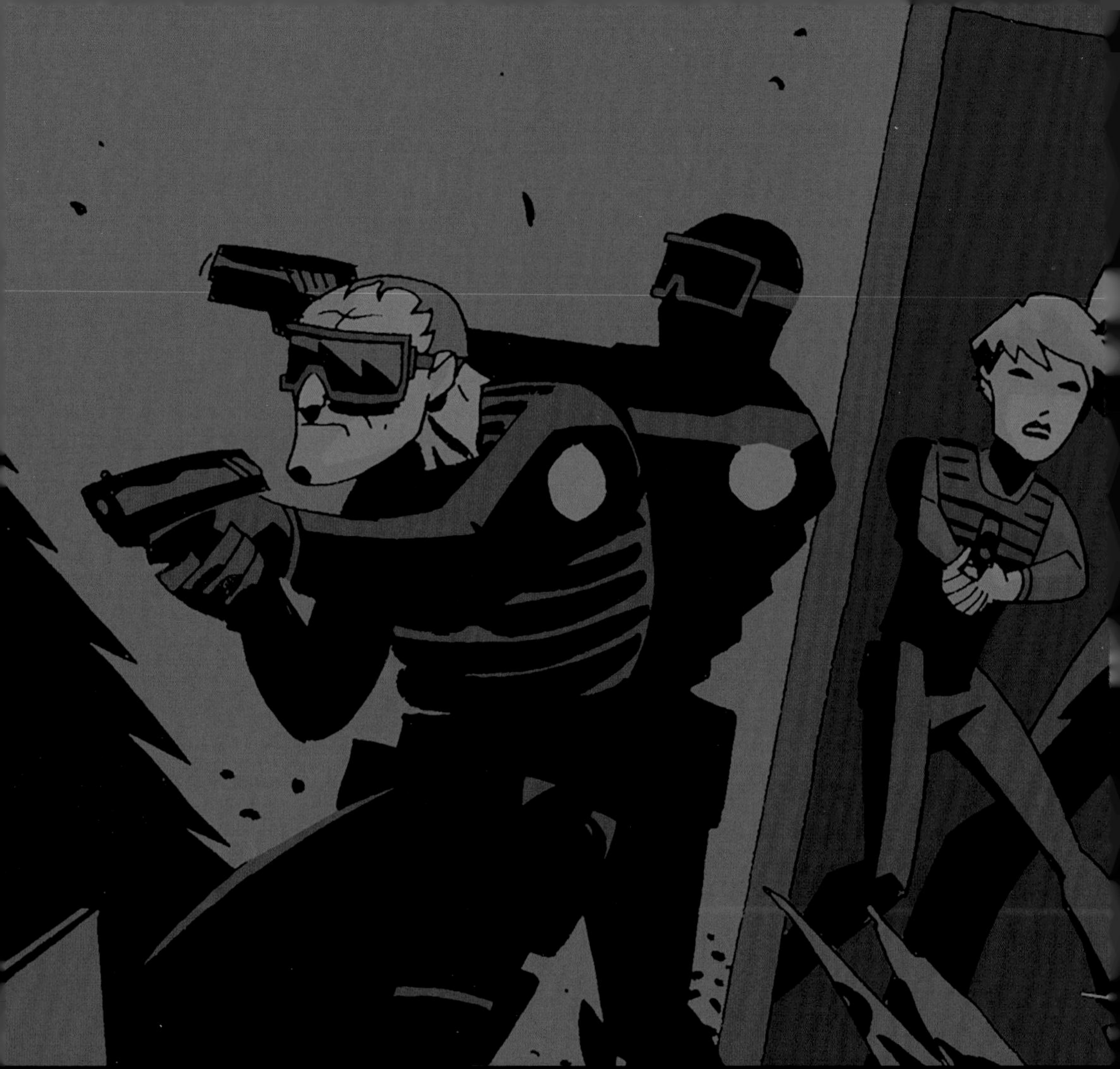

struck by an idea . . . actually, I was struck with an dea about a week ago, that sort of developed in my head . . . but now, I was struck with an idea to write you. Though I'll make it short.

Everybody together now: too late!!!

Why are there always the US heroes who get all the credits? Or rather, the heroes who are stationed n America (Superman isn't really American, nor s the Martian Manhunter). It's time that Norway showed what they're good for, showed the world that they're just as good as any other US team. You know what they say . . . "There's the wrong way, and there's Norway."

Hopefully, DC might be interested in such an idea, but I fear that they'd dismiss it before even listening to the plot itself, thinking that any comic book taking place in Norway gotta be too silly to ever be a hit. I'd rather be concerned about it being too brutal (indeed, it even features a Viking character that both Norwegians and foreigners love so much). But then I thought, it might work as a *Powers* mini-series as well, though it'd be quite a different comic—would only be set in the same world.

This just in: Bob Schreck just quit!

[redacted] I recently met Mike Oeming at a signing here in Buffalo. He was great guy.

He was hitting on you.

I was having trouble finding my artistic voice.

Oh don't worry about that—it's comics.

I have been recently criticized for my image use/work being to cliche/contemporary (this past friday at school). A college professor has challenged me

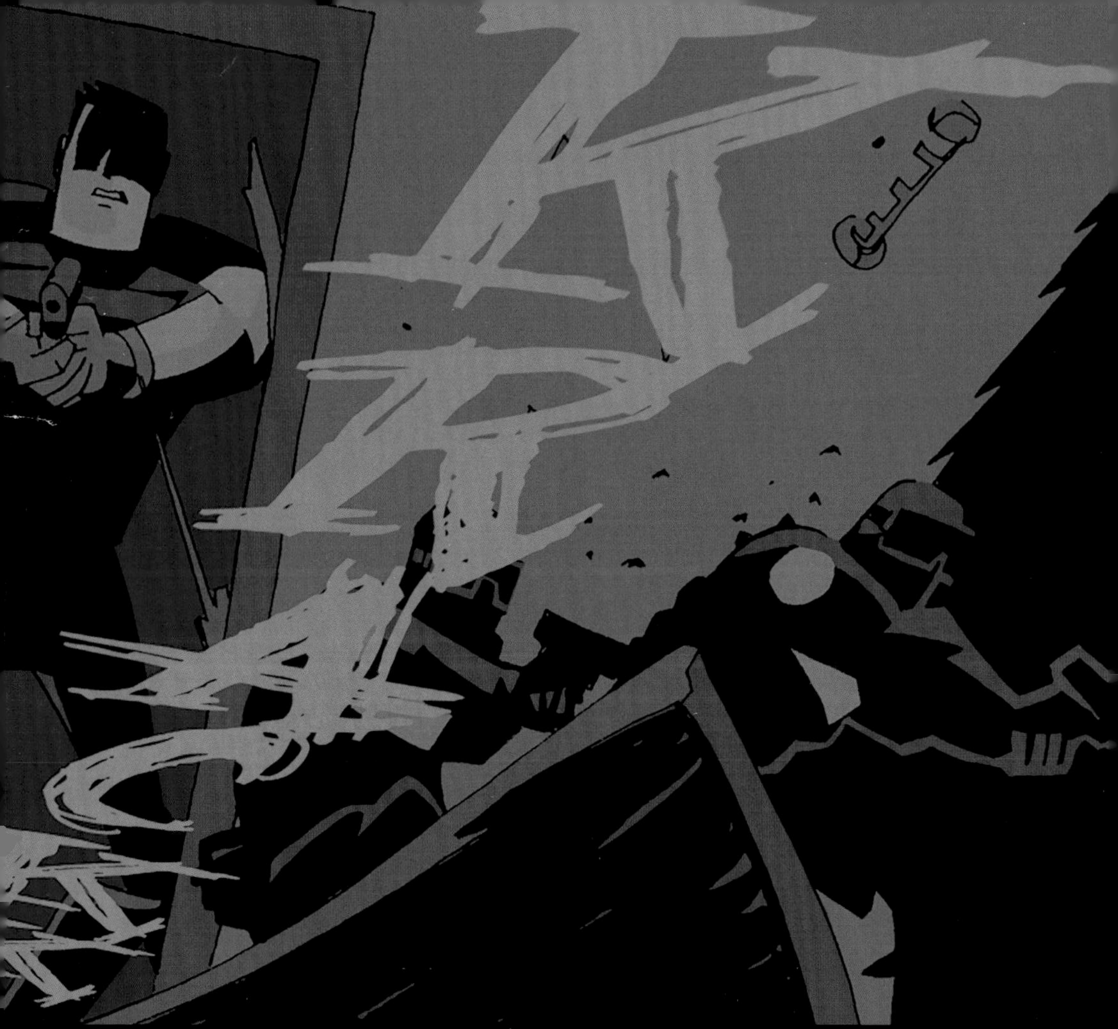

(during my illustration dept review at school) to be more aggressive in my image - concept relation in my art. She says I am talented but wants me to push my self-concept/communication between images wise in her illustration class next semester. She became annoyed every time I said and artist, she said I was a communicator, no an artist. Communicator is really what an artist is to her. Actually I agree, but never thought of it that way.

Tell your teacher I said to shut the fuck up with her bullshit *Oleanna* crap and let you create. God, I hated art school. No wonder I'm a writer now.

Mr. Bendis,

Your storytelling is impressive; and I think I know

Let's start with a shitty storyteller like Johr Byrne. The only thing that's just as goofy as tha absent-minded grin on his mug is the out of contro mop on his head. I think that a full head of hair is a negative for any comic writer.

I call it the Balding Writer Theory.

It goes as follows . . .

If you look at *Wizard*'s Top Ten Writers list it's a balding frenzy. What do you say we take a lool at some cats that are Hasselhof Challenged Jeph Loeb . . . great writer. Chris Claremont (pre *Sovereign Seven*) great writer. Peter David . . . gooc stuff. That J. Michael St-Straz-Stray-whatever the hell his name is, he's okay. Erik Larsen . . . well, witł the stuff he's been writing lately he may be growing his hair back. But you get my point; balding for a comic writer is a positive thing.

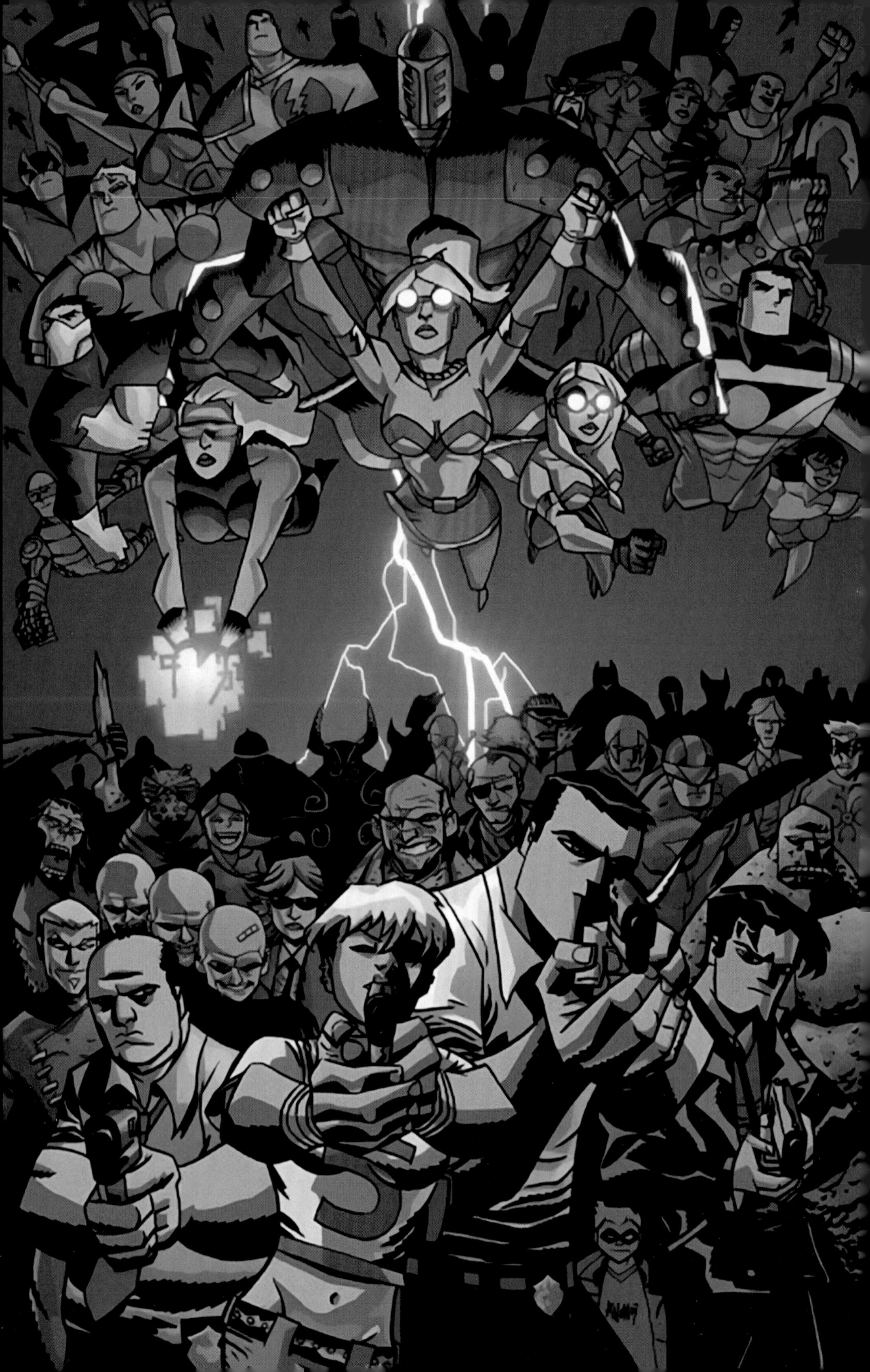